Bethan Davies 3H

Lytton

Oxford
Concise
School
Dictionary

Compiled by Joyce M. Hawkins, Andrew Delahunty
and Fred McDonald

OXFORD
UNIVERSITY PRESS

OXFORD
UNIVERSITY PRESS

Great Clarendon Street, Oxford OX2 6DP

Oxford University Press is a department of the University of Oxford.
It furthers the University's objective of excellence in research, scholarship,
and education by publishing worldwide in

Oxford New York

Auckland Bangkok Buenos Aires Cape Town Chennai
Dar es Salaam Delhi Hong Kong Istanbul Karachi Kolkata
Kuala Lumpur Madrid Melbourne Mexico City Mumbai Nairobi
São Paulo Shanghai Singapore Taipei Tokyo Toronto
with an associated company in Berlin

Oxford is a registered trade mark of Oxford University Press
in the UK and in certain other countries

British Library Cataloguing in Publication Data available

ISBN 0-19-910908-7

10 9 8 7 6 5 4 3 2 1

Typeset in MNimrod
by Pentacor PLC, High Wycombe
Printed in Italy by G. Canale & C. S.p.A.

Do you have a query about words, their origin, meaning, use, spelling,
pronunciation, or any other aspect of the English language? Visit our
website at www.askoxford.com where you will be able to find answers
to your queries.

Contents

Preface

This dictionary has been specially written for upper primary and lower secondary school students aged 10–14 years. It should serve as a working tool in the classroom and accustom its users to the style in which most adult dictionaries are written, but at the same time be easy to use because it avoids abbreviations and similar conventions.

Inflections of all verbs and plurals of nouns are spelt out in full, and comparatives and superlatives of many adjectives and adverbs are also given. Pronunciation of difficult words is given in a simple look-and-say system without special symbols. Definitions are clearly expressed, with careful explanations of difficult concepts (e.g. *hindsight, hypothesis, irony*), and many examples of words in use are provided. There are a number of notes on correct usage, grammatical points, and words that are easily confused (e.g. *alternate/alternative*). Direct opposites or parallel terms are sometimes indicated (e.g. *maximum/minimum, optimist/pessimist, libel/slander*).

Prefixes and suffixes are entered at the appropriate place in the alphabetical sequence; lists of them are contained in Appendix 1. Etymologies are given for a large number of words. The etymologies are intended to introduce the idea that words have a history as well as a meaning, to demonstrate the connection between related words and help with recognition of word elements, and to show the variety of languages that have contributed to English. It is hoped that the etymologies will also arouse the curiosity of users so that they will be encouraged to look in a larger dictionary for more detailed information.

Acknowledgements

The publisher and editors are indebted to all the people who helped in the production of this dictionary. We are grateful to the teachers who advised us in the initial stages, to John Butterworth and Clive Johnson for their helpful comments and to Richard Jeffery and Janet Foot for their careful proof-reading.

The English Language

English is the chief language of Britain, the USA, Australia, and a number of other countries. More than 300 million people speak it as their first or their only language, and millions more in all parts of the world learn it as a foreign language for use in communicating with people of other nations. It is the official language used between airline pilots and their air traffic controllers in all countries, and in shipping, and the main language of international business, science, medicine, and computing.

All languages have a history: they are constantly changing and evolving. It is probable that nearly all the languages of Europe, and some of those in the Middle East and India, came from one ancient community, who lived in Eastern Europe about 5,000 years ago. Scholars call the language of this community Indo-European. As people moved away to the east and west they lost contact with each other and developed new and different lifestyles. Naturally their language needs changed too. They invented new words and forgot old ones, and the grammar of the language also changed. Many varied languages grew from the original parent tongue, until the time came when people with the same ancestors would no longer have understood each other.

Invasions and conquests complicated the process. The English language shows this very well, for invaders brought their own languages to Britain, and British travellers took theirs to lands overseas. The earliest known inhabitants of Britain spoke a form of **Celtic**, related to modern Welsh and Gaelic. Very little of this Celtic survived the waves of invasion that drove its speakers into western and highland parts of the country, but the names of some cities, rivers, and hills date back to Celtic times (e.g. *Carlisle, Avon, Pendle*).

Old English

Old English, which is also called Anglo-Saxon, does not look very much like modern English (for example *Faeder ure, þu þe eart in heofonum* = Our Father, who is in heaven) but many words, especially the most frequently used ones, can be traced back to it. *Eat, drink, sleep, speak, work, play*, and *sing* are all from Old English; so are *house, door, meat, bread, milk, fish*; and *head, nose, eye, man, woman, husband, wife*. The prepositions and conjunctions that we use to join words together in sentences, such as *and, but, to, from*, come from Old English, and so do many common adverbs, for example *up, down, here, there, over, under*.

Old English did not originate in Britain. It was the language of the Angles, Saxons, and Jutes, Germanic tribes who came to Britain from the Continent in about AD 450. By about AD 700 the Anglo-Saxons had occupied most of the country and their language was the dominant one. Even the name of the country itself became 'England', which means 'land of the Angles', and from it came 'Englisc', the Old English spelling of 'English'.

The next great influence on Old English came from the Vikings, who arrived from Norway and Denmark in the 9th and 10th centuries and occupied much of northern and eastern England. They also settled in parts of Scotland, Wales, and Ireland. Their language was Old Norse, and from it we get many common words, such as *call, cast,* and *take,* and a number of words beginning with 'sc' or 'sk', including *scare, scrap, skirt,* and *sky.*

Middle English

In 1066 the Normans, led by William the Conqueror, invaded England. English life was greatly changed in the years that followed and the language changed too, so much so that, with a little practice, we can now read and understand the language of that time. These lines, for example, were written in about 1390: *This carpenter hadde wedded newe a wyf, Which that he lovede moore than his lyf.* We call this language 'Middle English' to distinguish it from Old English or Anglo-Saxon.

For much of this period the language used by the ruling classes was the French of the victorious Norman invaders, though most of the ordinary people still spoke English. Many words connected with government and law came into the language at this time through their French use, e.g. *advise, command, court, govern, people, reign, royalty, rule.*

Throughout all these centuries, although scholars in different countries spoke different languages, they all understood Latin, which had been the language of the ancient Roman Empire, and used it for writing about every subject that they studied. Some Latin words (e.g. *mint, pound, sack,* and *street*) had already been adopted by the Anglo-Saxons before they came to Britain, because they had lived on the fringe of the Roman Empire; others (e.g. *font, pope,* and *school*) arrived with the spread of Christianity. Then in the 14–16th centuries (the *Renaissance*) people throughout Europe became especially interested in Greek and Roman literature, philosophy, art, and buildings, and many more words from Greek and Latin were introduced into English (e.g. *architecture, column, comedy, educate, history, physics, tributary*). The Christian Church in all western countries had always used Latin, and continued to use this (not English or other local languages) in all its services.

Modern English

From about 1500 onwards the English language continued to change, and developed enormously. It adopted words from other languages with which people came into contact through trade or travel, and it was exported to other lands when English-speaking people travelled abroad. In the early 17th century colonies began to be established, first in North America and in India, then in the West Indies, and later in Australia, New Zealand, Hong Kong, and Africa. To each country the settlers took the English language of their own time, and in each country it changed, little by little, until it differed in various ways not only from the English of other settlements but from its parent form in Britain—where, of course, the language was changing too. Some words, such as names for birds and animals found only in one country, were adopted into the form of English used there and are not known elsewhere; others (e.g. *banana, potato*, and *tornado*) have made their way into international English and are known everywhere.

In the 20th century, people who came from the Caribbean and Asia to settle in England brought with them their own cultures and vocabulary, and many words from these have been adopted into standard English (e.g. *chapatti, reggae*).

Nowadays travel is not the only way in which people acquire words from other countries. Films made in one country are shown in many others, and television programmes from all over the world are received in people's homes. The result is that while American, Australian, and other vocabulary becomes familiar in Britain, British English continues to be exported.

Dialect

There are different forms of English not only in different parts of the world but within the British Isles. People from North Yorkshire, the Midlands, East Anglia, and Somerset have different words for different things, or use different grammatical forms. The varieties of English are called **dialects**. Each is known, understood, and regarded as standard in its own area, but not outside it.

The way that people of an area pronounce words is called an **accent**, and this too varies in different parts of the country.

Every language has a number of dialects and most languages have one dialect and style of pronunciation that is regarded as standard for the whole country. In Britain, 'Standard English' is based on the form of English used in southern England. It is the basis of the written language, known (unlike other dialects) in all parts of the country, spoken by all well-educated people, used for national news bulletins on radio and television, and learned by foreigners. People from outside southern England often speak Standard English with a local accent, and use it as well as their local dialect.

Formal and informal

We wear different clothes for different kinds of occasions, and often the words that we use when writing or speaking formally are different from those that we use informally to friends.

Very informal language (e.g. *nick* = to steal, *quid* = £1, *piffle* = nonsense) is called **slang**. It is used either for fun, or to express something in a more vivid or picturesque way than dignified words would do, or to shock people or attract their attention. Often, special slang words are used by members of a group, and they recognize others who use them as belonging to it too.

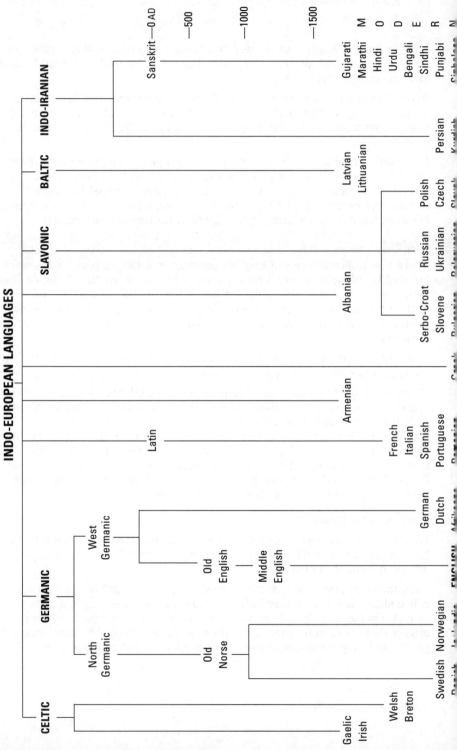

INDO-EUROPEAN LANGUAGES

CELTIC

Gaelic
Irish

Welsh
Breton

GERMANIC

North Germanic

Swedish Norwegian

Old Norse

West Germanic

German
Dutch

Old English — Middle English — ENGLISH

Latin

French
Italian
Spanish
Portuguese

Armenian

Albanian

SLAVONIC

Serbo-Croat
Slovene

Russian
Ukrainian

Polish
Czech

BALTIC

Latvian
Lithuanian

INDO-IRANIAN

Sanskrit — 0 AD

— 500

— 1000

— 1500

Gujarati
Marathi
Hindi
Urdu
Bengali
Sindhi
Punjabi

Persian

M
O
D
E
R
N

The dictionary

There are over 500,000 words in the English language, and the total is increasing all the time. Of these, about 3,000 are known and used by almost everyone whose native language is English. Most people know the meaning of at least another 5,000 words, though they may not use all of them in everyday speech or writing. In addition, those who specialize in a particular subject (e.g. music, chemistry, medicine, computers) have a wide vocabulary of words that are used by people working in that subject but are not generally known to others.

The biggest dictionary in the world is the *Oxford English Dictionary*, which fills twenty very large volumes, and it contains most of these words. Small dictionaries can find room for only a fraction of the whole language; they include most of the words that are in common use, but (in order to make the book a convenient size and not too expensive) they have to miss out a considerable number of words, and a larger dictionary must be consulted for information about these.

Notes on the use of the dictionary

Dictionary entries

Words defined are arranged in alphabetical order. The words derived from each word (*derivatives*) are often included in the same entry without definitions if their meaning can easily be worked out from the meaning of the main word.

Words with the same spelling but with a different meaning or origin (*homographs*) are given separate entries with a space between them, and numbered with a raised figure, e.g.

peer[1] *verb* (peers, peering, peered)
look at something closely or with difficulty. [from *appear*]

peer[2] *noun* (*plural* peers)
1 a noble. 2 someone who is equal to another in rank, merit, or age etc., *She had no peer.* **peeress** *noun*
[from Latin *par* = equal]

Pronunciation

Help is given with this when the word is difficult, or when two words with the same spelling are pronounced differently. The pronunciation is given in brackets with *say* or *rhymes with*, e.g.

toll (rhymes with *hole*) *noun*

chaos (*say* kay-oss) *noun*

Words are broken up into small units (usually of one syllable), and the syllable that is spoken with most stress is shown in thick black letters. In the pronunciation guide, note the following distinctions:

oo shows the sound as in *soon*
uu "   "   "   " " *book*
th "   "   "   " " *thin*
th "   "   "   " " *this*
zh "   "   "   " " *vision*

Word classes (parts of speech)

These are printed in italic or sloping print (e.g. *noun, adjective, verb*) after the word and before its definition. Some words can be used as more than one word class (part of speech). When these are defined, no space is left between the entries, e.g.

barricade *noun* (*plural* barricades)
a barrier, especially one put up hastily across a street or door.

barricade *verb* (barricades, barricading, barricaded)
block a street or door with a barricade.

Inflections and plurals

Derived forms of verbs, plurals of nouns, and some comparative and superlative forms of adjectives and adverbs are given after the word class (part of speech).

The first verb form given (ending in -s) is used for the present tense. The second form given (ending in -ing) is the present participle. When three verb forms are given, e.g.

admit *verb* (admits, admitting, admitted)

the third form is both the past tense (as in 'he *admitted* it') and the past participle ('it was *admitted*'). When four forms are given, e.g.

come *verb* (comes, coming, came, come)

freeze *verb* (freezes, freezing, froze, frozen)

the third is the past tense (as in 'he *came*'; 'it *froze*'), and the fourth is the past participle ('he had *come*'; 'it was *frozen*').

Meanings

Many words have more than one meaning. Each meaning is numbered separately.

Labels

Words that are not standard English are labelled as *informal* or *slang* etc.

Examples

Examples of words in use are given in italic or sloping print *like this* to help make a definition clearer, e.g.

beware *verb*
be careful, *Beware of pickpockets.*

Phrases

These are listed and defined under the word class (part of speech) to which they belong, e.g.

jump *verb* (jumps, jumping, jumped)
move up suddenly from the ground into the air.
jump at (*informal*) accept something eagerly.
jump the gun start before you should.
jump the queue not wait your turn.
jump *noun* (*plural* jumps)
a jumping movement.

Usage notes

The dictionary includes over 200 notes on correct usage, grammatical points, and words that are easily confused, e.g.

less *adjective & adverb*

USAGE: Do not use *less* when you mean *fewer*. You should use *fewer* when you are talking about a number of individual things, and *less* when you are talking about a quantity or mass of something: *The less batter you make, the fewer pancakes you'll get.*

Origins of words

The derivation (or *etymology*) of a word is given in square brackets at the end of the entry, e.g.

alligator *noun* (*plural* **alligators**)
a large reptile of the crocodile family.
[from Spanish *el lagarto* = the lizard]

These derivations often shed light on the word's meaning or how its meaning has changed, or show the connection between words that have the same set of letters in them (e.g. *attract, contract, extract*, and *tractor*) and also help to indicate the number of languages from which words have been taken into English. For instance, *alligator* comes from Spanish, *algebra* from Arabic, *mammoth* from Russian, *bungalow* from Hindi, *shawl* from Persian or Urdu, and *skunk* from a Native American language.

Other examples:

bread [from Old English, from Germanic]
butter [from Old English, taken via Latin from Greek]
cake [from a Scandinavian language]
cereal [from *Ceres*, the Roman goddess of farming]
cheese [from Old English, taken from Latin]
chocolate [via French or Spanish from Nahuatl (a Central American language spoken by the Aztecs)]
coffee [from Arabic *kahwa*]
cream [from old French]
liquorice [from Greek *glykys* = sweet + *rhiza* = root]
tea [via Dutch from Chinese]

No origin is given if the word is obviously related to another word nearby, for which there is an etymology (e.g. the origin of *determine* is given, but not those of *determination, determined*, or *determiner*). Etymology is not always given for words made up of two other words in the dictionary (e.g. *seafood, racecourse*), or of a word and a prefix or suffix (e.g. *regenerate, radiography, sleepless, unfortunate*). Some words have very complicated origins, and it is not always possible to show all the details; users who are interested in discovering more about word origins should look in a larger dictionary.

Aa

a *adjective* (called the *indefinite article* and
changing to **an** before most vowel sounds)
1 one (but not any special one), *Can you lend
me a book?* **2** each; per, *We see it once a day* or
once an hour.
[from Old English *an* = *one*]

a-¹ *prefix*
1 on; to; towards (as in *afoot, ashore, aside*).
2 in the process of (as in *a-hunting*).
[from the preposition *on*]

a-² *prefix* (**an-** is used before a vowel sound)
not; without (as in *asymmetrical, anarchy*).
[from Greek *a-* = not]

ab- *prefix* (changing to **abs-** before *c* and *t*)
away; from (as in *abduct, abnormal, abstract*).
[from Latin *ab* = away]

aback *adverb*
taken aback surprised.
[from Old English *on baec* = backwards]

abacus (*say* ab-a-kus) *noun* (*plural* **abacuses**)
a frame used for counting with beads sliding
on wires. [from Greek]

abandon *verb* (abandons, abandoning,
abandoned)
1 give up, *We never abandoned hope.* **2** leave
something without intending to return,
Abandon ship! **abandonment** *noun*
abandon *noun*
a careless and uncontrolled manner, *dancing
with great abandon.*

abbey *noun* (*plural* **abbeys**)
1 a monastery or convent. **2** a church that was
once part of a monastery, *Westminster Abbey.*
[same origin as *abbot*]

abbot *noun* (*plural* **abbots**)
the head of an abbey. [via Latin and Greek
from Aramaic (a language once spoken in the
Middle East), *abba* = father]

abbreviate *verb* (abbreviates, abbreviating,
abbreviated)
shorten something.
[from Latin *brevis* = short, brief]

abbreviation *noun* (*plural* **abbreviations**)
1 a shortened form of a word or words,
especially one using the initial letters, such as
GCSE, St., USA. **2** abbreviating something.

abdicate *verb* (abdicates, abdicating, abdicated)
1 resign from a throne. **2** give up an important
responsibility. **abdication** *noun*

abdomen (*say* ab-dom-en) *noun* (*plural*
abdomens)
1 the lower front part of a person's or animal's
body, containing the stomach, intestines, and

other digestive organs. **2** the rear section of an
insect's body.
abdominal (*say* ab-**dom**-in-al) *adjective*

abduct *verb* (abducts, abducting, abducted)
take a person away illegally; kidnap.
abduction *noun*, **abductor** *noun*

abhor *verb* (abhors, abhorring, abhorred)
(*formal*) hate something very much.
abhorrent *adjective*, **abhorrence** *noun*
[from Latin *abhorrere* = shrink away in
horror]

abide *verb* (abides, abiding, abided)
1 (*old use; past tense* **abode**) remain or dwell
somewhere. **2** bear or tolerate, *I can't abide
wasps.*
abide by keep a promise etc.

ability *noun* (*plural* **abilities**)
1 being able to do something. **2** cleverness or
talent.

ablaze *adjective*
blazing; on fire.

able *adjective*
1 having the power or skill or opportunity to
do something. **2** skilful or clever. **ably** *adverb*
[from old French]

-able *suffix* (*also* **-ble**, **-ible**, and **-uble**)
forms adjectives (e.g. *readable, legible*). The
nouns formed from these end in **-bility** (e.g.
readability, legibility). [from Latin]

abnormal *adjective*
not normal; unusual. **abnormally** *adverb*,
abnormality *noun* [from *ab-* + *normal*]

aboard *adverb* & *preposition*
on or into a ship or aircraft or train.

abolish *verb* (abolishes, abolishing, abolished)
put an end to a law or custom etc.
abolition (*say* ab-ol-**ish**-on) *noun*

abominable *adjective*
very bad or unpleasant. **abominably** *adverb*,
abomination *noun* [from Latin *abominari*
= regard as a bad omen]

aborigine (*say* ab-er-ij-in-ee) *noun* (*plural*
aborigines)
one of the original inhabitants of a country.
aboriginal *adjective* & *noun*
Aborigine one of the original inhabitants of
Australia.
[from Latin *ab origine* = from the beginning]

abort *verb* (aborts, aborting, aborted)
put an end to something before it has been
completed, *They aborted the space flight
because of problems.*

abortion *noun* (*plural* **abortions**)
removal of a baby from the womb before it has
developed enough to survive.

abortive *adjective*
unsuccessful, *an abortive attempt.*

abound *verb* (abounds, abounding, abounded)
1 be plentiful or abundant, *Fish abound in the river*. 2 have something in great quantities, *The river abounds in fish*.
[from Latin *abundare* = overflow]

about *preposition*
1 near in amount or size or time etc., *It costs about £5. Come about two o'clock*. 2 on the subject of; in connection with, *Tell me about your holiday*. 3 all round; in various parts of, *They ran about the playground*.

about *adverb*
1 in various directions, *They were running about*. 2 not far away, *He is somewhere about*.
be about to be going to do something.
[from *a-*[1] + Old English *butan* = outside]

above *preposition*
1 higher than. 2 more than.

above *adverb*
at or to a higher place. [from Old English]

abrasive *adjective*
1 that scrapes things away, *an abrasive wheel*. 2 harsh, *an abrasive manner*.

abreast *adverb*
1 side by side. 2 keeping up with something.
[from *a*[1] + *breast*]

abridge *verb* (abridges, abridging, abridged)
shorten a book etc. by using fewer words, *an abridged edition*. **abridgement** *noun* [same origin as *abbreviate*]

abroad *adverb*
in or to another country.

abrupt *adjective*
1 sudden or hasty, *his abrupt departure*. 2 rather rude and unfriendly; curt, *She has quite an abrupt manner*. **abruptly** *adverb*, **abruptness** *noun*
[from *ab-* + Latin *ruptum* = broken]

abs- *prefix*
away; from. see **ab-**.

abscess (*say* ab-sis) *noun* (*plural* abscesses)
an inflamed place where pus has formed in the body. [from Latin]

abscond *verb* (absconds, absconding, absconded)
go away secretly, *The cashier had absconded with the money*. [from Latin]

absent *adjective*
not here; not present, *absent from school*. **absence** *noun*

absent (*say* ab-sent) *verb* (absents, absenting, absented)
absent yourself stay away.
[from *abs-* + Latin *esse* = to be]

absentee *noun* (*plural* absentees)
a person who is absent. **absenteeism** *noun*

absent-minded *adjective*
having your mind on other things; forgetful.

absolute *adjective*
complete; not restricted. **absolutely** *adverb*
[same origin as *absolve*]

absolute zero *noun*
the lowest possible temperature, calculated as −273.15 °C.

absolve *verb* (absolves, absolving, absolved)
1 clear a person of blame or guilt. 2 release a person from a promise or obligation.
[from *ab-* + Latin *solvere* = set free]

absorb *verb* (absorbs, absorbing, absorbed)
1 soak up a liquid or gas. 2 receive something and reduce its effects, *The buffers absorbed most of the shock*. 3 take up a person's attention or time.

absorbent *adjective*
able to soak up liquids easily, *absorbent paper*.

abstain *verb* (abstains, abstaining, abstained)
1 keep yourself from doing something; refrain. 2 choose not to use your vote. **abstainer** *noun*, **abstention** *noun*

abstinence *noun*
abstaining, especially from alcohol.
abstinent *adjective* [same origin as *abstain*]

abstract (*say* ab-strakt) *adjective*
1 concerned with ideas, not solid objects, *Truth, hope, danger are all abstract*. 2 (of a painting or sculpture) showing the artist's ideas or feelings, not showing a recognizable person or thing.

absurd *adjective*
ridiculous or foolish.
absurdly *adverb*, **absurdity** *noun*

abundance *noun*
plenty. [same origin as *abound*]

abundant *adjective*
plentiful. **abundantly** *adverb*

abuse (*say* ab-yooz) *verb* (abuses, abusing, abused)
1 use something badly or wrongly; misuse. 2 ill-treat a person. 3 say unpleasant things about a person or thing.

abuse (*say* ab-yooss) *noun* (*plural* abuses)
1 a misuse, *the abuse of power*. 2 ill-treatment. 3 words abusing a person or thing; insults.
[from *ab-* + *use*]

abusive *adjective*
rude and insulting, *abusive remarks*.

abysmal (*say* ab-iz-mal) *adjective*
extremely bad, *abysmal ignorance*.

abyss (*say* ab-iss) *noun* (*plural* abysses)
an extremely deep pit.
[from Greek *abyssos* = bottomless]

ac- *prefix*
to; towards. see **ad-**.

academic 3 account

academic *adjective*
1 to do with education or studying, especially at a school or college or university. **2** theoretical; having no practical use, *an academic point.*
academic *noun* (*plural* **academics**)
a university or college teacher.

academy *noun* (*plural* **academies**)
1 a school or college, especially one for specialized training. **2** a society of scholars or artists, *The Royal Academy.*
[from *Akademeia*, the name of the garden where the Greek philosopher Plato taught his pupils]

accelerate *verb* (**accelerates, accelerating, accelerated**)
make or become quicker; increase speed.

acceleration *noun* (*plural* **accelerations**)
1 the rate at which the speed of something increases. **2** the rate of change of velocity.

accelerator *noun* (*plural* **accelerators**)
1 the pedal that a driver presses to make a motor vehicle go faster. **2** a thing used to increase the speed of something.

accent (*say* ak-sent) *noun* (*plural* **accents**)
1 the way a person pronounces words, *She has a French accent.* **2** emphasis or stress, *In 'fairy', the accent is on 'fair-'.* **3** a mark placed over a letter to show how it is pronounced, e.g. on *café.*

accept *verb* (**accepts, accepting, accepted**)
1 take a thing that is offered or presented. **2** say yes to an invitation, offer, etc.
acceptance *noun*

USAGE: Do not confuse with *except.*

acceptable *adjective*
good enough to accept; pleasing.
acceptably *adverb*, **acceptability** *noun*

access (*say* ak-sess) *noun*
1 a way to enter or reach something. **2** the right to use or look at something.
access *verb* (**accesses, accessing, accessed**)
find information that has been stored in a computer. [from Latin]

accessible *adjective*
able to be reached.
accessibly *adverb*, **accessibility** *noun*

accessory (*say* ak-sess-er-ee) *noun* (*plural* **accessories**)
1 an extra thing that goes with something. **2** a person who helps another with a crime.

accident *noun* (*plural* **accidents**)
an unexpected happening, especially one causing injury or damage. **accidental** *adjective*, **accidentally** *adverb*
by accident by chance; without its being arranged in advance.
[from Latin *accidere* = happen]

acclaim *verb* (**acclaims, acclaiming, acclaimed**)
welcome or applaud.
acclaim *noun*, **acclamation** *noun*
[from *ac-* + Latin *clamare* = to shout]

accommodate *verb* (**accommodates, accommodating, accommodated**)
1 provide somebody with a place to live, work, or sleep overnight. **2** help by providing something, *We can accommodate you with skis.*
[from Latin *accommodare* = make suitable for]

accommodation *noun*
somewhere to live, work, or sleep overnight.

accompanist *noun* (*plural* **accompanists**)
a pianist etc. who accompanies a singer or another musician.

accompany *verb* (**accompanies, accompanying, accompanied**)
1 go somewhere with somebody. **2** be present with something, *Thunder accompanied the storm.* **3** play music, especially on a piano, that supports a singer or another player etc.
accompaniment *noun*

accomplice (*say* a-kum-pliss) *noun* (*plural* **accomplices**)
a person who helps another in a crime etc.

accomplish *verb* (**accomplishes, accomplishing, accomplished**)
do something successfully.
accomplishment *noun*
[from *ac-* + Latin *complere* = to complete]

accomplished *adjective*
skilled.

accord *noun*
agreement; consent.
of your own accord voluntarily; without being asked or compelled.

according *adverb*
according to **1** as stated by, *According to him, we are stupid.* **2** in relation to, *Price the apples according to their size.*

accordingly *adverb*
1 in the way that is required, *I've given you your instructions and I expect you to act accordingly.* **2** therefore.

accordion *noun* (*plural* **accordions**)
a portable musical instrument like a large concertina. [via German from Italian *accordare* = to tune an instrument]

account *noun* (*plural* **accounts**)
1 a statement of money owed, spent, or received; a bill. **2** an arrangement to keep money in a bank etc. **3** a description or report.
on account of because of.
on no account under no circumstances; certainly not.
take something into account consider or include it when making a decision or calculation.

account *verb* (accounts, accounting, accounted)
account for make it clear why something happens.

accountable *adjective*
responsible; having to explain why you have done something.
accountability *noun*

accountant *noun* (*plural* accountants)
a person whose job is keeping or inspecting financial accounts.
accountancy *noun*

accumulate *verb* (accumulates, accumulating, accumulated)
collect; pile up. **accumulation** *noun*

accurate *adjective*
correct or exact. **accurately** *adverb*,
accuracy *noun* [from *ac-* + Latin *cura* = care]

accuse *verb* (accuses, accusing, accused)
say that a person has committed a crime etc.; blame. **accusation** *noun*, **accuser** *noun*

ace *noun* (*plural* aces)
1 a playing card with one spot. 2 a very skilful person or thing. 3 (in tennis) a serve that is too good for the other player to reach.
[from Latin *as* = unit]

ache *noun* (*plural* aches)
a dull continuous pain.
ache *verb* (aches, aching, ached)
have an ache. [from Old English]

achieve *verb* (achieves, achieving, achieved)
succeed in doing or producing something.
achievable *adjective*, **achievement** *noun*
[from old French *a chief* = to a head]

acid *noun* (*plural* acids)
a chemical substance that contains hydrogen and neutralizes alkalis.
acidic *adjective*, **acidity** *noun*
acid *adjective*
1 sharp-tasting; sour. 2 looking or sounding bitter, *an acid reply.* **acidly** *adverb*

acid rain *noun*
rain made acid by mixing with waste gases from factories etc.

acknowledge *verb* (acknowledges, acknowledging, acknowledged)
1 admit that something is true. 2 state that you have received or noticed something,
Acknowledge this letter. 3 express thanks or appreciation for something.
acknowledgement *noun*

acne (*say* ak-nee) *noun*
inflamed red pimples on the face and neck.

acorn *noun* (*plural* acorns)
the seed of the oak tree. [from Old English]

acoustic (*say* a-koo-stik) *adjective*
1 to do with sound or hearing. 2 (of a musical instrument) not electronic, *an acoustic guitar.*
acoustically *adverb*
[from Greek *akouein* = hear]

acoustics (*say* a-koo-stiks) *plural noun*
1 the qualities of a hall etc. that make it good or bad for carrying sound. 2 the properties of sound.

acquaint *verb* (acquaints, acquainting, acquainted)
tell somebody about something, *Acquaint him with the facts.*
be acquainted with know slightly.

acquaintance *noun* (*plural* acquaintances)
1 a person you know slightly. 2 being acquainted.

acquire *verb* (acquires, acquiring, acquired)
obtain. **acquisition** *noun*
[from *ac-* + Latin *quaerere* = seek]

acquit *verb* (acquits, acquitting, acquitted)
decide that somebody is not guilty, *The jury acquitted her.* **acquittal** *noun*
acquit yourself well perform or do something well.
[from *ac-* + Latin *quietus* = at rest]

acre (*say* ay-ker) *noun* (*plural* acres)
an area of land measuring 4,840 square yards or 0.405 hectares. **acreage** *noun*
[from Old English *aecer* = field]

acrobat *noun* (*plural* acrobats)
a person who performs spectacular gymnastic stunts for entertainment. **acrobatic** *adjective*,
acrobatics *plural noun*

acronym (*say* ak-ron-im) *noun* (*plural* acronyms)
a word or name that is formed from the initial letters of other words, *Nato is an acronym of North Atlantic Treaty Organization.*
[from Greek *akros* = top + *onyma* = name]

across *preposition* & *adverb*
1 from one side to the other, *Swim across the river. Are you across yet?* 2 on the opposite side, *the house across the street.* [from French *à croix* = crosswise]

acrylic (*say* a-kril-ik) *noun*
a kind of fibre, plastic, or resin made from an organic acid.

act *noun* (*plural* acts)
1 an action. 2 a law passed by a parliament.
3 one of the main divisions of a play or opera.
4 a short performance in a programme of entertainment, *a juggling act.* 5 a pretence, *She is only putting on an act.*
act *verb* (acts, acting, acted)
1 do something; perform actions. 2 perform a part in a play or film etc. 3 function; have an effect.
[from Latin *actus* = doing, performing]

action *noun* (*plural* actions)
1 doing something. 2 something done.
3 a battle; fighting, *He was killed in action.*

4 a lawsuit.
out of action not working or functioning.
take action do something.

activate verb (activates, activating, activated)
start something working.
activation noun, **activator** noun

active adjective
1 lively or energetic. 2 functioning or working; in operation, an active volcano. 3 radioactive. 4 (of a form of a verb) used when the subject of the verb is performing the action. In 'The shop sells sweets' the verb is active; in 'Sweets are sold by the shop' the verb is passive.
actively adverb, **activeness** noun

activist noun (plural activists)
a person who believes in vigorous action, especially in politics.

activity noun (plural activities)
1 an action or occupation, outdoor activities. 2 being active or lively.

actor noun (plural actors)
a person who acts a part in a play or film etc.

actress noun (plural actresses)
a woman who acts a part in a play or film etc.

actual adjective
real. **actually** adverb, **actuality** noun

acupuncture (say ak-yoo-punk-cher) noun
pricking parts of the body with needles to relieve pain or cure disease. **acupuncturist** noun
[from Latin acu = with a needle, + puncture]

acute adjective
1 sharp or strong, acute pain. 2 having a sharp mind. **acutely** adverb, **acuteness** noun

acute accent noun (plural acute accents)
a mark over a vowel, as over é in café.

acute angle noun (plural acute angles)
an angle of less than 90°.

AD abbreviation
Anno Domini (Latin = in the year of Our Lord), used in dates counted from the birth of Jesus Christ.

ad- prefix (changing to ac-, af-, ag-, al-, an-, ap-, ar-, as-, at- before certain consonants)
to; towards (as in adapt, admit).
[from Latin ad = to]

adamant (say ad-am-ant) adjective
firm and not giving way to requests.

adapt verb (adapts, adapting, adapted)
change something so that it is suitable for a new purpose or situation.
adaptable adjective, **adaptation** noun
[from ad- + Latin aptus = suitable, apt]

adaptor noun (plural adaptors)
a device to connect pieces of electrical or other equipment.

add verb (adds, adding, added)
1 put one thing with another. 2 make another remark.
add up 1 make or find a total. 2 (informal) make sense; seem reasonable.

adder noun (plural adders)
a small poisonous snake.
[from Old English; originally called a nadder, which became an adder]

addict noun (plural addicts)
a person who does or uses something that he or she cannot give up. **addicted** adjective, **addiction** noun [from Latin]

addictive adjective
causing people to become addicts, an addictive drug.

addition noun (plural additions)
1 the process of adding. 2 something added.
in addition also; as an extra thing.
additional adjective, **additionally** adverb

additive noun (plural additives)
a substance added to another in small amounts for a special purpose, e.g. as a flavouring.

address noun (plural addresses)
1 the details of the place where someone lives or of where letters etc. should be delivered to a person or firm. 2 a speech to an audience.
address verb (addresses, addressing, addressed)
1 write an address on a parcel etc. 2 make a speech or remark etc. to somebody.

adenoids plural noun
thick spongy flesh at the back of the nose and throat, which may hinder breathing.

adept (say a-dept) adjective
very skilful. [from Latin]

adequate adjective
enough or good enough. **adequately** adverb, **adequacy** noun [from Latin]

adhere verb (adheres, adhering, adhered)
stick to something. **adhesion** noun
[from ad- + Latin haerere = to stick]

adhesive adjective
sticky; causing things to stick together.
adhesive noun (plural adhesives)
a substance used to stick things together; glue.
[same origin as adhere]

adjacent adjective
near or next to, I waited in an adjacent room.
[from ad- + Latin jacens = lying]

adjective noun (plural adjectives)
a word that describes a noun or adds to its meaning, e.g. big, honest, strange, our.
adjectival adjective, **adjectivally** adverb

adjourn (say a-jern) verb (adjourns, adjourning, adjourned)
1 break off a meeting etc. until a later time.

2 break off and go somewhere else, *They adjourned to the library.* **adjournment** *noun* [from Latin, = to another day]

adjudicate (*say* a-joo-dik-ayt) *verb* (adjudicates, adjudicating, adjudicated) act as judge in a competition etc. **adjudication** *noun*, **adjudicator** *noun*

adjust *verb* (adjusts, adjusting, adjusted) 1 put a thing into its proper position or order. 2 alter something so that it fits or is suitable. **adjustable** *adjective*, **adjustment** *noun* [from *ad* + Latin *justa* = close to]

ad lib *verb* (ad libs, ad libbing, ad libbed) say or do something without any rehearsal or preparation. [from Latin *ad libitum* = according to pleasure]

administer *verb* (administers, administering, administered) 1 give or provide something, *He administered medicine.* 2 manage business affairs; **administrator** *noun*, **administrative** *adjective*, **administration** *noun*

admirable *adjective* worth admiring; excellent. **admirably** *adverb*

admiral *noun* (*plural* admirals) a naval officer of high rank. [from Arabic *amir* = commander]

admire *verb* (admires, admiring, admired) 1 look at something and enjoy it. 2 think that someone or something is very good. **admiration** *noun*, **admirer** *noun* [from *ad-* + Latin *mirari* = wonder at]

admission *noun* (*plural* admissions) 1 admitting. 2 the charge for being allowed to go in. 3 a statement admitting something; a confession.

admit *verb* (admits, admitting, admitted) 1 allow someone or something to come in. 2 state reluctantly that something is true; confess, *We admit that the task is difficult. He admitted his crime.*

admittance *noun* being allowed to go in, especially to a private place.

admonish *verb* (admonishes, admonishing, admonished) advise or warn someone firmly but mildly. **admonition** *noun*

adolescent *noun* (*plural* adolescents) a young person at the age between being a child and being an adult. **adolescence** *noun* **adolescent** *adjective*

adopt *verb* (adopts, adopting, adopted) 1 take someone into your family as your own child. 2 accept something; take something and use it, *They adopted new methods of working.* **adoption** *noun*

adore *verb* (adores, adoring, adored) love a person or thing very much. **adorable** *adjective*, **adoration** *noun*

adorn *verb* (adorns, adorning, adorned) decorate. **adornment** *noun* [from *ad-* + Latin *ornare* = furnish, decorate]

adrenalin (*say* a-dren-al-in) *noun* a hormone that stimulates the nervous system. [from *ad-* + *renal* (because adrenalin is made by the adrenal glands, above the kidneys)]

adrift *adjective* & *adverb* drifting. [from *a-*^{1} + *drift*]

adulation *noun* very great flattery. [from old French]

adult (*say* ad-ult) *noun* (*plural* adults) a fully grown or mature person. [from Latin *adultus* = grown up]

adultery *noun* being unfaithful to your wife or husband by having sexual intercourse with someone else. **adulterer** *noun*, **adulterous** *adjective* [from Latin]

advance *noun* (*plural* advances) 1 a forward movement; progress. 2 an increase. 3 a loan; payment made before it is due.
in advance beforehand; ahead.
advance *verb* (advances, advancing, advanced) 1 move forward; make progress. 2 lend or pay money ahead of the proper time, *Advance her a month's salary.* **advancement** *noun* [from old French]

advantage *noun* (*plural* advantages) 1 something useful or helpful. 2 the next point won after deuce in tennis. **advantageous** *adjective*
take advantage of use a person or thing profitably or unfairly.
to advantage making a good effect, *The painting can be seen to its best advantage here.*
to your advantage profitable or helpful to you.

Advent *noun* the period just before Christmas, when Christians celebrate the coming of Christ.

advent *noun* the arrival of a new person or thing, *the advent of computers.* [from *ad-* + Latin *ventum* = arrived]

adventure *noun* (*plural* adventures) 1 an exciting or dangerous experience. 2 willingness to take risks. **adventurer** *noun*, **adventurous** *adjective* [same origin as *advent*]

adverb *noun* (*plural* adverbs) a word that adds to the meaning of a verb or adjective or another adverb and tells how, when, or where something happens, e.g. *gently, soon,* and *upstairs.*
adverbial *adjective*, **adverbially** *adverb*

adversary (*say* ad-ver-ser-ee) *noun* (*plural* **adversaries**)
an opponent or enemy.

adverse *adjective*
unfavourable or harmful, *adverse effects*.
adversely *adverb*, **adversity** *noun*
[from Latin *adversus* = opposite, from *ad-* + *versus* = turned]

advert *noun* (*plural* **adverts**)
(*informal*) an advertisement.

advertise *verb* (**advertises, advertising, advertised**)
1 make something publicly known, *advertise a meeting*. 2 praise goods etc. in order to encourage people to buy or use them. 3 ask or offer by a public notice, *advertise for a secretary*. **advertiser** *noun*

advertisement *noun* (*plural* **advertisements**)
a public notice or announcement, especially one advertising goods or services in newspapers, on posters, or in broadcasts.

advice *noun*
1 telling a person what you think he or she should do. 2 a piece of information, *We received advice that the goods had been dispatched*.
[originally = opinion, point of view: from *ad-* + Latin *videre* = see]

USAGE: Do not confuse with the verb *advise*.

advisable *adjective*
that is the wise thing to do.
advisability *noun*

advise *verb* (**advises, advising, advised**)
1 give somebody advice; recommend. 2 inform.
adviser *noun*, **advisory** *adjective*

aerial *adjective*
1 in or from the air. 2 to do with aircraft.
aerial *noun* (*plural* **aerials**)
a wire or rod etc. for receiving or transmitting radio or television signals.

aero- *prefix*
to do with air or aircraft (as in *aeronautics*).
[from Greek *aer* = air]

aerobics *plural noun*
exercises to stimulate breathing and strengthen the heart and lungs. **aerobic** *adjective* [from *aero-* + Greek *bios* = life]

aerodrome *noun* (*plural* **aerodromes**)
an airfield. [from *aero-* + Greek *dromos* = running-track]

aerodynamic *adjective*
designed to move through the air quickly and easily.

aeronautics *noun*
the study of aircraft and flying.
aeronautic *adjective*, **aeronautical** *adjective*

aeroplane *noun* (*plural* **aeroplanes**)
a flying machine with wings.

aerosol *noun* (*plural* **aerosols**)
a container that holds a liquid under pressure and can let it out in a fine spray.
[from *aero-* + *solution*]

aesthetic (*say* iss-thet-ik) *adjective*
to do with the appreciation of beautiful things.
[from Greek *aisthesthai* = perceive]

af- *prefix*
to; towards. see **ad-**.

afar *adverb*
far away, *The din was heard from afar*.
[from *a-*[1] + *far*]

affair *noun* (*plural* **affairs**)
1 an event or matter, *The party was a grand affair*. 2 a temporary sexual relationship between two people who are not married to each other.
[from French *à faire* = to do]

affairs *plural noun*
the business and activities that are part of private or public life, *Keep out of my affairs*; *current affairs*.

affect *verb* (**affects, affecting, affected**)
1 have an effect on; influence. 2 pretend, *She affected ignorance*.
[from *af-* + Latin *facere* = do]

USAGE: The word *affect* is a verb. Do not confuse it with the noun *effect*.

affectation *noun* (*plural* **affectations**)
a pretence; behaviour that is put on for show and not natural.

affected *adjective*
pretended and unnatural.

affection *noun* (*plural* **affections**)
a strong liking for a person.

affectionate *adjective*
showing affection; loving. **affectionately** *adverb*
[from Latin *affectionatus* = devoted]

affirm *verb* (**affirms, affirming, affirmed**)
state something definitely or firmly.
affirmation *noun*

affirmative *adjective*
that says 'yes', *an affirmative reply*. (Compare *negative*.)

afflict *verb* (**afflicts, afflicting, afflicted**)
cause somebody to suffer, *He is afflicted with arthritis*. **affliction** *noun*

affluent (*say* af-loo-ent) *adjective*
rich. **affluence** *noun* [from Latin *affluens* = overflowing, from *af-* + *fluens* = flowing]

afford *verb* (**affords, affording, afforded**)
1 have enough money to pay for something. 2 have enough time or resources etc. to do something.

affront *verb* (**affronts, affronting, affronted**)
insult or offend someone.

affront noun (plural affronts)
an insult.

afloat adjective & adverb
floating; on the sea. [from a-^{1} + float]

afraid adjective
frightened or alarmed.
I'm afraid I regret, I'm afraid I'm late.
[past participle of an old word affray
= attack, frighten]

afresh adverb
again; in a new way, We must start afresh.
[from a-^{1} + fresh]

African adjective
to do with Africa or its people.
African noun (plural Africans)
an African person.

aft adverb
at or towards the back of a ship or aircraft.
[from Old English, related to after]

after preposition
1 later than, Come after tea. 2 behind in place
or order, Which letter comes after H? 3 trying to
catch; pursuing, Run after him. 4 in spite of, We
can come after all. 5 in imitation or honour of,
She is named after her aunt. 6 about or
concerning, He asked after you.
after adverb
1 behind, Jill came tumbling after. 2 later, It
came a week after. [from Old English]

afternoon noun (plural afternoons)
the time from noon or lunchtime to evening.

aftershave noun
a pleasant-smelling lotion that men put on
their skin after shaving.

afterwards adverb
at a later time. [from after + -wards]

ag- prefix
to; towards. see ad-.

again adverb
1 another time; once more, try again. 2 as
before, You will soon be well again. 3 besides;
moreover. [from Old English ongean = in the
opposite direction, back to the beginning]

against preposition
1 touching or hitting, He leant against the wall.
2 in opposition to; not in favour of, They voted
against the proposal. 3 in preparation for,
Protect them against the cold. [from again]

age noun (plural ages)
1 the length of time a person has lived or a
thing has existed. 2 a special period of history
or geology, the ice age.
ages plural noun (informal) a very long time,
We've been waiting for ages.
come of age reach the age at which you have an
adult's legal rights and obligations (now at 18
years; formerly 21).
age verb (ages, ageing, aged)
make or become old. [from old French]

aged adjective
1 (say ayjd) having the age of, a girl aged 9.
2 (say ay-jid) very old, an aged man.

agency noun (plural agencies)
1 the office or business of an agent, a travel
agency. 2 the means by which something is
done, Flowers are pollinated by the agency of
bees. [same origin as agent]

agenda (say a-jen-da) noun (plural agendas)
a list of things to be done or discussed, The
agenda is rather long.
[Latin, = things to be done]

agent noun (plural agents)
1 a person who organizes things for other
people. 2 a spy, a secret agent.
[from Latin agens = doing things]

aggravate verb (aggravates, aggravating,
aggravated)
1 make a thing worse or more serious.
2 annoy. **aggravation** noun

aggregate noun (plural aggregates)
a total amount or score.

aggression noun
starting an attack or war etc.; aggressive
behaviour. [from Latin aggredi = attack, from
ag- = against + gradi = step, move]

aggressive adjective
likely to attack people; forceful. **aggressively**
adverb, **aggressiveness** noun, **aggressor** noun

aggrieved (say a-greevd) adjective
resentful because of being treated unfairly.

aghast adjective
horrified. [from Old English]

agile adjective
moving quickly or easily. **agilely** adverb,
agility noun [from Latin agere = do]

agitate verb (agitates, agitating, agitated)
1 make someone feel upset or anxious. 2 stir
up public interest or concern; campaign, They
agitated for a new bypass. 3 shake something
about. **agitation** noun, **agitator** noun [from
Latin agitare = shake]

agnostic (say ag-nost-ik) noun (plural agnostics)
a person who believes that it is impossible to
know whether God exists. **agnosticism** noun
[from a-^{2} + Greek gnostikos = knowing]

ago adverb
in the past, long ago.
[from Middle English agone = gone by]

agog adjective
eager and excited.

agony noun (plural agonies)
extremely great pain or suffering.
agonizing adjective

agree verb (agrees, agreeing, agreed)
1 think or say the same as another person etc.
2 consent, She agreed to come. 3 suit a person's

health or digestion, *Curry doesn't agree with me.* **4** correspond in grammatical number, gender, or person. In 'They were good teachers', *they* agrees with *teachers* (both are plural forms) and *were* agrees with *they*; *was* would be incorrect because it is singular. [from old French]

agreeable *adjective*
1 willing, *We shall go if you are agreeable.* **2** pleasant, *an agreeable place.*
agreeably *adverb*

agreement *noun* (*plural* agreements)
1 agreeing. **2** an arrangement that people have agreed on.

agriculture *noun*
cultivating land on a large scale and rearing livestock; farming. **agricultural** *adjective*

aground *adverb* & *adjective*
stranded on the bottom in shallow water.

ahead *adverb*
1 further forward; in front. **2** forwards, *Full steam ahead!* [from *a-*¹ + *head*]

aid *noun* (*plural* aids)
1 help. **2** something that helps, *a hearing aid.* **3** money, food, etc. sent to another country to help it, *overseas aid.*
in aid of for the purpose of; to help something.
aid *verb* (aids, aiding, aided)
help. [from old French]

Aids *noun*
a disease that greatly weakens a person's ability to resist infections.
[from the initial letters of 'acquired immune deficiency syndrome']

ailing *adjective*
1 ill; in poor health. **2** in difficulties; not successful, *the ailing ship industry.*

ailment *noun* (*plural* ailments)
a slight illness.

aim *verb* (aims, aiming, aimed)
1 point a gun etc. in a particular direction. **2** throw or kick in a particular direction. **3** try or intend to do something.
aim *noun* (*plural* aims)
1 aiming a gun etc. **2** a purpose or intention. [via old French *amer* from Latin *aestimare* = estimate]

aimless *adjective*
without a purpose. **aimlessly** *adverb*

air *noun* (*plural* airs)
1 the mixture of gases that surrounds the earth and which everyone breathes. **2** the open space above the earth. **3** a tune or melody. **4** an appearance or impression of something, *an air of mystery.* **5** an impressive or haughty manner, *He puts on airs.*
by air in or by aircraft.
on the air on radio or television.

air *verb* (airs, airing, aired)
1 put clothes etc. in a warm place to finish drying. **2** ventilate a room. **3** express, *He aired his opinions.* [from old French]

air-conditioning *noun*
a system for controlling the temperature, purity, etc. of the air in a room or building.
air-conditioned *adjective*

aircraft *noun* (*plural* aircraft)
an aeroplane, glider, or helicopter etc.

aircraft carrier *noun* (*plural* aircraft carriers)
a large ship with a long deck where aircraft can take off and land.

airfield *noun* (*plural* airfields)
an area equipped with runways etc. where aircraft can take off and land.

air force (*plural* air forces)
the part of a country's armed forces that is equipped with aircraft.

airline *noun* (*plural* airlines)
a company that provides a regular service of transport by aircraft.

airliner *noun* (*plural* airliners)
a large aircraft for carrying passengers.

airlock *noun* (*plural* airlocks)
1 a compartment with an airtight door at each end, through which people can go in and out of a pressurized chamber. **2** a bubble of air that stops liquid flowing through a pipe.

airmail *noun*
mail carried by air.

airman *noun* (*plural* airmen)
a man who is a member of an air force or of the crew of an aircraft.

airport *noun* (*plural* airports)
an airfield for aircraft carrying passengers and goods.

air raid (*plural* air raids)
an attack by aircraft.

airstrip *noun* (*plural* airstrips)
a strip of ground prepared for aircraft to land and take off.

airtight *adjective*
not letting air in or out.

airy *adjective*
1 with plenty of fresh air. **2** light as air. **3** light-hearted and insincere, *airy promises.*
airily *adverb*

aisle (*say* I'll) *noun* (*plural* aisles)
1 a passage between or beside rows of seats or pews. **2** a side part of a church.

ajar *adverb* & *adjective*
slightly open, *Leave the door ajar.*
[literally = turned: from *a-*¹ + Old English *cerr* = a turn]

akin *adjective*
related or similar to, *a feeling akin to regret.*
[from Old English *a* = of, + *kin*]

al- *prefix*
to; towards. see **ad-**.

alarm *noun* (*plural* **alarms**)
1 a warning sound or signal; a piece of equipment for giving this. **2** a feeling of fear or worry. **3** an alarm clock.
alarm *verb* (**alarms, alarming, alarmed**)
make someone frightened or anxious.
alarming *adjective* [from Italian *all' arme!* = to arms!: compare this with *alert*]

alarm clock *noun* (*plural* **alarm clocks**)
a clock that can be set to make a sound at a fixed time to wake a sleeping person.

alas *interjection*
an exclamation of sorrow.

albatross *noun* (*plural* **albatrosses**)
a large seabird with very long wings.

albino (*say* al-**been**-oh) *noun* (*plural* **albinos**)
a person or animal with no colour in the skin and hair (which are white).

album *noun* (*plural* **albums**)
1 a book with blank pages in which to keep a collection of photographs, stamps, autographs, etc. **2** a collection of songs on a CD, record, or tape. [Latin, = white piece of stone etc. on which to write things]

alcohol *noun*
1 a colourless liquid made by fermenting sugar or starch. **2** drinks containing this liquid (e.g. wine, beer, whisky), that can make people drunk. [from Arabic]
alcoholic *adjective*
containing alcohol.
alcoholic *noun* (*plural* **alcoholics**)
a person who is seriously addicted to alcohol.
alcoholism *noun*

ale *noun* (*plural* **ales**)
beer. [from Old English]

alert *adjective*
watching for something; ready to act.
alertly *adverb*, **alertness** *noun*
alert *noun* (*plural* **alerts**)
a warning or alarm.
on the alert on the lookout; watchful.
alert *verb* (**alerts, alerting, alerted**)
warn someone of danger etc.; make someone aware of something.
[from Italian *all' erta!* = to the watchtower!: compare this with *alarm*]

A level *noun* (*plural* **A levels**)
advanced level in GCSE.

algae (*say* al-jee) *plural noun*
plants that grow in water, with no true stems or leaves. [Latin, = seaweed]

algebra (*say* al-jib-ra) *noun*
mathematics in which letters and symbols are used to represent quantities. **algebraic** (*say* al-jib-**ray**-ik) *adjective* [from Arabic *al-jabr* = putting together broken parts]

alias (*say* ay-lee-as) *noun* (*plural* **aliases**)
a false or different name.
alias *adverb*
also named, *Clark Kent, alias Superman.*

alibi (*say* al-ib-I) *noun* (*plural* **alibis**)
evidence that a person accused of a crime was somewhere else when it was committed.
[Latin, = at another place]

alien (*say* ay-lee-en) *noun* (*plural* **aliens**)
1 a person who is not a citizen of the country where he or she is living; a foreigner. **2** a being from another world.
alien *adjective*
1 foreign. **2** unnatural, *Cruelty is alien to her nature.* [from Latin *alius* = other]

alienate (*say* ay-lee-en-ayt) *verb* (**alienates, alienating, alienated**)
make a person become unfriendly or hostile.
alienation *noun*

alight *adjective*
1 on fire. **2** lit up. [from *a-*^{1} + *light*^{1}]

alike *adjective* & *adverb*
like one another; in the same way, *The twins are very alike. Treat them alike.*

alimony *noun*
money paid by someone to his or her wife or husband after they are separated or divorced; maintenance.
[from Latin *alimonia* = nourishment]

alive *adjective*
1 living. **2** alert, *Be alive to the possible dangers.*
[from Old English *on life* = in life]

alkali (*say* alk-al-I) *noun* (*plural* **alkalis**)
a substance that neutralizes acids.
alkaline *adjective*
[from Arabic *al-kali* = the ashes (because alkali was first obtained from the ashes of seaweed)]

all *adjective*
the whole number or amount of, *All my books are here; all day.*
all *noun*
1 everything, *That is all I know.* **2** everybody, *All are agreed.*
all *adverb*
1 completely, *She was dressed all in white.* **2** each team or competitor, *The score is fifteen all.*
all in (*informal*) exhausted, *I'm all in.*
all-in *adjective* including or allowing everything, *an all-in price.*
all there (*informal*) having an alert mind.
all the same in spite of this; making no difference, *I like him, all the same.*

Allah *noun*
the Muslim name of God.

allegation (*say* al-ig-**ay**-shon) *noun* (*plural* **allegations**)
a statement made without proof.

allege (*say* a-**lej**) *verb* (**alleges, alleging, alleged**)
say something without being able to prove it, *He alleged that I had cheated.* **allegedly** (*say* a-**lej**-id-lee) *adverb* [from old French]

allegiance (*say* a-**lee**-jans) *noun* (*plural* **allegiances**)
loyalty. [from old French; related to *liege*]

allegory (*say* **al**-ig-er-ee) *noun* (*plural* **allegories**)
a story in which the characters and events represent or symbolize a deeper meaning, e.g. to teach a moral lesson.
allegorical (*say* al-ig-o-**rik**-al) *adjective*

alleluia *interjection*
praise to God. [from Hebrew]

allergic *adjective*
very sensitive to something that may make you ill, *He is allergic to pollen, which gives him hay fever.* **allergy** (*say* **al**-er-jee) *noun*

alley *noun* (*plural* **alleys**)
1 a narrow street or passage. 2 a place where you can play bowls or skittles.
[from French *aller* = go]

alliance (*say* a-**leye**-ans) *noun* (*plural* **alliances**)
an association formed by countries or groups who wish to support each other.

allied *adjective*
1 joined as allies; on the same side. 2 of the same kind.

alligator *noun* (*plural* **alligators**)
a large reptile of the crocodile family. [from Spanish *el lagarto* = the lizard]

alliteration *noun*
having the same letter or sound at the beginning of several words, e.g. in *Sit in solemn silence.*
[from *al-* + Latin *littera* = letter]

allotment *noun* (*plural* **allotments**)
1 a small rented piece of public land used for growing vegetables, fruit, or flowers.
2 allotting; the amount allotted.

allow *verb* (**allows, allowing, allowed**)
1 permit, *Smoking is not allowed.* 2 permit someone to have something; provide with, *She was allowed £10 for books.* 3 agree, *I allow that you have been patient.* **allowable** *adjective* [from old French]

allowance *noun* (*plural* **allowances**)
an amount of money that is given regularly for a particular purpose.
make allowances be considerate; excuse, *Make allowances for his age.*

alloy *noun* (*plural* **alloys**)
a metal formed by mixing two or more metals etc.

all right *adjective* & *adverb*
1 satisfactory. 2 in good condition. 3 as desired. 4 yes, I consent.

all-round *adjective*
general; not specialist, *an all-round athlete.* **all-rounder** *noun*

allure *verb* (**allures, alluring, allured**)
attract or fascinate someone.
allure *noun*, **alluring** *adjective*
[from old French; related to *lure*]

ally (*say* **al**-eye) *noun* (*plural* **allies**)
1 a country in alliance with another.
2 a person who cooperates with another.
ally *verb* (**allies, allying, allied**)
form an alliance.
[from *al-* + Latin *ligare* = bind]

almighty *adjective*
1 having complete power. 2 (*informal*) very great, *an almighty din.*

almond (*say* **ah**-mond) *noun* (*plural* **almonds**)
an oval edible nut. [from Greek]

almost *adverb*
near to being something but not quite, *almost ready.* [from Old English]

alone *adjective*
without any other people or things; without help. [from *all one*]

along *preposition*
following the length of something, *Walk along the path.*
along *adverb*
1 on or onwards, *Push it along.*
2 accompanying somebody, *I've brought my brother along.* [from Old English]

alongside *preposition* & *adverb*
next to something; beside.

aloof *adverb*
apart; not taking part, *We stayed aloof from their quarrels.*
aloof *adjective*
distant and not friendly in manner, *She seemed aloof.* [from old French]

aloud *adverb*
in a voice that can be heard.
[from a^{-1} + *loud*]

alpha *noun*
the first letter of the Greek alphabet, = a.

alphabet *noun* (*plural* **alphabets**)
the letters used in a language, usually arranged in a set order. **alphabetical** *adjective*, **alphabetically** *adverb*
[from *alpha*, *beta*, the first two letters of the Greek alphabet]

already *adverb*
by now; before now. [from *all* + *ready*]

Alsatian (*say* al-**say**-shan) *noun* (*plural* **Alsatians**)
a German shepherd dog.
[from *Alsace*, in north-eastern France: the

name was adopted during the First World War, when British people disliked anything that was German]

also *adverb*
in addition; besides.

altar *noun* (*plural* **altars**)
a table or similar structure used in religious ceremonies.

USAGE: Do not confuse with the verb *alter*.

alter *verb* (**alters, altering, altered**)
make or become different; change.
alteration *noun*

USAGE: Do not confuse with the noun *altar*.

alternate (*say* ol-tern-at) *adjective*
1 happening or coming one after the other, *alternate layers of sponge and cream.* 2 one in every two, *We meet up on alternate Fridays.*
alternately *adverb*

USAGE: See the note at *alternative.*

alternate (*say* ol-tern-ayt) *verb* (**alternates, alternating, alternated**)
use or come alternately. **alternation** *noun*, **alternator** *noun* [from Latin *alternus* = every other one, from *alter* = other]

alternating current *noun* (*plural* **alternating currents**)
electric current that keeps reversing its direction at regular intervals.

alternative *adjective*
available instead of something else.
alternatively *adverb*

USAGE: Do not confuse *alternative* with *alternate*. If there are *alternative colours* it means that there is a choice of two or more colours, but *alternate colours* means that there is first one colour and then the other.

alternative *noun* (*plural* **alternatives**)
one of two or more possibilities.
no alternative no choice.

alternative medicine *noun*
types of medical treatment that are not based on ordinary medicine.

although *conjunction*
though. [from *all* + *though*]

altitude *noun* (*plural* **altitudes**)
the height of something, especially above sea level. [from Latin *altus* = high]

alto *noun* (*plural* **altos**)
1 an adult male singer with a very high voice. 2 a contralto. [Italian, = high]

altogether *adverb*
1 with all included; in total, *The outfit costs £20 altogether.* 2 completely, *The stream dries up*

altogether in summer. 3 on the whole, *Altogether, it was a good concert.*

USAGE: Do not confuse *altogether* and *all together.*

aluminium *noun*
a lightweight silver-coloured metal.

always *adverb*
1 at all times. 2 often, *You are always crying.* 3 whatever happens, *You can always sleep on the floor.*

Alzheimer's disease *noun*
a serious disease of the brain which affects some old people and makes them confused and forgetful.

a.m. *abbreviation*
ante meridiem [Latin, = before noon]

amalgamate *verb* (**amalgamates, amalgamating, amalgamated**)
mix or combine. **amalgamation** *noun* [from Latin]

amateur (*say* am-at-er) *noun* (*plural* **amateurs**)
a person who does something as a hobby, not as a professional. **amateurish** *adjective* [from Latin *amator* = lover]

amaze *verb* (**amazes, amazing, amazed**)
surprise somebody greatly; fill with wonder.
amazement *noun*

amazing *adjective*
very surprising or remarkable.

ambassador *noun* (*plural* **ambassadors**)
a person sent to a foreign country to represent his or her own government. [from old French; related to *embassy*]

amber *noun*
1 a hard clear yellowish substance used for making ornaments. 2 a yellow traffic light shown as a signal for caution, placed between red (= stop) and green (= go).

ambi- *prefix*
both; on both sides (as in *ambidextrous*). [from Latin *ambo* = both]

ambidextrous *adjective*
able to use either your left hand or your right hand equally well. [from *ambi-* + *dextrous* = skilful (related to *dexterity*)]

ambiguous *adjective*
having more than one possible meaning; unclear. **ambiguously** *adverb*, **ambiguity** *noun* [from Latin *ambiguus* = doubtful, shifting, from *ambi-* + *agere* = drive, go]

ambition *noun* (*plural* **ambitions**)
1 a strong desire to achieve something. 2 the thing desired.
[from Latin *ambire* = go around, especially to persuade people to vote for you]

ambitious *adjective*
full of ambition.

ambivalent

ambivalent (*say* am-biv-al-ent) *adjective*
having mixed feelings about something (e.g.
liking and disliking it). **ambivalence** *noun*
[from *ambi-* + Latin *valens* = strong]

amble *verb* (ambles, ambling, ambled)
walk at a slow easy pace.

ambulance *noun* (*plural* ambulances)
a vehicle equipped to carry sick or injured
people. [from French *hôpital ambulant*, a
mobile military hospital; from Latin *ambulare*
= walk]

ambush *noun* (*plural* ambushes)
a surprise attack from troops etc. who have
concealed themselves.
ambush *verb* (ambushes, ambushing, ambushed)
attack someone after lying in wait for them.
[from old French]

amen *interjection*
a word used at the end of a prayer or hymn,
meaning 'may it be so'.
[Hebrew, = certainly]

amend *verb* (amends, amending, amended)
alter something in order to improve it.
make amends make up for having done
something wrong; atone. **amendment** *noun*

American *adjective*
1 to do with the continent of America. **2** to do
with the United States of America.
American *noun*

amino acid (*say* a-**meen**-oh) *noun* (*plural* amino
acids)
an acid found in proteins. [from *ammonia*,
because the amino acids contain the same
group of atoms as ammonia]

amiss *adjective*
wrong or faulty, *She knew something was
amiss.*

ammonia *noun*
a colourless gas or liquid with a strong smell.
[from Latin]

ammunition *noun*
a supply of bullets, shells, grenades, etc. for use
in fighting. [from French *la munition*, wrongly
taken as *l'ammunition*]

amnesia (*say* am-**nee**-zee-a) *noun*
loss of memory.
[from Greek *a-* = without, + *-mnesis* = memory]

amnesty *noun* (*plural* amnesties)
a general pardon for people who have
committed a crime.

amoeba (*say* a-**mee**-ba) *noun* (*plural* amoebas)
a microscopic creature consisting of a single
cell which constantly changes shape. [from
Greek *amoibe* = change]

among or **amongst** *preposition*
1 surrounded by; in, *There were weeds among
the flowers.* **2** between, *Divide the sweets among
the children.*

amount *noun* (*plural* amounts)
1 a quantity. **2** a total.
amount *verb* (amounts, amounting, amounted)
amount to 1 add up to. **2** be equivalent to, *Their
reply amounts to a refusal.*
[from Latin *ad montem* = to the mountain,
upwards]

amp *noun* (*plural* amps)
1 an ampere. **2** (*informal*) an amplifier.

ampere (*say* am-pair) *noun* (*plural* amperes)
a unit for measuring electric current.

amphi- *prefix*
both; on both sides; in both places (as in
amphibian). [from Greek *amphi* = around]

amphibian *noun* (*plural* amphibians)
1 an amphibious animal; an animal (e.g. a frog)
that at first (as a tadpole) has gills and lives in
water but later develops lungs and breathes
air. **2** an amphibious aircraft or tank etc. [from
amphi- + Greek *bios* = life]

amphibious *adjective*
able to live or move both on land and in water.

ample *adjective*
1 quite enough, *ample provisions.* **2** large.
amply *adverb*
[from Latin *amplus* = large, plentiful]

amplifier *noun* (*plural* amplifiers)
a piece of equipment for making a sound or
electrical signal louder or stronger.

amplify *verb* (amplifies, amplifying, amplified)
1 make a sound or electrical signal louder or
stronger. **2** give more details about something,
Could you amplify that point?

amplitude *noun*
1 the strength of a sound wave or electronic
signal. **2** largeness or abundance.

amputate *verb* (amputates, amputating,
amputated)
cut off an arm or leg by a surgical operation.
amputation *noun* [from Latin *amb-* = around +
putare cut off, prune]

amuse *verb* (amuses, amusing, amused)
1 make a person laugh or smile. **2** make time
pass pleasantly for someone. **amusing** *adjective*

amusement *noun* (*plural* amusements)
1 being amused. **2** a way of passing time
pleasantly.

an *adjective* see **a**.

an-¹ *prefix*
not; without. see **a-**².

an-² *prefix*
to; towards. see **ad-**.

ana- *prefix*
up; back (as in *analysis*).
[Greek, = up]

anachronism (*say* an-**ak**-ron-izm) *noun* (*plural* **anachronisms**)
something wrongly placed in a particular historical period, or regarded as out of date, *Bows and arrows would be an anachronism in modern warfare.*
[from *ana-* + Greek *chronos* = time]

anaemia (*say* a-**nee**-mee-a) *noun*
a poor condition of the blood that makes a person pale. **anaemic** *adjective*
[from *an-*¹ + Greek *haima* = blood]

anaesthetic (*say* an-iss-**thet**-ik) *noun* (*plural* **anaesthetics**)
a substance or gas that makes you unable to feel pain. **anaesthesia** *noun*
[from *an-*¹ + Greek *aisthesis* = sensation]

anaesthetist (*say* an-**ees**-thet-ist) *noun* (*plural* **anaesthetists**)
a person trained to give anaesthetics. **anaesthetize** *verb*

anagram *noun* (*plural* **anagrams**)
a word or phrase made by rearranging the letters of another, *'Trap' is an anagram of 'part'.*

anal (*say* **ay**-nal) *adjective*
to do with the anus.

analogy (*say* a-**nal**-oj-ee) *noun* (*plural* **analogies**)
comparing two things that are alike in some ways, *the analogy between the human heart and a pump.* **analogous** *adjective*

analyse *verb* (**analyses, analysing, analysed**)
1 separate something into its parts. 2 examine and interpret something, *analyse the causes.*

analysis *noun* (*plural* **analyses**)
1 a separation of something into its parts. 2 a detailed examination of something.
analytic *adjective*, **analytical** *adjective*
[from Greek, = dissolving, loosening]

anarchist (*say* **an**-er-kist) *noun* (*plural* **anarchists**)
a person who believes that all forms of government are bad and should be abolished.

anarchy (*say* **an**-er-kee) *noun*
1 lack of government or control, resulting in lawlessness. 2 complete disorder.
[from *an-*¹ + *-archy*]

anatomy (*say* an-**at**-om-ee) *noun*
the study of the structure of the bodies of humans or animals. **anatomical** *adjective*, **anatomist** *noun*
[from *ana-* + Greek *tome* = cutting]

ancestor *noun* (*plural* **ancestors**)
anyone from whom a person is descended.
ancestral *adjective*, **ancestry** *noun*
[from Latin, literally = one who goes before]

anchor *noun* (*plural* **anchors**)
a heavy object joined to a ship by a chain or rope and dropped to the bottom of the sea to stop the ship from moving.
anchor *verb* (**anchors, anchoring, anchored**)
1 fix or be fixed by an anchor. 2 fix something firmly. [from Latin]

ancient *adjective*
1 very old. 2 belonging to the distant past, *ancient history.* [from old French]

and *conjunction*
1 together with; in addition to, *We had cakes and buns.* 2 so that; with this result, *Work hard and you will pass.* 3 to, *Go and buy a pen.* [from Old English]

anecdote *noun* (*plural* **anecdotes**)
a short amusing or interesting story about a real person or thing.
[from Greek *anekdota* = things that have not been published]

angel *noun* (*plural* **angels**)
1 an attendant or messenger of God. 2 a very kind or beautiful person.
angelic (*say* an-**jel**-ik) *adjective*
[from Greek *angelos* = messenger]

anger *noun*
a strong feeling that makes you want to quarrel or fight.
anger *verb* (**angers, angering, angered**)
make a person angry. [from Old Norse]

angle *noun* (*plural* **angles**)
1 the space between two lines or surfaces that meet; the amount by which a line or surface must be turned to make it lie along another. 2 a point of view.
angle *verb* (**angles, angling, angled**)
1 put something in a slanting position. 2 present news etc. from one point of view.
[from Latin *angulus* = corner]

angler *noun* (*plural* **anglers**)
a person who fishes with a fishing rod and line.
angling *noun*
[from Old English *angul* = fishing-hook]

Anglican *adjective*
to do with the Church of England.
Anglican *noun*

Anglo-Saxon *noun* (*plural* **Anglo-Saxons**)
1 an English person, especially of the time before the Norman conquest in 1066. 2 'Old English'. [from Old English *Angulseaxe* = an English Saxon (contrasted with the Old Saxons on the Continent)]

angry *adjective* (**angrier, angriest**)
feeling anger. **angrily** *adverb*

angular *adjective*
1 having angles or sharp corners. 2 (of a person) bony, not plump.

animal *noun* (*plural* **animals**)
1 a living thing that can feel and usually move about, *Horses, birds, fish, bees, and people are all animals.* 2 a brutish person; someone not worthy of being called human.

animate *verb* (**animates, animating, animated**)
1 make a thing lively. 2 produce something as an animated cartoon.
animation *noun*, **animator** *noun*

ankle *noun* (*plural* **ankles**)
the part of the leg where it joins the foot.

annihilate (*say* an-l-il-ayt) *verb* (**annihilates, annihilating, annihilated**)
destroy something completely.
annihilation *noun*
[from *an-*² + Latin *nihil* = nothing]

anniversary *noun* (*plural* **anniversaries**)
a day when you remember something special that happened on the same day in a previous year.

announce *verb* (**announces, announcing, announced**)
make something known, especially by saying it publicly or to an audience.
announcement *noun*, **announcer** *noun*
[from *an-*² + Latin *nuntius* = messenger]

annoy *verb* (**annoys, annoying, annoyed**)
1 make a person slightly angry. 2 be troublesome to someone. **annoyance** *noun*
[from Latin *in odio* = hateful]

annual *adjective*
1 happening or done once a year, *her annual visit.* 2 calculated over one year, *our annual income.* 3 living for one year or one season, *an annual plant.* **annually** *adverb*
annual *noun* (*plural* **annuals**)
1 a book that comes out once a year. 2 an annual plant. [from Latin *annus* = year]

anode *noun* (*plural* **anodes**)
the electrode by which electric current enters a device. (Compare *cathode.*)
[from *ana-* = up + Greek *hodos* = way]

anoint *verb* (**anoints, anointing, anointed**)
put oil or ointment on something, especially in a religious ceremony.

anon *adverb* (*old use*)
soon, *I will say more about this anon.*
[from Old English *on ane* = in one, at once]

anon. *abbreviation*
anonymous.

anonymous (*say* an-on-im-us) *adjective*
without the name of the person responsible being known or made public, *an anonymous donor.* **anonymously** *adverb*, **anonymity** (*say* an-on-im-it-ee) *noun*
[from *an-*¹ + Greek *onyma* = name]

anorak *noun* (*plural* **anoraks**)
a thick warm jacket with a hood.
[from an Eskimo word]

anorexia (*say* an-er-**eks**-ee-a) *noun*
an illness that makes a person so anxious to lose weight that he or she refuses to eat.
anorexic *adjective*

another *adjective* & *pronoun*
a different or extra person or thing, *another day; choose another.*

answer *noun* (*plural* **answers**)
1 a reply. 2 the solution to a problem.
answer *verb* (**answers, answering, answered**)
1 give or find an answer to; reply. 2 respond to a signal, *Answer the telephone.*
answer back reply cheekily.
answer for be responsible for.
answer to correspond to, *This answers to the description of the stolen bag.*

ant *noun* (*plural* **ants**)
a very small insect that lives as one of an organized group. [from Old English]

ant- *prefix*
against; preventing. see **anti-**.

antagonism (*say* an-**tag**-on-izm) *noun*
an unfriendly feeling; hostility.
antagonist *noun*, **antagonistic** *adjective*

antagonize *verb* (**antagonizes, antagonizing, antagonized**)
make a person feel hostile or angry.

ante- *prefix*
before (as in *ante-room*). [from Latin]

antelope *noun* (*plural* **antelope** or **antelopes**)
an animal like a deer. [from Greek]

antenatal (*say* an-tee-**nay**-tal) *adjective*
before birth; during pregnancy.

antenna *noun*
1 (*plural* **antennae**) a feeler on the head of an insect or crustacean. 2 (*plural* **antennas**) an aerial. [Latin]

anthem *noun* (*plural* **anthems**)
a religious or patriotic song, usually sung by a choir or group of people. [from Latin]

anthology *noun* (*plural* **anthologies**)
a collection of poems, stories, songs, etc. in one book. [from Greek *anthos* = flower + *-logia* = collection]

anthropoid *adjective*
like a human being, *Gorillas are anthropoid apes.*
[from Greek *anthropos* = human being]

anthropology *noun*
the study of human beings and their customs.
anthropological *adjective*, **anthropologist** *noun*

anti- *prefix* (changing to **ant-** before a vowel)
against; preventing (as in *antifreeze*).
[from Greek *anti* = against]

antibiotic *noun* (*plural* **antibiotics**)
a substance (e.g. penicillin) that destroys bacteria or prevents them from growing.

antibody *noun* (*plural* **antibodies**)
a protein that forms in the blood as a defence against certain substances which it then attacks and destroys.
[from *anti-* + *body* (sense 5)]

anticipate *verb* (anticipates, anticipating, anticipated)
1 do something before the proper time or before someone else, *Others may have anticipated Columbus in discovering America.*
2 foresee, *They had anticipated our needs.*
3 expect, *We anticipate that it will rain.*
anticipation *noun*, **anticipatory** *adjective* [from *ante-* + Latin *capere* = take]

USAGE: Many people regard use 3 as incorrect; it is better to avoid it and use 'expect'.

anticlimax *noun* (*plural* **anticlimaxes**)
a disappointing ending or result where something exciting had been expected.

anticlockwise *adverb* & *adjective*
moving in the direction opposite to clockwise.

antics *plural noun*
funny or foolish actions.

anticyclone *noun* (*plural* **anticyclones**)
an area where air pressure is high, usually producing fine settled weather.
[from *anti-* + *cyclone*, because the pressure at the centre of a cyclone is low]

antidote *noun* (*plural* **antidotes**)
something that acts against the effects of a poison or disease.
[from *anti-* + Greek *dotos* = given]

antifreeze *noun*
a liquid added to water to make it less likely to freeze.

antihistamine *noun* (*plural* **antihistamines**)
a drug that protects people against unpleasant effects when they are allergic to something.

antimony *noun*
a brittle silvery metal. [from Latin]

antiquarian (*say* anti-kwair-ee-an) *adjective*
to do with the study of antiques.

antiquated *adjective*
old-fashioned.

antique (*say* an-teek) *adjective*
very old; belonging to the distant past.
antique *noun* (*plural* **antiques**)
something that is valuable because it is very old. [from Latin *antiquus* = ancient, from *ante* = before]

antiquity (*say* an-tik-wit-ee) *noun*
ancient times.

anti-Semitic (*say* anti-sim-it-ik) *adjective*
unfriendly or hostile towards Jews.
anti-Semitism (*say* anti-sem-it-izm) *noun*

antiseptic *adjective*
1 able to destroy bacteria, especially those that cause things to become septic or to decay.
2 thoroughly clean and free from germs.
antiseptic *noun* (*plural* **antiseptics**)
a substance with an antiseptic effect.

antisocial *adjective*
unfriendly or inconsiderate towards other people.

antler *noun* (*plural* **antlers**)
the branching horn of a deer.

anus (*say* ay-nus) *noun* (*plural* **anuses**)
the opening at the lower end of the alimentary canal, through which solid waste matter is passed out of the body.

anvil *noun* (*plural* **anvils**)
a large block of iron on which a blacksmith hammers metal into shape.

anxious *adjective*
1 worried. 2 eager, *She is anxious to please us.*
anxiously *adverb*, **anxiety** *noun*

any *adjective* & *pronoun*
1 one or some, *Have you any wool? There isn't any.* 2 no matter which, *Come any day you like.*
3 every, *Any fool knows that!*
any *adverb*
at all; in some degree, *Is that any better?*

anybody *noun* & *pronoun*
any person.

anyhow *adverb*
1 anyway. 2 (*informal*) carelessly, *He does his work anyhow.*

anyone *noun* & *pronoun*
anybody.

anything *noun* & *pronoun*
any thing.

anyway *adverb*
whatever happens; whatever the situation may be.

anywhere *adverb*
in or to any place.
anywhere *pronoun*
any place, *Anywhere will do.*

aorta (*say* ay-or-ta) *noun* (*plural* **aortas**)
the main artery that carries blood away from the left side of the heart. [from Greek]

ap-¹ *prefix*
to; towards. see **ad-**.

ap-² *prefix*
from; out or away. see **apo-**.

apart *adverb*
1 away from each other; separately, *Keep your desks apart.* 2 into pieces, *It fell apart.*
3 excluded, *Joking apart, what do you think of it?* [from French *à* = to + *part* = side]

apartheid (*say* a-part-hayt) *noun*
the political policy that used to be practised in South Africa, of keeping people of different races apart.
[Afrikaans, = being apart]

apartment *noun* (*plural* **apartments**)
1 a set of rooms. 2 (*American*) a flat.

apathy (*say* ap-ath-ee) *noun*
lack of interest or concern. **apathetic** (*say* ap-a-thet-ik) *adjective*
[from *a-*² + Greek *pathos* = feeling]

ape *noun* (*plural* **apes**)
any of the four kinds of monkey (gorillas, chimpanzees, orang-utans, gibbons) that do not have a tail.
ape *verb* (**apes, aping, aped**)
imitate or mimic. [from Old English]

aperture *noun* (*plural* **apertures**)
an opening. [from Latin *aperire* = to open]

apex (*say* ay-peks) *noun* (*plural* **apexes**)
the tip or highest point. [Latin]

aplomb (*say* a-plom) *noun*
dignity and confidence, *She handled the press conference with aplomb.*
[from French = straight as a plumb line]

apo- *prefix* (changing to **ap-** before a vowel or h)
from; out or away (as in *Apostle*).
[from Greek *apo* = away from]

apologetic *adjective*
making an apology. **apologetically** *adverb*

apologize *verb* (**apologizes, apologizing, apologized**)
make an apology.

apology *noun* (*plural* **apologies**)
1 a statement saying that you are sorry for having done something wrong or badly.
2 something very poor, *this feeble apology for a meal.*

apoplexy (*say* ap-op-lek-see) *noun*
1 sudden loss of the ability to feel and move, caused by the blocking or breaking of a blood vessel in the brain. 2 (*informal*) rage or anger.
apoplectic *adjective*

Apostle *noun* (*plural* **Apostles**)
any of the twelve men sent out by Christ to preach the Gospel.
[from Greek *apostellein* = send out]

apostrophe (*say* a-poss-trof-ee) *noun* (*plural* **apostrophes**)
the punctuation mark ' used to show that letters have been missed out (as in *I can't* = I cannot) or to show possession (as in *the boy's book*; *the boys' books*).

appalling *adjective*
shocking; very unpleasant.
[from old French *apalir* = become pale]

apparatus *noun*
the equipment for a particular experiment or job etc.
[from Latin *apparare* = prepare, get ready]

apparent *adjective*
1 clear or obvious, *His embarrassment was apparent to everyone.* 2 seeming; appearing to be true but not really so, *I could not understand her apparent indifference.* **apparently** *adverb*
[same origin as *appear*]

apparition *noun* (*plural* **apparitions**)
1 a ghost. 2 something strange or surprising that appears.

appeal *verb* (**appeals, appealing, appealed**)
1 ask for something earnestly or formally, *They appealed for funds.* 2 ask for a decision to be changed, *He appealed against the prison sentence.* 3 seem attractive or interesting, *Cricket doesn't appeal to me.*
appeal *noun* (*plural* **appeals**)
1 the action of appealing for something or about a decision; an earnest or formal request. 2 attraction or interest.

appear *verb* (**appears, appearing, appeared**)
1 come into sight. 2 seem. 3 take part in a play, film, or show etc.
[from *ap-*¹ + Latin *parere* = come into]

appearance *noun* (*plural* **appearances**)
1 appearing. 2 what somebody looks like; what something appears to be.

appease *verb* (**appeases, appeasing, appeased**)
calm or pacify someone, especially by giving in to demands. **appeasement** *noun* [from French *à* = to + *paix* = peace]

appendage *noun* (*plural* **appendages**)
something added or attached; a thing that forms a natural part of something larger.
[from *ap-*¹ + Latin *pendere* = hang]

appendicitis *noun*
inflammation of the appendix.

appendix *noun*
1 (*plural* **appendixes**) a small tube leading off from the intestine. 2 (*plural* **appendices**) a section added at the end of a book. [same origin as *appendage*]

appetite *noun* (*plural* **appetites**)
1 desire for food. 2 an enthusiasm for something, *an appetite for violent films.* [from *ap-*¹ + Latin *petere* = seek]

appetizing *adjective*
(of food) looking and smelling good to eat.

applaud *verb* (**applauds, applauding, applauded**)
show that you like something, especially by clapping your hands.

applause *noun*
clapping.

apple *noun* (*plural* **apples**)
a round fruit with a red, yellow, or green skin.

appliance noun (plural appliances)
a device or piece of equipment, electrical appliances. [from apply]

applicable (say ap-lik-a-bul) adjective
able to be applied; suitable or relevant.

applicant noun (plural applicants)
a person who applies for a job or position.

application noun (plural applications)
1 the action of applying. 2 a formal request. 3 the ability to apply yourself.

applied adjective
put to practical use, applied maths.

apply verb (applies, applying, applied)
1 put one thing on another. 2 start using something. 3 concern; be relevant, This rule does not apply to you. 4 make a formal request, apply for a job.
apply yourself give all your attention to a job; work diligently.
[from ap-^{1} + Latin plicare = to fold]

appoint verb (appoints, appointing, appointed)
1 choose a person for a job. 2 arrange something officially, They appointed a time for the meeting. [from old French]

appointment noun (plural appointments)
1 an arrangement to meet or visit somebody at a particular time. 2 choosing somebody for a job. 3 a job or position.

apposition noun
placing things together, especially nouns and phrases in a grammatical relationship. In the reign of Elizabeth, our Queen, 'our Queen' is in apposition to 'Elizabeth'.

appreciable adjective
enough to be noticed or felt; perceptible.
appreciably adverb

appreciate verb (appreciates, appreciating, appreciated)
1 enjoy or value something. 2 understand. 3 increase in value. **appreciation** noun, **appreciative** adjective

apprehend verb (apprehends, apprehending, apprehended)
1 seize or arrest someone. 2 understand. 3 expect something with fear or worry. [from ap-^{1} + Latin prehendere = to grasp]

apprehension noun
1 fear or worry. 2 understanding. 3 the arrest of a person.

apprehensive adjective
anxious or worried.

apprentice noun (plural apprentices)
a person who is learning a trade or craft by a legal agreement with an employer.
apprenticeship noun

apprentice verb (apprentices, apprenticing, apprenticed)
place a person as an apprentice.
[from French apprendre = learn]

approach verb (approaches, approaching, approached)
1 come near. 2 go to someone with a request or offer, They approached me for help. 3 set about doing something or tackling a problem.
approach noun (plural approaches)
1 approaching. 2 a way or road.

appropriate (say a-proh-pree-at) adjective
suitable. **appropriately** adverb
appropriate (say a-proh-pree-ayt) verb
(appropriates, appropriating, appropriated)
take something and use it as your own.
appropriation noun

approval noun
approving somebody or something.
on approval received by a customer to examine before deciding to buy.

approve verb (approves, approving, approved)
say or think that a person or thing is good or suitable.
[from ap-^{1} + Latin probus = good]

approximate (say a-proks-im-at) adjective
almost exact or correct but not completely so.
approximately adverb
approximate (say a-proks-im-ayt) verb
(approximates, approximating, approximated)
make or be almost the same as something.
[from ap-^{1} + Latin proximus = very near]

apricot noun (plural apricots)
a juicy orange-coloured fruit with a stone in it. [from Spanish or Portuguese]

apron noun (plural aprons)
1 a piece of clothing worn over the front of the body, especially to protect other clothes. 2 a hard-surfaced area on an airfield where aircraft are loaded and unloaded. [originally a naperon, from French nappe = tablecloth]

apt adjective
1 likely, He is apt to be careless. 2 suitable, an apt quotation. **aptly** adverb, **aptness** noun

aptitude noun
a talent or skill, an aptitude for languages.

aquarium noun (plural aquariums)
a tank or building in which live fish and other water animals are displayed.
[from Latin aquarius = of water]

aquatic adjective
to do with water, aquatic sports.

aqueduct noun (plural aqueducts)
a bridge carrying a water-channel across low ground or a valley. [from Latin aqua = water + ducere = to lead]

ar- prefix
to; towards. see ad-.

Arab *noun* (*plural* **Arabs**)
a member of a people living in Arabia and
other parts of the Middle East and North
Africa. **Arabian** *adjective*
Arabic *adjective*
to do with the Arabs or their language.
Arabic *noun*
the language of the Arabs.

arabic numerals *plural noun*
the symbols 1, 2, 3, 4, etc. (Compare *Roman
numerals*.)

arable *adjective*
suitable for ploughing or growing crops on,
arable land. [from Latin *arare* = to plough]

arbitrary (*say* **ar**-bit-rer-ee) *adjective*
chosen or done on an impulse, not according to
a rule or law, *an arbitrary decision*.
arbitrarily *adverb*
[originally = according to a judge's decision,
not according to rules]

arbitration *noun*
settling a dispute by calling in someone from
outside to make a decision. **arbitrate** *verb*,
arbitrator *noun*
[from Latin *arbitrari* = to judge]

arbour (*say* ar-ber) *noun* (*plural* **arbours**)
a shady place among trees.

arc *noun* (*plural* **arcs**)
1 a curve; part of the circumference of a circle.
2 a luminous electric current passing between
two electrodes.

arcade *noun* (*plural* **arcades**)
a covered passage or area, especially for
shopping.
[French or Italian, from Latin *arcus* = curve
(because early arcades had curved roofs)]

arch[1] *noun* (*plural* **arches**)
1 a curved structure that helps to support a
bridge or other building etc. 2 something
shaped like this.
arch *verb* (**arches, arching, arched**)
form something into an arch; curve, *The cat
arched its back and hissed.*

arch[2] *adjective*
pretending to be playful; mischievous, *an arch
smile.* **archly** *adverb*
[from Greek *archos* = a chief]

arch- *prefix*
chief or principal (as in *arch-enemy*).

-arch and **-archy** *suffixes*
form nouns meaning 'ruler' or 'rule, ruling'
(e.g. *monarch, monarchy*).
[from Greek *archein* = to rule]

archaeology (*say* ar-kee-ol-oj-ee) *noun*
the study of the remains of ancient
civilizations. **archaeological** *adjective*,
archaeologist *noun*
[from Greek *archaios* = old, + *-logy*]

archaic (*say* ar-kay-ik) *adjective*
belonging to former or ancient times.
[from Greek *arche* = beginning]

archangel *noun* (*plural* **archangels**)
an angel of the highest rank.

archbishop *noun* (*plural* **archbishops**)
the chief bishop of a province of the Church.

arch-enemy *noun* (*plural* **arch-enemies**)
the chief enemy.

archer *noun* (*plural* **archers**)
a person who shoots with a bow and arrows.

archery *noun*
the sport of shooting at a target with a
bow and arrows.

archetype (*say* ark-i-typ) *noun* (*plural*
archetypes)
the original form or model from which others
are copied. [from *arch-* + *type*]

archipelago (*say* ark-i-pel-ag-oh) *noun* (*plural*
archipelagos)
a large group of islands, or the sea containing
these.

architect (*say* ark-i-tekt) *noun* (*plural* **architects**)
a person who designs buildings.
[from *arch-* + Greek *tekton* = builder]

architecture *noun*
1 the process of designing buildings. 2 a
particular style of building, *Elizabethan
architecture.* **architectural** *adjective*

archives (*say* ark-I'vz) *plural noun*
the historical documents etc. of an
organization or community.
[from Greek *archeia* = public records]

archway *noun* (*plural* **archways**)
an arched passage or entrance.

arc lamp or **arc light** *noun* (*plural* **arc lamps, arc
lights**)
a light using an electric arc.

arctic *adjective*
very cold, *The weather was arctic.* [from the
Arctic, the area round the North Pole]

ardour (*say* ar-der) *noun*
enthusiasm or passion.
[from old French]

arduous *adjective*
needing much effort; laborious. **arduously**
adverb [from Latin *arduus* = steep]

area *noun* (*plural* **areas**)
1 the extent or measurement of a surface. 2 a
particular region or piece of land.
3 a subject or activity.

arena (*say* a-reen-a) *noun* (*plural* **arenas**)
the level area in the centre of an amphitheatre
or sports stadium.
[Latin, = sand (because the floors of Roman
arenas were covered with sand)]

aren't (*mainly spoken*)
are not.
aren't I? (*informal*) am I not?

argue *verb* (**argues, arguing, argued**)
1 say that you disagree; exchange angry comments. 2 state that something is true and give reasons. [from Latin]

argument *noun* (*plural* **arguments**)
1 a disagreement or quarrel. 2 a reason or series of reasons put forward.

argumentative *adjective*
fond of arguing.

aria (*say* ar-ee-a) *noun* (*plural* **arias**)
a solo in an opera or oratorio.

-arian *suffix*
forms nouns and adjectives (e.g. *vegetarian*) showing members of a group.

arid *adjective*
dry and barren. [from Latin]

arise *verb* (**arises, arising, arose, arisen**)
1 come into existence; come to people's notice, *Problems arose.* 2 (*old use*) rise; stand up, *Arise, Sir Francis.*

aristocracy (*say* a-ris-tok-ra-see) *noun*
people of the highest social rank; members of the nobility.
[from Greek *aristos* = best, + -*cracy*]

aristocrat (*say* a-ris-tok-rat) *noun* (*plural* **aristocrats**)
a member of the aristocracy.
aristocratic *adjective*

arithmetic *noun*
the science or study of numbers; calculating with numbers. **arithmetical** *adjective* [from Greek *arithmos* = number]

ark *noun* (*plural* **arks**)
1 (in the Bible) the ship in which Noah and his family escaped the Flood. 2 a wooden box in which the writings of the Jewish Law were kept. [from Latin *arca* = box]

arm¹ *noun* (*plural* **arms**)
1 either of the two upper limbs of the body, between the shoulder and the hand. 2 a sleeve. 3 something shaped like an arm or jutting out from a main part. 4 the raised side part of a chair. **armful** *noun*
[Old English]

arm² *verb* (**arms, arming, armed**)
1 supply someone with weapons. 2 prepare for war. [from Latin *arma* = weapons]

armada (*say* ar-mah-da) *noun* (*plural* **armadas**)
a fleet of warships.
the Armada or **Spanish Armada** the warships sent by Spain to invade England in 1588. [Spanish, = navy, from Latin *armata* = armed]

armadillo *noun* (*plural* **armadillos**)
a small burrowing South American animal whose body is covered with a shell of bony plates. [Spanish, = little armed man]

armature *noun* (*plural* **armatures**)
the current-carrying part of a dynamo or electric motor. [from Latin]

armchair *noun* (*plural* **armchairs**)
a chair with arms.

armed forces or **armed services** *plural noun*
a country's military forces; the army, navy, and air force.

armistice *noun* (*plural* **armistices**)
an agreement to stop fighting in a war or battle. [from Latin *arma* = weapons + *sistere* = stop]

armour *noun*
1 a protective covering for the body, formerly worn in fighting. 2 a metal covering on a warship, tank, or car to protect it from missiles. **armoured** *adjective*

armpit *noun* (*plural* **armpits**)
the hollow underneath the top of the arm, below the shoulder.

arms *plural noun*
1 weapons. 2 a coat of arms.
up in arms protesting vigorously.

arms race *noun*
competition between nations in building up supplies of weapons, especially nuclear weapons.

army *noun* (*plural* **armies**)
1 a large number of people trained to fight on land. 2 a large group. [via old French *armée* from Latin *armata* = armed]

aroma (*say* a-roh-ma) *noun* (*plural* **aromas**)
a smell, especially a pleasant one. **aromatic** (*say* a-ro-mat-ik) *adjective*
[from Greek *aroma* = spice]

around *adverb* & *preposition*
all round; about. [from *a-*¹ + *round*]

arouse *verb* (**arouses, arousing, aroused**)
1 stir up a feeling in someone, *You've aroused my curiosity.* 2 wake someone up.

arpeggio (*say* ar-pej-ee-oh) *noun* (*plural* arpeggios)
the notes of a musical chord played one after the other instead of together.
[from Italian *arpa* = harp]

arrange *verb* (**arranges, arranging, arranged**)
1 put things into a certain order; adjust. 2 form plans for something, *We arranged to be there.* 3 prepare music for a particular purpose. **arrangement** *noun*

array *noun* (*plural* **arrays**)
1 a display. 2 an orderly arrangement. [from *ar-* + old form of *ready*]

arrears *plural noun*
1 money that is owing and ought to have been paid earlier. **2** a backlog of work etc.
in arrears behind with payments.
[from *ar-* + Latin *retro* = behind]

arrest *verb* (arrests, arresting, arrested)
1 seize a person by authority of the law. **2** stop a process or movement.
arrest *noun* (*plural* arrests)
1 arresting somebody, *The police made several arrests.* **2** stopping something.

arrive *verb* (arrives, arriving, arrived)
1 reach the end of a journey or a point on it. **2** come, *The great day arrived.* **arrival** *noun*
[from *ar-* + Latin *ripa* = shore]

arrogant *adjective*
behaving in an unpleasantly proud way because you think you are superior to other people. **arrogantly** *adverb*, **arrogance** *noun*
[from Latin *arrogare* = claim, demand]

arrow *noun* (*plural* arrows)
1 a pointed stick to be shot from a bow. **2** a sign with an outward-pointing V at the end, used to show direction or position. **arrowhead** *noun*
[from Old Norse]

arsenic *noun*
a very poisonous metallic substance.
[originally the name of arsenic sulphide, which is yellow; from Persian *zar* = gold]

arson *noun*
the crime of deliberately setting fire to a house or building. **arsonist** *noun*
[from Latin *ardere* = burn]

art *noun* (*plural* arts)
1 producing something beautiful, especially by painting or drawing; things produced in this way. **2** a skill, *the art of sailing.* [from Latin]

artery *noun* (*plural* arteries)
1 one of the tubes that carry blood away from the heart to all parts of the body. (Compare *vein.*) **2** an important road or route.
arterial (*say* ar-**teer**-ee-al) *adjective*

artesian well *noun* (*plural* artesian wells)
a well that is bored straight down into a place where water will rise easily to the surface.
[French *artésien* = of Artois, a region of France where wells of this type were first made]

artful *adjective*
crafty. **artfully** *adverb*

arthritis (*say* arth-**ry**-tiss) *noun*
a disease that makes joints in the body stiff and painful. **arthritic** (*say* arth-**rit**-ik) *adjective*
[from Greek *arthron* = joint]

arthropod *noun* (*plural* arthropods)
an animal of the group that includes insects, spiders, crabs, and centipedes. [from Greek *arthron* = joint + *podes* = feet (because arthropods have jointed limbs)]

artichoke *noun* (*plural* artichokes)
a kind of plant with a flower head used as a vegetable. [from Arabic]

article *noun* (*plural* articles)
1 a piece of writing published in a newspaper or magazine. **2** an object.
definite article the word 'the'.
indefinite article the word 'a' or 'an'.

articulate *adjective*
able to express things clearly and fluently.
articulate *verb* (articulates, articulating, articulated)
1 say or speak clearly. **2** connect by a joint.
articulation *noun* [from Latin *artus* = joint]

articulated *adjective*
(of a vehicle) in two sections that are connected by a flexible joint, *an articulated lorry.*

artificial *adjective*
not natural; made by human beings in imitation of a natural thing. **artificially** *adverb*, **artificiality** *noun*
[from Latin *ars* = art + *facere* = make]

artificial intelligence *noun*
the use of computers to perform tasks normally requiring human intelligence, e.g. decision-making.

artificial respiration *noun*
helping somebody to start breathing again after their breathing has stopped.

artillery *noun*
1 large guns. **2** the part of the army that uses large guns. [from old French]

artist *noun* (*plural* artists)
1 a person who produces works of art, especially a painter. **2** an entertainer.
artistry *noun*

artistic *adjective*
1 to do with art or artists. **2** having a talent for art. **artistically** *adverb*

arts *plural noun*
subjects (e.g. languages, literature, history) in which opinion and understanding are very important, as opposed to sciences where measurements and calculations are used.
the arts painting, music, and writing etc., considered together.

-ary *suffix*
to do with; of that kind: forms adjectives (e.g. *contrary*, *primary*) or nouns (e.g. *dictionary*, *January*). [from Latin]

as *adverb*
equally or similarly, *This is just as easy.*
as *preposition*
in the function or role of, *Use it as a handle.*
as *conjunction*
1 when or while, *She slipped as she got off the bus.* **2** because, *As he was late, we missed the*

train. **3** in a way that, *Leave it as it is.*
as for with regard to, *As for you, I despise you.*
as it were in a way, *She became, as it were, her own enemy.*
as well also.

as- *prefix*
to; towards. see **ad-**.

A/S *abbreviation*
advanced supplementary level in GCSE.

asbestos *noun*
a soft fireproof material.
[from Greek, = unquenchable]

ascend *verb* (**ascends, ascending, ascended**)
go up.
ascend the throne become king or queen.

ascent *noun* (*plural* **ascents**)
1 ascending. **2** a way up; an upward path or slope.

ascertain (*say* as-er-**tayn**) *verb* (**ascertains, ascertaining, ascertained**)
find something out by asking. **ascertainable** *adjective* [from old French]

ascetic (*say* a-**set**-ik) *adjective*
not allowing yourself pleasure and luxuries.
asceticism *noun* [from Greek *asketes* = hermit]

ascribe *verb* (**ascribes, ascribing, ascribed**)
regard something as belonging to or caused by; attribute, *She ascribes her success to good luck.*

asexual *adjective*
(in biology, to do with reproduction) by other than sexual methods.
[from *a-*^{2} = not + *sexual*]

ash^1 *noun* (*plural* **ashes**)
the powder that is left after something has been burned. **ashy** *adjective*
[from Old English *aesce*]

ash^2 *noun* (*plural* **ashes**)
a tree with silver-grey bark.
[from Old English *aesc*]

ashamed *adjective*
feeling shame.

Asian *adjective*
to do with Asia or its people.
Asian *noun* (*plural* **Asians**)
an Asian person.

Asiatic *adjective*
to do with Asia.

aside *adverb*
1 to or at one side, *pull it aside.* **2** away; in reserve.
aside *noun* (*plural* **asides**)
words spoken so that only certain people will hear.

ask *verb* (**asks, asking, asked**)
1 speak so as to find out or get something.
2 invite, *Ask her to the party.*

asleep *adverb* & *adjective*
sleeping.

asparagus *noun*
a plant whose young shoots are eaten as a vegetable. [from Greek]

aspect *noun* (*plural* **aspects**)
1 one part of a problem or situation, *Violence was the worst aspect of the crime.* **2** a person's or thing's appearance, *The forest had a sinister aspect.* **3** the direction a house etc. faces, *This room has a southern aspect.*
[from *as-* + Latin *specere* = to look]

asphalt (*say* **ass**-falt) *noun*
a sticky black substance like tar, often mixed with gravel to surface roads, etc. [from French]

asphyxiate (*say* ass-**fiks**-ee-ayt) *verb* (**asphyxiates, asphyxiating, asphyxiated**)
suffocate. **asphyxiation** *noun*
[from Greek *asphyxia* = stopping of the pulse]

aspidistra *noun* (*plural* **aspidistras**)
a house-plant with broad leaves.
[from Greek *aspis* = a shield]

aspirate (*say* **asp**-er-at) *noun* (*plural* **aspirates**)
the sound of 'h'.
[same origin as *aspire*]

aspiration *noun* (*plural* **aspirations**)
ambition; strong desire.

aspire *verb* (**aspires, aspiring, aspired**)
have an ambition to achieve something, *He aspired to be world champion.*
[from *ad-* = to + Latin *spirare* = breathe]

aspirin *noun* (*plural* **aspirins**)
a medicinal drug used to relieve pain or reduce fever. [German]

ass *noun* (*plural* **asses**)
1 a donkey. **2** (*informal*) a stupid person.

assassin *noun* (*plural* **assassins**)
a person who assassinates somebody. [from Arabic *hashishi* = hashish-takers, used as a name for a group of Muslims at the time of the Crusades, who were believed to take hashish before going out to kill Christian leaders]

assassinate *verb* (**assassinates, assassinating, assassinated**)
kill an important person deliberately and violently, especially for political reasons.
assassination *noun*

assault *noun* (*plural* **assaults**)
a violent or illegal attack.
assault *verb* (**assaults, assaulting, assaulted**)
make an assault on someone.

assemble *verb* (**assembles, assembling, assembled**)
1 bring or come together. **2** fit or put together the parts of something. **assemblage** *noun*
[from *as-* + Latin *simul* = together]

assembly *noun* (*plural* **assemblies**)
1 assembling. 2 a regular meeting, such as when everybody in a school meets together. 3 people who regularly meet for a special purpose; a parliament.

assent *verb* (**assents, assenting, assented**)
consent; say you agree.
assent *noun*
consent or approval.

assert *verb* (**asserts, asserting, asserted**)
state something firmly. **assertion** *noun*
assert yourself use firmness or forcefulness.

assertive *adjective*
asserting yourself; firm and forceful.

assess *verb* (**assesses, assessing, assessed**)
decide or estimate the value or quality of a person or thing. **assessment** *noun*, **assessor** *noun*
[from Latin *assessor* = an assistant judge]

asset *noun* (*plural* **assets**)
something useful. [from old French]

assets *plural noun*
a person's or firm's property, reckoned as having value.

assign *verb* (**assigns, assigning, assigned**)
1 give or allot. 2 appoint a person to perform a task.

assignment *noun* (*plural* **assignments**)
1 assigning. 2 something assigned; a task given to someone.

assimilate *verb* (**assimilates, assimilating, assimilated**)
take in and absorb something, e.g. nourishment into the body or knowledge into the mind. **assimilation** *noun*

assist *verb* (**assists, assisting, assisted**)
help. **assistance** *noun*
[from Latin *assistere* = stand by]

assistant *noun* (*plural* **assistants**)
1 a person who assists another; a helper. 2 a person who serves customers in a shop.
assistant *adjective*
helping a person and ranking next below him or her, *the assistant manager.*

associate *verb* (**associates, associating, associated**)
1 connect things in your mind, *I don't associate Ryan with fitness and healthy living.* 2 spend time or have dealings with a group of people.
associate *noun* (*plural* **associates**)
a colleague or companion; a partner.
associate *adjective*

association *noun* (*plural* **associations**)
1 an organization of people; a society. 2 associating. 3 a connection or link in your mind.

Association football *noun*
a form of football using a round ball that may not be handled during play except by the goalkeeper.

assonance (*say* ass-on-ans) *noun*
similarity of vowel sounds, e.g. in *vermin* and *furnish.*
[from *as-* + Latin *sonus* = sound]

assorted *adjective*
of various sorts put together; mixed, *assorted sweets.*

assortment *noun* (*plural* **assortments**)
a mixed collection of things.

assume *verb* (**assumes, assuming, assumed**)
1 accept (without proof or question) that something is true or sure to happen. 2 take on; undertake, *She assumed the extra responsibility.* 3 put on, *He assumed an innocent expression.*
assumed name a false name. **assumption** *noun*
[from *as-* + Latin *sumere* = take]

assurance *noun* (*plural* **assurances**)
1 a promise or guarantee that something is true or will happen. 2 life insurance. 3 self-confidence.

assure *verb* (**assures, assuring, assured**)
1 tell somebody confidently; promise. 2 make certain.

asterisk *noun* (*plural* **asterisks**)
a star-shaped sign * used to draw attention to something.
[from Greek *asteriskos* = little star]

asteroid *noun* (*plural* **asteroids**)
one of the small planets found mainly between the orbits of Mars and Jupiter.

asthma (*say* ass-ma) *noun*
a disease that makes breathing difficult.
asthmatic *adjective* & *noun* [Greek]

astonish *verb* (**astonishes, astonishing, astonished**)
surprise somebody greatly. **astonishment** *noun*
[same origin as *astound*]

astound *verb* (**astounds, astounding, astounded**)
astonish; shock somebody greatly.
[from old French; related to *stun*]

astray *adverb* & *adjective*
away from the right path or place or course of action.

astride *adverb* & *preposition*
with one leg on each side of something.

astringent *adjective*
1 causing skin or body tissue to contract. 2 harsh or severe, *astringent criticism.*

astrology *noun*
the study of how the stars and planets may influence people's lives. **astrologer** *noun*, **astrological** *adjective*
[from Greek *astron* = star, + *-logy*]

astronaut *noun* (*plural* **astronauts**)
a person who travels in a spacecraft.
astronautics *noun*
[from Greek *astron* = star + *nautes* = sailor]

astronomical *adjective*
1 to do with astronomy. 2 extremely large, *The restaurant's prices are astronomical.*

astronomy *noun*
the study of the stars and planets and their movements. **astronomer** *noun* [from Greek *astron* = star + *-nomia* = arrangement]

astute *adjective*
clever and good at understanding situations quickly; shrewd.
astutely *adverb*, **astuteness** *noun*
[from Latin *astus* = cleverness, cunning]

asylum *noun* (*plural* **asylums**)
1 refuge and safety; a place of refuge, *The defeated rebels sought political asylum in another country.* 2 (*old use*) a mental hospital. [from Greek *asylon* = refuge]

asymmetrical (*say* ay-sim-**et**-rik-al) *adjective*
not symmetrical. **asymmetrically** *adverb*

at *preposition*
This word is used to show 1 position (*at the top*), 2 time (*at midnight*), 3 condition (*Stand at ease*), 4 direction towards something (*Aim at the target*), 5 level or price etc. (*Sell them at £1 each*), 6 cause (*We were annoyed at his failure*).
at all in any way.
at it doing or working at something.
at once 1 immediately. 2 at the same time, *It all came out at once.*

at- *prefix*
to; towards. see **ad-**.

-ate *suffix*
forms 1 adjectives (e.g. *passionate*), 2 nouns showing status or function (e.g. *magistrate*) or (in scientific use) nouns meaning salts of certain acids (e.g. *nitrate*; compare **-ite**), 3 verbs (e.g. *create*, *fascinate*). [from Latin]

atheist (*say* **ayth**-ee-ist) *noun* (*plural* **atheists**)
a person who believes that there is no God.
atheism *noun* [from *a-²* + Greek *theos* = god]

athlete *noun* (*plural* **athletes**)
a person who is good at sport, especially athletics.
[from Greek *athlein* = compete for a prize]

athletic *adjective*
1 physically strong and active. 2 to do with athletes. **athletically** *adverb*

athletics *plural noun*
physical exercises and sports, e.g. running, jumping, and throwing.

-ation *suffix*
forms nouns, often from verbs (e.g. *creation*, *organization*, *starvation*). [from Latin]

atlas *noun* (*plural* **atlases**)
a book of maps. [named after Atlas, a giant in Greek mythology, who was made to support the universe on his shoulders]

atmosphere *noun* (*plural* **atmospheres**)
1 the air round the earth. 2 a feeling or mood given by surroundings, *the happy atmosphere of the fairground.*
atmospheric *adjective*
[from Greek *atmos* = vapour, + *sphere*]

atom *noun* (*plural* **atoms**)
the smallest particle of a substance.
[from Greek *atomos* = indivisible]

atom bomb *noun* (*plural* **atom bombs**)
a bomb using atomic energy.

atomic *adjective*
1 to do with an atom or atoms. 2 to do with atomic energy or atom bombs.

atomic number *noun* (*plural* **atomic numbers**)
the number of protons in the nucleus of the atom of a chemical element.

atrocity (*say* a-**tross**-it-ee) *noun* (*plural* **atrocities**)
something extremely bad or wicked; wickedness. [from Latin *atrox* = cruel]

attach *verb* (**attaches**, **attaching**, **attached**)
1 fix or join to something else. 2 regard as belonging to something, *We attach great importance to fitness.* **attachment** *noun*
attached to fond of.

attack *noun* (*plural* **attacks**)
1 a violent attempt to hurt or overcome somebody. 2 a piece of strong criticism.
3 sudden illness or pain.
attack *verb* (**attacks**, **attacking**, **attacked**)
make an attack. **attacker** *noun*

attain *verb* (**attains**, **attaining**, **attained**)
accomplish; succeed in doing or getting something. **attainable** *adjective*, **attainment** *noun* [from *at-* + Latin *tangere* = touch]

attempt *verb* (**attempts**, **attempting**, **attempted**)
make an effort to do something; try.
attempt *noun* (*plural* **attempts**)
an effort to do something; a try.

attend *verb* (**attends**, **attending**, **attended**)
1 give care and thought to something; look and listen, *Why don't you attend to your teacher?* 2 be present somewhere; go regularly to a meeting etc. 3 look after someone; be an attendant. **attendance** *noun*

attendant *noun* (*plural* **attendants**)
a person who helps or accompanies someone.

attention *noun*
1 giving concentration and careful thought, *Pay attention to what I'm saying.* 2 a position in which a soldier etc. stands with feet together and arms straight downwards.

attentive *adjective*
giving attention to something.
attentively *adverb*, **attentiveness** *noun*

attic *noun* (*plural* **attics**)
a room in the roof of a house.
[via French from Greek]

attitude *noun* (*plural* **attitudes**)
1 the position of the body or its parts; posture.
2 a way of thinking or behaving.

attract *verb* (**attracts, attracting, attracted**)
1 get someone's attention or interest; seem pleasant to someone. 2 pull something by an invisible force, *Magnets attract metal pins.*
attraction *noun*
[from *at-* + Latin *tractum* = pulled]

attractive *adjective*
1 pleasant or good-looking. 2 interesting or appealing, *an attractive plan.*
attractively *adverb*, **attractiveness** *noun*

attribute (*say* a-**trib**-yoot) *verb* (**attributes, attributing, attributed**)
regard something as belonging to or created by, *We attribute his success to hard work.*
attribution *noun*
attribute (*say* **at**-rib-yoot) *noun* (*plural* **attributes**)
a quality or characteristic, *Kindness is one of his attributes.*

attributive (*say* a-**trib**-yoo-tiv) *adjective*
expressing an attribute and placed before the word it describes, e.g. *old* in *the old dog.*
(Compare *predicative.*) **attributively** *adverb*

auburn *adjective*
(of hair) reddish-brown. [from old French]

auction *noun* (*plural* **auctions**)
a public sale where things are sold to the person who offers the most money for them.
auction *verb* (**auctions, auctioning, auctioned**)
sell something by auction. **auctioneer** *noun*
[from Latin *auctum* = increased]

audacious (*say* aw-**day**-shus) *adjective*
bold or daring. **audaciously** *adverb*, **audacity** *noun* [from Latin *audax* = bold]

audible *adjective*
loud enough to be heard. **audibly** *adverb*, **audibility** *noun* [from Latin *audire* = hear]

audience *noun* (*plural* **audiences**)
1 people who have gathered to hear or watch something. 2 a formal interview with an important person.

audio *noun*
reproduced sounds.

audio-visual *adjective*
using both sound and pictures to give information.

audit *noun* (*plural* **audits**)
an official examination of financial accounts to see that they are correct.
audit *verb* (**audits, auditing, audited**)
make an audit of accounts. **auditor** *noun*
[from Latin *audire* = hear (because originally the accounts were read out)]

audition *noun* (*plural* **auditions**)
a test to see if an actor or musician is suitable for a job.
audition *verb*

auditorium *noun* (*plural* **auditoriums**)
the part of a building where the audience sits.
[Latin, = place for hearing]

aunt *noun* (*plural* **aunts**)
the sister of your father or mother; your uncle's wife. [from Latin]

au pair (*say* oh pair) *noun* (*plural* **au pairs**)
a young person from overseas who works for a time in someone's home.

aura (*say* **or**-a) *noun* (*plural* **auras**)
a general feeling surrounding a person or thing, *an aura of happiness.*
[Greek, = breeze]

aural (*say* **or**-al) *adjective*
to do with the ear or hearing. **aurally** *adverb*
[from Latin *auris* = ear]

USAGE: Do not confuse with *oral.*

aurora (*say* aw-**raw**-ra) *noun* (*plural* **auroras**)
bands of coloured light appearing in the sky at night, the **aurora borealis** (*say* bor-ee-**ay**-liss) in the northern hemisphere and the **aurora australis** (*say* aw-**stray**-liss) in the southern hemisphere.
[Latin: *aurora* = dawn; *borealis* = of the north; *australis* = of the south]

auspices (*say* **aw**-spiss-eez) *plural noun*
protection or support, *under the auspices of the Red Cross.*
[originally = omens; later = influence, protection; same origin as *auspicious*]

auspicious (*say* aw-**spish**-us) *adjective*
fortunate or favourable, *an auspicious start.*
[from Latin *auspicium* = telling the future from the behaviour of birds, from *avis* = bird]

austere (*say* aw-**steer**) *adjective*
very simple and plain; without luxuries.
austerely *adverb*, **austerity** *noun*

aut- *prefix*
self-; of or by yourself or itself. see **auto-**.

authentic *adjective*
genuine, *an authentic signature.* **authentically** *adverb*, **authenticity** *noun*

author *noun* (*plural* **authors**)
the writer of a book, play, poem, etc.
authorship *noun*
[from Latin *auctor* = originator]

authoritative *adjective*
having proper authority or expert knowledge; official.

authority *noun* (*plural* **authorities**)
1 the right or power to give orders to other people. 2 a person or organization with the

authorize 26 awake

right to give orders. **3** an expert; a book etc. that gives reliable information, *an authority on spiders*.

authorize *verb* (authorizes, authorizing, authorized) give official permission for something. **authorization** *noun*

autistic (*say* aw-tist-ik) *adjective* unable to communicate with other people or respond to surroundings. **autism** *noun* [from *auto-*]

auto- *prefix* (changing to **aut-** before a vowel) self-; of or by yourself or itself (as in *autograph, automatic*). [from Greek *autos* = self]

autobiography *noun* (*plural* autobiographies) the story of a person's life written by himself or herself. **autobiographical** *adjective*

autocrat *noun* (*plural* autocrats) a ruler with unlimited power. **autocratic** *adjective*, **autocratically** *adverb* [from *auto-* + *-crat*]

autocue *noun* (*plural* autocues) (*trade mark*) a device that displays the script for a television presenter or newsreader to read.

autograph *noun* (*plural* autographs) a person's signature. **autograph** *verb* (autographs, autographing, autographed) sign your name on or in a book etc.

automatic *adjective* **1** working on its own without continuous attention or control by people. **2** done without thinking. **automatically** *adverb* [from Greek *automatos* = self-operating]

automation *noun* making processes automatic; using machines instead of people to do jobs.

automaton (*say* aw-tom-at-on) *noun* (*plural* automatons) **1** a robot. **2** a person who seems to act mechanically without thinking.

autonomy (*say* aw-ton-om-ee) *noun* **1** self-government. **2** the right to act independently without being told what to do. **autonomous** *adjective* [from *auto-* + Greek *-nomia* = arrangement]

autumn *noun* (*plural* autumns) the season between summer and winter. **autumnal** *adjective* [from old French]

auxiliary *adjective* giving help and support, *auxiliary services*. **auxiliary** *noun* (*plural* auxiliaries) a helper. [from Latin *auxilium* = help]

auxiliary verb *noun* (*plural* auxiliary verbs) a verb used in forming tenses etc. of other verbs, e.g. *have* in *I have finished*.

available *adjective* ready or able to be used; obtainable. **availability** *noun*

avalanche *noun* (*plural* avalanches) a mass of snow or rock falling down the side of a mountain. [French, from *avaler* = descend]

avenge *verb* (avenges, avenging, avenged) take vengeance for something done to harm you. **avenger** *noun*

avenue *noun* (*plural* avenues) **1** a wide street. **2** a road with trees along both sides. [from French *avenir* = approach]

average *noun* (*plural* averages) **1** the value obtained by adding several quantities together and dividing by the number of quantities. **2** the usual or ordinary standard. **average** *adjective* **1** worked out as an average, *Their average age is ten*. **2** of the usual or ordinary standard. **average** *verb* (averages, averaging, averaged) work out, produce, or amount to as an average. [from Arabic]

aversion *noun* a strong dislike.

avert *verb* (averts, averting, averted) **1** turn something away, *People averted their eyes from the accident*. **2** prevent, *We averted a disaster*.

aviary *noun* (*plural* aviaries) a large cage or building for keeping birds. [from Latin *avis* = bird]

aviation *noun* the flying of aircraft. **aviator** *noun* [from Latin *avis* = bird]

avocado (*say* av-ok-ah-doh) *noun* (*plural* avocados) a pear-shaped tropical fruit. [via Spanish from Nahuatl (a Central American language)]

avoid *verb* (avoids, avoiding, avoided) **1** keep yourself away from someone or something. **2** keep yourself from doing something; refrain from, *Avoid rash promises*. **avoidable** *adjective*, **avoidance** *noun* [from old French]

avoirdupois (*say* av-er-dew-poiz) *noun* a system of weights using the unit of 16 ounces = 1 pound. [French, = goods of weight (goods sold by weight)]

await *verb* (awaits, awaiting, awaited) wait for. [from old French]

awake *verb* (awakes, awaking, awoke, awoken) wake up. **awake** *adjective* not asleep. [from Old English]

award *verb* (awards, awarding, awarded)
give something officially as a prize, payment, or penalty.
award *noun* (*plural* awards)
something awarded, such as a prize or a sum of money. [from old French]

aware *adjective*
knowing or realizing something, *Were you aware of the danger?* **awareness** *noun*

away *adverb*
1 to or at a distance; not at the usual place.
2 out of existence, *The water had boiled away.*
3 continuously or persistently, *We worked away at it.*
away *adjective*
played on an opponent's ground, *an away match.* [from Old English]

awe *noun*
fearful or deeply respectful wonder, *The mountains always fill me with awe.*
awed *adjective*, **awesome** *adjective*,
awestricken *adjective*, **awestruck** *adjective*
[from Old English]

awful *adjective*
1 very bad, *an awful accident.* 2 (*informal*) very great, *That's an awful lot of money.*
awfully *adverb*
[from *awe* + *-ful*]

awkward *adjective*
1 difficult to use or deal with; not convenient.
2 clumsy; not skilful. **awkwardly** *adverb*,
awkwardness *noun*

awning *noun* (*plural* awnings)
a roof-like shelter made of canvas etc.

axe *noun* (*plural* axes)
1 a tool for chopping things. 2 (*informal*) being axed.
have an axe to grind have a personal interest in something and want to take care of it.
axe *verb* (axes, axing, axed)
1 cancel or abolish something. 2 reduce something greatly. [from Old English]

axis *noun* (*plural* axes)
1 a line through the centre of a spinning object.
2 a line dividing a thing in half.
[Latin, = axle]

axle *noun* (*plural* axles)
the rod through the centre of a wheel, on which the wheel turns. [from Old Norse]

ayatollah (*say* I-a-**tol**-a) *noun* (*plural* ayatollahs)
a Muslim religious leader in Iran.
[from Arabic *ayatu-llah* = sign from God]

aye (*say* I) *adverb*
yes. [origin unknown]

azure *adjective*
sky-blue. [via old French from Persian]

Bb

babble *verb* (babbles, babbling, babbled)
1 talk very quickly without making sense.
2 make a murmuring sound. **babble** *noun*,
babbler *noun* [imitating the sound]

baboon *noun* (*plural* baboons)
a kind of large monkey from Africa and Asia.
Baboons have long muzzles and short tails.
[from French]

baby *noun* (*plural* babies)
a very young child or animal. **babyish** *adjective*

babysitter *noun* (*plural* babysitters)
someone who looks after a child while its parents are out.

bachelor *noun* (*plural* bachelors)
a man who has not married.
Bachelor of Arts or **Science** a person who has taken a first degree in arts or science.
[from French]

back *noun* (*plural* backs)
1 the part that is furthest from the front. 2 the back part of the body from the shoulders to the buttocks. 3 the part of a chair etc. that your back rests against.
4 a defending player near the goal in football, hockey, etc.
back *adjective*
1 placed at or near the back. 2 to do with the back, *back pain.*
back *adverb*
1 to or towards the back. 2 to the place you have come from, *Go back home.* 3 to an earlier time or position, *Put the clocks back one hour.*
back *verb* (backs, backing, backed)
1 move backwards. 2 give someone support or help. 3 bet on something. 4 cover the back of something, *Back the rug with canvas.* **backer** *noun*
back out refuse to do what you agreed to do.
back up give support or help to a person or thing. **back-up** *noun*
[from Old English]

backbencher *noun* (*plural* backbenchers)
a Member of Parliament who does not hold an important position.

backbone *noun* (*plural* backbones)
the column of small bones down the centre of the back; the spine.

backfire *verb* (backfires, backfiring, backfired)
1 if a car backfires, it makes a loud noise, caused by an explosion in the exhaust pipe. 2 if a plan backfires, it goes wrong.

background *noun*
1 the back part of a scene or view etc.
2 the conditions influencing something. 3 a person's family, upbringing, and education.

backing *noun*
1 support. 2 material that is used to line the back of something. 3 musical accompaniment.

backlash *noun* (*plural* **backlashes**)
a violent reaction to an event.

backlog *noun* (*plural* **backlogs**)
an amount of work that should have been finished but is still waiting to be done.

backstroke *noun*
a way of swimming lying on your back.

backward *adjective*
1 going backwards. 2 slow at learning or developing. **backwardness** *noun*
backward *adverb*
backwards.

USAGE: The adverb *backward* is mainly used in American English.

backwards *adverb*
1 to or towards the back. 2 with the back end going first. 3 in reverse order, *Count backwards.*
backwards and forwards in each direction alternately; to and fro.

bacon *noun*
smoked or salted meat from the back or sides of a pig. [via French from Germanic; related to *back*]

bacterium *noun* (*plural* **bacteria**)
a microscopic organism. **bacterial** *adjective*
[from Greek *bakterion* = little cane]

USAGE: Note that it is a mistake to use the plural form *bacteria* as if it were the singular. It is incorrect to say 'a bacteria' or 'this bacteria'; correct usage is *this bacterium* or *these bacteria.*

bad *adjective* (**worse, worst**)
1 not having the right qualities; not good. 2 wicked or evil. 3 serious or severe, *a bad accident.* 4 ill or unhealthy. 5 harmful, *Sweets are bad for your teeth.* 6 decayed or rotten, *This meat has gone bad.* **badness** *noun*
not bad quite good.

badge *noun* (*plural* **badges**)
a button or sign that you wear to show people who you are or what school or club etc. you belong to. [origin unknown]

badger *noun* (*plural* **badgers**)
a grey burrowing animal with a black and white head.
badger *verb* (**badgers, badgering, badgered**)
keep asking someone to do something; pester. [perhaps from *badge* (because of the markings on a badger's head)]

badly *adverb* (**worse, worst**)
1 in a bad way; not well. 2 severely; causing much injury, *He was badly wounded.* 3 very much, *She badly wanted to win.*

baffle *verb* (**baffles, baffling, baffled**)
puzzle or confuse somebody. **bafflement** *noun*
[origin unknown]

bag *noun* (*plural* **bags**)
a container made of a soft material, for holding or carrying things.
bags (*informal*) plenty, *bags of room.*
bag *verb* (**bags, bagging, bagged**)
1 (*informal*) catch or claim something. 2 put something into bags.

baggage *noun*
luggage. [from old French]

baggy *adjective*
(of clothes) large and loose.

bagpipes *plural noun*
a musical instrument in which air is squeezed out of a bag into pipes. Bagpipes are played especially in Scotland.

bail[1] *noun*
money that is paid or promised as a guarantee that a person who is accused of a crime will return for trial if he or she is released in the meantime.
bail *verb* (**bails, bailing, bailed**)
provide bail for a person.

bail[2] *noun* (*plural* **bails**)
one of the two small pieces of wood placed on top of the stumps in cricket.
[from old French *bail* = palisade]

bail[3] *verb* (**bails, bailing, bailed**)
scoop out water that has got into a boat. [from French *baille* = bucket]

bailiff *noun* (*plural* **bailiffs**)
1 a law officer who helps a sheriff by serving writs and performing arrests. 2 an official who takes people's property when they owe money.

bait *noun*
1 food that is put on a hook or in a trap to catch fish or animals. 2 something that is meant to tempt someone.
bait *verb* (**baits, baiting, baited**)
1 put bait on a hook or in a trap. 2 try to make someone angry by teasing them. [from Old Norse; related to *bite*]

baize *noun*
the thick green cloth that is used for covering snooker tables.
[same origin as *bay*[5] (because the cloth was originally reddish-brown)]

bake *verb* (**bakes, baking, baked**)
1 cook in an oven. 2 make or become very hot. 3 make a thing hard by heating it.

baker *noun* (*plural* **bakers**)
a person who bakes and sells bread or cakes. **bakery** *noun*

balance *noun* (*plural* **balances**)
1 a steady position, with the weight or amount evenly distributed. 2 a machine for weighing things, with two containers hanging from a

bar. **3** the difference between money paid into an account and money taken out of it. **4** the money left after something has been paid for.
balance *verb* (**balances, balancing, balanced**) make or be steady or equal. [from Latin]

balcony *noun* (*plural* **balconies**)
1 a platform that sticks out from an outside wall of a building. **2** the upstairs part of a theatre or cinema. [from Italian]

bald *adjective*
1 without hair on the top of the head. **2** with no details; blunt, *a bald statement*. **baldly** *adverb*, **baldness** *noun*

ball[1] *noun* (*plural* **balls**)
1 a round object used in many games. **2** anything that has a round shape, *a ball of string*. [from Old Norse]

ball[2] *noun* (*plural* **balls**)
a formal party where people dance. [same origin as *ballet*]

ballad *noun* (*plural* **ballads**)
a simple song or poem that tells a story.

ballast (*say* bal-ast) *noun*
heavy material that is carried in a ship to keep it steady.

ball-bearings *plural noun*
small steel balls rolling in a groove on which machine parts can move easily.

ballerina (*say* bal-er-een-a) *noun* (*plural* **ballerinas**)
a female ballet dancer. [Italian, = female dancing teacher]

ballet (*say* bal-ay) *noun* (*plural* **ballets**)
a stage entertainment that tells a story with dancing, mime, and music.

ballistic missile *noun* (*plural* **ballistic missiles**)
a missile that is initially powered and guided and then falls under gravity on its target. [from Greek *ballein* = to throw]

balloon *noun* (*plural* **balloons**)
1 a bag made of thin rubber that can be inflated and used as a toy or decoration. **2** a large round bag inflated with hot air or light gases to make it rise in the air. **3** an outline round spoken words in a strip cartoon. [from French or Italian; related to *ball*[1]]

ballot *noun* (*plural* **ballots**)
1 a secret method of voting, usually by making a mark on a piece of paper. **2** a piece of paper on which a vote is made.
ballot *verb* (**ballots, balloting, balloted**) invite people to vote for something by a ballot. [from Italian *ballotta* = small ball (because one way of voting is by placing a ball in a box; the colour of the ball shows whether you are voting for something or against it)]

ballpoint pen *noun* (*plural* **ballpoint pens**)
a pen with a tiny ball round which the ink flows.

balm *noun*
1 a sweet-scented ointment. **2** something that soothes you. [from Latin *balsamum*]

balmy *adjective*
1 sweet-scented like balm. **2** soft and warm, *a balmy breeze*.

bamboo *noun* (*plural* **bamboos**)
1 a tall plant with hard hollow stems. **2** a stem of the bamboo plant. [via Dutch from Malay (a language spoken in Malaysia)]

ban *verb* (**bans, banning, banned**)
forbid something officially.
ban *noun* (*plural* **bans**)
an order that bans something.

banana *noun* (*plural* **bananas**)
a long curved fruit with a yellow or green skin.

band[1] *noun* (*plural* **bands**)
1 a strip or loop of something. **2** a range of values, wavelengths, etc. [via French from Germanic; related to *bind*]

band[2] *noun* (*plural* **bands**)
1 an organized group of people doing something together, *a band of robbers*. **2** a group of people playing music together.
band *verb* (**bands, banding, banded**) form an organized group. [from French]

bandage *noun* (*plural* **bandages**)
a strip of material for binding up a wound.
bandage *verb* [French; related to *band*[1]]

bandit *noun* (*plural* **bandits**)
a member of a gang of robbers who attack travellers. [from Latin *bannire* = banish]

bandwagon *noun*
jump or **climb on the bandwagon** join other people in something that is successful.

bandy *verb* (**bandies, bandying, bandied**)
if a word or story is bandied about, it is mentioned or told by a lot of different people. [probably from French]

bane *noun*
a cause of trouble or worry etc., *Exams are the bane of our lives!* [from Old English]

bang *noun* (*plural* **bangs**)
1 a sudden loud noise like that of an explosion. **2** a sharp blow or knock.
bang *verb* (**bangs, banging, banged**)
1 hit or shut something noisily. **2** make a sudden loud noise.
bang *adverb*
1 with a bang; suddenly. **2** (*informal*) exactly, *bang in the middle*. [imitating the sound]

banish *verb* (**banishes, banishing, banished**)
1 punish a person by ordering them to leave a place. **2** if you banish doubts or fears, you

drive them away.

banishment *noun*
[via French from Germanic; related to *ban*]

banisters *plural noun*
a handrail with upright supports beside a staircase. [from Italian]

banjo *noun* (*plural* banjos)
an instrument like a guitar with a round body. [a Black American word]

bank[1] *noun* (*plural* banks)
1 a slope. 2 a long piled-up mass of sand, snow, cloud, etc. 3 a row of lights or switches etc.
bank *verb* (banks, banking, banked)
1 build or form a bank. 2 tilt sideways while changing direction, *The plane banked as it prepared to land.*
[from Old Norse]

bank[2] *noun* (*plural* banks)
1 a business that looks after people's money. 2 a reserve supply, *a blood bank.*
bank *verb* (banks, banking, banked)
put money in a bank.
bank on rely on.
[from Italian]

banker *noun* (*plural* bankers)
a person who runs a bank.

bank holiday *noun* (*plural* bank holidays)
a public holiday, when banks are officially closed.

bankrupt *adjective*
a person or business that is bankrupt is unable to pay debts. **bankruptcy** *noun*
[from *bank*[2] + Latin *ruptum* = broken]

banner *noun* (*plural* banners)
1 a flag. 2 a strip of cloth with a design or slogan on it, carried on a pole or two poles in a procession or demonstration.

banquet *noun* (*plural* banquets)
a formal public meal. **banqueting** *noun*

banter *noun*
playful teasing or joking. **banter** *verb*

baptism *noun* (*plural* baptisms)
baptizing.

Baptist *noun* (*plural* Baptists)
a member of a group of Christians who believe that a person should not be baptized until he or she is old enough to understand what baptism means.

baptize *verb* (baptizes, baptizing, baptized)
receive a person into the Christian Church in a ceremony in which he or she is sprinkled with or dipped in water, and usually given a name or names.
[from Greek *baptizein* = to dip]

bar *noun* (*plural* bars)
1 a long piece of something hard, *a gold bar.* 2 a counter or room where refreshments, especially alcoholic drinks, are served. 3 a

barrier or obstruction. 4 one of the small equal sections into which music is divided, *three beats to the bar.*
the Bar barristers.
bar *verb* (bars, barring, barred)
1 fasten something with a bar or bars. 2 block or obstruct, *A man with a dog barred the way.* 3 forbid or ban.

barb *noun* (*plural* barbs)
the backward-pointing spike of a spear, arrow, or fish-hook, which makes the point stay in.
[from Latin *barba* = beard]

barbarian *noun* (*plural* barbarians)
an uncivilized or brutal person.
barbaric *adjective*, **barbarous** *adjective*, **barbarity** *noun*, **barbarism** *noun*
[from Greek *barbaros* = babbling, not speaking Greek]

barbecue *noun* (*plural* barbecues)
1 a metal frame for grilling food over an open fire outdoors. 2 a party where food is cooked in this way.
barbecue *verb* (barbecues, barbecuing, barbecued)
cook food on a barbecue.

barbed *adjective*
1 having a barb or barbs. 2 a barbed comment or remark is deliberately hurtful.

barbed wire *noun*
wire with small spikes in it, used to make fences.

barber *noun* (*plural* barbers)
a men's hairdresser.
[from Latin *barba* = beard]

bar chart *noun* (*plural* bar charts)
a diagram that shows amounts as bars of equal width but varying height.

bar code *noun* (*plural* bar codes)
a set of black lines that are printed on goods, library books, etc., and can be read by a computer to give information about the goods, books, etc.

bare *adjective*
1 without clothing or covering. 2 empty, *The cupboard was bare.* 3 plain; without details, *the bare facts.* 4 only just enough, *the bare necessities of life.*
barely *adverb*, **bareness** *noun*
bare *verb* (bares, baring, bared)
uncover or reveal, *The dog bared its teeth in a snarl.* [from Old English]

bargain *noun* (*plural* bargains)
1 an agreement about buying or selling or exchanging something. 2 something that you buy cheaply.
bargain *verb* (bargains, bargaining, bargained)
argue over the price to be paid or what you will do in return for something.
bargain for be prepared for or expect, *He got more than he bargained for.*

barge *noun* (*plural* **barges**)
a long flat-bottomed boat used on canals.
barge *verb* (**barges, barging, barged**)
push or knock against roughly.
barge in rush into a room rudely.
[from Latin *barca* = boat]

baritone *noun* (*plural* **baritones**)
a male singer with a voice between a tenor and
a bass.
[from Greek *barys* = heavy, + *tone*]

barium (*say* **bair**-ee-um) *noun*
a soft silvery-white metal. [from Greek]

bark[1] *noun* (*plural* **barks**)
the short harsh sound made by a dog or fox.
bark *verb* [from Old English *beorc*, imitating
the sound]

bark[2] *noun*
the outer covering of a tree's branches or
trunk. [from Old Norse]

barley *noun*
a cereal plant from which malt is made.

bar mitzvah *noun* (*plural* **bar mitzvahs**)
a religious ceremony for Jewish boys aged 13.
[Hebrew, = son of the commandment]

barn *noun* (*plural* **barns**)
a farm building for storing hay or grain etc.
barnyard *noun* [from Old English]

barnacle *noun* (*plural* **barnacles**)
a shellfish that attaches itself to rocks and the
bottoms of ships. [from Latin]

barometer (*say* ba-**rom**-it-er) *noun* (*plural*
barometers)
an instrument that measures air pressure,
used in forecasting the weather.
[from Greek *baros* = weight, + *meter*]

baron *noun* (*plural* **barons**)
1 a member of the lowest rank of noblemen. 2 a
powerful owner of an industry or business, *a
newspaper baron.* **barony** *noun*, **baronial** (*say*
ba-**roh**-nee-al) *adjective* [from Latin *baro* = man,
warrior]

baroness *noun* (*plural* **baronesses**)
a female baron or a baron's wife.

baronet *noun* (*plural* **baronets**)
a nobleman ranking below a baron but above a
knight. **baronetcy** *noun*

baroque (*say* ba-**rok**) *noun*
an elaborately decorated style of architecture
used in the 17th and 18th centuries. [from
French]

barracks *noun*
a large building or group of buildings for
soldiers to live in.

barrage (*say* ba-**rahzh**) *noun* (*plural* **barrages**)
1 a dam built across a river. 2 heavy gunfire.
3 a large amount of something, *a barrage of
questions.*

barrel *noun* (*plural* **barrels**)
1 a large rounded container with flat ends.
2 the metal tube of a gun, through which the
shot is fired.
[from Latin *barriculus* = a small cask]

barrel organ *noun* (*plural* **barrel organs**)
a musical instrument which you play by
turning a handle.

barricade *noun* (*plural* **barricades**)
a barrier, especially one put up hastily across a
street or door.
barricade *verb* (**barricades, barricading,
barricaded**)
block a street or door with a barricade.
[French, from Spanish *barrica* = barrel
(because barrels were sometimes used to build
barricades)]

barrier *noun* (*plural* **barriers**)
something that prevents people or things from
getting past; an obstacle.

barrister *noun* (*plural* **barristers**)
a lawyer who represents people in the higher
lawcourts.
[originally one who was allowed to pass the
bar, a partition separating qualified lawyers
from students]

barrow *noun* (*plural* **barrows**)
1 a wheelbarrow. 2 a small cart that is pushed
or pulled by hand.
[from Old English; related to *bear*[2]]

barter *verb* (**barters, bartering, bartered**)
trade by exchanging goods for other goods, not
for money.

USAGE: This word does not mean 'to
bargain'.

barter *noun* (*plural* **barters**)
the system of bartering.
[probably from old French]

basalt (*say* **bas**-awlt) *noun*
a kind of dark volcanic rock. [from Greek]

base[1] *noun* (*plural* **bases**)
1 the lowest part of something; the part on
which a thing stands. 2 a starting point or
foundation; a basis. 3 a headquarters. 4 each of
the four corners that must be reached by a
runner in baseball. 5 a substance that can
combine with an acid to form a salt. 6 the
number in terms of which other numbers can
be expressed in a number system. 10 is the base
of the decimal system and 2 is the base of the
binary system.
base *verb* (**bases, basing, based**)
use something as a starting point or
foundation, *The story is based on facts.* [same
origin as *basis*]

base[2] *adjective*
1 dishonourable, *base motives.* 2 not of great
value, *base metals.* **basely** *adverb*, **baseness**
noun [from French *bas* = low]

baseball *noun* (*plural* baseballs)
1 an American ball game rather like rounders.
2 the ball used in this game.

basement *noun* (*plural* basements)
a room or rooms below ground level.

bash *verb* (bashes, bashing, bashed)
hit hard.
bash *noun* (*plural* bashes)
1 a hard hit. 2 (*informal*) a try, *Have a bash at it.* [imitating the sound]

bashful *adjective*
shy and self-conscious. **bashfully** *adverb*

basic *adjective*
forming a basis or starting point; very important, *Bread is a basic food.*
[from *base*¹]

basin *noun* (*plural* basins)
1 a deep bowl. 2 a washbasin. 3 a sheltered area of water for mooring boats. 4 the area from which water drains into a river, *the Amazon basin.* [from old French]

basis *noun* (*plural* bases)
something to start from or add to; the main principle or ingredient.
[Greek, = step, stepping]

bask *verb* (basks, basking, basked)
sit or lie comfortably warming yourself in the sun. [origin unknown]

basket *noun* (*plural* baskets)
a container for holding or carrying things, made of strips of flexible material or wire woven together. [probably from Latin]

basketball *noun* (*plural* basketballs)
1 a game in which goals are scored by putting a ball through high nets. 2 the ball used in this game.

bass (*say* bayss) *adjective*
deep-sounding; the bass part of a piece of music is the lowest part.
bass *noun* (*plural* basses)
1 a male singer with a very deep voice. 2 a bass instrument or part. [from *base*² = low]

bassoon *noun* (*plural* bassoons)
a bass woodwind instrument.
[from Italian *basso* = low]

bastard *noun* (*plural* bastards)
1 (*old use*) an illegitimate child. 2 (*slang*) an unpleasant or difficult person or thing.
bastardy *noun* [from old French]

bat¹ *noun* (*plural* bats)
1 a shaped piece of wood used to hit the ball in cricket, baseball, etc. 2 a batsman, *their opening bat.*
off your own bat without help from other people.
bat *verb* (bats, batting, batted)
use a bat in cricket etc. [from Old English]

bat² *noun* (*plural* bats)
a flying animal that looks like a mouse with wings.

batch *noun* (*plural* batches)
a set of things or people dealt with together.
[from Old English; related to *bake*]

bath *noun* (*plural* baths)
1 washing your whole body while sitting in water. 2 a large container for water in which to wash your whole body; this water, *Your bath is getting cold.* 3 a liquid in which something is placed, *an acid bath.*
bath *verb* (baths, bathing, bathed)
wash in a bath.

bathe *verb* (bathes, bathing, bathed)
1 go swimming. 2 wash something gently.
bathe *noun*, **bather** *noun*, **bathing suit** *noun*

bathroom *noun* (*plural* bathrooms)
a room containing a bath.

baths *plural noun*
1 a building with rooms where people can bath. 2 a public swimming pool.

batsman *noun* (*plural* batsmen)
a player who uses a bat in cricket etc.

battalion *noun* (*plural* battalions)
an army unit containing two or more companies. [from Italian *battaglia* = battle]

batten *verb* (battens, battening, battened)
fasten something down firmly.

batter *verb* (batters, battering, battered)
hit hard and often.
batter *noun* (*plural* batters)
1 a beaten mixture of flour, eggs, and milk, used for making pancakes etc. 2 a batsman in baseball. [from Latin *battuere* = to beat]

battery *noun* (*plural* batteries)
1 a device for storing and supplying electricity. 2 a set of similar pieces of equipment; a group of large guns. 3 a series of cages in which poultry or animals are kept close together, *battery farming.*

battle *noun* (*plural* battles)
1 a fight between two armies. 2 a struggle.
battlefield *noun*, **battleground** *noun*
battle *verb* (battles, battling, battled)
fight or struggle. [same origin as *batter*]

battlements *plural noun*
the top of a castle wall, often with gaps from which the defenders could fire at the enemy.

battleship *noun* (*plural* battleships)
a heavily armed warship.

bawl *verb* (bawls, bawling, bawled)
1 shout. 2 cry noisily.

bay¹ *noun* (*plural* bays)
a place where the shore curves inwards. [from Spanish]

bay² *noun* (*plural* bays)
a recess. [from Latin *batare* = gape]

bay³ *noun* (*plural* **bays**)
the long deep cry of a hunting hound or other large dog.
at bay cornered but defiantly facing attackers, *a stag at bay.*
keep at bay prevent something from coming near or causing harm, *We need laws to keep poverty at bay.*
[from French]

bayonet *noun* (*plural* **bayonets**)
a blade that can be fixed to the end of a rifle and used for stabbing. [named after *Bayonne* in France, where it was first used]

bay window *noun* (*plural* **bay windows**)
a window that sticks out from the main wall of a house. [from *bay*²]

bazaar *noun* (*plural* **bazaars**)
1 a market place in an Eastern country.
2 a sale to raise money for a charity etc.
[from Persian *bazar* = market]

BBC *abbreviation*
British Broadcasting Corporation.

BC *abbreviation*
before Christ (used with dates counting back from the birth of Jesus Christ).

be *verb* (**am, are, is; was, were; being, been**)
1 exist; occupy a position, *The shop is on the corner.* 2 happen; take place, *The wedding is tomorrow.* This verb is also used 1 to join subject and complement (*He is my teacher*), 2 to form parts of other verbs (*It is raining. He was killed*).
have been have gone to or come to as a visitor etc., *We have been to Rome.*

be- *prefix*
used to form verbs (as in *befriend, belittle*) or strengthen their meaning (as in *begrudge*).
[from Old English]

beach *noun* (*plural* **beaches**)
the part of the seashore nearest to the water.
[probably from Old English]

beacon *noun* (*plural* **beacons**)
a light or fire used as a signal.
[from Old English; related to *beckon*]

bead *noun* (*plural* **beads**)
1 a small piece of a hard substance with a hole in it for threading with others on a string or wire, e.g. to make a necklace. 2 a drop of liquid, *a bead of sweat.*
[from Old English *gebed* = prayer (because people kept count of the prayers they said by moving the beads on a rosary)]

beady *adjective*
(of eyes) small and bright.

beak *noun* (*plural* **beaks**)
the hard horny part of a bird's mouth.

beaker *noun* (*plural* **beakers**)
1 a tall drinking-mug, often without a handle.
2 a glass container used for pouring liquids in a laboratory.

beam *noun* (*plural* **beams**)
1 a long thick bar of wood or metal. 2 a ray or stream of light or other radiation. 3 a happy smile.
beam *verb* (**beams, beaming, beamed**)
1 smile happily. 2 send out a beam of light or other radiation. [from Old English]

bean *noun* (*plural* **beans**)
1 a kind of plant with seeds growing in pods.
2 its seed or pod eaten as food. 3 the seed of coffee. [from Old English]

bear¹ *noun* (*plural* **bears**)
a large heavy animal with thick fur and large teeth and claws.
[from Old English *bera*]

bear² *verb* (**bears, bearing, bore, borne**)
1 carry or support. 2 have a mark etc., *She still bears the scar.* 3 endure or stand, *I can't bear this pain.* 4 produce or give birth to, *She bore him two sons.* **bearer** *noun*
bear out support or confirm.
[from Old English *beran*]

beard *noun* (*plural* **beards**)
hair on a man's chin. **bearded** *adjective*
beard *verb* (**beards, bearding, bearded**)
come face to face with a person and challenge him or her boldly.
[from Old English; the verb originally = to grab someone's beard]

bearing *noun* (*plural* **bearings**)
1 the way a person stands, walks, behaves, etc.
2 relevance, *My friendship with Tom has no bearing on his selection for the team.* 3 the direction or position of one thing in relation to another. 4 a device for preventing friction in a machine, *ball-bearings.*
get your bearings work out where you are in relation to things.

beast *noun* (*plural* **beasts**)
1 any large four-footed animal. 2 (*informal*) a cruel or vicious person. **beastly** *adjective* [from Latin *bestia*]

beat *verb* (**beats, beating, beat, beaten**)
1 hit often, especially with a stick. 2 shape or flatten something by beating it. 3 stir vigorously. 4 make repeated movements, *The heart beats.* 5 do better than somebody; overcome. **beater** *noun*
beat *noun* (*plural* **beats**)
1 a regular rhythm or stroke, *the beat of your heart.* 2 emphasis in rhythm; the strong rhythm of pop music. 3 a policeman's regular route.

beautiful *adjective*
attractive to your senses or your mind.
beautifully *adverb*

beautify *verb* (beautifies, beautifying, beautified)
make someone beautiful.
beautification *noun*

beauty *noun* (*plural* beauties)
1 a quality that gives pleasure to your senses or your mind. **2** a person or thing that has beauty. **3** an excellent example of something.
[from old French]

beaver *noun* (*plural* beavers)
an animal with soft brown fur and strong teeth; it builds its home in a deep pool which it makes by damming a stream.
beaver *verb* (beavers, beavering, beavered)
work hard, *beavering away*.

because *conjunction*
for the reason that.
because of for the reason of, *He limped because of his bad leg.*
[from *by* + *cause*]

beck *noun*
at someone's beck and call always ready and waiting to do what he or she asks.
[from *beckon*]

beckon *verb* (beckons, beckoning, beckoned)
make a sign to a person asking him or her to come.
[from Old English; related to *beacon*]

become *verb* (becomes, becoming, became, become)
1 come or grow to be; begin to be, *It became dark.* **2** be suitable for; make a person look attractive.
become of happen to, *What became of it?*

bed *noun* (*plural* beds)
1 a piece of furniture that you sleep or rest on, especially one with a mattress and coverings. **2** a piece of a garden where plants are grown. **3** the bottom of the sea or of a river. **4** a flat base; a foundation. **5** a layer of rock or soil.
[from Old English]

bedclothes *plural noun*
sheets, blankets, etc.

bedpan *noun* (*plural* bedpans)
a container for use as a lavatory by a bedridden person.

bedraggled (*say* bid-**rag**-eld) *adjective*
very untidy; wet and dirty.

bedridden *adjective*
too weak or ill to get out of bed.

bedrock *noun*
solid rock beneath soil.

bedroom *noun* (*plural* bedrooms)
a room for sleeping in.

bedtime *noun* (*plural* bedtimes)
the time for going to bed.

bee *noun* (*plural* bees)
a stinging insect with four wings that makes honey. [from Old English]

beech *noun* (*plural* beeches)
a tree with smooth bark and glossy leaves.

beef *noun*
meat from an ox, bull, or cow.
[from old French]

beefy *adjective*
having a solid muscular body.
beefiness *noun*

beehive *noun* (*plural* beehives)
a box or other container for bees to live in.

beeline *noun*
make a beeline for go straight or quickly towards something.
[because a bee was believed to fly in a straight line back to its hive]

beer *noun* (*plural* beers)
an alcoholic drink made from malt and hops.
beery *adjective*

beet *noun* (*plural* beet or beets)
a plant with a thick root used as a vegetable or for making sugar.

beetle *noun* (*plural* beetles)
an insect with hard shiny wing covers. [from Old English; related to *bite*]

beetroot *noun* (*plural* beetroot)
the dark red root of beet used as a vegetable.

before *adverb*
at an earlier time, *Have you been here before?*
before *preposition* & *conjunction*
1 earlier than, *I was here before you!*
2 in front of, *He came before the judge.*

beforehand *adverb*
earlier; in readiness. [from *before* + *hand* (with the idea of your hand doing something before someone else's does)]

befriend *verb* (befriends, befriending, befriended)
make friends with someone.

beg *verb* (begs, begging, begged)
1 ask to be given money, food, etc. **2** ask earnestly or humbly or formally.
beg the question argue in an illogical way by relying on the result that you are trying to prove.
go begging be available.
I beg your pardon I apologize; I did not hear what you said.

beggar *noun* (*plural* beggars)
1 a person who lives by begging. **2** (*informal*) a person, *You lucky beggar!* **beggary** *noun*

begin *verb* (begins, beginning, began, begun)
1 do the earliest or first part of something; start speaking. **2** come into existence, *The problem began last year.* **3** have something as its first part, *The word begins with B.*
[from Old English]

beginner *noun* (*plural* beginners)
a person who is just beginning to learn a subject.

begrudge *verb* (begrudges, begrudging, begrudged)
resent having to give or allow something; grudge.

beguile (*say* big-l'll) *verb* (beguiles, beguiling, beguiled)
1 amuse or fascinate. 2 deceive.

behalf *noun*
on behalf of for the benefit of someone else. on my behalf for me.
[from an old phrase *bi halve him* = on his side]

USAGE: Do not use *on behalf of* (= for someone else) when you mean *on the part of* (= by someone). For example, do not say: *This was the worst performance on behalf of Arsenal that I can remember.*

behave *verb* (behaves, behaving, behaved)
1 act in a particular way, *They behaved badly.* 2 show good manners, *Behave yourself!*
behaviour *noun*, **behavioural** *adjective*
[from *be-* + *have*]

behead *verb* (beheads, beheading, beheaded)
cut the head off a person or thing; execute a person in this way. [from Old English]

behind *adverb*
1 at or to the back; at a place people have left, *Don't leave it behind.* 2 not making good progress; late, *I'm behind with my rent.*
behind *preposition*
1 at or to the back of; on the further side of. 2 having made less progress than, *He is behind the others in French.* 3 supporting; causing, *What is behind all this trouble?*
behind a person's back kept secret from him or her deceitfully.
behind the times out of date.
behind *noun* (*plural* behinds) (*informal*)
a person's bottom. [from Old English]

behindhand *adverb* & *adjective*
1 late. 2 out of date.

beige (*say* bayzh) *noun* & *adjective*
a very light brown colour. [French]

being *noun* (*plural* beings)
1 existence. 2 a creature.

belated *adjective*
coming very late or too late.
belatedly *adverb*

belch *verb* (belches, belching, belched)
1 send out wind from your stomach through your mouth noisily. 2 send out fire or smoke etc. from an opening.
belch *noun* [from Old English]

belief *noun* (*plural* beliefs)
1 believing. 2 something a person believes.

believe *verb* (believes, believing, believed)
think that something is true or that someone is telling the truth.
believable *adjective*, **believer** *noun*

believe in think that something exists or is good or can be relied on.
[from Old English]

belittle *verb* (belittles, belittling, belittled)
make something seem of little value, *Do not belittle their success.* **belittlement** *noun*

bell *noun* (*plural* bells)
1 a cup-shaped metal instrument that makes a ringing sound when struck by the clapper hanging inside it. 2 any device that makes a ringing or buzzing sound to attract attention. 3 a bell-shaped object.

belligerent (*say* bil-ij-er-ent) *adjective*
1 aggressive; eager to fight. 2 fighting; engaged in a war. **belligerently** *adverb*, **belligerence** *noun*
[from Latin *bellum* = war + *gerens* = waging]

bellow *noun* (*plural* bellows)
1 the loud deep sound made by a bull or other large animal. 2 a deep shout.
bellow *verb* (bellows, bellowing, bellowed)
give a deep shout.

belly *noun* (*plural* bellies)
the abdomen; the stomach.

belong *verb* (belongs, belonging, belonged)
have a proper place, *The pans belong in the kitchen.*
belong to be the property of; be a member of, *We belong to the same club.*
[from *be-* + *long* = owing to, because of]

belongings *plural noun*
a person's possessions.

beloved *adjective*
dearly loved.

below *adverb*
at or to a lower position; underneath, *There's fire down below.*
below *preposition*
lower than; under, *The temperature was ten degrees below zero.*

belt *noun* (*plural* belts)
1 a strip of cloth or leather etc. worn round the waist. 2 a band of flexible material used in machinery. 3 a long narrow area, *a belt of rain.*
belt *verb* (belts, belting, belted)
1 put a belt round something. 2 (*slang*) hit or beat. 3 (*slang*) rush along.
[via Old English from Latin]

bench *noun* (*plural* benches)
1 a long seat. 2 a long table for working at. 3 the seat where judges or magistrates sit; the judges or magistrates hearing a lawsuit. [from Old English]

bend *verb* (bends, bending, bent)
1 change from being straight. 2 turn downwards; stoop, *She bent to pick it up.*
bend *noun* (*plural* bends)
a place where something bends; a curve or turn, *a bend in the road.*

bene- (*say* ben-ee) *prefix*
well (as in *benefit, benevolent*).
[from Latin *bene* = well]

beneath *preposition*
1 under. 2 unworthy of, *Cheating is beneath you.*
beneath *adverb*
underneath. [from Old English]

benefactor *noun* (*plural* **benefactors**)
a person who gives money or other help. [from *bene-* + Latin *factor* = doer]

beneficial *adjective*
having a good or helpful effect; advantageous. [from Latin *beneficium* = favour, support]

beneficiary (*say* ben-if-ish-er-ee) *noun* (*plural* **beneficiaries**)
a person who receives benefits, especially from a will. [same origin as *beneficial*]

benefit *noun* (*plural* **benefits**)
1 something that is helpful or profitable. 2 a payment to which a person is entitled from government funds or from an insurance policy.
benefit *verb* (**benefits, benefiting, benefited**)
1 do good to a person or thing. 2 receive a benefit. [from *bene-* + Latin *facere* = do]

benevolent *adjective*
1 kind and helpful. 2 formed for charitable purposes, *a benevolent fund.*
benevolently *adverb*, **benevolence** *noun*
[from *bene-* + Latin *volens* = wishing]

benign (*say* bin-I'n) *adjective*
1 kindly. 2 favourable. 3 (of a disease) mild, not malignant. **benignly** *adverb*
[from Latin *benignus* = kind-hearted]

benignant (*say* bin-ig-nant) *adjective*
kindly. [same origin as *benign*]

bent *adjective*
curved or crooked.
bent on intending to do something.
bent *noun*
a talent for something.

bequeath *verb* (**bequeaths, bequeathing, bequeathed**)
leave something to a person, especially in a will. [from *be-* + Old English *cwethan* = say]

bequest *noun* (*plural* **bequests**)
something left to a person, especially in a will.

bereaved *adjective*
deprived of a relative or friend who has died.
bereavement *noun* [from *be-* + an old word *reave* = take forcibly]

berry *noun* (*plural* **berries**)
any small round juicy fruit without a stone.
[from Old English]

berserk (*say* ber-serk) *adjective*
go berserk become uncontrollably violent.
[from Icelandic *berserkr* = wild warrior, from *ber-* = bear + *serkr* = coat]

berth *noun* (*plural* **berths**)
1 a sleeping place on a ship or train.
2 a place where a ship can moor.
give a wide berth keep at a safe distance from a person or thing.
berth *verb* (**berths, berthing, berthed**)
moor in a berth. [from *bear*^{2}]

beseech *verb* (**beseeches, beseeching, beseeched** or **besought**)
ask earnestly; implore. [from *be-* + *seek*]

beside *preposition*
1 by the side of; near. 2 compared with.
be beside himself or **herself** etc. be very excited or upset.
[from Old English *be sidan* = by the side]

besides *preposition* & *adverb*
in addition to; also, *Who came besides you? And besides, it's the wrong colour.*

besiege *verb* (**besieges, besieging, besieged**)
1 surround a place in order to capture it.
2 crowd round, *Fans besieged the singer after the concert.*

besotted *adjective*
too fond of something; fond in a silly way.

besought *past tense* of **beseech.**

best *adjective*
most excellent.
best *adverb*
1 in the best way; most. 2 most usefully; most wisely, *We had best go.*

best man *noun*
the bridegroom's chief attendant at a wedding.

bestow *verb* (**bestows, bestowing, bestowed**)
present to someone. **bestowal** *noun*

best-seller *noun* (*plural* **best-sellers**)
a book sold in large numbers.

bet *noun* (*plural* **bets**)
1 an agreement that you will pay money etc. if you are wrong in forecasting the result of a race etc. 2 the money that you agree to pay in this way.
bet *verb* (**bets, betting, bet** or **betted**)
1 make a bet. 2 (*informal*) think most likely; predict, *I bet he will forget.*

beta (*say* beet-a) *noun*
the second letter of the Greek alphabet, = b.

betray *verb* (**betrays, betraying, betrayed**)
1 be disloyal to a person or country etc.
2 reveal something that should have been kept secret. **betrayal** *noun*, **betrayer** *noun*

betrothed *adjective* (*formal*)
engaged to be married. **betroth** *verb*, **betrothal** *noun* [from *be-* + *troth*]

better *adjective*
1 more excellent; more satisfactory.
2 recovered from illness.
better *adverb*
1 in a better way; more. 2 more usefully; more wisely, *We had better go.*

better *verb* (betters, bettering, bettered)
1 improve something. 2 do better than.
betterment *noun* [from Old English]

between *preposition* & *adverb*
1 within two or more given limits, *between the walls.* 2 connecting two or more people, places, or things, *The train runs between London and Glasgow.* 3 shared by, *Divide this money between you.* 4 separating; comparing, *Can you tell the difference between them?* [from Old English]

USAGE: The preposition *between* should be followed by the object form of the pronoun (*me, her, him, them,* or *us*). The expression 'between you and I' is incorrect; say *between you and me.*

beverage *noun* (*plural* beverages)
any kind of drink. [from old French]

bewail *verb* (bewails, bewailing, bewailed)
mourn for something.

beware *verb*
be careful, *Beware of pickpockets.*
[from *be-* + *ware* = wary]

bewilder *verb* (bewilders, bewildering, bewildered)
puzzle someone hopelessly. **bewilderment** *noun* [from *be-* + an old word *wilder* = lose your way]

bewitch *verb* (bewitches, bewitching, bewitched)
1 put a magic spell on someone. 2 delight someone very much.
[from *be-* + *witch* = put under a spell]

beyond *preposition* & *adverb*
1 further than; further on, *Don't go beyond the fence.* 2 outside the range of; too difficult for, *The problem is beyond me.*

bi- *prefix*
1 two (as in *bicycle*). 2 twice (as in *biannual*).
[from Latin *bis* = twice]

bias *noun* (*plural* biases)
1 a feeling or influence for or against someone or something; a prejudice. 2 a tendency to swerve. 3 a slanting direction.

biased *adjective*
prejudiced.

bib *noun* (*plural* bibs)
1 a cloth or covering put under a baby's chin during meals. 2 the part of an apron above the waist.
[probably from Latin *bibere* = to drink]

Bible *noun* (*plural* Bibles)
the sacred book of the Jews (the Old Testament) and of the Christians (the Old and New Testament). [from Greek *biblia* = books (originally = rolls of papyrus from Byblos, a port now in Lebanon)]

biblical *adjective*
to do with or in the Bible.

bibliography (*say* bib-lee-og-ra-fee) *noun* (*plural* bibliographies)
1 a list of books about a subject or by a particular author. 2 the study of books and their history. **bibliographical** *adjective*
[from Greek *biblion* = book, + *-graphy*]

bicentenary (*say* by-sen-teen-er-ee) *noun* (*plural* bicentenaries)
a 200th anniversary.
bicentennial (*say* by-sen-ten-ee-al) *adjective*
[from *bi* + *centenary*]

biceps (*say* by-seps) *noun* (*plural* biceps)
the large muscle at the front of the arm above the elbow.
[Latin, = two-headed (because its end is attached at two points)]

bicker *verb* (bickers, bickering, bickered)
quarrel over unimportant things; squabble.

bicycle *noun* (*plural* bicycles)
a two-wheeled vehicle driven by pedals.
bicyclist *noun*
[from *bi-* + Greek *kyklos* = circle, wheel]

bid *noun* (*plural* bids)
1 the offer of an amount you are willing to pay for something, especially at an auction. 2 an attempt.
bid *verb* (bids, bidding, bid) make a bid. **bidder** *noun*
bid *verb* (bids, bidding, bid (or *old use* bade), bid or bidden)
1 command, *Do as you are bid* or *bidden.* 2 say as a greeting or farewell, *bidding them good night.*
[from two Old English words; *biddan* = to ask, and *beodan* = to announce or command]

bidding *noun*
if you do someone's bidding, you do what they tell you to do.

bide *verb* (bides, biding, bided)
if you bide your time, you wait for the right time to do something.

biennial *noun* (*plural* biennials)
a plant that lives for two years, flowering and dying in the second year.
[from Latin *biennis* = of two years]

bier (*say* beer) *noun* (*plural* biers)
a movable stand on which a coffin or a dead body is placed before it is buried.

bifocal (*say* by-foh-kal) *adjective*
(of spectacle lenses) made in two sections, with the upper part for looking at distant objects and the lower part for reading.

bifocals *plural noun*
bifocal spectacles.

big *adjective* (bigger, biggest)
1 large. 2 important, *the big match.* 3 more grown-up; elder, *my big sister.*

bigamy (*say* **big**-a-mee) *noun*
the crime of marrying a person when you are already married to someone else.
bigamous *adjective*, **bigamist** *noun*
[from *bi-* + Greek *-gamos* = married]

bigot *noun* (*plural* **bigots**)
a bigoted person. [French]

bigoted *adjective*
narrow-minded and intolerant.
bigotry *noun*

bike *noun* (*plural* **bikes**) (*informal*)
a bicycle or motorcycle.
[abbreviation of *bicycle*]

bikini *noun* (*plural* **bikinis**)
a woman's very small two-piece swimsuit.
[named after the island of Bikini in the Pacific Ocean, where an atomic bomb test was carried out in 1946, at about the time the bikini was first worn (both caused great excitement)]

bilateral *adjective*
1 of or on two sides. 2 between two people or groups, *a bilateral agreement.*
[from *bi-* + *lateral*]

bile *noun*
a bitter liquid produced by the liver, helping to digest fats. [from Latin]

bilingual (*say* by-**ling**-wal) *adjective*
1 written in two languages. 2 able to speak two languages.
[from *bi-* + Latin *lingua* = language]

bilious *adjective*
feeling sick; sickly. **biliousness** *noun*
[from *bile*]

-bility *suffix* see **-able**.

bill[1] *noun* (*plural* **bills**)
1 a written statement of charges for goods or services that have been supplied. 2 a poster. 3 a list; a programme of entertainment. 4 the draft of a proposed law to be discussed by Parliament. 5 (*American*) a banknote.
bill of fare a menu.
[same origin as *bull*[2]]

bill[2] *noun* (*plural* **bills**)
a bird's beak. [from Old English]

billabong *noun* (*plural* **billabongs**)
(in Australia) a backwater.
[an Aboriginal word]

billiards *noun*
a game in which three balls are struck with cues on a cloth-covered table (**billiard table**).
[from French *billard* = cue]

billion *noun* (*plural* **billions**)
1 a thousand million (1,000,000,000).
2 a million million (1,000,000,000,000).
billionth *adjective* & *noun*
[French, from *bi-* + *million*]

USAGE: Although the word originally meant a million million, nowadays it usually means a thousand million.

billow *noun* (*plural* **billows**)
a huge wave.

bin *noun* (*plural* **bins**)
a large or deep container.

binary (*say* **by**-ner-ee) *adjective*
involving sets of two; consisting of two parts.
[from Latin]

binary digit *noun* (*plural* **binary digits**)
either of the two digits (0 and 1) used in the system of numbers known as binary notation or the binary scale.

bind *verb* (**binds, binding, bound**)
1 fasten material round something. 2 fasten the pages of a book into a cover. 3 tie up or tie together. 4 make somebody agree to do something. **binder** *noun*
bind a person over make him or her agree not to break the law.
bind *noun* (*slang*)
a nuisance; a bore. [from Old English]

binding *noun* (*plural* **bindings**)
something that binds, especially the covers, glue, etc. of a book.
binding *adjective*
(of an agreement or promise) that must be carried out or obeyed.

binge *noun* (*plural* **binges**) (*slang*)
a time spent eating a lot of food.

bingo *noun*
a game using cards on which numbered squares are crossed out as the numbers are called out at random. [origin unknown]

binoculars *plural noun*
a device with lenses for both eyes, making distant objects seem nearer.
[from Latin *bini* = two together + *oculus* = eye]

bio- *prefix*
life (as in *biology*). [from Greek *bios* = life]

biochemistry *noun*
the study of the chemical composition and processes of living things.
biochemical *adjective*, **biochemist** *noun*

biodegradable *adjective*
able to be decomposed by bacteria, *This packaging is biodegradable.*

biography (*say* by-**og**-ra-fee) *noun* (*plural* **biographies**)
the story of a person's life.
biographical *adjective*, **biographer** *noun*

biology *noun*
the study of the life and structure of living things. **biological** *adjective*, **biologist** *noun*

bionic (*say* by-on-ik) *adjective*
(of a person or parts of the body) operated by electronic devices.
[from *bio-* + electro*nic*]

biopsy (*say* by-op-see) *noun* (*plural* **biopsies**)
examination of tissue from a living body.
[from *bio-* + auto*psy*]

biped (*say* by-ped) *noun* (*plural* **bipeds**)
a two-footed animal.
[from *bi-* + Latin *pedes* = feet]

birch *noun* (*plural* **birches**)
1 a deciduous tree with slender branches. 2 a bundle of birch branches for flogging people.
[from Old English]

bird *noun* (*plural* **birds**)
1 an animal with feathers, two wings, and two legs. 2 (*slang*) a young woman.
bird's-eye view a view from above.

birth *noun* (*plural* **births**)
1 the process by which a baby or young animal comes out from its mother's body. 2 origin; parentage, *He is of noble birth.*

birth control *noun*
ways of avoiding conceiving a baby.

birthday *noun* (*plural* **birthdays**)
the anniversary of the day a person was born.

birth rate *noun* (*plural* **birth rates**)
the number of children born in one year for every 1,000 people.

birthright *noun*
a right or privilege to which a person is entitled through being born into a particular family or country.

biscuit *noun* (*plural* **biscuits**)
a small flat kind of cake that has been baked until it is crisp. [from Latin *bis* = twice + *coctus* = cooked (because originally they were baked and then dried out in a cool oven to make them keep longer)]

bisect (*say* by-sekt) *verb* (**bisects, bisecting, bisected**)
divide something into two equal parts.
bisection *noun*, **bisector** *noun*
[from *bi-* + Latin *sectum* = cut]

bishop *noun* (*plural* **bishops**)
1 an important member of the clergy in charge of all the churches in a city or district. 2 a chess piece shaped like a bishop's mitre.
[via Old English from Latin *episcopus*]

bismuth *noun*
a greyish-white metal.

bison (*say* by-son) *noun* (*plural* **bison**)
a wild ox found in North America and Europe, with a large shaggy head.

bit[1] *noun* (*plural* **bits**)
1 a small piece or amount of something. 2 the metal part of a horse's bridle that is put into its mouth. 3 the part of a tool that cuts or grips things when twisted.
a bit 1 a short distance or time, *Wait a bit.* 2 slightly, *I'm a bit worried.*
bit by bit gradually.
[from Old English; related to *bite*]

bit[2] *past tense* of **bite**.

bit[3] *noun* (*plural* **bits**)
the smallest unit of information in a computer, expressed as a choice between two possibilities.
[from *bi*nary digi*t*]

bitch *noun* (*plural* **bitches**)
1 a female dog, fox, or wolf. 2 (*informal*) a spiteful woman. **bitchy** *adjective*

bite *verb* (**bites, biting, bit, bitten**)
1 cut or take something with your teeth. 2 penetrate; sting. 3 accept bait, *The fish are biting.*
bite the dust fall wounded and die.
bite *noun* (*plural* **bites**)
1 biting, *She took a bite.* 2 a mark or spot made by biting, *an insect bite.* 3 a snack.
[from Old English; related to *bit*[1]]

bitter *adjective*
1 tasting sharp, not sweet. 2 feeling or causing mental pain or resentment, *a bitter disappointment.* 3 very cold.
bitterly *adverb*, **bitterness** *noun*
[from Old English; related to *bite*]

bivalve *noun* (*plural* **bivalves**)
a shellfish (e.g. an oyster) that has a shell with two hinged parts.

bizarre (*say* biz-ar) *adjective*
very odd in appearance or effect.
[from Italian *bizarro* = angry]

Black *noun* (*plural* **Blacks**)
a person with a very dark or black skin.
Black *adjective*

USAGE: *Black* is the word generally preferred by African people and people of African descent.

black *noun* (*plural* **blacks**)
the very darkest colour, like coal or soot.
black *adjective*
1 of the colour black. 2 very dirty. 3 dismal; not hopeful, *The outlook is black.* 4 hostile; disapproving, *He gave me a black look.* 5 (of coffee or tea) without milk. **blackly** *adverb*, **blackness** *noun*
black *verb* (**blacks, blacking, blacked**)
make a thing black.
black out 1 cover windows etc. so that no light can penetrate. 2 faint, lose consciousness.
blackout *noun*

blackberry noun (plural blackberries)
a sweet black berry.

blackbird noun (plural blackbirds)
a European songbird, the male of which is
black.

blackboard noun (plural blackboards)
a dark board for writing on with chalk.

black box noun (plural black boxes)
a flight recorder.

blacken verb (blackens, blackening, blackened)
make or become black.

black eye noun (plural black eyes)
an eye with a bruise round it.

blackguard (say blag-erd) noun (plural
blackguards) (old use)
a wicked person.
[originally the black guard = the servants who
did the dirty jobs]

black hole noun (plural black holes)
a region in outer space with such a strong
gravitational field that no matter or radiation
can escape from it.

blacklist verb (blacklists, blacklisting, blacklisted)
put someone on a list of those who are
disapproved of.

blackmail verb (blackmails, blackmailing,
blackmailed)
demand money etc. from someone by threats.
blackmail noun, **blackmailer** noun [from black
+ mail²; literally = black armour or protection]

black market noun (plural black markets)
illegal trading.

blacksmith noun (plural blacksmiths)
a person who makes and repairs iron things,
especially one who makes and fits horseshoes.
[because of the dark colour of iron]

black spot noun (plural black spots)
a dangerous place.

bladder noun (plural bladders)
1 the bag-like part of the body in which urine
collects. 2 the inflatable bag inside a football.
[from Old English]

blade noun (plural blades)
1 the flat cutting-part of a knife, sword, axe,
etc. 2 the flat wide part of an oar, spade,
propeller, etc. 3 a flat narrow leaf, blades of
grass. 4 a broad flat bone, shoulder blade. [from
Old English]

blame verb (blames, blaming, blamed)
1 say that somebody or something has caused
what is wrong, They blamed me. 2 find fault
with someone, We can't blame them for wanting
a holiday.
blame noun (plural blames)
responsibility for what is wrong.

blancmange (say bla-monj) noun (plural
blancmanges)
a jelly-like pudding made with milk.
[from French blanc = white + mange = eat]

bland adjective
1 having a mild flavour rather than a strong
one. 2 gentle and casual; not irritating or
stimulating, a bland manner. **blandly** adverb,
blandness noun
[from Latin blandus = soft, smooth]

blank adjective
1 not written or printed on; unmarked.
2 without interest or expression, a blank look.
3 empty of thoughts, My mind's gone blank.
blankly adverb, **blankness** noun
blank noun (plural blanks)
1 an empty space. 2 a blank cartridge. [from
French blanc = white]

blanket noun (plural blankets)
1 a warm cloth covering used on a bed etc.
2 any thick soft covering, a blanket of snow.
blanket adjective
covering a wide range of conditions etc., a
blanket agreement.
[originally = woollen cloth which had not been
dyed; from French blanc = white]

blank verse noun
poetry without rhymes.

blare verb (blares, blaring, blared)
make a loud harsh sound. **blare** noun

blaspheme (say blas-feem) verb (blasphemes,
blaspheming, blasphemed)
talk or write irreverently about sacred things.

blasphemy (say blas-fim-ee) noun (plural
blasphemies)
irreverent talk about sacred things.
blasphemous adjective

blast noun (plural blasts)
1 a strong rush of wind or air. 2 a loud noise,
the blast of the trumpets.
blast verb (blasts, blasting, blasted)
blow up with explosives.
blast-off launch by the firing of rockets.
blast-off noun
[from Old English; related to blow¹]

blatant (say blay-tant) adjective
very obvious, a blatant lie. **blatantly** adverb
[from an old word meaning 'noisy']

blaze noun (plural blazes)
a very bright flame, fire, or light.
blaze verb (blazes, blazing, blazed)
1 burn or shine brightly. 2 show great feeling,
He was blazing with anger.

blazer noun (plural blazers)
a kind of jacket, often with a badge or in the
colours of a school or team etc.
[from blaze¹ (because originally blazers were
made in very bright colours and were thought
of as shining or 'blazing')]

-ble *suffix* see **-able**.

bleach *verb* (bleaches, bleaching, bleached)
make or become white.
bleach *noun* (*plural* bleaches)
a substance used to bleach things.

bleak *adjective*
1 bare and cold, *a bleak hillside*. 2 dreary or
miserable, *a bleak future*. **bleakly** *adverb*,
bleakness *noun*

bleary *adjective*
watery and not seeing clearly, *bleary eyes*.
blearily *adverb* [origin unknown]

bleat *noun* (*plural* bleats)
the cry of a lamb, goat, or calf.
bleat *verb* (bleats, bleating, bleated)
make a bleat. [imitating the sound]

bleed *verb* (bleeds, bleeding, bled)
1 lose blood. 2 draw blood or fluid from.
[from Old English; related to *blood*]

blemish *noun* (*plural* blemishes)
a flaw; a mark that spoils a thing's appearance.
blemish *verb* [from old French]

blench *verb* (blenches, blenching, blenched)
flinch. [from Old English]

blend *verb* (blends, blending, blended)
mix smoothly or easily.
blend *noun* (*plural* blends)
a mixture.

blender *noun* (*plural* blenders)
an electric machine used to mix food or turn it
into liquid.

bless *verb* (blesses, blessing, blessed)
1 make sacred or holy. 2 bring God's favour on
a person or thing.

blessing *noun* (*plural* blessings)
1 a prayer that blesses a person or thing; being
blessed. 2 something that people are glad of.

blind *adjective*
1 without the ability to see. 2 without any
thought or understanding, *blind obedience*.
3 (of a tube, passage, or road) closed at one end.
blindly *adverb*, **blindness** *noun*
blind *verb* (blinds, blinding, blinded)
make a person blind.
blind *noun* (*plural* blinds)
1 a screen for a window. 2 a deception;
something used to hide the truth, *His journey
was a blind*. [from Old English]

blind date *noun* (*plural* blind dates)
a date between a man and woman who have
not met before.

blindfold *noun* (*plural* blindfolds)
a strip of cloth tied round someone's eyes so
that they cannot see.
blindfold *verb* (blindfolds, blindfolding,
blindfolded)
cover someone's eyes with a blindfold. [from
Old English *blindfeld* = struck blind, from
blind + *fell²*]

blind spot *noun* (*plural* blind spots)
a subject that you do not understand or know
much about.

blink *verb* (blinks, blinking, blinked)
shut and open your eyes rapidly. **blink** *noun*
[from *blench*, influenced by Dutch *blinken*
= shine]

bliss *noun*
perfect happiness.
blissful *adjective*, **blissfully** *adverb*

blister *noun* (*plural* blisters)
a swelling like a bubble, especially on skin.
blister *verb* [origin unknown]

blizzard *noun* (*plural* blizzards)
a severe snowstorm. [origin unknown]

bloated *adjective*
swollen by fat, gas, or liquid.
[from Old Norse *blautr* = soft]

blob *noun* (*plural* blobs)
a small round mass of something, *blobs of
paint*.
[because *blob* sounds squelchy, like liquid]

block *noun* (*plural* blocks)
1 a solid piece of something. 2 an obstruction.
3 a large building divided into flats or offices.
4 a group of buildings.
block *verb* (blocks, blocking, blocked)
obstruct; prevent something from moving or
being used. **blockage** *noun*

blockade *noun* (*plural* blockades)
the blocking of a city or port etc. in order to
prevent people and goods from going in or out.
blockade *verb* (blockades, blockading, blockaded)
set up a blockade of a place. [from *block*]

block letters *plural noun*
plain capital letters.

blond or **blonde** *adjective*
fair-haired; fair.

blonde *noun* (*plural* blondes)
a fair-haired girl or woman.

blood *noun*
1 the red liquid that flows through veins and
arteries. 2 family relationship; ancestry, *He is
of royal blood*.
in cold blood deliberately and cruelly.
[from Old English; related to *bleed*]

blood bank *noun* (*plural* blood banks)
a place where supplies of blood and plasma for
transfusions are stored.

bloodbath *noun*
a massacre.

blood donor *noun* (*plural* blood donors)
a person who gives blood for use in
transfusions.

bloodhound *noun* (*plural* bloodhounds)
a large dog that was used to track people by
their scent.

bloodshed *noun*
the killing or wounding of people.

bloodshot *adjective*
(of eyes) streaked with red.

blood sport *noun* (*plural* **blood sports**)
a sport that involves wounding or killing animals.

bloodthirsty *adjective*
eager for bloodshed.

blood vessel *noun* (*plural* **blood vessels**)
a tube carrying blood in the body; an artery, vein, or capillary.

bloody *adjective* (**bloodier, bloodiest**)
1 bloodstained. 2 with much bloodshed, *a bloody battle*.
bloody-minded *adjective* deliberately awkward and not helpful.

bloom *noun* (*plural* **blooms**)
1 a flower. 2 the fine powder on fresh ripe grapes etc.
bloom *verb* (**blooms, blooming, bloomed**)
produce flowers. [from Old Norse]

blossom *noun* (*plural* **blossoms**)
a flower or mass of flowers, especially on a fruit tree.
blossom *verb* (**blossoms, blossoming, blossomed**)
1 produce flowers. 2 develop into something, *She blossomed into a fine singer.*

blot *noun* (*plural* **blots**)
1 a spot of ink. 2 a flaw or fault; something ugly, *a blot on the landscape.*
blot *verb* (**blots, blotting, blotted**)
1 make a blot or blots on something.
2 dry with blotting paper.
blot out 1 cross out thickly. 2 obscure, *Fog blotted out the view.*

blotch *noun* (*plural* **blotches**)
an untidy patch of colour. **blotchy** *adjective*

blotting paper *noun*
absorbent paper for soaking up ink from writing.

blouse *noun* (*plural* **blouses**)
a woman's garment like a shirt.

blow[1] *verb* (**blows, blowing, blew, blown**)
1 send out a current of air. 2 move in or with a current of air, *His hat blew off.* 3 make or sound something by blowing, *blow bubbles; blow the whistle.* 4 melt with too strong an electric current, *A fuse has blown.* 5 (*slang*) damn, *Blow you!*
blow up 1 inflate. 2 explode. 3 shatter by an explosion.
blow *noun* (*plural* **blows**)
the action of blowing. [from Old English]

blow[2] *noun* (*plural* **blows**)
1 a hard knock or hit. 2 a shock; a disaster. [origin unknown]

blubber *noun*
the fat of whales. [originally = sea foam; probably related to *bubble*]

bludgeon (*say* bluj-on) *noun* (*plural* **bludgeons**)
a short stick with a thickened end, used as a weapon.
bludgeon *verb* (**bludgeons, bludgeoning, bludgeoned**)
hit someone several times with a heavy stick or other object. [origin unknown]

blue *noun* (*plural* **blues**)
the colour of a cloudless sky.
out of the blue unexpectedly.
blue *adjective*
1 of the colour blue. 2 unhappy; depressed.
3 indecent; obscene, *blue films.* **blueness** *noun*
[via French from Germanic]

bluebottle *noun* (*plural* **bluebottles**)
a large bluish fly. [origin unknown]

blueprint *noun* (*plural* **blueprints**)
a detailed plan. [because copies of plans were made on blue paper]

blues *noun*
a slow sad jazz song or tune.
the blues a very sad feeling; depression.
[short for *blue devils*, spiteful demons believed to cause depression]

bluff[1] *verb* (**bluffs, bluffing, bluffed**)
deceive someone, especially by pretending to be someone else or to be able to do something.
bluff *noun* (*plural* **bluffs**)
bluffing; a threat that you make but do not intend to carry out.

bluff[2] *adjective*
frank and hearty in manner. **bluffness** *noun*
[originally a sailor's word to describe a blunt ship's bow]

blunder *noun* (*plural* **blunders**)
a stupid mistake.
blunder *verb* (**blunders, blundering, blundered**)
1 make a blunder. 2 move clumsily and uncertainly.

blunt *adjective*
1 not sharp. 2 speaking in plain terms; straightforward, *a blunt refusal.*
bluntly *adverb*, **bluntness** *noun*
blunt *verb* (**blunts, blunting, blunted**)
make a thing blunt.

blur *verb* (**blurs, blurring, blurred**)
make or become indistinct or smeared.
blur *noun* (*plural* **blurs**)
an indistinct appearance, *Without his glasses on, everything was a blur.*

blurt *verb* (**blurts, blurting, blurted**)
say something suddenly or tactlessly, *He blurted it out.* [origin unknown]

blush *verb* (**blushes, blushing, blushed**)
become red in the face because you are ashamed or embarrassed.

blush *noun* (*plural* **blushes**)
reddening in the face. [from Old English]

bluster *verb* (**blusters, blustering, blustered**)
1 blow in gusts; be windy. 2 talk loudly and aggressively. **blustery** *adjective*

BMX *abbreviation*
a kind of bicycle for use in racing on a dirt track. [short for bicycle *moto*-cross (*x* standing for *cross*)]

boar *noun* (*plural* **boars**)
1 a wild pig. 2 a male pig.

board *noun* (*plural* **boards**)
1 a flat piece of wood. 2 a flat piece of stiff material, e.g. a chessboard. 3 daily meals supplied in return for payment or work, *board and lodging*. 4 a committee.
on board on or in a ship, aircraft, etc.
board *verb* (**boards, boarding, boarded**)
1 go on board a ship, etc. 2 give or get meals and accommodation.
board up block with fixed boards.
[from Old English]

boarder *noun* (*plural* **boarders**)
1 a pupil who lives at a boarding school during the term. 2 a lodger who receives meals.

boarding school *noun* (*plural* **boarding schools**)
a school where pupils live during the term.

boast *verb* (**boasts, boasting, boasted**)
1 speak with great pride and try to impress people. 2 have something to be proud of, *The town boasts a fine park*. **boaster** *noun*, **boastful** *adjective*, **boastfully** *adverb*
boast *noun* (*plural* **boasts**)
a boastful statement. [origin unknown]

boat *noun* (*plural* **boats**)
a vehicle built to travel on water and carry people etc.
in the same boat in the same situation; suffering the same difficulties.

bob *verb* (**bobs, bobbing, bobbed**)
move quickly up and down.

bobsleigh or **bobsled** *noun* (*plural* **bobsleighs, bobsleds**)
a sledge with two sets of runners.

bodice *noun* (*plural* **bodices**)
the upper part of a dress. [from *body*]

body *noun* (*plural* **bodies**)
1 the structure consisting of bones and flesh etc. of a person or animal; the main part of this apart from the head and limbs. 2 a corpse. 3 the main part of something. 4 a group or quantity regarded as a unit, *the school's governing body*. 5 a distinct object or piece of matter, *Stars and planets are heavenly bodies*. **bodily** *adjective* & *adverb* [from Old English]

bodyguard *noun* (*plural* **bodyguards**)
a guard to protect a person's life.

bog *noun* (*plural* **bogs**)
an area of wet spongy ground. **boggy** *adjective*
bogged down stuck and unable to make any progress. [Scottish Gaelic, = soft]

bogus *adjective*
not real; sham.
[an American word; origin unknown]

boil[1] *verb* (**boils, boiling, boiled**)
1 make or become hot enough to bubble and give off steam. 2 cook or wash something in boiling water. 3 be very hot.
boil *noun*
boiling point, *bring the milk to the boil*. [from old French]

boil[2] *noun* (*plural* **boils**)
an inflamed swelling under the skin.
[from Old English]

boiler *noun* (*plural* **boilers**)
a container in which water is heated or clothes are boiled.

boisterous *adjective*
noisy and lively. [origin unknown]

bold *adjective*
1 brave; courageous. 2 impudent. 3 (of colours) strong and vivid. **boldly** *adverb*, **boldness** *noun* [from Old English]

bolster *noun* (*plural* **bolsters**)
a long pillow for placing across a bed under other pillows.
bolster *verb* (**bolsters, bolstering, bolstered**)
add extra support. [from Old English]

bolt *noun* (*plural* **bolts**)
1 a sliding bar for fastening a door. 2 a thick metal pin for fastening things together. 3 a sliding bar that opens and closes the breech of a rifle. 4 a shaft of lightning. 5 an arrow shot from a crossbow. 6 the action of bolting.
a bolt from the blue a surprise, usually an unpleasant one.
bolt upright quite upright.
bolt *verb* (**bolts, bolting, bolted**)
1 fasten with a bolt or bolts. 2 run away; (of a horse) run off out of control. 3 swallow food quickly. [from Old English]

bomb *noun* (*plural* **bombs**)
an explosive device.
the bomb an atomic or hydrogen bomb.
bomb *verb* (**bombs, bombing, bombed**)
attack a place with bombs.
[probably from Greek *bombos* = booming]

bombard *verb* (**bombards, bombarding, bombarded**)
1 attack with gunfire or many missiles. 2 direct a large number of questions or comments etc. at somebody. **bombardment** *noun* [same origin as *bomb*]

bomber *noun* (*plural* **bombers**)
1 someone who plants or sets off a bomb. 2 an aeroplane from which bombs are dropped.

bombshell *noun* (*plural* bombshells)
a great shock.

bonanza (*say* bon-an-za) *noun* (*plural* bonanzas)
sudden great wealth or luck.
[originally an American word; from Spanish, = good weather, prosperity]

bond *noun* (*plural* bonds)
1 a close friendship or connection between two or more people. 2 bonds ropes or chains used to tie someone up. 3 a document stating an agreement.
bond *verb* (bonds, bonding, bonded)
become closely linked or connected.

bondage *noun*
slavery; captivity.

bone *noun* (*plural* bones)
one of the hard parts of a person's or animal's body (excluding teeth, nails, horns, and cartilage).
bone *verb* (bones, boning, boned)
remove the bones from meat or fish.

bonfire *noun* (*plural* bonfires)
an outdoor fire to burn rubbish or celebrate something.
[originally *bone fire*, = a fire to dispose of people's or animals' bones]

bonnet *noun* (*plural* bonnets)
1 a hat with strings that tie under the chin. 2 a Scottish beret. 3 the hinged cover over a car engine. [from Latin *abonnis* = hat]

bonus (*say* boh-nus) *noun* (*plural* bonuses)
1 an extra payment in addition to a person's normal wages. 2 an extra benefit.
[from Latin *bonus* = good]

bony *adjective*
1 with large bones; having bones with little flesh on them. 2 full of bones. 3 like bones.

boo *verb* (boos, booing, booed)
shout 'boo' in disapproval. **boo** *noun*

booby *noun* (*plural* boobies)
a babyish or stupid person. [from Spanish]

booby prize *noun* (*plural* booby prizes)
a prize given as a joke to someone who comes last in a contest.

booby trap *noun* (*plural* booby traps)
something designed to hit or injure someone unexpectedly.

book *noun* (*plural* books)
a set of sheets of paper, usually with printing or writing on them, fastened together inside a cover. **bookseller** *noun*, **bookshop** *noun*, **bookstall** *noun*
book *verb* (books, booking, booked)
1 reserve a place in a theatre, hotel, train, etc. 2 enter a person in a police record, *The police booked him for speeding.*

bookcase *noun* (*plural* bookcases)
a piece of furniture with shelves for books.

bookkeeping *noun*
recording details of the money that is spent and received by a business.
bookkeeper *noun*

booklet *noun* (*plural* booklets)
a small thin book.

bookmaker *noun* (*plural* bookmakers)
a person whose business is taking bets.
[because the bets used to be written down in a notebook]

bookmark *noun* (*plural* bookmarks)
something to mark a place in a book.

bookworm *noun* (*plural* bookworms)
1 a grub that eats holes in books. 2 a person who loves reading.

boom *verb* (booms, booming, boomed)
1 make a deep hollow sound. 2 be growing and prospering, *Business is booming.*
boom *noun* (*plural* booms)
1 a deep hollow sound. 2 prosperity; growth.
[imitating the sound]

boomerang *noun* (*plural* boomerangs)
a curved piece of wood that can be thrown so that it returns to the thrower, originally used by Australian Aborigines.

boor *noun* (*plural* boors)
an ill-mannered person. **boorish** *adjective*

boost *verb* (boosts, boosting, boosted)
1 increase the strength, value, or reputation of a person or thing. 2 push something upwards.
booster *noun*
boost *noun* (*plural* boosts)
1 an increase. 2 an upward push.

boot *noun* (*plural* boots)
1 a shoe that covers the foot and ankle or leg. 2 the compartment for luggage in a car.
booted *adjective*

booty *noun*
valuable goods taken away by soldiers after a battle. [from old German *buite* = exchange, sharing out]

booze *verb* (boozes, boozing, boozed) (*slang*)
drink alcohol.
booze *noun* (*slang*)
alcoholic drink.

border *noun* (*plural* borders)
1 the boundary of a country; the part near this. 2 an edge. 3 something placed round an edge to strengthen or decorate it. 4 a strip of ground round a garden or part of it.
border *verb* (borders, bordering, bordered)
put or be a border to something.

borderline *noun* (*plural* borderlines)
a boundary.
borderline case something that is on the borderline between two different groups or kinds of things.

bore[1] *verb* (bores, boring, bored)
1 drill a hole. 2 get through by pushing.

bore^2 *verb* (bores, boring, bored)
make somebody feel uninterested by being
dull.
bore *noun* (*plural* bores)
a boring person or thing. **boredom** *noun*
bore^3 *past tense* of **bear**^{2}.

bored *adjective*
weary and uninterested because something is
so dull.

born *adjective*
1 having come into existence by birth. (See the
note on *borne*.) 2 having a certain natural
quality or ability, *a born leader*.

borne *past participle* of **bear**^{2}.

USAGE: The word *borne* is used before *by* or
after *have, has,* or *had,* e.g. *children borne by
Eve*; *she had borne him a son.* The word *born* is
used e.g. in *a son was born.*

borrow *verb* (borrows, borrowing, borrowed)
1 get something to use for a time, with the
intention to give it back afterwards. 2 obtain
money as a loan. **borrower** *noun*

USAGE: Do not confuse *borrow* with *lend,*
which means just the opposite.

bosom *noun* (*plural* bosoms)
a person's breast.
[from Old English]

boss *noun* (*plural* bosses) (*informal*)
a manager; a person whose job is to give orders
to workers etc.
boss *verb* (bosses, bossing, bossed) (*slang*)
order someone about.
[from Dutch *baas* = master]

bossy *adjective*
fond of ordering people about.
bossiness *noun*

botany *noun*
the study of plants.
botanical *adjective,* **botanist** *noun*
[from Greek *botane* = a plant]

both *adjective* & *pronoun*
the two; not only one, *Are both films good? Both
are old.*
both *adverb*
both ... and not only ... but also, *The house is
both small and ugly.* [from Old Norse]

bother *verb* (bothers, bothering, bothered)
1 cause somebody trouble or worry; pester.
2 take trouble; feel concern, *Don't bother to
reply.*
bother *noun*
trouble or worry.

bottle *noun* (*plural* bottles)
1 a narrow-necked container for liquids.
2 (*slang*) courage, *She showed a lot of bottle.*

bottle *verb* (bottles, bottling, bottled)
put or store something in bottles.
bottle up if you bottle up your feelings, you
keep them to yourself.

bottle bank *noun* (*plural* bottle banks)
a large container in which used glass bottles
are collected for recycling.

bottleneck *noun* (*plural* bottlenecks)
a narrow place where something, especially
traffic, cannot flow freely.

bottom *noun* (*plural* bottoms)
1 the lowest part; the base. 2 the part furthest
away, *the bottom of the garden.* 3 a person's
buttocks.
bottom *adjective*
lowest, *the bottom shelf.* [from Old English]

bough *noun* (*plural* boughs)
a large branch coming from the trunk of a tree.
[from Old English]

boulder *noun* (*plural* boulders)
a very large smooth stone.

bounce *verb* (bounces, bouncing, bounced)
1 spring back when thrown against something.
2 make a ball etc. bounce. 3 (of a cheque) be
sent back by the bank because there is not
enough money in the account. 4 jump
suddenly; move in a lively manner.
bounce *noun* (*plural* bounces)
1 the action or power of bouncing. 2 a lively
confident manner, *full of bounce.*
bouncy *adjective*
[origin unknown]

bound^1 *verb* (bounds, bounding, bounded)
jump or spring; run with jumping movements,
bounding along.
bound *noun* (*plural* bounds)
a bounding movement.

bound^2 *past tense* of **bind**.
bound *adjective*
bound to certain to, *He is bound to fail.*
bound up with closely connected with,
Happiness is bound up with success.

bound^3 *adjective*
going towards something, *We are bound for
Spain.* [from Old Norse]

bound^4 *verb* (bounds, bounding, bounded)
limit; be the boundary of, *Their land is bounded
by the river.*

boundary *noun* (*plural* boundaries)
1 a line that marks a limit. 2 a hit to the
boundary of a cricket field. [from *bound*^{4}]

bounds *plural noun*
limits.
out of bounds where you are not allowed
to go.
[from *bound*^{4}]

bouquet (*say* boh-**kay**) *noun* (*plural* bouquets)
a bunch of flowers.
[French, = group of trees]

bout *noun* (*plural* **bouts**)
1 a boxing or wrestling contest. 2 a period of exercise or work or illness, *a bout of flu.*

boutique (*say* boo-teek) *noun* (*plural* **boutiques**)
a small shop selling fashionable clothes.

bow[1] (rhymes with *go*) *noun* (*plural* **bows**)
1 a strip of wood curved by a tight string joining its ends, used for shooting arrows. 2 a wooden rod with horsehair stretched between its ends, used for playing a violin etc. 3 a knot made with loops.

bow[2] (rhymes with *cow*) *verb* (**bows, bowing, bowed**)
1 bend your body forwards to show respect or as a greeting. 2 bend downwards, *bowed by the weight.*
bow *noun* (*plural* **bows**)
bowing your body.

bow[3] (rhymes with *cow*) *noun* (*plural* **bows**)
the front part of a ship.

bowel *noun* (*plural* **bowels**)
the intestine.
[from Latin *botellus* = little sausage]

bowl[1] *noun* (*plural* **bowls**)
1 a rounded usually deep container for food or liquid. 2 the rounded part of a spoon or tobacco pipe etc.
[from Old English]

bowl[2] *noun* (*plural* **bowls**)
a ball used in the game of **bowls** or in bowling, when heavy balls are rolled towards skittles.
bowl *verb* (**bowls, bowling, bowled**)
1 send a ball to be played by a batsman. 2 get a batsman out by bowling. 3 send a ball etc. rolling. [from old French]

bow-legged *adjective*
having legs that curve outwards at the knees; bandy.

bowling *noun*
1 the game of bowls. 2 the game of knocking down skittles with a heavy ball.

bow tie *noun* (*plural* **bow ties**)
a man's necktie tied into a bow.

bow window *noun* (*plural* **bow windows**)
a curved window.

box[1] *noun* (*plural* **boxes**)
1 a container made of wood, cardboard, etc., usually with a top or lid. 2 a compartment in a theatre, lawcourt, etc., *witness box.* 3 a hut or shelter, *sentry box.* 4 a rectangular space to be filled in on a form or questionnaire. 5 a small evergreen shrub.
the box (*informal*) television.

box[2] *verb* (**boxes, boxing, boxed**)
fight with the fists. [origin unknown]

boxer *noun* (*plural* **boxers**)
1 a person who boxes. 2 a dog that looks like a bulldog.

Boxing Day *noun*
the first weekday after Christmas Day. [from the old custom of giving presents (*Christmas boxes*) to tradesmen and servants on that day]

box office *noun* (*plural* **box offices**)
an office for booking seats at a theatre or cinema etc.
[because boxes could be reserved there]

boy *noun* (*plural* **boys**)
1 a male child. 2 a young man. **boyhood** *noun*, **boyish** *adjective* [origin unknown]

boycott *verb* (**boycotts, boycotting, boycotted**)
refuse to use or have anything to do with, *They boycotted the buses when the fares went up.*
boycott *noun*
[from the name of Captain Boycott, a harsh landlord in Ireland whose tenants in 1880 refused to deal with him]

boyfriend *noun* (*plural* **boyfriends**)
a boy that a girl regularly goes out with.

bra *noun* (*plural* **bras**)
a piece of underwear worn by women to support their breasts.
[abbreviation of French *brassière*]

brace *verb* (**braces, bracing, braced**)
support; make a thing firm against something.
[from Latin *bracchia* = arms]

bracelet *noun* (*plural* **bracelets**)
an ornament worn round the wrist.
[same origin as *brace*]

braces *plural noun*
straps to hold trousers up, passing over the shoulders.

bracing *adjective*
making you feel refreshed and healthy, *the bracing sea breeze.*

bracken *noun*
1 a large fern. 2 a mass of ferns.
[from Old Norse]

bracket *noun* (*plural* **brackets**)
1 a mark used in pairs to enclose words or figures, *There are round brackets ( ) and square brackets [ ].* 2 a support attached to a wall etc. 3 a group or range between certain limits, *a high income bracket.*
bracket *verb* (**brackets, bracketing, bracketed**)
1 enclose in brackets. 2 put things together because they are similar.
[from Latin *bracae* = breeches]

brahmin *noun* (*plural* **brahmins**)
a member of the highest Hindu class, originally priests.
[from Sanskrit *brahman* = priest]

Braille *noun* (rhymes with *mail*)
a system of representing letters etc. by raised dots which blind people can read by feeling them. [named after Louis Braille, a blind French teacher who invented it in about 1830]

brain *noun* (*plural* brains)
1 the organ inside the top of the head that controls the body. 2 the mind; intelligence.

brainwash *verb* (brainwashes, brainwashing, brainwashed)
force a person to give up one set of ideas or beliefs and accept new ones; indoctrinate.

brainwave *noun* (*plural* brainwaves)
a sudden bright idea.

brainy *adjective*
clever; intelligent.

brake *noun* (*plural* brakes)
a device for slowing or stopping something.
brake *verb* (brakes, braking, braked)
use a brake. [origin unknown]

bramble *noun* (*plural* brambles)
a blackberry bush or a prickly bush like it. [from Old English; related to *broom*]

bran *noun*
ground-up husks of corn. [from old French]

branch *noun* (*plural* branches)
1 a woody arm-like part of a tree or shrub. 2 a part of a railway, road, or river etc. that leads off from the main part. 3 a shop or office etc. that belongs to a large organization.
branch *verb* (branches, branching, branched)
form a branch.
branch out start something new.
[from Latin *branca* = a paw]

brand *noun* (*plural* brands)
a particular make of goods.

brandish *verb* (brandishes, brandishing, brandished)
wave something about.

brand new *adjective*
completely new.

brandy *noun* (*plural* brandies)
a strong alcoholic drink, usually made from wine. [from Dutch *brandewijn* = burnt (distilled) wine]

brash *adjective*
1 impudent. 2 reckless. [origin unknown]

brass *noun* (*plural* brasses)
1 a metal that is an alloy of copper and zinc. 2 wind instruments made of brass, e.g. trumpets and trombones.
brass *adjective*, **brassy** *adjective*

bravado (*say* brav-ah-doh) *noun*
a display of boldness. [from Spanish]

brave *adjective*
having or showing courage. **bravely** *adverb*, **bravery** *noun*
brave *verb* (braves, braving, braved)
face and endure something bravely.
[from Latin *barbarus* = barbarous]

brawl *noun* (*plural* brawls)
a noisy quarrel or fight.

brawl *verb* (brawls, brawling, brawled)
take part in a brawl. [origin unknown]

brawny *adjective*
strong and muscular.

brazen *verb* (brazens, brazening, brazened)
brazen it out behave as if there is nothing to be ashamed of when you know you have done wrong.

breach *noun* (*plural* breaches)
1 the breaking of an agreement or rule etc. 2 a broken place; a gap.

bread *noun* (*plural* breads)
a food made by baking flour and water, usually with yeast. **breadcrumbs** *noun* [from Old English]

breadth *noun*
width; broadness. [from Old English]

break *verb* (breaks, breaking, broke, broken)
1 divide or fall into pieces by hitting or pressing. 2 fail to keep a promise or law etc. 3 stop for a time; end, *She broke her silence.* 4 change, *the weather broke.* 5 damage; stop working properly.
6 (of waves) fall in foam. 7 go suddenly or with force, *They broke through.* 8 appear suddenly, *Dawn had broken.* **breakage** *noun*
break a record do better than anyone else has done before.
break down 1 stop working properly. 2 collapse.
break out 1 begin suddenly. 2 escape.
break the news make something known.
break up 1 break into small parts. 2 separate at the end of a school term.
break *noun* (*plural* breaks)
1 a broken place; a gap. 2 an escape; a sudden dash. 3 a short rest from work.
4 a number of points scored continuously in snooker etc. 5 (*informal*) a piece of luck; an opportunity.
break of day dawn.

breakdown *noun* (*plural* breakdowns)
1 breaking down; failure. 2 a period of mental illness caused by anxiety or depression. 3 an analysis of accounts or statistics. 4 a sudden failure to work, esp. by a car, *We had a breakdown on the motorway; the breakdown of law and order.*

breakfast *noun* (*plural* breakfasts)
the first meal of the day.
[from *break* + *fast*²]

breakneck *adjective*
dangerously fast, *He had to drive at breakneck speed to get there on time.*

breakthrough *noun* (*plural* breakthroughs)
an important advance or achievement.

breast *noun* (*plural* **breasts**)
1 one of the two fleshy parts on the upper front of a woman's body that produce milk to feed a baby. 2 a person's or animal's chest.
[from Old English]

breastplate *noun* (*plural* **breastplates**)
a piece of armour covering the chest.

breath (*say* breth) *noun* (*plural* **breaths**)
1 air drawn into the lungs and sent out again.
2 a gentle blowing, *a breath of wind.*
out of breath panting. **take your breath away** surprise or delight you greatly.
under your breath in a whisper.

breathalyser *noun* (*plural* **breathalysers**)
a device for measuring the amount of alcohol in a person's breath.
breathalyse *verb* [from *breath* + *analyse*]

breathe (*say* bree*th*) *verb* (**breathes, breathing, breathed**)
1 take air into the body and send it out again.
2 speak or utter, *Don't breathe a word of this.*
[from *breath*]

breather (*say* bree-*th*er) *noun* (*plural* **breathers**)
a pause for rest, *Let's take a breather.*

breathless *adjective*
out of breath.

breed *verb* (**breeds, breeding, bred**)
1 produce young creatures. 2 keep animals in order to produce young ones from them.
3 bring up or train. 4 create or produce, *Poverty breeds illness.* **breeder** *noun*
breed *noun* (*plural* **breeds**)
a variety of animals with qualities inherited from their parents.
[from Old English; related to *brood*]

breeze *noun* (*plural* **breezes**)
a wind. **breezy** *adjective*

brevity *noun*
shortness; briefness. [same origin as *brief*]

brew *verb* (**brews, brewing, brewed**)
1 make beer or tea. 2 develop, *Trouble is brewing.*
brew *noun* (*plural* **brews**)
a brewed drink. [from Old English]

brewery *noun* (*plural* **breweries**)
a place where beer is brewed.

bribe *noun* (*plural* **bribes**)
money or a gift offered to a person to influence him or her.
bribe *verb* (**bribes, bribing, bribed**)
give someone a bribe. **bribery** *noun*
[from old French *briber* = beg]

brick *noun* (*plural* **bricks**)
1 a small hard block of baked clay etc. used to build walls. 2 a rectangular block of something.
brick *verb* (**bricks, bricking, bricked**)
close something with bricks, *We bricked up the gap in the wall.*

bricklayer *noun* (*plural* **bricklayers**)
a worker who builds with bricks.

bride *noun* (*plural* **brides**)
a woman on her wedding day. **bridal** *adjective*
[from Old English]

bridegroom *noun* (*plural* **bridegrooms**)
a man on his wedding day. [from Old English *brydguma* = bride's man]

bridesmaid *noun* (*plural* **bridesmaids**)
a girl or unmarried woman who attends the bride at a wedding.

bridge[1] *noun* (*plural* **bridges**)
1 a structure built over and across a river, railway, or road etc. to allow people to cross it.
2 a high platform above a ship's deck, for the officer in charge. 3 the bony upper part of the nose. 4 something that connects things.
bridge *verb* (**bridges, bridging, bridged**)
make or form a bridge over something.

bridge[2] *noun*
a card game rather like whist.

bridle *noun* (*plural* **bridles**)
the part of a horse's harness that fits over its head.

bridle path or **bridle road** *noun* (*plural* **bridle paths, bridle roads**)
a road suitable for horses but not for vehicles.

brief *adjective*
short. **briefly** *adverb*, **briefness** *noun*
in brief in a few words.
brief *noun* (*plural* **briefs**)
instructions and information given to someone, especially to a barrister.
brief *verb* (**briefs, briefing, briefed**)
1 give a brief to a barrister. 2 instruct or inform someone concisely in advance.
[from Latin *brevis* = short]

briefcase *noun* (*plural* **briefcases**)
a flat case for carrying documents etc.

briefing *noun* (*plural* **briefings**)
a meeting to give someone concise instructions or information.

briefs *plural noun*
very short knickers or underpants.

brigade *noun* (*plural* **brigades**)
1 a large unit of an army. 2 a group of people organized for a special purpose, *the fire brigade.*
[from Italian *brigata* = a troop]

bright *adjective*
1 giving a strong light; shining. 2 clever.
3 cheerful. **brightly** *adverb*, **brightness** *noun*

brighten *verb* (**brightens, brightening, brightened**)
make or become brighter.

brilliant *adjective*
1 very bright; sparkling. 2 very clever.
brilliantly *adverb*, **brilliance** *noun*

brim *noun* (*plural* **brims**)
1 the edge of a cup etc. 2 the bottom part of a hat that sticks out.
brim-full *adjective* completely full.
brim *verb* (**brims, brimming, brimmed**)
be full to the brim.
brim over overflow.

bring *verb* (**brings, bringing, brought**)
cause a person or thing to come; lead; carry.
bring about cause to happen.
bring off achieve; do something successfully.
bring up 1 look after and train growing children. 2 mention a subject. 3 vomit. 4 cause to stop suddenly.

brisk *adjective*
quick and lively. **briskly** *adverb*,
briskness *noun* [same origin as *brusque*]

bristle *noun* (*plural* **bristles**)
1 a short stiff hair. 2 one of the stiff pieces of hair, wire, or plastic etc. in a brush.
bristly *adjective*
bristle *verb* (**bristles, bristling, bristled**)
1 (of an animal) raise its bristles in anger or fear. 2 show indignation.
bristle with be full of, *The plan bristled with problems.*

Britain *noun*
the island made up of England, Scotland, and Wales, with the small adjacent islands; Great Britain.

USAGE: Note the difference in use between the terms *Britain, Great Britain*, the *United Kingdom*, and the *British Isles*. Great Britain (or Britain) is used to refer to the island made up of England, Scotland, and Wales. The United Kingdom includes Great Britain and Northern Ireland. The British Isles refers to the whole of the island group which includes Great Britain, Ireland, and all the smaller nearby islands.

British Isles *plural noun*
the island group which includes Great Britain, Ireland, and all the smaller nearby islands.

USAGE: See note at *Britain*.

brittle *adjective*
hard but easy to break or snap. **brittleness** *noun*
[from Old English]

broad *adjective*
1 large across; wide. 2 full and complete, *broad daylight.* 3 in general terms; not detailed, *We are in broad agreement.* 4 strong and unmistakable, *a broad hint; a broad accent.*
broadly *adverb*, **broadness** *noun*
[from Old English]

broad bean *noun* (*plural* **broad beans**)
a bean with large flat seeds.

broadcast *noun* (*plural* **broadcasts**)
a programme sent out on the radio or on television.
broadcast *verb* (**broadcasts, broadcasting, broadcast**)
send out a programme on the radio or on television. **broadcaster** *noun* [originally = to scatter widely: from *broad* + *cast*]

broaden *verb* (**broadens, broadening, broadened**)
make or become broader.

broad-minded *adjective*
tolerant; not easily shocked.

broccoli *noun* (*plural* **broccoli**)
a kind of cauliflower with greenish flowerheads. [Italian, = cabbage-heads]

brochure (*say* broh-shoor) *noun* (*plural* **brochures**)
a booklet or pamphlet containing information.
[from French, = stitching (because originally the pages were roughly stitched together)]

broke *adjective* (*informal*)
having spent all your money.
[old past participle of *break*]

broken-hearted *adjective*
overwhelmed with grief.

broken home *noun* (*plural* **broken homes**)
a family lacking one parent through divorce or separation.

bronchitis (*say* bronk-I-tiss) *noun*
a disease with bronchial inflammation, which makes you cough a lot.
[from Greek *bronchos* = windpipe, + *-itis*]

bronze *noun* (*plural* **bronzes**)
1 a metal that is an alloy of copper and tin. 2 something made of bronze. 3 a bronze medal. 4 yellowish-brown. **bronze** *adjective* [probably from Persian *birinj* = brass]

Bronze Age *noun*
the time when tools and weapons were made of bronze.

brooch *noun* (*plural* **brooches**)
an ornament with a hinged pin for fastening it on to clothes.
[a different spelling of *broach*]

brood *noun* (*plural* **broods**)
young birds that were hatched together.
brood *verb* (**broods, brooding, brooded**)
1 sit on eggs to hatch them. 2 keep thinking about something, especially with resentment.
[from Old English]

brook *noun* (*plural* **brooks**)
a small stream. [from Old English *broc*]

broom *noun* (*plural* **brooms**)
1 a brush with a long handle, for sweeping. 2 a shrub with yellow, white, or pink flowers.

broomstick *noun* (*plural* **broomsticks**)
a broom-handle.

broth *noun* (*plural* **broths**)
a kind of thin soup. [from Old English]

brother *noun* (*plural* **brothers**)
1 a son of the same parents as another person.
2 a man who is a fellow member of a Church, trade union, etc.
brotherly *adjective* [from Old English]

brother-in-law *noun* (*plural* **brothers-in-law**)
the brother of a married person's husband or wife; the husband of a person's sister.

brow *noun* (*plural* **brows**)
1 an eyebrow. 2 the forehead. 3 the ridge at the top of a hill; the edge of a cliff.

brown *noun* (*plural* **browns**)
a colour between orange and black.
brown *adjective*
1 of the colour brown. 2 having a brown skin; suntanned.

Brownie *noun* (*plural* **Brownies**)
a member of a junior branch of the Guides.

browse *verb* (**browses, browsing, browsed**)
1 read or look at something casually. 2 feed on grass or leaves. [from old French]

bruise *noun* (*plural* **bruises**)
a dark mark made on the skin by hitting it.
bruise *verb* (**bruises, bruising, bruised**)
give or get a bruise or bruises.
[from Old English]

brunette *noun* (*plural* **brunettes**)
a woman with dark-brown hair.
[from French *brun* = brown, + *-ette*]

brunt *noun*
the chief impact or strain, *They bore the brunt of the attack.* [origin unknown]

brush *noun* (*plural* **brushes**)
1 an implement used for cleaning or painting things or for smoothing the hair, usually with pieces of hair, wire, or plastic etc. set in a solid base. 2 a fox's bushy tail. 3 brushing, *Give it a good brush.* 4 a short fight, *They had a brush with the enemy.*
brush *verb* (**brushes, brushing, brushed**)
1 use a brush on something. 2 touch gently in passing.
brush up revise a subject.

brusque (*say* bruusk) *adjective*
curt and offhand in manner.
brusquely *adverb*

Brussels sprouts *plural noun*
the edible buds of a kind of cabbage.

brutal *adjective*
very cruel. **brutally** *adverb*, **brutality** *noun*

brute *noun* (*plural* **brutes**)
1 a brutal person. 2 an animal. **brutish** *adjective*
[from Latin *brutus* = stupid]

BSE *abbreviation*
bovine spongiform encephalopathy; a fatal disease of cattle that affects the nervous system and makes the cow stagger about. BSE is sometimes known as 'mad cow disease'.

bubble *noun* (*plural* **bubbles**)
1 a thin transparent ball of liquid filled with air or gas. 2 a small ball of air in something.
bubbly *adjective*
bubble *verb* (**bubbles, bubbling, bubbled**)
1 send up bubbles; rise in bubbles. 2 show great liveliness. [related to *burble*]

buccaneer *noun* (*plural* **buccaneers**)
a pirate. [from French]

buck *noun* (*plural* **bucks**)
a male deer, rabbit, or hare.
buck *verb* (**bucks, bucking, bucked**)
(of a horse) jump with its back arched.
buck up (*informal*) 1 hurry. 2 cheer up.

bucket *noun* (*plural* **buckets**)
a container with a handle, for carrying liquids etc. **bucketful** *noun* [from French]

buckle *noun* (*plural* **buckles**)
a device through which a belt or strap is threaded to fasten it.
buckle *verb* (**buckles, buckling, buckled**)
fasten something with a buckle.

bud *noun* (*plural* **buds**)
a flower or leaf before it opens.
[origin unknown]

Buddhism (*say* buud-izm) *noun*
a faith that started in Asia and follows the teachings of the Indian philosopher Gautama Buddha, who lived in the 5th century BC.
Buddhist *noun*
[from Sanskrit *Buddha* = enlightened one]

budge *verb* (**budges, budging, budged**)
if you cannot budge something, you cannot move it at all. [from French]

budgerigar *noun* (*plural* **budgerigars**)
an Australian bird often kept as a pet in a cage. [from Australian Aboriginal *budgeri* = good + *gar* = cockatoo]

budget *noun* (*plural* **budgets**)
1 a plan for spending money wisely. 2 an amount of money set aside for a purpose.
budgetary *adjective*
the Budget the Chancellor of the Exchequer's statement of plans to raise money (e.g. by taxes).

buffalo *noun* (*plural* **buffalo** or **buffaloes**)
a large ox. Different kinds are found in Asia, Africa, and North America (where they are also called *bison*).

buffer *noun* (*plural* **buffers**)
something that softens a blow, especially a device on a railway engine or wagon or at the

end of a track.
[from an old word *buff* = a blow (as in *blind man's buff*): related to *buffet*²]

buffet¹ (*say* buu-fay) *noun* (*plural* buffets)
1 a café at a station. 2 a meal where guests serve themselves. [from French = stool]

buffet² (*say* buf-it) *noun* (*plural* buffets)
a hit, especially with the hand.
buffet *verb* (buffets, buffeting, buffeted)
hit or knock, *Strong winds buffeted the aircraft.*
[from old French *buffe* = a blow]

buffoon *noun* (*plural* buffoons)
a person who plays the fool. **buffoonery** *noun*
[from Latin *buffo* = clown]

bug *noun* (*plural* bugs)
1 an insect. 2 an error in a computer program that prevents it working properly. 3 (*informal*) a germ or virus. 3 (*informal*) a secret hidden microphone.
bug *verb* (bugs, bugging, bugged) (*slang*)
1 fit with a secret hidden microphone.
2 annoy. [origin unknown]

bugbear *noun* (*plural* bugbears)
something you fear or dislike.
[from an old word *bug* = bogy]

build *verb* (builds, building, built)
make something by putting parts together.
build in include. **built-in** *adjective*
build up 1 establish gradually. **2** accumulate.
3 cover an area with buildings. **4** make stronger or more famous, *build up a reputation.*
built-up *adjective*
build *noun* (*plural* builds)
the shape of someone's body, *of slender build.*
[from Old English]

builder *noun* (*plural* builders)
someone who puts up buildings.

building *noun* (*plural* buildings)
1 the process of constructing houses etc. 2 a permanent built structure that people can go into.

building society *noun* (*plural* building societies)
an organization that accepts deposits of money and lends to people who want to buy houses etc.

bulb *noun* (*plural* bulbs)
1 a thick rounded part of a plant from which a stem grows up and roots grow down. 2 a rounded part of something, *the bulb of a thermometer.* 3 a glass globe that produces electric light. **bulbous** *adjective* [from Greek *bolbos* = onion]

bulge *noun* (*plural* bulges)
a rounded swelling; an outward curve.
bulgy *adjective*
bulge *verb* (bulges, bulging, bulged)
form or cause to form a bulge.

bulk *noun* (*plural* bulks)
1 the size of something, especially when it is large. 2 the greater portion; the majority, *The bulk of the population voted for it.*
in bulk in large amounts.
bulk *verb* (bulks, bulking, bulked)
increase the size or thickness of something, *bulk it out.* [from Old English]

bulky *adjective* (bulkier, bulkiest)
taking up a lot of space. **bulkiness** *noun*

bull *noun* (*plural* bulls)
the fully-grown male of cattle or of certain other large animals (e.g. elephant, whale, seal). [from Old Norse]

bulldog *noun* (*plural* bulldogs)
a dog of a powerful courageous breed with a short thick neck.
[because it was used for attacking tethered bulls in the sport of 'bull-baiting']

bulldozer *noun* (*plural* bulldozers)
a powerful tractor with a wide metal blade or scoop in front, used for shifting soil or clearing ground.

bullet *noun* (*plural* bullets)
a small lump of metal shot from a rifle or revolver. [from French *boulet* = little ball]

bulletin *noun* (*plural* bulletins)
a public statement giving news.

bullfight *noun* (*plural* bullfights)
a public entertainment in which bulls are tormented and killed in an arena.
bullfighter *noun*

bullock *noun* (*plural* bullocks)
a young castrated bull.
[from Old English *bulloc* = young bull]

bull's-eye *noun* (*plural* bull's-eyes)
the centre of a target

bully *verb* (bullies, bullying, bullied)
1 use strength or power to hurt or frighten a weaker person. 2 start play in hockey, when two opponents tap the ground and each other's stick, *bully off.*
bully *noun* (*plural* bullies)
someone who bullies people.

bulwark *noun* (*plural* bulwarks)
a wall of earth built as a defence; a protection. [from German or Dutch]

bumble-bee *noun* (*plural* bumble-bees)
a large bee with a loud hum.

bump *verb* (bumps, bumping, bumped)
1 knock against something. 2 move along with jolts.
bump into (*informal*) meet by chance.
bump off (*slang*) kill.
bump *noun* (*plural* bumps)
1 the action or sound of bumping. 2 a swelling or lump. **bumpy** *adjective*

bumper[1] *noun* (*plural* **bumpers**)
1 a bar along the front or back of a motor vehicle to protect it in collisions. 2 a ball in cricket that bounces high.

bumper[2] *adjective*
unusually large or plentiful, *a bumper crop.*

bumpkin *noun* (*plural* **bumpkins**)
a country person with awkward manners.

bun *noun* (*plural* **buns**)
1 a small round sweet cake. 2 hair twisted into a round bunch at the back of the head.

bunch *noun* (*plural* **bunches**)
a number of things joined or fastened together. [origin unknown]

bundle *noun* (*plural* **bundles**)
a number of things tied or wrapped together.
bundle *verb* (**bundles, bundling, bundled**)
1 make a number of things into a bundle. 2 push hurriedly or carelessly, *They bundled him into a taxi.*

bungalow *noun* (*plural* **bungalows**)
a house without any upstairs rooms. [from Hindi *bangla* = of Bengal]

bungle *verb* (**bungles, bungling, bungled**)
make a mess of doing something. **bungler** *noun* [because *bungle* sounds clumsy]

bunion *noun* (*plural* **bunions**)
a swelling at the side of the joint where the big toe joins the foot. [origin unknown]

bunk *noun* (*plural* **bunks**)
a bed built like a shelf. [origin unknown]

bunker *noun* (*plural* **bunkers**)
1 a container for storing fuel. 2 a sandy hollow built as an obstacle on a golf course. 3 an underground shelter.

bunny *noun* (*plural* **bunnies**) (*informal*)
a rabbit. [from dialect *bun* = rabbit]

Bunsen burner *noun* (*plural* **Bunsen burners**)
a small gas burner used in scientific work. [named after a German scientist, R. W. Bunsen]

bunting[1] *noun* (*plural* **buntings**)
a kind of small bird. [origin unknown]

bunting[2] *noun*
strips of small flags hung up to decorate streets and buildings. [origin unknown]

buoy (*say* boi) *noun* (*plural* **buoys**)
a floating object anchored to mark a channel or underwater rocks etc.

buoyant (*say* boi-ant) *adjective*
1 able to float. 2 light-hearted; cheerful.
buoyantly *adverb*, **buoyancy** *noun* [from French or Spanish; related to *buoy*]

bur *noun* (*plural* **burs**)
a plant's seed case or fruit that clings to hair or clothes.

burden *noun* (*plural* **burdens**)
1 a heavy load that you have to carry. 2 something troublesome that you have to bear, *Exams are a burden.*
burdensome *adjective*
burden *verb* (**burdens, burdening, burdened**)
put a burden on a person etc.

bureau (*say* bewr-oh) *noun* (*plural* **bureaux**)
1 a writing desk. 2 a business office, *They will tell you at the Information Bureau.* [French, = desk]

bureaucracy (*say* bewr-ok-ra-see) *noun*
the use of too many rules and forms by officials, especially in government departments.
bureaucratic (*say* bewr-ok-**rat**-ik) *adjective*

burglar *noun* (*plural* **burglars**)
a person who enters a building illegally, especially in order to steal things.
burglary *noun* [from French]

burgle *verb* (**burgles, burgling, burgled**)
rob a place as a burglar. [from *burglar*]

burgundy *noun* (*plural* **burgundies**)
a rich red or white wine. [originally made in Burgundy in France]

burial *noun* (*plural* **burials**)
burying somebody.

burlesque (*say* ber-**lesk**) *noun* (*plural* **burlesques**)
a comical imitation. [via French from Italian *burla* = ridicule, joke]

burly *adjective* (**burlier, burliest**)
having a strong heavy body. [from Old English]

burn *verb* (**burns, burning, burned** or **burnt**)
1 blaze or glow with fire; produce heat or light by combustion. 2 damage or destroy something by fire, heat, or chemicals. 3 be damaged or destroyed by fire etc. 4 feel very hot.

USAGE: The word *burnt* (not *burned*) is always used when an adjective is required, e.g. in *burnt wood.* As parts of the verb, either *burned* or *burnt* may be used, e.g. *the wood had burned* or *had burnt completely.*

burn *noun* (*plural* **burns**)
1 a mark or injury made by burning. 2 the firing of a spacecraft's rockets. [from Old English *birnan*]

burning *adjective*
1 intense, *a burning ambition.* 2 very important; hotly discussed, *a burning question.*

burr *noun* (*plural* **burrs**)
1 a bur. 2 a whirring sound. 3 a soft country accent. [a different spelling of *bur*]

burrow *noun* (*plural* **burrows**)
a hole or tunnel dug by a rabbit or fox etc. as a dwelling.

burrow *verb* (burrows, burrowing, burrowed)
1 dig a burrow. 2 push your way through or into something; search deeply, *She burrowed in her handbag.*

bursar *noun* (*plural* bursars)
a person who manages the finances and other business of a school or college.
[from Latin *bursa* = a bag]

burst *verb* (bursts, bursting, burst)
1 break or force apart. 2 come or start suddenly, *It burst into flame. They burst out laughing.* 3 be very full, *bursting with energy.*
burst *noun* (*plural* bursts)
1 bursting; a split. 2 something short and forceful, *a burst of gunfire.*

bury *verb* (buries, burying, buried)
1 place a dead body in the earth, a tomb, or the sea. 2 put underground; cover up.

bus *noun* (*plural* buses)
a large vehicle for passengers to travel in.
[short for *omnibus*]

bush *noun* (*plural* bushes)
1 a shrub. 2 wild uncultivated land, especially in Africa and Australia. **bushy** *adjective* [from old French or Old Norse]

bushel *noun* (*plural* bushels)
a measure for grain and fruit (8 gallons or 4 pecks). [from old French]

business (*say* biz-niss) *noun* (*plural* businesses)
1 a person's concern or responsibilities, *Mind your own business.* 2 an affair or subject, *I'm tired of the whole business.* 3 a shop or firm. 4 buying and selling things; trade.
businessman *noun*, **businesswoman** *noun*
[from Old English *bisignis* = busyness]

bust *noun* (*plural* busts)
1 a sculpture of a person's head, shoulders, and chest. 2 the upper front part of a woman's body. [from Latin]

bustle *verb* (bustles, bustling, bustled)
hurry in a busy or excited way.
bustle *noun*
hurried or excited activity.

busy *adjective* (busier, busiest)
1 having much to do; occupied. 2 full of activity. **busily** *adverb*, **busyness** *noun*
busy *verb* (busies, busying, busied)
busy yourself occupy yourself; keep busy.

busybody *noun* (*plural* busybodies)
a person who interferes.

but *conjunction*
however; nevertheless, *I wanted to go, but I couldn't.*
but *preposition*
except, *There is no one here but me.*
but *adverb*
only; no more than, *We can but try.*
[from Old English]

butcher *noun* (*plural* butchers)
1 a person who cuts up meat and sells it. 2 a person who kills cruelly or needlessly.
butchery *noun*
butcher *verb* (butchers, butchering, butchered)
kill cruelly or needlessly.

butt[1] *noun* (*plural* butts)
1 the thicker end of a weapon or tool. 2 a stub, *cigarette butts.*
[from Dutch *bot* = stumpy]

butt[2] *noun* (*plural* butts)
a large cask or barrel.
[from Latin *buttis* = cask]

butt[3] *noun* (*plural* butts)
a person or thing that is a target for ridicule or teasing, *He was the butt of their jokes.*
[from old French *but* = goal]

butt[4] *verb* (butts, butting, butted)
1 push or hit with the head as a ram or goat does. 2 place the edges of things together.
butt in interrupt or meddle.
[from old French *buter* = hit]

butter *noun*
a soft fatty food made by churning cream.
buttery *adjective* [from Old English]

buttercup *noun* (*plural* buttercups)
a wild plant with bright yellow cup-shaped flowers.

butterfly *noun* (*plural* butterflies)
1 an insect with large white or coloured wings. 2 a swimming stroke in which both arms are lifted at the same time.

buttock *noun* (*plural* buttocks)
either of the two fleshy rounded parts of your bottom. [from Old English]

button *noun* (*plural* buttons)
1 a knob or disc sewn on clothes as a fastening or ornament. 2 a small knob, *Press the button.*
button *verb* (buttons, buttoning, buttoned)
fasten something with a button or buttons.

buttonhole *noun* (*plural* buttonholes)
1 a slit through which a button passes to fasten clothes. 2 a flower worn on a lapel.
buttonhole *verb* (buttonholes, buttonholing, buttonholed)
stop somebody so that you can talk to him or her.

buttress *noun* (*plural* buttresses)
a support built against a wall.

buy *verb* (buys, buying, bought)
get something by paying for it. **buyer** *noun*
buy *noun* (*plural* buys)
something that is bought.

buzz *noun* (*plural* buzzes)
a vibrating humming sound.
buzz *verb* (buzzes, buzzing, buzzed)
1 make a buzz. 2 threaten an aircraft by deliberately flying close to it.

by *preposition*
This word is used to show **1** closeness (*Sit by me*), **2** direction or route (*We got here by a short cut*), **3** time (*They came by night*), **4** manner or method (*cooking by gas*), **5** amount (*You missed it by inches*).
by the way incidentally.
by yourself alone; without help.
by *adverb*
1 past, *I can't get by*. **2** in reserve; for future use, *Put it by*.
by and by soon; later on.
by and large on the whole.

by-election *noun* (*plural* **by-elections**)
an election to replace a Member of Parliament who has died or resigned. [from *by-* = extra (an 'extra' election between general elections)]

bygone *adjective*
belonging to the past.
let bygones be bygones forgive and forget.

bypass *noun* (*plural* **bypasses**)
1 a road taking traffic past a city etc. **2** a channel that allows something to flow when the main route is blocked.
bypass *verb* (**bypasses, bypassing, bypassed**)
avoid something by means of a bypass.

by-product *noun* (*plural* **by-products**)
something produced while something else is being made.
[from *by-* = at the side, besides]

byroad *noun* (*plural* **byroads**)
a minor road.

bystander *noun* (*plural* **bystanders**)
a person standing near but not taking part in something.

byte *noun* (*plural* **bytes**)
a fixed number of bits (= binary digits) in a computer, often representing a single character. [an invented word]

byword *noun* (*plural* **bywords**)
a person or thing spoken of as a famous example, *Their firm became a byword for quality*.
[from Old English *biwyrde* = proverb]

Cc

cab *noun* (*plural* **cabs**)
1 a taxi. **2** a compartment for the driver of a lorry, train, bus, or crane. [short for *cabriolet* = a light horsedrawn carriage]

cabaret (*say* **kab**-er-ay) *noun* (*plural* **cabarets**)
an entertainment, especially one provided for the customers in a restaurant or nightclub.
[from old French]

cabbage *noun* (*plural* **cabbages**)
a vegetable with green or purple leaves. [from old French *caboche* = head]

cabin *noun* (*plural* **cabins**)
1 a hut or shelter. **2** a compartment in a ship, aircraft, or spacecraft. **3** a driver's cab.
[from Latin]

Cabinet *noun*
the group of chief ministers, chosen by the Prime Minister, who meet to decide government policy.

cabinet *noun* (*plural* **cabinets**)
a cupboard or container with drawers or shelves. [from *cabin*]

cable *noun* (*plural* **cables**)
1 a thick rope of fibre or wire; a thick chain. **2** a covered group of wires laid underground for transmitting electrical signals. **3** a telegram sent overseas.
[from Latin *capulum* = halter]

cackle *noun* (*plural* **cackles**)
1 a loud silly laugh. **2** noisy chatter. **3** the loud clucking noise a hen makes.
cackle *verb*
[from old German or Dutch *kake* = jaw]

cactus *noun* (*plural* **cacti**)
a fleshy plant, usually with prickles, from a hot dry climate. [from Greek]

cad *noun* (*plural* **cads**)
a dishonourable person.
[short for *caddie* or *cadet*]

cadaverous (*say* kad-**av**-er-us) *adjective*
pale and gaunt.
[from Latin *cadaver* = corpse]

caddie *noun* (*plural* **caddies**)
a person who carries a golfer's clubs during a game. [from *cadet*]

cadence (*say* **kay**-denss) *noun* (*plural* **cadences**)
1 rhythm; the rise and fall of the voice in speaking. **2** the final notes of a musical phrase. [via French from Latin *cadere* = fall]

cadenza (*say* ka-**den**-za) *noun* (*plural* **cadenzas**)
an elaborate passage for a solo instrument or singer, to show the performer's skill. [via Italian from Latin *cadere* = fall]

cadet *noun* (*plural* **cadets**)
a young person being trained for the armed forces or the police.
[French, = younger son]

cadge *verb* (**cadges, cadging, cadged**)
get something by begging for it.
cadger *noun* [origin unknown]

cadmium *noun*
a metal that looks like tin. [from Latin]

Caesarean section (*say* siz-**air**-ee-an) (*plural* **Caesarean sections**)
a surgical operation for taking a baby out of

the mother's womb.
[so called because Julius Caesar is said to have
been born in this way]

café (*say* kaf-ay) *noun* (*plural* cafés)
a small restaurant.
[French, = coffee, coffee house]

caffeine (*say* kaf-een) *noun*
a stimulant substance found in tea and coffee.
[French, from *café* = coffee]

cage *noun* (*plural* cages)
1 a container with bars or wires, in which
birds or animals are kept. 2 the enclosed
platform of a lift. [from French]

cairn *noun* (*plural* cairns)
a pile of loose stones set up as a landmark or
monument. [from Scottish Gaelic]

cajole *verb* (cajoles, cajoling, cajoled)
persuade someone to do something by
flattering them; coax. [from French]

cake *noun* (*plural* cakes)
1 a baked food made from a mixture of flour,
fat, eggs, sugar, etc. 2 a shaped or hardened
mass, *a cake of soap; fish cakes.*

caked *adjective*
covered with dried mud etc.

calamine *noun*
a pink powder used to make a soothing lotion
for the skin. [from Latin]

calamity *noun* (*plural* calamities)
a disaster. **calamitous** *adjective* [from Latin]

calcium *noun*
a chemical substance found in teeth, bones,
and lime. [from Latin *calx* = lime^1]

calculate *verb* (calculates, calculating, calculated)
1 work something out by using mathematics.
2 plan something deliberately; intend, *Her
remarks were calculated to hurt me.*
calculable *adjective*, **calculation** *noun*
[same origin as *calculus*]

calculator *noun* (*plural* calculators)
a small electronic device for making
calculations.

calculus *noun*
mathematics for working out problems about
rates of change. [from Latin *calculus* = small
stone (used on an abacus)]

calendar *noun* (*plural* calendars)
something that shows the dates of the month or
year. [from Latin *kalendae* = the first day of the
month]

calf^1 *noun* (*plural* calves)
a young cow, whale, seal, etc.
[from Old English]

calf^2 *noun* (*plural* calves)
the fleshy back part of the leg below the knee.
[from Old Norse]

calibre (*say* kal-ib-er) *noun* (*plural* calibres)
1 the diameter of a tube or gun barrel, or of a
bullet etc. 2 ability; importance, *someone of
your calibre.* [French]

call *noun* (*plural* calls)
1 a shout or cry. 2 a visit. 3 telephoning
somebody. 4 a summons.

call *verb* (calls, calling, called)
1 shout or speak loudly, e.g. to attract
someone's attention. 2 telephone somebody.
3 name a person or thing, *They've decided to
call the baby Alexander.* 4 tell somebody to
come to you; summon. 5 make a short visit.
caller *noun*
call a person's bluff challenge a person to do
what was threatened, and expose the fact that
it was a bluff.
call for 1 come and collect. 2 require, *The
scandal calls for investigation.*
call up summon to join the armed forces.

calligraphy (*say* kal-ig-raf-ee) *noun*
the art of beautiful handwriting.
[from Greek *kalos* = beautiful, + *-graphy*]

calling *noun* (*plural* callings)
an occupation; a profession or trade.
[from the idea that God had called you to that
occupation]

callous (*say* kal-us) *adjective*
hard-hearted; unsympathetic.
callously *adverb*, **callousness** *noun*

calm *adjective*
1 quiet and still; not windy. 2 not excited or
agitated. **calmly** *adverb*, **calmness** *noun*
calm *verb* (calms, calming, calmed)
make or become calm. [from Greek *kauma*
= hot time of the day (when people rested)]

calorie *noun* (*plural* calories)
a unit for measuring an amount of heat or the
energy produced by food. **calorific** *adjective*
[from Latin *calor* = heat]

calypso *noun* (*plural* calypsos)
a West Indian song about current happenings.
[origin unknown]

calyx (*say* kay-liks) *noun* (*plural* calyces)
a ring of leaves (*sepals*) forming the outer case
of a bud. [from Greek]

camcorder *noun* (*plural* camcorders)
a combined video camera and sound recorder.
[from *camera* + *recorder*]

camel *noun* (*plural* camels)
a large animal with a long neck and either one
or two humps on its back, used in desert
countries for riding and for carrying goods.
[from Greek]

cameo (*say* kam-ee-oh) *noun* (*plural* cameos)
1 a small hard piece of stone carved with a
raised design in its upper layer. 2 a short well-
performed part in a play etc.

camera noun (plural **cameras**)
a device for taking photographs, films, or television pictures. **cameraman** noun
in camera in a judge's private room; in private. [Latin, = vault, chamber]

camouflage (say kam-off-lahzh) noun
a way of hiding things by making them look like part of their surroundings.
camouflage verb (**camouflages, camouflaging, camouflaged**)
hide by camouflage.
[from French camoufler = disguise]

camp noun (plural **camps**)
a place where people live in tents or huts etc. **campsite** noun
camp verb (**camps, camping, camped**)
make a camp; live in a camp. **camper** noun
[same origin as campus]

campaign noun (plural **campaigns**)
1 a series of battles in one area or with one purpose. 2 a planned series of actions, an advertising campaign.
campaign verb (**campaigns, campaigning, campaigned**)
take part in a campaign. **campaigner** noun
[from Latin campania = a piece of open ground]

camphor noun
a strong-smelling white substance used in medicine and mothballs and in making plastics. **camphorated** adjective

campus noun (plural **campuses**)
the grounds of a university or college.
[Latin, = field]

can[1] noun (plural **cans**)
1 a sealed tin in which food or drink is preserved. 2 a metal or plastic container for liquids.
can verb (**cans, canning, canned**)
preserve in a sealed can. **canner** noun [from Old English canne = container for liquids]

can[2] auxiliary verb (past tense **could**)
1 be able to, He can play the violin. 2 have permission to, You can go. [from Old English cunnan = know, know how to do]

USAGE: Some people object to can being used with the meaning 'have permission to' and insist that you should only use may for this meaning. Can is widely used in this meaning, however, and in most situations there is little reason to prefer may. May is appropriate, though, in formal or official writing.

canal noun (plural **canals**)
1 an artificial river cut through land so that boats can sail along it or so that it can drain or irrigate an area. 2 a tube through which something passes in the body, the alimentary canal. [same origin as channel]

canary noun (plural **canaries**)
a small yellow bird that sings.
[because it came from the Canary Islands]

cancel verb (**cancels, cancelling, cancelled**)
1 say that something planned will not be done or will not take place. 2 stop an order or instruction for something. 3 mark a stamp or ticket etc. so that it cannot be used again.
cancellation noun
cancel out stop each other's effect, The good and harm cancel each other out.

cancer noun (plural **cancers**)
1 a disease in which harmful growths form in the body. 2 a tumour, especially a harmful one.
cancerous adjective
[Latin, = crab, creeping ulcer]

candid adjective
frank. **candidly** adverb, **candour** noun
[from Latin candidus = white]

candidate noun (plural **candidates**)
1 a person who wants to be elected or chosen for a particular job or position etc. 2 a person taking an examination.
candidacy noun, **candidature** noun
[from Latin candidus = white (because Roman candidates for office had to wear a pure white toga)]

candle noun (plural **candles**)
a stick of wax with a wick through it, giving light when burning. **candlelight** noun
[Old English from Latin, from candere = be white, shine]

candyfloss noun (plural **candyflosses**)
a fluffy mass of very thin strands of spun sugar.

cane noun (plural **canes**)
1 the stem of a reed or tall grass etc. 2 a thin stick.
cane verb (**canes, caning, caned**)
beat someone with a cane. [from Greek]

canine (say kayn-I'n) adjective
to do with dogs.
canine tooth a pointed tooth.
canine noun (plural **canines**)
1 a dog. 2 a canine tooth.
[from Latin canis = dog]

canker noun
a disease that rots the wood of trees and plants or causes ulcers and sores on animals. [same origin as cancer]

cannabis noun
hemp, especially when smoked as a drug. [from Cannabis, the Latin name of the hemp plant]

cannibal noun (plural **cannibals**)
1 a person who eats human flesh. 2 an animal that eats animals of its own kind.
cannibalism noun

cannon *noun*
1 (*plural* **cannon**) a large heavy gun. 2 (*plural* **cannons**) the hitting of two balls in billiards by the third ball.
cannon *verb* (**cannons, cannoning, cannoned**) bump into something heavily. [via French from Italian *cannone* = large tube]

USAGE: Do not confuse with *canon*.

cannon ball *noun* (*plural* **cannon balls**) a large solid ball fired from a cannon.

cannot
can not.

canoe *noun* (*plural* **canoes**) a narrow lightweight boat.
canoe *verb* (**canoes, canoeing, canoed**) travel in a canoe. **canoeist** *noun*

canon *noun* (*plural* **canons**)
1 a clergyman of a cathedral. 2 a general principle; a rule.
[from Greek *kanon* = rule]

USAGE: Do not confuse with *cannon*.

canopy *noun* (*plural* **canopies**)
1 a hanging cover forming a shelter above a throne, bed, or person etc. 2 the part of a parachute that spreads in the air.
[from Greek *konopeion* = bed with a mosquito net]

cant *noun*
1 insincere talk. 2 jargon.
[from Latin *cantare* = sing]

can't (*mainly spoken*)
cannot.

cantankerous *adjective*
bad-tempered. [origin unknown]

canteen *noun* (*plural* **canteens**)
1 a restaurant for workers in a factory, office, etc. 2 a case or box containing a set of cutlery. 3 a soldier's or camper's water-flask.
[via French from Italian]

canter *noun*
a gentle gallop.
canter *verb* (**canters, cantering, cantered**) go or ride at a canter.
[short for 'Canterbury gallop', the gentle pace at which pilgrims were said to travel to Canterbury in the Middle Ages]

cantilever *noun* (*plural* **cantilevers**)
a beam or girder fixed at one end only and used to support a bridge etc.
[origin unknown]

canvas *noun* (*plural* **canvases**)
1 a kind of strong coarse cloth. 2 a piece of canvas for painting on; a painting.
[from Latin *cannabis* = hemp, from whose fibres cloth was made]

canvass *verb* (**canvasses, canvassing, canvassed**) visit people to ask for votes, opinions, etc.
canvasser *noun* [originally = to catch in a net or bag: from *canvas*]

canyon *noun* (*plural* **canyons**)
a deep valley, usually with a river running through it. [from Spanish *cañón* = tube]

cap *noun* (*plural* **caps**)
1 a soft hat without a brim but often with a peak. 2 a special headdress, e.g. that worn by a nurse. 3 a cap showing membership of a sports team. 4 a cap-like cover or top. 5 something that makes a bang when fired in a toy pistol.
cap *verb* (**caps, capping, capped**)
1 put a cap or cover on something; cover.
2 award a sports cap to a person chosen as a member of a team. 3 do better than something, *Can you cap that joke?*
[same origin as *cape*[1]]

capable *adjective*
able to do something.
capably *adverb*, **capability** *noun*
[from Latin; related to *capacity*]

capacious (*say* ka-**pay**-shus) *adjective*
roomy; able to hold a large amount.

capacity *noun* (*plural* **capacities**)
1 the amount that something can hold.
2 ability; capability. 3 the position that someone occupies, *In my capacity as your guardian I am responsible for you.*
[from Latin *capere* = take, hold]

cape[1] *noun* (*plural* **capes**)
a cloak. [from Latin *cappa* = hood]

cape[2] *noun* (*plural* **capes**)
a large piece of high land that sticks out into the sea. [from Latin *caput* = head]

caper *verb* (**capers, capering, capered**)
jump or run about playfully.
caper *noun* (*plural* **capers**)
1 capering. 2 (*slang*) an activity; an adventure.
[from Latin *caper* = goat]

capillary (*say* ka-**pil**-er-ee) *noun* (*plural* **capillaries**)
any of the very fine blood vessels that connect veins and arteries.

capital *adjective*
1 important. 2 (*informal*) excellent.
capital *noun* (*plural* **capitals**)
1 a capital city. 2 a capital letter. 3 the top part of a pillar. 4 money or property that can be used to produce more wealth.
[from Latin *caput* = head]

capital city *noun* (*plural* **capital cities**)
the most important city in a country.

capitalism (*say* **kap**-it-al-izm) *noun*
a system in which trade and industry are controlled by private owners for profit.
(Compare *Communism*.)

capitalist (*say* kap-it-al-ist) *noun* (*plural* capitalists)
1 a person who has much money or property being used to make more wealth; a very rich person. 2 a person who is in favour of capitalism.

capitalize (*say* kap-it-al-I'z) *verb* (capitalizes, capitalizing, capitalized)
1 write or print as a capital letter. 2 change something into capital; provide with capital (= money). **capitalization** *noun*
capitalize on profit by something; use it to your own advantage, *You could capitalize on your skill at drawing.*

capital letter *noun* (*plural* capital letters)
a large letter of the kind used at the start of a name or sentence.

capital punishment *noun*
punishing criminals by putting them to death.

capitulate *verb* (capitulates, capitulating, capitulated)
admit that you are defeated and surrender.
capitulation *noun* [from Latin]

capricious (*say* ka-prish-us) *adjective*
deciding or changing your mind in an impulsive way.
capriciously *adverb*, **capriciousness** *noun*

capsize *verb* (capsizes, capsizing, capsized)
overturn, *the boat capsized.*
[origin unknown]

capsule *noun* (*plural* capsules)
1 a hollow pill containing medicine. 2 a plant's seed-case that splits open when ripe. 3 a compartment that can be separated from the rest of a spacecraft. [same origin as *case*[1]]

captain *noun* (*plural* captains)
1 a person in command of a ship, aircraft, sports team, etc. 2 an army officer ranking next below a major; a naval officer ranking next below a commodore.
captaincy *noun*

caption *noun* (*plural* captions)
1 the words printed with a picture to describe it. 2 a short title or heading in a newspaper or magazine. [from Latin]

captious (*say* kap-shus) *adjective*
pointing out small mistakes or faults.

captivate *verb* (captivates, captivating, captivated)
charm or delight someone. **captivation** *noun*
[same origin as *captive*]

captive *noun* (*plural* captives)
someone taken prisoner.

captive *adjective*
taken prisoner; unable to escape. **captivity** *noun*
[from Latin *capere* = take, seize]

capture *verb* (captures, capturing, captured)
1 take someone prisoner. 2 take or obtain by force, trickery, skill, or attraction, *He captured her heart.*
capture *noun*
capturing. [same origin as *captive*]

car *noun* (*plural* cars)
1 a motor car. 2 a carriage, *dining car.* [from old French]

caramel *noun* (*plural* caramels)
1 a kind of toffee tasting like burnt sugar. 2 burnt sugar used for colouring and flavouring food. [via French from Spanish]

carat *noun* (*plural* carats)
1 a measure of weight for precious stones. 2 a measure of the purity of gold, *Pure gold is 24 carats.*
[via French and Italian from Arabic]

caravan *noun* (*plural* caravans)
1 an enclosed carriage equipped for living in, able to be towed by a motor vehicle or a horse. 2 a group of people travelling together across desert country. **caravanning** *noun*
[via French from Persian]

carbohydrate *noun* (*plural* carbohydrates)
a compound of carbon, oxygen, and hydrogen (e.g. sugar or starch). [from *carbon* + -*hydrate* = combined with water]

carbolic *noun*
a kind of disinfectant.
[from *carbon* (from which it is made)]

carbon *noun* (*plural* carbons)
1 a substance that is present in all living things and that occurs in its pure form as diamond and graphite. 2 carbon paper. 3 a carbon copy.
[from Latin *carbo* = coal]

carbonate *noun* (*plural* carbonates)
a compound that gives off carbon dioxide when mixed with acid.

carbon dioxide *noun*
a gas formed when things burn, or breathed out by animals.

carburettor *noun* (*plural* carburettors)
a device for mixing fuel and air in an engine.
[from *carbon* (which the fuel contains)]

carcass *noun* (*plural* carcasses)
1 the dead body of an animal. 2 the bony part of a bird's body after the meat has been eaten.
[from French]

carcinogen *noun* (*plural* carcinogens)
any substance that produces cancer.
[from Greek *karkinoma* = tumour]

card *noun* (*plural* cards)
1 a small usually oblong piece of stiff paper or of plastic. 2 a playing card. 3 cardboard.
cards *plural noun* a game using playing cards.
on the cards likely; possible.
[from Latin *charta* = papyrus leaf, paper]

cardboard *noun*
a kind of thin board made of layers of paper or wood-fibre.

cardiac (*say* kard-ee-ak) *adjective*
to do with the heart.
[from Greek *kardia* = heart]

cardigan *noun* (*plural* cardigans)
a knitted jacket. [named after the Earl of Cardigan, a commander in the Crimean War; cardigans were first worn by the troops in that war]

cardinal *noun* (*plural* cardinals)
a senior priest in the Roman Catholic Church.
cardinal *adjective*
1 chief; most important, *the cardinal features of our plan*. 2 deep scarlet (like a cardinal's cassock). [from old French]

cardinal numbers *plural noun*
the whole numbers one, two, three, etc. (Compare *ordinal*.)

cardinal points *plural noun*
the four main points of the compass (North, South, East, West).

care *noun* (*plural* cares)
1 serious attention and thought, *Plan your holiday with care*. 2 caution to avoid damage or loss, *Glass—handle with care*. 3 protection; supervision, *Leave the child in my care*. 4 worry; anxiety, *freedom from care*.
care *verb* (cares, caring, cared)
1 feel interested or concerned. 2 feel affection.
care for have in your care; be fond of.

career *noun* (*plural* careers)
1 progress through life, especially in work. 2 an occupation with opportunities for promotion.
career *verb* (careers, careering, careered)
rush along wildly.
[from Latin; related to *car*]

carefree *adjective*
without worries or responsibilities.

careful *adjective*
1 giving serious thought and attention to something. 2 avoiding damage or danger etc.; cautious.
carefully *adverb*, **carefulness** *noun*

careless *adjective*
not careful.
carelessly *adverb*, **carelessness** *noun*

caress *noun* (*plural* caresses)
a gentle loving touch.
caress *verb* (caresses, caressing, caressed)
touch lovingly. [from Latin *carus* = dear]

caretaker *noun* (*plural* caretakers)
a person employed to look after a school, block of flats, etc.

cargo *noun* (*plural* cargoes)
goods carried in a ship or aircraft.
[from Spanish]

Caribbean *adjective*
to do with or from the Caribbean Sea, a part of the Atlantic Ocean east of Central America.

caricature *noun* (*plural* caricatures)
an amusing or exaggerated picture of someone.
[from Italian *caricare* = exaggerate]

carnage *noun*
the killing of many people.
[same origin as *carnal*]

carnival *noun* (*plural* carnivals)
a festival, often with a procession in fancy dress. [from Latin *carnis* = of flesh (because originally this meant the festivities before Lent, when meat was given up until Easter)]

carnivorous (*say* kar-niv-er-us) *adjective*
meat-eating. (Compare *herbivorous*.)
carnivore *noun*
[from Latin *carnis* = of flesh + *vorare* = devour]

carol *noun* (*plural* carols)
a Christmas hymn. **caroller** *noun*, **carolling** *noun*
[from old French]

carp[1] *noun* (*plural* carp)
an edible freshwater fish.
[from Latin *carpa*]

carp[2] *verb* (carps, carping, carped)
keep finding fault.
[from Latin *carpere* = slander]

car park *noun* (*plural* car parks)
an area where cars may be parked.

carpenter *noun* (*plural* carpenters)
a person who makes things out of wood.
carpentry *noun* [from a Latin word meaning 'carriage-maker']

carpet *noun* (*plural* carpets)
a thick soft covering for a floor.
carpeted *adjective*, **carpeting** *noun*
[from old French]

carriage *noun* (*plural* carriages)
1 one of the separate parts of a train, where passengers sit. 2 a passenger vehicle pulled by horses. 3 carrying goods from one place to another; the cost of carrying goods, *Carriage is extra*. 4 a moving part carrying or holding something in a machine.
[same origin as *carry*]

carrier *noun* (*plural* carriers)
a person or thing that carries something.

carrot *noun* (*plural* carrots)
a plant with a thick orange-coloured root used as a vegetable. [from Greek]

carry *verb* (carries, carrying, carried)
1 take something from one place to another.
2 support the weight of something. 3 travel clearly, *Sound carries in the mountains*. 4 if a motion is carried, it is approved by most people at the meeting, *The motion was carried by ten votes to six*.
be carried away be very excited.

cart

cart 60 **casual**

carry on 1 continue. **2** (*informal*) behave
excitedly. **3** (*informal*) complain.
[from old French *carier*; related to *car*]

cart *noun* (*plural* **carts**)
an open vehicle for carrying loads.
cart *verb* (**carts, carting, carted**)
1 carry in a cart. **2** (*informal*) carry something
heavy or tiring, *I've carted these books all round
the school.* [from Old Norse]

carthorse *noun* (*plural* **carthorses**)
a large strong horse used for pulling heavy
loads.

cartilage *noun*
tough white flexible tissue attached to a bone.
[from Latin]

carton *noun* (*plural* **cartons**)
a cardboard or plastic container.
[French; related to *card*]

cartoon *noun* (*plural* **cartoons**)
1 an amusing drawing. **2** a comic strip (see
comic). **3** an animated film. **cartoonist** *noun*
[originally = a drawing on stiff paper; from
Italian, related to *card*]

cartridge *noun* (*plural* **cartridges**)
1 a case containing the explosive for a bullet or
shell. **2** a container holding film for a camera,
ink for a pen, etc. **3** the device that holds the
stylus of a record player.

cartwheel *noun* (*plural* **cartwheels**)
1 the wheel of a cart. **2** a handstand balancing
on each hand in turn with arms and legs
spread like spokes of a wheel.

carve *verb* (**carves, carving, carved**)
1 make something by cutting wood or stone
etc. **2** cut cooked meat into slices. **carver** *noun*
[from Old English]

case[1] *noun* (*plural* **cases**)
1 a container. **2** a suitcase.
[from Latin *capsa* = box]

case[2] *noun* (*plural* **cases**)
1 an example of something existing or
occurring; a situation, *In every case we found
that someone had cheated.* **2** something
investigated by police etc. or by a lawcourt, *a
murder case.* **3** a set of facts or arguments to
support something, *She put forward a good case
for equality.* **4** the form of a word that shows
how it is related to other words. *Fred's* is the
possessive case of *Fred*; *him* is the objective
case of *he*.
in any case anyway.
in case because something may happen.
[from Latin *casus* = a fall, an occasion]

cash *noun*
1 money in coin or notes. **2** immediate
payment for goods etc.
cash *verb* (**cashes, cashing, cashed**)
change a cheque etc. for cash. [originally
= a cash box; from Latin *capsa* = box]

cash dispenser *noun* (*plural* **cash dispensers**)
a machine, usually outside a bank, from which
people can draw out cash by using a cash card.

cashier *noun* (*plural* **cashiers**)
a person who takes in and pays out money in a
bank or takes payments in a shop.

cashpoint *noun* (*plural* **cashpoints**)
a cash dispenser.

casing *noun* (*plural* **casings**)
a protective covering. [from *case*[1]]

casino *noun* (*plural* **casinos**)
a public building or room for gambling.
[Italian, = little house]

cask *noun* (*plural* **casks**)
a barrel. [from French or Spanish]

casket *noun* (*plural* **caskets**)
a small box for jewellery etc.
[origin unknown]

casserole *noun* (*plural* **casseroles**)
1 a covered dish in which food is cooked and
served. **2** food cooked in a casserole.
[from Greek]

cassette *noun* (*plural* **cassettes**)
a small sealed case containing recording tape,
film, etc. [French, = little case]

cast *verb* (**casts, casting, cast**)
1 throw. **2** shed or throw off. **3** make a vote.
4 make something of metal or plaster in a
mould. **5** choose performers for a play or film
etc.
cast *noun* (*plural* **casts**)
1 a shape made by pouring liquid metal or
plaster into a mould. **2** all the performers in a
play or film. [from Old Norse]

castaway *noun* (*plural* **castaways**)
a shipwrecked person.
[originally = an outcast; from *cast* + *away*]

caste *noun* (*plural* **castes**)
(in India) one of the social classes into which
Hindus are born.
[from Spanish or Portuguese *casta*
= descent (from the same ancestors)]

casting vote *noun* (*plural* **casting votes**)
the vote that decides which group wins when
the votes on each side are equal.

castle *noun* (*plural* **castles**)
1 a large old fortified building. **2** a piece in
chess, also called a *rook*.
castles in the air daydreams.
[from Latin *castellum* = fort]

castor sugar *noun*
finely-ground white sugar.

castrate *verb* (**castrates, castrating, castrated**)
remove the testicles of a male animal.
(Compare *spay*.) **castration** *noun*

casual *adjective*
1 happening by chance; not planned. **2** not
careful; not methodical. **3** informal; suitable

for informal occasions, *casual clothes.* **4** not permanent, *casual work.* **casually** *adverb,* **casualness** *noun*
[same origin as *case*²]

casualty *noun* (*plural* **casualties**)
a person who is killed or injured in war or in an accident.
[originally = chance; same origin as *case*²]

cat *noun* (*plural* **cats**)
1 a small furry domestic animal. **2** an animal of the same family as the domestic cat, *Lions and tigers are cats.* **3** (*informal*) a spiteful girl or woman.
let the cat out of the bag reveal a secret.

cata- *prefix* (becoming **cat-** before a vowel; combining with an *h* to become **cath-**)
1 down (as in *catapult*). **2** thoroughly (as in *catalogue*). [from Greek *kata* = down]

cataclysm (*say* kat-a-klizm) *noun* (*plural* **cataclysms**)
a violent upheaval or disaster.
[from *cata-* + Greek *klyzein* = to wash]

catalogue *noun* (*plural* **catalogues**)
1 a list of things (e.g. of books in a library), usually arranged in order. **2** a book containing a list of things that can be bought, *Christmas catalogue.*
catalogue *verb* (**catalogues, cataloguing, catalogued**)
enter something in a catalogue.

catalyst (*say* kat-a-list) *noun* (*plural* **catalysts**)
something that starts or speeds up a change or reaction.
[from *cata-* + Greek *lysis* = loosening]

catalytic converter *noun* (*plural* **catalytic converters**)
a device fitted to a car's exhaust system, with a catalyst for converting pollutant gases into less harmful ones.

catapult *noun* (*plural* **catapults**)
1 a device with elastic for shooting small stones. **2** an ancient military device for hurling stones etc.
catapult *verb* (**catapults, catapulting, catapulted**)
hurl or rush violently.
[from *cata-* + Greek *pellein* = throw]

cataract *noun* (*plural* **cataracts**)
1 a large waterfall or rush of water. **2** a cloudy area that forms in the eye and prevents a person from seeing clearly.

catastrophe (*say* ka-tass-trof-ee) *noun* (*plural* **catastrophes**)
a sudden great disaster.
catastrophic (*say* kat-a-strof-ik) *adjective,* **catastrophically** *adverb*
[from *cata-* + Greek *strephein* = to turn]

catch *verb* (**catches, catching, caught**)
1 take and hold something. **2** capture. **3** overtake. **4** be in time to get on a bus or train etc. **5** be infected with an illness. **6** hear, *I didn't catch what he said.* **7** surprise or detect somebody, *caught in the act.* **8** trick somebody. **9** make or become fixed or unable to move; snag; entangle, *I caught my dress on a nail.* **10** hit; strike, *The blow caught him on the nose.*
catch fire start burning.
catch it (*informal*) be scolded or punished.
catch on (*informal*) **1** become popular. **2** understand.
catch *noun* (*plural* **catches**)
1 catching something. **2** something caught or worth catching. **3** a hidden difficulty. **4** a device for fastening something.
[same origin as *chase*]

catching *adjective*
infectious.

catchment area (*plural* **catchment areas**)
1 the whole area from which water drains into a river etc. **2** the area from which a school takes pupils or a hospital takes patients.

catchphrase *noun* (*plural* **catchphrases**)
a popular phrase.

catchy *adjective*
easy to remember; soon becoming popular, *a catchy tune.*

category *noun* (*plural* **categories**)
a set of people or things classified as being similar to each other.
[from Greek *kategoria* = statement, accusation]

cater *verb* (**caters, catering, catered**)
1 provide food, especially for a lot of people. **2** provide what is needed. **caterer** *noun*
[from old French *acateour* = a person who buys food etc.]

caterpillar *noun* (*plural* **caterpillars**)
the creeping worm-like creature that will turn into a butterfly or moth.
[from old French *chatepelose* = hairy cat]

cath- *prefix* see **cata-**.

cathedral *noun* (*plural* **cathedrals**)
the most important church of a district, usually containing the bishop's throne. [from Greek *kathedra* = seat]

Catherine wheel (*plural* **Catherine wheels**)
a firework that spins round.
[named after St Catherine, who was martyred on a spiked wheel]

cathode *noun* (*plural* **cathodes**)
the electrode by which electric current leaves a device. (Compare *anode*.)
[from *cata-* = down + Greek *hodos* = way]

Catholic *adjective*
1 of all Christians, *the Holy Catholic Church.* **2** Roman Catholic (see *Roman*).
Catholicism *noun*
Catholic *noun* (*plural* **Catholics**)
a Roman Catholic.

catholic *adjective*
including most things, *Her taste in literature is catholic.*
[from Greek *katholikos* = universal]

cattle *plural noun*
animals with horns and hoofs, kept by farmers for their milk and beef.

catty *adjective* (**cattier, cattiest**)
speaking or spoken spitefully.

cauldron *noun* (*plural* **cauldrons**)
a large deep pot for boiling things in.
[from Latin *caldarium* = hot bath]

cauliflower *noun* (*plural* **cauliflowers**)
a cabbage with a large head of white flowers.
[from French *chou fleuri* = flowered cabbage]

cause *noun* (*plural* **causes**)
1 a person or thing that makes something happen or produces an effect. **2** a reason, *There is no cause for worry.* **3** a purpose for which people work; an organization or charity.
cause *verb* (**causes, causing, caused**)
be the cause of; make something happen.

causeway *noun* (*plural* **causeways**)
a raised road across low or marshy ground.

caustic *adjective*
1 able to burn or wear things away by chemical action. **2** sarcastic. **caustically** *adverb*
[from Greek *kaustikos* = capable of burning]

caution *noun* (*plural* **cautions**)
1 care taken in order to avoid danger etc. **2** a warning.
caution *verb* (**cautions, cautioning, cautioned**)
warn someone. [from Latin *cavere* = beware]

cautionary *adjective*
giving a warning.

cautious *adjective*
showing caution.
cautiously *adverb*, **cautiousness** *noun*

Cavalier *noun* (*plural* **Cavaliers**)
a supporter of King Charles I in the English Civil War (1642–9).
[from French *chevalier* = knight, from Latin *caballus* = horse]

cavalry *noun*
soldiers who fight on horseback or in armoured vehicles. (Compare *infantry*.) [from Latin *caballus* = horse]

cave *noun* (*plural* **caves**)
a large hollow place in the side of a hill or cliff, or underground.
cave *verb* (**caves, caving, caved**)
cave in fall inwards; give way in an argument.
[from Latin *cavus* = hollow]

cavern *noun* (*plural* **caverns**)
a large cave. **cavernous** *adjective*
[same origin as *cave*]

cavity *noun* (*plural* **cavities**)
a hollow or hole. [same origin as *cave*]

cavort (*say* ka-**vort**) *verb* (**cavorts, cavorting, cavorted**)
jump or run about excitedly.

caw *noun* (*plural* **caws**)
the harsh cry of a crow etc.

cc *abbreviation*
cubic centimetre(s).

CD *abbreviation*
compact disc.

CD-ROM *abbreviation*
compact disc read-only memory; a compact disc on which large amounts of data can be stored and then displayed on a computer screen.

cease *verb* (**ceases, ceasing, ceased**)
stop or end.
cease *noun*
without cease not ceasing.

ceasefire *noun* (*plural* **ceasefires**)
a signal to stop firing.

ceaseless *adjective*
not ceasing.

cedar *noun* (*plural* **cedars**)
an evergreen tree with hard fragrant wood.
cedarwood *noun*
[from Greek]

cedilla (*say* sid-**il**-a) *noun* (*plural* **cedillas**)
a mark under *c* in certain languages to show that it is pronounced as *s*, e.g. in *façade*. [from Spanish, = a little *z*]

ceiling *noun* (*plural* **ceilings**)
1 the flat surface under the top of a room. **2** the highest limit that something can reach.
[origin unknown]

celebrate *verb* (**celebrates, celebrating, celebrated**)
1 do something special or enjoyable to show that a day or event is important. **2** perform a religious ceremony.
celebrant *noun*, **celebration** *noun*
[from Latin]

celebrated *adjective*
famous.

celebrity *noun* (*plural* **celebrities**)
1 a famous person. **2** fame; being famous.

celery *noun*
a vegetable with crisp white or green stems.
[from Greek]

celestial (*say* sil-**est**-ee-al) *adjective*
1 to do with the sky. **2** to do with heaven; divine.
celestial bodies stars etc.

cell *noun* (*plural* **cells**)
1 a small room where a prisoner is locked up. **2** a small room in a monastery. **3** a microscopic unit of living matter. **4** a compartment of a honeycomb. **5** a device for producing electric

current chemically. **6** a small group or unit in an organization etc.
[from Latin *cella* = storeroom]

cellar *noun* (*plural* **cellars**)
an underground room. [same origin as *cell*]

cello (*say* chel-oh) *noun* (*plural* **cellos**)
a musical instrument like a large violin, placed between the knees of a player. **cellist** *noun*
[from Italian *violoncello* = small double bass]

cellulose *noun*
1 tissue that forms the main part of all plants and trees. **2** paint made from cellulose.
[from Latin]

Celsius (*say* sel-see-us) *adjective*
(of a temperature scale) centigrade.
[named after A. Celsius, a Swedish astronomer, who invented it]

cement *noun*
1 a mixture of lime and clay used in building, to join bricks together, etc. **2** a strong glue.
cement *verb* (**cements, cementing, cemented**)
1 put cement on something. **2** join firmly; strengthen. [from Latin]

cemetery (*say* sem-et-ree) *noun* (*plural* **cemeteries**)
a place where people are buried.
[from Greek *koimeterion* = dormitory]

censor *noun* (*plural* **censors**)
a person who examines films, books, letters, etc. and removes or bans anything that seems harmful. **censor** *verb*, **censorship** *noun*
[Latin, = magistrate with power to ban unsuitable people from ceremonies; from *censere* = to judge]

USAGE: Do not confuse with *censure*.
---

censure (*say* sen-sher) *noun*
strong criticism or disapproval of something.
censure *verb*
[same origin as *census*]

USAGE: Do not confuse with *censor*.
---

census *noun* (*plural* **censuses**)
an official count or survey of the population of a country or area.
[from Latin *censere* = estimate, judge]

cent *noun* (*plural* **cents**)
a coin worth one-hundredth of a dollar. [from Latin *centum* = 100]

centenary (*say* sen-teen-er-ee) *noun* (*plural* **centenaries**)
a 100th anniversary. **centennial** (*say* sen-ten-ee-al) *adjective* [from Latin *centenarius* = containing a hundred]

centi- *prefix*
1 one hundred (as in *centipede*). **2** one-hundredth (as in *centimetre*).
[from Latin *centum* = 100]

centigrade *adjective*
measuring temperature on a scale using 100 degrees, where water freezes at 0° and boils at 100°.
[from *centi-* + Latin *gradus* = step]

centimetre *noun* (*plural* **centimetres**)
one-hundredth of a metre, about four-tenths of an inch.

centipede *noun* (*plural* **centipedes**)
a small crawling creature with a long body and many legs.
[from *centi-* + Latin *pedes* = feet]

central *adjective*
1 to do with or at the centre. **2** most important. **centrally** *adverb*

central heating *noun*
a system of heating a building from one source by circulating hot water or hot air or steam in pipes or by linked radiators.

centre *noun* (*plural* **centres**)
1 the middle point or part. **2** an important place, e.g. from which things are organized; a place where certain things happen, *shopping centre*.
centre *verb* (**centres, centring, centred**)
place something at the centre.
centre on or **centre around** be concentrated in; have as its main subject or concern.
[from Greek *kentron* = sharp point, point of a pair of compasses]

centre of gravity *noun* (*plural* **centres of gravity**)
the point in an object at which it balances perfectly.

century *noun* (*plural* **centuries**)
1 a period of one hundred years. **2** a hundred runs scored by a batsman in an innings at cricket.
[from Latin *centum* = 100]

ceramic *adjective*
to do with or made of pottery. [from Greek]

cereal *noun* (*plural* **cereals**)
1 a grass producing seeds which are used as food, e.g. wheat, barley, rice. **2** a breakfast food made from these seeds. [from *Ceres*, the Roman goddess of farming]

USAGE: Do not confuse with *serial*.
---

cerebral (*say* se-rib-ral) *adjective*
to do with the brain.
[from Latin *cerebrum* = brain]

cerebral palsy *noun*
a condition caused by brain damage before birth that makes a person suffer from spasms of the muscles and jerky movements.

ceremonial *adjective*
to do with or used in a ceremony; formal.
ceremonially *adverb*

ceremonious *adjective*
full of ceremony; elaborately performed.

ceremony *noun* (*plural* **ceremonies**)
the formal actions carried out on an important
occasion, e.g. at a wedding or a funeral.
[from Latin *caerimonia* = worship, ritual]

certain *adjective*
sure; without doubt.
a certain person or **thing** a person or thing that
is known but not named.

certainty *noun* (*plural* **certainties**)
1 something that is sure to happen. 2 being
sure.

certificate *noun* (*plural* **certificates**)
an official written or printed statement giving
information about a person etc.,
a birth certificate.

certitude *noun*
a feeling of certainty.

cervix *noun* (*plural* **cervices**, *say* ser-vis-ees)
the entrance to the womb. **cervical** *adjective*
[Latin, = neck]

cesspit or **cesspool** *noun* (*plural* **cesspits,
cesspools**)
a covered pit where liquid waste or sewage is
stored temporarily. [origin unknown]

CFC *abbreviation*
chlorofluorocarbon; a gas containing chlorine
and fluorine that is thought to be harmful to
the ozone layer in the Earth's atmosphere.

chaff[1] *noun*
husks of corn, separated from the seed. [from
Old English]

chaff[2] *verb*
tease someone.
[origin unknown]

chain *noun* (*plural* **chains**)
1 a row of metal rings fastened together. 2 a
connected series of things, *a chain of
mountains*; *a chain of events.*
chain *verb* (**chains, chaining, chained**)
fasten something with a chain or chains.

chain letter *noun* (*plural* **chain letters**)
a letter that you are asked to copy and send to
several other people.

chain reaction *noun* (*plural* **chain reactions**)
a series of happenings in which each causes
the next.

chain store *noun* (*plural* **chain stores**)
one of a number of similar shops owned by the
same firm.

chair *noun* (*plural* **chairs**)
1 a movable seat, with a back, for one person.
2 a position of authority at a meeting, *Mr
Bloggs was in the chair.*

chair *verb* (**chairs, chairing, chaired**)
be in control of a meeting, *Who will chair this
meeting?*
[from old French; related to *cathedral*]

chairman *noun* (*plural* **chairmen**)
the person who is in control of a meeting.
chairmanship *noun*

USAGE: The word *chairman* may be used of a
man or of a woman; they are addressed
formally as *Mr Chairman* and *Madam
Chairman.*

chairperson *noun* (*plural* **chairpersons**)
a chairman.

chalk *noun* (*plural* **chalks**)
1 a soft white or coloured stick used for writing
on blackboards or for drawing. 2 soft white
limestone. **chalky** *adjective*

challenge *noun* (*plural* **challenges**)
1 a demand to take part in a contest. 2 a task or
activity that is new and exciting but also
difficult.
challenge *verb* (**challenges, challenging,
challenged**)
1 make a challenge to someone. 2 question
whether something is true or correct.
challenger *noun* [from old French]

chamber *noun* (*plural* **chambers**)
1 (*old use*) a room. 2 a hall used for meetings of
a parliament etc.; the members of the group
using it. 3 a compartment in machinery etc.
[same origin as *camera*]

chambermaid *noun* (*plural* **chambermaids**)
a woman employed to clean bedrooms at a
hotel etc.

chamber music *noun*
music for a small group of players.

chamber pot *noun* (*plural* **chamber pots**)
a receptacle for urine etc., used in a bedroom.

chameleon (*say* kam-ee-lee-on) *noun* (*plural*
chameleons)
a small lizard that can change its colour to that
of its surroundings. [from Greek *khamaileon*,
literally = ground lion]

champagne (*say* sham-**payn**) *noun*
a bubbly white wine, especially from
Champagne in France.

champion *noun* (*plural* **champions**)
1 a person or thing that has defeated all the
others in a sport or competition etc. 2 someone
who supports a cause by fighting, speaking,
etc. **championship** *noun*
champion *verb* (**champions, championing,
championed**)
support a cause by fighting or speaking for it.
[from old French]

chance noun (plural **chances**)
1 an opportunity or possibility, *Now is your chance to escape.* 2 the way things happen without being planned, *I met her by chance.* **take a chance** take a risk.

chancellor noun (plural **chancellors**)
an important official.
Chancellor of the Exchequer the government minister in charge of a country's finances. [from Latin *cancellarius* = secretary]

change verb (**changes, changing, changed**)
1 make or become different. 2 exchange. 3 put on different clothes. 4 go from one train or bus etc. to another.
change noun (plural **changes**)
1 changing; a difference in doing something. 2 coins or notes of small values. 3 money given back to the payer when the price is less than the amount handed over. 4 a fresh set of clothes. 5 a variation in routine, *Let's walk home for a change.*

changeable adjective
likely to change; changing frequently, *changeable weather.*

channel noun (plural **channels**)
1 a stretch of water connecting two seas. 2 a way for water to flow along. 3 the part of a river or sea etc. that is deep enough for ships. 4 a broadcasting wavelength.
channel verb (**channels, channelling, channelled**)
1 make a channel in something. 2 direct something through a channel or other route. [from Latin *canalis* = canal]

chant noun (plural **chants**)
1 a tune to which words with no regular rhythm are fitted, e.g. one used in singing psalms. 2 a rhythmic call or shout.
chant verb (**chants, chanting, chanted**)
1 sing. 2 call out words in a rhythm. [from Latin *cantare* = sing]

chaos (say **kay**-oss) noun
great disorder.
chaotic adjective, **chaotically** adverb
[Greek, = bottomless pit]

chap noun (plural **chaps**) (*informal*)
a man. [short for *chapman*, an old word for a pedlar]

chapatti noun (plural **chapattis**)
a flat cake of unleavened bread, used in Indian cookery.
[Hindi, from *chapana* = flatten or roll out]

chapel noun (plural **chapels**)
1 a place used for Christian worship, other than a cathedral or parish church; a religious service in this. 2 a section of a large church, with its own altar.

chaplain noun (plural **chaplains**)
a member of the clergy who looks after a college or hospital or regiment etc.

chapped adjective
with skin split or cracked from cold etc.

chapter noun (plural **chapters**)
1 a division of a book. 2 the clergy of a cathedral or members of a monastery. The room where they meet is called a **chapter house**. [from Latin]

character noun (plural **characters**)
1 a person in a story, film, or play. 2 all the qualities that make a person or thing what he, she, or it is. 3 a letter of the alphabet. [from Greek]

characteristic noun (plural **characteristics**)
a quality that forms part of a person's or thing's character.
characteristic adjective
typical of a person or thing.
characteristically adverb

charade (say sha-**rahd**) noun (plural **charades**)
1 a scene in the game of *charades*, in which people try to guess a word from other people's acting. 2 a pretence. [French]

charcoal noun
a black substance made by burning wood slowly. Charcoal can be used for drawing with. [origin unknown]

charge noun (plural **charges**)
1 the price asked for something. 2 a rushing attack. 3 the amount of explosive needed to fire a gun etc. 4 electricity in something. 5 an accusation that someone has committed a crime. 6 a person or thing in someone's care. **in charge** in control; deciding what shall happen to a person or thing.
charge verb (**charges, charging, charged**)
1 ask a particular price. 2 rush forward in an attack. 3 give an electric charge to something. 4 accuse someone of committing a crime. 5 entrust someone with a responsibility or task.
[from Latin *carcare* = to load]

chariot noun (plural **chariots**)
a horse-drawn vehicle with two wheels, used in ancient times for fighting, racing, etc.
charioteer noun
[from old French; related to *car*]

charity noun (plural **charities**)
1 an organization set up to help people who are poor, ill, or disabled or have suffered a disaster. 2 giving money or help etc. to the needy. 3 kindness and sympathy towards others; being unwilling to think badly of people. **charitable** adjective, **charitably** adverb
[from Latin *caritas* = love]

charm noun (plural **charms**)
1 the power to please or delight people; attractiveness. 2 a magic spell. 3 a small object believed to bring good luck. 4 an ornament worn on a bracelet etc.

charm *verb* (charms, charming, charmed)
1 give pleasure or delight to people. **2** put a spell on someone; bewitch. **charmer** *noun* [from Latin *carmen* = song or spell]

chart *noun* (*plural* charts)
1 a map for people sailing ships or flying aircraft. **2** an outline map showing special information, *a weather chart*. **3** a diagram or list etc. giving information in an orderly way. **the charts** a list of the records that are most popular.
chart *verb* (charts, charting, charted)
make a chart of something; map.
[same origin as *card*]

charter *noun* (*plural* charters)
1 an official document giving somebody certain rights etc. **2** chartering an aircraft, ship, or vehicle.
charter *verb* (charters, chartering, chartered)
1 hire an aircraft, ship, or vehicle. **2** give a charter to someone. [same origin as *card*]

charwoman *noun* (*plural* charwomen)
a woman employed as a cleaner.
[from Old English *cerr* = task]

chase *verb* (chases, chasing, chased)
go quickly after a person or thing in order to capture or catch them up or drive them away.
chase *noun*
[from Latin *captare* = capture]

chasm (*say* kazm) *noun* (*plural* chasms)
a deep opening in the ground.
[from Greek *chasma* = gaping hollow]

chassis (*say* shas-ee) *noun* (*plural* chassis)
the framework under a car etc., on which other parts are mounted. [originally = window frame; related to *casement*]

chaste *adjective*
not having sexual intercourse at all, or only with the person to whom you are married.
chastity *noun*
[from Latin *castus* = pure]

chat *noun* (*plural* chats)
a friendly conversation.
chat *verb* (chats, chatting, chatted)
have a friendly conversation.
[from *chatter*]

chatter *verb* (chatters, chattering, chattered)
1 talk quickly about unimportant things; keep on talking. **2** if your teeth chatter, they make a rattling sound because you are cold or frightened. **chatterer** *noun*
chatter *noun*
chattering talk or sound.

chauvinism (*say* shoh-vin-izm) *noun*
1 prejudiced belief that your own country is superior to others. **2** the belief of some men that men are superior to women. **chauvinist** *noun*, **chauvinistic** *adjective*

cheap *adjective*
1 low in price; not expensive. **2** of poor quality; of low value. **cheaply** *adverb*, **cheapness** *noun* [from Old English *ceap* = a bargain]

cheapen *verb* (cheapens, cheapening, cheapened)
make or become cheap.

cheat *verb* (cheats, cheating, cheated)
1 trick or deceive somebody. **2** try to do well in an examination or game etc. by breaking rules.
cheat *noun* (*plural* cheats)
a person who cheats. [from old French]

check[1] *verb* (checks, checking, checked)
1 make sure that something is correct or in good condition. **2** make something stop or go slower.
check *noun* (*plural* checks)
1 checking something. **2** stopping or slowing; a pause. **3** a receipt; a bill in a restaurant. **4** the situation in chess when a king may be captured.

check[2] *noun* (*plural* checks)
a pattern of squares. **checked** *adjective*

checkmate *noun*
the winning situation in chess.
checkmate *verb*
[from Persian *shah mat* = the king is dead]

checkout *noun* (*plural* checkouts)
a place where goods are paid for in a self-service shop.

cheek *noun* (*plural* cheeks)
1 the side of the face below the eye. **2** rude or disrespectful behaviour; impudence.

cheeky *adjective*
rude or disrespectful; impudent.
cheekily *adverb*, **cheekiness** *noun*

cheer *noun* (*plural* cheers)
1 a shout of praise or pleasure or encouragement, especially 'hurray'. **2** cheerfulness, *full of good cheer*.
cheer *verb* (cheers, cheering, cheered)
1 give a cheer. **2** gladden or encourage somebody.
cheer up make or become cheerful.
[originally = a person's expression; from old French *chiere* = face]

cheerful *adjective*
1 looking or sounding happy. **2** pleasantly bright or colourful.
cheerfully *adverb*, **cheerfulness** *noun*

cheerless *adjective*
gloomy or dreary.

cheery *adjective*
bright and cheerful.

cheese *noun* (*plural* cheeses)
a solid food made from milk.

chemical *adjective*
to do with or produced by chemistry.

chemical *noun* (*plural* chemicals)
a substance obtained by or used in chemistry.

chemist *noun* (*plural* chemists)
1 a person who makes or sells medicines. 2 an expert in chemistry.

chemistry *noun*
1 the way that substances combine and react with one another. 2 the study of substances and their reactions etc.

chemotherapy *noun*
the treatment of disease, especially cancer, by the use of chemical substances.

cheque *noun* (*plural* cheques)
a printed form on which you write instructions to a bank to pay out money from your account. [a different spelling of *check*¹]

cherish *verb* (cherishes, cherishing, cherished)
1 look after a person or thing lovingly. 2 be fond of. [from French *cher* = dear]

cherry *noun* (*plural* cherries)
a small soft round fruit with a stone. [from old French]

chess *noun*
a game for two players with sixteen pieces each (called **chessmen**) on a board of 64 squares (a **chessboard**). [from old French *esches* = checks]

chest *noun* (*plural* chests)
1 the front part of the body between the neck and the waist. 2 a large strong box for storing things in. [from Old English]

chestnut *noun* (*plural* chestnuts)
1 a tree that produces hard brown nuts. 2 the nut of this tree. 3 an old joke or story. [from Greek]

chest of drawers *noun* (*plural* chests of drawers)
a piece of furniture with drawers for storing clothes etc.

chew *verb* (chews, chewing, chewed)
grind food between the teeth. **chewy** *adjective* [from Old English]

chewing gum *noun*
a sticky flavoured type of sweet for chewing.

chick *noun* (*plural* chicks)
a very young bird. [shortened form of *chicken*]

chicken *noun* (*plural* chickens)
1 a young bird, especially of the domestic fowl. 2 the flesh of a domestic fowl as food.
chicken *adjective* (*slang*)
afraid to do something; cowardly.
chicken *verb* (chickens, chickening, chickened)
chicken out (*slang*) not take part in something because you are afraid.

chickenpox *noun*
a disease that produces red spots on the skin. [probably because the disease is mild]

chief *noun* (*plural* chiefs)
a person with the highest rank or authority.
chief *adjective*
most important; main. **chiefly** *adverb* [from French]

chieftain *noun* (*plural* chieftains)
the chief of a tribe, band of robbers, etc.

child *noun* (*plural* children)
1 a young person; a boy or girl. 2 someone's son or daughter. [from Old English]

childhood *noun* (*plural* childhoods)
the time when a person is a child.

childish *adjective*
like a child; unsuitable for a grown person. **childishly** *adverb*

childminder *noun* (*plural* childminders)
a person who looks after children for payment.

chill *noun* (*plural* chills)
1 unpleasant coldness. 2 an illness that makes you shiver.
chill *verb* (chills, chilling, chilled)
make a person or thing cold.

chilli *noun* (*plural* chillies)
the hot-tasting pod of a red pepper. [via Spanish from Nahuatl (a Central American language)]

chilly *adjective*
1 rather cold. 2 unfriendly. **chilliness** *noun*

chime *noun* (*plural* chimes)
a series of notes sounded by a set of bells each making a different musical sound.

chimney *noun* (*plural* chimneys)
a tall pipe or structure that carries smoke away from a fire. [from French]

chimney pot *noun* (*plural* chimney pots)
a pipe fitted to the top of a chimney.

chimpanzee *noun* (*plural* chimpanzees)
an African ape, smaller than a gorilla. [via French from Kikongo (an African language)]

chin *noun* (*plural* chins)
the lower part of the face below the mouth.

china *noun*
thin delicate pottery. [from Persian *chini* = from China]

chink *noun* (*plural* chinks)
1 a narrow opening, *a chink in the curtains*. 2 a chinking sound.
chink *verb* (chinks, chinking, chinked)
make a sound like glasses or coins being struck together. [origin unknown]

chip *noun* (*plural* chips)
1 a thin piece cut or broken off something hard. 2 a fried oblong strip of potato. 3 a place where a small piece has been knocked off something. 4 a small counter used in games. 5 a microchip.

a chip off the old block a child who is very like his or her father.
have a chip on your shoulder have a grievance and feel bitter or resentful.
chip *verb* (chips, chipping, chipped)
1 knock small pieces off something. 2 cut a potato into chips. [from Old English]

chipolata *noun* (*plural* chipolatas)
a small spicy sausage.
[via French from Italian]

chiropody (*say* ki-rop-od-ee) *noun*
medical treatment of the feet, e.g. corns.
chiropodist *noun*
[from Greek *cheir* = hand + *podos* = of the foot (because chiropodists originally treated both hands and feet)]

chirp *verb* (chirps, chirping, chirped)
make short sharp sounds like a small bird.
chirp *noun* [imitating the sound]

chisel *noun* (*plural* chisels)
a tool with a sharp end for shaping wood, stone, etc.
chisel *verb* (chisels, chiselling, chiselled)
shape or cut something with a chisel.

chivalrous (*say* shiv-al-rus) *adjective*
being considerate and helpful towards people less strong than yourself. **chivalry** *noun* [= like a perfect knight (same origin as *Cavalier*)]

chlorine (*say* klor-een) *noun*
a greenish-yellow gas used to disinfect water etc. [from Greek *chloros* = green]

chloroform (*say* klo-ro-form) *noun*
a liquid that gives off a vapour that makes people unconscious.

chlorophyll (*say* klo-ro-fil) *noun*
the substance that makes plants green.
[from Greek *chloros* = green + *phyllon* = leaf]

chock-full *adjective*
crammed full.

chocolate *noun* (*plural* chocolates)
1 a solid brown food or powder made from roasted cacao seeds. 2 a drink made with this powder. 3 a sweet made of or covered with chocolate.
[via French or Spanish from Nahuatl (a Central American language)]

choice *noun* (*plural* choices)
1 choosing between things. 2 the range of things from which someone can choose, *There is a wide choice of holidays.* 3 a person or thing chosen, *This is my choice.*
choice *adjective*
of the best quality, *choice bananas.*

choir *noun* (*plural* choirs)
a group of people trained to sing together, especially in a church. **choirboy** *noun*
[from Latin *chorus* = choir]

choke *verb* (chokes, choking, choked)
1 cause somebody to stop breathing properly. 2 be unable to breathe properly. 3 clog.
choke *noun* (*plural* chokes)
a device controlling the flow of air into the engine of a motor vehicle.

cholera (*say* kol-er-a) *noun*
an infectious disease that is often fatal. [from Greek]

cholesterol (*say* kol-est-er-ol) *noun*
a fatty substance that can clog the arteries.
[from Greek *chole* = bile + *stereos* = stiff]

choose *verb* (chooses, choosing, chose, chosen)
decide which you are going to take from among a number of people or things. **choosy** *adjective*
[from Old English]

chop *verb* (chops, chopping, chopped)
cut or hit something with a heavy blow.
chop *noun* (*plural* chops)
1 a chopping blow. 2 a small thick slice of meat, usually on a rib. [origin unknown]

choppy *adjective* (choppier, choppiest)
(of the sea) not smooth; full of small waves.
choppiness *noun*

chopsticks *plural noun*
a pair of thin sticks used for lifting Chinese and Japanese food to your mouth. [from pidgin English, literally = quick sticks]

choral *adjective*
to do with or sung by a choir or chorus.

chord[1] (*say* kord) *noun* (*plural* chords)
a number of musical notes sounded together.
[from *accord*]

chord[2] (*say* kord) *noun* (*plural* chords)
a straight line joining two points on a curve.
[a different spelling of *cord*]

USAGE: Do not confuse with *cord*.

chore (*say* chor) *noun* (*plural* chores)
a regular or dull task.
[a different spelling of *char*]

choreography (*say* ko-ree-og-ra-fee) *noun*
the art of writing the steps for ballets or stage dances. **choreographer** *noun*
[from Greek *choreia* = dance, + *-graphy*]

chorus *noun* (*plural* choruses)
1 the words repeated after each verse of a song or poem. 2 music sung by a group of people. 3 a group singing together.
chorus *verb* (choruses, chorusing, chorused)
sing or speak in chorus.
[Latin, from Greek *choros*]

christen *verb* (christens, christening, christened)
1 baptize. 2 give a name or nickname to a person or thing. **christening** *noun*
[from Old English *cristnian* = make someone a Christian]

Christian *noun* (*plural* Christians)
a person who believes in Jesus Christ and his teachings.
Christian *adjective*
to do with Christians or their beliefs.
Christianity *noun*

Christian name *noun* (*plural* Christian names)
a name given to a person at his or her christening.

Christmas *noun* (*plural* Christmases)
the day (25 December) when Christians commemorate the birth of Jesus Christ; the days round it. [from Old English *Cristes maesse* = the feast day of Christ]

Christmas pudding *noun* (*plural* Christmas puddings)
a dark pudding containing dried fruit etc., eaten at Christmas.

Christmas tree *noun* (*plural* Christmas trees)
an evergreen or artificial tree decorated at Christmas.

chromatic (*say* krom-at-ik) *adjective*
to do with colours.
chromatic scale a musical scale going up or down in semitones.
[from Greek *chroma* = colour]

chromium (*say* kroh-mee-um) *noun*
a shiny silvery metal.
[from Greek *chroma* = colour (because its compounds have brilliant colours)]

chromosome (*say* kroh-mos-ohm) *noun* (*plural* chromosomes)
a tiny thread-like part of an animal cell or plant cell, carrying genes. [from Greek *chroma* = colour + *soma* = body]

chronic *adjective*
lasting for a long time, *a chronic illness*.
chronically *adverb*
[from Greek *chronikos* = to do with time]

chronicle *noun* (*plural* chronicles)
a record of events in the order that they happened. [same origin as *chronic*]

chronology (*say* kron-ol-oj-ee) *noun*
the arrangement of events in the order in which they happened, e.g. in history or geology. **chronological** *adjective*
[from Greek *chronos* = time, + *-logy*]

chrysalis *noun* (*plural* chrysalises)
a caterpillar that is changing into a butterfly or moth. [from Greek *chrysos* = gold (because some are this colour)]

chrysanthemum *noun* (*plural* chrysanthemums)
a garden flower that blooms in autumn.
[originally = a kind of marigold: from Greek *chrysos* = gold + *anthemon* = flower]

chubby *adjective* (chubbier, chubbiest)
plump. **chubbiness** *noun* [origin unknown]

chuckle *noun* (*plural* chuckles)
a quiet laugh.
chuckle *verb* (chuckles, chuckling, chuckled)
laugh quietly. [origin unknown]

chum *noun* (*plural* chums) (*informal*)
a friend. **chummy** *adjective*
[short for *chamber-fellow* = a person you share a room with]

chunk *noun* (*plural* chunks)
a thick piece of something. **chunky** *adjective*

church *noun* (*plural* churches)
1 a public building for Christian worship. 2 a religious service in a church, *I will see you after church*.
the Church all Christians; a group of these, *the Church of England*.
[via Old English from Greek *kyriakon* = Lord's house]

churlish *adjective*
ill-mannered and unfriendly; surly.
[= like a *churl* = a peasant]

churn *noun* (*plural* churns)
1 a large can in which milk is carried from a farm. 2 a machine in which milk is beaten to make butter.
churn *verb* (churns, churning, churned)
1 make butter in a churn. 2 stir or swirl vigorously.
churn out produce something in large quantities.

chute (*say* shoot) *noun* (*plural* chutes)
a steep channel for people or things to slide down. [French, = a fall]

chutney *noun* (*plural* chutneys)
a strong-tasting mixture of fruit, peppers, etc., eaten with meat. [from Hindi *chatni*]

-cide *suffix*
forms nouns meaning 'killing' or 'killer' (e.g. *homicide*). [from Latin *caedere* = kill]

cider *noun* (*plural* ciders)
an alcoholic drink made from apples.
[via French and Latin from Hebrew]

cigar *noun* (*plural* cigars)
a roll of compressed tobacco leaves for smoking. [from Spanish]

cigarette *noun* (*plural* cigarettes)
a small roll of shredded tobacco in thin paper for smoking. [French, = little cigar]

cinder *noun* (*plural* cinders)
a small piece of partly burnt coal or wood.

cine-camera (*say* sin-ee) *noun* (*plural* cine-cameras)
a camera used for taking moving pictures.
[from Greek *kinema* = movement, + *camera*]

cinema *noun* (*plural* cinemas)
a place where films are shown.
[from Greek *kinema* = movement]

cipher (*say* sy-fer) *noun* (*plural* ciphers)
1 a kind of code. 2 the symbol 0, representing nought or zero.
[from Arabic *sifr* = nought]

circle *noun* (*plural* circles)
1 a perfectly round flat shape or thing. 2 a number of people with similar interests. 3 the balcony of a cinema or theatre.
circle *verb* (circles, circling, circled)
move in a circle; go round something. [from Latin *circus*]

circuit (*say* ser-kit) *noun* (*plural* circuits)
1 a circular line or journey. 2 a motor-racing track. 3 the path of an electric current.
[from Latin *circum* = round + *itum* = gone]

circular *adjective*
1 shaped like a circle; round. 2 moving round a circle. **circularity** *noun*
circular *noun* (*plural* circulars)
a letter or advertisement etc. sent to a number of people.

circulate *verb* (circulates, circulating, circulated)
1 go round something continuously, *Blood circulates in the body.* 2 pass from place to place. 3 send something round to a number of people. **circulation** *noun*

circum- *prefix*
around (as in *circumference*).
[from Latin *circum* = around]

circumcise *verb* (circumcises, circumcising, circumcised)
cut off the fold of skin at the tip of the penis. **circumcision** *noun*

circumference *noun* (*plural* circumferences)
the line or distance round something, especially round a circle.

circumflex accent *noun* (*plural* circumflex accents)
a mark over a vowel, as over *e* in *fête*.

circumnavigate *verb* (circumnavigates, circumnavigating, circumnavigated)
sail completely round something. **circumnavigation** *noun*

circumscribe *verb* (circumscribes, circumscribing, circumscribed)
1 draw a line round something. 2 limit or restrict something, *Her powers are circumscribed by many regulations.*

circumspect *adjective*
cautious and watchful. **circumspection** *noun*
[from *circum-* + Latin *specere* = to look]

circumstance *noun* (*plural* circumstances)
a fact or condition connected with an event or person or action.

circumstantial (*say* ser-kum-**stan**-shal) *adjective*
consisting of facts that strongly suggest something but do not actually prove it, *circumstantial evidence.*

circus *noun* (*plural* circuses)
a travelling show with clowns, acrobats, animals, etc. [Latin, = ring]

cistern *noun* (*plural* cisterns)
a tank for storing water. [from Latin]

citizen *noun* (*plural* citizens)
a person belonging to a particular city or country and having certain rights and duties because of this. **citizenship** *noun* [same origin as *city*]

citrus fruit *noun* (*plural* citrus fruits)
a lemon, orange, grapefruit, or other sharp-tasting fruit. [Latin]

city *noun* (*plural* cities)
a large important town, usually with special rights given by a charter.
[from Latin *civitas* = city]

civic *adjective*
1 to do with a city or town. 2 to do with citizens. [from Latin *civis* = citizen]

civil *adjective*
1 to do with citizens. 2 to do with civilians; not military, *civil aviation.* 3 polite. **civilly** *adverb*
[from Latin]

civilian *noun* (*plural* civilians)
a person who is not serving in the armed forces. [from *civil*]

civility *noun* (*plural* civilities)
politeness.

civilization *noun* (*plural* civilizations)
1 a civilized condition or society. 2 making or becoming civilized.

civilize *verb* (civilizes, civilizing, civilized)
bring culture and education etc. to a primitive community. [from French]

Civil Service *noun*
people employed by the government in various departments other than the armed forces.

civil war *noun* (*plural* civil wars)
war between groups of people of the same country.

claim *verb* (claims, claiming, claimed)
1 ask for something to which you believe you have a right. 2 declare; state something without being able to prove it. **claimant** *noun*
claim *noun* (*plural* claims)
1 claiming. 2 something claimed. 3 a piece of ground claimed or assigned to someone for mining etc. [same origin as *clamour*]

clairvoyant *noun* (*plural* clairvoyants)
a person who is said to be able to predict future events or know about things that are happening out of sight. **clairvoyance** *noun*
[from French *clair* = clear + *voyant* = seeing]

clamber *verb* (clambers, clambering, clambered)
climb with difficulty.
[from *clamb*, the old past tense of *climb*]

clammy *adjective*
damp and slimy. [from Old English *claeman*
= smear, make sticky]

clamour *noun* (*plural* **clamours**)
1 a loud confused noise. 2 an outcry; a loud
protest or demand. **clamorous** *adjective*
clamour *verb* (**clamours, clamouring, clamoured**)
make a loud protest or demand.
[from Latin *clamare* = call out]

clamp *noun* (*plural* **clamps**)
a device for holding things tightly.
clamp *verb* (**clamps, clamping, clamped**)
1 fix something with a clamp. 2 fix something
firmly.
clamp down on 1 become stricter about
something. 2 put a stop to something.

clan *noun* (*plural* **clans**)
a group sharing the same ancestor, especially
in Scotland. [Scottish Gaelic]

clang *noun* (*plural* **clangs**)
a loud ringing sound. **clang** *verb*
[imitating the sound]

clank *noun* (*plural* **clanks**)
a sound like heavy pieces of metal banging
together. **clank** *verb* [imitating the sound]

clap *verb* (**claps, clapping, clapped**)
1 strike the palms of the hands together loudly,
especially as applause. 2 slap in a friendly way,
clapped him on the shoulder. 3 put quickly,
They clapped him into gaol.
clap *noun* (*plural* **claps**)
1 a sudden sharp noise, *a clap of thunder.*
2 clapping; applause. 3 a friendly slap.
[from Old English]

claret *noun* (*plural* **clarets**)
a kind of red wine.
[from old French *vin claret* = clear wine]

clarify *verb* (**clarifies, clarifying, clarified**)
make or become clear or easier to understand.
clarification *noun*
[from Latin *clarus* = clear]

clarinet *noun* (*plural* **clarinets**)
a woodwind instrument. **clarinettist** *noun* [from
French]

clarity *noun*
clearness. [same origin as *clarify*]

clash *verb* (**clashes, clashing, clashed**)
1 make a loud sound like that of cymbals
banging together. 2 conflict. 3 happen
inconveniently at the same time. 4 (of colours)
look unpleasant together. **clash** *noun*
[imitating the sound]

clasp *noun* (*plural* **clasps**)
1 a device for fastening things, with
interlocking parts. 2 a grasp.
clasp *verb* (**clasps, clasping, clasped**)
1 grasp or hold tightly. 2 fasten with a clasp.
[origin unknown]

class *noun* (*plural* **classes**)
1 a group of children, students, etc. who are
taught together. 2 a group of similar people,
animals, or things. 3 people of the same social
or economic level. 4 level of quality, *first class.*
class *verb* (**classes, classing, classed**)
arrange things in classes or groups; classify.
[from Latin *classis* = a social division of the
Roman people]

classic *adjective*
generally agreed to be excellent or important.
classic *noun* (*plural* **classics**)
a classic book, film, writer, etc.
[from Latin *classicus* = of the highest class]

classical *adjective*
1 to do with ancient Greek or Roman
literature, art. 2 serious or conventional in
style, *classical music.*

classified *adjective*
1 put into classes or groups. 2 (of information)
declared officially to be secret and available
only to certain people.

classify *verb* (**classifies, classifying, classified**)
arrange things in classes or groups.
classification *noun*, **classificatory** *adjective*

classroom *noun* (*plural* **classrooms**)
a room where a class of children or students is
taught.

clatter *verb* & *noun* (**clatters, clattering, clattered**)
rattle. [imitating the sound]

clause *noun* (*plural* **clauses**)
1 a single part of a treaty, law, or contract.
2 part of a complex sentence, with its own
verb, *There are two clauses in 'We choose what
we want'.*
[from Latin]

claustrophobia *noun*
fear of being inside an enclosed space. [from
Latin *claustrum* = enclosed space, + *phobia*]

claw *noun* (*plural* **claws**)
1 a sharp nail on a bird's or animal's foot. 2 a
claw-like part or device used for grasping
things.

clay *noun*
a kind of stiff sticky earth that becomes hard
when baked, used for making bricks and
pottery. **clayey** *adjective*

-cle *suffix* see **-cule.**

clean *adjective*
1 without any dirt or marks or stains. 2 fresh;
not yet used. 3 honourable; not unfair, *a clean
fight.* 4 not indecent. 5 a clean catch is one
made skilfully with no fumbling.
cleanness *noun*
clean *verb* (**cleans, cleaning, cleaned**)
make a thing clean.
clean *adverb*
completely, *I clean forgot.*

clear *adjective*
1 transparent; not muddy or cloudy. 2 easy to see or hear or understand; distinct. 3 free from obstacles or unwanted things; free from guilt, *a clear conscience*. 4 complete, *Give three clear days' notice.* **clearly** *adverb*, **clearness** *noun*
clear *adverb*
1 distinctly; clearly, *We heard you loud and clear.* 2 completely, *He got clear away.* 3 apart; not in contact, *Stand clear of the doors.*
clear *verb* (**clears, clearing, cleared**)
1 make or become clear. 2 show that someone is innocent or reliable. 3 jump over something without touching it. 4 get approval or authorization for something, *Clear this with the headmaster.*
clear away remove used plates etc. after a meal.
clear off or **out** (*informal*) go away.
clear up 1 make things tidy. **2** become better or brighter. **3** solve, *clear up the mystery.*
[same origin as *clarify*]

clearing *noun* (*plural* **clearings**)
an open space in a forest.

clef *noun* (*plural* **clefs**)
a symbol on a stave in music, showing the pitch of the notes, *treble clef*; *bass clef*. [French, = key]

cleft *noun* (*plural* **clefts**)
a split in something.

clemency *noun*
gentleness or mildness; mercy.

clench *verb* (**clenches, clenching, clenched**)
close teeth or fingers tightly.

clergy *noun*
the people who have been ordained as priests or ministers of the Christian Church.
clergyman *noun*
[same origin as *clerical*]

clerical *adjective*
1 to do with clerks or their work. 2 to do with the clergy.
[via Latin from Greek *klerikos* = belonging to the Christian Church]

clerk (*say* klark) *noun* (*plural* **clerks**)
a person employed to keep records or accounts, deal with papers in an office, etc. [originally = a Christian minister: same origin as *clerical*]

clever *adjective*
1 quick at learning and understanding things. 2 skilful. **cleverly** *adverb*, **cleverness** *noun*
[origin unknown]

cliché (*say* klee-shay) *noun* (*plural* **clichés**)
a phrase or idea that is used too often. [French, = stereotyped]

click *noun* (*plural* **clicks**)
a short sharp sound. **click** *verb*
[imitating the sound]

client *noun* (*plural* **clients**)
a person who gets help from a lawyer, accountant, or professional person other than a doctor; a customer.
[from Latin *cliens* = one who listens]

cliff *noun* (*plural* **cliffs**)
a steep rock face, especially on a coast. [from Old English]

climate *noun* (*plural* **climates**)
the regular weather conditions of an area.
climatic (*say* kly-mat-ik) *adjective*
[from Greek *klima* = zone, region]

climax *noun* (*plural* **climaxes**)
the most interesting or important point of a story, series of events, etc.
[from Greek *klimax* = ladder]

climb *verb* (**climbs, climbing, climbed**)
1 go up or over or down something. 2 grow upwards. 3 go higher. **climb** *noun*, **climber** *noun*
climb down admit that you have been wrong.

cling *verb* (**clings, clinging, clung**)
hold on tightly. [from Old English]

clinic *noun* (*plural* **clinics**)
a place where people see doctors etc. for treatment or advice. **clinical** *adjective*
[from Greek *klinike* = teaching (of medicine) at the bedside]

clink *noun* (*plural* **clinks**)
a thin sharp sound like glasses being struck together. **clink** *verb*

clip[1] *noun* (*plural* **clips**)
a fastener for keeping things together, usually worked by a spring.
clip *verb* (**clips, clipping, clipped**)
fasten with a clip.
[from Old English *clyppan* = embrace, hug]

clip[2] *verb* (**clips, clipping, clipped**)
1 cut with shears or scissors etc. 2 (*informal*) hit.
clip *noun* (*plural* **clips**)
1 a short piece of film shown on its own. 2 (*informal*) a hit on the head.
[from Old Norse]

clippers *plural noun*
an instrument for cutting hair.

clique (*say* kleek) *noun* (*plural* **cliques**)
a small group of people who stick together and keep others out. [French]

cloak *noun* (*plural* **cloaks**)
a sleeveless garment that hangs loosely from the shoulders.
cloak *verb* (**cloaks, cloaking, cloaked**)
cover or conceal. [from old French]

cloakroom *noun* (*plural* **cloakrooms**)
1 a place where people can leave outdoor clothes, luggage, etc. 2 a lavatory.

clock *noun* (*plural* **clocks**)
a device (other than a watch) that shows what the time is.

clock *verb* (clocks, clocking, clocked)
clock in or **out** register the time you arrive at work or leave work.
clock up reach a certain speed.
[from Latin *clocca* = bell]

clockwise *adverb* & *adjective*
moving round a circle in the same direction as a clock's hands.
[from *clock* + -*wise*]

clockwork *noun*
a mechanism with a spring that has to be wound up.
like clockwork very regularly.

clod *noun* (*plural* clods)
a lump of earth or clay.

clog *noun* (*plural* clogs)
a shoe with a wooden sole.
clog *verb* (clogs, clogging, clogged)
block up. [origin unknown]

cloister *noun* (*plural* cloisters)
a covered path along the side of a church or monastery etc., round a courtyard.
[from Latin *claustrum* = enclosed place]

clone *noun* (*plural* clones)
an animal or plant made from the cells of another animal or plant and therefore exactly like it.
[from Greek *klon* = a cutting from a plant]

close[1] (*say* klohss) *adjective*
1 near. 2 detailed or concentrated, *with close attention.* 3 tight; with little empty space, *a close fit.* 4 in which competitors are nearly equal, *a close contest.* 5 stuffy. **closely** *adverb*, **closeness** *noun*
close *adverb*
closely, *close behind.*
close *noun* (*plural* closes)
1 a cul-de-sac. 2 an enclosed area, especially round a cathedral.

close[2] (*say* klohz) *verb* (closes, closing, closed)
1 shut. 2 end.
close in 1 get nearer. 2 if the days are closing in, they are getting shorter.
close *noun*
end, *at the close of play.*

close-up *noun* (*plural* close-ups)
a photograph or piece of film taken at close range.

closure *noun* (*plural* closures)
closing.

clot *noun* (*plural* clots)
1 a small mass of blood, cream, etc. that has become solid. 2 (*slang*) a stupid person.
clot *verb* (clots, clotting, clotted)
form clots. [from Old English]

cloth *noun* (*plural* cloths)
1 woven material or felt. 2 a piece of this material. 3 a tablecloth. [from Old English]

clothes *plural noun*
things worn to cover the body. [from *cloth*]

clothing *noun*
clothes.

cloud *noun* (*plural* clouds)
1 a mass of condensed water-vapour floating in the sky. 2 a mass of smoke, dust, etc., in the air.

cloudy *adjective* (cloudier, cloudiest)
1 full of clouds. 2 not transparent, *The liquid became cloudy.* **cloudiness** *noun*

clover *noun*
a small plant usually with three leaves on each stalk.
in clover in ease and luxury.

clown *noun* (*plural* clowns)
1 a performer who does amusing tricks and actions, especially in a circus. 2 a person who does silly things.

cloying *adjective*
sickeningly sweet.
[from an old word *accloy* = overfill, disgust]

club *noun* (*plural* clubs)
1 a heavy stick used as a weapon. 2 a stick with a shaped head used to hit the ball in golf. 3 a group of people who meet because they are interested in the same thing; the building where they meet. 4 a playing card with black clover leaves on it.
club *verb* (clubs, clubbing, clubbed)
hit with a heavy stick.
club together join with other people in order to pay for something, *club together to buy a boat.*

cluck *verb* (clucks, clucking, clucked)
make a hen's throaty cry. **cluck** *noun*

clue *noun* (*plural* clues)
something that helps a person to solve a puzzle or a mystery.
not have a clue (*informal*) be stupid or helpless.

clump *noun* (*plural* clumps)
1 a cluster or mass of things. 2 a clumping sound.
clump *verb* (clumps, clumping, clumped)
1 form a cluster or mass. 2 walk with a heavy tread. [from old German]

clumsy *adjective* (clumsier, clumsiest)
1 heavy and ungraceful; likely to knock things over or drop things. 2 not skilful; not tactful, *a clumsy apology.*
clumsily *adverb*, **clumsiness** *noun*

cluster *noun* (*plural* clusters)
a small close group.
cluster *verb* (clusters, clustering, clustered)
form a cluster. [from Old English]

clutch *verb* (clutches, clutching, clutched)
grasp tightly.
clutch *noun* (*plural* clutches)
1 a tight grasp. 2 a device for connecting and disconnecting the engine of a motor vehicle from its gears. [from Old English]

clutter *noun*
things lying about untidily.
clutter *verb* (clutters, cluttering, cluttered)
fill with clutter, *Piles of books and papers
cluttered her desk.*

Co. *abbreviation*
Company.

c/o *abbreviation*
care of.

co- *prefix*
1 together, jointly (as in *coexistence, cooperate).*
2 joint (as in *co-pilot).*
[same origin as *com-*]

coach *noun* (*plural* **coaches**)
1 a bus used for long journeys. **2** a carriage of a
railway train. **3** a large horse-drawn carriage
with four wheels. **4** an instructor in sports. **5** a
teacher giving private specialized tuition.
coach *verb* (**coaches, coaching, coached**)
instruct or train somebody, especially in
sports. [from Hungarian *kocsi szekér* = cart
from *Kocs*, a town in Hungary]

coagulate *verb* (**coagulates, coagulating,
coagulated**)
change from liquid to semi-solid; clot.
coagulant *noun*, **coagulation** *noun*

coal *noun*
a hard black mineral substance used for
burning to supply heat; a piece of this.

coalesce (*say* koh-a-less) *verb* (**coalesces,
coalescing, coalesced**)
combine and form one whole thing.
coalescence *noun*, **coalescent** *adjective*
[from *co-* + Latin *alescere* = grow up]

coalition *noun* (*plural* **coalitions**)
a temporary alliance, especially of two or more
political parties in order to form a government.
[same origin as *coalesce*]

coarse *adjective*
1 not smooth, not delicate; rough. **2** composed
of large particles; not fine. **3** not refined;
vulgar. **coarsely** *adverb*, **coarseness** *noun*
[origin unknown]

coarsen *verb* (**coarsens, coarsening, coarsened**)
make or become coarse.

coast *noun* (*plural* **coasts**)
the seashore or the land close to it.
coastal *adjective*, **coastline** *noun*
the coast is clear there is no chance of being
seen or hindered.

coastguard *noun* (*plural* **coastguards**)
a person whose job is to keep watch on the
coast, detect or prevent smuggling, etc.

coat *noun* (*plural* **coats**)
1 an outdoor garment with sleeves. **2** the hair
or fur on an animal's body. **3** a coating, *a coat
of paint.*
coat *verb* (**coats, coating, coated**)
cover something with a coating.

coating *noun* (*plural* **coatings**)
a covering layer.

coax *verb* (**coaxes, coaxing, coaxed**)
persuade someone gently or patiently.

cobalt *noun*
a hard silvery-white metal.
[from German *Kobalt* = demon (because it was
believed to harm the silver ore with which it
was found)]

cobble *noun* (*plural* **cobbles**)
a rounded stone used for paving streets etc.
cobbled *adjective*

cobra (*say* koh-bra) *noun* (*plural* **cobras**)
a poisonous snake that can rear up.
[from Portuguese *cobra de capello* = snake with
a hood]

cobweb *noun* (*plural* **cobwebs**)
the thin sticky net made by a spider to trap
insects.
[from Old English *coppe* = spider, + *web*]

cocaine *noun*
a drug made from the leaves of a tropical plant
called *coca.*

cock *noun* (*plural* **cocks**)
1 a male chicken. **2** a male bird. **3** a stopcock.
4 a lever in a gun.
cock *verb* (**cocks, cocking, cocked**)
1 make a gun ready to fire by raising the cock.
2 turn something upwards or in a particular
direction, *The dog cocked its ears.* [from Old
English]

cockatoo *noun* (*plural* **cockatoos**)
a crested parrot. [via Dutch from Malay (a
language spoken in Malaysia)]

cockerel *noun* (*plural* **cockerels**)
a young male chicken. [from *cock*]

cocker spaniel *noun* (*plural* **cocker spaniels**)
a kind of small spaniel.
[because they were used to hunt woodcock]

cockpit *noun* (*plural* **cockpits**)
the compartment where the pilot of an aircraft
sits.
[from the pits where cock fights took place]

cockroach *noun* (*plural* **cockroaches**)
a beetle-like insect. [from Spanish]

cocksure *adjective*
very sure; too confident. [from *cock* (used to
avoid saying *God* in oaths)]

cocoa *noun* (*plural* **cocoas**)
1 a hot drink made from a powder of crushed
cacao seeds. **2** this powder.

coconut *noun* (*plural* **coconuts**)
1 a large round nut that grows on a kind of
palm tree. **2** its white lining, used in sweets
and cookery.
[from Spanish *coco* = grinning face (because
the base of the nut looks like a monkey's face)]

cocoon *noun* (*plural* cocoons)
1 the covering round a chrysalis. 2 a protective wrapping.

cod *noun* (*plural* cod)
a large edible sea fish. [origin unknown]

code *noun* (*plural* codes)
1 a word or phrase used to represent a message in order to keep its meaning secret. 2 a set of signs used in sending messages by machine etc., *the Morse code*. 3 a set of laws or rules, *the Highway Code*.
code *verb* (codes, coding, coded)
put a message into code.
[from Latin *codex* = book]

coeducation *noun*
educating boys and girls together.
coeducational *adjective*
[from *co-* + *education*]

coefficient *noun* (*plural* coefficients)
a number by which another number is multiplied; a factor. [from *co-* + *efficient* (because the numbers work together)]

coexist *verb* (coexists, coexisting, coexisted)
exist together or at the same time.
coexistence *noun*, **coexistent** *adjective*

coffee *noun* (*plural* coffees)
1 a hot drink made from the roasted ground seeds (*coffee beans*) of a tropical plant. 2 these seeds. [from Arabic *kahwa*]

coffin *noun* (*plural* coffins)
a long box in which a body is buried or cremated.

cog *noun* (*plural* cogs)
one of a number of tooth-like parts round the edge of a wheel, fitting into and pushing those on another wheel.

cogent (*say* koh-jent) *adjective*
convincing, *a cogent argument*.

cogitate *verb* (cogitates, cogitating, cogitated)
think deeply about something. **cogitation** *noun*
[from Latin]

coherent (*say* koh-heer-ent) *adjective*
clear, reasonable, and making sense.
coherently *adverb*

coil *noun* (*plural* coils)
something wound into a spiral.
coil *verb* (coils, coiling, coiled)
wind something into a coil.
[same origin as *collect*]

coin *noun* (*plural* coins)
a piece of metal, usually round, used as money.
coin *verb* (coins, coining, coined)
1 manufacture coins. 2 (*informal*) make a lot of money as profit. 3 invent a word or phrase.
[French, = die for stamping coins]

coincide *verb* (coincides, coinciding, coincided)
1 happen at the same time as something else. 2 be in the same place. 3 be the same, *My opinion coincided with hers*.
[from *co-* + Latin *incidere* = fall upon or into]

coincidence *noun* (*plural* coincidences)
the happening of similar events at the same time by chance.

col- *prefix*
with; together. see **com-**.

colander *noun* (*plural* colanders)
a bowl-shaped container with holes in it, used for straining water from vegetables etc. after cooking.
[from Latin *colare* = strain]

cold *adjective*
1 having or at a low temperature; not warm. 2 not friendly or loving; not enthusiastic.
coldly *adverb*, **coldness** *noun*
cold shoulder deliberate unfriendliness.
cold-shoulder *verb*
get cold feet feel afraid or reluctant to do something.
cold *noun* (*plural* colds)
1 lack of warmth; low temperature; cold weather. 2 an infectious illness that makes your nose run, your throat sore, etc.

cold-blooded *adjective*
1 having a body temperature that changes according to the surroundings. 2 callous; deliberately cruel.

collaborate *verb* (collaborates, collaborating, collaborated)
work together on a job.
collaboration *noun*, **collaborator** *noun*
[from *col-* + Latin *laborare* = to work]

collapse *verb* (collapses, collapsing, collapsed)
1 fall down or inwards suddenly; break. 2 become very weak or ill. 3 fold up.
collapse *noun* (*plural* collapses)
1 collapsing. 2 a breakdown.
[from *col-* + Latin *lapsum* = slipped]

collapsible *adjective*
able to be folded up, *a collapsible umbrella*.

collar *noun* (*plural* collars)
1 an upright or turned-over band round the neck of a garment etc. 2 a band that goes round the neck of a dog, cat, horse, etc.

colleague *noun* (*plural* colleagues)
a person you work with. [from Latin]

collect (*say* kol-ekt) *verb* (collects, collecting, collected)
1 bring people or things together from various places. 2 obtain examples of things as a hobby, *She collects stamps*. 3 come together. 4 ask for money or contributions etc. from people. 5 fetch, *Collect your coat from the cleaners*.
collector *noun*
[from *col-* + Latin *legere* = assemble, choose]

collection *noun* (*plural* **collections**)
1 collecting. 2 things collected. 3 money collected for a charity etc.

collective noun *noun* (*plural* **collective nouns**)
a noun that is singular in form but refers to many individuals taken as a unit, e.g. *army*, *herd*.

college *noun* (*plural* **colleges**)
a place where people can continue learning something after they have left school.

collide *verb* (**collides, colliding, collided**)
crash into something. **collision** *noun*
[from Latin *collidere* = clash together]

colloquial (*say* col-oh-kwee-al) *adjective*
suitable for conversation but not for formal speech or writing. **colloquially** *adverb*,
colloquialism *noun*
[from *col-* + Latin *loqui* = speak]

colon[1] *noun* (*plural* **colons**)
a punctuation mark (:), often used to introduce lists. [from Greek *kōlon* = clause]

colon[2] *noun* (*plural* **colons**)
the largest part of the intestine.
[from Greek *kolon*]

colonel (*say* ker-nel) *noun* (*plural* **colonels**)
an army officer in charge of a regiment. [via French from Italian]

colonial *adjective*
to do with a colony.

colonize *verb* (**colonizes, colonizing, colonized**)
establish a colony in a country. **colonist** *noun*,
colonization *noun*

colony *noun* (*plural* **colonies**)
1 an area of land that the people of another country settle in and control. 2 the people of a colony. 3 a group of people or animals of the same kind living close together.
[from Latin *colonia* = farm, settlement]

colossal *adjective*
immense; enormous.
[from the bronze statue of Apollo at Rhodes, called the *Colossus of Rhodes*]

colour *noun* (*plural* **colours**)
1 the effect produced by waves of light of a particular wavelength. 2 the use of various colours, not only black and white. 3 the colour of someone's skin. 4 a substance used to colour things. 5 the special flag of a ship or regiment.
colour *verb* (**colours, colouring, coloured**)
1 put colour on; paint or stain. 2 blush.
3 influence what someone says or believes.
colouring *noun* [from Latin]

colour-blind *adjective*
unable to see the difference between certain colours.

coloured *adjective*
1 having colour. 2 having a dark skin; Black.

colourful *adjective*
1 full of colour. 2 lively; with vivid details.

column *noun* (*plural* **columns**)
1 a pillar. 2 something long or tall and narrow, *a column of smoke*. 3 a vertical section of a page, *There are two columns on this page*. 4 a regular article in a newspaper. **columnist** *noun*
[from Latin]

com- *prefix* (becoming **col-** before *l*, **cor-** before *r*, **con-** before many other consonants)
with; together (as in *combine, connect*). [from Latin *cum* = with]

coma (*say* koh-ma) *noun* (*plural* **comas**)
a state of deep unconsciousness, especially in someone who is ill or injured.
[from Greek *koma* = deep sleep]

comb *noun* (*plural* **combs**)
1 a strip of wood or plastic etc. with teeth, used to tidy hair or hold it in place. 2 something used like this, e.g. to separate strands of wool.
3 the red crest on a fowl's head. 4 a honeycomb.
comb *verb* (**combs, combing, combed**)
1 tidy hair with a comb. 2 search thoroughly.
[from Old English]

combat *noun* & *verb* (**combats, combating, combated**)
fight. **combatant** (*say* kom-ba-tant) *noun*
[from *com-* + Latin *batuere* = fight]

combination *noun* (*plural* **combinations**)
1 combining. 2 a number of people or things that are combined. 3 a series of numbers or letters used to open a combination lock.

combine (*say* komb-l'n) *verb* (**combines, combining, combined**)
join or mix together.

combustion *noun*
the process of burning, a chemical process (accompanied by heat) in which substances combine with oxygen in air.

come *verb* (**comes, coming, came, come**)
This word is used to show 1 movement towards somewhere (*Come here!*), 2 arrival, reaching a place or condition or result (*They came to a city. We came to a decision*),
3 happening (*How did you come to lose it?*),
4 occurring (*It comes on the next page*),
5 resulting (*That's what comes of being careless*).
come by obtain.
come in for receive a share of.
come to 1 amount to. 2 become conscious again.
come to pass happen.

comedian *noun* (*plural* **comedians**)
someone who entertains people by making them laugh. [from French]

comedy noun (plural comedies)
1 a play or film etc. that makes people laugh.
2 humour.
[from Greek komos = having fun + oide = song]

comet noun (plural comets)
an object moving across the sky with a bright tail of light.
[from Greek kometes = long-haired (star)]

comfort noun (plural comforts)
1 a comfortable feeling or condition.
2 soothing somebody who is unhappy or in pain. 3 a person or thing that gives comfort.
comfort verb (comforts, comforting, comforted)
make a person less unhappy; soothe.
[from Latin confortare = strengthen]

comfortable adjective
1 at ease; relaxed. 2 making someone feel at ease or relaxed, comfortable shoes.
comfortably adverb

comic adjective
making people laugh. **comical** adjective, **comically** adverb
comic strip a series of drawings telling a comic story or a serial.
comic noun (plural comics)
1 a paper full of comic strips. 2 a comedian.
[from Greek; related to comedy]

comma noun (plural commas)
a punctuation mark (,) used to mark a pause in a sentence or to separate items in a list. [from Greek komma = short clause]

command noun (plural commands)
1 a statement telling somebody to do something; an order. 2 authority; control.
3 ability to use something; mastery, She has a good command of Spanish.
command verb (commands, commanding, commanded)
1 give a command to somebody; order. 2 have authority over. 3 deserve and get, They command our respect. **commander** noun
[from com- + Latin mandare = entrust or impose a duty]

commandeer verb (commandeers, commandeering, commandeered)
take or seize something for military purposes or for your own use.

commandment noun (plural commandments)
a sacred command, especially one of the Ten Commandments given to Moses.

commando noun (plural commandos)
a soldier trained for making dangerous raids.
[from Portuguese]

commemorate verb (commemorates, commemorating, commemorated)
be a celebration or reminder of some past event or person etc. **commemoration** noun, **commemorative** adjective
[from com- + Latin memor = memory]

commence verb (commences, commencing, commenced)
begin. **commencement** noun
[from com- + Latin initiare = initiate]

commend verb (commends, commending, commended)
1 praise, He was commended for bravery.
2 entrust, We commend him to your care.
commendation noun
[same origin as command]

comment noun (plural comments)
an opinion given about an event etc. or to explain something.
comment verb (comments, commenting, commented)
make a comment. [from Latin]

commentary verb (plural commentaries)
a set of comments, especially describing a sports event while it is happening.
commentate verb, **commentator** noun

commercial adjective
1 to do with commerce. 2 paid for by firms etc. whose advertisements are included, commercial radio. 3 profitable.
commercially adverb
commercial noun (plural commercials)
a broadcast advertisement.

commiserate verb (commiserates, commiserating, commiserated)
sympathize. **commiseration** noun
[from com- + Latin miserari = to pity]

commission noun (plural commissions)
1 authorization to do something; the task etc. authorized, a commission to paint a portrait.
2 an appointment to be an officer in the armed forces. 3 a group of people given authority to do or investigate something. 4 payment to someone for selling your goods etc.
commission verb (commissions, commissioning, commissioned)
give a commission to a person or for a task etc.
[same origin as commit]

commit verb (commits, committing, committed)
1 do or perform, commit a crime. 2 place in someone's care or custody, He was committed to prison. 3 promise that you will make your time etc. available for a particular purpose, Don't commit all your spare time to helping him.
[from com- + Latin mittere = put, send]

committee noun (plural committees)
a group of people appointed to deal with something.

commodity noun (plural commodities)
a useful thing; a product.
[from Latin commodus = convenient]

commodore noun (plural commodores)
1 a naval officer ranking next below a rear admiral. 2 the commander of part of a fleet.

common *adjective*
1 ordinary; usual; occurring frequently, *a common weed*. 2 of all or most people, *They worked for the common good*. 3 shared, *Music is their common interest*. 4 vulgar.
commonly *adverb*, **commonness** *noun*
in common shared by two or more people or things.

Common Market *noun*
a group of European countries that trade freely together.

commonplace *adjective*
ordinary; usual.

common sense *noun*
normal good sense in thinking or behaviour.

Commonwealth *noun*
1 an association of countries, *The Commonwealth consists of Britain and various other countries, including Canada, Australia, and New Zealand*. 2 a federal association of States, *the Commonwealth of Australia*. 3 the republic set up in Britain by Cromwell, lasting from 1649 to 1660.
[from *common* + an old sense of *wealth* = welfare]

commotion *noun*
an uproar; a fuss. [from *com-* + Latin *motio* = movement, motion]

commune (*say* kom-yoon) *noun* (*plural* communes)
1 a group of people sharing a home, food, etc. 2 a district of local government in France and some other countries.
[from Latin *communis* = common]

communicate *verb* (communicates, communicating, communicated)
1 pass news, information, etc. to other people. 2 (of rooms etc.) open into each other; connect.
[from Latin *communicare* = tell, share]

communication *noun* (*plural* communications)
1 communicating. 2 something communicated; a message.
communications *plural noun* links between places (e.g. roads, railways, telephones, radio).

communicative *adjective*
willing to talk.

communion *noun*
Communion or **Holy Communion** the Christian ceremony in which consecrated bread and wine are given to worshippers.
[same origin as *commune*]

Communism *noun*
a political system where the State controls property, production, trade, etc. (Compare *capitalism*.) **Communist** *noun*

community *noun* (*plural* communities)
1 the people living in one area. 2 a group with similar interests or origins.

commute *verb* (commutes, commuting, commuted)
1 travel a fairly long way by train, bus, or car to and from your daily work. 2 alter a punishment to something less severe.
[from *com-* + Latin *mutare* = change]

commuter *noun* (*plural* commuters)
a person who commutes to and from work.

compact *adjective*
1 closely or neatly packed together. 2 concise.
compactly *adverb*, **compactness** *noun*
compact *noun* (*plural* compacts)
a small flat container for face powder.

compact disc *noun* (*plural* compact discs)
a small disc from which recorded sound etc. is reproduced by means of a laser beam.

companion *noun* (*plural* companions)
1 a person who accompanies another. 2 one of a matching pair of things. 3 (in book-titles) a guidebook or reference book, *The Oxford Companion to Music*. **companionship** *noun*
[literally = someone you eat bread with: from *com-* + Latin *panis* = bread]

company *noun* (*plural* companies)
1 a number of people together. 2 a business firm. 3 having people with you; companionship. 4 visitors, *We've got company*. 5 a section of a battalion.
[same origin as *companion*]

comparative *adjective*
comparing a thing with something else, *They live in comparative comfort*.
comparatively *adverb*
comparative *noun* (*plural* comparatives)
the form of an adjective or adverb that expresses 'more', *The comparative of 'big' is 'bigger'*.

compare *verb* (compares, comparing, compared)
1 put things together so as to tell in what ways they are similar or different. 2 form the comparative and superlative of an adjective or adverb.
compare notes share information.
compare with 1 be similar to. 2 be as good as, *Our football pitch cannot compare with Wembley Stadium*.
[from *com-* + Latin *par* = equal]

USAGE: When *compare* is used with an object, it can be followed by either *to* or *with*. Traditionally, *to* is used when you are showing the similarity between two things: *She compared me to a pig*. *With* is used when you are looking at the similarities and differences between things: *Just compare this year's profits with last year's*.

comparison *noun* (*plural* comparisons)
comparing.

compartment noun (plural **compartments**)
one of the spaces into which something is divided; a separate room or enclosed space.
[from Latin compartiri = share with someone]

compass noun (plural **compasses**)
a device with a pointer that points north.
compasses or **pair of compasses** a device for drawing circles, usually with two rods hinged together at one end.

compassion noun
pity or mercy. **compassionate** adjective, **compassionately** adverb
[from com- + Latin passum = suffered]

compel verb (**compels, compelling, compelled**)
force somebody to do something.
[from com- + Latin pellere = drive]

compensate verb (**compensates, compensating, compensated**)
1 give a person money etc. to make up for a loss or injury. 2 have a balancing effect, This victory compensates for our earlier defeats.
compensation noun, **compensatory** adjective
[from Latin compensare = weigh one thing against another]

compete verb (**competes, competing, competed**)
take part in a competition.
[from com- + Latin petere = aim at]

competent adjective
able to do a particular thing.
competently adverb, **competence** noun
[from Latin, = suitable, sufficient]

competition noun (plural **competitions**)
1 a game or race or other contest in which people try to win. 2 competing. 3 the people competing with yourself. **competitive** adjective

competitor noun (plural **competitors**)
someone who competes; a rival.

compile verb (**compiles, compiling, compiled**)
put things together into a list or collection, e.g. to form a book. **compiler** noun, **compilation** noun [from French]

complacent adjective
self-satisfied. **complacently** adverb, **complacency** noun [from Latin]

complain verb (**complains, complaining, complained**)
say that you are annoyed or unhappy about something. [from Latin]

complaint noun (plural **complaints**)
1 a statement complaining about something. 2 an illness.

complement noun (plural **complements**)
1 the quantity needed to fill or complete something, The ship had its full complement of sailors. 2 the word or words used after verbs such as be and become to complete the sense. In She was brave and He became king of England, the complements are brave and king of England.

USAGE: Do not confuse with compliment.

---

complementary adjective
completing; forming a complement.

complementary angle noun (plural **complementary angles**)
either of two angles that add up to 90°.

complete adjective
1 having all its parts. 2 finished. 3 thorough; in every way, a complete stranger.
completely adverb, **completeness** noun
complete verb (**completes, completing, completed**)
make a thing complete; add what is needed.
completion noun
[from Latin completum = filled up]

complex adjective
1 made up of parts. 2 complicated. **complexity** noun
complex noun (plural **complexes**)
1 a set of buildings made up of related parts, a sports complex. 2 a group of feelings or ideas that influence a person's behaviour etc., a persecution complex.
[from Latin complexum = embraced, plaited]

complexion noun (plural **complexions**)
1 the natural colour and appearance of the skin of the face. 2 the way things seem, That puts a different complexion on the matter.
[from old French]

complicated adjective
1 made up of many parts. 2 difficult to understand or do.

complication noun (plural **complications**)
1 something that complicates things or adds difficulties. 2 a complicated condition.

compliment noun (plural **compliments**)
something said or done to show that you approve of a person or thing, pay compliments. **compliments** plural noun formal greetings given in a message.
compliment verb (**compliments, complimenting, complimented**)
pay someone a compliment; congratulate. [via French from Italian]

USAGE: Do not confuse with complement.

---

complimentary adjective
1 expressing a compliment. 2 given free of charge, complimentary tickets.

component noun (plural **components**)
each of the parts of which a thing is made up. [same origin as compound]

compose *verb* (composes, composing, composed)
1 form or make up, *The class is composed of 20 students.* 2 write music or poetry etc. 3 arrange in good order. 4 make calm, *compose yourself.*
[from French; related to *compound*]

composer *noun* (*plural* composers)
a person who composes music etc.

composite (*say* kom-poz-it) *adjective*
made up of a number of parts or different styles. [same origin as *compose*]

composition *noun* (*plural* compositions)
1 composing. 2 something composed, especially a piece of music. 3 an essay or story written as a school exercise. 4 the parts that make something, *the composition of the soil.*

compost *noun*
1 decayed leaves and grass etc. used as a fertilizer. 2 a soil-like mixture for growing seedlings, cuttings, etc.
[same origin as *compose*]

composure *noun*
calmness of manner.

compound *adjective*
made of two or more parts or ingredients.
compound *noun* (*plural* compounds)
a compound substance.
compound *verb* (compounds, compounding, compounded)
put together; combine.
[from Latin *componere* = put together]

comprehensible *adjective*
understandable.

comprehensive *adjective*
including all or many kinds of people or things.
comprehensive *noun* (*plural* comprehensives)
a comprehensive school.

comprehensive school *noun* (*plural* comprehensive schools)
a large secondary school for all or most of the children of an area.

compress (*say* kom-press) *verb* (compresses, compressing, compressed)
press together or into a smaller space.
compression *noun*, **compressor** *noun*

compromise (*say* kom-prom-I'z) *noun* (*plural* compromises)
settling a dispute by each side accepting less than it asked for.
compromise *verb* (compromises, compromising, compromised)
1 settle by a compromise. 2 expose someone to danger or suspicion etc., *His confession compromises his sister.*
[from *com-* + Latin *promittere* = to promise]

compulsion *noun* (*plural* compulsions)
a strong and uncontrollable desire to do something.

compulsory *adjective*
that must be done; not optional.
[same origin as *compel*]

compunction *noun*
a guilty feeling, *She felt no compunction about hitting the burglar.* [from *com-* + Latin *punctum* = pricked (by conscience)]

compute *verb* (computes, computing, computed)
calculate. **computation** *noun*

computer *noun* (*plural* computers)
an electronic machine for making calculations, storing and analysing information put into it, or controlling machinery automatically.

comrade *noun* (*plural* comrades)
a companion who shares in your activities.
comradeship *noun*
[from Spanish *camarada* = room-mate]

con- *prefix*
with; together. see **com-**.

concave *adjective*
curved like the inside of a ball or circle. (The opposite is *convex*.) **concavity** *noun*
[from *con-* + Latin *cavus* = hollow]

conceal *verb* (conceals, concealing, concealed)
hide; keep something secret.
concealment *noun*
[from *con-* + Latin *celare* = hide]

concede *verb* (concedes, conceding, conceded)
1 admit that something is true. 2 grant or allow something, *They conceded us the right to cross their land.* 3 admit that you have been defeated.

conceit *noun*
being too proud of yourself; vanity.
conceited *adjective*
[originally = idea, opinion; from *conceive*]

conceive *verb* (conceives, conceiving, conceived)
1 become pregnant; form a baby in the womb. 2 form an idea or plan; imagine, *I can't conceive why you want to come.*
[from Latin *concipere* = take in, contain]

concentrate *verb* (concentrates, concentrating, concentrated)
1 give your full attention or effort to something. 2 bring or come together in one place. 3 make a liquid etc. less dilute.
[from French; related to *centre*]

concentration *noun* (*plural* concentrations)
1 concentrating. 2 the amount dissolved in each part of a liquid.

concentric *adjective*
having the same centre, *concentric circles.*
[from Latin; related to *centre*]

concept *noun* (*plural* concepts)
an idea. [same origin as *conceive*]

conception *noun* (*plural* conceptions)
1 conceiving. 2 an idea.

concern *verb* (concerns, concerning, concerned)
1 be important to or affect somebody. 2 worry somebody. 3 be about; have as its subject, *The story concerns a group of rabbits.*
concern *noun* (*plural* concerns)
1 something that concerns you; a responsibility. 2 worry. 3 a business.

concert *noun* (*plural* concerts)
a musical entertainment.
[same origin as *concerto*]

concerto (*say* kon-chert-oh) *noun* (*plural* concertos)
a piece of music for a solo instrument and an orchestra.
[from Italian *concertare* = harmonize]

concession *noun* (*plural* concessions)
1 conceding. 2 something conceded. 3 a reduction in price for a certain category of person. **concessionary** *adjective*
[same origin as *concede*]

conciliate *verb* (conciliates, conciliating, conciliated)
1 win over an angry or hostile person by friendliness. 2 help people who disagree to come to an agreement. **conciliation** *noun*
[from Latin; related to *council*]

concise *adjective*
brief; giving much information in a few words.
concisely *adverb*, **conciseness** *noun*
[from con- + Latin *caedere* = cut]

conclude *verb* (concludes, concluding, concluded)
1 bring or come to an end. 2 decide; form an opinion by reasoning, *The jury concluded that he was guilty.*
[from con- + Latin *claudere* = shut]

conclusion *noun* (*plural* conclusions)
1 an ending. 2 an opinion formed by reasoning.

conclusive *adjective*
putting an end to all doubt.
conclusively *adverb*

concoct *verb* (concocts, concocting, concocted)
1 make something by putting ingredients together. 2 invent, *concoct an excuse.*
concoction *noun*
[from con- + Latin *coctum* = cooked]

concord *noun*
friendly agreement or harmony.
[from con- + Latin *cor* = heart]

concrete *noun*
cement mixed with sand and gravel, used in building.
concrete *adjective*
1 able to be touched and felt; not abstract.
2 definite, *We need concrete evidence, not theories.* [from Latin *concretus* = stiff, hard]

concurrent *adjective*
happening or existing at the same time.

concussion *noun*
a temporary injury to the brain caused by a hard knock. **concussed** *adjective*
[from Latin *concussum* = shaken violently]

condemn *verb* (condemns, condemning, condemned)
1 say that you strongly disapprove of something. 2 convict or sentence a criminal.
3 destine to something unhappy, *condemned to a lonely life.* 4 declare that houses etc. are not fit to be used. **condemnation** *noun*

condense *verb* (condenses, condensing, condensed)
1 make a liquid denser or more compact. 2 put something into fewer words. 3 change from gas or vapour to liquid, *Steam condenses on windows.* **condensation** *noun*, **condenser** *noun*

condescend *verb* (condescends, condescending, condescended)
1 behave in a way which shows that you feel superior. 2 allow yourself to do something that seems unsuitable for a person of your high rank. **condescension** *noun* [from Latin *condescendere* = stoop, lower yourself]

condition *noun* (*plural* conditions)
1 the state or fitness of a person or thing, *This bicycle is in good condition.* 2 the situation or surroundings etc. that affect something, *working conditions.* 3 something required as part of an agreement.
on condition that only if; on the understanding that something will be done.
condition *verb* (conditions, conditioning, conditioned)
1 put something into a proper condition.
2 train or accustom. [from Latin]

conditional *adjective*
containing a condition (see *condition* 3); depending. **conditionally** *adverb*

condom *noun* (*plural* condoms)
a rubber sheath worn on the penis as a contraceptive. [origin unknown]

condone *verb* (condones, condoning, condoned)
forgive or ignore wrongdoing, *Do not condone violence.* **condonation** *noun*

conduct (*say* kon-dukt) *verb* (conducts, conducting, conducted)
1 lead or guide. 2 be the conductor of an orchestra or choir. 3 manage or direct something, *conduct an experiment.* 4 allow heat, light, sound, or electricity to pass along or through. 5 behave, *They conducted themselves with dignity.*

conduction *noun*
the conducting of heat or electricity etc. (see *conduct* 4).

conductor *noun* (*plural* conductors)
1 a person who directs the performance of an orchestra or choir by movements of the arms.

2 a person who collects the fares on a bus etc.
3 something that conducts heat or electricity
etc. **conductress** *noun*

cone *noun* (*plural* **cones**)
1 an object that is circular at one end and
narrows to a point at the other end. **2** the dry
cone-shaped fruit of a pine, fir, or cedar tree.
[from Greek]

confectioner *noun* (*plural* **confectioners**)
someone who makes or sells sweets.
confectionery *noun*

confederate *adjective*
allied; joined by an agreement or treaty.
confederate *noun* (*plural* **confederates**)
1 a member of a confederacy. **2** an ally; an
accomplice.
[from *con-* + Latin *foederatum* = allied]

confederation *noun* (*plural* **confederations**)
1 the process of joining in an alliance. **2** a
group of people, organizations, or States joined
together by an agreement or treaty.

conference *noun* (*plural* **conferences**)
a meeting for holding a discussion.
[same origin as *confer*]

confess *verb* (**confesses, confessing, confessed**)
state openly that you have done something
wrong or have a weakness; admit.
confession *noun*
[from Latin]

confetti *noun*
tiny pieces of coloured paper thrown by
wedding guests at the bride and bridegroom.
[Italian, = sweets (which were traditionally
thrown at Italian weddings)]

confide *verb* (**confides, confiding, confided**)
1 tell confidentially, *confide a secret to someone*
or *confide in someone*. **2** entrust.
[from *con-* + Latin *fidere* = to trust]

confidence *noun* (*plural* **confidences**)
1 firm trust. **2** a feeling of certainty or
boldness; being sure that you can do
something. **3** something told confidentially.
in confidence as a secret.
in a person's confidence trusted with his or her
secrets.

confidence trick *noun* (*plural* **confidence tricks**)
swindling a person after persuading him or her
to trust you.

confident *adjective*
showing or feeling confidence; bold.
confidently *adverb*
[from Latin; related to *confide*]

confidential *adjective*
something that is confidential is meant to be
kept secret. **confidentially** *adverb*,
confidentiality *noun*

confine *verb* (**confines, confining, confined**)
1 keep something within limits; restrict, *Please
confine your remarks to the subject being
discussed.* **2** keep somebody in a place.
[from *con-* + Latin *finis* = limit, end]

confirm *verb* (**confirms, confirming, confirmed**)
1 prove that something is true or correct.
2 make a thing definite, *Please write to confirm
your booking.* **3** make a person a full member of
the Christian Church. **confirmation** *noun*,
confirmatory *adjective*
[from *con-* + Latin *firmare* = strengthen]

confiscate *verb* (**confiscates, confiscating,
confiscated**)
take something away as a punishment.
confiscation *noun* [from Latin]

conflagration *noun* (*plural* **conflagrations**)
a great and destructive fire.

conflict (*say* kon-flikt) *noun* (*plural* **conflicts**)
a fight, struggle, or disagreement.
conflict (*say* kon-**flikt**) *verb* (**conflicts, conflicting,
conflicted**)
have a conflict; differ or disagree.
[from *con-* = together + Latin *flictum* = struck]

conform *verb* (**conforms, conforming, conformed**)
keep to accepted rules or customs etc.
conformist *noun*, **conformity** *noun*
[from Latin *conformare* = shape evenly]

confound *verb* (**confounds, confounding,
confounded**)
1 astonish or puzzle someone. **2** confuse.

confront *verb* (**confronts, confronting,
confronted**)
1 come or bring face to face, especially in a
hostile way. **2** be present and have to be dealt
with, *Problems confront us.* **confrontation** *noun*
[from Latin]

confuse *verb* (**confuses, confusing, confused**)
1 make a person puzzled or muddled.
2 mistake one thing for another. **confusion**
noun [from old French; related to *confound*]

confute *verb* (**confutes, confuting, confuted**)
prove a person or statement to be wrong.
confutation *noun*

congeal (*say* kon-**jeel**) *verb* (**congeals, congealing,
congealed**)
become jelly-like instead of liquid, especially in
cooling, *congealed blood.*

congenital (*say* kon-**jen**-it-al) *adjective*
existing in a person from birth.
congenitally *adverb*
[from *con-* + Latin *genitus* = born]

congested *adjective*
crowded or blocked up, *congested streets,
congested lungs.* **congestion** *noun*
[from Latin *congestum* = heaped up]

conglomeration *noun* (*plural* **conglomerations**)
a mass of different things put together. [from
con- + Latin *glomus* = mass]

congratulate *verb* (congratulates, congratulating, congratulated)
tell a person that you are pleased about his or her success or good fortune.
congratulation *noun*, **congratulatory** *adjective*
[from *con-* + Latin *gratulari* = show joy]

congregate *verb* (congregates, congregating, congregated)
assemble; flock together.
[from *con-* + Latin *gregatum* = herded]

congregation *noun* (*plural* congregations)
a group who have gathered to take part in worship.

Congress *noun*
the parliament of the USA.

congruent *adjective*
congruent triangles have exactly the same shape and size. **congruence** *noun*

conic *adjective*
to do with a cone.

conical *adjective*
cone-shaped. **conically** *adverb*

conifer (*say* kon-if-er) *noun* (*plural* conifers)
an evergreen tree with cones.
coniferous *adjective*
[from *cone* + Latin *ferens* = bearing]

conjecture *noun* (*plural* conjectures)
a guess. **conjecture** *verb*, **conjectural** *adjective*
[from Latin]

conjugate *verb* (conjugates, conjugating, conjugated)
give all the different forms of a verb.
conjugation *noun*

conjunction *noun* (*plural* conjunctions)
1 a word that joins words or phrases or sentences, e.g. *and*, *but*. 2 combination, *The four armies acted in conjunction.*
[from Latin *conjunctum* = yoked together]

conjure *verb* (conjures, conjuring, conjured)
perform puzzling tricks. **conjuror** *noun*
conjure up produce in your mind, *Mention of the Arctic conjures up visions of snow.*

connect *verb* (connects, connecting, connected)
1 join together; link. 2 think of as being associated with each other.

connection *noun* (*plural* connections)
1 a point where two things are connected; a link, *We all know there is a connection between smoking and cancer.* 2 a train, bus, etc. that leaves a station soon after another arrives, so that passengers can change from one to the other.

connoisseur (*say* kon-a-ser) *noun* (*plural* connoisseurs)
a person with great experience and appreciation of something, *a connoisseur of wine.* [French, = one who knows]

conquer *verb* (conquers, conquering, conquered)
defeat or overcome. **conqueror** *noun*
[from old French]

conquest *noun* (*plural* conquests)
1 conquering. 2 conquered territory.

conscience (*say* kon-shens) *noun* (*plural* consciences)
knowing what is right and wrong, especially in your own actions.
[from Latin *conscientia* = knowledge]

conscientious (*say* kon-shee-en-shus) *adjective*
careful and honest, *conscientious workers.*
conscientiously *adverb*

conscientious objector *noun* (*plural* conscientious objectors)
a person who refuses to serve in the armed forces because he or she believes it is wrong.

conscious (*say* kon-shus) *adjective*
awake; aware of what is happening.
consciously *adverb*, **consciousness** *noun*
[from Latin *conscius* = knowing]

conscript (*say* kon-skript) *verb* (conscripts, conscripting, conscripted)
make a person join the armed forces.
conscription *noun*
conscript (*say* kon-skript) *noun* (*plural* conscripts)
a conscripted person. [from *con-* + Latin *scriptus* = written in a list, enlisted]

consecrate *verb* (consecrates, consecrating, consecrated)
officially say that a thing, especially a building, is holy. **consecration** *noun*

consecutive *adjective*
following one after another.
consecutively *adverb*
[from Latin *consequi* = follow closely]

consensus *noun* (*plural* consensuses)
general agreement; the opinion of most people.
[same origin as *consent*]

consent *noun*
agreement to what someone wishes; permission.
consent *verb* (consents, consenting, consented)
say that you are willing to do or allow what someone wishes.
[from *con-* + Latin *sentire* = feel]

consequence *noun* (*plural* consequences)
1 something that happens as the result of an event or action. 2 importance, *It is of no consequence.*

consequent *adjective*
happening as a result. **consequently** *adverb*
[same origin as *consecutive*]

conservation *noun*
conserving; preservation, especially of the natural environment. **conservationist** *noun*

Conservative *noun* (*plural* **Conservatives**)
a person who supports the Conservative Party,
a political party that favours private
enterprise and freedom from State control.
Conservative *adjective*

conservative *adjective*
1 liking traditional ways and disliking
changes. 2 (of an estimate) moderate; low.
conservatively *adverb*, **conservatism** *noun*

conserve *verb* (**conserves, conserving, conserved**)
prevent something valuable from being
changed, spoilt, or wasted.
[from *con-* + Latin *servare* = keep safe]

consider *verb* (**considers, considering, considered**)
1 think carefully about or give attention to
something, especially in order to make a
decision. 2 have an opinion; think to be,
Consider yourself lucky. [from Latin]

considerable *adjective*
fairly great, *a considerable amount.*
considerably *adverb*

considerate *adjective*
taking care not to inconvenience or hurt
others. **considerately** *adverb*

consideration *noun* (*plural* **considerations**)
1 being considerate. 2 careful thought or
attention. 3 a fact that must be kept in mind.
4 payment given as a reward.
take into consideration allow for.

considering *preposition*
taking something into consideration, *The car
runs well, considering its age.*

consist *verb* (**consists, consisting, consisted**)
be made up or composed of, *The flat consists of
three rooms.* [from Latin]

consistency *noun* (*plural* **consistencies**)
1 being consistent. 2 thickness or stiffness,
especially of a liquid.

consistent *adjective*
1 keeping to a regular pattern or style; not
changing. 2 not contradictory.
consistently *adverb*

consolation *noun* (*plural* **consolations**)
1 consoling. 2 something that consoles
someone.

console[1] (*say* kon-sohl) *verb* (**consoles, consoling,
consoled**)
comfort someone who is unhappy or
disappointed.
[from *con-* + Latin *solari* = soothe]

console[2] (*say* kon-sohl) *noun* (*plural* **consoles**)
1 a panel holding the controls of equipment.
2 a frame containing the keyboard and stops
etc. of an organ. 3 a cabinet for a radio or
television set. [French]

consolidate *verb* (**consolidates, consolidating,
consolidated**)
1 make or become secure and strong.

2 combine two or more organizations, funds,
etc. into one. **consolidation** *noun*
[from *con-* + Latin *solidare* = make solid]

consonant *noun* (*plural* **consonants**)
a letter that is not a vowel, *B, c, d, f, etc.* are
consonants.
[from *con-* + Latin *sonans* = sounding]

conspicuous *adjective*
easily seen; noticeable. **conspicuously** *adverb*,
conspicuousness *noun*
[from Latin *conspicere* = look at carefully]

conspiracy *noun* (*plural* **conspiracies**)
planning with others to do something illegal; a
plot. **conspirator** *noun*

constable *noun* (*plural* **constables**)
a police officer of the lowest rank.
[from Latin, originally = officer in charge of
the stable]

constant *adjective*
1 not changing; happening all the time.
2 faithful or loyal.
constantly *adverb*, **constancy** *noun*
constant *noun* (*plural* **constants**)
1 a thing that does not vary. 2 in mathematics,
a number or value that does not change.

constellation *noun* (*plural* **constellations**)
a group of stars.
[from *con-* + Latin *stella* = star]

constipated *adjective*
unable to empty the bowels easily or regularly.
constipation *noun*
[from Latin *constipare* = cram]

constituency *noun* (*plural* **constituencies**)
a district represented by a Member of
Parliament elected by the people who live
there.

constituent *noun* (*plural* **constituents**)
1 one of the parts that form a whole thing.
2 someone who lives in a particular
constituency. **constituent** *adjective*

constitute *verb* (**constitutes, constituting,
constituted**)
make up or form something, *Twelve months
constitute a year.*
[from *con-* + Latin *statuere* = set up]

constitution *noun* (*plural* **constitutions**)
1 the group of laws or principles that state how
a country is to be organized and governed.
2 the nature of the body in regard to
healthiness, *She has a strong constitution.*
3 constituting. 4 the composition of something.
constitutional *adjective*

constrict *verb* (**constricts, constricting,
constricted**)
squeeze or tighten something by making it
narrower. **constriction** *noun*

construct verb (constructs, constructing, constructed)
make something by placing parts together; build. **constructor** noun
[from con- + Latin structum = built]

construction noun (plural constructions)
1 constructing. 2 something constructed; a building. 3 two or more words put together to form a phrase or clause or sentence. 4 an explanation or interpretation, They put a bad construction on our refusal.

constructive adjective
constructing; being helpful, constructive suggestions.

consult verb (consults, consulting, consulted)
go to a person or book etc. for information or advice. **consultation** noun [from Latin consulere = take advice or counsel]

consultant noun (plural consultants)
a person who is qualified to give expert advice.

consume verb (consumes, consuming, consumed)
1 eat or drink something. 2 use up, Much time was consumed in waiting. 3 destroy, Fire consumed the building.
[from con- + Latin sumere = take up]

consumer noun (plural consumers)
a person who buys or uses goods or services.

consummate (say kon-sum-at) adjective
perfect; highly skilled, a consummate artist.
[from con- + Latin summus = highest]

consumption noun
1 consuming. 2 (old use) tuberculosis of the lungs.

contact noun (plural contacts)
1 touching. 2 being in touch; communication. 3 a person to communicate with when you need information or help.
contact verb (contacts, contacting, contacted)
get in touch with a person.
[from con- + Latin tactum = touched]

contact lens noun (plural contact lenses)
a tiny lens worn against the eyeball, instead of spectacles.

contagious adjective
spreading by contact with an infected person, a contagious disease.
[from con- + Latin tangere = to touch]

contain verb (contains, containing, contained)
1 have inside, The box contains chocolates. 2 consist of, A gallon contains 8 pints. 3 restrain; hold back, Try to contain your laughter. [from con- + Latin tenere = hold]

container noun (plural containers)
1 a box or bottle etc. designed to contain something. 2 a large box-like object of standard design in which goods are transported.

contaminate verb (contaminates, contaminating, contaminated)
make a thing dirty or impure or diseased etc.; pollute. **contamination** noun
[from Latin; related to contagion]

contemplate verb (contemplates, contemplating, contemplated)
1 look at something thoughtfully. 2 consider or think about doing something, We are contemplating a visit to London.
contemplation noun, **contemplative** adjective
[from Latin]

contemporary adjective
1 belonging to the same period, Dickens was contemporary with Thackeray. 2 modern; up-to-date, contemporary furniture.
contemporary noun (plural contemporaries)
a person who is contemporary with another or who is about the same age, She was my contemporary at college.
[from con- + Latin tempus = time]

contempt noun
a feeling of despising a person or thing.

contemptible adjective
deserving contempt, Hurting her feelings like that was a contemptible thing to do.

contemptuous adjective
feeling or showing contempt, She gave me a contemptuous look. **contemptuously** adverb

content[1] (say kon-tent) adjective
contented. **contentment** noun

content[2] (say kon-tent) noun or **contents** plural noun
what something contains.
[from Latin contenta = things contained]

contented adjective
happy with what you have; satisfied.
contentedly adverb

contest (say kon-test) noun (plural contests)
a competition; a struggle in which rivals try to obtain something or to do best.

contestant noun (plural contestants)
a person taking part in a contest; a competitor.

context noun (plural contexts)
1 the words that come before and after a particular word or phrase and help to fix its meaning. 2 the background to an event that helps to explain it.
[from con- + Latin textum = woven]

continent noun (plural continents)
one of the main masses of land in the world, The continents are Europe, Asia, Africa, North America, South America, Australia, and Antarctica.
continental adjective
the Continent the mainland of Europe, not including the British Isles.
[from Latin terra continens = continuous land]

continual *adjective*
happening all the time, usually with breaks in between, *Stop this continual quarrelling!*
continually *adverb*

USAGE: Do not confuse with *continuous*. *Continual* is used to describe something that happens very frequently (*there were continual interruptions*) while *continuous* is used to describe something that happens without a pause (*there was continuous rain all day*).

continue *verb* (continues, continuing, continued)
1 do something without stopping. **2** begin again after stopping, *The game will continue after lunch.* **continuation** *noun*

continuous *adjective*
going on and on; without a break.
continuously *adverb*, **continuity** *noun*

USAGE: See note at *continual*.

contort *verb* (contorts, contorting, contorted)
twist or force out of the usual shape.
contortion *noun*
[from *con-* + Latin *tortum* = twisted]

contortionist *noun* (*plural* contortionists)
a person who can twist his or her body into unusual positions.

contour *noun* (*plural* contours)
1 a line on a map joining the points that are the same height above sea level. **2** an outline.

contra- *prefix*
against. [Latin]

contraband *noun*
smuggled goods.
[from *contra-* + Italian *banda* = a ban]

contraception *noun*
preventing conception; birth control.
[from *contra-* + *conception*]

contraceptive *noun* (*plural* contraceptives)
a substance or device that prevents conception.

contract (*say* kon-trakt) *noun* (*plural* contracts)
1 a formal agreement to do something. **2** a document stating the terms of an agreement.
contract (*say* kon-trakt) *verb* (contracts, contracting, contracted)
1 make or become smaller. **2** make a contract. **3** get an illness, *She contracted measles.*
[from *con-* + Latin *tractum* = pulled]

contraction *noun* (*plural* contractions)
1 contracting. **2** a shortened form of a word or words. *Can't* is a contraction of *cannot*.

contractor *noun* (*plural* contractors)
a person who makes a contract, especially for building.

contradict *verb* (contradicts, contradicting, contradicted)
1 say that something said is not true or that someone is wrong. **2** say the opposite of, *These*

rumours contradict previous ones. **contradiction** *noun*, **contradictory** *adjective*
[from *contra-* + Latin *dicere* = say]

contraflow *noun* (*plural* contraflows)
a flow of road traffic travelling in the opposite direction to the usual flow and close beside it.
[from *contra-* + *flow*]

contralto *noun* (*plural* contraltos)
a female singer with a low voice.
[Italian, from *contra-* + *alto*]

contraption *noun* (*plural* contraptions)
a strange-looking device or machine. [origin unknown]

contrary *adjective*
1 (*say* kon-tra-ree) of the opposite kind or direction etc.; opposed; unfavourable. **2** (*say* kon-trair-ee) awkward and obstinate.
contrary (*say* kon-tra-ree) *noun*
the opposite.
on the contrary the opposite is true.

contrast *noun* (*plural* contrasts)
1 a difference clearly seen when things are compared. **2** something showing a clear difference.
contrast *verb* (contrasts, contrasting, contrasted)
1 compare or oppose two things in order to show that they are clearly different. **2** be clearly different when compared.
[from *contra-* + Latin *stare* = to stand]

contravene *verb* (contravenes, contravening, contravened)
act against a rule or law. **contravention** *noun*
[from *contra-* + Latin *venire* = come]

contribute *verb* (contributes, contributing, contributed)
1 give money or help etc. when others are doing the same. **2** write something for a newspaper or magazine etc. **3** help to cause something. **contribution** *noun*, **contributor** *noun*, **contributory** *adjective*
[from *con-* + Latin *tribuere* = bestow]

contrite *adjective*
very sorry for having done wrong.
[from Latin *contritus* = ground down]

contrive *verb* (contrives, contriving, contrived)
plan cleverly; find a way of doing or making something. [from old French]

control *verb* (controls, controlling, controlled)
1 have the power to make someone or something do what you want. **2** hold something, especially anger, in check; restrain.
controller *noun*
control *noun*
controlling a person or thing; authority.
out of control no longer able to be controlled.
[from old French]

controls *plural noun*
the switches etc. used to control a machine.

controversial *adjective*
causing controversy.

controversy (*say* kon-tro-ver-see or kon-**trov**-er-see) *noun* (*plural* **controversies**)
a long argument or disagreement.
[from *contra-* + Latin *versum* = turned]

conundrum *noun* (*plural* **conundrums**)
a riddle; a hard question. [origin unknown]

convalesce *verb* (**convalesces, convalescing, convalesced**)
be recovering from an illness.
convalescence *noun*, **convalescent** *adjective* & *noun*
[from *con-* + Latin *valescere* = grow strong]

convection *noun*
the passing on of heat within liquid, air, or gas by circulation of the warmed parts. [from *con-* + Latin *vectum* = carried]

convenience *noun* (*plural* **conveniences**)
1 being convenient. 2 something that is convenient. 3 a public lavatory.
at your convenience whenever you find convenient; as it suits you.

convenient *adjective*
easy to use or deal with or reach.
conveniently *adverb*
[from Latin *convenire* = to suit]

conventional *adjective*
1 done or doing things in the accepted way; traditional. 2 (of weapons) not nuclear.
conventionally *adverb*, **conventionality** *noun*

conversation *noun* (*plural* **conversations**)
talk between people.
conversational *adjective*

convert (*say* kon-**vert**) *verb* (**converts, converting, converted**)
1 change. 2 cause a person to change his or her beliefs. 3 kick a goal after scoring a try at Rugby football.
converter *noun*, **conversion** *noun*

convex *adjective*
curved like the outside of a ball or circle. (The opposite is *concave*.) **convexity** *noun* [from Latin *convexus* = arched]

convey *verb* (**conveys, conveying, conveyed**)
1 transport. 2 communicate a message or idea etc. **conveyor** *noun*
[from old French *conveier* = lead, escort]

conveyor belt (*plural* **conveyor belts**)
a continuous moving belt for conveying objects.

convict (*say* kon-**vikt**) *verb* (**convicts, convicting, convicted**)
prove or declare that a certain person is guilty of a crime.
convict (*say* kon-vikt) *noun* (*plural* **convicts**)
a convicted person who is in prison.
[from *con-* + Latin *victum* = conquered]

conviction *noun* (*plural* **convictions**)
1 convicting or being convicted of a crime. 2 being convinced. 3 a firm opinion or belief.
carry conviction be convincing.

convince *verb* (**convinces, convincing, convinced**)
make a person feel certain that something is true.
[from *con-* + Latin *vincere* = conquer]

convoy *noun* (*plural* **convoys**)
a group of ships or lorries travelling together.
[same origin as *convey*]

convulsion *noun* (*plural* **convulsions**)
1 a violent movement of the body. 2 a violent upheaval.

coo *verb* (**coos, cooing, cooed**)
make a dove's soft murmuring sound.
coo *noun*

cook *verb* (**cooks, cooking, cooked**)
make food ready to eat by heating it.
cook up (*informal*) if you cook up a story or plan, you invent it.
cook *noun* (*plural* **cooks**)
a person who cooks. [from Latin]

cookery *noun*
the skill of cooking food.

cool *adjective*
1 fairly cold; not hot or warm. 2 calm; not enthusiastic. **coolly** *adverb*, **coolness** *noun*
cool *verb* (**cools, cooling, cooled**)
make or become cool. **cooler** *noun*

cooperate *verb* (**cooperates, cooperating, cooperated**)
work helpfully with other people.
cooperation *noun*, **cooperative** *adjective*

coordinate *verb* (**coordinates, coordinating, coordinated**)
organize people or things to work properly together.
coordination *noun*, **coordinator** *noun*
coordinate *noun* (*plural* **coordinates**)
either of the pair of numbers or letters used to fix the position of a point on a graph or map.
[from *co-* + Latin *ordinare* = arrange]

cope *verb* (**copes, coping, coped**)
manage or deal with something successfully.
[from French; related to *coup*]

copious *adjective*
plentiful; in large amounts. **copiously** *adverb*
[same origin as *copy*]

copper *noun* (*plural* **coppers**)
1 a reddish-brown metal used to make wire, coins, etc. 2 a reddish-brown colour. 3 a coin made of copper or metal of this colour.
copper *adjective*
[via Old English from Latin *cyprium* = Cyprus metal (because the Romans got most of their copper from Cyprus)]

copse *noun* (*plural* **copses**)
a small group of trees.

copulate *verb* (copulates, copulating, copulated)
have sexual intercourse with someone.
copulation *noun*
[from Latin *copulare* = link or join together]

copy *noun* (*plural* copies)
1 a thing made to look like another.
2 something written or typed out again from
its original form. 3 one of a number of
specimens of the same book or newspaper etc.
copy *verb* (copies, copying, copied)
1 make a copy of something. 2 do the same as
someone else; imitate. **copyist** *noun*
[from Latin *copia* = plenty, abundance]

copyright *noun*
the legal right to print a book, reproduce a
picture, record a piece of music, etc.

cor- *prefix*
with; together. see **com-**.

coral *noun*
1 a hard red, pink, or white substance formed
by the skeletons of tiny sea-creatures massed
together. 2 a pink colour.

cord *noun* (*plural* cords)
1 a long thin flexible strip of twisted threads or
strands. 2 a piece of flex. 3 a cord-like
structure in the body, *the spinal cord.*
4 corduroy. [from Greek]

USAGE: Do not confuse with *chord.*

cordial *adjective*
warm and friendly. **cordially** *adverb*, **cordiality**
noun [from Latin *cordis* = of the heart (a
cordial was originally a drink given to
stimulate the heart)]

corduroy *noun*
cotton cloth with velvety ridges. [from *cord*
+ *duroy* = a kind of woollen material]

core *noun* (*plural* cores)
1 the part in the middle of something. 2 the
hard central part of an apple or pear etc.,
containing the seeds. [origin unknown]

corgi *noun* (*plural* corgis)
a small dog with short legs and upright ears.
[from Welsh *cor* = dwarf + *ci* = dog]

cork *noun* (*plural* corks)
1 the lightweight bark of a kind of oak tree. 2 a
stopper for a bottle, made of cork or other
material.
cork *verb* (corks, corking, corked)
close something with a cork.

corkscrew *noun* (*plural* corkscrews)
1 a device for removing corks from bottles. 2 a
spiral.

corn[1] *noun*
1 the seed of wheat and similar plants. 2 a
plant, such as wheat, grown for its grain.
[from Old English]

corn[2] *noun* (*plural* corns)
a small hard lump on the foot.
[from Latin *cornu* = horn]

cornea *noun* (*plural* corneas)
the transparent covering over the pupil of the
eye. **corneal** *adjective* [from Latin]

corner *noun* (*plural* corners)
1 the angle or area where two lines or sides or
walls meet or where two streets join. 2 a free
hit or kick from the corner of a hockey or
football field. 3 a region, *a quiet corner of the
world.*
corner *verb* (corners, cornering, cornered)
1 drive someone into a corner or other position
from which it is difficult to escape. 2 travel
round a corner. 3 obtain possession of all or
most of something, *corner the market.*
[from Latin *cornu* = horn, tip]

cornet *noun* (*plural* cornets)
1 a cone-shaped wafer etc. holding ice cream.
2 a musical instrument rather like a trumpet.
[French, = small horn]

cornflakes *plural noun*
toasted maize flakes eaten as a breakfast
cereal.

cornucopia *noun*
1 a horn-shaped container overflowing with
fruit and flowers. 2 a plentiful supply of good
things.
[from Latin *cornu* = horn + *copiae* = of plenty]

corny *adjective* (cornier, corniest) (*informal*)
1 repeated so often that people are bored, *corny
jokes.* 2 sentimental.
[originally = rustic, simple: from *corn*[1]]

corollary (*say* ker-ol-er-ee) *noun* (*plural*
corollaries)
a fact etc. that logically results from another,
The work is difficult and, as a corollary, tiring.
[from Latin]

coronary *noun* (*plural* coronaries)
short for **coronary thrombosis**, blockage of an
artery carrying blood to the heart.
[from *corona* (because the coronary arteries
encircle the heart like a crown)]

coronation *noun* (*plural* coronations)
the crowning of a king or queen.

corporal *noun* (*plural* corporals)
a soldier ranking next below a sergeant.

corporal punishment *noun*
punishment by being whipped or beaten.

corps (*say* kor) *noun* (*plural* corps (*say* korz))
1 a special army unit, *the Medical Corps.* 2 a
large group of soldiers. 3 a set of people doing
the same job, *the diplomatic corps.*
[French, from Latin *corpus* = body]

corpse *noun* (*plural* corpses)
a dead body. [from Latin *corpus* = body]

corpuscle *noun* (*plural* **corpuscles**)
one of the red or white cells in blood.
[from Latin *corpusculum* = little body]

correct *adjective*
1 true; accurate; without any mistakes.
2 proper; done or said in an approved way.
correctly *adverb*, **correctness** *noun*
correct *verb* (**corrects, correcting, corrected**)
1 make a thing correct by altering or adjusting
it. **2** mark the mistakes in something. **3** point
out or punish a person's faults. **correction** *noun*,
corrective *adjective*, **corrector** *noun*
[from *cor-* + Latin *rectus* = straight]

correspond *verb* (**corresponds, corresponding,
corresponded**)
1 write letters to each other. **2** agree; match,
Your story corresponds with his. **3** be similar or
equivalent, *Their assembly corresponds to our
parliament.*

correspondence *noun*
1 letters; writing letters. **2** similarity;
agreement.

corridor *noun* (*plural* **corridors**)
a passage in a building.
[via French from Italian]

corroborate *verb* (**corroborates, corroborating,
corroborated**)
help to confirm a statement etc.
corroboration *noun*
[from *cor-* + Latin *roborare* = strengthen]

corrode *verb* (**corrodes, corroding, corroded**)
destroy metal gradually by chemical action.
corrosion *noun*, **corrosive** *adjective*
[from *cor-* + Latin *rodere* = gnaw]

corrugated *adjective*
shaped into alternate ridges and grooves,
corrugated iron.
[from *cor-* + Latin *ruga* = wrinkle]

corrupt *adjective*
1 dishonest; accepting bribes. **2** wicked.
3 decaying.
corrupt *verb* (**corrupts, corrupting, corrupted**)
1 cause someone to become dishonest or
wicked. **2** spoil; cause something to decay.
corruption *noun*, **corruptible** *adjective*
[from *cor-* + Latin *ruptum* = broken]

cosine *noun* (*plural* **cosines**)
(in a right-angled triangle) the ratio of the
length of a side adjacent to one of the acute
angles to the length of the hypotenuse.
(Compare *sine.*) [from *co-* + *sine*]

cosmetic *noun* (*plural* **cosmetics**)
a substance (e.g. face powder, lipstick) put on
the skin to make it look more attractive. [from
Greek *kosmein* = arrange, decorate]

cosmetic surgery *noun*
surgery carried out to make people look more
attractive.

cosmic *adjective*
1 to do with the universe. **2** to do with outer
space, *cosmic rays.* [from *cosmos*]

cosmopolitan *adjective*
from many countries; containing people from
many countries.
[from *cosmos* + Greek *polites* = citizen]

cosmos (*say* koz-moss) *noun*
the universe. [from Greek, = the world]

cost *noun* (*plural* **costs**)
the price of something.
cost *verb* (**costs, costing, cost**)
1 have a certain price. **2** (*past tense* is **costed**)
estimate the cost of something.

costly *adjective* (**costlier, costliest**)
expensive. **costliness** *noun*

costume *noun* (*plural* **costumes**)
clothes, especially for a particular purpose or
of a particular place or period.
[via French from Italian; related to *custom*]

cosy *adjective* (**cosier, cosiest**)
warm and comfortable.
cosily *adverb*, **cosiness** *noun*

cot *noun* (*plural* **cots**)
a baby's bed with high sides.
[from Hindi *khat* = bedstead]

cottage *noun* (*plural* **cottages**)
a small simple house, especially in the country.
[from Old English]

cotton *noun*
1 a soft white substance covering the seeds of a
tropical plant; the plant itself. **2** thread made
from this substance. **3** cloth made from cotton
thread.
[via French from Arabic]

cotton wool *noun*
soft fluffy wadding originally made from
cotton.

couch *noun* (*plural* **couches**)
1 a long soft seat like a sofa but with only one
end raised. **2** a sofa or settee.
couch *verb* (**couches, couching, couched**)
express in words of a certain kind, *The request
was couched in polite terms.*
[from French *coucher* = lay down flat]

cough (*say* kof) *verb* (**coughs, coughing, coughed**)
send out air from the lungs with a sudden
sharp sound.
cough *noun* (*plural* **coughs**)
1 the act or sound of coughing. **2** an illness that
makes you cough.

could *past tense* of **can**[2].

couldn't (*mainly spoken*)
could not.

council *noun* (*plural* **councils**)
a group of people chosen or elected to organize

or discuss something, especially those elected
to organize the affairs of a town or county.
[from Latin *concilium* = assembly]

USAGE: Do not confuse with *counsel.*

councillor *noun* (*plural* **councillors**)
a member of a town or county council.

council tax *noun* (*plural* **council taxes**)
a tax paid to a local authority to pay for local
services, based on the estimated value of
someone's house or flat.

counsel *noun* (*plural* **counsels**)
1 advice, *give counsel.* 2 a barrister or group of
barristers representing someone in a lawsuit.
take counsel with consult.

USAGE: Do not confuse with *council.*

counsel *verb* (**counsels, counselling, counselled**)
give advice to someone; recommend.
[from Latin *consulere* = consult]

count[1] *verb* (**counts, counting, counted**)
1 say numbers in their proper order. 2 find the
total of something by using numbers. 3 include
in a total, *There are six of us, counting the dog.*
4 be important, *It's what you do that counts.*
5 regard; consider, *I should count it an honour
to be invited.*
count on rely on.
count *noun* (*plural* **counts**)
1 counting. 2 a number reached by counting; a
total. 3 any of the points being considered, e.g.
in accusing someone of crimes, *guilty on all
counts.*
[via French from Latin *computare* = compute]

count[2] *noun* (*plural* **counts**)
a foreign nobleman. [from old French]

countdown *noun* (*plural* **countdowns**)
counting numbers backwards to zero before an
event, especially the launching of a space
rocket.

counter[1] *noun* (*plural* **counters**)
1 a flat surface over which customers are
served in a shop, bank, etc. 2 a small round
playing piece used in certain board games. 3 a
device for counting things.
under the counter sold or obtained in an
underhand way.
[same origin as *count*[1]]

counter[2] *verb* (**counters, countering, countered**)
1 counteract. 2 counter-attack; return an
opponent's blow by hitting back.
[via old French from Latin *contra* = against]

counter- *prefix*
1 against; opposing; done in return (as in
counter-attack). 2 corresponding (as in
countersign).
[from Latin *contra* = against]

counteract *verb* (**counteracts, counteracting,
counteracted**)
act against something and reduce or prevent
its effects. **counteraction** *noun*

counterbalance *noun* (*plural* **counterbalances**)
a weight or influence that balances another.
counterbalance *verb*

counterfeit (*say* **kownt-er-feet**) *adjective*
fake; not genuine.
counterfeit *verb* (**counterfeits, counterfeiting,
counterfeited**)
forge or make an imitation of something. [from
old French *countrefait* = made in opposition]

counterfoil *noun* (*plural* **counterfoils**)
a section of a cheque or receipt etc. that is torn
off and kept as a record. [from *counter-* + an old
sense of *foil*[1] = sheet of paper]

counterpart *noun* (*plural* **counterparts**)
a person or thing that corresponds to another,
*Their President is the counterpart of our Prime
Minister.*

countless *adjective*
too many to count.

country *noun* (*plural* **countries**)
1 the land occupied by a nation. 2 all the
people of a country. 3 the countryside.

countryside *noun*
an area with fields, woods, villages, etc. away
from towns.

county *noun* (*plural* **counties**)
each of the main areas that a country is
divided into for local government.
[originally = the land of a count (*count*[2])]

coup (*say* koo) *noun* (*plural* **coups**)
a sudden action taken to win power; a clever
victory. [French, = a blow]

couple *noun* (*plural* **couples**)
two people or things considered together; a
pair.
couple *verb* (**couples, coupling, coupled**)
fasten or link two things together.
[same origin as *copulate*]

couplet *noun* (*plural* **couplets**)
a pair of lines in rhyming verse.

coupon *noun* (*plural* **coupons**)
a piece of paper that gives you the right to
receive or do something.
[French, = piece cut off]

courage *noun*
the ability to face danger or difficulty or pain
even when you are afraid; bravery.
courageous *adjective*
[from Latin *cor* = heart]

courier (*say* **koor-ee-er**) *noun* (*plural* **couriers**)
1 a messenger. 2 a person employed to guide
and help a group of tourists.
[old French, = runner]

course noun (plural **courses**)
1 the direction in which something goes; a route, *the ship's course.* **2** a series of events or actions etc., *Your best course is to start again.* **3** a series of lessons, exercises, etc. **4** part of a meal, *the meat course.* **5** a racecourse. **6** a golf course.
of course without a doubt; as we expected.

court noun (plural **courts**)
1 the royal household. **2** a lawcourt; the judges etc. in a lawcourt. **3** an enclosed area for games such as tennis or netball. **4** a courtyard.
court verb (**courts, courting, courted**)
try to win somebody's love or support.
courtship noun [from old French]

courteous (say ker-tee-us) adjective
polite. **courteously** adverb, **courtesy** noun
[from old French, = having manners suitable for a royal court]

courtier noun (plural **courtiers**) (old use)
one of a king's or queen's companions at court.

courtly adjective
dignified and polite.

courtyard noun (plural **courtyards**)
a space surrounded by walls or buildings.

cousin noun (plural **cousins**)
a child of your uncle or aunt.
[from old French]

cover verb (**covers, covering, covered**)
1 place one thing over or round another; conceal. **2** travel a certain distance, *We covered ten miles a day.* **3** aim a gun at somebody, *I've got you covered.* **4** protect by insurance or a guarantee, *These goods are covered against fire or theft.* **5** be enough money to pay for something, *£5 should cover my fare.* **6** deal with or include, *The book covers all kinds of farming.*
coverage noun
cover noun (plural **covers**)
1 a thing used for covering something else; a lid, wrapper, envelope, etc. **2** the binding of a book. **3** something that hides or shelters or protects you. [from old French]

cow noun (plural **cows**)
the fully-grown female of cattle or of certain other large animals (e.g. elephant, whale, seal).
[from Old English]

coward noun (plural **cowards**)
a person who has no courage and shows fear in a shameful way.
cowardice noun, **cowardly** adjective
[from old French]

cowboy noun (plural **cowboys**)
a man in charge of grazing cattle on a ranch in the USA.

cower verb (**cowers, cowering, cowered**)
crouch or shrink back in fear.

coy adjective
pretending to be shy or modest; bashful.
coyly adverb, **coyness** noun
[from old French; related to *quiet*]

crab noun (plural **crabs**)
a shellfish with ten legs. [from Old English]

crab apple noun (plural **crab apples**)
a small sour apple.
[probably from a Scandinavian language]

crack noun (plural **cracks**)
1 a line on the surface of something where it has broken but not come completely apart. **2** a narrow gap. **3** a sudden sharp noise. **4** a knock, *a crack on the head.* **5** (informal) a joke; a wisecrack. **6** a drug made from cocaine.
crack adjective (informal)
first-class, *He is a crack shot.*
crack verb (**cracks, cracking, cracked**)
1 make or get a crack; split. **2** make a sudden sharp noise. **3** break down, *He cracked under the strain.*
crack a joke tell a joke.
crack down on (informal) stop something that is illegal or against rules.
get cracking (informal) get busy.

cracker noun (plural **crackers**)
1 a paper tube that bangs when pulled apart. **2** a firework that explodes with a crack. **3** a thin biscuit.

crackle verb (**crackles, crackling, crackled**)
make small cracking sounds, *The fire crackled in the grate.* **crackle** noun

-cracy suffix
forms nouns meaning 'ruling' or 'government' (e.g. *democracy*).
[from Greek *-kratia* = rule]

cradle noun (plural **cradles**)
1 a small cot for a baby. **2** a supporting framework.
cradle verb (**cradles, cradling, cradled**)
hold gently. [from Old English]

craft noun (plural **crafts**)
1 a job that needs skill, especially with the hands. **2** skill. **3** cunning; trickery. **4** (plural is **craft**) a ship or boat; an aircraft or spacecraft.
[from Old English]

craftsman noun (plural **craftsmen**)
a person who is good at a craft.
craftsmanship noun

crafty adjective (**craftier, craftiest**)
cunning. **craftily** adverb, **craftiness** noun
[originally = skilful: from *craft*]

crag noun (plural **crags**)
a steep piece of rough rock. **craggy** adjective, **cragginess** noun [a Celtic word]

cram *verb* (crams, cramming, crammed)
1 push many things into something so that it is very full. 2 learn as many facts as you can in a short time just before an examination. [from Old English]

cramp *noun* (*plural* cramps)
pain caused by a muscle tightening suddenly.
cramp *verb* (cramps, cramping, cramped)
1 keep in a space that is too small. 2 hinder someone's freedom or growth etc.

crane *noun* (*plural* cranes)
1 a machine for lifting and moving heavy objects. 2 a large wading bird with long legs and neck.
crane *verb* (cranes, craning, craned)
stretch your neck to try and see something.

crank *noun* (*plural* cranks)
1 an L-shaped part used for changing the direction of movement in machinery. 2 a person with strange or fanatical ideas.
cranky *adjective*

cranny *noun* (*plural* crannies)
a crevice. [from old French]

crash *noun* (*plural* crashes)
1 the loud noise of something breaking or colliding. 2 a violent collision or fall. 3 a sudden drop or failure.
crash *verb* (crashes, crashing, crashed)
1 make or have a crash; cause to crash. 2 move with a crash.
crash *adjective*
intensive, *a crash course.*

crash helmet *noun* (*plural* crash helmets)
a padded helmet worn to protect the head in a crash.

crass *adjective*
1 very obvious or shocking; gross, *crass ignorance.* 2 very stupid.
[from Latin *crassus* = thick]

-crat *suffix*
forms nouns meaning 'ruler' or 'believer in some type of government'.
[same origin as *-cracy*]

crate *noun* (*plural* crates)
1 a packing case made of strips of wood. 2 an open container with compartments for carrying bottles. [origin unknown]

crater *noun* (*plural* craters)
1 a bowl-shaped cavity or hollow. 2 the mouth of a volcano.
[from Greek *krater* = bowl]

craving *noun* (*plural* cravings)
a strong desire; a longing.

crawl *verb* (crawls, crawling, crawled)
1 move with the body close to the ground or other surface, or on hands and knees. 2 move slowly. 3 be covered with crawling things.
crawler *noun*

crawl *noun*
1 a crawling movement. 2 a very slow pace. 3 an overarm swimming stroke.

crayon *noun* (*plural* crayons)
a stick or pencil of coloured wax etc. for drawing. [French]

craze *noun* (*plural* crazes)
a temporary enthusiasm.

crazy *adjective* (crazier, craziest)
1 insane. 2 very foolish, *this crazy idea.*
crazily *adverb*, **craziness** *noun*
[from *craze*]

crazy paving *noun*
paving made of oddly-shaped pieces of stone etc.

creak *noun* (*plural* creaks)
a harsh squeak like that of a stiff door-hinge.
creaky *adjective*
creak *verb* (creaks, creaking, creaked)
make a creak. [imitating the sound]

cream *noun* (*plural* creams)
1 the fatty part of milk. 2 a yellowish-white colour. 3 a food containing or looking like cream, *chocolate cream.* 4 a soft substance, *shoe cream.* 5 the best part.
creamy *adjective*
cream *verb* (creams, creaming, creamed)
make creamy; beat butter etc. until it is soft like cream.
cream off remove the best part of something.

crease *noun* (*plural* creases)
1 a line made in something by folding, pressing, or crushing it. 2 a line on a cricket pitch marking a batsman's or bowler's position.
crease *verb* (creases, creasing, creased)
make a crease or creases in something.

create *verb* (creates, creating, created)
1 bring into existence; make or produce, especially something that no one has made before. 2 (*slang*) make a fuss; grumble.
creation *noun*, **creative** *adjective*, **creativity** *noun*, **creator** *noun*
[from Latin]

creature *noun* (*plural* creatures)
a person or animal.
[from Latin *creatura* = a created being]

crèche (*say* kresh) *noun* (*plural* crèches)
a place where babies and young children are looked after while their parents are at work.
[French]

credentials *plural noun*
documents showing a person's identity, qualifications, etc.

credible *adjective*
able to be believed; convincing.

credibly *adverb*, **credibility** *noun*
[same origin as *credit*]

USAGE: Do not confuse with *creditable* or *credulous*.

credit *noun* (*plural* **credits**)
1 honour; acknowledgement. 2 an arrangement trusting a person to pay for something later on. 3 an amount of money in someone's account at a bank etc., or entered in an account-book as paid in. (Compare *debit*.)
4 belief or trust, *I put no credit in this rumour*.
credits or **credit titles** a list of people who have helped to produce a film or television programme.
credit *verb* (**credits, crediting, credited**)
1 believe. 2 attribute; say that a person has done or achieved something, *Columbus is credited with the discovery of America.* 3 enter something as a credit in an account-book. (Compare *debit*.)
[from Latin *credere* = believe, trust]

credit card *noun* (*plural* **credit cards**)
a card authorizing a person to buy on credit.

creditor *noun* (*plural* **creditors**)
a person to whom money is owed.

credulous *adjective*
too ready to believe things; gullible.
[from Latin *credulus* = trusting]

USAGE: Do not confuse with *credible*.

creed *noun* (*plural* **creeds**)
a set or formal statement of beliefs.
[from Latin *credo* = I believe]

creep *verb* (**creeps, creeping, crept**)
1 move along close to the ground. 2 move quietly. 3 come gradually. 4 prickle with fear, *It makes my flesh creep.*
creep *noun* (*plural* **creeps**)
1 a creeping movement. 2 (*slang*) an unpleasant person, especially one who seeks to win favour.
the creeps (*informal*) a nervous feeling caused by fear or dislike.

creeper *noun* (*plural* **creepers**)
a plant that grows along the ground or up a wall etc.

creepy *adjective* (**creepier, creepiest**)
frightening and sinister.

cremate *verb* (**cremates, cremating, cremated**)
burn a dead body to ashes. **cremation** *noun*
[from Latin *cremare* = to burn]

crematorium *noun* (*plural* **crematoria**)
a place where corpses are cremated.

crescendo (*say* krish-end-oh) *noun* (*plural* **crescendos**)
a gradual increase in loudness.
[Italian, = increasing]

crescent *noun* (*plural* **crescents**)
1 a narrow curved shape coming to a point at each end. 2 a curved street.
[originally = the new moon: from Latin *crescens* = growing]

cress *noun*
a plant with hot-tasting leaves, used in salads and sandwiches. [from Old English]

crest *noun* (*plural* **crests**)
1 a tuft of hair, skin, or feathers on an animal's or bird's head. 2 the top of a hill or wave etc.
3 a design used on notepaper etc.
crested *adjective*

crestfallen *adjective*
disappointed or dejected.

crevasse (*say* kri-vass) *noun* (*plural* **crevasses**)
a deep open crack, especially in a glacier.
[same origin as *crevice*]

crevice *noun* (*plural* **crevices**)
a narrow opening, especially in a rock or wall.
[from old French *crever* = burst, split]

crew[1] *noun* (*plural* **crews**)
1 the people working in a ship or aircraft. 2 a group working together, *the camera crew.*
[from old French]

crew[2] *past tense* of **crow**[2].

crib *noun* (*plural* **cribs**)
1 a baby's cot. 2 a framework holding fodder for animals. 3 a model representing the Nativity of Jesus Christ. 4 something cribbed.
5 a translation for use by students.
crib *verb* (**cribs, cribbing, cribbed**)
copy someone else's work.

crick *noun* (*plural* **cricks**)
painful stiffness in the neck or back.

cricket[1] *noun*
a game played outdoors between teams with a ball, bats, and two wickets. **cricketer** *noun*
[origin unknown]

cricket[2] *noun* (*plural* **crickets**)
a brown insect like a grasshopper.
[from old French *criquer* = crackle (imitating the sound it makes)]

crime *noun* (*plural* **crimes**)
1 an action that breaks the law. 2 law-breaking. [from Latin]

criminal *noun* (*plural* **criminals**)
a person who has committed a crime or crimes.
criminal *adjective*, **criminally** *adverb*

crimson *adjective*
deep-red. **crimson** *noun*
[from Arabic *kirmiz* = an insect which was used to make crimson dye]

cringe *verb* (**cringes, cringing, cringed**)
shrink back in fear; cower. [from Old English *crincan* = yield, fall in battle]

cripple *noun* (*plural* **cripples**)
a person who is permanently lame.

cripple *verb* (cripples, crippling, crippled)
1 make a person lame. 2 weaken or damage something seriously.

crisis *noun* (*plural* crises)
an important and dangerous or difficult situation. [from Greek]

crisp *adjective*
1 very dry so that it breaks with a snap. 2 fresh and stiff, *a crisp £5 note*. 3 cold and dry, *a crisp morning*. 4 brisk and sharp, *a crisp manner*.
crisply *adverb*, **crispness** *noun*
crisp *noun* (*plural* crisps)
a very thin fried slice of potato. Crisps are usually sold in packets. [from Latin]

criss-cross *adjective* & *adverb*
with crossing lines. [from *Christ-cross* (the cross on which Christ died)]

criterion (*say* kry-teer-ee-on) *noun* (*plural* criteria)
a standard by which something is judged. [from Greek, = means of judging]

critic *noun* (*plural* critics)
1 a person who gives opinions on books, plays, films, music, etc. 2 a person who criticizes. [from Greek *krites* = judge]

critical *adjective*
1 criticizing. 2 to do with critics or criticism. 3 to do with or at a crisis; very serious.
critically *adverb*

criticism *noun* (*plural* criticisms)
1 criticizing; pointing out faults. 2 the work of a critic.

criticize *verb* (criticizes, criticizing, criticized)
say that a person or thing has faults.

croak *noun* (*plural* croaks)
a deep hoarse sound like that of a frog.
croak *verb* [imitating the sound]

crockery *noun*
household china.

crocodile *noun* (*plural* crocodiles)
1 a large tropical reptile with a thick skin, long tail, and huge jaws. 2 a long line of schoolchildren walking in pairs.
crocodile tears sorrow that is not sincere (so called because the crocodile was said to weep while it ate its victim).

crocus *noun* (*plural* crocuses)
a small plant with yellow, purple, or white flowers. [from Greek]

crony *noun* (*plural* cronies)
a close friend or companion. [from Greek]

crook *noun* (*plural* crooks)
1 a shepherd's stick with a curved end. 2 something bent or curved. 3 (*informal*) a person who makes a living dishonestly.

crooked *adjective*
1 bent or twisted; not straight. 2 dishonest.

croon *verb* (croons, crooning, crooned)
sing softly and gently.

crop *noun* (*plural* crops)
1 something grown for food, *a good crop of wheat*. 2 a whip with a loop instead of a lash. 3 part of a bird's throat. 4 a very short haircut.
crop *verb* (crops, cropping, cropped)
1 cut or bite off, *sheep were cropping the grass*. 2 produce a crop.
crop up happen unexpectedly.

croquet (*say* kroh-kay) *noun*
a game played with wooden balls and mallets. [origin unknown]

cross *noun* (*plural* crosses)
1 a mark or shape made like + or ×. 2 an upright post with another piece of wood across it, used in ancient times for crucifixion; **the Cross** the cross on which Christ was crucified, used as a symbol of Christianity. 3 a mixture of two different things.
cross *verb* (crosses, crossing, crossed)
1 go across something. 2 draw a line or lines across something. 3 make the sign or shape of a cross, *Cross your fingers for luck*. 4 produce something from two different kinds.
cross out draw a line across something because it is unwanted, wrong, etc.
cross *adjective*
1 going from one side to another. 2 annoyed; bad-tempered. **crossly** *adverb*, **crossness** *noun* [via Old Norse and old Irish from Latin]

cross- *prefix*
1 across; crossing something (as in *crossbar*). 2 from two different kinds (as in *cross-breed*).

crossbar *noun* (*plural* crossbars)
a horizontal bar, especially between two uprights.

cross-breed *verb* (cross-breeds, cross-breeding, cross-bred)
breed by mating an animal with one of a different kind. **cross-breed** *noun* (Compare *hybrid*.)

cross-examine *verb* (cross-examines, cross-examining, cross-examined)
cross-question someone, especially in a lawcourt. **cross-examination** *noun*

cross-eyed *adjective*
with eyes that look or seem to look towards the nose.

crossing *noun* (*plural* crossings)
a place where people can cross a road, railway, etc.

cross-legged *adjective* & *adverb*
with ankles crossed and knees spread apart.

cross-question *verb* (cross-questions, cross-questioning, cross-questioned)
question someone carefully in order to test answers given to previous questions.

cross-reference *noun* (*plural* **cross-references**)
a note telling people to look at another part of a book etc. for more information.

crossroads *noun* (*plural* **crossroads**)
a place where two or more roads cross one another.

cross-section *noun* (*plural* **cross-sections**)
1 a drawing of something as if it has been cut through. **2** a typical sample.

crossword *noun* (*plural* **crosswords**)
short for **crossword puzzle**, a puzzle in which words have to be guessed from clues and then written into the blank squares in a diagram.

crotchet *noun* (*plural* **crotchets**)
a note in music, which usually represents one beat (written ♩).
[from French, = small hook]

crouch *verb* (**crouches, crouching, crouched**)
lower your body, with your arms and legs bent.
[origin unknown]

crow[1] *noun* (*plural* **crows**)
a large black bird.
as the crow flies in a straight line.
[from Old English]

crow[2] *verb* (**crows, crowing, crowed** or **crew**)
1 make a shrill cry as a cock does. **2** boast; be triumphant. **crow** *noun*
[imitating the sound]

crowbar *noun* (*plural* **crowbars**)
an iron bar used as a lever. [because the end is shaped like a crow's beak]

crowd *noun* (*plural* **crowds**)
a large number of people in one place.

crowd *verb* (**crowds, crowding, crowded**)
1 come together in a crowd. **2** cram; fill uncomfortably full. [from Old English]

crown *noun* (*plural* **crowns**)
1 an ornamental headdress worn by a king or queen. **2** (often **Crown**) the sovereign, *This land belongs to the Crown.* **3** the highest part, *the crown of the road.* **4** a former coin worth 5 shillings (25p).
Crown Prince or **Crown Princess** the heir to the throne.

crown *verb* (**crowns, crowning, crowned**)
1 place a crown on someone as a symbol of royal power or victory. **2** form or cover or decorate the top of something. **3** reward; make a successful end to something, *Our efforts were crowned with victory.* **4** (*slang*) hit someone on the head.
[from Latin *corona* = garland or crown]

crucial (*say* kroo-shal) *adjective*
most important. **crucially** *adverb*
[from Latin *crucis* = of a cross]

crucifix *noun* (*plural* **crucifixes**)
a model of the Cross or of Jesus Christ on the Cross. [same origin as *crucify*]

crucify *verb* (**crucifies, crucifying, crucified**)
put a person to death by nailing or binding the hands and feet to a cross.
crucifixion *noun*
[from Latin *crucifigere* = fix to a cross]

crude *adjective*
1 in a natural state; not yet refined, *crude oil.* **2** not well finished; rough, *a crude carving.* **3** vulgar. **crudely** *adverb*, **crudity** *noun*
[from Latin *crudus* = raw, rough]

cruel *adjective* (**crueller, cruellest**)
causing pain or suffering.
cruelly *adverb*, **cruelty** *noun*
[from old French; related to *crude*]

cruise *noun* (*plural* **cruises**)
a pleasure trip in a ship.

cruise *verb* (**cruises, cruising, cruised**)
1 sail or travel at a moderate speed. **2** have a cruise. [from Dutch *kruisen* = to cross]

cruiser *noun* (*plural* **cruisers**)
1 a fast warship. **2** a large motor boat.

crumb *noun* (*plural* **crumbs**)
a tiny piece of bread, etc.

crumble *verb* (**crumbles, crumbling, crumbled**)
break or fall into small fragments.
crumbly *adjective*

crumpet *noun* (*plural* **crumpets**)
a soft flat cake made with yeast, eaten toasted with butter. [origin unknown]

crumple *verb* (**crumples, crumpling, crumpled**)
1 crush or become crushed into creases. **2** collapse loosely.
[from Old English *crump* = crooked]

crunch *verb* (**crunches, crunching, crunched**)
crush something noisily, for example between your teeth.

crunch *noun* (*plural* **crunches**)
a crunching sound. **crunchy** *adjective*
the crunch (*informal*) a crucial event or turning point.

Crusade *noun* (*plural* **Crusades**)
a military expedition made by Christians in the Middle Ages to recover Palestine from the Muslims who had conquered it. **Crusader** *noun*

crusade *noun* (*plural* **crusades**)
a campaign against something bad.
[from Latin *crux* = cross]

crush *verb* (**crushes, crushing, crushed**)
1 press something so that it gets broken or harmed. **2** squeeze tightly. **3** defeat.

crush *noun* (*plural* **crushes**)
1 a crowd of people pressed together. **2** a drink made with crushed fruit.

crust *noun* (*plural* **crusts**)
1 the hard outer layer of something, especially bread. **2** the rocky outer layer of the earth.
[from Latin *crusta* = rind, shell]

crustacean (*say* krust-ay-shon) *noun* (*plural* crustaceans)
an animal with a shell, e.g. a crab. [same origin as *crust*]

crutch *noun* (*plural* crutches)
a support like a long walking stick for helping a lame person to walk.

cry *noun* (*plural* cries)
1 a loud wordless sound expressing pain, grief, joy, etc. 2 a shout. 3 crying, *Have a good cry.*
cry *verb* (cries, crying, cried)
1 shed tears; weep. 2 call out loudly.

cryptic *adjective*
hiding its meaning in a puzzling way.
cryptically *adverb*
[from Greek *kryptos* = hidden]

crystal *noun* (*plural* crystals)
1 a transparent colourless mineral rather like glass. 2 very clear high-quality glass. 3 a small solid piece of certain substances, *crystals of snow and ice.* **crystalline** *adjective*
[from Greek *krystallos* = ice]

crystallize *verb* (crystallizes, crystallizing, crystallized)
1 form into crystals. 2 become definite in form. **crystallization** *noun*

cub *noun* (*plural* cubs)
a young lion, tiger, fox, bear, etc.

Cub or **Cub Scout** (*plural* Cubs, Cub Scouts)
a member of the junior branch of the Scout Association.

cubby hole *noun* (*plural* cubby holes)
a small compartment.
[from an old word *cub* = coop, hutch]

cube *noun* (*plural* cubes)
1 something that has six equal square sides. 2 the number produced by multiplying something by itself twice, *The cube of 3 is 3 × 3 × 3 = 27.*
cube *verb* (cubes, cubing, cubed)
1 multiply a number by itself twice, *4 cubed is 4 × 4 × 4 = 64.* 2 cut something into small cubes. [from Greek]

cube root *noun* (*plural* cube roots)
the number that gives a particular number if it is multiplied by itself twice, *The cube root of 27 is 3.*

cubic *adjective*
three-dimensional.
cubic foot, cubic metre, etc., the volume of a cube with sides that are one foot or one metre etc. long.

cubicle *noun* (*plural* cubicles)
a compartment of a room. [originally = bedroom: from Latin *cubare* = lie down]

cuckoo *noun* (*plural* cuckoos)
a bird that makes a sound like 'cuck-oo'.

cucumber *noun* (*plural* cucumbers)
a long green-skinned vegetable eaten raw or pickled. [from Latin]

cuddle *verb* (cuddles, cuddling, cuddled)
put your arms closely round a person or animal that you love. **cuddly** *adjective*

cue[1] *noun* (*plural* cues)
something said or done that acts as a signal for an actor etc. to say or do something. [origin unknown]

cue[2] *noun* (*plural* cues)
a long stick for striking the ball in billiards or snooker. [a different spelling of *queue* (because of its long, thin shape)]

cuff *noun* (*plural* cuffs)
1 the end of a sleeve that fits round the wrist. 2 hitting somebody with your hand; a slap.
cuff *verb* (cuffs, cuffing, cuffed)
hit somebody with your hand.

cul-de-sac *noun* (*plural* culs-de-sac)
a street with an opening at one end only; a dead end.
[French, = bottom of a sack]

-cule *suffix*
forms diminutives (e.g. *molecule* = little mass). [from Latin]

cull *verb* (culls, culling, culled)
1 select and use, *culling lines from several poems.* 2 pick out and kill surplus animals from a flock. **cull** *noun*
[from Latin *colligere* = collect]

culpable *adjective*
deserving blame.
[from Latin *culpare* = to blame]

culprit *noun* (*plural* culprits)
the person who has done something wrong.

cult *noun* (*plural* cults)
1 a religious sect. 2 devotion to a person or a thing by a lot of people.
[from Latin *cultus* = worship]

cultivate *verb* (cultivates, cultivating, cultivated)
1 use land to grow crops. 2 grow or develop things by looking after them. **cultivation** *noun*, **cultivator** *noun*

culture *noun* (*plural* cultures)
1 appreciation and understanding of literature, art, music, etc. 2 customs and traditions, *West Indian culture.* 3 improvement by care and training, *physical culture.* 4 cultivating things. **cultural** *adjective*
[from Latin *colere* = cultivate, look after, worship]

cumbersome *adjective*
clumsy to carry or manage.
[from *encumber* + *-some*]

cumulative *adjective*
accumulating; increasing by continuous additions. [from Latin *cumulus* = heap]

cunning *adjective*
1 clever at deceiving people. 2 cleverly designed or planned.
cunning *noun*
1 skill in deceiving people; craftiness. 2 skill or ingenuity. [from Old Norse]

cup *noun* (*plural* **cups**)
1 a small bowl-shaped container for drinking from. 2 anything shaped like a cup. 3 a goblet-shaped ornament given as a prize. **cupful** *noun*
cup *verb* (**cups, cupping, cupped**)
form into the shape of a cup, *cup your hands.*
[from Latin]

cupboard *noun* (*plural* **cupboards**)
a piece of furniture with a door, for storing things.
[originally = sideboard: from *cup* + *board*]

cur *noun* (*plural* **curs**)
a scruffy or bad-tempered dog.

curate *noun* (*plural* **curates**)
a member of the clergy who helps a vicar.
[from Latin *cura* = care]

curator (*say* kewr-ay-ter) *noun* (*plural* **curators**)
a person in charge of a museum or other collection. [same origin as *cure*]

curb *verb* (**curbs, curbing, curbed**)
restrain, *curb your impatience.*
curb *noun* (*plural* **curbs**)
a restraint, *Put a curb on spending.*

USAGE: Do not confuse with *kerb.*

curd *noun* or **curds** *plural noun*
a thick substance formed when milk turns sour. [origin unknown]

curdle *verb* (**curdles, curdling, curdled**)
form into curds.
make someone's blood curdle horrify or terrify them.

cure *verb* (**cures, curing, cured**)
1 get rid of someone's illness. 2 stop something bad. 3 treat something in order to preserve it, *Fish can be cured in smoke.*
cure *noun* (*plural* **cures**)
1 something that cures a person or thing; a remedy. 2 curing; being cured, *We cannot promise a cure.*
[from Latin *curare* = care for, cure]

curfew *noun* (*plural* **curfews**)
a time or signal after which people must remain indoors until the next day.

curiosity *noun* (*plural* **curiosities**)
1 being curious. 2 something unusual and interesting.

curious *adjective*
1 wanting to find out about things; inquisitive. 2 strange; unusual.
curiously *adverb*

curl *noun* (*plural* **curls**)
a curve or coil, e.g. of hair.

curl *verb* (**curls, curling, curled**)
form into curls.
curl up sit or lie with knees drawn up.

curly *adjective*
having curls.

currant *noun* (*plural* **currants**)
1 a small black dried grape used in cookery. 2 a small round red, black, or white berry.
[from old French *raisins de Courauntz* = grapes from Corinth (a city in Greece)]

USAGE: Do not confuse with *current.*

currency *noun* (*plural* **currencies**)
1 the money in use in a country. 2 the general use of something, *Some words have no currency now.* [from *current*]

current *adjective*
happening now; used now. **currently** *adverb*
current *noun* (*plural* **currents**)
1 water or air etc. moving in one direction. 2 the flow of electricity along a wire etc. or through something.
[from Latin *currens* = running]

USAGE: Do not confuse with *currant.*

curriculum *noun* (*plural* **curricula**)
a course of study in a school or university.
[Latin, = running, course]

curry[1] *noun* (*plural* **curries**)
food cooked with spices that taste hot.
curried *adjective* [from Tamil *kari* = sauce]

curry[2] *verb* (**curries, currying, curried**)
curry favour seek to win favour by flattering someone.
[from old French]

curse *noun* (*plural* **curses**)
1 a call or prayer for a person or thing to be harmed; the evil produced by this. 2 something very unpleasant. 3 an angry word or words.
curse *verb* (**curses, cursing, cursed**)
1 make a curse. 2 use a curse against a person or thing.
be cursed with something suffer from it.

cursor *noun* (*plural* **cursors**)
a movable indicator, usually a flashing light, on a VDU screen.
[Latin, = runner]

curt *adjective*
brief and hasty or rude, *a curt reply.*
curtly *adverb*, **curtness** *noun*
[from Latin *curtus* = cut short]

curtain *noun* (*plural* **curtains**)
1 a piece of material hung at a window or door. 2 the large cloth screen hung at the front of a stage. [from old French]

curtsy *noun* (*plural* **curtsies**)
a movement of respect made by women and girls, putting one foot behind the other and bending the knees.

curtsy *verb* (curtsies, curtsying, curtsied)
make a curtsy.
[a different spelling of *courtesy*]

curvature *noun* (*plural* curvatures)
curving; a curved shape.

curve *verb* (curves, curving, curved)
bend smoothly.
curve *noun* (*plural* curves)
a curved line or shape. **curvy** *adjective*

cushion *noun* (*plural* cushions)
1 a bag, usually of cloth, filled with soft
material so that it is comfortable to sit on or
lean against. 2 anything soft or springy that
protects or supports something, *The hovercraft
travels on a cushion of air.*
cushion *verb* (cushions, cushioning, cushioned)
1 supply with cushions, *cushioned seats.*
2 protect from the effects of a knock or shock
etc., *His fur hat cushioned the blow.*

custard *noun* (*plural* custards)
1 a sweet yellow sauce made with milk. 2 a
pudding made with beaten eggs and milk.
[from old French]

custody *noun*
1 care and supervision; guardianship.
2 imprisonment.
take into custody arrest.
[from Latin *custos* = guardian]

custom *noun* (*plural* customs)
1 the usual way of behaving or doing
something. 2 regular business from customers.
[from Latin *consuescere* = become accustomed]

customary *adjective*
according to custom; usual.
customarily *adverb*

customer *noun* (*plural* customers)
a person who uses a shop, bank, or other
business. [originally a person who customarily
used the same shop etc.]

customs *plural noun*
1 taxes charged on goods brought into a
country. 2 the place at a port or airport where
officials examine your luggage.
[= taxes customarily charged, from *custom*]

cut *verb* (cuts, cutting, cut)
1 divide or wound or separate something by
using a knife, axe, scissors, etc. 2 make a thing
shorter or smaller; remove part of something,
They are cutting all their prices. 3 divide a pack
of playing cards. 4 hit a ball with a chopping
movement. 5 go through or across something.
6 stay away from something deliberately, *She
cut her music lesson.* 7 make a sound recording.
8 switch off electrical power or an engine etc.
cut a corner pass round it very closely.
cut and dried already decided.
cut in interrupt.

cut *noun* (*plural* cuts)
1 cutting; the result of cutting. 2 a small
wound. 3 (*slang*) a share.
be a cut above something be superior.

cute *adjective* (*informal*)
1 attractive. 2 clever.
cutely *adverb*, **cuteness** *noun* [from *acute*]

cutlass *noun* (*plural* cutlasses)
a short sword with a broad curved blade. [same
origin as *cutlery*]

cutlery *noun*
knives, forks, and spoons.
[from Latin *culter* = knife]

cutlet *noun* (*plural* cutlets)
a thick slice of meat for cooking.

cutting *noun* (*plural* cuttings)
1 a steep-sided passage cut through high
ground for a road or railway. 2 something cut
out of a newspaper or magazine. 3 a piece cut
from a plant to form a new plant.

-cy *suffix*
forms nouns showing action or condition etc.
(e.g. *piracy, infancy*).
[from Latin or Greek]

cycle *noun* (*plural* cycles)
1 a bicycle or motorcycle. 2 a series of events
that are regularly repeated in the same order.
cyclic *adjective*, **cyclical** *adjective*
cycle *verb* (cycles, cycling, cycled)
ride a bicycle or tricycle. **cyclist** *noun*
[from Greek *kyklos* = circle]

cyclone *noun* (*plural* cyclones)
a wind that rotates round a calm central area.
cyclonic *adjective*
[from Greek *kykloma* = wheel]

cygnet (*say* sig-nit) *noun* (*plural* cygnets)
a young swan. [from Latin *cycnus* = swan]

cylinder *noun* (*plural* cylinders)
an object with straight sides and circular ends.
cylindrical *adjective*
[from Greek *kylindros* = roller]

cymbal *noun* (*plural* cymbals)
a percussion instrument consisting of a metal
plate that is hit to make a ringing sound. [from
Greek]

USAGE: Do not confuse with *symbol*.

cynic (*say* sin-ik) *noun* (*plural* cynics)
a person who believes that people's reasons for
doing things are selfish or bad, and shows this
by sneering at them.
cynical *adjective*, **cynically** *adverb*, **cynicism** *noun*
[from Greek *kynikos* = surly]

cypress *noun* (*plural* cypresses)
an evergreen tree with dark leaves.

Dd

dab *noun* (*plural* **dabs**)
1 a quick gentle touch, usually with something wet. 2 a small lump, *a dab of butter*.
dab *verb* (**dabs, dabbing, dabbed**)
touch something quickly and gently.

dabble *verb* (**dabbles, dabbling, dabbled**)
1 splash something about in water. 2 do something as a hobby, *dabble in chemistry*.

dachshund (*say* daks-huund) *noun* (*plural* **dachshunds**)
a small dog with a long body and very short legs. [German, = badger-dog (because dachshunds were used to dig badgers out of their sets)]

daffodil *noun* (*plural* **daffodils**)
a yellow flower that grows from a bulb. [from *asphodel*, another plant with yellow flowers]

daft *adjective* (*informal*)
silly or stupid. [from Old English]

dagger *noun* (*plural* **daggers**)
a pointed knife with two sharp edges, used as a weapon. [from old French]

daily *adverb* & *adjective*
every day.

dainty *adjective* (**daintier, daintiest**)
small, delicate, and pretty. **daintily** *adverb*, **daintiness** *noun* [via old French from Latin *dignitas* = value, beauty]

dairy *noun* (*plural* **dairies**)
a place where milk, butter, etc. are produced or sold. [from Old English]

daisy *noun* (*plural* **daisies**)
a small flower with white petals and a yellow centre.
[from *day's eye* (because the daisy opens in daylight and closes at night)]

dam[1] *noun* (*plural* **dams**)
a wall built to hold water back.
dam *verb* (**dams, damming, dammed**)
hold water back with a dam.
[from Old English]

dam[2] *noun* (*plural* **dams**)
the mother of a horse or dog etc. (Compare *sire*.) [from *dame*]

damage *noun*
harm or injury done to something.
damage *verb* (**damages, damaging, damaged**)
harm or spoil something.
[from Latin *damnum* = loss]

damages *plural noun*
money paid as compensation for an injury or loss.

Dame *noun* (*plural* **Dames**)
the title of a lady who has been given the equivalent of a knighthood.
dame *noun* (*plural* **dames**)
a comic middle-aged woman in a pantomime, usually played by a man. [from Latin *domina* = lady]

damn *verb* (**damns, damning, damned**)
curse. [from Latin *damnare* = condemn]

damnation *noun*
being condemned to hell.

damned *adjective*
hateful or annoying.

damp *adjective*
slightly wet; not quite dry. **damply** *adverb*, **dampness** *noun*
damp *noun*
moisture in the air or on a surface or all through something.

damp course *noun* (*plural* **damp courses**)
a layer of material built into a wall to prevent dampness in the ground from rising.

dampen *verb* (**dampens, dampening, dampened**)
1 make something damp. 2 reduce the strength of something.

damsel *noun* (*plural* **damsels**) (*old use*)
a young woman. [from old French]

dance *verb* (**dances, dancing, danced**)
move about in time to music.
dance *noun* (*plural* **dances**)
1 a set of movements used in dancing. 2 a piece of music for dancing to. 3 a party or gathering where people dance. **dancer** *noun*
[from old French]

dandelion *noun* (*plural* **dandelions**)
a yellow wild flower with jagged leaves. [from French *dent-de-lion* = tooth of a lion (because the jagged edges of the leaves looked like lion's teeth)]

dandruff *noun*
tiny white flakes of dead skin in a person's hair. [origin unknown]

danger *noun* (*plural* **dangers**)
something that is not safe or could harm you. [from old French]

dangerous *adjective*
likely to kill or harm you.
dangerously *adverb*

dangle *verb* (**dangles, dangling, dangled**)
hang or swing loosely.

dappled *adjective*
marked with patches of a different colour. [probably from Old Norse *depill* = spot]

dare *verb* (**dares, daring, dared**)
1 be brave or bold enough to do something.
2 challenge a person to do something risky.
dare *noun* (*plural* **dares**)
a challenge to do something risky.

dark *adjective*
1 with little or no light. 2 not light in colour, *a dark suit.* 3 having dark hair. 4 sinister or evil.
darkly *adverb,* **darkness** *noun*
dark *noun*
1 absence of light, *Cats can see in the dark.*
2 the time when darkness has come, *She went out after dark.* [from Old English]

darken *verb* (**darkens, darkening, darkened**)
make or become dark.

darling *noun* (*plural* **darlings**)
someone who is loved very much.
[from Old English *deorling* = little dear]

darn *verb* (**darns, darning, darned**)
mend a hole by weaving threads across it.
darn *noun* (*plural* **darns**)
a place that has been darned.
[from Old English *diernan* = hide]

dart *noun* (*plural* **darts**)
1 an object with a sharp point, thrown at a target. 2 a darting movement. 3 a tapering tuck stitched in something to make it fit.
dart *verb* (**darts, darting, darted**)
run suddenly and quickly.

darts *noun*
a game in which darts are thrown at a circular board (**dartboard**).

dash *verb* (**dashes, dashing, dashed**)
1 run quickly; rush. 2 throw a thing violently against something, *The storm dashed the ship against the rocks.*
dash *noun* (*plural* **dashes**)
1 a short quick run; a rush. 2 energy or liveliness. 3 a small amount, *Add a dash of brandy.* 4 a short line (—) used in writing or printing. [origin unknown]

dashboard *noun* (*plural* **dashboards**)
a panel with dials and controls in front of the driver of a car etc. [originally a board on the front of a carriage to keep out mud, which dashed against it]

dashing *adjective*
lively and showy.

data (*say* **day**-ta) *noun*
pieces of information.

USAGE: Strictly speaking, this word is a plural noun (the singular is *datum*), so it should be used with a plural verb: *Here are the data.* However, the word is widely used nowadays as if it were a singular noun and most people do not regard this as wrong: *Here is the data.*

---

database *noun* (*plural* **databases**)
a store of information held in a computer.

date[1] *noun* (*plural* **dates**)
1 the time when something happens or happened or was written, stated as the day,

month, and year (or any of these). 2 an appointment to meet someone, especially someone of the opposite sex.
date *verb* (**dates, dating, dated**)
1 give a date to something. 2 have existed from a particular time, *The church dates from 1684.* 3 seem old-fashioned.
[from Latin *data* = given (at a certain time)]

date[2] *noun* (*plural* **dates**)
a small sweet brown fruit that grows on a kind of palm tree. [from Greek]

daub *verb* (**daubs, daubing, daubed**)
paint or smear something clumsily.
daub *noun*
[from Latin *dealbare* = whitewash, plaster]

daughter *noun* (*plural* **daughters**)
a girl or woman who is someone's child.

daughter-in-law *noun* (*plural* **daughters-in-law**)
a son's wife.

daunt *verb* (**daunts, daunting, daunted**)
make somebody afraid or discouraged. [from Latin *domitare* = to tame]

dawdle *verb* (**dawdles, dawdling, dawdled**)
go slowly and lazily. **dawdler** *noun*

dawn *noun* (*plural* **dawns**)
the time when the sun rises.
dawn *verb* (**dawns, dawning, dawned**)
1 begin to grow light in the morning. 2 begin to be realized, *The truth dawned on them.*
[from Old English]

day *noun* (*plural* **days**)
1 the 24 hours between midnight and the next midnight. 2 the light part of this time. 3 a particular day, *sports day.* 4 a period of time, *in Queen Victoria's day.*

daybreak *noun*
dawn.

daydream *noun* (*plural* **daydreams**)
pleasant thoughts of something you would like to happen.
daydream *verb* (**daydreams, daydreaming, daydreamed**)
have daydreams.

dazed *adjective*
unable to think or see clearly. **daze** *noun* [from Old Norse *dasathr* = weary]

dazzle *verb* (**dazzles, dazzling, dazzled**)
1 make a person unable to see clearly because of too much bright light. 2 amaze or impress a person by a splendid display. [from *daze*]

de- *prefix*
1 removing (as in *defrost*). 2 down, away (as in *descend*). 3 completely (as in *denude*).
[from old French; related to *dis-*]

dead *adjective*
1 no longer alive. 2 not lively. 3 not functioning; no longer in use. 4 exact or complete, *a dead loss.* [from Old English]

deaden *verb* (deadens, deadening, deadened)
make pain or noise etc. weaker.

dead end *noun* (*plural* dead ends)
1 a road or passage with one end closed. 2 a
situation where there is no chance of making
progress.

dead heat *noun* (*plural* dead heats)
a race in which two or more winners finish
exactly together.

deadline *noun* (*plural* deadlines)
a time limit.
[originally this meant a line round an
American military prison; if prisoners went
beyond it they could be shot]

deadlock *noun* (*plural* deadlocks)
a situation in which no progress can be made.
[from *dead* + *lock*¹]

deadly *adjective* (deadlier, deadliest)
likely to kill.

deaf *adjective*
1 unable to hear. 2 unwilling to hear.
deafness *noun* [from Old English]

deafen *verb* (deafens, deafening, deafened)
make somebody become deaf, especially by a
very loud noise.

deal *verb* (deals, dealing, dealt)
1 hand something out; give. 2 give out cards
for a card game. 3 do business; trade, *He deals
in scrap metal.* **dealer** *noun*
deal with 1 be concerned with, *This book deals
with words and meanings.* 2 do what is needed,
deal with the problem.
deal *noun* (*plural* deals)
1 an agreement or bargain. 2 someone's turn
to deal at cards.
a good deal or **a great deal** a large amount.
[from Old English *daelan* = divide, share out]

dear *adjective*
1 loved very much. 2 a polite greeting in
letters, *Dear Sir.* 3 expensive. **dearly** *adverb*
[from Old English]

death *noun* (*plural* deaths)
dying; the end of life. [from Old English]

debatable *adjective*
questionable; that can be argued against.

debate *noun* (*plural* debates)
a formal discussion.
debate *verb* (debates, debating, debated)
hold a debate. **debater** *noun*

debilitating *adjective*
causing weakness.

debit *noun* (*plural* debits)
an entry in an account-book showing how
much money is owed. (Compare *credit.*)

debris (*say* deb-ree) *noun*
scattered broken pieces of something; rubbish
left behind.
[from French *débris* = broken down]

debt (*say* det) *noun* (*plural* debts)
something that you owe someone.
in debt owing money etc.
[same origin as *debit*]

debtor (*say* det-or) *noun* (*plural* debtors)
a person who owes money to someone.

deca- *prefix*
ten (as in *decathlon*). [from Greek]

decade (*say* dek-ayd) *noun* (*plural* decades)
a period of ten years. [from old French]

decadent (*say* dek-a-dent) *adjective*
falling to a lower standard of morality.
decadence *noun* [same origin as *decay*]

decaffeinated *adjective*
(of coffee or tea) with the caffeine removed.

decapitate *verb* (decapitates, decapitating,
decapitated)
cut someone's head off; behead.
decapitation *noun*
[from *de-* + Latin *caput* = head]

decathlon *noun* (*plural* decathlons)
an athletic contest in which each competitor
takes part in ten events.
[from *deca-* + Greek *athlon* = contest]

decay *verb* (decays, decaying, decayed)
1 go bad; rot. 2 become less good or less strong.
decay *noun*
[from old French *decaoir* = fall down]

deceased *adjective*
dead.

deceit (*say* dis-eet) *noun* (*plural* deceits)
making a person believe something that is not
true.
deceitful *adjective*, **deceitfully** *adverb*

deceive *verb* (deceives, deceiving, deceived)
make a person believe something that is not
true. **deceiver** *noun* [from Latin]

decent *adjective*
1 respectable and honest. 2 reasonable or
adequate. 3 (*informal*) kind. **decently** *adverb*,
decency *noun* [from Latin]

deception *noun* (*plural* deceptions)
deceiving someone.
deceptive *adjective*, **deceptively** *adverb*

deci- (*say* dess-ee) *prefix*
one-tenth (as in *decimetre*).
[same origin as *decimal*]

decibel (*say* dess-ib-el) *noun* (*plural* decibels)
a unit for measuring the loudness of sound.
[originally one-tenth of the unit called a *bel*]

decide *verb* (decides, deciding, decided)
1 make up your mind; make a choice. 2 settle a
contest or argument.
decider *noun* [from Latin]

decided *adjective*
1 having clear and definite opinions.
2 noticeable, *a decided difference*.
decidedly *adverb*

deciduous (*say* dis-**id**-yoo-us) *adjective*
a deciduous tree is one that loses its leaves in
autumn. [from Latin *decidere* = fall off]

decimal *adjective*
using tens or tenths.
decimal *noun* (*plural* decimals)
a decimal fraction.
[from Latin *decimus* = tenth]

decimal fraction *noun* (*plural* decimal fractions)
a fraction with tenths shown as numbers after
a dot ($\frac{3}{10}$ is 0.3; $1\frac{1}{2}$ is 1.5).

decimal point *noun* (*plural* decimal points)
the dot in a decimal fraction.

decipher (*say* dis-**I**-fer) *verb* (deciphers,
deciphering, deciphered)
1 decode. 2 work out the meaning of something
written badly.

decision *noun* (*plural* decisions)
1 deciding; what you have decided.
2 determination.

decisive (*say* dis-**I**-siv) *adjective*
1 that settles or ends something, *a decisive
battle*. 2 full of determination; resolute.
decisively *adverb*, **decisiveness** *noun*

deck *noun* (*plural* decks)
1 a floor on a ship or bus. 2 a pack of playing
cards. 3 a turntable on a record player.

deckchair *noun* (*plural* deckchairs)
a folding chair with a canvas or plastic seat.
[because they were used on the decks of
passenger ships]

declaim *verb* (declaims, declaiming, declaimed)
make a speech etc. loudly and dramatically.
declamation *noun*
[from *de-* + Latin *clamare* = to shout]

declare *verb* (declares, declaring, declared)
1 say something clearly or firmly. 2 tell
customs officials that you have goods on which
you ought to pay duty. 3 end a cricket innings
before all the batsmen are out. **declaration** *noun*
declare war announce that you are starting a
war against someone.
[from *de-* + Latin *clarare* = make clear]

decline *verb* (declines, declining, declined)
1 refuse. 2 become weaker or smaller. 3 slope
downwards. 4 state the forms of a noun,
pronoun, or adjective that correspond to
particular cases, numbers, and genders.
decline *noun* (*plural* declines)
a gradual decrease or loss of strength. [from *de-*
+ Latin *clinare* = bend]

decode *verb* (decodes, decoding, decoded)
work out the meaning of something written in
code. **decoder** *noun*

decompose *verb* (decomposes, decomposing,
decomposed)
decay. **decomposition** *noun*

decorate *verb* (decorates, decorating, decorated)
1 make something look more beautiful or
colourful. 2 put fresh paint or paper on walls.
3 give somebody a medal. **decoration** *noun*,
decorator *noun*, **decorative** *adjective*
[from Latin *decor* = beauty]

decorous (*say* **dek**-er-us) *adjective*
polite and dignified. **decorously** *adverb* [from
Latin *decorus* = suitable, proper]

decoy (*say* **dee**-koi) *noun* (*plural* decoys)
something used to tempt a person or animal
into a trap or into danger.
decoy (*say* dik-**oi**) *verb* (decoys, decoying,
decoyed)
tempt a person or animal into a trap etc.

decrease *verb* (decreases, decreasing, decreased)
make or become smaller or fewer.
decrease *noun* (*plural* decreases)
decreasing; the amount by which something
decreases.
[from *de-* + Latin *crescere* = grow]

decree *noun* (*plural* decrees)
an official order or decision.
decree *verb* (decrees, decreeing, decreed)
make a decree. [from Latin *decretum*
= what has been decided]

decrepit (*say* dik-**rep**-it) *adjective*
old and weak. **decrepitude** *noun*
[from Latin *decrepitus* = creaking]

dedicate *verb* (dedicates, dedicating, dedicated)
1 devote to a special use, *She dedicated herself
to her work*. 2 name a person as a mark of
respect, e.g. at the beginning of a book.
dedication *noun* [from Latin]

deduce *verb* (deduces, deducing, deduced)
work something out by reasoning.
deducible *adjective*
[from *de-* + Latin *ducere* = to lead]

deduct *verb* (deducts, deducting, deducted)
subtract part of something.
[same origin as *deduce*]

deduction *noun* (*plural* deductions)
1 deducting; something deducted. 2 deducing;
something deduced.

deed *noun* (*plural* deeds)
1 something that someone has done; an act. 2 a
legal document. [from Old English]

deep *adjective*
1 going a long way down or back or in, *a deep
well*; *deep cupboards*. 2 measured from top to
bottom or front to back, *a hole six feet deep*.
3 intense or strong, *deep colours*; *deep feelings*.
4 low-pitched, not shrill, *a deep voice*.
deeply *adverb*, **deepness** *noun*

deepen *verb* (deepens, deepening, deepened)
make or become deeper.

deer *noun* (*plural* **deer**)
a fast-running graceful animal, the male of which usually has antlers.
[from Old English *deor* = an animal]

deface *verb* (**defaces, defacing, defaced**)
spoil the surface of something, e.g. by scribbling on it. **defacement** *noun*

defeat *verb* (**defeats, defeating, defeated**)
1 win a victory over someone. 2 baffle; be too difficult for someone.
defeat *noun* (*plural* **defeats**)
1 defeating someone. 2 being defeated; a lost game or battle.
[from Latin *disfacere* = undo, destroy]

defect (*say* dif-**ekt** or **dee**-fekt) *noun* (*plural* **defects**)
a flaw.
defect (*say* dif-**ekt**) *verb* (**defects, defecting, defected**)
desert your own country etc. and join the enemy. **defection** *noun*, **defector** *noun*
[from Latin *deficere* = fail, leave, undo]

defective *adjective*
having defects; incomplete.
defectiveness *noun*

defence *noun* (*plural* **defences**)
1 defending something. 2 something that defends or protects. 3 a reply put forward by a defendant.

defend *verb* (**defends, defending, defended**)
1 protect, especially against an attack. 2 try to prove that a statement is true or that an accused person is not guilty. **defender** *noun*
[from Latin]

defendant *noun* (*plural* **defendants**)
a person accused of something in a lawcourt.

defensive *adjective*
used or done for defence; protective.
defensively *adverb*
on the defensive ready to defend yourself.

defer[1] *verb* (**defers, deferring, deferred**)
postpone. **deferment** *noun*, **deferral** *noun* [from old French; related to *differ*]

defer[2] *verb* (**defers, deferring, deferred**)
give way to a person's wishes or authority; yield. [from Latin]

deference (*say* **def**-er-ens) *noun*
polite respect. **deferential** (*say* def-er-**en**-shal) *adjective*, **deferentially** *adverb*
[from *defer*[2]]

defiant *adjective*
defying; openly disobedient.
defiantly *adverb*, **defiance** *noun*

deficiency *noun* (*plural* **deficiencies**)
1 a lack or shortage. 2 a defect.
deficient *adjective* [same origin as *defect*]

defile *verb* (**defiles, defiling, defiled**)
make a thing dirty or impure.
defilement *noun* [from an old word *defoul*]

define *verb* (**defines, defining, defined**)
1 explain what a word or phrase means.
2 show clearly what something is; specify.
3 show a thing's outline. **definable** *adjective*
[from *de-* + Latin *finis* = limit]

definite *adjective*
1 clearly stated; exact, *Fix a definite time.*
2 certain or settled, *Is it definite that we are to move?* **definitely** *adverb*
definite article the word 'the'.
[from Latin *definitus* = defined]

definition *noun* (*plural* **definitions**)
1 a statement of what a word or phrase means or of what a thing is. 2 being distinct; clearness of outline (e.g. in a photograph).

deflate *verb* (**deflates, deflating, deflated**)
1 let out air from a tyre or balloon etc. 2 make someone feel less proud or less confident.
3 reduce or reverse inflation. **deflation** *noun*, **deflationary** *adjective*
[from *de-* + *inflate*]

deflect *verb* (**deflects, deflecting, deflected**)
make something turn aside. **deflection** *noun*, **deflector** *noun*
[from *de-* + Latin *flectere* = to bend]

deforest *verb* (**deforests, deforesting, deforested**)
clear away the trees from an area.
deforestation *noun*

deform *verb* (**deforms, deforming, deformed**)
spoil a thing's shape or appearance.
deformation *noun*
[from *de-* + Latin *forma* = shape, form]

deft *adjective*
skilful and quick. **deftly** *adverb*,
deftness *noun* [from Old English]

defuse *verb* (**defuses, defusing, defused**)
1 remove the fuse from a bomb etc. 2 make a situation less dangerous or tense.

defy *verb* (**defies, defying, defied**)
1 resist something openly; refuse to obey, *They defied the law.* 2 challenge a person to do something you believe cannot be done, *I defy you to prove this.* 3 prevent something being done, *The door defied all efforts to open it.*
[from *de-* + Latin *fidus* = faithful]

degenerate *verb* (**degenerates, degenerating, degenerated**)
become worse, especially morally.
degeneration *noun*
degenerate *adjective*
having become immoral or bad.
degeneracy *noun* [from Latin]

degrade *verb* (degrades, degrading, degraded)
1 humiliate or dishonour someone. 2 reduce to a simpler molecular form.
degradation (*say* deg-ra-**day**-shon) *noun*
[from *de-* + Latin *gradus* = grade]

degree *noun* (*plural* degrees)
1 a unit for measuring temperature. 2 a unit for measuring angles. 3 extent, *to some degree*. 4 an award to someone at a university or college who has successfully finished a course. [from *de-* + Latin *gradus* = grade]

dehydrated *adjective*
dried up, with all moisture removed.
dehydration *noun*
[from *de-* + Greek *hydor* = water]

deity (*say* **dee**-it-ee or **day**-it-ee) *noun* (*plural* deities)
a god or goddess. [from Latin *deus* = god]

dejected *adjective*
sad or depressed.
dejectedly *adverb*, **dejection** *noun*
[from *de-* + Latin *-jectum* = cast]

delay *verb* (delays, delaying, delayed)
1 make someone or something late. 2 postpone.
delay *noun* (*plural* delays)
delaying; the time for which something is delayed, *a two-hour delay*.

delegate (*say* **del**-ig-at) *noun* (*plural* delegates)
a person who represents others and acts on their instructions.
delegate (*say* **del**-ig-ayt) *verb* (delegates, delegating, delegated)
1 appoint someone as a delegate, *We delegated Jones to represent us*. 2 entrust, *We delegated the work to Jones*.
[from Latin *delegare* = entrust]

delegation (*say* del-ig-**ay**-shon) *noun* (*plural* delegations)
1 delegating. 2 a group of delegates.

deliberate (*say* dil-**ib**-er-at) *adjective*
1 done on purpose; intentional. 2 slow and careful. **deliberately** *adverb*
deliberate (*say* dil-**ib**-er-ayt) *verb* (deliberates, deliberating, deliberated)
discuss or think carefully. **deliberation** *noun*
[from *de-* + Latin *librare* = weigh]

delicacy *noun* (*plural* delicacies)
1 being delicate. 2 a delicious food.

delicate *adjective*
1 fine and graceful, *delicate embroidery*. 2 fragile and easily damaged. 3 pleasant and not strong or intense. 4 becoming ill easily. 5 using or needing great care, *a delicate situation*. **delicately** *adverb*, **delicateness** *noun*
[from Latin]

delicious *adjective*
tasting or smelling very pleasant.
deliciously *adverb* [from Latin]

delight *verb* (delights, delighting, delighted)
1 please someone greatly. 2 take great pleasure in something.
delight *noun* (*plural* delights)
great pleasure.
delightful *adjective*, **delightfully** *adverb*
[from Latin *delectare* = entice]

delinquent (*say* dil-**ing**-kwent) *noun* (*plural* delinquents)
someone who breaks the law or commits an offence. **delinquent** *adjective*, **delinquency** *noun*
[from Latin *delinquere* = offend]

delirium (*say* dil-**irri**-um) *noun*
1 a state of mental confusion and agitation during a feverish illness. 2 wild excitement.
delirious *adjective*, **deliriously** *adverb*
[Latin, = deranged]

deliver *verb* (delivers, delivering, delivered)
1 take letters or goods etc. to someone's house or place of work. 2 give a speech or lecture etc. 3 help with the birth of a baby. 4 aim or strike a blow or an attack. 5 rescue; set free.
deliverer *noun*, **deliverance** *noun*, **delivery** *noun*
[from *de-* + Latin *liberare* = set free]

delta *noun* (*plural* deltas)
a triangular area at the mouth of a river where it spreads into branches. [shaped like the Greek letter delta (= D), written Δ]

delude *verb* (deludes, deluding, deluded)
deceive or mislead someone.
[from Latin *deludere* = play unfairly]

deluge *noun* (*plural* deluges)
1 a large flood. 2 a heavy fall of rain. 3 something coming in great numbers, *a deluge of questions*.
deluge *verb* (deluges, deluging, deluged)
overwhelm by a deluge. [from old French]

delusion *noun* (*plural* delusions)
a false belief.

demagogue (*say* **dem**-a-gog) *noun* (*plural* demagogues)
a leader who wins support by making emotional speeches rather than by careful reasoning. [from Greek *demos* = people + *agogos* = leading]

demand *verb* (demands, demanding, demanded)
1 ask for something firmly or forcefully. 2 need, *It demands skill*.
demand *noun* (*plural* demands)
1 a firm or forceful request. 2 a desire to have or buy something, *There is a great demand for computers*.
in demand wanted or needed.
[from *de-* + Latin *mandare* = to order]

demarcation (*say* dee-mar-**kay**-shon) *noun*
marking the boundary or limits of something.
[from Spanish]

demented *adjective*
driven mad; crazy.
[from *de-* + Latin *mentis* = of the mind]

demi- *prefix*
half (as in *demisemiquaver*). [from French]

demigod *noun* (*plural* **demigods**)
a partly divine being.

democracy *noun* (*plural* **democracies**)
1 government of a country by representatives elected by the whole people. 2 a country governed in this way. **democrat** *noun*, **democratic** *adjective*, **democratically** *adverb*
[from Greek *demos* = people, + *-cracy*]

Democrat *noun* (*plural* **Democrats**)
a member of the Democratic Party in the USA.

demolish *verb* (**demolishes, demolishing, demolished**)
1 knock a building down and break it up. 2 destroy something completely. **demolition** *noun*
[from *de-* + Latin *moliri* = build]

demon *noun* (*plural* **demons**)
1 a devil; an evil spirit. 2 a fierce or forceful person. **demonic** (*say* dim-on-ik) *adjective*
[from Greek *daimon* = a spirit]

demonstrate *verb* (**demonstrates, demonstrating, demonstrated**)
1 show or prove something. 2 take part in a demonstration. **demonstrator** *noun*
[from *de-* + Latin *monstrare* = to show]

demonstration *noun* (*plural* **demonstrations**)
1 demonstrating; showing how to do or work something. 2 a meeting or procession etc. held to show everyone what you think about something.

demonstrative (*say* dim-on-strat-iv) *adjective*
1 showing or proving something. 2 showing feelings or affections openly. 3 (in grammar) pointing out the person or thing referred to. *This, that, these,* and *those* are demonstrative adjectives and pronouns. **demonstratively** *adverb*, **demonstrativeness** *noun*

demoralize *verb* (**demoralizes, demoralizing, demoralized**)
dishearten someone; weaken someone's confidence or morale. **demoralization** *noun*
[from *de-* + *morale*]

demote *verb* (**demotes, demoting, demoted**)
reduce a person to a lower position or rank. **demotion** *noun* [from *de-* + *promote*]

demure *adjective*
shy and modest. **demurely** *adverb*, **demureness** *noun* [origin unknown]

den *noun* (*plural* **dens**)
1 a lair. 2 a person's private room. 3 a place where something illegal happens, *a gambling den.* [from Old English]

denial *noun* (*plural* **denials**)
denying or refusing something.

denim *noun*
a kind of strong, usually blue, cotton cloth used to make jeans etc.
[from French *serge de Nim* = serge from Nimes (a town in southern France)]

denomination *noun* (*plural* **denominations**)
1 a name or title. 2 a religious group with a special name, *Baptists, Methodists, and other denominations.* 3 a unit of weight or of money, *coins of small denomination.*
[from *de-* + Latin *nominare* = to name]

denominator *noun* (*plural* **denominators**)
the number below the line in a fraction, showing how many parts the whole is divided into, e.g. 4 in $\frac{1}{4}$. (Compare *numerator.*)

denounce *verb* (**denounces, denouncing, denounced**)
speak strongly against something; accuse, *They denounced him as a spy.*
denunciation *noun*
[from *de-* + Latin *nuntiare* = announce]

dense *adjective*
1 thick; packed close together, *dense fog.* 2 stupid. **densely** *adverb* [from Latin]

density *noun* (*plural* **densities**)
1 thickness. 2 (in physics) the proportion of mass to volume.

dent *noun* (*plural* **dents**)
a hollow left in a surface where something has pressed or hit it.
dent *verb* (**dents, denting, dented**)
make a dent in something.

dental *adjective*
to do with the teeth or with dentistry. [from Latin *dentalis* = to do with a tooth]

dentist *noun* (*plural* **dentists**)
a person who is trained to treat teeth, fill or extract them, fit false ones, etc. **dentistry** *noun* [from French *dent* = tooth]

denture *noun* (*plural* **dentures**)
a set of false teeth. [French]

denude *verb* (**denudes, denuding, denuded**)
make bare or naked; strip something away. **denudation** *noun*
[from *de-* + Latin *nudare* = to bare]

denunciation *noun* (*plural* **denunciations**)
denouncing.

deny *verb* (**denies, denying, denied**)
1 say that something is not true. 2 refuse to give or allow something, *deny a request.*
[from *de-* + Latin *negare* = say no]

deodorant (*say* dee-oh-der-ant) *noun* (*plural* **deodorants**)
a substance that removes smells.

depart *verb* (**departs, departing, departed**)
go away; leave. **departure** *noun*
[from old French *départir* = separate]

department *noun* (*plural* **departments**)
one section of a large organization or shop.
departmental *adjective*
[from French *département* = division]

depend *verb* (**depends, depending, depended**)
depend on 1 rely on, *We depend on your help.* **2**
be controlled by something else, *Whether we
can picnic depends on the weather.*
[from *de-* + Latin *pendere* = hang]

dependant *noun* (*plural* **dependants**)
a person who depends on another, especially
financially, *She has two dependants.*

USAGE: Note that the spelling ends in *-ant* for
this noun but *-ent* for the adjective *dependent.*

dependent *adjective*
depending, *She has two dependent children; they
are dependent on her.* **dependence** *noun*

deplore *verb* (**deplores, deploring, deplored**)
be very upset or annoyed by something.
deplorable *adjective*, **deplorably** *adverb*
[from *de-* + Latin *plorare* = weep]

deport *verb* (**deports, deporting, deported**)
send an unwanted foreign person out of a
country. **deportation** *noun*
[from *de-* + Latin *portare* = carry]

depose *verb* (**deposes, deposing, deposed**)
remove a person from power.
[from old French *deposer* = put down]

deposit *noun* (*plural* **deposits**)
1 an amount of money paid into a bank etc.
2 money paid as a first instalment. **3** a layer of
solid matter in or on the earth.
deposit *verb* (**deposits, depositing, deposited**)
1 put something down. **2** pay money as a
deposit. **depositor** *noun*
[from *de-* + Latin *positum* = placed]

depot (*say* dep-oh) *noun* (*plural* **depots**)
1 a place where things are stored. **2** a
headquarters.
[same origin as *deposit*]

depraved *adjective*
behaving wickedly; of bad character.
depravity *noun*
[from *de-* + Latin *pravus* = perverse, wrong]

depress *verb* (**depresses, depressing, depressed**)
1 make somebody sad. **2** lower the value of
something, *Threat of war depressed prices.*
3 press down, *Depress the lever.*
depressive *adjective*

depression *noun* (*plural* **depressions**)
1 a great sadness or feeling of hopelessness. **2** a
long period when trade is very slack because
no one can afford to buy things. **3** a shallow
hollow in the ground or on a surface. **4** an area
of low air pressure which may bring rain.
5 pressing something down.

deprive *verb* (**deprives, depriving, deprived**)
take or keep something away from somebody.
deprival *noun*, **deprivation** *noun*
[from *de-* + Latin *privare* = rob]

depth *noun* (*plural* **depths**)
1 being deep; how deep something is. **2** the
deepest or lowest part.
in depth thoroughly.
out of your depth 1 in water that is too deep to
stand in. **2** trying to do something that is too
difficult for you.
[from *deep*]

deputation *noun* (*plural* **deputations**)
a group of people sent as representatives of
others.

deputy *noun* (*plural* **deputies**)
a person appointed to act as a substitute for
another.

deranged *adjective*
insane. **derangement** *noun*
[from *de-* + French *rang* = rank]

derelict (*say* derri-likt) *adjective*
abandoned and left to fall into ruin.
dereliction *noun*
[from *de-* + Latin *relictum* = left behind]

deride *verb* (**derides, deriding, derided**)
laugh at with contempt or scorn; ridicule.
derision *noun* [from *de-* + Latin *ridere* = to
laugh]

derive *verb* (**derives, deriving, derived**)
1 obtain something from a source, *She derived
great enjoyment from music.* **2** form or originate
from something, *Some English words are
derived from Latin words.* **derivation** *noun*,
derivative *adjective*
[from *de-* + Latin *rivus* = a stream]

descend *verb* (**descends, descending, descended**)
go down. **descent** *noun*
be descended from have as an ancestor; come
by birth from a certain person or family.
[from *de-* + Latin *scandere* = climb]

descendant *noun* (*plural* **descendants**)
a person who is descended from someone.

describe *verb* (**describes, describing, described**)
1 say what someone or something is like.
2 draw in outline; move in a pattern, *The orbit
of the Earth around the Sun describes an ellipse.*
description *noun*, **descriptive** *adjective*
[from *de-* + Latin *scribere* = write]

desert (*say* dez-ert) *noun* (*plural* **deserts**)
a large area of dry often sandy land.
desert (*say* diz-ert) *verb* (**deserts, deserting,
deserted**)
abandon; leave a person or place without
intending to return.
deserter *noun*, **desertion** *noun*
[from Latin *desertus* = abandoned]

desert island *noun* (*plural* **desert islands**)
an uninhabited island.

deserve *verb* (deserves, deserving, deserved)
have a right to something; be worthy of
something. **deservedly** *adverb* [from Latin
deservire = serve someone well]

design *noun* (*plural* **designs**)
1 a drawing that shows how something is to be
made. 2 the way something is made or
arranged. 3 lines and shapes that form a
decoration; a pattern. 4 a mental plan or
scheme.
have designs on plan to get hold of.
design *verb* (designs, designing, designed)
1 draw a design for something. 2 plan or
intend something for a special purpose.
designer *noun*
[from *de-* + Latin *signare* = mark out]

desirable *adjective*
1 causing people to desire it; worth having.
2 worth doing; advisable. **desirability** *noun*

desire *noun* (*plural* **desires**)
a feeling of wanting something very much.
desirous *adjective*
desire *verb* (desires, desiring, desired)
have a desire for something. [from Latin]

desk *noun* (*plural* **desks**)
1 a piece of furniture with a flat top and often
drawers, used when writing or reading etc. 2 a
counter at which a cashier or receptionist sits.
[from Latin]

desolate *adjective*
1 lonely and sad. 2 uninhabited.
desolation *noun*
[from Latin *desolare* = abandon]

despair *noun*
a feeling of hopelessness.
despair *verb* (despairs, despairing, despaired)
feel despair.
[from *de-* + Latin *sperare* = to hope]

desperate *adjective*
1 extremely serious; hopeless, *a desperate
situation.* 2 reckless and ready to do anything.
desperately *adverb*, **desperation** *noun*
[same origin as *despair*]

despise *verb* (despises, despising, despised)
think someone or something is inferior or
worthless. [from *de-* + Latin *-spicere* = to look]

despite *preposition*
in spite of. [same origin as *despise*]

despondent *adjective*
sad or gloomy. **despondently** *adverb*,
despondency *noun*
[from Latin *despondere* = give up, resign]

dessert (*say* diz-ert) *noun* (*plural* **desserts**)
fruit or a sweet food served as the last course of
a meal.
[from French *desservir* = clear the table]

destination *noun* (*plural* **destinations**)
the place to which a person or thing is
travelling. [same origin as *destiny*]

destined *adjective*
having as a destiny; intended.

destiny *noun* (*plural* **destinies**)
what will happen or has happened to somebody
or something; fate.
[from Latin *destinare* = fix, settle]

destitute *adjective*
left without anything; living in extreme
poverty. **destitution** *noun*
[from Latin *destitutus* = left in the lurch]

destroy *verb* (destroys, destroying, destroyed)
ruin or put an end to something. **destruction**
noun, **destructive** *adjective*
[from *de-* + Latin *struere* = pile up]

destroyer *noun* (*plural* **destroyers**)
a fast warship.

detach *verb* (detaches, detaching, detached)
unfasten or separate. **detachable** *adjective*,
detachment *noun* [from *de-* + *attach*]

detached *adjective*
1 separated. 2 not prejudiced; not involved in
something.

detail *noun* (*plural* **details**)
1 a very small part of a design or plan
or decoration etc. 2 a small piece of
information. **detailed** *adjective*
[from *de-* + French *tailler* = cut in pieces]

detain *verb* (detains, detaining, detained)
1 keep someone waiting. 2 keep someone at a
place. **detention** *noun*
[from *de-* + Latin *tenere* = hold]

detect *verb* (detects, detecting, detected)
discover. **detection** *noun*, **detector** *noun* [from
de- + Latin *tegere* = cover]

detective *noun* (*plural* **detectives**)
a person who investigates crimes.

detention *noun* (*plural* **detentions**)
1 detaining; being detained. 2 being made to
stay late in school as a punishment.
[same origin as *detain*]

deter *verb* (deters, deterring, deterred)
discourage or prevent a person from doing
something. **deterrent** *noun*
[from *de-* + Latin *terrere* = frighten]

detergent *noun* (*plural* **detergents**)
a substance used for cleaning or washing
things. [from *de-* + Latin *tergere* = to clean]

deteriorate (*say* dit-eer-ee-er-ayt) *verb*
(deteriorates, deteriorating, deteriorated)
become worse. **deterioration** *noun*
[from Latin *deterior* = worse]

determination *noun*
1 the firm intention to achieve what you have
decided to achieve. 2 determining or deciding
something.

determine *verb* (determines, determining, determined)
1 decide, *determine what is to be done.* 2 find out; calculate, *determine the height of the mountain.*
[from *de-* + Latin *terminare* = to limit]

determined *adjective*
full of determination; with your mind firmly made up.

detest *verb* (detests, detesting, detested)
dislike something very much; loathe.
detestable *adjective*, **detestation** *noun*

detonate (*say* det-on-ayt) *verb* (detonates, detonating, detonated)
explode or cause something to explode.
detonation *noun*, **detonator** *noun*
[from *de-* + Latin *tonare* = to thunder]

detour (*say* dee-toor) *noun* (*plural* detours)
a roundabout route instead of the normal one.
[from French *détourner* = turn away]

detriment (*say* det-rim-ent) *noun*
harm or disadvantage, *She worked long hours, to the detriment of her health.*
[from Latin *detrimentum* = worn away]

detrimental (*say* det-rim-en-tal) *adjective*
harmful or disadvantageous.
detrimentally *adverb*

deuce *noun* (*plural* deuces)
a score in tennis where both sides have 40 points and must gain two consecutive points to win. [from old French *deus* = two]

devalue *verb* (devalues, devaluing, devalued)
1 reduce a thing's value. 2 reduce the value of a country's currency in relation to other currencies or to gold. **devaluation** *noun*

devastate *verb* (devastates, devastating, devastated)
ruin or cause great destruction to something.
devastation *noun* [from Latin]

develop *verb* (develops, developing, developed)
1 make or become bigger or better. 2 come gradually into existence, *Storms developed.* 3 begin to have or use, *They developed bad habits.* 4 use an area of land for building houses, shops, factories, etc. 5 treat photographic film with chemicals so that pictures appear.
developer *noun*, **development** *noun*
[from French]

deviate (*say* dee-vee-ayt) *verb* (deviates, deviating, deviated)
turn aside from a course or from what is usual or true. **deviation** *noun*
[from *de-* + Latin *via* = way]

device *noun* (*plural* devices)
1 something made for a particular purpose, *a device for opening tins.* 2 a design used as a decoration or emblem.

leave someone to their own devices leave them to do as they wish.
[same origin as *devise*]

devil *noun* (*plural* devils)
1 an evil spirit. 2 a wicked, cruel, or annoying person. **devilish** *adjective*, **devilry** *noun* [via Old English from Latin]

devilment *noun*
mischief.

devious (*say* dee-vee-us) *adjective*
1 roundabout; not direct, *a devious route.* 2 not straightforward; underhand. **deviously** *adverb*, **deviousness** *noun*
[same origin as *deviate*]

devise *verb* (devises, devising, devised)
invent or plan. [from old French]

devoid *adjective*
lacking or without something, *His work is devoid of merit.*
[from *de-* + old French *voider* = make void]

devolution *noun*
handing over power from central government to local or regional government. [same origin as *devolve*]

devolve *verb* (devolves, devolving, devolved)
pass or be passed to a deputy or successor.
[from Latin *devolvere* = roll down]

devote *verb* (devotes, devoting, devoted)
give completely, *He devoted his time to sport.*
[from *de-* + Latin *vovere* = to vow]

devoted *adjective*
very loving or loyal.

devotee (*say* dev-o-tee) *noun* (*plural* devotees)
a person who is devoted to something; an enthusiast.

devotion *noun*
great love or loyalty.

devotions *plural noun*
prayers.

devour *verb* (devours, devouring, devoured)
eat or swallow something hungrily or greedily.
[from *de-* + Latin *vorare* = to swallow]

devout *adjective*
earnestly religious or sincere.
devoutly *adverb*, **devoutness** *noun*
[same origin as *devote*]

dew *noun*
tiny drops of water that form during the night on surfaces of things in the open air.
dewdrop *noun*, **dewy** *adjective*
[from Old English]

dexterity (*say* deks-terri-tee) *noun*
skill in handling things.
[from Latin *dexter* = on the right-hand side]

dhoti *noun* (*plural* dhotis)
the loincloth worn by male Hindus. [Hindi]

di-¹ *prefix*
two; double (as in *dioxide*).
[from Greek *dis* = twice]

di-² *prefix*
1 not; the reverse of. 2 apart; separated. see **dis-**.

dia- *prefix*
through (as in *diarrhoea*); across (as in *diagonal*). [from Greek *dia* = through]

diabetes (*say* dy-a-**bee**-teez) *noun*
a disease in which there is too much sugar in a person's blood.
diabetic (*say* dy-a-**bet**-ik) *adjective* & *noun*
[from Greek]

diabolical *adjective*
1 like a devil; very wicked. 2 very clever or annoying. [from Latin *diabolus* = devil]

diadem (*say* **dy**-a-dem) *noun* (*plural* **diadems**)
a crown or headband worn by a royal person.
[from Greek]

diagnose *verb* (**diagnoses, diagnosing, diagnosed**)
find out what disease a person has or what is wrong.
diagnosis *noun*, **diagnostic** *adjective*
[from *dia-* + Greek *gignoskein* = know]

diagonal (*say* dy-**ag**-on-al) *noun* (*plural* **diagonals**)
a straight line joining opposite corners.
diagonal *adjective*, **diagonally** *adverb*
[from *dia-* + Greek *gonia* = angle]

diagram *noun* (*plural* **diagrams**)
a kind of drawing or picture that shows the parts of something or how it works.
[from *dia-* + *-gram*]

dial *noun* (*plural* **dials**)
a circular object with numbers or letters round it.
dial *verb* (**dials, dialling, dialled**)
telephone a number by turning a telephone dial or pressing numbered buttons. [from Latin *diale* = clock-face, from *dies* = day]

dialect *noun* (*plural* **dialects**)
the words and pronunciations used by people in one district but not in the rest of a country.
[from Greek *dialektos* = way of speaking]

dialogue *noun* (*plural* **dialogues**)
a conversation. [from Greek]

dialysis (*say* dy-**al**-iss-iss) *noun*
a way of removing harmful substances from the blood by letting it flow through a machine.
[from *dia-* + Greek *lysis* = loosening]

diameter (*say* dy-**am**-it-er) *noun* (*plural* **diameters**)
1 a line drawn straight across a circle or sphere and passing through its centre. 2 the length of this line.
[from Greek *diametros* = measuring across]

diametrically *adverb*
completely, *diametrically opposite*.

diamond *noun* (*plural* **diamonds**)
1 a very hard precious stone, a form of carbon, that looks like clear glass. 2 a shape with four equal sides and four angles that are not right angles. 3 a playing card with red diamond shapes on it.
[from Greek *adamas* = adamant (= a very hard stone)]

diaper *noun* (*plural* **diapers**)
(*American*) a baby's nappy. [from Greek *diaspros* = made of white cloth]

diaphanous (*say* dy-**af**-an-us) *adjective*
(of fabric) almost transparent.
[from *dia-* + Greek *phainein* = to show]

diaphragm (*say* **dy**-a-fram) *noun* (*plural* **diaphragms**)
1 the muscular layer inside the body that separates the chest from the abdomen and is used in breathing. 2 a dome-shaped contraceptive device that fits over the cervix.
[from *dia-* + Greek *phragma* = fence]

diarist *noun* (*plural* **diarists**)
a person who keeps a diary.

diarrhoea (*say* dy-a-**ree**-a) *noun*
too frequent and too watery emptying of the bowels.
[from *dia-* + Greek *rhoia* = a flow]

diary *noun* (*plural* **diaries**)
a book in which someone writes down what happens each day.
[from Latin *dies* = day]

diatribe *noun* (*plural* **diatribes**)
a strong verbal attack. [French]

dice *noun*
(strictly this is the plural of **die²**, but it is often used as a singular, plural **dice**) a small cube marked with dots (1 to 6) on its sides, used in games.
dice *verb* (**dices, dicing, diced**)
1 play gambling games using dice. 2 cut meat, vegetables, etc. into small cubes. [plural of *die²*]

dictate *verb* (**dictates, dictating, dictated**)
1 speak or read something aloud for someone else to write down. 2 give orders in a bossy way. **dictation** *noun*
[from Latin *dictare* = keep saying]

dictates (*say* **dik**-tayts) *plural noun*
orders or commands.

dictator *noun* (*plural* **dictators**)
a ruler who has unlimited power.
dictatorial (*say* dik-ta-**tor**-ee-al) *adjective*,
dictatorship *noun*

diction *noun*
a person's way of speaking words, *clear diction*.
[from Latin *dictio* = saying, word]

dictionary noun (plural **dictionaries**)
a book that contains words in alphabetical
order so that you can find out how to spell
them and what they mean.
[same origin as diction]

didactic (say dy-**dak**-tik) adjective
having the manner of someone who is
lecturing people. **didactically** adverb
[from Greek didaktikos = teaching]

diddle verb (diddles, diddling, diddled) (slang)
cheat or swindle.
[origin unknown]

didn't (mainly spoken)
did not.

die[1] verb (dies, dying, died)
1 stop living or existing. 2 stop burning or
functioning, The fire had died down.
[from Old Norse]

die[2] noun singular of dice. [from old French]

die[3] noun (plural dies)
a device that stamps a design on coins etc. or
that cuts or moulds metal.
[from old French]

diehard noun (plural diehards)
a person who obstinately refuses to give up old
ideas or policies.
[from die hard = die painfully]

diesel (say dee-zel) noun (plural diesels)
1 an engine that works by burning oil in
compressed air. 2 fuel for this kind of engine.
[named after R. Diesel, a German engineer,
who invented it]

diet[1] noun (plural diets)
1 special meals that someone eats in order to
be healthy or to become less fat. 2 the sort of
foods usually eaten by a person or animal.
diet verb (diets, dieting, dieted)
keep to a diet.
[from Greek diaita = way of life]

diet[2] noun (plural diets)
the parliament of certain countries (e.g.
Japan). [from Latin dieta = day's business]

dietitian (say dy-it-ish-an) noun (plural dietitians)
an expert in diet and nutrition.

dif- prefix
1 not; the reverse of. 2 apart; separated. see **dis-**.

differ verb (differs, differing, differed)
1 be different. 2 disagree.
[from dif- + Latin ferre = carry]

difference noun (plural differences)
1 being different; the way in which things
differ. 2 the remainder left after one number is
subtracted from another, The difference
between 8 and 3 is 5. 3 a disagreement.

different adjective
unlike; not the same. **differently** adverb

USAGE: It is regarded as more acceptable to
say different from rather than different to,
which is common in less formal use. The
phrase different than is used in American
English but not in standard British English.

differential noun (plural differentials)
1 a difference in wages between one group of
workers and another. 2 a differential gear.

differential gear noun (plural differential gears)
a system of gears that makes a vehicle's
driving wheels revolve at different speeds
when going round corners.

differentiate verb (differentiates, differentiating,
differentiated)
1 make different, These things differentiate one
breed from another. 2 distinguish; recognize
differences, We do not differentiate between
them.
differentiation noun

difficult adjective
needing a lot of effort or skill; not easy.
difficulty noun
[from dif- + Latin facilis = easy]

diffident (say dif-id-ent) adjective
shy and not self-confident; hesitating to put
yourself or your ideas forward.
diffidently adverb, **diffidence** noun
[from dif- + Latin fidentia = confidence]

diffract verb (diffracts, diffracting, diffracted)
break up a beam of light etc.
diffraction noun
[from dif- + Latin fractum = broken]

diffuse (say dif-yooz) verb (diffuses, diffusing,
diffused)
1 spread something widely or thinly, diffused
lighting. 2 mix slowly, diffusing gases.
diffusion noun
diffuse (say dif-yooss) adjective
1 spread widely; not concentrated. 2 using
many words; not concise.
diffusely adverb, **diffuseness** noun
[from dif- + Latin fusum = poured]

dig verb (digs, digging, dug)
1 break up soil and move it; make a hole or
tunnel by moving soil. 2 poke something in,
Dig a knife into it. 3 seek or discover by
investigating, We dug up some facts.
digger noun
dig noun (plural digs)
1 a piece of digging, especially an
archaeological excavation. 2 a poke.
[probably from Old English]

digest (say dy-jest) verb (digests, digesting,
digested)
1 soften and change food in the stomach etc. so

that the body can absorb it. **2** take information into your mind and think it over.
digestible *adjective*, **digestion** *noun*
digest (*say* dy-jest) *noun* (*plural* **digests**)
a summary of news, information, etc.
[from Latin]

digestive *adjective*
to do with digestion, *the digestive system*.

digestive biscuit *noun* (*plural* **digestive biscuits**)
a wholemeal biscuit (because it is supposed to be easy to digest).

digit (*say* dij-it) *noun* (*plural* **digits**)
1 any of the numbers from 0 to 9. **2** a finger or toe. [from Latin *digitus* = finger or toe]

digital *adjective*
to do with or using digits.

digital clock *noun* (*plural* **digital clocks**)
a clock that shows the time with a row of figures.

digital watch *noun* (*plural* **digital watches**)
a watch that shows the time with a row of figures.

dignified *adjective*
having dignity.

dignitary *noun* (*plural* **dignitaries**)
an important official.
[same origin as *dignity*]

dignity *noun*
a calm and serious manner.
beneath your dignity not considered worthy enough for you to do.
[from Latin *dignus* = worthy]

dilapidated *adjective*
falling to pieces. **dilapidation** *noun*
[from Latin]

dilemma (*say* dil-em-a) *noun* (*plural* **dilemmas**)
a situation where someone has to choose between two or more possible actions, each of which will bring difficulties.
[from Greek, = double proposal]

USAGE: Do not use *dilemma* to mean simply a problem or difficult situation. There should be some idea of choosing between two (or perhaps more) things.

---

diligent (*say* dil-ij-ent) *adjective*
hard-working. **diligently** *adverb*, **diligence** *noun*
[from Latin *diligens* = careful, conscientious]

dilute *verb* (**dilutes, diluting, diluted**)
make a liquid weaker by adding water or other liquid. **dilution** *noun*
dilute *adjective*
diluted, *a dilute acid*.
[from Latin *diluere* = wash away]

dim *adjective* (**dimmer, dimmest**)
1 not bright or clear; only faintly lit.
2 (*informal*) stupid. **dimly** *adverb*,
dimness *noun*

dim *verb* (**dims, dimming, dimmed**)
make or become dim. **dimmer** *noun*

dimension *noun* (*plural* **dimensions**)
1 a measurement such as length, width, area, or volume. **2** size or extent.
dimensional *adjective*
[from Latin *dimensio* = measuring out]

diminish *verb* (**diminishes, diminishing, diminished**)
make or become smaller. **diminution** *noun*
[same origin as *diminutive*]

diminutive (*say* dim-in-yoo-tiv) *adjective*
very small. [from Latin *diminuere* = lessen]

dimple *noun* (*plural* **dimples**)
a small hollow or dent, especially in the skin.
dimpled *adjective*

din *noun*
a loud annoying noise.

dine *verb* (**dines, dining, dined**) (*formal*)
have dinner. **diner** *noun*
[from old French *disner*]

dinghy (*say* ding-ee) *noun* (*plural* **dinghies**)
a kind of small boat.
[from Hindi *dingi* = a small river boat]

dingy (*say* din-jee) *adjective*
dirty-looking. **dingily** *adverb*, **dinginess** *noun*
[origin unknown]

dinner *noun* (*plural* **dinners**)
the main meal of the day, either at midday or in the evening. [same origin as *dine*]

dinosaur (*say* dy-noss-or) *noun* (*plural* **dinosaurs**)
a prehistoric lizard-like animal, often of enormous size. [from Greek *deinos* = terrible + *sauros* = lizard]

diocese (*say* dy-oss-iss) *noun* (*plural* **dioceses**)
a district under the care of a bishop.

dioxide *noun*
an oxide with two atoms of oxygen to one of another element, *carbon dioxide*.
[from *di-*[1] + *oxide*]

dip *verb* (**dips, dipping, dipped**)
put down or go down, especially into a liquid.
dip *noun* (*plural* **dips**)
1 dipping. **2** a downward slope. **3** a quick swim. **4** a substance into which things are dipped. [from Old English]

diploma *noun* (*plural* **diplomas**)
a certificate awarded by a college etc. for skill in a particular subject. [Latin, from Greek, literally = folded paper]

diplomacy *noun*
1 the work of making agreements with other countries. **2** skill in dealing with people and gently persuading them to agree to things; tact.

diplomat *noun* (*plural* **diplomats**)
1 a person employed in diplomacy on behalf of his or her country. **2** a tactful person.

diplomatic *adjective*
[from Latin *diploma* = an official letter given to travellers, saying who they were]

direct *adjective*
1 as straight as possible. 2 going straight to the point; frank. 3 exact, *the direct opposite.*
directly *adverb* & *conjunction*,
directness *noun*
direct *verb* (directs, directing, directed)
1 tell someone the way. 2 guide or aim in a certain direction. 3 control or manage. 4 order, *He directed his troops to advance.* **director** *noun*
[from Latin *directum* = kept straight]

direct current *noun*
electric current flowing only in one direction.

direction *noun* (*plural* directions)
1 directing. 2 the line along which something moves or faces.
directional *adjective*

direct object *noun* (*plural* direct objects)
the word that receives the action of the verb. In *'she hit him'*, 'him' is the direct object.

directory *noun* (*plural* directories)
a book containing a list of people with their telephone numbers, addresses, etc.
[from Latin *directorius* = guiding]

dirge *noun* (*plural* dirges)
a slow sad song. [from the first word of a song, which used to be part of the Roman Catholic service for a dead person]

dirt *noun*
earth, soil; anything that is not clean.

dirty *adjective* (dirtier, dirtiest)
1 not clean; soiled. 2 unfair; dishonourable, *a dirty trick.* 3 indecent; obscene. **dirtily** *adverb*,
dirtiness *noun*

dis- *prefix* (changing to dif- before words beginning with *f*, and to di- before some consonants)
1 not; the reverse of (as in *dishonest*). 2 apart; separated (as in *disarm, disperse*). [from Latin]

disabled *adjective*
unable to use part of your body properly because of illness or injury. **disability** *noun*,
disablement *noun*

disadvantage *noun* (*plural* disadvantages)
something that hinders or is unhelpful.

disagree *verb* (disagrees, disagreeing, disagreed)
1 have or express a different opinion from someone. 2 have a bad effect, *Rich food disagrees with me.* **disagreement** *noun*

disagreeable *adjective*
unpleasant. [from old French]

disappear *verb* (disappears, disappearing, disappeared)
stop being visible; vanish.
disappearance *noun*

disappoint *verb* (disappoints, disappointing, disappointed)
fail to do what someone hopes for.
disappointment *noun*
[originally = to dismiss someone from an important position: from *dis-* + *appoint*]

disapprove *verb* (disapproves, disapproving, disapproved)
have an unfavourable opinion of something; not approve. **disapproval** *noun*

disarm *verb* (disarms, disarming, disarmed)
1 reduce the size of armed forces. 2 take away someone's weapons. 3 overcome a person's anger or doubt, *Her friendliness disarmed their suspicions.* **disarmament** *noun* [from old French]

disaster *noun* (*plural* disasters)
1 a very bad accident or misfortune. 2 a complete failure. **disastrous** *adjective*,
disastrously *adverb*

disbelief *noun* (*plural* disbeliefs)
refusal or unwillingness to believe something.

disc *noun* (*plural* discs)
1 any round flat object. 2 (in computers, usually **disk**) a storage device consisting of magnetically coated plates. 3 a gramophone record.
[from Latin *discus* = disc]

discerning *adjective*
perceptive; showing good judgement.

discharge *verb* (discharges, discharging, discharged)
1 release a person. 2 send something out, *discharge smoke.* 3 pay or do what was agreed, *discharge the debt.*

disciple *noun* (*plural* disciples)
1 a person who accepts the teachings of another whom he or she regards as a leader. 2 any of the original followers of Jesus Christ.
[from Latin *discipulus* = learner]

discipline *noun* (*plural* disciplines)
1 orderly and obedient behaviour. 2 a subject for study.
disciplinary (*say* dis-ip-lin-er-ee) *adjective*
[from Latin *disciplina* = training]

disco *noun* (*plural* discos)
a place where CDs or records are played for dancing.
[from French *discothèque* = record-library]

discolour *verb* (discolours, discolouring, discoloured)
spoil a thing's colour; stain.
discoloration *noun*
[from *dis-* + Latin *colorare* = to colour]

disconcert (*say* dis-kon-sert) *verb* (disconcerts, disconcerting, disconcerted)
make a person feel uneasy. [from *dis-* + French *concerter* = make harmonious]

disconnect *verb* (disconnects, disconnecting, disconnected)
break a connection; detach.
disconnection *noun*

disconsolate (*say* dis-kon-sol-at) *adjective*
disappointed.
[from *dis-* + Latin *consolatus* = consoled]

discontent *noun*
lack of contentment; dissatisfaction.
discontented *adjective*,
discontentment *noun*

discontinue *verb* (discontinues, discontinuing, discontinued)
put an end to something.
[from *dis-* + Latin *continuare* = continue]

discord *noun* (*plural* discords)
1 disagreement; quarrelling. 2 musical notes sounded together and producing a harsh or unpleasant sound.
discordant *adjective*
[from *dis-* + Latin *cordis* = of the heart]

discount *noun* (*plural* discounts)
an amount by which a price is reduced.
discount *verb* (discounts, discounting, discounted)
ignore or disregard something, *We cannot discount the possibility.* [from old French]

discourage *verb* (discourages, discouraging, discouraged)
1 take away someone's enthusiasm or confidence. 2 try to persuade someone not to do something. **discouragement** *noun*
[from old French]

discover *verb* (discovers, discovering, discovered)
1 find. 2 be the first person to find something.
discoverer *noun*, **discovery** *noun*
[from *dis-* + Latin *cooperire* = to cover]

discredit *verb* (discredits, discrediting, discredited)
1 destroy people's confidence in a person or thing; disgrace. 2 distrust.
discredit *noun*
1 disgrace. 2 distrust. **discreditable** *adjective*
[from *dis-* + *credit*]

discreet *adjective*
1 not giving away secrets. 2 not showy.
discreetly *adverb*
[from Latin *discernere* = be discerning]

USAGE: Do not confuse with *discrete*.

discrepancy (*say* dis-krep-an-see) *noun* (*plural* discrepancies)
difference; lack of agreement, *There are several discrepancies in the two accounts.* [from Latin *discrepantia* = discord]

discrete *adjective*
separate; distinct from each other.
[from Latin *discretus* = separated]

USAGE: Do not confuse with *discreet*.

discretion (*say* dis-kresh-on) *noun*
1 being discreet; keeping secrets. 2 power to take action according to your own judgement, *The treasurer has full discretion.* [from *discreet*]

discriminate *verb* (discriminates, discriminating, discriminated)
1 notice the differences between things; distinguish; prefer one thing to another. 2 treat people differently or unfairly, e.g. because of their race, sex, or religion.
discrimination *noun*
[same origin as *discern*]

discus *noun* (*plural* discuses)
a thick heavy disc thrown in athletic contests.
[Latin]

discuss *verb* (discusses, discussing, discussed)
talk with other people about a subject.
discussion *noun* [from Latin]

disease *noun* (*plural* diseases)
an unhealthy condition; an illness.
diseased *adjective* [from *dis-* + *ease*]

disembark *verb* (disembarks, disembarking, disembarked)
put or go ashore. **disembarkation** *noun*

disentangle *verb* (disentangles, disentangling, disentangled)
free from tangles or confusion.

disfigure *verb* (disfigures, disfiguring, disfigured)
spoil a person's or thing's appearance.
disfigurement *noun*
[from *dis-* + Latin *figura* = a shape]

disgrace *noun*
1 shame; loss of approval or respect. 2 something that causes shame.
disgraceful *adjective*, **disgracefully** *adverb*
disgrace *verb* (disgraces, disgracing, disgraced)
bring disgrace upon someone.
[from *dis-* + Latin *gratia* = grace]

disguise *verb* (disguises, disguising, disguised)
make a person or thing look different in order to deceive people.
disguise *noun* (*plural* disguises)
something used for disguising.

disgust *noun*
a feeling that something is very unpleasant or disgraceful.
disgust *verb* (disgusts, disgusting, disgusted)
cause disgust.
disgusted *adjective*, **disgusting** *adjective*
[from *dis-* + Latin *gustare* = to taste]

dish *noun* (*plural* dishes)
1 a plate or bowl for food. 2 food prepared for eating. 3 a satellite dish.

dish *verb* (dishes, dishing, dished) (*informal*)
dish out give out portions of something to people.

dishevelled (*say* dish-ev-eld) *adjective*
ruffled and untidy. **dishevelment** *noun* [from *dis-* + old French *chevel* = hair]

dishonest *adjective*
not honest. **dishonestly** *adverb*, **dishonesty** *noun* [from old French]

dishonour *noun* & *verb* (dishonours, dishonouring, dishonoured)
disgrace. **dishonourable** *adjective*

disillusion *verb* (disillusions, disillusioning, disillusioned)
get rid of someone's pleasant but wrong beliefs. **disillusionment** *noun*

disinclined *adjective*
unwilling to do something.

disinfect *verb* (disinfects, disinfecting, disinfected)
destroy the germs in something. **disinfection** *noun* [from French]

disinfectant *noun* (*plural* disinfectants)
a substance used for disinfecting things.

disintegrate *verb* (disintegrates, disintegrating, disintegrated)
break up into small parts or pieces. **disintegration** *noun*

disinterested *adjective*
impartial; not biased; not influenced by hope of gaining something yourself, *She gave us some disinterested advice.*

USAGE: It is not accepted as part of standard English to use this word as if it meant 'not interested' or 'bored'. If this is what you mean, use *uninterested*.

disjointed *adjective*
disconnected.
[from *dis-* + Latin *jungere* = join]

disk *noun* (*plural* disks)
a disc. [the American spelling of *disc*]

dislike *verb* (dislikes, disliking, disliked)
not to like somebody or something.

dislocate *verb* (dislocates, dislocating, dislocated)
1 move or force a bone from its proper position in one of the joints. 2 disrupt, *Fog dislocated the traffic.* **dislocation** *noun*
[from *dis-* + Latin *locare* = to place]

dislodge *verb* (dislodges, dislodging, dislodged)
move or force something from its place. [from French]

disloyal *adjective*
not loyal. **disloyally** *adverb*, **disloyalty** *noun* [from French]

dismal *adjective*
1 gloomy. 2 of poor quality. **dismally** *adverb* [from Latin *dies mali* = unlucky days]

dismantle *verb* (dismantles, dismantling, dismantled)
take something to pieces.
[from *dis-* + old French *manteler* = fortify]

dismay *noun*
a feeling of surprise and discouragement. **dismayed** *adjective* [from *dis-* + *may*[1]]

dismiss *verb* (dismisses, dismissing, dismissed)
1 send someone away. 2 tell a person that you will no longer employ him or her. 3 stop considering an idea etc. 4 get a batsman or cricket side out. **dismissal** *noun*, **dismissive** *adjective* [from *dis-* + Latin *missum* = sent]

dismount *verb* (dismounts, dismounting, dismounted)
get off a horse or bicycle.

disobey *verb* (disobeys, disobeying, disobeyed)
not to obey; disregard orders. **disobedient** *adjective*, **disobedience** *noun*

disorder *noun* (*plural* disorders)
1 untidiness. 2 a disturbance. 3 an illness. **disorderly** *adjective*

disorganized *adjective*
muddled and badly organized. **disorganization** *noun* [from French]

dispatch *verb* (dispatches, dispatching, dispatched)
1 send off to a destination. 2 kill.
dispatch *noun* (*plural* dispatches)
1 dispatching. 2 a report or message sent. 3 promptness; speed.

dispel *verb* (dispels, dispelling, dispelled)
drive away; scatter, *Wind dispels fog.*
[from *dis-* + Latin *pellere* = to drive]

dispensary *noun* (*plural* dispensaries)
a place where medicines are dispensed.

dispense *verb* (dispenses, dispensing, dispensed)
1 distribute; deal out. 2 prepare medicine according to prescriptions. **dispensation** *noun*, **dispenser** *noun*
dispense with do without something.
[from Latin *dispensare* = weigh out]

disperse *verb* (disperses, dispersing, dispersed)
scatter. **dispersal** *noun*, **dispersion** *noun* [from Latin *dispersum* = scattered]

displace *verb* (displaces, displacing, displaced)
1 shift from its place. 2 take a person's or thing's place. **displacement** *noun*

display *verb* (displays, displaying, displayed)
show; arrange something so that it can be clearly seen.
display *noun* (*plural* displays)
1 the displaying of something; an exhibition. 2 something displayed.
[from *dis-* = separately + Latin *plicare* = to fold]

disposable *adjective*
made to be thrown away after it has been used.

dispose *verb* (disposes, disposing, disposed)
1 place in position; arrange, *Dispose your troops in two lines.* 2 make a person ready or willing to do something, *I feel disposed to help him.*
be well disposed be friendly.
dispose of get rid of.
[from old French; related to *deposit*]

disposition *noun* (*plural* dispositions)
1 a person's nature or qualities. 2 arrangement.

disproportionate *adjective*
out of proportion; too large or too small.

disprove *verb* (disproves, disproving, disproved)
show that something is not true.

dispute *verb* (disputes, disputing, disputed)
1 argue; debate. 2 quarrel. 3 raise an objection to, *We dispute their claim.*
dispute *noun* (*plural* disputes)
1 an argument or debate. 2 a quarrel.
in dispute being argued about.
[from *dis-* + Latin *putare* = settle]

disqualify *verb* (disqualifies, disqualifying, disqualified)
bar someone from a competition etc. because he or she has broken the rules or is not properly qualified to take part.
disqualification *noun*

disregard *verb* (disregards, disregarding, disregarded)
ignore.
disregard *noun*
the act of ignoring something.

disrepair *noun*
bad condition caused by not doing repairs, *The old mill is in a state of disrepair.*

disreputable *adjective*
not respectable. [from *disrepute*]

disrespect *noun*
lack of respect; rudeness.
disrespectful *adjective*, **disrespectfully** *adverb*

disrupt *verb* (disrupts, disrupting, disrupted)
put into disorder; interrupt a continuous flow, *Fog disrupted traffic.* **disruption** *noun*, **disruptive** *adjective* [from *dis-* + Latin *ruptum* = broken]

dissatisfied *adjective*
not satisfied. **dissatisfaction** *noun*

dissect (*say* dis-sekt) *verb* (dissects, dissecting, dissected)
cut something up in order to examine it.
dissection *noun* [from *dis-* + Latin *sectum* = cut]

dissent *noun*
disagreement.
dissent *verb* (dissents, dissenting, dissented)
disagree. [from *dis-* + Latin *sentire* = feel]

dissident *noun* (*plural* dissidents)
a person who disagrees, especially someone who opposes their government.
dissident *adjective*, **dissidence** *noun*
[from Latin *dissidere* = sit by yourself]

dissolute *adjective*
having an immoral way of life.
[from Latin *dissolutus* = loose]

dissolution *noun* (*plural* dissolutions)
1 putting an end to a marriage or partnership etc. 2 formally ending a parliament or assembly.
[from Latin]

dissolve *verb* (dissolves, dissolving, dissolved)
1 mix something with a liquid so that it becomes part of the liquid. 2 make or become liquid; melt. 3 put an end to a marriage or partnership etc. 4 formally end a parliament or assembly, *Parliament was dissolved and a general election was held.*
[from *dis-* = separate + Latin *solvere* = loosen]

dissuade *verb* (dissuades, dissuading, dissuaded)
persuade somebody not to do something.
dissuasion *noun*
[from *dis-* + Latin *suadere* = persuade]

distance *noun* (*plural* distances)
the amount of space between two places.
in the distance far away.

distant *adjective*
1 far away. 2 not friendly; not sociable.
distantly *adverb*
[from *dis-* + Latin *stans* = standing]

distaste *noun*
dislike.

distasteful *adjective*
unpleasant.

distemper *noun*
1 a disease of dogs and certain other animals. 2 a kind of paint. [from Latin]

distil *verb* (distils, distilling, distilled)
purify a liquid by boiling it and condensing the vapour. **distillation** *noun*
[from *dis-* + Latin *stillare* = drip down]

distinct *adjective*
1 easily heard or seen; noticeable. 2 clearly separate or different. **distinctly** *adverb*, **distinctness** *noun*
[from Latin *distinctus* = separated]

USAGE: See note at *distinctive*.

distinction *noun* (*plural* distinctions)
1 a difference. 2 excellence or honour. 3 an award for excellence; a high mark in an examination.

distinctive *adjective*
that distinguishes one thing from another or others, *The school has a distinctive uniform.*
distinctively *adverb*

USAGE: Do not confuse this word with *distinct*. A *distinct* mark is a clear mark; a *distinctive* mark is one that is not found anywhere else.

distinguish *verb* (distinguishes, distinguishing, distinguished)
1 make or notice differences between things. 2 see or hear something clearly. 3 bring honour to, *He distinguished himself by his bravery.* **distinguishable** *adjective* [from Latin *distinguere* = to separate]

distort *verb* (distorts, distorting, distorted)
1 pull or twist out of its normal shape. 2 misrepresent; give a false account of something, *distort the truth.* **distortion** *noun* [from *dis-* + Latin *tortum* = twisted]

distract *verb* (distracts, distracting, distracted)
take a person's attention away from something.
[from *dis-* + Latin *tractum* = pulled]

distraction *noun* (*plural* distractions)
1 something that distracts a person's attention. 2 an amusement. 3 great worry or distress.

distress *noun* (*plural* distresses)
great sorrow, pain, or trouble.

distribute *verb* (distributes, distributing, distributed)
1 deal or share out. 2 spread or scatter. **distribution** *noun*, **distributor** *noun* [from *dis-* = + Latin *tributum* = given]

district *noun* (*plural* districts)
part of a town or country. [French]

distrust *noun*
lack of trust; suspicion. **distrustful** *adjective*
distrust *verb* (distrusts, distrusting, distrusted)
not to trust.

disturb *verb* (disturbs, disturbing, disturbed)
1 spoil someone's peace or rest. 2 cause someone to worry. 3 move a thing from its position. **disturbance** *noun*
[from *dis-* = thoroughly + Latin *turbare* = confuse, upset]

disuse *noun*
the state of being no longer used.
disused *adjective*

ditch *noun* (*plural* ditches)
a trench dug to hold water or carry it away, or to serve as a boundary.

ditto *noun*
(used in lists) the same again.
[from Italian *detto* = said]

dive *verb* (dives, diving, dived)
1 go under water, especially head first. 2 move down quickly. **dive** *noun*
[from Old English]

diverse (*say* dy-verss) *adjective*
varied; of several different kinds.
diversity *noun*

diversify *verb* (diversifies, diversifying, diversified)
make or become varied; involve yourself in different kinds of things.
diversification *noun*

diversion *noun* (*plural* diversions)
1 diverting something from its course. 2 an alternative route for traffic when a road is closed. 3 a recreation or entertainment.

divert *verb* (diverts, diverting, diverted)
1 turn something aside from its course. 2 entertain or amuse.
[from *di-²* + Latin *vertere* = to turn]

divide *verb* (divides, dividing, divided)
1 separate from something or into smaller parts; split up. 2 find how many times one number is contained in another, *Divide six by three (6 ÷ 3 = 2).* **divider** *noun*

divine *adjective*
1 belonging to or coming from God. 2 like a god. 3 (*informal*) excellent; extremely beautiful. **divinely** *adverb*
[from Latin *divus* = god]

division *noun* (*plural* divisions)
1 dividing. 2 a dividing line; a partition. 3 one of the parts into which something is divided. 4 (in Parliament) separation of members into two sections for counting votes.
divisional *adjective*
[from Latin *dividere* = divide]

divisive (*say* div-I-siv) *adjective*
causing disagreement within a group.

divorce *noun* (*plural* divorces)
the legal ending of a marriage.
divorce *verb* (divorces, divorcing, divorced)
1 end a marriage by divorce. 2 separate; think of things separately.
[French; related to *divert*]

Diwali (*say* di-**wah**-lee) *noun*
a Hindu religious festival at which lamps are lit, held in October or November.
[from Sanskrit *dipavali* = row of lights]

DIY *abbreviation*
do-it-yourself.

dizzy *adjective* (dizzier, dizziest)
having or causing the feeling that everything is spinning round; giddy. **dizzily** *adverb*, **dizziness** *noun* [from Old English]

DJ *abbreviation*
disc jockey.

DNA *abbreviation*
deoxyribonucleic acid; a substance in chromosomes that stores genetic information.

do *verb* (**does, doing, did, done**)
This word has many different uses, most of which mean performing or dealing with something (*Do your best. I can't do this. She is doing well at school*) or being suitable or enough (*This will do*). The verb is also used with other verbs **1** in questions (*Do you want this?*), **2** in statements with 'not' (*He does not want it*), **3** for emphasis (*I do like nuts*), **4** to avoid repeating a verb that has just been used (*We work as hard as they do*).
do away with get rid of.
do up 1 fasten, *Do your coat up*. **2** repair or redecorate, *Do up the spare room*.

dock¹ *noun* (*plural* **docks**)
a part of a harbour where ships are loaded, unloaded, or repaired.
dock *verb* (**docks, docking, docked**)
1 bring or come into a dock. **2** when two spacecraft dock, they join together in space. [from old German or old Dutch]

dock² *noun*
an enclosure for the prisoner on trial in a lawcourt. [from Flemish *dok* = cage]

dock³ *noun*
a weed with broad leaves.
[from Old English]

dock⁴ *verb* (**docks, docking, docked**)
1 cut short an animal's tail. **2** reduce or take away part of someone's wages or supplies etc. [origin unknown]

docker *noun* (*plural* **dockers**)
a labourer who loads and unloads ships.

doctor *noun* (*plural* **doctors**)
1 a person who is trained to treat sick or injured people. **2** a person who holds an advanced degree (a **doctorate**) at a university, *Doctor of Music*.
[Latin, = teacher]

doctrine *noun* (*plural* **doctrines**)
a belief held by a religious, political, or other group. **doctrinal** *adjective*
[from Latin *doctrina* = teaching]

document *noun* (*plural* **documents**)
a written or printed paper giving information or evidence about something.
documentation *noun*
[from Latin *documentum* = lesson, official paper]

documentary *adjective*
1 consisting of documents, *documentary evidence*. **2** showing real events or situations.
documentary *noun* (*plural* **documentaries**)
a film giving information about real events.
[same origin as *document*]

dodge *verb* (**dodges, dodging, dodged**)
move quickly to avoid someone or something.
dodge *noun* (*plural* **dodges**)
1 a dodging movement. **2** (*informal*) a trick; a clever way of doing something.

dodgy *adjective* (*informal*)
1 awkward or tricky. **2** not working properly. **3** dishonest.

dodo *noun* (*plural* **dodos**)
a large heavy bird that used to live on an island in the Indian Ocean but has been extinct for over 200 years.
[from Portuguese *doudo* = fool (because the bird had no fear of man)]

doe *noun* (*plural* **does**)
a female deer, rabbit, or hare.
[from Old English]

doesn't (*mainly spoken*)
does not.

dog *noun* (*plural* **dogs**)
a four-legged animal that barks, often kept as a pet.
dog *verb* (**dogs, dogging, dogged**)
follow closely or persistently, *Reporters dogged his footsteps*. [from Old English]

dog-eared *adjective*
(of a book) having the corners of the pages bent from constant use.

dogged (*say* dog-id) *adjective*
persistent or obstinate. **doggedly** *adverb*

dogma *noun* (*plural* **dogmas**)
a belief or principle that a Church or other authority declares is true and must be accepted. [Greek, = opinion, decree]

dogmatic *adjective*
expressing ideas in a very firm authoritative way. **dogmatically** *adverb*

do-it-yourself *adjective*
suitable for an amateur to do or make at home.

dole *verb* (**doles, doling, doled**)
dole out distribute.
dole *noun* (*informal*)
money paid by the State to unemployed people.
[from Old English]

doll *noun* (*plural* **dolls**)
a toy model of a person.
[pet form of *Dorothy*]

dollar *noun* (*plural* **dollars**)
a unit of money in the USA and some other countries.
[from German *thaler* = a silver coin]

dolphin *noun* (*plural* **dolphins**)
a sea animal like a small whale with a beaklike snout. [from Greek]

-dom *suffix*
forms nouns showing rank, office, territory, or condition (e.g. *kingdom, freedom*). [from Old English]

domain (*say* dom-ayn) *noun* (*plural* domains)
1 a kingdom. 2 an area of knowledge, interest, etc.
[from French; related to *dominion*]

dome *noun* (*plural* domes)
a roof shaped like the top half of a ball.
domed *adjective* [via French from Italian]

domestic *adjective*
1 to do with the home or household. 2 (of animals) kept by people, not wild.
domestically *adverb*, **domesticated** *adjective*
[from Latin *domesticus* = to do with the home]

dominate *verb* (dominates, dominating, dominated)
1 control by being stronger or more powerful.
2 be conspicuous or prominent, *The mountain dominated the whole landscape.*
dominant *adjective*, **dominance** *noun*, **domination** *noun*
[from Latin *dominus* = master]

domineer *verb* (domineers, domineering, domineered)
behave in a dominating way.
domineering *adjective*
[same origin as *dominate*]

dominion *noun* (*plural* dominions)
1 authority to rule others; control. 2 an area over which someone rules; a domain.
[from Latin *dominium* = property]

domino *noun* (*plural* dominoes)
a small flat oblong piece of wood or plastic with dots (1 to 6) or a blank space at each end, used in the game of dominoes.

donkey *noun* (*plural* donkeys)
an animal that looks like a small horse with long ears. [origin unknown]

donor *noun* (*plural* donors)
someone who gives something, *a blood donor.*
[from old French]

don't (*mainly spoken*)
do not.

doom *noun*
a grim fate that you cannot avoid, especially death or destruction, *a sense of impending doom.*
doom *verb* (dooms, dooming, doomed)
destine to a grim fate. [from Old English]

door *noun* (*plural* doors)
a movable barrier on hinges (or one that slides or revolves), used to open or close an entrance.
doorknob *noun*, **doormat** *noun*

doorstep *noun* (*plural* doorsteps)
the step or piece of ground just outside a door.

doorway *noun* (*plural* doorways)
the opening into which a door fits.

dope *noun* (*plural* dopes)
1 (*informal*) a drug, especially one taken or given illegally. 2 (*informal*) a stupid person.
dopey *adjective*
dope *verb* (dopes, doping, doped) (*informal*)
give a drug to a person or animal.
[from Dutch *doop* = sauce]

dormant *adjective*
1 sleeping. 2 living or existing but not active; not extinct, *a dormant volcano.*
[French, = sleeping]

dormitory *noun* (*plural* dormitories)
a room for several people to sleep in, especially in a school or institution.
dormitory town or **suburb** a place from which people travel to work elsewhere.
[from Latin *dormire* = to sleep]

dormouse *noun* (*plural* dormice)
an animal like a large mouse that hibernates in winter. [origin unknown]

dose *noun* (*plural* doses)
an amount of medicine etc. taken at one time.
[from Greek *dosis* = something given]

dot *noun* (*plural* dots)
a tiny spot.
dot *verb* (dots, dotting, dotted)
mark something with dots.

double *adjective*
1 twice as much; twice as many. 2 having two things or parts that form a pair, *a double-barrelled gun.* 3 suitable for two people, *a double bed.* **doubly** *adverb*
double *noun* (*plural* doubles)
1 a double quantity or thing. 2 a person or thing that looks exactly like another.
double *verb* (doubles, doubling, doubled)
1 make or become twice as much or as many.
2 bend or fold in two. 3 turn back sharply, *The fox doubled back on its tracks.*
[from old French]

double bass *noun* (*plural* double basses)
a musical instrument with strings, like a large cello. [from *double* + *bass*[1]]

double-cross *verb* (double-crosses, double-crossing, double-crossed)
deceive or cheat someone who thinks you are working with them.

doubt *noun* (*plural* doubts)
a feeling of not being sure about something.
doubt *verb* (doubts, doubting, doubted)
feel doubt. **doubter** *noun*
[from Latin *dubitare* = hesitate]

doubtful *adjective*
1 feeling doubt. 2 making you feel doubt.
doubtfully *adverb*

dough *noun*
1 a thick mixture of flour and water used for making bread, pastry, etc. 2 (*slang*) money.
doughy *adjective*

doughnut noun (plural **doughnuts**)
a round bun that has been fried and covered in sugar.

dour (say doo-er) adjective
stern and gloomy-looking. **dourly** adverb [from Scottish Gaelic dur = dull, obstinate]

dove noun (plural **doves**)
a kind of pigeon. [from Old Norse]

dovetail noun (plural **dovetails**)
a wedge-shaped joint used to join two pieces of wood.
dovetail verb (**dovetails, dovetailing, dovetailed**)
1 join pieces of wood with a dovetail. 2 fit neatly together, My plans dovetailed with hers. [because the wedge-shape looks like a dove's tail]

dowager noun (plural **dowagers**)
a woman who holds a title or property after her husband has died, the dowager duchess. [from old French douage = widow's share]

dowdy adjective (**dowdier, dowdiest**)
shabby; unfashionable. **dowdily** adverb

down[1] adverb
1 to or in a lower place or position or level, It fell down. 2 to a source or place etc., Track them down. 3 in writing, Take down these instructions. 4 as a payment, We will pay £5 down and the rest later.
be down on disapprove of, She is down on smoking.
down preposition
downwards through or along or into, Pour it down the drain.
[from Old English adune]

down[2] noun
very fine soft feathers or hair. **downy** adjective [from Old Norse]

down[3] noun (plural **downs**)
a grass-covered hill, the South Downs.
downland noun [from Old English dun]

downhill adverb & adjective
down a slope.

download verb (**downloads, downloading, downloaded**)
transfer data from a large computer system to a smaller one.

downright adverb & adjective
complete or completely, a downright lie.

Down's syndrome noun
a medical condition caused by a chromosome defect in which a baby is born with reduced intelligence and physical abnormalities.

downward adjective & adverb
going towards what is lower.
downwards adverb

dowry noun (plural **dowries**)
property or money brought by a bride to her husband when she marries him. [from old French; related to endow]

doze verb (**dozes, dozing, dozed**)
sleep lightly.
doze noun
a light sleep. **dozy** adjective

dozen noun (plural **dozens**)
a set of twelve. [from old French]

USAGE: Correct use is ten dozen (not ten dozens).

drab adjective (**drabber, drabbest**)
1 not colourful. 2 dull or uninteresting, a drab life. **drably** adverb, **drabness** noun

draft noun (plural **drafts**)
1 a rough sketch or plan. 2 a written order for a bank to pay out money.
draft verb (**drafts, drafting, drafted**)
1 prepare a draft. 2 select for a special duty, She was drafted to our office in Paris. [a different spelling of draught]

USAGE: This is also the American spelling of draught.

drag verb (**drags, dragging, dragged**)
1 pull something heavy along. 2 search a river or lake etc. with nets and hooks. 3 continue slowly and dully.
drag noun
1 a hindrance; something boring. 2 (slang) women's clothes worn by men.

dragon noun (plural **dragons**)
1 a mythological monster, usually with wings and able to breathe out fire. 2 a fierce person. [from Greek drakon = serpent]

dragonfly noun (plural **dragonflies**)
an insect with a long thin body and two pairs of transparent wings.

drain noun (plural **drains**)
1 a pipe or ditch etc. for taking away water or other liquid. 2 something that takes away strength or resources. **drainpipe** noun
drain verb (**drains, draining, drained**)
1 take away water etc. through a drain. 2 flow or trickle away. 3 empty liquid out of a container. 4 take away strength etc.; exhaust. **drainage** noun [from Old English]

drake noun (plural **drakes**)
a male duck. [from West Germanic]

drama noun (plural **dramas**)
1 a play. 2 writing or performing plays. 3 a series of exciting events. **dramatic** adjective, **dramatist** noun, **dramatize** verb [from Greek]

drape verb (**drapes, draping, draped**)
hang cloth etc. loosely over something. [from French drap = cloth]

draper noun (plural **drapers**)
a shopkeeper who sells cloth or clothes. [same origin as drape]

drastic adjective
having a strong or violent effect.
drastically adverb [from Greek]

draught (say drahft) noun (plural **draughts**)
1 a current of usually cold air indoors. 2 a haul of fish in a net. 3 the depth of water needed to float a ship. 4 a swallow of liquid.
draughty adjective [from Old Norse]

draughts noun
a game played with 24 round pieces on a chessboard. [from draught in an old sense = way of moving]

draw verb (**draws, drawing, drew, drawn**)
1 produce a picture or outline by making marks on a surface. 2 pull. 3 take out, draw water. 4 attract, The fair drew large crowds. 5 end a game or contest with the same score on both sides. 6 move or come, The ship drew nearer. 7 write out a cheque to be cashed.
draw a conclusion form an opinion about something by thinking about the evidence.
draw noun (plural **draws**)
1 the drawing of lots (see lot). 2 the drawing out of a gun etc., He was quick on the draw. 3 an attraction. 4 a drawn game. [from Old English]

USAGE: Do not confuse this word with drawer.

drawback noun (plural **drawbacks**)
a disadvantage.
[from draw back = hesitate]

drawbridge noun (plural **drawbridges**)
a bridge over a moat, hinged at one end so that it can be raised or lowered.

drawer noun (plural **drawers**)
1 a sliding box-like compartment in a piece of furniture. 2 a person who draws something. 3 someone who draws (= writes out) a cheque.

drawing noun (plural **drawings**)
a picture or outline drawn.

drawing pin noun (plural **drawing pins**)
a short pin with a flat top to be pressed with your thumb, used for fastening paper etc. to a surface.

drawing room noun (plural **drawing rooms**)
a sitting room. [short for withdrawing room = a private room in a hotel etc., to which guests could withdraw]

drawl verb (**drawls, drawling, drawled**)
speak very slowly or lazily.
drawl noun (plural **drawls**)
a drawling way of speaking. [from old German or old Dutch dralen = delay]

dread noun
great fear.

dread verb (**dreads, dreading, dreaded**)
fear something greatly. [from Old English]

dreadful adjective (informal)
very bad, dreadful weather.
dreadfully adverb

dreadlocks plural noun
hair worn in many ringlets or plaits, especially by Rastafarians.
[from dread + lock² (because the style was copied from pictures of Ethiopian warriors)]

dream noun (plural **dreams**)
1 things a person seems to see while sleeping. 2 something imagined; an ambition or ideal.
dreamy adjective, **dreamily** adverb
dream verb (**dreams, dreaming, dreamt or dreamed**)
1 have a dream or dreams. 2 have an ambition. 3 think something might happen, I never dreamt she would leave. **dreamer** noun
[from Middle English]

dreary adjective (**drearier, dreariest**)
1 dull or boring. 2 gloomy. **drearily** adverb, **dreariness** noun [from Old English]

dredge verb (**dredges, dredging, dredged**)
drag something up, especially by scooping at the bottom of a river or the sea. **dredger** noun [origin unknown]

dregs plural noun
worthless bits that sink to the bottom of a liquid.

drench verb (**drenches, drenching, drenched**)
make wet all through; soak.

dress noun (plural **dresses**)
1 a woman's or girl's garment with a bodice and skirt. 2 clothes; costume, fancy dress.
dress verb (**dresses, dressing, dressed**)
1 put clothes on. 2 arrange a display in a window etc.; decorate, dress the shop windows. 3 prepare food for cooking or eating. 4 put a dressing on a wound. **dresser** noun
[from French dresser = prepare]

dresser noun (plural **dressers**)
a sideboard with shelves at the top for dishes etc. [same origin as dress]

dressing noun (plural **dressings**)
1 a bandage, plaster, or ointment etc. for a wound. 2 a sauce of oil, vinegar, etc. for a salad. 3 manure or other fertilizer for spreading on the soil.

dressing gown noun (plural **dressing gowns**)
a loose garment for wearing when you are not fully dressed.

dress rehearsal noun (plural **dress rehearsals**)
a rehearsal at which the cast wear their costumes.

dribble *verb* (dribbles, dribbling, dribbled)
1 let saliva trickle out of your mouth. 2 move the ball forward in football or hockey with slight touches of your feet or stick.
[from *drib*, a different spelling of *drip*]

drift *verb* (drifts, drifting, drifted)
1 be carried gently along by water or air.
2 move along slowly and casually. 3 live casually with no definite objective.
drifter *noun*
drift *noun* (*plural* drifts)
1 a drifting movement. 2 a mass of snow or sand piled up by the wind. 3 the general meaning of a speech etc. [from Old Norse]

driftwood *noun*
wood floating on the sea or washed ashore by it.

drill *noun* (*plural* drills)
1 a tool for making holes; a machine for boring holes or wells. 2 repeated exercises in gymnastics, military training, etc.
drill *verb* (drills, drilling, drilled)
1 make a hole etc. with a drill. 2 do repeated exercises; make people do exercises. [from old Dutch]

drink *verb* (drinks, drinking, drank, drunk)
1 swallow liquid. 2 drink a lot of alcoholic drinks. **drinker** *noun*
drink *noun* (*plural* drinks)
1 a liquid for drinking; an amount of liquid swallowed. 2 an alcoholic drink.

drip *verb* (drips, dripping, dripped)
fall or let something fall in drops.
drip *noun* (*plural* drips)
1 liquid falling in drops; the sound it makes.
2 apparatus for dripping liquid into the veins of a sick person.
[from Old English]

drip-dry *adjective*
made of material that dries easily and does not need ironing.

dripping *noun*
fat melted from roasted meat and allowed to set.

drive *verb* (drives, driving, drove, driven)
1 make something or someone move. 2 operate a motor vehicle or a train etc. 3 force or compel someone to do something, *Hunger drove them to steal.* 4 force someone into a state, *She is driving me crazy.* 5 rush; move rapidly, *Rain drove against the window.* **driver** *noun*
drive *noun* (*plural* drives)
1 a journey in a vehicle. 2 a hard stroke in cricket or golf etc. 3 the transmitting of power to machinery, *four-wheel drive.* 4 energy or enthusiasm. 5 an organized effort, *a sales drive.* 6 a track for vehicles through the grounds of a house.
[from Old English]

drive-in *adjective*
that you can use without getting out of your car.

drivel *noun*
silly talk; nonsense.
[from Old English *dreflian* = dribble]

drizzle *noun*
very fine rain.
[from Old English *dreosan* = to fall]

drone *verb* (drones, droning, droned)
1 make a deep humming sound. 2 talk in a boring voice.
drone *noun* (*plural* drones)
1 a droning sound. 2 a male bee.

drool *verb* (drools, drooling, drooled)
dribble.
drool over be very emotional about liking something.
[from *drivel*]

droop *verb* (droops, drooping, drooped)
hang down weakly. [from Old Norse]

drop *noun* (*plural* drops)
1 a tiny amount of liquid. 2 a fall or decrease.
3 a descent. 4 a small round sweet. 5 a hanging ornament.
drop *verb* (drops, dropping, dropped)
1 fall. 2 let something fall. 3 put down a passenger etc., *Drop me at the station.*
drop in visit someone casually.
drop out stop taking part in something.
drop-out *noun*

drought (*say* drout) *noun* (*plural* droughts)
a long period of dry weather.
[from Old English]

drown *verb* (drowns, drowning, drowned)
1 die or kill by suffocation under water. 2 flood or drench. 3 make so much noise that another sound cannot be heard.
[from Old Norse]

drowsy *adjective*
sleepy. **drowsily** *adverb*, **drowsiness** *noun*

drudge *noun* (*plural* drudges)
a person who does dull work. **drudgery** *noun*
[origin unknown]

drug *noun* (*plural* drugs)
1 a substance used in medicine. 2 a substance that affects your senses or your mind, *a drug addict.*
drug *verb* (drugs, drugging, drugged)
give a drug to someone, especially to make them unconscious. [from French]

drum *noun* (*plural* drums)
1 a musical instrument made of a cylinder with a skin or parchment stretched over one or both ends. 2 a cylindrical object or container, *an oil drum.*
drum *verb* (drums, drumming, drummed)
1 play a drum or drums. 2 tap repeatedly on something. **drummer** *noun*

drumstick *noun* (*plural* **drumsticks**)
1 a stick for beating a drum. **2** the lower part of a cooked bird's leg.

drunk *adjective*
not able to control your behaviour through drinking too much alcohol.
drunk *noun* (*plural* **drunks**)
a person who is drunk.
[past participle of *drink*]

drunkard *noun* (*plural* **drunkards**)
a person who is often drunk.

drunken *adjective*
1 drunk, *a drunken man*. **2** caused by drinking alcohol, *a drunken brawl*.

dry *adjective* (**drier, driest**)
1 without water or moisture. **2** thirsty.
3 boring or dull. **4** (of remarks or humour) said in a matter-of-fact or ironical way, *dry wit*.
drily *adverb*, **dryness** *noun*
dry *verb* (**dries, drying, dried**)
make or become dry.
[from Old English]

dry-cleaning *noun*
a method of cleaning clothes etc. using a liquid that evaporates quickly.

dual carriageway *noun* (*plural* **dual carriageways**)
a road with a dividing strip between lanes of traffic in opposite directions.

dubious (*say* **dew-bee-us**) *adjective*
doubtful. **dubiously** *adverb*
[from Latin *dubium* = doubt]

duchess *noun* (*plural* **duchesses**)
a duke's wife or widow. [from Latin]

duchy *noun* (*plural* **duchies**)
the territory of a duke, *the duchy of Cornwall*.
[from old French]

duck *noun* (*plural* **ducks**)
1 a swimming bird with a flat beak; the female of this. **2** a batsman's score of nought at cricket. **3** a ducking movement.
duck *verb* (**ducks, ducking, ducked**)
1 bend down quickly to avoid something. **2** go or push quickly under water. **3** dodge; avoid doing something. [from Old English]

duckling *noun* (*plural* **ducklings**)
a young duck.

duct *noun* (*plural* **ducts**)
a tube or channel through which liquid, gas, air, or cables can pass.
[from Latin *ductus* = leading]

ductile *adjective*
(of metal) able to be drawn out into fine strands. [from Latin]

due *adjective*
1 expected; scheduled to do something or to arrive, *The train is due in ten minutes*. **2** owing;

needing to be paid. **3** that ought to be given; rightful, *Treat her with due respect*.
due to as a result of.

USAGE: Traditionally, correct use is as in *His lateness was due to an accident*. Some people object to the use of 'due to' without a preceding noun (e.g. 'lateness') to which it refers. However, such uses as 'He was late, due to an accident' are nowadays widely regarded as acceptable. But if you prefer, you can use *because of* or *owing to* instead.

---

due *adverb*
exactly, *We sailed due east*.
due *noun* (*plural* **dues**)
1 something you deserve or have a right to; proper respect, *Give him his due*. **2** a fee, *harbour dues*.
[from French *dû* = what is owed]

duel *noun* (*plural* **duels**)
a fight between two people, especially with pistols or swords. **duelling** *noun*, **duellist** *noun*
[from Italian]

duet *noun* (*plural* **duets**)
a piece of music for two players or singers.
[from Italian *duo* = two]

duffel coat (*plural* **duffel coats**)
a thick overcoat with a hood, fastened with toggles. [named after *Duffel*, a town in Belgium, where the cloth for it was made]

duffer *noun* (*plural* **duffers**)
a person who is stupid or not good at doing something. [origin unknown]

duke *noun* (*plural* **dukes**)
a member of the highest rank of noblemen.
dukedom *noun* [from Latin *dux* = leader]

dull *adjective*
1 not bright or clear, *dull weather*. **2** stupid.
3 boring, *a dull concert*. **4** not sharp, *a dull pain*; *a dull thud*. **dully** *adverb*, **dullness** *noun*
[from Old English]

dumb *adjective*
1 without the ability to speak. **2** silent.
3 (*informal*) stupid. **dumbly** *adverb*, **dumbness** *noun* [from Old English]

dumbfound *verb* (**dumbfounds, dumbfounding, dumbfounded**)
astonish; strike a person dumb with surprise.
[from *dumb* + *confound*]

dummy *noun* (*plural* **dummies**)
1 something made to look like a person or thing. **2** an imitation teat given to a baby to suck. [from *dumb*]

dump *noun* (*plural* **dumps**)
1 a place where something (especially rubbish) is left or stored. **2** (*informal*) a dull or unattractive place.
dump *verb* (**dumps, dumping, dumped**)
1 get rid of something that is not wanted. **2** put something down carelessly.

dumpling *noun* (*plural* **dumplings**)
a lump of dough cooked in a stew etc. or baked with fruit inside.
[same origin as *dumpy*]

dumpy *adjective*
short and fat.
[from an old word *dump* = dumpy person]

dunce *noun* (*plural* **dunces**)
a person who is slow at learning.
[from John Duns Scotus, a Scottish philosopher in the Middle Ages (because his opponents said that his followers could not understand new ideas)]

dune *noun* (*plural* **dunes**)
a mound of loose sand shaped by the wind.

dung *noun*
solid waste matter excreted by an animal.

dungarees *plural noun*
overalls made of thick strong cloth.
[from Hindi *dungri* = the cloth they were made of]

dungeon (*say* dun-jon) *noun* (*plural* **dungeons**)
an underground cell for prisoners.
[from old French]

duodenum (*say* dew-o-**deen**-um) *noun* (*plural* **duodenums**)
the part of the small intestine that is just below the stomach. **duodenal** *adjective* [from Latin *duodecim* = twelve (because its length is about twelve times the breadth of a finger)]

dupe *verb* (**dupes, duping, duped**)
deceive. [French]

duplicate (*say* dyoop-lik-at) *noun* (*plural* **duplicates**)
1 something that is exactly the same as something else. 2 an exact copy.
duplicate (*say* dyoop-lik-ayt) *verb* (**duplicates, duplicating, duplicated**)
make or be a duplicate.
duplication *noun*, **duplicator** *noun*
[from Latin *duplex* = double]

duplicity (*say* dew-**plis**-it-ee) *noun*
deceitfulness. [same origin as *duplicate*]

durable *adjective*
strong and likely to last.
durably *adverb*, **durability** *noun*
[from Latin *durare* = endure]

during *preposition*
while something else is going on.
[from Latin *durans* = lasting, enduring]

dusk *noun* (*plural* **dusks**)
twilight in the evening. [from Old English]

dust *noun*
tiny particles of earth or other solid material.
dust *verb* (**dusts, dusting, dusted**)
1 wipe away dust. 2 sprinkle with dust or something powdery. [from Old English]

dustbin *noun* (*plural* **dustbins**)
a bin for household rubbish.

dustman *noun* (*plural* **dustmen**)
a person employed to empty dustbins and cart away rubbish.

dustpan *noun* (*plural* **dustpans**)
a pan into which dust is brushed from a floor.

dusty *adjective* (**dustier, dustiest**)
1 covered with dust. 2 like dust.

dutiful *adjective*
doing your duty; obedient. **dutifully** *adverb*
[from *duty* + *-ful*]

duty *noun* (*plural* **duties**)
1 what you ought to do or must do. 2 a task that must be done. 3 a tax charged on imports and on certain other things.
on duty actually doing what is your regular work.
[same origin as *due*]

duvet (*say* doo-vay) *noun* (*plural* **duvets**)
a kind of quilt used instead of other bedclothes.
[French, = down^2]

dwarf *noun* (*plural* **dwarfs** or **dwarves**)
a very small person or thing.
dwarf *verb* (**dwarfs, dwarfing, dwarfed**)
make something seem small by contrast, *The ocean liner dwarfed the tugs that were towing it.*
[from Old English]

dwelling *noun* (*plural* **dwellings**)
a house etc. to live in.

dwindle *verb* (**dwindles, dwindling, dwindled**)
get smaller gradually. [from Old English]

dye *verb* (**dyes, dyeing, dyed**)
colour something by putting it into a liquid.
dyer *noun*
dye *noun* (*plural* **dyes**)
a substance used to dye things.
[from Old English]

dynamic *adjective*
energetic or forceful. **dynamically** *adverb* [from Greek *dynamis* = power]

dynamite *noun*
1 a powerful explosive. 2 something likely to make people very excited or angry. [same origin as *dynamic*]

dynamo *noun* (*plural* **dynamos**)
a machine that makes electricity.

dynasty (*say* din-a-stee) *noun* (*plural* **dynasties**)
a succession of rulers all from the same family.
dynastic *adjective*
[same origin as *dynamic*]

dys- *prefix*
bad; difficult. [from Greek]

dyslexia (*say* dis-**leks**-ee-a) *noun*
unusually great difficulty in being able to read and spell. **dyslexic** *adjective*
[from *dys-* + Greek *lexis* = speech (which was confused with Latin *legere* = read)]

dystrophy (*say* dis-trof-ee) *noun*
a disease that weakens the muscles.
[from *dys-* + Greek *-trophia* = nourishment]

E. *abbreviation*
east; eastern.

e- *prefix*
1 out; away. 2 up, upwards; thoroughly.
3 formerly. see **ex-**.

each *adjective & pronoun*
every; every one, *each child*; *each of you*. [from Old English]

USAGE: In standard English, the pronoun *each* should be used with a singular verb and singular pronouns: *Each has chosen her own outfit.*

eager *adjective*
strongly wanting to do something; enthusiastic. **eagerly** *adverb*, **eagerness** *noun*
[from Latin]

eagle *noun* (*plural* **eagles**)
a large bird of prey with very strong sight.

ear[1] *noun* (*plural* **ears**)
1 the organ of the body that is used for hearing. 2 hearing ability, *She has a good ear for music.*
[from Old English *eare*]

ear[2] *noun* (*plural* **ears**)
the spike of seeds at the top of a stalk of corn.
[from Old English *ear*]

eardrum *noun* (*plural* **eardrums**)
a membrane in the ear that vibrates when sounds reach it.

earl *noun* (*plural* **earls**)
a British nobleman. **earldom** *noun*

early *adjective & adverb* (**earlier**, **earliest**)
1 before the usual or expected time. 2 near the beginning, *early in the book.*
earliness *noun* [from *ere* + *-ly*]

earmark *verb* (**earmarks**, **earmarking**, **earmarked**)
put something aside for a particular purpose. [from the custom of marking an animal's ear to identify it]

earn *verb* (**earns**, **earning**, **earned**)
get something by working or in return for what you have done. [from Old English]

earnest *adjective*
showing serious feelings or intentions.
earnestly *adverb*, **earnestness** *noun*

earshot *noun*
the distance within which a sound can be heard. [from *ear* + *shot* in the sense 'as far as something can reach']

earth *noun* (*plural* **earths**)
1 the planet (*Earth*) that we live on. 2 the ground; soil. 3 the hole where a fox or badger lives. 4 connection to the ground to complete an electrical circuit.
earth *verb* (**earths**, **earthing**, **earthed**)
connect an electrical circuit to the ground.

earthenware *noun*
pottery made of coarse baked clay.

earthly *adjective*
concerned with life on earth rather than with life after death.

earthquake *noun* (*plural* **earthquakes**)
a violent movement of part of the earth's surface.

earthy *adjective*
1 like earth or soil. 2 crude and vulgar.

earwig *noun* (*plural* **earwigs**)
a crawling insect with pincers at the end of its body. [so named because it was thought to crawl into people's ears]

ease *noun*
freedom from trouble or effort or pain, *She climbed the tree with ease.*

easel *noun* (*plural* **easels**)
a stand for supporting a blackboard or a painting. [from Dutch *ezel* = donkey (which carries a load)]

easily *adverb*
1 without difficulty; with ease. 2 by far, *easily the best.* 3 very likely, *He could easily be lying.*

east *noun*
1 the direction where the sun rises. 2 the eastern part of a country, city, etc.
east *adjective & adverb*
towards or in the east; coming from the east.
easterly *adjective*, **eastern** *adjective*, **easterner** *noun*, **easternmost** *adjective*
[from Old English]

Easter *noun*
the Sunday (in March or April) when Christians commemorate the resurrection of Christ; the days around it. [named after *Eastre*, an Anglo-Saxon goddess whose feast was celebrated in spring]

eastward *adjective & adverb*
towards the east. **eastwards** *adverb*

easy *adjective* (**easier**, **easiest**)
able to be done or used or understood without trouble. **easiness** *noun*
easy *adverb*
with ease; comfortably, *Take it easy!*

eat *verb* (eats, eating, ate, eaten)
1 chew and swallow as food. 2 have a meal,
When do we eat? 3 use up; destroy gradually,
Extra expenses ate up our savings.
[from Old English]

eaves *plural noun*
the overhanging edges of a roof.

eavesdrop *verb* (eavesdrops, eavesdropping,
eavesdropped)
listen secretly to a private conversation.
eavesdropper *noun*
[as if you are listening outside a wall, where
water drops from the eaves]

ebb *noun* (*plural* ebbs)
1 the movement of the tide when it is going
out, away from the land. 2 a low point, *Our
courage was at a low ebb.*

EC *abbreviation*
European Community.

eccentric (*say* ik-sen-trik) *adjective*
behaving strangely. **eccentrically** *adverb*,
eccentricity (*say* ek-sen-**triss**-it-ee) *noun* [from
Greek *ekkentros* = away from the centre]

ecclesiastical (*say* ik-lee-zee-**ast**-ik-al) *adjective*
to do with the Church or the clergy.
[from Greek *ekklesia* = church]

echo *noun* (*plural* echoes)
a sound that is heard again as it is reflected off
something.
echo *verb* (echoes, echoing, echoed)
1 make an echo. 2 repeat a sound or saying.
[from Greek *eche* = sound]

éclair (*say* ay-**klair**) *noun* (*plural* éclairs)
a finger-shaped cake of pastry with a creamy
filling. [French]

eclipse *noun* (*plural* eclipses)
the blocking of the sun's or moon's light when
the moon or the earth is in the way.

eco- *prefix*
to do with ecology or the environment. [from
ecology]

ecology (*say* ee-**kol**-o-jee) *noun*
the study of living things in relation to each
other and to where they live.
ecological *adjective*, **ecologically** *adverb*,
ecologist *noun*
[from Greek *oikos* = house, + *-logy*]

economic (*say* ee-kon-**om**-ik) *adjective*
1 to do with economy or economics.
2 profitable.

economical *adjective*
using as little as possible.
economically *adverb*

economics *noun*
the study of how money is used and how goods
and services are provided and used.
economist *noun*

economize *verb* (economizes, economizing,
economized)
be economical; use or spend less.

economy *noun* (*plural* economies)
1 a country's or household's income (e.g. from
what it sells or earns) and the way this is spent
(e.g. on goods and services). 2 being
economical. 3 a saving, *We made economies.*
[from Greek *oikos* = house + *-nomia*
= management]

ecstasy (*say* ek-sta-see) *noun*
1 a feeling of great delight. 2 an illegal drug
that makes people feel very energetic and can
cause hallucinations.
ecstatic (*say* ik-**stat**-ik) *adjective*,
ecstatically *adverb*
[from Greek, = standing outside yourself]

-ed *suffix*
can form a past tense or past participle of a
verb (e.g. *paint/painted*), or an adjective (e.g.
diseased). [from Old English]

eddy *noun* (*plural* eddies)
a swirling patch of water or air or smoke etc.

edge *noun* (*plural* edges)
1 the part along the side or end of something.
2 the sharp part of a knife or axe or other
cutting instrument.
be on edge be tense and irritable.

edgy *adjective*
tense and irritable. **edginess** *noun*

edible *adjective*
suitable for eating, not poisonous, *edible fruits.*
[from Latin *edere* = eat]

edit *verb* (edits, editing, edited)
1 be the editor of a newspaper or other
publication. 2 make written material ready for
publishing. 3 choose and put the parts of a film
or tape recording etc. into order.
[from *editor*]

edition *noun* (*plural* editions)
1 the form in which something is published, *a
paperback edition.* 2 all the copies of a book etc.
issued at the same time, *the first edition.* 3 an
individual television or radio programme in a
series.

editor *noun* (*plural* editors)
1 the person in charge of a newspaper or a
section of it. 2 a person who edits something.
[Latin, = producer]

editorial *adjective*
to do with editing or editors.
editorial *noun* (*plural* editorials)
a newspaper article giving the editor's
comments on something.

educate *verb* (educates, educating, educated)
provide people with education. **educative**
adjective, **educator** *noun* [from Latin]

education *noun*
the process of training people's minds and abilities so that they acquire knowledge and develop skills. **educational** *adjective*, **educationally** *adverb*, **educationist** *noun*

-ee *suffix*
forms nouns meaning 'person affected by or described as' (e.g. *absentee, employee, refugee*). [from French]

EEC *abbreviation*
European Economic Community (= the Common Market).

eel *noun* (*plural* **eels**)
a long fish that looks like a snake.

eerie *adjective* (**eerier, eeriest**)
strange in a frightening or mysterious way. **eerily** *adverb*, **eeriness** *noun*

ef- *prefix*
1 out; away. 2 up, upwards; thoroughly. 3 formerly. see **ex-**.

effect *noun* (*plural* **effects**)
1 a change that is produced by an action or cause; a result. 2 an impression that is produced by something, *a cheerful effect.*

USAGE: Do not confuse with *affect.*

effective *adjective*
1 producing the effect that is wanted. 2 impressive and striking. **effectively** *adverb*, **effectiveness** *noun*

effeminate *adjective*
(of a man) having qualities that are thought to be feminine. **effeminacy** *noun*

efficient *adjective*
doing work well; effective. **efficiently** *adverb*, **efficiency** *noun*

effort *noun* (*plural* **efforts**)
1 the use of energy; the energy used. 2 something difficult or tiring. 3 an attempt, *This painting is a good effort.*

e.g. *abbreviation*
for example. [short for Latin *exempli gratia* = for the sake of an example]

egg[1] *noun* (*plural* **eggs**)
1 a more or less round object produced by the female of birds, fishes, reptiles, and insects, which may develop into a new individual if fertilized. 2 a hen's or duck's egg used as food. 3 an ovum. [from Old Norse]

egg[2] *verb* (**eggs, egging, egged**)
encourage someone with taunts or dares etc., *We egged him on.* [from Old Norse *eggja* = sharpen]

ego (*say* eeg-oh) *noun* (*plural* **egos**)
a person's self or self-respect. [Latin, = I]

Eid (*say* eed) *noun*
a Muslim festival. Eid ul-Fitr marks the end of the fast of Ramadan. [from Arabic *'id* = feast]

eiderdown *noun* (*plural* **eiderdowns**)
a quilt stuffed with soft material. [originally the soft down of the *eider*, a kind of duck]

eight *noun* & *adjective* (*plural* **eights**)
the number 8. **eighth** *adjective* & *noun*

eighteen *noun* & *adjective* (*plural* **eighteens**)
the number 18. **eighteenth** *adjective* & *noun*

eighty *noun* & *adjective* (*plural* **eighties**)
the number 80. **eightieth** *adjective* & *noun*

either *adjective* & *pronoun*
1 one or the other of two, *Either team can win*; *either of them.* 2 both of two, *There are fields on either side of the river.*
either *adverb*
also; similarly, *If you won't go, I won't either.*
either *conjunction* (used with *or*)
the first of two possibilities, *He is either ill or drunk. Either come right in or go away.*

ejaculate *verb* (**ejaculates, ejaculating, ejaculated**)
1 (of a man) produce semen from the penis. 2 suddenly say something. **ejaculation** *noun* [from *e-* + Latin *jacere* = to throw]

eject *verb* (**ejects, ejecting, ejected**)
1 send something out forcefully. 2 force someone to leave. 3 (of a pilot) be thrown out of an aircraft in a special seat in an emergency. **ejection** *noun*, **ejector** *noun* [from *e-* + Latin *-jectum* = thrown]

elaborate (*say* il-ab-er-at) *adjective*
having many parts or details; complicated. **elaborately** *adverb*, **elaborateness** *noun*
elaborate (*say* il-ab-er-ayt) *verb* (**elaborates, elaborating, elaborated**)
explain or work something out in detail. **elaboration** *noun* [from *e-* + Latin *laborare* = to work]

elastic *noun*
cord or material woven with strands of rubber etc. so that it can stretch.
elastic *adjective*
able to be stretched or squeezed and then go back to its original length or shape. **elasticity** *noun* [from Greek]

elbow *noun* (*plural* **elbows**)
the joint in the middle of the arm.
elbow *verb* (**elbows, elbowing, elbowed**)
push with the elbow. [from Old English]

elder[1] *adjective*
older, *my elder brother.*
elder *noun* (*plural* **elders**)
1 an older person, *Respect your elders!* 2 an official in certain Churches. [an old spelling of *older*]

elder[2] *noun* (*plural* **elders**)
a tree with white flowers and black berries. **elderberry** *noun* [from Old English]

elderly *adjective*
rather old. [from *elder*[1] + *-ly*]

eldest *adjective*
oldest. [an old spelling of *oldest*]

elect *verb* (elects, electing, elected)
1 choose by voting. 2 choose to do something; decide.
[from *e-* + Latin *lectum* = chosen]

election *noun* (*plural* elections)
electing; the process of electing Members of Parliament.

electorate *noun* (*plural* electorates)
all the electors.

electric *adjective*
1 to do with or worked by electricity. 2 causing sudden excitement, *The news had an electric effect.* **electrical** *adjective*, **electrically** *adverb*
[from Greek *elektron* = amber (which is easily given a charge of static electricity)]

electric chair *noun*
an electrified chair used for capital punishment in the USA.

electrician *noun* (*plural* electricians)
a person whose job is to deal with electrical equipment.

electricity *noun*
a form of energy carried by certain particles of matter (electrons and protons), used for lighting and heating and for making machines work.

electrify *verb* (electrifies, electrifying, electrified)
1 give an electric charge to something.
2 supply something with electric power; cause something to work with electricity. 3 thrill with sudden excitement. **electrification** *noun*

electro- *prefix*
to do with or using electricity.

electrocute *verb* (electrocutes, electrocuting, electrocuted)
kill by electricity. **electrocution** *noun*
[from *electro-* + *execute*]

electrode *noun* (*plural* electrodes)
a solid conductor through which electricity enters or leaves a vacuum tube.
[from *electro-* + Greek *hodos* = way]

electromagnet *noun* (*plural* electromagnets)
a magnet worked by electricity.
electromagnetic *adjective*

electron *noun* (*plural* electrons)
a particle of matter with a negative electric charge. [same origin as *electric*]

electronic *adjective*
produced or worked by a flow of electrons.
electronically *adverb*

electronic mail *noun*
messages sent from one computer to others.

electronics *noun*
the use or study of electronic devices.

elegant *adjective*
graceful and dignified. **elegantly** *adverb*, **elegance** *noun* [from Latin]

element *noun* (*plural* elements)
1 each of the parts that make up a whole thing.
2 each of about 100 substances composed of atoms that have the same number of protons.
3 a basic or elementary principle, *the elements of algebra.* 4 a wire or coil that gives out heat in an electric fire or cooker etc. 5 the environment or circumstances that suit you best, *Karen is really in her element at parties.*
the elements the forces of weather, such as rain, wind, and cold.

elementary *adjective*
dealing with the simplest stages of something; easy.

elephant *noun* (*plural* elephants)
a very large animal with a trunk and tusks.
[from Greek *elephas* = ivory (which its tusks are made of)]

elevate *verb* (elevates, elevating, elevated)
lift or raise something to a higher position.
elevation *noun*
[from *e-* + Latin *levare* = to lift]

eleven *adjective* & *noun* (*plural* elevens)
the number 11. **eleventh** *adjective* & *noun*

elicit (*say* ill-**iss**-it) *verb* (elicits, eliciting, elicited)
draw out information by reasoning or questioning. [from Latin]

eligible (*say* el-ij-ib-ul) *adjective*
qualified or suitable for something.
eligibility *noun*
[from Latin *eligere* = choose]

eliminate *verb* (eliminates, eliminating, eliminated)
get rid of something. **elimination** *noun*
[from *e-* + Latin *limen* = entrance]

elision (*say* il-**lizh**-on) *noun*
omitting part of a word in pronouncing it, e.g. in saying *I'm* for *I am.*
[from Latin *elidere* = to push out]

élite (*say* ay-**leet**) *noun*
a group of people given privileges which are not given to others.
[from old French *élit* = chosen]

ellipse (*say* il-**ips**) *noun* (*plural* ellipses)
an oval shape. [same origin as *elliptical*]

elliptical (*say* il-**ip**-tik-al) *adjective*
1 shaped like an ellipse. 2 with some words omitted, *an elliptical phrase.* **elliptically** *adverb*
[from Greek *elleipsis* = fault]

elm *noun* (*plural* elms)
a tall tree with rough leaves.

elocution (*say* el-o-kew-shon) *noun*
the art of speaking clearly and correctly. [same
origin as *eloquent*]

elongated *adjective*
made longer; lengthened. **elongation** *noun*
[from *e-* + Latin *longus* = long]

elope *verb* (elopes, eloping, eloped)
run away secretly to get married.
elopement *noun* [from old French]

eloquent *adjective*
speaking fluently and expressing ideas vividly.
eloquently *adverb*, **eloquence** *noun*
[from *e-* + Latin *loqui* = speak]

else *adverb*
1 besides; other, *Nobody else knows.*
2 otherwise; if not, *Run or else you'll be late.*
[from Old English]

elsewhere *adverb*
somewhere else.

elude (*say* il-**ood**) *verb* (eludes, eluding, eluded)
avoid being caught by someone, *The fox eluded
the hounds.* **elusive** *adjective*
[from *e-* + Latin *ludere* = to play]

USAGE: Do not confuse with *allude*.

em- *prefix*
1 in; into. 2 on. see **en-**.

e-mail *noun*
electronic mail.

emancipate (*say* im-an-sip-ayt) *verb*
(emancipates, emancipating, emancipated)
set free from slavery or other restraints.
emancipation *noun*
[from *e-* + Latin *mancipium* = slave]

embalm *verb* (embalms, embalming, embalmed)
preserve a corpse from decay by using spices
or chemicals. [from *em-* + *balm*]

embankment *noun* (*plural* embankments)
a long bank of earth or stone to hold back
water or support a road or railway.
[from *em-* + *bank*[1]]

embargo *noun* (*plural* embargoes)
a ban. [from Spanish *embargar* = restrain]

embark *verb* (embarks, embarking, embarked)
put or go on board a ship or aircraft.
embarkation *noun*
embark on begin, *They embarked on a
dangerous exercise.*
[from *em-* + French *barque* = a sailing ship]

embarrass *verb* (embarrasses, embarrassing,
embarrassed)
make someone feel awkward or ashamed.
embarrassment *noun*

embassy *noun* (*plural* embassies)
1 an ambassador and his or her staff.
2 the building where they work.
[from old French; related to *ambassador*]

embellish *verb* (embellishes, embellishing,
embellished)
ornament something; add details to it.
embellishment *noun*
[from *em-* + French *bel* = beautiful]

embers *plural noun*
small pieces of glowing coal or wood in a dying
fire.
[from Old English]

embezzle *verb* (embezzles, embezzling,
embezzled)
take dishonestly money that was left in your
care. **embezzlement** *noun*

emblem *noun* (*plural* emblems)
a symbol that represents something, *The crown
is a royal emblem.*
emblematic *adjective*
[from Latin]

embody *verb* (embodies, embodying, embodied)
1 express principles or ideas in a visible form,
The house embodies our idea of a modern home.
2 include or contain, *Parts of the old treaty are
embodied in the new one.*
embodiment *noun*

embrace *verb* (embraces, embracing, embraced)
1 hold someone closely in your arms. 2 include
a number of things. 3 accept or adopt a cause
or belief.
embrace *noun* (*plural* embraces)
a hug.
[from *em-* + Latin *bracchium* = an arm]

embroider *verb* (embroiders, embroidering,
embroidered)
1 decorate cloth with needlework. 2 add made-
up details to a story to make it more
interesting. **embroidery** *noun*

embryo (*say* em-bree-oh) *noun* (*plural* embryos)
1 a baby or young animal as it starts to grow in
the womb; a young bird growing in an egg.
2 anything in its earliest stages of
development.
embryonic (*say* em-bree-on-ik) *adjective*
[from *em-* + Greek *bryein* = grow]

emend *verb* (emends, emending, emended)
remove errors from a piece of writing.
[from *e-* + Latin *menda* = a fault]

emerald *noun* (*plural* emeralds)
1 a bright-green precious stone. 2 its colour.
[from old French]

emerge *verb* (emerges, emerging, emerged)
1 come out or appear. 2 become known.
emergence *noun*, **emergent** *adjective*
[from *e-* + Latin *mergere* = plunge]

emergency *noun* (*plural* emergencies)
a sudden serious happening needing prompt
action. [same origin as *emerge*]

emigrate *verb* (emigrates, emigrating, emigrated)
leave your own country and go and live in
another. **emigration** *noun*, **emigrant** *noun* [from
e- + Latin *migrare* = migrate]

USAGE: People are *emigrants* from the
country they leave and *immigrants* in the
country where they settle.

eminent *adjective*
famous and respected. **eminence** *noun*,
eminently *adverb*

emit *verb* (emits, emitting, emitted)
send out light, heat, fumes, etc. **emission** *noun*
[from *e-* + Latin *mittere* = send]

emotion *noun* (*plural* emotions)
a strong feeling in the mind, such as love or
hate. **emotional** *adjective*, **emotionally** *adverb*
[from French]

emperor *noun* (*plural* emperors)
a man who rules an empire.
[from Latin *imperator* = commander]

emphasis (*say* em-fa-sis) *noun* (*plural* emphases)
1 special importance given to something.
2 stress put on a word or part of a word.
emphasize *verb* [from *em-* + Greek *phanein* = to
show]

emphatic (*say* im-fat-ik) *adjective*
using emphasis. **emphatically** *adverb*

empire *noun* (*plural* empires)
1 a group of countries controlled by one person
or government. 2 a set of shops or firms under
one control. [from Latin]

employ *verb* (employs, employing, employed)
1 pay a person to work for you. 2 make use of,
Our doctor employs the most modern methods.
employer *noun*, **employment** *noun*

employee *noun* (*plural* employees)
a person employed by someone (who is the
employer).

empress *noun* (*plural* empresses)
1 a woman who rules an empire. 2 an
emperor's wife. [from old French]

empty *adjective*
1 with nothing in it. 2 with nobody in it. 3 with
no meaning or no effect, *empty promises.*
emptily *adverb*, **emptiness** *noun*
empty *verb* (empties, emptying, emptied)
make or become empty. [from Old English]

en- *prefix* (changing to em- before words
beginning with *b*, *m*, or *p*)
1 in; into. 2 on. [from Latin or Greek, = in]

enable *verb* (enables, enabling, enabled)
give the means or ability to do something.

enamel *noun* (*plural* enamels)
1 a shiny substance for coating metal. 2 paint
that dries hard and shiny. 3 the shiny surface
of teeth.

encamp *verb* (encamps, encamping, encamped)
settle in a camp.

encampment *noun* (*plural* encampments)
a camp.

enchant *verb* (enchants, enchanting, enchanted)
1 put someone under a magic spell. 2 fill
someone with intense delight. **enchanter** *noun*,
enchantment *noun*, **enchantress** *noun*
[from old French; related to *incantation*]

encircle *verb* (encircles, encircling, encircled)
surround. **encirclement** *noun*

enclose *verb* (encloses, enclosing, enclosed)
1 put a wall or fence round; shut in on all sides.
2 put something into a box or envelope etc.
[from old French; related to *include*]

enclosure *noun* (*plural* enclosures)
1 enclosing. 2 an enclosed area. 3 something
enclosed with a letter or parcel.

encore (*say* on-kor) *noun* (*plural* encores)
an extra item performed at a concert etc. after
previous items have been applauded.

encounter *verb* (encounters, encountering,
encountered)
1 meet someone unexpectedly. 2 experience,
We encountered some difficulties.
encounter *noun* (*plural* encounters)
1 an unexpected meeting. 2 a battle.
[from *en-* + Latin *contra* = against]

encourage *verb* (encourages, encouraging,
encouraged)
1 give confidence or hope; hearten. 2 try to
persuade; urge. 3 stimulate; help to develop,
Encourage healthy eating. **encouragement** *noun*
[from *en-* + old French *corage* = courage]

encroach *verb* (encroaches, encroaching,
encroached)
intrude upon someone's rights; go further than
the proper limits, *The extra work would
encroach on their free time.* **encroachment** *noun*

encrust *verb* (encrusts, encrusting, encrusted)
cover with a crust or layer. **encrustation** *noun*
[from Latin]

encumber *verb* (encumbers, encumbering,
encumbered)
be a burden to; hamper. **encumbrance** *noun*
[from *en-* + old French *combre* = dam]

encyclopedia *noun* (*plural* encyclopedias)
a book or set of books containing all kinds of
information. **encyclopedic** *adjective*
[from Greek *enkyklopaideia* = general
education]

end *noun* (*plural* ends)
1 the last part or extreme point of something.
2 the half of a sports pitch or court defended or
occupied by one team or player. 3 destruction
or death. 4 purpose, *She did it to gain her own
ends.*
end *verb* (ends, ending, ended)
bring or come to an end.

endanger *verb* (endangers, endangering, endangered)
cause danger to.

endless *adjective*
1 never stopping. 2 with the ends joined to make a continuous strip for use in machinery etc., *an endless belt.*
endlessly *adverb*

endow *verb* (endows, endowing, endowed)
1 provide a source of income to establish something, *She endowed a scholarship.*
2 provide with an ability or quality, *He was endowed with great talent.* **endowment** *noun*
[from old French; related to *dowry*]

endure *verb* (endures, enduring, endured)
1 suffer or put up with pain or hardship etc. 2 continue to exist; last.
endurable *adjective*, **endurance** *noun*
[from *en-* + Latin *durus* = hard]

enemy *noun* (*plural* enemies)
1 one who hates and opposes or seeks to harm another. 2 a nation or army etc. at war with another. [from old French]

energetic *adjective*
full of energy. **energetically** *adverb*

energy *noun* (*plural* energies)
1 strength to do things, liveliness. 2 the ability of matter or radiation to do work. Energy is measured in joules.
[from *en-* + Greek *ergon* = work]

enforce *verb* (enforces, enforcing, enforced)
compel people to obey a law or rule.
enforcement *noun*, **enforceable** *adjective*

engage *verb* (engages, engaging, engaged)
1 arrange to employ or use, *Engage a typist.*
2 occupy the attention of, *They engaged her in conversation.* 3 begin a battle with, *We engaged the enemy.*

engaged *adjective*
1 having promised to marry somebody. 2 in use; occupied.

engagement *noun* (*plural* engagements)
1 engaging something. 2 a promise to marry somebody. 3 an arrangement to meet somebody or do something. 4 a battle.

engaging *adjective*
attractive or charming.

engine *noun* (*plural* engines)
1 a machine that provides power. 2 a vehicle that pulls a railway train; a locomotive.
[from old French; related to *ingenious*]

engineer *noun* (*plural* engineers)
an expert in engineering.
engineer *verb* (engineers, engineering, engineered)
plan and construct or cause to happen, *He engineered a meeting between them.*

engineering *noun*
the design and building or control of machinery or of structures such as roads and bridges.

engrave *verb* (engraves, engraving, engraved)
carve words or lines etc. on a surface.
engraver *noun*, **engraving** *noun*
[from *en-* + Old English *grafan* = carve]

enigma (*say* in-ig-ma) *noun* (*plural* enigmas)
something very difficult to understand; a puzzle. [from Greek]

enigmatic (*say* en-ig-mat-ik) *adjective*
mysterious and puzzling.
enigmatically *adverb*

enjoy *verb* (enjoys, enjoying, enjoyed)
get pleasure from something.
enjoyable *adjective*, **enjoyment** *noun*
[from *en-* + old French *joir* = rejoice]

enlarge *verb* (enlarges, enlarging, enlarged)
make or become bigger. **enlargement** *noun*

enlighten *verb* (enlightens, enlightening, enlightened)
give more knowledge or information to a person. **enlightenment** *noun*

enlist *verb* (enlists, enlisting, enlisted)
1 join the armed forces. 2 obtain someone's support or services etc., *enlist their help.*
enlistment *noun*

enmity *noun*
being somebody's enemy; hostility.

enormous *adjective*
very large; huge.
enormously *adverb*, **enormousness** *noun*
[from *e-* + Latin *norma* = standard]

enough *adjective* & *noun* & *adverb*
as much or as many as necessary, *enough food*; *I have had enough*; *Are you warm enough?*
[from Old English]

enquire *verb* (enquires, enquiring, enquired)
1 ask for information, *He enquired if I was well.*
2 investigate something carefully.
[same origin as *inquire*]

USAGE: See the note at *inquire*.

enquiry *noun* (*plural* enquiries)
1 a question. 2 an investigation.

enrage *verb* (enrages, enraging, enraged)
make someone very angry.

enrich *verb* (enriches, enriching, enriched)
make richer. **enrichment** *noun*

enrol *verb* (enrols, enrolling, enrolled)
1 become a member of a society etc. 2 make someone into a member. **enrolment** *noun*
[from *en-* + old French *rolle* = roll]

ensemble (*say* on-**sombl**) *noun* (*plural* ensembles)
1 a group of things that go together. 2 a group of musicians. 3 a matching outfit of clothes. [French]

enslave *verb* (enslaves, enslaving, enslaved) make a slave of someone; force someone into slavery. **enslavement** *noun*

ensure *verb* (ensures, ensuring, ensured) make certain of; guarantee, *Good food will ensure good health.* [from old French]

USAGE: Do not confuse with *insure.*

entail *verb* (entails, entailing, entailed) make a thing necessary; involve, *This plan entails danger.* **entailment** *noun* [from *en-* + old French *taillir* = bequeath]

entangle *verb* (entangles, entangling, entangled) tangle. **entanglement** *noun*

enter *verb* (enters, entering, entered)
1 come in or go in. 2 put something into a list or book. 3 type something into a computer. 4 register as a competitor. [from Latin *intra* = within]

enterprise *noun* (*plural* enterprises)
1 being enterprising; adventurous spirit. 2 an undertaking or project. 3 business activity, *private enterprise.* [from *en-* + Latin *prehendere* = take]

enterprising *adjective* willing to undertake new or adventurous projects.

entertain *verb* (entertains, entertaining, entertained)
1 amuse. 2 have people as guests and give them food and drink. 3 consider, *He refused to entertain the idea.* **entertainer** *noun*

entertainment *noun* (*plural* entertainments)
1 entertaining; being entertained. 2 something performed before an audience to amuse or interest them.

enthusiasm *noun* (*plural* enthusiasms) a strong liking, interest, or excitement. **enthusiast** *noun*, **enthusiastic** *adjective* [from Greek *enthousiazein* = be possessed by a god]

entire *adjective* whole or complete. **entirely** *adverb* [from old French; related to *integer*]

entirety (*say* int-**I**-rit-ee) *noun* the whole of something.
in its entirety in its complete form.

entitle *verb* (entitles, entitling, entitled) give the right to have something, *This coupon entitles you to a ticket.* **entitlement** *noun* [from old French]

entitled *adjective* having as a title, *a short poem entitled 'Spring'.*

entomology (*say* en-tom-ol-ojee) *noun* the study of insects. **entomologist** *noun* [from Greek *entomon* = insect, + *-logy*]

entrance[1] (*say* en-trans) *noun* (*plural* entrances)
1 the way into a place. 2 entering, *Her entrance is the signal for applause.* [from old French]

entrance[2] (*say* in-**trahns**) *verb* (entrances, entrancing, entranced) fill with intense delight; enchant. [from *en-* + *trance*]

entrant *noun* (*plural* entrants) someone who enters for an examination or contest etc. [from French]

entrench *verb* (entrenches, entrenching, entrenched)
1 fix or establish firmly, *These ideas are entrenched in his mind.* 2 settle in a well-defended position. **entrenchment** *noun*

entrust *verb* (entrusts, entrusting, entrusted) place a person or thing in someone's care.

entry *noun* (*plural* entries)
1 an entrance. 2 something entered in a list or in a diary etc.

entwine *verb* (entwines, entwining, entwined) twine round.

enumerate *verb* (enumerates, enumerating, enumerated) count; list one by one. [from *e-* + Latin *numerare* = to number]

envelop (*say* en-**vel**-op) *verb* (envelops, enveloping, enveloped) cover or wrap round something completely. [from old French]

envelope (*say* en-vel-ohp) *noun* (*plural* envelopes) a wrapper or covering, especially a folded cover for a letter. [from French]

envious *adjective* feeling envy. **enviously** *adverb*

environment *noun* (*plural* environments)
1 surroundings, especially as they affect people's lives. 2 the natural world of the land, sea, and air. **environmental** *adjective* [from old French *environer* = surround, enclose]

environmentalist *noun* (*plural* environmentalists) a person who wishes to protect or improve the environment.

environmentally-friendly *adjective* not harmful to the environment.

envy *noun*
1 a feeling of discontent you have when someone possesses things that you would like to have for yourself. 2 something causing this, *Their car is the envy of all their friends.*

envy *verb* (envies, envying, envied)
feel envy towards someone.
[from French; related to *invidious*]

enzyme *noun* (*plural* enzymes)
a kind of substance that assists chemical
processes.
[from Greek *enzymos* = leavened]

epi- *prefix*
on; above; in addition.
[from Greek *epi* = on]

epic *noun* (*plural* epics)
1 a long poem or story about heroic deeds or
history. **2** a spectacular film.
[from Greek *epos* = song]

epicentre *noun* (*plural* epicentres)
the point where an earthquake reaches the
earth's surface.
[from *epi-* + Greek *kentros* = centre]

epidemic *noun* (*plural* epidemics)
an outbreak of a disease that spreads quickly
among the people of an area.
[from *epi-* + Greek *demos* = people]

epigram *noun* (*plural* epigrams)
a short witty saying. [from *epi-* + *-gram*]

epilepsy *noun*
a disease of the nervous system, causing
convulsions. **epileptic** *adjective* & *noun* [from
Greek *epilambanein* = seize, attack]

epilogue (*say* ep-il-og) *noun* (*plural* epilogues)
a short section at the end of a book or
play etc.
[from *epi-* + Greek *logos* = speech]

episode *noun* (*plural* episodes)
1 one event in a series of happenings. **2** one
programme in a radio or television serial.

epitaph *noun* (*plural* epitaphs)
words written on a tomb or describing a person
who has died.
[from *epi-* + Greek *taphos* = tomb]

epithet *noun* (*plural* epithets)
an adjective; words expressing something
special about a person or thing, e.g. 'the Great'
in *Alfred the Great*.
[from Greek *epithetos* = attributed]

equal *adjective*
1 the same in amount, size, or value etc.
2 having the necessary strength, courage, or
ability etc., *She was equal to the task*.
equally *adverb*
equal *noun* (*plural* equals)
a person or thing that is equal to another, *She
has no equal*.
equal *verb* (equals, equalling, equalled)
be the same in amount, size, or value etc.

equality *noun*
being equal.

equalize *verb* (equalizes, equalizing, equalized)
make things equal. **equalization** *noun*

equation *noun* (*plural* equations)
a statement that two amounts etc. are equal,
e.g. 3 + 4 = 2 + 5.

equator *noun* (*plural* equators)
an imaginary line round the Earth at an equal
distance from the North and South Poles. [from
Latin *circulus aequator diei et noctis* = circle
equalizing day and night]

equatorial (*say* ek-wa-**tor**-ee-al) *adjective*
to do with or near the equator.

equi- *prefix*
equal; equally. [from Latin *aequus* = equal]

equilateral (*say* ee-kwi-**lat**-er-al) *adjective*
(of a triangle) having all sides equal.

equilibrium (*say* ee-kwi-**lib**-ree-um) *noun*
1 a balance between different forces,
influences, etc. **2** a balanced state of mind.
[from *equi-* + Latin *libra* = balance]

equinox (*say* ek-win-oks) *noun* (*plural*
equinoxes)
the time of year when day and night are equal
in length (about 20 March in spring, about 22
September in autumn). **equinoctial** *adjective*
[from *equi-* + Latin *nox* = night]

equip *verb* (equips, equipping, equipped)
supply with what is needed. [from French]

equipment *noun*
the things needed for a particular purpose.

equivalent *adjective*
equal in importance, meaning, value, etc.
equivalence *noun*
[from *equi-* + Latin *valens* = worth]

-er[1] and **-ier** *suffix*
can form the comparative of adjectives and
adverbs (e.g. *high/higher, lazy/lazier*). [from
Old English *-re*]

-er[2] *suffix*
can form nouns meaning 'a person or thing
that does something' (e.g. *farmer, computer*).
[from Old English *-ere*; in a few words (e.g.
butler, mariner) from Latin: compare *-or*]

era (*say* eer-a) *noun* (*plural* eras)
a period of history. [from Latin]

eradicate *verb* (eradicates, eradicating,
eradicated)
get rid of something; remove all traces of it.
eradication *noun*
[from Latin *eradicare* = root out]

erase *verb* (erases, erasing, erased)
1 rub something out. **2** wipe out a recording on
magnetic tape. **eraser** *noun*
[from *e-* + Latin *rasum* = scraped]

erect *adjective*
standing straight up.
erect *verb* (erects, erecting, erected)
set up or build something. **erection** *noun*,
erector *noun* [from Latin]

erosion *noun*
the wearing away of the earth's surface by the action of water, wind, etc.

erotic *adjective*
arousing sexual feelings. **erotically** *adverb*
[from Greek *eros* = sexual love]

errand *noun* (*plural* **errands**)
a short journey to take a message or fetch goods etc. [from Old English]

erratic (*say* ir-**at**-ik) *adjective*
1 not regular. 2 not reliable. **erratically** *adverb*
[from Latin *erraticus* = wandering]

error *noun* (*plural* **errors**)
a mistake. [same origin as *err*]

erupt *verb* (**erupts, erupting, erupted**)
1 burst out. 2 when a volcano erupts, it shoots out lava. **eruption** *noun*
[from *e-* + Latin *ruptum* = burst]

escalate *verb* (**escalates, escalating, escalated**)
make or become greater, more serious or more intense, *The riots escalated into a war.*
escalation *noun* [from *escalator*]

escalator *noun* (*plural* **escalators**)
a staircase with an endless line of steps moving up or down. [from French *escalade* = scaling a wall with ladders]

escapade (*say* eska-**payd**) *noun* (*plural* **escapades**)
a reckless adventure. [French, = an escape]

escape *verb* (**escapes, escaping, escaped**)
1 get yourself free; get out or away. 2 avoid something, *He escaped punishment.*
escape *noun* (*plural* **escapes**)
1 escaping. 2 a way to escape.
[from French]

escapist *noun* (*plural* **escapists**)
a person who likes to avoid thinking about serious matters by occupying his or her mind in entertainments, daydreams, etc.
escapism *noun*

escort (*say* **ess**-kort) *noun* (*plural* **escorts**)
a person or group accompanying a person or thing, especially as a protection.
escort (*say* iss-**kort**) *verb* (**escorts, escorting, escorted**)
act as an escort to somebody or something.

especial *adjective*
special. [from French]

especially *adverb*
specially; more than anything else.

espionage (*say* **ess**-pee-on-ah*zh*) *noun*
spying. [from French *espion* = spy]

espresso *noun* (*plural* **espressos**)
coffee made by forcing steam through ground coffee beans.
[Italian, = pressed out]

Esq. *abbreviation*
(short for **Esquire**) a title written after a man's surname where no title is used before his name. [an *esquire* was originally a knight's attendant; from Latin *scutarius* = shield-bearer)]

-esque *suffix*
forms adjectives meaning 'like' or 'in the style of' (e.g. *picturesque*). [French]

-ess *suffix*
forms feminine nouns (e.g. *lioness, princess*).
[from French]

essay (*say* **ess**-ay) *noun* (*plural* **essays**)
1 a short piece of writing in prose. 2 an attempt.

essence *noun* (*plural* **essences**)
1 the most important quality or element of something. 2 a concentrated liquid.
[from Latin *esse* = to be]

essential *adjective*
not able to be done without.
essentially *adverb*
essential *noun* (*plural* **essentials**)
an essential thing. [same origin as *essence*]

-est and **-iest** *suffix*
can form the superlative of adjectives and adverbs (e.g. *high/highest, lazy/laziest*). [from Old English]

establish *verb* (**establishes, establishing, established**)
1 set up a business, government, or relationship etc. on a firm basis. 2 show something to be true; prove, *He established his innocence.*
the established Church a country's national Church, established by law.
[from old French; related to *stable*[1]]

establishment *noun* (*plural* **establishments**)
1 establishing something. 2 a business firm or other institution.
the Establishment people who are established in positions of power and influence.

estate *noun* (*plural* **estates**)
1 an area of land with a set of houses or factories on it. 2 a large area of land owned by one person. 3 all that a person owns when he or she dies. 4 (*old use*) a condition or status, *the holy estate of matrimony.* [from old French; related to *state*]

estate agent *noun* (*plural* **estate agents**)
a person whose business is selling or letting houses and land.

esteem *verb* (**esteems, esteeming, esteemed**)
think that a person or thing is excellent.
esteem *noun*
respect and admiration.
[same origin as *estimate*]

estimable *adjective*
worthy of esteem.

estimate (*say* ess-tim-at) *noun* (*plural* **estimates**)
a rough calculation or guess about an amount or value.
estimate (*say* ess-tim-ayt) *verb* (**estimates, estimating, estimated**)
make an estimate. **estimation** *noun*
[from Latin *aestimare* = to put a value on something]

estuary (*say* ess-tew-er-ee) *noun* (*plural* **estuaries**)
the mouth of a river where it reaches the sea and the tide flows in and out.
[from Latin *aestus* = tide]

etc. *abbreviation*
(short for **et cetera**) and other similar things; and so on.
[from Latin *et* = and + *cetera* = the other things]

etch *verb* (**etches, etching, etched**)
1 engrave a picture with acid on a metal plate, especially for printing. 2 if something is etched on your mind or memory, it has made a deep impression and you will never forget it.
etcher *noun* [from Dutch]

eternal *adjective*
lasting for ever; not ending or changing.
eternally *adverb*, **eternity** *noun*
[from old French]

ether (*say* ee-ther) *noun*
1 a colourless liquid that evaporates easily into fumes that are used as an anaesthetic. 2 the upper air. [from Greek]

ethereal (*say* ith-eer-ee-al) *adjective*
light and delicate. **ethereally** *adverb*
[from Latin *aetherius* = belonging to the upper air]

ethical (*say* eth-ik-al) *adjective*
1 to do with ethics. 2 morally right; honourable. **ethically** *adverb*

ethics (*say* eth-iks) *plural noun*
standards of right behaviour; moral principles.
[from Greek *ethos* = character]

ethnic *adjective*
belonging to a particular racial group within a larger set of people.
[from Greek *ethnos* = nation]

ethnic cleansing *noun*
the mass killing of people from other ethnic or religious groups within a certain area.

etiquette (*say* et-ik-et) *noun*
the rules of correct behaviour.

-ette *suffix*
forms diminutives which mean 'little' (e.g. *cigarette, kitchenette*). [from French]

etymology (*say* et-im-ol-oj-ee) *noun* (*plural* **etymologies**)
1 an account of the origin of a word and its meaning. 2 the study of the origins of words.
etymological *adjective*
[from Greek *etymon* = original word, + *-logy*]

EU *abbreviation*
European Union.

eu- (*say* yoo) *prefix*
well. [from Greek]

Eucharist (*say* yoo-ker-ist) *noun*
the Christian sacrament in which bread and wine are consecrated and swallowed, commemorating the Last Supper of Christ and his disciples.
[from Greek *eucharistia* = thanksgiving]

eulogy (*say* yoo-loj-ee) *noun* (*plural* **eulogies**)
a piece of praise for a person or thing.
[from *eu-* + Greek *-logia* = speaking]

euphemism (*say* yoo-fim-izm) *noun* (*plural* **euphemisms**)
a mild word or phrase used instead of an offensive or frank one; *'to pass away'* is a euphemism for *'to die'*. **euphemistic** *adjective*, **euphemistically** *adverb*
[from *eu-* + Greek *pheme* = speech]

euro *noun* (*plural* **euros** or **euro**)
the single currency introduced in the EU in 1999.

European *adjective*
to do with Europe or its people.
European *noun*

euthanasia (*say* yooth-an-ay-zee-a) *noun*
the act of causing somebody to die gently and without pain, especially when they are suffering from a painful incurable disease.
[from *eu-* + Greek *thanatos* = death]

evacuate *verb* (**evacuates, evacuating, evacuated**)
1 move people away from a dangerous place. 2 make a thing empty of air or other contents.
evacuation *noun*
[from *e-* + Latin *vacuus* = empty]

evacuee *noun* (*plural* **evacuees**)
a person who has been evacuated.

evade *verb* (**evades, evading, evaded**)
avoid a person or thing by cleverness or trickery. [from *e-* + Latin *vadere* = go]

evaluate *verb* (**evaluates, evaluating, evaluated**)
estimate the value of something; assess.
evaluation *noun*
[from French]

evaporate *verb* (**evaporates, evaporating, evaporated**)
1 change from liquid into steam or vapour. 2 cease to exist, *Their enthusiasm had evaporated.* **evaporation** *noun*
[from *e-* = out + Latin *vapor* = steam]

evasion *noun* (*plural* **evasions**)
1 evading. 2 an evasive answer or excuse.

evasive *adjective*
evading something; not frank or straightforward.
evasively *adverb*, **evasiveness** *noun*

even[1] *adjective*
1 level and smooth. 2 not varying. 3 calm; not easily upset, *an even temper.* 4 equal, *Our scores were even.* 5 able to be divided exactly by two, *Six and fourteen are even numbers.* (Compare *odd.*)
evenly *adverb*, **evenness** *noun*
even *verb* (evens, evening, evened)
make or become even.

even *adverb*
(used to emphasize a word or statement) *She ran even faster.*
even so although that is correct.

evening *noun* (*plural* evenings)
the time at the end of the day before most people go to bed.
[from Old English]

event *noun* (*plural* events)
1 something that happens, especially something important. 2 a race or competition that forms part of a sports contest.
[from Latin *evenire* = happen]

eventful *adjective*
full of happenings.

eventual *adjective*
happening at last, *his eventual success.*
eventually *adverb*
[from Latin *eventus* = result, event]

ever *adverb*
1 at any time, *the best thing I ever did.*
2 always, *ever hopeful.* 3 (*informal*, used for emphasis), *Why ever didn't you tell me?*

evergreen *adjective*
having green leaves all the year.
evergreen *noun*

every *adjective*
each without any exceptions, *We enjoyed every minute.*
every one each one.
every other day or **week** etc., each alternate one; every second one.

USAGE: Follow with a singular verb, e.g. *Every one of them is growing* (not 'are growing').

everybody *pronoun*
every person.

everyday *adjective*
ordinary; usual, *everyday clothes.*

everyone *pronoun*
everybody.

everything *pronoun*
1 all things; all. 2 the only or most important thing, *Beauty is not everything.*

everywhere *adverb*
in every place.

evict *verb* (evicts, evicting, evicted)
make people move out from where they are living. **eviction** *noun*
[from Latin *evictum* = expelled]

evidence *noun*
1 anything that gives people reason to believe something. 2 statements made or objects produced in a lawcourt to prove something.
[same origin as *evident*]

evident *adjective*
obvious; clearly seen. **evidently** *adverb*
[from *e-* + Latin *videre* = see]

evil *adjective*
morally bad; wicked. **evilly** *adverb*
evil *noun* (*plural* evils)
1 wickedness. 2 something unpleasant or harmful. [from Old English]

evolution (*say* ee-vol-oo-shon) *noun*
1 evolving; gradual change into something different. 2 the development of animals and plants from earlier or simpler forms.
evolutionary *adjective*

evolve *verb* (evolves, evolving, evolved)
develop gradually or naturally.
[from *e-* + Latin *volvere* = to roll]

ewe (*say* yoo) *noun* (*plural* ewes)
a female sheep. [from Old English]

ex- *prefix* (changing to **ef-** before words beginning with *f*; shortened to **e-** before many consonants)
1 out; away (as in *extract*). 2 up, upwards; thoroughly (as in *excel*). 3 formerly (as in *ex-president*). [from Latin *ex* = out of]

exact *adjective*
1 correct. 2 clearly stated; giving all details, *exact instructions.*
exactly *adverb*, **exactness** *noun*
exact *verb* (exacts, exacting, exacted)
insist on something and obtain it, *He exacted obedience from the recruits.*
exaction *noun*
[from *ex-* + Latin *actum* = performed]

exaggerate *verb* (exaggerates, exaggerating, exaggerated)
make something seem bigger, better, or worse etc. than it really is.
exaggeration *noun*
[from *ex-* + Latin *aggerare* = heap up]

examination *noun* (*plural* examinations)
1 a test of a person's knowledge or skill. 2 examining something; an inspection.

examine *verb* (examines, examining, examined)
1 test a person's knowledge or skill. 2 inspect; look at something closely. **examiner** *noun*
[from Latin *examinare* = weigh accurately]

example 136 **excuse**

example *noun* (*plural* **examples**)
1 anything that shows what others of the same kind are like or how they work. **2** a person or thing good enough to be worth imitating. [from Latin]

exasperate *verb* (**exasperates, exasperating, exasperated**)
annoy someone greatly. **exasperation** *noun* [from *ex-* + Latin *asper* = rough]

excavate *verb* (**excavates, excavating, excavated**)
dig out; uncover by digging. **excavation** *noun*, **excavator** *noun* [from *ex-* + Latin *cavus* = hollow]

exceed *verb* (**exceeds, exceeding, exceeded**)
1 be greater than; surpass. **2** do more than you need or ought to do; go beyond a thing's limits, *He has exceeded his authority.* [from *ex-* + Latin *cedere* = go]

excel *verb* (**excels, excelling, excelled**)
be better than others at doing something. [from *ex-* + Latin *celsus* = lofty]

Excellency *noun* (*plural* **Excellencies**)
the title of high officials such as ambassadors and governors. [from Latin]

excellent *adjective*
extremely good. **excellently** *adverb*, **excellence** *noun* [from Latin]

except *preposition*
excluding; not including, *They all left except me.*

except *verb* (**excepts, excepting, excepted**)
exclude; leave out, *I blame you all, no one is excepted.* [from *ex-* + Latin *-ceptum* = taken]

USAGE: Do not confuse with *accept.*

exception *noun* (*plural* **exceptions**)
a person or thing that is left out or does not follow the general rule.
take exception raise objections to something.
with the exception of except.

exceptional *adjective*
1 forming an exception; very unusual. **2** outstandingly good. **exceptionally** *adverb*

excess *noun* (*plural* **excesses**)
too much of something. **excessive** *adjective* [same origin as *exceed*]

exchange *verb* (**exchanges, exchanging, exchanged**)
give something and receive something else for it. **exchangeable** *adjective*
exchange *noun* (*plural* **exchanges**)
1 exchanging. **2** a place where things (especially stocks and shares) are bought and sold, *a stock exchange.* **3** a place where telephone lines are connected to each other when a call is made. [from old French]

exchequer *noun* (*plural* **exchequers**)
a national treasury into which public funds (such as taxes) are paid.

[from Latin *scaccarium* = chessboard (because the Norman kings kept their accounts by means of counters placed on a chequered tablecloth)]

excitable *adjective*
easily excited.

excite *verb* (**excites, exciting, excited**)
1 rouse a person's feelings; make eager, *The thought of finding gold excited them.* **2** cause a feeling; arouse, *The invention excited great interest.* **excitedly** *adverb* [from *ex-* + Latin *citum* = woken, stirred]

excitement *noun* (*plural* **excitements**)
a strong feeling of eagerness or pleasure.

exclaim *verb* (**exclaims, exclaiming, exclaimed**)
shout or cry out in eagerness or surprise. [from *ex-* + Latin *clamare* = cry]

exclamation *noun* (*plural* **exclamations**)
1 exclaiming. **2** a word or words cried out expressing joy or pain or surprise etc.

exclamation mark *noun* (*plural* **exclamation marks**)
the punctuation mark ! placed after an exclamation.

exclude *verb* (**excludes, excluding, excluded**)
1 keep somebody or something out. **2** leave something out, *Do not exclude the possibility of rain.* **exclusion** *noun* [from *ex-* + Latin *claudere* = shut]

exclusive *adjective*
1 allowing only certain people to be members etc., *an exclusive club.* **2** not shared with others, *This newspaper has an exclusive report.* **exclusively** *adverb*, **exclusiveness** *noun*
exclusive of excluding, not including, *This is the price exclusive of meals.*

excrete *verb* (**excretes, excreting, excreted**)
get rid of waste matter from the body. **excretion** *noun*, **excretory** *adjective* [from *ex-* + Latin *cretum* = separated]

excruciating (*say* iks-**kroo**-shee-ayt-ing) *adjective*
extremely painful; agonizing.
excruciatingly *adverb* [from *ex-* + Latin *cruciatum* = tortured]

excursion *noun* (*plural* **excursions**)
a short journey made for pleasure. [from *ex-* + Latin *cursus* = course]

excuse (*say* iks-**kewz**) *verb* (**excuses, excusing, excused**)
1 forgive. **2** allow someone not to do something or to leave a room etc., *Please may I be excused swimming?*
excuse (*say* iks-**kewss**) *noun* (*plural* **excuses**)
a reason given to explain why something wrong has been done. [from *ex-* + Latin *causa* = accusation]

execute *verb* (executes, executing, executed)
1 put someone to death as a punishment.
2 perform or produce something, *She executed the somersault perfectly*. **execution** *noun* [from Latin *executare* = to carry out]

executive (*say* ig-zek-yoo-tiv) *noun* (*plural* executives)
a senior person with authority in a business or government organization.

exempt *adjective*
not having to do something that others have to do, *Charities are exempt from paying tax.*
exemption *noun*

exercise *noun* (*plural* exercises)
1 using your body to make it strong and healthy. **2** a piece of work done for practice.
exercise *verb* (exercises, exercising, exercised)
1 do exercises. **2** give exercise to an animal etc.
3 use, *exercise patience.*
[from Latin *exercere* = keep someone working]

exert *verb* (exerts, exerting, exerted)
use power or influence etc., *He exerted all his strength.* **exertion** *noun*
exert yourself make an effort.

exhale *verb* (exhales, exhaling, exhaled)
breathe out. **exhalation** *noun*
[from *ex-* + Latin *halare* = breathe]

exhaust *verb* (exhausts, exhausting, exhausted)
1 make somebody very tired. **2** use up something completely. **exhaustion** *noun*
exhaust *noun* (*plural* exhausts)
1 the waste gases or steam from an engine.
2 the pipe etc. through which they are sent out.
[from *ex-* + Latin *haustum* = drained]

exhaustive *adjective*
thorough; trying everything possible, *We made an exhaustive search.*
exhaustively *adverb*

exhibit *verb* (exhibits, exhibiting, exhibited)
show or display something in public.
exhibitor *noun*
exhibit *noun* (*plural* exhibits)
something on display in a gallery or museum.
[from *ex-* + Latin *habere* = hold]

exhibition *noun* (*plural* exhibitions)
a collection of things put on display for people to look at.

exhilarate (*say* ig-zil-er-ayt) *verb* (exhilarates, exhilarating, exhilarated)
make someone very happy and excited.
exhilaration *noun*
[from *ex-* + Latin *hilaris* = cheerful]

exhort (*say* ig-zort) *verb* (exhorts, exhorting, exhorted)
urge someone earnestly. **exhortation** *noun*
[from *ex-* + Latin *hortari* = encourage]

exile *verb* (exiles, exiling, exiled)
banish.

exile *noun* (*plural* exiles)
1 a banished person. **2** having to live away from your own country, *He was in exile for ten years.* [from Latin]

exist *verb* (exists, existing, existed)
1 be present as part of what is real, *Do ghosts exist?* **2** stay alive, *We cannot exist without food.*
existence *noun*, **existent** *adjective*
[from *ex-* + Latin *sistere* = stand]

exit *noun* (*plural* exits)
1 the way out of a building. **2** going off the stage, *The actress made her exit.*
exit *verb*
(in stage directions) he or she leaves the stage.
[Latin, = he or she goes out]

exorcize *verb* (exorcizes, exorcizing, exorcized)
get rid of an evil spirit.
exorcism *noun*, **exorcist** *noun* [from Greek]

exotic *adjective*
1 very unusual, *exotic clothes*. **2** from another part of the world, *exotic plants*.
exotically *adverb*
[from Greek *exo* = outside]

expand *verb* (expands, expanding, expanded)
make or become larger or fuller.
expansion *noun*, **expansive** *adjective*
[from *ex-* + Latin *pandere* = to spread]

expect *verb* (expects, expecting, expected)
1 think or believe that something will happen or that someone will come. **2** think that something ought to happen, *She expects obedience.*
[from *ex-* + Latin *spectare* = to look]

expectant *adjective*
1 expecting something to happen; hopeful. **2** an expectant mother is a woman who is pregnant.
expectantly *adverb*, **expectancy** *noun*

expectation *noun* (*plural* expectations)
1 expecting something; being hopeful.
2 something you expect to happen or get.

expedient (*say* iks-pee-dee-ent) *adjective*
1 suitable or convenient. **2** useful and practical though perhaps unfair. **expediently** *adverb*,
expediency *noun*
expedient *noun* (*plural* expedients)
a means of doing something, especially when in difficulty.

expedition *noun* (*plural* expeditions)
1 a journey made in order to do something.
2 speed or promptness. **expeditionary** *adjective*
[from French; related to *expedite*]

expel *verb* (expels, expelling, expelled)
1 send or force something out, *This fan expels stale air.* **2** make a person leave a school or country etc. **expulsion** *noun*
[from *ex-* + Latin *pellere* = drive]

expendable *adjective*
able to be sacrificed or got rid of in order to gain something.

expenditure *noun* (*plural* expenditures)
the spending or using up of money or effort etc.

expense *noun* (*plural* expenses)
the cost of doing something.

expensive *adjective*
costing a lot.
expensively *adverb*, **expensiveness** *noun*

experience *noun* (*plural* experiences)
1 what you learn from doing or seeing things.
2 something that has happened to you.
experience *verb* (experiences, experiencing, experienced)
have something happen to you.
[same origin as *experiment*]

experienced *adjective*
having great skill or knowledge from much experience.

experiment *noun* (*plural* experiments)
a test made in order to find out what happens or to prove something. **experimental** *adjective*, **experimentally** *adverb*
experiment *verb* (experiments, experimenting, experimented)
carry out an experiment. **experimentation** *noun*
[from Latin *experiri* = to test]

expert *noun* (*plural* experts)
a person with great knowledge or skill in something.
expert *adjective*
having great knowledge or skill.
expertly *adverb*, **expertness** *noun*
[from Latin *expertus* = experienced]

expire *verb* (expires, expiring, expired)
1 come to an end; stop being usable, *Your season ticket has expired.* 2 die. 3 breathe out air. **expiration** *noun*, **expiry** *noun*
[from *ex-* + Latin *spirare* = breathe]

explain *verb* (explains, explaining, explained)
1 make something clear to somebody else; show its meaning. 2 account for something, *That explains his absence.* **explanation** *noun*
[from *ex-* + Latin *planare* = make level or plain]

explicit (*say* iks-**pliss**-it) *adjective*
stated or stating something openly and exactly. (Compare *implicit*.) **explicitly** *adverb* [from Latin *explicitus* = unfolded]

explode *verb* (explodes, exploding, exploded)
1 burst or suddenly release energy with a loud noise. 2 cause a bomb to go off. 3 increase suddenly or quickly.
[originally = to drive a player off the stage by clapping or hissing; from *ex-* + Latin *plaudere* = clap]

exploit (*say* iks-**ploit**) *verb* (exploits, exploiting, exploited)
1 use or develop resources. 2 use a person or thing selfishly. **exploitation** *noun*

explore *verb* (explores, exploring, explored)
1 travel through a country etc. in order to learn about it. 2 examine a subject or idea carefully, *We explored the possibilities.*
exploration *noun*, **explorer** *noun*,
exploratory *adjective*
[from Latin *explorare* = search out]

explosion *noun* (*plural* explosions)
1 the exploding of a bomb etc.; the noise made by exploding. 2 a sudden great increase.

explosive *adjective*
able to explode.
explosive *noun* (*plural* explosives)
an explosive substance.

exponent *noun* (*plural* exponents)
1 a person who expounds something.
2 someone who uses a certain technique. 3 the raised number etc. written to the right of another (e.g. 3 in 2^3) showing how many times the first one is to be multiplied by itself; index.

export *verb* (exports, exporting, exported)
send goods abroad to be sold.
exportation *noun*, **exporter** *noun*
export *noun* (*plural* exports)
1 exporting things. 2 something exported.
[from *ex-* + Latin *portare* = carry]

expose *verb* (exposes, exposing, exposed)
1 reveal or uncover. 2 allow light to reach a photographic film so as to take a picture.
exposure *noun* [from old French]

express *adjective*
1 going or sent quickly. 2 clearly stated, *This was done against my express orders.*
express *noun* (*plural* expresses)
a fast train stopping at only a few stations.
express *verb* (expresses, expressing, expressed)
1 put ideas etc. into words; make your feelings known. 2 press or squeeze out, *Express the juice.* [from old French]

expression *noun* (*plural* expressions)
1 the look on a person's face that shows his or her feelings. 2 a word or phrase etc. 3 a way of speaking or of playing music etc. so as to show your feelings. 4 expressing, *this expression of opinion.*

expressive *adjective*
full of expression.

expulsion *noun* (*plural* expulsions)
expelling or being expelled.

exquisite (*say* eks-**kwiz**-it) *adjective*
very beautiful. **exquisitely** *adverb*
[from Latin *exquisitus* = sought out]

extend *verb* (extends, extending, extended)
1 stretch out. 2 make something become longer or larger. 3 offer or give, *Extend a warm welcome to our friends.*
extendible *adjective*, **extensible** *adjective*
[from *ex-* + Latin *tendere* = to stretch]

extension *noun* (*plural* **extensions**)
1 extending or being extended. **2** something added on; an addition to a building. **3** one of a set of telephones in an office or house etc.

extensive *adjective*
covering a large area or range, *extensive gardens.* **extensively** *adverb*, **extensiveness** *noun*

extent *noun* (*plural* **extents**)
1 the area or length over which something extends. **2** the amount, level, or scope of something, *the full extent of his power.* [from Latin *extenta* = extended]

exterior *adjective*
outer.
exterior *noun* (*plural* **exteriors**)
the outside of something.
[Latin, = further out]

exterminate *verb* (**exterminates, exterminating, exterminated**)
destroy or kill all the members or examples. **extermination** *noun*, **exterminator** *noun* [originally = banish; from *ex-* + Latin *terminus* = boundary]

external *adjective*
outside. **externally** *adverb* [from Latin]

extinct *adjective*
1 not existing any more, *The dodo is an extinct bird.* **2** not burning; not active, *an extinct volcano.* [same origin as *extinguish*]

extinction *noun*
1 making or becoming extinct.
2 extinguishing; being extinguished.

extinguish *verb* (**extinguishes, extinguishing, extinguished**)
1 put out a fire or light. **2** put an end to; destroy, *Our hopes of victory were extinguished.* [from *ex-* + Latin *stinguere* = quench]

extort *verb* (**extorts, extorting, extorted**)
obtain something by force or threats.
extortion *noun*
[from *ex-* + Latin *tortum* = twisted]

extortionate *adjective*
charging or demanding far too much.
[from *extort*]

extra *adjective*
additional; more than is usual, *extra strength.*
extra *adverb*
more than usually, *extra strong.*
extra *noun* (*plural* **extras**)
1 an extra person or thing. **2** a person acting as part of a crowd in a film or play.
[probably from *extraordinary*]

extra- *prefix*
outside; beyond (as in *extraterrestrial*). [from Latin]

extract (*say* iks-**trakt**) *verb* (**extracts, extracting, extracted**)
take out; remove. **extractor** *noun*

extract (*say* eks-**trakt**) *noun* (*plural* **extracts**)
1 a passage taken from a book, speech, film, etc. **2** a substance separated or obtained from another.
[from *ex-* + Latin *tractum* = pulled]

extraction *noun*
1 extracting. **2** someone's descent, *He is of Chinese extraction.*

extraordinary *adjective*
very unusual or strange. **extraordinarily** *adverb* [from Latin *extra ordinem* = out of the ordinary]

extrasensory *adjective*
outside the range of the known human senses.

extraterrestrial *adjective*
from beyond the earth's atmosphere; from outer space.
extraterrestrial *noun* (*plural* **extraterrestrials**)
a being from outer space.

extravagant *adjective*
spending or using too much.
extravagantly *adverb*, **extravagance** *noun*
[from *extra-* + Latin *vagans* = wandering]

extreme *adjective*
1 very great or intense, *extreme cold.* **2** furthest away, *the extreme north.* **3** going to great lengths in actions or opinions; not moderate.
extremely *adverb*
extreme *noun* (*plural* **extremes**)
1 something extreme. **2** either end of something.
[from Latin *extremus* = furthest out]

extricate (*say* eks-**trik-ayt**) *verb* (**extricates, extricating, extricated**)
release from a difficult position.
extrication *noun*
[from *ex-* + Latin *tricae* = entanglements]

extrovert *noun* (*plural* **extroverts**)
a person who is generally friendly and likes company. (The opposite is *introvert.*)

exuberant (*say* ig-**zew**-ber-ant) *adjective*
very lively.
exuberantly *adverb*, **exuberance** *noun*
[from Latin *exuberare* = grow thickly]

exude *verb* (**exudes, exuding, exuded**)
1 give off like sweat or a smell etc. **2** ooze out. [from *ex-* + Latin *sudare* = to sweat]

exult *verb* (**exults, exulting, exulted**)
rejoice greatly.
exultant *adjective*, **exultation** *noun*
[from Latin *exsilire* = leap up]

eye *noun* (*plural* **eyes**)
1 the organ of the body that is used for seeing. **2** the power of seeing, *She has sharp eyes.* **3** the small hole in a needle. **4** the centre of a storm.
eye *verb* (**eyes, eyeing, eyed**)
look at something with interest.
[from Old English]

eyeball *noun* (*plural* eyeballs)
the ball-shaped part of the eye inside the eyelids.

eyebrow *noun* (*plural* eyebrows)
the fringe of hair growing on the face above the eye.

eyelash *noun* (*plural* eyelashes)
one of the short hairs that grow on an eyelid.

eyelid *noun* (*plural* eyelids)
either of the two folds of skin that can close over the eyeball.

eyepiece *noun* (*plural* eyepieces)
the lens of a telescope or microscope etc. that you put to your eye.

eyesight *noun*
the ability to see.

eyewitness *noun* (*plural* eyewitnesses)
a person who actually saw an accident or crime etc.

Ff

fable *noun* (*plural* fables)
a short story that teaches about behaviour, often with animals as characters.
[from Latin *fabula* = story]

fabric *noun* (*plural* fabrics)
1 cloth. 2 the framework of a building (walls, floors, and roof). [from Latin]

fabricate *verb* (fabricates, fabricating, fabricated)
1 construct or manufacture something.
2 invent, *fabricate an excuse*.
fabrication *noun*
[from Latin *fabricare* = to make or forge]

fabulous *adjective*
1 wonderful. 2 incredibly great, *fabulous wealth*. 3 told of in fables. **fabulously** *adverb*
[same origin as *fable*]

façade (*say* fas-**ahd**) *noun* (*plural* façades)
1 the front of a building. 2 an outward appearance, especially a deceptive one.
[French; related to *face*]

face *noun* (*plural* faces)
1 the front part of the head. 2 the expression on a person's face. 3 the front or upper side of something. 4 a surface, *A cube has six faces*.
face *verb* (faces, facing, faced)
1 look or have the front towards something, *Our room faced the sea*. 2 meet and have to deal with something; encounter, *Explorers face many dangers*. 3 cover a surface with a layer of different material.
[from Latin *facies* = appearance]

facetious (*say* fas-ee-**shus**) *adjective*
trying to be funny at an unsuitable time, *facetious remarks*. **facetiously** *adverb*
[from Latin *facetus* = witty]

facilitate (*say* fas-il-it-**ayt**) *verb* (facilitates, facilitating, facilitated)
make something easy or easier.
facilitation *noun*

facility (*say* fas-il-**it-ee**) *noun* (*plural* facilities)
1 something that provides you with the means to do things, *There are sports facilities*.
2 easiness.

facsimile (*say* fak-**sim**-il-ee) *noun* (*plural* facsimiles)
1 an exact reproduction of a document etc. 2 a fax.
[from Latin *fac* = make + *simile* = a likeness]

fact *noun* (*plural* facts)
something that is certainly true.
the facts of life information about how babies are conceived.
[from Latin *factum* = thing done]

faction *noun* (*plural* factions)
a small united group within a larger one, especially in politics. [from Latin]

-faction *suffix*
forms nouns (e.g. *satisfaction*) from verbs that end in *-fy*. [from Latin]

factor *noun* (*plural* factors)
1 something that helps to bring about a result, *Hard work was a factor in her success*. 2 a number by which a larger number can be divided exactly, *2 and 3 are factors of 6*.
[from Latin *facere* = do or make]

factory *noun* (*plural* factories)
a large building where machines are used to make things. [from Latin *factorium* = place where things are made]

faculty *noun* (*plural* faculties)
1 any of the powers of the body or mind (e.g. sight, speech, understanding). 2 a department teaching a particular subject in a university, *the faculty of music*.

fad *noun* (*plural* fads)
1 a person's particular like or dislike.
2 a temporary fashion or craze. **faddy** *adjective*
[originally a dialect word; origin unknown]

fade *verb* (fades, fading, faded)
1 lose or cause to lose colour or freshness or strength. 2 disappear gradually. 3 make a sound etc. become gradually weaker (*fade it out*) or stronger (*fade it in* or *up*).

faeces (*say* **fee**-seez) *plural noun*
solid waste matter passed out of the body.
[plural of Latin *faex* = dregs]

Fahrenheit *adjective*
measuring temperature on a scale where water freezes at 32° and boils at 212°. [named after G. D. Fahrenheit, a German scientist, who invented the mercury thermometer]

fail *verb* (fails, failing, failed)
1 try to do something but be unable to do it. 2 become weak or useless; break down, *The brakes failed.* 3 not do something, *He failed to warn me.* 4 not get enough marks to pass an examination. 5 judge that someone has not passed an examination.
fail *noun*
without fail for certain; whatever happens. [from Latin *fallere* = disappoint, deceive]

failing *noun* (*plural* failings)
a weakness or a fault.

failure *noun* (*plural* failures)
1 not being able to do something. 2 a person or thing that has failed.

faint *adjective*
1 pale or dim; not distinct. 2 weak or giddy; nearly unconscious. 3 slight, *a faint hope.* faintly *adverb*, faintness *noun*
faint *verb* (faints, fainting, fainted)
become unconscious. [same origin as *feint*]

USAGE: Do not confuse with *feint.*

fair¹ *adjective*
1 right or just; according to the rules, *a fair fight.* 2 (of hair or skin) light in colour; (of a person) having fair hair. 3 (*old use*) beautiful. 4 fine or favourable, *fair weather.* 5 moderate; quite good, *a fair number of people.* fairness *noun*
fair *adverb*
fairly, *Play fair!* [from Old English]

fair² *noun* (*plural* fairs)
1 a group of entertainments such as roundabouts and sideshows. 2 an exhibition or market. [from Latin *feriae* = holiday]

fairly *adverb*
1 justly; according to the rules. 2 moderately, *It is fairly hard.*

fairy *noun* (*plural* fairies)
an imaginary very small creature with magic powers. fairyland *noun*, fairy tale *noun* [from an old word *fay*, from Latin *fata* = the Fates, three goddesses who were believed to control people's lives]

faith *noun* (*plural* faiths)
strong belief; trust.
in good faith with honest intentions. [from old French; related to *fidelity*]

faithful *adjective*
1 loyal and trustworthy. 2 sexually loyal to one partner.
faithfully *adverb*, faithfulness *noun*
Yours faithfully see *yours.*

fake *noun* (*plural* fakes)
something that looks genuine but is not; a forgery.
fake *verb* (fakes, faking, faked)
1 make something that looks genuine, in order to deceive people. 2 pretend, *They faked illness.* faker *noun*

falcon *noun* (*plural* falcons)
a kind of hawk often used in the sport of hunting other birds or game. falconry *noun*

fall *verb* (falls, falling, fell, fallen)
1 come or go down without being pushed or thrown etc. 2 decrease; become lower, *Prices fell.* 3 be captured or overthrown, *The city fell.* 4 die in battle. 5 happen, *Silence fell.* 6 become, *She fell asleep.*
fall back retreat.
fall back on use for support or in an emergency.
fall for 1 be attracted by a person.
2 be taken in by a deception.
fall out quarrel.
fall through fail, *plans fell through.*
fall *noun* (*plural* falls)
1 the action of falling. 2 (*American*) autumn, when leaves fall.

fallacy (*say* fal-a-see) *noun* (*plural* fallacies)
a false idea or belief. fallacious (*say* fal-ay-shus) *adjective* [same origin as *fail*]

Fallopian tube *noun* (*plural* Fallopian tubes)
one of the two tubes in a woman's body along which the eggs travel from the ovaries to the uterus.

fallout *noun*
particles of radioactive material carried in the air after a nuclear explosion.

false *adjective*
1 untrue or incorrect. 2 not genuine; faked. 3 treacherous or deceitful.
falsely *adverb*, falseness *noun*, falsity *noun* [same origin as *fail*]

falter *verb* (falters, faltering, faltered)
1 hesitate when you move or speak. 2 become weaker; begin to give way, *His courage faltered.* [origin unknown]

fame *noun*
being famous. famed *adjective* [from Latin *fama* = report, rumour]

familiar *adjective*
1 well-known; often seen or experienced. 2 knowing something well, *Are you familiar with this book?* 3 very friendly.
familiarly *adverb*, familiarity *noun* [from Latin *familias* = family]

family *noun* (*plural* families)
1 parents and their children, sometimes including grandchildren and other relations. 2 a group of things that are alike in some way. [from Latin]

family planning *noun*
birth control.

family tree *noun* (*plural* **family trees**)
a diagram showing how people in a family are related.

famine *noun* (*plural* **famines**)
a very bad shortage of food in an area. [from Latin *fames* = hunger]

famished *adjective*
very hungry. **famishing** *adjective*
[same origin as *famine*]

famous *adjective*
known to very many people.
[same origin as *fame*]

famously *adverb* (*informal*)
very well, *They get on famously.*

fan[1] *noun* (*plural* **fans**)
an object or machine for making air move about so as to cool people or things.
fan *verb* (**fans, fanning, fanned**)
send a current of air on something.
fan out spread out in the shape of a fan.

fan[2] *noun* (*plural* **fans**)
an enthusiast; a great admirer or supporter.
[short for *fanatic*]

fanatic *noun* (*plural* **fanatics**)
a person who is very enthusiastic or too enthusiastic about something.
fanatical *adjective*, **fanatically** *adverb*,
fanaticism *noun*
[from Latin *fanaticus* = inspired by a god]

fanciful *adjective*
1 imagining things. 2 imaginary.

fancy *noun* (*plural* **fancies**)
1 a liking or desire for something.
2 imagination.
fancy *adjective*
decorated or elaborate; not plain.
fancy *verb* (**fancies, fancying, fancied**)
1 believe, *I fancy it's raining.* 2 imagine. 3 have a liking or desire for something.
[short for *fantasy*]

fancy dress *noun*
unusual costume worn for a party, often to make you look like a famous person.

fantastic *adjective*
1 (*informal*) excellent. 2 designed in a very fanciful way. **fantastically** *adverb*
[from Greek *phantazesthai* = imagine]

fantasy *noun* (*plural* **fantasies**)
something imaginary or fantastic.
[same origin as *fantastic*]

far *adverb*
1 at or to a great distance, *We didn't go far.*
2 much; by a great amount, *This is far better.*
far *adjective*
distant or remote, *On the far side of the river.*
[from Old English]

fare *noun* (*plural* **fares**)
1 the price charged for a passenger to travel.
2 food and drink, *There was only very plain fare.*

farewell *interjection* & *noun* (*plural* **farewells**)
goodbye.

farm *noun* (*plural* **farms**)
1 an area of land where someone grows crops or keeps animals for food or other use. 2 the farmer's house. **farmhouse** *noun*, **farmyard** *noun*
farm *verb* (**farms, farming, farmed**)
1 grow crops or keep animals for food etc.
2 use land for growing crops; cultivate.

farmer *noun* (*plural* **farmers**)
a person who owns or manages a farm.

farther *adverb* & *adjective*
at or to a greater distance; more distant.
[a different spelling of *further*]

USAGE: *Farther* and *farthest* are used only in connection with distance (e.g. *She lives farther from the school than I do*), but even in such cases many people prefer to use *further*. Only *further* can be used to mean 'additional', e.g. in *We must make further inquiries*. If you are not sure which is right, use *further*.

farthest *adverb* & *adjective*
at or to the greatest distance; most distant.

USAGE: See the note at *farther*.

farthing *noun* (*plural* **farthings**)
a former British coin worth one-quarter of a penny.
[from Old English *feorthing* = one-fourth]

fascinate *verb* (**fascinates, fascinating, fascinated**)
be very attractive or interesting to somebody.
fascination *noun*, **fascinator** *noun* [from Latin *fascinum* = a spell]

fashion *noun* (*plural* **fashions**)
1 the style of clothes or other things that most people like at a particular time. 2 a way of doing something, *Continue in the same fashion.*
fashionable *adjective*, **fashionably** *adverb*

fast[1] *adjective*
1 moving or done quickly; rapid. 2 allowing fast movement, *a fast road.* 3 showing a time later than the correct time, *Your watch is fast.*
4 firmly fixed or attached. 5 not likely to fade, *fast colours.* **fastness** *noun*
fast *adverb*
1 quickly, *Run fast!* 2 firmly, *His leg was stuck fast in the mud.*
fast asleep in a deep sleep.
[from Old English *faest*]

fast[2] *verb* (**fasts, fasting, fasted**)
go without food. **fast** *noun*
[from Old English *faestan*]

fasten *verb* (fastens, fastening, fastened)
fix one thing firmly to another. **fastener** *noun*,
fastening *noun* [from Old English]

fat *noun* (*plural* fats)
1 the white greasy part of meat. 2 oil or grease
used in cooking.
the fat of the land the best food.
fat *adjective* (fatter, fattest)
1 having a very thick round body. 2 thick, *a fat
book*. 3 full of fat. **fatness** *noun*

fatal *adjective*
causing death or disaster, *a fatal accident*.
fatally *adverb* [from Latin *fatalis* = by fate]

fate *noun* (*plural* fates)
1 a power that is thought to make things
happen. 2 what will happen or has happened to
somebody or something; destiny. [from Latin
fatum, literally = that which has been spoken]

father *noun* (*plural* fathers)
1 a male parent. 2 the title of certain priests.
fatherly *adjective*

father-in-law *noun* (*plural* fathers-in-law)
the father of a married person's husband or
wife.

fatigue *noun*
1 tiredness. 2 weakness in metals, caused by
stress. **fatigued** *adjective*
[from Latin *fatigare* = make weary]

fatten *verb* (fattens, fattening, fattened)
make or become fat.

fatty *adjective*
like fat; containing fat.

fatuous *adjective*
silly or foolish. **fatuously** *adverb*,
fatuousness *noun*, **fatuity** *noun* [from Latin]

fault *noun* (*plural* faults)
1 anything that makes a person or thing
imperfect; a flaw or mistake. 2 the
responsibility for something wrong, *It wasn't
your fault*. 3 a break in a layer of rock.
faulty *adjective*
fault *verb* (faults, faulting, faulted)
1 find faults in something. 2 form a fault. [from
old French; related to *fail*]

fauna *noun*
the animals of a certain area or period of time.
(Compare *flora*.) [from the name of Fauna, an
ancient Roman country goddess, sister of
Faunus (see *faun*)]

favour *noun* (*plural* favours)
1 a kind or helpful act. 2 approval; goodwill.
3 friendly support shown to one person or
group but not to another, *without fear or
favour*.
favour *verb* (favours, favouring, favoured)
be in favour of something; show favour to a
person. [from Latin]

favourable *adjective*
1 showing approval. 2 helpful or
advantageous. **favourably** *adverb*

favourite *adjective*
liked more than others. **favourite** *noun*

fax *noun* (*plural* faxes)
1 a machine that sends an exact copy of a
document electronically. 2 a copy produced by
this.
fax *verb* (faxes, faxing, faxed)
send a copy of a document using a fax machine.
[from *facsimile*]

fear *noun* (*plural* fears)
a feeling that something unpleasant may
happen.
fear *verb* (fears, fearing, feared)
feel fear; be afraid of somebody or something.
[from Old English]

fearful *adjective*
1 feeling fear; afraid. 2 causing fear or horror,
a fearful monster. 3 (*informal*) very great or
bad. **fearfully** *adverb*

fearsome *adjective*
frightening.

feasible *adjective*
1 able to be done; possible. 2 likely or probable,
a feasible explanation.
feasibly *adverb*, **feasibility** *noun*
[from French *faire* = do]

USAGE: The use of *feasible* to mean 'likely or
probable' has not become generally accepted
in standard English, so it is better to avoid it
in writing or formal situations.

feast *noun* (*plural* feasts)
1 a large splendid meal. 2 a religious festival.
feast *verb*
[from old French; related to *fête*]

feather *noun* (*plural* feathers)
one of the very light coverings that grow from
a bird's skin. **feathery** *adjective*
feather *verb* (feathers, feathering, feathered)
cover or line something with feathers.

feature *noun* (*plural* features)
1 any part of the face (e.g. mouth, nose, eyes).
2 an important or noticeable part; a
characteristic. 3 a special newspaper article or
programme that deals with a particular
subject. 4 the main film in a cinema
programme. [from Latin *factura* = a creation]

fed *past tense* of **feed**.
fed up (*informal*) discontented.

federal *adjective*
to do with a system in which several States are
ruled by a central government but are
responsible for their own internal affairs.
federation *noun*
[from Latin *foederis* = of a treaty]

fee *noun* (*plural* fees)
a charge for something. [from old French]

feeble *adjective*
weak; without strength. **feebly** *adverb,*
feebleness *noun*
[from Latin *flebilis* = wept over]

feed *verb* (feeds, feeding, fed)
1 give food to a person or animal. 2 take food.
3 supply something to a machine etc.
feeder *noun*
feed *noun*
food for animals or babies.

feedback *noun*
1 the response you get from people to
something you have done. 2 the harsh noise
produced when some of the sound from an
amplifier goes back into it.

feel *verb* (feels, feeling, felt)
1 touch something to find out what it is like.
2 be aware of something; have an opinion.
3 experience an emotion. 4 give a certain
sensation, *It feels warm.*
feel like want.

feeler *noun* (*plural* feelers)
1 a long thin projection on an insect's or
crustacean's body, used for feeling; an antenna.
2 a cautious question or suggestion etc. to test
people's reactions.

feeling *noun* (*plural* feelings)
1 the ability to feel things; the sense of touch.
2 what a person feels.

feint (*say* faynt) *noun* (*plural* feints)
a pretended attack or punch meant to deceive
an opponent.
feint *verb* (feints, feinting, feinted)
make a feint. [old French, = feigned]

USAGE: Do not confuse with *faint.*

fell[1] *past tense* of **fall**.

fell[2] *verb* (fells, felling, felled)
make something fall; cut or knock down, *They
were felling the trees.*

fellow *noun* (*plural* fellows)
1 a friend or companion; one who belongs to
the same group. 2 a man or boy. 3 a member of
a learned society.
fellow *adjective*
of the same group or kind, *Her fellow teachers
supported her.* [from Old Norse]

fellowship *noun* (*plural* fellowships)
1 friendship. 2 a group of friends; a society.

felt[1] *past tense* of **feel**.

felt[2] *noun*
a thick fabric made of fibres of wool or fur etc.
pressed together. [from Old English]

female *adjective*
of the sex that can bear offspring or produce
eggs or fruit.

female *noun* (*plural* females)
a female person, animal, or plant.
[from Latin *femina* = woman]

feminine *adjective*
1 to do with or like women; suitable for
women. 2 (in some languages) belonging to the
class of words which includes the words
referring to women. **femininity** *noun*
[same origin as *female*]

feminist *noun* (*plural* feminists)
a person who believes that women should be
given the same rights and status as men.
feminism *noun*

fence *noun* (*plural* fences)
1 a barrier made of wood or wire etc. round an
area. 2 a structure for a horse to jump over. 3 a
person who buys stolen goods and sells them
again.
fence *verb* (fences, fencing, fenced)
1 put a fence round or along something. 2 fight
with long narrow swords (called *foils*) as a
sport. **fencer** *noun*
[shortened from *defence*]

fend *verb* (fends, fending, fended)
fend for provide things for someone.
fend off keep a person or thing away from
yourself.
[shortened from *defend*]

ferment (*say* fer-**ment**) *verb* (ferments,
fermenting, fermented)
bubble and change chemically by the action of
a substance such as yeast. **fermentation** *noun*
ferment (*say* **fer**-ment) *noun*
1 fermenting. 2 an excited or agitated
condition. [from Latin *fermentum* = yeast]

fern *noun* (*plural* ferns)
a plant with feathery leaves and no flowers.
[from Old English]

ferocious *adjective*
fierce or savage. **ferociously** *adverb,*
ferocity *noun* [from Latin *ferox* = fierce]

-ferous and **-iferous** *suffix*
form nouns meaning 'carrying' or 'providing'
(e.g. *carboniferous*).
[from Latin *ferre* = carry]

ferry *verb* (ferries, ferrying, ferried)
transport people or things, especially across
water.
ferry *noun* (*plural* ferries)
a boat or aircraft used in ferrying.

fertile *adjective*
1 producing good crops, *fertile soil.* 2 able to
produce offspring. 3 able to produce ideas, *a
fertile imagination.* **fertility** *noun*

fertilize *verb* (fertilizes, fertilizing, fertilized)
1 add substances to the soil to make it more
fertile. 2 put pollen into a plant or sperm into
an egg or female animal so that it develops seed
or young.
fertilization *noun,* **fertilizer** *noun*

festival *noun* (*plural* festivals)
a time when people arrange special
celebrations, performances, etc.
[from Latin]

festivity *noun* (*plural* festivities)
a festive occasion or celebration.

festoon *noun* (*plural* festoons)
a chain of flowers or ribbons etc. hung as a
decoration.
festoon *verb* (festoons, festooning, festooned)
decorate something with ornaments.
[via French from Italian *festone* = festive
ornament]

fetch *verb* (fetches, fetching, fetched)
1 go for and bring back, *fetch some milk*; *fetch a
doctor*. 2 be sold for a particular price, *The
chairs fetched £20*.

fête (*say* fayt) *noun* (*plural* fêtes)
an outdoor entertainment with stalls and
sideshows.
[from old French *feste* = feast]

fetter *noun* (*plural* fetters)
a chain or shackle put round a prisoner's
ankle.

feud (*say* fewd) *noun* (*plural* feuds)
a long-lasting quarrel, especially between two
families. [via old French from Germanic;
related to *foe*]

feudal (*say* few-dal) *adjective*
to do with the system used in the Middle Ages
in which people could farm land in exchange
for work done for the owner. **feudalism** *noun*
[from Latin]

fever *noun* (*plural* fevers)
1 an abnormally high body temperature,
usually with an illness. 2 excitement or
agitation. **fevered** *adjective*, **feverish** *adjective*,
feverishly *adverb* [from Latin]

few *adjective*
not many. **fewness** *noun*
few *noun*
a small number of people or things.

fiancé (*say* fee-ahn-say) *noun* (*plural* fiancés)
a man who is engaged to be married.
[French, = betrothed]

fiancée (*say* fee-ahn-say) *noun* (*plural* fiancées)
a woman who is engaged to be married.

fiasco (*say* fee-as-koh) *noun* (*plural* fiascos)
a complete failure. [Italian]

fibre *noun* (*plural* fibres)
1 a very thin thread. 2 a substance made of
thin threads. 3 indigestible material in certain
foods that stimulates the action of the
intestines. **fibrous** *adjective*

fibreglass *noun*
1 fabric made from glass fibres. 2 plastic
containing glass fibres.

fickle *adjective*
constantly changing; not loyal to one person or
group etc. **fickleness** *noun*

fiction *noun* (*plural* fictions)
1 writings about events that have not really
happened; stories and novels. 2 something
imagined or untrue. **fictional** *adjective* [same
origin as *feign*]

fiddle *noun* (*plural* fiddles)
1 (*informal*) a violin. 2 (*slang*) a swindle.
fiddle *verb* (fiddles, fiddling, fiddled)
1 (*informal*) play the violin. 2 fidget or tinker
with something, using your fingers. 3 (*slang*)
swindle; get or change something dishonestly.
fiddler *noun*
[from Old English]

fidget *verb* (fidgets, fidgeting, fidgeted)
make small restless movements.
fidgety *adjective*

field *noun* (*plural* fields)
1 a piece of land with grass or crops growing
on it. 2 an area of interest or study, *recent
advances in the field of science*. 3 those who are
taking part in a race or outdoor game etc.
field *verb* (fields, fielding, fielded)
1 stop or catch the ball in cricket etc. 2 be on
the side not batting in cricket etc. 3 put a team
into a match etc., *They fielded their best players*.
fielder *noun*, **fieldsman** *noun*

fieldwork *noun*
practical work or research done in various
places, not in a library or museum or
laboratory etc.

fiend (*say* feend) *noun* (*plural* fiends)
1 an evil spirit; a devil. 2 a very wicked or
cruel person. 3 an enthusiast, *a fresh-air fiend*.
fiendish *adjective* [from Old English]

fierce *adjective*
1 angry and violent or cruel. 2 intense, *fierce
heat*. **fiercely** *adverb*, **fierceness** *noun* [from
Latin *ferus* = untamed]

fifteen *noun* & *adjective* (*plural* fifteens)
1 the number 15. 2 a team in Rugby Union
football. **fifteenth** *adjective* & *noun*
[from Old English]

fifth *adjective* & *noun* (*plural* fifths)
next after the fourth. **fifthly** *adverb*
[from Old English]

fifty *noun* & *adjective* (*plural* fifties)
the number 50. **fiftieth** *adjective* & *noun* [from
Old English]

fifty-fifty *adjective* & *adverb*
1 shared equally between two people or
groups. 2 evenly balanced, *a fifty-fifty chance*.

fig *noun* (*plural* figs)
a soft fruit full of small seeds. [from Latin]

fight *noun* (*plural* **fights**)
1 a struggle against somebody using hands, weapons, etc. **2** an attempt to achieve or overcome something, *the fight against poverty*.
fight *verb* (**fights, fighting, fought**)
1 have a fight. **2** attempt to achieve or overcome something. **fighter** *noun*

figure *noun* (*plural* **figures**)
1 the symbol of a number. **2** an amount or value. **3** a diagram or illustration. **4** a shape. **5** the shape of a person's, especially a woman's, body. **6** a person. **7** a representation of a person or animal in painting, sculpture, etc.
figure *verb* (**figures, figuring, figured**)
appear or take part in something.
figure out work something out.

figurehead *noun* (*plural* **figureheads**)
1 a carved figure decorating the prow of a sailing ship. **2** a person who is head of a country or organization but has no real power.

figure of speech *noun* (*plural* **figures of speech**)
a word or phrase used for dramatic effect and not intended literally, e.g. 'a *flood of letters*'.

filament *noun* (*plural* **filaments**)
a thread or thin wire, especially one in a light bulb. [from Latin *filum* = thread]

file[1] *noun* (*plural* **files**)
a metal tool with a rough surface that is rubbed on things to shape them or make them smooth.
file *verb* (**files, filing, filed**)
shape or smooth something with a file. [from Old English]

file[2] *noun* (*plural* **files**)
1 a folder or box etc. for keeping papers in order. **2** a collection of data stored under one name in a computer. **3** a line of people one behind the other.
file *verb* (**files, filing, filed**)
1 put something into a file. **2** walk in a file, *They filed out*. [from Latin *filum* = thread (because a string or wire was put through papers to hold them in order)]

filings *plural noun*
tiny pieces of metal rubbed off by a file, *iron filings*.

fill *verb* (**fills, filling, filled**)
1 make or become full. **2** block up a hole or cavity. **filler** *noun*
fill *noun*
enough to fill a person or thing, *We ate our fill*. [from Old English]

film *noun* (*plural* **films**)
1 a motion picture, such as those shown in cinemas or on television. **2** a rolled strip or sheet of thin plastic coated with material that is sensitive to light, used for taking photographs or making a motion picture. **3** a very thin layer, *a film of grease*.
film *verb* (**films, filming, filmed**)
make a film of a story etc.
[from Old English *filmen* = thin skin]

filter *noun* (*plural* **filters**)
1 a device for holding back dirt or other unwanted material from a liquid or gas etc. that passes through it. **2** a system for filtering traffic.
filter *verb* (**filters, filtering, filtered**)
1 pass through a filter. **2** move gradually, *They filtered into the hall*. **3** move in a particular direction while other traffic is held up.
[from old French]

filth *noun*
disgusting dirt. [from Old English]

filthy *adjective* (**filthier, filthiest**)
disgustingly dirty. **filthiness** *noun*

fin *noun* (*plural* **fins**)
1 a thin flat part sticking out from a fish's body, that helps it to swim. **2** a small part that sticks out on an aircraft or rocket etc., for helping its balance. [from Old English]

final *adjective*
1 coming at the end; last. **2** that puts an end to an argument etc., *You must go, and that's final!*
finally *adverb*, **finality** *noun*
final *noun* (*plural* **finals**)
the last in a series of contests.
[from Latin *finis* = end]

finalist *noun* (*plural* **finalists**)
a competitor in a final.

finance *noun*
the use or management of money.
financial *adjective*
finances *plural noun* money resources; funds.
finance *verb* (**finances, financing, financed**)
provide the money for something. **financier** *noun* [from old French *finer* = settle a debt]

find *verb* (**finds, finding, found**)
1 get or see something by looking for it or by chance. **2** learn something by experience, *He found that digging was hard work*.
find out get or discover some information.
find *noun* (*plural* **finds**)
something found. [from Old English]

fine[1] *adjective*
1 of high quality; excellent. **2** dry and clear; sunny, *fine weather*. **3** very thin; consisting of small particles. **4** in good health; well, *I'm fine*.
finely *adverb*,
fineness *noun*
fine *adverb*
1 finely, *chop it fine*. **2** (*informal*) very well, *That will suit me fine*.
[same origin as *finish*]

fine[2] *noun* (*plural* **fines**)
money which has to be paid as a punishment.
fine *verb* (**fines, fining, fined**)
make somebody pay a fine. [from Latin *finis* = end (in the Middle Ages it referred to the sum paid to settle a lawsuit)]

finger noun (plural fingers)
1 one of the separate parts of the hand. 2 a narrow piece of something, fish fingers.
finger verb (fingers, fingering, fingered) touch or feel something with your fingers.

fingerprint noun (plural fingerprints)
a mark made by the tiny ridges on the fingertip, used as a way of identifying someone.

finish verb (finishes, finishing, finished)
bring or come to an end.
finish noun (plural finishes)
1 the last stage of something; the end.
2 the surface or coating on woodwork etc.
[from Latin finis = end]

finite (say fy-nyt) adjective
limited; not infinite, We have only a finite supply of coal. [from Latin finitus = finished]

finite verb noun (plural finite verbs)
a verb that agrees with its subject in person and number; 'was', 'went', and 'says' are finite verbs; 'going' and 'to say' are not.

fir noun (plural firs)
an evergreen tree with needle-like leaves, that produces cones. [from Old Norse]

fire noun (plural fires)
1 the process of burning that produces light and heat. 2 coal and wood etc. burning in a grate or furnace to give heat. 3 a device using electricity or gas to heat a room. 4 the shooting of guns, Hold your fire!
on fire burning.
set fire to start something burning.
fire verb (fires, firing, fired)
1 set fire to. 2 bake pottery or bricks etc. in a kiln. 3 shoot a gun; send out a bullet or missile. 4 dismiss someone from a job. 5 excite, fire them with enthusiasm. **firer** noun
[from Old English]

firearm noun (plural firearms)
a small gun; a rifle, pistol, or revolver.

fire brigade noun (plural fire brigades)
a team of people organized to fight fires.

fire engine noun (plural fire engines)
a large vehicle that carries firemen and equipment to put out large fires.

fire escape noun (plural fire escapes)
a special staircase by which people may escape from a burning building etc.

fire extinguisher noun (plural fire extinguishers)
a metal cylinder from which water or foam can be sprayed to put out a fire.

firefighter noun (plural firefighters)
a member of a fire brigade.

fireplace noun (plural fireplaces)
an open structure for holding a fire in a room.

firewood noun
wood for use as fuel.

firework noun (plural fireworks)
a device containing chemicals that burn or explode attractively and noisily.

firing squad noun (plural firing squads)
a group ordered to shoot a condemned person.

firm noun (plural firms)
a business organization.
firm adjective
1 not giving way when pressed; hard or solid.
2 steady; not shaking or moving. 3 definite and not likely to change, a firm belief. **firmly** adverb, **firmness** noun
firm verb (firms, firming, firmed)
make something become firm. [from Latin]

first adjective
coming before all others in time or order or importance. **firstly** adverb
first adverb
before everything else, Finish this work first.

first aid noun
treatment given to an injured person before a doctor comes.

fish noun (plural fish or fishes)
an animal with gills and fins that always lives and breathes in water.
fish verb (fishes, fishing, fished)
1 try to catch fish. 2 search for something; try to get something, He is only fishing for praise. [from Old English]

fisherman noun (plural fishermen)
a person who tries to catch fish.

fishmonger noun (plural fishmongers)
a shopkeeper who sells fish.
[from fish + an old word monger = trader]

fishy adjective (fishier, fishiest)
1 smelling or tasting of fish. 2 (informal) causing doubt or suspicion, a fishy excuse. **fishily** adverb, **fishiness** noun

fission noun
1 splitting something. 2 splitting the nucleus of an atom so as to release energy.
fissionable adjective
[from Latin fissum = split]

fist noun (plural fists)
a tightly closed hand with the fingers bent into the palm. [from Old English]

fit[1] adjective (fitter, fittest)
1 suitable or good enough, a meal fit for a king.
2 healthy, Keep fit! 3 ready or likely, They worked till they were fit to collapse. **fitly** adverb, **fitness** noun
fit verb (fits, fitting, fitted)
1 be the right size and shape for something; be suitable. 2 put something into place, Fit a lock on the door. 3 alter something to make it the right size and shape. 4 make suitable for something, His training fits him for the job. **fitter** noun

fit *noun*
the way something fits, *a good fit.*
[origin unknown]

fit² *noun* (*plural* fits)
1 a sudden illness, especially one that makes you move violently or become unconscious.
2 an outburst, *a fit of rage.* [from Old English]

fitful *adjective*
happening in short periods, not steadily.
fitfully *adverb* [from *fit²* + *-ful*]

fitting *adjective*
proper or appropriate, *This statue is a fitting memorial to an extraordinary woman.*

five *noun* & *adjective* (*plural* fives)
the number 5. [from Old English]

fix *verb* (fixes, fixing, fixed)
1 fasten or place firmly. 2 make permanent and unable to change. 3 decide or arrange, *We fixed a date for the party.* 4 repair; put into working condition, *He is fixing my bike.*
fixer *noun*
fix up arrange or organize something.

fixedly *adverb*
in a fixed way.

fixture *noun* (*plural* fixtures)
1 something fixed in its place. 2 a sports event planned for a particular day.

fizz *verb* (fizzes, fizzing, fizzed)
make a hissing or spluttering sound; produce a lot of small bubbles.
[imitating the sound]

fizzy *adjective*
(of a drink) having a lot of small bubbles.
fizziness *noun*

flabby *adjective*
fat and soft, not firm.
flabbily *adverb,* **flabbiness** *noun* [related to *flap*]

flag¹ (*plural* flags)
1 a piece of cloth with a coloured pattern or shape on it, used as a sign or signal.
2 a small piece of paper or plastic that looks like a flag. **flagpole** *noun,*
flagstaff *noun*
flag *verb* (flags, flagging, flagged)
1 become weak; droop. 2 signal with a flag or by waving.
[from an old word *flag* = drooping]

flag² *noun* (*plural* flags)
a flat slab of stone used for paving.
[from Old Norse *flaga* = slab of stone]

flagrant (*say* flay-grant) *adjective*
very bad and noticeable, *flagrant disobedience.*
flagrantly *adverb,* **flagrancy** *noun* [from Latin *flagrans* = blazing]

flagship *noun* (*plural* flagships)
1 a ship that carries an admiral and flies his flag. 2 the best and most important product that a company produces.

flair *noun*
a natural ability or talent, *Ian has a flair for languages.*
[French, = power to smell things]

USAGE: Do not confuse with *flare.*

flake *noun* (*plural* flakes)
1 a very light thin piece of something.
2 a small flat piece of falling snow.
flaky *adjective*

flamboyant *adjective*
very showy in appearance or manner. [French, = blazing]

flame *noun* (*plural* flames)
a tongue-shaped portion of fire or burning gas.
flame *verb* (flames, flaming, flamed)
1 produce flames. 2 become bright red.

flamingo *noun* (*plural* flamingoes)
a wading bird with long legs, a long neck, and pinkish feathers. [from Spanish]

flammable *adjective*
able to be set on fire. **flammability** *noun* [from Latin *flamma* = flame]

USAGE: See note at *inflammable.*

flank *noun* (*plural* flanks)
the side of something, especially an animal's body or an army.

flannel *noun* (*plural* flannels)
1 a soft cloth for washing yourself. 2 a soft woollen material.
[from Welsh *gwlanen* = woollen]

flap *verb* (flaps, flapping, flapped)
1 wave about. 2 (*slang*) panic or fuss about something.
flap *noun* (*plural* flaps)
1 a part that is fixed at one edge onto something else, often to cover an opening.
2 the action or sound of flapping.
3 (*slang*) a panic or fuss, *in a flap.*

flare *verb* (flares, flaring, flared)
1 blaze with a sudden bright flame. 2 become angry suddenly. 3 become gradually wider, *flaring nostrils.*
flare *noun* (*plural* flares)
1 a sudden bright flame or light, especially one used as a signal. 2 a gradual widening. [origin unknown]

USAGE: Do not confuse with *flair.*

flash *noun* (*plural* flashes)
1 a sudden bright flame or light. 2 a device for making a sudden bright light for taking photographs. 3 a sudden display of anger, wit, etc. 4 a short item of news.
flash *verb* (flashes, flashing, flashed)
1 make a flash. 2 appear suddenly; move quickly, *The train flashed past us.*

flashback *noun* (*plural* flashbacks)
going back in a film or story to something that
happened earlier.

flashy *adjective*
gaudy or showy.

flask *noun* (*plural* flasks)
1 a bottle with a narrow neck. 2 a vacuum
flask.

flat *adjective* (flatter, flattest)
1 with no curves or bumps; smooth and level.
2 spread out; lying at full length, *Lie flat on the
ground.* 3 (of a tyre) with no air inside. 4 (of
feet) without the normal arch underneath.
5 absolute, *a flat refusal.* 6 dull; not changing.
7 (of a drink) no longer fizzy. 8 (of a battery)
unable to produce any more electric current.
9 (in music) one semitone lower than the
natural note, *E flat.*
flatly *adverb,* **flatness** *noun*
flat *noun* (*plural* flats)
1 a set of rooms for living in, usually on one
floor of a building. 2 (in music) a note one
semitone lower than the natural note; the sign
(♭) that indicates this. 3 a punctured tyre.
[from Old Norse]

flatten *verb* (flattens, flattening, flattened)
make or become flat.

flatter *verb* (flatters, flattering, flattered)
1 praise somebody more than he or she
deserves. 2 make a person or thing seem better
or more attractive than they really are.
flatterer *noun,* **flattery** *noun*
[from old French *flater* = smooth down]

flaunt *verb* (flaunts, flaunting, flaunted)
display something proudly in a way that
annoys people; show it off, *He liked to flaunt his
expensive clothes and cars.*

USAGE: Do not confuse this word with *flout*,
which has a different meaning.

flavour *noun* (*plural* flavours)
the taste of something.
flavour *verb* (flavours, flavouring, flavoured)
give something a flavour; season it.
flavouring *noun* [from old French]

flaw *noun* (*plural* flaws)
something that makes a person or thing
imperfect. **flawed** *adjective*

flea *noun* (*plural* fleas)
a small jumping insect that sucks blood.

fleck *noun* (*plural* flecks)
1 a very small patch of colour. 2 a particle; a
speck, *flecks of dirt.* **flecked** *adjective*

fledged *adjective*
(of young birds) having grown feathers and
able to fly.
fully-fledged *adjective* fully trained, *a fully-
fledged engineer.*

fledgeling *noun* (*plural* fledgelings)
a young bird that is just fledged.
[from *fledge* = become fledged, + *-ling*]

fleece *noun* (*plural* fleeces)
the woolly hair of a sheep or similar animal.
fleecy *adjective*
fleece *verb* (fleeces, fleecing, fleeced)
1 shear the fleece from a sheep. 2 swindle
a person out of some money.

fleet *noun* (*plural* fleets)
a number of ships, aircraft, or vehicles owned
by one country or company.

fleeting *adjective*
passing quickly; brief.

flesh *noun*
1 the soft substance of the bodies of people and
animals, consisting of muscle and fat. 2 the
pulpy part of fruits and vegetables.
fleshy *adjective* [from Old English]

flex *verb* (flexes, flexing, flexed)
bend or stretch something that is flexible, *flex
your muscles.*
flex *noun* (*plural* flexes)
flexible insulated wire for carrying electric
current. [from Latin *flexum* = bent]

flexible *adjective*
1 easy to bend or stretch. 2 able to be changed
or adapted, *Our plans are flexible.*
flexibility *noun*

flick *noun* (*plural* flicks)
a quick light hit or movement.
flick *verb* (flicks, flicking, flicked)
hit or move with a flick.

flicker *verb* (flickers, flickering, flickered)
1 burn or shine unsteadily. 2 move quickly to
and fro.
flicker *noun* (*plural* flickers)
a flickering light or movement.

flight[1] *noun* (*plural* flights)
1 flying. 2 a journey in an aircraft etc. 3 a
series of stairs. 4 the feathers or fins on a dart
or arrow. [from Old English]

flight[2] *noun* (*plural* flights)
fleeing; an escape. [from Middle English]

flimsy *adjective* (flimsier, flimsiest)
made of something thin or weak. **flimsily**
adverb, **flimsiness** *noun* [origin unknown]

flinch *verb* (flinches, flinching, flinched)
move or shrink back because you are afraid;
wince. **flinch** *noun*

fling *verb* (flings, flinging, flung)
throw something violently or carelessly.
fling *noun* (*plural* flings)
1 the movement of flinging. 2 a vigorous
dance, *the Highland fling.* 3 a short time of
enjoyment, *have a fling.*
[origin unknown]

flint *noun* (*plural* flints)
1 a very hard kind of stone. 2 a piece of flint or hard metal used to produce sparks.
flinty *adjective* [from Old English]

flip *verb* (flips, flipping, flipped)
1 flick. 2 (*slang*) become crazy or very angry.
flip *noun* (*plural* flips)
a flipping movement. [origin unknown]

flippant *adjective*
not showing proper seriousness.
flippantly *adverb*, **flippancy** *noun* [from *flip*]

flirt *verb* (flirts, flirting, flirted)
behave lovingly towards somebody to amuse yourself. **flirtation** *noun*
flirt *noun* (*plural* flirts)
a person who flirts. **flirtatious** *adjective*, **flirtatiously** *adverb* [origin unknown]

float *verb* (floats, floating, floated)
1 stay or move on the surface of a liquid or in air. 2 make something float. **floater** *noun*
float *noun* (*plural* floats)
1 a device designed to float. 2 a vehicle with a platform used for delivering milk or for carrying a display in a parade etc. 3 a small amount of money kept for paying small bills or giving change etc.

flock *noun* (*plural* flocks)
a group of sheep, goats, or birds.
flock *verb* (flocks, flocking, flocked)
gather or move in a crowd.

flog *verb* (flogs, flogging, flogged)
1 beat a person or animal hard with a whip or stick as a punishment. 2 (*slang*) sell.
flogging *noun* [from Latin]

flood *noun* (*plural* floods)
1 a large amount of water spreading over a place that is usually dry. 2 a great amount, *a flood of requests*. 3 the movement of the tide when it is coming in towards the land.
flood *verb* (floods, flooding, flooded)
1 cover with a flood. 2 come in great amounts, *Letters flooded in*.

floodlight *noun* (*plural* floodlights)
a lamp that makes a broad bright beam to light up a stage, stadium, important building, etc.
floodlit *adjective*

floor *noun* (*plural* floors)
1 the part of a room that people walk on. 2 a storey of a building; all the rooms at the same level.

USAGE: In Britain, the *ground floor* of a building is the one at street level, and the one above it is the *first floor*. In the USA, the *first floor* is the one at street level, and the one above it is the *second floor*.

floor *verb* (floors, flooring, floored)
1 put a floor into a building. 2 knock a person down. 3 baffle somebody.
[from Old English]

flop *verb* (flops, flopping, flopped)
1 fall or sit down clumsily. 2 hang or sway heavily and loosely. 3 (*slang*) be a failure.
floppy *adjective*

floppy disk *noun* (*plural* floppy disks)
a flexible disc holding data for use in a computer.

flora *noun*
the plants of a particular area or period. (Compare *fauna*.) [from the name of *Flora*, the ancient Roman goddess of flowers; her name comes from Latin *flores* = flowers]

florist *noun* (*plural* florists)
a shopkeeper who sells flowers.
[same origin as *flora*]

flotsam *noun*
wreckage or cargo found floating after a shipwreck.
flotsam and jetsam odds and ends.
[from old French *floter* = float]

flounce *verb* (flounces, flouncing, flounced)
go in an impatient or annoyed manner, *She flounced out of the room*. **flounce** *noun*

flounder *verb* (flounders, floundering, floundered)
1 move clumsily and with difficulty. 2 make mistakes or become confused when trying to do something. [from old French]

flour *noun*
a fine powder of wheat or other grain, used in cooking. **floury** *adjective*
[old spelling of *flower*]

flourish *verb* (flourishes, flourishing, flourished)
1 grow or develop strongly. 2 be successful; prosper. 3 wave something about dramatically.
flourish *noun* (*plural* flourishes)
a showy or dramatic sweeping movement, curve, or passage of music.
[from Latin *florere* = to flower]

flout *verb* (flouts, flouting, flouted)
disobey a rule or instruction openly and scornfully, *She shaved her head one day, just because she loved to flout convention*. [probably from Dutch *fluiten* = whistle, hiss]

USAGE: Do not confuse this word with *flaunt*, which has a different meaning.

flow *verb* (flows, flowing, flowed)
1 move along smoothly or continuously. 2 gush out, *Water flowed from the tap*. 3 hang loosely, *flowing hair*. 4 (of the tide) come in towards the land.
flow *noun* (*plural* flows)
1 a flowing movement or mass. 2 the movement of the tide when it is coming in towards the land, *the ebb and flow of the tide*.

flower noun (plural **flowers**)
1 the part of a plant from which seed and fruit develops. 2 a blossom and its stem used for decoration, usually in groups. (Compare *flora*.)
flower verb (**flowers, flowering, flowered**)
produce flowers.
[from old French; related to *flora*]

flowery adjective
1 full of flowers. 2 full of ornamental phrases.

flu noun
influenza.

fluctuate verb (**fluctuates, fluctuating, fluctuated**)
rise and fall; vary, *Prices fluctuated.*
fluctuation noun
[from Latin *fluctus* = a wave]

fluent (say floo-ent) adjective
1 skilful at speaking clearly and without hesitating. 2 able to speak a foreign language easily and well. **fluently** adverb, **fluency** noun
[from Latin *fluens* = flowing]

fluff noun
a fluffy substance. [probably from Flemish]

fluffy adjective
having a mass of soft fur or fibres.
fluffiness noun

fluid noun (plural **fluids**)
a substance that is able to flow freely as liquids and gases do.
fluid adjective
1 able to flow freely. 2 not fixed, *My plans for Christmas are fluid.* **fluidity** noun
[from Latin *fluere* = to flow]

fluke noun (plural **flukes**)
a piece of good luck that makes you able to do something you thought you could not do.
[origin unknown]

fluorescent (say floo-er-ess-ent) adjective
creating light from radiation, *a fluorescent lamp.* **fluorescence** noun
[from *fluorspar*, a fluorescent mineral]

fluoridation noun
adding fluoride to drinking water in order to help prevent tooth decay.

fluoride noun
a chemical substance that is thought to prevent tooth decay. [from Latin]

flurry noun (plural **flurries**)
1 a sudden whirling gust of wind, rain, or snow. 2 an excited or flustered disturbance.
[from an old word *flurr* = to throw about]

flush[1] verb (**flushes, flushing, flushed**)
1 blush. 2 clean or remove something with a fast flow of water.
flush noun (plural **flushes**)
1 a blush. 2 a fast flow of water.
[imitating the sound of water]

flush[2] adjective
1 level with the surrounding surface, *The doors are flush with the walls.* 2 having plenty of money. [origin unknown]

fluster verb (**flusters, flustering, flustered**)
make somebody nervous and confused.
fluster noun [origin unknown]

flute noun (plural **flutes**)
a musical instrument consisting of a long pipe with holes that are stopped by fingers or keys.
[from old French]

flutter verb (**flutters, fluttering, fluttered**)
1 flap wings quickly. 2 move or flap quickly and irregularly.
flutter noun (plural **flutters**)
1 a fluttering movement. 2 a nervously excited condition. 3 (*informal*) a small bet, *Have a flutter!* [from Old English]

fly[1] noun (plural **flies**)
1 a small flying insect with two wings. 2 a real or artificial fly used as bait in fishing. [from Old English *flycge*]

fly[2] verb (**flies, flying, flew, flown**)
1 move through the air by means of wings or in an aircraft. 2 travel through the air or through space. 3 wave in the air, *Flags were flying.* 4 make something fly, *They flew model aircraft.* 5 move or pass quickly, *Time flies.* 6 flee from, *You must fly the country!* **flyer** noun
fly noun (plural **flies**)
the front opening of a pair of trousers. [from Old English *fleogan*]

flying saucer noun (plural **flying saucers**)
a mysterious saucer-shaped object reported to have been seen in the sky and believed by some people to be an alien spacecraft.

flyleaf noun (plural **flyleaves**)
a blank page at the beginning or end of a book.

flyover noun (plural **flyovers**)
a bridge that carries one road or railway over another.

flywheel noun (plural **flywheels**)
a heavy wheel used to regulate machinery.

foal noun (plural **foals**)
a young horse.

foam noun
1 a white mass of tiny bubbles on a liquid; froth. 2 a spongy kind of rubber or plastic.
foamy adjective
foam verb (**foams, foaming, foamed**)
form foam. [from Old English]

fob verb (**fobs, fobbing, fobbed**)
fob off get rid of someone by an excuse or a trick.

focal adjective
to do with or at a focus.

focus noun (plural **focuses** or **foci**)
1 the distance from an eye or lens at which an object appears clearest. 2 the point at which

rays etc. seem to meet. **3** something that is a centre of interest or attention etc.
in focus appearing clearly.
out of focus not appearing clearly.
focus *verb* (**focuses, focusing, focused**)
1 use or adjust a lens so that objects appear clearly. **2** concentrate, *She focused her attention on it.* [Latin, = hearth (the central point of a household)]

fodder *noun*
food for horses and farm animals.

foetus (*say* fee-tus) *noun* (*plural* **foetuses**)
a developing embryo, especially an unborn human baby. **foetal** *adjective* [Latin]

fog *noun*
thick mist. **foggy** *adjective*

foghorn *noun* (*plural* **foghorns**)
a loud horn for warning ships in fog.

foil¹ *noun* (*plural* **foils**)
1 a very thin sheet of metal. **2** a person or thing that makes another look better in contrast. [same origin as *foliage*]

foil² *noun* (*plural* **foils**)
a long narrow sword used in the sport of fencing. [origin unknown]

foil³ *verb* (**foils, foiling, foiled**)
prevent something from being successful, *We foiled his evil plan.*
[from old French *fouler* = trample]

foist *verb* (**foists, foisting, foisted**)
make a person accept something inferior or unwelcome, *They foisted the job on me.*

fold *verb* (**folds, folding, folded**)
bend or move so that one part lies on another part.
fold *noun* (*plural* **folds**)
a line where something is folded.
[from Old English *fealdan*]

-fold *suffix*
forms adjectives and adverbs meaning 'multiplied by' (e.g *twofold, fourfold, manifold*).
[from Old English]

folder *noun* (*plural* **folders**)
a folding cover for loose papers.

folk *noun*
people. [from Old English]

folk dance *nouns* (*plural* **folk dances**)
a dance in the traditional style of a country.

folklore *noun*
old beliefs and legends.

folk song *noun* (*plural* **folk songs**)
a song in the traditional style of a country.

follow *verb* (**follows, following, followed**)
1 go or come after. **2** do a thing after something else. **3** take a person or thing as a guide or example. **4** take an interest in the progress of

events or a sport or team etc. **5** understand, *Did you follow what he said?* **6** result from something. **follower** *noun* [from Old English]

following *preposition*
after, as a result of, *Following the burglary, we had new locks fitted.*

folly *noun* (*plural* **follies**)
foolishness; a foolish action etc.
[from French *folie* = madness]

fond *adjective*
1 loving or liking a person or thing. **2** foolishly hopeful, *fond hopes.*
fondly *adverb*, **fondness** *noun*
[from an old word *fon* = fool]

fondle *verb* (**fondles, fondling, fondled**)
touch or stroke lovingly. [from *fond*]

food *noun* (*plural* **foods**)
any substance that a plant or animal can take into its body to help it to grow and be healthy. [from Old English]

food chain *noun* (*plural* **food chains**)
a series of plants and animals each of which serves as food for the one above it in the series.

fool *noun* (*plural* **fools**)
1 a stupid person; someone who acts unwisely. **2** a jester or clown, *Stop playing the fool.* **3** a creamy pudding with crushed fruit in it, *gooseberry fool.*
fool's errand a useless errand.
fool's paradise happiness that comes only from being mistaken about something.
fool *verb* (**fools, fooling, fooled**)
1 behave in a joking way; play about. **2** trick or deceive someone.

foolish *adjective*
without good sense or judgement; unwise.
foolishly *adverb*, **foolishness** *noun*

foolproof *adjective*
easy to use or do correctly.

foot *noun* (*plural* **feet**)
1 the lower part of the leg below the ankle. **2** any similar part, e.g. one used by certain animals to move or attach themselves to things. **3** the lowest part, *the foot of the hill.* **4** a measure of length, 12 inches or about 30 centimetres, *a ten-foot pole; it is ten feet long.* **5** a unit of rhythm in a line of poetry, e.g. each of the four divisions in *Jack / and Jill / went up / the hill.*
on foot walking.

foot-and-mouth disease *noun*
a serious contagious disease that affects cattle, sheep, and other animals.

football *noun* (*plural* **footballs**)
1 a game played by two teams which try to kick an inflated leather ball into their opponents' goal. **2** the ball used in this game.
footballer *noun*

foothill *noun* (*plural* **foothills**)
a low hill near the bottom of a mountain or range of mountains.

foothold *noun* (*plural* **footholds**)
1 a place to put your foot when climbing. 2 a small but firm position from which you can advance in business etc.

footing *noun*
1 having your feet placed on something; a foothold, *He lost his footing and slipped.* 2 the status or nature of a relationship, *We are on a friendly footing with that country.*

footlights *plural noun*
a row of lights along the front of the floor of a stage.

footnote *noun* (*plural* **footnotes**)
a note printed at the bottom of the page.

footpath *noun* (*plural* **footpaths**)
a path for pedestrians.

footprint *noun* (*plural* **footprints**)
a mark made by a foot or shoe.

footstep *noun* (*plural* **footsteps**)
1 a step taken in walking or running. 2 the sound of this.

for *preposition*
This word is used to show 1 purpose or direction (*This letter is for you; We set out for home*), 2 distance or time (*Walk for six miles or two hours*), 3 price or exchange (*We bought it for £2; New lamps for old*), 4 cause (*She was fined for speeding*), 5 defence or support (*He fought for his country; Are you for us or against us?*), 6 reference (*For all her wealth, she is bored*), 7 similarity or correspondence (*We took him for a fool*),
for ever for all time; always.

for *conjunction*
because, *They hesitated, for they were afraid.* [from Old English]

for- *prefix*
1 away, off (as in *forgive*). 2 prohibiting (as in *forbid*). 3 abstaining or neglecting (as in *forgo, forsake*). [from Old English]

forbear *verb* (**forbears, forbearing, forbore, forborne**)
1 refrain from something, *We forbore to mention it.* 2 be patient or tolerant. **forbearance** *noun* [from Old English]

forbid *verb* (**forbids, forbidding, forbade, forbidden**)
1 order someone not to do something. 2 refuse to allow, *We shall forbid the marriage.* [from Old English]

forbidding *adjective*
looking stern or unfriendly.

force *noun* (*plural* **forces**)
1 strength or power. 2 (in science) an influence, which can be measured, that causes something to move. 3 an organized group of police, soldiers, etc.
in or **into force** in or into effectiveness, *The new law comes into force next week.*
the forces a country's armed forces.

force *verb* (**forces, forcing, forced**)
1 use force in order to get or do something, or to make somebody obey. 2 break something open by force. 3 cause plants to grow or bloom earlier than is normal, *You can force them in a greenhouse.*
[from Latin *fortis* = strong]

forceful *adjective*
strong and vigorous. **forcefully** *adverb*

forcible *adjective*
done by force; forceful. **forcibly** *adverb*

ford *noun* (*plural* **fords**)
a shallow place where you can walk across a river.

ford *verb* (**fords, fording, forded**)
cross a river at a ford. [from Old English]

fore *adjective & adverb*
at or towards the front, *fore and aft.*

fore *noun*
the front part.
to the fore to or at the front; in or to a prominent position.

fore- *prefix*
before (as in *forecast*); in front (as in *foreleg*).

forearm[1] *noun* (*plural* **forearms**)
the arm from the elbow to the wrist or fingertips. [from *fore-* + *arm*[1]]

forearm[2] *verb* (**forearms, forearming, forearmed**)
prepare in advance against possible danger. [from *fore-* + *arm*[2]]

forecast *noun* (*plural* **forecasts**)
a statement that tells in advance what is likely to happen.

forecast *verb* (**forecasts, forecasting, forecast**)
make a forecast. **forecaster** *noun*
[from *fore-* + *cast*]

forefinger *noun* (*plural* **forefingers**)
the finger next to the thumb.

foregone conclusion (*plural* **foregone conclusions**)
a result that can be foreseen easily and with certainty.

foreground *noun*
the front part of a scene or view etc.

forehand *noun* (*plural* **forehands**)
a stroke made in tennis etc. with the palm of the hand turned forwards.

forehead (*say* **forrid** or **for**-hed) *noun* (*plural* **foreheads**)
the part of the face above the eyes.

foreign *adjective*
1 belonging to or in another country. 2 not belonging naturally to a place or to someone's nature, *Lying is foreign to her nature.* [from old French]

foreigner *noun* (*plural* **foreigners**)
a person from another country.

foreman *noun* (*plural* **foremen**)
1 a worker in charge of a group of other workers. 2 a member of a jury who is in charge of the jury's discussions and who speaks on its behalf.

foremost *adjective & adverb*
first in position or rank; most important.

forensic (*say* fer-en-sik) *adjective*
to do with or used in lawcourts.
[from Latin; related to *forum*]

forensic medicine *noun*
medical knowledge needed in legal matters.

forerunner *noun* (*plural* **forerunners**)
a person or thing that comes before another; a sign of what is to come.

foresee *verb* (**foresees, foreseeing, foresaw, foreseen**)
realize what is going to happen.

foreshadow *verb* (**foreshadows, foreshadowing, foreshadowed**)
be a sign of something that is to come.

foreshorten *verb* (**foreshortens, foreshortening, foreshortened**)
show an object in a drawing etc. with some lines shortened to give an effect of distance or depth.

foresight *noun*
the ability to foresee and prepare for future needs.

forest *noun* (*plural* **forests**)
trees and undergrowth covering a large area.
forested *adjective* [from old French]

forestry *noun*
planting forests and looking after them.
forester *noun*

foretaste *noun* (*plural* **foretastes**)
an experience of something that is to come in the future.

foretell *verb* (**foretells, foretelling, foretold**)
tell in advance; prophesy.

forethought *noun*
careful thought and planning for the future.

foreword *noun* (*plural* **forewords**)
a preface.

forfeit (*say* for-fit) *verb* (**forfeits, forfeiting, forfeited**)
pay or give up something as a penalty.
forfeiture *noun*
forfeit *noun* (*plural* **forfeits**)
something forfeited. [from old French]

forge[1] *noun* (*plural* **forges**)
a place where metal is heated and shaped; a blacksmith's workshop.

forge *verb* (**forges, forging, forged**)
1 shape metal by heating and hammering. 2 copy something in order to deceive people.
forger *noun*, **forgery** *noun*
[from old French]

forge[2] *verb* (**forge, forging, forged**)
forge ahead move forward by a strong effort.
[probably a different spelling of *force*]

forget *verb* (**forgets, forgetting, forgot, forgotten**)
1 fail to remember. 2 stop thinking about, *Forget your troubles.*
forget yourself behave rudely or thoughtlessly.

forgetful *adjective*
tending to forget. **forgetfully** *adverb*, **forgetfulness** *noun*

forgive *verb* (**forgives, forgiving, forgave, forgiven**)
stop feeling angry with somebody about something. **forgiveness** *noun*

fork *noun* (*plural* **forks**)
1 a small device with prongs for lifting food to your mouth. 2 a large device with prongs used for digging or lifting things. 3 a place where something separates into two or more parts, *a fork in the road.*
fork *verb* (**forks, forking, forked**)
1 lift or dig with a fork. 2 form a fork by separating into two branches. 3 follow one of these branches, *Fork left.*
fork out (*slang*) pay out money.
[via Old English from Latin]

fork-lift truck (*plural* **fork-lift trucks**)
a truck with two metal bars at the front for lifting and moving heavy loads.

forlorn *adjective*
left alone and unhappy.
forlorn hope the only faint hope left.
[from *for-* + an old word *lorn* = lost]

form *noun* (*plural* **forms**)
1 the shape, appearance, or condition of something. 2 the way something exists, *Ice is a form of water.* 3 a class in school. 4 a bench. 5 a piece of paper with spaces to be filled in.
form *verb* (**forms, forming, formed**)
1 shape or construct something; create. 2 come into existence; develop, *Icicles formed.*
[from Latin]

formal *adjective*
1 strictly following the accepted rules or customs; ceremonious, *a formal occasion*; *formal dress.* 2 rather serious and stiff in your manner. **formally** *adverb*
[from Latin *formalis* = having a set form]

format *noun* (*plural* **formats**)
the shape and size of something; the way it is arranged.
[from Latin *formatus* = formed, shaped]

formation *noun* (*plural* **formations**)
1 the act of forming something. **2** a thing formed. **3** a special arrangement or pattern, *flying in formation*.
[from Latin *formare* = to mould]

former *adjective*
of an earlier time. **formerly** *adverb*
the former the first of two people or things just mentioned.
[from Old English; related to *fore*]

formidable (*say* for-mid-a-bul) *adjective*
1 frightening. **2** difficult to deal with or do, *a formidable task*. **formidably** *adverb*
[from Latin *formidare* = to fear]

formula *noun* (*plural* **formulae**)
1 a set of chemical symbols showing what a substance consists of. **2** a rule or statement expressed in symbols or numbers. **3** a list of substances needed for making something. **4** a fixed wording for a ceremony etc. **5** one of the groups into which racing cars are placed according to the size of their engines, *Formula One*. [Latin, = small form]

formulate *verb* (**formulates, formulating, formulated**)
express an idea or plan clearly and exactly.
formulation *noun* [from *formula*]

fort *noun* (*plural* **forts**)
a fortified building.
[from Latin *fortis* = strong]

forth *adverb*
1 out; into view. **2** onwards or forwards, *from this day forth*.
and so forth and so on.

forthcoming *adjective*
1 happening soon, *forthcoming events*. **2** made available when needed, *Money for the trip was not forthcoming*. **3** willing to give information.

forthright *adjective*
frank and outspoken.

fortification *noun* (*plural* **fortifications**)
1 fortifying something. **2** a wall or building constructed to make a place strong against attack.

fortify *verb* (**fortifies, fortifying, fortified**)
1 make a place strong against attack, especially by building fortifications. **2** strengthen. [same origin as *fort*]

fortnight *noun* (*plural* **fortnights**)
a period of two weeks.
fortnightly *adverb* & *adjective*
[from Old English *feowertene niht* = fourteen nights]

fortress *noun* (*plural* **fortresses**)
a fortified building or town.
[from French *forteresse* = strong place]

fortunate *adjective*
lucky. **fortunately** *adverb*
[same origin as *fortune*]

fortune *noun* (*plural* **fortunes**)
1 luck, especially good luck. **2** a great amount of money.
tell someone's fortune predict what will happen to them in the future.
[from Latin *fortuna* = luck]

forty *noun* & *adjective* (*plural* **forties**)
the number 40. **fortieth** *adjective* & *noun*
forty winks a short sleep; a nap.

forward *adjective*
1 going forwards. **2** placed in the front.
3 having made more than the normal progress.
4 too eager or bold.
forwardness *noun*
forward *adverb*
forwards.
forward *noun* (*plural* **forwards**)
a player in the front line of a team in football, hockey, etc.

forwards *adverb*
1 to or towards the front. **2** in the direction you are facing.

fossil *noun* (*plural* **fossils**)
the remains or traces of a prehistoric animal or plant that has been buried in the ground for a very long time and become hardened in rock.
fossilized *adjective*
[from Latin *fossilis* = dug up]

foul *adjective*
1 disgusting; tasting or smelling unpleasant.
2 (of weather) rough; stormy. **3** unfair; breaking the rules of a game. **4** colliding or entangled with something. **foully** *adverb*, **foulness** *noun*
foul *noun* (*plural* **fouls**)
an action that breaks the rules of a game.
foul *verb* (**fouls, fouling, fouled**)
1 make or become foul, *Smoke had fouled the air*. **2** commit a foul against a player in a game.
[from Old English]

found[1] *past tense* of **find**.

found[2] *verb* (**founds, founding, founded**)
1 establish; provide money for starting, *They founded a hospital*. **2** base, *This novel is founded on fact*.
[from Latin *fundus* = bottom]

foundation *noun* (*plural* **foundations**)
1 the founding of something. **2** a base or basis.
3 the solid base on which a building is built up.
foundation stone *noun*

founder[1] *noun* (*plural* **founders**)
a person who founds something, *the founder of the hospital*.

founder[2] *verb* (**founders, foundering, foundered**)
1 fill with water and sink, *The ship foundered*.

2 stumble or fall. **3** fail completely, *Their plans foundered.*
[same origin as *found²*]

fountain *noun* (*plural* **fountains**)
an ornamental structure in which a jet of water shoots up into the air.

four *noun* & *adjective* (*plural* **fours**)
the number 4.
on all fours on hands and knees.

fourteen *noun* & *adjective* (*plural* **fourteens**)
the number 14. **fourteenth** *adjective* & *noun*

fourth *adjective*
next after the third. **fourthly** *adverb*
fourth *noun* (*plural* **fourths**)
1 the fourth person or thing. **2** one of four equal parts; a quarter.

fowl *noun* (*plural* **fowls**)
a bird, especially one kept on a farm etc. for its eggs or meat. [from Old English]

fox *noun* (*plural* **foxes**)
a wild animal that looks like a dog with a long furry tail. **foxy** *adjective*

fraction *noun* (*plural* **fractions**)
1 a number that is not a whole number, e.g. ½, 0.5. **2** a tiny part. **fractional** *adjective*,
fractionally *adverb* [Latin, = breaking]

fracture *noun* (*plural* **fractures**)
the breaking of something, especially of a bone.
fracture *verb* (**fractures, fracturing, fractured**)
break. [from Latin *fractus* = broken]

fragile *adjective*
easy to break or damage. **fragilely** *adverb*,
fragility *noun* [from Latin]

fragment *noun* (*plural* **fragments**)
1 a small piece broken off. **2** a small part.
fragmentary *adjective*, **fragmentation** *noun*,
fragmented *adjective* [from Latin]

fragrant *adjective*
having a pleasant smell. **fragrance** *noun* [from Latin *fragrare* = smell sweet]

frail *adjective*
1 (of things) fragile. **2** (of people) not strong or healthy, *a frail old man.* **frailty** *noun* [from Latin *fragilis* = fragile]

frame *noun* (*plural* **frames**)
1 a holder that fits round the outside of a picture. **2** a rigid structure that supports something. **3** a human or animal body, *He has a small frame.* **4** a single exposure on a cinema film.
frame of mind the way you think or feel for a while.
frame *verb* (**frames, framing, framed**)
1 put a frame on or round. **2** construct, *They framed the question badly.* **3** make an innocent person seem guilty by arranging false evidence. **frame-up** *noun*

framework *noun* (*plural* **frameworks**)
1 a frame supporting something. **2** a basic plan or system.

franc *noun* (*plural* **francs**)
a unit of money in France, Switzerland, and many other countries.
[from Latin *Francorum rex* = King of the Franks, which was stamped on French gold coins in the Middle Ages]

frank *adjective*
making your thoughts and feelings clear to people; candid. **frankly** *adverb*,
frankness *noun*

frantic *adjective*
wildly agitated or excited. **frantically** *adverb*
[from old French; related to *frenzy*]

fraud *noun* (*plural* **frauds**)
1 a dishonest trick; a swindle. **2** an impostor; a person or thing that is not what it pretends to be. **fraudulent** *adjective*, **fraudulently** *adverb*,
fraudulence *noun*

fray¹ *noun* (*plural* **frays**)
a fight or conflict, *ready for the fray.* [shortened from *affray*; compare *afraid*]

fray² *verb* (**frays, fraying, frayed**)
1 make or become ragged so that loose threads show. **2** (of tempers or nerves) become strained or upset.
[from French; related to *friction*]

freak *noun* (*plural* **freaks**)
a very strange or abnormal person, animal, or thing. **freakish** *adjective*

freckle *noun* (*plural* **freckles**)
a small brown spot on the skin.
freckled *adjective* [from Old Norse]

free *adjective* (**freer, freest**)
1 able to do what you want to do or go where you want to go. **2** not costing anything. **3** not fixed, *Leave one end free.* **4** not having or being affected by something, *The harbour is free of ice.* **5** available; not being used or occupied.
6 generous, *She is very free with her money.*
freely *adverb*
free *verb* (**frees, freeing, freed**)
set free. [from Old English]

freedom *noun* (*plural* **freedoms**)
being free; independence.

freehand *adjective*
(of a drawing) done without a ruler or compasses etc.

free-range *adjective*
1 free-range hens are not kept in small cages but are allowed to move about freely. **2** free-range eggs are ones laid by these hens.

freewheel *verb* (**freewheels, freewheeling, freewheeled**)
ride a bicycle without needing to pedal.

freeze *verb* (freezes, freezing, froze, frozen)
1 turn into ice; become covered with ice.
2 make or be very cold. 3 keep wages or prices etc. at a fixed level. 4 suddenly stand completely still.

freezer *noun* (*plural* freezers)
a refrigerator in which food can be frozen quickly and stored.

French window (*plural* French windows)
a long window that serves as a door on an outside wall.

frenzy *noun*
wild excitement or agitation.
frenzied *adjective*, **frenziedly** *adverb*
[from Greek *phren* = the mind]

frequency *noun* (*plural* frequencies)
1 being frequent. 2 how often something happens. 3 the number of oscillations per second of a wave of sound or light etc.

frequent (*say* freek-went) *adjective*
happening often. **frequently** *adverb*
frequent (*say* frik-went) *verb* (frequents, frequenting, frequented)
be in or go to a place often, *They frequented the club.* [from Latin *frequens* = crowded]

fresh *adjective*
1 newly made or produced or arrived; not stale, *fresh bread*. 2 not tinned or preserved, *fresh fruit*. 3 cool and clean, *fresh air*. 4 (of water) not salty. **freshly** *adverb*, **freshness** *noun*
[from Old English]

freshen *verb* (freshens, freshening, freshened)
make or become fresh.

fret[1] *verb* (frets, fretting, fretted)
worry or be upset about something.
fretful *adjective*, **fretfully** *adverb*
[from Old English]

fret[2] *noun* (*plural* frets)
a bar or ridge on the fingerboard of a guitar etc. [origin unknown]

friar *noun* (*plural* friars)
a man who is a member of certain Roman Catholic religious orders, who has vowed to live a life of poverty. **friary** *noun*
[from French *frère* = brother]

friction *noun*
1 rubbing. 2 bad feeling between people; quarrelling. **frictional** *adjective*
[from Latin *fricare* = to rub]

fridge *noun* (*plural* fridges) (*informal*)
a refrigerator.

friend *noun* (*plural* friends)
1 a person you like who likes you. 2 a helpful or kind person.

friendly *adjective*
behaving like a friend. **friendliness** *noun*

friendship *noun* (*plural* friendships)
being friends.

frieze (*say* freez) *noun* (*plural* friezes)
a strip of designs or pictures round the top of a wall. [from Latin]

fright *noun* (*plural* frights)
1 sudden great fear. 2 a person or thing that looks ridiculous. [from Old English]

frighten *verb* (frightens, frightening, frightened)
make or become afraid.
be frightened of be afraid of.

frightful *adjective*
awful; very great or bad. **frightfully** *adverb*

frill *noun* (*plural* frills)
1 a decorative gathered or pleated trimming on a dress, curtain, etc. 2 something extra that is pleasant but unnecessary, *a simple life with no frills*. **frilled** *adjective*, **frilly** *adjective*

fringe *noun* (*plural* fringes)
1 a decorative edging with many threads hanging down loosely. 2 a straight line of hair hanging down over the forehead. 3 the edge of something. **fringed** *adjective*

frisk *verb* (frisks, frisking, frisked)
1 jump or run about playfully. 2 search somebody by running your hands over his or her clothes. **frisky** *adjective*, **friskily** *adverb*, **friskiness** *noun*
[from old French *frisque* = lively]

fritter[1] *noun* (*plural* fritters)
a slice of meat or fruit or potato etc. coated in batter and fried.
[from Latin *frictum* = fried]

fritter[2] *verb* (fritters, frittering, frittered)
waste something gradually; spend money or time on trivial things.
[from an old word *fritters* = fragments]

frivolous *adjective*
seeking pleasure in a light-hearted way; not serious. **frivolously** *adverb*, **frivolity** *noun* [from Latin]

frizzy *adjective*
(of hair) in tight curls. **frizziness** *noun*

fro *adverb*
to and fro backwards and forwards.

frock *noun* (*plural* frocks)
a girl's or woman's dress.

frog *noun* (*plural* frogs)
a small jumping animal that can live both in water and on land.
a frog in your throat hoarseness.

frolic *noun* (*plural* frolics)
a lively cheerful game or entertainment.
frolicsome *adjective*
frolic *verb* (frolics, frolicking, frolicked)
play about in a lively cheerful way.
[from Dutch *vrolijk* = joyously]

from *preposition*
This word is used to show 1 starting point in space or time or order (*We flew from London to*

Paris. We work from 9 to 5
o'clock. Count from one to ten), **2** source or
origin (Get water from the tap), **3** separation or
release (Take the gun from him. She was freed
from prison), **4** difference (Can you tell
margarine from butter?), **5** cause (I suffer from
headaches). [from Old English]

frond noun (plural **fronds**)
a leaf-like part of a fern, palm tree, etc. [from
Latin frondis = of a leaf]

front noun (plural **fronts**)
1 the part or side that comes first or is the most
important or furthest forward. **2** a road or
promenade along the seashore. **3** the place
where fighting is happening in a war.
frontal adjective
front adjective
of the front; in front.
[from Latin frons = forehead, front]

frontier noun (plural **frontiers**)
the boundary between two countries or
regions. [from old French; related to front]

frontispiece noun (plural **frontispieces**)
an illustration opposite the title-page of a book.
[from French]

frost noun (plural **frosts**)
1 powdery ice that forms on things in freezing
weather. **2** weather with a temperature below
freezing point.
frost verb (**frosts, frosting, frosted**)
cover with frost or frosting.
[from Old English]

frostbite noun
harm done to the body by very cold weather.
frostbitten adjective

frosty adjective
1 cold with frost. **2** unfriendly and
unwelcoming, a frosty look.
frostily adverb

froth noun
a white mass of tiny bubbles on a liquid.
frothy adjective [from Old Norse]

frown verb (**frowns, frowning, frowned**)
wrinkle your forehead because you are angry
or worried.
frown noun (plural **frowns**)
a frowning movement or look.
[from old French]

fruit noun (plural **fruits** or **fruit**)
1 the seed-container that grows on a tree or
plant and is often used as food. **2** the result of
doing something, the fruits of his efforts.
fruity adjective
fruit verb (**fruits, fruiting, fruited**)
produce fruit. [same origin as fruition]

fruitful adjective
producing good results, fruitful discussions.
fruitfully adverb

fruitless adjective
producing no results. **fruitlessly** adverb

frustrate verb (**frustrates, frustrating, frustrated**)
prevent somebody from doing something;
prevent something from being successful,
frustrate their wicked plans. **frustration** noun
[from Latin frustra = in vain]

fry verb (**fries, frying, fried**)
cook something in very hot fat. **fryer** noun

fudge noun
a soft sugary sweet. [origin unknown]

fuel noun (plural **fuels**)
something that is burnt to produce heat or
power.
fuel verb (**fuels, fuelling, fuelled**)
supply something with fuel.
[from old French; related to focus]

fugitive (say few-jit-iv) noun (plural **fugitives**)
a person who is running away from something.
[from Latin fugere = flee]

-ful suffix
forms **1** adjectives meaning 'full of' or 'having
this quality' (e.g. beautiful, truthful), **2** nouns
meaning 'the amount required to fill
something' (e.g. handful). [from full]

fulcrum noun (plural **fulcrums** or **fulcra**)
the point on which a lever rests. [Latin]

fulfil verb (**fulfils, fulfilling, fulfilled**)
1 do what is required; satisfy; carry out, You
must fulfil your promises. **2** make something
come true, It fulfilled an ancient prophecy.
3 give you satisfaction. **fulfilment** noun [from
Old English fullfyllan = fill up, satisfy]

full adjective
1 containing as much or as many as possible.
2 having many people or things, full of ideas.
3 complete, the full story. **4** the greatest
possible, at full speed. **5** fitting loosely; with
many folds, a full skirt. **6** when there is a full
moon, you can see its whole disc.
fully adverb, **fullness** noun
full adverb
completely and directly, It hit him full in the
face. [from Old English]

full-blown adjective
fully developed.

full stop noun (plural **full stops**)
the dot used as a punctuation mark at the end
of a sentence or an abbreviation.

fully adverb
completely.

fumble verb (**fumbles, fumbling, fumbled**)
hold or handle something clumsily.

fume noun or **fumes** plural noun
strong-smelling smoke or gas.
fume verb (**fumes, fuming, fumed**)
1 give off fumes. **2** be very angry.
[from Latin fumus = smoke]

fumigate (*say* few-mig-ayt) *verb* (fumigates, fumigating, fumigated)
disinfect something by fumes.
fumigation *noun*

fun *noun*
amusement or enjoyment.
make fun of make people laugh at a person or thing.

function *noun* (*plural* functions)
1 what somebody or something is there to do, *The function of a knife is to cut things.* 2 an important event or party. 3 a basic operation in a computer. 4 a variable quantity whose value depends on the value of other variable quantities, *X is a function of Y and Z.*
function *verb* (functions, functioning, functioned)
perform a function; work properly.
[from Latin *functum* = performed]

fund *noun* (*plural* funds)
1 money collected or kept for a special purpose. 2 a stock or supply.
fund *verb* (funds, funding, funded)
supply with money. [same origin as *found²*]

fundamental *adjective*
basic. **fundamentally** *adverb*
[from Latin *fundamentum* = foundation]

funeral *noun* (*plural* funerals)
the ceremony when a dead person is buried or cremated.
[from Latin *funeris* = of a burial]

fungus *noun* (*plural* fungi, *say* fung-I
a plant without leaves or flowers that grows on other plants or on decayed material, *Mushrooms are fungi.* [Latin]

funnel *noun* (*plural* funnels)
1 a metal chimney on a ship or steam engine. 2 a tube that is wide at the top and narrow at the bottom to help you pour things into a narrow opening.
[from Latin *fundere* = pour]

funny *adjective* (funnier, funniest)
1 that makes you laugh or smile. 2 strange or odd, *a funny smell.* **funnily** *adverb*

fur *noun* (*plural* furs)
1 the soft hair that covers some animals. 2 animal skin with the fur on it, used for clothing; fabric that looks like animal fur.

furious *adjective*
1 very angry. 2 violent or intense, *furious heat.* **furiously** *adverb* [from Latin]

furnace *noun* (*plural* furnaces)
a device in which great heat can be produced, e.g. for melting metals or making glass. [from Latin *furnus* = oven]

furnish *verb* (furnishes, furnishing, furnished)
1 provide a place with furniture. 2 provide or supply with something.

furniture *noun*
tables, chairs, and other movable things that you need in a house or school or office etc.

furrow *noun* (*plural* furrows)
1 a long cut in the ground made by a plough or other implement. 2 a groove. 3 a deep wrinkle in the skin.

furry *adjective*
like fur; covered with fur.

further *adverb* & *adjective*
1 at or to a greater distance; more distant. 2 more; additional, *We made further enquiries.*

USAGE: See the note at *farther.*

further *verb* (furthers, furthering, furthered)
help something to progress, *This success will further your career.* **furtherance** *noun*

further education *noun*
education for people above school age.

furthest *adverb* & *adjective*
at or to the greatest distance; most distant.

fury *noun*
wild anger; rage. [from Latin *furia* = rage; an avenging spirit]

fuse¹ *noun* (*plural* fuses)
a safety device containing a short piece of wire that melts if too much electricity is passed through it.
fuse *verb* (fuses, fusing, fused)
1 stop working because a fuse has melted. 2 blend together, especially through melting. [from Latin *fusum* = melted]

fuse² *noun* (*plural* fuses)
a length of material that burns easily, used for setting off an explosive.
[from Latin *fusus* = spindle (because originally the material was put in a tube)]

fusion *noun*
1 the action of blending or uniting things. 2 the uniting of atomic nuclei, usually releasing energy.

fuss *noun* (*plural* fusses)
1 unnecessary excitement or bustle. 2 an agitated protest.
fuss *verb* (fusses, fussing, fussed)
make a fuss about something.

fussy *adjective* (fussier, fussiest)
1 fussing; inclined to make a fuss. 2 choosing very carefully; hard to please. 3 full of unnecessary details or decorations. **fussily** *adverb*, **fussiness** *noun*

future *noun*
the time that will come; what is going to happen then.
future *adjective*
belonging or referring to the future.

fuzz *noun*
something fluffy or frizzy.

fuzzy *adjective*
1 like fuzz; covered with fuzz. **2** blurred; not clear. **fuzzily** *adverb*, **fuzziness** *noun*

-fy *suffix*
forms verbs meaning 'make' or 'bring into a certain condition' (e.g. *beautify, purify*). [from Latin *-ficare* = make]

Gg

gabble *verb* (**gabbles, gabbling, gabbled**)
talk so quickly that it is difficult to know what is being said. [from old Dutch]

gadget *noun* (*plural* **gadgets**)
any small useful tool. **gadgetry** *noun*

Gaelic (*say* **gay**-lik) *noun*
the Celtic languages of Scotland and Ireland.

gag *noun* (*plural* **gags**)
1 something put into a person's mouth or tied over it to prevent him or her speaking. **2** a joke.
gag *verb* (**gags, gagging, gagged**)
1 put a gag on a person. **2** prevent someone from making comments, *We cannot gag the press*. **3** retch.
[imitating the sound of someone retching]

gaiety *noun*
1 cheerfulness. **2** brightly coloured appearance.
(see *gay* for origin and usage note.)

gaily *adverb*
in a cheerful way.

gain *verb* (**gains, gaining, gained**)
1 get something that you did not have before; obtain. **2** a clock or watch gains when it becomes ahead of the correct time. **3** reach; arrive at, *At last we gained the shore*.
gain on come closer to a person or thing when chasing them or in a race.
gain *noun* (*plural* **gains**)
something gained; a profit or improvement.
gainful *adjective*

galaxy *noun* (*plural* **galaxies**)
a very large group of stars.
galactic (*say* ga-**lak**-tik) *adjective*
[originally = the Milky Way: from Greek *galaxias* = milky]

gale *noun* (*plural* **gales**)
a very strong wind. [origin unknown]

gallant (*say* **gal**-lant) *adjective*
1 brave or chivalrous. **2** fine and stately, *our gallant ship*. **gallantly** *adverb*, **gallantry** *noun*
[originally = spendidly dressed: from old French *galant* = celebrating]

gallery *noun* (*plural* **galleries**)
1 a platform jutting out from the wall in a church or hall. **2** the highest balcony in a cinema or theatre. **3** a long room or passage. **4** a room or building for showing works of art.
[from Italian *galleria* = gallery, church porch, perhaps from *Galilee* (a church porch furthest from the altar was called a *galilee*, as Galilee was the province furthest from Jerusalem)]

gallon (*plural* **gallons**)
a unit used to measure liquids, 8 pints or 4.546 litres. [from old French]

gallop *noun* (*plural* **gallops**)
1 the fastest pace that a horse can go. **2** a fast ride on a horse.
gallop *verb* (**gallops, galloping, galloped**)
go or ride at a gallop.
[from old French; related to *wallop*]

gallows *noun* (*plural* **gallows** or **gallowses**)
a framework with a noose for hanging criminals. [from Old English]

galoshes *plural noun*
a pair of waterproof shoes worn over ordinary shoes. [from old French]

galvanize *verb* (**galvanizes, galvanizing, galvanized**)
1 stimulate someone into sudden activity. **2** coat iron with zinc to protect it from rust. **galvanization** *noun*
[named after an Italian scientist, Luigi Galvani, who discovered that muscles move because of electricity in the body]

gambit *noun* (*plural* **gambits**)
1 a kind of opening move in chess. **2** an action or remark intended to gain an advantage. [from Italian *gambetto* = tripping up]

gamble *verb* (**gambles, gambling, gambled**)
1 bet on the result of a game, race, or other event. **2** take great risks in the hope of gaining something. **gambler** *noun*
gamble *noun* (*plural* **gambles**)
1 a bet or chance, *a gamble on the lottery*. **2** a risky attempt.
[from Old English *gamenian* = play games]

gambol *verb* (**gambols, gambolling, gambolled**)
jump or skip about in play. [from French]

game *noun* (*plural* **games**)
1 a form of play or sport, especially one with rules, *a game of football, a computer game*. **2** a section of a long game such as tennis or whist. **3** a scheme or plan; a trick, *Whatever his game is, he won't succeed*. **4** wild animals or birds hunted for sport or food.
give the game away reveal a secret.
game *adjective*
1 able and willing to do something, *'Shall we swim to the island?' 'I'm game!'* **2** brave.
gamely *adverb*
[from Old English]

gamekeeper *noun* (*plural* gamekeepers)
a person employed to protect game birds and animals, especially from poachers.

gamma *noun*
the third letter of the Greek alphabet, = g.

gamma rays *plural noun*
very short X-rays.

gander *noun* (*plural* ganders)
a male goose. [from Old English]

gang *noun* (*plural* gangs)
a number of people who do things together, *a gang of criminals, a roadmending gang.*
gang *verb* (gangs, ganging, ganged)
join in a gang, *gang up.* [from Old Norse]

gangling *adjective*
tall, thin, and awkward-looking.

gangplank *noun* (*plural* gangplanks)
a plank placed so that people can walk into or out of a boat.
[from Old Norse *gangr* = walking, going]

gangrene (*say* gang-green) *noun*
decay of body tissue in a living person.

gangster *noun* (*plural* gangsters)
a member of a gang of violent criminals.

gangway *noun* (*plural* gangways)
1 a gap left for people to pass between rows of seats or through a crowd. **2** a movable bridge placed so that people can walk into or out of a ship. [same origin as *gangplank*]

gaol (*say* jayl) *noun* (*plural* gaols)
a different spelling of *jail.*
gaol *verb,* **gaoler** *noun*

gap *noun* (*plural* gaps)
1 a break or opening in something continuous such as a hedge or fence. **2** an interval. **3** a wide difference in ideas.

gape *verb* (gapes, gaping, gaped)
1 have your mouth open. **2** stare with your mouth open. **3** be open wide.

garage (*say* ga-rah*zh* or ga-rij) *noun* (*plural* garages)
1 a building in which a motor vehicle or vehicles may be kept. **2** a place where motor vehicles are repaired or serviced and where petrol is sold.
[French, = a shelter]

garbage *noun*
rubbish, especially household rubbish.

garble *verb* (garbles, garbling, garbled)
give a confused account of a story or message so that it is misunderstood.
[from Arabic *garbala* = sift, select (because the real facts are 'sifted out')]

garden *noun* (*plural* gardens)
a piece of ground where flowers, fruit, or vegetables are grown.
gardener *noun,* **gardening** *noun*

gargle *verb* (gargles, gargling, gargled)
hold a liquid at the back of the mouth and breathe air through it to wash the inside of the throat. **gargle** *noun*
[from French *gargouille* = throat]

gargoyle *noun* (*plural* gargoyles)
an ugly or comical face or figure carved on a building, especially on a waterspout. [from French *gargouille* = throat (because the water passes through the throat of the figure)]

garland *noun* (*plural* garlands)
a wreath of flowers worn or hung as a decoration. **garland** *verb* [from old French]

garlic *noun*
a plant with a bulb divided into smaller bulbs (cloves), which have a strong smell and taste and are used for flavouring food.

garment *noun* (*plural* garments)
a piece of clothing.
[from French *garnement* = equipment]

garnish *verb* (garnishes, garnishing, garnished)
decorate something, especially food.
garnish *noun*
something used to decorate food or give it extra flavour.

garret *noun* (*plural* garrets)
an attic.
[from old French *garite* = watchtower]

garrison *noun* (*plural* garrisons)
1 troops who stay in a town or fort to defend it. **2** the building they occupy. **garrison** *verb*
[from old French *garison* = defence]

garter *noun* (*plural* garters)
a band of elastic to hold up a sock or stocking.
[from old French]

gas[1] *noun* (*plural* gases)
1 a substance that (like air) can move freely and is not liquid or solid at ordinary temperatures. **2** a gas that can be burned, used for lighting, heating, or cooking.
gas *verb* (gasses, gassing, gassed)
1 kill or injure someone with gas. **2** (*informal*) talk idly for a long time.
[an invented word suggested by the Greek word *chaos*]

gas[2] *noun* (*American*)
gasoline. [abbreviation]

gaseous (*say* gas-ee-us) *adjective*
in the form of a gas.

gash *noun* (*plural* gashes)
a long deep cut or wound.
gash *verb* (gashes, gashing, gashed)
make a gash in something.

gasoline *noun* (*American*)
petrol. [from *gas* + Latin *oleum* = oil]

gasp *verb* (gasps, gasping, gasped)
1 breathe in suddenly when you are shocked or surprised. **2** struggle to breathe with your

mouth open when you are tired or ill. **3** speak in a breathless way. **gasp** *noun* [from Old Norse]

gassy *adjective*
fizzy.

gastric *adjective*
to do with the stomach.
[from Greek *gaster* = stomach]

gastronomy (*say* gas-tron-om-ee) *noun*
the art of science of good eating.
gastronomic *adjective* [from Greek *gaster* = stomach + *-nomia* = management]

gastropod *noun* (*plural* **gastropods**)
an animal (e.g. a snail) that moves by means of a fleshy 'foot' on its stomach. [from Greek *gaster* = stomach + *podos* = of the foot]

gate *noun* (*plural* **gates**)
1 a movable barrier, usually on hinges, used as a door in a wall or fence. **2** the opening it covers. **3** a barrier for controlling the flow of water in a dam or lock. **4** the number of people attending a football match etc.
[from Old English]

gatecrash *verb* (**gatecrashes, gatecrashing, gatecrashed**)
go to a private party without being invited.
gatecrasher *noun*

gateway *noun* (*plural* **gateways**)
1 an opening containing a gate. **2** a way to reach something, *The gateway to success.*

gather *verb* (**gathers, gathering, gathered**)
1 come or bring together. **2** collect; obtain gradually, *gather information.* **3** collect as harvest; pluck, *Gather the corn when it is ripe*; *gather flowers.* **4** understand or learn, *We gather you have been on holiday.* **5** pull cloth into folds by running a thread through it. **6** a sore gathers when it swells up and forms pus.
[from Old English]

gathering *noun* (*plural* **gatherings**)
1 an assembly of people. **2** a swelling that forms pus.

gaudy *adjective*
too showy and bright.
gaudily *adverb*, **gaudiness** *noun*
[from Latin *gaudere* = rejoice]

gauge (*say* gayj) *noun* (*plural* **gauges**)
1 a standard measurement. **2** the distance between a pair of rails on a railway. **3** a measuring instrument.
gauge *verb* (**gauges, gauging, gauged**)
1 measure. **2** estimate; form a judgement.

gaunt *adjective*
1 a gaunt person is lean and haggard. **2** a gaunt place is grim or desolate-looking.
gauntness *noun* [origin unknown]

gauntlet *noun*
run the gauntlet have to suffer continuous severe criticism or risk.
[from a former military and naval punishment in which the victim was made to pass between two rows of men who struck him as he passed; the word is from Swedish *gatlopp* = passage]

gauze *noun*
1 thin transparent woven material. **2** fine wire mesh. **gauzy** *adjective* [from *Gaza*, a town in Palestine, where it was first made]

gay *adjective*
1 homosexual. **2** cheerful. **3** brightly coloured.
gayness *noun* [from French]

USAGE: Nowadays the most common meaning of *gay* is 'homosexual'. The older meanings 'cheerful' and 'brightly coloured' can still be used but are becoming less and less common in everyday use. *Gayness* is the noun from meaning 1 of *gay*. The noun that relates to the other two meanings is *gaiety*.

gaze *verb* (**gazes, gazing, gazed**)
look at something steadily for a long time.
gaze *noun* (*plural* **gazes**)
a long steady look. [origin unknown]

gazetteer (*say* gaz-it-eer) *noun* (*plural* **gazetteers**)
a list of place names.
[originally = journalist; the first gazetteer was intended to help journalists]

GCSE *abbreviation*
General Certificate of Secondary Education.

gear *noun* (*plural* **gears**)
1 a cogwheel, especially one of a set in a motor vehicle that turn power from the engine into movement of the wheels. **2** equipment or apparatus, *camping gear.*
gear *verb* (**gears, gearing, geared**)
gear to make something match something else, *Health care should be geared to people's needs, not to whether they can pay.*
gear up get ready for, *We were all geared up to play cricket, but then it rained.*

Geiger counter (*say* gy-ger) *noun* (*plural* **Geiger counters**)
an instrument that detects and measures radioactivity.
[named after a German scientist, H. W. Geiger, who helped to develop it]

gelatine *noun*
a clear jelly-like substance made by boiling animal tissue and used to make jellies and other foods and in photographic film.
gelatinous (*say* jil-at-in-us) *adjective*
[from Italian *gelata* = jelly]

gem *noun* (*plural* **gems**)
1 a precious stone. **2** an excellent person or thing. [via Old English from Latin]

-gen *suffix*
used in scientific language to form nouns meaning 'producing' or 'produced' (e.g. *oxygen, hydrogen*).

gender *noun* (*plural* **genders**)
1 the group in which a noun is classed in the grammar of some languages (e.g. *masculine, feminine, neuter*). **2** a person's sex, *Jobs should be open to all, regardless of race or gender*.
[from Latin *genus* = a kind]

gene (*say* jeen) *noun* (*plural* **genes**)
the part of a living cell that controls which characteristics (such as the colour of hair or eyes) are inherited from parents.
[from Greek *genos* = kind, race]

genealogy (*say* jeen-ee-al-o-jee) *noun* (*plural* **genealogies**)
1 a statement or diagram showing how people are descended from an ancestor; a pedigree. **2** the study of family history and ancestors.
genealogical (*say* jeen-ee-a-loj-ik-al) *adjective*
[from Greek *genea* = race of people, + -*logy*]

genera (*say* jen-e-ra)
plural of **genus**.

general *adjective*
1 to do with or involving most people or things, *This drug is now in general use*. **2** not detailed; broad, *I've got the general idea*. **3** chief or head, *the general manager*.
general *noun* (*plural* **generals**)
a senior army officer. [from Latin]

general election *noun* (*plural* **general elections**)
an election of Members of Parliament for the whole country.

generally *adverb*
1 usually. **2** in a general sense; without regard to details, *I was speaking generally*.

general practitioner *noun* (*plural* **general practitioners**)
a doctor who treats all kinds of diseases. He or she is the first doctor that people see when they are ill.

generate *verb* (generates, generating, generated)
produce or create.
[from Latin *generatus* = fathered]

generation *noun* (*plural* **generations**)
1 generating. **2** a single stage in a family, *Three generations were included: children, parents, and grandparents*. **3** all the people born at about the same time, *our parents' generation*.

generator *noun* (*plural* **generators**)
1 an apparatus for producing gases or steam. **2** a machine for converting mechanical energy into electricity.

generous *adjective*
1 willing to give things or share them. **2** given freely; plentiful, *a generous helping*.
generously *adverb*, **generosity** *noun*
[from Latin *generosus* = noble]

genetic (*say* jin-et-ik) *adjective*
1 to do with genes. **2** to do with characteristics inherited from parents or ancestors.
genetically *adverb* [from *genesis*]

genial (*say* jee-nee-al) *adjective*
kindly and cheerful. **genially** *adverb*,
geniality (*say* jee-nee-al-it-ee) *noun*
[from Latin *genialis* = joyous]

genital (*say* jen-it-al) *adjective*
to do with animal reproduction or reproductive organs.
[from old French; related to *generate*]

genitals (*say* jen-it-alz) *plural noun*
external sexual organs.

genius *noun* (*plural* **geniuses**)
1 an unusually clever person. **2** a very great natural ability, *He has a real genius for music*.
[Latin, = a spirit]

genocide (*say* jen-o-syd) *noun*
deliberate extermination of a race of people.
[from Greek *genos* = kind, race, + -*cide*]

gentle *adjective*
kind and quiet; not rough or severe.
gently *adverb*, **gentleness** *noun*
[from Latin *gentilis* = from a good family]

gentleman (*plural* **gentlemen**)
1 a well-mannered or honourable man. **2** a man of good social position. **3** (*in polite use*) a man.

genuine *adjective*
real; not faked or pretending. **genuinely** *adverb*,
genuineness *noun*
[from Latin *genu* = knee (because a father would take a baby onto his knee to show that he accepted it as his)]

genus (*say* jee-nus) *noun* (*plural* **genera**, *say* jen-er-a)
a group of similar animals or plants, *Lions and tigers belong to the same genus*.
[Latin, = family or race]

geo- *prefix*
earth. [from Greek *ge* = earth]

geography (*say* jee-og-ra-fee) *noun*
the study of the earth's surface and of its climate, peoples, and products. **geographer** *noun*, **geographical** *adjective*, **geographically** *adverb* [from *geo-* + -*graphy*]

geology (*say* jee-ol-o-jee) *noun*
the study of the structure of the earth's crust and its layers.
geological *adjective*, **geologically** *adverb*,
geologist *noun*
[from *geo-* + -*logy*]

geometry (*say* jee-om-it-ree) *noun*
the study of lines, angles, surfaces, and solids in mathematics. **geometric** *adjective*, **geometrical** *adjective*, **geometrically** *adverb* [from *geo-* + Greek *-metria* = measurement]

gerbil (*say* jer-bil) *noun* (*plural* **gerbils**)
a small brown animal with long hind legs, from Africa and Asia. One sort of gerbil, which originally came from Mongolia, is often kept as a pet. [from Latin]

geriatric (*say* je-ree-at-rik) *adjective*
to do with the care of old people and their health. [from Greek *geras* = old age + *iatros* = doctor]

germ *noun* (*plural* **germs**)
1 a micro-organism, especially one that can cause disease. 2 a tiny living structure from which a plant or animal may develop. 3 part of the seed of a cereal plant.
[from Latin *germen* = seed or sprout]

German measles *noun*
rubella.

German shepherd dog *noun* (*plural* **German shepherd dogs**)
a large strong dog, often used by the police.

germinate *verb* (**germinates, germinating, germinated**)
when a seed germinates, it begins to develop, and roots and shoots grow from it.
germination *noun* [same origin as *germ*]

gesticulate (*say* jes-tik-yoo-layt) *verb* (**gesticulates, gesticulating, gesticulated**)
make expressive movements with your hands and arms.
gesticulation *noun*
[same origin as *gesture*]

gesture (*say* jes-cher) *noun* (*plural* **gestures**)
1 a movement that expresses what a person feels. 2 an action that shows goodwill, *It would be a nice gesture to send her some flowers.*

gesture *verb* (**gestures, gesturing, gestured**)
tell a person something by making a gesture, *She gestured me to be quiet.*
[from Latin *gestus* = action, way of standing or moving]

get *verb* (**gets, getting, got**)
This word has many different uses, including
1 obtain or receive, *She got first prize.*
2 become, *Don't get angry!* 3 reach a place, *We got there by midnight.* 4 put or move, *I can't get my shoe on.* 5 prepare, *Will you get the tea?*
6 persuade or order, *Get him to wash up.*
7 catch or suffer from an illness. 8 (*informal*) understand, *Do you get what I mean?*
get away with 1 escape with something. 2 avoid being punished for what you have done.
get by (*informal*) manage.
get on 1 make progress. 2 be friendly with somebody.

get over recover from an illness etc.
get up 1 stand up. 2 get out of your bed in the morning. 3 prepare or organize, *We got up a concert.*
get your own back (*informal*) have your revenge.
have got to must.

geyser (*say* gee-zer or gy-zer) *noun* (*plural* **geysers**)
1 a natural spring that shoots up columns of hot water. 2 a kind of water heater.
[from *Geysir* = gusher, the name of a geyser in Iceland]

ghastly *adjective*
1 very unpleasant or bad. 2 looking pale and ill. **ghastliness** *noun*
[from Old English *gaestan* = terrify]

ghost *noun* (*plural* **ghosts**)
the spirit of a dead person that appears to the living. **ghostly** *adjective*

ghoulish (*say* gool-ish) *adjective*
enjoying things that are grisly or unpleasant.
ghoulishly *adverb*, **ghoulishness** *noun* [from Arabic *gul* = a demon that eats dead bodies]

giant *noun* (*plural* **giants**)
1 (in myths or fairy tales) a creature like a huge man. 2 a man, animal, or plant that is much larger than the usual size.

gibberish (*say* jib-er-ish) *noun*
meaningless speech; nonsense.

gibbet (*say* jib-it) *noun* (*plural* **gibbets**)
1 a gallows. 2 an upright post with an arm from which a criminal's body was hung after execution, as a warning to others.

gibbon *noun* (*plural* **gibbons**)
a small ape from south-east Asia. Gibbons have very long arms to help them swing through the trees where they live. [French]

giddy *adjective*
1 feeling that everything is spinning round and that you might fall. 2 causing this feeling, *We looked down from the giddy height of the cliff.* **giddily** *adverb*, **giddiness** *noun*
[from Old English]

gift *noun* (*plural* **gifts**)
1 a present. 2 a talent, *She has a gift for music.*
[from Old Norse]

gigantic (*say* jy-gan-tik) *adjective*
extremely large; huge.
[from Latin *gigantis* = of a giant]

giggle *verb* (**giggles, giggling, giggled**)
laugh in a silly way.
giggle *noun* (*plural* **giggles**)
1 a silly laugh. 2 (*informal*) something amusing; a bit of fun. [imitating the sound]

gild *verb* (**gilds, gilding, gilded**)
cover something with a thin layer of gold or gold paint. [from Old English]

gills *plural noun*
the part of the body through which fishes and certain other water animals breathe.

gilt *noun*
a thin covering of gold or gold paint.

gimmick *noun* (*plural* **gimmicks**)
something unusual or silly done or used just to attract people's attention.

gin *noun*
a colourless alcoholic drink flavoured with juniper berries. [from the name of Geneva, a city in Switzerland]

ginger *noun*
1 the hot-tasting root of a tropical plant, or a flavouring made from this root, used especially in drinks and Eastern cooking. 2 liveliness or energy. 3 a reddish-yellow colour. *ginger adjective*
ginger *verb* (**gingers, gingering, gingered**)
make something more lively, *This will ginger things up!* [via Old English, Latin, and Greek from Dravidian (a group of languages spoken in southern India)]

gingerly *adverb*
cautiously. [origin unknown]

giraffe *noun* (*plural* **giraffe** or **giraffes**)
an African animal, the world's tallest mammal, which reaches up to 5.5 metres in height. The giraffe's neck makes up nearly half its height. [from Arabic]

girder *noun* (*plural* **girders**)
a metal beam supporting part of a building or a bridge.

girdle *noun* (*plural* **girdles**)
a belt or cord worn round the waist.

girl *noun* (*plural* **girls**)
1 a female child. 2 a young woman. **girlhood** *noun*, **girlish** *adjective*

giro (*say* jy-roh) *noun*
a system of arranging payment for customers, run by a post office or bank.

gist (*say* jist) *noun*
the essential points or general sense of a speech, conversation, etc.

give *verb* (**gives, giving, gave, given**)
1 let someone have something. 2 make or do something, *He gave a laugh.* 3 be flexible or springy; bend or collapse when pressed. **giver** *noun*
give in acknowledge that you are defeated; yield.
give up 1 stop trying. 2 end a habit.

given *adjective*
named or stated in advance, *All the people in a given area.*

glacial (*say* glay-shal) *adjective*
icy; made of or produced by ice. **glacially** *adverb* [from Latin *glacies* = ice]

glacier (*say* glas-ee-er) *noun* (*plural* **glaciers**)
a mass of ice that moves very slowly down a mountain valley. [same origin as *glacial*]

glad *adjective*
1 pleased; expressing joy. 2 giving pleasure, *We brought the glad news.*
gladly *adverb*, **gladness** *noun*
glad of grateful for or pleased with something.

gladden *verb* (**gladdens, gladdening, gladdened**)
make a person glad.

glade *noun* (*plural* **glades**)
an open space in a forest. [origin unknown]

gladiator (*say* glad-ee-ay-ter) *noun* (*plural* **gladiators**)
a man trained to fight for public entertainment in ancient Rome. **gladiatorial** (*say* glad-ee-at-or-ee-al) *adjective* [from Latin *gladius* = sword]

glamorous *adjective*
excitingly attractive.

glamour *noun*
attractiveness, romantic charm. [from an old meaning of *grammar* = magic]

glance *verb* (**glances, glancing, glanced**)
1 look at something briefly. 2 strike something at an angle and slide off it, *The ball glanced off his bat.* **glance** *noun*

gland *noun* (*plural* **glands**)
an organ of the body that separates substances from the blood so that they can be used or secreted (passed out of the body). **glandular** *adjective* [from Latin]

glare *verb* (**glares, glaring, glared**)
1 shine with an unpleasant dazzling light. 2 stare angrily or fiercely. **glare** *noun*

glasnost *noun*
the open reporting of news or giving of information, especially in the former Soviet Union. [Russian, = openness]

glass *noun* (*plural* **glasses**)
1 a hard brittle substance that is usually transparent. 2 a container made of glass for drinking from. 3 a mirror. 4 a lens. **glassy** *adjective* [from Old English]

glasses *plural noun*
1 spectacles. 2 binoculars.

glaze *verb* (**glazes, glazing, glazed**)
1 fit a window or building with glass. 2 give a shiny surface to something. 3 become glassy. [from *glass*]

gleam *noun* (*plural* **gleams**)
1 a beam of soft light, especially one that comes and goes. 2 a small amount of hope, humour, etc.
gleam *verb* (**gleams, gleaming, gleamed**)
shine brightly, especially after cleaning or polishing. [from Old English]

glib *adjective*
speaking or writing readily but not sincerely or thoughtfully. **glibly** *adverb*, **glibness** *noun*
[from an old word *glibbery* = slippery]

glide *verb* (glides, gliding, glided)
1 move along smoothly. 2 fly without using an engine. 3 birds glide when they fly without beating their wings. **glide** *noun*

glider *noun* (*plural* gliders)
an aeroplane without an engine that flies by floating on warm air currents called thermals.

glimmer *noun* (*plural* glimmers)
1 a faint light. 2 a small sign or trace of something, *a glimmer of hope.*
glimmer *verb* (glimmers, glimmering, glimmered)
shine with a faint, flickering light.

glimpse *noun* (*plural* glimpses)
a brief view.
glimpse *verb* (glimpses, glimpsing, glimpsed)
see something briefly.

glint *noun* (*plural* glints)
a very brief flash of light.
glint *verb* (glints, glinting, glinted)
shine with a flash of light.
[probably from a Scandinavian language]

glisten (*say* glis-en) *verb* (glistens, glistening, glistened)
shine like something wet or oily.

glitter *verb* (glitters, glittering, glittered)
shine with tiny flashes of light; sparkle.
glitter *noun*
tiny sparkling pieces used for decoration.

gloat *verb* (gloats, gloating, gloated)
be pleased in an unkind way that you have succeeded or that someone else has been hurt or upset. [origin unknown]

global *adjective*
1 to do with the whole world; worldwide. 2 to do with the whole of a system. **globally** *adverb*
[from *globe*]

global warming *noun*
the increase in the temperature of the earth's atmosphere, caused by the greenhouse effect.

globe *noun* (*plural* globes)
1 something shaped like a ball, especially one with a map of the whole world on it. 2 the world, *She has travelled all over the globe.* 3 a hollow round glass object.

gloom *noun*
1 darkness. 2 sadness or despair.

gloomy *adjective* (gloomier, gloomiest)
1 almost dark. 2 depressed or depressing.
gloomily *adverb*, **gloominess** *noun*

glorify *verb* (glorifies, glorifying, glorified)
1 give great praise or great honour to. 2 make a thing seem more splendid or attractive than it really is, *It is a film that glorifies war.*
glorification *noun*

glorious *adjective*
splendid or magnificent. **gloriously** *adverb*

glory *noun* (*plural* glories)
1 fame and honour. 2 praise. 3 beauty or magnificence.
glory *verb* (glories, glorying, gloried)
rejoice; pride yourself, *They gloried in victory.*
[from Latin]

gloss[1] *noun* (*plural* glosses)
the shine on a smooth surface.
gloss *verb* (glosses, glossing, glossed)
make a thing glossy. [origin unknown]

gloss[2] *verb* (glosses, glossing, glossed)
gloss over mention a fault or mistake etc. only briefly to make it seem less serious than it really is.
[from old French *gloser* = flatter or deceive]

glossary *noun* (*plural* glossaries)
a list of difficult words with their meanings explained.
[from Greek *glossa* = tongue, language]

glossy *adjective* (glossier, glossiest)
smooth and shiny. **glossily** *adverb*, **glossiness** *noun*

glove *noun* (*plural* gloves)
a covering for the hand, usually with separate divisions for each finger and thumb.
gloved *adjective* [from Old English]

glow *noun*
1 brightness and warmth without flames. 2 a warm or cheerful feeling, *We felt a glow of pride.*
glow *verb* (glows, glowing, glowed)
shine with a soft, warm light.

glue *noun* (*plural* glues)
a sticky substance used for joining things together. **gluey** *adjective*
glue *verb* (glues, gluing, glued)
1 stick with glue. 2 attach or hold closely, *His ear was glued to the keyhole.*
[from French; related to *gluten*]

glum *adjective*
miserable or depressed. **glumly** *adverb*, **glumness** *noun*
[from dialect *glum* = to frown]

glut *noun* (*plural* gluts)
an excessive supply.
[from Latin *gluttire* = to swallow]

glutinous (*say* gloo-tin-us) *adjective*
glue-like or sticky.

glutton *noun* (*plural* gluttons)
a person who eats too much.
gluttonous *adjective*, **gluttony** *noun*
glutton for punishment a person who seems to enjoy doing something difficult or unpleasant.
[from old French; related to *glut*]

gm *abbreviation*
gram.

GMT *abbreviation*
Greenwich Mean Time.

gnarled (*say* narld) *adjective*
twisted and knobbly, like an old tree.

gnash (*say* nash) *verb* (**gnashes, gnashing, gnashed**)
grind your teeth together.

gnat (*say* nat) *noun* (*plural* **gnats**)
a tiny fly that bites. [from Old English]

gnaw (*say* naw) *verb* (**gnaws, gnawing, gnawed**)
keep on biting something hard so that it wears away. [from Old English]

gnome (*say* nohm) *noun* (*plural* **gnomes**)
a kind of dwarf in fairy tales, usually living underground. [from Latin]

go *verb* (**goes, going, went, gone**)
This word is used to show **1** movement, especially away from somewhere (*Where are you going?*), **2** direction (*The road goes to Bristol*), **3** change (*Milk went sour*), **4** progress or result (*The gun went bang*), **5** place (*Plates go on that shelf*), **6** sale (*The house went very cheaply*).
go off 1 explode. **2** become stale. **3** stop liking something.
go on continue.
go out stop burning or shining.
go *noun* (*plural* **goes**)
1 a turn or try, *May I have a go?* **2** (*informal*) energy or liveliness, *She is full of go.*
make a go of make a success of something.
on the go active; always working or moving.

goad *noun* (*plural* **goads**)
a stick with a pointed end for prodding cattle to move onwards.
goad *verb* (**goads, goading, goaded**)
stir into action by being annoying, *He goaded me into fighting.* [from Old English]

goal *noun* (*plural* **goals**)
1 the place where a ball must go to score a point in football, hockey, etc. **2** a point scored in this way. **3** something that you are trying to reach or achieve.

goalkeeper *noun* (*plural* **goalkeepers**)
the player who stands in the goal to try and keep the ball from entering.

goat *noun* (*plural* **goats**)
a mammal with horns and a beard, closely related to the sheep. Domestic goats are kept for their milk. [from Old English]

gobble *verb* (**gobbles, gobbling, gobbled**)
eat quickly and greedily.
[from old French *gober* = to swallow]

go-between *noun* (*plural* **go-betweens**)
a person who acts as a messenger or negotiator between others.

God *noun*
the creator of the universe in Christian, Jewish, and Muslim belief.

god *noun* (*plural* **gods**)
a male being that is worshipped, *Mars was a Roman god.*

goddess *noun* (*plural* **goddesses**)
a female being that is worshipped.

godparent *noun* (*plural* **godparents**)
a person at a child's christening who promises to see that it is brought up as a Christian.
godchild *noun*, **god-daughter** *noun*, **godfather** *noun*, **godmother** *noun*, **godson** *noun*

godsend *noun* (*plural* **godsends**)
a piece of unexpected good luck. [from an old phrase *God's send* = what God has sent]

goggle *verb* (**goggles, goggling, goggled**)
stare with wide-open eyes.

going *present participle* of **go**.
be going to do something be ready or likely to do it.

gold *noun* (*plural* **golds**)
1 a precious yellow metal. **2** a deep yellow colour. **3** a gold medal, usually given as first prize. **gold** *adjective*

golden *adjective*
1 made of gold. **2** coloured like gold. **3** precious or excellent, *a golden opportunity.*

golden wedding *noun* (*plural* **golden weddings**)
a couple's fiftieth wedding anniversary.

goldfish *noun* (*plural* **goldfish**)
a small red or orange fish, often kept as a pet.

golf *noun*
an outdoor game played by hitting a small white ball with a club into a series of holes on a specially prepared ground (a **golf course** or **golf links**) and taking as few strokes as possible.
golfer *noun*, **golfing** *noun*

-gon *suffix*
used to form nouns meaning 'having a certain number of angles (and sides)' (e.g. *hexagon*).
[from Greek *gonia* = angle]

gong *noun* (*plural* **gongs**)
a large metal disc that makes an echoing sound when it is hit.
[from Malay (a language spoken in Malaysia)]

good *adjective* (**better, best**)
1 having the right qualities; of the kind that people like, *a good book.* **2** kind, *It was good of you to help us.* **3** well-behaved, *Be a good boy.* **4** skilled or talented, *a good pianist.* **5** healthy; giving benefit, *Exercise is good for you.* **6** thorough, *Give it a good clean.* **7** large; considerable, *It's a good distance from the shops.*

good *noun*
1 something good, *Do good to others.* 2 benefit, *It's for your own good.*
for good for ever. **no good** useless.

USAGE: In standard English, *good* cannot be used as an adverb. You can say *She's a good player* but not *She played good.* The adverb that goes with *good* is *well*.

goodbye *interjection*
a word used when you leave somebody or at the end of a phone call.
[short for *God be with you*]

goods *plural noun*
1 things that are bought and sold. 2 things that are carried on trains or lorries.

goose *noun* (*plural* **geese**)
a long-necked water bird with webbed feet, larger than a duck. [from Old English]

gooseberry *noun* (*plural* **gooseberries**)
1 a small green fruit that grows on a prickly bush. 2 (*informal*) an unwanted extra person.
[probably from French dialect *gozell*]

goose-flesh *noun* or **goose pimples** *plural noun*
skin that has turned rough with small bumps on it because a person is cold or afraid.
[because it looks like the skin of a plucked goose]

gorge *noun* (*plural* **gorges**)
a narrow valley with steep sides.
gorge *verb* (**gorges, gorging, gorged**)
eat greedily; stuff with food.
[French, = throat]

gorgeous *adjective*
magnificent or beautiful. **gorgeously** *adverb*
[from old French]

gorilla *noun* (*plural* **gorillas**)
an African ape, the largest of all the apes. Males are about 1.8 metres tall and can weigh up to 300kg. [from Latin, probably from an African word = hairy woman]

USAGE: Do not confuse with *guerrilla*, which can be pronounced in the same way.

gospel *noun*
the Gospels the first four books of the New Testament, telling of the life and teachings of Jesus Christ.
[from Old English *god* = good + *spel* = news]

gossip *verb* (**gossips, gossiping, gossiped**)
talk a lot about other people.
gossip *noun* (*plural* **gossips**)
1 talk, especially rumours, about other people. 2 a person who enjoys gossiping.
gossipy *adjective*
[from Old English *godsibb* = close friend (literally = god-brother or sister), someone to gossip with]

got *past tense* of **get**.
have got possess, *Have you got a car?*
have got to must.

Gothic *noun*
the style of building common in the 12th–16th centuries, with pointed arches and much decorative carving.
[from the Goths, whom the Romans regarded as barbarians (because some people thought this style was barbaric compared to Greek or Roman styles)]

gouge (*say* gowj) *verb* (**gouges, gouging, gouged**)
scoop or force out by pressing.
[from Latin *gubia* = a kind of chisel]

gourmet (*say* goor-may) *noun* (*plural* **gourmets**)
a person who understands and appreciates good food and drink.
[French, = wine taster]

govern *verb* (**governs, governing, governed**)
be in charge of the public affairs of a country or region.
[from Latin *gubernare* = steer or direct]

governess *noun* (*plural* **governesses**)
a woman employed to teach children in a private household.

government *noun* (*plural* **governments**)
1 the group of people who are in charge of the public affairs of a country. 2 the process of governing.
governmental *adjective*

governor *noun* (*plural* **governors**)
1 a person who governs a State or a colony etc. 2 a member of the governing body of a school or other institution. 3 the person in charge of a prison.

gown *noun* (*plural* **gowns**)
a loose flowing garment.
[from Latin *gunna* = a fur-lined robe]

GP *abbreviation*
general practitioner.

grab *verb* (**grabs, grabbing, grabbed**)
take hold of something suddenly or greedily.
[from old German or old Dutch]

grace *noun*
1 beauty, especially of movement. 2 goodwill or favour. 3 dignity or good manners, *At least he had the grace to apologize.* 4 a short prayer of thanks before or after a meal. 5 the title of a duke, duchess, or archbishop, *His Grace the Duke of Kent.*
grace *verb* (**graces, gracing, graced**)
bring honour or dignity to something, *The mayor himself graced us with his presence.*
[from Latin *gratus* = pleasing]

graceful *adjective*
beautiful and elegant in movement or shape.
gracefully *adverb*, **gracefulness** *noun*

gracious *adjective*
behaving kindly and honourably.
graciously *adverb*, **graciousness** *noun*

grade *noun* (*plural* **grades**)
1 a step in a scale of quality or value or rank.
2 a mark showing the quality of a student's work.
grade *verb* (**grades, grading, graded**)
arrange in grades.
[from Latin *gradus* = a step]

gradient (*say* gray-dee-ent) *noun* (*plural* **gradients**)
a slope or the steepness of a slope.

gradual *adjective*
happening slowly but steadily.
gradually *adverb*

graduate (*say* grad-yoo-at) *noun* (*plural* **graduates**)
a person who has a university or college degree. [same origin as *grade*]

graffiti *noun*
words or drawings scribbled or sprayed on a wall. [Italian, = scratchings]

USAGE: Strictly speaking, this word is a plural noun (the singular is *graffito*), so it should be used with a plural verb: *There are graffiti all over the wall*. However, the word is widely used nowadays as if it were a singular noun and most people do not regard this as wrong: *There is graffiti all over the wall*.

graft *noun* (*plural* **grafts**)
1 a shoot from one plant or tree fixed into another to form a new growth. 2 a piece of living tissue transplanted by a surgeon to replace what is diseased or damaged, *a skin graft*.
graft *verb* (**grafts, grafting, grafted**)
insert or transplant as a graft.
[from Greek *grapheion* = pointed writing stick (because of the pointed shape of the end of the shoot)]

grain *noun* (*plural* **grains**)
1 a small hard seed or similar particle. 2 cereal plants when they are growing or after being harvested. 3 a very small amount, *a grain of truth*. 4 the pattern of lines made by the fibres in a piece of wood or paper. **grainy** *adjective*
[from Latin]

gram *noun* (*plural* **grams**)
a unit of mass or weight in the metric system.
[from Latin *gramma* = a small weight]

-gram *suffix*
used to form nouns meaning something written or drawn etc. (e.g. *diagram*).
[from Greek *gramma* = thing written]

grammar *noun* (*plural* **grammars**)
1 the rules for using words correctly. 2 a book about these rules. **grammatical** *adjective*
[from Greek, = the art of letters]

grammar school *noun* (*plural* **grammar schools**)
a secondary school for children with academic ability.

grand *adjective*
1 splendid and impressive. 2 most important or highest-ranking. 3 including everything; complete. **grandly** *adverb*, **grandness** *noun*
[from Latin *grandis* = fully-grown]

grandchild *noun* (*plural* **grandchildren**)
the child of a person's son or daughter.
granddaughter *noun*, **grandson** *noun*

grandeur (*say* grand-yer) *noun*
impressive beauty; splendour.

grandfather *noun* (*plural* **grandfathers**)
the father of a person's father or mother.

grandiose (*say* grand-ee-ohss) *adjective*
large and impressive; trying to seem impressive. [via French from Italian]

grandmother *noun* (*plural* **grandmothers**)
the mother of a person's father or mother.

grandparent *noun* (*plural* **grandparents**)
a grandfather or grandmother.

grand piano *noun* (*plural* **grand pianos**)
a large piano with the strings fixed horizontally.

grandstand *noun* (*plural* **grandstands**)
a building with a roof and rows of seats for spectators at a racecourse or sports ground.

grand total *noun*
the sum of other totals.

granite *noun*
a very hard kind of rock used for building.
[from Italian *granito* = like grains (because of the small particles you can see in the rock)]

grant *verb* (**grants, granting, granted**)
1 give or allow someone what he or she has asked for, *grant a request*. 2 admit; agree that something is true.
take for granted assume that something is true or will always be available.
grant *noun* (*plural* **grants**)
something granted, especially a sum of money.
[from old French]

Granth (*say* grunt) *noun*
the sacred scriptures of the Sikhs.
[from Sanskrit]

grape *noun* (*plural* **grapes**)
a small green or purple berry that grows in bunches on a vine. Grapes are used to make wine. [from old French]

grapefruit *noun* (*plural* **grapefruit**)
a large round yellow citrus fruit.
[because they grow in clusters, like grapes]

grapevine noun (plural grapevines)
1 a vine on which grapes grow. 2 a way by which news spreads unofficially, with people passing it on from one to another.

graph noun (plural graphs)
a diagram showing how two quantities or variables are related.
[from Greek graphein = to write or draw]

-graph suffix
used to form nouns and verbs meaning
1 something written, drawn, or recorded in some way (e.g. photograph). 2 a machine which records (e.g. telegraph, seismograph).
[same origin as graph]

graphic adjective
1 to do with drawing or painting, a graphic artist. 2 giving a lively description.
graphically adverb [same origin as graph]

-graphy suffix
used to form names of 1 sciences (e.g. geography), 2 methods of writing, drawing, or recording (e.g. photography).
[same origin as graph]

grapple verb (grapples, grappling, grappled)
1 struggle or wrestle. 2 seize or hold firmly.
3 try to deal with a problem etc., I've been grappling with this essay all day.

grasp verb (grasps, grasping, grasped)
1 seize and hold firmly. 2 understand.
grasp noun
1 the power of understanding something. 2 a firm hold.

grasping adjective
greedy for money or possessions.

grass noun (plural grasses)
1 a plant with green blades and stalks that are eaten by animals. 2 ground covered with grass; lawn.
grassy adjective

grasshopper noun (plural grasshoppers)
a jumping insect that makes a shrill noise.

grass roots plural noun
the ordinary people in a political party or other group.

grate[1] noun (plural grates)
1 a metal framework that keeps fuel in a fireplace. 2 a fireplace.
[from old French or Spanish]

grate[2] verb (grates, grating, grated)
1 shred something into small pieces by rubbing it on a rough surface. 2 make an unpleasant noise by rubbing. 3 sound harshly.
grate on have an irritating effect.
[via old French from Germanic]

grateful adjective
feeling or showing that you are thankful for something that has been done for you.
gratefully adverb
[from Latin gratus = thankful, pleasing]

gratify verb (gratifies, gratifying, gratified)
1 give pleasure. 2 satisfy a feeling or desire, Please gratify our curiosity.
gratification noun
[from Latin gratus = pleasing]

grating noun (plural gratings)
a framework of metal bars placed across an opening.
[from grate[1]]

gratitude noun
being grateful.

grave[1] noun (plural graves)
the place where a corpse is buried.
[from Old English]

grave[2] adjective
serious or solemn. **gravely** adverb
[from Latin gravis = heavy]

grave accent (rhymes with starve) noun (plural grave accents)
a mark over a vowel, as over a in vis-à-vis.
[from French; related to grave[2]]

gravel noun
small stones mixed with coarse sand, used to make paths.
gravelled adjective, **gravelly** adjective
[from old French]

graveyard noun (plural graveyards)
a burial ground.

gravity noun
1 the force that pulls all objects in the universe towards each other. 2 the force that pulls everything towards the earth. 3 seriousness.
[same origin as grave[2]]

gravy noun
a hot brown sauce made from meat juices.

graze verb (grazes, grazing, grazed)
1 feed on growing grass. 2 scrape your skin slightly, I grazed my elbow on the wall. 3 touch something lightly in passing.
graze noun (plural grazes)
a raw place where skin has been scraped. [from Old English graes = grass]

grease noun
melted fat; any thick oily substance.
greasy adjective
grease verb (greases, greasing, greased)
put grease on something.
[from Latin crassus = thick, fat]

great adjective
1 very large; much above average. 2 very important or talented, a great composer.
3 (informal) very good or enjoyable, It's great to see you again. 4 older or younger by one generation, great-grandfather.
greatly adverb, **greatness** noun

Great Britain *noun*
the island made up of England, Scotland, and Wales, with the small adjacent islands.

USAGE: See the note at *Britain.*

greed *noun*
being greedy. [from *greedy*]

greedy *adjective*
wanting more food, money, or other things than you need. **greedily** *adverb*, **greediness** *noun*
[from Old English]

green *noun* (*plural* **greens**)
1 the colour of grass, leaves, etc. 2 an area of grassy land, *the village green*; *a putting green.*
green *adjective*
1 of the colour green. 2 concerned with protecting the natural environment. 3 inexperienced and likely to make mistakes. **greenness** *noun*

green belt *noun* (*plural* **green belts**)
an area kept as open land round a city.

greenery *noun*
green leaves or plants.

greengrocer *noun* (*plural* **greengrocers**)
a person who keeps a shop that sells fruit and vegetables. **greengrocery** *noun*

greenhouse *noun* (*plural* **greenhouses**)
a glass building where plants are protected from cold.

greenhouse effect *noun*
the warming up of the earth's surface when radiation from the sun is trapped by the atmosphere.

greens *plural noun*
green vegetables, such as cabbage and spinach.

Greenwich Mean Time (*say* gren-ich)
the time on the line of longitude which passes through Greenwich in London, used as a basis for calculating time throughout the world.

greet *verb* (**greets, greeting, greeted**)
1 speak to a person who arrives. 2 receive, *They greeted the song with applause.* 3 present itself to, *A strange sight greeted our eyes.*
[from Old English]

greeting *noun*
words or actions used to greet somebody.

grey *noun* (*plural* **greys**)
the colour between black and white, like ashes or dark clouds. **grey** *adjective*, **greyness** *noun*
[from Old English]

greyhound *noun* (*plural* **greyhounds**)
a slender dog with smooth hair, used in racing. [from Old English *grighund*, probably = bitch-hound]

grid *noun* (*plural* **grids**)
a framework or pattern of bars or lines crossing each other.

grid reference *noun* (*plural* **grid references**)
a set of numbers that allows you to describe the exact position of something on a map.

grief *noun*
deep sorrow, especially at a person's death.
come to grief suffer a disaster.
[same origin as *grieve*]

grievance *noun* (*plural* **grievances**)
something that people are discontented about.
[old French, = injury or hardship]

grieve *verb* (**grieves, grieving, grieved**)
1 feel deep sorrow, especially at a person's death. 2 make a person feel very sad.
[from old French *grever* = to burden; related to *grave*²]

grill *noun* (*plural* **grills**)
1 a heated element on a cooker, for sending heat downwards. 2 food cooked under this. 3 a grille.
grill *verb* (**grills, grilling, grilled**)
1 cook under a grill. 2 question closely and severely, *The police grilled him for an hour.*

grim *adjective* (**grimmer, grimmest**)
1 stern or severe. 2 unpleasant or unattractive, *a grim prospect.* **grimly** *adverb*, **grimness** *noun*
[from Old English]

grimace (*say* grim-**ayss** or grim-as) *noun* (*plural* **grimaces**)
a twisted expression on the face made in pain or disgust.
grimace *verb* (**grimaces, grimacing, grimaced**)
make a grimace.
[from Spanish *grima* = fright]

grime *noun*
dirt in a layer on a surface or on the skin.
grimy *adjective*
[from old German or old Dutch]

grin *noun* (*plural* **grins**)
a broad smile showing your teeth.
grin *verb* (**grins, grinning, grinned**)
smile broadly showing your teeth.
[from Old English]

grind *verb* (**grinds, grinding, ground**)
1 crush something into tiny pieces or powder. 2 sharpen or smooth something by rubbing it on a rough surface. 3 rub harshly together, *He ground his teeth in fury.* 4 move with a harsh grating noise, *The bus ground to a halt.*
grinder *noun*

grip *verb* (**grips, gripping, gripped**)
1 hold something firmly. 2 hold a person's attention, *The opening chapter really gripped me.*
grip *noun* (*plural* **grips**)
1 a firm hold. 2 a handle, especially on a sports racket, bat, etc. 3 (*American*) a travelling bag. 4 control or power, *The country is in the grip of lottery fever.*
get to grips with begin to deal with successfully.

gristle *noun*
tough rubbery tissue in meat. **gristly** *adjective* [from Old English]

grit *noun*
1 tiny pieces of stone or sand. 2 courage and endurance.
gritty *adjective*, **grittiness** *noun*
grit *verb* (grits, gritting, gritted)
1 spread a road or path with grit. 2 clench your teeth when in pain or trouble.

grizzled *adjective*
streaked with grey hairs.
[from old French *grisel* = grey]

grizzly bear *noun* (*plural* grizzly bears)
a large fierce bear of North America.
[from *grizzled* (the bear has brown fur with white-tipped hairs)]

groan *verb* (groans, groaning, groaned)
1 make a long deep sound in pain, distress, or disapproval. 2 creak loudly under a heavy load. **groan** *noun*, **groaner** *noun*

grocer *noun* (*plural* grocers)
a person who keeps a shop that sells food and household goods.
[originally = wholesaler; from Latin *grossus* = gross (because a wholesaler buys goods *in the gross* = in large quantities)]

groceries *plural noun*
goods sold by a grocer.

groom *noun* (*plural* grooms)
1 a person whose job is to look after horses. 2 a bridegroom.
groom *verb* (grooms, grooming, groomed)
1 clean and brush a horse or other animal. 2 make something neat and trim. 3 train a person for a certain job or position, *Evans is being groomed for the captaincy.*

groove *noun* (*plural* grooves)
a long narrow furrow or channel cut in the surface of something. **grooved** *adjective* [from old Dutch *groeve* = furrow or ditch]

grope *verb* (gropes, groping, groped)
feel about for something you cannot see.

gross (*say* grohss) *adjective*
1 fat and ugly. 2 having bad manners; vulgar. 3 very obvious or shocking, *gross stupidity.* 4 total; without anything being deducted, *our gross income.* (Compare *net²*.)
grossly *adverb*, **grossness** *noun*
gross *noun* (*plural* gross)
twelve dozen (144) of something, *ten gross* = 1440. [from Latin]

grotesque (*say* groh-**tesk**) *adjective*
fantastically ugly or very strangely shaped.
grotesquely *adverb*, **grotesqueness** *noun*

ground¹ *past tense* of grind.

ground² *noun* (*plural* grounds)
1 the solid surface of the earth. 2 a sports field.

ground *verb* (grounds, grounding, grounded)
1 prevent a plane from flying, *All aircraft are grounded because of the fog.* 2 give a good basic training, *Ground them in the rules of spelling.* 3 base, *This theory is grounded on reliable evidence.*

grounds *plural noun*
1 the gardens of a large house. 2 solid particles that sink to the bottom, *coffee grounds.* 3 reasons, *There are grounds for suspicion.*

group *noun* (*plural* groups)
1 a number of people, animals, or things that come together or belong together in some way. 2 a band of musicians.
group *verb* (groups, grouping, grouped)
put together or come together in a group or groups.

grouse¹ *noun* (*plural* grouse)
a bird with feathered feet, hunted as game.
[origin unknown]

grouse² *verb* (grouses, grousing, groused)
(*informal*)
grumble or complain. **grouse** *noun*,
grouser *noun* [origin unknown]

grove *noun* (*plural* groves)
a group of trees; a small wood.

grovel *verb* (grovels, grovelling, grovelled)
1 crawl on the ground, especially in a show of fear or humility. 2 act in an excessively humble way, for example by apologizing a lot.
groveller *noun*
[from Old Norse *a grufu* = face downwards]

grow *verb* (grows, growing, grew, grown)
1 become bigger or greater. 2 develop. 3 cultivate; plant and look after, *She grows roses.* 4 become, *He grew rich.* **grower** *noun*

growl *verb* (growls, growling, growled)
make a deep angry sound in the throat.
growl *noun* [imitating the sound]

grown-up *noun* (*plural* grown-ups)
an adult person.
grown-up *adjective* like or suitable for an adult.

growth *noun* (*plural* growths)
1 growing or developing. 2 something that has grown. 3 a lump that has grown on or inside a person's body; a tumour.

grub *noun* (*plural* grubs)
1 a tiny worm-like creature that will become an insect; a larva. 2 (*slang*) food.
grub *verb* (grubs, grubbing, grubbed)
1 dig up by the roots. 2 turn things over or move them about while looking for something; rummage. [origin unknown]

grubby *adjective* (grubbier, grubbiest)
rather dirty. **grubbiness** *noun*

grudge *noun* (*plural* grudges)
a feeling of resentment or ill will, *She isn't the sort of person who bears a grudge.*

grudge *verb* (grudges, grudging, grudged)
resent having to give or allow something. [from old French *grouchier* = grumble]

gruff *adjective*
having a rough unfriendly voice or manner. **gruffly** *adverb*, **gruffness** *noun* [from Dutch *grof* = coarse or rude]

grumble *verb* (grumbles, grumbling, grumbled)
complain in a bad-tempered way. **grumble** *noun*, **grumbler** *noun* [origin unknown]

grunt *verb* (grunts, grunting, grunted)
1 make a pig's gruff snort. 2 speak or say gruffly. **grunt** *noun* [from Old English *grunnettan*, imitating the sound]

guarantee *noun* (*plural* guarantees)
a formal promise to do something or to repair an object if it breaks or goes wrong.
guarantee *verb* (guarantees, guaranteeing, guaranteed)
give a guarantee; promise. **guarantor** *noun*

guard *verb* (guards, guarding, guarded)
1 protect; keep safe. 2 watch over and prevent from escaping.
guard *noun* (*plural* guards)
1 guarding; protection, *Keep the prisoners under close guard.* 2 someone who guards a person or place. 3 a group of soldiers or police officers etc. acting as a guard. 4 a railway official in charge of a train. 5 a protecting device, *a fireguard.* [via old French from Germanic; related to *ward*]

guardian *noun* (*plural* guardians)
1 someone who guards. 2 a person who is legally in charge of a child whose parents cannot look after him or her.
guardianship *noun* [via old French from Germanic; related to *warden*]

guerrilla (*say* ger-il-a) *noun* (*plural* guerrillas)
a member of a small unofficial army who fights by making surprise attacks. [Spanish, = little war]

USAGE: Do not confuse with *gorilla.*

guess *noun* (*plural* guesses)
an opinion or answer that you give without making careful calculations or without certain knowledge.
guess *verb* (guesses, guessing, guessed)
make a guess. **guesser** *noun*

guest *noun* (*plural* guests)
1 a person who is invited to visit or stay at another's house. 2 a person staying at a hotel. 3 a person who takes part in another's show as a visiting performer.

guidance *noun*
1 guiding. 2 advising or advice on problems.

Guide *noun* (*plural* Guides)
a member of the Girl Guides Association, an organization for girls.

guide *noun* (*plural* guides)
1 a person who shows others the way or points out interesting sights. 2 a book giving information about a place or subject.
guide *verb* (guides, guiding, guided)
show someone the way or how to do something. [via old French from Germanic; related to *wit*]

guide dog *noun* (*plural* guide dogs)
a dog trained to lead a blind person.

guile (rhymes with *mile*) *noun*
craftiness. [via old French from Old Norse]

guillotine (*say* gil-ot-een) *noun* (*plural* guillotines)
a machine with a heavy blade for beheading criminals, used in France.
[named after Dr Guillotin, who suggested its use in France in 1789]

guilt *noun*
1 the fact that you have committed an offence. 2 a feeling that you are to blame for something that has happened.
[from Old English *gylt* = a crime or sin]

guilty *adjective*
1 having done wrong. 2 feeling or showing guilt. **guiltily** *adverb*

guinea pig *noun* (*plural* guinea pigs)
1 a small furry animal without a tail. 2 a person who is used as the subject of an experiment.
[from *Guinea* in west Africa, probably by mistake for Guiana, in South America, where the guinea pig comes from]

guitar *noun* (*plural* guitars)
a musical instrument played by plucking its strings. **guitarist** *noun*
[from Greek *kithara*, a small harp]

gulf *noun* (*plural* gulfs)
1 a large area of the sea that is partly surrounded by land. 2 a wide gap; a great difference. [from Greek]

gull *noun* (*plural* gulls)
a seagull. [a Celtic word]

gullible *adjective*
easily deceived.
[from an old word *gull* = fool or deceive]

gulp *verb* (gulps, gulping, gulped)
1 swallow hastily or greedily. 2 make a loud swallowing noise, especially because of fear.
gulp *noun* (*plural* gulps)
1 the act of gulping. 2 a large mouthful of liquid. [imitating the sound]

gum[1] *noun* (*plural* gums)
the firm flesh in which your teeth are rooted. [from Old English]

gum[2] *noun* (*plural* gums)
1 a sticky substance produced by some trees and shrubs, used as glue. 2 a sweet made with

gum or gelatine, *a fruit gum*. **3** chewing gum. **4** a gum tree.
gummy *adjective*
gum *verb* (**gums, gumming, gummed**)
cover or stick something with gum. [via old French, Latin, and Greek from Egyptian]

gum tree *noun* (*plural* **gum trees**)
a eucalyptus.

gun *noun* (*plural* **guns**)
1 a weapon that fires shells or bullets from a metal tube. **2** a starting pistol. **3** a device that forces a substance out of a tube, *a grease gun*.
gunfire *noun*, **gunshot** *noun*
gun *verb* (**guns, gunning, gunned**)
gun down shoot someone with a gun.
[probably from the Swedish girl's name *Gunnhildr*, from *gunnr* = war]

gunpowder *noun*
an explosive made from a powdered mixture of potassium nitrate, charcoal, and sulphur.

gurgle *verb* (**gurgles, gurgling, gurgled**)
make a low bubbling sound. **gurgle** *noun*

guru *noun* (*plural* **gurus**)
1 a Hindu religious leader. **2** an influential teacher; a mentor.
[from Sanskrit]

gush *verb* (**gushes, gushing, gushed**)
1 flow suddenly or quickly. **2** talk too enthusiastically or emotionally. **gush** *noun*

gust *noun* (*plural* **gusts**)
a sudden rush of wind, rain, or smoke. **gusty** *adjective*, **gustily** *adverb*
gust *verb* (**gusts, gusting, gusted**)
blow in gusts. [from Old Norse]

gut *noun* (*plural* **guts**)
the lower part of the digestive system; the intestine.
gut *verb* (**guts, gutting, gutted**)
1 remove the guts from a dead fish or other animal. **2** remove or destroy the inside of something, *The fire gutted the factory*.

guts *plural noun*
1 the digestive system; the inside parts of a person or thing. **2** (*informal*) courage.

gutted *adjective* (*informal*)
extremely disappointed or upset.

gutter *noun* (*plural* **gutters**)
a long narrow channel at the side of a street, or along the edge of a roof, for carrying away rainwater.
gutter *verb* (**gutters, guttering, guttered**)
a candle gutters when it burns unsteadily so that melted wax runs down.
[from Latin *gutta* = a drop]

guttural (*say* gut-er-al) *adjective*
throaty and harsh-sounding, *a guttural voice*.
[from Latin *guttur* = throat]

guy[1] *noun* (*plural* **guys**)
1 a figure representing Guy Fawkes, burnt on 5 November in memory of the Gunpowder Plot which planned to blow up Parliament on that day in 1605. **2** (*informal*) a man.

guy[2] or **guy-rope** *noun* (*plural* **guys, guy-ropes**)
a rope used to hold something in place, especially a tent.
[probably from old German]

gym (*say* jim) *noun* (*plural* **gyms**) (*informal*)
1 a gymnasium. **2** gymnastics.

gymkhana (*say* jim-kah-na) *noun* (*plural* **gymkhanas**)
a series of horse-riding contests and other sports events. [from Urdu]

gymnasium *noun* (*plural* **gymnasia, gymnasiums**)
a place equipped for gymnastics.
[from Greek *gymnos* = naked (because Greek men exercised naked)]

gymnastics *plural noun*
exercises performed to develop the muscles or to show the performer's agility.
gymnastic *adjective*

gypsy *noun* (*plural* **gypsies**)
a member of a people who live in caravans and wander from place to place, especially a Romany.
[from *Egyptian*, because gypsies were originally thought to have come from Egypt]

gyrate (*say* jy-rayt) *verb* (**gyrates, gyrating, gyrated**)
revolve; move in circles or spirals.
gyration *noun*
[from Greek *gyros* = a ring or circle]

gyroscope (*say* jy-ro-skohp) *noun* (*plural* **gyroscopes**)
a device that keeps steady because of a heavy wheel spinning inside it.
[same origin as *gyrate*]

Hh

haberdashery *noun*
small articles used in sewing, e.g. ribbons, buttons, thread. [origin unknown]

habit *noun* (*plural* **habits**)
1 something that you do without thinking because you have done it so often; a settled way of behaving. **2** the long dress worn by a monk or nun. **habitual** *adjective*, **habitually** *adverb*
[from Latin]

habitat *noun* (*plural* **habitats**)
where an animal or plant lives naturally.
[Latin, literally = inhabits]

habitation noun (plural habitations)
1 a dwelling. 2 inhabiting a place.
[from Latin habitare = inhabit]

hack verb (hacks, hacking, hacked)
1 chop or cut roughly. 2 (informal) break into
a computer system. [from Old English]

hackles plural noun
with his or her hackles up angry and ready to
fight.
[hackles are the long feathers on some birds'
necks]

haddock noun (plural haddock)
a sea fish like cod but smaller, used as food.

hadn't (mainly spoken)
had not.

haemoglobin (say heem-a-**gloh**-bin) noun
the red substance that carries oxygen in the
blood.
[from Greek haima = blood + globule (because
of the shape of haemoglobin cells)]

haemophilia (say heem-o-**fil**-ee-a) noun
a disease that causes people to bleed
dangerously from even a slight cut.
haemophiliac noun
[from Greek haima = blood + philia = loving]

haemorrhage (say **hem**-er-ij) noun
bleeding, especially inside a person's body.
[from Greek haima = blood + rhegnunai
= burst]

hag noun (plural hags)
an ugly old woman. [from Old English]

haggard adjective
looking ill or very tired. [from old French]

haggis noun (plural haggises)
a Scottish food made from sheep's offal.

hail[1] noun
frozen drops of rain. **hail** verb, **hailstone** noun,
hailstorm noun [from Old English]

hail[2] interjection
an exclamation of greeting.
hail verb (hails, hailing, hailed)
call out to somebody.
hail from come from, He hails from Ireland.
[from Old Norse]

hair noun (plural hairs)
1 a soft covering that grows on the heads and
bodies of people and animals. 2 one of the
threads that make up this covering.
hairbrush noun, **haircut** noun
keep your hair on (informal) do not lose your
temper.
split hairs make petty or unimportant
distinctions of meaning. **hair-splitting** noun

hairdresser noun (plural hairdressers)
a person whose job is to cut and arrange
people's hair.

hairpin noun (plural hairpins)
a U-shaped pin for keeping hair in place.

hairpin bend noun (plural hairpin bends)
a sharp bend in a road.

hair-raising adjective
terrifying.

hairy adjective
1 with a lot of hair. 2 (informal) dangerous or
risky.

halal noun
meat prepared according to Muslim law.
[Arabic, = according to religious law]

halcyon (say **hal**-see-on) adjective
happy and peaceful, halcyon days.
[from Greek alkyon = a bird which was once
believed to build its nest on the sea, which
magically stayed calm]

half noun (plural halves)
one of the two equal parts or amounts into
which something is or can be divided.
half adverb
partly; not completely, This meat is only half
cooked.
not half (slang) extremely, Was she cross? Not
half!

half-brother noun (plural half-brothers)
a brother to whom you are related by one
parent but not by both parents.

half-hearted adjective
not very enthusiastic. **half-heartedly** adverb

half-life noun (plural half-lives)
the time taken for the radioactivity of a
substance to fall to half its original value.

halfpenny (say **hayp**-nee) noun (plural
halfpennies for separate coins, halfpence for a
sum of money)
a former coin worth half a penny.

half-sister noun (plural half-sisters)
a sister to whom you are related by one parent
but not by both parents.

half-term noun (plural half-terms)
a short holiday in the middle of a term.

halfway adjective & adverb
between two others and equally distant from
each.

hall noun (plural halls)
1 a space or passage into which the front
entrance of a house etc. opens. 2 a very large
room or building used for meetings, concerts,
etc. [from Old English]

Hallowe'en noun
31 October, traditionally a time when ghosts
and witches are believed to appear. [from All
Hallow Even, the evening before the Christian
festival honouring all the hallows = saints]

hallucination noun (plural hallucinations)
something you think you can see or hear that
is not really there.
[from Latin alucinari = wander in your mind]

halo *noun* (*plural* **haloes**)
a circle of light round something, especially
round the head of a saint etc. in paintings.
[from Greek]

halt *verb* (**halts, halting, halted**)
stop.
halt *noun* (*plural* **halts**)
1 a stop, *Work came to a halt.* **2** a small
stopping place on a railway.

halve *verb* (**halves, halving, halved**)
1 divide something into halves. **2** reduce
something to half its size. [from *half*]

ham *noun* (*plural* **hams**)
1 meat from a pig's leg. **2** (*slang*) an actor who
overacts. **3** (*informal*) someone who operates a
radio to send and receive messages as a hobby.
[from Old English]

hamburger *noun* (*plural* **hamburgers**)
a flat round cake of minced beef served fried,
often in a bread roll. [named after Hamburg in
Germany (not after *ham*)]

hammer *noun* (*plural* **hammers**)
a tool with a heavy metal head used for driving
nails in, breaking things, etc.
hammer *verb* (**hammers, hammering, hammered**)
1 hit something with a hammer. **2** strike
loudly. **3** (*informal*) defeat.

hammock *noun* (*plural* **hammocks**)
a bed made of a strong net or piece of cloth
hung by cords. [via Spanish from Taino (a
South American language)]

hamper[1] *noun* (*plural* **hampers**)
a large box-shaped basket with a lid.
[from old French]

hamper[2] *verb* (**hampers, hampering, hampered**)
hinder; prevent from moving or working
freely. [origin unknown]

hamster *noun* (*plural* **hamsters**)
a small furry animal with cheek pouches for
carrying grain. [from German]

hand *noun* (*plural* **hands**)
1 the end part of the arm below the wrist. **2** a
pointer on a clock or dial. **3** a worker; a
member of a ship's crew, *All hands on deck!*
4 the cards held by one player in a card game.
5 side or direction, *on the other hand.* **6** help or
aid, *Give me a hand with these boxes.*
at hand near.
by hand using your hand or hands.
give or **receive a big hand** applaud or be
applauded.
hands down winning easily.
in good hands in the care or control of someone
who can be trusted.
in hand in your possession; being dealt with.
on hand available.
out of hand out of control.

hand *verb* (**hands, handing, handed**)
give or pass something to somebody, *Hand it
over.*
hand down pass something from one
generation to another.

handbag *noun* (*plural* **handbags**)
a small bag for holding a purse and personal
articles.

handbook *noun* (*plural* **handbooks**)
a small book that gives useful facts about
something.

handcuff *noun* (*plural* **handcuffs**)
one of a pair of metal rings linked by a chain,
for fastening wrists together.
handcuff *verb* (**handcuffs, handcuffing,
handcuffed**)
fasten with handcuffs.

handful *noun* (*plural* **handfuls**)
1 as much as can be carried in one hand. **2** a
few people or things. **3** (*informal*) a
troublesome person or task.

handicap *noun* (*plural* **handicaps**)
1 a disadvantage. **2** a physical or mental
disability. **handicapped** *adjective* [from *hand in
cap* (from an old game in which forfeit money
was deposited in a cap)]

handkerchief *noun* (*plural* **handkerchiefs**)
a small square of cloth for wiping the nose or
face.

handle *noun* (*plural* **handles**)
the part of a thing by which it is carried or
controlled.
handle *verb* (**handles, handling, handled**)
1 touch or feel something with your hands.
2 deal with; manage, *Will you handle the
catering?* **handler** *noun* [from Old English]

handlebar *noun* or **handlebars** *plural noun*
the bar, with a handle at each end, that steers a
bicycle or motorcycle etc.

handsome *adjective*
1 good-looking. **2** generous.
handsomely *adverb* [originally = easy to handle
or use: from *hand* + *-some*]

handstand *noun* (*plural* **handstands**)
balancing on your hands with your feet in the
air.

handwriting *noun*
writing done by hand.
handwritten *adjective*

handy *adjective* (**handier, handiest**)
1 convenient or useful. **2** good at using the
hands. **handily** *adverb*, **handiness** *noun*

hang *verb* (**hangs, hanging, hung**)
1 fix the top or side of something to a hook or
nail etc.; be supported in this way. **2** stick
wallpaper to a wall. **3** decorate
with drapery or hanging ornaments etc., *The
tree was hung with lights.* **4** droop or lean,
People hung over the gate. **5** (with *past tense* &

past participle **hanged**) execute someone by hanging them from a rope that tightens round the neck, *He was hanged in 1950.*
hang about 1 loiter. **2** not go away.
hang back hesitate to go forward or to do something.
hang on 1 hold tightly. **2** (*informal*) wait.
hang up end a telephone conversation by putting back the receiver.
hang *noun*
get the hang of (*informal*) learn how to do or use something.

hang-glider *noun* (*plural* **hang-gliders**)
a framework in which a person can glide through the air. **hang-gliding** *noun*

hangover *noun* (*plural* **hangovers**)
an unpleasant feeling after drinking too much alcohol.

hank *noun* (*plural* **hanks**)
a coil or piece of wool, thread, etc.

hanker *verb* (**hankers, hankering, hankered**)
feel a longing for something.

haphazard *adjective*
done or chosen at random, not by planning. [from an old word *hap* = luck, + *hazard*]

happen *verb* (**happens, happening, happened**)
1 take place; occur. **2** do something by chance, *I happened to see him.*
[from an old word *hap* = luck]

happy *adjective* (**happier, happiest**)
1 pleased or contented. **2** fortunate, *a happy coincidence.* **happily** *adverb*, **happiness** *noun*
[same origin as *happen*]

harangue (*say* ha-**rang**) *verb* (**harangues, haranguing, harangued**)
make a long speech to somebody.
harangue *noun* [from Latin]

harass (*say* ha-**ras**) *verb* (**harasses, harassing, harassed**)
trouble or annoy somebody often.
harassment (*say* ha-**ras**-ment) *noun*
[from French *harer* = set a dog on someone]

harbour *noun* (*plural* **harbours**)
a place where ships can shelter or unload.

hard *adjective*
1 firm or solid; not soft. **2** difficult, *hard sums.* **3** severe or stern. **4** causing suffering, *hard luck.* **5** using great effort, *a hard worker.* **6** hard drugs are strong and addictive ones.
hardness *noun*
hard of hearing slightly deaf.
hard up (*informal*) short of money.
hard *adverb*
1 so as to be hard, *The ground froze hard.* **2** with great effort; intensively, *We worked hard. It is raining hard.* **3** with difficulty, *hard-earned.* [from Old English]

hard disk *noun* (*plural* **hard disks**)
a disk fixed inside a computer, able to store large amounts of data.

harden *verb* (**hardens, hardening, hardened**)
make or become hard or hardy.
hardener *noun*

hardly *adverb*
only just; only with difficulty, *She can hardly walk.*

USAGE: It is not acceptable in standard English to use 'not' with *hardly*, as in 'she can't hardly walk'.

hardship *noun* (*plural* **hardships**)
difficult conditions that cause discomfort or suffering, *a life of hardship.*

hardware *noun*
1 metal implements and tools etc.; machinery. **2** the machinery of a computer as opposed to the software. (Compare *software*.)

hard water *noun*
water containing minerals that prevent soap from making much lather.

hardy *adjective* (**hardier, hardiest**)
able to endure cold or difficult conditions.
hardiness *noun*
[from French *hardi* = bold or daring]

hare *noun* (*plural* **hares**)
an animal like a rabbit but larger.

harm *verb* (**harms, harming, harmed**)
damage or injure.
harm *noun*
damage or injury. **harmful** *adjective*, **harmless** *adjective* [from Old English]

harmonica *noun* (*plural* **harmonicas**)
a mouth organ. [from Latin *harmonicus* = to do with melody]

harmonious *adjective*
1 combining together in a pleasant and attractive way. **2** peaceful and friendly.

harmony *noun* (*plural* **harmonies**)
1 a pleasant combination, especially of musical notes. **2** being friendly to each other and not quarrelling.
[from Latin *harmonia* = agreement]

harness *noun* (*plural* **harnesses**)
the straps put round a horse's head and neck for controlling it.
harness *verb* (**harnesses, harnessing, harnessed**)
1 put a harness on a horse. **2** control and use something, *Could we harness the power of the wind?* [via French from Old Norse]

harp *noun* (*plural* **harps**)
a musical instrument made of strings stretched across a frame and plucked by the fingers.
harpist *noun*

harpoon *noun* (*plural* **harpoons**)
a spear attached to a rope, used for catching whales etc. **harpoon** *verb*

harrowing *adjective*
very upsetting or distressing.

harsh *adjective*
1 rough and unpleasant. 2 severe or cruel.
harshly *adverb*, **harshness** *noun*
[from old German *horsch* = rough or hairy]

harvest *noun* (*plural* **harvests**)
1 the time when farmers gather in the corn, fruit, or vegetables that they have grown. 2 the crop that is gathered in.

hash *noun*
a mixture of small pieces of meat and vegetables, usually fried.
make a hash of (*informal*) make a mess of something; bungle.
[from French *hacher* = cut up small]

hasn't (*mainly spoken*)
has not.

haste *noun*
a hurry.
make haste act quickly.

hasten *verb* (**hastens, hastening, hastened**)
hurry.

hasty *adjective*
hurried; done too quickly. **hastily** *adverb*, **hastiness** *noun*

hat *noun* (*plural* **hats**)
a shaped covering for the head.
keep it under your hat keep it secret.

hatch[1] *noun* (*plural* **hatches**)
an opening in a floor, wall, or door, usually with a covering. [from Old English]

hatch[2] *verb* (**hatches, hatching, hatched**)
1 break out of an egg. 2 keep an egg warm until a baby bird comes out. 3 plan, *They hatched a plot.* [origin unknown]

hatchet *noun* (*plural* **hatchets**)
a small axe.

hate *verb* (**hates, hating, hated**)
dislike very strongly.
hate *noun*
extreme dislike. [from Old English]

hatred *noun*
extreme dislike.

hat-trick *noun* (*plural* **hat-tricks**)
getting three goals, wickets, victories, etc. one after the other.

haughty *adjective*
proud of yourself and looking down on other people. **haughtily** *adverb*, **haughtiness** *noun*
[from French *haut* = high]

haul *verb* (**hauls, hauling, hauled**)
pull or drag with great effort. **haulage** *noun*

haul *noun* (*plural* **hauls**)
1 hauling. 2 the amount obtained by an effort; booty, *The robbers made a good haul.* 3 a distance to be covered, *a long haul.*

haunt *verb* (**haunts, haunting, haunted**)
1 (of ghosts) appear often in a place or to a person. 2 visit a place often. 3 stay in your mind, *Memories haunt me.*
haunt *noun* (*plural* **haunts**)
a place that you often visit.

have *verb* (**has, having, had**)
This word has many uses, including 1 possess or own, *We have two dogs.* 2 contain, *This tin has sweets in it.* 3 experience, *He had a shock.* 4 be obliged to do something, *We have to go now.* 5 allow, *I won't have him bullied.* 6 receive or accept, *Will you have a sweet?* 7 get something done, *I'm having my watch mended.* 8 (*slang*) cheat or deceive, *We've been had!*
have somebody on (*informal*) fool him or her.
have *auxiliary verb*
used to form the past tense of verbs, e.g. *He has gone.* [from Old English]

haven *noun* (*plural* **havens**)
a refuge. [from Old Norse]

haven't (*mainly spoken*)
have not.

havoc *noun*
great destruction or disorder. [from old French *havot*, an order to begin looting]

hawk *noun* (*plural* **hawks**)
a bird of prey with very strong eyesight.

hawthorn *noun* (*plural* **hawthorns**)
a thorny tree with small red berries (called *haws*).

hay *noun*
dried grass for feeding to animals.

hay fever *noun*
irritation of the nose, throat, and eyes, caused by pollen or dust.

hazard *noun* (*plural* **hazards**)
1 a danger or risk. 2 an obstacle.
hazardous *adjective*
[via French from Persian or Turkish *zar* = dice]

hazy *adjective*
1 misty. 2 vague or uncertain.
hazily *adverb*, **haziness** *noun*

he *pronoun*
1 the male person or animal being talked about. 2 a person (male or female), *He who hesitates is lost.* [from Old English]

head *noun* (*plural* **heads**)
1 the part of the body containing the brains, eyes, and mouth. 2 your brains or mind; intelligence, *Use your head!* 3 a talent or ability, *She has a good head for figures.* 4 the side of a coin on which someone's head is shown. 5 a person, *It costs £2 per head.* 6 the

top, *a pinhead*; the leading part of something, *at the head of the procession*. **7** the chief; the person in charge. **8** a headteacher.
come to a head reach a crisis point.
keep your head stay calm.
head *verb* (heads, heading, headed)
1 be at the top or front of something. **2** hit a ball with your head. **3** move in a particular direction, *We headed for the coast*. **4** force someone to turn by getting in front, *head him off*. [from Old English]

headache *noun* (*plural* headaches)
1 a pain in the head. **2** (*informal*) a worrying problem.

heading *noun* (*plural* headings)
a word or words put at the top of a piece of printing or writing.

headland *noun* (*plural* headlands)
a large piece of high land that sticks out into the sea; a promontory.

headlight *noun* (*plural* headlights)
a powerful light at the front of a car, engine, etc.

headline *noun* (*plural* headlines)
a heading in a newspaper.
the headlines the main items of news.

headlong *adverb* & *adjective*
1 head first. **2** in a hasty or thoughtless way.

headmaster *noun* (*plural* headmasters)
a male headteacher.

headmistress *noun* (*plural* headmistresses)
a female headteacher.

head-on *adverb* & *adjective*
with the front parts colliding, *a head-on collision*.

headquarters *noun* or *plural noun*
the place from which an organization is controlled.

headstrong *adjective*
determined to do as you want.

headteacher *noun* (*plural* headteachers)
the person in charge of a school.

headway *noun*
make headway make progress.

heal *verb* (heals, healing, healed)
1 make or become healthy flesh again, *The wound healed*. **2** (*old use*) cure, *healing the sick*.

health *noun*
1 the condition of a person's body or mind, *His health is bad*. **2** being healthy, *in sickness and in health*.

healthy *adjective* (healthier, healthiest)
1 having good health; free from illness. **2** producing good health, *Fresh air is healthy*.
healthily *adverb*, **healthiness** *noun*

heap *noun* (*plural* heaps)
a pile, especially an untidy one.
heaps *plural noun* (*informal*) a great amount; plenty, *There's heaps of time*.
heap *verb* (heaps, heaping, heaped)
1 make things into a heap. **2** put on large amounts, *She heaped the plate with food*.

hear *verb* (hears, hearing, heard)
1 take in sounds through the ears. **2** receive news or information etc.
hearer *noun*
hear! hear! (in a debate) I agree.

hearing *noun* (*plural* hearings)
1 the ability to hear. **2** a chance to be heard; a trial in a lawcourt.

hearing aid *noun* (*plural* hearing aids)
a device to help a deaf person to hear.

heart *noun* (*plural* hearts)
1 the organ of the body that makes the blood circulate. **2** a person's feelings or emotions; sympathy. **3** enthusiasm; courage, *Take heart*. **4** the middle or most important part. **5** a curved shape representing a heart. **6** a playing card with red heart shapes on it.
break a person's heart make him or her very unhappy. **heartbroken** *adjective*
by heart memorized.

heart attack *noun* (*plural* heart attacks)
a sudden failure of the heart to work properly, which results in great pain or sometimes death.

hearten *verb* (heartens, heartening, heartened)
make a person feel encouraged.

heartfelt *adjective*
felt deeply.

hearth *noun* (*plural* hearths)
the floor of or near a fireplace.

heartless *adjective*
without pity or sympathy.

hearty *adjective*
1 strong and vigorous. **2** enthusiastic and sincere, *hearty congratulations*. **3** (of a meal) large.
heartily *adverb*, **heartiness** *noun*

heat *noun* (*plural* heats)
1 hotness or (in scientific use) the form of energy causing this. **2** hot weather. **3** a race or contest to decide who will take part in the final.
heat *verb* (heats, heating, heated)
make or become hot. [from Old English]

heathen *noun* (*plural* heathens)
a person who does not believe in one of the chief religions. [from Old English]

heather *noun*
an evergreen plant with small purple, pink, or white flowers. [from Old English]

heatwave *noun* (*plural* heatwaves)
a long period of hot weather.

heave *verb* (heaves, heaving, heaved)
1 lift or move something heavy. 2 (*informal*)
throw. 3 rise and fall. 4 if your stomach
heaves, you feel like vomiting.
heave *noun*
heave a sigh utter a deep sigh.

heaven *noun* (*plural* heavens)
1 the place where God and angels are thought
to live. 2 a very pleasant place or condition.
the heavens the sky.

heavy *adjective* (heavier, heaviest)
1 having great weight; difficult to lift or carry.
2 great in amount or force etc., *heavy rain; a
heavy penalty*. 3 needing much effort, *heavy
work*. 4 full of sadness or worry, *with a heavy
heart*. **heavily** *adverb*, **heaviness** *noun*
[from Old English]

heavyweight *noun* (*plural* heavyweights)
1 a heavy person. 2 a boxer of the heaviest
weight. **heavyweight** *adjective*

Hebrew *noun*
the language of the Jews in ancient Palestine
and modern Israel.

hectare (*say* hek-tar) *noun* (*plural* hectares)
a unit of area equal to 10,000 square metres or
nearly 2½ acres.
[from Greek *hekaton* = hundred, + French *are*
= a hundred square metres]

hecto- *prefix*
one hundred (as in *hectogram* = 100 grams).
[from Greek]

hedge *noun* (*plural* hedges)
a row of bushes forming a barrier or boundary.

hedgehog *noun* (*plural* hedgehogs)
a small animal covered with long prickles.
[because of the grunting noises it makes]

heed *noun*
take or **pay heed** give attention to something.
heedful *adjective*, **heedless** *adjective* [from Old
English]

heel *noun* (*plural* heels)
1 the back part of the foot. 2 the part round or
under the heel of a sock or shoe etc.
take to your heels run away.
[from Old English *hela*]

hefty *adjective* (heftier, heftiest)
large and strong. **heftily** *adverb*

height *noun* (*plural* heights)
1 how high something is; the distance from the
base to the top or from head to foot. 2 a high
place. 3 the highest or most intense part, *at the
height of the holiday season*.

heighten *verb* (heightens, heightening,
heightened)
make or become higher or more intense.

heir (*say as* air) *noun* (*plural* heirs)
a person who inherits something.

heiress (*say* air-ess) *noun* (*plural* heiresses)
a female heir, especially to great wealth.

heirloom (*say* air-loom) *noun* (*plural* heirlooms)
a valued possession that has been handed
down in a family for several generations.
[from *heir* + Old English *geloma* = tool]

helicopter *noun* (*plural* helicopters)
a kind of aircraft with a large horizontal
propeller or rotor.
[from *helix* + Greek *pteron* = wing]

helium (*say* hee-lee-um) *noun*
a light colourless gas that does not burn. [from
Greek *helios* = sun]

helix (*say* hee-liks) *noun* (*plural* helices, *say* hee-
liss-eez)
a spiral. [Greek, = coil]

hell *noun*
1 a place where wicked people are thought to
be punished after they die. 2 a very unpleasant
place. 3 (*informal*) an exclamation of anger.
hell for leather (*informal*) at high speed.

hello *interjection*
a word used to greet somebody or to attract
their attention.

helmet *noun* (*plural* helmets)
a strong covering worn to protect the head.

help *verb* (helps, helping, helped)
1 do part of another person's work for him or
her. 2 benefit; make something better or
easier, *This will help you to sleep*. 3 if you
cannot help doing something, you cannot avoid
doing it, *I can't help coughing*. 4 serve food etc.
to somebody.
helper *noun*, **helpful** *adjective*, **helpfully** *adverb*
help *noun*
1 helping somebody. 2 a person or thing that
helps. [from Old English]

helping *noun* (*plural* helpings)
a portion of food.

helpless *adjective*
not able to do things. **helplessly** *adverb*,
helplessness *noun*

helpline *noun* (*plural* helplines)
a telephone service providing help with
problems.

hem *noun* (*plural* hems)
the edge of a piece of cloth that is folded over
and sewn down.
hem *verb* (hems, hemming, hemmed)
put a hem on something.
hem in surround and restrict.

hemisphere *noun* (*plural* hemispheres)
1 half a sphere. 2 half the earth.
hemispherical *adjective*
[from Greek *hemi-* = half, + *sphere*]

hen *noun* (*plural* hens)
1 a female bird. 2 a female fowl.

hence *adverb*
1 henceforth. 2 therefore. 3 (*old use*) from here.
[from Old English]

henchman *noun* (*plural* **henchmen**)
a trusty supporter. [origin unknown]

hepta- *prefix*
seven. [from Greek]

her *pronoun*
the form of *she* used as the object of a verb or
after a preposition.
her *adjective*
belonging to her, *her book.*

herald *noun* (*plural* **heralds**)
an official in former times who made
announcements and carried messages for a
king or queen.

heraldry *noun*
the study of coats of arms.
heraldic (*say* hir-**al**-dik) *adjective*
[because a herald decided who could have a
coat of arms and what should be on it]

herb *noun* (*plural* **herbs**)
a plant used for flavouring or for making
medicine. **herbal** *adjective* [from Latin]

herbivorous (*say* her-**biv**-er-us) *adjective*
plant-eating. (Compare *carnivorous.*)
herbivore *noun*
[from Latin *herba* = grass, + *-vorous*]

herd *noun* (*plural* **herds**)
1 a group of cattle or other animals that feed
together. 2 a mass of people; a mob.
herdsman *noun*
herd *verb* (**herds, herding, herded**)
1 gather or move or send in a herd, *We all
herded into the dining room.* 2 look after a herd
of animals.

here *adverb*
in or to this place etc.
here and there in various places or directions.

hereby *adverb*
by this act or decree etc.

hereditary *adjective*
1 inherited, *a hereditary disease.* 2 inheriting a
position, *Our Queen is a hereditary monarch.*

heredity (*say* hir-**ed**-it-ee) *noun*
inheriting characteristics from parents or
ancestors.
[from Latin *heredis* = to do with an heir]

heresy (*say* **herri**-see) *noun* (*plural* **heresies**)
an opinion that disagrees with the beliefs
accepted by the Christian Church or other
authority.
[from Greek *hairesis* = choice]

heretic (*say* **herri**-tik) *noun* (*plural* **heretics**)
a person who supports a heresy.
heretical (*say* hi-**ret**-ik-al) *adjective*

heritage *noun*
the things that someone has inherited. [from
Latin *hereditare* = inherit]

hermetically *adverb*
so as to be airtight, *The tin is hermetically
sealed.* [from Latin]

hermit *noun* (*plural* **hermits**)
a person who lives alone and keeps away from
people.
[from Greek *eremos* = alone or deserted]

hero *noun* (*plural* **heroes**)
1 a man or boy who is admired for doing
something very brave or great. 2 the chief
male character in a story etc.
heroic *adjective*, **heroically** *adverb*, **heroism** *noun*
[from Greek *heros* = a very strong or brave
man, whom the gods love]

heroin *noun*
a very strong drug, made from morphine.

heroine *noun* (*plural* **heroines**)
1 a woman or girl who is admired for doing
something very brave or great. 2 the chief
female character in a story etc.
[Greek, feminine of *heros* = hero]

heron *noun* (*plural* **herons**)
a wading bird with long legs and a long neck.
[via old French from Germanic]

herring *noun* (*plural* **herring** or **herrings**)
a sea fish used as food.

hers *possessive pronoun*
belonging to her, *Those books are hers.* [from
her]

USAGE: It is incorrect to write *her's.*

herself *pronoun*
she or her and nobody else. The word is used to
refer back to the subject of a sentence (e.g. *She
cut herself*) or for emphasis (e.g. *She herself has
said it*).
by herself alone; on her own.

hertz *noun* (*plural* **hertz**)
a unit of frequency of electromagnetic waves,
= one cycle per second.
[named after a German scientist, H. R. Hertz,
who discovered radio waves]

hesitate *verb* (**hesitates, hesitating, hesitated**)
be slow or uncertain in speaking, moving, etc.
hesitant *adjective*, **hesitation** *noun*
[from Latin *haesitare* = get stuck]

hetero- *prefix*
other; different.
[from Greek *heteros* = other]

heterogeneous (*say* het-er-o-**jeen**-ee-us) *adjective*
composed of people or things of different kinds.
[from *hetero-* + Greek *genos* = a kind]

heterosexual *adjective*
attracted to people of the opposite sex; not
homosexual. **heterosexual** *noun*

hexa- *prefix*
six. [from Greek]

hexagon *noun* (*plural* hexagons)
a flat shape with six sides and six angles.
hexagonal *adjective*
[from *hexa-* + Greek *gonia* = angle]

hibernate *verb* (hibernates, hibernating, hibernated)
spend the winter in a state like deep sleep.
hibernation *noun*
[from Latin *hibernus* = wintry]

hiccup *noun* (*plural* hiccups)
1 a high gulping sound made when your breath is briefly interrupted. 2 a brief hitch.
hiccup *verb* [imitating the sound]

hide[1] *verb* (hides, hiding, hid, hidden)
1 keep a person or thing from being seen; conceal. 2 get into a place where you cannot be seen. 3 keep a thing secret.
[from Old English *hydan*]

hide[2] *noun* (*plural* hides)
an animal's skin. [from Old English *hyd*]

hide-and-seek *noun*
a game in which one person looks for others who are hiding.

hideous *adjective*
very ugly or unpleasant. **hideously** *adverb*

hiding[1] *noun*
being hidden, *She went into hiding.*
hiding place *noun*

hiding[2] *noun* (*plural* hidings)
a thrashing or beating. [from an old word *hide* = to beat the hide (skin)]

hierarchy (*say* hyr-ark-ee) *noun* (*plural* hierarchies)
an organization that ranks people one above another according to the power or authority that they hold.
[from Greek *hieros* = sacred, + *-archy*]

hieroglyphics (*say* hyr-o-glif-iks) *plural noun*
pictures or symbols used in ancient Egypt to represent words.
[from Greek *hieros* = sacred + *glyphe* = carving]

hi-fi *noun* (*plural* hi-fis) (*informal*)
1 high fidelity. 2 equipment for reproducing recorded sound with very little distortion.

higgledy-piggledy *adverb* & *adjective*
completely mixed up; in great disorder.
[nonsense word based on *pig* (because of the way pigs huddle together)]

high *adjective*
1 reaching a long way upwards, *high hills.*
2 far above the ground or above sea level, *high clouds.* 3 measuring from top to bottom, *two metres high.* 4 above average level in importance, quality, amount, etc., *high rank;*
high prices. 5 (of meat) beginning to go bad.
6 (*slang*) affected by a drug.
high time fully time, *it's high time we left.*
high *adverb*
at or to a high level or position etc., *They flew high above us.* [from Old English]

highbrow *adjective*
intellectual.
[from *highbrowed* = having a high forehead (thought to be a sign of intelligence)]

higher education *noun*
education at a university, polytechnic, or college.

high fidelity *noun*
reproducing recorded sound with very little distortion.

high jump *noun*
an athletic contest in which competitors try to jump over a high bar.

highlight *noun* (*plural* highlights)
1 the most interesting part of something, *The highlight of the holiday was the trip to Pompeii.*
2 a light area in a painting etc. 3 a light-coloured streak in a person's hair.

highly *adverb*
1 extremely, *highly amusing.* 2 very favourably, *We think highly of her.*

Highness *noun* (*plural* Highnesses)
the title of a prince or princess.

high road *noun* (*plural* high roads)
the main road.

high school *noun* (*plural* high schools)
a secondary school.

high street *noun* (*plural* high streets)
a town's main street.

high tea *noun*
an evening meal with tea and meat or other cooked food.

highway *noun* (*plural* highways)
a main road or route.

highwayman *noun* (*plural* highwaymen)
a man who robbed travellers on highways in former times.

hijack *verb* (hijacks, hijacking, hijacked)
seize control of an aircraft or vehicle during a journey. **hijack** *noun*, **hijacker** *noun*

hike *noun* (*plural* hikes)
a long walk. **hike** *verb*, **hiker** *noun*

hilarious *adjective*
very funny. **hilariously** *adverb*, **hilarity** *noun*
[from Greek *hilaros* = cheerful]

hill *noun* (*plural* hills)
a piece of land that is higher than the ground around it. **hillside** *noun*, **hilly** *adjective*
[from Old English]

hilt *noun* (*plural* hilts)
the handle of a sword or dagger etc.
to the hilt completely.

him *pronoun*
the form of *he* used as the object of a verb or
after a preposition. [from Old English]

himself *pronoun*
he or him and nobody else. (Compare *herself*.)

hind *adjective*
at the back, *the hind legs*.
[probably from *behind*]

hinder *verb* (hinders, hindering, hindered)
get in someone's way; make it difficult for a
person to do something quickly or for
something to happen. **hindrance** *noun*

hindquarters *plural noun*
an animal's hind legs and rear parts.

hindsight *noun*
looking back on an event with knowledge or
understanding that you did not have at the
time.

Hindu *noun* (*plural* Hindus)
a person who believes in Hinduism, which is
one of the religions of India.

hinge *noun* (*plural* hinges)
a joining device on which a lid or door etc.
turns when it opens.

hinge *verb* (hinges, hinging, hinged)
1 fix something with a hinge. 2 depend,
Everything hinges on this meeting.

hint *noun* (*plural* hints)
1 a slight indication or suggestion, *Give me a
hint of what you want*. 2 a useful suggestion,
household hints.

hint *verb* (hints, hinting, hinted)
make a hint. [from an old word *hent*
= getting hold, especially of an idea]

hip¹ *noun* (*plural* hips)
the bony part at the side of the body between
the waist and the thigh.
[from Old English *hype*]

hip² *noun* (*plural* hips)
the fruit of the wild rose.
[from Old English *heope*]

hippopotamus *noun* (*plural* hippopotamuses)
a very large African animal that lives near
water. [from Greek *hippos ho potamios*
= horse of the river]

hire *verb* (hires, hiring, hired)
1 pay to borrow something. 2 lend for
payment, *He hires out bicycles*. **hirer** *noun*
hire *noun*
hiring, *for hire*. [from Old English]

hire purchase *noun*
buying something by paying in instalments.

his *adjective* & *possessive pronoun*
belonging to him, *That is his book. That book is
his*. [from Old English]

hiss *verb* (hisses, hissing, hissed)
make a sound like an *s*, *The snakes were
hissing*. **hiss** *noun* [imitating the sound]

histogram *noun* (*plural* histograms)
a chart consisting of rectangles of varying
sizes. [from Greek *histos* = mast, + *-gram*]

historian *noun* (*plural* historians)
a person who writes or studies history.

historic *adjective*
famous or important in history; likely to be
remembered, *a historic town; a historic
meeting*.

USAGE: Do not confuse with *historical*.

historical *adjective*
1 to do with history. 2 that actually existed or
took place in the past, *The novel is based on
historical events*.

USAGE: Do not confuse with *historic*.

history *noun* (*plural* histories)
1 what happened in the past. 2 study of past
events. 3 a description of important events.
[from Greek *historia* = learning or finding out]

hit *verb* (hits, hitting, hit)
1 come forcefully against a person or thing;
knock or strike. 2 have a bad effect on, *Famine
has hit the poor countries*. 3 reach, *I can't hit
that high note*.
hit on discover something by chance.

hit *noun* (*plural* hits)
1 hitting; a knock or stroke. 2 a shot
that hits the target. 3 a success.
4 a successful song, show, etc.

hitch *verb* (hitches, hitching, hitched)
1 raise or pull with a slight jerk. 2 fasten with
a loop or hook etc. 3 hitch-hike.
hitch *noun* (*plural* hitches)
1 a hitching movement. 2 a knot.
3 a difficulty causing delay.

hitch-hike *verb* (hitch-hikes, hitch-hiking, hitch-
hiked)
travel by getting lifts from passing vehicles.
hitch-hiker *noun*

hi-tech *adjective*
using the most advanced technology, especially
electronic devices and computers.

hither *adverb*
to or towards this place.

hitherto *adverb*
until this time.

HIV *abbreviation*
human immunodeficiency virus; a virus that
causes Aids.
[from the initial letters of *human
immunodeficiency virus*]

hive noun (plural **hives**)
1 a beehive. 2 the bees living in a beehive.
hive of industry a place full of people working busily.

hoard noun (plural **hoards**)
a carefully saved store of money, treasure, food, etc.
hoard verb (**hoards, hoarding, hoarded**)
store something away. **hoarder** noun

USAGE: Do not confuse with *horde*.

hoarding noun (plural **hoardings**)
a tall fence covered with advertisements.

hoar frost noun
a white frost. [from Old English *har* = grey-haired, + *frost*]

hoarse adjective
with a rough voice. **hoarsely** adverb,
hoarseness noun [from Old English]

hoax verb (**hoaxes, hoaxing, hoaxed**)
deceive somebody as a joke.
hoax noun, **hoaxer** noun
[probably from *hocus-pocus*, used by conjurors as a 'magic' word]

hobble verb (**hobbles, hobbling, hobbled**)
limp. [probably from old German]

hobby noun (plural **hobbies**)
something you do for pleasure in your spare time. [from *hobby horse*]

hobby horse noun (plural **hobby horses**)
1 a stick with a horse's head, used as a toy. 2 a subject that a person likes to talk about whenever he or she gets the chance.

hobgoblin noun (plural **hobgoblins**)
a mischievous or evil spirit.

hockey noun
a game played by two teams with curved sticks and a hard ball. [origin unknown]

hoe noun (plural **hoes**)
a tool for scraping up weeds.
hoe verb (**hoes, hoeing, hoed**)
scrape or dig with a hoe.

hog noun (plural **hogs**)
1 a male pig. 2 (*informal*) a greedy person.
go the whole hog (*slang*) do something completely or thoroughly.

Hogmanay noun
New Year's Eve in Scotland.

hoist verb (**hoists, hoisting, hoisted**)
lift; raise something by using ropes and pulleys etc. [probably from Dutch]

hold verb (**holds, holding, held**)
This word has many uses, including 1 have and keep, especially in your hands, 2 have room for (*The jug holds two pints*), 3 support (*This plank won't hold my weight*), 4 stay unbroken; continue (*Will the fine weather hold?*), 5 believe or consider (*We shall hold you*

responsible), 6 cause something to take place (*hold a meeting*), 7 restrain or stop (*Hold everything!*).
hold forth make a long speech.
hold out refuse to give in.
hold up 1 hinder. 2 stop and rob somebody by threats or force.
hold with approve of, *We don't hold with bullying.*
hold your tongue (*informal*) stop talking.
hold noun (plural **holds**)
1 holding something; a grasp. 2 something to hold on to for support. 3 the part of a ship where cargo is stored, below the deck.
get hold of 1 grasp. 2 obtain. 3 make contact with a person.

hold-up noun (plural **hold-ups**)
1 a delay. 2 a robbery with threats or force.

hole noun (plural **holes**)
1 a hollow place; a gap or opening. 2 a burrow. 3 one of the small holes into which you have to hit the ball in golf. 4 (*informal*) an unpleasant place. **holey** adjective
in a hole in an awkward situation.
hole verb (**holes, holing, holed**)
1 make a hole or holes in something. 2 hit a golf ball into one of the holes.

holiday noun (plural **holidays**)
1 a day or week etc. when people do not go to work or to school. 2 a time when you go away to enjoy yourself.
[from *holy* + *day* (because holidays were originally religious festivals)]

holiness noun
being holy or sacred.
His Holiness the title of the pope.

hollow adjective
with an empty space inside; not solid.
hollowly adverb
hollow noun (plural **hollows**)
a hollow or sunken place.
hollow verb (**hollows, hollowing, hollowed**)
make a thing hollow. [from Old English]

holly noun (plural **hollies**)
an evergreen bush with shiny prickly leaves and red berries. [from Old English]

holocaust noun (plural **holocausts**)
an immense destruction, especially by fire, *the nuclear holocaust.*
the Holocaust the mass murder of the Jews by the Nazis from 1939 to 1945.
[from Greek *holos* = whole + *kaustos* = burnt]

hologram noun (plural **holograms**)
a type of photograph made by laser beams that produces a three-dimensional image.

holy adjective (**holier, holiest**)
1 belonging or devoted to God. 2 consecrated, *holy water.* **holiness** noun

homage noun (plural **homages**)
an act or expression of respect or honour, We paid homage to his achievements.

home noun (plural **homes**)
1 the place where you live. 2 the place where you were born or where you feel you belong. 3 a place where those who need help are looked after, an old people's home. 4 the place to be reached in a race or in certain games.

home adjective
1 of a person's own home or country, home industries. 2 played on a team's own ground, a home match.

home adverb
1 to or at home, Is she home yet? 2 to the point aimed at, Push the bolt home.
bring something home to somebody make him or her realize it.

home verb (**homes, homing, homed**)
make for a target, The missile homed in.

home economics noun
the study of household management.

homely adverb
simple and ordinary, a homely meal.
homeliness noun

home-made adjective
made at home, not bought from a shop.

homeopathy noun
the treatment of disease by tiny doses of drugs that in a healthy person would produce symptoms of the disease. **homeopathic** adjective [from Greek homoios = similar + -pathos = suffering]

homesick adjective
sad because you are away from home.
homesickness noun

homeward adjective & adverb
going towards home. **homewards** adverb

homework noun
school work that has to be done at home.

homicide noun (plural **homicides**)
the killing of one person by another.
homicidal adjective
[from Latin homo = person, + -cide]

homo- prefix
same. [from Greek]

homogeneous (say hom-o-jeen-ee-us) adjective
composed of people or things of the same kind. [from homo- + Greek genos = a kind]

homograph noun (plural **homographs**)
a word that is spelt like another but has a different meaning or origin, e.g. bat (a flying animal) and bat (for hitting a ball). [from homo- + -graph]

homonym (say hom-o-nim) noun (plural **homonyms**)
a homograph or homophone. [from homo- + Greek onyma = name]

homophone noun (plural **homophones**)
a word with the same sound as another, e.g. son, sun. [from homo- + Greek phone = sound]

Homo sapiens noun
human beings regarded as a species of animal. [Latin, = wise man or person]

homosexual adjective
attracted to people of the same sex.
homosexual noun, **homosexuality** noun

honest adjective
not stealing or cheating or telling lies; truthful.
honestly adverb, **honesty** noun [from old French; related to honour]

honey noun
a sweet sticky food made by bees.

honeycomb noun (plural **honeycombs**)
a wax structure of small six-sided sections made by bees to hold their honey and eggs.

honeycombed adjective
with many holes or tunnels.

honeymoon noun (plural **honeymoons**)
a holiday spent together by a newly-married couple. [from honey + moon (because the first intensely passionate feelings gradually wane)]

honeysuckle noun
a climbing plant with fragrant yellow or pink flowers. [because people sucked the flowers for their sweet nectar]

honk noun (plural **honks**)
a loud sound like that made by a goose or an old-fashioned car horn. **honk** verb

honorary adjective
1 given or received as an honour, an honorary degree. 2 unpaid, the honorary treasurer of the club.

USAGE: Do not confuse with honourable.

honour noun (plural **honours**)
1 great respect. 2 a person or thing that brings honour. 3 honesty and loyalty, a man of honour. 4 an award for distinction.

honour verb (**honours, honouring, honoured**)
1 feel or show honour for a person. 2 acknowledge and pay a cheque etc. 3 keep to the terms of an agreement or promise. [from Latin]

honourable adjective
deserving honour; honest and loyal.
honourably adverb

USAGE: Do not confuse with honorary.

hood noun (plural **hoods**)
1 a covering of soft material for the head and neck. 2 a folding roof or cover.
hooded adjective

-hood *suffix*
forms nouns meaning condition or quality (e.g.
childhood). [from Old English]

hoodwink *verb* (**hoodwinks, hoodwinking,
hoodwinked**)
deceive. [originally = to blindfold with a hood:
from *hood* + an old sense of *wink*
= close the eyes]

hoof *noun* (*plural* **hoofs** or **hooves**)
the horny part of the foot of a horse etc.

hook *noun* (*plural* **hooks**)
a bent or curved piece of metal etc. for hanging
things on or for catching hold of something.
hook *verb* (**hooks, hooking, hooked**)
1 catch something with a hook. **2** fasten
something with or on a hook. **3** send a ball in a
curving direction.
be hooked on something (*slang*) be addicted to
it.

hooked *adjective*
hook-shaped.

hooligan *noun* (*plural* **hooligans**)
a rough and violent young person.
hooliganism *noun* [the surname of a rowdy
Irish family in a cartoon]

hoop *noun* (*plural* **hoops**)
a ring made of metal or wood.

hoot *noun* (*plural* **hoots**)
1 the sound made by an owl or a vehicle's horn
or a steam whistle. **2** a cry of scorn or
disapproval. **3** laughter. **4** something funny.
hoot *verb*, **hooter** *noun*

hop[1] *verb* (**hops, hopping, hopped**)
1 jump on one foot. **2** (of an animal) spring
from all feet at once. **3** (*informal*) move
quickly, *Here's the car—hop in!*
hop it (*slang*) go away.
hop *noun* (*plural* **hops**)
a hopping movement.
[from Old English]

hop[2] *noun* (*plural* **hops**)
a climbing plant used to give beer its flavour.
[from old German or old Dutch]

hope *noun* (*plural* **hopes**)
1 a wish for something to happen. **2** a person
or thing that gives hope, *You are our only hope.*
hope *verb* (**hopes, hoping, hoped**)
feel hope; want and expect something.

hopeful *adjective*
1 feeling hope. **2** likely to be good or successful.

hopefully *adverb*
1 it is to be hoped; I hope that. **2** in a hopeful
way.

USAGE: Some people say it is incorrect to use
hopefully to mean 'I hope that' or 'let's hope',
and say that it should only be used to mean 'in
a hopeful way'. This first use is very common

in informal language but you should probably
avoid it when you are writing or speaking
formally.

hopeless *adjective*
1 without hope. **2** very bad at something.
hopelessly *adverb*, **hopelessness** *noun*

hopscotch *noun*
a game of hopping into squares drawn on the
ground. [from *hop* + an old word *scotch* = a cut
or scratch]

horde *noun* (*plural* **hordes**)
a large group or crowd. [via Polish from
Turkish *ordu* = royal camp]

USAGE: Do not confuse with *hoard*.

horizon *noun* (*plural* **horizons**)
the line where the earth and the sky seem to
meet.
[from Greek *horizein* = form a boundary]

horizontal *adjective*
level, so as to be parallel to the horizon; going
across from left to right. (The opposite is
vertical.) **horizontally** *adverb*

hormone *noun* (*plural* **hormones**)
a substance that stimulates an organ of the
body or of a plant. **hormonal** *adjective*
[from Greek *horman* = set something going]

horn *noun* (*plural* **horns**)
1 a hard substance that grows into a point on
the head of a bull, cow, ram, etc. **2** a pointed
part. **3** a brass instrument played by blowing.
4 a device for making a warning sound.
horned *adjective*, **horny** *adjective*
[from Old English]

horoscope *noun* (*plural* **horoscopes**)
an astrologer's forecast of future events.
[from Greek *hora* = hour (of birth) + *skopos*
= observer]

horrendous *adjective*
horrifying. [from Latin *horrendus* = making
your hair stand on end]

horrible *adjective*
1 horrifying. **2** very unpleasant. **horribly**
adverb [from Latin]

horrid *adjective*
horrible. **horridly** *adverb* [from Latin *horridus*
= rough, shaggy, or wild]

horrify *verb* (**horrifies, horrifying, horrified**)
1 make somebody feel great fear and dislike.
2 shock.
[from Latin *horrificare* = make someone shiver
with cold or fear]

horror *noun* (*plural* **horrors**)
1 great fear and dislike or dismay.
2 a person or thing causing horror.

horse noun (plural **horses**)
1 a large four-legged animal used for riding on and for pulling carts etc. 2 a framework for hanging clothes on to dry. 3 a vaulting horse.
on horseback mounted on a horse.

horse chestnut noun (plural **horse chestnuts**)
a large tree that produces dark-brown nuts (conkers).

horsepower noun
a unit for measuring the power of an engine.
[because the unit was based on the amount of work a horse could do]

horseshoe noun (plural **horseshoes**)
a U-shaped piece of metal nailed to a horse's hoof.

horticulture noun
the art of cultivating gardens.
horticultural adjective
[from Latin hortus = garden, + culture]

hose noun (plural **hoses**)
1 (also **hosepipe**) a flexible tube for taking water to something. 2 (old use) breeches, doublet and hose.

hospitable adjective
welcoming; liking to give hospitality.
hospitably adverb [from Latin]

hospital noun (plural **hospitals**)
a place providing medical and surgical treatment for people who are ill or injured.
[from Latin hospitalis = hospitable]

hospitality noun
welcoming people and giving them food and entertainment. [from Latin]

host[1] noun (plural **hosts**)
a person who has guests and looks after them.
[from Latin hospes]

host[2] noun (plural **hosts**)
a large number of people or things.
[from Latin hostis = enemy or army]

host[3] noun (plural **hosts**)
the bread consecrated at Holy Communion.
[from Latin hostia = sacrifice]

hostage noun (plural **hostages**)
a person who is held prisoner until the holder gets what he or she wants.

hostel noun (plural **hostels**)
a building where travellers, students, or other groups can stay or live.
[from old French; related to hospital]

hostess noun (plural **hostesses**)
a woman who has guests and looks after them.
[from old French]

hostile adjective
1 to do with an enemy. 2 unfriendly, a hostile glance. **hostility** noun
[same origin as host[2]]

hot adjective (**hotter, hottest**)
1 having great heat or a high temperature.
2 giving a burning sensation when tasted.
3 passionate or excitable, a hot temper.
hotly adverb, **hotness** noun
in hot water (informal) in trouble or disgrace.

hotel noun (plural **hotels**)
a building where people pay to have meals and stay for the night.
[from French; related to hostel]

hound noun (plural **hounds**)
a dog used in hunting or racing.

hour noun (plural **hours**)
1 one twenty-fourth part of a day and night; sixty minutes. 2 a time, Why are you up at this hour?
hours plural noun a fixed period for work, Office hours are 9 a.m. to 5 p.m.

hourly adverb & adjective
every hour.

house (say howss) noun (plural **houses**)
1 a building made for people to live in, usually designed for one family. 2 a building or establishment for a special purpose, the opera house. 3 a building for a government assembly; the assembly itself, the House of Commons; the House of Lords. 4 each of the divisions of a school for sports competitions etc. 5 a family or dynasty, the royal house of Tudor.

house (say howz) verb (**houses, housing, housed**)
provide accommodation or room for someone or something.

household noun (plural **households**)
all the people who live together in the same house.
[from house + an old sense of hold = possession]

householder noun (plural **householders**)
a person who owns or rents a house.

housekeeper noun (plural **housekeepers**)
a person employed to look after a household.

housekeeping noun
1 looking after a household. 2 (informal) the money for a household's food and other necessities.

housemaid noun (plural **housemaids**)
a woman servant in a house, especially one who cleans rooms.

house-proud adjective
very careful to keep a house clean and tidy.

house-trained adjective
(of an animal) trained to be clean in the house.

housewife noun (plural **housewives**)
a woman who does the housekeeping for her family.

housework noun
the cleaning and cooking etc. done in housekeeping.

housing *noun* (*plural* **housings**)
1 accommodation; houses. 2 a stiff cover or guard for a piece of machinery.

housing estate *noun* (*plural* **housing estates**)
a set of houses planned and built together in one area.

hovel *noun* (*plural* **hovels**)
a small shabby house. [origin unknown]

hover *verb* (**hovers, hovering, hovered**)
1 stay in one place in the air. 2 wait about near someone or something; linger.

hovercraft *noun* (*plural* **hovercraft**)
a vehicle that travels just above the surface of land or water, supported by a strong current of air sent downwards from its engines.

how *adverb*
1 in what way; by what means, *How did you do it?* 2 to what extent or amount etc., *How high can you jump?* 3 in what condition, *How are you?*
how about would you like, *How about a game of football?*
how do you do? a formal greeting.

however *adverb*
1 in whatever way; to whatever extent, *You will never catch him, however hard you try.* 2 all the same; nevertheless, *Later, however, he decided to go.*

howl *noun* (*plural* **howls**)
a long loud sad-sounding cry or sound, such as that made by a dog or wolf.

howl *verb* (**howls, howling, howled**)
1 make a howl. 2 weep loudly.

howler *noun* (*plural* **howlers**)
(*informal*) a foolish mistake.

hub *noun* (*plural* **hubs**)
1 the central part of a wheel. 2 the central point of interest or activity.

hubbub *noun*
a loud confused noise of voices.
[probably from Irish]

huddle *verb* (**huddles, huddling, huddled**)
1 crowd together into a small space. 2 curl your body closely. **huddle** *noun*

huff *noun*
in a huff offended or sulking about something, *She went away in a huff.*
huffy *adjective*

hug *verb* (**hugs, hugging, hugged**)
1 clasp someone tightly in your arms; embrace. 2 keep close to something, *The ship hugged the shore.*

hug *noun* (*plural* **hugs**)
a tight embrace.

huge *adjective*
extremely large; enormous. **hugely** *adverb*, **hugeness** *noun* [from old French]

hulk *noun* (*plural* **hulks**)
1 the body or wreck of an old ship. 2 a large clumsy person or thing. **hulking** *adjective* [from Old English]

hull *noun* (*plural* **hulls**)
the framework of a ship.

hullabaloo *noun* (*plural* **hullabaloos**)
an uproar. [origin unknown]

hum *verb* (**hums, humming, hummed**)
1 sing a tune with your lips closed. 2 make a low continuous sound as some flying insects do.

human *adjective*
to do with human beings. [from Latin]

human being *noun* (*plural* **human beings**)
a creature distinguished from other animals by its better mental development, power of speech, and upright posture.

humane (*say* hew-**mayn**) *adjective*
kind-hearted and merciful. **humanely** *adverb* [old spelling of *human*]

humanitarian *adjective*
concerned with people's welfare and the reduction of suffering. **humanitarian** *noun*

humanity *noun*
1 human beings; people. 2 being human. 3 being humane.
humanities *plural noun* arts subjects.

humble *adjective*
1 modest; not proud or showy. 2 of low rank or importance. **humbly** *adverb*, **humbleness** *noun* [from Latin *humilis* = near the ground, low]

humbug *noun* (*plural* **humbugs**)
1 insincere or dishonest talk or behaviour. 2 a hard peppermint sweet.

humdrum *adjective*
dull and not exciting; commonplace.

humid (*say* hew-mid) *adjective*
(of air) moist. **humidity** *noun* [from Latin]

humiliate *verb* (**humiliates, humiliating, humiliated**)
make a person feel disgraced. **humiliation** *noun* [same origin as *humble*]

humility *noun*
being humble. [same origin as *humble*]

hummingbird *noun* (*plural* **hummingbirds**)
a small tropical bird that makes a humming sound by moving its wings rapidly.

humorous *adjective*
full of humour.

humour *noun*
1 being amusing; what makes people laugh. 2 the ability to enjoy comical things, *a sense of humour.* 3 a mood, *in a good humour.*

humour *verb* (**humours, humouring, humoured**)
keep a person contented by doing what he or she wants. [from Latin]

hump *noun* (*plural* **humps**)
1 a rounded lump or mound. **2** an abnormal outward curve at the top of a person's back.

humpback bridge *noun* (*plural* **humpback bridges**) a small bridge that steeply curves upwards in the middle.

humus (*say* hew-mus) *noun* rich earth made by decayed plants. [Latin, = soil]

hunch[1] *noun* (*plural* **hunches**) a feeling that you can guess what will happen. [origin unknown]

hunch[2] *verb* (**hunches, hunching, hunched**) bend into a hump, *He hunched his shoulders.* [origin unknown]

hunchback *noun* (*plural* **hunchbacks**) someone with a hump on their back. **hunchbacked** *adjective*

hundred *noun* & *adjective* (*plural* **hundreds**) the number 100. **hundredth** *adjective* & *noun* [from Old English]

hundredweight *noun* (*plural* **hundredweight**) a unit of weight, 112 pounds (= 50.8 kilograms). [probably originally = 100 pounds]

hunger *noun* the feeling that you have when you have not eaten for some time; need for food.

hunger strike *noun* (*plural* **hunger strikes**) refusing to eat, as a way of making a protest.

hungry *adjective* (**hungrier, hungriest**) feeling hunger. **hungrily** *adverb*

hunk *noun* (*plural* **hunks**) **1** a large piece of something. **2** (*informal*) a muscular, good-looking man.

hunt *verb* (**hunts, hunting, hunted**) **1** chase and kill animals for food or as a sport. **2** search for something. **hunter** *noun*, **huntsman** *noun*

hurdle *noun* (*plural* **hurdles**) **1** an upright frame to be jumped over in hurdling. **2** an obstacle. [from Old English]

hurdling *noun* racing in which the runners jump over hurdles. **hurdler** *noun*

hurl *verb* (**hurls, hurling, hurled**) throw something violently.

hurrah or **hurray** *interjection* a shout of joy or approval; a cheer.

hurricane *noun* (*plural* **hurricanes**) a storm with violent wind.

hurry *verb* (**hurries, hurrying, hurried**) **1** move quickly; do something quickly. **2** try to make somebody or something be quick. **hurried** *adjective*, **hurriedly** *adverb*
hurry *noun* hurrying; a need to hurry.

hurt *verb* (**hurts, hurting, hurt**) cause pain or damage or injury.
hurt *noun* pain or injury. **hurtful** *adjective*

hurtle *verb* (**hurtles, hurtling, hurtled**) move rapidly, *The train hurtled along.* [from an old sense of *hurt* = knock or dash against something]

husband *noun* (*plural* **husbands**) the man to whom a woman is married. [from Old Norse *husbondi* = master of the house]

husk *noun* (*plural* **husks**) the dry outer covering of some seeds and fruits. [probably from old German]

husky *adjective* (**huskier, huskiest**) **1** hoarse. **2** big and strong; burly. **huskily** *adverb*, **huskiness** *noun*

hustle *verb* (**hustles, hustling, hustled**) hurry or bustle. **hustle** *noun*, **hustler** *noun* [from Dutch *husselen* = shake or toss]

hut *noun* (*plural* **huts**) a small roughly-made house or shelter.

hutch *noun* (*plural* **hutches**) a box-like cage for a pet rabbit etc.

hybrid *noun* (*plural* **hybrids**) **1** a plant or animal produced by combining two different species or varieties. **2** something that combines parts or characteristics of two different things.

hydr- *prefix* **1** water. **2** containing hydrogen. see **hydro-**.

hydrant *noun* (*plural* **hydrants**) a special water-tap to which a large hose can be attached for fire-fighting or street-cleaning etc. [same origin as *hydro-*]

hydraulic *adjective* worked by the force of water or other fluid, *hydraulic brakes.* [from *hydr-* + Greek *aulos* = pipe]

hydro- *prefix* (**hydr-** before a vowel) **1** water (as in *hydroelectric*). **2** (in chemical names) containing hydrogen (as in *hydrochloric*). [from Greek *hydor* = water]

hydrochloric acid *noun* a colourless acid containing hydrogen and chlorine.

hydroelectric *adjective* using water-power to produce electricity. **hydroelectricity** *noun*

hydrogen *noun* a lightweight gas that combines with oxygen to form water. [from *hydro-* + *-gen* = producing]

hydrogen bomb *noun* (*plural* **hydrogen bombs**) a very powerful bomb using energy created by the fusion of hydrogen nuclei.

hyena *noun* (*plural* **hyenas**)
a wild animal that looks like a wolf and makes a shrieking howl. [from Greek]

hygiene (*say* hy-jeen) *noun*
keeping things clean in order to remain healthy and prevent disease.
hygienic *adjective*, **hygienically** *adverb*
[from Greek *hygies* = healthy]

hymn *noun* (*plural* **hymns**)
a religious song, usually of praise to God.
hymn book *noun* [from Greek]

hyper- *prefix*
over or above; excessive.
[from Greek *hyper* = over]

hyperbola (*say* hy-per-bol-a) *noun* (*plural* **hyperbolas**)
a kind of curve. [same origin as *hyperbole*]

hyphen *noun* (*plural* **hyphens**)
a short dash used to join words or parts of words together (e.g. in *hitch-hiker*).
[from Greek, = together]

hypnosis (*say* hip-noh-sis) *noun*
a condition like a deep sleep in which a person's actions may be controlled by someone else.
[from Greek *hypnos* = sleep]

hypnotize *verb* (**hypnotizes, hypnotizing, hypnotized**)
produce hypnosis in somebody.
hypnotism *noun*, **hypnotic** *adjective*, **hypnotist** *noun*

hypo- *prefix*
below; under. [from Greek *hypo* = under]

hypochondriac (*say* hy-po-kon-dree-ak) *noun* (*plural* **hypochondriacs**)
a person who constantly imagines that he or she is ill. **hypochondria** *noun*
[from Greek *hypochondrios* = under the breastbone (because the organs there were once thought to be the source of depression and anxiety)]

hypocrite (*say* hip-o-krit) *noun* (*plural* **hypocrites**)
a person who pretends to be more virtuous than he or she really is.
hypocrisy (*say* hip-ok-riss-ee) *noun*, **hypocritical** *adjective*
[from Greek *hypokrites* = actor or pretender]

hypodermic *adjective*
injecting something under the skin, *a hypodermic syringe*.
[from *hypo-* + Greek *derma* = skin]

hypotenuse (*say* hy-pot-i-newz) *noun* (*plural* **hypotenuses**)
the side opposite the right angle in a right-angled triangle. [from Greek]

hypothermia *noun*
being too cold; the condition in which someone's temperature is below normal. [from *hypo-* + Greek *therme* = heat]

hypothesis (*say* hy-poth-i-sis) *noun* (*plural* **hypotheses**)
a suggestion or guess that tries to explain something. **hypothetical** *adjective*
[from *hypo-* + Greek *thesis* = placing]

hysteria *noun*
wild uncontrollable excitement, panic, or emotion. **hysterics** *noun*
[from Greek *hystera* = womb (once thought to be the cause of hysteria)]

hysterical *adjective*
1 in a state of hysteria. 2 (*informal*) extremely funny. **hysterically** *adverb*

Ii

I *pronoun*
a word used by a person to refer to himself or herself. [from Old English]

-ible see **-able**.

-ic *suffix*
forms 1 adjectives, some of which are used as nouns (e.g. *comic, domestic, public*), 2 names of arts (e.g. *music, magic*).
[from Latin *-icus* or Greek *-ikos*]

-ical *suffix*
forms adjectives from or similar to words ending in *-ic* (e.g. *comical, musical*).

ice *noun* (*plural* **ices**)
1 frozen water, a brittle transparent solid substance. 2 an ice cream.

ice age *noun* (*plural* **ice ages**)
a period in the past when most of the earth's surface was covered with ice.

iceberg *noun* (*plural* **icebergs**)
a large mass of ice floating in the sea with most of it under water. [from Dutch]

ice cream *noun* (*plural* **ice creams**)
a sweet creamy frozen food.

ice hockey *noun*
a form of hockey played on ice.

ice rink *noun* (*plural* **ice rinks**)
a place made for skating.

-ician *suffix*
forms nouns meaning 'person skilled in something' (e.g. *musician*).

icicle *noun* (*plural* **icicles**)
a pointed hanging piece of ice formed when dripping water freezes. [from Old English]

icing *noun*
a sugary substance for decorating cakes.

-icity *suffix*
forms nouns (e.g. *publicity*) from words ending in *-ic*.

-ics *suffix*
forms nouns which are plural in form but are often used with a singular verb (e.g. *mathematics*, *gymnastics*).

icy *adjective* (**icier**, **iciest**)
1 covered with ice. 2 very cold.
icily *adverb*, **iciness** *noun*

idea *noun* (*plural* **ideas**)
1 a plan or thought formed in the mind. 2 an opinion or belief. [Greek]

ideal *adjective*
perfect; completely suitable. **ideally** *adverb*
ideal *noun* (*plural* **ideals**)
a person or thing regarded as perfect or as worth trying to achieve.
[from Latin, related to *idea*]

identical *adjective*
exactly the same. **identically** *adverb*
[same origin as *identity*]

identify *verb* (**identifies**, **identifying**, **identified**)
1 recognize as being a certain person or thing.
2 treat something as being identical to something else, *Don't identify wealth with happiness.* 3 think of yourself as sharing someone's feelings etc., *We can identify with the hero of this play.* **identification** *noun*

identity *noun* (*plural* **identities**)
1 who or what a person or thing is. 2 being identical; sameness. 3 distinctive character.
[from Latin *idem* = same]

idiom *noun* (*plural* **idioms**)
a phrase that means something different from the meanings of the words in it, e.g. *in hot water* (= in disgrace), *hell for leather* (= at high speed).
idiomatic *adjective*, **idiomatically** *adverb*
[from Greek *idios* = your own]

idiosyncrasy (*say* id-ee-o-**sink**-ra-see) *noun* (*plural* **idiosyncrasies**)
one person's own way of behaving or doing something.
[from Greek *idios* = your own + *syn-* + *krasis* = mixture]

idiot *noun* (*plural* **idiots**)
1 a stupid or foolish person. 2 a person who is mentally deficient. **idiocy** *noun*, **idiotic** *adjective*, **idiotically** *adverb*
[from Greek *idiotes* = private citizen, uneducated person]

idle *adjective*
1 doing no work; lazy. 2 not in use, *The machines were idle.* 3 useless; with no special purpose, *idle gossip.* **idly** *adverb*, **idleness** *noun*

idol *noun* (*plural* **idols**)
1 a statue or image that is worshipped as a god.
2 a person who is admired intensely.
[from Greek *eidolon* = image]

idolize *verb* (**idolizes**, **idolizing**, **idolized**)
admire someone intensely. **idolization** *noun*

i.e. *abbreviation*
that is, *The world's highest mountain (i.e. Mount Everest) is in the Himalayas.*
[short for Latin *id est* = that is]

USAGE: Do not confuse with *e.g.*

-ie see **-y**.

-ier see **-er**.

-iest see **-est**.

if *conjunction*
1 on condition that; supposing that, *He will do it if you pay him.* 2 even though, *I'll finish this job if it kills me.* 3 whether, *Do you know if dinner is ready?*
if only I wish, *If only I were rich!*

-iferous see **-ferous**.

-ification *suffix*
forms nouns of action (e.g. *purification*) from verbs that end in *-ify*.
[from Latin *-ficare* = make]

ignition *noun* (*plural* **ignitions**)
1 igniting. 2 the part of a motor engine that starts the fuel burning.

ignominious *adjective*
humiliating; with disgrace. **ignominy** *noun*

ignorant *adjective*
not knowing about something or about many things. **ignorantly** *adverb*, **ignorance** *noun*
[same origin as *ignore*]

ignore *verb* (**ignores**, **ignoring**, **ignored**)
take no notice of a person or thing.
[from Latin *ignorare* = not know]

il- *prefix*
1 in; into. 2 on; towards. 3 not. see **in-**.

ilk *noun*
of that ilk (*informal*) of that kind.
[from Old English *ilca* = same]

ill *adjective*
1 unwell; in bad health. 2 bad or harmful, *There were no ill effects.*
ill *adverb*
badly, *She was ill-treated.*
ill at ease uncomfortable or embarrassed.

illegal *adjective*
not legal; against the law.
illegally *adverb*, **illegality** *noun*

illegible *adjective*
impossible to read.
illegibly *adverb*, **illegibility** *noun*

illegitimate *adjective*
born when the parents are not married to each other.
illegitimately *adverb*, **illegitimacy** *noun*

illiterate *adjective*
unable to read or write.
illiterately *adverb*, **illiteracy** *noun*

illness *noun* (*plural* **illnesses**)
1 being ill. 2 a particular form of bad health; a disease.

illogical *adjective*
not logical; not reasoning correctly.
illogically *adverb*, **illogicality** *noun*

illuminate *verb* (**illuminates, illuminating, illuminated**)
1 light something up. 2 decorate streets etc. with lights. 3 decorate a manuscript with coloured designs. 4 clarify or help to explain something. **illumination** *noun*
[from *il-* + Latin *lumen* = light]

illusion *noun* (*plural* **illusions**)
something unreal or imaginary; a false impression, *The train went so fast that we had the illusion that it was flying.* (Compare *delusion.*) **illusive** *adjective*, **illusory** *adjective*
[from Latin *illudere* = mock]

illustrate *verb* (**illustrates, illustrating, illustrated**)
1 show something by pictures, examples, etc. 2 put illustrations in a book. **illustrator** *noun*
[from Latin *illustrare* = add light or brilliance]

illustration *noun* (*plural* **illustrations**)
1 a picture in a book etc. 2 illustrating something. 3 an example that helps to explain something.

illustrious *adjective*
famous and distinguished. [from Latin]

im- *prefix*
1 in; into. 2 on; towards. 3 not. see **in-**.

image *noun* (*plural* **images**)
1 a picture or statue of a person or thing. 2 the appearance of something as seen in a mirror or through a lens etc. 3 a person or thing that is very much like another, *He is the image of his father.* 4 a person's public reputation.
[from Latin]

imaginary *adjective*
existing only in the imagination; not real.

imagination *noun* (*plural* **imaginations**)
the ability to imagine things, especially in a creative or inventive way.
imaginative *adjective*

imagine *verb* (**imagines, imagining, imagined**)
form pictures or ideas in your mind.

imitate *verb* (**imitates, imitating, imitated**)
copy or mimic something. **imitation** *noun*, **imitator** *noun*, **imitative** *adjective*

immaculate *adjective*
1 perfectly clean; spotless. 2 without any fault or blemish. **immaculately** *adverb*
[from *im-* + Latin *macula* = spot or blemish]

immature *adjective*
not mature. **immaturity** *noun*

immediate *adjective*
1 happening or done without any delay.
2 nearest; with nothing or no one between, *our immediate neighbours.*
immediately *adverb*, **immediacy** *noun*
[from *im-* + Latin *mediatus* = coming between]

immense *adjective*
exceedingly great; huge. **immensely** *adverb*, **immensity** *noun*
[from *im-* + Latin *mensum* = measured]

immersion heater *noun* (*plural* **immersion heaters**)
a device that heats up water by means of an electric element in the water in a tank etc.
[from *im-* + Latin *mersum* = dipped]

immigrate *verb* (**immigrates, immigrating, immigrated**)
come into a country to live there.
immigration *noun*, **immigrant** *noun*

USAGE: See the note at *emigrate.*

imminent *adjective*
likely to happen at any moment, *an imminent storm.* **imminence** *noun*
[from Latin *imminere* = hang over]

immobilize *verb* (**immobilizes, immobilizing, immobilized**)
stop a thing from moving or working.
immobilization *noun*

immoral *adjective*
morally wrong; wicked.
immorally *adverb*, **immorality** *noun*

immortal *adjective*
1 living for ever; not mortal. 2 famous for all time. **immortal** *noun*, **immortality** *noun*, **immortalize** *verb*

immune *adjective*
safe from or protected against something, *immune from* (or *against* or *to*) *infection* etc.
immunity *noun*
[from Latin *immunis* = exempt]

immunize *verb* (**immunizes, immunizing, immunized**)
make a person immune from a disease etc., e.g. by vaccination. **immunization** *noun*

impact *noun* (*plural* **impacts**)
1 a collision; the force of a collision. 2 an influence or effect, *the impact of computers on our lives.*
[from *im-* + Latin *pactum* = driven]

impale *verb* (impales, impaling, impaled)
pierce or fix something on a sharp pointed object. **impalement** *noun*
[from *im-* + Latin *palus* = a stake]

impartial *adjective*
not favouring one side more than the other; not biased. **impartially** *adverb*, **impartiality** *noun*

impatient *adjective*
not patient.
impatiently *adverb*, **impatience** *noun*

impel *verb* (impels, impelling, impelled)
1 urge or drive someone to do something, *Curiosity impelled her to investigate.* 2 drive forward; propel.
[from *im-* + Latin *pellere* = to drive]

impending *adjective*
soon to happen; imminent.
[from *im-* + Latin *pendere* = hang]

impenetrable *adjective*
1 impossible to get through.
2 incomprehensible.

imperative *adjective*
1 expressing a command. 2 essential, *Speed is imperative.*
imperative *noun* (*plural* imperatives)
a command; the form of a verb used in making commands (e.g. 'come' in *Come here!*). [from Latin *imperare* = to command]

imperceptible *adjective*
if something is imperceptible it is so slight or gradual that it is almost impossible to notice.

imperfect *adjective*
1 not perfect. 2 (of a tense of a verb) showing a continuous action, e.g. *She was singing.*
imperfectly *adverb*, **imperfection** *noun*

imperial *adjective*
1 to do with an empire or its rulers. 2 (of weights and measures) fixed by British law; non-metric, *an imperial gallon.*
imperially *adverb*
[from Latin *imperium* = supreme power]

imperious *adjective*
haughty and bossy.
[same origin as *imperial*]

impermeable *adjective*
not allowing liquid to pass through it.

impersonal *adjective*
1 not affected by personal feelings; showing no emotion. 2 not referring to a particular person.
impersonally *adverb*

impersonal verb *noun* (*plural* impersonal verbs)
a verb used only with 'it', e.g. in *It is raining* or *It is hard to find one.*

impertinent *adjective*
insolent; not showing proper respect.
impertinently *adverb*, **impertinence** *noun*

imperturbable *adjective*
not excitable; calm. **imperturbably** *adverb*

impervious *adjective*
1 not allowing water, heat, etc. to pass through, *impervious to water.* 2 not able to be affected by something, *impervious to criticism.*
[from *im-* + Latin *per* = through + *via* = way]

impetuous *adjective*
acting hastily without thinking; rash. [same origin as *impetus*]

impetus *noun*
1 the force that makes an object start moving and that keeps it moving. 2 the influence that causes something to develop more quickly.
[Latin, = an attack]

implacable *adjective*
not able to be placated; relentless.
implacably *adverb*
[from *im-* + *placate* + *-able*]

implant *verb* (implants, implanting, implanted)
insert; fix something in. **implantation** *noun*
implant *noun* (*plural* implants)
an organ or piece of tissue inserted in the body.
[from *im-* + Latin *plantare* = to plant]

implement *noun* (*plural* implements)
a tool.

implicate *verb* (implicates, implicating, implicated)
involve a person in a crime etc.; show that a person is involved, *His evidence implicates his sister.*
[from Latin *implicare* = to fold in]

implication *noun* (*plural* implications)
1 implicating. 2 implying; something that is implied.

implicit (*say* im-pliss-it) *adjective*
1 implied but not stated openly. (Compare *explicit.*) 2 absolute; unquestioning, *She expects implicit obedience.* **implicitly** *adverb*
[from Latin *implicitus* = entangled]

implore *verb* (implores, imploring, implored)
beg somebody to do something; entreat. [from Latin *implorare* = ask tearfully]

imply *verb* (implies, implying, implied)
suggest something without actually saying it.
implication *noun*
[from old French; related to *implicate*]

impolite *adjective*
not polite.

import *verb* (imports, importing, imported)
bring in goods etc. from another country.
import *noun* (*plural* imports)
1 importing; something imported. 2 (*formal*) meaning or importance, *The message was of great import.*
[from *im-* + Latin *portare* = carry]

important *adjective*
1 having or able to have a great effect. **2** having great authority or influence.
importantly *adverb*, **importance** *noun*

impose *verb* (imposes, imposing, imposed)
put or inflict, *It imposes a strain upon us.*
impose on somebody put an unfair burden on him or her.
[from *im-* + Latin *positum* = placed]

imposing *adjective*
impressive.

imposition *noun* (*plural* **impositions**)
1 something imposed; an unfair burden or inconvenience. **2** imposing something.

impossible *adjective*
1 not possible. **2** (*informal*) very annoying; unbearable, *He really is impossible!*
impossibly *adverb*, **impossibility** *noun*

impostor *noun* (*plural* **impostors**)
a person who dishonestly pretends to be someone else. [from French]

impotent *adjective*
1 powerless; unable to take action. **2** (of a man) unable to have sexual intercourse.
impotently *adverb*, **impotence** *noun*

impoverish *verb* (impoverishes, impoverishing, impoverished)
1 make a person poor. **2** make a thing poor in quality, *impoverished soil.*
impoverishment *noun*
[from *im-* + old French *povre* = poor]

impracticable *adjective*
not able to be done in practice.

impractical *adjective*
not practical.

imprecise *adjective*
not precise.

impregnable *adjective*
strong enough to be safe against attack. [from *im-* + old French *prendre* = take]

impregnate *verb* (impregnates, impregnating, impregnated)
1 fertilize; make pregnant. **2** saturate; fill throughout, *The air was impregnated with the scent.* **impregnation** *noun*
[from *im-* + Latin *pregnare* = be pregnant]

impress *verb* (impresses, impressing, impressed)
1 make a person admire something or think it is very good. **2** fix something firmly in the mind, *He impressed on them the need for secrecy.* **3** press a mark into something.
[from *im-* + old French *presser* = to press]

impression *noun* (*plural* **impressions**)
1 an effect produced on the mind. **2** a vague idea. **3** an imitation of a person or a sound etc. **4** a reprint of a book.

impressionable *adjective*
easily influenced or affected.

impressive *adjective*
making a strong impression; seeming to be very good.

imprison *verb* (imprisons, imprisoning, imprisoned)
put someone in prison; shut someone up in a place. **imprisonment** *noun*

improbable *adjective*
unlikely.
improbably *adverb*, **improbability** *noun*

impromptu *adjective* & *adverb*
done without any rehearsal or preparation.
[from Latin *in promptu* = in readiness]

improper *adjective*
1 unsuitable or wrong. **2** indecent.
improperly *adverb*,
impropriety (*say* im-pro-**pry**-it-ee) *noun*

improper fraction *noun* (*plural* **improper fractions**)
a fraction that is greater than 1, with the numerator greater than the denominator, e.g. $\frac{5}{3}$.

improve *verb* (improves, improving, improved)
make or become better. **improvement** *noun*
[from old French *emprouer* = make a profit]

improvise *verb* (improvises, improvising, improvised)
1 compose or perform something without any rehearsal or preparation. **2** make something quickly with whatever is available.
improvisation *noun*
[from *im-* + Latin *provisus* = provided for]

imprudent *adjective*
unwise.

impudent *adjective*
cheeky or disrespectful.
impudently *adverb*, **impudence** *noun*
[from *im-* + Latin *pudens* = ashamed]

impulse *noun* (*plural* **impulses**)
1 a sudden desire to do something. **2** a push; impetus. **3** (in physics) a force acting for a very short time, *electrical impulses.* [same origin as *impel*]

impulsive *adjective*
done or acting on impulse, not after careful thought.
impulsively *adverb*, **impulsiveness** *noun*

impure *adjective*
not pure. **impurity** *noun*

in *preposition*
This word is used to show position or condition, e.g. **1** at or inside; within the limits of something (*in a box; in two hours*), **2** into (*He fell in a puddle*), **3** arranged as; consisting of (*a serial in four parts*), **4** occupied with; a member of (*He is in the army*), **5** by means of (*We paid in cash*).
in all in total number; altogether.

in *adverb*
1 so as to be in something or inside (*Get in*),
2 inwards (*The top caved in*), 3 at home;
indoors (*Is anybody in?*), 4 in action; (in
cricket) batting; (of a fire) burning, 5 having
arrived (*The train is in*).
in for likely to get, *You're in for a shock.*
in on (*informal*) aware of or sharing in, *I want
to be in on this project.*

in- *prefix* (changing to **il-** before *l*, **im-** before *b*, *m*,
p, **ir-** before *r*)
1 in; into; on; towards (as in *include, invade*).
[from Latin] 2 not (as in *incorrect, indirect*).
[usually from Latin; in a few words from
Germanic *un-*]

inability *noun*
being unable.

inaccessible *adjective*
not accessible.

inaccurate *adjective*
not accurate.

inadequate *adjective*
1 not enough. 2 not capable enough.
inadequately *adverb*, **inadequacy** *noun*

inadvisable *adjective*
not advisable.

inanimate *adjective*
1 not living. 2 not moving.

inappropriate *adjective*
not appropriate.

inarticulate *adjective*
1 not able to speak or express yourself clearly,
inarticulate with rage. 2 not expressed in
words, *an inarticulate cry.*

inaudible *adjective*
unable to be heard.
inaudibly *adverb*, **inaudibility** *noun*

inaugurate *verb* (inaugurates, inaugurating,
inaugurated)
1 start or introduce something new and
important. 2 formally establish a person in
office, *inaugurate a new President.*
inaugural *adjective*, **inauguration** *noun*,
inaugurator *noun* [from Latin]

inborn *adjective*
present in a person or animal from birth, *an
inborn ability.*

inbred *adjective*
1 inborn. 2 produced by inbreeding.

inbreeding *noun*
breeding from closely related individuals.

incalculable *adjective*
not able to be calculated or predicted.
[from *in-* + *calculate* + *-able*]

incandescent *adjective*
giving out light when heated; shining.
incandescence *noun* [from *in-* + Latin
candescere = become white]

incantation *noun* (*plural* incantations)
a spoken spell or charm; the chanting of this.
[from *in-* = in + Latin *cantare* = sing]

incapable *adjective*
not able to do something, *incapable of working
alone.*

incapacitate *verb* (incapacitates, incapacitating,
incapacitated)
make a person or thing unable to do
something; disable.
[from *in-* + *capacity* + *-ate*]

incarnate *adjective*
having a body or human form, *a devil
incarnate.* **incarnation** *noun*
the Incarnation the embodiment of God in
human form as Jesus Christ.
[from *in-* + Latin *carnis* = of flesh]

incautious *adjective*
rash.

incendiary *adjective*
starting or designed to start a fire, *an
incendiary bomb.* [same origin as *incense*]

incentive *noun* (*plural* incentives)
something that encourages a person to do
something or to work harder.
[from Latin *incentivus* = setting the tune]

incest *noun*
sexual intercourse between two people who are
so closely related that they cannot marry each
other. **incestuous** *adjective* [from *in-* + Latin
castus = pure]

inch *noun* (*plural* inches)
a measure of length, one-twelfth of a foot (about
2½ centimetres). [from Old English]

incident *noun* (*plural* incidents)
an event. [from Latin *incidere* = fall upon or
happen to]

incidental *adjective*
happening as a minor part of something else,
incidental expenses. [from *incident*]

incidentally *adverb*
by the way.

incinerate *verb* (incinerates, incinerating,
incinerated)
destroy something by burning. **incineration**
noun [from *in-* + Latin *cineris* = of ashes]

incinerator *noun* (*plural* incinerators)
a device for burning rubbish.

incision *noun* (*plural* incisions)
a cut, especially one made in a surgical
operation. [from *in-* + Latin *caesum* = cut]

incisive *adjective*
clear and sharp, *incisive comments.*

incisor (*say* in-sy-zer) *noun* (*plural* incisors)
each of the sharp-edged front teeth in the upper
and lower jaws.

incite *verb* (incites, inciting, incited)
urge a person to do something; stir up, *They
incited a riot.* **incitement** *noun*
[from *in-* = towards + Latin *citare* = rouse]

inclination *noun* (*plural* inclinations)
1 a tendency. 2 a liking or preference.
3 a slope or slant.

incline *verb* (inclines, inclining, inclined)
1 lean or slope. 2 bend the head or body
forward, as in a nod or bow. 3 cause or
influence, *Her frank manner inclines me to
believe her.*
be inclined have a tendency, *The door is
inclined to bang.* [from Latin *inclinare* = to
bend]

include *verb* (includes, including, included)
make or consider something as part of a group
of things.
[from Latin *includere* = enclose]

incoherent *adjective*
not speaking or reasoning in an orderly way.

income *noun* (*plural* incomes)
money received regularly from wages,
investments, etc. [from *in* (adverb) + *come*]

income tax *noun*
tax charged on income.

incomparable *adjective*
without an equal; unsurpassed, *incomparable
beauty.*
[from *in-* + Latin *comparabilis* = comparable]

incompetent *adjective*
not competent.

incomplete *adjective*
not complete.

incomprehensible *adjective*
not able to be understood.
incomprehension *noun* [from *in-* + Latin
comprehensibilis = comprehensible]

incongruous *adjective*
out of place or unsuitable.
incongruously *adverb*, **incongruity** *noun*
[from *in-* + Latin *congruus* = agreeing or
suitable]

inconsiderate *adjective*
not considerate.

inconsistent *adjective*
not consistent. **inconsistently** *adverb*,
inconsistency *noun*

inconspicuous *adjective*
not conspicuous. **inconspicuously** *adverb*

incontinent *adjective*
not able to control the bladder or bowels.
incontinence *noun* [from *in-* + Latin *continentia*
= restraining, keeping in]

incontrovertible *adjective*
unable to be denied; indisputable.
[from *in-* + Latin *controversus* = disputed]

inconvenience *noun* (*plural* inconveniences)
being inconvenient.
inconvenience *verb* (inconveniences,
inconveniencing, inconvenienced)
cause inconvenience or slight difficulty to
someone.

inconvenient *adjective*
not convenient.

incorporate *verb* (incorporates, incorporating,
incorporated)
include something as a part.
incorporation *noun*
[from *in-* + Latin *corpus* = body]

incorporated *adjective*
(of a business firm) formed into a legal
corporation.

incorrect *adjective*
not correct. **incorrectly** *adverb*

incorruptible *adjective*
1 not able to decay. 2 not able to be bribed.

increase *verb* (increases, increasing, increased)
make or become larger or more.
increase *noun* (*plural* increases)
increasing; the amount by which a thing
increases.
[from *in-* + Latin *crescere* = grow]

incredible *adjective*
unbelievable.
incredibly *adverb*, **incredibility** *noun*

USAGE: Do not confuse with *incredulous.*

incredulous *adjective*
not believing somebody; showing disbelief.
incredulously *adverb*, **incredulity** *noun*

USAGE: Do not confuse with *incredible.*

incriminate *verb* (incriminates, incriminating,
incriminated)
show a person to have been involved in a crime
etc. **incrimination** *noun*
[from *in-* + Latin *criminare* = accuse of a crime]

incubate *verb* (incubates, incubating, incubated)
1 hatch eggs by keeping them warm. 2 cause
bacteria or a disease etc. to develop.
incubation *noun*
[from *in-* + Latin *cubare* = lie]

incubator *noun* (*plural* incubators)
1 a device for incubating eggs etc. 2 a device in
which a baby born prematurely can be kept
warm and supplied with oxygen.

indebted *adjective*
owing money or gratitude to someone.

indecent *adjective*
not decent; improper.
indecently *adverb*, **indecency** *noun*

indecisive *adjective*
not decisive.

indeed *adverb*
1 really; truly, *I am indeed surprised*; (used to strengthen a meaning), *very nice indeed*. 2 admittedly, *It is, indeed, his first attempt*. [from *in deed* = in action or fact]

indefensible *adjective*
unable to be defended or justified, *an indefensible decision*.

indefinite *adjective*
not definite; vague.
indefinite article the word 'a' or 'an'.

indefinitely *adverb*
for an indefinite or unlimited time.

indelible *adjective*
impossible to rub out or remove.
indelibly *adverb*
[from *in-* + Latin *delere* = destroy]

indelicate *adjective*
1 slightly indecent. 2 tactless.
indelicacy *noun*

independent *adjective*
1 not dependent; not controlled by any other person or thing. 2 (of a country) governing itself. 3 (of broadcasting) not financed by money from licences. **independently** *adverb*, **independence** *noun*

indestructible *adjective*
unable to be destroyed. **indestructibility** *noun*
[from *in-* + Latin *destruere* = destroy]

indeterminate *adjective*
not fixed or decided exactly; left vague. [from *in-* + Latin *determinare* = define or determine]

index *noun*
1 (*plural* **indexes**) an alphabetical list of things, especially at the end of a book. 2 a number showing how prices or wages have changed from a previous level. 3 (*plural* **indices**) the raised number etc. written to the right of another (e.g. 3 in 2^3) showing how many times the first one is to be multiplied by itself. [Latin, = pointer]

Indian *adjective*
1 to do with India or its people. 2 to do with Native Americans. **Indian** *noun*

USAGE: The preferred term for the descendants of the original inhabitants of North and South America is *Native American*. *American Indian* is usually acceptable but the term *Red Indian* is now regarded as offensive and should not be used.

india rubber *noun* (*plural* **india rubbers**)
a rubber.
[because it was made of rubber from India]

indicate *verb* (**indicates**, **indicating**, **indicated**)
1 point something out or make it known. 2 be a sign of. 3 when drivers indicate, they signal which direction they are turning by using their indicators. **indication** *noun*
[from Latin; related to *index*]

indicative *adjective*
giving an indication.
indicative *noun*
the form of a verb used in making a statement (e.g. 'he said' or 'he is coming'), not in a command or question etc.

indicator *noun* (*plural* **indicators**)
1 a thing that indicates or points to something. 2 a flashing light used to signal that a motor vehicle is turning.

indifferent *adjective*
1 not caring about something; not interested. 2 not very good, *an indifferent cricketer*. **indifferently** *adverb*, **indifference** *noun*
[from *in-* + Latin *differre* = recognize differences]

indigenous (*say* in-**dij**-in-us) *adjective*
growing or originating in a particular country; native, *The koala bear is indigenous to Australia*.
[from Latin *indigena* = born in a country]

indigestible *adjective*
difficult or impossible to digest.

indigestion *noun*
pain caused by difficulty in digesting food.
[from *in-* + Latin *digerere* = digest]

indignant *adjective*
angry at something that seems unfair or wicked. **indignantly** *adverb*, **indignation** *noun*
[from Latin *indignari* = regard as unworthy]

indignity *noun* (*plural* **indignities**)
treatment that makes a person feel undignified or humiliated; an insult.
[from *in-* + Latin *dignus* worthy]

indirect *adjective*
not direct. **indirectly** *adverb*

indiscreet *adjective*
1 not discreet; revealing secrets. 2 not cautious; rash.
indiscreetly *adverb*, **indiscretion** *noun*

indiscriminate *adjective*
showing no discrimination; not making a careful choice. **indiscriminately** *adverb*

indispensable *adjective*
not able to be dispensed with; essential.
indispensability *noun*

indisputable *adjective*
undeniable.
[from *in-* + Latin *disputare* = dispute]

indistinct *adjective*
not distinct.
indistinctly *adverb*, **indistinctness** *noun*

indistinguishable *adjective*
not able to be told apart; not distinguishable.

individual *adjective*
1 of or for one person. 2 single or separate, *Count each individual word.*
individually *adverb*
individual *noun* (*plural* **individuals**)
one person, animal, or plant.
[from *in-* + Latin *dividuus* = able to be divided]

individuality *noun*
the things that make one person or thing different from another; distinctive identity.

indivisible *adjective*
not able to be divided or separated.
indivisibly *adverb*
[from *in-* + Latin *divisum* = divided]

indoctrinate *verb* (**indoctrinates, indoctrinating, indoctrinated**)
fill a person's mind with particular ideas or beliefs, especially so that he or she comes to accept them without thinking.
indoctrination *noun*
[from *in-* = in, + *doctrine*]

indomitable *adjective*
not able to be overcome or conquered. [from *in-* + Latin *domitare* = to tame]

indoor *adjective*
used or placed or done etc. inside a building, *indoor games.*

indoors *adverb*
inside a building.

induce *verb* (**induces, inducing, induced**)
1 persuade. 2 produce or cause, *Some substances induce sleep.* 3 if a pregnant woman is induced, labour is brought on artificially with the use of drugs. **induction** *noun*
[from *in-* + Latin *ducere* = to lead]

indulge *verb* (**indulges, indulging, indulged**)
allow a person to have or do what he or she wishes.
indulgence *noun*, **indulgent** *adjective*
indulge in allow yourself to have or do something that you like.

industrial *adjective*
to do with industry; working or used in industry. **industrially** *adverb*

industrial action *noun*
striking or working to rule.

industrialized *adjective*
(of a country or district) having many industries. **industrialization** *noun*

Industrial Revolution *noun*
the expansion of British industry by the use of machines in the late 18th and early 19th century.

industrious *adjective*
working hard. **industriously** *adverb*

industry *noun* (*plural* **industries**)
1 making or producing goods etc., especially in factories. 2 a particular branch of this, *the motor industry.* 3 being industrious.
[from Latin *industria* = hard work]

ineffective *adjective*
not effective; inefficient.
ineffectively *adverb*

ineffectual *adjective*
not achieving anything.

inefficient *adjective*
not efficient.
inefficiently *adverb*, **inefficiency** *noun*

inert *adjective*
not moving or reacting. **inertly** *adverb* [from Latin *iners* = idle]

inert gas *noun* (*plural* **inert gases**)
a gas that almost never combines with other substances.

inertia (*say* in-er-sha) *noun*
1 inactivity; being inert or slow to take action. 2 the tendency for a moving thing to keep moving in a straight line.
[same origin as *inert*]

inevitable *adjective*
unavoidable; sure to happen.
inevitably *adverb*, **inevitability** *noun*
[from *in-* + Latin *evitare* = avoid]

inexhaustible *adjective*
so great that it cannot be used up completely, *Ben has an inexhaustible supply of jokes.*

inexorable (*say* in-eks-er-a-bul) *adjective*
1 relentless. 2 not able to be persuaded by requests or entreaties. **inexorably** *adverb*
[from *in-* + Latin *exorare* = plead]

inexperience *noun*
lack of experience. **inexperienced** *adjective*

infallible *adjective*
1 never wrong. 2 never failing, *an infallible remedy.*
infallibly *adverb*, **infallibility** *noun*
[from *in-* + Latin *fallere* = deceive]

infancy *noun*
1 early childhood; babyhood. 2 an early stage of development.

infant *noun* (*plural* **infants**)
a baby or young child.
[from Latin *infans* = unable to speak]

infantile *adjective*
1 to do with infants. 2 very childish.

infantry *noun*
soldiers who fight on foot. (Compare *cavalry.*)
[from Italian *infante* = a youth]

infatuated *adjective*
filled with foolish or unreasoning love.
infatuation *noun*
[from *in-* + Latin *fatuus* = foolish]

infect *verb* (infects, infecting, infected)
pass on a disease or bacteria etc. to a person, animal, or plant.
[from Latin *infectum* = tainted]

infection *noun* (*plural* infections)
1 infecting. 2 an infectious disease or condition.

infectious *adjective*
1 (of a disease) able to be spread by air or water etc. (Compare *contagious*.) 2 quickly spreading to others, *His fear was infectious*.

inferior *adjective*
less good or less important; low or lower in position, quality, etc. **inferiority** *noun* [Latin, = lower]

infernal *adjective*
1 to do with or like hell, *the infernal regions*. 2 (*informal*) detestable or tiresome, *that infernal noise*. **infernally** *adverb*
[from Latin *infernus* = below, used by Christians to mean 'hell']

inferno *noun* (*plural* infernos)
a terrifying fire.
[same origin as *infernal*]

infertile *adjective*
not fertile. **infertility** *noun*

infest *verb* (infests, infesting, infested)
(of pests) be numerous and troublesome in a place. **infestation** *noun*
[from Latin *infestus* = hostile]

infidelity *noun*
unfaithfulness.

infiltrate *verb* (infiltrates, infiltrating, infiltrated)
get into a place or organization gradually and without being noticed. **infiltration** *noun*, **infiltrator** *noun*
[from *in-* + Latin *filtrare* = to filter]

infinite *adjective*
1 endless; without a limit. 2 too great to be measured. **infinitely** *adverb*
[from Latin *infinitus* = unlimited]

infinitesimal *adjective*
extremely small. **infinitesimally** *adverb*

infinitive *noun* (*plural* infinitives)
a form of a verb that does not indicate a particular tense or number or person, in English used with or without *to*, e.g. *go* in 'Let him go' or 'Allow him to go'.
[from *in-* + Latin *finitivus* = definite]

infinity *noun*
an infinite number or distance or time.

inflame *verb* (inflames, inflaming, inflamed)
1 produce strong feelings or anger in people. 2 cause redness, heat, and swelling in a part of the body.
[from *in-* + Latin *flamma* = flame]

inflammable *adjective*
able to be set on fire.
[same origin as *inflame*]

USAGE: This word means the same as *flammable*. If you want to say that something is not able to be set on fire, use *non-flammable*.

inflammation *noun*
painful redness or swelling in a part of the body.

inflate *verb* (inflates, inflating, inflated)
1 fill something with air or gas so that it expands. 2 increase something too much. 3 raise prices or wages etc. more than is justifiable. [from *in-* + Latin *flatum* = blown]

inflation *noun*
1 inflating. 2 a general rise in prices and fall in the purchasing power of money. **inflationary** *adjective*

inflect *verb* (inflects, inflecting, inflected)
1 change the ending or form of a word to show its tense or its grammatical relation to other words, e.g. *sing* changes to *sang* or *sung*, *child* changes to *children*. 2 alter the voice in speaking. [originally = bend inwards: from *in-* + Latin *flectere* = to bend]

inflection *noun* (*plural* inflections)
an ending or form of a word used to inflect, e.g. *-ed*.

inflexible *adjective*
not able to be bent or changed or persuaded. **inflexibly** *adverb*, **inflexibility** *noun*
[from *in-* + Latin *flexibilis* = flexible]

influence *noun* (*plural* influences)
1 the power to produce an effect. 2 a person or thing with this power.
influence *verb* (influences, influencing, influenced)
have influence on a person or thing; affect. [from *in-* + Latin *fluentia* = flowing]

influential *adjective*
having influence.

influenza *noun*
an infectious disease that causes fever, catarrh, and pain.
[Italian, literally = influence]

inform *verb* (informs, informing, informed)
give information to somebody. **informant** *noun*
[from Latin *informare* = form an idea of something]

informal *adjective*
not formal.
informally *adverb*, **informality** *noun*

USAGE: In this dictionary, words marked *informal* are used in talking but not when you are writing or speaking formally.

information *noun*
facts told or heard or discovered, or put into a computer etc.
[from Latin *informatio* = idea]

informative *adjective*
giving a lot of useful information.

informed *adjective*
knowing about something.

infra- *prefix*
below. [Latin]

infra-red *adjective*
below or beyond red in the spectrum.

infuriate *verb* (infuriates, infuriating, infuriated)
make a person very angry; enrage.
infuriation *noun*
[from *in-* + Latin *furia* = fury]

-ing *suffix*
forms nouns and adjectives showing the action of a verb (e.g. *hearing, tasting, telling*).

ingenious *adjective*
1 clever at inventing things. 2 cleverly made.
ingeniously *adverb*, **ingenuity** *noun*
[from Latin *ingenium* = genius]

ingrained *adjective*
1 (of dirt) marking a surface deeply. 2 (of feelings or habits etc.) firmly fixed.
[from *in the grain* (of wood)]

ingratiate *verb* (ingratiates, ingratiating, ingratiated)
ingratiate yourself get yourself into favour with someone, especially by flattering them or always agreeing with them. **ingratiation** *noun*
[from Latin *in gratiam* = into favour]

ingratitude *noun*
lack of gratitude.

ingredient *noun* (*plural* ingredients)
one of the parts of a mixture; one of the things used in a recipe.
[from Latin *ingrediens* = going in]

inhabit *verb* (inhabits, inhabiting, inhabited)
live in a place. **inhabitant** *noun*
[from *in-* + Latin *habitare* = occupy]

inhale *verb* (inhales, inhaling, inhaled)
breathe in. **inhalation** *noun*
[from *in-* + Latin *halare* = breathe]

inhaler *noun* (*plural* inhalers)
a device used for relieving asthma etc. by inhaling.

inherent (*say* in-heer-ent) *adjective*
existing in something as one of its natural or permanent qualities.
inherently *adverb*, **inherence** *noun*
[from *in-* + Latin *haerere* = to stick]

inherit *verb* (inherits, inheriting, inherited)
1 receive money, property, or a title etc. when its previous owner dies. 2 get certain qualities etc. from parents or predecessors.
inheritance *noun*, **inheritor** *noun*
[from *in-* + Latin *heres* = heir]

inhibition *noun* (*plural* inhibitions)
a feeling of embarrassment or worry that prevents you from doing something or expressing your emotions. **inhibited** *adjective*
[from *in-* + Latin *habere* = to hold]

inhuman *adjective*
cruel; without pity or kindness.
inhumanity *noun*
[from *in-* + Latin *humanus* = human]

inimitable *adjective*
impossible to imitate.

initial *noun* (*plural* initials)
the first letter of a word or name.
initial *adjective*
at the beginning, *the initial stages.*
initially *adverb*
[from Latin *initium* = the beginning]

initiative (*say* in-ish-a-tiv) *noun*
the power or courage to get something started; enterprising ability.
take the initiative take action to start something happening.

inject *verb* (injects, injecting, injected)
1 put a medicine or drug into the body by means of a hollow needle. 2 put liquid into something by means of a syringe etc. 3 add a new quality, *Inject some humour into the story.*
injection *noun*
[from *in-* + Latin *jacere* = to throw]

injure *verb* (injures, injuring, injured)
harm or hurt someone. **injury** *noun*, **injurious** (*say* in-joor-ee-us) *adjective* [originally = treat someone unfairly: from *in-* + Latin *juris* = of right]

injustice *noun* (*plural* injustices)
1 lack of justice. 2 an unjust action or treatment.

ink *noun* (*plural* inks)
a black or coloured liquid used in writing and printing. [from Greek]

inky *adjective*
1 stained with ink. 2 black like ink, *inky darkness.*

inland *adjective* & *adverb*
in or towards the interior of a country; away from the coast.

Inland Revenue *noun*
the government department responsible for collecting taxes and similar charges inland (not at a port).

in-laws *plural noun* (*informal*)
relatives by marriage. [from French *en loi de mariage* = in law of marriage]

inlet noun (plural **inlets**)
1 a strip of water reaching into the land from a sea or lake. 2 a passage that lets something in (e.g. to a tank).

inmost adjective
most inward.

inn noun (plural **inns**)
a hotel or public house, especially in the country. **innkeeper** noun

inner adjective
inside; nearer to the centre.
innermost adjective

innings noun (plural **innings**)
the time when a cricket team or player is batting.
[from an old verb in = put or get in, + -ing]

innocent adjective
1 not guilty. 2 not wicked. 3 harmless.
innocently adverb, **innocence** noun
[from in- + Latin nocens = doing harm]

innocuous adjective
harmless.
[from in- + Latin nocuus = harmful]

innovation noun (plural **innovations**)
1 introducing new things or new methods.
2 something newly introduced.
innovative adjective, **innovator** noun
[from in- + Latin novus = new]

innumerable adjective
countless. [from in- + Latin numerare = to count or number]

inoculate verb (**inoculates, inoculating, inoculated**)
inject or treat someone with a vaccine or serum as a protection against a disease.
inoculation noun
[from Latin inoculare = implant]

USAGE: Note the spelling of this word. It has one 'n' and one 'c'.

inoffensive adjective
harmless.

inorganic adjective
not of living organisms; of mineral origin.

input noun
what is put into something (e.g. data into a computer). **input** verb

inquest noun (plural **inquests**)
an official inquiry to find out how a person died.
[from old French; related to inquire]

inquire verb (**inquires, inquiring, inquired**)
1 investigate something carefully. 2 ask for information.
[from in- + Latin quaerere = seek]

USAGE: You can spell this word inquire or enquire in either of its meanings. It is probably more common for inquire to be used for 'investigate' and enquire to be used for 'ask for information', but there is no real need to follow this distinction.

inquiry noun (plural **inquiries**)
1 an investigation. 2 a question.

inquisitive adjective
always asking questions or trying to look at things; prying.
inquisitively adverb
[same origin as inquire]

inroads plural noun
make inroads on or **into** use up large quantities of stores etc.
[from in (adverb) + an old sense of road = riding]

insane adjective
not sane; mad.
insanely adverb, **insanity** noun

insanitary adjective
unclean and likely to be harmful to health.

insatiable (say in-say-sha-bul) adjective
impossible to satisfy, an insatiable appetite.
[from in- + Latin satiare = satiate]

inscribe verb (**inscribes, inscribing, inscribed**)
write or carve words etc. on something. [from in- + Latin scribere = write]

inscription noun (plural **inscriptions**)
1 words or names inscribed on a monument, coin, stone, etc. 2 inscribing.

insect noun (plural **insects**)
a small animal with six legs, no backbone, and a body divided into three parts (head, thorax, abdomen).
[from Latin insectum = cut up]

insecticide noun (plural **insecticides**)
a substance for killing insects.
[from insect + -cide]

insectivorous adjective
feeding on insects and other small invertebrate creatures.
insectivore noun

insecure adjective
not secure; unsafe.
insecurely adverb, **insecurity** noun

inseminate verb (**inseminates, inseminating, inseminated**)
insert semen into the womb.
insemination noun
[from in- + Latin seminare = to sow]

insensitive adjective
not sensitive.
insensitively adverb, **insensitivity** noun

inseparable *adjective*
1 not able to be separated. 2 liking to be constantly together, *inseparable friends*.
inseparably *adverb*

insert *verb* (inserts, inserting, inserted)
put a thing into something else. **insertion** *noun*
[from *in-* + Latin *serere* = to plant]

inside *noun* (*plural* insides)
the inner side, surface, or part.
inside out with the inside turned to face outwards.

inside *adverb & preposition*
on or to the inside of something; in, *Come inside. It's inside that box.*

insider *noun* (*plural* insiders)
a member of a certain group, especially someone with access to private information.

insight *noun* (*plural* insights)
being able to perceive the truth about things; understanding.

insignificant *adjective*
not important or influential.
insignificance *noun*

insincere *adjective*
not sincere.
insincerely *adverb*, **insincerity** *noun*

insinuate *verb* (insinuates, insinuating, insinuated)
1 hint something unpleasant. 2 introduce a thing or yourself gradually or craftily into a place. **insinuation** *noun*
[from *in-* + Latin *sinuare* = to curve]

insist *verb* (insists, insisting, insisted)
be very firm in saying or asking for something.
insistent *adjective*, **insistence** *noun*
[from *in-* + Latin *sistere* = to stand]

insolent *adjective*
very impudent; insulting.
insolently *adverb*, **insolence** *noun*
[from Latin *insolentia* = pride]

insoluble *adjective*
1 impossible to solve, *an insoluble problem.*
2 impossible to dissolve. **insolubility** *noun*
[from *in-* + Latin *solubilis* = soluble]

insomnia *noun*
being unable to sleep. **insomniac** *noun*
[from *in-* + Latin *somnus* = sleep]

inspect *verb* (inspects, inspecting, inspected)
examine something carefully and critically.
inspection *noun*
[from *in-* + Latin *specere* = to look]

inspector *noun* (*plural* inspectors)
1 a person whose job is to inspect or supervise things. 2 a police officer ranking next above a sergeant.

inspiration *noun* (*plural* inspirations)
1 a sudden brilliant idea. 2 inspiring; an inspiring influence.

inspire *verb* (inspires, inspiring, inspired)
fill a person with enthusiasm or creative feelings or ideas, *The applause inspired us with confidence.*
[from *in-* + Latin *spirare* = breathe]

install *verb* (installs, installing, installed)
1 put something in position and ready to use, *They installed central heating.* 2 put a person into an important position with a ceremony, *He was installed as pope.* **installation** *noun*
[from *in-* + Latin *stallum* = a place or position]

instalment *noun* (*plural* instalments)
each of the parts in which something is given or paid for gradually, *an instalment of a serial.*
[from old French]

instance *noun* (*plural* instances)
an example, *for instance.* [from Latin]

instant *adjective*
1 happening immediately, *instant success.* 2 (of food) designed to be prepared quickly and easily, *instant coffee.* **instantly** *adverb*
instant *noun* (*plural* instants)
a moment, *not an instant too soon.*
[from Latin *instans* = urgent]

instantaneous *adjective*
happening immediately.
instantaneously *adverb*

instead *adverb*
in place of something else.
[from *in-* + *stead* = a place]

instinct *noun* (*plural* instincts)
a natural tendency or ability, *Birds fly by instinct.* **instinctive** *adjective*, **instinctively** *adverb*
[from Latin *instinguere* = urge on]

institute *noun* (*plural* institutes)
a society or organization; the building used by this.

institution *noun* (*plural* institutions)
1 an institute; a public organization; e.g. a hospital or university. 2 a habit or custom.
3 instituting something.
institutional *adjective*

instruct *verb* (instructs, instructing, instructed)
1 teach a person a subject or skill. 2 inform.
3 tell a person what he or she must do.
instruction *noun*,
instructional *adjective*, **instructor** *noun*
[from Latin *instruere* = to build up or prepare]

instrument *noun* (*plural* instruments)
1 a device for producing musical sounds. 2 a tool used for delicate or scientific work. 3 a measuring-device.
[same origin as *instruct*]

instrumental *adjective*
1 performed on musical instruments, without singing. 2 being the means of doing something, *She was instrumental in getting me a job.*

insubordinate *adjective*
disobedient or rebellious.
insubordination *noun*

insufferable *adjective*
unbearable.

insular *adjective*
1 to do with or like an island. 2 narrow-minded. [same origin as *insulate*]

insulate *verb* (insulates, insulating, insulated)
cover or protect something to prevent heat, cold, or electricity etc. from passing in or out.
insulation *noun*, **insulator** *noun*
[from Latin *insula* = island]

insulin *noun*
a substance that controls the amount of sugar in the blood. The lack of insulin causes diabetes. [from Latin]

insult (*say* in-sult) *verb* (insults, insulting, insulted)
hurt a person's feelings or pride.
insult (*say* in-sult) *noun* (*plural* insults)
an insulting remark or action. [from Latin]

insuperable *adjective*
unable to be overcome, *an insuperable difficulty.*
[from *in-* + Latin *superare* = to overcome]

insurance *noun*
an agreement to compensate someone for a loss, damage, or injury etc., in return for a payment (called a *premium*) made in advance.

insure *verb* (insures, insuring, insured)
protect with insurance, *Is your jewellery insured?* [a different spelling of *ensure*]

USAGE: Do not confuse with *ensure.*

intact *adjective*
not damaged; complete.
[from *in-* + Latin *tactum* = touched]

intake *noun* (*plural* intakes)
1 taking something in. 2 the number of people or things taken in.

integer *noun* (*plural* integers)
a whole number (e.g. 0, 3, 19), not a fraction.
[Latin, = whole]

integral (*say* in-tig-ral) *adjective*
1 being an essential part of a whole thing, *An engine is an integral part of a car.* 2 whole or complete.
[same origin as *integer*]

integrate *verb* (integrates, integrating, integrated)
1 make parts into a whole; combine. 2 join together harmoniously into a single community. **integration** *noun*
[from Latin *integrare* = make whole]

integrity (*say* in-teg-rit-ee) *noun*
honesty. [from Latin *integritas* = wholeness or purity]

intellect *noun* (*plural* intellects)
the ability to think (contrasted with *feeling* and *instinct*). [same origin as *intelligent*]

intellectual *adjective*
1 to do with or using the intellect. 2 having a good intellect and a liking for knowledge.
intellectually *adverb*
intellectual *noun* (*plural* intellectuals)
an intellectual person.

intelligence *noun*
1 being intelligent. 2 information, especially of military value; the people who collect and study this information.

intelligent *adjective*
able to learn and understand things; having great mental ability.
intelligently *adverb*
[from Latin *intelligere* = understand]

intend *verb* (intends, intending, intended)
have something in mind as what you want to do; plan.
[from Latin *intendere* = stretch, aim]

intense *adjective*
1 very strong or great. 2 feeling things very strongly and seriously, *He's a very intense young man.*
intensely *adverb*, **intensity** *noun*
[from Latin *intensus* = stretched tight]

intent *noun* (*plural* intents)
intention.
intent *adjective*
with concentrated attention; very interested.
intently *adverb*
[same origin as *intend*]

intention *noun* (*plural* intentions)
what a person intends; a purpose or plan.

intentional *adjective*
deliberate, not accidental.
intentionally *adverb*

inter- *prefix*
between; among. [from Latin]

interact *verb* (interacts, interacting, interacted)
have an effect upon one another. **interaction** *noun*

interbreed *verb* (interbreeds, interbreeding, interbred)
breed with each other; cross-breed.

intercept *verb* (intercepts, intercepting, intercepted)
stop or catch a person or thing that is going from one place to another. **interception** *noun*
[from *inter-* + Latin *captum* = seized]

interchange *verb* (interchanges, interchanging, interchanged)
1 put each of two things into the other's place. 2 exchange things. 3 alternate.
interchangeable *adjective*

interchange *noun* (*plural* **interchanges**)
1 interchanging. **2** a road junction where vehicles can move from one motorway etc. to another.

intercourse *noun*
1 communication or dealings between people. **2** sexual intercourse.
[from Latin *intercursus* = running between]

interdependent *adjective*
dependent upon each other.

interest *noun* (*plural* **interests**)
1 a feeling of wanting to know about or help with something. **2** a thing that interests somebody, *Science fiction is one of my interests.* **3** an advantage or benefit, *She looks after her own interests.* **4** money paid regularly in return for money lent or deposited.
interest *verb* (**interests, interesting, interested**)
attract a person's interest.
interested *adjective*, **interesting** *adjective*
[Latin, = it matters]

interfere *verb* (**interferes, interfering, interfered**)
1 take part in something that has nothing to do with you. **2** get in the way; obstruct.
interference *noun*
[from *inter-* + Latin *ferire* = to strike]

interior *adjective*
inner.
interior *noun* (*plural* **interiors**)
the inside of something; the central or inland part of a country.
[Latin, = further in]

interjection *noun* (*plural* **interjections**)
a word or words exclaimed expressing joy or pain or surprise, such as *oh!* or *wow!* or *good heavens!* [from *inter-* + Latin *jactum* = thrown]

interlude *noun* (*plural* **interludes**)
1 an interval. **2** something happening in an interval or between other events.
[from *inter-* + Latin *ludus* = game]

intermediate *adjective*
coming between two things in time, place, or order.
[from *inter-* + Latin *medius* = middle]

interminable *adjective*
endless; long and boring. **interminably** *adverb*
[from *in-* + Latin *terminare* = to limit or end]

intermission *noun* (*plural* **intermissions**)
an interval, especially between parts of a film.
[same origin as *intermittent*]

intermittent *adjective*
happening at intervals; not continuous.
intermittently *adverb*
[from *inter-* + Latin *mittere* = to let go]

internal *adjective*
inside. **internally** *adverb* [from Latin]

internal-combustion engine *noun* (*plural* **internal-combustion engines**)
an engine that produces power by burning fuel inside the engine itself.

international *adjective*
to do with or belonging to more than one country; agreed between nations.
internationally *adverb*
international *noun* (*plural* **internationals**)
1 a sports contest between teams representing different countries. **2** a sports player who plays for his or her country.

Internet *noun*
an international computer network that allows users all over the world to interchange information.

interplanetary *adjective*
between planets.

interpolate *verb* (**interpolates, interpolating, interpolated**)
1 interject a remark in a conversation. **2** insert words; put terms into a mathematical series.
interpolation *noun* [from Latin *interpolare* = redecorate or smarten up]

interpose *verb* (**interposes, interposing, interposed**)
place something between two things.
[from *inter-* + Latin *positum* = put]

interpret *verb* (**interprets, interpreting, interpreted**)
1 explain what something means. **2** translate what someone says into another language orally.
interpretation *noun*, **interpreter** *noun*

interrogate *verb* (**interrogates, interrogating, interrogated**)
question someone closely or formally.
interrogation *noun*, **interrogator** *noun*
[from *inter-* + Latin *rogare* = ask]

interrogative *adjective*
questioning; expressing a question.
interrogatory *adjective*

interrupt *verb* (**interrupts, interrupting, interrupted**)
1 break in on a person's speech etc. by inserting a remark. **2** prevent something from continuing. **interruption** *noun*
[from *inter-* + Latin *ruptum* = broken]

intersect *verb* (**intersects, intersecting, intersected**)
1 divide a thing by passing or lying across it. **2** (of lines or roads etc.) cross each other.
intersection *noun*
[from *inter-* + Latin *sectum* = cut]

interval *noun* (*plural* **intervals**)
1 a time between two events or parts of a play etc. **2** a space between two things.
at intervals with some time or distance between

each one.
[from Latin *intervallum* = space between
ramparts]

intervene *verb* (intervenes, intervening,
intervened)
1 come between two events, *in the intervening
years.* 2 interrupt a discussion or fight etc. to
try and stop it or change its result.
intervention *noun*
[from *inter-* + Latin *venire* = come]

interview *noun* (*plural* interviews)
a formal meeting with someone to ask him or
her questions or to obtain information.
interview *verb* (interviews, interviewing,
interviewed)
hold an interview with someone.
interviewer *noun*
[from *inter-* + French *voir* = see]

intestine *noun* (*plural* intestines)
the long tube along which food passes while
being absorbed by the body, between the
stomach and the anus. **intestinal** *adjective*
[from Latin *intestinus* = internal]

intimate (*say* in-tim-at) *adjective*
1 very friendly with someone. 2 private and
personal, *intimate thoughts.* 3 detailed, *an
intimate knowledge of the country.*
intimately *adverb*, **intimacy** *noun*
[from Latin *intimus* = close friend]

intimidate *verb* (intimidates, intimidating,
intimidated)
frighten a person by threats into doing
something. **intimidation** *noun*
[from *in-* + Latin *timidus* = timid]

into *preposition*
used to express 1 movement to the inside (*Go
into the house*), 2 change of condition or
occupation etc. (*It broke into pieces. She went
into politics*), 3 (in division) *4 into 20* = 20
divided by 4.

intolerable *adjective*
unbearable. **intolerably** *adverb*

intoxicate *verb* (intoxicates, intoxicating,
intoxicated)
make a person drunk or very excited.
intoxication *noun*
[from *in-* + Latin *toxicum* = poison]

intra- *prefix*
within. [from Latin]

intransitive *adjective*
(of a verb) used without a direct object after it,
e.g. *hear* in *we can hear* (but not in *we can hear
you*). Compare *transitive*. **intransitively** *adverb*
[from *in-* + Latin *transitivus* = passing over]

intravenous (*say* in-tra-**veen**-us) *adjective*
into a vein.
[from *intra-* + Latin *vena* = vein]

intricate *adjective*
very complicated.
intricately *adverb*, **intricacy** *noun*
[from Latin *intricatus* = entangled]

intrigue (*say* in-**treeg**) *verb* (intrigues, intriguing,
intrigued)
1 plot with someone in an underhand way.
2 interest someone very much, *The subject
intrigues me.* [from Italian; related to *intricate*]

intro- *prefix*
into; inwards. [from Latin]

introduce *verb* (introduces, introducing,
introduced)
1 make a person known to other people.
2 announce a broadcast, speaker, etc. 3 bring
something into use or for consideration.
[from *intro-* + Latin *ducere* = to lead]

introduction *noun* (*plural* introductions)
1 introducing somebody or something. 2 an
explanation put at the beginning of a book or
speech etc. **introductory** *adjective*

introvert *noun* (*plural* introverts)
a shy person who does not like to talk about his
or her own thoughts and feelings with other
people. (The opposite is *extrovert*.)

intrude *verb* (intrudes, intruding, intruded)
come in or join in without being wanted.
intrusion *noun*, **intrusive** *adjective*
[from *in-* + Latin *trudere* = to push]

intruder *noun* (*plural* intruders)
1 someone who intrudes. 2 a burglar.

intuition *noun*
the power to know or understand things
without having to think hard or without being
taught. **intuitive** *adjective*, **intuitively** *adverb*
[from *in-* + Latin *tueri* = to look]

Inuit (*say* in-yoo-it) *noun* (*plural* Inuit)
1 a member of a people living in northern
Canada and Greenland; an Eskimo. 2 the
language of the Inuit. [Inuit, = people]

USAGE: See note at *Eskimo*.

inundate *verb* (inundates, inundating, inundated)
flood or overwhelm a place, *We've been
inundated with letters about the programme.*
inundation *noun*
[from *in-* + Latin *unda* = a wave]

invade *verb* (invades, invading, invaded)
1 attack and enter a country etc. 2 crowd into a
place, *Tourists invade Oxford in summer.*
invader *noun*
[from *in-* + Latin *vadere* = go]

invalid (*say* in-va-leed) *noun* (*plural* invalids)
a person who is ill or who is weakened by
illness.
invalid (*say* in-**val**-id) *adjective*
not valid, *This passport is invalid.*
invalidity *noun*
[from *in-* + Latin *validus* = strong or powerful]

invaluable *adjective*
having a value that is too great to be measured;
extremely valuable.
[from *in-* + *value* + *-able*]

invariable *adjective*
not variable; never changing.
invariably *adverb*

invasion *noun* (*plural* **invasions**)
attacking and entering a country etc.
[same origin as *invade*]

invent *verb* (**invents, inventing, invented**)
1 be the first person to make or think of a
particular thing. 2 make up a false story etc.,
invent an excuse. **invention** *noun*, **inventor** *noun*,
inventive *adjective*
[from *in-* + Latin *venire* = come]

invertebrate *noun* (*plural* **invertebrates**)
an animal without a backbone.
invertebrate *adjective*

inverted commas *plural noun*
punctuation marks " " or ' ' put round
quotations and spoken words.

invest *verb* (**invests, investing, invested**)
1 use money to make a profit, e.g. by lending it
in return for interest to be paid, or by buying
stocks and shares or property. 2 give
somebody a rank, medal, etc. in a formal
ceremony.
investment *noun*, **investor** *noun*
[from Latin *investire* = to clothe]

investigate *verb* (**investigates, investigating,
investigated**)
find out as much as you can about something;
make a systematic inquiry. **investigation** *noun*,
investigator *noun*, **investigative** *adjective* [from
Latin]

invigilate *verb* (**invigilates, invigilating,
invigilated**)
supervise candidates at an examination.
invigilation *noun*, **invigilator** *noun*
[from *in-* + Latin *vigilare* = to watch]

invigorate *verb* (**invigorates, invigorating,
invigorated**)
give a person strength or courage. (Compare
vigour.)
[from *in-* + Latin *vigor* = vigour]

invincible *adjective*
not able to be defeated; unconquerable.
invincibly *adverb*, **invincibility** *noun*
[from *in-* + Latin *vincere* = conquer]

invisible *adjective*
not visible; not able to be seen.
invisibly *adverb*, **invisibility** *noun*

invite *verb* (**invites, inviting, invited**)
1 ask a person to come or do something. 2 be
likely to cause something to happen, *You are
inviting disaster.* **invitation** *noun*

invoice *noun* (*plural* **invoices**)
a list of goods sent or work done, with the
prices charged.
[from French *envoyer* = send]

involuntary *adjective*
not deliberate; unintentional.
involuntarily *adverb*

involve *verb* (**involves, involving, involved**)
1 have as a part; make a thing necessary, *The
job involves hard work.* 2 make someone share
in something, *They involved us in their charity
work.* **involvement** *noun* [from *in-* + Latin
volvere = to roll]

inward *adjective*
1 on the inside. 2 going or facing inwards.
inward *adverb*
inwards. [from Old English]

inwards *adverb*
towards the inside.

iodine *noun*
a chemical substance used as an antiseptic.
[from Greek *iodes* = violet-coloured (because it
gives off violet-coloured vapour)]

ion *noun* (*plural* **ions**)
an electrically charged particle.

-ion, -sion, -tion, and **-xion** *suffixes*
form nouns meaning 'condition or action' (e.g.
*dominion, dimension, attraction, pollution,
inflexion*).

ionosphere (*say* I-on-os-feer) *noun*
a region of the upper atmosphere, containing
ions.

IQ *abbreviation*
intelligence quotient; a number showing how a
person's intelligence compares with that of an
average person.

ir- *prefix*
1 in; into. 2 on; towards. 3 not. see **in-**.

IRA *abbreviation*
Irish Republican Army.

iridescent *adjective*
showing rainbow-like colours. **iridescence** *noun*
[from Greek *iris* = iris or rainbow]

iron *noun* (*plural* **irons**)
1 a hard grey metal. 2 a device with a flat base
that is heated for smoothing clothes or cloth.
3 a tool etc. made of iron.
iron *adjective*
iron *verb* (**irons, ironing, ironed**)
smooth clothes or cloth with an iron.

Iron Age *noun*
the time when tools and weapons were made of
iron.

ironic (*say* I-ron-ik) *adjective*
using irony; full of irony.
ironical *adjective*, **ironically** *adverb*

ironmonger *noun* (*plural* **ironmongers**)
a shopkeeper who sells tools and other metal objects. **ironmongery** *noun*
[from *iron* + an old word *monger* = trader]

irony (*say* I-ron-ee) *noun* (*plural* **ironies**)
1 saying the opposite of what you mean in order to emphasize it, e.g. saying 'What a lovely day' when it is pouring with rain. 2 an oddly contradictory situation, *The irony of it is that I tripped while telling someone else to be careful.*
[from Greek *eiron* = someone who pretends not to know]

irrational *adjective*
not rational; illogical. **irrationally** *adverb*

irregular *adjective*
1 not regular; uneven. 2 against the rules or usual custom. 3 (of troops) not in the regular armed forces.
irregularly *adverb*, **irregularity** *noun*

irrepressible *adjective*
unable to be repressed; always lively and cheerful. **irrepressibly** *adverb*

irreproachable *adjective*
blameless or faultless.
irreproachably *adverb*
[from *ir-* + French *reprocher* = reproach]

irresistible *adjective*
unable to be resisted; very attractive.
irresistibly *adverb*

irrespective *adjective*
not taking something into account, *Prizes are awarded to winners, irrespective of age.*

irresponsible *adjective*
not showing a proper sense of responsibility.
irresponsibly *adverb*, **irresponsibility** *noun*

irrigate *verb* (**irrigates, irrigating, irrigated**)
supply land with water so that crops etc. can grow. **irrigation** *noun*
[from *ir-* + Latin *rigare* = to water]

irritable *adjective*
easily annoyed; bad-tempered.
irritably *adverb*, **irritability** *noun*

irritate *verb* (**irritates, irritating, irritated**)
1 annoy. 2 cause itching. **irritation** *noun*,
irritant *adjective* & *noun* [from Latin]

-ise *suffix* see -ize.

-ish *suffix*
forms nouns meaning 1 'of a certain nature' (e.g. *foolish*), 2 'rather' (e.g. *greenish*, *yellowish*).

Islam *noun*
the religion of Muslims. **Islamic** *adjective*
[Arabic, = submission to God]

island *noun* (*plural* **islands**)
1 a piece of land surrounded by water.
2 something that resembles an island because it is isolated. [from Old English]

-ism *suffix*
forms nouns showing action from verbs ending in *-ize* (e.g. *baptism, criticism*), or condition (e.g. *heroism*).

isn't (*mainly spoken*)
is not.

iso- *prefix*
equal (as in *isobar*). [from Greek]

isobar (*say* I-so-bar) *noun* (*plural* **isobars**)
a line (on a map) connecting places that have the same atmospheric pressure.
[from *iso-* + Greek *baros* = weight]

isolate *verb* (**isolates, isolating, isolated**)
place a person or thing apart or alone; separate. **isolation** *noun*
[from Latin *insulatus* = made into an island]

isosceles (*say* I-soss-il-eez) *adjective*
an isosceles triangle has two sides of equal length. [from *iso-* + Greek *skelos* = leg]

isotope *noun* (*plural* **isotopes**)
a form of an element that differs from other forms in its nuclear properties but not in its chemical properties.
[from *iso-* + Greek *topos* = place (because they appear in the same place in the table of chemical elements)]

issue *verb* (**issues, issuing, issued**)
1 come or go out; flow out. 2 supply; give out, *We issued one blanket to each refugee.* 3 put out for sale; publish. 4 send out, *They issued a gale warning.* 5 result.

issue *noun* (*plural* **issues**)
1 a subject for discussion or concern, *What are the real issues?* 2 a result, *Await the issue of the trial.* 3 a particular edition of a newspaper or magazine, *The Christmas issue of Radio Times.* 4 issuing something, *The issue of passports is held up.*
[from old French; related to *exit*]

-ist *suffix*
forms nouns meaning 'person who does something or believes in or supports something' (e.g. *cyclist, Communist*).

isthmus (*say* iss-mus) *noun* (*plural* **isthmuses**)
a narrow strip of land connecting two larger pieces of land. [from Greek]

IT *abbreviation*
information technology.

it *pronoun*
1 the thing being talked about. 2 the player who has to catch others in a game. The word is also used 3 in statements about the weather (*It is raining*) or about circumstances etc. (*It is six miles to York*), 4 as an indefinite object (*Run for it!*), 5 to refer to a phrase (*It is unlikely that she will fail*).

italic (*say* it-al-ik) *adjective*
printed with sloping letters (called **italics**) *like
this.*
[because this style was first used in Italy]

itch *verb* (**itches, itching, itched**)
1 have or feel a tickling sensation in the skin
that makes you want to scratch it. **2** long to do
something.

-ite *suffix*
(in scientific use) forms names of minerals (e.g.
anthracite), explosives (e.g. *dynamite*), and salts
of certain acids (e.g. *nitrite*; compare **-ate**).

item *noun* (*plural* **items**)
1 one thing in a list or group of things. **2** one
piece of news, article etc. in a newspaper or
bulletin.
[Latin, = just so, similarly (used to introduce
each item on a list)]

-itis *suffix*
forms nouns meaning inflammation of part of
the body (as in *bronchitis*). [Greek]

its *possessive pronoun*
belonging to it, *The cat hurt its paw.*

USAGE: Do not put an apostrophe into *its*
unless you mean 'it is' or 'it has' (see the next
entry).

it's (*mainly spoken*)
1 it is, *It's very hot.* **2** it has, *It's broken all
records.*

USAGE: Do not confuse with *its*.

itself *pronoun*
it and nothing else. (Compare *herself*.)
by itself on its own; alone.

ITV *abbreviation*
Independent Television.

-ive *suffix*
forms adjectives, chiefly from verbs (e.g. *active,
explosive*).

ivory *noun*
1 the hard creamy-white substance that forms
elephants' tusks. **2** a creamy-white colour.
[from Latin]

ivy *noun* (*plural* **ivies**)
a climbing evergreen plant with shiny leaves.
[from Old English]

-ize or **-ise** *suffix*
forms verbs meaning 'bring or come into a
certain condition' (e.g. *civilize*), or 'treat in a
certain way' (e.g. *pasteurize*), or 'have a certain
feeling' (e.g. *sympathize*).
[from the Greek verb-ending *-izein*, or French *-
iser*]

jab *verb* (**jabs, jabbing, jabbed**)
poke roughly; push a thing into something.

jack *noun* (*plural* **jacks**)
1 a device for lifting something heavy off the
ground. **2** a playing card with a picture of a
young man. **3** a small white ball aimed at in
bowls.
jack of all trades someone who can do many
different kinds of work. [the name *Jack*, used
for various sorts of tool (as though it was a
person helping you)]

jackdaw *noun* (*plural* **jackdaws**)
a kind of small crow. [from the name *Jack*
+ Middle English *dawe* = jackdaw]

jacket *noun* (*plural* **jackets**)
1 a short coat, usually reaching to the hips. **2** a
cover to keep the heat in a water-tank etc. **3** a
paper wrapper for a book. **4** the skin of a potato
that is baked without being peeled.
[from old French]

jackpot *noun* (*plural* **jackpots**)
an amount of prize money that increases until
someone wins it.
hit the jackpot 1 win a large prize. **2** have
remarkable luck or sucess.
[originally = a kitty which could be won only
by playing a pair of jacks or cards of higher
value: from *jack* + *pot*[1]]

jagged (*say* jag-id) *adjective*
having an uneven edge with sharp points.
[from Scots *jag* = stab]

jaguar *noun* (*plural* **jaguars**)
a large fierce South American animal rather
like a leopard.
[via Portuguese from a South American
language]

jail *noun* (*plural* **jails**)
a prison. [from old French *jaiole* = cage or
prison]

jam *noun* (*plural* **jams**)
1 a sweet food made of fruit boiled with sugar
until it is thick. **2** a lot of people, cars, or logs
etc. crowded together so that movement is
difficult.
in a jam in a difficult situation.

jam *verb* (**jams, jamming, jammed**)
1 crowd or squeeze into a space. **2** make or
become fixed and difficult to move. **3** push
something forcibly, *jam the brakes on.* **4** block
a broadcast by causing interference with the
transmission.

jamboree *noun* (*plural* **jamborees**)
a large party or celebration

jangle *verb* (jangles, jangling, jangled)
make a loud harsh ringing sound.
jangle *noun* [from old French]

janitor *noun* (*plural* janitors)
a caretaker. [originally = doorkeeper: from
Latin *janua* = door]

jar¹ *noun* (*plural* jars)
a container made of glass or pottery.
[via French from Arabic]

jar² *verb* (jars, jarring, jarred)
1 cause an unpleasant jolt or shock. 2 sound
harshly.
jar *noun* (*plural* jars)
a jarring effect. [imitating the sound]

jargon *noun*
special words used by a group of people,
scientists' jargon. [from French]

jaunt *noun* (*plural* jaunts)
a short trip. **jaunting** *noun*

jaunty *adjective* (jauntier, jauntiest)
lively and cheerful.
jauntily *adverb*, **jauntiness** *noun*
[originally = stylish, elegant: from French,
related to *gentle*]

javelin *noun* (*plural* javelins)
a lightweight spear. [from French]

jaw *noun* (*plural* jaws)
1 either of the two bones that form the
framework of the mouth. 2 the lower part of
the face. 3 something shaped like the jaws or
used for gripping things. 4 (*slang*) talking.
[from old French]

jazz *noun*
a kind of music with strong rhythm.
jazzy *adjective*

jealous *adjective*
1 unhappy or resentful because you feel that
someone is your rival or is better or luckier
than yourself. 2 careful in keeping something,
He is very jealous of his own rights.
jealously *adverb*, **jealousy** *noun*

jeans *plural noun*
trousers made of strong cotton fabric. [from
Genoa, a city in Italy, where such a cloth was
once made]

jeer *verb* (jeers, jeering, jeered)
laugh or shout at somebody rudely or
scornfully. **jeer** *noun* [origin unknown]

jelly *noun* (*plural* jellies)
1 a soft transparent food. 2 any soft slippery
substance. **jellied** *adjective*
[from Latin *gelare* = freeze]

jellyfish *noun* (*plural* jellyfish)
a sea animal with a body like jelly.

jerk *verb* (jerks, jerking, jerked)
1 make a sudden sharp movement. 2 pull
something suddenly.

jerk *noun* (*plural* jerks)
1 a sudden sharp movement. 2 (*slang*) a stupid
person. **jerky** *adjective*, **jerkily** *adverb*

jerkin *noun* (*plural* jerkins)
a sleeveless jacket. [origin unknown]

jersey *noun* (*plural* jerseys)
1 a pullover with sleeves. 2 a plain machine-
knitted material used for making clothes.
[originally = a woollen cloth made in *Jersey*,
one of the Channel Islands]

jest *noun* (*plural* jests)
a joke. [from Middle English *gest* = a story]

jester *noun* (*plural* jesters)
a professional entertainer at a royal court in
the Middle Ages.

jet *noun* (*plural* jets)
1 a stream of water, gas, flame, etc. shot out
from a narrow opening. 2 a spout or nozzle
from which a jet comes. 3 an aircraft driven by
engines that send out a high-speed jet of hot
gases at the back.
[from French *jeter* = to throw]

jet lag *noun*
extreme tiredness that a person feels after a
long flight between different time zones.

jettison *verb* (jettisons, jettisoning, jettisoned)
1 throw something overboard. 2 get rid of
something that is no longer wanted. 3 release
or drop something from an aircraft or
spacecraft in flight.
[same origin as *jet*]

jetty *noun* (*plural* jetties)
a small landing stage. [same origin as *jet*]

Jew *noun* (*plural* Jews)
a member of a people descended from the
ancient tribes of Israel, or who believes in the
religion of this people. **Jewish** *adjective* [from
Hebrew *yehudi* = belonging to the tribe of
Judah (the founder of one of the ten tribes of
ancient Israel)]

jewel *noun* (*plural* jewels)
1 a precious stone. 2 an ornament containing
precious stones.
jewelled *adjective* [from old French]

jewellery *noun*
jewels and similar ornaments for wearing.

jigsaw *noun* (*plural* jigsaws)
1 a saw that can cut curved shapes. 2 a jigsaw
puzzle.

jigsaw puzzle *noun* (*plural* jigsaw puzzles)
a picture cut into irregular pieces which are
then shuffled and fitted together again for
amusement.

jilt *verb* (jilts, jilting, jilted)
abandon a boyfriend or girlfriend, especially
after promising to marry him or her. [origin
unknown]

jingle *verb* (jingles, jingling, jingled)
make or cause to make a tinkling sound.
jingle *noun* (*plural* jingles)
1 a jingling sound. **2** a very simple verse or tune, especially one used in advertising.

jitters *plural noun* (*informal*)
nervousness. **jittery** *adjective*

job *noun* (*plural* jobs)
1 work that someone does regularly to earn a living. **2** a piece of work to be done.
3 (*informal*) a difficult task, *You'll have a job to lift that box.* **4** (*informal*) a thing; a state of affairs, *It's a good job you're here.*

jockey *noun* (*plural* jockeys)
a person who rides horses in races.
[pet form of the name *Jock*]

jodhpurs (*say* jod-perz) *plural noun*
trousers for horse riding, fitting closely from the knee to the ankle.
[named after *Jodhpur*, a city in India, where similar trousers are worn]

jog *verb* (jogs, jogging, jogged)
1 run or trot slowly, especially for exercise.
2 give something a slight push. **jogger** *noun*
jog someone's memory help him or her to remember something. [same origin as *jagged*]

jogtrot *noun*
a slow steady trot.

join *verb* (joins, joining, joined)
1 put or come together; fasten or connect. **2** do something together with others, *We all joined in the chorus.* **3** become a member of a group or organization etc., *Join the Navy.*
join up enlist in the armed forces.

joint *noun* (*plural* joints)
1 a join. **2** the place where two bones fit together. **3** a large piece of meat cut ready for cooking.
joint *adjective*
shared or done by two or more people, nations, etc., *a joint project.* **jointly** *adverb*

joke *noun* (*plural* jokes)
something said or done to make people laugh.

joker *noun* (*plural* jokers)
1 someone who jokes. **2** an extra playing card with a jester on it.

jolly *adjective* (jollier, jolliest)
cheerful and good-humoured. **jollity** *noun*
jolly *adverb* (*informal*)
very, *jolly good.*

jolt *verb* (jolts, jolting, jolted)
1 shake or dislodge something with a sudden sharp movement. **2** move along jerkily, e.g. on a rough road. **3** give someone a shock.
jolt *noun* (*plural* jolts)
1 a jolting movement. **2** a shock.

jostle *verb* (jostles, jostling, jostled)
push roughly, especially in a crowd.

jot *verb* (jots, jotting, jotted)
write something quickly, *jot it down.*

jotter *noun* (*plural* jotters)
a notepad or notebook.

joule (*say* jool) *noun* (*plural* joules)
a unit of work or energy. [named after an English scientist, James Joule]

journal *noun* (*plural* journals)
1 a newspaper or magazine. **2** a diary.
[from Latin, = by day]

journalist *noun* (*plural* journalists)
a person who writes for a newspaper or magazine.
journalism *noun*, **journalistic** *adjective*

journey *noun* (*plural* journeys)
1 going from one place to another. **2** the distance or time taken to travel somewhere, *two days' journey.*
journey *verb* (journeys, journeying, journeyed)
make a journey. [from French *journée*
= a day's travel, from *jour* = day]

jovial *adjective*
cheerful and good-humoured.
jovially *adverb*, **joviality** *noun*
[from Latin *jovialis* = to do with Jupiter (because people born under its influence were said to be cheerful)]

joy *noun* (*plural* joys)
1 a feeling of great pleasure; gladness.
2 a thing that causes joy.
joyful *adjective*, **joyfully** *adverb*, **joyfulness** *noun*, **joyous** *adjective*, **joyously** *adverb*

joyride *noun* (*plural* joyrides)
a drive in a stolen car for amusement.
joyrider *noun*, **joyriding** *noun*

joystick *noun* (*plural* joysticks)
1 the control lever of an aircraft. **2** a device for moving a cursor etc. on a VDU screen.

JP *abbreviation*
Justice of the Peace.

jubilant *adjective*
rejoicing or triumphant.
jubilantly *adverb*, **jubilation** *noun*
[from Latin *jubilans* = shouting for joy]

jubilee (*say* joo-bil-ee) *noun* (*plural* jubilees)
a special anniversary, *silver* (25th), *golden*
(50th), *and diamond* (60th) *jubilee.* [from Hebrew *yobel* = a year when slaves were freed and property returned to its owners, held in ancient Israel every 50 years]

Judaism (*say* joo-day-izm) *noun*
the religion of the Jewish people.
[from Greek *Ioudaios* = Jew]

judge *noun* (*plural* judges)
1 a person appointed to hear cases in a lawcourt and decide what should be done.

2 a person deciding who has won a contest or competition, or the value or quality of something.
judge *verb* (judges, judging, judged)
1 act as a judge. **2** form and give an opinion. **3** estimate, *He judged the distance carefully.*
[from Latin *judex* = a judge, from *jus* = law + *-dicus* = saying]

judgement *noun* (*plural* judgements)
1 judging. **2** the decision made by a lawcourt. **3** someone's opinion. **4** the ability to judge wisely. **5** something considered as a punishment from God, *It's a judgement on you!*

judicial *adjective*
to do with lawcourts, judges, or judgements, *the British judicial system.* **judicially** *adverb*

USAGE: Do not confuse with *judicious.*

judicious (*say* joo-**dish**-us) *adjective*
having or showing good sense or good judgement. **judiciously** *adverb*
[same origin as *judge*]

USAGE: Do not confuse with *judicial.*

judo *noun*
a Japanese method of self-defence without using weapons.
[from Japanese *ju* = gentle + *do* = way]

jug *noun* (*plural* jugs)
a container for holding and pouring liquids, with a handle and a lip.
[pet form of *Joan* or *Jenny*]

juggernaut *noun* (*plural* juggernauts)
a huge lorry.
[named after a Hindu god whose image was dragged in procession on a huge wheeled vehicle]

juggle *verb* (juggles, juggling, juggled)
1 toss and keep a number of objects in the air, for entertainment. **2** rearrange or alter things skilfully or in order to deceive people.
juggler *noun* [from old French]

jugular *adjective*
to do with the throat or neck, *the jugular veins.*
[from Latin *jugulum* = throat]

juice *noun* (*plural* juices)
1 the liquid from fruit, vegetables, or other food. **2** a liquid produced by the body, *the digestive juices.* **juicy** *adjective* [from Latin]

jukebox *noun* (*plural* jukeboxes)
a machine that automatically plays a record you have selected when you put a coin in.

jumble *verb* (jumbles, jumbling, jumbled)
mix things up into a confused mass.
jumble *noun*
a confused mixture of things; a muddle.

jumble sale *noun* (*plural* jumble sales)
a sale of second-hand goods.

jumbo *noun* (*plural* jumbos)
1 something very large; a jumbo jet. **2** an elephant. [the name of a very large elephant in London Zoo]

jumbo jet *noun* (*plural* jumbo jets)
a very large jet aircraft.

jump *verb* (jumps, jumping, jumped)
1 move up suddenly from the ground into the air. **2** go over something by jumping, *jump the fence.* **3** pass over something; miss out part of a book etc. **4** move suddenly in surprise. **5** pass quickly to a different place or level.
jump at (*informal*) accept something eagerly.
jump the gun start before you should.
jump the queue not wait your turn.
jump *noun* (*plural* jumps)
1 a jumping movement. **2** an obstacle to jump over. **3** a sudden rise or change.

jumper *noun* (*plural* jumpers)
a jersey. [from French *jupe* = tunic]

jumpy *adjective*
nervous.

junction *noun* (*plural* junctions)
1 a join. **2** a place where roads or railway lines meet. [from Latin *junctum* = joined]

jungle *noun* (*plural* jungles)
a thick tangled forest, especially in the tropics.
jungly *adjective* [from Hindi]

junior *adjective*
1 younger. **2** for young children, *a junior school.* **3** lower in rank or importance, *junior officers.* [Latin, = younger]

junk *noun*
rubbish; things of no value.

junk food *noun*
food that is not nourishing.

jury *noun* (*plural* juries)
a group of people (usually twelve) appointed to give a verdict about a case in a lawcourt.
juryman *noun*, **jurywoman** *noun*
[from Latin *jurare* = take an oath]

just *adjective*
1 giving proper consideration to everyone's claims. **2** deserved; right in amount etc., *a just reward.*
justly *adverb*, **justness** *noun*
just *adverb*
1 exactly, *It's just what I wanted.* **2** only; simply, *I just wanted to see him.* **3** barely; by only a small amount, *just below the knee.* **4** at this moment or only a little while ago, *She has just gone.*
[from Latin *justus* = rightful]

justice *noun* (*plural* justices)
1 being just; fair treatment. **2** legal proceedings, *a court of justice.* **3** a judge or magistrate.

jut *verb* (juts, jutting, jutted)
stick out. [a different spelling of *jet*]

jute *noun*
fibre from tropical plants, used for making sacks etc. [from Bengali (a language spoken in Bangladesh and West Bengal)]

juvenile *adjective*
to do with or for young people.
[from Latin *juvenis* = young person]

juvenile delinquent *noun* (*plural* **juvenile delinquents**)
a young person who has broken the law.

Kk

kaleidoscope (*say* kal-I-dos-kohp) *noun* (*plural* **kaleidoscopes**)
a tube that you look through to see brightly coloured patterns which change as you turn the end of the tube. **kaleidoscopic** *adjective*
[from Greek *kalos* = beautiful + *eidos* = form + *skopein* = look at]

kangaroo *noun* (*plural* **kangaroos**)
an Australian animal that jumps along on its strong hind legs. (See *marsupial*.)
[an Australian Aboriginal word]

karaoke *noun*
a form of entertainment in which people sing well-known songs against a pre-recorded backing. [Japanese]

karate (*say* ka-rah-tee) *noun*
a Japanese method of self-defence in which the hands and feet are used as weapons. [from Japanese *kara* = empty + *te* = hand]

keel *noun* (*plural* **keels**)
the long piece of wood or metal along the bottom of a boat.
on an even keel steady.
keel *verb* (**keels, keeling, keeled**)
keel over fall down or overturn, *The ship keeled over.*

keen *adjective*
1 enthusiastic; very interested in or eager to do something, *a keen swimmer*. 2 sharp, *a keen edge*. 3 piercingly cold, *a keen wind*.
keenly *adverb*, **keenness** *noun*

keep *verb* (**keeps, keeping, kept**)
This word has many uses, including 1 have something and look after it or not get rid of it, 2 stay or cause to stay in the same condition etc. (*keep still*; *keep it hot*), 3 do something continually (*She keeps laughing*), 4 respect and not break (*keep a promise*), 5 make entries in (*keep a diary*).
keep up 1 make the same progress as others. 2 continue something.

keep *noun* (*plural* **keeps**)
1 maintenance; the food etc. that you need to live, *She earns her keep*. 2 a strong tower in a castle.
for keeps (*informal*) permanently; to keep, *Is this football mine for keeps?*

keeper *noun* (*plural* **keepers**)
1 a person who looks after an animal, building, etc., *the park keeper*. 2 a goalkeeper or wicketkeeper.

keeping *noun*
care; looking after something, *in safe keeping*.

keg *noun* (*plural* **kegs**)
a small barrel. [from Old Norse]

kelvin *noun* (*plural* **kelvins**)
the SI unit of thermodynamic temperature. [named after a British scientist, Lord Kelvin, who invented it]

kennel *noun* (*plural* **kennels**)
a shelter for a dog. [from Latin *canis* = dog]

kerb *noun* (*plural* **kerbs**)
the edge of a pavement.
[a different spelling of *curb*]

kernel *noun* (*plural* **kernels**)
the part inside the shell of a nut etc.

ketchup *noun*
a thick sauce made from tomatoes and vinegar etc. [probably from Chinese *k'e chap* = tomato juice]

kettle *noun* (*plural* **kettles**)
a container with a spout and handle, for boiling water in. [from Old English]

key *noun* (*plural* **keys**)
1 a piece of metal shaped so that it will open a lock. 2 a device for winding up a clock or clockwork toy etc. 3 a small lever to be pressed by a finger, e.g. on a piano, typewriter, or computer. 4 a system of notes in music, *the key of C major*. 5 a fact or clue that explains or solves something, *the key to the mystery*.
key *verb* (**keys, keying, keyed**)
key in type information into a computer using a keyboard.

keyboard *noun* (*plural* **keyboards**)
the set of keys on a piano, typewriter, computer, etc.

keyhole *noun* (*plural* **keyholes**)
the hole through which a key is put into a lock.

kg *abbreviation*
kilogram.

khaki *noun*
a dull yellowish-brown colour, used for military uniforms.
[from Urdu *khaki* = dust-coloured]

kibbutz *noun* (*plural* **kibbutzim**)
a commune in Israel, especially for farming.
[from Hebrew *qibbus* = gathering]

kick *verb* (**kicks, kicking, kicked**)
1 hit or move a person or thing with your foot.
2 move your legs about vigorously. 3 (of a gun)
recoil when fired.
kick out get rid of; dismiss.
kick up (*informal*) make a noise or fuss.
kick *noun* (*plural* **kicks**)
1 a kicking movement. 2 the recoiling
movement of a gun. 3 (*informal*) a thrill.
4 (*informal*) an interest or activity, *He's on a
health kick.*
[origin unknown]

kid *noun* (*plural* **kids**)
1 (*informal*) a child. 2 a young goat. 3 fine
leather made from goat's skin.

kidnap *verb* (**kidnaps, kidnapping, kidnapped**)
take someone away by force, especially in
order to obtain a ransom. **kidnapper** *noun*
[from *kid* + an old word *napper* = thief]

kidney *noun* (*plural* **kidneys**)
either of the two organs in the body that
remove waste products from the blood and
excrete urine into the bladder.

kill *verb* (**kills, killing, killed**)
1 make a person or thing die. 2 destroy or put
an end to something. **killer** *noun*
kill time occupy time idly while waiting.

kilo *noun* (*plural* **kilos**)
a kilogram.

kilo- *prefix*
one thousand (as in *kilolitre* = 1,000 litres,
kilohertz = 1,000 hertz).
[from Greek *chilioi* = thousand]

kilogram *noun* (*plural* **kilograms**)
a unit of mass or weight equal to 1,000 grams
(about 2.2 pounds).

kilometre (*say* kil-o-meet-er or kil-**om**-it-er) *noun*
(*plural* **kilometres**)
a unit of length equal to 1,000 metres (about $\frac{3}{5}$ of
a mile).

kilowatt *noun* (*plural* **kilowatts**)
a unit of electrical power equal to 1,000
watts.

kilt *noun* (*plural* **kilts**)
a kind of pleated skirt worn especially by
Scotsmen.
kilted *adjective*
[probably from a Scandinavian language]

-kin *suffix*
forms diminutives (e.g. *lambkin* = little lamb).
[from old Dutch]

kind[1] *noun* (*plural* **kinds**)
a class of similar things or animals; a sort or
type.

payment in kind payment in goods not in
money. [from Old English *cynd* = nature]

USAGE: Correct use is *this kind of thing* or
these kinds of things (not 'these kind of
things').

kind[2] *adjective*
friendly and helpful; considerate.
kind-hearted *adjective*, **kindness** *noun*
[from Old English *gecynd* = natural or proper]

kindergarten *noun* (*plural* **kindergartens**)
a school or class for very young children.
[from German *Kinder* = children + *Garten*
= garden]

kindle *verb* (**kindles, kindling, kindled**)
1 start a flame; set light to something. 2 begin
burning. [from Old Norse]

kinetic *adjective*
to do with or produced by movement, *kinetic
energy.*
[from Greek *kinetikos* = moving]

king *noun* (*plural* **kings**)
1 a man who is the ruler of a country through
inheriting the position. 2 a person or thing
regarded as supreme, *the lion is the king of
beasts.* 3 the most important piece in chess. 4 a
playing card with a picture of a king.
kingly *adjective*, **kingship** *noun*
[from Old English]

kingdom *noun* (*plural* **kingdoms**)
a country ruled by a king or queen.

kingfisher *noun* (*plural* **kingfishers**)
a small bird with blue feathers that dives to
catch fish.

kink *noun* (*plural* **kinks**)
1 a short twist in a rope, wire, piece of hair,
etc. 2 a peculiarity. [from old German]

kinky *adjective*
involving peculiar sexual behaviour.

kiosk *noun* (*plural* **kiosks**)
1 a telephone box. 2 a small hut or stall where
newspapers, sweets, etc. are sold.
[via French and Turkish from Persian]

kiss *noun* (*plural* **kisses**)
touching somebody with your lips as a sign of
affection.
kiss *verb* (**kisses, kissing, kissed**)
give somebody a kiss. [from Old English]

kiss of life *noun*
blowing air from your mouth into another
person's to help the other person to start
breathing again, especially after an accident.

kit *noun* (*plural* **kits**)
1 equipment or clothes for a particular
occupation. 2 a set of parts sold ready to be
fitted together. [from old Dutch]

kitchen *noun* (*plural* kitchens)
a room in which meals are prepared and
cooked. [from Old English]

kite *noun* (*plural* kites)
1 a light framework covered with cloth, paper,
etc. and flown in the wind on the end of a long
piece of string. 2 a large hawk.
[from Old English]

kitten *noun* (*plural* kittens)
a very young cat.
[from old French *chitoun* = small cat]

kleptomania *noun*
an uncontrollable urge to steal things.
kleptomaniac *noun*
[from Greek *kleptes* = thief, + *mania*]

km *abbreviation*
kilometre.

knack *noun*
a special skill, *There's a knack to putting up a
deckchair.*

knapsack *noun* (*plural* knapsacks)
a bag carried on the back by soldiers, hikers,
etc. [from Dutch]

knave *noun* (*plural* knaves)
1 (*old use*) a dishonest man; a rogue. 2 a jack in
playing cards. [from Old English *cnafa* = a boy
or male servant]

knead *verb* (kneads, kneading, kneaded)
press and stretch something soft (especially
dough) with your hands.

knee *noun* (*plural* knees)
the joint in the middle of the leg.

kneecap *noun* (*plural* kneecaps)
the small bone covering the front of the knee
joint.

kneel *verb* (kneels, kneeling, knelt)
be or get yourself in a position on your knees.
[from Old English]

knickers *plural noun*
a woman's or girl's undergarment worn on the
lower part of the body.

knife *noun* (*plural* knives)
a cutting instrument consisting of a sharp
blade set in a handle.

knight *noun* (*plural* knights)
1 a man who has been given the rank that
allows him to put 'Sir' before his name. 2 a
piece in chess, with a horse's head.
knighthood *noun*
[from Old English *cniht* = young man]

knit *verb* (knits, knitting, knitted or knit)
make something by looping together wool or
other yarn, using long needles or a machine.
knitter *noun*, **knitting needle** *noun*
knit your brow frown.
[from Old English *cnyttan* = tie in knots]

knob *noun* (*plural* knobs)
1 the round handle of a door, drawer, etc. 2 a
round lump on something. 3 a small round
piece of something, *a knob of butter*.
knobbly *adjective*, **knobby** *adjective*

knock *verb* (knocks, knocking, knocked)
1 hit a thing hard or so as to make a noise.
2 produce by hitting, *knock a hole in it.*
3 (*slang*) criticize unfavourably, *Stop knocking
Britain!*
knock off 1 (*informal*) stop working. 2 deduct
something from a price. 3 (*slang*) steal.
knock out make a person unconscious,
especially by a blow to the head.

knockout *noun* (*plural* knockouts)
1 knocking somebody out. 2 a contest in which
the loser in each round has to drop out.
3 (*slang*) an amazing person or thing.

knot *noun* (*plural* knots)
1 a place where a piece of string, rope, or
ribbon etc. is twisted round itself or another
piece. 2 a tangle; a lump. 3 a round spot on a
piece of wood where a branch joined it. 4 a
cluster of people or things. 5 a unit for
measuring the speed of ships and aircraft, 2,025
yards (= 1,852 metres or 1 nautical mile) per
hour.
knot *verb* (knots, knotting, knotted)
1 tie or fasten with a knot. 2 entangle.

know *verb* (knows, knowing, knew, known)
1 have something in your mind that you have
learnt or discovered. 2 recognize or be familiar
with a person or place, *I've known him for
years.* 3 understand, *She knows how to please
us.* [from Old English]

knowing *adjective*
showing that you know something, *a knowing
look.*

knowingly *adverb*
1 in a knowing way. 2 deliberately.

knowledge *noun*
1 knowing. 2 all that a person knows. 3 all that
is known.
to my knowledge as far as I know.
[from *know* + Old English *lac* = practice]

knowledgeable *adjective*
well-informed. **knowledgeably** *adverb*

knuckle *noun* (*plural* knuckles)
a joint in the finger.
knuckle *verb* (knuckles, knuckling, knuckled)
knuckle down to buckle down to.
knuckle under be submissive.

koala (*say* koh-ah-la) *noun* (*plural* koalas)
an Australian animal that looks like a small
bear.
[an Australian Aboriginal word]

Koran (*say* kor-**ahn**) *noun*
the sacred book of Islam, written in Arabic,
believed by Muslims to contain the words of
Allah revealed to the prophet Muhammad.
[from Arabic *kur'an* = reading]

kosher *adjective*
keeping to Jewish laws about food, *kosher
meat*.
[from Hebrew *kasher* = suitable or proper]

kw *abbreviation*
kilowatt.

Ll

label *noun* (*plural* **labels**)
a small piece of paper, cloth, or metal etc. fixed
on or beside something to show what it is or
what it costs, or its owner or destination, etc.
label *verb* (**labels, labelling, labelled**)
put a label on something. [from old French]

laboratory *noun* (*plural* **laboratories**)
a room or building equipped for scientific
experiments.
[from Latin *laboratorium* = workplace]

laborious *adjective*
1 needing or using a lot of hard work.
2 explaining something at great length and
with obvious effort. **laboriously** *adverb*

Labour *noun*
the Labour Party, a socialist political party.

labour *noun* (*plural* **labours**)
1 hard work. 2 a task. 3 the contractions of the
womb when a baby is being born.
labour *verb* (**labours, labouring, laboured**)
1 work hard. 2 explain something at great
length and with obvious effort, *Don't labour the
point*. [from Latin *labor* = work, trouble, or
suffering]

labourer *noun* (*plural* **labourers**)
a person who does hard manual work,
especially outdoors.

laburnum *noun* (*plural* **laburnums**)
a tree with hanging yellow flowers. [Latin]

labyrinth *noun* (*plural* **labyrinths**)
a complicated arrangement of passages or
paths; a maze. [from Greek]

lace *noun* (*plural* **laces**)
1 net-like material with decorative patterns of
holes in it. 2 a piece of thin cord or leather for
fastening a shoe, etc.
lacy *adjective*

lack *noun*
being without something.
lack *verb* (**lacks, lacking, lacked**)
be without something, *He lacks courage*.

lacquer *noun*
a hard glossy varnish. **lacquered** *adjective*

lacrosse *noun*
a game using a stick with a net on it
(a *crosse*) to catch and throw a ball.
[from French *la crosse* = the crosse]

lacy *adjective*
made of lace or like lace.

lad *noun* (*plural* **lads**)
a boy or youth. [origin unknown]

ladder *noun* (*plural* **ladders**)
1 two upright pieces of wood or metal etc. and
crosspieces (*rungs*), for use in climbing. 2 a
vertical ladder-like flaw in a stocking etc.
where a stitch has become undone.

ladle *noun* (*plural* **ladles**)
a large deep spoon with a long handle, used for
lifting and pouring liquids.

lady *noun* (*plural* **ladies**)
1 a well-mannered woman. 2 a woman of good
social position. 3 (in polite use) a woman.
ladylike *adjective*, **ladyship** *noun*
Lady *noun* the title of a noblewoman.
[from Old English *hlaefdige* = person who
makes the bread (compare *lord*)]

ladybird *noun* (*plural* **ladybirds**)
a small flying beetle, usually red with black
spots.

lag[1] *verb* (**lags, lagging, lagged**)
go too slowly and fail to keep up with others.
[origin unknown]

lag[2] *verb* (**lags, lagging, lagged**)
wrap pipes or boilers etc. in insulating
material (**lagging**) to keep them warm.
[probably from a Scandinavian language]

lager (*say* **lah**-ger) *noun* (*plural* **lagers**)
a light beer.
[from German *Lager* = storehouse (because the
beer was kept to mature)]

lagoon *noun* (*plural* **lagoons**)
a salt-water lake separated from the sea by
sandbanks or reefs.
[from Latin *lacuna* = pool]

laid *past tense* of **lay**.

lain *past participle* of **lie**[2].

lair *noun* (*plural* **lairs**)
a sheltered place where a wild animal lives.
[from Old English]

lake *noun* (*plural* **lakes**)
a large area of water entirely surrounded by
land. [from Latin]

lamb *noun* (*plural* **lambs**)
1 a young sheep. 2 meat from a lamb.
lambswool *noun* [from Old English]

lame *adjective*
1 unable to walk normally. 2 weak; not convincing, *a lame excuse.* **lamely** *adverb,* **lameness** *noun* [from Old English]

lament *noun* (*plural* laments)
a statement, song, or poem expressing grief or regret.
lament *verb* (laments, lamenting, lamented)
express grief or regret about something.
lamentation *noun*
[from Latin *lamentari* = weep]

lamentable (*say* lam-in-ta-bul) *adjective*
regrettable or deplorable.

lamp *noun* (*plural* lamps)
a device for producing light from electricity, gas, or oil.
lamplight *noun,* **lampshade** *noun*
[from Greek *lampas* = torch]

lamp-post *noun* (*plural* lamp-posts)
a tall post in a street etc., with a lamp at the top.

lance *noun* (*plural* lances)
a long spear.

lance corporal *noun* (*plural* lance corporals)
a soldier ranking between a private and a corporal. [origin unknown]

land *noun* (*plural* lands)
1 the part of the earth's surface not covered by sea. 2 the ground or soil; an area of country, *forest land.* 3 the area occupied by a nation; a country.
land *verb* (lands, landing, landed)
1 arrive or put on land from a ship or aircraft etc. 2 reach the ground after jumping or falling. 3 bring a fish out of the water. 4 obtain, *She landed an excellent job.* 5 arrive or cause to arrive at a certain place or position etc., *They landed up in gaol.* 6 present with a problem, *He landed me with this task.* [from Old English]

landing *noun* (*plural* landings)
1 bringing or coming to land. 2 a place where people can get on and off a boat. 3 the level area at the top of stairs.

landing stage *noun* (*plural* landing stages)
a platform on which people and goods are taken on and off a boat.

landlady *noun* (*plural* landladies)
1 a woman who lets rooms to lodgers. 2 a woman who looks after a public house.

landlord *noun* (*plural* landlords)
1 a person who lets a house, room, or land to a tenant. 2 a person who looks after a public house.

landmark *noun* (*plural* landmarks)
1 an object that is easily seen in a landscape. 2 an important event in the history of something.

landowner *noun* (*plural* landowners)
a person who owns a large amount of land.

landscape *noun* (*plural* landscapes)
the scenery or a picture of the countryside.

landslide *noun* (*plural* landslides)
1 a huge mass of soil and rocks sliding down a slope. 2 an overwhelming victory in an election, *She won the General Election by a landslide.*

lane *noun* (*plural* lanes)
1 a narrow road, especially in the country. 2 a strip of road for a single line of traffic. 3 a strip of track or water for one runner, swimmer, etc. in a race. [from Old English]

language *noun* (*plural* languages)
1 words and their use. 2 the words used in a particular country or by a particular group of people.
[from Latin *lingua* = tongue]

languid *adjective*
slow because of tiredness, weakness, or laziness. **languidly** *adverb,* **languor** *noun* [same origin as *languish*]

languish *verb* (languishes, languishing, languished)
1 become weak or listless and depressed. 2 live in miserable conditions; be neglected.
[from Latin *languere* = be faint or weak]

lank *adjective*
(of hair) long and limp. [from Old English]

lanky *adjective* (lankier, lankiest)
awkwardly thin and tall. **lankiness** *noun*

lantern *noun* (*plural* lanterns)
a transparent case for holding a light and shielding it from the wind.
[from Latin; related to *lamp*]

lap¹ *noun* (*plural* laps)
1 the level place formed by the front of the legs above the knees when a person is sitting down. 2 going once round a racecourse. 3 one section of a journey, *the last lap.*
lap *verb* (laps, lapping, lapped)
be a lap ahead of someone in a race.
[from Old English *laeppa*]

lap² *verb* (laps, lapping, lapped)
1 take up liquid by moving the tongue, as a cat does. 2 make a gentle splash against something, *Waves lapped the shore.*
[from Old English *lapian*]

lapel (*say* la-pel) *noun* (*plural* lapels)
a flap folded back at the front edge of a coat etc.
[from *lap*¹]

lapse *noun* (*plural* lapses)
1 a slight mistake or failure, *a lapse of memory.* 2 an amount of time elapsed, *after a lapse of six months.*
lapse *verb* (lapses, lapsing, lapsed)
1 pass or slip gradually, *He lapsed into unconsciousness.* 2 be no longer valid, through

not being renewed, *My insurance policy has
lapsed.*
[from Latin *lapsus* = sliding]

larch *noun* (*plural* **larches**)
a tall deciduous tree that bears small cones.
[via old German from Latin]

lard *noun*
a white greasy substance prepared from pig-fat
and used in cooking.
[French, = bacon]

larder *noun* (*plural* **larders**)
a cupboard or small room for storing food.
[from Latin]

large *adjective*
of more than the ordinary or average size; big.
largeness *noun*
at large 1 free to roam about, not captured, *The
escaped prisoners are still at large.* **2** in general,
as a whole, *She is respected by the country at
large.*
[from Latin *largus* = abundant or generous]

largely *adverb*
to a great extent, *You are largely responsible for
the accident.*

lark[1] *noun* (*plural* **larks**)
a small sandy-brown bird; the skylark. [from
Old English]

lark[2] *noun* (*plural* **larks**) (*informal*)
something amusing; a bit of fun, *We did it for a
lark.* [origin unknown]

larva *noun* (*plural* **larvae**)
an insect in the first stage of its life, after it
comes out of the egg. **larval** *adjective*
[Latin, = ghost or mask]

laser *noun* (*plural* **lasers**)
a device that makes a very strong narrow beam
of light or other electromagnetic radiation.
[from the initials of 'light amplification (by)
stimulated emission (of) radiation']

lash *noun* (*plural* **lashes**)
1 a stroke with a whip etc. **2** the cord or cord-
like part of a whip. **3** an eyelash.
lash *verb* (**lashes, lashing, lashed**)
1 strike with a whip; beat violently. **2** tie with
cord etc., *Lash the sticks together.*
lash down (of rain or wind) pour or beat down
forcefully.
lash out 1 speak or hit out angrily. **2** spend
money extravagantly.

lass *noun* (*plural* **lasses**)
a girl or young woman. **lassie** *noun*

lasso *noun* (*plural* **lassoes** or **lassos**)
a rope with a sliding noose at the end, used for
catching cattle etc. [from Spanish]

last[1] *adjective* & *adverb*
1 coming after all others; final. **2** latest; most
recent, *last night.* **3** least likely, *She is the last
person I'd have chosen.*
the last straw a final thing that makes problems
unbearable.
last *noun*
1 a person or thing that is last. **2** the end, *He
was brave to the last.*
at last or **at long last** finally; after much delay.
[from Old English *latost*]

last[2] *verb* (**lasts, lasting, lasted**)
1 continue; go on existing or living or being
usable. **2** be enough for, *The food will last us for
three days.*
[from Old English *laestan*]

lasting *adjective*
able to last for a long time, *a lasting peace.*

lastly *adverb*
in the last place; finally.

latch *noun* (*plural* **latches**)
a small bar fastening a door or gate, lifted by a
lever or spring. **latchkey** *noun*
latch *verb* (**latches, latching, latched**)
fasten with a latch.
latch onto 1 meet someone and follow them
around all the time. **2** understand something.

late *adjective* & *adverb*
1 after the usual or expected time. **2** near the
end, *late in the afternoon.* **3** recent, *the latest
news.* **4** who has died recently, *the late king.*
of late recently.

lately *adverb*
recently.

latent heat *noun*
the heat needed to change a solid into a liquid
or vapour, or a liquid into a vapour, without a
change in temperature.
[from Latin *latens* = lying hidden]

lathe (*say* lay*th*) *noun* (*plural* **lathes**)
a machine for holding and turning pieces of
wood while they are being shaped.

lather *noun*
a mass of froth.
lather *verb* (**lathers, lathering, lathered**)
1 cover with lather. **2** form a lather.

Latin *noun*
the language of the ancient Romans.
[from *Latium*, an ancient district of Italy
including Rome]

Latin America *noun*
the parts of Central and South America where
the main language is Spanish or Portuguese.
[because these languages developed from
Latin]

latitude *noun* (*plural* **latitudes**)
1 the distance of a place from the equator,
measured in degrees. **2** freedom from
restrictions on what people can do or believe.
[from Latin *latitudo* = breadth]

latrine (*say* la-treen) *noun* (*plural* **latrines**)
a lavatory in a camp or barracks etc. [French, related to *lavatory*]

latter *adjective*
later, *the latter part of the year.*
the latter the second of two people or things just mentioned. (Compare *former*.)

lattice *noun* (*plural* **lattices**)
a framework of crossed laths or bars with spaces between. [from French]

laugh *verb* (**laughs, laughing, laughed**)
make the sounds that show you think something is funny.
laugh *noun* (*plural* **laughs**)
the sound of laughing. [from Old English]

laughable *adjective*
deserving to be laughed at.

laughing stock *noun* (*plural* **laughing stocks**)
a person or thing that is the object of ridicule and scorn.

laughter *noun*
the act, sound, or manner of laughing.

launch¹ *verb* (**launches, launching, launched**)
1 send a ship from the land into the water.
2 set a thing moving by throwing or pushing it.
3 send a rocket etc. into space. 4 start into action, *launch an attack.* [from old French]

launch² *noun* (*plural* **launches**)
a large motor boat. [from Spanish]

launderette *noun* (*plural* **launderettes**)
a place fitted with washing machines that people pay to use. [from *laundry* + *-ette*]

laundry *noun* (*plural* **laundries**)
1 a place where clothes etc. are washed and ironed for customers. 2 clothes etc. sent to or from a laundry.
[from Latin *lavandaria* = things to be washed]

laureate (*say* lorri-at) *adjective*
Poet Laureate a person appointed to write poems for national occasions.
[from *laurel*, because a laurel wreath was worn in ancient times as a sign of victory]

laurel *noun* (*plural* **laurels**)
an evergreen shrub with smooth shiny leaves. [from Latin]

lava *noun*
molten rock that flows from a volcano; the solid rock formed when it cools.
[from Latin *lavare* = to wash]

lavatory *noun* (*plural* **lavatories**)
1 a toilet. 2 a room containing a toilet.
[from Latin *lavatorium* = a basin or bath for washing]

lavender *noun*
1 a shrub with sweet-smelling purple flowers.
2 light-purple colour. [from Latin]

lavish *adjective*
1 generous. 2 plentiful.
lavishly *adverb*, **lavishness** *noun*
[from old French *lavasse* = heavy rain]

law *noun* (*plural* **laws**)
1 a rule or set of rules that everyone must obey. 2 (*informal*) the police. 3 a scientific statement of something that always happens, *the law of gravity.*

law-abiding *adjective*
obeying the law.

lawcourt *noun* (*plural* **lawcourts**)
a room or building in which a judge or magistrate hears evidence and decides whether someone has broken the law.

lawful *adjective*
allowed or accepted by the law.
lawfully *adverb*

lawless *adjective*
1 not obeying the law. 2 without proper laws, *a lawless country.*
lawlessly *adverb*, **lawlessness** *noun*

lawn *noun* (*plural* **lawns**)
an area of closely-cut grass in a garden or park. [from old French]

lawnmower *noun* (*plural* **lawnmowers**)
a machine for cutting the grass of lawns.

lawn tennis *noun*
tennis played on an outdoor grass or hard court.

lawsuit *noun* (*plural* **lawsuits**)
a dispute or claim etc. that is brought to a lawcourt to be settled.

lawyer *noun* (*plural* **lawyers**)
a person who is qualified to give advice in matters of law.

laxative *noun* (*plural* **laxatives**)
a medicine that stimulates the bowels to empty. [from Latin *laxare* = loosen]

lay¹ *verb* (**lays, laying, laid**)
1 put something down in a particular place or way. 2 arrange things, especially for a meal, *lay the table.* 3 place, *He laid the blame on his sister.* 4 prepare or arrange, *We laid our plans.* 5 produce an egg.
lay off 1 stop employing somebody for a while. 2 (*informal*) stop doing something.
lay on supply or provide.
lay out 1 arrange or prepare. 2 knock a person unconscious. 3 prepare a corpse for burial.
[from Old English]

USAGE: Do not confuse *lay/laid/laying* = 'put down', with *lie/lay/lain/lying* = 'be in a flat position'. Correct uses are as follows: *Go and lie down; she went and lay down; please lay it on the floor.* 'Go and lay down' is incorrect.

lay² *past tense* of **lie**².

lay³ *adjective*
1 not belonging to the clergy, *a lay preacher.*
2 not professionally qualified, *lay opinion.*
[from Greek *laos* = people]

lay-by *noun* (*plural* lay-bys)
a place where vehicles can stop beside a main road.

layer *noun* (*plural* layers)
a single thickness or coating. [from *lay¹*]

layman *noun* (*plural* laymen)
1 a person who does not have specialized knowledge or training (e.g. as a doctor or lawyer). 2 a person who is not ordained as a member of the clergy. [from *lay³* + *man*]

layout *noun* (*plural* layouts)
an arrangement of parts of something according to a plan.

lazy *adjective* (lazier, laziest)
not wanting to work; doing little work. **lazily** *adverb*, **laziness** *noun*

lead¹ (*say* leed) *verb* (leads, leading, led)
1 take or guide someone, especially by going in front. 2 be winning in a race or contest etc.; be ahead. 3 be in charge of a group of people. 4 be a way or route, *This path leads to the beach.* 5 play the first card in a card game. 6 live or experience, *He leads a dull life.*
lead to result in; cause.
lead (*say* leed) *noun* (*plural* leads)
1 guidance or example, *Give us a lead.* 2 a leading place or part or position, *She took the lead.* 3 a strap or cord for leading a dog or other animal. 4 an electrical wire attached to something.
[from Old English *laedan*]

lead² (*say* led) *noun* (*plural* leads)
1 a soft heavy grey metal. 2 the writing substance (graphite) in a pencil. **lead** *adjective*
[from Old English *lead*]

leader *noun* (*plural* leaders)
1 the person in charge of a group of people; a chief. 2 the person who is winning.
leadership *noun*

leaf *noun* (*plural* leaves)
1 a flat usually green part of a plant, growing out from its stem, branch, or root. 2 the paper forming one page of a book. 3 a very thin sheet of metal, *gold leaf.* 4 a flap that makes a table larger.
leafy *adjective*, **leafless** *adjective*
turn over a new leaf make a fresh start and improve your behaviour.
[from Old English]

leaflet *noun* (*plural* leaflets)
1 a piece of paper printed with information. 2 a small leaf.

league¹ *noun* (*plural* leagues)
1 a group of people or nations who agree to work together. 2 a group of teams who compete

against each other for a championship.
in league with working or plotting together.
[from Latin *legare* = bind]

league² *noun* (*plural* leagues)
an old measure of distance, about 3 miles.
[from Greek]

leak *noun* (*plural* leaks)
1 a hole or crack etc. through which liquid or gas accidentally escapes. 2 the revealing of secret information. **leaky** *adjective*
leak *verb* (leaks, leaking, leaked)
1 get out or let out through a leak. 2 reveal secret information. **leakage** *noun*

lean¹ *adjective*
1 with little or no fat, *lean meat.* 2 thin, *a lean body.*
[from Old Engligh *hlaene*]

lean² *verb* (leans, leaning, leaned or leant)
1 bend your body towards or over something. 2 put or be in a sloping position. 3 rest against something.
[from Old English *hleonian*]

leaning *noun* (*plural* leanings)
a tendency or preference.

leap *verb* (leaps, leaping, leaped or leapt)
jump vigorously. **leap** *noun*

leapfrog *noun*
a game in which each player jumps with legs apart over another who is bending down.

leap year *noun* (*plural* leap years)
a year with an extra day in it (29 February).
[probably because the dates from March onwards 'leap' a day of the week; a date which would fall on a Monday in an ordinary year will be on Tuesday in a leap year]

learn *verb* (learns, learning, learned or learnt)
get knowledge or skill; find out about something. [from Old English]

USAGE: It is not acceptable in standard English to use *learn* to mean 'to teach'.

learned (*say* ler-nid) *adjective*
having much knowledge obtained by study.

learner *noun* (*plural* learners)
a person who is learning something, especially to drive a car.

learning *noun*
knowledge obtained by study.

lease *noun* (*plural* leases)
an agreement to allow someone to use a building or land etc. for a fixed period in return for payment. **leaseholder** *noun*
lease *verb* (leases, leasing, leased)
allow or obtain the use of something by lease.
[from old French]

leash *noun* (*plural* leashes)
a dog's lead. [from old French]

least *adjective* & *adverb*
very small in amount etc., *the least bit; the least expensive bike.*

leather *noun*
material made from animal skins.
leathery *adjective* [from Old English]

leave *verb* (**leaves, leaving, left**)
1 go away from a person or place. 2 stop belonging to a group. 3 cause or allow something to stay where it is or as it is, *You left the door open.* 4 go away without taking something, *I left my book at home.* 5 put something to be collected or passed on, *leave a message.*
leave off cease.
leave out omit; not include.
leave *noun*
1 permission. 2 official permission to be away from work; the time for which this permission lasts, *three days leave.*

lecture *noun* (*plural* **lectures**)
1 a talk about a subject to an audience or a class. 2 a long serious warning or rebuke.
lecture *verb* (**lectures, lecturing, lectured**)
give a lecture. **lecturer** *noun* [from Latin *lectura* = reading, or something to be read]

led *past tense* of **lead**¹.

ledge *noun* (*plural* **ledges**)
a narrow shelf, *a window ledge; a mountain ledge.* [origin unknown]

ledger *noun* (*plural* **ledgers**)
an account-book. [probably from Dutch]

leech *noun* (*plural* **leeches**)
a small blood-sucking worm that lives in water. [from Old English]

leek *noun* (*plural* **leeks**)
a long green and white vegetable of the onion family. [from Old English]

leer *verb* (**leers, leering, leered**)
look at someone in an insulting, sly, or unpleasant way. **leer** *noun*

leeway *noun*
1 extra space or time available. 2 a drift to leeward or off course.
make up leeway make up lost time; regain a lost position.

left¹ *adjective* & *adverb*
1 on or towards the west if you think of yourself as facing north. 2 (of political groups) in favour of socialist reforms.
left-hand *adjective*
left *noun*
the left-hand side or part etc.
[from Old English *lyft* = weak]

left² *past tense* of **leave**.

left-handed *adjective*
using the left hand in preference to the right hand.

leg *noun* (*plural* **legs**)
1 one of the limbs on a person's or animal's body, on which it stands or moves. 2 the part of a piece of clothing covering a leg. 3 each of the supports of a chair or other piece of furniture. 4 one part of a journey. 5 one of a pair of matches between the same teams.
[from Old Norse]

legacy *noun* (*plural* **legacies**)
something left to a person in a will.

legal *adjective*
1 lawful. 2 to do with the law or lawyers.
legally *adverb*, **legality** *noun*
[from Latin]

legend *noun* (*plural* **legends**)
an old story handed down from the past, which may or may not be true. (Compare *myth.*)
legendary *adjective*
[from Latin *legenda* = things to be read]

legible *adjective*
clear enough to read.
legibly *adverb*, **legibility** *noun*
[from Latin *legere* = to read]

legion *noun* (*plural* **legions**)
1 a division of the ancient Roman army. 2 a group of soldiers or former soldiers.

legislate *verb* (**legislates, legislating, legislated**)
make laws. **legislation** *noun*, **legislator** *noun*
[from Latin *legis* = of a law + *latio* = proposing]

legitimate *adjective*
1 lawful. 2 born when parents are married to each other. **legitimately** *adverb*, **legitimacy** *noun*
[from Latin *legitimare* = make something lawful]

leisure *noun*
time that is free from work, when you can do what you like.
leisured *adjective*, **leisurely** *adjective*
at leisure having leisure; not hurried.
at your leisure when you have time.

lemming *noun* (*plural* **lemmings**)
a small mouse-like animal of Arctic regions that migrates in large numbers and is said to run headlong into the sea and drown.

lemon *noun* (*plural* **lemons**)
1 an oval yellow citrus fruit with a sour taste. 2 pale-yellow colour.
[same origin as *lime*²]

lemonade *noun*
a lemon-flavoured drink.

lemur (*say* lee-mer) *noun* (*plural* **lemurs**)
a monkey-like animal. [from Latin]

lend *verb* (**lends, lending, lent**)
1 allow a person to use something of yours for a short time. 2 provide someone with money that they must repay, usually in return for payments (called *interest*).

lender *noun*
lend a hand help somebody.
[from Old English]

USAGE: Do not confuse *lend* with *borrow*, which means just the opposite.

length *noun* (*plural* **lengths**)
1 how long something is. **2** a piece of cloth, rope, wire, etc. cut from a larger piece. **3** the amount of thoroughness in an action, *They went to great lengths to make us comfortable.*
at length 1 after a long time. **2** taking a long time; in detail.

lengthen *verb* (**lengthens, lengthening, lengthened**)
make or become longer.

lengthy *adjective*
1 very long. **2** long and boring.
lengthily *adverb*

lenient (*say* **lee-nee-ent**) *adjective*
merciful; not severe.
leniently *adverb*, **lenience** *noun*
[from Latin *lenis* = gentle]

lens *noun* (*plural* **lenses**)
1 a curved piece of glass or plastic used to focus things. **2** the transparent part of the eye, immediately behind the pupil.
[Latin, = lentil (because of its shape)]

Lent *noun*
a time of fasting and penitence observed by Christians for about six weeks before Easter.
Lenten *adjective*
[from Old English *lencten* = the spring]

lent *past tense* of **lend.**

lentil *noun* (*plural* **lentils**)
a kind of small bean.
[from old French; related to *lens*]

leopard (*say* **lep-erd**) *noun* (*plural* **leopards**)
a large lion-like spotted wild animal, also called a panther. **leopardess** *noun*

leper *noun* (*plural* **lepers**)
a person who has leprosy.

leprosy *noun*
an infectious disease that makes parts of the body waste away. **leprous** *adjective*
[from Greek *lepros* = scaly (because white scales form on the skin)]

lesbian *noun* (*plural* **lesbians**)
a homosexual woman.
[named after the Greek island of Lesbos (because Sappho, a poetess who lived there about 600 BC, was said to be homosexual)]

less *adjective* & *adverb*
smaller in amount; not so much, *Make less noise. It is less important.*

USAGE: Do not use *less* when you mean *fewer.* You should use *fewer* when you are talking about a number of individual things, and *less* when you are talking about a quantity or mass of something: *The less batter you make, the fewer pancakes you'll get.*

less *noun*
a smaller amount.
less *preposition*
minus; deducting, *She earned £100, less tax.*

-less *suffix*
forms adjectives meaning 'without' (e.g. *colourless*) or 'unable to be …' (e.g. *countless*).
[from Old English]

lesser *adjective*
not so great as the other, *the lesser evil.*

lesson *noun* (*plural* **lessons**)
1 an amount of teaching given at one time. **2** something to be learnt by a pupil. **3** an example or experience from which you should learn, *Let this be a lesson to you!* **4** a passage from the Bible read aloud as part of a church service.
[from old French; related to *lecture*]

lest *conjunction* (*old use*)
so that something should not happen, *Remind us, lest we forget.*

let *verb* (**lets, letting, let**)
1 allow somebody or something to do something; not prevent or forbid, *Let me see it.* **2** cause to, *Let us know what happens.* **3** allow or cause to come or go or pass, *Let me out!* **4** allow someone to use a house or building etc. in return for payment (*rent*). **5** leave, *Let it alone.*
let down 1 deflate. **2** disappoint somebody.
let off 1 cause to explode. **2** excuse somebody from a duty or punishment etc.
let up (*informal*) relax. **let-up** *noun*

lethal (*say* **lee-thal**) *adjective*
deadly; causing death. **lethally** *adverb*
[from Latin *letum* = death]

lethargy (*say* **leth-er-jee**) *noun*
extreme lack of energy or vitality; sluggishness. **lethargic** (*say* **lith-ar-jik**) *adjective*
[from Greek *lethargos* = forgetful]

letter *noun* (*plural* **letters**)
1 a symbol representing a sound used in speech. **2** a written message, usually sent by post. [from Latin]

letter box *noun* (*plural* **letter boxes**)
1 a slot in a door, through which letters are delivered. **2** a postbox.

lettering *noun*
letters drawn or painted.

lettuce *noun* (*plural* **lettuces**)
a garden plant with broad crisp leaves used in salads. [from Latin]

leukaemia (*say* lew-**kee**-mee-a) *noun*
a disease in which there are too many white corpuscles in the blood.
[from Greek *leukos* = white + *haima* = blood]

level *adjective*
1 flat or horizontal. 2 at the same height or position etc. as others.
level *noun* (*plural* **levels**)
1 height, depth, position, or value etc., *Fix the shelves at eye level.* 2 a level surface. 3 a device that shows whether something is level.
on the level (*informal*) honest.
level *verb* (**levels**, **levelling**, **levelled**)
1 make or become level. 2 aim a gun or missile. 3 direct an accusation at a person.
[from Latin *libra* = balance]

level crossing *noun* (*plural* **level crossings**)
a place where a road crosses a railway at the same level.

lever *noun* (*plural* **levers**)
1 a bar that turns on a fixed point (the *fulcrum*) in order to lift something or force something open. 2 a bar used as a handle to operate machinery etc., *a gear lever.*
lever *verb* (**levers**, **levering**, **levered**)
lift or move something by means of a lever.
[from Latin *levare* = raise]

leverage *noun*
1 the force you need when you use a lever. 2 influence.

levity *noun*
being humorous, especially at an unsuitable time; frivolity.
[from Latin *levis* = lightweight]

levy *verb* (**levies**, **levying**, **levied**)
1 impose or collect a tax or other payment by the use of authority or force. 2 enrol, *levy an army.*
levy *noun* (*plural* **levies**)
an amount of money paid in tax.
[same origin as *lever*]

liability *noun* (*plural* **liabilities**)
1 being liable. 2 a debt or obligation. 3 a disadvantage or handicap.

liable *adjective*
1 likely to do or get something, *She is liable to colds. The cliff is liable to crumble.* 2 legally responsible for something.

liaison (*say* lee-ay-zon) *noun* (*plural* **liaisons**)
1 communication and cooperation between people or groups. 2 a person who is a link or go-between.
[from French *lier* = bind]

liar *noun* (*plural* **liars**)
a person who tells lies. [from Old English]

libel (*say* **ly**-bel) *noun* (*plural* **libels**)
an untrue written, printed, or broadcast statement that damages a person's reputation. (Compare *slander*)
libellous *adjective*
libel *verb* (**libels**, **libelling**, **libelled**)
make a libel against someone.
[from Latin *libellus* = little book]

liberal *adjective*
1 giving generously. 2 given in large amounts. 3 not strict; tolerant.
liberally *adverb*, **liberality** *noun*
[same origin as *liberty*]

Liberal Democrat *noun* (*plural* **Liberal Democrats**)
a member of the Liberal Democrat political party.

liberate *verb* (**liberates**, **liberating**, **liberated**)
set free. **liberation** *noun*, **liberator** *noun*

liberty *noun* (*plural* **liberties**)
freedom.
take liberties behave too casually or in too familiar a way.
[from Latin *liber* = free]

librarian *noun* (*plural* **librarians**)
a person in charge of or assisting in a library.
librarianship *noun*

library (*say* **ly**-bra-ree) *noun* (*plural* **libraries**)
1 a place where books are kept for people to use or borrow. 2 a collection of books, records, films, etc.
[from Latin *libraria* = bookshop]

lice *plural* of **louse**.

licence *noun* (*plural* **licences**)
1 an official permit to do or use or own something, *a driving licence.* 2 special freedom to avoid the usual rules or customs. [from Latin *licere* = be allowed]

license *verb* (**licenses**, **licensing**, **licensed**)
give a licence to a person; authorize, *We are licensed to sell tobacco.*

lichen (*say* **ly**-ken or **lich**-en) *noun* (*plural* **lichens**)
a dry-looking plant that grows on rocks, walls, trees, etc.

lick *verb* (**licks**, **licking**, **licked**)
1 move your tongue over something. 2 (of a wave or flame) move like a tongue; touch lightly. 3 (*slang*) defeat.

lid *noun* (*plural* **lids**)
1 a cover for a box or pot etc. 2 an eyelid.

lie[1] *noun* (*plural* **lies**)
a statement that the person who makes it knows to be untrue.
lie *verb* (**lies**, **lying**, **lied**)
tell a lie or lies; be deceptive.
[from Old English *leogan*]

lie[2] *verb* (**lays, lying, lay, lain**)
1 be or get in a flat or resting position, *He lay on the grass. The cat has lain here all night.* **2** be or remain, *The island lies near the coast. The machinery lay idle.*
lie low keep yourself hidden. [from Old English *licgan*]

USAGE: See the note at **lay**[1].

lieutenant (*say* lef-**ten**-ant) *noun* (*plural* **lieutenants**)
1 an officer in the army or navy. **2** a deputy or chief assistant. [from French *lieu* = place + *tenant* = holding]

life *noun* (*plural* **lives**)
1 the ability to function and grow. **2** the period between birth and death. **3** living things, *Is there life on Mars?* **4** liveliness, *full of life.* **5** a biography.

lifebelt *noun* (*plural* **lifebelts**)
a ring of material that will float, used to support someone's body in water.

lifeboat *noun* (*plural* **lifeboats**)
a boat for rescuing people at sea.

life cycle *noun* (*plural* **life cycles**)
the series of changes in the life of a living thing.

lifeguard *noun* (*plural* **lifeguards**)
someone whose job is to rescue swimmers who are in difficulty.

life jacket *noun* (*plural* **life jackets**)
a jacket of material that will float, used to support someone's body in water.

lifeless *adjective*
1 without life. **2** unconscious.
lifelessly *adverb*

lifelike *adjective*
looking exactly like a real person or thing.

lifetime *noun* (*plural* **lifetimes**)
the time for which someone is alive.

lift *verb* (**lifts, lifting, lifted**)
1 raise or pick up something. **2** rise or go upwards. **3** (*informal*) steal. **4** remove or abolish something, *The ban has been lifted.*
lift *noun* (*plural* **lifts**)
1 lifting. **2** a device for taking people or goods from one floor or level to another in a building. **3** a free ride in somebody else's vehicle, *Can you give me a lift to the station?*

ligament *noun* (*plural* **ligaments**)
a piece of the tough flexible tissue that holds your bones together. [from Latin *ligare* = bind]

light[1] *noun* (*plural* **lights**)
1 radiation that stimulates the sense of sight and makes things visible. **2** something that

provides light, especially an electric lamp. **3** a flame.
bring or **come to light** make or become known.
light *adjective*
1 full of light; not dark. **2** pale, *light blue.*
light *verb* (**lights, lighting, lit** or **lighted**)
1 start a thing burning; kindle. **2** provide the light.
light up 1 put lights on, especially at dusk. **2** make or become light or bright.
[from Old English *leoht*]

USAGE: Say *He lit the lamps; the lamps were lit* (not 'lighted'), but *She carried a lighted torch* (not 'a lit torch').

light[2] *adjective*
1 having little weight; not heavy. **2** small in amount or force etc., *light rain; a light punishment.* **3** needing little effort, *light work.* **4** cheerful, not sad, *with a light heart.* **5** not serious or profound, *light music.* **lightly** *adverb*, **lightness** *noun*
light *adverb*
lightly; with only a small load, *We were travelling light.* [from Old English *liht*]

lighten[1] *verb* (**lightens, lightening, lightened**)
make or become lighter or brighter.

lighten[2] *verb* (**lightens, lightening, lightened**)
make or become lighter or less heavy.

light-hearted *adjective*
1 cheerful and free from worry. **2** not serious.

lighthouse *noun* (*plural* **lighthouses**)
a tower with a bright light at the top to guide or warn ships.

lightning *noun*
a flash of bright light produced by natural electricity during a thunderstorm.
like lightning with very great speed.

lightning conductor *noun* (*plural* **lightning conductors**)
a metal rod or wire fixed on a building to divert lightning into the earth.

light year *noun* (*plural* **light years**)
the distance that light travels in one year (about 9.5 million million km).

like[1] *verb* (**likes, liking, liked**)
1 think a person or thing is pleasant or satisfactory. **2** wish, *I should like to come.* [from Old English]

like[2] *adjective*
similar; having some or all of the qualities of another person or thing, *They are as like as two peas.*
like *noun*
a similar person or thing, *We shall not see his like again.*

like *preposition*
1 similar to; in the manner of, *He swims like a fish.* 2 in a suitable state for, *It looks like rain. I feel like a cup of tea.*
[from Old Norse]

likelihood *noun*
being likely; probability.

likely *adjective* (likelier, likeliest)
1 probable; expected to happen or be true etc., *Rain is likely.* 2 expected to be successful, *a likely lad; a likely spot.*
[from *like²*]

liken *verb* (likens, likening, likened)
compare, *He likened the human heart to a pump.*

likeness *noun* (*plural* likenesses)
1 a similarity in appearance; a resemblance. 2 a portrait.

liking *noun*
a feeling that you like something, *She has a liking for ice cream.*

lilac *noun*
1 a bush with fragrant purple or white flowers. 2 pale purple.
[from Persian *lilak* = bluish]

lilt *noun* (*plural* lilts)
a light pleasant rhythm. **lilting** *adjective*

lily *noun* (*plural* lilies)
a garden plant with trumpet-shaped flowers, growing from a bulb. [from Greek]

limb *noun* (*plural* limbs)
1 a leg, arm, or wing. 2 a large branch of a tree.
out on a limb isolated; without any support.

limber *verb* (limbers, limbering, limbered)
limber up exercise in preparation for an athletic activity.

lime¹ *noun*
a white substance (calcium oxide) used in making cement and as a fertilizer.
[from Old English *lim*]

lime² *noun* (*plural* limes)
a green fruit like a small round lemon.
lime juice *noun*
[from Arabic *lima* = citrus fruit]

lime³ *noun* (*plural* limes)
a tree with yellow flowers.
[from Old English *lind*]

limelight *noun*
in the limelight receiving a lot of publicity and attention.
[from *lime¹* which gives a bright light when heated, formerly used to light up the stage of a theatre]

limerick *noun* (*plural* limericks)
a type of amusing poem with five lines. [named after Limerick, a town in Ireland]

limestone *noun*
a kind of rock from which lime (calcium oxide) is obtained.

limit *noun* (*plural* limits)
1 a line, point, or level where something ends. 2 the greatest amount allowed, *the speed limit.*
limit *verb* (limits, limiting, limited)
1 keep something within certain limits. 2 be a limit to something. **limitation** *noun* [from Latin *limes* = boundary]

limited company *noun* (*plural* limited companies)
a business company whose shareholders would have to pay only some of its debts.

limp¹ *verb* (limps, limping, limped)
walk lamely.
limp *noun* (*plural* limps)
a limping walk.

limp² *adjective*
1 not stiff or firm. 2 without strength or energy. **limply** *adverb*, **limpness** *noun*

limpet *noun* (*plural* limpets)
a small shellfish that attaches itself firmly to rocks. [via Old English from Latin]

line¹ *noun* (*plural* lines)
1 a long thin mark. 2 a row or series of people or things; a row of words. 3 a length of rope, string, wire, etc. used for a special purpose, *a fishing line.* 4 a railway; a line of railway track. 5 a system of ships, aircraft, buses, etc. 6 a way of doing things or behaving; a type of business.
in line 1 forming a straight line. 2 conforming.
line *verb* (lines, lining, lined)
1 mark something with lines, *Use lined paper.* 2 form something into a line or lines, *Line them up.*
[from Old English]

line² *verb* (lines, lining, lined)
cover the inside of something.
[from *linen* (used for linings)]

lineage (*say* lin-ee-ij) *noun* (*plural* lineages)
ancestry; a line of descendants from an ancestor.

linear (*say* lin-ee-er) *adjective*
1 arranged in a line. 2 to do with a line or length.

linen *noun*
1 cloth made from flax. 2 shirts, sheets, and tablecloths etc. (which were formerly made of linen). [from Latin *linum* = flax]

liner *noun* (*plural* liners)
a large ship or aircraft on a regular route, usually carrying passengers. [from *line¹*]

-ling *suffix*
forms nouns meaning 'having a certain quality' (e.g. *weakling*) or diminutives meaning 'little' (e.g. *duckling*).
[from Old English]

linger *verb* (**lingers, lingering, lingered**)
stay for a long time, as if unwilling to leave; be slow to leave. [from Old English]

lingerie (*say* **lan-***zher*-ee) *noun*
women's underwear.
[French, from *linge* = linen]

linguistics *noun*
the study of languages. **linguistic** *adjective*

lining *noun* (*plural* **linings**)
a layer that covers the inside of something.
[from *line²*]

link *noun* (*plural* **links**)
1 one ring or loop of a chain. **2** a connection.
link *verb* (**links, linking, linked**)
join things together; connect. **linkage** *noun*

links *noun* or *plural noun*
a golf course. [from Old English *hlinc*
= sandy ground near the seashore (where golf was often played)]

linoleum *noun*
a stiff shiny floor covering.
[from Latin *linum* = flax + *oleum* = oil (because linseed oil is used to make linoleum)]

linseed *noun*
the seed of flax, from which oil is obtained.
[from Latin *linum* = flax, + *seed*]

lint *noun*
a soft material for covering wounds. [probably from old French *lin* = flax (from which lint was originally made)]

lion *noun* (*plural* **lions**)
a large strong flesh-eating animal found in Africa and India. **lioness** *noun* [from Greek]

lip *noun* (*plural* **lips**)
1 either of the two fleshy edges of the mouth. **2** the edge of something hollow, such as a cup or crater. **3** the pointed part at the top of a jug etc., from which you pour things.
[from Old English]

lip-reading *noun*
understanding what a person says by watching the movements of his or her lips, not by hearing.

lipstick *noun* (*plural* **lipsticks**)
a stick of a waxy substance for colouring the lips.

liqueur (*say* lik-**yoor**) *noun* (*plural* **liqueurs**)
a strong sweet alcoholic drink.
[French, = liquor]

liquid *noun* (*plural* **liquids**)
a substance (such as water or oil) that flows freely but is not a gas.
liquid *adjective*
1 in the form of a liquid; flowing freely. **2** easily converted into cash, *the firm's liquid assets*. **liquidity** *noun*
[from Latin *liquidus* = flowing]

liquor *noun*
1 alcoholic drink. **2** juice produced in cooking; liquid in which food has been cooked.
[from Latin]

liquorice (*say* lick-er-iss) *noun*
1 a black substance used in medicine and as a sweet. **2** the plant from whose root this substance is obtained.
[from Greek *glykys* = sweet + *rhiza* = root]

lisp *noun* (*plural* **lisps**)
a fault in speech in which *s* and *z* are pronounced like *th*. **lisp** *verb*

list *noun* (*plural* **lists**)
a number of names, items, or figures etc. written or printed one after another.
list *verb* (**lists, listing, listed**)
make a list of people or things.

listen *verb* (**listens, listening, listened**)
pay attention in order to hear something.
listener *noun* [from Old English]

listless *adjective*
too tired to be active or enthusiastic.
listlessly *adverb*, **listlessness** *noun*
[from an old word *list* = desire, + *-less*]

lit *past tense* of **light¹**.

literacy *noun*
the ability to read and write.

literal *adjective*
1 meaning exactly what is said, not metaphorical or exaggerated. **2** word for word, *a literal translation*.
[from Latin *littera* = letter]

literally *adverb*
really; exactly as stated, *The noise made me literally jump out of my seat*.

literature *noun*
books and other writings, especially those considered to have been written well. [same origin as *literal*]

litigation *noun* (*plural* **litigations**)
a lawsuit; the process of carrying on a lawsuit.

litmus *noun*
a blue substance that is turned red by acids and can be turned back to blue by alkalis.
[from Old Norse *litr* = dye + *mosi* = moss (because litmus is obtained from some kinds of moss)]

litmus paper *noun*
paper stained with litmus.

litre *noun* (*plural* **litres**)
a measure of liquid, about $1\frac{3}{4}$ pints.

litter *noun* (*plural* **litters**)
1 rubbish or untidy things left lying about. **2** straw etc. put down as bedding for animals. **3** the young animals born to one mother at one time. **4** a kind of stretcher.

litter *verb* (**litters, littering, littered**)
1 make a place untidy with litter. 2 spread
straw etc. for animals.
[from old French *litière* = bed]

little *adjective* (**less, least**)
small in amount or size or intensity etc.; not
great or big or much.
little by little gradually; by a small amount at a
time.

little *adverb*
not much, *I eat very little.*

live[1] (rhymes with *give*) *verb* (**lives, living, lived**)
1 have life; be alive. 2 have your home, *She
lives in Glasgow.* 3 pass your life in a certain
way, *He lived as a hermit.*
live down if you cannot live down a mistake or
embarrassment, you cannot make people
forget it.
live on use something as food; depend on for
your living.
[from Old English]

live[2] (rhymes with *hive*) *adjective*
1 alive. 2 burning, *live coals.* 3 carrying
electricity. 4 broadcast while it is actually
happening, not from a recording.
[from *alive*]

livelihood *noun* (*plural* **livelihoods**)
a way of earning money or providing enough
food to support yourself. [from Old English *lif*
= life + *lad* = course or way]

lively *adjective* (**livelier, liveliest**)
full of life or action; vigorous and cheerful.
liveliness *noun*

liver *noun* (*plural* **livers**)
1 a large organ of the body, found in the
abdomen, that processes digested food and
purifies the blood. 2 an animal's liver used as
food. [from Old English]

livestock *noun*
farm animals.

livid *adjective*
1 bluish-grey, *a livid bruise.* 2 furiously angry.
[from Latin]

living *noun*
1 being alive. 2 the way that a person lives, *a
good standard of living.* 3 a way of earning
money or providing enough food to support
yourself.

living room *noun* (*plural* **living rooms**)
a room for general use during the day.

lizard *noun* (*plural* **lizards**)
a reptile with a rough or scaly skin, four legs,
and a long tail. [from Latin]

load *noun* (*plural* **loads**)
1 something carried; a burden. 2 the quantity
that can be carried. 3 the total amount of
electric current supplied. 4 (*informal*) a large
amount, *It's a load of nonsense. You could earn
loads of money.*

load *verb* (**loads, loading, loaded**)
1 put a load in or on something. 2 fill heavily.
3 weight with something heavy, *loaded dice.*
4 put a bullet or shell into a gun; put a film into
a camera. 5 enter data etc. into a computer.
[from Old English]

loaf[1] *noun* (*plural* **loaves**)
1 a shaped mass of bread baked in one piece.
2 minced or chopped meat etc. moulded into an
oblong shape.
use your loaf think; use common sense.
[from Old English]

loaf[2] *verb* (**loafs, loafing, loafed**)
spend time idly; loiter or stand about.
loafer *noun*
[probably from German *Landläufer* = a tramp]

loam *noun*
rich soil containing clay, sand, and decayed
leaves etc. **loamy** *adjective*

loan *noun* (*plural* **loans**)
1 something lent, especially money. 2 lending;
being lent, *These books are on loan from the
library.*

loathe (rhymes with *clothe*) *verb* (**loathes,
loathing, loathed**)
feel great hatred and disgust for something;
detest. **loathing** *noun*

loathsome *adjective*
making you feel great hatred and disgust;
detestable.

lobby *noun* (*plural* **lobbies**)
1 an entrance hall. 2 a group who lobby
Members of Parliament etc.
lobby *verb* (**lobbies, lobbying, lobbied**)
try to influence a Member of Parliament etc. in
favour of a special interest.
[same origin as *lodge*: the lobby of the Houses
of Parliament is where members of the public
can meet Members]

lobster *noun* (*plural* **lobsters**)
a large shellfish with eight legs and two long
claws. [via Old English from Latin]

local *adjective*
belonging to a particular place or a small area.
locally *adverb*
local *noun* (*plural* **locals**) (*informal*)
1 someone who lives in a particular district.
2 a public house near a person's home.
[from Latin *locus* = a place]

local anaesthetic *noun* (*plural* **local
anaesthetics**)
an anaesthetic affecting only the part of the
body where it is applied.

localized *adjective*
restricted to a particular place, *localized
showers.*

locate *verb* (locates, locating, located)
1 discover where something is, *locate the electrical fault*. **2** situate something in a particular place, *The cinema is located in High Street*. [from Latin *locare* = to place]

location *noun* (*plural* locations)
1 the place where something is situated. **2** discovering where something is; locating.
on location filmed in natural surroundings, not in a studio.

lock[1] *noun* (*plural* locks)
1 a fastening that is opened with a key or other device. **2** a section of a canal or river fitted with gates and sluices so that boats can be raised or lowered to the level beyond each gate. **3** a wrestling-hold that keeps an opponent's arm or leg from moving.
lock, stock, and barrel completely.

lock *verb* (locks, locking, locked)
1 fasten or secure something by means of a lock. **2** store something away securely. **3** become fixed in one place; jam.
[from Old English *loc*]

lock[2] *noun* (*plural* locks)
a clump of hair. [from Old English *locc*]

locker *noun* (*plural* lockers)
a small cupboard or compartment where things can be stowed safely.

locket *noun* (*plural* lockets)
a small ornamental case for holding a portrait or lock of hair etc., worn on a chain round the neck. [from old French *locquet* = small latch or lock]

locks *plural noun*
the hair of the head.

locomotive *noun* (*plural* locomotives)
a railway engine.
locomotive *adjective*
to do with movement or the ability to move, *locomotive power*. **locomotion** *noun*
[from Latin *locus* = place + *motivus* = moving]

locus (*say* loh-kus) *noun* (*plural* loci, *say* loh-sy)
1 the exact place of something. **2** (in geometry) the path traced by a moving point, or made by points placed in a certain way. [Latin, = place]

locust *noun* (*plural* locusts)
a kind of grasshopper that travels in large swarms which eat all the plants in an area.

lodge *noun* (*plural* lodges)
1 a small house, especially at the gates of a park. **2** a porter's room at the entrance to a college, factory, etc. **3** a beaver's or otter's lair.
lodge *verb* (lodges, lodging, lodged)
1 stay somewhere as a lodger. **2** provide a person with somewhere to live temporarily. **3** become stuck or caught somewhere, *The ball lodged in the tree*. **lodging house** *noun*
lodge a complaint complain formally.
[from old French *loge* = hut, from Germanic]

lodger *noun* (*plural* lodgers)
a person who pays to live in another person's house.

loft *noun* (*plural* lofts)
a room or storage space under the roof of a house or barn etc. [from Old Norse]

lofty *adjective*
1 tall. **2** noble. **3** haughty.
loftily *adverb*, **loftiness** *noun*
[from an old sense of *loft* = sky]

log[1] *noun* (*plural* logs)
1 a large piece of a tree that has fallen or been cut down; a piece cut off this. **2** a detailed record of a ship's voyage, aircraft's flight, etc. kept in a logbook.
log *verb* (logs, logging, logged)
enter facts in a logbook.
log in (or **on**), **log out** (or **off**) connect and disconnect a terminal correctly to or from a computer system.

log[2] *noun* (*plural* logs)
a logarithm, *log tables*.

logarithm *noun* (*plural* logarithms)
one of a series of numbers set out in tables which make it possible to do sums by adding and subtracting instead of multiplying and dividing. [from Greek *logos* = reckoning + *arithmos* = number]

loggerheads *plural noun*
at loggerheads disagreeing or quarrelling. [from an old word *loggerhead* = a stupid person]

logic *noun*
1 reasoning; a system of reasoning. **2** the principles used in designing a computer; the circuits involved in this.
[from Greek *logos* = word, reason]

logical *adjective*
using logic; reasoning or reasoned correctly.
logically *adverb*, **logicality** *noun*

-logical *suffix*
forms adjectives (e.g. *biological*) from nouns ending in *-logy*.

-logist *suffix*
forms nouns meaning 'an expert in or student of something' (e.g. *biologist*).
[same origin as *-logy*]

logo (*say* loh-goh or log-oh) *noun* (*plural* logos)
a printed symbol used by a business company etc. as its emblem.
[short for *logograph*, from Greek *logos* = word, + *-graph*]

-logy and **-ology** *suffixes*
form nouns meaning a subject of study (e.g. *biology*). [from Greek *-logia* = study]

loiter *verb* (loiters, loitering, loitered)
linger or stand about idly. **loiterer** *noun*

lollipop *noun* (*plural* **lollipops**)
a large round hard sweet on a stick.
[origin unknown]

lonely *adjective* (**lonelier, loneliest**)
1 sad because you are on your own. 2 solitary.
3 far from inhabited places; not often visited or
used, *a lonely road.* **loneliness** *noun* [from *lone*]

long[1] *adjective*
1 measuring a lot from one end to the other.
2 taking a lot of time, *a long holiday.* 3 having a
certain length, *The river is 10 miles long.*

long *adverb*
1 for a long time, *Have you been waiting long?*
2 at a long time before or after, *They left long
ago.* 3 throughout a time, *all night long.*
as long as or **so long as** provided that; on
condition that.
[from Old English *lang*]

long[2] *verb* (**longs, longing, longed**)
feel a strong desire.
[from Old English *langian*]

long division *noun*
dividing one number by another and writing
down all the calculations.

longing *noun* (*plural* **longings**)
a strong desire.

longitude *noun* (*plural* **longitudes**)
the distance east or west, measured in degrees,
from the Greenwich meridian. [from Latin
longitudo = length]

long jump *noun*
an athletic contest in which competitors jump
as far as possible along the ground in one leap.

long-sighted *adjective*
able to see distant things clearly but not things
close to you.

long-winded *adjective*
talking or writing at great length.

look *verb* (**looks, looking, looked**)
1 use your eyes; turn your eyes in a particular
direction. 2 face in a particular direction.
3 have a certain appearance; seem, *You look
sad.*
look after 1 protect or take care of someone.
2 be in charge of something.
look down on despise.
look forward to be waiting eagerly for
something you expect.
look into investigate.
look out be careful.
look up 1 search for information about
something. 2 improve in prospects, *Things are
looking up.*
look up to admire or respect.

look *noun* (*plural* **looks**)
1 the act of looking; a gaze or glance.
2 appearance, *I don't like the look of this place.*
[from Old English]

looking-glass *noun* (*plural* **looking-glasses**)
a glass mirror.

lookout *noun* (*plural* **lookouts**)
1 looking out or watching for something. 2 a
place from which you can keep watch. 3 a
person whose job is to keep watch. 4 a future
prospect, *It's a poor lookout for us.* 5 (*informal*)
a person's own concern, *If he wastes his money,
that's his lookout.*

loom[1] *noun* (*plural* **looms**)
a machine for weaving cloth.
[from Old English]

loom[2] *verb* (**looms, looming, loomed**)
appear suddenly; seem large or close and
threatening, *An iceberg loomed up through the
fog.* [probably from old Dutch]

loop *noun* (*plural* **loops**)
the shape made by a curve crossing itself; a
piece of string, ribbon, wire, etc. made into this
shape.

loophole *noun* (*plural* **loopholes**)
1 a way of avoiding a law or rule or promise
etc. without actually breaking it. 2 a narrow
opening in the wall of a fort etc.

loose *adjective*
1 not tight; not firmly fixed, *a loose tooth.* 2 not
tied up or shut in, *There's a lion loose!* 3 not
packed in a box or packet etc. 4 not exact, *a
loose translation.*
loosely *adverb*, **looseness** *noun*
at a loose end with nothing to do.

loosen *verb* (**loosens, loosening, loosened**)
make or become loose or looser.

loot *noun*
stolen things; goods taken from an enemy.
loot *verb* (**loots, looting, looted**)
1 rob a place or an enemy, especially in a time
of war or disorder. 2 take something as loot.
looter *noun* [from Hindi]

lop *verb* (**lops, lopping, lopped**)
cut away branches or twigs; cut off.

lopsided *adjective*
with one side lower than the other; uneven.

lord *noun* (*plural* **lords**)
1 a nobleman, especially one who is allowed to
use the title 'Lord' in front of his name. 2 a
master or ruler.
lordly *adjective*, **lordship** *noun*
Lord Mayor the mayor of a large city.
Our Lord Jesus Christ.
the Lord God. [from Old English *hlaford*
= person who keeps the bread (compare *lady*)]

lorry *noun* (*plural* **lorries**)
a large strong motor vehicle for carrying heavy
goods or troops. [origin unknown]

lose *verb* (**loses, losing, lost**)
1 be without something that you once had,
especially because you cannot find it. 2 fail to
keep or obtain something, *We lost control.* 3 be

defeated in a contest or argument etc. **4** cause
the loss of, *That fall lost us the game.* **5** (of a
clock or watch) become behind the correct
time. **loser** *noun*
be lost or lose your way not know where you are
or which is the right path.
lose your life be killed.
lost cause an idea or policy etc. that is failing.

loss *noun* (*plural* **losses**)
1 losing something. **2** something lost.
be at a loss not know what to do or say.

lot *noun* (*plural* **lots**)
1 a number of people or things. **2** one of a set of
objects used in choosing or deciding something
by chance, *We drew lots to see who should go
first.* **3** a person's share or fate. **4** something for
sale at an auction. **5** a piece of land.
the lot or the whole lot everything; all.
[from Old English]

lotion *noun* (*plural* **lotions**)
a liquid for putting on the skin.
[from Latin *lotio* = washing]

lottery *noun* (*plural* **lotteries**)
a way of raising money by selling numbered
tickets and giving prizes to people who hold
winning numbers, which are chosen by a
method depending on chance (compare *lot* 2).

loud *adjective*
1 easily heard; producing much noise.
2 unpleasantly bright; gaudy, *loud colours.*
loudly *adverb*, **loudness** *noun*

loudspeaker *noun* (*plural* **loudspeakers**)
a device that changes electrical signals into
sound.

lounge *noun* (*plural* **lounges**)
a sitting room.
lounge *verb* (**lounges, lounging, lounged**)
sit or stand in a lazy and relaxed way.

louse *noun* (*plural* **lice**)
a small insect that lives as a parasite on
animals or plants. [from Old English]

lousy *adjective* (**lousier, lousiest**)
1 full of lice. **2** (*slang*) very bad or unpleasant.

lout *noun* (*plural* **louts**)
a bad-mannered man. [origin unknown]

lovable *adjective*
easy to love.

love *noun* (*plural* **loves**)
1 great liking or affection. **2** sexual affection or
passion. **3** a loved person; a sweetheart. **4** (in
tennis) no score; nil.
in love feeling strong love.
make love have sexual intercourse.
love *verb* (**loves, loving, loved**)
feel love for a person or thing. **lover** *noun*,
lovingly *adverb* [from Old English]

love affair *noun* (*plural* **love affairs**)
a romantic or sexual relationship between two
people in love.

lovely *adjective* (**lovelier, loveliest**)
1 beautiful. **2** very pleasant or enjoyable.
loveliness *noun*

lover *noun* (*plural* **lovers**)
a person who someone is having a sexual
relationship with but is not married to.

lovesick *adjective*
longing for someone you love, especially
someone who does not love you.

low *adjective*
not high. **lowness** *noun*
low *adverb*
at or to a low level or position etc., *The plane
was flying low.* [from Old Norse]

lower *adjective* & *adverb*
less high.
lower *verb* (**lowers, lowering, lowered**)
make or become lower.

loyal *adjective*
always firmly supporting your friends or
group or country etc. **loyally** *adverb*,
loyalty *noun* [from old French]

lozenge *noun* (*plural* **lozenges**)
1 a small flavoured tablet, especially one
containing medicine. **2** a diamond shape.

Ltd. *abbreviation*
limited.

lubricant *noun* (*plural* **lubricants**)
a lubricating substance.

lubricate *verb* (**lubricates, lubricating, lubricated**)
oil or grease something so that it moves
smoothly. **lubrication** *noun*
[from Latin *lubricus* = slippery]

lucid *adjective*
1 clear and easy to understand. **2** sane.
lucidly *adverb*, **lucidity** *noun*
[from Latin *lucidus* = bright]

luck *noun*
1 the way things happen without being
planned; chance. **2** good fortune, *It will bring
you luck.* [from old German]

lucky *adjective* (**luckier, luckiest**)
having or bringing or resulting from good luck.
luckily *adverb*

ludicrous *adjective*
ridiculous. **ludicrously** *adverb*
[from Latin *ludere* = to play or have fun]

luggage *noun*
suitcases and bags etc. holding things for
taking on a journey. [from *lug*]

lukewarm *adjective*
1 only slightly warm; tepid. **2** not very
enthusiastic, *lukewarm applause.*
[from an old word *luke* = tepid, + *warm*]

lull *verb* (**lulls, lulling, lulled**)
soothe or calm; send someone to sleep.

lull *noun* (*plural* **lulls**)
a short period of quiet or inactivity. [imitating the sounds you make to soothe a child]

lullaby *noun* (*plural* **lullabies**)
a song that is sung to send a baby to sleep. [from *lull* + *bye* as in *bye-byes*, a child's word for bed or sleep]

lumbago *noun*
pain in the muscles of the lower back.

lumber *noun*
1 unwanted furniture etc.; junk. 2 (*American*) timber.
lumber *verb* (**lumbers, lumbering, lumbered**)
1 leave someone with an unwanted or unpleasant task. 2 move in a heavy clumsy way. [origin unknown]

luminous *adjective*
glowing in the dark. **luminosity** *noun*

lump[1] *noun* (*plural* **lumps**)
1 a solid piece of something. 2 a swelling. **lumpy** *adjective*
lump *verb* (**lumps, lumping, lumped**)
put or treat things together in a group because you regard them as alike in some way. [origin unknown]

lump[2] *verb* (**lumps, lumping, lumped**)
lump it (*informal*) put up with something you dislike.
[from an old word *lump* = look sulky]

lump sum *noun* (*plural* **lump sums**)
a single payment, especially one covering a number of items.

lunacy *noun* (*plural* **lunacies**)
insanity or great foolishness.

lunatic *noun* (*plural* **lunatics**)
an insane person. **lunatic** *adjective*
[from Latin *luna* = moon (because formerly people were thought to be affected by changes of the moon)]

lunch *noun* (*plural* **lunches**)
a meal eaten in the middle of the day.
lunch *verb* [short for *luncheon*]

lung *noun* (*plural* **lungs**)
either of the two parts of the body, in the chest, used in breathing.

lunge *verb* (**lunges, lunging, lunged**)
thrust the body forward suddenly.
lunge *noun*
[from French *allonger* = lengthen]

lupin *noun* (*plural* **lupins**)
a garden plant with tall spikes of flowers.

lurch[1] *verb* (**lurches, lurching, lurched**)
stagger; lean suddenly to one side. **lurch** *noun*
[originally a sailor's word: origin unknown]

lurch[2] *noun*
leave somebody in the lurch leave somebody in difficulties.
[from old French]

lure *verb* (**lures, luring, lured**)
tempt a person or animal into a trap; entice.
lure *noun*

lurid (*say* lewr-id) *adjective*
1 in very bright colours; gaudy. 2 sensational and shocking, *the lurid details of the murder*.
luridly *adverb*, **luridness** *noun* [from Latin]

lurk *verb* (**lurks, lurking, lurked**)
wait where you cannot be seen.

luscious (*say* lush-us) *adjective*
delicious. **lusciously** *adverb*, **lusciousness** *noun*
[origin unknown]

lush *adjective*
1 growing thickly and strongly, *lush grass*.
2 luxurious. **lushly** *adverb*, **lushness** *noun*

lust *noun* (*plural* **lusts**)
powerful desire, especially sexual desire.
lustful *adjective*
lust *verb* (**lusts, lusting, lusted**)
have a powerful desire for a person or thing, *people who lust after power*.
[Old English, = pleasure]

lusty *adjective* (**lustier, lustiest**)
strong and vigorous.
lustily *adverb*, **lustiness** *noun*
[originally = lively and cheerful: same origin as *lust*]

luxuriant *adjective*
growing abundantly.
[same origin as *luxury*]

USAGE: Do not confuse with *luxurious*.

luxury *noun* (*plural* **luxuries**)
1 something expensive that you enjoy but do not really need. 2 expensive and comfortable surroundings, *a life of luxury*.
luxurious *adjective*, **luxuriously** *adverb*
[from Latin *luxus* = plenty]

-ly *suffix*
forms 1 adjectives (e.g. *friendly, heavenly, sickly*), 2 adverbs from adjectives (e.g. *boldly, sweetly, thoroughly*).
[from Old English]

lying *present participle* of **lie**[1] and **lie**[2].

lynch *verb* (**lynches, lynching, lynched**)
join together to execute or punish someone violently without a proper trial, especially by hanging them. [named after William Lynch, an American judge who allowed this kind of punishment in about 1780]

lyric (*say* li-rik) *noun* (*plural* **lyrics**)
1 a short poem that expresses thoughts and feelings. 2 the words of a song.
lyrical *adjective*, **lyrically** *adverb*
[from Greek *lyrikos* = to be sung to a kind of small harp called a *lyre*]

Mm

MA *abbreviation*
Master of Arts.

mac *noun* (*plural* **macs**) (*informal*)
a mackintosh.

macaroni *noun*
flour-paste (*pasta*) formed into tubes.

macaroon *noun* (*plural* **macaroons**)
a small sweet cake or biscuit made with ground almonds.

machine *noun* (*plural* **machines**)
something with parts that work together to do a job. [from Greek *mechane* = device]

machine-gun *noun* (*plural* **machine-guns**)
a gun that can keep firing bullets quickly one after another.

machinery *noun*
1 machines. 2 mechanism. 3 an organized system for doing something.

mackerel *noun* (*plural* **mackerel**)
a sea fish used as food. [from old French]

mackintosh *noun* (*plural* **mackintoshes**)
a raincoat.
[named after the Scottish inventor of a waterproof material, C. Macintosh]

mad *adjective* (**madder, maddest**)
1 having something wrong with the mind; insane. 2 extremely foolish. 3 very keen, *He is mad about football.* 4 (*informal*) very excited or annoyed. **madly** *adverb*, **madness** *noun*, **madman** *noun*
like mad (*informal*) with great speed, energy, or enthusiasm.

madam *noun*
a word used when speaking politely to a woman, *Can I help you, madam?*
[from French *ma dame* = my lady]

mad cow disease *noun*
BSE.

madden *verb* (**maddens, maddening, maddened**)
make a person mad or angry.

mafia *noun*
1 a large organization of criminals in Italy, Sicily, and the United States of America. 2 any group of people believed to act together in a sinister way.
[Italian, = bragging]

magazine *noun* (*plural* **magazines**)
1 a paper-covered publication that comes out regularly, with articles or stories etc. by a number of writers. 2 the part of a gun that holds the cartridges. 3 a store for weapons and ammunition or for explosives. 4 a device that holds film for a camera or slides for a projector.
[from Arabic *makhazin* = storehouses]

magenta (*say* ma-**jen**-ta) *noun*
a colour between bright red and purple.
[named after Magenta, a town in north Italy, where Napoleon III won a battle in the year when the dye was discovered (1859)]

maggot *noun* (*plural* **maggots**)
the larva of some kinds of fly.
maggoty *adjective* [origin unknown]

magic *noun*
the art or pretended art of making things happen by secret or unusual powers. **magic** *adjective*, **magical** *adjective*, **magically** *adverb*
[from old Persian *magus* = priest; later = astrologer or wizard]

magician *noun* (*plural* **magicians**)
1 a person who does magic tricks. 2 a wizard.

magistrate *noun* (*plural* **magistrates**)
an official who hears and judges minor cases in a local court. **magistracy** *noun* [from Latin *magister* = master]

magnanimous (*say* mag-**nan**-im-us) *adjective*
generous and forgiving, not petty-minded.
magnanimously *adverb*, **magnanimity** *noun*
[from Latin *magnus* = great + *animus* = mind]

magnate *noun* (*plural* **magnates**)
a wealthy influential person, especially in business. [from Latin *magnus* = great]

magnesium *noun*
a silvery-white metal that burns with a very bright flame.

magnet *noun* (*plural* **magnets**)
a piece of iron or steel that can attract iron and that points north and south when it is hung up.
magnetism *noun*

magnetic *adjective*
having the powers of a magnet.
magnetically *adverb*

magnetize *verb* (**magnetizes, magnetizing, magnetized**)
1 make into a magnet. 2 attract like a magnet.
magnetization *noun*

magneto (*say* mag-**neet**-oh) *noun* (*plural* **magnetos**)
a small electric generator using magnets.

magnificent *adjective*
1 grand or splendid in appearance etc. 2 excellent.
magnificently *adverb*, **magnificence** *noun*
[from Latin *magnificus* = splendid]

magnify *verb* (**magnifies, magnifying, magnified**)
make something look or seem bigger than it really is. **magnification** *noun*, **magnifier** *noun*
[from Latin *magnus* = great + *facere* = make]

magnifying glass *noun* (*plural* magnifying glasses)
a lens that magnifies things.

magnitude *noun* (*plural* magnitudes)
1 size or extent. **2** importance.
[from Latin *magnus* = great]

magpie *noun* (*plural* magpies)
a noisy bird with black and white feathers, related to the crow. [from *Mag* (short for Margaret) + an old word *pie* = magpie]

mahogany *noun*
a hard brown wood. [origin unknown]

maid *noun* (*plural* maids)
1 a female servant. **2** (*old use*) a girl.
maidservant *noun* [short for *maiden*]

maiden *noun* (*plural* maidens) (*old use*)
a girl. **maidenhood** *noun*
maiden *adjective*
1 not married, *a maiden aunt*. **2** first, *a maiden voyage*. [from Old English]

maiden name *noun* (*plural* maiden names)
a woman's family name before she married.

maiden over *noun* (*plural* maiden overs)
a cricket over in which no runs are scored.

mail[1] *noun*
letters or parcels etc. sent by post.
mail order ordering goods by post.
[from old French *male* = a bag]

mail[2] *noun*
armour made of metal rings joined together, *a suit of chain mail*.
[from Latin *macula* = mesh]

mailing list *noun* (*plural* mailing lists)
a list of names and addresses of people to whom an organization sends information from time to time.

mail order *noun*
a system for buying and selling goods by post.

main *adjective*
largest or most important.
main *noun*
1 the main pipe or cable in a public system carrying water, gas, or (usually called mains) electricity to a building. **2** (*old use*) the seas, *Drake sailed the Spanish main*.

main clause *noun* (*plural* main clauses)
a clause that can be used as a complete sentence. (Compare *subordinate clause*.)

mainland *noun*
the main part of a country or continent, not the islands round it.

mainly *adverb*
1 chiefly. **2** almost completely. **3** usually.

mainstream *noun*
the most widely accepted ideas or opinions about something, *Fascism is not in the mainstream of British politics*.

maintain *verb* (maintains, maintaining, maintained)
1 cause something to continue; keep in existence. **2** keep a thing in good condition. **3** provide money for a person to live on. **4** state that something is true. **maintenance** *noun*
[from Latin *manu* = by hand + *tenere* = to hold]

maize *noun*
a tall kind of corn with large seeds on cobs.

majestic *adjective*
1 stately and dignified. **2** imposing.
majestically *adverb*

majesty *noun* (*plural* majesties)
1 the title of a king or queen, *Her Majesty the Queen*. **2** being majestic.
[from old French; related to *major*]

major *adjective*
1 greater; very important, *major roads*. **2** of the musical scale that has a semitone after the 3rd and 7th notes. (Compare *minor*.)
major *noun* (*plural* majors)
an army officer ranking next above a captain.
[Latin, = larger, greater]

majority *noun* (*plural* majorities)
1 the greatest part of a group of people or things. (Compare *minority*.) **2** the difference between numbers of votes, *She had a majority of 25 over her opponent*. **3** the age at which a person becomes an adult according to the law (now 18, formerly 21 years of age), *He attained his majority*. [same origin as *major*]

make *verb* (makes, making, made)
1 bring something into existence, especially by putting things together. **2** gain or earn, *She makes £5,000 a year*. **3** cause or compel, *Make him repeat it*. **4** achieve, *The swimmer just made the shore*. **5** reckon, *What do you make the time?* **6** perform an action etc., *make an effort*. **7** arrange for use, *make the beds*. **8** cause to be successful or happy, *Her visit made my day*.
make do manage with something that is not what you really want.
make for go towards.
make love 1 have sexual intercourse. **2** (*old use*) try to win someone's love.
make off go away quickly.
make out 1 manage to see, hear, or understand something. **2** claim or pretend that something is true.
make up 1 build or put together. **2** invent a story etc. **3** compensate for something. **4** put on make-up.
make up your mind decide.
make *noun* (*plural* makes)
1 making; how something is made. **2** a brand of goods; something made by a particular firm.

makeshift *adjective*
improvised or used because you have nothing better, *We used a box as a makeshift table*.
[from an old phrase *make shift* = manage somehow, put up with]

make-up *noun*
1 cosmetics. 2 the way something is made up.
3 a person's character.

mal- *prefix*
1 bad. 2 badly (as in *malnourished*).
[from Latin *male* = badly]

maladjusted *adjective*
unable to fit in or cope with other people or
your own circumstances.
[from *mal-* + *adjust*]

malapropism *noun* (*plural* malapropisms)
a comical confusion of words, e.g. using
hooligan instead of *hurricane*. [named after
Mrs Malaprop in Sheridan's play *The Rivals*,
who made mistakes of this kind]

malaria *noun*
a feverish disease spread by mosquitoes.
malarial *adjective*
[from Italian *mala aria* = bad air, which was
once thought to cause the disease]

male *adjective*
1 belonging to the sex that reproduces by
fertilizing egg-cells produced by the female.
2 of men, *a male voice choir*.
male *noun* (*plural* males)
a male person, animal, or plant.
[from old French; related to *masculine*]

male chauvinist *noun* (*plural* male chauvinists)
a man who thinks that women are not as good
as men.

malevolent (*say* ma-**lev**-ol-ent) *adjective*
wishing to harm people.
malevolently *adverb*, **malevolence** *noun*
[from *mal-* + Latin *volens* = wishing]

malfunction *noun* (*plural* malfunctions)
faulty functioning, *a malfunction in the
computer*.
malfunction *verb* (malfunctions, malfunctioning,
malfunctioned)
fail to work properly.

malice *noun*
the desire to harm others or to tease.
malicious *adjective*, **maliciously** *adverb*
[from Latin *malus* = evil]

malign (*say* mal-**l'n**) *adjective*
1 harmful, *a malign influence*. 2 showing
malice. **malignity** (*say* mal-**ig**-nit-ee) *noun*
[from Latin *malignare* = plot wickedly]

malignant *adjective*
1 (of a tumour) growing uncontrollably. 2 full
of malice. **malignantly** *adverb*, **malignancy** *noun*
[same origin as *malign*]

malleable *adjective*
1 able to be pressed or hammered into shape.
2 easy to influence; adaptable. **malleability** *noun*
[from Latin *malleare* = to hammer]

mallet *noun* (*plural* mallets)
1 a large hammer, usually made of wood. 2 an
implement with a long handle, used in croquet
or polo for striking the ball.
[from Latin *malleus* = a hammer]

malnutrition *noun*
bad health because you do not have enough
food or the right kind of food.
malnourished *adjective*

malt *noun*
dried barley used in brewing, making vinegar,
etc. **malted** *adjective*

maltreat *verb* (maltreats, maltreating,
maltreated)
ill-treat. **maltreatment** *noun*

mammal *noun* (*plural* mammals)
any animal which gives birth to live babies
which are fed with milk from the mother's
body. **mammalian** (*say* mam-**ay**-lee-an) *adjective*
[from Latin *mamma* = breast]

mammoth *noun* (*plural* mammoths)
an extinct elephant with a hairy skin and
curved tusks.
mammoth *adjective*
huge. [from Russian]

man *noun* (*plural* men)
1 a grown-up male human being. 2 an
individual person. 3 mankind. 4 a piece used
in chess etc.
man *verb* (mans, manning, manned)
supply with people to work something, *Man the
pumps!* [from Old English]

manacle *noun* (*plural* manacles)
a fetter or handcuff.
manacle *verb* (manacles, manacling, manacled)
fasten with manacles.
[from Latin *manus* = hand]

manage *verb* (manages, managing, managed)
1 be able to cope with something difficult. 2 be
in charge of a shop, factory, etc.
manageable *adjective*
[from Italian *maneggiare* = to handle]

management *noun*
1 managing. 2 managers; the people in charge.

manager *noun* (*plural* managers)
a person who manages something. **manageress**
noun, **managerial** (*say* man-a-**jeer**-ee-al) *adjective*

mandarin *noun* (*plural* mandarins)
1 an important official. 2 a kind of small
orange.
[via Portuguese and Malay (a language spoken
in Malaysia) from Sanskrit]

mane *noun* (*plural* manes)
the long hair on a horse's or lion's neck.

manganese *noun*
a hard brittle metal.

manger *noun* (*plural* mangers)
a trough in a stable etc., for horses or cattle to
feed from. [from French *manger* = eat]

mangle *verb* (mangles, mangling, mangled)
damage something by crushing or cutting it
roughly. [from old French]

mango *noun* (*plural* mangoes)
a tropical fruit with yellow pulp.

manhandle *verb* (manhandles, manhandling,
manhandled)
treat or push roughly.

manhole *noun* (*plural* manholes)
a space or opening, usually with a cover, by
which a person can get into a sewer or boiler
etc. to inspect or repair it.

manhood *noun*
1 the condition of being a man. 2 manly
qualities.

mania *noun* (*plural* manias)
1 violent madness. 2 great enthusiasm, *a
mania for sport.* **maniac** *noun*, **manic** *adjective*
[Greek, = madness]

manicure *noun* (*plural* manicures)
care and treatment of the hands and nails.
manicure *verb*, **manicurist** *noun*
[from Latin *manus* = hand + *cura* = care]

manifest *adjective*
clear and obvious. **manifestly** *adverb*

manifesto *noun* (*plural* manifestos)
a public statement of a group's or person's
policy or principles.

manifold *adjective*
of many kinds; very varied.
[from *many* + *-fold*]

manipulate *verb* (manipulates, manipulating,
manipulated)
handle or arrange something cleverly or
cunningly.
manipulation *noun*, **manipulator** *noun* [from
Latin *manus* = hand]

mankind *noun*
human beings in general.

manly *adjective*
1 suitable for a man. 2 brave and strong.
manliness *noun*

manner *noun*
1 the way something happens or is done. 2 a
person's way of behaving. 3 sort, *all manner of
things.* [from old French]

mannerism *noun* (*plural* mannerisms)
a person's own particular gesture or way of
speaking.

manners *plural noun*
how a person behaves with other people;
politeness.

manœuvre (*say* man-oo-ver) *noun* (*plural*
manœuvres)
a difficult or skilful or cunning action.

manœuvre *verb* (manœuvres, manœuvring,
manœuvred)
move carefully and skilfully.
manœuvrable *adjective* [via French from Latin
manu operari = work by hand]

manor *noun* (*plural* manors)
1 a manor house. 2 the land belonging to a
manor house. **manorial** *adjective*
[from old French; related to *mansion*]

manor house *noun* (*plural* manor houses)
a large important house in the country.

manpower *noun*
the number of people who are working or
needed or available for work on something.

mansion *noun* (*plural* mansions)
a large stately house. [from Latin *mansio*
= a place to stay, a dwelling]

manslaughter *noun*
killing a person unlawfully but without
meaning to.

mantelpiece *noun* (*plural* mantelpieces)
a shelf above a fireplace. [same origin as
mantle (because it goes over the fireplace)]

mantle *noun* (*plural* mantles)
1 a cloak. 2 a covering, *a mantle of snow.*

manual *adjective*
worked by or done with the hands,
a manual typewriter, manual work.
manually *adverb*
manual *noun* (*plural* manuals)
a handbook. [from Latin *manus* = hand]

manufacture *verb* (manufactures, manufacturing,
manufactured)
make things.
manufacture *noun*, **manufacturer** *noun*
[from Latin *manu* = by hand + *facere* = make]

manure *noun*
fertilizer, especially dung.

manuscript *noun* (*plural* manuscripts)
something written or typed but not printed.
[from Latin *manu* = by hand
+ *scriptum* = written]

Manx *adjective*
to do with the Isle of Man.

many *adjective* (more, most)
great in number; numerous, *many people.*
many *noun*
many people or things, *Many were found.*

Maori (rhymes with *flowery*) *noun* (*plural*
Maoris)
1 a member of the aboriginal people of New
Zealand. 2 their language.

map *noun* (*plural* maps)
a diagram of part or all of the earth's surface or
of the sky.

map 235 **marrow**

map *verb* (maps, mapping, mapped)
make a map of an area.
map out plan the details of something.
[from Latin *mappa mundi* = sheet of the world]

marathon *noun* (*plural* marathons)
a long-distance race for runners. [named after
Marathon in Greece, from which a messenger
is said to have run to Athens (about 40
kilometres) to announce that the Greeks had
defeated the Persian army]

marauding *adjective*
going about in search of plunder or prey.
marauder *noun*
[from French *maraud* = rogue]

marble *noun* (*plural* marbles)
1 a small glass ball used in games. 2 a kind of
limestone polished and used in sculpture or
building.
[from Greek *marmaros* = shining stone]

march *verb* (marches, marching, marched)
1 walk with regular steps. 2 make somebody
walk somewhere, *He marched them up the hill.*
marcher *noun*
march *noun* (*plural* marches)
1 marching. 2 music suitable for marching to.
[from old French]

mare *noun* (*plural* mares)
a female horse or donkey.

mare's nest *noun*
a discovery that seems interesting but turns
out to be false or worthless.

margarine (*say* mar-ja-**reen** or mar-ga-**reen**) *noun*
a substance used like butter, made from
animal or vegetable fats. [from French]

margin *noun* (*plural* margins)
1 an edge or border. 2 the blank space between
the edge of a page and the writing or pictures
etc. on it. 3 the difference between two scores
or prices etc., *She won by a narrow margin.*
[from Latin]

marginal *adjective*
1 in a margin, *marginal notes*. 2 very slight, *a
marginal difference.*
marginally *adverb*

marginal seat *noun* (*plural* marginal seats)
a constituency where a Member of Parliament
was elected with only a small majority and
may be defeated in the next election.

marine (*say* ma-**reen**) *adjective*
of or concerned with the sea.
marine *noun* (*plural* marines)
a member of the troops who are trained to
serve at sea as well as on land.
[from Latin *mare* = sea]

marionette *noun* (*plural* marionettes)
a puppet worked by strings or wires. [French,
= little Mary]

maritime *adjective*
1 to do with the sea or ships. 2 found near the
sea. [same origin as *marine*]

mark[1] *noun* (*plural* marks)
1 a spot, dot, line, or stain etc. on something.
2 a number or letter etc. put on a piece of work
to show how good it is. 3 a distinguishing
feature. 4 a symbol, *They all stood as a mark of
respect.* 5 a target.
on your marks! a command to runners to get
ready to begin a race.
up to the mark of the normal or expected
standard.
mark *verb* (marks, marking, marked)
1 put a mark on something. 2 give a mark to a
piece of work; correct. 3 pay attention to
something, *Mark my words!* 4 keep close to an
opposing player in football etc. **marker** *noun*
[from Old English *merc*]

mark[2] *noun* (*plural* marks)
a German unit of money.

marked *adjective*
noticeable, *a marked improvement.*
markedly *adverb*

market *noun* (*plural* markets)
1 a place where things are bought and sold,
usually from stalls in the open air. 2 demand
for things; trade.
market place *noun* [via Old English from Latin
merx = goods, merchandise]

market research *noun*
the study of what people need or want to buy.

marksman *noun* (*plural* marksmen)
an expert in shooting at a target.
marksmanship *noun*

mark time *verb*
1 march on one spot without moving forward.
2 occupy your time without making any
progress.

marmalade *noun*
jam made from oranges, lemons, or other
citrus fruit. [via French from Portuguese
marmelo = quince (from which marmalade was
first made)]

maroon *verb* (maroons, marooning, marooned)
abandon or isolate somebody in a deserted
place; strand. [via French from Spanish
cimarrón = runaway slave]

marquee (*say* mar-**kee**) *noun* (*plural* marquees)
a large tent used for a party or exhibition etc.
[from French; related to *marquis*]

marquis *noun* (*plural* marquises)
a nobleman ranking next above an earl.

marriage *noun* (*plural* marriages)
1 the state of being married. 2 a wedding.

marrow *noun* (*plural* marrows)
1 a large gourd eaten as a vegetable. 2 the soft
substance inside bones.

marry *verb* (marries, marrying, married)
1 become a person's husband or wife. 2 unite a man and woman legally for the purpose of living together.
[from Latin *maritus* = husband]

marsh *noun* (*plural* marshes)
an area of very wet ground. **marshy** *adjective*
[from Old English]

marshal *noun* (*plural* marshals)
1 an official who supervises a contest or ceremony etc. 2 an officer of very high rank, *a Field Marshal.*

marshmallow *noun* (*plural* marshmallows)
a soft spongy sweet, usually pink or white.
[originally made from the root of the marshmallow, a pink flower that grows in marshes]

marsupial (*say* mar-soo-pee-al) *noun* (*plural* marsupials)
an animal such as a kangaroo or wallaby. The female has a pouch on the front of its body in which its babies are carried.
[from Greek *marsypion* = pouch]

martial *adjective*
to do with war; warlike.
[Latin, = belonging to Mars, the Roman god of war]

martial arts *plural noun*
fighting sports, such as judo and karate.

martial law *noun*
government of a country by the armed forces during a crisis.

martyr *noun* (*plural* martyrs)
a person who is killed or made to suffer because of his or her beliefs.
martyrdom *noun*

marvel *noun* (*plural* marvels)
a wonderful thing. **marvellous** *adjective*
[from old French; related to *miracle*]

marzipan *noun*
a soft sweet food made of ground almonds, eggs, and sugar. [via German from Italian]

mascot *noun* (*plural* mascots)
a person, animal, or thing that is believed to bring good luck. [from French]

masculine *adjective*
1 to do with men. 2 typical of or suitable for men. 3 (in some languages) belonging to the class of words which includes the words referring to men, such as *garçon* and *livre* in French. **masculinity** *noun*
[from Latin *masculus* = male]

mash *verb* (mashes, mashing, mashed)
crush into a soft mass.

mask *noun* (*plural* masks)
a covering worn over the face to disguise or protect it.

masochist (*say* mas-ok-ist) *noun* (*plural* masochists)
a person who enjoys things that seem painful or tiresome. **masochism** *noun* [named after an Austrian novelist, L. von Sacher-Masoch, who wrote about masochism]

mason *noun* (*plural* masons)
a person who builds or works with stone.

masonry *noun*
1 the stone parts of a building; stonework. 2 a mason's work.

masquerade *noun* (*plural* masquerades)
a pretence.
masquerade *verb* (masquerades, masquerading, masqueraded)
pretend to be something, *He masqueraded as a policeman.*
[via French from Italian *mascara* = mask]

Mass *noun* (*plural* masses)
the Communion service in a Roman Catholic church.

mass *noun* (*plural* masses)
1 a large amount. 2 a heap or other collection of matter. 3 (in scientific use) the quantity of matter that a thing contains. In non-scientific use this is called *weight.*
mass *adjective*
involving a large number of people, *mass murder.*

massacre *noun* (*plural* massacres)
the killing of a large number of people.
massacre *verb* [from French, = butchery]

massage (*say* mas-ah*zh*) *verb* (massages, massaging, massaged)
rub and press the body to make it less stiff or less painful. **massage** *noun*, **masseur** *noun*, **masseuse** *noun* [from French]

massive *adjective*
large and heavy; huge.
[from French; related to *mass*]

mass media *noun*
the media.

mass production *noun*
manufacturing goods in large quantities.
mass-produced *adjective*

mast *noun* (*plural* masts)
a tall pole that holds up a ship's sails or a flag or an aerial. [from Old English]

master *noun* (*plural* masters)
1 a man who is in charge of something. 2 a male teacher. 3 a great artist, composer, sportsman, etc. 4 something from which copies are made. 5 Master a title put before a boy's name. [same origin as *magistrate*]

masterful *adjective*
1 domineering. 2 very skilful.
masterfully *adverb*

master key *noun* (*plural* master keys)
a key that will open several different locks.

masterly *adjective*
very skilful.

Master of Arts *noun* (*plural* Masters of Arts)
a person who has taken the next degree after Bachelor of Arts.

master of ceremonies *noun* (*plural* masters of ceremonies)
a person who introduces the speakers at a formal event, or the entertainers at a variety show.

Master of Science *noun* (*plural* Masters of Science)
a person who has taken the next degree after Bachelor of Science.

masterpiece *noun* (*plural* masterpieces)
1 an excellent piece of work. 2 a person's best piece of work.

mastery *noun*
complete control or thorough knowledge or skill in something.

mastiff *noun* (*plural* mastiffs)
a large kind of dog. [from old French]

masturbate *verb* (masturbates, masturbating, masturbated)
excite yourself by fingering your genitals.
masturbation *noun* [from Latin]

mat *noun* (*plural* mats)
1 a small carpet. 2 a doormat. 3 a small piece of material put on a table to protect the surface.
[from Old English]

matador *noun* (*plural* matadors)
a bullfighter who fights on foot.
[Spanish, from *matar* = kill]

match[1] *noun* (*plural* matches)
a small thin stick with a head made of a substance that gives a flame when rubbed on something rough. **matchbox** *noun*,
matchstick *noun* [from old French]

match[2] *noun* (*plural* matches)
1 a game or contest between two teams or players. 2 one person or thing that matches another. 3 a marriage.
match *verb* (matches, matching, matched)
1 be equal or similar to another person or thing. 2 put teams or players to compete against each other. 3 find something that is similar or corresponding.
[from Old English]

mate[1] *noun* (*plural* mates)
1 a companion or friend. 2 one of a mated pair. 3 an officer on a merchant ship.
mate *verb* (mates, mating, mated)
1 come or put together so as to have offspring. 2 put things together as a pair or because they correspond.
[from old German]

mate[2] *noun* & *verb* (*in chess*)
checkmate.

material *noun* (*plural* materials)
1 anything used for making something else. 2 cloth or fabric.
[from Latin *materia* = matter]

materialize *verb* (materializes, materializing, materialized)
1 become visible; appear, *The ghost didn't materialize.* 2 become a fact; happen, *The trip did not materialize.*
materialization *noun*

maternal *adjective*
1 to do with a mother. 2 motherly.
maternally *adverb*
[from Latin *mater* = mother]

maternity *noun*
motherhood.
maternity *adjective*
to do with having a baby, *maternity ward.*
[same origin as *maternal*]

mathematics *noun*
the study of numbers, measurements, and shapes. **mathematical** *adjective*,
mathematically *adverb*, **mathematician** *noun*
[from Greek *mathema* = science]

matriarch (*say* may-tree-ark) *noun* (*plural* matriarchs)
a woman who is head of a family or tribe.
(Compare *patriarch.*) **matriarchal** *adjective*,
matriarchy *noun*
[from Latin *mater* = mother, + -*arch*]

matrix (*say* may-triks) *noun* (*plural* matrices, *say* may-tri-seez)
1 an array of mathematical quantities etc. in rows and columns. 2 a mould or framework in which something is made or allowed to develop. [from Latin]

matron *noun* (*plural* matrons)
1 a mature married woman. 2 a woman in charge of nursing in a school etc. or (formerly) of the nursing staff in a hospital.
matronly *adjective*

matted *adjective*
tangled into a mass. [from *mat*]

matter *noun* (*plural* matters)
1 something you can touch or see, not spirit or mind or qualities etc. 2 things of a certain kind, *printed matter.* 3 something to be thought about or done, *It's a serious matter.* 4 a quantity, *in a matter of minutes.*
no matter it does not matter.
what is the matter? what is wrong?
matter *verb* (matters, mattering, mattered)
be important.
[same origin as *material*]

matter of course *noun*
the natural or expected thing, *I always lock my bike up, as a matter of course.*

matter-of-fact *adjective*
keeping to facts; not imaginative or emotional, *She talked about death in a very matter-of-fact way.*

mattress *noun* (*plural* **mattresses**)
soft or springy material in a fabric covering, used on or as a bed.
[via French from Arabic]

mature *adjective*
1 fully grown or developed. 2 grown-up.
maturely *adverb*, **maturity** *noun*
mature *verb* (**matures, maturing, matured**)
make or become mature.
[from Latin *maturus* = ripe]

maul *verb* (**mauls, mauling, mauled**)
injure by handling or clawing, *He was mauled by a lion.*
[originally = knock down: from Latin *malleus* = a hammer]

mauve (*say* mohv) *noun*
pale purple.
[from Latin *malva* = a plant with mauve flowers]

maxim *noun* (*plural* **maxims**)
a short saying giving a general truth or rule of behaviour, e.g. 'Waste not, want not'.
[from Latin *maxima propositio* = greatest statement]

maximize *verb* (**maximizes, maximizing, maximized**)
increase something to a maximum.

maximum *noun* (*plural* **maxima** or **maximums**)
the greatest possible number or amount. (The opposite is *minimum.*)
[Latin, = greatest thing]

may[1] *auxiliary verb* (**may, might**)
used to express 1 permission (*You may go now*), 2 possibility (*It may be true*), 3 wish (*Long may she reign*), 4 uncertainty (*whoever it may be*).
[from Old English]

USAGE: See note at *can.*

may[2] *noun*
hawthorn blossom.
[because the hawthorn blooms in the month of May]

maybe *adverb*
perhaps; possibly.

mayfly *noun* (*plural* **mayflies**)
an insect that lives for only a short time, in spring.

mayhem *noun*
violent confusion or damage, *The mob caused mayhem.*

mayonnaise *noun*
a creamy sauce made from eggs, oil, vinegar, etc., eaten with salad.

[French, named after Mahón on Minorca, which the French had just captured when mayonnaise was invented]

mayor *noun* (*plural* **mayors**)
the person in charge of the council in a town or city. **mayoral** *adjective*, **mayoress** *noun* [from old French; related to *major*]

maze *noun* (*plural* **mazes**)
a network of paths, especially one designed as a puzzle in which to try and find your way.
[from *amaze*]

me *pronoun*
the form of *I* used as the object of a verb or after a preposition. [from Old English]

meadow (*say* med-oh) *noun* (*plural* **meadows**)
a field of grass. [from Old English]

meagre *adjective*
scanty in amount; barely enough, *a meagre diet.* [from French]

meal[1] *noun* (*plural* **meals**)
food served and eaten at one sitting.
[from Old English *mael*]

meal[2] *noun*
coarsely-ground grain. **mealy** *adjective* [from Old English *melu*]

mean[1] *verb* (**means, meaning, meant** (*say* ment))
1 have as an equivalent, '*Maybe' means 'perhaps'.* 2 have as a purpose; intend, *I mean to win.* 3 indicate, *Dark clouds mean rain.*
[from Old English *maenan*]

mean[2] *adjective* (**meaner, meanest**)
1 not generous; miserly. 2 unkind or spiteful, *a mean trick.* 3 poor in quality or appearance, *a mean little house.*
meanly *adverb*, **meanness** *noun*
[from Old English *maene*]

mean[3] *noun* (*plural* **means**)
a middle point or condition.
mean *adjective*
average.
[from old French; related to *medial*]

meander (*say* mee-an-der) *verb* (**meanders, meandering, meandered**)
take a winding course; wander. **meander** *noun* [named after the Meander, a river in Turkey (now Mendere or Menderes)]

meaning *noun* (*plural* **meanings**)
what something means.
meaningful *adjective*, **meaningless** *adjective*

means *noun*
a way of achieving something or producing a result, *a means of transport.*
by all means certainly.
by means of by this method; using this.
by no means not at all.
means *plural noun*
money or other wealth.
live beyond your means spend more than you

can afford.
[from *mean*[3], in an old sense = someone in the middle, a go-between]

meantime *noun*
in the meantime the time between two events or while something else is happening.
[from *mean*[3] + *time*]

meanwhile *adverb*
in the time between two events or while something else is happening.
[from *mean*[3] + *while*]

measles *noun*
an infectious disease that causes small red spots on the skin. [probably from old German *masele* = pimple]

measure *verb* (measures, measuring, measured)
1 find how big or heavy something is by comparing it with a unit of standard size or weight. 2 be a certain size, *The room measures 3×4 metres.*
measurable *adjective*, **measurement** *noun*
measure *noun* (*plural* measures)
1 a unit used for measuring, *A kilometre is a measure of length.* 2 a device used in measuring. 3 the size or quantity of something. 4 something done for a particular purpose, *We took measures to stop vandalism.*
[from Latin]

meat *noun*
animal flesh used as food. **meaty** *adjective*
[from Old English *mete* = food]

mechanic *noun* (*plural* mechanics)
a person who maintains or repairs machinery.

mechanical *adjective*
1 to do with machines. 2 produced or worked by machines. 3 done or doing things without thought. **mechanically** *adverb*
[from Greek *mechane* = machine]

mechanics *noun*
1 the study of movement and force. 2 the study or use of machines.

mechanism *noun* (*plural* mechanisms)
1 the moving parts of a machine. 2 the way a machine works.

medal *noun* (*plural* medals)
a piece of metal shaped like a coin, star, or cross, given to a person for bravery or for achieving something. [from French]

meddle *verb* (meddles, meddling, meddled)
1 interfere. 2 tinker, *Don't meddle with it.*
meddler *noun*, **meddlesome** *adjective*
[from old French; related to *mix*]

media *plural* of **medium** *noun*
the media newspapers, radio, and television,

which convey information and ideas to the public. (See *medium*.)

USAGE: This word is a plural. Although it is commonly used with a singular verb, this is not generally approved of. Say *The media are* (not 'is') *very influential*. It is incorrect to speak of one of them (e.g. television) as 'this media'.

mediate *verb* (mediates, mediating, mediated)
negotiate between the opposing sides in a dispute. **mediation** *noun*, **mediator** *noun*

medical *adjective*
to do with the treatment of disease.
medically *adverb*
[from Latin *medicus* = doctor]

medicine *noun* (*plural* medicines)
1 a substance, usually swallowed, used to try to cure a disease. 2 the study and treatment of diseases. **medicinal** (*say* med-**iss**-in-al) *adjective*, **medicinally** *adverb*
[same origin as *medical*]

medieval (*say* med-ee-**ee**-val) *adjective*
belonging to or to do with the Middle Ages.
[from Latin *medius* = middle + *aevum* = age]

mediocre (*say* mee-dee-**oh**-ker) *adjective*
not very good; of only medium quality.
mediocrity *noun*
[from Latin *mediocris* = of medium height]

meditate *verb* (meditates, meditating, meditated)
think deeply and quietly. **meditation** *noun*, **meditative** *adjective* [from Latin]

Mediterranean *adjective*
to do with the Mediterranean Sea (which lies between Europe and Africa) or the countries round it. [from Latin *Mare Mediterraneum* = sea in the middle of land, from *medius* = middle + *terra* = land]

medium *adjective*
neither large or small; moderate.
medium *noun* (*plural* media)
1 a thing in which something exists, moves, or is expressed, *Air is the medium in which sound travels. Television is used as a medium for advertising.* (See *media*.) 2 (with plural mediums) a person who claims to be able to communicate with the dead. [Latin, = middle thing]

meek *adjective* (meeker, meekest)
quiet and obedient. **meekly** *adverb*,
meekness *noun* [from Old Norse]

meet *verb* (meets, meeting, met)
1 come together from different places. 2 get to know someone, *We met at a party.* 3 come into contact; touch. 4 go to receive an arrival, *We will meet your train.* 5 pay a bill or the cost of something. 6 satisfy, *I hope this meets your needs.*

meet *noun* (*plural* **meets**)
a gathering of riders and hounds for a hunt.
[from Old English *metan*]

meeting *noun* (*plural* **meetings**)
1 coming together. 2 a number of people who
have come together for a discussion, contest,
etc.

mega- *prefix*
1 large or great (as in *megaphone*). 2 one
million (as in *megahertz* = one million hertz).
[from Greek *megas* = great]

megalomania *noun*
an exaggerated idea of your own importance.
megalomaniac *noun*
[from *mega-* + *mania*]

megaphone *noun* (*plural* **megaphones**)
a funnel-shaped device for amplifying a
person's voice.
[from *mega-* + Greek *phone* = voice]

melancholy *adjective*
sad; gloomy.
melancholy *noun*
sadness or depression.
[from Greek *melas* = black + *chole* = bile
(because black bile in the body was once
thought to cause melancholy)]

mellow *adjective* (**mellower, mellowest**)
1 not harsh; soft and rich in flavour, colour, or
sound. 2 kindly and genial. **mellowness** *noun*
mellow *verb* (**mellows, mellowing, mellowed**)
make or become mellow. [origin unknown]

melodious *adjective*
like a melody; pleasant to listen to.

melodrama *noun* (*plural* **melodramas**)
a play full of dramatic excitement and emotion.
melodramatic *adjective*
[from Greek *melos* = music + French *drame*
= drama (because melodramas were originally
musicals)]

melody *noun* (*plural* **melodies**)
a tune, especially a pleasing tune.
[from Greek *melos* = music + *oide* = song]

melt *verb* (**melts, melting, melted**)
1 make or become liquid by heating.
2 disappear slowly. 3 soften.

melting pot *noun* (*plural* **melting pots**)
a place where people of many different races
and cultures live and influence each other.

member *noun* (*plural* **members**)
1 a person or thing that belongs to a particular
society or group. 2 a part of something.
membership *noun*
[from Latin *membrum* = limb]

membrane *noun* (*plural* **membranes**)
a thin skin or similar covering.
membranous *adjective* [from Latin]

memoir (*say* mem-wahr) *noun* (*plural* **memoirs**)
a biography, especially one written by
someone who knew the person.
[from French *mémoire* = memory]

memorable *adjective*
1 worth remembering. 2 easy to remember.
memorably *adverb*

memorandum *noun* (*plural* **memoranda** or
memorandums)
1 a note to remind yourself of something. 2 a
note from one person to another in the same
firm.
[Latin, = thing to be remembered]

memorial *noun* (*plural* **memorials**)
something to remind people of a person or
event, *a war memorial.* **memorial** *adjective*
[from Latin *memoria* = memory]

memorize *verb* (**memorizes, memorizing,
memorized**)
get something into your memory.
[from *memory*]

memory *noun* (*plural* **memories**)
1 the ability to remember things. 2 something
that you remember. 3 the part of a computer
where information is stored.
[from Latin *memor* = remembering]

menace *noun* (*plural* **menaces**)
1 a threat or danger. 2 a troublesome person or
thing.
menace *verb* (**menaces, menacing, menaced**)
threaten with harm or danger.
[from Latin *minax* = threatening]

mend *verb* (**mends, mending, mended**)
1 repair. 2 make or become better; improve.
mender *noun*
mend *noun* (*plural* **mends**)
a repair.

menopause *noun*
the time of life when a woman gradually ceases
to menstruate. [from Greek *menos*
= of a month + *pausis* = stopping]

menstruate *verb* (**menstruates, menstruating,
menstruated**)
bleed from the womb about once a month, as
girls and women normally do from their teens
until middle age.
menstruation *noun*, **menstrual** *adjective*
[from Latin *menstruus* = monthly]

mental *adjective*
1 to do with or in the mind. 2 (*informal*) mad.
mentally *adverb*
[from Latin *mentis* = of the mind]

mentality *noun* (*plural* **mentalities**)
a person's mental ability or attitude.

mention *verb* (**mentions, mentioning, mentioned**)
speak or write about a person or thing briefly;
refer to.

mention *noun* (*plural* **mentions**)
an example of mentioning something, *Our school got a mention in the local paper.*

menu (*say* men-yoo) *noun* (*plural* **menus**)
1 a list of the food available in a restaurant or served at a meal. 2 a list of things, shown on a screen, from which you decide what you want a computer to do.

MEP *abbreviation*
Member of the European Parliament.

mercenary *adjective*
working only for money or some other reward.
mercenary *noun* (*plural* **mercenaries**)
a soldier hired to serve in a foreign army.
[from Latin *merces* = wages]

merchandise *noun*
goods for sale.
[from French *marchand* = merchant]

merchant *noun* (*plural* **merchants**)
a person involved in trade.
[from Latin *mercari* = to trade]

merchant navy *noun*
the ships and sailors that carry goods for trade.

merciful *adjective*
showing mercy. **mercifully** *adverb*

mercury *noun*
a heavy silvery metal (also called *quicksilver*) that is usually liquid, used in thermometers.
mercuric *adjective*
[from the name of the planet Mercury]

mercy *noun* (*plural* **mercies**)
1 kindness or pity shown in not punishing a wrongdoer severely or not harming a defeated enemy etc. 2 something to be thankful for.
[from old French]

mere *adjective*
not more than, *He's a mere child.*

merely *adverb*
only; simply.

merge *verb* (**merges, merging, merged**)
combine or blend.
[from Latin *mergere* = dip]

merger *noun* (*plural* **mergers**)
the combining of two business companies etc. into one.

meridian *noun* (*plural* **meridians**)
a line on a map or globe from the North Pole to the South Pole. The meridian that passes through Greenwich is shown on maps as 0° longitude. [from Latin]

meringue (*say* mer-ang) *noun* (*plural* **meringues**)
a crisp cake made from egg white and sugar.
[French]

merit *noun* (*plural* **merits**)
1 a quality that deserves praise. 2 excellence.
meritorious *adjective*
[from Latin *meritum* = value]

mermaid *noun* (*plural* **mermaids**)
a mythical sea creature with a woman's body but with a fish's tail instead of legs.
merman *noun*
[from Old English *mere* = sea, + *maid*]

merry *adjective* (**merrier, merriest**)
cheerful and lively. **merrily** *adverb*,
merriment *noun* [from Old English]

merry-go-round *noun* (*plural* **merry-go-rounds**)
a roundabout at a fair.

mesh *noun* (*plural* **meshes**)
1 the open spaces in a net, sieve, or other criss-cross structure. 2 material made like a net; network.

mesmerize *verb* (**mesmerizes, mesmerizing, mesmerized**)
1 (*old use*) hypnotize. 2 fascinate or hold a person's attention completely. **mesmerism** *noun*
[named after an Austrian doctor, F. A. Mesmer, who made hypnosis famous]

mess *noun* (*plural* **messes**)
1 a dirty or untidy condition or thing. 2 a difficult or confused situation; trouble. 3 (in the armed forces) a dining room.
make a mess of bungle.
mess *verb* (**messes, messing, messed**)
mess about 1 behave stupidly. 2 potter.
mess up 1 make a thing dirty or untidy.
2 bungle; spoil by muddling, *They messed up our plans.*
mess with interfere or tinker with.
[from old French *mes* = a portion of food]

message *noun* (*plural* **messages**)
a piece of information etc. sent from one person to another.
[from old French; related to *missile*]

messenger *noun* (*plural* **messengers**)
a person who carries a message.

Messiah (*say* mis-I-a) *noun* (*plural* **Messiahs**)
1 the saviour expected by the Jews. 2 Jesus Christ, who Christians believe was this saviour. **Messianic** *adjective*
[from Hebrew *mashiah* = anointed]

messy *adjective* (**messier, messiest**)
dirty and untidy.
messily *adverb*, **messiness** *noun*

metabolism (*say* mit-ab-ol-izm) *noun*
the process by which food is built up into living material in a plant or animal, or used to supply it with energy.
metabolic *adjective*, **metabolize** *verb*
[from Greek *metabole* = change]

metal *noun* (*plural* **metals**)
a hard mineral substance (e.g. gold, silver, copper, iron) that melts when it is heated.
metallic *adjective* [from Latin]

metamorphosis (*say* met-a-mor-fo-sis) *noun*
(*plural* **metamorphoses**, *say* met-a-mor-fo-seez
a change of form or character.
metamorphose *verb*
[same origin as *metamorphic*]

metaphor *noun* (*plural* **metaphors**)
using a word or phrase in a way that is not
literal, e.g. 'The pictures of starving people
touched our hearts'. **metaphorical** *adjective*,
metaphorically *adverb*
[from Greek *metapherein* = transfer]

meteor (*say* meet-ee-er) *noun* (*plural* **meteors**)
a piece of rock or metal that moves through
space and burns up when it enters the earth's
atmosphere.
[from Greek *meteoros* = high in the air]

meteorite *noun* (*plural* **meteorites**)
the remains of a meteor that has landed on the
earth.

meter *noun* (*plural* **meters**)
a device for measuring something, e.g. the
amount supplied, *a gas meter*. **meter** *verb*
[from *mete*]

USAGE: Do not confuse with *metre*.

methane (*say* mee-thayn) *noun*
an inflammable gas produced by decaying
matter. [from *methyl*, a chemical which
methane contains]

method *noun* (*plural* **methods**)
1 a procedure or way of doing something.
2 methodical behaviour; orderliness.
[from Greek *methodos* = pursuit of knowledge]

methodical *adjective*
doing things in an orderly or systematic way.
methodically *adverb*

methylated spirit or **spirits** *noun*
a liquid fuel made from alcohol.
[from *methyl*, a chemical added to make alcohol
nasty to drink]

metre *noun* (*plural* **metres**)
1 a unit of length in the metric system, about
$39\frac{1}{2}$ inches. 2 rhythm in poetry.
[from Greek *metron* = a measure]

USAGE: Do not confuse with *meter*.

metric *adjective*
1 to do with the metric system. 2 to do with
metre in poetry. **metrically** *adverb*

metric system *noun*
a measuring system based on decimal units
(the metre, litre, and gram).

metric ton *noun* (*plural* **metric tons**)
1,000 kilograms.

metronome *noun* (*plural* **metronomes**)
a device that makes a regular clicking noise to
help a person keep in time when practising
music.
[from Greek *metron* = measure + *nomos* = law]

mew *verb* (**mews**, **mewing**, **mewed**)
make a cat's cry. **mew** *noun*

mice *plural* of **mouse**.

micro- *prefix*
very small (as in *microfilm*).
[from Greek *mikros* = small]

microbe *noun* (*plural* **microbes**)
a micro-organism.
[from *micro-* + Greek *bios* = life]

microchip *noun* (*plural* **microchips**)
a very small piece of silicon etc. made to work
like a complex wired electric circuit.

microcosm *noun* (*plural* **microcosms**)
a world in miniature; something regarded as
resembling something else on a very small
scale.
[from Greek *mikros kosmos* = little world]

microfilm *noun*
a length of film on which written or printed
material is photographed in greatly reduced
size.

micron *noun* (*plural* **microns**)
a unit of measurement, one millionth of a
metre. [same origin as *micro-*]

microphone *noun* (*plural* **microphones**)
an electrical device that picks up sound waves
for recording, amplifying, or broadcasting.
[from *micro-* + Greek *phone* = sound]

microscope *noun* (*plural* **microscopes**)
an instrument with lenses that magnify tiny
objects or details.
[from *micro-* + Greek *skopein* = look at]

microscopic *adjective*
1 extremely small; too small to be seen without
the aid of a microscope. 2 to do with a
microscope.

microwave *noun* (*plural* **microwaves**)
1 a very short electromagnetic wave. 2 a
microwave oven.

microwave oven *noun* (*plural* **microwave ovens**)
an oven that uses microwaves to heat or cook
food very quickly.

midday *noun*
the middle of the day; noon.

middle *noun* (*plural* **middles**)
1 the place or part of something that is at the
same distance from all its sides or edges or
from both its ends. 2 someone's waist.
middle *adjective*
1 placed or happening in the middle.
2 moderate in size or rank etc.

Middle Ages *noun*
the period in history from about AD 1000 to 1400.

middle class or **classes** *noun*
the class of people between the upper class and the working class, including business and professional people such as teachers, doctors, and lawyers. **middle-class** *adjective*

Middle East *noun*
the countries from Egypt to Iran inclusive.

Middle English *noun*
the English language from about 1150 to 1500.

middle school *noun* (*plural* **middle schools**)
a school for children aged from about 9 to 13.

middling *adjective*
of medium size or quality.
middling *adverb*
fairly or moderately.

midge *noun* (*plural* **midges**)
a small insect like a gnat.

midget *noun* (*plural* **midgets**)
an extremely small person or thing.
midget *adjective* [from *midge*]

midland *adjective*
1 to do with the middle part of a country. 2 to do with the Midlands.

Midlands *plural noun*
the central part of England.

midnight *noun*
twelve o'clock at night.

midst *noun*
in the midst of in the middle of or surrounded by.
in our midst among us.

midsummer *noun*
the middle of summer, about 21 June in the northern hemisphere.

midway *adverb*
halfway.

midwife *noun* (*plural* **midwives**)
a person trained to look after a woman who is giving birth to a baby. **midwifery** *noun*
[from Old English *mid* = with + *wif* = woman]

might[1] *noun*
great strength or power.
with all your might using all your strength and determination.
[from Old English]

might[2] *auxiliary verb*
used 1 as the past tense of *may*[1] (*We told her she might go*), 2 to express possibility (*It might be true*).

mighty *adjective*
very strong or powerful.
mightily *adverb*, **mightiness** *noun*

migraine (*say* mee-grayn or my-grayn) *noun*
(*plural* **migraines**)
a severe kind of headache. [French]

migrate *verb* (**migrates, migrating, migrated**)
1 leave one place or country and settle in another. 2 (of birds or animals) move periodically from one area to another.
migration *noun*, **migratory** *adjective*

mild *adjective* (**milder, mildest**)
1 gentle; not harsh or severe. 2 not strongly flavoured. **mildly** *adverb*, **mildness** *noun*
[from Old English]

mildew *noun*
a tiny fungus that forms a white coating on things kept in damp conditions. **mildewed** *adjective* [from Old English]

mile *noun* (*plural* **miles**)
a measure of distance, 1,760 yards (about 1.6 kilometres).
[from Latin *mille* = thousand (paces)]

milestone *noun* (*plural* **milestones**)
1 a stone of a kind that used to be fixed beside a road to mark the distance between towns. 2 an important event in life or history.

militant *adjective*
1 eager to fight. 2 forceful or aggressive, *a militant protest*. **militant** *noun*, **militancy** *noun*
[same origin as *militate*]

military *adjective*
to do with soldiers or the armed forces. [from Latin *miles* = soldier]

milk *noun*
1 a white liquid that female mammals produce in their bodies to feed their babies. 2 the milk of cows, used as food by human beings. 3 a milky liquid, e.g. that in a coconut.
milk *verb* (**milks, milking, milked**)
get the milk from a cow or other animal.

milkman *noun* (*plural* **milkmen**)
a man who delivers milk to customers' houses.

milky *adjective* (**milkier, milkiest**)
1 like milk. 2 white.

Milky Way *noun*
the broad band of stars formed by our galaxy.

mill *noun* (*plural* **mills**)
1 machinery for grinding corn to make flour; a building containing this machinery. 2 a grinding machine, *a coffee mill*. 3 a factory for processing certain materials, *a paper mill*.
[via Old English from Latin *molere* = grind]

millennium *noun* (*plural* **millenniums**)
a period of 1,000 years. [from Latin *mille* = thousand + *annus* = year]

milli- *prefix*
1 one thousand (as in *millepede*). 2 one-thousandth (as in *milligram, millilitre, millimetre*). [from Latin *mille* = thousand]

million *noun* (*plural* millions)
one thousand thousand (1,000,000). **millionth**
adjective & *noun*
[French, related to *milli-*]

millionaire *noun* (*plural* millionaires)
an extremely rich person.

millstone *noun* (*plural* millstones)
either of a pair of large circular stones between
which corn is ground.
a millstone around someone's neck a heavy
responsibility or burden.

mimic *verb* (mimics, mimicking, mimicked)
imitate. **mimicry** *noun*
mimic *noun* (*plural* mimics)
a person who mimics others, especially to
amuse people. [same origin as *mime*]

mince *verb* (minces, mincing, minced)
1 cut into very small pieces in a machine.
2 walk in an affected way. **mincer** *noun*
not to mince matters speak bluntly.
mince *noun*
minced meat.
[from French; related to *minute*^{2}]

mincemeat *noun*
a sweet mixture of currants, raisins, apple, etc.
used in pies.
[from *mince* + an old sense of *meat* = food]

mince pie *noun* (*plural* mince pies)
a pie containing mincemeat.

mind *noun* (*plural* minds)
1 the ability to think, feel, understand, and
remember, originating in the brain. **2** a
person's thoughts and feelings or opinion, *I
changed my mind.*
mind *verb* (minds, minding, minded)
1 look after, *He was minding the baby.* **2** be
careful about, *Mind the step.* **3** be sad or upset
about something; object to, *We don't mind
waiting.* **minder** *noun*

mine^1 *possessive pronoun*
belonging to me.
[from Old English]

mine^2 *noun* (*plural* mines)
1 a place where coal, metal, precious stones,
etc. are dug out of the ground. **2** an explosive
placed in or on the ground or in the sea etc. to
destroy people or things that come close to it.
mine *verb* (mines, mining, mined)
1 dig from a mine. **2** lay explosive mines
in a place.
[from old French]

minefield *noun* (*plural* minefields)
1 an area where explosive mines have been
laid. **2** something with hidden dangers or
problems.

miner *noun* (*plural* miners)
a person who works in a mine.

mineral *noun* (*plural* minerals)
1 a hard inorganic substance found in the
ground. **2** a cold fizzy non-alcoholic drink.
[from Latin *minera* = ore]

mingle *verb* (mingles, mingling, mingled)
mix. [from Old English]

mingy *adjective* (mingier, mingiest) (*informal*)
not generous; mean.
[probably from *mean*^{2} + *stingy*]

mini- *prefix*
miniature; very small.
[short for *miniature*]

miniature *adjective*
1 very small. **2** copying something on a very
small scale, *a miniature railway.*
miniature *noun* (*plural* miniatures)
1 a very small portrait. **2** a small-scale model.
[from Italian]

minim *noun* (*plural* minims)
a note in music, lasting twice as long as a
crotchet (written ♩).
[same origin as *minimum*]

minimize *verb* (minimizes, minimizing,
minimized)
reduce something to a minimum.

minimum *noun* (*plural* minima or minimums)
the lowest possible number or amount. (The
opposite is *maximum*.) **minimal** *adjective*
[Latin, = least thing]

minister *noun* (*plural* ministers)
1 a person in charge of a government
department. **2** a member of the clergy.
ministerial *adjective* [Latin, = servant]

ministry *noun* (*plural* ministries)
1 a government department, *the Ministry of
Defence.* **2** the work of the clergy.
[same origin as *minister*]

minnow *noun* (*plural* minnows)
a tiny freshwater fish.

minor *adjective*
1 not very important, especially when
compared to something else. **2** to do with the
musical scale that has a semitone after the
second note. (Compare *major*.)
[Latin, = smaller, lesser]

minority *noun* (*plural* minorities)
1 the smallest part of a group of people or
things. **2** a small group that is different from
others. (Compare *majority*.)
[same origin as *minor*]

minstrel *noun* (*plural* minstrels)
a travelling singer and musician in the Middle
Ages.

mint^1 *noun* (*plural* mints)
1 a plant with fragrant leaves that are used for
flavouring things. **2** peppermint or a sweet
flavoured with this.
[from Latin *mentha* = mint]

mint[2] *noun* (*plural* mints)
the place where a country's coins are made.
in mint condition in perfect condition, as
though it had never been used.
mint *verb* (mints, minting, minted)
make coins.
[from Latin *moneta* = coins; a mint]

minus *preposition*
with the next number or thing subtracted, *Ten
minus four equals six* (10 − 4 = 6).
minus *adjective*
less than zero, *temperatures of minus ten
degrees* (−10°). [Latin, = less]

minute[1] (*say* min-it) *noun* (*plural* minutes)
1 one-sixtieth of an hour. **2** a very short time; a
moment. **3** a particular time, *Come here this
minute!* **4** one-sixtieth of a degree (used in
measuring angles). [from Latin *pars minuta
prima* = first little part]

minute[2] (*say* my-newt) *adjective*
1 very small, *a minute insect.* **2** very detailed, *a
minute examination.* **minutely** *adverb*
[from Latin *minutus* = little]

minutes *plural noun*
a written summary of what was said at a
meeting. [probably from Latin *minuta
scriptura* = small writing]

miracle *noun* (*plural* miracles)
something wonderful and good that happens,
especially something believed to have a
supernatural or divine cause.
miraculous *adjective*, **miraculously** *adverb*
[same origin as *mirror*]

mirage (*say* mi-rahzh) *noun* (*plural* mirages)
an illusion; something that seems to be there
but is not, especially when a lake seems to
appear in a desert. [French, from *se mirer* = be
reflected or mirrored]

mirror *noun* (*plural* mirrors)
a device or surface of reflecting material,
usually glass.
mirror *verb* (mirrors, mirroring, mirrored)
reflect in or like a mirror.
[from Latin *mirari* = to look at or wonder at]

mis- *prefix*
badly or wrongly. (Compare *amiss.*)
[from Old English *mis-* (related to *amiss*), or old
French *mes-* (related to *minus*)]

misbehave *verb* (misbehaves, misbehaving,
misbehaved)
behave badly. **misbehaviour** *noun*

miscalculate *verb* (miscalculates, miscalculating,
miscalculated)
calculate incorrectly. **miscalculation** *noun*

miscarriage *noun* (*plural* miscarriages)
1 the birth of a baby before it has developed
enough to live. **2** failure to achieve the right
result, *a miscarriage of justice.* [from *miscarry*
= to be lost, destroyed, or badly managed]

miscellaneous (*say* mis-el-ay-nee-us) *adjective*
of various kinds; mixed.
miscellany (*say* mis-el-an-ee) *noun*
[from Latin *miscellus* = mixed]

mischief *noun*
1 naughty or troublesome behaviour. **2** trouble
caused by this. **mischievous** *adjective*,
mischievously *adverb* [from old French
meschever = come to a bad end]

misconception *noun* (*plural* misconceptions)
a mistaken idea.

misconduct *noun*
bad behaviour by someone in a responsible
position, *professional misconduct.*

miser *noun* (*plural* misers)
a person who hoards money and spends as
little as possible. **miserly** *adjective*,
miserliness *noun* [same origin as *misery*]

miserable *adjective*
1 full of misery; very unhappy, poor, or
uncomfortable. **2** disagreeable or unpleasant,
miserable weather. **miserably** *adverb*
[same origin as *misery*]

misery *noun* (*plural* miseries)
1 great unhappiness or discomfort or
suffering, especially lasting for a long time.
2 (*informal*) a discontented or disagreeable
person. [from Latin *miser* = wretched]

misfire *verb* (misfires, misfiring, misfired)
1 fail to fire. **2** fail to function correctly or to
have the required effect, *The joke misfired.*

misfit *noun* (*plural* misfits)
a person who does not fit in well with other
people or who is not well suited to his or her
work.

misfortune *noun* (*plural* misfortunes)
1 bad luck. **2** an unlucky event or accident.

misgiving *noun* (*plural* misgivings)
a feeling of doubt or slight fear or mistrust.
[from an old word *misgive* = give someone bad
feelings about something]

misguided *adjective*
guided by mistaken ideas or beliefs.

mishap (*say* mis-hap) *noun* (*plural* mishaps)
an unlucky accident.
[from *mis-* + Middle English *hap* = luck]

misinterpret *verb* (misinterprets, misinterpreting,
misinterpreted)
interpret incorrectly.
misinterpretation *noun*

mislay *verb* (mislays, mislaying, mislaid)
lose something for a short time because you
cannot remember where you put it.

mislead *verb* (misleads, misleading, misled)
give somebody a wrong idea; deceive.

misnomer *noun* (*plural* misnomers)
an unsuitable name for something.
[from *mis-* + Latin *nomen* = name]

misogynist (*say* mis-oj-in-ist) *noun* (*plural* misogynists)
a person who hates women. **misogyny** *noun*
[from Greek *misos* = hatred + *gyne* = woman]

misplaced *adjective*
1 placed wrongly. 2 inappropriate, *misplaced sympathy*. **misplacement** *noun*

misprint *noun* (*plural* misprints)
a mistake in printing.

misrepresent *verb* (misrepresents, misrepresenting, misrepresented)
represent in a false or misleading way.
misrepresentation *noun*

Miss *noun* (*plural* Misses)
a title put before a girl's or unmarried woman's name. [short for *mistress*]

miss *verb* (misses, missing, missed)
1 fail to hit, reach, catch, see, hear, or find something. 2 be sad because someone or something is not with you. 3 notice that something has gone.
miss *noun* (*plural* misses)
missing something, *Was that shot a hit or a miss?* [from Old English]

misshapen *adjective*
badly shaped. [from *mis-* + *shapen*, the old past participle of *shape*]

missile *noun* (*plural* missiles)
a weapon or other object for firing or throwing at a target.
[from Latin *missum* = sent]

missing *adjective*
1 lost; not in the proper place. 2 absent.

mission *noun* (*plural* missions)
1 an important job that somebody is sent to do or feels he or she must do. 2 a place or building where missionaries work.
[from Latin *missio* = sending someone out]

missionary *noun* (*plural* missionaries)
a person who is sent to another country to spread a religious faith.

mist *noun* (*plural* mists)
1 damp cloudy air near the ground.
2 condensed water vapour on a window, mirror, etc. [from Old English]

mistake *noun* (*plural* mistakes)
1 something done wrongly. 2 an incorrect opinion.
mistake *verb* (mistakes, mistaking, mistook, mistaken)
1 misunderstand, *Don't mistake my meaning.*
2 choose or identify wrongly, *We mistook her for her sister.*
[from *mis-* + Old Norse *taka* = take]

mistaken *adjective*
1 incorrect. 2 having an incorrect opinion.

mistletoe *noun*
a plant with white berries that grows as a parasite on trees. [from Old English]

mistress *noun* (*plural* mistresses)
1 a woman who is in charge of something. 2 a woman teacher. 3 a woman who is a man's lover but not his wife.
[from old French *maistresse*, feminine form of *maistre* = master]

mistrust *verb* (mistrusts, mistrusting, mistrusted)
feel no trust in somebody or something.
mistrust *noun*

misty *adjective* (mistier, mistiest)
1 full of mist. 2 not clear or distinct.
mistily *adverb*, **mistiness** *noun*

misunderstand *verb* (misunderstands, misunderstanding, misunderstood)
get a wrong idea or impression of something.

mitigating circumstances *plural noun*
facts that may partially excuse wrongdoing.
[from Latin *mitigare* = make mild]

mitten *noun* (*plural* mittens)
a kind of glove without separate parts for the fingers. [from French]

mix *verb* (mixes, mixing, mixed)
1 put different things together so that the substances etc. are no longer distinct; blend or combine. 2 (of a person) get together with others. **mixer** *noun*
mix up 1 mix thoroughly. 2 confuse.
mix *noun* (*plural* mixes)
a mixture. [from *mixed*]

mixed *adjective*
containing two or more kinds of things or people. [from Latin *mixtus* = mingled]

mixture *noun* (*plural* mixtures)
1 something made of different things mixed together. 2 the process of mixing.

mnemonic (*say* nim-on-ik) *noun* (*plural* mnemonics)
a verse or saying that helps you to remember something. [from Greek *mnemonikos* = for the memory]

moan *verb* (moans, moaning, moaned)
1 make a long low sound of pain or suffering.
2 grumble. **moan** *noun*

moat *noun* (*plural* moats)
a deep wide ditch round a castle, usually filled with water. **moated** *adjective*

mob *noun* (*plural* mobs)
1 a large disorderly crowd; a rabble. 2 a gang.
[from Latin *mobile vulgus* = excitable crowd]

mobile *adjective*
moving easily. **mobility** *noun*

mobile *noun* (*plural* mobiles)
a decoration for hanging up so that its parts move in currents of air.
[from Latin *movere* = move]

mobile home *noun* (*plural* mobile homes)
a large caravan permanently parked and used for living in.

mobilize *verb* (mobilizes, mobilizing, mobilized)
assemble people or things for a particular purpose, especially for war.
mobilization *noun*

mock *verb* (mocks, mocking, mocked)
1 make fun of a person or thing. 2 imitate someone or something to make people laugh.
mockery *noun*
mock *adjective*
imitation, not real, *mock exams.*

mock-up *noun* (*plural* mock-ups)
a model of something, made in order to test or study it.

mode *noun* (*plural* modes)
1 the way a thing is done. 2 what is fashionable. [from Latin]

model *noun* (*plural* models)
1 a copy of an object, usually on a smaller scale. 2 a particular design. 3 a person who poses for an artist or displays clothes by wearing them. 4 a person or thing that is worth copying.
model *verb* (models, modelling, modelled)
1 make a model of something. 2 make according to a model. 3 work as an artist's model or a fashion model.
[from Latin *modulus* = a small measure]

modem (*say* moh-dem) *noun* (*plural* modems)
a device that links a computer to a telephone line. [from *mo*dulator + *dem*odulator]

moderate *adjective*
1 medium; not extremely small or great or hot etc., *a moderate climate.* 2 not extreme or unreasonable, *moderate opinions.*
moderately *adverb*
moderate (*say* mod-er-ayt) *verb* (moderates, moderating, moderated)
make or become moderate.
moderation *noun*
in moderation in moderate amounts.
[from Latin *moderari* = restrain]

modern *adjective*
1 belonging to the present or recent times. 2 in fashion now. **modernity** *noun*
[from Latin *modo* = just now]

modernize *verb* (modernizes, modernizing, modernized)
make a thing more modern.
modernization *noun*

modest *adjective*
1 not vain or boastful. 2 moderate, *a modest income.* 3 not showy or splendid. 4 behaving or dressing decently or decorously.
modestly *adverb*, **modesty** *noun*
[from Latin, = keeping the proper measure]

modify *verb* (modifies, modifying, modified)
1 change something slightly. 2 describe a word or limit its meaning, *Adjectives modify nouns.*
modification *noun*
[from Latin *modificare* = to limit]

modulate *verb* (modulates, modulating, modulated)
1 adjust or regulate. 2 vary in pitch or tone etc. 3 alter an electronic wave to allow signals to be sent. **modulation** *noun*, **modulator** *noun*
[same origin as *model*]

module *noun* (*plural* modules)
1 an independent part of a spacecraft, building, etc. 2 a unit; a section of a course of study.
modular *adjective*
[same origin as *model*]

moist *adjective*
slightly wet; damp. **moistly** *adverb*,
moistness *noun* [from old French]

moisten *verb* (moistens, moistening, moistened)
make or become moist.

moisture *noun*
water in the air or making a thing moist.

mole[1] *noun* (*plural* moles)
1 a small furry animal that burrows under the ground. 2 a person who secretly gives confidential information to an enemy or rival.
[probably from old Dutch]

mole[2] *noun* (*plural* moles)
a small dark spot on skin.
[from Old English]

molecule *noun* (*plural* molecules)
the smallest part into which a substance can be divided without changing its chemical nature; a group of atoms. **molecular** *adjective*
[from Latin *molecula* = little mass]

molehill *noun* (*plural* molehills)
a small pile of earth thrown up by a burrowing mole.

mollusc *noun* (*plural* molluscs)
an animal with no backbone and a soft body protected by a shell; snails and many shellfish are molluscs.
[from Latin *molluscus* = soft thing]

molten *adjective*
melted; made liquid by great heat.
[the old past participle of *melt*]

moment *noun* (*plural* moments)
1 a very short time. 2 a particular time, *Call me the moment she arrives.*
[from Latin *movere* = move]

momentary *adjective*
lasting for only a moment.
momentarily *adverb*

momentous (*say* mo-ment-us) *adjective*
very important.
[from an old sense of *moment* = importance]

momentum *noun*
amount or force of movement, *The stone gathered momentum as it rolled downhill.*
[Latin, = movement]

monarch *noun* (*plural* monarchs)
a king, queen, emperor, or empress ruling a country. **monarchic** *adjective* [from Greek *monos* = alone + *archein* = to rule]

monarchy *noun* (*plural* monarchies)
a country ruled by a monarch.
monarchist *noun*

monastery *noun* (*plural* monasteries)
a building where monks live and work.
monastic *adjective*
[from Greek *monazein* = live alone]

monetary *adjective*
to do with money.

money *noun*
1 coins and banknotes. 2 wealth.
[same origin as *mint*²]

mongrel (*say* mung-rel) *noun* (*plural* mongrels)
a dog of mixed breeds. [related to *mingle*]

monitor *noun* (*plural* monitors)
1 a device for watching or testing how something is working. 2 a pupil who is given a special responsibility in a school.
monitor *verb* (monitors, monitoring, monitored)
watch or test how something is working. [from Latin *monere* = warn]

monk *noun* (*plural* monks)
a member of a community of men who live according to the rules of a religious organization. (Compare *nun*.)
[via Old English from Greek *monachos* = single or solitary]

monkey *noun* (*plural* monkeys)
1 an animal with long arms, hands with thumbs, and often a tail. 2 a mischievous person. [origin unknown]

mono- *prefix*
1 one. 2 single. [from Greek *monos* = alone]

monocle *noun* (*plural* monocles)
a lens worn over one eye, like half of a pair of spectacles.
[from *mono-* + Latin *oculus* = eye]

monogram *noun* (*plural* monograms)
a design made up of a letter or letters, especially a person's initials.
monogrammed *adjective*
[from *mono-* + *-gram*]

monolith *noun* (*plural* monoliths)
a large single upright block of stone.
[from *mono-* + Greek *lithos* = stone]

monolithic *adjective*
1 consisting of monoliths. 2 to do with or like a monolith. 3 huge and difficult to move or change.

monologue *noun* (*plural* monologues)
a speech by one person.
[from *mono-* + Greek *logos* = word]

monopolize *verb* (monopolizes, monopolizing, monopolized)
take the whole of something for yourself, *One girl monopolized my attention.*
monopolization *noun* [from *monopoly*]

monopoly *noun* (*plural* monopolies)
complete possession or control of something by one group, *The company had a monopoly in supplying electricity.*
[from *mono-* + Greek *polein* = sell]

monosyllable *noun* (*plural* monosyllables)
a word with only one syllable.
monosyllabic *adjective*

monotone *noun*
a level unchanging tone of voice in speaking or singing.

monotonous *adjective*
boring because it does not change.
monotonously *adverb*, **monotony** *noun*
[from *mono-* + Greek *tonos* = tone]

monsoon *noun* (*plural* monsoons)
1 a strong wind in and near the Indian Ocean, bringing heavy rain in summer. 2 the rainy season brought by this wind.
[via Dutch from Arabic *mawsim* = a season]

monster *noun* (*plural* monsters)
1 a large frightening creature. 2 a huge thing. 3 a wicked or cruel person.
monster *adjective*
huge. [from Latin *monstrum* = marvel]

monstrosity *noun* (*plural* monstrosities)
a monstrous thing.

monstrous *adjective*
1 like a monster; huge. 2 very shocking or outrageous.

month *noun* (*plural* months)
each of the twelve parts into which a year is divided. [from Old English; related to *moon* (because time was measured by the changes in the moon's appearance)]

monthly *adjective* & *adverb*
happening or done once a month.

monument *noun* (*plural* monuments)
a statue, building, or column etc. put up as a memorial of some person or event.
[from Latin *monumentum* = a memorial]

monumental *adjective*
1 built as a monument. 2 very large or important.

moo *verb* (moos, mooing, mooed)
make the low deep sound of a cow. **moo** *noun*
[imitating the sound]

mood *noun* (*plural* moods)
the way someone feels, *She is in a cheerful mood.* [from Old English]

moody *adjective* (moodier, moodiest)
1 gloomy or sullen. 2 having sudden changes of mood for no apparent reason. **moodily** *adverb*, **moodiness** *noun*

moon *noun* (*plural* moons)
1 the natural satellite of the earth that can be seen in the sky at night. 2 a satellite of any planet. **moonbeam** *noun*, **moonlight** *noun*, **moonlit** *adjective*

moor[1] *noun* (*plural* moors)
an area of rough land covered with heather, bracken, and bushes. **moorland** *noun* [from Old English]

moor[2] *verb* (moors, mooring, moored)
fasten a boat etc. to a fixed object by means of a cable. [probably from old German]

mooring *noun* (*plural* moorings)
a place where a boat can be moored.

mop *noun* (*plural* mops)
1 a bunch or pad of soft material fastened on the end of a stick, used for cleaning floors etc. 2 a thick mass of hair.
mop *verb* (mops, mopping, mopped)
clean or wipe with a mop etc.
mop up 1 wipe or soak up liquid. 2 deal with the last parts of something, *The army is mopping up the last of the rebels.*

mope *verb* (mopes, moping, moped)
be sad.

moped (*say* moh-ped) *noun* (*plural* mopeds)
a kind of small motorcycle that can be pedalled. [from *motor* + *pedal*]

moral *adjective*
1 connected with what is right and wrong in behaviour. 2 virtuous.
morally *adverb*, **morality** *noun*
moral support encouragement.
moral *noun* (*plural* morals)
a lesson in right behaviour taught by a story or event.
[from Latin *mores* = customs]

USAGE: Do not confuse with *morale*.

morale (*say* mor-ahl) *noun*
the level of confidence and good spirits in a person or group of people, *Morale was high after the victory.* [same origin as *moral*]

USAGE: Do not confuse with *moral*.

morals *plural noun*
standards of behaviour.

morbid *adjective*
1 thinking about gloomy or unpleasant things. 2 unhealthy.
morbidly *adverb*, **morbidity** *noun*
[from Latin *morbus* = disease]

more *adjective* (comparative of **much** and **many**)
greater in amount etc.
more *noun*
a greater amount.
more *adverb*
1 to a greater extent, *more beautiful.* 2 again, *once more.*
more or less 1 approximately. 2 nearly or practically.

moreover *adverb*
besides; in addition to what has been said.

Mormon *noun* (*plural* Mormons)
a member of a religious group founded in the USA. [the name of a prophet who they believe wrote their sacred book]

morning *noun* (*plural* mornings)
the early part of the day, before noon or before lunchtime. [from *morn*]

moron *noun* (*plural* morons) (*informal*)
a very stupid person. **moronic** *adjective* [from Greek *moros* = foolish]

morose (*say* mo-rohss) *adjective*
bad-tempered and miserable. **morosely** *adverb*, **moroseness** *noun* [from Latin]

Morse code
a signalling code using short and long sounds or flashes of light (dots and dashes) to represent letters. [named after its American inventor, S. F. B. Morse]

morsel *noun* (*plural* morsels)
a small piece of food. [from old French]

mortal *adjective*
1 not living for ever, *All of us are mortal.* 2 causing death; fatal, *a mortal wound.* 3 deadly, *mortal enemies.*
mortally *adverb*, **mortality** *noun*
mortal *noun* (*plural* mortals)
a human being, as compared to a god or immortal spirit.
[from Latin *mortis* = of death]

mortar *noun* (*plural* mortars)
1 a mixture of sand, cement, and water used in building to stick bricks together. 2 a hard bowl in which substances are pounded with a pestle. 3 a short cannon.

mortgage (*say* mor-gij) *noun* (*plural* mortgages)
an arrangement to borrow money to buy a house, with the house as security for the loan.
mortgage *verb* (mortgages, mortgaging, mortgaged)
offer a house etc. as security in return for a loan. [from old French]

mortify *verb* (mortifies, mortifying, mortified)
humiliate someone or make them feel very
ashamed. **mortification** *noun*
[originally = kill or destroy: from Latin *mors*
= death]

mortuary *noun* (*plural* mortuaries)
a place where dead bodies are kept before
being buried. [from Latin *mortuus* = dead]

mosaic (*say* mo-**zay**-ik) *noun* (*plural* mosaics)
a picture or design made from small coloured
pieces of stone or glass.
[via old French from Italian]

mosque (*say* mosk) *noun* (*plural* mosques)
a building where Muslims worship.
[via French and Italian from Arabic]

mosquito *noun* (*plural* mosquitoes)
a kind of gnat that sucks blood.
[Spanish or Portuguese, = little fly]

moss *noun* (*plural* mosses)
a plant that grows in damp places and has no
flowers. **mossy** *adjective*

most *adjective* (superlative of **much** and **many**)
greatest in amount etc., *Most people came by
bus.*
most *noun*
the greatest amount, *Most of the food was eaten.*
most *adverb*
1 to the greatest extent; more than any other,
most beautiful. 2 very or extremely, *most
impressive.* [from Old English]

-most *suffix*
forms superlative adjectives (e.g. *hindmost,
uppermost*). [from Old English *-mest*]

mostly *adverb*
mainly.

motel *noun* (*plural* motels)
a hotel providing accommodation for motorists
and their cars.
[from *motor* + ho*tel*]

moth *noun* (*plural* moths)
an insect rather like a butterfly, that usually
flies at night. [from Old English]

mother *noun* (*plural* mothers)
a female parent. **motherhood** *noun*
mother *verb* (mothers, mothering, mothered)
look after someone in a motherly way.

mother-in-law *noun* (*plural* mothers-in-law)
the mother of a married person's husband or
wife.

motherly *adjective*
kind and gentle like a mother.
motherliness *noun*

motion *noun* (*plural* motions)
1 a way of moving; movement. 2 a formal
statement to be discussed and voted on at a
meeting.
motion *verb* (motions, motioning, motioned)
signal by a gesture, *She motioned him to sit
beside her.* [from Latin *motio* = movement]

motive *noun* (*plural* motives)
what makes a person do something, *a motive
for murder.* [from Latin *motivus* = moving]

motor *noun* (*plural* motors)
a machine providing power to drive
machinery etc.; an engine.
motor *verb* (motors, motoring, motored)
go or take someone in a car.
[Latin, = mover]

motorist *noun* (*plural* motorists)
a person who drives a car.

motorway *noun* (*plural* motorways)
a wide road for fast long-distance traffic.

motto *noun* (*plural* mottoes)
1 a short saying used as a guide for behaviour,
Their motto is 'Who dares, wins'. 2 a short verse
or riddle etc. found inside a cracker. [Italian]

mould[1] *noun* (*plural* moulds)
a hollow container of a particular shape, in
which a liquid or soft substance is put to set
into this shape.
mould *verb* (moulds, moulding, moulded)
make something have a particular shape or
character.
[from Latin *modulus* = little measure]

mould[2] *noun*
a fine furry growth of very small fungi.
mouldy *adjective* [from Old Norse]

moulder *verb* (moulders, mouldering, mouldered)
rot away or decay into dust.

moult *verb* (moults, moulting, moulted)
shed feathers, hair, or skin etc. while a new
growth forms. [from Latin *mutari* = to change,
probably via Old English]

mound *noun* (*plural* mounds)
1 a pile of earth or stones etc. 2 a small hill.

mount *verb* (mounts, mounting, mounted)
1 climb or go up; ascend. 2 get on a horse or
bicycle etc. 3 increase in amount, *Our costs
mounted.* 4 place or fix in position for use or
display, *Mount your photos in an album.*
mount *noun* (*plural* mounts)
1 a mountain, *Mount Everest.* 2 something on
which an object is mounted. 3 a horse etc. for
riding.
[from Latin *mons* = mountain]

mountain *noun* (*plural* mountains)
1 a very high hill. 2 a large heap or pile or
quantity. **mountainous** *adjective*
[from old French; related to *mount*]

mountaineer *noun* (*plural* mountaineers)
a person who climbs mountains.
mountaineering *noun*

mounted *adjective*
serving on horseback, *mounted police.*

mourn *verb* (mourns, mourning, mourned)
be sad, especially because someone has died.
mourner *noun* [from Old English]

mournful *adjective*
sad and sorrowful. **mournfully** *adverb*

mouse *noun* (*plural* **mice**)
1 a small animal with a long thin tail and a pointed nose. 2 (*plural* **mouses** or **mice**) a small device which you move around on a mat to control a computer.
mousetrap *noun*, **mousy** *adjective*
[from Old English]

mousse (*say* mooss) *noun* (*plural* **mousses**)
1 a creamy pudding flavoured with fruit or chocolate. 2 a frothy creamy substance put on the hair so that it can be styled more easily.
[French, = froth]

moustache (*say* mus-tahsh) *noun* (*plural* **moustaches**)
hair allowed to grow on a man's upper lip.

mouth *noun* (*plural* **mouths**)
1 the opening through which food is taken into the body. 2 the place where a river enters the sea. 3 an opening or outlet. **mouthful** *noun*

mouth organ *noun* (*plural* **mouth organs**)
a small musical instrument that you play by blowing and sucking while passing it along your lips.

move *verb* (**moves, moving, moved**)
1 take or go from one place to another; change a person's or thing's position. 2 affect a person's feelings, *Their sad story moved us deeply.* 3 put forward a formal statement (a *motion*) to be discussed and voted on at a meeting.
mover *noun*
move *noun* (*plural* **moves**)
1 a movement. 2 a player's turn to move a piece in chess etc.
get a move on (*informal*) hurry up.
on the move moving or making progress.

movement *noun* (*plural* **movements**)
1 moving or being moved. 2 a group of people working together to achieve something. 3 one of the main divisions of a symphony or other long musical work.

mow *verb* (**mows, mowing, mowed, mown**)
cut down grass etc.
mower *noun*
mow down knock down and kill.

MP *abbreviation*
Member of Parliament.

Mr (*say* mist-er) *noun* (*plural* **Messrs**)
a title put before a man's name.
[short for *mister*]

Mrs (*say* mis-iz) *noun* (*plural* **Mrs**)
a title put before a married woman's name.
[short for *mistress*]

Ms (*say* miz) *noun*
a title put before a woman's name.
[from *Mrs* and *Miss*]

USAGE: You put *Ms* before the name of a woman if she does not wish to be called 'Miss' or 'Mrs', or if you do not know whether she is married.

M.Sc. *abbreviation*
Master of Science.

Mt *abbreviation*
mount or mountain.

much *adjective* (**more, most**)
existing in a large amount, *much noise.*
much *noun*
a large amount of something.
much *adverb*
1 greatly or considerably, *much to my surprise.*
2 approximately, *It is much the same.*
[from Old English]

muck *noun*
1 farmyard manure. 2 (*informal*) dirt or filth.
3 (*informal*) a mess. **mucky** *adjective*
muck *verb*
muck about (*informal*) mess about.
muck out clean out the place where an animal is kept.
muck up (*informal*) 1 make dirty. 2 make a mess of; spoil.
[probably from a Scandinavian language]

mud *noun*
wet soft earth. **muddy** *adjective*, **muddiness** *noun* [probably from old German]

muddle *verb* (**muddles, muddling, muddled**)
1 jumble or mix things up. 2 confuse.
muddler *noun*
muddle *noun* (*plural* **muddles**)
a muddled condition or thing; confusion or disorder. [origin unknown]

mudguard *noun* (*plural* **mudguards**)
a curved cover over the top part of the wheel of a bicycle etc. to protect the rider from the mud and water thrown up by the wheel.

muff *noun* (*plural* **muffs**)
a short tube-shaped piece of warm material into which the hands are pushed from opposite ends. [from Dutch]

muffin *noun* (*plural* **muffins**)
1 a flat bun eaten toasted and buttered. 2 a small sponge cake, usually containing fruit, chocolate chips, etc.

muffle *verb* (**muffles, muffling, muffled**)
1 cover or wrap something to protect it or keep it warm. 2 deaden the sound of something, *a muffled scream.*

muffler *noun* (*plural* **mufflers**)
a warm scarf. [from *muffle*]

mug *noun* (*plural* **mugs**)
1 a kind of large cup, usually used without a saucer. **2** (*slang*) a fool; a person who is easily deceived. **3** (*slang*) a person's face.
mug *verb* (**mugs, mugging, mugged**)
attack and rob somebody in the street.
mugger *noun*

mule *noun* (*plural* **mules**)
an animal that is the offspring of a donkey and a mare, known for being stubborn. **mulish** *adjective* [from Old English]

mull[1] *verb* (**mulls, mulling, mulled**)
heat wine or beer with sugar and spices, as a drink, *mulled ale*. [origin unknown]

mull[2] *verb* (**mulls, mulling, mulled**)
mull something over think about something carefully; ponder.
[probably related to *mill*]

multi- *prefix*
many (as in *multicoloured* = with many colours). [from Latin *multus* = many]

multicultural *adjective*
made up of people of many different races, religions, and cultures.

multilateral *adjective*
(of an agreement or treaty) made between three or more people or countries etc. [from Latin *multilaterus* = many sided]

multimedia *adjective*
using more than one medium, *a multimedia show with pictures, lights, and music.*
multimedia *noun*
a computer program with sound and still and moving pictures linked to the text.

multimillionaire *noun* (*plural* **multimillionaires**)
a person with a fortune of several million pounds.

multinational *noun* (*plural* **multinationals**)
a large business company which works in several countries.

multiple *adjective*
having many parts.
multiple *noun* (*plural* **multiples**)
a number that contains another number (a *factor*) an exact amount of times with no remainder, *8 and 12 are multiples of 4.* [same origin as *multiply*]

multiple sclerosis *noun*
a disease of the nervous system which makes a person unable to control their movements, and may affect their sight.

multiply *verb* (**multiplies, multiplying, multiplied**)
1 take a number a given quantity of times, *Five multiplied by four equals twenty* (5 × 4 = 20).
2 make or become many; increase.
multiplication *noun*, **multiplier** *noun*
[from Latin *multiplex* = many-sided]

multiracial *adjective*
consisting of people of many different races.

multitude *noun* (*plural* **multitudes**)
a great number of people or things.
multitudinous *adjective*
[from Latin *multus* = many]

mumble *verb* (**mumbles, mumbling, mumbled**)
speak indistinctly so that you are not easy to hear. **mumble** *noun*, **mumbler** *noun*

mumbo-jumbo *noun*
talk or ceremony that has no real meaning.
[probably from a West African language]

mummy *noun* (*plural* **mummies**)
a corpse wrapped in cloth and treated with oils etc. before being buried so that it does not decay, as was the custom in ancient Egypt.
mummify *verb* [from Arabic]

mumps *noun*
an infectious disease that causes the neck to swell painfully. [from an old word *mump* = pull a face (because the glands in the face sometimes swell)]

munitions *plural noun*
military weapons and ammunition etc. [from Latin *munitum* = fortified]

mural *adjective*
on or to do with a wall.
mural *noun* (*plural* **murals**)
a wall painting. [from Latin *murus* = wall]

murder *verb* (**murders, murdering, murdered**)
kill a person unlawfully and deliberately.
murderer *noun*, **murderess** *noun*
murder *noun* (*plural* **murders**)
the murdering of somebody.
murderous *adjective* [from Old English]

murky *adjective* (**murkier, murkiest**)
dark and gloomy. **murk** *noun*,
murkiness *noun* [from Old English]

murmur *verb* (**murmurs, murmuring, murmured**)
1 make a low continuous sound. **2** speak in a soft voice. **murmur** *noun* [from Latin]

muscle *noun* (*plural* **muscles**)
1 a band or bundle of fibrous tissue that can contract and relax and so produce movement in parts of the body. **2** the power of muscles; strength. **muscular** *adjective*, **muscularity** *noun*
[from Latin]

museum *noun* (*plural* **museums**)
a place where interesting, old, or valuable objects are displayed for people to see. [from Greek *mouseion* = place of Muses (goddesses of the arts and sciences)]

mush *noun*
soft pulp. **mushy** *adjective*
[different spelling of *mash*]

mushroom *noun* (*plural* **mushrooms**)
an edible fungus with a stem and a dome-shaped top.

music *noun*
1 a pattern of pleasant or interesting sounds made by instruments or by the voice. 2 printed or written symbols which stand for musical sounds. [from Greek *mousike* = of the Muses (see *museum*)]
musical *adjective*
1 to do with music. 2 producing music. 3 good at music or interested in it. **musically** *adverb*
musical *noun* (*plural* musicals)
a play or film containing a lot of songs.

musician *noun* (*plural* musicians)
someone who plays a musical instrument.

Muslim *noun* (*plural* Muslims)
a person who follows the religious teachings of Muhammad (who lived in about 570–632), set out in the Koran. [Arabic, = someone who submits to God]

must *auxiliary verb*
used to express 1 necessity or obligation (*You must go*), 2 certainty (*You must be joking!*) [from Old English]

mustard *noun*
a yellow paste or powder used to give food a hot taste.
mustard and cress small green plants eaten in salads.

muster *noun* (*plural* musters)
an assembly of people or things.
pass muster be up to the required standard. [from Latin *monstrare* = to show]

mustn't (*mainly spoken*)
must not.

musty *adjective* (mustier, mustiest)
smelling or tasting mouldy or stale.
mustiness *noun* [probably from *moist*]

mutation *noun* (*plural* mutations)
a change in the form of a living creature because of changes in its genes.

mute *adjective*
1 silent; not speaking or able to speak. 2 not pronounced, *The g in 'gnat' is mute.*
mutely *adverb*, **muteness** *noun*

mutilate *verb* (mutilates, mutilating, mutilated)
damage something by breaking or cutting off part of it. **mutilation** *noun*
[from Latin *mutilus* = maimed]

mutineer *noun* (*plural* mutineers)
a person who mutinies.

mutiny *noun* (*plural* mutinies)
rebellion against authority, especially refusal by members of the armed forces to obey orders. **mutinous** *adjective*, **mutinously** *adverb*
mutiny *verb* (mutinies, mutinying, mutinied)
take part in a mutiny. [from old French]

mutter *verb* (mutters, muttering, muttered)
1 speak in a low voice. 2 grumble. **mutter** *noun*
[related to *mute*]

mutton *noun*
meat from a sheep. [from old French]

mutual (*say* mew-tew-al) *adjective*
1 given or done to each other, *mutual destruction.* 2 felt by each for the other, *mutual affection.* **mutually** *adverb*

muzzle *noun* (*plural* muzzles)
1 an animal's nose and mouth. 2 a cover put over an animal's nose and mouth so that it cannot bite. 3 the open end of a gun.
muzzle *verb* (muzzles, muzzling, muzzled)
1 put a muzzle on an animal. 2 silence; prevent a person from expressing opinions. [from old French]

my *adjective*
belonging to me. [originally, the form of *mine*[1] used before consonants]

myself *pronoun*
I or me and nobody else. (Compare *herself.*)

mysterious *adjective*
full of mystery; puzzling. **mysteriously** *adverb*

mystery *noun* (*plural* mysteries)
something that cannot be explained or understood; something puzzling. [from Greek *mysterion* = a secret thing or ceremony]

mystic *adjective*
1 having a spiritual meaning. 2 mysterious and filling people with wonder. **mystical** *adjective*, **mystically** *adverb*, **mysticism** *noun*
mystic *noun* (*plural* mystics)
a person who seeks to obtain spiritual contact with God by deep religious meditation. [from Greek *mystikos* = secret]

mystify *verb* (mystifies, mystifying, mystified)
puzzle or bewilder. **mystification** *noun*

myth (*say* mith) *noun* (*plural* myths)
1 an old story containing ideas about ancient times or about supernatural beings. (Compare *legend.*) 2 an untrue story or belief. [from Greek *mythos* = story]

mythical *adjective*
imaginary; found only in myths, *a mythical animal.*

mythology *noun*
myths or the study of myths.
mythological *adjective*

Nn

N. *abbreviation*
1 north. 2 northern.

nag *verb* (nags, nagging, nagged)
1 pester a person by keeping on criticizing, complaining, or asking for things. 2 keep on hurting, *a nagging pain.*

nail noun (plural **nails**)
1 the hard covering over the end of a finger or toe. 2 a small sharp piece of metal hammered in to fasten pieces of wood etc. together.
nail verb (**nails, nailing, nailed**)
1 fasten with a nail or nails. 2 catch; arrest.
[from Old English]

naked adjective
without any clothes or coverings on.
nakedly adverb, **nakedness** noun

naked eye noun
the eye when it is not helped by a telescope or microscope etc.

name noun (plural **names**)
1 the word or words by which a person, animal, place, or thing is known. 2 a reputation.
name verb (**names, naming, named**)
1 give a name to. 2 state the name or names of.
name the day decide when something, especially a wedding, is to take place or happen, Have you two named the day yet?

namely adverb
that is to say, My two favourite subjects are sciences, namely chemistry and biology.

nap noun (plural **naps**)
a short sleep.
catch a person napping catch a person unprepared for something or not alert.

napkin noun (plural **napkins**)
1 a piece of cloth or paper used to keep your clothes clean or to wipe your lips or fingers; a serviette, a table napkin. 2 a nappy.
[from French nappe = tablecloth, + -kin]

nappy noun (plural **nappies**)
a piece of cloth or other fabric put round a baby's bottom.

narcotic noun (plural **narcotics**)
a drug that makes a person sleepy or unconscious. **narcotic** adjective, **narcosis** noun
[from Greek narke = numbness]

narrative noun (plural **narratives**)
a spoken or written account of something.

narrow adjective
1 not wide or broad. 2 uncomfortably close; with only a small margin of safety, a narrow escape. **narrowly** adverb

narrow-minded adjective
not tolerant of other people's beliefs and ways.

nasty adjective (**nastier, nastiest**)
1 unpleasant. 2 unkind. **nastily** adverb, **nastiness** noun [origin unknown]

nation noun (plural **nations**)
a large community of people most of whom have the same ancestors, language, history, and customs, and who usually live in the same part of the world under one government.
national adjective & noun, **nationally** adverb
[from Latin natio = birth or race]

national anthem noun (plural **national anthems**)
a nation's official song, which is played or sung on important occasions.

national curriculum noun
the subjects that must be taught by state schools in England and Wales.

nationalist noun (plural **nationalists**)
1 a person who is very patriotic. 2 a person who wants his or her country to be independent and not to form part of another country, Scottish Nationalists.
nationalism noun, **nationalistic** adjective

nationality noun (plural **nationalities**)
the condition of belonging to a particular nation, What is his nationality?

nationalize verb (**nationalizes, nationalizing, nationalized**)
put an industry etc. under public ownership.
nationalization noun

national park noun (plural **national parks**)
an area of natural beauty which is protected by the government and which the public may visit.

native noun (plural **natives**)
a person born in a particular place, He is a native of Sweden.
native adjective
1 belonging to a person because of the place of his or her birth, my native country. 2 natural; belonging to a person by nature, native ability.
[from Latin nativus = natural or innate]

Native American noun (plural **Native Americans**)
one of the original inhabitants of North and South America.

USAGE: See note at **Indian**.

natural adjective
1 produced or done by nature, not by people or machines. 2 normal; not surprising. 3 (of a note in music) neither sharp nor flat.
naturally adverb, **naturalness** noun
natural noun (plural **naturals**)
1 a person who is naturally good at something. 2 a natural note in music; a sign (♮) that shows this.

natural history noun
the study of plants and animals.

naturalist noun (plural **naturalists**)
an expert in natural history.

natural science noun
the study of physics, chemistry, and biology.

natural selection noun
Charles Darwin's theory that only the plants and animals best suited to their surroundings will survive and breed.

nature noun (plural **natures**)
1 everything in the world that was not made by people. 2 the qualities and characteristics of a person or thing, *She has a loving nature.* 3 a kind or sort of thing, *He likes things of that nature.*

naughty adjective (**naughtier, naughtiest**)
1 badly behaved or disobedient. 2 slightly rude or indecent, *naughty pictures.* **naughtily** adverb, **naughtiness** noun [originally = poor: from *naught*]

nausea (say naw-zee-a) noun
a feeling of sickness or disgust.
nauseous adjective, **nauseating** adjective [from Greek *nausia* = seasickness]

nautical adjective
of ships or sailors.
[from Greek *nautes* = sailor]

nautical mile noun (plural **nautical miles**)
a measure of distance used at sea, 2025 yards (1.852 kilometres).

naval adjective
to do with a navy. [from Latin *navis* = ship]

navel noun (plural **navels**)
the small hollow in the centre of the abdomen, where the umbilical cord was attached. [from Old English]

navigate verb (**navigates, navigating, navigated**)
1 sail in or through a river or sea etc., *The ship navigated the Suez Canal.* 2 make sure that a ship, aircraft, or vehicle is going in the right direction.
navigation noun, **navigator** noun
[from Latin *navis* = ship + *agere* = to drive]

navy noun (plural **navies**)
1 a country's warships and the people trained to use them. 2 (also **navy blue**) very dark blue, the colour of naval uniform. [from old French *navie* = a ship or fleet; related to *naval*]

Nazi (say nah-tsee) noun (plural **Nazis**)
a member of the National Socialist Party in Germany in Hitler's time, with Fascist beliefs.
Nazism noun [from the German pronunciation of *Nationalsozialist*]

NB abbreviation
take note that (Latin *nota bene* = note well).

NE abbreviation
1 north-east. 2 north-eastern.

near adverb & adjective
not far away.
near by not far away, *They live near by.*
near preposition
not far away from, *near the shops.*

nearby adjective
near, *a nearby house.*

nearly adverb
1 almost, *We have nearly finished.* 2 closely, *They are nearly related.*

neat adjective (**neater, neatest**)
1 simple and clean and tidy. 2 skilful. 3 undiluted, *neat whisky.*
neatly adverb, **neatness** noun
[from Latin *nitidus* = clean, shining]

neaten verb (**neatens, neatening, neatened**)
make or become neat.

nebula noun (plural **nebulae**)
a bright or dark patch in the sky, caused by a distant galaxy or a cloud of dust or gas.
[Latin, = mist]

nebulous adjective
indistinct or vague, *nebulous ideas.*
[same origin as *nebula*]

necessary adjective
not able to be done without; essential.
necessarily adverb [from Latin]

necessity noun (plural **necessities**)
1 need, *the necessity of buying food and clothing.* 2 something necessary.

neck noun (plural **necks**)
1 the part of the body that joins the head to the shoulders. 2 the part of a garment round the neck. 3 a narrow part of something, especially of a bottle.

necklace noun (plural **necklaces**)
an ornament worn round the neck.

necktie noun (plural **neckties**)
a strip of material worn passing under the collar of a shirt and knotted in front.

need verb (**needs, needing, needed**)
1 be without something you should have; require, *We need two more chairs.* 2 (as an *auxiliary verb*) have to do something, *You need not answer.*
need noun (plural **needs**)
1 something needed; a necessary thing. 2 a situation where something is necessary, *There is no need to cry.* 3 great poverty or hardship.
needful adjective, **needless** adjective
[from Old English]

needle noun (plural **needles**)
1 a very thin pointed piece of steel used in sewing. 2 something long and thin and sharp, *a knitting needle, pine needles.* 3 the pointer of a meter or compass.

needlework noun
sewing or embroidery.

needy adjective (**needier, neediest**)
very poor; lacking things necessary for life.
neediness noun

negative adjective
1 that says 'no', *a negative answer.* 2 not definite or positive. 3 less than nought; minus.

4 to do with the kind of electric charge carried by electrons.
negatively *adverb*

USAGE: The opposite of sense 1 is *affirmative*, and of senses 2, 3, 4 *positive*.

negative *noun* (*plural* **negatives**)
1 a negative statement. **2** a photograph on film with the dark parts light and the light parts dark, from which a positive print (with the dark and light or colours correct) can be made.

neglect *verb* (**neglects, neglecting, neglected**)
1 not look after or attend to a person or thing. **2** not do something; forget, *He neglected to shut the door.*
neglect *noun*
neglecting or being neglected.
neglectful *adjective*
[from Latin *nec* = not + *legere* = choose]

negligence *noun*
lack of proper care or attention; carelessness.
negligent *adjective*, **negligently** *adverb* [same origin as *neglect*]

negligible *adjective*
not big enough or important enough to be worth bothering about.
[from French *négliger* = neglect]

negotiable *adjective*
1 able to be changed after being discussed, *The salary is negotiable.* **2** (of a cheque) able to be changed for cash or transferred to another person. [from *negotiate*]

negotiate *verb* (**negotiates, negotiating, negotiated**)
1 bargain or discuss with others in order to reach an agreement. **2** arrange after discussion, *They negotiated a treaty.* **3** get over an obstacle or difficulty.
negotiation *noun*, **negotiator** *noun*
[from Latin *negotium* = business]

neigh *verb* (**neighs, neighing, neighed**)
make the high-pitched cry of a horse.
neigh *noun*

neighbour *noun* (*plural* **neighbours**)
a person who lives next door or near to another. **neighbouring** *adjective*, **neighbourly** *adjective*
[from Old English *neahgebur* = near dweller]

neighbourhood *noun* (*plural* **neighbourhoods**)
1 the surrounding district or area. **2** a part of a town where people live, *a quiet neighbourhood.*

neither (*say* ny-*ther* or nee-*ther*) *adjective* & *pronoun*
not either.

USAGE: Correct use is *Neither of them likes it. Neither he nor his children like it.* Use a singular verb (e.g. *likes*) unless one of its subjects is plural (e.g. *children*).

neither *adverb* & *conjunction*
neither ... nor not one thing and not the other, *She neither knew nor cared.*
[from Old English]

USAGE: Say *I don't know that either* (not 'neither').

neo- *prefix*
new. [from Greek]

neolithic (*say* nee-o-lith-ik) *adjective*
belonging to the later part of the Stone Age.
[from *neo-* + Greek *lithos* = stone]

neon *noun*
a gas that glows when electricity passes through it, used in glass tubes to make illuminated signs. [from Greek *neos* = new]

nephew *noun* (*plural* **nephews**)
the son of a person's brother or sister.

nerve *noun* (*plural* **nerves**)
1 any of the fibres in the body that carry messages to and from the brain, so that parts of the body can feel and move. **2** courage; calmness in a dangerous situation, *Don't lose your nerve.* **3** impudence, *You've got a nerve!*
nerves *plural noun* nervousness.
nerve *verb* (**nerves, nerving, nerved**)
give strength or courage to someone.
[from Latin *nervus* = sinew]

nervous *adjective*
1 easily upset or agitated; excitable. **2** slightly afraid; timid. **3** of the nerves, *a nervous illness.*
nervously *adverb*, **nervousness** *noun*

nervous breakdown *noun* (*plural* **nervous breakdowns**)
a state of severe depression and anxiety, so that the person cannot cope with life.

nervous system *noun* (*plural* **nervous systems**)
the system, consisting of the brain, spinal cord, and nerves, which sends electrical messages from one part of the body to another.

-ness *suffix*
forming nouns from adjectives (e.g. *kindness, sadness*). [from Old English]

nest *noun* (*plural* **nests**)
1 a structure or place in which a bird lays its eggs and feeds its young. **2** a place where some small creatures (e.g. mice, wasps) live. **3** a set of similar things that fit inside each other, *a nest of tables.*
nest *verb* (**nests, nesting, nested**)
1 have or make a nest. **2** fit inside something.
[from Old English]

nest egg *noun* (*plural* **nest eggs**)
a sum of money saved up for future use.
[originally = an egg left in the nest to encourage a hen to lay more]

nestle *verb* (**nestles, nestling, nestled**)
curl up comfortably.
[from Old English *nestlian* = to nest]

net[1] *noun* (*plural* **nets**)
1 material made of pieces of thread, cord, or wire etc. joined together in a criss-cross pattern with holes between. 2 something made of this.
net *verb* (**nets, netting, netted**)
cover or catch with a net.
[from Old English]

net[2] *adjective*
remaining when nothing more is to be deducted, *The net weight, without the box, is 100 grams.* (Compare *gross*.)
net *verb* (**nets, netting, netted**)
obtain or produce as net profit.
[from French *net* = neat]

netball *noun*
a game in which two teams try to throw a ball into a high net hanging from a ring.

netting *noun*
a piece of net.

nettle *noun* (*plural* **nettles**)
a wild plant with leaves that sting when they are touched.
nettle *verb* (**nettles, nettling, nettled**)
annoy or provoke someone.

network *noun* (*plural* **networks**)
1 a net-like arrangement of connected lines or parts, *the railway network.* 2 a group of radio or television stations which broadcast the same programmes. 3 a set of computers which are linked to each other.

neurotic (*say* newr-ot-ik) *adjective*
always very worried about something. [from Greek *neuron* = nerve]

neuter *adjective*
1 neither masculine nor feminine. 2 (in some languages) belonging to the class of words which are neither masculine nor feminine, such as *Fenster* in German.
neuter *verb* (**neuters, neutering, neutered**)
remove an animal's sex organs so that it cannot breed. [Latin, = neither]

neutral *adjective*
1 not supporting either side in a war or quarrel. 2 not very distinctive, *a neutral colour such as grey.* 3 neither acid nor alkaline.
neutrally *adverb*, **neutrality** *noun*
[same origin as *neuter*]

neutral gear *noun*
a gear that is not connected to the driving parts of an engine.

neutron *noun* (*plural* **neutrons**)
a particle with no electric charge.
[from *neutral*]

never *adverb*
1 at no time; not ever. 2 not at all.
[from Old English *naefre* = not ever]

nevertheless *adverb* & *conjunction*
in spite of this; although this is a fact.

new *adjective*
not existing before; just made, invented, discovered, or received etc.
newly *adverb*, **newness** *noun*
new *adverb*
newly, *newborn; new-laid.*

newcomer *noun* (*plural* **newcomers**)
a person who has arrived recently.

newfangled *adjective*
disliked because it is new in method or style.
[from *new* + Middle English *fang* = seize]

newly *adverb*
1 recently. 2 in a new way.

new moon *noun* (*plural* **new moons**)
the moon at the beginning of its cycle, when only a thin crescent can be seen.

news *noun*
1 information about recent events or a broadcast report of this. 2 a piece of new information.

newsagent *noun* (*plural* **newsagents**)
a shopkeeper who sells newspapers.

newspaper *noun* (*plural* **newspapers**)
1 a daily or weekly publication on large sheets of paper, containing news reports, articles, etc. 2 the sheets of paper forming a newspaper, *Wrap it in newspaper.*

newt *noun* (*plural* **newts**)
a small animal rather like a lizard, that lives near or in water.
[from Old English: originally *an ewt*]

newton *noun* (*plural* **newtons**)
a unit for measuring force. [named after an English scientist, Isaac Newton]

New Year's Day *noun*
1 January.

next *adjective*
nearest; coming immediately after, *on the next day.*
next *adverb*
1 in the next place. 2 on the next occasion, *What happens next?* [from Old English]

next door *adverb* & *adjective*
in the next house or room.

nib *noun* (*plural* **nibs**)
the pointed metal part of a pen.

nibble *verb* (**nibbles, nibbling, nibbled**)
take small, quick, or gentle bites.

nice *adjective* (**nicer, nicest**)
1 pleasant or kind. 2 precise or careful, *Dictionaries make nice distinctions between meanings of words.* **nicely** *adverb*, **niceness** *noun*
[originally = stupid: from Latin *nescius* = ignorant]

nick noun (plural **nicks**)
1 a small cut or notch. 2 (slang) a police station or prison.
in good nick (informal) in good condition.
in the nick of time only just in time.

nickel noun (plural **nickels**)
1 a silvery-white metal. 2 (American) a 5-cent coin. [from German]

nickname noun (plural **nicknames**)
a name given to a person instead of his or her real name.
[originally an eke-name: from Middle English eke = addition, + name]

nicotine noun
a poisonous substance found in tobacco. [from the name of J. Nicot, who introduced tobacco into France in 1560]

niece noun (plural **nieces**)
the daughter of a person's brother or sister. [from French; related to nephew]

niggardly adjective
mean or stingy. **niggardliness** noun [from Middle English nig = a mean person]

night noun (plural **nights**)
1 the dark hours between sunset and sunrise. 2 a particular night or evening, the first night of the play.

nightclub noun (plural **nightclubs**)
a place that is open at night where people go to drink and dance.

nightdress noun (plural **nightdresses**)
a loose dress that girls or women wear in bed.

nightingale noun (plural **nightingales**)
a small brown bird that sings sweetly. [from Old English nihtegala = night-singer (because it often sings until late in the evening)]

nightmare noun (plural **nightmares**)
1 a frightening dream. 2 an unpleasant experience, the journey was a nightmare.
nightmarish adjective [from night + Middle English mare = an evil spirit]

nil noun
nothing or nought.
[from Latin nihil = nothing]

nimble adjective
able to move quickly; agile. **nimbly** adverb

nine noun & adjective (plural **nines**)
the number 9. **ninth** adjective & noun

nineteen noun & adjective
the number 19. **nineteenth** adjective & noun

ninety noun & adjective (plural **nineties**)
the number 90. **ninetieth** adjective & noun

nip verb (**nips**, **nipping**, **nipped**)
1 pinch or bite quickly. 2 (informal) go quickly.

nip noun (plural **nips**)
1 a quick pinch or bite. 2 sharp coldness, There's a nip in the air. 3 a small drink of a spirit, a nip of brandy.

nippers plural noun
pincers.

nipple noun (plural **nipples**)
a small projecting part, especially at the front of a person's breast.

nirvana noun
(in Buddhism and Hinduism) the highest state of knowledge and understanding, achieved by meditation. [Sanskrit]

nit noun (plural **nits**)
a parasitic insect or its egg, found in people's hair. [from Old English]

nit-picking noun
pointing out very small faults.

nitrate noun (plural **nitrates**)
1 a chemical compound containing nitrogen. 2 potassium or sodium nitrate, used as a fertilizer.

nitrogen (say ny-tro-jen) noun
a gas that makes up about four-fifths of the air. [from nitre = a substance once thought to be a vital part of the air]

no adjective
not any, We have no money.
no adverb
1 used to deny or refuse something, Will you come? No. 2 not at all, She is no better. [from none]

No. or **no.** abbreviation (plural **Nos.** or **nos.**)
number. [from Latin numero = by number]

noble adjective (**nobler**, **noblest**)
1 of high social rank; aristocratic. 2 having a very good character or qualities, a noble king. 3 stately or impressive, a noble building.
nobly adverb, **nobility** noun
noble noun (plural **nobles**)
a person of high social rank. **nobleman** noun, **noblewoman** noun [from Latin]

nobody pronoun
no person; no one.
nobody noun (plural **nobodies**) (informal)
an unimportant or unimpressive person; a nonentity.

nocturnal adjective
1 happening at night. 2 active at night, nocturnal animals.
[from Latin noctis = of night]

nod verb (**nods**, **nodding**, **nodded**)
1 move the head up and down, especially as a way of agreeing with somebody or as a greeting. 2 be drowsy. **nod** noun

noise noun (plural **noises**)
a sound, especially one that is loud or unpleasant. **noisy** adjective, **noisily** adverb, **noiseless** adjective [from French]

nomad *noun* (*plural* **nomads**)
a member of a tribe that moves from place to place looking for pasture for their animals.
nomadic *adjective*
[from Greek *nomas* = roaming]

no man's land *noun*
an area that does not belong to anybody, especially the land between opposing armies.

nominate *verb* (**nominates, nominating, nominated**)
name a person or thing to be appointed or chosen. **nomination** *noun*, **nominator** *noun*
[from Latin *nominare* = to name]

non- *prefix*
not. [from Latin]

non-commissioned officer *noun* (*plural* **non-commissioned officers**)
a member of the armed forces, such as a corporal or sergeant, who has not been commissioned as an officer but has been promoted from the ranks of ordinary soldiers.

non-committal *adjective*
not committing yourself; not showing what you think.

nondescript *adjective*
having no special or distinctive qualities and therefore difficult to describe.

none *pronoun*
1 not any. 2 no one, *None can tell.*
[from Old English *nan* = not one]

USAGE: It is better to use a singular verb (e.g. *None of them is here*), but the plural is not incorrect (e.g. *None of them are here*).

nonentity (*say* non-en-tit-ee) *noun* (*plural* **nonentities**)
an unimportant person.
[from *non-* + *entity*]

non-existent *adjective*
not existing or unreal.

non-fiction *noun*
writings that are not fiction; books about real people and things and true events.

non-flammable *adjective*
not able to be set on fire.

USAGE: See note at *inflammable*.

nonplussed *adjective*
puzzled or confused.
[from Latin *non plus* = not further]

nonsense *noun*
1 words put together in a way that does not mean anything. 2 stupid ideas or behaviour.
nonsensical (*say* non-sens-ik-al) *adjective*
[from *non-* + *sense*]

non-stop *adjective* & *adverb*
1 not stopping, *They talked non-stop for hours.*
2 not stopping between two main stations, *a non-stop train.*

noodles *plural noun*
pasta made in narrow strips, used in soups etc.
[from German]

nook *noun* (*plural* **nooks**)
a sheltered corner; a recess.

noon *noun*
twelve o'clock midday.
[via Old English from Latin]

no one *noun*
no person; nobody.

noose *noun* (*plural* **nooses**)
a loop in a rope that gets smaller when the rope is pulled. [origin unknown]

nor *conjunction*
and not, *She cannot do it; nor can I.*

normal *adjective*
1 usual or ordinary. 2 natural and healthy; without a physical or mental illness.
normally *adverb*, **normality** *noun*

Norman *noun* (*plural* **Normans**)
a member of the people of Normandy in northern France, who conquered England in 1066. **Norman** *adjective*
[from Old Norse *northmathr* = man from the north (because the Normans were partly descended from the Vikings)]

north *noun*
1 the direction to the left of a person who faces east. 2 the northern part of a country, city, etc.
north *adjective* & *adverb*
towards or in the north. **northerly** *adjective*, **northern** *adjective*, **northerner** *noun*, **northernmost** *adjective* [from Old English]

north-east *noun*, *adjective*, & *adverb*
midway between north and east.
north-easterly *adjective*, **north-eastern** *adjective*

northward *adjective* & *adverb*
towards the north. **northwards** *adverb*

north-west *noun*, *adjective*, & *adverb*
midway between north and west.
north-westerly *adjective*, **north-western** *adjective*

Nos. or **nos.** *plural* of **No.** or **no.**

nose *noun* (*plural* **noses**)
1 the part of the face that is used for breathing and for smelling things. 2 the front end or part.

nosedive *noun* (*plural* **nosedives**)
a steep downward dive, especially of an aircraft. **nosedive** *verb*

nostalgia (*say* nos-tal-ja) *noun*
sentimental remembering or longing for the past. **nostalgic** *adjective*, **nostalgically** *adverb*
[originally = homesickness: from Greek *nostos* = return home + *algos* = pain]

nostril noun (plural **nostrils**)
either of the two openings in the nose. [from
Old English nosthryl = nose-hole]

nosy adjective (**nosier, nosiest**)
inquisitive. **nosily** adverb, **nosiness** noun [from
sticking your nose in = being inquisitive]

not adverb
used to change the meaning of something to its
opposite or absence. [from nought]

notation noun (plural **notations**)
a system of symbols representing numbers,
quantities, musical notes, etc.

notch noun (plural **notches**)
a small V-shape cut into a surface.

note noun (plural **notes**)
1 something written down as a reminder or as
a comment or explanation. **2** a short letter. **3** a
banknote, a £5 note. **4** a single sound in music.
5 any of the black or white keys on a piano etc.
(see key 3). **6** a sound or quality that indicates
something, a note of warning. **7** notice or
attention, Take note.
note verb (**notes, noting, noted**)
1 make a note about something; write down.
2 notice or pay attention to, Note what we say.
[from Latin nota = a mark]

notebook noun (plural **notebooks**)
a book with blank pages on which to write
notes.

notepaper noun
paper for writing letters.

nothing noun
1 no thing; not anything. **2** no amount; nought.
for nothing 1 without payment, free. **2** without
a result. [from no thing]

notice noun (plural **notices**)
1 something written or printed and displayed
for people to see. **2** attention, It escaped my
notice. **3** information that something is going to
happen; warning that you are about to end an
agreement or a person's employment etc., We
gave him a month's notice.
notice verb (**notices, noticing, noticed**)
see or become aware of something.
[from Latin notus = known]

noticeable adjective
easily seen or noticed. **noticeably** adverb

notion noun (plural **notions**)
an idea, especially one that is vague or
incorrect.
[from Latin notio = getting to know]

notorious adjective
well-known for something bad.
notoriously adverb, **notoriety** (say noh-ter-I-it-
ee) noun [same origin as notice]

notwithstanding preposition
in spite of.

nought (say nawt) noun
1 the figure 0. **2** nothing.
[from Old English nowiht = not anything]

noun noun (plural **nouns**)
a word that stands for a person, place, or thing.
Common nouns are words such as boy, dog,
river, sport, table, which are used of a whole
kind of people or things; proper nouns are
words such as Charles, Thames, and London
which name a particular person or thing.
[from Latin nomen = name]

nourish verb (**nourishes, nourishing, nourished**)
keep a person, animal, or plant alive and well
by means of food. **nourishment** noun [from old
French; related to nutrient]

novel noun (plural **novels**)
a story that fills a whole book.
novel adjective
of a new and unusual kind, a novel experience.
[from Latin novus = new]

novelist noun (plural **novelists**)
a person who writes novels.

novelty noun (plural **novelties**)
1 newness and originality. **2** something new
and unusual. **3** a small and unusual object,
suitable as a small gift.

novice noun (plural **novices**)
1 a beginner. **2** a person preparing to be a
monk or nun.
[from French; related to novel]

now adverb
1 at this time. **2** by this time. **3** immediately,
You must go now. **4** I wonder, or I am telling
you, Now why didn't I think of that?
now and again or **now and then** sometimes;
occasionally.
now conjunction
as a result of or at the same time as something,
Now that you have come, we'll start.
now noun
this moment, They will be at home by now.

nowadays adverb
at the present time, as contrasted with years
ago.

nowhere adverb
not anywhere.
nowhere noun
no place, Nowhere is as beautiful as Scotland.

nozzle noun (plural **nozzles**)
the spout of a hose or pipe etc.
[= little nose]

nuclear adjective
1 to do with a nucleus or nuclei. **2** using the
energy that is created by reactions in the
nuclei of atoms.

nucleus noun (plural **nuclei**)
1 the part in the centre of something, round
which other things are grouped. **2** the central
part of an atom or of a seed or a biological cell.
[Latin, = kernel]

nude *adjective*
not wearing any clothes; naked. **nudity** *noun*
[from Latin *nudus* = bare]

nudge *verb* (nudges, nudging, nudged)
1 poke a person gently with your elbow. 2 push slightly or gradually. **nudge** *noun* [origin unknown]

nugget *noun* (*plural* nuggets)
a rough lump of gold or platinum found in the earth. [origin unknown]

nuisance *noun* (*plural* nuisances)
an annoying person or thing.
[from French *nuire* = to hurt someone]

numb *adjective*
unable to feel or move.
numbly *adverb*, **numbness** *noun*

number *noun* (*plural* numbers)
1 a symbol or word indicating how many; a numeral or figure. 2 a numeral given to a thing to identify it, *a telephone number.* 3 a quantity of people or things, *the number of people present.* 4 one issue of a magazine or newspaper. 5 a song or piece of music.

USAGE: Note that *a number of*, meaning 'several', should be followed by a plural verb: *A number of problems remain.*

number *verb* (numbers, numbering, numbered)
1 mark with numbers. 2 count. 3 amount to, *The crowd numbered 10,000.*
[from old French; related to *numeral*]

numeral *noun* (*plural* numerals)
a symbol that represents a certain number; a figure. [from Latin *numerus* = number]

numerate (*say* new-mer-at) *adjective*
having a good basic knowledge of mathematics. **numeracy** *noun*
[same origin as *numeral*]

numerator *noun* (*plural* numerators)
the number above the line in a fraction, showing how many parts are to be taken, e.g. 2 in $\frac{2}{3}$. (Compare *denominator.*)

numerical (*say* new-merri-kal) *adjective*
of a number or series of numbers, *in numerical order.* **numerically** *adverb*
[same origin as *numeral*]

numerous *adjective*
many. [same origin as *numeral*]

nun *noun* (*plural* nuns)
a member of a community of women who live according to the rules of a religious organization. (Compare *monk.*)
[via Old English from Latin *nonna*, feminine of *nonnus* = monk]

nunnery *noun* (*plural* nunneries)
a convent.

nurse *noun* (*plural* nurses)
1 a person trained to look after people who are ill or injured. 2 a woman employed to look after young children.

nurse *verb* (nurses, nursing, nursed)
1 look after someone who is ill or injured. 2 hold carefully. 3 feed a baby.
[from *nourish*]

nursemaid *noun* (*plural* nursemaids)
a young woman employed to look after young children.

nursery *noun* (*plural* nurseries)
1 a place where young children are looked after or play. 2 a place where young plants are grown and usually for sale.

nursery rhyme *noun* (*plural* nursery rhymes)
a simple rhyme or song of the kind that young children like.

nursery school *noun* (*plural* nursery schools)
a school for children below primary school age.

nursing home *noun* (*plural* nursing homes)
a small hospital or home for invalids.

nut *noun* (*plural* nuts)
1 a fruit with a hard shell. 2 a kernel. 3 a small piece of metal with a hole in the middle, for screwing onto a bolt. 4 (*slang*) the head. 5 (*slang*) a mad or eccentric person.
nutty *adjective* [from Old English]

nutcrackers *plural noun*
pincers for cracking nuts.

nutrition (*say* new-trish-on) *noun*
1 nourishment. 2 the study of what nourishes people.
nutritional *adjective*, **nutritionally** *adverb*

nutritious (*say* new-trish-us) *adjective*
nourishing; giving good nourishment.
nutritiousness *noun*

nutshell *noun* (*plural* nutshells)
the shell of a nut.
in a nutshell stated very briefly.

nuzzle *verb* (nuzzles, nuzzling, nuzzled)
rub gently with the nose. [from *nose*]

NW *abbreviation*
1 north-west. 2 north-western.

nylon *noun*
a synthetic, strong, lightweight cloth or fibre.
[invented to go with *rayon* and *cotton*]

NZ *abbreviation*
New Zealand.

Oo

O *interjection*
oh.

oaf *noun* (*plural* **oafs**)
a stupid lout. [from Old Norse]

oak *noun* (*plural* **oaks**)
a large deciduous tree with seeds called acorns.
oaken *adjective* [from Old English]

oar *noun* (*plural* **oars**)
a pole with a flat blade at one end, used for rowing a boat. **oarsman** *noun*, **oarsmanship** *noun* [from Old English]

oasis (*say* oh-**ay**-sis) *noun* (*plural* **oases**)
a fertile place in a desert, with a spring or well of water. [from Greek]

oath *noun* (*plural* **oaths**)
1 a solemn promise to do something or that something is true, appealing to God or a holy person as witness. **2** a swear word.

oats *plural noun*
a cereal used to make food (*oats* for horses, *oatmeal* for people). [from Old English]

ob- *prefix* (changing to **oc-** before *c*, **of-** before *f*, **op-** before *p*)
1 to; towards (as in *observe*). **2** against (as in *opponent*). **3** in the way; blocking (as in *obstruct*).
[from Latin *ob* = towards, against]

obedient *adjective*
doing what you are told; willing to obey.
obediently *adverb*, **obedience** *noun*

obey *verb* (**obeys, obeying, obeyed**)
do what you are told to do by a person, law, etc.
[from *ob-* + Latin *audire* = listen or hear]

obituary *noun* (*plural* **obituaries**)
a notice in a newspaper of a person's death, often with a short account of his or her life. [from Latin *obitus* = death]

object (*say* ob-jikt) *noun* (*plural* **objects**)
1 something that can be seen or touched. **2** a purpose or intention. **3** (in grammar) the word or words naming who or what is acted upon by a verb or by a preposition, e.g. *him* in *the dog bit him* and *against him*.
object (*say* ob-**jekt**) *verb* (**objects, objecting, objected**)
say that you are not in favour of something or do not agree; protest. **objector** *noun*
[from *ob-* + Latin *-jectum* = thrown]

objection *noun* (*plural* **objections**)
1 objecting to something. **2** a reason for objecting.

objectionable *adjective*
unpleasant or nasty. **objectionably** *adverb*

objective *noun* (*plural* **objectives**)
what you are trying to reach or do; an aim.
objective *adjective*
1 real or actual, *Dreams have no objective existence.* **2** not influenced by personal feelings or opinions, *an objective account of the quarrel.*
(Compare *subjective.*) **objectively** *adverb*, **objectivity** *noun*

obligation *noun* (*plural* **obligations**)
1 being obliged to do something. **2** what you are obliged to do; a duty.
under an obligation owing gratitude to someone who has helped you.

obligatory (*say* ob-**lig**-a-ter-ee) *adjective*
compulsory, not optional.

oblige *verb* (**obliges, obliging, obliged**)
1 force or compel. **2** help and please someone, *Can you oblige me with a loan?*
be obliged to someone feel gratitude to a person who has helped you.
[from *ob-* + Latin *ligare* = bind]

obliging *adjective*
polite and helpful.

oblique (*say* ob-**leek**) *adjective*
1 slanting. **2** not saying something straightforwardly, *an oblique reply.*
obliquely *adverb* [from Latin]

obliterate *verb* (**obliterates, obliterating, obliterated**)
blot out; destroy and remove all traces of something. **obliteration** *noun*
[from Latin *obliterare* = cross out, from *ob-* + *littera* = letter]

oblong *adjective*
rectangular in shape and longer than it is wide.
oblong *noun* [from Latin]

obnoxious *adjective*
very unpleasant; objectionable.
[from *ob-* + Latin *noxa* = harm]

oboe *noun* (*plural* **oboes**)
a high-pitched woodwind instrument. **oboist** *noun*
[from French *haut* = high + *bois* = wood]

obscene (*say* ob-**seen**) *adjective*
indecent in a very offensive way.
obscenely *adverb*, **obscenity** *noun* [from Latin]

obscure *adjective*
1 difficult to see or to understand; not clear.
2 not well-known.
obscurely *adverb*, **obscurity** *noun*
obscure *verb* (**obscures, obscuring, obscured**)
make a thing obscure; darken or conceal, *Clouds obscured the sun.*
[from Latin *obscurus* = dark]

observant *adjective*
quick at observing or noticing things.
observantly *adverb*

observation *noun* (*plural* **observations**)
1 observing or watching. **2** a comment or remark.

observatory *noun* (*plural* **observatories**)
a building with telescopes etc. for observing the stars or weather.

observe *verb* (**observes, observing, observed**)
1 see and notice; watch carefully. **2** obey a law. **3** keep or celebrate a custom or religious festival etc. **4** make a remark.
observer *noun*
[from *ob-* + Latin *servare* = to watch or keep]

obsolescent *adjective*
becoming obsolete; going out of use or fashion.
obsolescence *noun*

obsolete *adjective*
not used any more; out of date.
[from Latin *obsoletus* = worn out]

obstacle *noun* (*plural* **obstacles**)
something that stands in the way or obstructs progress.
[from *ob-* + Latin *stare* = to stand]

obstinate *adjective*
keeping firmly to your own ideas or ways, even though they may be wrong. **obstinately** *adverb*, **obstinacy** *noun*
[from Latin *obstinare* = keep on, persist]

obstreperous (*say* ob-**strep**-er-us) *adjective*
noisy and unruly.
[from *ob-* + Latin *strepere* = make a noise]

obstruct *verb* (**obstructs, obstructing, obstructed**)
stop a person or thing from getting past; hinder. **obstruction** *noun*, **obstructive** *adjective*
[from *ob-* + Latin *structum* = built]

obtain *verb* (**obtains, obtaining, obtained**)
get something by buying, taking, or being given it. **obtainable** *adjective*
[from *ob-* + Latin *tenere* = to hold]

obtrusive *adjective*
unpleasantly noticeable. **obtrusiveness** *noun*

obtuse angle *noun* (*plural* **obtuse angles**)
an angle of more than 90° but less than 180°. (Compare *acute angle*.)

obvious *adjective*
easy to see or understand. **obviously** *adverb*
[from Latin *ob viam* = in the way]

oc- *prefix*
1 to; towards. **2** against. **3** in the way; blocking. see *ob-*.

occasion *noun* (*plural* **occasions**)
1 the time when something happens. **2** a special event. **3** a suitable time; an opportunity.

occasional *adjective*
1 happening at intervals. **2** for special occasions, *occasional music*.
occasionally *adverb*

occult *adjective*
to do with the supernatural or magic, *occult powers*.
[from Latin *occultum* = hidden]

occupation *noun* (*plural* **occupations**)
1 a person's job or profession. **2** something you do to pass your time. **3** capturing a country etc. by military force.

occupational *adjective*
caused by an occupation, *an occupational disease*.

occupational therapy *noun*
creative work designed to help people to recover from certain illnesses.

occupy *verb* (**occupies, occupying, occupied**)
1 live in a place; inhabit. **2** fill a space or position. **3** capture a country etc. and place troops there. **4** keep somebody busy.
occupier *noun* [from Latin]

occur *verb* (**occurs, occurring, occurred**)
1 happen or exist. **2** be found; appear, *These plants occur in ponds*. **3** come into a person's mind, *An idea occurred to me*.

ocean *noun* (*plural* **oceans**)
the seas that surround the continents of the earth, especially one of the large named areas of this, *the Pacific Ocean*.
oceanic *adjective*
[from Oceanus, the river that the ancient Greeks thought surrounded the world]

o'clock *adverb*
by the clock, *Lunch is at one o'clock*.
[short for *of the clock*]

octa- or **octo-** *prefix*
eight. [from Greek]

octagon *noun* (*plural* **octagons**)
a flat shape with eight sides and eight angles.
octagonal *adjective*
[from *octa-* + Greek *gonia* = angle]

octave *noun* (*plural* **octaves**)
the interval of eight steps between one musical note and the next note of the same name above or below it.
[from Latin *octavus* = eighth]

octo- *prefix*
eight. see **octa-**.

octopus *noun* (*plural* **octopuses**)
a sea creature with eight long tentacles. [from *octo-* + Greek *pous* = foot]

oculist *noun* (*plural* **oculists**)
a doctor who treats diseases of the eye.

odd *adjective*
1 strange or unusual. **2** (of a number) not able to be divided exactly by 2; not even. **3** left over from a pair or set, *I've got one odd sock*. **4** of various kinds; not regular, *odd jobs*.
oddly *adverb*, **oddness** *noun*, **oddity** *noun*
[from Old Norse]

oddments *plural noun*
small things of various kinds.

odds *plural noun*
the chances that a certain thing will happen; a measure of this, *When the odds are 10 to 1, you will win £10 if you bet £1.*
odds and ends oddments.

odious (*say* oh-dee-us) *adjective*
hateful. **odiously** *adverb*, **odiousness** *noun*

odour *noun* (*plural* **odours**)
a smell. **odorous** *adjective*, **odourless** *adjective*
[Latin *odor* = smell]

odyssey (*say* od-iss-ee) *noun* (*plural* **odysseys**)
a long adventurous journey. [named after the *Odyssey*, a Greek poem telling of the wanderings of Odysseus]

o'er *preposition* & *adverb* (*poetic*)
over.

oesophagus (*say* ee-sof-a-gus) *noun* (*plural* **oesophagi**)
the tube from the throat to the stomach.

of *preposition*
(used to indicate relationships) **1** belonging to, *the mother of the child.* **2** concerning; about, *news of the disaster.* **3** made from, *built of stone.* **4** from, *north of the town.* [from Old English]

of- *prefix*
1 to; towards. **2** against. **3** in the way; blocking. see **ob-**.

off *preposition*
1 not on; away or down from, *He fell off the ladder.* **2** not taking or wanting, *She is off her food.* **3** deducted from, *£5 off the price.*
off *adverb*
1 away or down from something, *His hat blew off.* **2** not working or happening, *The heating is off. The match is off because of snow.* **3** to the end; completely, *Finish it off.* **4** as regards money or supplies, *How are you off for cash?* **5** behind or at the side of a stage, *There were noises off.* **6** (of food) beginning to go bad.

offal *noun*
the organs of an animal (e.g. liver, kidneys) sold as food. [originally = waste products: from *off* + *fall*]

offence *noun* (*plural* **offences**)
1 an illegal action. **2** a feeling of annoyance or resentment.

offend *verb* (**offends, offending, offended**)
1 cause offence to someone; hurt a person's pride. **2** do wrong, *offend against the law.*
offender *noun*
[from *ob-* + Latin *fendere* = to strike]

offensive *adjective*
1 causing offence; insulting. **2** disgusting, *an offensive smell.* **3** used in attacking, *offensive weapons.*
offensively *adverb*, **offensiveness** *noun*

offensive *noun* (*plural* **offensives**)
an attack.
take the offensive be the first to attack.

offer *verb* (**offers, offering, offered**)
1 present something so that people can accept it if they want to. **2** say that you are willing to do or give something or to pay a certain amount.
offer *noun* (*plural* **offers**)
1 offering something. **2** an amount offered.

offhand *adjective*
1 said or done without preparation. **2** rather casual and rude; curt.
offhanded *adjective*

office *noun* (*plural* **offices**)
1 a room or building used for business, especially for clerical work; the people who work there. **2** a government department, *the Foreign and Commonwealth Office.* **3** an important job or position.
be in office hold an official position.
[from Latin *officium* = a service or duty]

officer *noun* (*plural* **officers**)
1 a person who is in charge of others, especially in the armed forces. **2** an official. **3** a member of the police.

official *adjective*
1 done or said by someone with authority. **2** done as part of your job or position, *official duties.* **officially** *adverb*
official *noun* (*plural* **officials**)
a person who holds a position of authority.

offing *noun*
in the offing likely to happen soon.

off-licence *noun* (*plural* **off-licences**)
a shop with a licence to sell alcohol to be drunk somewhere else.

offshoot *noun* (*plural* **offshoots**)
1 a side shoot on a plant. **2** a by-product.

offside *adjective* & *adverb*
(of a player in football etc.) in a position where the rules do not allow him or her to play the ball.

often *adverb*
many times; in many cases.

ogre *noun* (*plural* **ogres**)
1 a cruel giant in fairy tales. **2** a terrifying person. [French]

oh *interjection*
an exclamation of pain, surprise, delight, etc., or used for emphasis (*Oh yes I will!*).

ohm *noun* (*plural* **ohms**)
a unit of electrical resistance.
[named after a German scientist, G. S. Ohm, who studied electric currents]

oil *noun* (*plural* oils)
1 a thick slippery liquid that will not dissolve in water. 2 a kind of petroleum used as fuel.
  oil well *noun*
oil *verb* (oils, oiling, oiled)
put oil on something, especially to make it work smoothly. [from Latin]

oilfield *noun*
an area where oil is found.

oily *adjective*
1 containing or like oil; covered or soaked with oil. 2 behaving in an insincerely polite way.
  oiliness *noun*

ointment *noun* (*plural* ointments)
a cream or slippery paste for putting on sore skin and cuts. [from old French]

OK or **okay** *adverb* & *adjective* (*informal*)
all right. [perhaps from the initials of *oll* (or *orl*) *korrect*, a humorous spelling of *all correct*, first used in the USA in 1839]

old *adjective*
1 not new; born or made or existing from a long time ago. 2 of a particular age, *I'm ten years old.* 3 former or original, *in its old place.* 4 (*informal*, used casually or for emphasis), *good old mum!* **oldness** *noun*

Old English *noun*
the English language from about 700 to 1150, also called *Anglo-Saxon.*

old-fashioned *adjective*
of the kind that was usual a long time ago; no longer fashionable.

Old Norse *noun*
the language spoken by the Vikings, the ancestor of modern Scandinavian languages.

olive *noun* (*plural* olives)
1 an evergreen tree with a small bitter fruit. 2 this fruit, from which an oil (*olive oil*) is made. 3 a shade of green like an unripe olive. [from Greek]

olive branch *noun* (*plural* olive branches)
something you do or offer that shows you want to make peace.
[from a story in the Bible, where the dove brings Noah an olive branch as a sign that God is no longer angry with man]

-ology *suffix* see -logy.

Olympic Games or **Olympics** *plural noun*
a series of international sports contests held every fourth year in a different part of the world. [from the name of Olympia, a city in Greece where they were held in ancient times]

omega (*say* oh-meg-a) *noun*
the last letter of the Greek alphabet, a long *o.* [from Greek *o mega* = big O]

omelette *noun* (*plural* omelettes)
eggs beaten together and cooked in a pan, often with a filling. [French]

omen *noun* (*plural* omens)
an event regarded as a sign of what is going to happen. [Latin]

ominous *adjective*
suggesting that trouble is coming. **ominously** *adverb*
[from Latin *ominosus* = acting as an omen]

omit *verb* (omits, omitting, omitted)
1 miss something out. 2 fail to do something. **omission** *noun* [from Latin]

omni- *prefix*
all. [from Latin]

omnibus *noun* (*plural* omnibuses)
1 a book containing several stories or books that were previously published separately. 2 (*old use*) a bus.
[Latin, = for everybody]

omniscient (*say* om-niss-ee-ent) *adjective*
knowing everything. **omniscience** *noun* [from *omni-* + Latin *sciens* = knowing]

omnivorous (*say* om-niv-er-us) *adjective*
feeding on all kinds of food. (Compare *carnivorous, herbivorous.*)
[from *omni-* + Latin *vorare* = devour]

on *preposition*
1 supported by; covering; added or attached to, *the sign on the door.* 2 close to; towards, *The army advanced on Paris.* 3 during; at the time of, *on my birthday.* 4 by reason of, *Arrest him on suspicion.* 5 concerning, *a book on butterflies.* 6 in a state of; using or showing, *The house was on fire.*
on *adverb*
1 so as to be on something, *Put it on.* 2 further forward, *Move on.* 3 working; in action, *Is the heater on?*
  on and off not continually.

once *adverb*
1 for one time or on one occasion only, *They came only once.* 2 formerly, *They once lived here.*
once *noun*
one time, *Once is enough.*
once *conjunction*
as soon as, *You can go once I have taken your names.* [from *one*]

oncoming *adjective*
approaching; coming towards you, *oncoming traffic.*

one *adjective*
1 single. 2 individual or united.
one *noun*
1 the smallest whole number, 1. 2 a person or thing alone.
  one another each other.
one *pronoun*
a person; any person, *One likes to help.*
oneself *pronoun*

one-sided *adjective*
1 with one side or person in a contest, conversation etc. being much stronger or doing a lot more than the other, *a one-sided match.*
2 showing only one point of view in an unfair way, *This is a very one-sided account of the conflict.*

onion *noun* (*plural* **onions**)
a round vegetable with a strong flavour.
oniony *adjective* [from old French]

onlooker *noun* (*plural* **onlookers**)
a spectator.

only *adjective*
being the one person or thing of a kind; sole, *my only wish.*
only child a child who has no brothers or sisters.
only *adverb*
no more than; and that is all, *There are only three cakes left.*
only *conjunction*
but then; however, *He makes promises, only he never keeps them.* [from Old English]

onomatopoeia (*say* on-om-at-o-**pee**-a) *noun*
the formation of words that imitate what they stand for, e.g. *cuckoo, plop.*
onomatopoeic *adjective*
[from Greek *onoma* = name + *poiein* = make]

onshore *adjective*
from the sea towards the land, *an onshore breeze.*

onslaught *noun* (*plural* **onslaughts**)
a fierce attack.
[from old Dutch *aan* = on + *slag* = a blow]

onto *preposition*
to a position on.

onward *adverb* & *adjective*
going forward; further on. **onwards** *adverb*

ooze *verb* (**oozes, oozing, oozed**)
1 flow out slowly; trickle. 2 allow something to flow out slowly, *The wound oozed blood.*
ooze *noun*
mud at the bottom of a river or sea.

op- *prefix*
1 to; towards. 2 against. 3 in the way; blocking. see **ob-**.

opal *noun* (*plural* **opals**)
a kind of stone with a rainbow sheen.
opalescent *adjective*

opaque (*say* o-**payk**) *adjective*
not able to be seen through; not transparent or translucent.
[from Latin *opacus* = shady or dark]

open *adjective*
1 allowing people or things to go in and out; not closed or fastened. 2 not covered or blocked up. 3 spread out; unfolded. 4 not limited or restricted, *an open championship.* 5 letting in visitors or customers. 6 with wide empty

spaces, *open country.* 7 honest and frank; not secret or secretive, *Be open about the danger.*
8 not decided, *an open mind.* **openness** *noun*
in the open air not inside a house or building.
open-air *adjective*
open *verb* (**opens, opening, opened**)
1 make or become open or more open. 2 begin.
opener *noun* [from Old English]

opencast *adjective*
(of a mine) worked by removing layers of earth from the surface, not underground.

opening *noun* (*plural* **openings**)
1 a space or gap; a place where something opens. 2 the beginning of something. 3 an opportunity.

openly *adverb*
without secrecy.

opera *noun* (*plural* **operas**)
a play in which all or most of the words are sung. **operatic** *adjective* [Latin, = work]

operate *verb* (**operates, operating, operated**)
1 make a machine work. 2 be in action; work.
3 perform a surgical operation on somebody.
operable *adjective*
[from Latin *operari* = to work]

operation *noun* (*plural* **operations**)
1 a piece of work or method of working.
2 something done to the body to take away or repair a part of it. 3 a planned military activity.
in operation working or in use, *When does the new system come into operation?*
operational *adjective*

operator *noun* (*plural* **operators**)
a person who works something, especially a telephone switchboard or exchange.

opinion *noun* (*plural* **opinions**)
what you think of something; a belief or judgement. [from Latin *opinari* = believe]

opinion poll *noun* (*plural* **opinion polls**)
an estimate of what people think, made by questioning a sample of them.

opium *noun*
a drug made from the juice of certain poppies, used in medicine.
[from Greek *opion* = poppy juice]

opponent *noun* (*plural* **opponents**)
a person or group opposing another in a contest or war.
[from Latin *opponere* = to set against]

opportunist *noun* (*plural* **opportunists**)
a person who is quick to seize opportunities.

opportunity *noun* (*plural* **opportunities**)
a good chance to do a particular thing.

oppose *verb* (**opposes, opposing, opposed**)
1 argue or fight against; resist. 2 contrast, *'Soft' is opposed to 'hard'.*
[from French; related to *opponent*]

opposite *adjective*
1 placed on the other or further side; facing, *on the opposite side of the road*. 2 moving away from or towards each other, *The trains were travelling in opposite directions*. 3 completely different, *opposite characters*.
opposite *noun* (*plural* **opposites**)
an opposite person or thing.
opposite *preposition*
opposite to, *They live opposite the school*. [from Latin *oppositus* = set or placed against]

opposition *noun*
1 opposing something; resistance. 2 the people who oppose something; **the Opposition** the chief political party opposing the one that is in power.

oppress *verb* (**oppresses, oppressing, oppressed**)
1 govern or treat somebody cruelly or unjustly. 2 weigh somebody down with worry or sadness.
oppression *noun*, **oppressive** *adjective*, **oppressor** *noun*
[from *op-* + Latin *pressus* = pressed]

opt *verb* (**opts, opting, opted**)
choose.
opt out decide not to take part in something.
[from Latin *optare* = wish for]

optical *adjective*
to do with sight; aiding sight, *optical instruments*. **optically** *adverb* [from Greek *optos* = seen]

optical illusion *noun* (*plural* **optical illusions**)
a deceptive appearance that makes you see something wrongly.

optician *noun* (*plural* **opticians**)
a person who makes or sells spectacles etc.

optimist *noun* (*plural* **optimists**)
a person who expects that things will turn out well. (Compare *pessimist*.) **optimism** *noun*, **optimistic** *adjective*, **optimistically** *adverb* [from French, related to *optimum*]

optimum *adjective*
best; most favourable. **optimum** *noun*, **optimal** *adjective* [Latin, = best thing]

option *noun* (*plural* **options**)
1 the right or power to choose something. 2 something chosen or that may be chosen. [same origin as *opt*]

optional *adjective*
that you can choose, not compulsory.
optionally *adverb*

or *conjunction*
used to show that there is a choice or an alternative, *Do you want a bun or a biscuit?* [from *other*]

-or *suffix*
forms nouns meaning 'a person or thing that does something' (e.g. *tailor, refrigerator*). [from Latin or old French]

oracle *noun* (*plural* **oracles**)
1 a shrine where the ancient Greeks consulted one of their gods for advice or a prophecy. 2 a wise or knowledgeable adviser.
oracular (*say* or-**ak**-yoo-ler) *adjective*
[from Latin *orare* = speak]

oral *adjective*
1 spoken, not written. 2 to do with or using the mouth. **orally** *adverb*
[from Latin *oris* = of the mouth]

USAGE: Do not confuse with *aural*.

orange *noun* (*plural* **oranges**)
1 a round juicy citrus fruit with reddish-yellow peel. 2 a reddish-yellow colour.

orangeade *noun*
an orange-flavoured drink.

orang-utan *noun* (*plural* **orang-utans**)
a large ape of Borneo and Sumatra.
[from Malay *orang hutan* = man of the forest (Malay is spoken in Malaysia)]

orator *noun* (*plural* **orators**)
a person who makes speeches.
oratorical *adjective*

orbit *noun* (*plural* **orbits**)
1 the curved path taken by something moving round a planet etc. in space. 2 the range of someone's influence or control. **orbital** *adjective*
orbit *verb* (**orbits, orbiting, orbited**)
move in an orbit round something, *The spacecraft orbited the earth*.

orchard *noun* (*plural* **orchards**)
a piece of ground planted with fruit trees.

orchestra *noun* (*plural* **orchestras**)
a large group of people playing various musical instruments together. **orchestral** *adjective*
[Greek, = the space where the chorus danced during a play]

orchid *noun* (*plural* **orchids**)
a kind of flower, often with unevenly shaped petals. [from Latin]

ordain *verb* (**ordains, ordaining, ordained**)
1 make a person a member of the clergy in the Christian Church, *He was ordained in 1981*. 2 declare or order something by law.
[from old French; related to *order*]

ordeal *noun* (*plural* **ordeals**)
a difficult or horrific experience.

order *noun* (*plural* **orders**)
1 a command. 2 a request for something to be supplied. 3 the way things are arranged, *in alphabetical order*. 4 a neat arrangement; a proper arrangement or condition, *in working order*. 5 obedience to rules or laws, *law and order*. 6 a kind or sort, *She showed courage of the highest order*. 7 a group of monks or nuns who live by certain religious rules.
in order that or **in order to** for the purpose of.

order *verb* (orders, ordering, ordered)
1 command. **2** ask for something to be supplied. **3** put something into order; arrange neatly. [from Latin *ordo* = a row, series, or arrangement]

orderly *adjective*
1 arranged neatly or well; methodical. **2** well-behaved and obedient.
orderliness *noun*

ordinal number *noun* (*plural* ordinal numbers)
a number that shows a thing's position in a series, e.g. *first, fifth, twentieth*. (Compare *cardinal numbers*.)
[from Latin *ordinalis* = showing the order]

ordinary *adjective*
normal or usual; not special.
ordinarily *adverb*
[from Latin *ordinarius* = orderly or usual]

ordination *noun* (*plural* ordinations)
ordaining or being ordained as a member of the clergy.

Ordnance Survey *noun*
an official survey organization that makes detailed maps of the British Isles.

ore *noun* (*plural* ores)
rock with metal or other useful substances in it, *iron ore*. [from Old English]

organ *noun* (*plural* organs)
1 a musical instrument from which sounds are produced by air forced through pipes, played by keys and pedals. **2** a part of the body with a particular function, *the digestive organs*.
[from Greek *organon* = tool]

organic *adjective*
1 to do with the organs of the body, *organic diseases*. **2** to do with or formed from living things, *organic matter*. **3** organic food is grown or produced without the use of chemical fertilizers, pesticides, etc., *organic farming*.
organically *adverb*

organism *noun* (*plural* organisms)
a living thing; an individual animal or plant.
[from Greek]

organist *noun* (*plural* organists)
a person who plays the organ.

organization *noun* (*plural* organizations)
1 an organized group of people, such as a business, charity, government department, etc. **2** the organizing of something.
organizational *adjective*

organize *verb* (organizes, organizing, organized)
1 plan and prepare something, *We organized a picnic*. **2** form people into a group to work together. **3** put things in order. **organizer** *noun*
[same origin as *organ*]

orgasm *noun* (*plural* orgasms)
the climax of sexual excitement.

orgy *noun* (*plural* orgies)
1 a wild party that involves a lot of drinking and sex. **2** an extravagant activity, *an orgy of spending*.
[from Latin *orgia* = secret rites (held in honour of Bacchus, the Greek and Roman god of wine)]

oriental *adjective*
to do with the countries east of the Mediterranean Sea, especially China and Japan.

orientate *verb* (orientates, orientating, orientated)
place something or face in a certain direction.
orientation *noun*

origami (*say* o-rig-ah-mee) *noun*
folding paper into decorative shapes.
[from Japanese *ori* = fold + *kami* = paper]

origin *noun* (*plural* origins)
1 the start of something; the point or cause from which something began. **2** the point where two or more axes on a graph meet. [from Latin *oriri* = to rise]

original *adjective*
1 existing from the start; earliest, *the original inhabitants*. **2** new in its design etc.; not a copy. **3** producing new ideas; inventive.
originally *adverb*, **originality** *noun*

originate *verb* (originates, originating, originated)
1 cause something to begin; create. **2** have its origin, *The quarrel originated in rivalry*.
origination *noun*, **originator** *noun*

ornament *noun* (*plural* ornaments)
an object displayed or worn as a decoration.
ornamental *adjective*
ornament *verb* (ornaments, ornamenting, ornamented)
decorate something with beautiful things.
ornamentation *noun*

ornithology *noun*
the study of birds.
ornithologist *noun*, **ornithological** *adjective*
[from Greek *ornithos* = of a bird, + *-logy*]

orphan *noun* (*plural* orphans)
a child whose parents are dead.

ortho- *prefix*
right; straight; correct.
[from Greek *orthos* = straight]

orthodox *adjective*
holding beliefs that are correct or generally accepted. **orthodoxy** *noun*
[from *ortho-* + Greek *doxa* = opinion]

Orthodox Church *noun*
the Christian Churches of eastern Europe.

orthopaedics (*say* orth-o-pee-diks) *noun*
the treatment of deformities and injuries to bones and muscles. **orthopaedic** *adjective* [from

ortho- + Greek *paideia* = rearing of children (because the treatment was originally of children)]

oscillate *verb* (oscillates, oscillating, oscillated)
1 move to and fro like a pendulum; vibrate. **2** waver or vary. **oscillation** *noun*, **oscillator** *noun* [from Latin *oscillare* = to swing]

-osis *suffix*
1 a diseased condition (as in *tuberculosis*). **2** an action or process (as in *metamorphosis*). [from Latin or Greek]

osmosis *noun*
the passing of fluid through a porous partition into another more concentrated fluid. [from Greek *osmos* = a push]

ostentatious *adjective*
making a showy display of something to impress people. **ostentatiously** *adverb*, **ostentation** *noun* [same origin as *ostensible*]

osteopath *noun* (*plural* **osteopaths**)
a person who treats certain diseases etc. by manipulating a patient's bones and muscles. **osteopathy** *noun*, **osteopathic** *adjective* [from Greek *osteon* = bone + *-patheia* = suffering]

ostrich *noun* (*plural* **ostriches**)
a large long-legged African bird that can run very fast but cannot fly. It was said to bury its head in the sand when pursued, believing that it cannot then be seen.

other *adjective*
1 different, *some other tune.* **2** remaining, *Try the other shoe.* **3** additional, *my other friends.* **4** just recent or past, *I saw him the other day.*
other *noun* & *pronoun* (*plural* **others**)
the other person or thing, *Where are the others?* [from Old English]

otherwise *adverb*
1 if things happen differently; if you do not, *Write it down, otherwise you'll forget.* **2** in other ways, *It rained, but otherwise the holiday was good.* **3** differently, *We could not do otherwise.* [from *other* + *-wise*]

otter *noun* (*plural* **otters**)
a fish-eating animal with webbed feet, a flat tail, and thick brown fur, living near water. [from Old English]

ought *auxiliary verb*
expressing duty (*We ought to feed them*), rightness or advisability (*You ought to take more exercise*), or probability (*At this speed, we ought to be there by noon*). [from Old English *ahte* = owed]

oughtn't (*mainly spoken*)
ought not.

ounce *noun* (*plural* **ounces**)
a unit of weight equal to $\frac{1}{16}$ of a pound (about 28 grams). [from Latin]

our *adjective*
belonging to us. [from Old English]

ours *possessive pronoun*
belonging to us, *These seats are ours.* [from *our*]

USAGE: It is incorrect to write *our's.*

ourselves *pronoun*
we or us and nobody else. (Compare *herself.*)

out *adverb*
1 away from or not in a particular place or position or state etc.; not at home. **2** into the open; into existence or sight etc., *The sun came out.* **3** not in action or use etc.; (of a batsman) having had the innings ended; (of a fire) not burning. **4** to or at an end; completely, *sold out; tired out.* **5** without restraint; boldly or loudly, *Speak out!*
be out for or **out to** be seeking or wanting, *They are out to make trouble.*
out of date 1 old-fashioned. **2** not valid any more.
out of doors in the open air.
out of the way remote.

out- *prefix*
1 out of; away from (as in *outcast*). **2** external; separate (as in *outhouse*). **3** more than; so as to defeat or exceed (as in *outdo*).

out and out *adjective*
thorough or complete, *an out and out villain.*

outboard motor *noun* (*plural* **outboard motors**)
a motor fitted to the outside of a boat's stern.

outbreak *noun* (*plural* **outbreaks**)
the start of a disease or war or anger etc.

outburst *noun* (*plural* **outbursts**)
the bursting out of anger or laughter etc.

outcast *noun* (*plural* **outcasts**)
a person who has been rejected by family, friends, or society.

outcrop *noun* (*plural* **outcrops**)
a piece of rock from a lower level that sticks out on the surface of the ground. [from *out*, + *crop* = outcrop]

outcry *noun* (*plural* **outcries**)
a strong protest.

outdo *verb* (outdoes, outdoing, outdid, outdone)
do better than another person etc.

outdoors *adverb*
in the open air.

outer *adjective*
outside or external; nearer to the outside. **outermost** *adjective*

outer space *noun*
the universe beyond the earth's atmosphere.

outfit *noun* (*plural* **outfits**)
1 a set of clothes worn together. **2** a set of equipment. **3** (*informal*) a team or organization.

outgrow *verb* (outgrows, outgrowing, outgrew, outgrown)
1 grow out of clothes or habits etc. 2 grow faster or larger than another person or thing.

outhouse *noun* (*plural* **outhouses**)
a small building (e.g. a shed or barn) that belongs to a house but is separate from it.

outing *noun* (*plural* **outings**)
a journey for pleasure.

outlandish *adjective*
looking or sounding strange or foreign.
[from Old English *utland* = a foreign land]

outlast *verb* (outlasts, outlasting, outlasted)
last longer than something else.

outlaw *noun* (*plural* **outlaws**)
a person who is punished by being excluded from legal rights and the protection of the law.

outlay *noun* (*plural* **outlays**)
what is spent on something.

outlet *noun* (*plural* **outlets**)
1 a way for something to get out. 2 a market for goods.

outline *noun* (*plural* **outlines**)
1 a line round the outside of something, showing its boundary or shape. 2 a summary.

outlook *noun* (*plural* **outlooks**)
1 a view on which people look out. 2 a person's mental attitude to something. 3 future prospects, *The outlook is bleak.*

outlying *adjective*
far from the centre; remote, *the outlying districts.*

outmoded *adjective*
out of date.

outnumber *verb* (outnumbers, outnumbering, outnumbered)
be more numerous than another group.

outpatient *noun* (*plural* **outpatients**)
a person who visits a hospital for treatment but does not stay there.

outpost *noun* (*plural* **outposts**)
a distant settlement. [from *out* + *post*³]

output *noun* (*plural* **outputs**)
1 the amount produced. 2 the information or results produced by a computer.

outrage *noun* (*plural* **outrages**)
1 something that shocks people by being very wicked or cruel. 2 great anger.
outrageous *adjective*, **outrageously** *adverb*
outrage *verb* (outrages, outraging, outraged)
shock and anger people greatly.
[from old French *outrer* = go beyond, exaggerate, influenced by *rage*]

outright *adverb*
1 completely; not gradually, *This drug should be banned outright.* 2 frankly, *We told him this outright.*

outright *adjective*
thorough or complete, *an outright fraud.*

outset *noun*
the beginning of something, *from the outset of his career.*

outside *noun* (*plural* **outsides**)
the outer side, surface, or part.
at the outside at the most, *a mile at the outside.*
outside *adjective*
1 on or coming from the outside, *the outside edge.* 2 greatest possible, *the outside price.* 3 remote or slight, *an outside chance.*
outside *adverb*
on or to the outside; outdoors, *Leave it outside. It's cold outside.*
outside *preposition*
on or to the outside of, *Leave it outside the door.*

outside broadcast *noun* (*plural* **outside broadcasts**)
a broadcast made on location and not in a studio.

outsider *noun* (*plural* **outsiders**)
1 a person who does not belong to a certain group. 2 a horse or person thought to have no chance of winning a race or competition.

outsize *adjective*
much larger than average.

outskirts *plural noun*
the outer parts or districts, especially of a town.

outspoken *adjective*
speaking or spoken very frankly.

outstanding *adjective*
1 extremely good or distinguished. 2 not yet paid or dealt with.

outstrip *verb* (outstrips, outstripping, outstripped)
1 run faster or further than another; outrun. 2 surpass in achievement or success. [from *out-* + Middle English *strypen* = move quickly]

outward *adjective*
1 going outwards. 2 on the outside.
outwardly *adverb*, **outwards** *adverb*

outwit *verb* (outwits, outwitting, outwitted)
deceive somebody by being crafty.

ova *plural* of **ovum**.

oval *adjective*
shaped like a 0, rounded and longer than it is broad. **oval** *noun*
[from Latin *ovum* = egg]

ovary *noun* (*plural* **ovaries**)
1 either of the two organs in which ova or egg-cells are produced in a woman's or female animal's body. 2 part of the pistil in a plant, from which fruit is formed.
[from Latin *ovum* = egg]

oven *noun* (*plural* **ovens**)
a closed space in which things are cooked or heated.

over *preposition*
1 above. 2 more than, *It's over a mile away.*
3 concerning, *They quarrelled over money.*
4 across the top of; on or to the other side of, *They rowed the boat over the lake.* 5 during, *We can talk over dinner.* 6 in superiority or preference to, *their victory over United.*

over *adverb*
1 out and down from the top or edge; from an upright position, *He fell over.* 2 so that a different side shows, *Turn it over.* 3 at or to a place; across, *Walk over to our house.*
4 remaining, *There is nothing left over.* 5 all through; thoroughly, *Think it over.* 6 at an end, *The lesson is over.*
over and over many times; repeatedly.

over *noun* (*plural* **overs**)
a series of six balls bowled in cricket.

over- *prefix*
1 over (as in *overturn*). 2 too much; too (as in *over-anxious*).

overact *verb* (**overacts**, **overacting**, **overacted**)
(of an actor) act in an exaggerated manner.

overall *adjective*
including everything; total, *the overall cost.*

overalls *plural noun*
a garment, like a shirt and trousers combined, worn over other clothes to protect them.

overarm *adjective* & *adverb*
with the arm lifted above shoulder level and coming down in front of the body, *bowling overarm.*

overawe *verb* (**overawes**, **overawing**, **overawed**)
overcome a person with awe.

overbalance *verb* (**overbalances**, **overbalancing**, **overbalanced**)
lose balance and fall over.

overbearing *adjective*
domineering.

overblown *adjective*
1 exaggerated or pretentious. 2 (of a flower) too fully open; past its best.

overboard *adverb*
from in or on a ship into the water, *She jumped overboard.*

overcast *adjective*
covered with cloud.

overcoat *noun* (*plural* **overcoats**)
a warm outdoor coat.

overcome *verb* (**overcomes**, **overcoming**, **overcame**, **overcome**)
1 win a victory over somebody; defeat. 2 make a person helpless, *He was overcome by the fumes.* 3 find a way of dealing with a problem etc.

overdo *verb* (**overdoes**, **overdoing**, **overdid**, **overdone**)
1 do something too much. 2 cook food for too long.

overdose *noun* (*plural* **overdoses**)
too large a dose of a drug.

overdraft *noun* (*plural* **overdrafts**)
the amount by which a bank account is overdrawn.

overdraw *verb* (**overdraws**, **overdrawing**, **overdrew**, **overdrawn**)
draw more money from a bank account than the amount you have in it.

overdue *adjective*
late; not paid or arrived etc. by the proper time.

overhaul *verb* (**overhauls**, **overhauling**, **overhauled**)
1 examine something thoroughly and repair it if necessary. 2 overtake.
overhaul *noun*

overhead *adjective* & *adverb*
1 above the level of your head. 2 in the sky.

overheads *plural noun*
the expenses of running a business.

overhear *verb* (**overhears**, **overhearing**, **overheard**)
hear something accidentally or without the speaker intending you to hear it.

overjoyed *adjective*
filled with great joy.

overlap *verb* (**overlaps**, **overlapping**, **overlapped**)
1 lie across part of something. 2 happen partly at the same time. **overlap** *noun*
[from *over* + *lap*[1]]

overlay *verb* (**overlays**, **overlaying**, **overlaid**)
cover with a layer; lie on top of something.

overlook *verb* (**overlooks**, **overlooking**, **overlooked**)
1 not notice or consider something. 2 not punish an offence. 3 have a view over something.

overpower *verb* (**overpowers**, **overpowering**, **overpowered**)
overcome.

overpowering *adjective*
very strong.

overrate *verb* (**overrates**, **overrating**, **overrated**)
have too high an opinion of something.

override *verb* (**overrides**, **overriding**, **overrode**, **overridden**)
1 overrule. 2 be more important than, *Safety overrides all other considerations.*

overrule *verb* (**overrules**, **overruling**, **overruled**)
reject a suggestion etc. by using your authority, *We voted for having a disco but the headteacher overruled the idea.*

overrun *verb* (overruns, overrunning, overran, overrun)
1 spread over and occupy or harm something, *Mice overran the place.* 2 go on for longer than it should, *The broadcast overran its time.*

oversee *verb* (oversees, overseeing, oversaw, overseen)
watch over or supervise people working.
overseer *noun*

oversight *noun* (*plural* oversights)
a mistake made by not noticing something.

overtake *verb* (overtakes, overtaking, overtook, overtaken)
1 pass a moving vehicle or person etc. 2 catch up with someone.

overthrow *verb* (overthrows, overthrowing, overthrew, overthrown)
remove someone from power by force, *They overthrew the king.*

overtime *noun*
time spent working outside the normal hours; payment for this.

overture *noun* (*plural* overtures)
1 a piece of music written as an introduction to an opera, ballet, etc. 2 a friendly attempt to start a discussion, *They made overtures of peace.*
[from old French, = opening]

overturn *verb* (overturns, overturning, overturned)
1 turn over or upside down. 2 reverse a legal decision.

overwhelm *verb* (overwhelms, overwhelming, overwhelmed)
1 bury or drown beneath a huge mass. 2 overcome completely.

ovum (*say* oh-vum) *noun* (*plural* ova)
a female cell that can develop into a new individual when it is fertilized.
[Latin, = egg]

owe *verb* (owes, owing, owed)
1 have a duty to pay or give something to someone, especially money. 2 have something because of the action of another person or thing, *They owed their lives to the pilot's skill.*
owing to because of; caused by.

USAGE: The use of *owing to* as a preposition meaning 'because of' is entirely acceptable, unlike this use of *due to*, which some people object to. See note at *due*.

owl *noun* (*plural* owls)
a bird of prey with large eyes, usually flying at night.

own *adjective*
belonging to yourself or itself.
get your own back get revenge.
on your own alone.

own *verb* (owns, owning, owned)
1 possess; have something as your property. 2 acknowledge or admit something, *I own that I made a mistake.*
own up confess; admit guilt.

owner *noun* (*plural* owners)
the person who owns something.
ownership *noun*

ox *noun* (*plural* oxen)
a large animal kept for its meat and for pulling carts.

oxide *noun* (*plural* oxides)
a compound of oxygen and one other element.

oxygen *noun*
a colourless odourless tasteless gas that exists in the air and is essential for living things.
[from French]

oyster *noun* (*plural* oysters)
a kind of shellfish whose shell sometimes contains a pearl.

ozone *noun*
a form of oxygen with a sharp smell.
[from Greek *ozein* = to smell]

ozone layer *noun*
a layer of ozone high in the atmosphere, protecting the world from harmful amounts of the sun's rays.

Pp

p *abbreviation*
penny or pence.

p. *abbreviation* (*plural* pp.)
page.

pace *noun* (*plural* paces)
1 one step in walking, marching, or running. 2 speed, *He set a fast pace.* [from Latin *passus*, literally = a stretch of the leg]

pacemaker *noun* (*plural* pacemakers)
1 a person who sets the pace for another in a race. 2 an electrical device to keep the heart beating.

pacifist (*say* pas-if-ist) *noun* (*plural* pacifists)
a person who believes that war is always wrong. **pacifism** *noun*

pacify *verb* (pacifies, pacifying, pacified)
1 calm a person down. 2 bring peace to a country etc. **pacification** *noun*
[from Latin *pacis* = of peace]

pack *noun* (*plural* packs)
1 a bundle; a collection of things wrapped or tied together. 2 a set of playing cards (usually 52). 3 a group of hounds or wolves etc. 4 a group of people; a group of Brownies or Cub

Scouts. **5** a large amount, *a pack of lies.* **6** a mass of pieces of ice floating in the sea, *pack ice.*
pack *verb* (**packs, packing, packed**)
1 put things into a suitcase, bag, or box etc. in order to move or store them. **2** crowd together; fill tightly.
pack off send a person away.
send a person packing dismiss him or her.

package *noun* (*plural* **packages**)
1 a parcel or packet. **2** a number of things offered or accepted together. **packaging** *noun* [from *pack*]

package holiday *noun* (*plural* **package holidays**) a holiday with everything arranged and included in the price.

packet *noun* (*plural* **packets**)
a small parcel. [from *pack*]

pad *noun* (*plural* **pads**)
1 a soft thick mass of material, used e.g. to protect or stuff something. **2** a piece of soft material worn to protect your leg in cricket and other games. **3** a set of sheets of paper fastened together at one edge. **4** the soft fleshy part under an animal's foot or the end of a finger or toe. **5** a flat surface from which rockets are launched or where helicopters take off and land.
pad *verb* (**pads, padding, padded**)
put a pad on or in something.

padding *noun*
material used to pad things.

paddle[1] *verb* (**paddles, paddling, paddled**)
walk about in shallow water. **paddle** *noun* [probably from old Dutch]

paddle[2] *noun* (*plural* **paddles**)
a short oar with a broad blade; something shaped like this.
paddle *verb* (**paddles, paddling, paddled**)
move a boat along with a paddle or paddles; row gently. [origin unknown]

paddock *noun* (*plural* **paddocks**)
a small field where horses are kept.

padlock *noun* (*plural* **padlocks**)
a detachable lock with a metal loop that passes through a ring or chain etc.

paediatrics (*say* peed-ee-**at**-riks) *noun*
the study of children's diseases.
paediatric *adjective*, **paediatrician** *noun* [from Greek *paidos* = of a child + *iatros* = doctor]

pagan (*say* **pay**-gan) *noun* (*plural* **pagans**)
a person who does not believe in one of the chief religions; a heathen. **pagan** *adjective* [same origin as *peasant*]

page[1] *noun* (*plural* **pages**)
a piece of paper that is part of a book or newspaper etc.; one side of this. [from Latin]

page[2] *noun* (*plural* **pages**)
a boy or man employed to go on errands or be an attendant.
[from Greek *paidion* = small boy]

pageant *noun* (*plural* **pageants**)
1 a play or entertainment about historical events and people. **2** a procession of people in costume as an entertainment. **pageantry** *noun* [origin unknown]

pagoda (*say* pag-**oh**-da) *noun* (*plural* **pagodas**)
a Buddhist tower, or a Hindu temple shaped like a pyramid, in India and the Far East. [via Portuguese from Persian]

paid *past tense* of **pay**.
put paid to (*informal*) put an end to someone's activity or hope etc.

pail *noun* (*plural* **pails**)
a bucket. [from Old English]

pain *noun* (*plural* **pains**)
1 an unpleasant feeling caused by injury or disease. **2** suffering in the mind.
painful *adjective*, **painfully** *adverb*, **painless** *adjective*
take pains make a careful effort with work etc. [from Latin *poena* = punishment]

painkiller *noun* (*plural* **painkillers**)
a medicine or drug that relieves pain.

painstaking *adjective*
very careful and thorough.

paint *noun* (*plural* **paints**)
a liquid substance put on something to colour it. **paintbox** *noun*, **paintbrush** *noun*
paint *verb* (**paints, painting, painted**)
1 put paint on something. **2** make a picture with paints. [from Latin]

painting *noun* (*plural* **paintings**)
a painted picture.

pair *noun* (*plural* **pairs**)
1 a set of two things or people; a couple.
2 something made of two joined parts, *a pair of scissors.* [from Latin *paria* = equal things]

palace *noun* (*plural* **palaces**)
a mansion where a king, queen, or other important person lives. [from *Palatium*, the name of a hill on which the house of the emperor Augustus stood in ancient Rome]

palatable *adjective*
tasting pleasant.

palate *noun* (*plural* **palates**)
1 the roof of your mouth. **2** a person's sense of taste. [from Latin]

pale[1] *adjective*
1 almost white, *a pale face.* **2** not bright in colour or light, *pale green; the pale moonlight.*
palely *adverb*, **paleness** *noun* [from Latin *pallidus* = pallid]

pale² *noun* (*plural* **pales**)
a boundary.
beyond the pale beyond the limits of good taste or behaviour etc.
[from Latin *palus* = a stake or fence post]

palindrome *noun* (*plural* **palindromes**)
a word or phrase that reads the same backwards as forwards, e.g. *radar*. [from Greek *palindromos* = running back again]

paling *noun* (*plural* **palings**)
a fence made of wooden posts or railings; one of its posts. [from *pale²*]

pall¹ (*say* pawl) *noun* (*plural* **palls**)
1 a cloth spread over a coffin. 2 a dark covering, *A pall of smoke lay over the town.* [from Latin *pallium* = cloak]

pall² (*say* pawl) *verb* (**palls, palling, palled**)
become uninteresting or boring to someone, *The novelty of the new computer game soon began to pall.* [from *appal*]

palliative *noun* (*plural* **palliatives**)
something that lessens pain or suffering.
palliative *adjective*

palm *noun* (*plural* **palms**)
1 the inner part of the hand, between the fingers and the wrist. 2 a palm tree.
palm off deceive a person into accepting something.

palm tree *noun* (*plural* **palm trees**)
a tropical tree with large leaves and no branches.

palpitate *verb* (**palpitates, palpitating, palpitated**)
1 (of the heart) beat hard and quickly. 2 (of a person) quiver with fear or excitement.
palpitation *noun* [from Latin]

pampas *noun*
wide grassy plains in South America.

pamper *verb* (**pampers, pampering, pampered**)
treat or look after someone very kindly and indulgently; coddle.

pamphlet *noun* (*plural* **pamphlets**)
a leaflet or booklet giving information on a subject. [from *Pamphilet*, the name of a long 12th-century poem in Latin]

pan *noun* (*plural* **pans**)
1 a wide container with a flat base, used for cooking etc. 2 something shaped like this. 3 the bowl of a lavatory. [from Old English]

pan- *prefix*
1 all (as in *panorama*). 2 to do with the whole of a continent or group etc. (as in *pan-African*). [from Greek]

pancake *noun* (*plural* **pancakes**)
a thin round cake of batter fried on both sides. [from *pan* + *cake*]

panda *noun* (*plural* **pandas**)
a large bear-like black-and-white animal found in China. [from the name given to a related animal in Nepal]

pandemonium *noun*
uproar and complete confusion.
[from *pan-* + *demon*]

pane *noun* (*plural* **panes**)
a sheet of glass in a window. [from Latin]

panel *noun* (*plural* **panels**)
1 a long flat piece of wood, metal, etc. that is part of a door, wall, piece of furniture, etc. 2 a group of people chosen to discuss or decide something.
panelled *adjective*, **panelling** *noun*
[from old French, related to *pane*]

pang *noun* (*plural* **pangs**)
a sudden sharp pain. [from *prong*]

panic *noun*
sudden uncontrollable fear.
panic-stricken *adjective*, **panicky** *adjective*
panic *verb* (**panics, panicking, panicked**)
fill or be filled with panic. [from the name of Pan, an ancient Greek god thought to be able to cause sudden fear]

panorama *noun* (*plural* **panoramas**)
a view or picture of a wide area.
panoramic *adjective*
[from *pan-* + Greek *horama* = view]

pant *verb* (**pants, panting, panted**)
take short quick breaths, usually after running or working hard.

panther *noun* (*plural* **panthers**)
a leopard. [from Greek]

pantomime *noun* (*plural* **pantomimes**)
1 a Christmas entertainment, usually based on a fairy tale. 2 mime.
[from *pan-* + *mime* (because in its most ancient form an actor mimed the different parts)]

pantry *noun* (*plural* **pantries**)
a small room for storing food; a larder.
[from old French *paneterie*, literally = bread-store]

pants *plural noun* (*informal*)
1 trousers. 2 underpants or knickers.

paper *noun* (*plural* **papers**)
1 a substance made in thin sheets from wood, rags, etc. and used for writing or printing or drawing on or for wrapping things. 2 a newspaper. 3 wallpaper. 4 a document.
paper *verb* (**papers, papering, papered**)
cover a wall or room with wallpaper.

paperback *noun* (*plural* **paperbacks**)
a book with a thin flexible cover.

papier mâché (*say* pap-yay mash-ay)
paper made into pulp and moulded to make models, ornaments, etc.
[French, = chewed paper]

para-[1] *prefix*
1 beside (as in *parallel*). 2 beyond (as in *paradox*). [from Greek]

para-[2] *prefix*
protecting from (as in *parasol*).
[from Italian]

parable *noun* (*plural* **parables**)
a story told to teach people something, especially one of those told by Jesus Christ.
[from Greek *paraballein* = put beside or compare: related to *parabola*]

parabola (*say* pa-**rab**-ol-a) *noun* (*plural* **parabolas**)
a curve like the path of an object thrown into the air and falling down again.
parabolic *adjective*
[from *para-*[1] + Greek *bole* = a throw]

parachute *noun* (*plural* **parachutes**)
an umbrella-like device on which people or things can float slowly to the ground from an aircraft. **parachuting** *noun*, **parachutist** *noun*
[from *para-*[2] + French *chute* = a fall]

parade *noun* (*plural* **parades**)
1 a procession that displays people or things. 2 an assembly of troops for inspection, drill, etc.; a ground for this. 3 a public square, promenade, or row of shops.
parade *verb* (**parades, parading, paraded**)
1 move in a parade. 2 assemble for a parade.
[from Spanish or Italian, = display]

paradise *noun*
1 heaven; a heavenly place. 2 the Garden of Eden.
[from ancient Persian *pairidaeza* = garden]

paradox *noun* (*plural* **paradoxes**)
a statement that seems to contradict itself but which contains a truth, e.g. 'More haste, less speed'.
paradoxical *adjective*, **paradoxically** *adverb*
[from *para-*[1] + Greek *doxa* = opinion]

paraffin *noun*
a kind of oil used as fuel.
[via German from Latin *parum* = hardly + *affinis* = related (because paraffin does not combine readily with other substances)]

paragraph *noun* (*plural* **paragraphs**)
one or more sentences on a single subject, forming a section of a piece of writing and beginning on a new line, usually slightly in from the margin of the page.
[from *para-*[1] + *-graph*]

parallel *adjective*
1 (of lines etc.) always at the same distance from each other, like the rails on which a train runs. 2 similar or corresponding, *When petrol prices rise there is a parallel rise in bus fares.*
parallelism *noun*

parallel *noun* (*plural* **parallels**)
1 something similar or corresponding. 2 a comparison, *You can draw a parallel between the two situations.* 3 a line etc. that is parallel to another. 4 a line of latitude.
[from *para-*[1] + Greek *allelos* = one another]

USAGE: Take care with the spelling of this word: one 'r', two 'l's, then one 'l'.

parallelogram *noun* (*plural* **parallelograms**)
a quadrilateral with its opposite sides equal and parallel. [from *parallel* + *-gram*]

paralyse *verb* (**paralyses, paralysing, paralysed**)
1 cause paralysis in a person etc. 2 make something be unable to move, *She was paralysed with fear.*
[from French, related to *paralysis*]

paralysis *noun*
being unable to move, especially because of a disease or an injury to the nerves.
paralytic (*say* pa-ra-**lit**-ik) *adjective*
[from Greek *para* = on one side + *lysis* = loosening]

parameter (*say* pa-**ram**-it-er) *noun* (*plural* **parameters**)
a quantity or quality etc. that is variable and affects other things by its changes.
[from *para-*[1] + Greek *metron* = measure]

USAGE: Do not confuse with *perimeter*.

paramount *adjective*
more important than anything else, *Secrecy is paramount.*
[from old French *paramont* = above]

parapet *noun* (*plural* **parapets**)
a low wall along the edge of a balcony, bridge, roof, etc. [via French from Italian]

paraphernalia *noun*
numerous pieces of equipment, belongings, etc.
[originally = the personal belongings a woman could keep after her marriage (as opposed to her dowry, which went to her husband): from *para-*[1] + Greek *pherne* = dowry]

paraphrase *verb* (**paraphrases, paraphrasing, paraphrased**)
give the meaning of something by using different words. **paraphrase** *noun*
[from *para-*[1] + *phrase*]

parasite *noun* (*plural* **parasites**)
an animal or plant that lives in or on another, from which it gets its food. **parasitic** *adjective*
[from Greek *parasitos* = guest at a meal]

paratroops *plural noun*
troops trained to be dropped from aircraft by parachute. **paratrooper** *noun*
[from *parachute* + *troops*]

parcel *noun* (*plural* **parcels**)
something wrapped up to be sent by post or carried.

parcel *verb* (parcels, parcelling, parcelled)
1 wrap something up as a parcel. **2** divide something into portions, *parcel out the work*. [from old French, related to *particle*]

parched *adjective*
very dry or thirsty. [origin unknown]

parchment *noun* (*plural* parchments)
a kind of heavy paper, originally made from animal skins. [from the city of Pergamum, now in Turkey, where parchment was made in ancient times]

pardon *noun*
forgiveness.
pardon *verb* (pardons, pardoning, pardoned)
1 forgive somebody. **2** excuse somebody kindly.
pardonable *adjective*, **pardonably** *adverb*
pardon *interjection*
used to mean 'I didn't hear or understand what you said' or 'I apologize'.

parent *noun* (*plural* parents)
1 a father or mother; a living thing that has produced others of its kind. **2** a source from which others are derived, *the parent company*.
parenthood *noun*, **parenting** *noun*, **parental** (*say* pa-rent-al) *adjective*
[from Latin *parens* = producing offspring]

parenthesis (*say* pa-ren-thi-sis) (*plural* parentheses)
1 something extra that is inserted in a sentence, usually between brackets or dashes. **2** either of the pair of brackets (like these) used to mark off words from the rest of a sentence.
parenthetical *adjective* [Greek, = putting in besides]

parish *noun* (*plural* parishes)
a district with its own church.
parishioner *noun*
[from Greek *paroikia* = neighbourhood, from *para-*[1] = beside + *oikos* = house]

park *noun* (*plural* parks)
1 a large garden or recreation ground for public use. **2** an area of grassland or woodland belonging to a country house.
park *verb* (parks, parking, parked)
leave a vehicle somewhere for a time.

parliament *noun* (*plural* parliaments)
the assembly that makes a country's laws.
parliamentary *adjective*
[same origin as *parley*]

parlour *noun* (*plural* parlours) (*old use*)
a sitting room. [originally = a room in a monastery where the monks were allowed to talk: from French *parler* = speak]

parody *noun* (*plural* parodies)
an imitation that makes fun of a person or thing.
parody *verb* (parodies, parodying, parodied)
make or be a parody of a person or thing. [from *para-*[1] + Greek *oide* = song]

parole *noun*
the release of a prisoner before the end of his or her sentence on condition of good behaviour, *He was on parole*.
[French, = word of honour]

paroxysm (*say* pa-roks-izm) *noun* (*plural* paroxysms)
a sudden outburst of rage, jealousy, laughter, etc. [from Greek *paroxynein* = to annoy or exasperate]

parrot *noun* (*plural* parrots)
a brightly-coloured tropical bird that can learn to repeat words etc. [from French]

parsley *noun*
a plant with crinkled green leaves used to flavour and decorate food.

parsnip *noun* (*plural* parsnips)
a plant with a pointed pale-yellow root used as a vegetable. [from old French]

parson *noun* (*plural* parsons)
a member of the clergy, especially a rector or vicar.
[from old French *persone* = person]

part *noun* (*plural* parts)
1 some but not all of a thing or number of things; anything that belongs to something bigger. **2** the character played by an actor or actress. **3** the words spoken by a character in a play. **4** one side in an agreement or in a dispute or quarrel.
take in good part not be offended at something.
take part join in an activity.
part *verb* (parts, parting, parted)
separate or divide.
part with give away or get rid of something.

part exchange *noun*
giving something that you own, as part of the price of what you are buying.

partial *adjective*
1 not complete or total, *a partial eclipse*. **2** favouring one side more than the other; biased or unfair.
partially *adverb*, **partiality** *noun*
be partial to be fond of something.

participate *verb* (participates, participating, participated)
take part or have a share in something.
participant *noun*, **participation** *noun*, **participator** *noun*
[from Latin *pars* = part + *capere* = take]

participle *noun* (*plural* participles)
a word formed from a verb (e.g. *gone, going*; *guided, guiding*) and used with an auxiliary verb to form certain tenses (e.g. *It has gone. It is going*) or the passive (e.g. *We were guided to our seats*), or as an adjective (e.g. *a guided missile*; *a guiding light*). The **past participle** (e.g. *gone, guided*) describes a completed action or past

condition. The **present participle** (which ends in -*ing*) describes a continuing action or condition. [from Latin *particeps* = taking part]

particle *noun* (*plural* particles)
a very small portion or amount.
[from Latin, = little part]

particular *adjective*
1 of this one and no other; individual, *This particular stamp is very rare.* 2 special, *Take particular care of it.* 3 giving something close attention; choosing carefully, *He is very particular about his clothes.*
particularly *adverb*, **particularity** *noun*
particular *noun* (*plural* particulars)
a single fact; a detail, *Can you give me the particulars of the case?*
in particular 1 especially, *We liked this one in particular.* 2 special, *We did nothing in particular.*
[same origin as *particle*]

parting *noun* (*plural* partings)
1 leaving or separation. 2 a line where hair is combed away in different directions.

partisan *noun* (*plural* partisans)
1 a strong supporter of a party or group etc. 2 a member of an organization resisting the authorities in a conquered country.

partition *noun* (*plural* partitions)
1 a thin wall that divides a room or space.
2 dividing something, especially a country, into separate parts.
partition *verb* (partitions, partitioning, partitioned)
1 divide something into separate parts.
2 divide a room or space by means of a partition. [from Latin *partitio* = division]

partly *adverb*
to some extent but not completely.

partner *noun* (*plural* partners)
1 one of a pair of people who do something together, e.g. in business or dancing or playing a game. 2 the person that someone is married to or is having a sexual relationship with.
partnership *noun*
[from Latin *partiri* = to divide or share]

part of speech *noun* (*plural* parts of speech)
any of the groups into which words are divided in grammar (noun, pronoun, adjective, verb, adverb, preposition, conjunction, interjection).

partridge *noun* (*plural* partridges)
a game bird with brown feathers.

part-time *adjective* & *adverb*
working for only some of the normal hours.
part-timer *noun*

party *noun* (*plural* parties)
1 a gathering of people to enjoy themselves, *a birthday party.* 2 a group working or travelling together. 3 an organized group of people with similar political beliefs, *the Labour Party.* 4 a

person who is involved in an action or lawsuit etc., *the guilty party.*
[from old French; related to *part*]

pass *verb* (passes, passing, passed)
1 go past something; go onwards. 2 move something in a certain direction, *Pass the cord through the ring.* 3 give or transfer something to another person, *Pass the butter to your father.* 4 be successful in a test or examination.
5 approve or accept, *They passed a law.*
6 occupy time. 7 happen, *We heard what passed when they met.* 8 come to an end. 9 utter, *Pass a remark.* 10 let your turn go by at cards or in a competition etc., *Pass!*
pass out 1 complete your military training.
2 faint.
pass *noun* (*plural* passes)
1 passing something. 2 a permit to go in or out of a place. 3 a route through a gap in a range of mountains. 4 a critical state of affairs, *Things have come to a pretty pass!*
[from Latin *passus* = pace]

passage *noun* (*plural* passages)
1 a way through something; a corridor. 2 a journey by sea or air. 3 a section of a piece of writing or music. 4 passing, *the passage of time.*
passageway *noun*
[old French, = passing]

passenger *noun* (*plural* passengers)
a person who is driven or carried in a car, train, ship, or aircraft etc.
[same origin as *passage*]

passer-by *noun* (*plural* passers-by)
a person who happens to be going past something.

passion *noun* (*plural* passions)
1 strong emotion. 2 great enthusiasm.
the Passion the sufferings of Jesus Christ at the Crucifixion.
[from Latin *passio* = suffering]

passionate *adjective*
full of passion. **passionately** *adverb*

passive *adjective*
1 not resisting or fighting against something.
2 acted upon and not active. 3 (of a form of a verb) used when the subject of the sentence receives the action, e.g. *was hit* in 'She was hit on the head'. (Compare *active.*)
passively *adverb*, **passiveness** *noun*,
passivity *noun*
[from Latin *passivus* = capable of suffering]

Passover *noun*
a Jewish religious festival commemorating the freeing of the Jews from slavery in Egypt.
[from *pass over*, because God spared the Jews from the fate which affected the Egyptians]

passport *noun* (*plural* passports)
an official document that entitles the person holding it to travel abroad.
[from *pass* + *port*[1]]

password *noun* (*plural* **passwords**)
1 a secret word or phrase used to distinguish friends from enemies. 2 a word you need to key in to gain access to certain computer files.

past *adjective*
of the time gone by, *during the past week*.
past *noun*
the time gone by.
past *preposition*
1 beyond, *Walk past the school*. 2 after, *It is past midnight*.
past it (*slang*) too old to be able to do something.
[the old past participle of *pass*]

paste *noun* (*plural* **pastes**)
1 a soft and moist or gluey substance. 2 a hard glassy substance used to make imitation jewellery.
paste *verb* (**pastes, pasting, pasted**)
1 stick something onto a surface by using paste. 2 coat something with paste. 3 (*slang*) beat or thrash someone.

pastel *noun* (*plural* **pastels**)
1 a crayon that is like chalk. 2 a light delicate colour.
[from Latin *pastellus* = woad]

pasteurize *verb* (**pasteurizes, pasteurizing, pasteurized**)
purify milk by heating and then cooling it.
[named after a French scientist, Louis Pasteur, who invented the process]

pastille *noun* (*plural* **pastilles**)
a small flavoured sweet for sucking.
[from Latin *pastillus* = lozenge]

pastime *noun* (*plural* **pastimes**)
something you do to make time pass pleasantly; a hobby or game.

pastoral *adjective*
to do with country life, *a pastoral scene*.

pastry *noun* (*plural* **pastries**)
1 dough made with flour, fat, and water, rolled flat and baked. 2 something made of pastry.
[from *paste*]

pasture *noun* (*plural* **pastures**)
land covered with grass etc. that cattle, sheep, or horses can eat.
pasture *verb* (**pastures, pasturing, pastured**)
put animals to graze in a pasture.
[from Latin *pastum* = fed]

pasty[1] (*say* **pas**-tee) *noun* (*plural* **pasties**)
pastry with a filling of meat and vegetables, baked without a dish to shape it. [from old French *pasté* = paste or pastry]

pasty[2] (*say* **pay**-stee) *adjective*
looking pale and unhealthy. [from *paste*]

pat *verb* (**pats, patting, patted**)
tap gently with the open hand or with something flat.

pat *noun* (*plural* **pats**)
1 a patting movement or sound. 2 a small piece of butter or other soft substance.
a pat on the back praise.

patch *noun* (*plural* **patches**)
1 a piece of material or metal etc. put over a hole or damaged place. 2 an area that is different from its surroundings. 3 a piece of ground, *the cabbage patch*. 4 a small area or piece of something, *There are patches of fog*.
not a patch on (*informal*) not nearly as good as.
patch *verb* (**patches, patching, patched**)
put a patch on something.
patch up 1 repair something roughly. 2 settle a quarrel.
[probably from old French *pieche* = piece]

patchwork *noun*
needlework in which small pieces of different cloth are sewn edge to edge.

patchy *adjective*
occurring in patches; uneven.
patchily *adverb*, **patchiness** *noun*

pâté (*say* **pat**-ay) *noun* (*plural* **pâtés**)
paste made of meat or fish. [French]

pâté de foie gras (*say* **pat**-ay der fwah **grah**) *noun*
a paste or pie of goose-liver.
[French, = paste of fat liver]

patent (*say* **pat**-ent or **pay**-tent) *noun* (*plural* **patents**)
the official right given to an inventor to make or sell his or her invention and to prevent other people from copying it.
patent *verb* (**patents, patenting, patented**)
get a patent for something.
[originally, in *letters patent*, an open letter from a monarch or government recording a contract or granting a right: from Latin *patens* = lying open]

paternalistic *adjective*
treating people in a paternal way, providing for their needs but giving them no responsibility. **paternalism** *noun*

paternity *noun*
1 fatherhood. 2 being the father of a particular baby. [from Latin *pater* = father]

path *noun* (*plural* **paths**)
1 a narrow way along which people or animals can walk. 2 a line along which a person or thing moves. [from Old English]

pathetic *adjective*
1 making you feel pity or sympathy.
2 miserably inadequate or useless, *a pathetic attempt*. **pathetically** *adverb*
[same origin as *pathos*]

pathos (*say* **pay**-thoss) *noun*
a quality of making people feel pity or sympathy. [Greek, = feeling or suffering]

-pathy *suffix*
forms nouns meaning 'feeling or suffering something' (e.g. *sympathy, telepathy*).
[from Greek *patheia* = feeling or suffering]

patience *noun*
1 being patient. 2 a card game for one person.

patient *adjective*
1 able to wait or put up with annoyances without becoming angry. 2 able to persevere.
patiently *adverb*
patient *noun* (*plural* patients)
a person who has treatment from a doctor or dentist etc.
[from Latin *patiens* = suffering]

patio *noun* (*plural* patios)
a paved area beside a house.
[Spanish, = courtyard]

patriarch (*say* pay-tree-ark) *noun* (*plural* patriarchs)
1 the male who is head of a family or tribe. 2 a bishop of high rank in the Orthodox Christian churches. **patriarchal** *adjective* [from Greek *patria* = family + *archein* = to rule]

patriot (*say* pay-tree-ot or pat-ree-ot) *noun* (*plural* patriots)
a person who loves his or her country and supports it loyally. **patriotic** *adjective*, **patriotically** *adverb*, **patriotism** *noun*
[from Greek *patris* = fatherland]

patrol *verb* (patrols, patrolling, patrolled)
walk or travel regularly over an area in order to guard it and see that all is well.
patrol *noun* (*plural* patrols)
1 a patrolling group of people, ships, aircraft, etc. 2 a group of Scouts or Guides.
on patrol patrolling.
[from French *patrouiller* = paddle in mud]

patron (*say* pay-tron) *noun* (*plural* patrons)
1 someone who supports a person or cause with money or encouragement. 2 a regular customer. **patronage** (*say* pat-ron-ij) *noun* [from Latin *patronus* = protector]

patronize (*say* pat-ron-I'z) *verb* (patronizes, patronizing, patronized)
1 be a regular customer of a particular shop, restaurant, etc. 2 talk to someone in a way that shows you think they are stupid or inferior to you.

patter[1] *noun*
a series of light tapping sounds.
patter *verb* (patters, pattering, pattered)
make light tapping sounds, *Rain pattered on the window panes*. [from *pat*]

patter[2] *noun*
the quick talk of a comedian, conjuror, salesperson, etc.
[originally = recite a prayer: from Latin *pater noster* = Our Father, the first words of a Christian prayer]

pattern *noun* (*plural* patterns)
1 a repeated arrangement of lines, shapes, or colours etc. 2 a thing to be copied in order to make something, *a dress pattern*. 3 the regular way in which something happens, *James Bond films follow a set pattern*. 4 an excellent example or model. [same origin as *patron*]

paunch *noun* (*plural* paunches)
a large belly. [from old French]

pauper *noun* (*plural* paupers)
a person who is very poor. [Latin, = poor]

pause *noun* (*plural* pauses)
a temporary stop in speaking or doing something.
pause *verb* (pauses, pausing, paused)
stop speaking or doing something for a short time. [from Greek *pauein* = to stop]

pave *verb* (paves, paving, paved)
lay a hard surface on a road or path etc.
paving-stone *noun*
pave the way prepare for something.
[from Latin *pavire* = ram down]

pavement *noun* (*plural* pavements)
a paved path along the side of a street.

pavilion *noun* (*plural* pavilions)
1 a building for use by players and spectators etc., especially at a cricket ground. 2 an ornamental building or shelter used for dances, concerts, exhibitions, etc.
[from French *pavillon* = tent]

paw *noun* (*plural* paws)
the foot of an animal that has claws.
paw *verb* (paws, pawing, pawed)
touch or scrape something with a hand or foot.
[from old French]

pawn[1] *noun* (*plural* pawns)
1 the least valuable piece in chess. 2 a person whose actions are controlled by somebody else.
[from Latin *pedo* = foot-soldier]

pawn[2] *verb* (pawns, pawning, pawned)
leave something with a pawnbroker as security for a loan.
[from old French *pan* = pledge]

pawnbroker *noun* (*plural* pawnbrokers)
a shopkeeper who lends money to people in return for objects that they leave as security.
pawnshop *noun*

pay *verb* (pays, paying, paid)
1 give money in return for goods or services. 2 give what is owed, *pay your debts*; *pay the rent*. 3 be profitable or worthwhile, *It pays to advertise*. 4 give or express, *pay attention*; *pay them a visit*; *pay compliments*. 5 suffer a penalty. 6 let out a rope by loosening it gradually. **payer** *noun*
pay off 1 pay in full what you owe. **2** be worthwhile or have good results, *All the preparation she did really paid off*.
pay up pay the full amount you owe.

pay *noun*
salary or wages.
[from Latin *pacare* = appease]

payable *adjective*
that must be paid.

payment *noun* (*plural* payments)
1 paying. 2 money paid.

PC *abbreviation*
1 personal computer. 2 police constable.

PE *abbreviation*
physical education.

pea *noun* (*plural* peas)
the small round green seed of a climbing plant,
growing inside a pod and used as a vegetable.
[via Old English from Greek]

peace *noun*
1 a time when there is no war, violence, or
disorder. 2 quietness and calm.

peaceable *adjective*
fond of peace; not quarrelsome or warlike.
peaceably *adverb*

peaceful *adjective*
quiet and calm.
peacefully *adverb*, **peacefulness** *noun*

peach *noun* (*plural* peaches)
1 a round soft juicy fruit with a pinkish or
yellowish skin and a large stone. 2 (*informal*) a
thing of great quality, *a peach of a shot*. [from
old French]

peacock *noun* (*plural* peacocks)
a male bird with a long brightly-coloured tail
that it can spread out like a fan. **peahen** *noun*
[via Old English from Latin]

peak *noun* (*plural* peaks)
1 a pointed top, especially of a mountain. 2 the
highest or most intense part of something,
Traffic reaches its peak at 5 p.m. 3 the part of a
cap that sticks out in front. **peaked** *adjective*
peak *verb* (peaks, peaking, peaked)
reach its highest point or value.

peal *noun* (*plural* peals)
1 the loud ringing of a bell or set of bells. 2 a
loud burst of thunder or laughter.
peal *verb* (peals, pealing, pealed)
(of bells) ring loudly. [from *appeal*]

peanut *noun* (*plural* peanuts)
a small round nut that grows in a pod in the
ground.

pear *noun* (*plural* pears)
a juicy fruit that gets narrower near the stalk.
[via Old English from Latin]

pearl *noun* (*plural* pearls)
a small shiny white ball found in the shells of
some oysters and used as a jewel.
pearly *adjective* [from French]

peasant *noun* (*plural* peasants)
a person who belongs to a farming community,
especially in poor areas of the world.
peasantry *noun* [from Latin *paganus* = villager]

peat *noun*
rotted plant material that can be dug out of the
ground and used as fuel or in gardening.
peaty *adjective* [from Latin *peta*, probably from
a Celtic word]

pebble *noun* (*plural* pebbles)
a small round stone. **pebbly** *adjective* [origin
unknown]

peck *verb* (pecks, pecking, pecked)
1 bite at something quickly with the beak.
2 kiss someone lightly on the cheek.
peck *noun* (*plural* pecks)
1 a quick bite by a bird. 2 a light kiss on the
cheek. [probably from old German]

peckish *adjective* (*informal*)
hungry. [from *peck* + *-ish*]

peculiar *adjective*
1 strange or unusual. 2 belonging to a
particular person, place, or thing; restricted,
This custom is peculiar to this tribe. 3 special,
This point is of peculiar interest.
peculiarly *adverb*, **peculiarity** *noun*
[from Latin *peculium* = private property]

pedal *noun* (*plural* pedals)
a lever pressed by the foot to operate a bicycle,
car, machine, etc. or in certain musical
instruments.
pedal *verb* (pedals, pedalling, pedalled)
use a pedal; move or work something,
especially a bicycle, by means of pedals.
[from Latin *pedis* = of a foot]

pedantic *adjective*
being very careful and strict about exact
meanings and facts etc. in learning.
pedantically *adverb*

peddle *verb* (peddles, peddling, peddled)
1 go from house to house selling small things.
2 sell illegal drugs. 3 try to get people to accept
an idea, way of life, etc. [from *pedlar*]

pedestal *noun* (*plural* pedestals)
the raised base on which a statue or pillar etc.
stands.
put someone on a pedestal admire him or her
greatly.
[from Italian *piede* = foot, + *stall*[1]]

pedestrian *noun* (*plural* pedestrians)
a person who is walking.
pedestrian *adjective*
ordinary and dull. [same origin as *pedal*]

pedestrian crossing *noun* (*plural* pedestrian
crossings)
a place where pedestrians can cross the road
safely.

pedigree *noun* (*plural* pedigrees)
a list of a person's or animal's ancestors,
especially to show how well an animal has
been bred. [from old French *pé de grue*
= crane's foot (from the shape made by the
lines on a family tree)]

pedlar *noun* (*plural* pedlars)
a person who goes from house to house selling
small things. [from Middle English *ped* = a
hamper or basket (in which a pedlar carried
his goods)]

peel *noun* (*plural* peels)
the skin of certain fruits and vegetables.
peel *verb* (peels, peeling, peeled)
1 remove the peel or covering from something.
2 come off in strips or layers. 3 lose a covering
or skin. [Middle English; related to Latin *pilare*
= cut off the hair]

peelings *plural noun*
strips of skin peeled from potatoes etc.

peep *verb* (peeps, peeping, peeped)
1 look quickly or secretly. 2 look through a
narrow opening. 3 come slowly or briefly into
view, *The moon peeped out from behind the
clouds.* **peep** *noun*, **peephole** *noun* [origin
unknown]

peer[1] *verb* (peers, peering, peered)
look at something closely or with difficulty.
[origin unknown]

peer[2] *noun* (*plural* peers)
1 a noble. 2 someone who is equal to another
in rank, merit, or age etc., *She had no peer.*
peeress *noun*, **peerage** *noun*
[from Latin *par* = equal]

peerless *adjective*
without an equal; better than the others.

peevish *adjective*
irritable. [origin unknown]

peg *noun* (*plural* pegs)
a piece of wood or metal or plastic for fastening
things together or for hanging things on.
peg *verb* (pegs, pegging, pegged)
1 fix something with pegs. 2 keep wages or
prices at a fixed level.
peg away work diligently; persevere.
peg out (*slang*) die.

Pekingese *noun* (*plural* Pekingese)
a small kind of dog with short legs, a flat face,
and long silky hair. [from *Peking*, the old name
of Beijing, the capital of China (where the
breed came from)]

pelican *noun* (*plural* pelicans)
a large bird with a pouch in its long beak for
storing fish. [from Greek]

pelican crossing *noun* (*plural* pelican crossings)
a place where pedestrians can cross a street
safely by operating lights that signal traffic to
stop.

pellet *noun* (*plural* pellets)
a tiny ball of metal, food, paper, etc.
[from Latin *pila* = ball]

pelt[1] *verb* (pelts, pelting, pelted)
1 throw a lot of things at someone. 2 run fast.
3 rain very hard. [origin unknown]

pelt[2] *noun* (*plural* pelts)
an animal skin, especially with the fur still on
it. [from Latin *pellis* = skin or leather]

pen[1] *noun* (*plural* pens)
an instrument with a point for writing with
ink.
[from Latin *penna* = feather (because a pen was
originally a sharpened quill)]

pen[2] *noun* (*plural* pens)
an enclosure for cattle, sheep, hens, or other
animals.
pen *verb* (pens, penning, penned)
shut animals etc. into a pen or other enclosed
space. [from Old English]

penalize *verb* (penalizes, penalizing, penalized)
punish; put a penalty on someone.
penalization *noun*

penalty *noun* (*plural* penalties)
1 a punishment. 2 a point or advantage given
to one side in a game when a member of the
other side has broken a rule.

pence *plural noun* see **penny**.
[from *pennies*]

pencil *noun* (*plural* pencils)
an instrument for drawing or writing, made of
a thin stick of graphite or coloured chalk etc.
enclosed in a cylinder of wood or metal.
[from Latin *penicillum* = paintbrush]

pendant *noun* (*plural* pendants)
an ornament worn hanging on a cord or chain
round the neck.
[from Latin *pendens* = hanging]

pending *preposition*
1 until, *Please take charge, pending his return.*
2 during, *pending these discussions.*
pending *adjective*
waiting to be decided or settled.

pendulum *noun* (*plural* pendulums)
a weight hung so that it can swing to and fro,
especially in the works of a clock. [from Latin,
= something hanging down]

penetrate *verb* (penetrates, penetrating,
penetrated)
make or find a way through or into something;
pierce.
penetration *noun*, **penetrative** *adjective*
[from Latin *penitus* = inside]

penfriend *noun* (*plural* penfriends)
a friend to whom you write without meeting.

penguin *noun* (*plural* penguins)
an Antarctic seabird that cannot fly but uses its wings as flippers for swimming. [origin unknown]

penicillin *noun*
an antibiotic obtained from mould.
[from the Latin name of the mould used]

peninsula *noun* (*plural* peninsulas)
a piece of land that is almost surrounded by water. **peninsular** *adjective*
[from Latin *paene* = almost + *insula* = island]

penis (*say* peen-iss) *noun* (*plural* penises)
the part of the body with which a male urinates and has sexual intercourse. [Latin, = tail]

penitence *noun*
regret for having done wrong. **penitent** *adjective*, **penitently** *adverb* [from Latin *paenitere* = to make someone sorry]

penknife *noun* (*plural* penknives)
a small folding knife.
[originally used for sharpening quill pens]

pen-name *noun* (*plural* pen-names)
a name used by an author instead of his or her real name.

penniless *adjective*
having no money; very poor.

penny *noun* (*plural* pennies for separate coins, pence for a sum of money)
1 a British coin worth $\frac{1}{100}$ of a pound. 2 a former coin worth $\frac{1}{12}$ of a shilling.
[from Old English]

pension *noun* (*plural* pensions)
an income consisting of regular payments made by a government or firm to someone who is retired, widowed, or disabled.
[from Latin *pensio* = payment]

pensioner *noun* (*plural* pensioners)
a person who receives a pension.

penta- *prefix*
five. [from Greek]

pentagon *noun* (*plural* pentagons)
a flat shape with five sides and five angles.
pentagonal (*say* pent-**ag**-on-al) *adjective*
the Pentagon a five-sided building in Washington, headquarters of the leaders of the American armed forces.
[from *penta-* + Greek *gonia* = angle]

pentameter *noun* (*plural* pentameters)
a line of verse with five rhythmic beats. [from *penta-* + Greek *metron* = measure]

pentathlon *noun* (*plural* pentathlons)
an athletic contest consisting of five events.
[from *penta-* + Greek *athlon* = contest]

Pentecost *noun*
1 the Jewish harvest festival, fifty days after Passover. 2 Whit Sunday.
[from Greek *pentekoste* = fiftieth (day)]

pent-up *adjective*
shut in, *pent-up feelings*.
[old past participle of *pen*²]

penultimate *adjective*
last but one.
[from Latin *paene* = almost, + *ultimate*]

peony *noun* (*plural* peonies)
a plant with large round red, pink, or white flowers. [named after Paion, physician of the Greek gods (because the plant was once used in medicines)]

people *plural noun*
human beings; persons, especially those belonging to a particular country, area, or group etc.

people *noun* (*plural* peoples)
a community or nation, *a warlike people*; *the English-speaking peoples*.

pepper *noun* (*plural* peppers)
1 a hot-tasting powder used to flavour food. 2 a bright green, red, or yellow vegetable.
peppery *adjective*
pepper *verb* (peppers, peppering, peppered)
1 sprinkle with pepper. 2 pelt with many small objects. [from Old English]

peppermint *noun* (*plural* peppermints)
1 a kind of mint used for flavouring. 2 a sweet flavoured with this mint.
[because of its sharp taste]

per *preposition*
for each, *The charge is £2 per person*.
[from Latin, = through]

per- *prefix*
1 through (as in *perforate*). 2 thoroughly (as in *perturb*). 3 away entirely; towards badness (as in *pervert*). [from Latin]

perceive *verb* (perceives, perceiving, perceived)
see, notice, or understand something. [from Latin *percipere* = seize, understand]

per cent *adverb*
for or in every hundred, *three per cent* (3%).
[from *per* + Latin *centum* = hundred]

percentage *noun* (*plural* percentages)
an amount or rate expressed as a proportion of 100.

perceptible *adjective*
able to be seen or noticed.
perceptibly *adverb*, **perceptibility** *noun*

perception *noun* (*plural* perceptions)
the ability to see, notice, or understand something. [same origin as *perceive*]

perceptive *adjective*
quick to notice or understand things.

perch¹ *noun* (*plural* perches)
1 a place where a bird sits or rests. 2 a seat high up.
perch *verb* (perches, perching, perched)
rest or place on a perch.
[from Latin *pertica* = pole]

perch[2] *noun* (*plural* **perch**)
an edible freshwater fish. [from Greek]

percolate *verb* (**percolates, percolating, percolated**)
flow through small holes or spaces.
percolation *noun*
[from *per-* + Latin *colum* = strainer]

percolator *noun* (*plural* **percolators**)
a pot for making coffee, in which boiling water percolates through coffee grounds.

percussion *noun*
1 musical instruments (e.g. drums, cymbals) played by being struck or shaken. 2 the striking of one thing against another.
percussive *adjective*
[from Latin *percussum* = hit]

perdition *noun*
eternal damnation.
[from Latin *perditum* = destroyed]

peregrine *noun* (*plural* **peregrines**)
a kind of falcon. [from Latin *peregrinus* = travelling (because it migrates)]

perennial *adjective*
lasting for many years; keeping on recurring.
perennially *adverb*
perennial *noun* (*plural* **perennials**)
a plant that lives for many years.
[from *per-* + Latin *annus* = year]

perfect (*say* per-fikt) *adjective*
1 so good that it cannot be made any better. 2 complete, *a perfect stranger.*
perfectly *adverb*
perfect (*say* per-fekt) *verb* (**perfects, perfecting, perfected**)
make a thing perfect. **perfection** *noun*
to perfection perfectly.
[from Latin *perfectum* = completed]

perfectionist *noun* (*plural* **perfectionists**)
a person who likes everything to be done perfectly.

perfect tense *noun*
a tense of a verb showing a completed action, e.g. *He has arrived.*

perforate *verb* (**perforates, perforating, perforated**)
1 make tiny holes in something, especially so that it can be torn off easily. 2 pierce.
perforation *noun*
[from *per-* + Latin *forare* = bore through]

perform *verb* (**performs, performing, performed**)
1 do something in front of an audience, *perform a play.* 2 do something, *perform an operation.* **performance** *noun*, **performer** *noun*
[from old French]

perfume *noun* (*plural* **perfumes**)
1 a pleasant smell. 2 a liquid for giving something a pleasant smell; scent.
perfume *verb*, **perfumery** *noun*

[originally used of smoke from something burning: via French from old Italian *parfumare* = to smoke through]

perfunctory *adjective*
done without much care or interest, *a perfunctory glance.* **perfunctorily** *adverb* [from Latin]

perhaps *adverb*
it may be; possibly.
[from *per* + Middle English *hap* = luck]

peri- *prefix*
around (as in *perimeter*). [from Greek]

peril *noun* (*plural* **perils**)
danger. **perilous** *adjective*, **perilously** *adverb*
[from Latin *periculum* = danger]

perimeter *noun* (*plural* **perimeters**)
1 the outer edge or boundary of something. 2 the distance round the edge.
[from *peri-* + Greek *metron* = measure]

USAGE: Do not confuse with *parameter.*

period *noun* (*plural* **periods**)
1 a length of time. 2 the time when a woman menstruates. 3 (in punctuation) a full stop.
[from Greek *periodos* = course or cycle (of events)]

periodic *adjective*
occurring at regular intervals.
periodically *adverb*

periodical *noun* (*plural* **periodicals**)
a magazine published at regular intervals (e.g. monthly).

periodic table *noun*
a table in which the chemical elements are arranged in order of increasing atomic number.

periscope *noun* (*plural* **periscopes**)
a device with a tube and mirrors with which a person in a trench or submarine etc. can see things that are otherwise out of sight.
[from *peri-* + Greek *skopein* = look at]

perish *verb* (**perishes, perishing, perished**)
1 die; be destroyed. 2 rot, *The rubber ring has perished.* **perishable** *adjective*
[from *per-* + Latin *ire* = go]

perjure *verb* (**perjures, perjuring, perjured**)
perjure yourself commit perjury.

perjury *noun*
telling a lie while you are on oath to speak the truth.
[from Latin *perjurare* = break an oath]

perk[1] *verb* (**perks, perking, perked**)
perk up make or become more cheerful.
[from *perch*[1]]

perk[2] *noun* (*plural* **perks**) (*informal*)
something extra given to a worker, *Free bus travel is one of the perks of the job.*
[from *perquisite*, from Latin]

perky *adjective*
lively and cheerful. **perkily** *adverb*
[from *perk*¹]

permanent *adjective*
lasting for always or for a very long time.
permanently *adverb*, **permanence** *noun* [from
per- + Latin *manens* = remaining]

permanent wave *noun* (*plural* **permanent
waves**)
treatment of the hair to give it long-lasting
waves.

permeate *verb* (**permeates, permeating,
permeated**)
spread into every part of something; pervade,
Smoke had permeated the hall. **permeation** *noun*
[from *per-* + Latin *meare* = to pass]

permissible *adjective*
allowable.

permission *noun*
the right to do something, given by someone in
authority; authorization. [same origin as
permit]

permissive *adjective*
letting people do what they wish; tolerant or
liberal.

permit (*say* per-mit) *verb* (**permits, permitting,
permitted**)
give permission or consent or a chance to do
something; allow.

permit (*say* per-mit) *noun* (*plural* **permits**)
written or printed permission to do something
or go somewhere.
[from *per-* + Latin *mittere* = send or let go]

permutation *noun* (*plural* **permutations**)
1 changing the order of a set of things. 2 a
changed order, *3, 1, 2 is a permutation of 1, 2, 3*.
[from *per-* + Latin *mutare* = to change]

peroxide *noun*
a chemical used for bleaching hair.
[from *per-* + *oxide*]

perpendicular *adjective*
upright; at a right angle (90°) to a line or
surface.
[from Latin *perpendiculum* = plumb line]

perpetrate *verb* (**perpetrates, perpetrating,
perpetrated**)
commit or be guilty of, *perpetrate a crime or an
error*. **perpetration** *noun*, **perpetrator** *noun*
[from *per-* + Latin *patrare* = make something
happen]

perpetual *adjective*
lasting for a long time; continual.
perpetually *adverb*
[from Latin *perpes* = uninterrupted]

perplex *verb* (**perplexes, perplexing, perplexed**)
bewilder or puzzle somebody. **perplexity** *noun*
[from *per-* + Latin *plexus* = twisted together]

persecute *verb* (**persecutes, persecuting,
persecuted**)
be continually cruel to somebody, especially
because you disagree with his or her beliefs.
persecution *noun*, **persecutor** *noun* [from Latin
persecutum = pursued]

persevere *verb* (**perseveres, persevering,
persevered**)
go on doing something even though it is
difficult. **perseverance** *noun*
[from *per-* + Latin *severus* = strict]

Persian *adjective*
to do with or belonging to Persia, a country in
the Middle East now called Iran.

Persian *noun*
the language of Persia.

persist *verb* (**persists, persisting, persisted**)
1 continue firmly or obstinately, *She persists in
breaking the rules*. 2 continue to exist, *The
custom persists in some countries*.
persistent *adjective*, **persistently** *adverb*,
persistence *noun*, **persistency** *noun*
[from *per-* + Latin *sistere* = to stand]

person *noun* (*plural* **people** or **persons**)
1 a human being; a man, woman, or child. 2 (in
grammar) any of the three groups of personal
pronouns and forms taken by verbs. The **first
person** (= *I, me, we, us*) refers to the person(s)
speaking; the **second person** (= *you*) refers to
the person(s) spoken to; the **third person** (= *he,
him, she, her, it, they, them*) refers to the
person(s) spoken about.
in person being actually present oneself, *She
was there in person*.
[from Latin *persona* = mask used by an actor]

personal *adjective*
1 belonging to, done by, or concerning a
particular person, *personal belongings*.
2 criticizing a person, *making personal
remarks*. **personally** *adverb*

USAGE: Do not confuse with *personnel*.

personality *noun* (*plural* **personalities**)
1 a person's character, *She has a cheerful
personality*. 2 a well-known person, *a TV
personality*.

personify *verb* (**personifies, personifying,
personified**)
represent a quality or idea etc. as a person.
personification *noun*

personnel *noun*
the people employed by a firm or other large
organization. [French, = personal]

USAGE: Do not confuse with *personal*.

perspective *noun* (*plural* **perspectives**)
the impression of depth and space in a picture
or scene.

in perspective giving a well-balanced view of things.
[from Latin *perspicere* = look at closely]

perspire *verb* (perspires, perspiring, perspired) sweat. **perspiration** *noun*
[from *per-* + Latin *spirare* = breathe]

persuade *verb* (persuades, persuading, persuaded)
make someone believe or agree to do something. **persuasion** *noun*, **persuasive** *adjective*
[from *per-* + Latin *suadere* = advise or induce]

pert *adjective*
cheeky. **pertly** *adverb*, **pertness** *noun*

perturb *verb* (perturbs, perturbing, perturbed)
worry someone. **perturbation** *noun*
[from *per-* + Latin *turbare* = disturb]

pervade *verb* (pervades, pervading, pervaded)
spread all through something; permeate.
pervasion *noun*, **pervasive** *adjective*
[from *per-* + Latin *vadere* = go]

perverse *adjective*
obstinately doing something different from what is reasonable or required.
perversely *adverb*, **perversity** *noun*
[same origin as *pervert*]

pervert (*say* per-vert) *verb* (perverts, perverting, perverted)
1 turn something from the right course of action, *By false evidence they perverted the course of justice.* **2** cause a person to behave wickedly or abnormally. **perversion** *noun*
pervert (*say* per-vert) *noun* (*plural* perverts)
a person whose sexual behaviour is thought to be unnatural or disgusting. [from *per-* + Latin *vertere* = to turn]

pessimist *noun* (*plural* pessimists)
a person who expects that things will turn out badly. (Compare *optimist*.) **pessimism** *noun*, **pessimistic** *adjective*, **pessimistically** *adverb*
[from Latin *pessimus* = worst]

pest *noun* (*plural* pests)
1 a destructive insect or animal, such as a locust or a mouse. **2** a nuisance.
[from Latin *pestis* = plague]

pester *verb* (pesters, pestering, pestered)
keep annoying someone by frequent questions or requests. [from French *empestrer* = infect with plague]

pesticide *noun* (*plural* pesticides)
a substance for killing harmful insects and other pests. [from *pest* + *-cide*]

pestilence *noun* (*plural* pestilences)
a deadly epidemic. [same origin as *pest*]

pet *noun* (*plural* pets)
1 a tame animal kept for companionship and pleasure. **2** a person treated as a favourite, *teacher's pet.*

pet *adjective*
favourite, *Science fiction is my pet subject.*
pet *verb* (pets, petting, petted)
treat or fondle someone affectionately.

petal *noun* (*plural* petals)
one of the separate coloured outer parts of a flower. [from Greek *petalos* = spread out, unfolded]

peter *verb* (peters, petering, petered)
peter out become gradually less and cease to exist.
[origin unknown]

petition *noun* (*plural* petitions)
a formal request for something, especially a written one signed by many people.
[from Latin *petere* = claim or ask for]

petrify *verb* (petrifies, petrifying, petrified)
1 make someone so terrified that he or she cannot move. **2** turn to stone. **petrifaction** *noun*
[from Greek *petra* = rock]

petrol *noun*
a liquid made from petroleum, used as fuel for engines.

petroleum *noun*
an oil found underground that is refined to make fuel (e.g. petrol, paraffin) or for use in dry-cleaning etc.
[from Greek *petra* = rock + Latin *oleum* = oil]

petticoat *noun* (*plural* petticoats)
a woman's or girl's dress-length undergarment.
[from *petty* = little, + *coat*]

petting *noun*
affectionate touching or fondling.

petty *adjective* (pettier, pettiest)
1 unimportant or trivial, *petty regulations.*
2 mean and small-minded.
pettily *adverb*, **pettiness** *noun*
[from French *petit* = small]

petty cash *noun*
cash kept by an office for small payments.

pew *noun* (*plural* pews)
a long wooden seat, usually fixed in rows, in a church.
[from old French; related to *podium*]

pewter *noun*
a grey alloy of tin and lead.

pH *noun*
a measure of the acidity or alkalinity of a solution. Pure water has a pH of 7, acids have a pH between 0 and 7, and alkalis have a pH between 7 and 14.
[from the initial letter of German *Potenz* = power, + H, the symbol for hydrogen]

phantom *noun* (*plural* phantoms)
a ghost; something that is not real.

Pharaoh (*say* fair-oh) *noun* (*plural* Pharaohs)
the title of the king of ancient Egypt.
[from ancient Egyptian *pr-'o* = great house]

pharmacy *noun* (*plural* pharmacies)
1 a shop selling medicines; a dispensary. 2 the job of preparing medicines.
[from Greek *pharmakon* = drug]

phase *noun* (*plural* phases)
a stage in the progress or development of something.
phase *verb* (phases, phasing, phased)
do something in stages, not all at once, *a phased withdrawal*. [from Latin]

Ph.D. *abbreviation*
Doctor of Philosophy; a university degree awarded to someone who has done advanced research in their subject.

pheasant (*say* fez-ant) *noun* (*plural* pheasants)
a game bird with a long tail. [from Greek]

phenomenal *adjective*
amazing or remarkable.
phenomenally *adverb*

phenomenon *noun* (*plural* phenomena)
an event or fact, especially one that is remarkable. [from Greek *phainomenon* = something appearing]

USAGE: Note that *phenomena* is a plural. It is incorrect to say 'this phenomena' or 'these phenomenas'.

phial *noun* (*plural* phials)
a small glass bottle. [from Greek]

phil- *prefix*
1 fond of. 2 a lover of. see **philo-**.

philanthropy *noun*
love of mankind, especially as shown by kind and generous acts that benefit large numbers of people. **philanthropist** *noun*,
philanthropic *adjective*
[from *phil-* + Greek *anthropos* = mankind]

philistine (*say* fil-ist-I'n) *noun* (*plural* philistines)
a person who dislikes art, poetry, etc.
[from the Philistines in the Bible, who were enemies of the Israelites]

philo- *prefix*
1 fond of. 2 a lover of.
[from Greek *philein* = to love]

philosopher *noun* (*plural* philosophers)
an expert in philosophy.

philosophical *adjective*
1 to do with philosophy. 2 calm and not upset after a misfortune or disappointment, *Be philosophical about losing*.
philosophically *adverb*

philosophy *noun* (*plural* philosophies)
1 the study of truths about life, morals, etc. 2 a set of ideas or principles or beliefs.
[from *philo-* + Greek *sophia* = wisdom]

phobia (*say* foh-bee-a) *noun* (*plural* phobias)
great or abnormal fear of something.
[from Greek *phobos* = fear]

-phobia *suffix*
forms nouns meaning 'fear or great dislike of something' (e.g. *hydrophobia*).

phone *noun* (*plural* phones)
a telephone.
phone *verb* (phones, phoning, phoned)
telephone. [short for *telephone*]

phonetic (*say* fon-et-ik) *adjective*
1 to do with speech-sounds. 2 representing speech-sounds. **phonetically** *adverb*
[from Greek *phonein* = speak]

phosphorus *noun*
a chemical substance that glows in the dark.
[from Greek *phos* = light + *-phoros* = bringing]

photo *noun* (*plural* photos)
a photograph.

photo- *prefix*
light (as in *photograph*). [from Greek]

photograph *noun* (*plural* photographs)
a picture made by the effect of light or other radiation on film or special paper.
photograph *verb* (photographs, photographing, photographed)
take a photograph of a person or thing.
photographer *noun*

photography *noun*
taking photographs. **photographic** *adjective*

photosynthesis *noun*
the process by which green plants use sunlight to turn carbon dioxide and water into complex substances, giving off oxygen.

phrase *noun* (*plural* phrases)
1 a group of words that form a unit in a sentence or clause, e.g. *in the garden* in 'The Queen was in the garden'. 2 a short section of a tune. [from Greek *phrazein* = declare]

physical *adjective*
1 to do with the body rather than the mind or feelings. 2 to do with things that you can touch or see. 3 to do with physics. **physically** *adverb*
[same origin as *physics*]

physical education or **physical training** *noun*
gymnastics or other exercises done to keep the body healthy.

physician *noun* (*plural* physicians)
a doctor, especially one who is not a surgeon.
[from old French *fisicien* = physicist]

physicist (*say* fiz-i-sist) *noun* (*plural* physicists)
an expert in physics.

physics (*say* fiz-iks) *noun*
the study of the properties of matter and energy (e.g. heat, light, sound, movement).
[from Greek *physikos* = natural]

physiotherapy (*say* fiz-ee-o-th'erra-pee) *noun*
the treatment of a disease or weakness by
massage, exercises, etc.
physiotherapist *noun*
[from Greek *physis* = nature, + *therapy*]

physique (*say* fiz-**eek**) *noun* (*plural* **physiques**)
a person's build. [French, = physical]

pi *noun*
the symbol (π) of the ratio of the circumference
of a circle to its diameter. The value of pi is
approximately 3.142.
[the name of the sixteenth letter (π) of the
Greek alphabet]

pianist *noun* (*plural* **pianists**)
a person who plays the piano.

piano *noun* (*plural* **pianos**)
a large musical instrument with a keyboard.
[short for *pianoforte*, from Italian *piano* = soft
+ *forte* = loud (because it can produce soft notes
and loud notes)]

piccolo *noun* (*plural* **piccolos**)
a small high-pitched flute. [Italian, = small]

pick[1] *verb* (**picks, picking, picked**)
1 separate a flower or fruit from its plant, *We
picked apples.* **2** choose; select carefully. **3** pull
bits off or out of something. **4** open a lock by
using something pointed, not with a key.
pick a quarrel deliberately provoke a quarrel
with somebody.
pick holes in find fault with.
pick on keep criticizing or harassing a
particular person.
pick someone's pocket steal from it.
pick up 1 lift or take up. **2** collect. **3** take
someone into a vehicle. **4** manage to hear
something. **5** get better or recover.
pick *noun*
1 choice, *take your pick.* **2** the best of a group.
[origin unknown]

pick[2] *noun* (*plural* **picks**)
1 a pickaxe. **2** a plectrum.
[a different spelling of *pike*]

pickaxe *noun* (*plural* **pickaxes**)
a heavy pointed tool with a long handle, used
for breaking up hard ground etc. [from old
French *picois*, later confused with *axe*]

picket *noun* (*plural* **pickets**)
1 a striker or group of strikers who try to
persuade other people not to go into a place of
work during a strike. **2** a pointed post as part
of a fence.
picket *verb* (**pickets, picketing, picketed**)
stand outside a place of work to try to persuade
other people not to go in during a strike. [from
French *picquet* = small pike]

pickle *noun* (*plural* **pickles**)
1 a strong-tasting food made of pickled
vegetables. **2** (*informal*) a mess.
pickle *verb* (**pickles, pickling, pickled**)
preserve food in vinegar or salt water.

pickpocket *noun* (*plural* **pickpockets**)
a thief who steals from people's pockets or
bags.

pick-up *noun* (*plural* **pick-ups**)
1 the part of a record player that holds the
stylus. **2** an open truck for carrying small
loads.

picnic *noun* (*plural* **picnics**)
a meal eaten in the open air away from home.
picnic *verb* (**picnics, picnicking, picnicked**)
have a picnic. **picnicker** *noun* [from French]

picture *noun* (*plural* **pictures**)
1 a representation of a person or thing made
by painting, drawing, or photography. **2** a film
at the cinema. **3** how something seems; an
impression.
picture *verb* (**pictures, picturing, pictured**)
1 show in a picture. **2** imagine.
[from Latin *pictum* = painted]

picturesque *adjective*
1 forming an attractive scene, *a picturesque
village.* **2** vividly described; expressive,
picturesque language. **picturesquely** *adverb*

pie *noun* (*plural* **pies**)
a baked dish of meat, fish, or fruit covered with
pastry.
[perhaps from *magpie* (because the contents of
a pie look like the bits and pieces a magpie
collects in its nest)]

piece *noun* (*plural* **pieces**)
1 a part or portion of something; a fragment.
2 a separate thing or example, *a fine piece of
work.* **3** something written, composed, or
painted etc., *a piece of music.* **4** one of the
objects used to play a game on a board, *a chess-
piece.*
piece *verb* (**pieces, piecing, pieced**)
put pieces together to make something.

piecemeal *adjective* & *adverb*
done or made one piece at a time.
[from *piece* + Old English *mael* = a measure]

pie chart *noun* (*plural* **pie charts**)
a circle divided into sectors to represent the
way in which a quantity is divided up.

pier *noun* (*plural* **piers**)
1 a long structure built out into the sea for
people to walk on. **2** a pillar supporting a
bridge or arch. [from Latin]

pierce *verb* (**pierces, piercing, pierced**)
make a hole through something; penetrate.

piety *noun*
being very religious and devout; piousness.
[from Latin *pietas* = dutiful behaviour]

pig *noun* (*plural* **pigs**)
1 a fat animal with short legs and a blunt
snout, kept for its meat. **2** (*informal*) someone
greedy, dirty, or unpleasant. **piggy** *adjective* &
noun [origin unknown]

pigeon *noun* (*plural* pigeons)
a bird with a fat body and a small head. [from old French *pijon* = young bird]

pigeon-hole *noun* (*plural* pigeon-holes)
a small compartment above a desk etc., used for holding letters or papers.
pigeon-hole *verb* (pigeon-holes, pigeon-holing, pigeon-holed)
decide that a person belongs to a particular category, *She doesn't want to be pigeon-holed simply as a pop singer.*

piggyback *adverb*
carried on somebody else's back or shoulders.
piggyback *noun*
[from *pick-a-back*]

pig-headed *adjective*
obstinate.

piglet *noun* (*plural* piglets)
a young pig.

pigment *noun* (*plural* pigments)
a substance that colours something.
pigmented *adjective*, **pigmentation** *noun*
[from Latin *pingere* = to paint]

pigsty *noun* (*plural* pigsties)
1 a partly-covered pen for pigs. 2 a filthy room or house.

pigtail *noun* (*plural* pigtails)
a plait of hair worn hanging at the back of the head.

pike *noun* (*plural* pikes)
1 a heavy spear. 2 (*plural* pike) a large freshwater fish. [origin unknown]

pile¹ *noun* (*plural* piles)
1 a number of things on top of one another. 2 (*informal*) a large quantity; a lot of money. 3 a tall building.
pile *verb* (piles, piling, piled)
put things into a pile; make a pile.
[from Latin *pila* = pillar]

pile² *noun* (*plural* piles)
a heavy beam made of metal, concrete, or timber driven into the ground to support something. [from Old English]

pile³ *noun*
a raised surface on fabric, made of upright threads, *a carpet with a thick pile.*
[from Latin *pilus* = hair]

pile-up *noun* (*plural* pile-ups)
a road accident that involves a number of vehicles.

pilfer *verb* (pilfers, pilfering, pilfered)
steal small things. **pilferer** *noun*,
pilferage *noun* [from old French]

pilgrim *noun* (*plural* pilgrims)
a person who travels to a holy place for religious reasons. **pilgrimage** *noun*

pill *noun* (*plural* pills)
a small solid piece of medicine for swallowing.
the pill a contraceptive pill.
[from Latin *pila* = ball]

pillage *verb* (pillages, pillaging, pillaged)
carry off goods using force, especially in a war; plunder. **pillage** *noun*
[from Latin *pilare* = cut the hair from]

pillar *noun* (*plural* pillars)
a tall stone or wooden post.
[same origin as *pile*¹]

pillar box *noun* (*plural* pillar boxes)
a postbox standing in a street.
[because many of them are shaped like a short pillar]

pillion *noun* (*plural* pillions)
a seat behind the driver on a motorcycle. [from Scottish Gaelic *pillean* = cushion]

pillow *noun* (*plural* pillows)
a cushion for a person's head to rest on, especially in bed.

pillowcase or **pillowslip** *noun* (*plural* pillowcases, pillowslips)
a cloth cover for a pillow.

pilot *noun* (*plural* pilots)
1 a person who works the controls for flying an aircraft. 2 a person qualified to steer a ship in and out of a port or through a difficult stretch of water. 3 a guide.
pilot *verb* (pilots, piloting, piloted)
1 be pilot of an aircraft or ship. 2 guide or steer.
pilot *adjective*
testing on a small scale how something will work, *a pilot scheme.*
[from Greek *pedon* = oar or rudder]

pilot light *noun* (*plural* pilot lights)
1 a small flame that lights a larger burner on a gas cooker etc. 2 an electric indicator light.

pimp *noun* (*plural* pimps)
a man who gets clients for prostitutes and lives off their earnings. [origin unknown]

pimple *noun* (*plural* pimples)
a small round raised spot on the skin.
pimply *adjective*

PIN *abbreviation*
personal identification number; a number used as a person's password so that he or she can use a cash dispenser, computer, etc.

pin *noun* (*plural* pins)
1 a short thin piece of metal with a sharp point and a rounded head, used to fasten pieces of cloth or paper etc. together. 2 a pointed device for fixing or marking something.
pins and needles a prickling feeling.

pin *verb* (pins, pinning, pinned)
1 fasten something with a pin or pins. 2 make a person or thing unable to move, *He was pinned under the wreckage.* 3 fix, *They pinned the blame on her.*

pincer *noun* (*plural* pincers)
the claw of a shellfish such as a lobster. [from old French *pincier* = to pinch]

pincers *plural noun*
a tool with two parts that are pressed together for gripping and holding things.

pinch *verb* (pinches, pinching, pinched)
1 squeeze something tightly or painfully between two things, especially between the finger and thumb. 2 (*informal*) steal.
pinch *noun* (*plural* pinches)
1 a pinching movement. 2 the amount that can be held between the tips of the thumb and forefinger, *a pinch of salt.*
at a pinch in time of difficulty; if necessary.
feel the pinch suffer from lack of money.
[same origin as *pincer*]

pincushion *noun* (*plural* pincushions)
a small pad into which pins are stuck to keep them ready for use.

pine[1] *noun* (*plural* pines)
an evergreen tree with needle-shaped leaves. [from Latin]

pine[2] *verb* (pines, pining, pined)
1 feel an intense longing for somebody or something. 2 become weak through longing for somebody or something.
[from Old English]

pineapple *noun* (*plural* pineapples)
a large tropical fruit with a tough prickly skin and yellow flesh. [from *pine*[1] + *apple* (because it looks like a pine cone)]

ping-pong *noun*
table tennis.
[from the sound of the bats hitting the ball]

pinion *noun* (*plural* pinions)
a bird's wing, especially the outer end.
pinion *verb* (pinions, pinioning, pinioned)
1 clip a bird's wings to prevent it from flying. 2 hold or fasten someone's arms or legs in order to prevent them from moving. [from Latin *pinna* = pin, arrow, or feather]

pink *adjective*
pale red. **pinkness** *noun*
pink *noun* (*plural* pinks)
1 pink colour. 2 a garden plant with fragrant flowers, often pink or white.

pinnacle *noun* (*plural* pinnacles)
1 a pointed ornament on a roof. 2 a high mountain top. 3 the highest point of something, *It was the pinnacle of her career.*

pinpoint *adjective*
exact or precise, *with pinpoint accuracy.*

pinpoint *verb* (pinpoints, pinpointing, pinpointed)
find or identify something precisely.

pinstripe *noun* (*plural* pinstripes)
one of the very narrow stripes that form a pattern in cloth. **pinstriped** *adjective*

pint *noun* (*plural* pints)
a measure for liquids, one-eighth of a gallon. [from old French]

pin-up *noun* (*plural* pin-ups) (*informal*)
a picture of an attractive or famous person for pinning on a wall.

pioneer *noun* (*plural* pioneers)
one of the first people to go to a place or do or investigate something. **pioneer** *verb* [from French *pionnier* = foot soldier, later = one of the troops who went ahead of the army to prepare roads etc.]

pious *adjective*
very religious; devout.
piously *adverb*, **piousness** *noun*
[from Latin *pius* = dutiful]

pip *noun* (*plural* pips)
1 a small hard seed of an apple, pear, orange, etc. 2 one of the stars on the shoulder of an army officer's uniform. 3 a short high-pitched sound, *She heard the six pips of the time signal on the radio.*
pip *verb* (pips, pipping, pipped) (*informal*)
defeat someone by a small amount.

pipe *noun* (*plural* pipes)
1 a tube through which water or gas etc. can flow from one place to another. 2 a short narrow tube with a bowl at one end in which tobacco can burn for smoking. 3 a tube forming a musical instrument or part of one.
the pipes bagpipes.
pipe *verb* (pipes, piping, piped)
1 send something along pipes. 2 transmit music or other sound by wire or cable. 3 play music on a pipe or the bagpipes. 4 decorate a cake with thin lines of icing, cream, etc.
pipe down (*informal*) be quiet.
pipe up begin to say something.

pipe dream *noun* (*plural* pipe dreams)
an impossible wish. [perhaps from dreams produced by smoking opium]

pipeline *noun* (*plural* pipelines)
a pipe for carrying oil or water etc. a long distance.
in the pipeline in the process of being made or organized.

piping *noun*
1 pipes; a length of pipe. 2 a decorative line of icing, cream, etc. on a cake or other dish. 3 a long narrow pipe-like fold decorating clothing, upholstery, etc.
piping *adjective*
shrill, *a piping voice.*
piping hot very hot.

pirate *noun* (*plural* **pirates**)
1 a person on a ship who robs other ships at sea or makes a plundering raid on the shore. 2 someone who produces or publishes or broadcasts without authorization, *a pirate radio station*; *pirate videos*. **piratical** *adjective*, **piracy** *noun*
[from Greek *peiraein* = to attack]

pirouette (*say* pir-oo-et) *noun* (*plural* **pirouettes**)
a spinning movement of the body made while balanced on the point of the toe or on one foot. **pirouette** *verb*
[French, = spinning top]

pistol *noun* (*plural* **pistols**)
a small handgun.

piston *noun* (*plural* **pistons**)
a disc or cylinder that fits inside a tube in which it moves up and down as part of an engine or pump etc.
[via French from Italian *pestone* = pestle]

pit *noun* (*plural* **pits**)
1 a deep hole. 2 a hollow. 3 a coal mine. 4 the part of a racecourse where racing cars are refuelled and repaired during a race.
pit *verb* (**pits, pitting, pitted**)
1 make holes or hollows in something, *The ground was pitted with holes.* 2 put somebody in competition with somebody else, *He was pitted against the champion.*

pitch[1] *noun* (*plural* **pitches**)
1 a piece of ground marked out for cricket, football, or another game. 2 the highness or lowness of a voice or a musical note. 3 intensity or strength, *Excitement was at fever pitch.* 4 the steepness of a slope, *the pitch of the roof.*
pitch *verb* (**pitches, pitching, pitched**)
1 throw or fling. 2 fix a tent etc. 3 fall heavily, *He pitched forward as the bus braked suddenly.* 4 move up and down on a rough sea. 5 set something at a particular level, *They pitched their hopes high.* 6 (of a bowled ball in cricket) strike the ground.
pitch in (*informal*) start working or eating vigorously.

pitch[2] *noun*
a black sticky substance rather like tar.
pitch-black or **pitch-dark** *adjectives* very black or very dark.

pitched battle *noun* (*plural* **pitched battles**)
a battle between troops in prepared positions.

pitcher *noun* (*plural* **pitchers**)
a large jug. [from old French *pichier* – pot]

pitchfork *noun* (*plural* **pitchforks**)
a large fork with two prongs, used for lifting hay.

pitchfork *verb* (**pitchforks, pitchforking, pitchforked**)
1 lift something with a pitchfork. 2 put a person somewhere suddenly.
[originally *pickfork*: from *pick*[1]]

pitfall *noun* (*plural* **pitfalls**)
an unsuspected danger or difficulty.

pitiable *adjective*
making you feel pity; pitiful.

pitiful *adjective*
making you feel pity; pathetic.
pitifully *adverb*

pity *noun*
1 the feeling of being sorry because someone is in pain or trouble. 2 a cause for regret, *It's a pity that you can't come.*
take pity on feel sorry for someone and help them.
pity *verb* (**pities, pitying, pitied**)
feel pity for someone. [same origin as *piety*]

pivot *noun* (*plural* **pivots**)
a point or part on which something turns or balances. **pivotal** *adjective*
pivot *verb* (**pivots, pivoting, pivoted**)
turn or place something to turn on a pivot.

pixie *noun* (*plural* **pixies**)
a small fairy; an elf. [origin unknown]

pizza (*say* peets-a) *noun* (*plural* **pizzas**)
an Italian food that consists of a layer of dough baked with a savoury topping. [Italian, = pie]

pizzicato (*say* pits-i-kah-toh) *adjective* & *adverb*
plucking the strings of a musical instrument. [Italian, = pinched or twitched]

placard *noun* (*plural* **placards**)
a poster or notice, especially one carried at a demonstration.
[from old French *plaquier* = to lay flat]

place *noun* (*plural* **places**)
1 a particular part of space, especially where something belongs; an area or position. 2 a seat, *Save me a place.* 3 a job; employment. 4 a building; a home, *Come round to our place.* 5 a duty or function, *It's not my place to interfere.* 6 a point in a series of things, *In the first place, the date is wrong.*
in place 1 in the right position. 2 suitable.
out of place 1 in the wrong position. 2 unsuitable.
place *verb* (**places, placing, placed**)
put something in a particular place.
placement *noun*
[from Greek *plateia* = broad way]

placid *adjective*
calm and peaceful; not easily made anxious or upset. **placidly** *adverb*, **placidity** *noun* [from Latin *placidus* = gentle]

plagiarize (*say* play-jee-er-I'z) *verb* (**plagiarizes, plagiarizing, plagiarized**)
copy and use someone else's writings or ideas

etc. as if they were your own. **plagiarism** *noun*, **plagiarist** *noun*
[from Latin *plagiarius* = kidnapper]

plague *noun* (*plural* plagues)
1 a dangerous illness that spreads very quickly. 2 a large number of pests, *a plague of locusts*.
plague *verb* (plagues, plaguing, plagued)
pester or annoy, *We've been plagued by wasps all afternoon*. [from Latin]

plain *adjective*
1 simple; not decorated or elaborate. 2 not beautiful. 3 easy to see or hear or understand. 4 frank and straightforward. **plainly** *adverb*, **plainness** *noun*
plain *noun* (*plural* plains)
a large area of flat country.
[from Latin *planus* = flat]

USAGE: Do not confuse with *plane*.

plain clothes *noun*
civilian clothes worn instead of a uniform, e.g. by police.

plaintiff *noun* (*plural* plaintiffs)
the person who brings a complaint against somebody else to a lawcourt. (Compare *defendant*.) [same origin as *plaintive*]

plaintive *adjective*
sounding sad. [from French *plaintif* = grieving or complaining]

plait (*say* plat) *verb* (plaits, plaiting, plaited)
weave three or more strands of hair or rope to form one length.
plait *noun* (*plural* plaits)
a length of hair or rope that has been plaited.
[from Latin *plicatum* = folded]

plan *noun* (*plural* plans)
1 a way of doing something thought out in advance. 2 a drawing showing the arrangement of parts of something. 3 a map of a town or district.
plan *verb* (plans, planning, planned)
make a plan for something. **planner** *noun*
[French, = flat surface, plan of a building: related to *plain*]

plane¹ *noun* (*plural* planes)
1 an aeroplane. 2 a tool for making wood smooth by scraping its surface. 3 a flat or level surface.
plane *verb* (planes, planing, planed)
smooth wood with a plane.
plane *adjective*
flat or level, *a plane surface*.
[same origin as *plain*]

USAGE: Do not confuse with *plain*.

plane² *noun* (*plural* planes)
a tall tree with broad leaves. [from Greek]

planet *noun* (*plural* planets)
one of the bodies that move in an orbit round the sun, *The main planets are Mercury, Venus, Earth, Mars, Jupiter, Saturn, Uranus, Neptune, and Pluto.* **planetary** *adjective*
[from Greek *planetes* = wanderer (because planets seem to move in relation to the stars)]

plank *noun* (*plural* planks)
a long flat piece of wood. [from Latin]

plankton *noun*
microscopic plants and animals that float in the sea, lakes, etc.
[Greek, = wandering or drifting]

plant *noun* (*plural* plants)
1 a living thing that cannot move and that makes its food from chemical substances, *Flowers, trees, and shrubs are plants.* 2 a small plant, not a tree or shrub. 3 a factory or its equipment. 4 (*slang*) something planted to deceive people (see *plant* verb 3).
plant *verb* (plants, planting, planted)
1 put something in soil for growing. 2 fix something firmly in place. 3 place something where it will be found, usually to mislead people or cause trouble. **planter** *noun* [from Latin]

plantation *noun* (*plural* plantations)
1 a large area of land where cotton, tobacco, or tea etc. is planted. 2 a group of planted trees.

plaque (*say* plak) *noun* (*plural* plaques)
1 a flat piece of metal or porcelain fixed on a wall as an ornament or memorial. 2 a filmy substance that forms on teeth and gums, where bacteria can live.

plaster *noun* (*plural* plasters)
1 a mixture of lime, sand, and water etc. for covering walls and ceilings. 2 plaster of Paris. 3 a piece of sticking plaster.
plaster *verb* (plasters, plastering, plastered)
1 cover a wall etc. with plaster. 2 cover something thickly; daub.

plastic *noun* (*plural* plastics)
a strong light synthetic substance that can be moulded into a permanent shape.
plastic *adjective*
1 made of plastic. 2 soft and easy to mould, *Clay is a plastic substance.*
plasticity *noun*
[from Greek *plastos* = moulded or formed]

plastic surgery *noun*
surgery to repair deformed or injured parts of the body. **plastic surgeon** *noun*

plate *noun* (*plural* plates)
1 an almost flat usually circular object from which food is eaten or served. 2 a thin flat sheet of metal, glass, or other hard material. 3 an illustration on special paper in a book. **plateful** *noun*

plate 292 **plight**

plate *verb* (plates, plating, plated)
1 coat metal with a thin layer of gold, silver, tin, etc. 2 cover something with sheets of metal.
[from Latin *platus* = broad or flat]

plateau (*say* plat-oh) *noun* (*plural* plateaux, *say* plat-ohz)
a flat area of high land.
[French, related to *plate*]

platform *noun* (*plural* platforms)
1 a flat surface that is above the level of the ground or the rest of the floor, e.g. in a hall or beside a railway line at a station. 2 the policies that a political party puts forward when there is an election.
[from French *plateforme* = a flat surface]

platinum *noun*
a valuable silver-coloured metal that does not tarnish. [from Spanish *plata* = silver]

platitude *noun* (*plural* platitudes)
a trite or hackneyed remark.
platitudinous *adjective* [French, from *plat* = flat]

plausible *adjective*
seeming to be honest or worth believing but perhaps deceptive, *a plausible excuse*.
plausibly *adverb*, **plausibility** *noun*
[from Latin *plausibilis* = deserving applause]

play *verb* (plays, playing, played)
1 take part in a game, sport, or other amusement. 2 make music or sound with a musical instrument, record player, etc. 3 perform a part in a play or film.
player *noun*
play down give people the impression that something is not important.
play up (*informal*) be mischievous or annoying.
play *noun* (*plural* plays)
1 a story acted on a stage or on radio or television. 2 playing. [from Old English]

playful *adjective*
1 wanting to play; full of fun. 2 done in fun; not serious.
playfully *adverb*, **playfulness** *noun*

playground *noun* (*plural* playgrounds)
a piece of ground for children to play on.

playgroup *noun* (*plural* playgroups)
a group of very young children who play together regularly, supervised by adults.

playing card *noun* (*plural* playing cards)
each of a set of cards (usually 52) used for playing games.

playing field *noun* (*plural* playing fields)
a field used for outdoor games.

playmate *noun* (*plural* playmates)
a person you play games with.

play-off *noun* (*plural* play-offs)
a match that is played to decide a draw or tie.

plaything *noun* (*plural* playthings)
a toy.

playwright *noun* (*plural* playwrights)
a dramatist.
[from *play* + *wright* = maker]

PLC or **p.l.c.** *abbreviation*
public limited company.

plea *noun* (*plural* pleas)
1 a request or appeal, *a plea for mercy*. 2 an excuse, *He stayed at home on the plea of a headache*. 3 a formal statement of 'guilty' or 'not guilty' made in a lawcourt by someone accused of a crime.

plead *verb* (pleads, pleading, pleaded)
1 beg someone to do something. 2 state formally in a lawcourt that you are guilty or not guilty of a crime. 3 give something as an excuse, *She didn't come on holiday with us, pleading poverty*.

pleasant *adjective*
pleasing; giving pleasure.
pleasantly *adverb*, **pleasantness** *noun*
[from French *plaisant* = pleasing]

please *verb* (pleases, pleasing, pleased)
1 make a person feel satisfied or glad. 2 (used to make a request or an order polite), *Please ring the bell*. 3 like; think suitable, *Do as you please*.
[from Latin *placere* = satisfy]

pleasure *noun* (*plural* pleasures)
1 a feeling of satisfaction or gladness; enjoyment. 2 something that pleases you.
[from French *plaisir* = to please]

plectrum *noun* (*plural* plectra)
a small piece of metal or bone etc. for plucking the strings of a musical instrument.
[from Greek *plektron* = something to strike with]

pledge *noun* (*plural* pledges)
1 a solemn promise. 2 a thing handed over as security for a loan or contract.
pledge *verb* (pledges, pledging, pledged)
1 promise solemnly to do or give something. 2 hand something over as security.
[from old French]

plenty *noun*
quite enough; as much as is needed or wanted.
plenty *adverb* (*informal*)
quite or fully, *It's plenty big enough*.
[from Latin *plenitas* = fullness]

pliable *adjective*
1 easy to bend; flexible. 2 easy to influence or control. **pliability** *noun*
[French, from *plier* = to bend]

pliers *plural noun*
pincers that have jaws with flat surfaces for gripping things. [from *ply*^{2}]

plight *noun* (*plural* plights)
a difficult situation. [from old French]

plimsoll *noun* (*plural* plimsolls)
a canvas sports shoe with a rubber sole. [same origin as *Plimsoll line* (because the thin sole reminded people of a Plimsoll line)]

Plimsoll line *noun* (*plural* Plimsoll lines)
a mark on a ship's side showing how deeply it may legally go down in the water when loaded. [named after an English politician, S. Plimsoll, who in the 1870s protested about ships being overloaded]

PLO *abbreviation*
Palestine Liberation Organization.

plod *verb* (plods, plodding, plodded)
1 walk slowly and heavily. 2 work slowly but steadily. **plodder** *noun*

plop *noun* (*plural* plops)
the sound of something dropping into water.
plop *verb* [imitating the sound]

plot *noun* (*plural* plots)
1 a secret plan. 2 the story in a play, novel, or film. 3 a small piece of land.
plot *verb* (plots, plotting, plotted)
1 make a secret plan. 2 make a chart or graph of something, *We plotted the ship's route on our map.* [origin unknown]

plough *noun* (*plural* ploughs)
a farming implement for turning the soil over.
plough *verb* (ploughs, ploughing, ploughed)
1 turn over soil with a plough. 2 go through something with great effort or difficulty, *He ploughed through the book.* **ploughman** *noun*
plough back reinvest profits in the business that produced them.

pluck *verb* (plucks, plucking, plucked)
1 pick a flower or fruit. 2 pull the feathers off a bird. 3 pull something up or out. 4 pull a string (e.g. on a guitar) and let it go again.
pluck up courage summon up courage and overcome fear.

plucky *adjective* (pluckier, pluckiest)
brave or spirited. **pluckily** *adverb*

plug *noun* (*plural* plugs)
1 something used to stop up a hole. 2 a device that fits into a socket to connect wires to a supply of electricity. 3 (*informal*) a piece of publicity for something.
plug *verb* (plugs, plugging, plugged)
1 stop up a hole. 2 (*informal*) publicize something.
plug in put a plug into an electrical socket.

plum *noun* (*plural* plums)
1 a soft juicy fruit with a pointed stone in the middle. 2 (*old use*) a dried grape or raisin used in cooking, *plum pudding.* 3 reddish-purple colour. 4 (*informal*) something good, *a plum job.*
[via Old English from Latin]

plumb *verb* (plumbs, plumbing, plumbed)
1 measure how deep something is. 2 get to the bottom of a matter, *We could not plumb the mystery.* 3 fit a room or building with a plumbing system.
plumb *adjective*
exactly upright; vertical, *The wall was plumb.*
plumb *adverb* (*informal*)
exactly, *It fell plumb in the middle.*
[from Latin *plumbum* = lead² (originally *plumb* = the lead weight on a plumb line)]

plumber *noun* (*plural* plumbers)
a person who fits and mends plumbing.

plumbing *noun*
1 the water pipes, water tanks, and drainage pipes in a building. 2 the work of a plumber.
[from *plumb* (because water pipes used to be made of lead)]

plume *noun* (*plural* plumes)
1 a large feather. 2 something shaped like a feather, *a plume of smoke.*
plume *verb* (plumes, pluming, plumed)
if a bird plumes its feathers, it smooths them with its beak; preen.
[from Latin *pluma* = feather]

plummet *noun* (*plural* plummets)
a plumb line or the weight on its end.
plummet *verb* (plummets, plummeting, plummeted)
drop downwards quickly.
[from old French; related to *plumb*]

plump¹ *adjective*
slightly fat; rounded. **plumpness** *noun*
plump *verb* (plumps, plumping, plumped)
make something rounded, *plump up a cushion.*
[from old German *plumpich* = bulky]

plump² *verb* (plumps, plumping, plumped)
plump for (*informal*) choose.
[from old German *plompen* = to plop]

plunder *verb* (plunders, plundering, plundered)
rob a person or place using force; loot.
plunderer *noun*
plunder *noun*
1 plundering. 2 goods etc. that have been plundered; loot. [from old German]

plunge *verb* (plunges, plunging, plunged)
1 go or push forcefully into something; dive. 2 fall or go downwards suddenly. 3 go or force into action etc., *They plunged the world into war.*
plunge *noun* (*plural* plunges)
a sudden fall or dive.
take the plunge start a bold course of action.
[from old French; related to *plumb*]

plural *noun* (*plural* plurals)
the form of a noun or verb used when it stands for more than one person or thing, *The plural of 'child' is 'children'.* (Compare *singular.*)
plural *adjective*, **plurality** *noun*
[from Latin *pluralis* = of many]

plus *preposition*
with the next number or thing added, *2 plus 2 equals four* (2 + 2 = 4).
[Latin, = more]

plush *noun*
a thick velvety cloth used in furnishings.
plushy *adjective* [from Latin *pilus* = hair]

plutonium *noun*
a radioactive substance used in nuclear weapons and reactors.
[named after the planet Pluto]

ply[1] *noun* (*plural* **plies**)
1 a thickness or layer of wood or cloth etc. 2 a strand in yarn, *4-ply wool*.
[from French *pli* = a fold]

ply[2] *verb* (**plies, plying, plied**)
1 use or wield a tool or weapon. 2 work at, *Tailors plied their trade.* 3 keep offering, *They plied her with food* or *with questions.* 4 go regularly, *The boat plies between the two harbours.* 5 drive or wait about looking for custom, *Taxis are allowed to ply for hire.*
[from *apply*]

plywood *noun*
strong thin board made of layers of wood glued together.

PM *abbreviation*
Prime Minister.

p.m. *abbreviation*
post meridiem (Latin, = after noon).

pneumatic (*say* new-mat-ik) *adjective*
filled with or worked by compressed air, *a pneumatic drill.* **pneumatically** *adverb*
[from Greek *pneuma* = wind]

pneumonia (*say* new-moh-nee-a) *noun*
a serious illness caused by inflammation of one or both lungs.
[from Greek *pneumon* = lung]

PO *abbreviation*
1 Post Office. 2 postal order.

poach *verb* (**poaches, poaching, poached**)
1 cook an egg (removed from its shell) in or over boiling water. 2 cook fish or fruit etc. in a small amount of liquid. 3 steal game or fish from someone else's land or water. 4 take something unfairly, *One club was poaching members from another.*
poacher *noun*
[same origin as *pouch*]

pocket *noun* (*plural* **pockets**)
1 a small bag-shaped part, especially in a garment. 2 a person's supply of money, *The expense is beyond my pocket.* 3 an isolated part or area, *small pockets of rain.*
pocketful *noun*
be out of pocket have spent more money than you have gained.

pocket *adjective*
small enough to carry in a pocket, *a pocket calculator.*
pocket *verb* (**pockets, pocketing, pocketed**)
put something into a pocket.
[from old French *pochet* = little pouch]

pocket money *noun*
money given to a child to spend as he or she likes.

pod *noun* (*plural* **pods**)
a long seed-container of the kind found on a pea or bean plant. [origin unknown]

poem *noun* (*plural* **poems**)
a piece of poetry.
[from Greek *poiema* = thing made]

poet *noun* (*plural* **poets**)
a person who writes poetry. **poetess** *noun*
[from Greek *poietes* = maker]

poetry *noun*
writing arranged in short lines, usually with a particular rhythm and sometimes with rhymes. **poetic** *adjective*,
poetical *adjective*, **poetically** *adverb*

poignant (*say* poin-yant) *adjective*
very distressing; affecting the feelings, *poignant memories.* **poignancy** *noun*
[from French, = pricking]

point *noun* (*plural* **points**)
1 the narrow or sharp end of something. 2 a dot, *the decimal point.* 3 a particular place or time, *At this point she was winning.* 4 a detail or characteristic, *He has his good points.* 5 the important or essential idea, *Keep to the point!* 6 purpose or value, *There is no point in hurrying.* 7 an electrical socket. 8 a device for changing a train from one track to another.
point *verb* (**points, pointing, pointed**)
1 aim or direct, *She pointed a gun at me.* 2 show where something is, especially by holding out a finger etc. towards it. 3 fill in the parts between bricks with mortar or cement.
point out draw attention to something.
[from Latin *punctum* = pricked]

point-blank *adjective*
1 aimed or fired from close to the target.
2 direct and straightforward, *a point-blank refusal.*
point-blank *adverb*
in a point-blank manner, *He refused point-blank.* [from to *point* + *blank* = the white centre of a target]

pointed *adjective*
1 with a point at the end. 2 clearly directed at a person, *a pointed remark.*
pointedly *adverb*

pointer *noun* (*plural* **pointers**)
1 a stick, rod, or mark etc. used to point at something. 2 a dog that points with its muzzle towards birds that it scents. 3 an indication or hint.

pointless *adjective*
without a point; with no purpose. **pointlessly** *adverb*

poise *verb* (poises, poising, poised)
balance.
poise *noun*
1 a dignified self-confident manner. 2 balance.
[from old French]

poison *noun* (*plural* poisons)
a substance that can harm or kill a living thing. **poisonous** *adjective*
poison *verb* (poisons, poisoning, poisoned)
1 give poison to; kill somebody with poison.
2 put poison in something. 3 corrupt or spoil something, *He poisoned their minds*.
poisoner *noun*

poke *verb* (pokes, poking, poked)
1 prod or jab. 2 push out or forward; stick out.
3 search, *I was poking about in the attic*.
poke fun at ridicule.
poke *noun* (*plural* pokes)
a poking movement; a prod.

poker¹ *noun* (*plural* pokers)
a stiff metal rod for poking a fire.

poker² *noun*
a card game in which players bet on who has the best cards.
[probably from German *pochen* = to brag]

polar *adjective*
1 to do with or near the North Pole or South Pole. 2 to do with either pole of a magnet.
polarity *noun*

polar bear *noun* (*plural* polar bears)
a white bear living in Arctic regions.

polarize *verb* (polarizes, polarizing, polarized)
1 keep vibrations of light-waves etc. to a single direction. 2 divide into two groups of completely opposite extremes of feeling or opinion, *Opinions had polarized*.
polarization *noun* [from *pole*²]

Polaroid camera *noun* (*plural* Polaroid cameras) (*trade mark*)
a camera that takes a picture and produces the finished photograph a few seconds later.

pole¹ *noun* (*plural* poles)
a long slender rounded piece of wood or metal.
[same origin as *pale*²]

pole² *noun* (*plural* poles)
1 a point on the earth's surface that is as far north (**North Pole**) or as far south (**South Pole**) as possible. 2 either of the ends of a magnet.
3 either terminal of an electric cell or battery.
[from Greek *polos* = axis]

pole star *noun*
the star above the North Pole.

pole vault *noun*
an athletic contest in which competitors jump over a high bar with the help of a long pole.

police *noun*
the people whose job is to catch criminals and make sure that the law is kept. **policeman** *noun*, **policewoman** *noun*
police *verb* (polices, policing, policed)
keep order in a place by means of police. [same origin as *political*]

policy¹ *noun* (*plural* policies)
the aims or plan of action of a person or group.
[same origin as *political*]

policy² *noun* (*plural* policies)
a document stating the terms of a contract of insurance.
[from Greek *apodeixis* = evidence]

polish *verb* (polishes, polishing, polished)
1 make a thing smooth and shiny by rubbing.
2 make a thing better by making corrections and alterations. **polisher** *noun*
polish off finish off.
polish *noun* (*plural* polishes)
1 a substance used in polishing. 2 a shine.
3 elegance of manner. [from Latin]

polite *adjective*
having good manners. **politely** *adverb*, **politeness** *noun*
[from Latin *politus* = polished]

political *adjective*
connected with the governing of a country, city, or county. **politically** *adverb*
[from Greek *politeia* = citizenship or government]

politician *noun* (*plural* politicians)
a person who is involved in politics.

politics *noun*
political matters.

poll (*say as* pole) *noun* (*plural* polls)
1 voting or votes at an election. 2 an opinion poll. 3 (*old use*) the head.
poll *verb* (polls, polling, polled)
1 vote at an election. 2 receive a stated number of votes in an election.
polling booth *noun*, **polling station** *noun*
[probably from old Dutch word *polle* = head. In some polls those voting yes stand apart from those voting no, and the decision is reached by counting the heads in the two groups]

pollen *noun*
powder produced by the anthers of flowers, containing male cells for fertilizing other flowers. [Latin, = fine flour]

pollen count *noun* (*plural* pollen counts)
a measurement of the amount of pollen in the air, given as a warning for people who are allergic to pollen.

pollinate *verb* (pollinates, pollinating, pollinated)
fertilize a plant with pollen.
pollination *noun*

poll tax *noun* (*plural* **poll taxes**)
a tax on each person; the community charge.

pollute *verb* (**pollutes, polluting, polluted**)
make a place or thing dirty or impure.
pollutant *noun*, **pollution** *noun* [from Latin]

poly- *prefix*
many (as in *polytechnic*). [from Greek]

polygamy (*say* pol-ig-a-mee) *noun*
having more than one wife at a time.
polygamous *adjective*
[from *poly-* + Greek *gamos* = marriage]

polygon *noun* (*plural* **polygons**)
a shape with many sides, *Hexagons and octagons are polygons.* **polygonal** *adjective* [from *poly-* + Greek *gonia* = corner]

polyhedron *noun* (*plural* **polyhedrons**)
a solid shape with many sides.
[from *poly-* + Greek *hedra* = base]

polytechnic *noun* (*plural* **polytechnics**)
a college giving instruction in many subjects at degree level or below. In 1992 the British polytechnics were able to change their names and call themselves universities.
[from *poly-* + Greek *techne* = skill]

polythene *noun*
a lightweight plastic used to make bags, wrappings, etc. [from *polyethylene*, a polymer from which it is made]

pomegranate *noun* (*plural* **pomegranates**)
a tropical fruit with many seeds.
[from Latin *pomum* = apple + *granatum* = having many seeds]

pomp *noun*
the ceremonial splendour that is traditional on important public occasions. [from Greek *pompe* = solemn procession]

pompous *adjective*
full of excessive dignity and self-importance.
pompously *adverb*, **pomposity** *noun*
[from *pomp*]

pond *noun* (*plural* **ponds**)
a small lake. [from *pound*²]

ponder *verb* (**ponders, pondering, pondered**)
think deeply and seriously; muse.
[from Latin *ponderare* = weigh]

ponderous *adjective*
1 heavy and awkward. 2 laborious and dull, *He writes in a ponderous style.* **ponderously** *adverb*
[from Latin *ponderis* = of weight]

pontificate *verb* (**pontificates, pontificating, pontificated**)
speak or write pompously. **pontification** *noun*

pony *noun* (*plural* **ponies**)
a small horse.
[from French *poulenet* = small foal]

ponytail *noun* (*plural* **ponytails**)
a bunch of long hair tied at the back of the head.

poodle *noun* (*plural* **poodles**)
a dog with thick curly hair.
[from German *Pudelhund* = water-dog]

pooh *interjection*
an exclamation of contempt.

pool¹ *noun* (*plural* **pools**)
1 a pond. 2 a puddle. 3 a swimming pool.
[from Old English]

pool² *noun* (*plural* **pools**)
1 the fund of money staked in a gambling game. 2 a group of things shared by several people.
the pools gambling based on the results of football matches.
pool *verb* (**pools, pooling, pooled**)
put money or things together for sharing.
[from French]

poor *adjective*
1 with very little money or other resources.
2 not good; inadequate, *a poor piece of work.*
3 unfortunate; deserving pity, *Poor fellow!*
poorness *noun*
[from old French; related to *pauper*]

poorly *adverb*
1 in a poor way, *We've played poorly this season.* 2 rather ill.

pop¹ *noun* (*plural* **pops**)
1 a small explosive sound. 2 a fizzy drink.
pop *verb* (**pops, popping, popped**)
1 make a pop. 2 (*informal*) go or put quickly, *Pop down to the shop. I'll just pop this pie into the microwave.*
[imitating the sound]

pop² *noun*
modern popular music. [short for *popular*]

Pope *noun* (*plural* **Popes**)
the leader of the Roman Catholic Church.
[from Greek *papas* = father]

pop-eyed *adjective*
with bulging eyes.

poplar *noun* (*plural* **poplars**)
a tall slender tree. [from Latin]

poppy *noun* (*plural* **poppies**)
a plant with large red flowers.

popular *adjective*
1 liked or enjoyed by many people. 2 intended for the general public.
popularly *adverb*, **popularity** *noun*
[from Latin *populus* = people]

populate *verb* (**populates, populating, populated**)
supply with a population; inhabit.
[same origin as *popular*]

population *noun* (*plural* **populations**)
the people who live in a district or country; the total number of these people.

porcelain *noun*
the finest kind of china. [from French]

porch *noun* (*plural* **porches**)
a shelter outside the entrance to a building.

porcupine *noun* (*plural* **porcupines**)
a small animal covered with long prickles.
[from old French *porc espin* = spiny pig]

pore[1] *noun* (*plural* **pores**)
a tiny opening on the skin through which
moisture can pass in or out.
[from Greek *poros* = passage]

pore[2] *verb* (**pores, poring, pored**)
pore over study with close attention, *He was
poring over his books.*
[origin unknown]

USAGE: Do not confuse with *pour*.

---

pork *noun*
meat from a pig. [from Latin *porcus* = pig]

pornography (*say* porn-**og**-ra-fee) *noun*
obscene pictures or writings.
pornographic *adjective*
[from Greek *porne* = prostitute, + *-graphy*]

porpoise (*say* por-pus) *noun* (*plural* **porpoises**)
a sea animal rather like a small whale. [from
Latin *porcus* = pig + *piscis* = fish]

porridge *noun*
a food made by boiling oatmeal to a thick paste.
[from an old word *pottage* = soup]

port[1] *noun* (*plural* **ports**)
1 a harbour. **2** a city or town with a harbour.
3 the left-hand side of a ship or aircraft when
you are facing forward. (Compare *starboard*.)
[from Latin *portus* = harbour]

port[2] *noun*
a strong red Portuguese wine.
[from the city of Oporto in Portugal]

portable *adjective*
able to be carried.
[from Latin *portare* = carry]

portcullis *noun* (*plural* **portcullises**)
a strong heavy vertical grating that can be
lowered in grooves to block the gateway to a
castle. [from old French *porte coleice*
= sliding door]

porter[1] *noun* (*plural* **porters**)
a person whose job is to carry luggage or other
goods. [from Latin *portare* = carry]

porter[2] *noun* (*plural* **porters**)
a person whose job is to look after the entrance
to a large building.
[from Latin *porta* = gate]

porthole *noun* (*plural* **portholes**)
a small window in the side of a ship or aircraft.
[from Latin *porta* = gate, + *hole*]

portion *noun* (*plural* **portions**)
a part or share given to somebody.

portion *verb* (**portions, portioning, portioned**)
divide something into portions, *Portion it out.*
[from Latin]

portly *adjective* (**portlier, portliest**)
stout and dignified. **portliness** *noun*
[originally = dignified: from Middle English
port = bearing, deportment]

portrait *noun* (*plural* **portraits**)
a picture of a person or animal.

pose *noun* (*plural* **poses**)
1 a position or posture of the body, e.g. for a
portrait or photograph. **2** a pretence;
unnatural and affected behaviour to impress
people.
pose *verb* (**poses, posing, posed**)
1 take up a pose. **2** put someone into a pose.
3 pretend. **4** put forward or present, *It poses
several problems for us.*

posh *adjective* (*informal*)
1 very smart; high-class, *a posh restaurant.*
2 upper-class, *a posh accent.*

position *noun* (*plural* **positions**)
1 the place where something is or should be.
2 the way a person or thing is placed or
arranged, *in a sitting position.* **3** a situation or
condition, *I am in no position to help you.* **4** paid
employment; a job.
positional *adjective*

positive *adjective*
1 definite or certain, *We have positive proof
that he is guilty.* **2** agreeing; saying 'yes', *We
received a positive reply.* **3** greater than nought.
4 of the kind of electric charge that lacks
electrons. **5** (of an adjective or adverb) in the
simple form, not comparative or superlative,
*The positive form is 'big', the comparative is
'bigger', the superlative is 'biggest'.*
positively *adverb*

USAGE: The opposite of senses 1–4 is
negative.

---

possess *verb* (**possesses, possessing, possessed**)
1 have or own something. **2** control someone's
thoughts or behaviour, *I don't know what
possessed you to do such a thing!* **possessor** *noun*
[from Latin]

possessed *adjective*
seeming to be controlled by strong emotion or
an evil spirit, *He fought like a man possessed.*

possession *noun* (*plural* **possessions**)
1 something you possess or own. **2** possessing.

possessive *adjective*
1 wanting to possess and keep things for
yourself. **2** showing that somebody owns
something, *a possessive pronoun* (see *pronoun*).

possibility *noun* (*plural* **possibilities**)
1 being possible. **2** something that may exist or
happen etc.

possible *adjective*
able to exist, happen, be done, or be used. [from Latin *posse* = be able]

possibly *adverb*
1 in any way, *I can't possibly do it.* 2 perhaps.

post[1] *noun* (*plural* **posts**)
1 an upright piece of wood, concrete, or metal etc. set in the ground. 2 the starting point or finishing point of a race, *He was left at the post.*
post *verb* (**posts, posting, posted**)
put up a notice or poster etc. to announce something. [from Latin *postis* = post]

post[2] *noun*
1 the collecting and delivering of letters, parcels, etc. 2 these letters and parcels etc.
post *verb* (**posts, posting, posted**)
put a letter or parcel etc. into a postbox for collection.
keep me posted keep me informed.
[from French; related to *post*[3] (because originally mail was carried in relays by riders posted along the route)]

post[3] *noun* (*plural* **posts**)
1 a position of paid employment; a job. 2 the place where someone is on duty, *a sentry-post.* 3 a place occupied by soldiers, traders, etc.
post *verb* (**posts, posting, posted**)
place someone on duty, *We posted sentries.*
[from Latin *positum* = placed]

post- *prefix*
after (as in *post-war*). [from Latin]

postage *noun*
the charge for sending something by post.

postage stamp *noun* (*plural* **postage stamps**)
a stamp for sticking on things to be posted, showing the amount paid.

postal *adjective*
to do with or by the post.

postal order *noun* (*plural* **postal orders**)
a document bought from a post office for sending money by post.

postbox *noun* (*plural* **postboxes**)
a box into which letters are put for collection.

postcard *noun* (*plural* **postcards**)
a card for sending messages by post without an envelope.

postcode *noun* (*plural* **postcodes**)
a group of letters and numbers included in an address to help in sorting the post.

poster *noun* (*plural* **posters**)
a large sheet of paper announcing or advertising something, for display in a public place. [from *post*[1]]

posterity *noun*
future generations of people, *These letters and diaries should be preserved for posterity.*
[from Latin *posterus* = following, future]

postman *noun* (*plural* **postmen**)
a person who delivers or collects letters etc.

postmark *noun* (*plural* **postmarks**)
an official mark put on something sent by post to show where and when it was posted.

post-mortem *noun* (*plural* **post-mortems**)
an examination of a dead body to discover the cause of death. [Latin, = after death]

post office *noun* (*plural* **post offices**)
a building or room where postal business is carried on.

postpone *verb* (**postpones, postponing, postponed**)
fix a later time for something, *They postponed the meeting for a fortnight.* **postponement** *noun*
[from *post-* + Latin *ponere* = to place]

postscript *noun* (*plural* **postscripts**)
something extra added at the end of a letter (after the writer's signature) or at the end of a book.
[from *post-* + Latin *scriptum* = written]

posture *noun* (*plural* **postures**)
the way a person stands, sits, or walks; a pose.
posture *verb* (**postures, posturing, postured**)
pose, especially to impress people. [from Latin *positura* = position or situation]

post-war *adjective*
happening during the time after a war.

pot[1] *noun* (*plural* **pots**)
1 a deep usually round container. 2 (*informal*) a lot of something, *He has got pots of money.*
go to pot (*informal*) lose quality; be ruined.
take pot luck (*informal*) take whatever is available.
pot *verb* (**pots, potting, potted**)
put into a pot. [from Old English]

pot[2] *noun* (*slang*)
marijuana. [short for Spanish *potiguaya* = drink of grief]

potassium *noun*
a soft silvery-white metal substance that is essential for living things.

potato *noun* (*plural* **potatoes**)
a starchy white tuber growing underground, used as a vegetable.

potentate (*say* poh-ten-tayt) *noun* (*plural* **potentates**)
a powerful monarch or ruler.
[from Latin *potentatus* = power or rule]

potential (*say* po-ten-shal) *adjective*
capable of happening or being used or developed, *a potential winner.*
potentially *adverb*, **potentiality** *noun*
potential *noun*
the ability of a person or thing to develop in the future. [from Latin *potentia* = power]

pothole *noun* (*plural* **potholes**)
1 a deep natural hole in the ground. 2 a hole in a road.

potion *noun* (*plural* **potions**)
a liquid for drinking as a medicine etc. [from Latin *potio* = a drink]

potted *adjective*
shortened or abridged, *a potted account of the story.*

potter[1] *noun* (*plural* **potters**)
a person who makes pottery.

potter[2] *verb* (**potters, pottering, pottered**)
work or move about in a leisurely way, *I spent the afternoon pottering around in the garden.* [from an old word *pote* = push or poke]

pottery *noun* (*plural* **potteries**)
1 cups, plates, ornaments, etc. made of baked clay. 2 a place where a potter works.

pouch *noun* (*plural* **pouches**)
1 a small bag. 2 something shaped like a bag. [from French *poche* = bag or pocket]

poultry *noun*
birds (e.g. chickens, geese, turkeys) kept for their eggs and meat.
[from old French *poulet* = pullet]

pounce *verb* (**pounces, pouncing, pounced**)
jump or swoop down quickly on something.
pounce *noun* [from old French]

pound[1] *noun* (*plural* **pounds**)
1 a unit of money (in Britain = 100 pence). 2 a unit of weight equal to 16 ounces or about 454 grams. [from Old English *pund*]

pound[2] *noun* (*plural* **pounds**)
1 a place where stray animals are taken. 2 a public enclosure for vehicles officially removed. [origin unknown]

pound[3] *verb* (**pounds, pounding, pounded**)
1 hit something often, especially in order to crush it. 2 run or go heavily, *pounding along.* 3 thump, *My heart was pounding.* [from Old English *punian*]

pour *verb* (**pours, pouring, poured**)
1 flow or make something flow. 2 rain heavily, *It poured all day.* 3 come or go in large amounts, *Letters poured in.* **pourer** *noun* [origin unknown]

USAGE: Do not confuse with *pore.*

pout *verb* (**pouts, pouting, pouted**)
push out your lips when you are annoyed or sulking. **pout** *noun*
[probably from a Scandinavian language]

poverty *noun*
being poor.
[from old French; related to *pauper*]

powder *noun* (*plural* **powders**)
1 a mass of fine dry particles of something. 2 a medicine or cosmetic etc. made as a powder. 3 gunpowder, *Keep your powder dry.*
powdery *adjective*

powder *verb* (**powders, powdering, powdered**)
1 put powder on something. 2 make something into powder.
[from old French; related to *pulverize*]

power *noun* (*plural* **powers**)
1 strength or energy. 2 the ability to do something, *the power of speech.* 3 political authority or control. 4 a powerful country, person, or organization. 5 mechanical or electrical energy; the electricity supply, *There was a power failure after the storm.* 6 (in mathematics) the product of a number multiplied by itself a given number of times, *The third power of 2 = 2 × 2 × 2 = 8.*
powered *adjective*, **powerless** *adjective*

powerful *adjective*
having great power, strength, or influence.
powerfully *adverb*

power station *noun* (*plural* **power stations**)
a building where electricity is produced.

pp. *abbreviation*
pages.

practicable *adjective*
able to be done. [French, from *pratiquer* = put into practice]

USAGE: Do not confuse with *practical.*

practical *adjective*
1 able to do useful things, *a practical person.* 2 likely to be useful, *a very practical invention.* 3 actually doing something, *She has had practical experience.* **practicality** *noun*

USAGE: Do not confuse with *practicable.*

practical *noun* (*plural* **practicals**)
a lesson or examination in which you actually do or make something rather than reading or writing about it, *a chemistry practical.* [from Greek *prattein* = do]

practical joke *noun* (*plural* **practical jokes**)
a trick played on somebody.

practically *adverb*
1 in a practical way. 2 almost, *I've practically finished.*

practice *noun* (*plural* **practices**)
1 practising, *Have you done your piano practice?* 2 actually doing something; action, not theory, *It works well in practice.* 3 the professional business of a doctor, dentist, lawyer, etc. 4 a habit or custom, *It is his practice to work until midnight.*
out of practice no longer skilful because you have not practised recently.
[from *practise*]

USAGE: See the note on *practise.*

practise *verb* (**practises, practising, practised**)
1 do something repeatedly in order to become

better at it. **2** do something actively or habitually, *Practise what you preach.* **3** work as a doctor, dentist, or lawyer.
[from Latin *practicare* = carry out, perform]

USAGE: Note the spelling: *practice* is a noun, *practise* is a verb.

practised *adjective*
experienced or expert.

prairie *noun* (*plural* prairies)
a large area of flat grass-covered land in North America.
[French, from Latin *pratum* = meadow]

praise *verb* (praises, praising, praised)
1 say that somebody or something is very good. **2** honour God in words.
praise *noun*
words that praise somebody or something.
praiseworthy *adjective*
[from Latin *pretium* = value]

pram *noun* (*plural* prams)
a four-wheeled carriage for a baby, pushed by a person walking.

prance *verb* (prances, prancing, pranced)
move about in a lively or happy way.

prank *noun* (*plural* pranks)
a trick played for mischief; a practical joke.
prankster *noun*

prattle *verb* (prattles, prattling, prattled)
chatter like a young child. **prattle** *noun*

prawn *noun* (*plural* prawns)
an edible shellfish like a large shrimp.

pray *verb* (prays, praying, prayed)
1 talk to God. **2** ask earnestly for something. **3** (*formal*) please, *Pray be seated.*
[from old French]

prayer *noun* (*plural* prayers)
praying; words used in praying.

pre- *prefix*
before (as in *prehistoric*). [from Latin]

preach *verb* (preaches, preaching, preached)
give a religious or moral talk. **preacher** *noun*
[from old French]

precarious (*say* pri-kair-ee-us) *adjective*
not very safe or secure. **precariously** *adverb*
[from Latin *precarius* = uncertain]

precaution *noun* (*plural* precautions)
something done to prevent future trouble or danger. **precautionary** *adjective*
[from *pre-* + Latin *cavere* = take care]

precede *verb* (precedes, preceding, preceded)
come or go before or in front of another thing.
[from *pre-* + Latin *cedere* = go]

USAGE: Do not confuse with *proceed.*

precedent (*say* press-i-dent) *noun* (*plural* precedents)
a previous case that is taken as an example to be followed.

precinct (*say* pree-sinkt) *noun* (*plural* precincts)
1 the area round a place, especially round a cathedral. **2** a part of a town where traffic is not allowed, *a shopping precinct.*
[from *pre-* + Latin *cinctum* = surrounded]

precious *adjective*
1 very valuable. **2** greatly loved. **preciousness** *noun*
precious *adverb* (*informal*)
very, *We have precious little time.*
[from Latin *pretium* = value]

precipice *noun* (*plural* precipices)
a very steep place, such as the face of a cliff.
[from Latin *praeceps* = headlong]

précis (*say* pray-see) *noun* (*plural* précis, *say* pray-seez
a summary. [French, = precise]

precise *adjective*
exact; clearly stated.
precisely *adverb*, **precision** *noun*
[from Latin *praecisum* = cut short]

precocious (*say* prik-oh-shus) *adjective*
(of a child) very advanced or developed for his or her age.
precociously *adverb*, **precocity** *noun*
[from Latin *praecox* = ripe very early]

predator (*say* pred-a-ter) *noun* (*plural* predators)
an animal that hunts or preys upon others.
predatory *adjective*
[from Latin *praedator* = plunderer]

predecessor (*say* pree-dis-ess-er) *noun* (*plural* predecessors)
an earlier person or thing, e.g. an ancestor or the former holder of a job. [from *pre-* + Latin *decessor* = person departed]

predicate *noun* (*plural* predicates)
the part of a sentence that says something about the subject, e.g. 'is short' in *life is short.*
[from Latin *praedicare* = proclaim]

predicative (*say* prid-ik-a-tiv) *adjective*
forming part of the predicate, e.g. *old* in *The dog is old.* (Compare *attributive.*)
predicatively *adverb*

predict *verb* (predicts, predicting, predicted)
say what will happen in the future; foretell or prophesy. **predictable** *adjective*, **prediction** *noun*, **predictor** *noun*
[from *pre-* + Latin *dicere* = say]

predispose *verb* (predisposes, predisposing, predisposed)
influence you in advance so that you are likely to do or be in favour of something, *We are predisposed to pity the refugees.*
predisposition *noun*

predominate *verb* (predominates, predominating, predominated)
be the largest or most important or most powerful.
predominant *adjective*, **predominance** *noun*
[from *pre-* + Latin *dominari* = rule, dominate]

pre-eminent *adjective*
excelling others; outstanding.
pre-eminently *adverb*, **pre-eminence** *noun*

preen *verb* (preens, preening, preened)
1 (of a bird) smooth its feathers with its beak.
2 (of a person) smarten.
preen yourself congratulate yourself.

preface (*say* pref-as) *noun* (*plural* prefaces)
an introduction at the beginning of a book or speech. **preface** *verb* [from Latin *praefatio* = something said beforehand]

prefect *noun* (*plural* prefects)
1 a school pupil given authority to help to keep order. 2 a district official in France, Japan, and other countries.
[from Latin *praefectus* = overseer]

prefer *verb* (prefers, preferring, preferred)
1 like one person or thing more than another.
2 put forward, *They preferred charges of forgery against him.*
preference *noun*
[from *pre-* + Latin *ferre* = carry]

preferable (*say* pref-er-a-bul) *adjective*
liked better; more desirable.
preferably *adverb*

prefix *noun* (*plural* prefixes)
a word or syllable joined to the front of a word to change or add to its meaning, as in *dis*order, *out*stretched, *un*happy.

pregnant *adjective*
having a baby developing in the womb.
pregnancy *noun*
[from *pre-* + Latin *gnasci* = be born]

prehensile *adjective*
(of an animal's foot or tail etc.) able to grasp things.
[from Latin *prehendere* = seize]

prehistoric *adjective*
belonging to very ancient times, before written records of events were made. **prehistory** *noun*

prejudice *noun* (*plural* prejudices)
a fixed opinion formed without examining the facts fairly. **prejudiced** *adjective*
[from *pre-* + Latin *judicium* = judgement]

preliminary *adjective*
coming before an important action or event and preparing for it.
[from *pre-* + Latin *limen* = threshold]

prelude *noun* (*plural* preludes)
1 a thing that introduces or leads up to something else. 2 a short piece of music.
[from *pre-* + Latin *ludere* = to play]

premature *adjective*
too early; coming before the usual or proper time. **prematurely** *adverb*
[from *pre-* + Latin *maturus* = mature]

premeditated *adjective*
planned beforehand, *a premeditated crime.*
[from *pre-* + Latin *meditare* = meditate]

premier *noun* (*plural* premiers)
a prime minister or other head of government.
[French, = first]

première (*say* prem-yair) *noun* (*plural* premières)
the first public performance of a play or film.
[French, feminine of *premier* = first]

premises *plural noun*
a building and its grounds. [originally, the buildings etc. previously mentioned on a deed: from Latin *praemittere* = put before]

premium *noun* (*plural* premiums)
1 an amount or instalment paid to an insurance company. 2 an extra payment; a bonus.
at a premium above the normal price; highly valued.
[from Latin *praemium* = reward]

Premium Bond *noun* (*plural* Premium Bonds)
a savings certificate that gives the person who holds it a chance to win a prize of money.

premonition *noun* (*plural* premonitions)
a feeling that something is about to happen, especially something bad.
[from *pre-* + Latin *monere* = warn]

preoccupied *adjective*
having your thoughts completely busy with something. **preoccupation** *noun*

prep *noun*
homework. [short for *preparation*]

preparation *noun* (*plural* preparations)
1 preparing. 2 something prepared.

preparatory school *noun* (*plural* preparatory schools)
a school that prepares pupils for a higher school.

prepare *verb* (prepares, preparing, prepared)
make ready; get ready.
be prepared to be ready and willing to do something.
[from *pre-* + Latin *parare* = get something ready]

preposition *noun* (*plural* prepositions)
a word used with a noun or pronoun to show place, position, time, or means, e.g. *at* home, *in* the hall, *on* Sunday, *by* train. [from *pre-* + Latin *positio* = placing]

preposterous *adjective*
very absurd; outrageous.
[from Latin *praeposterus* = back to front, from *prae* = before + *posterus* = behind]

prep school noun (plural **prep schools**)
a preparatory school.

Presbyterian (say prez-bit-**eer**-ee-an) noun
(plural **Presbyterians**)
a member of a Church that is governed by
people called elders or presbyters who are
chosen by the congregation.
[from Greek presbyteros = elder]

prescribe verb (prescribes, prescribing,
prescribed)
1 advise a person to use a particular medicine
or treatment etc. 2 say what should be done.
[from pre- + Latin scribere = write]

prescription noun (plural **prescriptions**)
1 a doctor's written order for a medicine. 2 the
medicine prescribed. 3 prescribing.

presence noun
1 being present in a place, Your presence is
required. 2 if someone has presence, they have
an impressive personality or manner.

presence of mind noun
the ability to act quickly and sensibly in an
emergency.

present[1] adjective
1 in a particular place, No one else was present.
2 belonging or referring to what is happening
now; existing now, the present Queen.
present noun
present times or events.
[from Latin praesens = being at hand]

present[2] noun (plural **presents**)
something given or received without payment;
a gift.
present (say priz-ent) verb (presents, presenting,
presented)
1 give something, especially with a ceremony,
Who is to present the prizes? 2 introduce
someone to another person or to an audience.
3 put on a play or other entertainment. 4 show.
5 cause or provide something, Writing a
dictionary presents many problems.
presentation noun, **presenter** noun
[from Latin praesentare = place before
someone]

presently adverb
1 soon, I shall be with you presently. 2 now, the
person who is presently in charge.
[from present[1]]

preserve verb (preserves, preserving, preserved)
keep something safe or in good condition.
preserver noun, **preservation** noun,
preservative adjective & noun
preserve noun (plural **preserves**)
1 jam. 2 an activity that belongs to a particular
person or group.
[from pre- + Latin servare = keep]

preside verb (presides, presiding, presided)
be in charge of a meeting etc.
[from pre- + Latin -sidere = sit]

president noun (plural **presidents**)
1 the person in charge of a club, society, or
council etc. 2 the head of a republic.
presidency noun, **presidential** adjective
[from Latin praesidens = sitting in front]

press verb (presses, pressing, pressed)
1 put weight or force steadily on something;
squeeze. 2 make something by pressing.
3 make clothes smooth by ironing them.
4 urge; make demands, They pressed for an
increase in wages.
press noun (plural **presses**)
1 a device for pressing things, a trouser press.
2 a machine for printing things. 3 a firm that
prints or publishes books etc., Oxford
University Press. 4 newspapers; journalists.
[from Latin pressum = squeezed]

pressure noun (plural **pressures**)
1 continuous pressing. 2 the force with which
something presses. 3 an influence that
persuades or compels you to do something.
[from Latin]

pressure cooker noun (plural **pressure cookers**)
a large air-tight pan used for cooking food
quickly under steam pressure.

prestige (say pres-**teej**) noun
good reputation. **prestigious** adjective
[from Latin praestigium = an illusion]

presumably adverb
according to what you may presume.

presume verb (presumes, presuming, presumed)
1 suppose; assume something to be true. 2 take
the liberty of doing something; venture, May
we presume to advise you? **presumption** noun
[from pre- + Latin sumere = take]

presumptuous adjective
too bold or confident.
presumptuously adverb

presuppose verb (presupposes, presupposing,
presupposed)
suppose or assume something beforehand.
presupposition noun [from French]

pretence noun (plural **pretences**)
an attempt to pretend that something is true.
false pretences pretending to be something that
you are not, in order to deceive people, You've
invited me here under false pretences.

pretend verb (pretends, pretending, pretended)
1 behave as if something is true or real when
you know that it is not, either in play or so as
to deceive people. 2 put forward a claim, The
son of King James II was called the Old
Pretender because he pretended to the British
throne. **pretender** noun [from Latin praetendere
= put forward or claim]

pretentious *adjective*
1 showy or ostentatious. 2 claiming to have great merit or importance.
pretentiously *adverb*, **pretentiousness** *noun*
[from French; related to *pretend*]

pretext *noun* (*plural* **pretexts**)
a reason put forward to conceal the true reason. [from Latin *praetextus* = an outward display]

pretty *adjective* (**prettier, prettiest**)
attractive in a delicate way.
prettily *adverb*, **prettiness** *noun*
pretty *adverb*
quite, *It's pretty cold.* [from Old English]

prevent *verb* (**prevents, preventing, prevented**)
1 stop something from happening. 2 stop a person from doing something.
preventable *adjective*, **prevention** *noun*,
preventive or **preventative** *adjective* & *noun*
[from Latin *praevenire* = come first, anticipate]

preview *noun* (*plural* **previews**)
a showing of a film or play etc. before it is shown to the general public.

previous *adjective*
coming before this; preceding.
previously *adverb*
[from *pre-* + Latin *via* = way]

prey (*say as* pray) *noun*
an animal that is hunted or killed by another for food.
bird or **beast of prey** one that kills and eats other birds or four-footed animals.
prey *verb* (**preys, preying, preyed**)
prey on 1 hunt or take as prey. 2 cause to worry, *The problem preyed on his mind.*

price *noun* (*plural* **prices**)
1 the amount of money for which something is bought or sold. 2 what must be given or done in order to achieve something.
[from old French: related to *praise*]

priceless *adjective*
1 very valuable. 2 (*informal*) very amusing.

prick *verb* (**pricks, pricking, pricked**)
1 make a tiny hole in something. 2 hurt somebody with a pin or needle etc.
prick *noun*
prick up your ears start listening suddenly.

prickle *noun* (*plural* **prickles**)
1 a small thorn. 2 a sharp spine on a hedgehog or cactus. 3 a feeling that something is pricking you. **prickly** *adjective*
prickle *verb* (**prickles, prickling, prickled**)
feel or cause a pricking feeling.

pride *noun* (*plural* **prides**)
1 being proud. 2 something that makes you feel proud. 3 a group of lions.
pride of place the most important or most honoured position.

pride *verb* (**prides, priding, prided**)
pride yourself on be proud of.
[from *proud*]

priest *noun* (*plural* **priests**)
1 a member of the clergy. 2 a person who conducts religious ceremonies. **priestess** *noun*,
priesthood *noun*, **priestly** *adjective*

prig *noun* (*plural* **prigs**)
a self-righteous person. **priggish** *adjective*

prim *adjective* (**primmer, primmest**)
formal and correct in manner; disliking anything rough or rude. **primly** *adverb*,
primness *noun* [origin unknown]

primary *adjective*
first; most important. (Compare *secondary*.)
primarily (*say* pry-mer-il-ee) *adverb* [same origin as *prime*]

primary colour *noun* (*plural* **primary colours**)
one of the colours from which all others can be made by mixing (red, yellow, and blue for paint; red, green, and blue for light).

primary school *noun* (*plural* **primary schools**)
a school for the first stage of a child's education.

primate (*say* pry-mat) *noun* (*plural* **primates**)
1 an archbishop. 2 an animal of the group that includes human beings, apes, and monkeys.
[from Latin *primas* = of the first rank]

prime *adjective*
1 chief; most important, *the prime cause.*
2 excellent; first-rate, *prime beef.*
prime *noun*
the best time or stage of something, *in the prime of life.*
prime *verb* (**primes, priming, primed**)
1 prepare something for use or action. 2 put a coat of liquid on something to prepare it for painting. 3 equip a person with information.
[from Latin *primus* = first]

prime minister *noun* (*plural* **prime ministers**)
the leader of a government.

prime number *noun* (*plural* **prime numbers**)
a number (e.g. 2, 3, 5, 7, 11) that can be divided exactly only by itself and one.

primeval (*say* pry-mee-val) *adjective*
belonging to the earliest times of the world.
[from Latin *primus* = first + *aevum* = age]

primitive *adjective*
1 at an early stage of civilization. 2 at an early stage of development; not complicated or sophisticated.

primrose *noun* (*plural* **primroses**)
a pale-yellow flower that blooms in spring.
[from Latin *prima rosa* = first rose]

prince *noun* (*plural* **princes**)
1 the son of a king or queen. 2 a man or boy in a royal family. **princely** *adjective* [from Latin *princeps* = chieftain]

princess noun (plural **princesses**)
1 the daughter of a king or queen. 2 a woman or girl in a royal family. 3 the wife of a prince. [from French]

principal adjective
chief; most important. **principally** adverb
principal noun (plural **principals**)
the head of a college or school. [from Latin principalis = first or chief]

USAGE: Do not confuse with principle.

principle noun (plural **principles**)
1 a general truth, belief, or rule, She taught me the principles of geometry. 2 a rule of conduct, Cheating is against his principles.
in principle in general, not in details.
on principle because of your principles of behaviour. [from Latin principium = source]

USAGE: Do not confuse with principal.

print verb (prints, printing, printed)
1 put words or pictures on paper by using a machine. 2 write with letters that are not joined together. 3 press a mark or design etc. on a surface. 4 make a picture from the negative of a photograph. **printer** noun
print noun (plural **prints**)
1 printed lettering or words. 2 a mark made by something pressing on a surface. 3 a printed picture, photograph, or design. [from old French priente = pressed]

printout noun (plural **printouts**)
information etc. produced in printed form by a computer.

priority noun (plural **priorities**)
1 being earlier or more important than something else; precedence. 2 something considered more important than other things, Safety is a priority.

prise verb (prises, prising, prised)
lever something out or open, Prise the lid off the crate. [French, = seized]

prism (say prizm) noun (plural **prisms**)
1 a solid shape with ends that are triangles or polygons which are equal and parallel. 2 a glass prism that breaks up light into the colours of the rainbow. **prismatic** adjective [from Greek]

prison noun (plural **prisons**)
a place where criminals are kept as a punishment. [from old French]

prisoner noun (plural **prisoners**)
1 a person kept in prison. 2 a captive.

private adjective
1 belonging to a particular person or group, private property. 2 confidential, private talks. 3 secluded. 4 not holding public office, a private citizen. 5 independent; not organized by

a government, private medicine; a private detective. **privately** adverb, **privacy** (say priv-a-see) noun
in private where only particular people can see or hear; not in public.
private noun (plural **privates**)
a soldier of the lowest rank. [from Latin privus = single or individual]

privatize verb (privatizes, privatizing, privatized)
transfer a nationalized industry etc. to a private organization. **privatization** noun

privilege noun (plural **privileges**)
a special right or advantage given to one person or group. **privileged** adjective [from Latin privus = an individual + legis = of law]

Privy Council noun
a group of distinguished people who advise the sovereign.

prize noun (plural **prizes**)
an award given to the winner of a game or competition etc.
prize verb (prizes, prizing, prized)
value something greatly. [a different spelling of price]

pro noun (plural **pros**) (informal)
a professional.

pro- prefix
1 favouring or supporting (as in pro-British). 2 deputizing or substituted for (as in pronoun). 3 onwards; forwards (as in proceed). [from Latin pro = for; in front of]

probable adjective
likely to happen or be true.
probably adverb, **probability** noun [from Latin probare = prove]

probation noun
the testing of a person's character and abilities. **probationary** adjective
on probation being supervised by a probation officer instead of being sent to prison. [same origin as prove]

probation officer noun (plural **probation officers**)
an official who supervises the behaviour of a convicted criminal who is not in prison.

probe noun (plural **probes**)
1 an instrument for exploring something. 2 an investigation.
probe verb (probes, probing, probed)
1 explore something with a probe. 2 investigate. [from Latin proba = proof]

problem noun (plural **problems**)
1 something difficult to deal with or understand. 2 something that has to be done or answered.
problematic or **problematical** adjective [from Greek]

procedure noun (plural procedures)
an orderly way of doing something. [French, from procéder = proceed]

proceed verb (proceeds, proceeding, proceeded)
1 go forward or onward. 2 continue; go on to do something, She proceeded to explain the plan. [from pro- + Latin cedere = go]

USAGE: Do not confuse with precede.

proceedings plural noun
1 things that happen; activities. 2 a lawsuit.

proceeds plural noun
the money made from a sale or show etc.; profit.

process (say proh-sess) noun (plural processes)
a series of actions for making or doing something.
in the process of in the course of doing something.
process verb (processes, processing, processed)
put something through a manufacturing or other process, processed cheese.
[same origin as proceed]

procession noun (plural processions)
a number of people or vehicles etc. moving steadily forward following each other. [from Latin processio = an advance]

processor noun (plural processors)
1 a machine that processes things. 2 the part of a computer that controls all its operations.

proclaim verb (proclaims, proclaiming, proclaimed)
announce something officially or publicly.
proclamation noun
[from pro- + Latin clamare = to shout]

prod verb (prods, prodding, prodded)
1 poke. 2 stimulate someone into action.
prod noun [origin unknown]

prodigal adjective
wasteful or extravagant.
prodigally adverb, **prodigality** noun
[from Latin prodigus = lavish, generous]

prodigious adjective
wonderful or enormous. **prodigiously** adverb
[same origin as prodigy]

prodigy noun (plural prodigies)
1 a person with wonderful abilities. 2 a wonderful thing.
[from Latin prodigium = good omen]

produce verb (produces, producing, produced)
1 make or create something; bring something into existence. 2 bring something out so that it can be seen. 3 organize the performance of a play, making of a film, etc. 4 extend a line further, Produce the base of the triangle.
producer noun
produce (say prod-yooss) noun
things produced, especially by farmers. [from pro- + Latin ducere = to lead]

product noun (plural products)
1 something produced. 2 the result of multiplying two numbers. (Compare quotient.)
[from Latin productum = produced]

production noun (plural productions)
1 producing. 2 the thing or amount produced.

productive adjective
producing a lot of things. **productivity** noun

profanity noun (plural profanities)
words or language that show disrespect for religion.

profession noun (plural professions)
1 an occupation that needs special education and training, The professions include being a doctor, nurse, or lawyer. 2 a declaration, They made professions of loyalty.
[from Latin professio = public declaration]

professional adjective
1 to do with a profession. 2 doing a certain kind of work as a full-time job for payment, not as an amateur, a professional footballer.
professional noun, **professionally** adverb

professor noun (plural professors)
a university lecturer of the highest rank.
professorship noun [same origin as profess]

profile noun (plural profiles)
1 a side view of a person's face. 2 a short description of a person's character or career.
keep a low profile not make yourself noticeable.
[from old Italian profilare = draw in outline]

profit noun (plural profits)
1 the extra money obtained by selling something for more than it cost to buy or make. 2 an advantage gained by doing something.
profitable adjective, **profitably** noun
profit verb (profits, profiting, profited)
gain an advantage or benefit from something.
[from old French]

profiteer noun (plural profiteers)
a person who makes a great profit unfairly.
profiteering noun

profound adjective
1 very deep or intense, We take a profound interest in it. 2 showing or needing great study.
profoundly adverb, **profundity** noun
[from pro- + Latin fundus = bottom]

prognosis (say prog-noh-sis) noun (plural prognoses)
a forecast or prediction, especially about a disease. **prognostication** noun
[from Greek pro- = before + gnosis = knowing]

program noun (plural programs)
a series of coded instructions for a computer to carry out.

program *verb* (programs, programming, programmed)
prepare a computer by means of a program. **programmer** *noun*
[the American spelling of *programme*]

programme *noun* (*plural* programmes)
1 a list of planned events. 2 a leaflet giving details of a play, concert, etc. 3 a show, play or talk etc. on radio or television.
[from Greek *programma* = public notice]

progress (*say* proh-gress) *noun*
1 forward movement; an advance. 2 a development or improvement.
progress (*say* pro-gress) *verb* (progresses, progressing, progressed)
1 move forward. 2 improve.
progression *noun*, **progressive** *adjective*
[from *pro-* + Latin *gressus* = going]

prohibit *verb* (prohibits, prohibiting, prohibited)
forbid or ban, *Smoking is prohibited.*
prohibition *noun* [from Latin]

prohibitive *adjective*
1 prohibiting. 2 (of prices) so high that people will not buy things.

project (*say* proj-ekt) *noun* (*plural* projects)
1 a plan or scheme. 2 the task of finding out as much as you can about something and writing about it.
project (*say* pro-jekt) *verb* (projects, projecting, projected)
1 stick out. 2 show a picture on a screen. 3 give people a particular impression, *He likes to project an image of absent-minded brilliance.*
projection *noun*
[from *pro-* + Latin *-jectum* = thrown]

projectile *noun* (*plural* projectiles)
a missile.

projector *noun* (*plural* projectors)
a machine for showing films or photographs on a screen.

prolific *adjective*
producing a lot, *a prolific author.*
prolifically *adverb*

prologue (*say* proh-log) *noun* (*plural* prologues)
an introduction to a poem or play etc. [from Greek *pro-* = before + *logos* = speech]

prolong *verb* (prolongs, prolonging, prolonged)
make a thing longer or make it last for a long time. **prolongation** *noun*
[from *pro-* + Latin *longus* = long]

prom *noun* (*plural* proms) (*informal*)
1 a promenade. 2 a promenade concert.

promenade (*say* prom-in-ahd) *noun* (*plural* promenades)
1 a place suitable for walking, especially beside the seashore. 2 a leisurely walk.
promenade *verb*
[French, from *se promener* = to walk]

promenade concert (*plural* promenade concerts)
a concert where part of the audience may stand or walk about.

prominent *adjective*
1 sticking out; projecting. 2 conspicuous. 3 important.
prominently *adverb*, **prominence** *noun*
[from Latin]

promiscuous *adjective*
1 having many casual sexual relationships. 2 indiscriminate. **promiscuously** *adverb*, **promiscuity** *noun*

promise *noun* (*plural* promises)
1 a statement that you will definitely do or not do something. 2 an indication of future success or good results, *His work shows promise.*
promise *verb* (promises, promising, promised)
make a promise.
[from Latin]

promote *verb* (promotes, promoting, promoted)
1 move a person to a higher rank or position. 2 help the progress or sale of something, *He has done much to promote the cause of peace.*
promoter *noun*, **promotion** *noun*
[from *pro-* + Latin *motum* = moved]

prompt *adjective*
1 without delay, *a prompt reply.* 2 punctual. **promptly** *adverb*, **promptness** *noun*, **promptitude** *noun*
prompt *verb* (prompts, prompting, prompted)
1 cause or encourage a person to do something. 2 remind an actor or speaker of words when he or she has forgotten them. **prompter** *noun*
[from Latin *promptum* = produced]

prong *noun* (*plural* prongs)
one of the spikes on a fork.
pronged *adjective*

pronoun *noun* (*plural* pronouns)
a word used instead of a noun.
demonstrative pronouns are *this, that, these, those*; **interrogative pronouns** are *who? what? which?*, etc.; **personal pronouns** are *I, me, we, us, thou, thee, you, ye, he, him, she, her, it, they, them*; **possessive pronouns** are *mine, yours, theirs*, etc.; **reflexive pronouns** are *myself, yourself*, etc.; **relative pronouns** are *who, what, which, that.*
[from *pro-* = in place of + *noun*]

pronounce *verb* (pronounces, pronouncing, pronounced)
1 say a sound or word in a particular way, *'Two' is pronounced like 'too'.* 2 declare something formally, *I now pronounce you man and wife.*
[from *pro-* + Latin *nuntiare* = announce]

pronounced *adjective*
noticeable, *This street has a pronounced slope.*

pronunciation *noun* (*plural* **pronunciations**)
1 the way a word is pronounced. 2 the way a person pronounces words.

USAGE: Note the spelling; this word should not be written or spoken as 'pronounciation'.

proof *noun* (*plural* **proofs**)
1 a fact or thing that shows something is true.
2 a printed copy of a book or photograph etc. made for checking before other copies are printed.
proof *adjective*
able to resist something or not be penetrated, *a bulletproof jacket.*
[from old French; related to *prove*]

prop[1] *noun* (*plural* **props**)
a support, especially one made of a long piece of wood or metal.
prop *verb* (**props, propping, propped**)
support something by leaning it against something else. [probably from old Dutch]

prop[2] *noun* (*plural* **props**)
an object or piece of furniture used on a theatre stage or in a film. [from *property*]

propaganda *noun*
publicity intended to make people believe something.
[Italian, = propagating, spreading]

propel *verb* (**propels, propelling, propelled**)
push something forward.
[from *pro-* + Latin *pellere* = to drive]

propeller *noun* (*plural* **propellers**)
a device with blades that spin round to drive an aircraft or ship.

proper *adjective*
1 suitable or right, *the proper way to hold a bat.*
2 respectable, *prim and proper.* 3 (*informal*) complete or thorough, *You're a proper nuisance!* **properly** *adverb*
[from Latin *proprius* = your own, special]

proper fraction *noun* (*plural* **proper fractions**)
a fraction that is less than 1, with the numerator less than the denominator, e.g. $\frac{3}{5}$.

proper noun *noun* (*plural* **proper nouns**)
the name of one person or thing, e.g. *Mary, London, Spain.*

property *noun* (*plural* **properties**)
1 a thing or things that belong to somebody.
2 a building or someone's land. 3 a quality or characteristic, *It has the property of becoming soft when heated.* [same origin as *proper*]

prophecy *noun* (*plural* **prophecies**)
1 a statement that prophesies something. 2 the action of prophesying.

prophesy *verb* (**prophesies, prophesying, prophesied**)
say what will happen in the future; foretell.
[from Greek *pro* = before + *phanai* = speak]

prophet *noun* (*plural* **prophets**)
1 a person who makes prophecies. 2 a religious teacher who is believed to be inspired by God.
prophetess *noun*, **prophetic** *adjective*
the Prophet Muhammad, who founded the Muslim faith.
[from Greek *prophetes* = someone who speaks for a god]

proportion *noun* (*plural* **proportions**)
1 a part or share of a whole thing. 2 a ratio.
3 the correct relationship in size, amount, or importance between two things, *You've drawn his head out of proportion.*
proportional *adjective*, **proportionally** *adverb*, **proportionate** *adjective*
proportions *plural noun* size, *a ship of large proportions.*
[from *pro-* + Latin *portio* = portion or share]

proportional representation *noun*
a system in which each political party has a number of Members of Parliament in proportion to the number of votes for all its candidates.

propose *verb* (**proposes, proposing, proposed**)
1 suggest an idea or plan etc. 2 ask a person to marry you. **proposal** *noun*
[from old French; related to *proponent*]

proposition *noun* (*plural* **propositions**)
1 a suggestion or offer. 2 a statement.
3 (*informal*) an undertaking or problem, *a difficult proposition.*
[same origin as *proponent*]

proprietor *noun* (*plural* **proprietors**)
the owner of a shop or business.
proprietress *noun* [from *proprietary*]

prosaic *adjective*
plain or dull and ordinary. **prosaically** *adverb*
[from *prose*]

prose *noun*
writing or speech that is not in verse.
[from Latin *prosa* = straightforward, plain]

prosecute *verb* (**prosecutes, prosecuting, prosecuted**)
1 make someone go to a lawcourt to be tried for a crime. 2 continue with something; pursue, *prosecuting their trade.* **prosecution** *noun*, **prosecutor** *noun*
[from Latin *prosecutus* = pursued]

prospect *noun* (*plural* **prospects**)
1 a possibility or expectation of something, *There is no prospect of success.* 2 a wide view.
prospect (*say* pro-**spekt**) *verb* (**prospects, prospecting, prospected**)
explore in search of something, *prospecting for gold.* **prospector** *noun*
[from *pro-* + Latin *-spicere* = to look]

prospective *adjective*
expected to be or to happen; possible, *prospective customers.*

prospectus *noun* (*plural* prospectuses)
a booklet describing and advertising a school,
business company, etc.
[Latin, = view or prospect]

prosperous *adjective*
successful or rich. **prosperity** *noun*

prostitute *noun* (*plural* prostitutes)
a person who takes part in sexual acts for
payment. **prostitution** *noun*
[from Latin *prostitutus* = for sale]

protect *verb* (protects, protecting, protected)
keep safe from harm or injury.
protection *noun*, **protective** *adjective*,
protector *noun*
[from *pro-* + Latin *tectum* = covered]

protein *noun* (*plural* proteins)
a substance that is found in all living things
and is an essential part of the food of animals.
[from Greek *proteios* = primary, most
important]

protest (*say* proh-test) *noun* (*plural* protests)
a statement or action showing that you
disapprove of something.
protest (*say* pro-test) *verb* (protests, protesting,
protested)
1 make a protest. 2 declare firmly, *They
protested their innocence.* **protestation** *noun*
[from *pro-* + Latin *testari* = say on oath]

Protestant *noun* (*plural* Protestants)
a member of any of the western Christian
Churches separated from the Roman Catholic
Church.
[because in the 16th century many people
protested (= declared firmly) their opposition
to the Catholic Church]

proto- *prefix*
1 first. 2 at an early stage of development.
[from Greek *protos* = first or earliest]

proton *noun* (*plural* protons)
a particle of matter with a positive electric
charge. [same origin as *proto-*]

prototype *noun* (*plural* prototypes)
the first model of something, from which
others are copied or developed.

protractor *noun* (*plural* protractors)
a device for measuring angles, usually a
semicircle marked off in degrees.

proud *adjective*
1 very pleased with yourself or with someone
else who has done well. 2 causing pride, *This is
a proud moment for us.* 3 full of self-respect and
independence, *They were too proud to ask for
help.*
proudly *adverb*
[via Old English from old French *prud*
= brave]

prove *verb* (proves, proving, proved)
1 show that something is true. 2 turn out, *The
forecast proved to be correct.*
provable *adjective*
[from Latin *probare* = to test]

proverb *noun* (*plural* proverbs)
a short well-known saying that states a truth,
e.g. 'Many hands make light work'.
[from *pro-* + Latin *verbum* = word]

proverbial *adjective*
1 referred to in a proverb. 2 well-known.

provide *verb* (provides, providing, provided)
1 make something available; supply. 2 prepare
for something, *Try to provide against
emergencies.* **provider** *noun*
[from Latin *providere* = foresee]

provided *conjunction*
on condition, *You can stay provided that you
help.*

providing *conjunction*
provided.

province *noun* (*plural* provinces)
1 a section of a country. 2 the area of a
person's special knowledge or responsibility,
*Repairing stereos is outside my province, I'm
afraid.* **provincial** *adjective*
the provinces the parts of a country outside its
capital city.
[from Latin]

provision *noun* (*plural* provisions)
1 providing something. 2 a statement in a
document, *the provisions of the treaty.*
[from Latin *provisum* = provided]

provisional *adjective*
arranged or agreed upon temporarily but
possibly to be altered later.
provisionally *adverb*

provisions *plural noun*
supplies of food and drink.

provoke *verb* (provokes, provoking, provoked)
1 make a person angry. 2 cause or give rise to
something, *The joke provoked laughter.*
provocation *noun*, **provocative** *adjective*
[from *pro-* + Latin *vocare* = summon]

prow *noun* (*plural* prows)
the front end of a ship. [from French]

prowl *verb* (prowls, prowling, prowled)
move about quietly or cautiously, like a
hunter. **prowl** *noun*, **prowler** *noun*

proxy *noun* (*plural* proxies)
a person authorized to represent or act for
another person, *I will be abroad, so I have
arranged to vote by proxy.* [from Latin]

prude *noun* (*plural* prudes)
a person who is easily shocked.
prudish *adjective*, **prudery** *noun*
[from old French]

prudent *adjective*
careful, not rash or reckless. **prudently** *adverb*, **prudence** *noun*, **prudential** *adjective* [from French; related to *provide*]

prune[1] *noun* (*plural* **prunes**)
a dried plum. [from Greek]

prune[2] *verb* (**prunes, pruning, pruned**)
cut off unwanted parts of a tree or bush etc. [from old French]

pry *verb* (**pries, prying, pried**)
look or ask inquisitively.

PS *abbreviation*
postscript.

psalm (*say* sahm) *noun* (*plural* **psalms**)
a religious song, especially one from the Book of Psalms in the Bible. **psalmist** *noun*
[via Old English from Greek *psalmos* = song sung to the harp]

pseudo- (*say* s'yood-oh) *prefix*
false; pretended. [from Greek]

pseudonym *noun* (*plural* **pseudonyms**)
a false name used by an author.
[from *pseudo-* + Greek *onyma* = name]

psychiatrist (*say* sy-ky-a-trist) *noun* (*plural* **psychiatrists**)
a doctor who treats mental illnesses.
psychiatry *noun*, **psychiatric** *adjective*
[from *psycho-* + Greek *iatreia* = healing]

psychic (*say* sy-kik) *adjective*
1 supernatural. 2 having supernatural powers, especially being able to predict the future. 3 to do with the mind or soul. **psychical** *adjective*
[same origin as *psycho-*]

psycho- *prefix*
to do with the mind.
[from Greek *psyche* = life or soul]

psychoanalysis *noun*
investigation of a person's mental processes, especially in psychotherapy.

psychology *noun*
the study of the mind and how it works.
psychological *adjective*, **psychologist** *noun*
[from *psycho-* + *-logy*]

PT *abbreviation*
physical training.

pterodactyl (*say* te-ro-dak-til) *noun* (*plural* **pterodactyls**)
an extinct flying reptile.
[from Greek *pteron* = wing + *daktylos* = finger (because one of the 'fingers' on its front leg was enlarged to support its wing)]

PTO *abbreviation*
please turn over.

pub *noun* (*plural* **pubs**) (*informal*)
a public house.

puberty (*say* pew-ber-tee) *noun*
the time when a young person is developing physically into an adult.

public *adjective*
belonging to or known by everyone, not private. **publicly** *adverb*
public *noun*
people in general.
in public openly, not in private.
[from Latin *publicus* = of the people]

publication *noun* (*plural* **publications**)
1 publishing. 2 a published book or newspaper etc.

public house *noun* (*plural* **public houses**)
a building licensed to serve alcoholic drinks to the public.

publicity *noun*
public attention; doing things (e.g. advertising) to draw people's attention to something.

public school *noun* (*plural* **public schools**)
1 a secondary school that charges fees. 2 (in Scotland and the USA) a school run by a local authority or by the State.

publish *verb* (**publishes, publishing, published**)
1 have something printed and sold to the public. 2 announce something in public.
publisher *noun*
[from Latin *publicare* = make public]

pucker *verb* (**puckers, puckering, puckered**)
wrinkle. [origin unknown]

pudding *noun* (*plural* **puddings**)
1 a food made in a soft mass, especially in a mixture of flour and other ingredients. 2 the sweet course of a meal. [from French]

puddle *noun* (*plural* **puddles**)
a shallow patch of liquid, especially of rainwater on a road. [from Old English]

puff *noun* (*plural* **puffs**)
1 a short blowing of breath, wind, or smoke etc. 2 a soft pad for putting powder on the skin. 3 a cake of very light pastry filled with cream.
puff *verb* (**puffs, puffing, puffed**)
1 blow out puffs of smoke etc. 2 breathe with difficulty; pant. 3 inflate or swell something, *He puffed out his chest.*

puffy *adjective*
puffed out; swollen. **puffiness** *noun*

pugnacious *adjective*
wanting to fight; aggressive.
pugnaciously *adverb*, **pugnacity** *noun*
[from Latin *pugnare* = to fight]

pull *verb* (**pulls, pulling, pulled**)
1 make a thing come towards or after you by using force on it. 2 move by a driving force, *The car pulled out into the road.*
pull *noun*
pull a face make a strange face.
pull off achieve something.

pull somebody's leg tease him or her.
pull through recover from an illness.
pull yourself together become calm or sensible.

pulley *noun* (*plural* **pulleys**)
a wheel with a rope, chain, or belt over it, used for lifting or moving heavy things.

pullover *noun* (*plural* **pullovers**)
a knitted piece of clothing for the top half of the body.

pulp *noun*
1 the soft moist part of fruit. 2 any soft moist mass. **pulpy** *adjective* [from Latin]

pulpit *noun* (*plural* **pulpits**)
a small enclosed platform for the preacher in a church or chapel. [from Latin *pulpitum* = a platform, stage, or scaffold]

pulsate *verb* (**pulsates, pulsating, pulsated**)
expand and contract rhythmically; vibrate.
pulsation *noun* [from Latin]

pulse[1] *noun* (*plural* **pulses**)
1 the rhythmical movement of the arteries as blood is pumped through them by the beating of the heart, *The pulse can be felt in a person's wrists.* 2 a throb.
pulse *verb* (**pulses, pulsing, pulsed**)
throb or pulsate.
[from Latin *pulsum* = driven, beaten]

pulse[2] *noun* (*plural* **pulses**)
the edible seed of peas, beans, lentils, etc. [from Latin]

pulverize *verb* (**pulverizes, pulverizing, pulverized**)
crush something into powder.
pulverization *noun* [from Latin *pulveris* = of dust]

pump[1] *noun* (*plural* **pumps**)
a device that pushes air or liquid into or out of something, or along pipes.
pump *verb* (**pumps, pumping, pumped**)
1 move air or liquid with a pump. 2 (*informal*) question a person to obtain information.
pump up inflate.
[originally a sailors' word: origin unknown]

pump[2] *noun* (*plural* **pumps**)
a canvas sports shoe with a rubber sole. [origin unknown]

pumpkin *noun* (*plural* **pumpkins**)
a very large round fruit with a hard orange skin.
[from Greek *pepon*, a kind of large melon]

pun *noun* (*plural* **puns**)
a joking use of a word sounding the same as another, e.g. 'Deciding where to bury him was a *grave* decision'.

punch[1] *verb* (**punches, punching, punched**)
1 hit someone with your fist. 2 make a hole in something.

punch *noun* (*plural* **punches**)
1 a hit with a fist. 2 a device for making holes in paper, metal, leather, etc. 3 vigour. [same origin as *puncture*]

punch[2] *noun*
a drink made by mixing wine or spirits and fruit juice in a bowl.
[from Sanskrit *pañca* = five (the number of ingredients in the traditional recipe: spirits, fruit juice, water, sugar, and spice)]

punchline *noun* (*plural* **punchlines**)
words that give the climax of a joke or story.

punctual *adjective*
doing things exactly at the time arranged; not late. **punctually** *adverb*, **punctuality** *noun* [from Latin *punctum* = a point]

punctuate *verb* (**punctuates, punctuating, punctuated**)
1 put punctuation marks into something. 2 put something in at intervals, *His speech was punctuated with cheers.* [from Latin *punctuare* = mark with points or dots]

punctuation *noun*
marks such as commas, full stops, and brackets put into a piece of writing to make it easier to read.

puncture *noun* (*plural* **punctures**)
a small hole made by something sharp, especially in a tyre.
puncture *verb* (**punctures, puncturing, punctured**)
make a puncture in something.

pungent (*say* pun-jent) *adjective*
1 having a strong taste or smell. 2 (of remarks) sharp.
pungently *adverb*, **pungency** *noun*
[from Latin *pungere* = to prick]

punish *verb* (**punishes, punishing, punished**)
make a person suffer because he or she has done something wrong.
punishable *adjective*, **punishment** *noun* [same origin as *pain*]

punk *noun* (*plural* **punks**)
1 (also **punk rock**) a loud aggressive style of rock music. 2 a person who likes this music. [origin unknown]

punt[1] *noun* (*plural* **punts**)
a flat-bottomed boat, usually moved by pushing a pole against the bottom of a river while standing in the punt.
punt *verb* (**punts, punting, punted**)
move a punt with a pole.
[from Latin *ponto* = pontoon[1]]

punt[2] *verb* (**punts, punting, punted**)
kick a football after dropping it from your hands and before it touches the ground. [origin unknown]

pupa (*say* pew-pa) *noun* (*plural* **pupae**)
a chrysalis. [from Latin; related to *pupil*]

pupil *noun* (*plural* **pupils**)
1 someone who is being taught by another person, especially at school. 2 the opening in the centre of the eye. [from Latin *pupilla* = little girl or doll (the use in sense 2 refers to the tiny images of people and things that can be seen in the eye)]

puppet *noun* (*plural* **puppets**)
1 a kind of doll that can be made to move by fitting it over your hand or working it by strings or wires. 2 a person whose actions are controlled by someone else. **puppetry** *noun* [probably related to *pupil*]

puppy *noun* (*plural* **puppies**)
a young dog.
[from old French; related to *pupil*]

purchase *verb* (**purchases, purchasing, purchased**)
buy. **purchaser** *noun*
purchase *noun* (*plural* **purchases**)
1 something bought. 2 buying. 3 a firm hold to pull or raise something.

pure *adjective*
1 not mixed with anything else; clean. 2 mere; nothing but, *pure nonsense.* **purely** *adverb*, **pureness** *noun*, **purity** *noun* [from Latin]

purée (*say* pewr-ay) *noun* (*plural* **purées**)
fruit or vegetables made into pulp.
[French, = squeezed]

purge *verb* (**purges, purging, purged**)
get rid of unwanted people or things.
purge *noun* [from Latin *purgare* = make pure]

purify *verb* (**purifies, purifying, purified**)
make a thing pure.
purification *noun*, **purifier** *noun*

Puritan *noun* (*plural* **Puritans**)
a Protestant in the 16th and 17th centuries who wanted simpler religious ceremonies and strictly moral behaviour.

purple *noun*
deep reddish-blue colour.

purpose *noun* (*plural* **purposes**)
1 what you intend to do; a plan or aim.
2 determination.
purposeful *adjective*, **purposefully** *adverb*
on purpose by intention, not by accident.
[from old French; related to *propose*]

purr *verb* (**purrs, purring, purred**)
make the low murmuring sound that a cat does when it is pleased. **purr** *noun*

purse *noun* (*plural* **purses**)
a small pouch for carrying money.
purse *verb* (**purses, pursing, pursed**)
draw something into folds, *She pursed up her lips.* [from Latin *bursa* = a bag]

pursue *verb* (**pursues, pursuing, pursued**)
1 chase someone in order to catch them.
2 continue with something; work at, *We are pursuing our enquiries.* **pursuer** *noun*
[from old French; related to *prosecute*]

pursuit *noun* (*plural* **pursuits**)
1 pursuing. 2 a regular activity.

pus *noun*
a thick yellowish substance produced in inflamed or infected tissue, e.g. in an abscess or boil. [Latin]

push *verb* (**pushes, pushing, pushed**)
1 make a thing go away from you by using force on it. 2 move yourself by using force, *He pushed in front of me.* 3 try to force someone to do or use something; urge.
push off (*slang*) go away.
push *noun* (*plural* **pushes**)
a pushing movement or effort.
at a push if necessary but only with difficulty. [from French; related to *pulse*[1]]

pusher *noun* (*plural* **pushers**)
a person who sells illegal drugs.

pushy *adjective*
unpleasantly self-confident and eager to do things.

puss *noun* (*informal*)
a cat.

put *verb* (**puts, putting, put**)
This word has many uses, including 1 move a person or thing to a place or position (*Put the lamp on the table*), 2 cause a person or thing to do or experience something or be in a certain condition (*Put the light on. Put her in a good mood*), 3 express in words (*She put it tactfully*).
be hard put have difficulty in doing something.
put off 1 postpone. 2 dissuade. 3 stop someone wanting something, *The smell puts me off.*
put out 1 stop a fire from burning or a light from shining. 2 annoy or inconvenience, *Our lateness has put her out.*
put up 1 build. 2 raise. 3 give someone a place to sleep; provide, *Who will put up the money?*
put up with endure or tolerate.

putt *verb* (**putts, putting, putted**)
hit a golf ball gently towards the hole.
putt *noun*, **putter** *noun*, **putting green** *noun*
[a different spelling of *put*]

putty *noun*
a soft paste that sets hard, used for fitting the glass into a window frame.

puzzle *noun* (*plural* **puzzles**)
1 a difficult question or problem. 2 a game or toy that sets a problem or difficult task. 3 a jigsaw puzzle.
puzzle *verb* (**puzzles, puzzling, puzzled**)
1 give someone a problem so that they have to think hard. 2 think patiently about how to solve something. **puzzlement** *noun*
[origin unknown]

pygmy (*say* pig-mee) *noun* (*plural* **pygmies**)
1 a very small person or thing. 2 a member of a race of very small people in Central Africa.
[from Greek]

pyjamas *plural noun*
a loose jacket and trousers worn in bed.
[from Persian or Urdu *pay* = leg + *jamah*
= clothing]

pylon *noun* (*plural* **pylons**)
a tall framework made of strips of steel,
supporting electric cables. [from Greek]

pyramid *noun* (*plural* **pyramids**)
1 a structure with a square base and with
sloping sides that meet in a point at the top.
2 an ancient Egyptian tomb shaped like this.
pyramidal (*say* pir-**am**-id-al) *adjective* [from
Greek]

python *noun* (*plural* **pythons**)
a large snake that kills its prey by coiling
round and crushing it.
[the name of a large serpent or monster in
Greek legend, killed by Apollo]

QC *abbreviation*
Queen's Counsel.

QED *abbreviation*
quod erat demonstrandum (Latin, = which was
the thing that had to be proved).

quack[1] *verb* (**quacks, quacking, quacked**)
make the harsh cry of a duck. **quack** *noun*
[imitating the sound]

quack[2] *noun* (*plural* **quacks**)
a person who falsely claims to have medical
skill or have remedies to cure diseases. [from
Dutch *quacken* = to boast]

quadratic equation *noun* (*plural* **quadratic
equations**)
an equation that involves quantities or
variables raised to the power of two, but no
higher than two.
[from Latin *quadrare* = to square]

quadri- *prefix*
four. [from Latin]

quadrilateral *noun* (*plural* **quadrilaterals**)
a flat geometric shape with four sides.

quadruped *noun* (*plural* **quadrupeds**)
an animal with four feet.
[from *quadri-* + Latin *pedis* = of a foot]

quagmire *noun* (*plural* **quagmires**)
a bog or marsh.
[from an old word *quag* = marsh, + *mire*]

quail[1] *noun* (*plural* **quail** or **quails**)
a bird related to the partridge.
[from old French]

quail[2] *verb* (**quails, quailing, quailed**)
flinch; feel or show fear. [origin unknown]

quaint *adjective*
attractively odd or old-fashioned.
quaintly *adverb*, **quaintness** *noun*

quake *verb* (**quakes, quaking, quaked**)
tremble; shake with fear.

Quaker *noun* (*plural* **Quakers**)
a member of a religious group called the
Society of Friends, founded by George Fox in
the 17th century.
[originally an insult, probably from George
Fox's saying that people should 'tremble at the
name of the Lord']

qualify *verb* (**qualifies, qualifying, qualified**)
1 make or become able to do something
through having certain qualities or training,
or by passing a test. **2** make a statement less
extreme; limit its meaning. **3** (of an adjective)
add meaning to a noun. **qualification** *noun*
[from Latin *qualis* = of what kind?, of a
particular kind]

quality *noun* (*plural* **qualities**)
1 how good or bad something is. **2** a
characteristic; something that is special in a
person or thing. [same origin as *qualify*]

qualm (*say* kwahm) *noun* (*plural* **qualms**)
a misgiving or scruple. [origin unknown]

quandary *noun* (*plural* **quandaries**)
a difficult situation where you are uncertain
what to do. [origin unknown]

quantity *noun* (*plural* **quantities**)
1 how much there is of something; how many
things there are of one sort. **2** a large amount.
[from Latin *quantus* = how big?, how much?]

quarantine *noun*
keeping a person or animal isolated in case
they have a disease which could spread to
others. [from Italian *quaranta* = forty (the
original period of isolation was 40 days)]

quarrel *noun* (*plural* **quarrels**)
an angry disagreement.
quarrel *verb* (**quarrels, quarrelling, quarrelled**)
have a quarrel. **quarrelsome** *adjective*
[from Latin *querela* = complaint]

quarry[1] *noun* (*plural* **quarries**)
an open place where stone or slate is dug or cut
out of the ground.
quarry *verb* (**quarries, quarrying, quarried**)
dig or cut from a quarry. [from Latin]

quarry[2] *noun* (*plural* **quarries**)
an animal etc. being hunted or pursued. [from
old French]

quart *noun* (*plural* **quarts**)
two pints, a quarter of a gallon.
[from old French; related to *quarter*]

quarter *noun* (*plural* **quarters**)
1 each of four equal parts into which a thing is
or can be divided. **2** three months, one-fourth
of a year. **3** a district or region, *People came*

from every quarter.
at close quarters very close together.
give no quarter show no mercy.
quarter *verb* (quarters, quartering, quartered)
1 divide something into quarters. 2 put soldiers etc. into lodgings.
[from Latin *quartus* = fourth]

quarters *plural noun*
lodgings.

quartet *noun* (*plural* quartets)
1 a group of four musicians. 2 a piece of music for four musicians. 3 a set of four people or things.
[via French from Italian *quarto* = fourth]

quartz *noun*
a hard mineral. [via German from Polish]

quasi- (*say* kwayz-I) *prefix*
seeming to be something but not really so, *a quasi-scientific explanation.*
[from Latin *quasi* = as if]

quaver *verb* (quavers, quavering, quavered)
tremble or quiver.
quaver *noun* (*plural* quavers)
1 a quavering sound. 2 a note in music (♪) lasting half as long as a crotchet.

quay (*say* kee) *noun* (*plural* quays)
a landing-place where ships can be tied up for loading and unloading; a wharf. **quayside** *noun*
[from old French]

queasy *adjective*
feeling slightly sick. **queasily** *adverb*, **queasiness** *noun* [origin unknown]

queen *noun* (*plural* queens)
1 a woman who is the ruler of a country through inheriting the position. 2 the wife of a king. 3 a female bee or ant that produces eggs. 4 an important piece in chess. 5 a playing card with a picture of a queen on it.
queenly *adjective*

Queen's Counsel *noun* (*plural* Queen's Counsels)
a senior barrister.

queer *adjective*
1 strange or eccentric. 2 slightly ill or faint.
queerly *adverb*, **queerness** *noun*
queer *verb* (queers, queering, queered)
queer a person's pitch spoil his or her chances beforehand.

quell *verb* (quells, quelling, quelled)
1 crush a rebellion. 2 stop yourself from feeling fear, anger etc.; suppress.
[from Old English]

quench *verb* (quenches, quenching, quenched)
1 satisfy your thirst by drinking. 2 put out a fire or flame. [from Old English]

query (*say* kweer-ee) *noun* (*plural* queries)
1 a question. 2 a question mark.
[from Latin *quaere* = ask!]

quest *noun* (*plural* quests)
a long search for something, *the quest for gold.*
[same origin as *question*]

question *noun* (*plural* questions)
1 a sentence asking something. 2 a problem to be discussed or solved, *Parliament debated the question of education.* 3 doubt, *Whether we shall win is open to question.*
in question being discussed or disputed, *His honesty is not in question.*
out of the question impossible.
question *verb* (questions, questioning, questioned)
1 ask someone questions. 2 say that you are doubtful about something. **questioner** *noun*
[from Latin *quaesitum* = sought for]

questionable *adjective*
causing doubt; not certainly true or honest or advisable.

question mark *noun* (*plural* question marks)
the punctuation mark ? placed after a question.

questionnaire *noun* (*plural* questionnaires)
a list of questions.

queue (*say* kew) *noun* (*plural* queues)
a line of people or vehicles waiting for something.
queue *verb* (queues, queueing, queued)
wait in a queue. [French]

quibble *noun* (*plural* quibbles)
a trivial complaint or objection.
quibble *verb* (quibbles, quibbling, quibbled)
make trivial complaints or objections.
[probably from Latin *quibus* = what?, for which, for whom (because *quibus* often appeared in legal documents)]

quick *adjective*
1 taking only a short time to do something. 2 done in a short time. 3 able to notice or learn or think quickly. 4 (*old use*) alive, *the quick and the dead.*
quickly *adverb*, **quickness** *noun*
[from Old English]

quicksand *noun* (*plural* quicksands)
an area of loose wet sand which is so deep that heavy objects sink into it.
[from *quick* in sense 4 (because the sand moves as if it were alive and 'eats' things)]

quid *noun* (*plural* quid) (*slang*)
£1. [origin unknown]

quiet *adjective*
1 silent, *Be quiet!* 2 with little sound; not loud or noisy. 3 calm and peaceful; without disturbance, *a quiet life.* 4 (of colours) not bright. **quietly** *adverb*, **quietness** *noun*
quiet *noun*
quietness. [from Latin *quietus* = calm]

quieten *verb* (quietens, quietening, quietened)
make or become quiet.

quill *noun* (*plural* **quills**)
1 a large feather. 2 a pen made from a large feather. 3 one of the spines on a hedgehog.

quilt *noun* (*plural* **quilts**)
a padded bedcover.
[from Latin *culcita* = mattress or cushion]

quintet *noun* (*plural* **quintets**)
1 a group of five musicians. 2 a piece of music for five musicians.
[from Italian *quinto* = fifth]

quirk *noun* (*plural* **quirks**)
1 a peculiarity of a person's behaviour. 2 a trick of fate. [origin unknown]

quit *verb* (**quits, quitting, quitted** or **quit**)
1 leave or abandon. 2 (*informal*) stop doing something. **quitter** *noun* [same origin as *quiet*]

quite *adverb*
1 completely or entirely, *I am quite all right.* 2 somewhat; to some extent, *She is quite a good swimmer.* 3 really, *It's quite a change.*
[same origin as *quiet*]

quits *adjective*
even or equal after retaliating or paying someone, *I think you and I are quits now.*

quiver[1] *noun* (*plural* **quivers**)
a container for arrows.
[via old French from Germanic]

quiver[2] *verb* (**quivers, quivering, quivered**)
tremble. **quiver** *noun* [from Old English]

quiz *noun* (*plural* **quizzes**)
a series of questions, especially as an entertainment or competition.
quiz *verb* (**quizzes, quizzing, quizzed**)
question someone closely.

quoit (*say* koit) *noun* (*plural* **quoits**)
a ring thrown at a peg in the game of **quoits**.
[origin unknown]

quota *noun* (*plural* **quotas**)
1 a fixed share that must be given or received or done. 2 a limited amount.
[from Latin *quot* = how many?]

quotation *noun* (*plural* **quotations**)
1 quoting. 2 something quoted. 3 a statement of the price.

quotation marks *plural noun*
inverted commas.

quote *verb* (**quotes, quoting, quoted**)
1 repeat words that were first written or spoken by someone else. 2 mention something as proof. 3 state the price of goods or services that you can supply.
quote *noun* (*plural* **quotes**)
a quotation. [from Latin *quotare* = to number]

quotient (*say* kwoh-shent) *noun* (*plural* **quotients**)
the result of dividing one number by another. (Compare *product*.)
[from Latin *quotiens* = how many times?]

Rr

rabbi (*say* rab-I) *noun* (*plural* **rabbis**)
a Jewish religious leader.
[Hebrew, = my master]

rabbit *noun* (*plural* **rabbits**)
a furry animal with long ears that digs burrows. [origin unknown]

rabble *noun* (*plural* **rabbles**)
a disorderly crowd; a mob.

rabid (*say* rab-id) *adjective*
1 fanatical, *a rabid tennis fan.* 2 suffering from rabies.

rabies (*say* ray-beez) *noun*
a fatal disease that affects dogs, cats, etc. and can infect people.
[Latin, from *rabere* = to be mad]

race[1] *noun* (*plural* **races**)
1 a competition to be the first to reach a particular place or to do something. 2 a strong fast current of water, *the tidal race.*
race *verb* (**races, racing, raced**)
1 compete in a race. 2 move very fast.
racer *noun* [from Old Norse]

race[2] *noun* (*plural* **races**)
a very large group of people thought to have the same ancestors and with physical characteristics (e.g. colour of skin and hair, shape of eyes and nose) that differ from those of other groups. **racial** *adjective* [via French from Italian]

racism (*say* ray-sizm) *noun*
1 belief that a particular race of people is better than others. 2 hostility towards people of other races. **racist** *noun*

rack[1] *noun* (*plural* **racks**)
1 a framework used as a shelf or container. 2 a bar or rail with cogs into which the cogs of a gear or wheel etc. fit. 3 an ancient device for torturing people by stretching them.
rack *verb* (**racks, racking, racked**)
torment, *He was racked with pain.*
rack your brains think hard in trying to solve a problem.
[from old German or old Dutch]

rack[2] *noun*
destruction, *The place has gone to rack and ruin.* [a different spelling of *wreck*]

racket[1] *noun* (*plural* **rackets**)
a bat with strings stretched across a frame, used in tennis and similar games.
[from Arabic *rahat* = palm of the hand]

racket[2] *noun* (*plural* **rackets**)
1 a loud noise; a din. 2 a dishonest business; a swindle. [origin unknown]

racy *adjective* (**racier, raciest**)
lively and slightly shocking in style, *She gave a racy account of her travels*. [originally = having a particular quality: from *race²*]

radar *noun*
a system or apparatus that uses radio waves to show on a screen etc. the position of objects that cannot be seen because of darkness, fog, distance, etc.
[from the initial letters of *radio detection and ranging*]

radiant *adjective*
1 radiating light or heat etc. 2 radiated, *radiant heat*. 3 looking very bright and happy.
radiantly *adverb*, **radiance** *noun*

radiate *verb* (**radiates, radiating, radiated**)
1 send out light, heat, or other energy in rays. 2 spread out from a central point like the spokes of a wheel.
[same origin as *radium*]

radiation *noun*
1 the process of radiating. 2 light, heat, or other energy radiated. 3 the energy or particles sent out by a radioactive substance.

radiator *noun* (*plural* **radiators**)
1 a device that gives out heat, especially a metal case that is heated electrically or through which steam or hot water flows. 2 a device that cools the engine of a motor vehicle.
[from *radiate*]

radical *adjective*
1 basic and thorough, *radical changes*. 2 wanting to make great reforms, *a radical politician*. **radically** *adverb*
radical *noun* (*plural* **radicals**)
a person who wants to make great reforms.
[from Latin *radicis* = of a root]

radio *noun* (*plural* **radios**) (also called *wireless*)
1 the process of sending and receiving sound or pictures by means of electromagnetic waves without a connecting wire. 2 an apparatus for receiving sound (a *receiver*) or sending it out (a *transmitter*) in this way. 3 sound broadcasting.
[same origin as *radium*]

radio- *prefix*
1 to do with rays or radiation. 2 to do with radio.

radioactive *adjective*
having atoms that break up and send out radiation which produces electrical and chemical effects and penetrates things.
radioactivity *noun*

radiocarbon dating *noun*
the use of a kind of radioactive carbon that decays at a steady rate, to find out how old something is.

radio telescope *noun* (*plural* **radio telescopes**)
an instrument that can detect radio waves from space.

radiotherapy *noun*
the use of radioactive substances in treating diseases.

radish *noun* (*plural* **radishes**)
a small hard round red vegetable, eaten raw in salads. [from Latin *radix* = root]

radium *noun*
a radioactive metal, often used in radiotherapy.
[from Latin *radius* = a spoke or ray]

radius *noun* (*plural* **radii** or **radiuses**)
1 a straight line from the centre of a circle or sphere to the circumference; the length of this line. 2 a range or distance from a central point, *The school takes pupils living within a radius of ten kilometres*.
[Latin, = a spoke or ray]

raffle *noun* (*plural* **raffles**)
a kind of lottery, usually to raise money for a charity.
raffle *verb* (**raffles, raffling, raffled**)
offer something as a prize in a raffle.

raft *noun* (*plural* **rafts**)
a flat floating structure made of wood etc., used as a boat. [from Old Norse]

rafter *noun* (*plural* **rafters**)
any of the long sloping pieces of wood that hold up a roof. [from Old English]

rag¹ *noun* (*plural* **rags**)
1 an old or torn piece of cloth. 2 a piece of ragtime music. [from *ragged*]

rag² *noun* (*plural* **rags**)
a carnival held by students to collect money for charity.
rag *verb* (**rags, ragging, ragged**) (*slang*)
tease. [origin unknown]

rage *noun* (*plural* **rages**)
1 great or violent anger. 2 a craze, *Skateboarding was all the rage*.
rage *verb* (**rages, raging, raged**)
1 be very angry. 2 be violent or noisy, *A storm was raging*.
[from old French; related to *rabies*]

ragged *adjective*
1 torn or frayed. 2 wearing torn clothes. 3 jagged. 4 irregular or uneven, *a ragged performance*.
[from Old Norse *roggvathr* = tufted]

raid *noun* (*plural* **raids**)
1 a sudden attack. 2 a surprise visit by police etc. to arrest people or seize illegal goods.
raid *verb* (**raids, raiding, raided**)
make a raid on a place. **raider** *noun*

rail¹ *noun* (*plural* **rails**)
1 a level or sloping bar for hanging things on or forming part of a fence, banisters, etc. 2 a long metal bar forming part of a railway track.
by rail on a train.
[from old French; related to *rule*]

rail² *verb* (rails, railing, railed)
protest angrily or bitterly.
[via French from Portuguese]

railings *plural noun*
a fence made of metal bars.

railway *noun*
1 the parallel metal bars that trains travel on.
2 (*plural* **railways**) a system of transport using rails.

rain *noun*
drops of water that fall from the sky.
rainy *adjective*
rain *verb* (rains, raining, rained)
1 fall as rain or like rain. 2 send down like rain, *They rained blows on him.*

rainbow *noun* (*plural* **rainbows**)
a curved band of colours seen in the sky when the sun shines through rain.

rainfall *noun*
the amount of rain that falls in a particular place or time.

rainforest *noun* (*plural* **rainforests**)
a dense tropical forest in an area of very heavy rainfall.

raise *verb* (raises, raising, raised)
1 move something to a higher place or an upright position. 2 increase the amount or level of something. 3 collect; manage to obtain, *They raised £100 for Oxfam.* 4 bring up young children or animals, *raise a family.* 5 rouse or cause, *She raised a laugh with her joke.* 6 put forward, *We raised objections.* 7 end a siege.
[from Old Norse]

raisin *noun* (*plural* **raisins**)
a dried grape. [French, = grape]

rake *noun* (*plural* **rakes**)
a gardening tool with a row of short spikes fixed to a long handle.
rake *verb* (rakes, raking, raked)
1 gather or smooth with a rake. 2 search.
3 gather; collect, *raking it in.*
rake up 1 collect. 2 remind people of an old scandal etc., *Don't rake that up.*

rally *noun* (*plural* **rallies**)
1 a large meeting to support something or share an interest. 2 a competition to test skill in driving, *the Monte Carlo Rally.* 3 a series of strokes in tennis before a point is scored. 4 a recovery.
rally *verb* (rallies, rallying, rallied)
1 bring or come together for a united effort, *They rallied support. People rallied round.*
2 revive; recover strength.

RAM *abbreviation*
random-access memory (in a computer), with contents that can be retrieved or stored directly without having to read through items already stored.

ram *noun* (*plural* **rams**)
1 a male sheep. 2 a device for ramming things.
ram *verb* (rams, ramming, rammed)
push one thing hard against another.

Ramadan *noun*
the ninth month of the Muslim year, when Muslims do not eat or drink between sunrise and sunset.
[Arabic, from *ramida* = to be parched]

ramble *noun* (*plural* **rambles**)
a long walk in the country.
ramble *verb* (rambles, rambling, rambled)
1 go for a ramble; wander. 2 talk or write a lot without keeping to the subject. **rambler** *noun*
[origin unknown]

ramifications *plural noun*
1 the branches of a structure. 2 the many effects of a plan or action.
[from Latin *ramificare* = to branch out]

ramp *noun* (*plural* **ramps**)
a slope joining two different levels.
[from French *ramper* = to climb]

rampage *verb* (rampages, rampaging, rampaged)
rush about wildly or destructively.
on the rampage rampaging.

rampant *adjective*
1 growing or increasing unrestrained, *Disease was rampant in the poorer districts.* 2 (of an animal on coats of arms) standing upright on a hind leg, *a lion rampant.* [same origin as *ramp*]

rampart *noun* (*plural* **ramparts**)
a wide bank of earth built as a fortification or a wall on top of this.
[from French *remparer* = fortify]

ramshackle *adjective*
badly made and rickety, *a ramshackle hut.*
[from *ransack*]

ranch *noun* (*plural* **ranches**)
a large cattle-farm in America.

rancid *adjective*
smelling or tasting unpleasant like stale fat.
[from Latin]

random *noun*
at random using no particular order or method, *In bingo, numbers are chosen at random.*
random *adjective*
done or taken at random, *a random sample.*

range *noun* (*plural* **ranges**)
1 a line or series of things, *a range of mountains.* 2 the limits between which things exist or are available; an extent, *a wide range of goods.* 3 the distance that a gun can shoot, an aircraft can travel, a sound can be heard, etc.
4 a place with targets for shooting-practice. 5 a large open area of grazing-land or hunting-ground. 6 a kitchen fireplace with ovens.

range *verb* (ranges, ranging, ranged)
1 exist between two limits; extend, *Prices ranged from £1 to £50.* **2** arrange. **3** move over a wide area; wander.
[from old French; related to *rank*[1]]

ranger *noun* (*plural* rangers)
someone who looks after or patrols a park, forest, etc. [from *range*]

rank[1] *noun* (*plural* ranks)
1 a line of people or things. **2** a place where taxis stand to await customers. **3** a position in a series of different levels, *He holds the rank of sergeant.*
rank *verb* (ranks, ranking, ranked)
1 arrange in a rank or ranks. **2** have a certain rank or place, *She ranks among the greatest novelists.*
[via old French from Germanic]

rank[2] *adjective* (ranker, rankest)
1 growing too thickly and coarsely. **2** smelling very unpleasant. **3** unmistakably bad, *rank injustice.*
rankly *adverb*, **rankness** *noun*
[from Old English]

rank and file *noun*
the ordinary people or soldiers, not the leaders.

ransack *verb* (ransacks, ransacking, ransacked)
1 search thoroughly or roughly. **2** rob or pillage a place. [from Old Norse]

ransom *noun* (*plural* ransoms)
money that has to be paid for a prisoner to be set free.
hold to ransom hold someone captive or in your power and demand ransom.
ransom *verb* (ransoms, ransoming, ransomed)
1 free someone by paying a ransom. **2** get a ransom for someone.
[from old French; related to *redeem*]

rant *verb* (rants, ranting, ranted)
speak loudly and violently. [from Dutch]

rap *verb* (raps, rapping, rapped)
1 knock loudly. **2** (*informal*) reprimand. **3** (*slang*) chat. **4** speak rhymes with a backing of rock music.
rap *noun* (*plural* raps)
1 a rapping movement or sound. **2** (*informal*) blame or punishment, *take the rap.* **3** (*slang*) a chat. **4** rhymes spoken with a backing of rock music.

rapacious (*say* ra-pay-shus) *adjective*
1 greedy. **2** using threats or force to get everything you can.
rapaciously *adverb*, **rapacity** *noun*
[from Latin *rapax* = grasping]

rape *noun* (*plural* rapes)
the act of having sexual intercourse with a person without her or his consent.

rape *verb* (rapes, raping, raped)
force someone to have sexual intercourse.
rapist *noun*
[from Latin *rapere* = take by force]

rapid *adjective*
moving very quickly; swift. **rapidly** *adverb*, **rapidity** *noun* [from Latin]

rapids *plural noun*
part of a river where the water flows very quickly.

rapt *adjective*
very intent and absorbed; enraptured.
raptly *adverb* [from Latin *raptum* = seized]

rapture *noun*
very great delight.
rapturous *adjective*, **rapturously** *adverb*
[from old French; related to *rapt*]

rare[1] *adjective* (rarer, rarest)
1 unusual; not often found or happening. **2** (of air) thin; below normal pressure. **rarely** *adverb*, **rareness** *noun*, **rarity** *noun* [from Latin]

rare[2] *adjective*
(of meat) only lightly cooked; undercooked.
[from Old English]

rarefied *adjective*
1 (of air) rare. **2** remote from everyday life, *the rarefied atmosphere of the university.*

rascal *noun* (*plural* rascals)
a dishonest or mischievous person; a rogue.
rascally *adjective* [from old French]

rash[1] *adjective*
doing something or done without thinking of the possible risks or effects.
rashly *adverb*, **rashness** *noun*
[probably from Old English]

rash[2] *noun* (*plural* rashes)
1 an outbreak of spots or patches on the skin. **2** a number of (usually unwelcome) events happening in a short time, *a rash of accidents.*
[probably from old French]

rasher *noun* (*plural* rashers)
a slice of bacon. [origin unknown]

rasp *noun* (*plural* rasps)
1 a file with sharp points on its surface. **2** a rough grating sound.
rasp *verb* (rasps, rasping, rasped)
1 scrape roughly. **2** make a rough grating sound or effect.

raspberry *noun* (*plural* raspberries)
a small soft red fruit. [origin unknown]

Rastafarian *noun* (*plural* Rastafarians)
a member of a religious group that started in Jamaica. [from *Ras Tafari* (*ras* = chief), the title of a former Ethiopian king whom the group reveres]

rat *noun* (*plural* rats)
1 an animal like a large mouse. **2** an unpleasant or treacherous person.

rate *noun* (*plural* **rates**)
1 speed, *The train travelled at a great rate.* **2** a measure of cost, value, etc., *Postage rates went up.* **3** quality or standard, *first-rate.*
at any rate anyway.
rate *verb* (**rates, rating, rated**)
1 put a value on something. **2** regard as, *He rated me among his friends.*
[from Latin *ratum* = reckoned]

rather *adverb*
1 slightly or somewhat, *It's rather dark.*
2 preferably or more willingly, *I would rather not go.* **3** more exactly, *He is lazy rather than stupid.* **4** (*informal*) definitely, yes, *'Will you come?' 'Rather!'*
[from Old English]

rating *noun* (*plural* **ratings**)
1 the way something is rated. **2** a sailor who is not an officer. [from *rate*]

ratio (*say* ray-shee-oh) *noun* (*plural* **ratios**)
1 the relationship between two numbers, given by the quotient, *The ratio of 2 to 10* = $2:10 = \frac{2}{10} = \frac{1}{5}$. **2** proportion, *Mix flour and butter in the ratio of two to one* (= two measures of flour to one measure of butter).
[Latin, = reasoning, reckoning]

ration *noun* (*plural* **rations**)
an amount allowed to one person.
ration *verb* (**rations, rationing, rationed**)
share something out in fixed amounts.
[French; related to *ratio*]

rational *adjective*
1 reasonable or sane. **2** able to reason, *Plants are not rational.* **rationally** *adverb*,
rationality *noun* [same origin as *ratio*]

rationalize *verb* (**rationalizes, rationalizing, rationalized**)
1 make a thing logical and consistent, *Attempts to rationalize English spelling have failed.*
2 invent a reasonable explanation of something, *She rationalized her meanness by calling it economy.* **3** make an industry etc. more efficient by reorganizing it.
rationalization *noun*

rations *plural noun*
a fixed daily amount of food issued to a soldier etc.

rattle *verb* (**rattles, rattling, rattled**)
1 make a series of short sharp hard sounds.
2 make a person nervous or flustered.
rattle off say or recite rapidly.
rattle *noun* (*plural* **rattles**)
1 a rattling sound. **2** a device or baby's toy that rattles. [imitating the sound]

rattlesnake *noun* (*plural* **rattlesnakes**)
a poisonous American snake with a tail that rattles.

raucous (*say* raw-kus) *adjective*
loud and harsh, *a raucous voice.*
[from Latin *raucus* = hoarse]

rave *verb* (**raves, raving, raved**)
1 talk wildly or angrily or madly. **2** talk rapturously about something.
rave *noun* (*plural* **raves**)
a big party or event with loud fast music and flashing lights. [from old French]

ravenous *adjective*
very hungry. **ravenously** *adverb*
[from French *raviner* = rush, ravage]

ravine (*say* ra-veen) *noun* (*plural* **ravines**)
a deep narrow gorge or valley.
[French, = a rush of water (because a ravine is cut by rushing water)]

ravishing *adjective*
very beautiful.

raw *adjective*
1 not cooked. **2** in the natural state; not yet processed, *raw materials.* **3** without experience, *raw recruits.* **4** with the skin removed, *a raw wound.* **5** cold and damp, *a raw morning.* **rawness** *noun*

raw material *noun* (*plural* **raw materials**)
natural substances used in industry, *rich in iron ore, coal, and other raw materials.*

ray *noun* (*plural* **rays**)
1 a thin line of light, heat, or other radiation.
2 each of a set of lines or parts extending from a centre.
[from Latin *radius*]

razor *noun* (*plural* **razors**)
a device with a very sharp blade, especially one used for shaving. [same origin as *raze*]

re- *prefix*
1 again (as in *rebuild*). **2** back again, to an earlier condition (as in *reopen*). **3** in return; to each other (as in *react*). **4** against (as in *rebel*). **5** away or down (as in *recede*). [from Latin]

reach *verb* (**reaches, reaching, reached**)
1 go as far as; arrive at a place or thing.
2 stretch out your hand to get or touch something. **reachable** *adjective*
reach *noun* (*plural* **reaches**)
1 the distance a person or thing can reach. **2** a distance you can easily travel, *We live within reach of the sea.* **3** a straight stretch of a river or canal. [from Old English]

react *verb* (**reacts, reacting, reacted**)
respond to something; have a reaction. [from *re-* + Latin *agere* = act or do]

reaction *noun* (*plural* **reactions**)
1 an effect or feeling etc. produced in one person or thing by another. **2** a chemical change caused when substances act upon each other.

reactionary *adjective*
opposed to progress or reform.

reactor *noun* (*plural* **reactors**)
an apparatus for producing nuclear power in a controlled way.

read *verb* (reads, reading, read (*say as* red))
1 look at something written or printed and understand it or say it aloud. 2 (of a computer) copy, search, or extract data. 3 indicate or register, *The thermometer reads 20° Celsius.* **readable** *adjective*

reader *noun* (*plural* readers)
1 a person who reads. 2 a book that helps you learn to read.

readily (*say* red-il-ee) *adverb*
1 willingly. 2 easily; without any difficulty.

reading *noun* (*plural* readings)
1 reading books. 2 the figure shown on a meter or gauge. 3 a gathering of people at which something is read aloud, *a poetry reading.*

ready *adjective* (readier, readiest)
able or willing to do something or be used immediately; prepared. **readiness** *noun*
at the ready ready for use or action.
ready *adverb*
beforehand, *This meat is ready cooked.*
ready-made *adjective* [from Old English]

real *adjective*
1 existing or true; not imaginary. 2 genuine; not an imitation, *real pearls.* 3 (of food) regarded as superior because it is produced by traditional methods, *real ale.* [from Latin]

realism *noun*
seeing or showing things as they really are.
realist *noun*, **realistic** *adjective*, **realistically** *adverb*

reality *noun* (*plural* realities)
1 what is real, *You must face reality.*
2 something real, *Her worst fears had become a reality.*

realize *verb* (realizes, realizing, realized)
1 be fully aware of something; accept something as true. 2 make a hope or plan etc. happen, *She realized her ambition to become a racing driver.* 3 obtain money in exchange for something by selling it. **realization** *noun*
[from *real* + *-ize*]

really *adverb*
1 truly or in fact. 2 very, *She's really clever.*

realm (*say* relm) *noun* (*plural* realms)
1 a kingdom. 2 an area of knowledge, interest, etc., *in the realms of science.*
[from old French; related to *regiment*]

reams *plural noun*
a large quantity of writing.

reap *verb* (reaps, reaping, reaped)
1 cut down and gather corn when it is ripe.
2 obtain as the result of something done, *They reaped great benefit from their training.*
reaper *noun* [from Old English]

rear¹ *noun*
the back part.

rear *adjective*
placed at the rear.
[from Latin *retro-* = back]

rear² *verb* (rears, rearing, reared)
1 bring up young children or animals. 2 rise up; raise itself on hind legs, *The horse reared in fright.* 3 build or set up a monument etc.
[from Old English]

rearguard *noun* (*plural* rearguards)
troops protecting the rear of an army.
fight a rearguard action go on defending or resisting something even though you are losing.

rearrange *verb* (rearranges, rearranging, rearranged)
arrange in a different way or order.
rearrangement *noun*

reason *noun* (*plural* reasons)
1 a cause or explanation of something.
2 reasoning; common sense, *Listen to reason.*

USAGE: Do not use the phrase *the reason is* with the word *because* (which means the same thing). Correct usage is *We cannot come. The reason is that we both have flu* (not 'The reason is because ...').

reason *verb* (reasons, reasoning, reasoned)
1 use your ability to think and draw conclusions. 2 try to persuade someone by giving reasons, *We reasoned with the rebels.*
[from old French; related to *ratio*]

reasonable *adjective*
1 ready to use or listen to reason; sensible or logical. 2 fair or moderate; not expensive, *reasonable prices.* 3 acceptable or fairly good, *a reasonable standard of living.*
reasonably *adverb*

reassure *verb* (reassures, reassuring, reassured)
restore someone's confidence by removing doubts and fears.
reassurance *noun*

rebel (*say* rib-el) *verb* (rebels, rebelling, rebelled)
refuse to obey someone in authority, especially the government; fight against the rulers of your own country.
rebel (*say* reb-el) *noun* (*plural* rebels)
someone who rebels against the government, or against accepted standards of behaviour.
rebellion *noun*, **rebellious** *adjective*
[from *re-* + Latin *bellum* = war (originally referring to a defeated enemy who began to fight again)]

rebound *verb* (rebounds, rebounding, rebounded)
bounce back after hitting something.
rebound *noun*

rebuff *noun* (*plural* rebuffs)
an unkind refusal; a snub. **rebuff** *verb*
[from *re-* + Italian *buffo* = a gust]

rebuke *verb* (rebukes, rebuking, rebuked)
speak severely to a person who has done
wrong. **rebuke** *noun*
[originally = to force back: from *re-* + old
French *buker* = to hit]

recalcitrant *adjective*
disobedient or uncooperative.
recalcitrance *noun*
[from Latin *recalcitrare* = to kick back]

recall *verb* (recalls, recalling, recalled)
1 ask a person to come back. **2** ask for
something to be returned. **3** bring back into the
mind; remember.

recapitulate *verb* (recapitulates, recapitulating,
recapitulated)
state again the main points of what has been
said. **recapitulation** *noun*
[from *re-* + Latin *capitulare* = arrange under
headings]

recapture *verb* (recaptures, recapturing,
recaptured)
1 capture again; recover. **2** bring or get back a
mood or feeling. **recapture** *noun*

receipt (*say* ris-eet) *noun* (*plural* receipts)
1 a written statement that money has been
paid or something has been received.
2 receiving something.

receive *verb* (receives, receiving, received)
1 take or get something that is given or sent.
2 greet someone who comes.
[from *re-* + Latin *capere* = take]

receiver *noun* (*plural* receivers)
1 a person or thing that receives something.
2 a person who buys and sells stolen goods.
3 an official who takes charge of a bankrupt
person's property. **4** a radio or television set
that receives broadcasts. **5** the part of a
telephone that receives the sound and is held to
a person's ear.

recent *adjective*
happening or made or done a short time ago.
recently *adverb* [from Latin]

reception *noun* (*plural* receptions)
1 the way a person or thing is received. **2** a
formal party to receive guests, *a wedding
reception*. **3** a place in a hotel or office etc.
where visitors are received and registered.

receptionist *noun* (*plural* receptionists)
a person whose job is to receive and direct
visitors, patients, etc.

receptive *adjective*
quick or willing to receive ideas etc.

recession *noun* (*plural* recessions)
1 receding from a point. **2** a reduction in trade
or prosperity.

recipe (*say* ress-ip-ee) *noun* (*plural* recipes)
instructions for preparing or cooking food.
[Latin, = take (used at the beginning of a list of
ingredients)]

reciprocal (*say* ris-ip-rok-al) *adjective*
given and received; mutual, *reciprocal help*.
reciprocally *adverb*, **reciprocity** *noun*
reciprocal *noun* (*plural* reciprocals)
a reversed fraction, $\frac{3}{2}$ *is the reciprocal of* $\frac{2}{3}$.
[from Latin *reciprocus* = moving backwards
and forwards]

recital *noun* (*plural* recitals)
1 reciting something. **2** a musical
entertainment given by one performer or
group.

recite *verb* (recites, reciting, recited)
say a poem etc. aloud from memory.
recitation *noun*
[from Latin *recitare* = to read aloud]

reckless *adjective*
rash; ignoring risk or danger.
recklessly *adverb*, **recklessness** *noun*
[from an old word *reck* = heed, + *-less*]

reckon *verb* (reckons, reckoning, reckoned)
1 calculate or count up. **2** have as an opinion;
feel confident, *I reckon we shall win*.
reckon with think about or deal with, *We didn't
reckon with the train strike when we planned
our journey*.

reclaim *verb* (reclaims, reclaiming, reclaimed)
1 claim or get something back. **2** make a thing
usable again, *reclaimed land*. **reclamation** *noun*

recognize *verb* (recognizes, recognizing,
recognized)
1 know who someone is or what something is
because you have seen that person or thing
before. **2** realize, *We recognize the truth of what
you said*. **3** accept something as genuine,
welcome, or lawful etc., *Nine countries
recognized the island's new government*.
recognition *noun*, **recognizable** *adjective*
[from *re-* + Latin *cognoscere* = know]

recoil *verb* (recoils, recoiling, recoiled)
1 move back suddenly in shock or disgust.
2 (of a gun) jerk backwards when it is fired.

recollect *verb* (recollects, recollecting,
recollected)
remember. **recollection** *noun*
[from *re-* + Latin *colligere* = collect]

recommend *verb* (recommends, recommending,
recommended)
say that a person or thing would be a good one
to do a job or achieve something.
recommendation *noun*
[from *re-* + Latin *commendare* = commend]

reconcile *verb* (reconciles, reconciling, reconciled)
1 make people who have quarrelled become
friendly again. **2** persuade a person to put up
with something, *New frames reconciled him to*

wearing glasses. **3** make things agree, *I cannot reconcile what you say with what you do.*
reconciliation *noun*
[from *re-* + Latin *conciliare* = conciliate]

recondition *verb* (reconditions, reconditioning, reconditioned)
overhaul and repair.

reconnaissance (*say* rik-on-i-sans) *noun*
an exploration of an area, especially in order to gather information about it for military purposes. [French, = recognition]

reconstruct *verb* (reconstructs, reconstructing, reconstructed)
1 construct or build something again. **2** create or act past events again, *Police reconstructed the robbery.*
reconstruction *noun*

record (*say* rek-ord) *noun* (*plural* records)
1 information kept in a permanent form, e.g. written or printed. **2** a disc on which sound has been recorded. **3** facts known about a person's past life or career etc., *She has a good school record.* **4** the best performance in a sport etc., or the most remarkable event of its kind, *He holds the record for the high jump.*
record (*say* rik-ord) *verb* (records, recording, recorded)
1 put something down in writing or other permanent form. **2** store sounds or scenes (e.g. television pictures) on a disc or magnetic tape etc. so that you can play or show them later. [from French]

recorder *noun* (*plural* recorders)
1 a kind of flute held downwards from the player's mouth. **2** a person or thing that records something.

recover *verb* (recovers, recovering, recovered)
1 get something back again after losing it; regain. **2** get well again after being ill or weak.
recovery *noun*
[from old French; related to *recuperate*]

recreation *noun* (*plural* recreations)
1 refreshing your mind or body after work through an enjoyable pastime. **2** a game or hobby etc. that is an enjoyable pastime.
recreational *adjective*
[from *re-* + Latin *creatio* = creation]

recruit *noun* (*plural* recruits)
1 a person who has just joined the armed forces. **2** a new member of a society or group etc.
recruit *verb* (recruits, recruiting, recruited)
enlist recruits. **recruitment** *noun*
[from French *recroître* = to increase again]

rectangle *noun* (*plural* rectangles)
a shape with four sides and four right angles.
rectangular *adjective*
[from Latin *rectus* = straight or right, + *angle*]

rectum *noun* (*plural* rectums or recta)
the last part of the large intestine, ending at the anus. [Latin, = straight (intestine)]

recuperate *verb* (recuperates, recuperating, recuperated)
get better after an illness. **recuperation** *noun*
[from Latin]

recur *verb* (recurs, recurring, recurred)
happen again; keep on happening.
recurrent *adjective*, **recurrence** *noun*
[from *re-* + Latin *currere* = to run]

recycle *verb* (recycles, recycling, recycled)
convert waste material into a form in which it can be reused.

red *adjective* (redder, reddest)
1 of the colour of blood or a colour rather like this. **2** to do with Communists; favouring Communism. **redness** *noun*
red *noun*
1 red colour. **2** a Communist.
in the red in debt (because debts were entered in red in account-books).

redden *verb* (reddens, reddening, reddened)
make or become red.

redeem *verb* (redeems, redeeming, redeemed)
1 buy something back or pay off a debt. **2** save a person from damnation, *Christians believe that Christ redeemed us all.* **3** make up for faults, *His one redeeming feature is his kindness.*
redeemer *noun*, **redemption** *noun*
[from *re-* + Latin *emere* = buy]

red-handed *adjective*
catch red-handed catch while actually committing a crime.

red herring *noun* (*plural* red herrings)
something that draws attention away from the main subject; a misleading clue. [because a red herring (= a kipper) drawn across a fox's path put hounds off the scent]

red-hot *adjective*
very hot; so hot that it has turned red.

Red Indian *noun* (*plural* Red Indians)
(*old use*) a Native American from North America.

USAGE: see note at *Indian.*

red tape *noun*
use of too many rules and forms in official business. [because bundles of official papers are tied up with red or pink tape]

reduce *verb* (reduces, reducing, reduced)
1 make or become smaller or less. **2** force someone into a condition or situation, *He was reduced to borrowing the money.* **reduction** *noun*
[from *re-* + Latin *ducere* = bring]

redundant *adjective*
not needed, especially for a particular job.
redundancy *noun* [same origin as *redound*]

re-echo *verb* (re-echoes, re-echoing, re-echoed)
echo; go on echoing.

reed *noun* (*plural* reeds)
1 a tall plant that grows in water or marshy ground. 2 a thin strip that vibrates to make the sound in a clarinet, saxophone, oboe, etc. [from Old English]

reef *noun* (*plural* reefs)
a ridge of rock or sand etc., especially one near the surface of the sea. [via old German or old Dutch from Old Norse]

reek *verb* (reeks, reeking, reeked)
smell strongly or unpleasantly. **reek** *noun*

reel *noun* (*plural* reels)
1 a spool. 2 a lively Scottish dance.
reel *verb* (reels, reeling, reeled)
1 wind something onto or off a reel. 2 stagger.
reel off say something quickly.

refer *verb* (refers, referring, referred)
pass a problem etc. to someone else, *My doctor referred me to a specialist.*
referral *noun*
refer to 1 mention or speak about, *I wasn't referring to you.* 2 look in a book etc. for information, *We referred to our dictionary.*
[from *re-* + Latin *ferre* = bring]

referee *noun* (*plural* referees)
someone appointed to see that people keep to the rules of a game.
[literally = someone who is referred to]

reference *noun* (*plural* references)
1 referring to something, *There was no reference to recent events.* 2 a direction to a book or page or file etc. where information can be found. 3 a testimonial.
in or **with reference to** concerning or about.

reference book *noun* (*plural* reference books)
a book (such as a dictionary or encyclopedia) that gives information systematically.

referendum *noun* (*plural* referendums or referenda)
voting by all the people of a country (not by Parliament) to decide whether something shall be done. It is also called a *plebiscite.*
[Latin, = referring]

refill *verb* (refills, refilling, refilled)
fill again.
refill *noun* (*plural* refills)
a container holding a substance which is used to refill something, *this pen needs another refill.*

refine *verb* (refines, refining, refined)
1 purify. 2 improve something, especially by making small changes.
[from *re-* + Middle English *fine* = make pure]

refined *adjective*
1 purified. 2 cultured; having good taste or good manners.

refinement *noun* (*plural* refinements)
1 the action of refining. 2 being refined.
3 something added to improve a thing.

refinery *noun* (*plural* refineries)
a factory for refining something, *an oil refinery.*

reflect *verb* (reflects, reflecting, reflected)
1 send back light, heat, or sound etc. from a surface. 2 form an image of something as a mirror does. 3 think something over; consider. 4 be influenced by something, *Prices reflect the cost of producing things.*
reflection *noun,* **reflective** *adjective,* **reflector** *noun*
[from *re-* + Latin *flectere* = to bend]

reflex *noun* (*plural* reflexes)
a movement or action done without any conscious thought. [same origin as *reflect*]

reflexive pronoun *noun* (*plural* reflexive pronouns)
any of the pronouns *myself, herself, himself,* etc. (as in 'She cut *herself*'), which refer back to the subject of the verb.

reflexive verb *noun* (*plural* reflexive verbs)
a verb where the subject and the object are the same person or thing, as in 'She cut *herself*', 'The cat *washed itself*'.

reform *verb* (reforms, reforming, reformed)
make or become better by removing faults.
reformer *noun,* **reformative** *adjective,* **reformatory** *adjective*
reform *noun* (*plural* reforms)
1 reforming. 2 a change made in order to improve something.
[from *re-* + Latin *formare* = to form]

reformation *noun*
reforming.
the Reformation a religious movement in Europe in the 16th century intended to reform certain teachings and practices of the Roman Catholic Church, which resulted in the establishment of the Reformed or Protestant Churches.

refract *verb* (refracts, refracting, refracted)
bend a ray of light at the point where it enters water or glass etc. at an angle.
refraction *noun,* **refractor** *noun,* **refractive** *adjective*
[from *re-* + Latin *fractum* = broken]

refrain[1] *verb* (refrains, refraining, refrained)
stop yourself from doing something, *Refrain from talking.*
[from Latin *refrenare* = to bridle]

refrain[2] *noun* (*plural* refrains)
the chorus of a song. [from French]

refresh *verb* (refreshes, refreshing, refreshed)
make a tired person etc. feel fresh and strong again.

refreshing *adjective*
1 producing new strength, *a refreshing sleep.*
2 pleasantly different or unusual, *refreshing honesty.*

refreshments *plural noun*
drinks and snacks provided at an event.

refrigerator *noun* (*plural* **refrigerators**)
a cabinet or room in which food is stored at a very low temperature.
[from *re-* + Latin *frigus* = cold]

refuge *noun* (*plural* **refuges**)
a place where a person is safe from pursuit or danger.
take refuge go somewhere or do something so that you are protected.
[from *re-* + Latin *fugere* = flee]

refugee *noun* (*plural* **refugees**)
a person who has had to leave home and seek refuge somewhere, e.g. because of war or persecution or famine.

refund *verb* (**refunds, refunding, refunded**)
pay money back.
refund *noun*
money paid back. [from Latin *refundere* = pour back]

refuse (*say* ri-**fewz**) *verb* (**refuses, refusing, refused**)
say that you are unwilling to do or give or accept something. **refusal** *noun*
refuse (*say* **ref**-yooss) *noun*
waste material, *Lorries collected the refuse.*

regain *verb* (**regains, regaining, regained**)
1 get something back after losing it. 2 reach a place again.

regalia (*say* rig-**ayl**-i-a) *plural noun*
the emblems of royalty or rank, *The royal regalia include the crown, sceptre, and orb.*

regard *verb* (**regards, regarding, regarded**)
1 look or gaze at. 2 think of in a certain way; consider to be, *We regard the matter as serious.*
regard *noun*
1 a gaze. 2 consideration; heed, *You acted without regard to people's safety.* 3 respect, *We have a great regard for her.*
with regard to concerning.
[from *re-* + French *garder* = to guard]

regarding *preposition*
concerning, *There are laws regarding drugs.*

regardless *adverb*
without considering something, *Do it, regardless of the cost.*

regards *plural noun*
kind wishes sent in a message, *Give him my regards.*

regatta *noun* (*plural* **regattas**)
a meeting for boat or yacht races.
[from Italian]

regenerate *verb* (**regenerates, regenerating, regenerated**)
give new life or strength to something.
regeneration *noun*

regent *noun* (*plural* **regents**)
a person appointed to rule a country while the monarch is too young or unable to rule. [from Latin *regens* = ruling]

reggae (*say* **reg**-ay) *noun*
a West Indian style of music with a strong beat.
[origin unknown]

regime (*say* ray-**zheem**) *noun* (*plural* **regimes**)
a system of government or organization, *a Communist regime.*
[French; related to *regiment*]

regiment *noun* (*plural* **regiments**)
an army unit, usually divided into battalions or companies.
regimental *adjective*
[from Latin *regimentum* = rule, governing]

region *noun* (*plural* **regions**)
an area; a part of a country or of the world, *in tropical regions.*
regional *adjective*, **regionally** *adverb*
in the region of near, *The cost will be in the region of £100.*
[from Latin *regio* = boundary]

register *noun* (*plural* **registers**)
1 an official list of things or names etc. 2 a book in which information about school attendances is recorded. 3 the range of a voice or musical instrument.
register *verb* (**registers, registering, registered**)
1 list something in a register. 2 indicate; show, *The thermometer registered 100˚.* 3 make an impression on someone's mind. 4 pay extra for a letter or parcel to be sent with special care.
registration *noun*

regret *noun* (*plural* **regrets**)
a feeling of sorrow or disappointment about something that has happened or been done.
regretful *adjective*, **regretfully** *adverb*
regret *verb* (**regrets, regretting, regretted**)
feel regret about something.
regrettable *adjective*, **regrettably** *adverb* [from old French *regreter* = mourn for the dead]

regular *adjective*
1 always happening or doing something at certain times. 2 even or symmetrical, *regular teeth.* 3 normal, standard, or correct, *the regular procedure.* 4 belonging to a country's permanent armed forces, *a regular soldier.*
regularly *adverb*, **regularity** *noun* [from Latin *regula* = a rule]

regulate *verb* (**regulates, regulating, regulated**)
1 control, especially by rules. 2 make a machine work at a certain speed.
regulator *noun* [same origin as *regular*]

regulation *noun*
1 regulating. 2 a rule or law.

rehabilitation *noun*
restoring a person to a normal life or a building etc. to a good condition.
rehabilitate *verb*
[from *re-* + Latin *habilitare* = enable]

rehearse *verb* (**rehearses, rehearsing, rehearsed**)
practise something before performing to an audience. **rehearsal** *noun*

reign *verb*
1 rule a country as king or queen. 2 be supreme; be the strongest influence, *Silence reigned.*
reign *noun*
the time when someone reigns.
[from Latin *regnum* = royal authority]

reimburse *verb* (**reimburses, reimbursing, reimbursed**)
repay money that has been spent, *Your travelling expenses will be reimbursed.*
reimbursement *noun*
[from *re-* + an old word *imburse* = pay]

rein *noun* (*plural* **reins**)
a strap used to guide a horse.
[from old French; related to *retain*]

reincarnation *noun*
being born again into a new body.
[from *re-* + *incarnation* (see *incarnate*)]

reindeer *noun* (*plural* **reindeer**)
a kind of deer that lives in Arctic regions.

reinforce *verb* (**reinforces, reinforcing, reinforced**)
strengthen by adding extra people or supports etc. [from *re-* + old French *enforcer* = enforce]

reinforcements *plural noun*
extra troops or ships etc. sent to strengthen a force.

reiterate *verb* (**reiterates, reiterating, reiterated**)
say something again and again.
reiteration *noun*
[from *re-* + Latin *iterare* = repeat]

reject *verb* (**rejects, rejecting, rejected**)
1 refuse to accept a person or thing. 2 throw away or discard. **rejection** *noun*
[from *re-* + Latin *-jectum* = thrown]

rejoice *verb* (**rejoices, rejoicing, rejoiced**)
feel or show great joy. [from old French]

rejuvenate *verb* (**rejuvenates, rejuvenating, rejuvenated**)
make a person seem young again.
rejuvenation *noun*
[from *re-* + Latin *juvenis* = young]

relapse *verb* (**relapses, relapsing, relapsed**)
return to a previous condition; become worse after improving. **relapse** *noun*
[from *re-* + Latin *lapsum* = slipped]

relate *verb* (**relates, relating, related**)
1 narrate. 2 connect or compare one thing with another. 3 understand and get on well with, *Some people cannot relate to animals.*

related *adjective*
belonging to the same family.

relation *noun* (*plural* **relations**)
1 a relative. 2 the way one thing is related to another.

relationship *noun* (*plural* **relationships**)
1 how people or things are related. 2 how people get on with each other. 3 a close association with strong feelings.

relative *noun* (*plural* **relatives**)
a person who is related to another.
relative *adjective*
connected or compared with something; compared with the average, *They live in relative comfort.* **relatively** *adverb*
relative pronoun see *pronoun.*

relax *verb* (**relaxes, relaxing, relaxed**)
1 become less strict or stiff. 2 stop working; rest.
relaxation *noun* [from *re-* + Latin *laxus* = loose]

relay (*say* ri-lay) *verb* (**relays, relaying, relayed**)
pass on a message or broadcast.
relay *noun* (*say* re-lay) (*plural* **relays**)
1 a fresh group taking the place of another, *The firemen worked in relays.* 2 a relay race. 3 a device for relaying a broadcast.

relay race *noun* (*plural* **relay races**)
a race between teams in which each person covers part of the distance.

release *verb* (**releases, releasing, released**)
1 set free or unfasten. 2 let a thing fall or fly or go out. 3 make a film or record etc. available to the public.
release *noun* (*plural* **releases**)
1 being released. 2 something released. 3 a device that unfastens something.
[from old French; related to *relax*]

relegate *verb* (**relegates, relegating, relegated**)
1 put into a less important place. 2 put a sports team into a lower division of a league.
relegation *noun*
[from *re-* + Latin *legatum* = sent]

relent *verb* (**relents, relenting, relented**)
become less severe or more merciful.
[from *re-* + Latin *lentare* = bend, soften]

relentless *adjective*
not stopping or relenting; pitiless.
relentlessly *adverb*

relevant *adjective*
connected with what is being discussed or dealt with. (The opposite is *irrelevant.*)
relevance *noun* [from Latin]

reliable *adjective*
able to be relied on; trustworthy.
reliably *adverb*, **reliability** *noun*

relic *noun* (*plural* **relics**)
something that has survived from an earlier time. [from Latin *reliquus* = remaining]

relief *noun* (*plural* **reliefs**)
1 the ending or lessening of pain, trouble, boredom, etc. **2** something that gives relief or help. **3** a person who takes over a turn of duty when another finishes. **4** a method of making a design etc. that stands out from a surface.

relief map *noun* (*plural* **relief maps**)
a map that shows hills and valleys by shading or moulding.

relieve *verb* (**relieves, relieving, relieved**)
give relief to a person or thing.
relieve of take something from a person, *The thief relieved him of his wallet.*
[from *re-* + Latin *levare* = raise, lighten]

religion *noun* (*plural* **religions**)
1 what people believe about God or gods, and how they worship. **2** a particular system of beliefs and worship.
[from Latin *religio* = reverence]

religious *adjective*
1 to do with religion. **2** believing firmly in a religion and taking part in its customs.
religiously *adverb*

relish *noun* (*plural* **relishes**)
1 great enjoyment. **2** something tasty that adds flavour to plainer food.
relish *verb* (**relishes, relishing, relished**)
enjoy greatly. [from old French]

reluctant *adjective*
unwilling or not keen.
reluctantly *adverb*, **reluctance** *noun*
[from *re-* + Latin *luctatus* = struggling]

rely *verb* (**relies, relying, relied**)
rely on trust a person or thing to help or support you.
[from old French *relier* = bind together]

remain *verb* (**remains, remaining, remained**)
1 be there after other parts have gone or been dealt with; be left over. **2** continue to be in the same place or condition; stay. [from *re-* + Latin *manere* = to stay]

remainder *noun*
1 the remaining part or people or things. **2** the number left after subtraction or division.

remains *plural noun*
1 all that is left over after other parts have been removed or destroyed. **2** ancient ruins or objects; relics. **3** a dead body.

remand *verb* (**remands, remanding, remanded**)
send a prisoner back into custody while further evidence is sought. **remand** *noun*
on remand in prison while waiting for a trial.
[from *re-* + Latin *mandare* = entrust]

remark *noun* (*plural* **remarks**)
something said; a comment.
remark *verb* (**remarks, remarking, remarked**)
1 make a remark; say. **2** notice.
[from French]

remarkable *adjective*
unusual or extraordinary. **remarkably** *adverb*
[from *remark*]

remedy *noun* (*plural* **remedies**)
something that cures or relieves a disease etc. or that puts a matter right.
[from *re-* + Latin *mederi* = heal]

remember *verb* (**remembers, remembering, remembered**)
1 keep something in your mind. **2** bring something back into your mind.
remembrance *noun*
[from *re-* + Latin *memor* = mindful, remembering]

remind *verb* (**reminds, reminding, reminded**)
help or make a person remember something.
reminder *noun*
[from *re-* + an old sense of *mind* = put into someone's mind, mention]

reminisce (*say* rem-in-**iss**) *verb* (**reminisces, reminiscing, reminisced**)
think or talk about things that you remember.
reminiscence *noun*, **reminiscent** *adjective* [from Latin *reminisci* = remember]

remiss *adjective*
negligent; careless about doing what you ought to do. [same origin as *remit*]

remnant *noun* (*plural* **remnants**)
a part or piece left over from something. [from old French; related to *remain*]

remonstrate *verb* (**remonstrates, remonstrating, remonstrated**)
make a protest, *We remonstrated with him about his behaviour.*
[from *re-* + Latin *monstrare* = to show]

remorse *noun*
deep regret for having done wrong.
remorseful *adjective*, **remorsefully** *adverb*
[from *re-* + Latin *morsum* = bitten]

remote *adjective*
1 far away or isolated. **2** some but very little; unlikely, *a remote chance.*
remotely *adverb*, **remoteness** *noun*
[from Latin *remotum* = removed]

remote control *noun*
controlling something from a distance, usually by electricity or radio.

removal *noun*
removing or moving something.

remove *verb* (**removes, removing, removed**)
take something away or off.
remove *noun* (*plural* **removes**)
a distance or degree away from something, *That is several removes from the truth.*
[from *re-* + Latin *movere* = move]

Renaissance (*say* ren-**ay**-sans) *noun*
the revival of classical styles of art and literature in Europe in the 14th–16th centuries.
[French, = rebirth]

render *verb* (renders, rendering, rendered)
1 (*formal*) give or perform something, *render help to the victims.* **2** cause to become, *The shock rendered us speechless.*

rendezvous (*say* rond-ay-voo) *noun* (*plural* rendezvous, *say* rond-ay-vooz)
1 a meeting with somebody. **2** a place arranged for this.
[French, = present yourselves]

renew *verb* (renews, renewing, renewed)
1 restore something to its original condition or replace it with something new. **2** begin or make or give again, *We renewed our request.*
renewal *noun*

renewable resource *noun* (*plural* renewable resources)
a resource (such as power from the sun, wind, or waves) that can never be used up, or which can be renewed.

renounce *verb* (renounces, renouncing, renounced)
give up or reject. **renunciation** *noun*
[from *re-* + Latin *nuntiare* = announce]

renovate *verb* (renovates, renovating, renovated)
repair a thing and make it look new.
renovation *noun*
[from *re-* + Latin *novus* = new]

renowned *adjective*
well-known because of something good. [from *re-* + French *nomer* = to name]

rent[1] *noun* (*plural* rents)
a regular payment for the use of something, especially a house that belongs to another person.
rent *verb* (rents, renting, rented)
have or allow the use of something in return for rent. [from French]

rent[2] *noun* (*plural* rents)
a torn place; a split.

repair *verb* (repairs, repairing, repaired)
put something into good condition after it has been damaged or broken etc.
repairable *adjective*
repair *noun* (*plural* repairs)
1 repairing, *closed for repair.* **2** a mended place, *the repair is hardly visible.*
in good repair in good condition; well maintained.
[from *re-* + Latin *parare* = get something ready]

repartee *noun*
witty replies and remarks.
[from French *repartir* = answer back]

repatriate *verb* (repatriates, repatriating, repatriated)
send a person back to his or her own country.
repatriation *noun*
[from *re-* + Latin *patria* = native country]

repeal *verb* (repeals, repealing, repealed)
cancel a law officially. **repeal** *noun*
[from *re-* + French *appeler* = to appeal]

repeat *verb* (repeats, repeating, repeated)
say or do the same thing again.
repeatedly *adverb*
repeat *noun* (*plural* repeats)
1 the action of repeating. **2** something that is repeated. [from *re-* + Latin *petere* = seek]

repel *verb* (repels, repelling, repelled)
1 drive away or repulse, *repel the attack.*
2 disgust somebody. **repellent** *adjective* & *noun*
[from *re-* + Latin *pellere* = to drive]

repent *verb* (repents, repenting, repented)
be sorry for what you have done.
repentance *noun*, **repentant** *adjective*
[from old French; related to *penitent*]

repercussion *noun* (*plural* repercussions)
a result or reaction produced indirectly by something.
[from *re-* + Latin *percutere* = to strike]

repertoire (*say* rep-er-twahr) *noun*
a stock of songs or plays etc. that a person or company knows and can perform. [French; related to *repertory*]

repetition *noun* (*plural* repetitions)
1 repeating. **2** something repeated.
repetitious *adjective*

repetitive *adjective*
full of repetitions. **repetitively** *adverb*

replace *verb* (replaces, replacing, replaced)
1 put a thing back in its place. **2** take the place of another person or thing. **3** put a new or different thing in place of something.
replacement *noun*

replica *noun* (*plural* replicas)
an exact copy. [from Italian]

reply *noun* (*plural* replies)
something said or written to deal with a question, letter, etc.; an answer.
reply *verb* (replies, replying, replied)
give a reply to; answer. [from old French]

report *verb* (reports, reporting, reported)
1 describe something that has happened or that you have done or studied. **2** make a complaint or accusation against somebody.
3 go and tell somebody that you have arrived or are ready for work.
report *noun* (*plural* reports)
1 a description or account of something. **2** a regular statement of how someone has worked or behaved, e.g. at school. **3** an explosive sound.
[from *re-* + Latin *portare* = carry]

reporter *noun* (*plural* reporters)
a person whose job is to collect and report news for a newspaper, radio or television programme, etc.

repose *noun*
calm, rest, or sleep.
repose *verb* (reposes, reposing, reposed)
rest or lie somewhere. [from *re-* + Latin
pausare = to pause]

repossess *verb* (repossesses, repossessing,
repossessed)
take something back because it has not been
paid for.

reprehensible *adjective*
extremely bad and deserving blame or rebuke.
[from Latin *reprehendere* = blame, rebuke]

represent *verb* (represents, representing,
represented)
1 show a person or thing in a picture or play
etc. 2 symbolize or stand for, *In Roman
numerals, V represents 5.* 3 be an example or
equivalent of something. 4 help someone by
speaking or doing something on their behalf.
representation *noun*
[from *re-* + Latin *praesentare* = to present]

representative *noun* (*plural* representatives)
a person or thing that represents another or
others.
representative *adjective*
1 representing others. 2 typical of a group.

repress *verb* (represses, repressing, repressed)
1 keep down; control by force. 2 restrain or
suppress. **repression** *noun*, **repressive** *adjective*
[from Latin]

reprieve *noun* (*plural* reprieves)
postponement or cancellation of a punishment
etc., especially the death penalty. [from old
French]

reprimand *noun* (*plural* reprimands)
a rebuke, especially a formal or official one.
reprimand *verb* (reprimands, reprimanding,
reprimanded)
give someone a reprimand.
[from French; related to *repress*]

reprisal *noun* (*plural* reprisals)
an act of revenge. [from old French]

reproach *verb* (reproaches, reproaching,
reproached)
tell someone you are upset and disappointed by
something he or she has done. **reproach** *noun*,
reproachful *adjective*, **reproachfully** *adverb*
[from old French]

reproduce *verb* (reproduces, reproducing,
reproduced)
1 cause to be seen or heard or happen again.
2 make a copy of something. 3 produce
offspring.
reproduction *noun*, **reproductive** *adjective*

reprove *verb* (reproves, reproving, reproved)
rebuke or reproach. **reproof** *noun*
[from Latin *reprobare* = disapprove]

reptile *noun* (*plural* reptiles)
a cold-blooded animal that has a backbone and
very short legs or no legs at all, e.g. a snake,
lizard, crocodile, or tortoise.
[from Latin *reptilis* = crawling]

republic *noun* (*plural* republics)
a country that has a president, especially one
who is elected. (Compare *monarchy*.)
republican *adjective*
[from Latin *res publica* = public affairs]

repudiate *verb* (repudiates, repudiating,
repudiated)
reject or deny. **repudiation** *noun*
[from Latin *repudiare* = to divorce]

repulsive *adjective*
1 disgusting. 2 repelling things. (The opposite
is *attractive*.)
repulsively *adverb*, **repulsiveness** *noun*

reputable (*say* rep-yoo-ta-bul) *adjective*
having a good reputation; respected.
reputably *adverb*

reputation *noun* (*plural* reputations)
what people say about a person or thing.
[from Latin *reputare* = consider]

reputed *adjective*
said or thought to be something, *This is reputed
to be the best hotel.* **reputedly** *adverb*

request *verb* (requests, requesting, requested)
1 ask for a thing. 2 ask a person to do
something.
request *noun* (*plural* requests)
1 asking for something. 2 a thing asked for.
[from old French; related to *require*]

require *verb* (requires, requiring, required)
1 need. 2 make somebody do something;
oblige, *Drivers are required to pass a test.*
[from *re-* + Latin *quaerere* = seek]

requirement *noun* (*plural* requirements)
what is required; a need.

rescue *verb* (rescues, rescuing, rescued)
save from danger, harm, etc.; free from
captivity. **rescuer** *noun*
rescue *noun* (*plural* rescues)
the action of rescuing. [from old French]

research *noun*
careful study or investigation to discover facts
or information.
research (*say* ri-serch) *verb* (researches,
researching, researched)
do research into something.
[from old French *recerche* = careful search]

resemblance *noun* (*plural* resemblances)
likeness or similarity.

resemble *verb* (resembles, resembling,
resembled)
be like another person or thing.
[from old French; related to *similar*]

resent *verb* (resents, resenting, resented)
feel indignant about or insulted by something.
resentful *adjective*,
resentfully *adverb*, **resentment** *noun*
[from *re-* + Latin *sentire* = feel]

reservation *noun* (*plural* reservations)
1 reserving. 2 something reserved. 3 an area of
land kept for a special purpose. 4 a limit on
how far you agree with something, *I believe
most of his story, but I have some reservations.*

reserve *verb* (reserves, reserving, reserved)
1 keep or order something for a particular
person or a special use. 2 postpone, *reserve
judgement.*
reserve *noun* (*plural* reserves)
1 a person or thing kept ready to be used if
necessary. 2 an area of land kept for a special
purpose, *a nature reserve.* 3 shyness; being
reserved.
[from *re-* + Latin *servare* = keep]

reservoir (*say* rez-er-vwar) *noun* (*plural*
reservoirs)
a place where water is stored, especially an
artificial lake.
[from French *réservoir*; related to *reserve*]

residence *noun* (*plural* residences)
a place where a person lives.

resident *noun* (*plural* residents)
a person living in a particular place.
resident *adjective*
[from *re-* + Latin *-sidens* = sitting]

residential *adjective*
1 containing people's homes, *a residential area.*
2 making it necessary to live in a particular
place, *residential care.*

residue *noun* (*plural* residues)
what is left over. **residual** *adjective*
[from Latin *residuus* = remaining]

resign *verb* (resigns, resigning, resigned)
give up your job or position.
resignation *noun*
be resigned or **resign yourself to something**
accept that you must put up with it.
[from Latin *resignare* = unseal]

resist *verb* (resists, resisting, resisted)
oppose; fight or act against something. [from
re- + Latin *sistere* = stand firmly]

resistance *noun*
1 resisting. 2 the ability of a substance to
hinder the flow of electricity.
resistant *adjective*

resolute *adjective*
showing great determination. **resolutely** *adverb*
[same origin as *resolve*]

resolution *noun* (*plural* resolutions)
1 being resolute. 2 something you have
resolved to do, *New Year resolutions.* 3 a formal
decision made by a committee etc. 4 the
solving of a problem etc.

resolve *verb* (resolves, resolving, resolved)
1 decide firmly or formally. 2 solve a problem
etc. 3 overcome doubts or disagreements.
resolve *noun*
1 something you have decided to do; a
resolution. 2 great determination.
[from *re-* + Latin *solvere* = loosen]

resort *verb* (resorts, resorting, resorted)
turn to or make use of something, *They
resorted to violence.*
resort *noun* (*plural* resorts)
1 a place where people go for relaxation or
holidays. 2 resorting, *without resort to
cheating.*
the last resort something to be tried when
everything else has failed.
[from *re-* + French *sortir* = go out]

resounding *adjective*
1 loud and echoing. 2 very great; outstanding,
a resounding victory.

resource *noun* (*plural* resources)
1 something that can be used; an asset, *The
country's natural resources include coal and oil.*
2 an ability; ingenuity. [from old French;
related to *resurgence*]

resourceful *adjective*
clever at finding ways of doing things.
resourcefully *adverb*, **resourcefulness** *noun*

respect *noun* (*plural* respects)
1 admiration for a person's or thing's good
qualities. 2 politeness or consideration, *Have
respect for people's feelings.* 3 a detail or aspect,
In this respect he is like his sister. 4 reference,
*The rules with respect to bullying are quite
clear.*
respect *verb* (respects, respecting, respected)
have respect for a person or thing. [from Latin
respicere = look back at, consider]

respectable *adjective*
1 having good manners and character etc.
2 fairly good, *a respectable score.*
respectably *adverb*, **respectability** *noun*

respectful *adjective*
showing respect.
respectfully *adverb*

respective *adjective*
of or for each individual, *We went to our
respective rooms.* **respectively** *adverb*

respiration *noun*
breathing. **respiratory** *adjective*

respirator *noun* (*plural* respirators)
1 a device that fits over a person's nose and
mouth to purify air before it is breathed. 2 an
apparatus for giving artificial respiration.

resplendent *adjective*
brilliant with colour or decorations.
[from *re-* + Latin *splendens* = glittering]

respond *verb* (responds, responding, responded)
1 reply. 2 act in answer to, or because of,
something; react.
[from *re-* + Latin *spondere* = to promise]

response *noun* (*plural* responses)
1 a reply. 2 a reaction.

responsibility *noun* (*plural* responsibilities)
1 being responsible. 2 something for which a
person is responsible.

responsible *adjective*
1 looking after a person or thing and having to
take the blame if something goes wrong.
2 reliable and trustworthy. 3 with important
duties, *a responsible job.* 4 causing something,
*His carelessness was responsible for their
deaths.* **responsibly** *adverb* [same origin as
respond]

rest¹ *noun* (*plural* rests)
1 a time of sleep or freedom from work as a
way of regaining strength. 2 a support, *an
armrest.* 3 an interval of silence between notes
in music.

rest *verb* (rests, resting, rested)
1 have a rest; be still. 2 allow to rest, *Sit down
and rest your feet.* 3 support; be supported. 4 be
left without further investigation etc., *And
there the matter rests.* [from Old English]

rest² *noun*
the rest the remaining part; the others.

rest *verb* (rests, resting, rested)
remain, *Rest assured, it will be a success.*
rest with be left to someone to deal with, *It rests
with you to suggest a date.*
[from Latin *restare* = stay behind]

restaurant *noun* (*plural* restaurants)
a place where you can buy a meal and eat it.
[French, literally = restoring]

restful *adjective*
giving rest or a feeling of rest.

restive *adjective*
restless or impatient because of delay,
boredom, etc. [earlier (of a horse)
= refusing to move: from *rest*¹]

restless *adjective*
unable to rest or keep still. **restlessly** *adverb*

restore *verb* (restores, restoring, restored)
put something back to its original place or
condition. **restoration** *noun* [from Latin]

restrain *verb* (restrains, restraining, restrained)
hold a person or thing back; keep under
control. **restraint** *noun*
[from Latin *restringere* = tie up firmly, confine]

restrict *verb* (restricts, restricting, restricted)
limit or control.
restriction *noun,* **restrictive** *adjective*
[from Latin *restrictus* = restrained]

result *noun* (*plural* results)
1 something produced by an action or
condition etc.; an effect or consequence. 2 the
score or situation at the end of a game,
competition, or race etc. 3 the answer to a sum
or calculation.

result *verb* (results, resulting, resulted)
1 happen as a result. 2 have a particular result.
resultant *adjective* [from Latin]

resurrect *verb* (resurrects, resurrecting,
resurrected)
bring back into use or existence, *resurrect an
old custom.* [from *resurrection*]

resurrection *noun*
1 coming back to life after being dead. 2 the
revival of something.
the Resurrection in the Christian religion, the
resurrection of Jesus Christ three days after
his death.

resuscitate *verb* (resuscitates, resuscitating,
resuscitated)
revive a person from unconsciousness or
apparent death. **resuscitation** *noun*
[from *re-* + Latin *suscitare* = revive]

retail *noun*
selling to the general public. (Compare
wholesale.) **retailer** *noun*
[from old French *retaille* = a piece cut off]

retain *verb* (retains, retaining, retained)
1 continue to have something; keep in your
possession or memory etc. 2 hold something in
place.
[from *re-* + Latin *tenere* = to hold]

retaliate *verb* (retaliates, retaliating, retaliated)
repay an injury or insult etc. with a similar
one; counter-attack. **retaliation** *noun*
[from *re-* + Latin *talis* = the same kind]

reticent (*say* ret-i-sent) *adjective*
not telling people what you feel or think;
discreet. **reticence** *noun*
[from Latin *reticere* = keep silent]

retina *noun* (*plural* retinas)
a layer of membrane at the back of the eyeball,
sensitive to light. [from Latin]

retinue *noun* (*plural* retinues)
a group of people accompanying an important
person. [from old French *retenue* = restrained,
in someone's service]

retire *verb* (retires, retiring, retired)
1 give up your regular work because you are
getting old. 2 retreat. 3 go to bed or to your
private room. **retirement** *noun*
[from *re-* + French *tirer* = to draw]

retiring *adjective*
shy; avoiding company.

retort *noun* (*plural* retorts)
1 a quick or witty or angry reply. 2 a glass
bottle with a long downward-bent neck, used in
distilling liquids. 3 a receptacle used in
making steel etc.

retort *verb* (retorts, retorting, retorted)
make a quick, witty, or angry reply.
[from *re-* + Latin *tortum* = twisted]

retract *verb* (retracts, retracting, retracted)
1 pull back or in, *The snail retracts its horns.*
2 withdraw an offer or statement.
retraction *noun*, **retractable** *adjective*,
retractile *adjective*
[from *re-* + Latin *tractum* = pulled]

retreat *verb* (retreats, retreating, retreated)
go back after being defeated or to avoid danger
or difficulty etc.; withdraw.
retreat *noun* (*plural* retreats)
1 retreating. 2 a quiet place to which someone
can withdraw.
[from old French; related to *retract*]

retribution *noun* (*plural* retributions)
a deserved punishment.
[from *re-* + Latin *tributum* = assigned]

retrieve *verb* (retrieves, retrieving, retrieved)
1 bring or get something back. 2 rescue.
retrievable *adjective*, **retrieval** *noun*
[from old French *retrover* = find again]

retriever *noun* (*plural* retrievers)
a kind of dog that is often trained to retrieve
game.

retro- *prefix*
1 back. 2 backward (as in *retrograde*). [from
Latin]

retrograde *adjective*
1 going backwards. 2 becoming less good.
[from *retro-* + Latin *gradus* = a step]

retrospect *noun*
in retrospect when you look back at what has
happened. [from *retro-* + *prospect*]

retrospective *adjective*
1 looking back on the past. 2 applying to the
past as well as the future, *The law could not be
made retrospective.*
retrospection *noun*

return *verb* (returns, returning, returned)
1 come back or go back. 2 bring, give, put, or
send back.
return *noun* (*plural* returns)
1 returning. 2 something returned. 3 profit, *He
gets a good return on his savings.* 4 a return
ticket.
[from *re-* + Latin *tornare* = to turn]

return ticket *noun* (*plural* return tickets)
a ticket for a journey to a place and back again.

reunion *noun* (*plural* reunions)
1 reuniting. 2 a meeting of people who have
not met for some time.

reunite *verb* (reunites, reuniting, reunited)
unite again after being separated.

reuse *verb* (reuses, reusing, reused)
use again. **reusable** *adjective*
reuse *noun*
using again.

reveal *verb* (reveals, revealing, revealed)
let something be seen or known.
[from Latin *revelare* = unveil]

revel *verb* (revels, revelling, revelled)
1 take great delight in something. 2 hold
revels. **reveller** *noun*
[from old French; related to *rebel*]

revelation *noun* (*plural* revelations)
1 revealing. 2 something revealed, especially
something surprising.

revels *plural noun*
noisy festivities.

revenge *noun*
harming somebody in return for harm that
they have caused.
revenge *verb* (revenges, revenging, revenged)
avenge; take vengeance.
[from old French; related to *vindicate*]

revenue *noun* (*plural* revenues)
1 a country's income from taxes etc., used for
paying public expenses. 2 a company's income.
[French, = returned]

reverberate *verb* (reverberates, reverberating,
reverberated)
resound or re-echo. **reverberation** *noun* [from
re- + Latin *verberare* = to beat]

reverence *noun*
a feeling of awe and deep or religious respect.

Reverend *noun*
the title of a member of the clergy, *the Reverend
John Smith.* [from Latin *reverendus* = someone
to be respected]

USAGE: Do not confuse with *reverent*.

reverent *adjective*
feeling or showing reverence. **reverently** *adverb*

USAGE: Do not confuse with *Reverend*.

reverie (*say* rev-er-ee) *noun* (*plural* reveries)
a daydream. [from French]

reversal *noun* (*plural* reversals)
1 reversing or being reversed. 2 a piece of bad
luck; a reverse.

reverse *adjective*
opposite in direction, order, or manner etc.
reverse *noun* (*plural* reverses)
1 the reverse side, order, manner, etc. 2 a piece
of misfortune, *They suffered several reverses.*
in reverse the opposite way round.
reverse *verb* (reverses, reversing, reversed)
1 turn in the opposite direction or order etc.;
turn something inside out or upside down.
2 move backwards. 3 cancel a decision or
decree. **reversible** *adjective* [same origin as
revert]

reverse gear *noun*
a gear that allows a vehicle to be driven
backwards.

review noun (plural reviews)
1 an inspection or survey. 2 a published description and opinion of a book, film, play, etc.
review verb (reviews, reviewing, reviewed) make a review of something.
reviewer noun

USAGE: Do not confuse with revue.

revise verb (revises, revising, revised)
1 go over work that you have already done, especially in preparing for an examination.
2 alter or correct something. **revision** noun [from re- + Latin visere = examine]

revive verb (revives, reviving, revived) come or bring back to life, strength, activity, or use etc. **revival** noun [from re- + Latin vivere = to live]

revolt verb (revolts, revolting, revolted)
1 rebel. 2 disgust somebody.
revolt noun (plural revolts)
1 a rebellion. 2 a feeling of disgust.
[same origin as revolve]

revolting adjective
disgusting.

revolution noun (plural revolutions)
1 a rebellion that overthrows the government.
2 a complete change. 3 revolving; rotation; one complete turn of a wheel, engine, etc.
revolutionary adjective

revolve verb (revolves, revolving, revolved) turn or keep on turning round.
[from re- + Latin volvere = to roll]

revolver noun (plural revolvers)
a pistol with a revolving mechanism that makes it possible to fire it a number of times without reloading.

revue noun (plural revues)
an entertainment consisting of songs, sketches, etc., often about current events.
[French, = review]

USAGE: Do not confuse with review.

reward noun (plural rewards)
something given in return for a useful action or a merit.
reward verb (rewards, rewarding, rewarded) give a reward to someone. [originally = consider, take notice: related to regard]

rewarding adjective
giving satisfaction and a feeling of achievement, a rewarding job.

rhetorical question noun (plural rhetorical questions)
something put as a question so that it sounds dramatic, not to get an answer, e.g. 'Who cares?' (= nobody cares).

rheumatism noun
a disease that causes pain and stiffness in joints and muscles.
rheumatic adjective, **rheumatoid** adjective [from Greek rheuma, a substance in the body which was once believed to cause rheumatism]

rhinoceros noun (plural rhinoceros or rhinoceroses)
a large heavy animal with a horn or two horns on its nose.
[from Greek rhinos = of the nose + keras = horn]

rhododendron noun (plural rhododendrons)
an evergreen shrub with large trumpet-shaped flowers.
[from Greek rhodon = rose + dendron = tree]

rhombus noun (plural rhombuses)
a shape with four equal sides but no right angles, like the diamond on playing cards.
[from Greek]

rhubarb noun
a plant with thick reddish stalks that are used as fruit. [from Latin]

rhyme noun (plural rhymes)
1 a similar sound in the endings of words, e.g. bat/fat/mat, batter/fatter/matter. 2 a poem with rhymes. 3 a word that rhymes with another.
rhyme verb (rhymes, rhyming, rhymed)
1 form a rhyme. 2 have rhymes.
[from old French; related to rhythm (originally used of a kind of rhythmic verse which also usually rhymed)]

rhythm noun (plural rhythms)
a regular pattern of beats, sounds, or movements. **rhythmic** adjective, **rhythmical** adjective, **rhythmically** adverb [from Greek]

rib noun (plural ribs)
1 each of the curved bones round the chest. 2 a curved part that looks like a rib or supports something, the ribs of an umbrella.
ribbed adjective

ribbon noun (plural ribbons)
1 a narrow strip of silk or nylon etc. used for decoration or for tying something. 2 a long narrow strip of inked material used in a typewriter etc.

rice noun
a cereal plant grown in flooded fields in hot countries, or its seeds. [from Greek]

rich adjective
1 having a lot of money or property or resources etc.; wealthy. 2 full of goodness, quality, etc. 3 expensive or luxurious.
richly adverb, **richness** noun

rickety adjective
shaky; likely to break or fall down.

rickshaw *noun* (*plural* **rickshaws**)
a two-wheeled carriage pulled by one or more people, used in the Far East.
[from Japanese *jin-riki-sha* = person-power-vehicle]

ricochet (*say* rik-osh-ay) *verb* (**ricochets, ricocheting, ricocheted**)
bounce off something; rebound, *The bullets ricocheted off the wall.* **ricochet** *noun*
[French, = the skipping of a flat stone on water]

rid *verb* (**rids, ridding, rid**)
make a person or place free from something unwanted, *He rid the town of rats.*
get rid of cause to go away.

riddle¹ *noun* (*plural* **riddles**)
a puzzling question, especially as a joke.
[from Old English *raedels*]

riddle² *verb* (**riddles, riddling, riddled**)
pierce with many holes, *They riddled the target with bullets.*

ride *verb* (**rides, riding, rode, ridden**)
1 sit on a horse, bicycle, etc. and be carried along on it. 2 travel in a car, bus, train, etc. 3 float or be supported on something, *The ship rode the waves.*
ride *noun* (*plural* **rides**)
1 a journey on a horse, bicycle, etc. or in a vehicle. 2 a roundabout etc. that you ride on at a fair. [from Old English]

ridge *noun* (*plural* **ridges**)
a long narrow part higher than the rest of something. **ridged** *adjective*

ridicule *verb* (**ridicules, ridiculing, ridiculed**)
make fun of a person or thing. **ridicule** *noun*
[from Latin *ridere* = to laugh]

ridiculous *adjective*
so silly that it makes people laugh or despise it.
ridiculously *adverb*

rifle *noun* (*plural* **rifles**)
a long gun with spiral grooves (called *rifling*) inside the barrel that make the bullet spin and so travel more accurately.
rifle *verb* (**rifles, rifling, rifled**)
search and rob, *They rifled his desk.*

rift valley *noun* (*plural* **rift valleys**)
a steep-sided valley formed where the land has sunk.

rig *verb* (**rigs, rigging, rigged**)
1 provide a ship with ropes, spars, sails, etc. 2 set something up quickly or out of makeshift materials.
rig out provide with clothes or equipment.
rig-out *noun*
rig *noun* (*plural* **rigs**)
1 a framework supporting the machinery for drilling an oil well. 2 the way a ship's masts and sails etc. are arranged. 3 (*informal*) an outfit of clothes.
[probably from a Scandinavian language]

rigging *noun*
the ropes etc. that support a ship's mast and sails.

right *adjective*
1 on or towards the east, if you think of yourself as facing north. 2 correct; true, *the right answer.* 3 morally good; fair or just, *Is it right to cheat?* 4 (of political groups) conservative; not in favour of socialist reforms. **right-hand** *adjective*, **rightly** *adverb*, **rightness** *noun*
right *adverb*
1 on or towards the right-hand side, *Turn right.* 2 straight, *Go right on.* 3 completely, *Go right round it.* 4 exactly, *right in the middle.* 5 rightly, *You did right to tell me.*
right away immediately.
right *noun* (*plural* **rights**)
1 the right-hand side or part etc. 2 what is morally good or fair or just. 3 something that people are allowed to do or have, *People over 18 have the right to vote in elections.*
right *verb* (**rights, righting, righted**)
make a thing right or upright, *They righted the boat.* [from Old English]

right angle *noun*
an angle of 90°.

rightful *adjective*
deserved or proper, *in her rightful place.*
rightfully *adverb*

right hand *noun* (*plural* **right hands**)
the hand that most people use more than the left, on the right side of the body.

right-handed *adjective*
using the right hand in preference to the left hand.

right of way *noun* (*plural* **rights of way**)
1 a public path across private land. 2 the right of one vehicle to pass or cross a junction etc. before another.

rigid *adjective*
1 stiff or firm; not bending, *a rigid support.* 2 strict, *rigid rules.* **rigidly** *adverb*, **rigidity** *noun*
[from Latin]

rigmarole *noun* (*plural* **rigmaroles**)
1 a long rambling statement. 2 a complicated procedure. [from Middle English *ragman* = a legal document]

rigorous *adjective*
1 strict or severe. 2 careful and thorough.
rigorously *adverb*

rim *noun* (*plural* **rims**)
the outer edge of a cup, wheel, or other round object. [from Old English]

rind *noun*
the tough skin on bacon, cheese, or fruit.

ring[1] *noun* (*plural* rings)
1 a circle. 2 a thin circular piece of metal worn on a finger. 3 the space where a circus performs. 4 a square area in which a boxing match or wrestling match takes place.
ring *verb* (rings, ringing, ringed)
put a ring round something; encircle.
[from Old English *hring*]

ring[2] *verb* (rings, ringing, rang, rung)
1 cause a bell to sound. 2 make a loud clear sound like that of a bell. 3 be filled with sound, *The hall rang with cheers.* 4 telephone, *Please ring me tomorrow.* **ringer** *noun*
ring *noun* (*plural* rings)
the act or sound of ringing.
give someone a ring (*informal*) telephone someone.
[from Old English *hringan*]

ringleader *noun* (*plural* ringleaders)
a person who leads others in rebellion, mischief, crime, etc. [from *ring*[1]]

ringmaster *noun* (*plural* ringmasters)
the person in charge of a performance in a circus ring.

ring road *noun* (*plural* ring roads)
a road that runs around the edge of a town so that traffic does not have to go through the centre.

rink *noun* (*plural* rinks)
a place made for skating. [origin unknown]

rinse *verb* (rinses, rinsing, rinsed)
1 wash something lightly. 2 wash in clean water to remove soap.
rinse *noun* (*plural* rinses)
1 rinsing. 2 a liquid for colouring the hair.

riot *noun* (*plural* riots)
wild or violent behaviour by a crowd of people.
riot *verb* (riots, rioting, rioted)
take part in a riot.
[from old French *rihoter* = to quarrel]

riotous *adjective*
1 disorderly or unruly. 2 boisterous, *riotous laughter.*

RIP *abbreviation*
may he or she (or they) rest in peace.
[short for Latin *requiescat* (or *requiescant*) *in pace*]

rip *verb* (rips, ripping, ripped)
1 tear roughly. 2 rush.
rip *noun*
a torn place. [origin unknown]

ripe *adjective* (riper, ripest)
1 ready to be harvested or eaten. 2 ready and suitable, *The time is ripe for revolution.*
ripeness *noun*
a ripe old age a great age.

ripen *verb* (ripens, ripening, ripened)
make or become ripe.

ripple *noun* (*plural* ripples)
a small wave or series of waves.
ripple *verb* (ripples, rippling, rippled)
form ripples. [origin unknown]

rise *verb* (rises, rising, rose, risen)
1 go upwards. 2 get up from lying, sitting, or kneeling. 3 get out of bed. 4 rebel, *They rose in revolt against the tyrant.* 5 (of a river) begin its course. 6 (of the wind) begin to blow more strongly.
rise *noun* (*plural* rises)
1 the action of rising; an upward movement. 2 an increase in amount etc. or in wages. 3 an upward slope.
give rise to cause.

rising *noun* (*plural* risings)
a revolt.

risk *noun* (*plural* risks)
a chance of danger or loss.
risk *verb* (risks, risking, risked)
take the chance of damaging or losing something. [via French from Italian]

risky *adjective* (riskier, riskiest)
full of risk.

rissole *noun* (*plural* rissoles)
a fried cake of minced meat or fish.

ritual *noun* (*plural* rituals)
the series of actions used in a religious or other ceremony. **ritual** *adjective*, **ritually** *adverb*
[from Latin *ritus*]

rival *noun* (*plural* rivals)
a person or thing that competes with another or tries to do the same thing. **rivalry** *noun*
[from Latin *rivalis* = someone using the same stream (from *rivus* = stream)]

river *noun* (*plural* rivers)
a large stream of water flowing in a natural channel. [from Latin *ripa* = bank]

rivet *noun* (*plural* rivets)
a strong nail or bolt for holding pieces of metal together. The end opposite the head is flattened to form another head when it is in place.
rivet *verb* (rivets, riveting, riveted)
1 fasten with rivets. 2 hold firmly, *He stood riveted to the spot.* 3 fascinate, *The concert was riveting.* **riveter** *noun* [from old French]

road *noun* (*plural* roads)
1 a level way with a hard surface made for traffic to travel on. 2 a way or course, *the road to success.* [from Old English]

roadworthy *adjective*
safe to be used on roads.

roam *verb* (roams, roaming, roamed)
wander. **roam** *noun* [origin unknown]

roar *noun* (*plural* roars)
a loud deep sound like that made by a lion.
roar *verb* (roars, roaring, roared)
make a roar.
a roaring trade brisk selling of something.

roast *verb* (roasts, roasting, roasted)
1 cook meat etc. in an oven or by exposing it to heat. 2 make or be very hot.
roast *adjective*
roasted, *roast beef.*
roast *noun* (*plural* roasts)
1 meat for roasting. 2 roast meat.
[via old French from Germanic]

rob *verb* (robs, robbing, robbed)
take or steal from somebody, *He robbed me of my watch.* **robber** *noun*, **robbery** *noun*

robe *noun* (*plural* robes)
a long loose garment.

robin *noun* (*plural* robins)
a small brown bird with a red breast.
[from old French, = Robert]

robot *noun* (*plural* robots)
1 a machine that looks or acts like a person. 2 a machine operated by remote control.
robotic *adjective*
[from Czech *robota* = forced labour]

robust *adjective*
strong and vigorous.
robustly *adverb*, **robustness** *noun*
[from Latin *robur* = strength, an oak tree]

rock[1] *noun* (*plural* rocks)
1 a large stone or boulder. 2 the hard part of the earth's crust, under the soil. 3 a hard sweet usually shaped like a stick and sold at the seaside. [from old French]

rock[2] *verb* (rocks, rocking, rocked)
1 move gently backwards and forwards while supported on something. 2 shake violently, *The earthquake rocked the city.*
rock *noun*
1 a rocking movement. 2 rock music.
[from Old English]

rock-bottom *adjective*
at the lowest level, *rock-bottom prices.*

rockery *noun* (*plural* rockeries)
a mound or bank in a garden, where plants are made to grow between large rocks.

rocket *noun* (*plural* rockets)
1 a firework that shoots high into the air. 2 a structure that flies by expelling burning gases, used to send up a missile or a spacecraft.
rocketry *noun*
rocket *verb* (rockets, rocketing, rocketed)
move quickly upwards or away.
[from Italian *rocchetto* = small distaff (because of the shape)]

rocking horse *noun* (*plural* rocking horses)
a model of a horse that can be rocked by a child sitting on it.

rock music *noun*
popular music with a heavy beat.

rocky[1] *adjective* (rockier, rockiest)
1 like rock. 2 full of rocks.

rocky[2] *adjective* (rockier, rockiest)
unsteady. **rockiness** *noun*

rod *noun* (*plural* rods)
1 a long thin stick or bar. 2 a stick with a line attached for fishing.

rodent *noun* (*plural* rodents)
an animal that has large front teeth for gnawing things, *Rats, mice, and squirrels are rodents.* [from Latin *rodens* = gnawing]

rodeo (*say* roh-day-oh) *noun* (*plural* rodeos)
a display of cowboys' skill in riding, controlling horses, etc.
[Spanish, from *rodear* = go round]

roe[1] *noun*
a mass of eggs or reproductive cells in a fish's body.
[from old German or old Dutch]

roe[2] *noun* (*plural* roes or roe)
a kind of small deer of Europe and Asia. The male is called a **roebuck**.
[from Old English]

rogue *noun* (*plural* rogues)
1 a dishonest person. 2 a mischievous person.
roguery *noun* [origin unknown]

role *noun* (*plural* roles)
1 a performer's part in a play or film etc.
2 someone's or something's purpose or function, *the role of computers in education.*
[from French *rôle* = roll (originally the roll of paper on which an actor's part was written)]

role model *noun* (*plural* role models)
a person who is regarded as an example of how to behave, *fathers are role models to their sons.*

roll *verb* (rolls, rolling, rolled)
1 move along by turning over and over, like a ball or wheel. 2 form something into the shape of a cylinder or ball. 3 flatten something by rolling a rounded object over it. 4 rock from side to side. 5 pass steadily, *The years rolled on.* 6 make a long vibrating sound, *The thunder rolled.*
roll *noun* (*plural* rolls)
1 a cylinder made by rolling something up. 2 a small individual portion of bread baked in a rounded shape. 3 an official list of names. 4 a long vibrating sound, *a drum roll.*
[from Latin *rotula* = little wheel]

roll-call *noun* (*plural* roll-calls)
the calling of a list of names to check that everyone is present.

roller *noun* (*plural* rollers)
1 a cylinder for rolling over things, or on which something is wound. 2 a long swelling sea-wave.

Rollerblade *noun* (*plural* Rollerblades)
(*trade mark*) a boot like an ice-skating boot, with a line of wheels in place of the skate, for rolling smoothly on hard ground.
rollerblading *noun*

roller coaster *noun* (*plural* **roller coasters**)
a switchback at a fair etc.

roller skate *noun* (*plural* **roller skates**)
a framework with wheels, fitted under a shoe so that the wearer can roll smoothly over the ground. **roller-skating** *noun*

rolling pin *noun*
a heavy cylinder for rolling over pastry to flatten it.

ROM *abbreviation*
read-only memory (in a computer), with contents that can be searched or copied but not changed.

Roman *adjective*
1 of ancient or modern Rome or its people.
2 Roman Catholic. **Roman** *noun*

Roman alphabet *noun*
this alphabet, in which most European languages are written.

Roman Catholic *adjective*
belonging to or to do with the Church that has the Pope (bishop of Rome) as its leader.
Roman Catholic *noun* (*plural* **Roman Catholics**)
a member of this Church.

romance (*say* ro-manss) *noun* (*plural* **romances**)
1 tender feelings, experiences, and qualities connected with love. 2 a love story. 3 a love affair. 4 an imaginative story about the adventures of heroes, *a romance of King Arthur's court.*

Roman numerals *plural noun*
letters that represent numbers (I = 1, V = 5, X = 10, etc.), used by the ancient Romans. (Compare *arabic numerals.*)

romantic *adjective*
1 to do with romance. 2 sentimental or idealistic; not realistic or practical.
romantically *adverb*

romp *verb* (**romps, romping, romped**)
play in a lively way. **romp** *noun*

roof *noun* (*plural* **roofs**)
1 the part that covers the top of a building, shelter, or vehicle. 2 the top inside surface of something, *the roof of the mouth.*

rook[1] *noun* (*plural* **rooks**)
a black crow that nests in large groups.
rook *verb* (**rooks, rooking, rooked**) (*informal*)
swindle; charge people an unnecessarily high price. [from Old English]

rook[2] *noun* (*plural* **rooks**)
a chess piece shaped like a castle.
[from Arabic]

room *noun* (*plural* **rooms**)
1 a part of a building with its own walls and ceiling. 2 enough space, *Is there room for me?*
roomful *noun* [from Old English]

roost *verb* (**roosts, roosting, roosted**)
(of birds) perch or settle for sleep.

roost *noun* (*plural* **roosts**)
a place where birds roost.

root[1] *noun* (*plural* **roots**)
1 that part of a plant that grows under the ground and absorbs water and nourishment from the soil. 2 a source or basis, *The love of money is the root of all evil.* 3 a number in relation to the number it produces when multiplied by itself, *9 is the square root of 81* (9 × 9 = 81).
take root 1 grow roots. 2 become established.
root *verb* (**roots, rooting, rooted**)
1 take root; cause something to take root. 2 fix firmly, *Fear rooted us to the spot.*
root out get rid of something.
[from Old Norse]

root[2] *verb* (**roots, rooting, rooted**)
rummage; (of an animal) turn up ground in search of food. [from Old English]

rope *noun* (*plural* **ropes**)
a strong thick cord made of twisted strands of fibre.
show someone the ropes show him or her how to do something.
rope *verb* (**ropes, roping, roped**)
fasten with a rope.
rope in persuade a person to take part in something.

rose[1] *noun* (*plural* **roses**)
1 a shrub that has showy flowers often with thorny stems. 2 deep pink colour. 3 a sprinkling-nozzle with many holes, e.g. on a watering can or hosepipe.
[via Old English from Greek]

rose[2] *past tense* of **rise.**

roster *noun* (*plural* **rosters**)
a list showing people's turns to be on duty etc.

rosy *adjective* (**rosier, rosiest**)
1 deep pink. 2 hopeful or cheerful, *a rosy future.* **rosiness** *noun*

rot *verb* (**rots, rotting, rotted**)
go soft or bad and become useless; decay.
rot *noun*
1 rotting or decay. 2 (*informal*) nonsense.

rota (*say* roh-ta) *noun* (*plural* **rotas**)
a list of people to do things or of things to be done in turn. [Latin, = wheel]

rotate *verb* (**rotates, rotating, rotated**)
1 go round like a wheel; revolve. 2 arrange or happen in a series; take turns at doing something. **rotation** *noun*, **rotary** *adjective*, **rotatory** *adjective* [same origin as *rota*]

rote *noun*
by rote from memory or by routine, without full understanding of the meaning, *We used to learn French songs by rote.* [origin unknown]

rotor *noun* (*plural* **rotors**)
a rotating part of a machine or helicopter.
[from *rotate*]

rotten *adjective*
1 rotted, *rotten apples*. 2 (*informal*) worthless or unpleasant. **rottenness** *noun*

rouble (*say* roo-bul) *noun* (*plural* **roubles**)
the unit of money in Russia.

rouge (*say* roozh) *noun*
a reddish cosmetic for colouring the cheeks.
rouge *verb* [French, = red]

rough *adjective* (**rougher, roughest**)
1 not smooth; uneven. 2 not gentle or careful; violent, *a rough push*. 3 not exact, *a rough guess*.
roughly *adverb*, **roughness** *noun*
rough *verb* (**roughs, roughing, roughed**)
rough it do without ordinary comforts.
rough out draw or plan something roughly.
rough up (*slang*) treat a person violently.

roughen *verb* (**roughens, roughening, roughened**)
make or become rough.

round *adjective*
1 shaped like a circle or ball or cylinder; curved. 2 full or complete, *a round dozen*. 3 returning to the start, *a round trip*.
roundness *noun*
in round figures approximately, without giving exact units.
round *adverb*
1 in a circle or curve; round something, *Go round to the back of the house*. 2 in every direction, *Hand the cakes round*. 3 in a new direction, *Turn your chair round*. 4 to someone's house or office etc., *Go round after dinner*.
come round become conscious again.
round about 1 near by. 2 approximately.
round *preposition*
1 on all sides of, *Put a fence round the field*. 2 in a curve or circle at an even distance from, *The earth moves round the sun*. 3 to all parts of, *Show them round the house*. 4 on the further side of, *The shop is round the corner*.
round *noun* (*plural* **rounds**)
1 a round object. 2 a whole slice of bread; a sandwich made with two slices of bread. 3 a series of visits made by a doctor, postman, etc. 4 one section or stage in a competition, *Winners go on to the next round*. 5 a shot or volley of shots from a gun; ammunition for this. 6 a song in which people sing the same words but start at different times.
round *verb* (**rounds, rounding, rounded**)
1 make or become round. 2 travel round, *The car rounded the corner*.
round off finish something.
round up gather people or animals together.
[from old French; related to *rotund*]

roundabout *noun* (*plural* **roundabouts**)
1 a road junction where traffic has to pass round a circular structure in the road. 2 a circular revolving ride at a fair.

roundabout *adjective*
indirect; not using the shortest way of going or of saying or doing something, *I heard the news in a roundabout way*.

rounders *noun*
a game in which players try to hit a ball and run round a circuit.

round-the-clock *adjective*
lasting or happening all day and all night.

round trip *noun* (*plural* **round trips**)
a trip to one or more places and back to where you started.

round-up *noun* (*plural* **round-ups**)
1 a gathering up of cattle or people, *a police round-up of suspects*. 2 a summary, *a round-up of the news*.

rouse *verb* (**rouses, rousing, roused**)
1 make or become awake. 2 cause to become active or excited.

rousing *adjective*
loud or exciting, *three rousing cheers*.

rout *verb* (**routs, routing, routed**)
defeat and chase away an enemy. **rout** *noun*

route (*say as* root) *noun* (*plural* **routes**)
the way taken to get to a place.

routine (*say* roo-teen) *noun* (*plural* **routines**)
a regular way of doing things. **routinely** *adverb*
[French; related to *route*]

row[1] (rhymes with *go*) *noun* (*plural* **rows**)
a line of people or things.
[from Old English *raw*]

row[2] (rhymes with *go*) *verb* (**rows, rowing, rowed**)
make a boat move by using oars.
rower *noun*, **rowing boat** *noun*
[from Old English *rowan*]

row[3] (rhymes with *cow*) *noun* (*plural* **rows**)
1 a loud noise. 2 a quarrel. 3 a scolding.
[origin unknown]

rowdy *adjective* (**rowdier, rowdiest**)
noisy and disorderly. **rowdiness** *noun*

royal *adjective*
to do with a king or queen. **royally** *adverb*

royalty *noun*
1 being royal. 2 a royal person or persons, *in the presence of royalty*. 3 (*plural* **royalties**) a payment made to an author or composer etc. for each copy of a work sold or for each performance.

RSVP *abbreviation*
répondez s'il vous plaît (French, = please reply).

rub *verb* (**rubs, rubbing, rubbed**)
move something backwards and forwards while pressing it on something else.
rub *noun*
rub out remove something by rubbing.

rubber *noun* (*plural* **rubbers**)
1 a strong elastic substance used for making tyres, balls, hoses, etc. 2 a piece of rubber for rubbing out pencil or ink marks.
rubbery *adjective*

rubbish *noun*
1 things that are worthless or not wanted. 2 nonsense. [from old French]

rubble *noun*
broken pieces of brick or stone.

ruby *noun* (*plural* **rubies**)
a red jewel. [from Latin *rubeus* = red]

rucksack *noun* (*plural* **rucksacks**)
a bag on straps for carrying on the back.
[from German *Rücken* = back + *Sack* = sack[1]]

rudder *noun* (*plural* **rudders**)
a hinged upright piece at the back of a ship or aircraft, used for steering.

ruddy *adjective* (**ruddier, ruddiest**)
red and healthy-looking, *a ruddy complexion*.
[from Old English]

rude *adjective* (**ruder, rudest**)
1 impolite. 2 indecent or improper. 3 roughly made; crude, *a rude shelter*. 4 vigorous and hearty, *in rude health*.
rudely *adverb*, **rudeness** *noun*
[from Latin *rudis* = raw, wild]

rudimentary *adjective*
1 to do with rudiments; elementary. 2 not fully developed, *Penguins have rudimentary wings*.

rudiments (*say* rood-i-ments) *plural noun*
the elementary principles of a subject, *Learn the rudiments of chemistry*.
[same origin as *rude*]

ruff *noun* (*plural* **ruffs**)
1 a starched pleated frill worn round the neck in the 16th century. 2 a collar-like ring of feathers or fur round a bird's or animal's neck.
[a different spelling of *rough*]

ruffian *noun* (*plural* **ruffians**)
a violent lawless person. **ruffianly** *adjective*

ruffle *verb* (**ruffles, ruffling, ruffled**)
1 disturb the smoothness of a thing. 2 upset or annoy someone.
ruffle *noun* (*plural* **ruffles**)
a gathered ornamental frill.

rug *noun* (*plural* **rugs**)
1 a thick mat for the floor. 2 a piece of thick fabric used as a blanket.

Rugby or **Rugby football** *noun*
a kind of football game using an oval ball that players may carry or kick.
[named after Rugby School in Warwickshire, where it was first played]

rugged *adjective*
1 having an uneven surface or outline; craggy. 2 sturdy.

rugger *noun*
Rugby football.

ruin *noun* (*plural* **ruins**)
1 severe damage or destruction to something. 2 a building that has fallen down.
ruin *verb* (**ruins, ruining, ruined**)
damage a thing so severely that it is useless; destroy. **ruination** *noun*
[from Latin *ruere* = to fall]

ruinous *adjective*
1 causing ruin. 2 in ruins; ruined.

rule *noun* (*plural* **rules**)
1 something that people have to obey. 2 ruling; governing, *under French rule*. 3 a carpenter's ruler.
as a rule usually; more often than not.
rule *verb* (**rules, ruling, ruled**)
1 govern; reign. 2 make a decision, *The referee ruled that it was a foul*. 3 draw a straight line with a ruler or other straight edge.
[from old French; related to *regulate*]

ruler *noun* (*plural* **rulers**)
1 a person who governs. 2 a strip of wood, metal, or plastic with straight edges, used for measuring and drawing straight lines.

ruling *noun* (*plural* **rulings**)
a judgement.

rum *noun*
a strong alcoholic drink made from sugar or molasses.

rumble *verb* (**rumbles, rumbling, rumbled**)
make a deep heavy continuous sound like thunder. **rumble** *noun*

ruminant *adjective*
ruminating.
ruminant *noun* (*plural* **ruminants**)
an animal that chews the cud (see *cud*).

ruminate *verb* (**ruminates, ruminating, ruminated**)
1 chew the cud. 2 meditate or ponder.
rumination *noun*, **ruminative** *adjective*

rummage *verb* (**rummages, rummaging, rummaged**)
turn things over or move them about while looking for something. **rummage** *noun*

rumour *noun* (*plural* **rumours**)
information that spreads to a lot of people but may not be true.
rumour *verb*
be rumoured be spread as a rumour.
[from Latin *rumor* = noise]

rump *noun* (*plural* **rumps**)
the hind part of an animal.

rumple *verb* (**rumples, rumpling, rumpled**)
crumple; make a thing untidy.

rump steak *noun* (*plural* **rump steaks**)
a piece of meat from the rump of a cow.

rumpus *noun* (*plural* **rumpuses**) (*informal*)
an uproar; an angry protest.

run *verb* (runs, running, ran, run)
1 move with quick steps so that both or all feet leave the ground at each stride. 2 go or travel; flow, *Tears ran down his cheeks.* 3 produce a flow of liquid, *Run some water into it.* 4 work or function, *The engine was running smoothly.* 5 manage or organize, *She runs a grocery shop.* 6 compete in a contest, *He ran for President.* 7 extend, *A fence runs round the estate.* 8 go or take in a vehicle, *I'll run you to the station.*
run away leave a place secretly or quickly.
run down 1 run over. 2 stop gradually; decline. 3 (*informal*) say unkind or unfair things about someone.
run into 1 collide with. 2 happen to meet.
run out 1 have used up your stock of something. 2 knock over the wicket of a running batsman.
run over knock down or crush with a moving vehicle.
run through examine or rehearse.
run *noun* (*plural* runs)
1 the action of running; a time spent running, *Go for a run.* 2 a point scored in cricket or baseball. 3 a continuous series of events, etc., *She had a run of good luck.* 4 an enclosure for animals, *a chicken run.* 5 a track, *a ski run.*
on the run running away from pursuit or capture.

runaway *noun* (*plural* runaways)
someone who has run away.
runaway *adjective*
1 having run away or out of control. 2 won easily, *a runaway victory.*

rundown *adjective*
1 tired and in bad health. 2 in bad condition; dilapidated.

rung[1] *noun* (*plural* rungs)
a crosspiece in a ladder.
[from Old English]

rung[2] *past participle* of **ring**[2].

runner *noun* (*plural* runners)
1 a person or animal that runs, especially in a race. 2 a stem that grows away from a plant and roots itself. 3 a groove, rod, or roller for a thing to move on; each of the long strips under a sledge. 4 a long narrow strip of carpet or covering.

runner bean *noun* (*plural* runner beans)
a kind of climbing bean with long green pods which are eaten.

runner-up *noun* (*plural* runners-up)
someone who comes second in a competition.

running *present participle* of **run**.
in the running competing and with a chance of winning.
running *adjective*
continuous or consecutive; without an interval, *It rained for four days running.*

runny *adjective* (runnier, runniest)
1 flowing like liquid, *runny honey.* 2 producing a flow of liquid, *a runny nose.*

runway *noun* (*plural* runways)
a long hard surface on which aircraft take off and land.

rural *adjective*
to do with or belonging to the countryside.
[from Latin *ruris* = of the country]

ruse *noun* (*plural* ruses)
a deception or trick. [from French]

rush[1] *verb* (rushes, rushing, rushed)
1 hurry. 2 move or flow quickly. 3 attack or capture by rushing.
rush *noun* (*plural* rushes)
1 a hurry. 2 a sudden movement towards something. 3 a sudden great demand for something. [from old French]

rush[2] *noun* (*plural* rushes)
a plant with a thin stem that grows in marshy places. [from Old English]

rush hour *noun* (*plural* rush hours)
the time when traffic is busiest.

rusk *noun* (*plural* rusks)
a kind of hard, dry biscuit, especially for feeding babies.

rust *noun*
1 a red or brown substance that forms on iron or steel exposed to damp and corrodes it. 2 reddish-brown colour.
rust *verb* (rusts, rusting, rusted)
make or become rusty. [from Old English]

rustic *adjective*
1 rural. 2 made of rough timber or branches, *a rustic bridge.*
[same origin as *rural*]

rustle *verb* (rustles, rustling, rustled)
1 make a sound like paper being crumpled. 2 (*American*) steal horses or cattle, *cattle rustling.* **rustle** *noun*, **rustler** *noun*
rustle up (*informal*) produce, *rustle up a meal.*

rusty *adjective* (rustier, rustiest)
1 coated with rust. 2 weakened by lack of use or practice, *My French is a bit rusty.*
rustiness *noun*

rut *noun* (*plural* ruts)
1 a deep track made by wheels in soft ground. 2 a settled and usually dull way of life, *We are getting into a rut.* **rutted** *adjective*
[probably related to *route*]

ruthless *adjective*
pitiless, merciless, or cruel.
ruthlessly *adverb*, **ruthlessness** *noun*
[from Middle English *ruth* = pity]

rye *noun*
a cereal used to make bread, biscuits, etc.

Ss

S. *abbreviation*
1 south. 2 southern.

sabbath *noun* (*plural* **sabbaths**)
a weekly day for rest and prayer, Saturday for Jews, Sunday for Christians. [from Hebrew *shabat* = rest]

sabotage *noun*
deliberate damage or disruption to hinder an enemy, employer, etc.
sabotage *verb*, **saboteur** *noun* [from French *saboter* = make a noise with *sabots* (= wooden clogs)]

saccharin (*say* sak-er-in) *noun*
a very sweet substance used as a substitute for sugar. [from Greek *saccharon* = sugar]

sack[1] *noun* (*plural* **sacks**)
a large bag made of strong material.
sacking *noun*
the sack (*informal*) dismissal from a job, *He got the sack*.
sack *verb* (*informal*) (**sacks, sacking, sacked**)
dismiss someone from a job. [via Old English from Latin]

sack[2] *verb* (**sacks, sacking, sacked**) (*old use*)
plunder a captured town in a violent destructive way. **sack** *noun* [from French *mettre à sac* = put in a sack]

sacrament *noun* (*plural* **sacraments**)
an important Christian religious ceremony such as baptism or Holy Communion. [same origin as *sacred*]

sacred *adjective*
holy; to do with God or a god. [from Latin]

sacrifice *noun* (*plural* **sacrifices**)
1 giving something that you think will please a god. 2 giving up a thing you value, so that something good may happen. 3 a thing sacrificed. **sacrificial** *adjective*
sacrifice *verb* (**sacrifices, sacrificing, sacrificed**)
give something as a sacrifice. [from Latin *sacrificare* = make something holy]

sacrilege (*say* sak-ril-ij) *noun*
disrespect or damage to something people regard as sacred. **sacrilegious** *adjective* [from Latin *sacer* = sacred + *legere* = take away]

sad *adjective* (**sadder, saddest**)
unhappy; showing or causing sorrow.
sadly *adverb*, **sadness** *noun* [from Old English]

sadden *verb* (**saddens, saddening, saddened**)
make a person sad.

saddle *noun* (*plural* **saddles**)
1 a seat for putting on the back of a horse or other animal. 2 the seat of a bicycle. 3 a ridge of high land between two peaks.

saddle *verb* (**saddles, saddling, saddled**)
put a saddle on a horse etc.

sadist (*say* say-dist) *noun* (*plural* **sadists**)
a person who enjoys hurting or humiliating other people.
sadism *noun*, **sadistic** *adjective* [named after a French novelist, the Marquis de Sade, noted for the cruelties in his stories]

safari *noun* (*plural* **safaris**)
an expedition to see or hunt wild animals. [from Arabic *safar* = a journey]

safe *adjective*
1 not in danger. 2 not dangerous.
safely *adverb*, **safeness** *noun*, **safety** *noun*
safe *noun* (*plural* **safes**)
a strong cupboard or box in which valuables can be locked safely. [from old French; related to *save*]

safeguard *noun* (*plural* **safeguards**)
a protection.

safety pin *noun* (*plural* **safety pins**)
a U-shaped pin with a clip fastening over the point.

sag *verb* (**sags, sagging, sagged**)
go down in the middle because something heavy is pressing on it; droop. **sag** *noun*

sage[1] *noun*
a kind of herb used in cooking and formerly used in medicine. [from Latin *salvia* = healing plant]

sage[2] *adjective*
wise. **sagely** *adverb*
sage *noun* (*plural* **sages**)
a wise and respected person. [from Latin *sapere* = to be wise]

sago *noun*
a starchy white food used to make puddings. [from Malay (a language spoken in Malaysia)]

said past tense of **say**.

sail *noun* (*plural* **sails**)
1 a large piece of strong cloth attached to a mast etc. to catch the wind and make a ship or boat move. 2 a short voyage. 3 an arm of a windmill.
sail *verb* (**sails, sailing, sailed**)
1 travel in a ship or boat. 2 start a voyage, *We sail at noon.* 3 control a ship or boat. 4 move quickly and smoothly. **sailing ship** *noun* [from Old English]

sailor *noun* (*plural* **sailors**)
a person who sails; a member of a ship's crew or of a navy.

saint *noun* (*plural* **saints**)
a holy or very good person.
saintly *adverb*, **saintliness** *noun* [via Old English from Latin *sanctus* = holy]

sake *noun*
for the sake of so as to help or please a person, get a thing, etc.

salad *noun* (*plural* salads)
a mixture of vegetables eaten raw or cold.

salary *noun* (*plural* salaries)
a regular wage, usually for a year's work, paid in monthly instalments.
salaried *adjective*
[from Latin *salarium* = salt-money, money given to Roman soldiers to buy salt]

sale *noun* (*plural* sales)
1 selling. 2 a time when things are sold at reduced prices. [from Old Norse]

salient (*say* say-lee-ent) *adjective*
1 jutting out; projecting. 2 most noticeable, *the salient features of the plan*.
[from Latin *saliens* = leaping]

saliva *noun*
the natural liquid in a person's or animal's mouth. **salivary** *adjective* [Latin]

sallow *adjective*
(of the skin) slightly yellow. **sallowness** *noun*
[from Old English]

salmon (*say* sam-on) *noun* (*plural* salmon)
a large edible fish with pink flesh.

salon *noun* (*plural* salons)
1 a large elegant room. 2 a room or shop where a hairdresser etc. receives customers. [French]

saloon *noun* (*plural* saloons)
1 a car with a hard roof and a separate boot. 2 a room where people can sit, drink, etc. [from French *salon*]

salt *noun* (*plural* salts)
1 sodium chloride, the white substance that gives sea water its taste and is used for flavouring food. 2 a chemical compound of a metal and an acid. **salty** *adjective*
salt *verb* (salts, salting, salted)
flavour or preserve food with salt.

salt cellar *noun* (*plural* salt cellars)
a small dish or perforated pot holding salt for use at meals.
[*cellar* from old French *salier* = salt-box]

salute *verb* (salutes, saluting, saluted)
1 raise your right hand to your forehead as a sign of respect. 2 greet. 3 say that you respect or admire something, *We salute this achievement.*
salute *noun* (*plural* salutes)
1 the act of saluting. 2 the firing of guns as a sign of greeting or respect.

salvage *verb* (salvages, salvaging, salvaged)
save or rescue something so that it can be used again. **salvage** *noun*
[from Latin *salvare* = save]

salvation *noun*
1 saving from loss or damage etc. 2 (in Christian teaching) saving the soul from sin and its consequences.
[same origin as *salvage*]

same *adjective*
1 of one kind, exactly alike or equal. 2 not changing; not different. **sameness** *noun*

sample *noun* (*plural* samples)
a small amount that shows what something is like; a specimen.
sample *verb* (samples, sampling, sampled)
take a sample of something.
[from old French *essample* = example]

sanatorium *noun* (*plural* sanatoriums or sanatoria)
a hospital for treating chronic diseases or convalescents. [from Latin *sanare* = heal]

sanctimonious *adjective*
making a show of being virtuous or pious.
[from Latin *sanctimonia* = holiness, piety]

sanction *noun* (*plural* sanctions)
1 permission or authorization. 2 action taken against a nation that is considered to have broken an international law etc., *Sanctions against that country include refusing to trade with it.*
sanction *verb* (sanctions, sanctioning, sanctioned)
permit or authorize.
[from Latin *sancire* = make holy]

sanctity *noun*
being sacred; holiness.

sanctuary *noun* (*plural* sanctuaries)
1 a safe place; a refuge. 2 a sacred place; the part of a church where the altar stands.

sand *noun*
the tiny particles that cover the ground in deserts, seashores, etc.
sand *verb* (sands, sanding, sanded)
smooth or polish with sandpaper or some other rough material. **sander** *noun*
[from Old English]

sandal *noun* (*plural* sandals)
a lightweight shoe with straps over the foot.
sandalled *adjective*
[from Greek *sandalon* = wooden shoe]

sandpaper *noun*
strong paper coated with sand or a similar substance, rubbed on rough surfaces to make them smooth.

sandwich *noun* (*plural* sandwiches)
two or more slices of bread with jam, meat, or cheese etc. between them.
sandwich *verb* (sandwiches, sandwiching, sandwiched)
put a thing between two other things.
[invented by the Earl of Sandwich (1718–92) so that he could eat while gambling]

sandy *adjective*
1 like sand. 2 covered with sand. 3 yellowish-red, *sandy hair*. **sandiness** *noun*

sane *adjective*
1 having a healthy mind; not mad. 2 sensible. **sanely** *adverb*, **sanity** *noun*
[from Latin *sanus* = healthy]

sanitary *adjective*
1 free from germs and dirt; hygienic. 2 to do with sanitation.
[from Latin *sanitas* = health]

sanitary towel *noun* (*plural* **sanitary towels**)
an absorbent pad worn during menstruation.

sanitation *noun*
arrangements for drainage and the disposal of sewage. [from *sanitary*]

sanity *noun*
being sane.

sap *noun*
the liquid inside a plant, carrying food to all its parts.

sap *verb* (**saps, sapping, sapped**)
take away a person's strength gradually.

sapling *noun* (*plural* **saplings**)
a young tree. [from *sap*]

sapphire *noun* (*plural* **sapphires**)
a bright-blue jewel. [from Latin]

sarcastic *adjective*
saying amusing or contemptuous things that hurt someone's feelings.
sarcastically *adverb*, **sarcasm** *noun*
[from Greek *sarkazein* = tear the flesh]

sardine *noun* (*plural* **sardines**)
a small sea fish, usually sold in tins, packed tightly in oil. [from French]

sari *noun* (*plural* **saris**)
a length of cloth worn wrapped round the body as a dress, especially by Indian women and girls. [from Hindi]

sash *noun* (*plural* **sashes**)
a strip of cloth worn round the waist or over one shoulder.
[from Arabic *shash* = turban]

satchel *noun* (*plural* **satchels**)
a bag worn on the shoulder or the back, especially for carrying books to and from school. [from Latin *saccellus* = little sack]

satellite *noun* (*plural* **satellites**)
1 a planet or spacecraft etc. that moves in an orbit round a planet, *The moon is a satellite of the earth.* 2 a country that is under the influence of a more powerful country; a hanger-on.
[from Latin *satelles* = a guard]

satin *noun*
a silky material that is shiny on one side.
satiny *adjective*

satire *noun* (*plural* **satires**)
1 using humour or exaggeration to show what is bad about a person or thing. 2 a play or poem etc. that does this. **satirical** *adjective*, **satirically** *adverb*, **satirist** *noun*, **satirize** *verb* [from Latin]

satisfaction *noun*
1 satisfying. 2 being satisfied and pleased because of this. 3 something that satisfies a desire etc.
[from Latin *satis* = enough + *facere* = make]

satisfactory *adjective*
good enough; sufficient.
satisfactorily *adverb*

satisfy *verb* (**satisfies, satisfying, satisfied**)
1 give a person etc. what is needed or wanted. 2 make someone feel certain; convince, *The firemen were satisfied that the fire was out.*
[same origin as *satisfaction*]

saturate *verb* (**saturates, saturating, saturated**)
1 make a thing very wet. 2 make something take in as much as possible of a substance or goods etc. **saturation** *noun* [from Latin *satur* = full, satiated]

sauce *noun* (*plural* **sauces**)
1 a thick liquid served with food to add flavour. 2 (*informal*) being cheeky; impudence.
[from Latin *salsus* = salted]

saucepan *noun* (*plural* **saucepans**)
a metal cooking pan with a handle at the side.

saucer *noun* (*plural* **saucers**)
a small shallow object on which a cup etc. is placed. [from old French *saussier* = container for sauce]

saucy *adjective* (**saucier, sauciest**)
cheeky or impudent.
saucily *adverb*, **sauciness** *noun*

sauna *noun* (*plural* **saunas**)
a room or compartment filled with steam, used as a kind of bath. [Finnish]

saunter *verb* (**saunters, sauntering, sauntered**)
walk slowly and casually. **saunter** *noun*

sausage *noun* (*plural* **sausages**)
a tube of skin or plastic stuffed with minced meat and other filling.
[from old French; related to *sauce*]

savage *adjective*
wild and fierce; cruel. **savagely** *adverb*, **savageness** *noun*, **savagery** *noun*
savage *noun* (*plural* **savages**)
1 a savage person. 2 (*old use*) a member of a primitive people.
savage *verb* (**savages, savaging, savaged**)
attack by biting, scratching, or trampling, *The sheep was savaged by a dog.*
[from Latin *silvaticus* = of the woods, wild]

save *verb* (**saves, saving, saved**)
1 keep safe; free a person or thing from danger or harm. 2 keep something, especially money, so that it can be used later. 3 avoid wasting something, *This will save time.* 4 (in sports) prevent an opponent from scoring.
save *noun*, **saver** *noun*
[from old French; related to *salvage*]

savings *plural noun*
money saved.

saviour *noun* (*plural* saviours)
a person who saves someone.
the or **our Saviour** (in Christianity) Jesus
Christ.

savoury *adjective*
1 tasty but not sweet. 2 having an appetizing
taste or smell.

saw¹ *noun* (*plural* saws)
a tool with a zigzag edge for cutting wood or
metal etc.
saw *verb* (saws, sawing, sawed, sawn)
1 cut something with a saw. 2 move to and fro
as a saw does. [from Old English]

saw² *past tense* of see.

sawdust *noun*
powder that comes from wood cut by a saw.

saxophone *noun* (*plural* saxophones)
a brass wind instrument with a reed in the
mouthpiece. **saxophonist** *noun*
[named after a Belgian instrument maker,
Adolphe Sax, who invented it]

say *verb* (says, saying, said)
1 speak or express something in words. 2 give
an opinion.
say *noun*
the power to decide something, *I have no say in
the matter.* [from Old English]

saying *noun* (*plural* sayings)
a well-known phrase or proverb or other
statement.

scab *noun* (*plural* scabs)
1 a hard crust that forms over a cut or graze
while it is healing. 2 (*offensive*) a blackleg.
scabby *adjective* [from Old Norse]

scaffold *noun* (*plural* scaffolds)
a platform on which criminals are executed.

scaffolding *noun*
a structure of poles or tubes and planks
making platforms for workers to stand on
while building or repairing a house etc.

scald *verb* (scalds, scalding, scalded)
1 burn yourself with very hot liquid or steam.
2 heat milk until it is nearly boiling. 3 clean
pans etc. with boiling water. **scald** *noun*
[from Latin *excaldare* = wash in hot water]

scale¹ *noun* (*plural* scales)
1 a series of units, degrees, or qualities etc. for
measuring something. 2 a series of musical
notes going up or down in a fixed pattern.
3 proportion or ratio, *The scale of this map is
one centimetre to the kilometre.* 4 the relative
size or importance of something, *They
entertain friends on a large scale.*
to scale with the parts in the same proportions
as those of an original, *The architect's plans
were drawn to scale.*

scale *verb* (scales, scaling, scaled)
climb, *She scaled the ladder.*
scale down or **up** reduce or increase at a fixed
rate, or in proportion to something else.
[from Latin *scala* = ladder]

scale² *noun* (*plural* scales)
1 each of the thin overlapping parts on the
outside of fish, snakes, etc.; a thin flake or part
like this. 2 a hard substance formed in a kettle
or boiler by hard water, or on teeth.
scaly *adjective*
scale *verb* (scales, scaling, scaled)
remove scales or scale from something. [from
old French; related to *scales*]

scale model *noun* (*plural* scale models)
a model of something, made to scale.

scales *plural noun*
a device for weighing things.
[from Old Norse *skal* = bowl]

scalp *noun* (*plural* scalps)
the skin on the top of the head.

scamp *noun* (*plural* scamps)
a rascal. [same origin as *scamper*]

scamper *verb* (scampers, scampering, scampered)
run quickly, lightly, or playfully. **scamper** *noun*
[originally = run away, decamp; probably via
old Dutch from Latin *ex-* = away + *campus*
= field]

scan *verb* (scans, scanning, scanned)
1 look at every part of something. 2 glance at
something. 3 count the beats of a line of poetry;
be correct in rhythm, *This line doesn't scan.*
4 sweep a radar or electronic beam over an
area to examine it or in search of something.
scan *noun* (*plural* scans)
1 scanning. 2 an examination using a scanner.
[from Latin]

scandal *noun* (*plural* scandals)
1 something shameful or disgraceful. 2 gossip
about people's faults and wrongdoing.
scandalous *adjective*
[from Greek *skandalon* = stumbling block]

scandalize *verb* (scandalizes, scandalizing,
scandalized)
shock a person by something considered
shameful or disgraceful.

scanner *noun* (*plural* scanners)
1 a machine that examines things by means of
light or other rays. 2 a machine that converts
printed text, pictures, etc. into machine-
readable form.

scanty *adjective* (scantier, scantiest)
small in amount or extent; meagre, *a scanty
harvest.* **scantily** *adverb*, **scantiness** *noun*

scapegoat *noun* (*plural* scapegoats)
a person who is made to bear the blame or
punishment for what others have done.

[named after the *goat* which the ancient Jews allowed to *escape* into the desert after the priest had symbolically laid the people's sins upon it]

scar noun (*plural* **scars**)
the mark left by a cut or burn etc. after it has healed.
scar verb (**scars, scarring, scarred**)
make a scar or scars on skin etc.

scarce adjective (**scarcer, scarcest**)
1 not enough to supply people. **2** rare.
scarcity noun
make yourself scarce (*informal*) go away; keep out of the way.

scarcely adverb
only just; only with difficulty, *She could scarcely walk.*

scare verb (**scares, scaring, scared**)
frighten.
scare noun (*plural* **scares**)
1 a fright. **2** alarm, mistaken or unnecessary anxiety. [from Old Norse]

scarecrow noun (*plural* **scarecrows**)
a figure of a person dressed in old clothes, set up to frighten birds away from crops.

scarf noun (*plural* **scarves**)
a strip of material worn round the neck or head. [from old French]

scarlet adjective & noun
bright red.

scathing (*say* skayth-ing) adjective
severely criticizing a person or thing. [from Old Norse *skatha* = injure or damage]

scatter verb (**scatters, scattering, scattered**)
throw or send or move in various directions. [a different spelling of *shatter*]

scavenge verb (**scavenges, scavenging, scavenged**)
1 search for useful things amongst rubbish. **2** (of a bird or animal) search for decaying flesh as food. **scavenger** noun

scene noun (*plural* **scenes**)
1 the place where something has happened, *the scene of the crime.* **2** a part of a play or film. **3** a view as seen by a spectator. **4** an angry or noisy outburst, *He made a scene about the money.* **5** stage scenery.
[from Greek *skene* = stage]

scenery noun
1 the natural features of a landscape. **2** things put on a stage to make it look like a place.

scent noun (*plural* **scents**)
1 a pleasant smell. **2** a liquid perfume. **3** an animal's smell that other animals can detect.
scented adjective [from Latin]

sceptical (*say* skep-tik-al) adjective
inclined to question things; not believing easily. **sceptically** adverb, **scepticism** noun
[from Greek *skeptikos* = thoughtful]

sceptre noun (*plural* **sceptres**)
a rod carried by a king or queen as a symbol of power. [from old French]

schedule (*say* shed-yool) noun (*plural* **schedules**)
a programme or timetable of planned events or work. [from Latin *scedula* = little piece of paper]

schematic (*say* skee-mat-ik) adjective
in the form of a diagram or chart.
[same origin as *scheme*]

scheme noun (*plural* **schemes**)
a plan of action.
scheme verb (**schemes, scheming, schemed**)
make plans; plot. **schemer** noun
[from Greek *schema* = form]

scholar noun (*plural* **scholars**)
1 a person who has studied a subject thoroughly. **2** a person who has been awarded a scholarship. **scholarly** adjective [from Latin *scholaris* = to do with a school]

scholarship noun (*plural* **scholarships**)
1 a grant of money given to someone to help to pay for his or her education. **2** scholars' knowledge or methods; advanced study.

school[1] noun (*plural* **schools**)
1 a place where teaching is done, especially of pupils aged 5–18. **2** the pupils in a school. **3** the time when teaching takes place in a school, *School begins at 9 a.m.* **4** a group of people who have the same beliefs or style of work etc.
school verb (**schools, schooling, schooled**)
train, *She was schooling her horse for the competition.* [from Greek]

school[2] noun (*plural* **schools**)
a shoal of fish or whales etc. [from old German or old Dutch *schole* = a troop]

schoolchild noun (*plural* **schoolchildren**)
a child who goes to school.
schoolboy noun, **schoolgirl** noun

schooling noun
1 training. **2** education, especially in a school.

schoolteacher noun (*plural* **schoolteachers**)
a person who teaches in a school.
schoolmaster noun, **schoolmistress** noun

science noun
the study of chemistry, physics, plants and animals, etc.
[from Latin *scientia* = knowledge]

science fiction noun
stories about imaginary scientific discoveries or space travel and life on other planets.

scientific adjective
1 to do with science or scientists. **2** studying things systematically and testing ideas carefully. **scientifically** adverb

scientist noun (*plural* **scientists**)
1 an expert in science. **2** someone who uses scientific methods.

scintillate *verb* (scintillates, scintillating, scintillated)
1 sparkle. 2 be lively and witty.
scintillation *noun* [from Latin *scintilla* = spark]

scissors *plural noun*
a cutting instrument used with one hand, with two blades pivoted so that they can close against each other.
[from Latin *scissum* = cut]

scoff *verb* (scoffs, scoffing, scoffed)
jeer; speak contemptuously. **scoffer** *noun*

scold *verb* (scolds, scolding, scolded)
to speak angrily; to tell someone off.
scolding *noun* [probably from Old Norse]

scone (*say* skon *or* skohn) *noun* (*plural* scones)
a soft flat cake, usually eaten with butter.

scoop *noun* (*plural* scoops)
1 a kind of deep spoon for serving ice cream etc. 2 a deep shovel for lifting grain, sugar, etc. 3 a scooping movement. 4 an important piece of news published by only one newspaper.
scoop *verb* (scoops, scooping, scooped)
lift or hollow something out with a scoop.

scoot *verb* (scoots, scooting, scooted)
1 propel a bicycle or scooter by sitting or standing on it and pushing it along with one foot. 2 run or go away quickly.

scooter *noun* (*plural* scooters)
1 a kind of motorcycle with small wheels. 2 a board with wheels and a long handle, which you ride on by scooting. [from *scoot*]

scope *noun*
1 opportunity to work, *This job gives scope for your musical abilities.* 2 the range or extent of a subject.
[from Greek *skopos* = target]

scorch *verb* (scorches, scorching, scorched)
make something go brown by burning it slightly. [origin unknown]

scorched-earth policy *noun*
the burning of crops and destruction of anything that might be useful to an opposing army.

score *noun* (*plural* scores or, in sense 2, score)
1 the number of points or goals made in a game; a result. 2 (*old use*) twenty, *'Three score years and ten' means 3 × 20 + 10 = 70 years.* 3 written or printed music.
on that score for that reason, because of that, *You needn't worry on that score.*
score *verb* (scores, scoring, scored)
1 get a point or goal in a game. 2 keep a count of the score. 3 mark with lines or cuts. 4 write out a musical score. **scorer** *noun* [from Old Norse]

scores *plural noun*
many; a large number.

scorn *noun*
contempt.
scornful *adjective*, **scornfully** *adverb*
scorn *verb* (scorns, scorning, scorned)
1 treat someone with contempt. 2 refuse something scornfully.

scorpion *noun* (*plural* scorpions)
an animal that looks like a tiny lobster, with a poisonous sting. [from Greek]

Scot *noun* (*plural* Scots)
a person who comes from Scotland.

scotch[1] *noun*
whisky made in Scotland. [from *Scottish*]

scotch[2] *verb* (scotches, scotching, scotched)
put an end to an idea or rumour etc.
[origin unknown]

scot-free *adjective*
without harm or punishment.
[from *scot* = a form of tax + *free*]

Scots *adjective*
from or belonging to Scotland.

USAGE: See note at *Scottish*.

Scottish *adjective*
to do with or belonging to Scotland.

USAGE: *Scottish* is the most widely used word for describing things to do with Scotland: *Scottish education, Scottish mountains. Scots* is less common and is mainly used to describe people: *a Scots girl. Scotch* is only used in fixed expressions like *Scotch egg* and *Scotch terrier.*

scoundrel *noun* (*plural* scoundrels)
a wicked or dishonest person.

scour[1] *verb* (scours, scouring, scoured)
1 rub something until it is clean and bright. 2 clear a channel or pipe by the force of water flowing through it.
scourer *noun*
[from *ex-* + *curare* = take care of, clean]

scour[2] *verb* (scours, scouring, scoured)
search thoroughly. [origin unknown]

scourge (*say* skerj) *noun* (*plural* scourges)
1 a whip for flogging people. 2 something that inflicts suffering or punishment.
[from *ex-* + Latin *corrigia* = whip]

Scout *noun* (*plural* Scouts)
a member of the Scout Association, an organization for boys.

scout *noun* (*plural* scouts)
someone sent out to collect information.
scout *verb* (scouts, scouting, scouted)
1 act as a scout. 2 search an area thoroughly.
[from Latin *auscultare* = listen]

scowl *noun* (*plural* scowls)
a bad-tempered frown.

scowl verb (scowls, scowling, scowled)
make a scowl.

scrabble verb (scrabbles, scrabbling, scrabbled)
1 scratch or claw at something with the hands
or feet. 2 grope or struggle to get something.
[from old Dutch]

scraggy adjective
thin and bony. [origin unknown]

scramble verb (scrambles, scrambling, scrambled)
1 move quickly and awkwardly. 2 struggle to
do or get something. 3 (of aircraft or their
crew) hurry and take off quickly. 4 cook eggs
by mixing them up and heating them in a pan.
5 mix things together. 6 alter a radio or
telephone signal so that it cannot be used
without a decoding device. **scrambler** noun
scramble noun (plural scrambles)
1 a climb or walk over rough ground. 2 a
struggle to do or get something. 3 a motor-cycle
race over rough ground.

scrap¹ noun (plural scraps)
1 a small piece. 2 rubbish; waste material,
especially metal that is suitable for
reprocessing.
scrap verb (scraps, scrapping, scrapped)
get rid of something that is useless or
unwanted. [from Old Norse]

scrap² noun (plural scraps) (informal)
a fight.
scrap verb (scraps, scrapping, scrapped)
(informal)
fight. [probably from scrape]

scrape verb (scrapes, scraping, scraped)
1 clean or smooth or damage something by
passing something hard over it. 2 remove by
scraping, Scrape the mud off your shoes. 3 pass
with difficulty, We scraped through. 4 get
something by great effort or care, They scraped
together enough money for a holiday.
scraper noun
scrape noun (plural scrapes)
1 a scraping movement or sound. 2 a mark etc.
made by scraping. 3 an awkward situation
caused by mischief or foolishness.
[from Old English]

scrappy adjective
1 made of scraps or bits or disconnected
things. 2 carelessly done. **scrappiness** noun

scratch verb (scratches, scratching, scratched)
1 mark or cut the surface of a thing with
something sharp. 2 rub the skin with
fingernails or claws because it itches.
3 withdraw from a race or competition.
scratch noun (plural scratches)
1 a mark made by scratching. 2 the action of
scratching. **scratchy** adjective
start from scratch start from the beginning or
with nothing prepared.
up to scratch up to the proper standard.

scrawl noun (plural scrawls)
untidy handwriting.

scrawl verb (scrawls, scrawling, scrawled)
write in a scrawl. [origin unknown]

scrawny adjective
scraggy.

scream noun (plural screams)
1 a loud cry of pain, fear, anger, or excitement.
2 a loud piercing sound. 3 (informal) a very
amusing person or thing.
scream verb (screams, screaming, screamed)
make a scream. [origin unknown]

screech noun (plural screeches)
a harsh high-pitched scream or sound.
screech verb [imitating the sound]

screen noun (plural screens)
1 a thing that protects, hides, or divides
something. 2 a surface on which films or
television pictures are shown. 3 a windscreen.
screen verb (screens, screening, screened)
1 protect, hide, or divide with a screen. 2 show
a film or television pictures on a screen.
3 examine carefully, e.g. to check whether a
person is suitable for a job or whether a
substance is present in something. 4 sift gravel
etc.

screenplay noun (plural screenplays)
the script of a film, with instructions to the
actors etc.

screw noun (plural screws)
1 a metal pin with a spiral ridge (the thread)
round it, holding things together by being
twisted in. 2 a twisting movement.
3 something twisted. 4 a propeller, especially
for a ship or motor boat.
screw verb (screws, screwing, screwed)
1 fasten with a screw or screws. 2 twist.

screwdriver noun (plural screwdrivers)
a tool for turning screws.

scribble verb (scribbles, scribbling, scribbled)
1 write quickly or untidily or carelessly.
2 make meaningless marks. **scribble** noun
[from Latin scribere = write]

script noun (plural scripts)
1 handwriting. 2 the text of a play, film,
broadcast talk, etc.
[from Latin scriptum = written]

scripture noun (plural scriptures)
1 sacred writings. 2 (in Christianity)
the Bible. [same origin as script]

scroll noun (plural scrolls)
1 a roll of paper or parchment used for writing
on. 2 a spiral design.
scroll verb (scrolls, scrolling, scrolled)
move the display on a computer screen up or
down to see what comes before or after it.
[from old French]

scrounge verb (scrounges, scrounging,
scrounged)
cadge. **scrounger** noun [from an old word
scringe = squeeze roughly]

scrub¹ *verb* (scrubs, scrubbing, scrubbed)
1 rub with a hard brush, especially to clean something. 2 (*informal*) cancel.
scrub *noun*
[probably from old German or old Dutch]

scrub² *noun*
1 low trees and bushes. 2 land covered with these. [from *shrub*]

scrubby *adjective*
undersized and shabby or wretched. [from *scrub²*]

scruff *noun*
the back of the neck. [from Old Norse]

scruffy *adjective*
shabby and untidy.
scruffily *adverb*, **scruffiness** *noun*
[a different spelling of *scurfy*]

scrum *noun* (*plural* scrums)
1 (also **scrummage**) a group of players from each side in Rugby football who push against each other and try to heel out the ball which is thrown between them. 2 a crowd pushing against each other.

scruple *noun* (*plural* scruples)
a feeling of doubt or hesitation when your conscience tells you that an action would be wrong.
scruple *verb* (scruples, scrupling, scrupled)
have scruples, *He would not scruple to betray us.* [from Latin]

scrupulous *adjective*
1 very careful and conscientious. 2 strictly honest or honourable. **scrupulously** *adverb*
[from *scruple*]

scrutinize *verb* (scrutinizes, scrutinizing, scrutinized)
examine or look at something carefully.
scrutiny *noun* [from Latin *scrutari*
= examine, (originally) = sort rags]

scuba diving *noun*
swimming underwater using a tank of air strapped to your back.
[from the initials of *self-contained underwater breathing apparatus*]

scuff *verb* (scuffs, scuffing, scuffed)
1 drag your feet while walking. 2 scrape with your foot; mark or damage something by doing this. [origin unknown]

scuffle *noun* (*plural* scuffles)
a confused fight or struggle.
scuffle *verb* (scuffles, scuffling, scuffled)
take part in a scuffle.
[probably from a Scandinavian language]

scullery *noun* (*plural* sculleries)
a room where dishes etc. are washed up. [from Latin *scutella* = small dish]

sculptor *noun* (*plural* sculptors)
a person who makes sculptures.

sculpture *noun* (*plural* sculptures)
1 making shapes by carving wood or stone or casting metal. 2 a shape made in this way.
sculpture *verb*
[from Latin *sculpere* = carve]

scum *noun*
1 froth or dirt on top of a liquid. 2 worthless people.

scuttle¹ *noun* (*plural* scuttles)
a bucket or container for coal in a house. [via Old Norse from Latin *scutella* = dish]

scuttle² *verb* (scuttles, scuttling, scuttled)
scurry; hurry away. [from *scud*]

scuttle³ *verb* (scuttles, scuttling, scuttled)
sink a ship deliberately by letting water into it. [probably from Spanish *escotar* = cut out]

scythe *noun* (*plural* scythes)
a tool with a long curved blade for cutting grass or corn.
scythe *verb* (scythes, scything, scythed)
cut with a scythe. [from Old English]

SE *abbreviation*
1 south-east. 2 south-eastern.

se- *prefix*
1 apart or aside (as in *secluded*). 2 without (as in *secure*). [Latin]

sea *noun* (*plural* seas)
1 the salt water that covers most of the earth's surface; a part of this. 2 a large lake, *the Sea of Galilee.* 3 a large area of something, *a sea of faces.*
at sea 1 on the sea. **2** not knowing what to do.

sea anemone *noun* (*plural* sea anemones)
a sea creature with short tentacles round its mouth.

seaboard *noun* (*plural* seaboards)
a coastline or coastal region.

sea breeze *noun* (*plural* sea breezes)
a breeze blowing from the sea onto the land.

seafaring *adjective* & *noun*
working or travelling on the sea.
seafarer *noun*

seafood *noun*
fish or shellfish from the sea eaten as food.

seagull *noun* (*plural* seagulls)
a seabird with long wings.

seal¹ *noun* (*plural* seals)
a sea mammal with thick fur or bristles, that breeds on land. [from Old English]

seal² *noun* (*plural* seals)
1 a piece of metal with an engraved design for pressing on a soft substance to leave an impression. 2 this impression. 3 something designed to close an opening and prevent air or liquid etc. from getting in or out. 4 a small decorative sticker, *Christmas seals.*

seal *verb* (seals, sealing, sealed)
1 close something by sticking two parts together. 2 close securely; stop up. 3 press a seal on something.
seal off prevent people getting to an area. [from old French; related to *sign*]

sea level *noun*
the level of the sea halfway between high and low tide.

sealing-wax *noun*
a substance that is soft when heated but hardens when cooled, used for sealing documents or for marking with a seal.

sea lion *noun* (*plural* **sea lions**)
a kind of large seal that lives in the Pacific Ocean.

seam *noun* (*plural* **seams**)
1 the line where two edges of cloth or wood etc. join. 2 a layer of coal in the ground. [from Old English]

seamanship *noun*
skill in seafaring.

seamy *adjective*
seamy side the less attractive side or part, *Police see a lot of the seamy side of life.* [originally, the 'wrong' side of a piece of sewing, where the rough edges of the seams show]

sear *verb* (sears, searing, seared)
scorch or burn the surface of something.

search *verb* (searches, searching, searched)
look very carefully in a place etc. in order to find something. **search** *noun*, **searcher** *noun* [from old French]

searchlight *noun* (*plural* **searchlights**)
a light with a strong beam that can be turned in any direction.

search party *noun* (*plural* **search parties**)
a group of people organized to search for a missing person or thing.

search warrant *noun* (*plural* **search warrants**)
an official document giving the police permission to search private property.

seasick *adjective*
sick because of the movement of a ship.
seasickness *noun*

seaside *noun*
a place by the sea where people go for holidays.

season *noun* (*plural* **seasons**)
1 each of the four main parts of the year (spring, summer, autumn, winter). 2 the time of year when something happens, *the football season.*
in season available and ready for eating, *Strawberries are in season in the summer.*
season *verb* (seasons, seasoning, seasoned)
1 give extra flavour to food by adding salt, pepper, or other strong-tasting substances.

2 dry and treat timber etc. to make it ready for use. [from Latin *satio* = time for sowing seed]

seasonable *adjective*
suitable for the season, *Hot weather is seasonable in summer.* **seasonably** *adverb*

USAGE: Do not confuse with *seasonal.*

seasonal *adjective*
1 for or to do with a season. 2 happening in a particular season, *Fruit-picking is seasonal work.* **seasonally** *adverb*

USAGE: Do not confuse with *seasonable.*

seasoning *noun* (*plural* **seasonings**)
a substance used to season food.

season ticket *noun* (*plural* **season tickets**)
a ticket that can be used as often as you like throughout a period of time.

seat *noun* (*plural* **seats**)
1 a thing made or used for sitting on. 2 the right to be a member of a council, committee, parliament, etc., *She won the seat ten years ago.* 3 the buttocks; the part of a skirt or trousers covering these. 4 the place where something is based or located, *London is the seat of our government.*
seat *verb* (seats, seating, seated)
1 place in or on a seat. 2 have seats for, *The theatre seats 3,000 people.*

seat belt *noun* (*plural* **seat belts**)
a strap to hold a person securely in a seat.

seating *noun*
1 the seats in a place, *seating for 400.* 2 the arrangement of seats, *a seating plan.*

seaweed *noun*
a plant or plants that grow in the sea.

seaworthy *adjective*
(of a ship) fit for a sea voyage.
seaworthiness *noun*

secateurs *plural noun*
clippers held in the hand for pruning plants. [French, from Latin *secare* = to cut]

secluded *adjective*
screened or sheltered from view.
seclusion *noun*
[from *se-* + Latin *claudere* = shut]

second[1] *adjective*
1 next after the first. 2 another, *a second chance.* 3 less good, *second quality.*
secondly *adverb*
second *noun* (*plural* **seconds**)
1 a person or thing that is second. 2 an attendant of a fighter in a boxing match, duel, etc. 3 a thing that is of second (not the best) quality. 4 one-sixtieth of a minute of time or of a degree used in measuring angles.

second

second *verb* (seconds, seconding, seconded)
1 assist someone. 2 support a proposal, motion, etc. **seconder** *noun*
[from Latin *secundus* = next]

second[2] (*say* sik-ond) *verb* (seconds, seconding, seconded)
transfer a person temporarily to another job or department etc. **secondment** *noun* [from French *en second* = in the second rank (because officers seconded to another company served under officers who belonged to that company)]

secondary *adjective*
1 coming after or from something. 2 less important. 3 (of education etc.) for children of more than about 11 years old, *a secondary school.* (Compare *primary.*)

second-hand *adjective*
1 bought or used after someone else has owned it. 2 selling used goods, *a second-hand shop.*

second nature *noun*
behaviour that has become automatic or a habit, *Lying is second nature to him.*

second-rate *adjective*
inferior; not very good.

secret *adjective*
1 that must not be told or shown to other people. 2 not known by everybody. 3 working secretly.
secretly *adverb*, **secrecy** *noun*
secret *noun* (*plural* secrets)
something secret.
[from Latin *secretum* = set apart]

secretary (*say* sek-rit-ree) *noun* (*plural* secretaries)
1 a person whose job is to help with letters, answer the telephone, and make business arrangements for a person or organization. 2 the chief assistant of a government minister or ambassador.
secretarial *adjective*
[from Latin *secretarius* = an officer or servant allowed to know your secrets]

secrete (*say* sik-reet) *verb* (secretes, secreting, secreted)
1 hide something. 2 produce a substance in the body, *Saliva is secreted in the mouth.*
secretion *noun* [same origin as *secret*]

secretive (*say* seek-rit-iv) *adjective*
liking or trying to keep things secret.
secretively *adverb*, **secretiveness** *noun*

secret police *noun*
a police force which works in secret for political purposes, not to deal with crime.

secret service *noun*
a government department responsible for espionage.

sect *noun* (*plural* sects)
a group whose beliefs differ from those of others in the same religion; a faction.

section *noun* (*plural* sections)
1 a part of something. 2 a cross-section. [from Latin *sectum* = cut]

sector *noun* (*plural* sectors)
1 one part of an area. 2 a part of something, *the private sector of industry.*
[from Latin *secare* = to cut]

secular *adjective*
to do with worldly affairs, not spiritual or religious matters.
[from Latin *saecularis* = worldly]

secure *adjective*
1 safe, especially against attack. 2 certain not to slip or fail. 3 reliable. **securely** *adverb*
secure *verb* (secures, securing, secured)
1 make a thing secure. 2 obtain, *We secured two tickets for the show.*
[from *se-* + Latin *cura* = care]

security *noun* (*plural* securities)
1 being secure; safety. 2 precautions against theft or spying etc. 3 something given as a guarantee that a promise will be kept or a debt repaid. 4 investments such as stocks and shares.

security guard *noun* (*plural* security guards)
a person employed to guard a building or its contents against theft and vandalism.

security risk *noun* (*plural* security risks)
a person or situation thought likely to threaten the security of a country.

sedate *adjective*
calm and dignified.
sedately *adverb*, **sedateness** *noun*
sedate *verb* (sedates, sedating, sedated)
give a sedative to. **sedation** *noun*
[from Latin *sedatum* = made calm]

sedative (*say* sed-a-tiv) *noun* (*plural* sedatives)
a medicine that makes a person calm. [from Latin *sedare* = settle]

sedentary (*say* sed-en-ter-ee) *adjective*
done sitting down, *sedentary work.*
[from Latin *sedens* = sitting]

sedge *noun*
a grass-like plant growing in marshes or near water. [from Old English]

sediment *noun*
fine particles of solid matter that float in liquid or sink to the bottom of it.
[from Latin *sedere* = sit]

sedimentary *adjective*
formed from particles that have settled on a surface, *sedimentary rocks.*

sedition *noun*
speeches or actions intended to make people rebel against the authority of the State.
seditious *adjective*
[from *se-* + Latin *itio* = going]

seduce *verb* (seduces, seducing, seduced)
1 persuade a person to have sexual intercourse. 2 attract or lead astray by offering temptations. **seducer** *noun*, **seduction** *noun*, **seductive** *adjective*
[from *se-* + Latin *ducere* = to lead]

see *verb* (sees, seeing, saw, seen)
1 perceive with the eyes. 2 meet or visit somebody, *See a doctor about your cough.*
3 understand, *She saw what I meant.*
4 imagine, *Can you see yourself as a teacher?*
5 consider, *I will see what can be done.* 6 make sure, *See that the windows are shut.* 7 discover, *See who is at the door.* 8 escort, *See her to the door.*
see through not be deceived by something.
see to attend to.

seed *noun* (*plural* seeds or seed)
1 a fertilized part of a plant, capable of growing into a new plant. 2 (*old use*) descendants. 3 a seeded player.
seed *verb* (seeds, seeding, seeded)
1 plant or sprinkle seeds in something. 2 name the best players and arrange for them not to play against each other in the early rounds of a tournament.

seedling *noun* (*plural* seedlings)
a very young plant growing from a seed.

seedy *adjective* (seedier, seediest)
1 full of seeds. 2 shabby and disreputable.
seediness *noun*

seeing *conjunction*
considering, *Seeing that we have all finished, let's go.*

seek *verb* (seeks, seeking, sought)
1 search for. 2 try to obtain.

seem *verb* (seems, seeming, seemed)
give the impression of being something, *She seems worried about her work.*
seemingly *adverb* [from Old Norse]

seemly *adjective* (*old use*)
(of behaviour etc.) proper or suitable.
seemliness *noun*
[from an old sense of *seem* = be suitable]

seep *verb* (seeps, seeping, seeped)
ooze slowly out or through something.
seepage *noun* [probably from Old English]

see-saw *noun* (*plural* see-saws)
a plank balanced in the middle so that two people can sit, one on each end, and make it go up and down.
[from an old rhyme which imitated the rhythm of a saw going to and fro, later used by children on a see-saw]

seethe *verb* (seethes, seething, seethed)
1 bubble and surge like water boiling. 2 be very angry or excited. [from Old English]

segment *noun* (*plural* segments)
a part that is cut off or separates naturally from other parts, *the segments of an orange.*
segmented *adjective* [from Latin]

segregate *verb* (segregates, segregating, segregated)
1 separate people of different religions, races, etc. 2 isolate a person or thing. **segregation** *noun*
[from *se-* + Latin *gregis* = from a flock]

seismic (*say* sy-zmik) *adjective*
to do with earthquakes or other vibrations of the earth.
[from Greek *seismos* = earthquake]

seize *verb* (seizes, seizing, seized)
1 take hold of a person or thing suddenly or forcibly. 2 take eagerly, *Seize your chance!*
3 have a sudden effect on, *Panic seized us.*
seize up become jammed, especially because of friction or overheating.
[via old French from Germanic]

seizure *noun* (*plural* seizures)
1 seizing. 2 a sudden fit, as in epilepsy or a heart attack.

seldom *adverb*
rarely; not often. [from Old English]

select *verb* (selects, selecting, selected)
choose a person or thing. **selector** *noun*
select *adjective*
1 carefully chosen, *a select group of pupils.* 2 (of a club etc.) choosing its members carefully; exclusive.
[from *se-* + Latin *lectus* = collected]

selection *noun* (*plural* selections)
1 selecting; being selected. 2 a person or thing selected. 3 a group selected from a larger group. 4 a range of goods from which to choose.

self *noun* (*plural* selves)
1 a person as an individual. 2 a person's particular nature, *She has recovered and is her old self again.* 3 a person's own advantage, *He always puts self first.*
[from Old English]

self- *prefix*
1 of or to or done by yourself or itself.
2 automatic (as in *self-loading*).

self-assured *adjective*
confident.

self-centred *adjective*
selfish.

self-confident *adjective*
confident of your own abilities.

self-conscious *adjective*
embarrassed or unnatural because you know that people are watching you.

self-contained *adjective*
(of accommodation) complete in itself; containing all the necessary facilities.

self-control *noun*
the ability to control your own behaviour.
self-controlled *adjective*

self-denial *noun*
deliberately going without things you would like to have.

self-determination *noun*
a country's right to rule itself and choose its own government.

self-employed *adjective*
working independently, not for an employer.

self-esteem *noun*
your own opinion of yourself and your own worth.

self-evident *adjective*
obvious and not needing proof or explanation.

self-important *adjective*
pompous.

selfish *adjective*
doing what you want and not thinking of other people; keeping things for yourself.
selfishly *adverb*, **selfishness** *noun*

selfless *adjective*
unselfish.

self-made *adjective*
rich or successful because of your own efforts.

self-pity *noun*
too much sorrow and pity for yourself and your own problems.

self-possessed *adjective*
calm and dignified.

self-raising *adjective*
(of flour) making cakes rise without needing to have baking powder etc. added.

self-respect *noun*
your own proper respect for yourself.

self-righteous *adjective*
smugly sure that you are behaving virtuously.

self-service *adjective*
where customers help themselves to things and pay a cashier for what they have taken.

self-sufficient *adjective*
able to produce or provide what you need without help from others.

self-supporting *adjective*
earning enough to keep yourself without needing money from others.

sell *verb* (**sells, selling, sold**)
exchange something for money. **seller** *noun*
sell out 1 sell all your stock of something.
2 (*informal*) betray someone.
sell *noun*
1 (*informal*) a deception. **2** the manner of selling something.
hard sell *noun* forceful selling; putting pressure

on someone to buy.
soft sell selling by suggestion or gentle persuasion.

sell-out *noun* (*plural* **sell-outs**)
an entertainment, sporting event, etc. for which all the tickets have been sold.

selves *plural* of **self**.

semaphore *noun*
a system of signalling by holding the arms in positions that indicate letters of the alphabet.
[from Greek *sema* = sign + *-phoros* = carrying]

semen (*say* **seem**-en) *noun*
a white liquid produced by males and containing sperm.
[Latin, from *semere* = to sow]

semi *noun* (*plural* **semis**) (*informal*)
a semi-detached house.

semi- *prefix*
1 half. **2** partly. [from Latin]

semibreve *noun* (*plural* **semibreves**)
the longest musical note normally used (**o**), lasting four times as long as a crotchet.

semicircle *noun* (*plural* **semicircles**)
half a circle. **semicircular** *adjective*

semicolon *noun* (*plural* **semicolons**)
a punctuation mark (;) used to mark a break that is more than that marked by a comma.

semiconductor *noun* (*plural* **semiconductors**)
a substance that can conduct electricity but not as well as most metals do.

semi-detached *adjective*
(of a house) joined to another house on one side only.

semifinal *noun* (*plural* **semifinals**)
a match or round whose winner will take part in the final.

seminar *noun* (*plural* **seminars**)
a meeting for advanced discussion and research on a subject.
[German; related to *seminary*]

semiquaver *noun* (*plural* **semiquavers**)
a note in music (♪), equal in length to one quarter of a crotchet.

Semitic (*say* sim-it-ik) *adjective*
to do with the Semites, the group of people that includes the Jews and Arabs.
Semite (*say* see-my't) *noun*

semitone *noun* (*plural* **semitones**)
half a tone in music.

semolina *noun*
hard round grains of wheat used to make milk puddings and pasta.
[from Italian *semola* = bran]

senate *noun* (*plural* **senates**)
1 the governing council in ancient Rome. **2** the upper house of the parliament of the United

States, France, and certain other countries.

senator *noun*
[from Latin *senatus* = council of elders]

send *verb* (sends, sending, sent)
1 make a person or thing go somewhere.
2 cause to become, *It sent them mad.*
sender *noun*
send for order a person or thing to come or be brought to you.
send up (*informal*) make fun of something by imitating it.

senile (*say* seen-I'll) *adjective*
weak or confused and forgetful because of old age. **senility** *noun*
[from Latin *senilis* = old]

senior *adjective*
1 older than someone else. 2 higher in rank.
3 for older children, *a senior school.*
seniority *noun*
senior *noun* (*plural* seniors)
1 a person who is older or higher in rank than you are, *He is my senior.* 2 a member of a senior school. [Latin, = older]

senior citizen *noun* (*plural* senior citizens)
an elderly person, especially a pensioner.

sensation *noun* (*plural* sensations)
1 a feeling, *a sensation of warmth.* 2 a very excited condition; something causing this, *The news caused a great sensation.*
[from Latin *sensus* = sense]

sensational *adjective*
1 causing great excitement, interest, or shock.
2 (*informal*) very good; wonderful.
sensationally *adverb*

sense *noun* (*plural* senses)
1 the ability to see, hear, smell, touch, or taste things. 2 the ability to feel or appreciate something; awareness, *a sense of humour.* 3 the power to think or make wise decisions, *He hasn't got the sense to come in out of the rain.*
4 meaning, *The word 'run' has many senses.*
make sense 1 have a meaning. 2 be a sensible idea.
sense *verb* (senses, sensing, sensed)
1 feel; get an impression, *I sensed that she did not like me.* 2 detect something, *This device senses radioactivity.* [from Latin]

senseless *adjective*
1 stupid; not showing good sense.
2 unconscious.

senses *plural noun*
sanity, *He is out of his senses.*

sensible *adjective*
wise; having or showing good sense.
sensibly *adverb*

sensitive *adjective*
1 receiving impressions quickly and easily, *sensitive fingers.* 2 easily hurt or offended, *She is very sensitive about her age.* 3 affected by

something, *Photographic paper is sensitive to light.*
sensitively *adverb*, **sensitivity** *noun*

sensor *noun* (*plural* sensors)
a device or instrument for detecting a physical property such as light, heat, or sound.

sentence *noun* (*plural* sentences)
1 a group of words that express a complete thought and form a statement, question, exclamation, or command. 2 the punishment announced to a convicted person in a lawcourt.
sentence *verb* (sentences, sentencing, sentenced)
give someone a sentence in a lawcourt, *The judge sentenced him to a year in prison.*
[from Latin *sententia* = opinion]

sententious *adjective*
giving moral advice in a pompous way.
[same origin as *sentence*]

sentiment *noun* (*plural* sentiments)
1 an opinion. 2 sentimentality.
[from Latin *sentire* = feel]

sentimental *adjective*
showing or arousing tenderness or romantic feeling or foolish emotion.
sentimentally *adverb*, **sentimentality** *noun*

sentinel *noun* (*plural* sentinels)
a sentry. [via French from Italian]

sentry *noun* (*plural* sentries)
a soldier guarding something.

separate *adjective*
1 not joined to anything. 2 not shared.
separately *adverb*
separate *verb* (separates, separating, separated)
1 make or keep separate; divide. 2 become separate. 3 stop living together as a married couple. **separation** *noun*, **separator** *noun*
[from se- + Latin *parare* = prepare]

septic *adjective*
infected with harmful bacteria that cause pus to form.
[from Greek *septikos* = made rotten]

sepulchre (*say* sep-ul-ker) *noun* (*plural* sepulchres)
a tomb. [from Latin *sepultum* = buried]

sequel *noun* (*plural* sequels)
1 a book or film etc. that continues the story of an earlier one. 2 something that follows or results from an earlier event.
[from Latin *sequi* = follow]

sequence *noun* (*plural* sequences)
1 the following of one thing after another; the order in which things happen. 2 a series of things.
[from Latin *sequens* = following]

seraph *noun* (*plural* seraphim or seraphs)
a kind of angel. [from Hebrew]

serenade *noun* (*plural* serenades)
a song or tune played by a lover to his lady.

serenade *verb* (serenades, serenading, serenaded)
sing or play a serenade to someone.
[via French from Italian *sereno* = serene]

serene *adjective*
calm and cheerful.
serenely *adverb*, **serenity** *noun*

serf *noun* (*plural* serfs)
a farm labourer who worked for a landowner in the Middle Ages, and who was not allowed to leave. **serfdom** *noun* [same origin as *servant*]

sergeant (*say* sar-jent) *noun* (*plural* sergeants)
a soldier or policeman who is in charge of others. [from old French; related to *serve*]

sergeant major *noun* (*plural* sergeant majors)
a soldier who is one rank higher than a sergeant. [from *sergeant* + *major* = greater]

serial *noun* (*plural* serials)
a story or film etc. that is presented in separate parts. [from *series*]

USAGE: Do not confuse with *cereal*.

---

serial killer *noun* (*plural* serial killers)
a person who commits a series of murders for no apparent reason.

serial number *noun* (*plural* serial numbers)
a number put onto an object, usually by the manufacturers, to distinguish it from other identical objects.

series *noun* (*plural* series)
1 a number of things following or connected with each other. 2 a number of games or matches between the same competitors. 3 a number of separate radio or television programmes with the same characters or on the same subject.
[Latin, = row or chain]

serious *adjective*
1 solemn and thoughtful; not smiling. 2 sincere; not casual; not light-hearted, *a serious attempt*. 3 causing anxiety, not trivial, *a serious accident*.
seriously *adverb*, **seriousness** *noun* [from Latin]

sermon *noun* (*plural* sermons)
a talk given by a preacher, especially as part of a religious service.
[from Latin *sermo* = talk, conversation]

serpent *noun* (*plural* serpents)
a snake. [from Latin *serpens* = creeping]

serried *adjective*
arranged in rows close together, *serried ranks of troops*.
[from Latin *serere* = join together]

servant *noun* (*plural* servants)
a person whose job is to work or serve in someone else's house.
[from Latin *servus* = slave]

serve *verb* (serves, serving, served)
1 work for a person or organization or country etc. 2 sell things to people in a shop. 3 give out food to people at a meal. 4 spend time in something; undergo, *He served a prison sentence.* 5 be suitable for something, *This will serve our purpose.* 6 start play in tennis etc. by hitting the ball. **server** *noun*
it serves you right you deserve it.

serve *noun* (*plural* serves)
a service in tennis etc.
[same origin as *servant*]

service *noun* (*plural* services)
1 working for a person or organization or country etc. 2 something that helps people or supplies what they want, *a bus service.* 3 the army, navy, or air force, *the armed services.* 4 a religious ceremony. 5 providing people with goods, food, etc., *quick service.* 6 a set of dishes and plates etc. for a meal, *a dinner service.* 7 the servicing of a vehicle or machine etc. 8 the action of serving in tennis etc.

service *verb* (services, servicing, serviced)
1 repair or keep a vehicle or machine etc. in working order. 2 supply with services. [from Latin *servitium* = slavery]

serviceable *adjective*
usable; suitable for ordinary use or wear.

services *plural noun*
an area beside a main road with a garage, shop, restaurant, lavatories, etc. for travellers to use.

serviette *noun* (*plural* serviettes)
a piece of cloth or paper used to keep your clothes or hands clean at a meal.
[French, from *servir* = to serve]

serving *noun* (*plural* servings)
a helping of food.

session *noun* (*plural* sessions)
1 a meeting or series of meetings, *The Queen will open the next session of Parliament.* 2 a time spent doing one thing, *a recording session.*
[from Latin *sessio* = sitting]

set *verb* (sets, setting, set)
This word has many uses, including 1 put or fix (*Set the vase on the table. Set a date for the wedding*), 2 make or become firm or hard (*Leave the jelly to set*), 3 give someone a task (*This sets us a problem*), 4 put into a condition (*Set them free*), 5 go down below the horizon (*The sun was setting*).
set about 1 start doing something. 2 (*informal*) attack somebody.
set off 1 begin a journey. 2 start something happening. 3 cause something to explode.
set out 1 begin a journey. 2 display or make known.
set sail begin a voyage.
set to 1 begin doing something vigorously. 2 begin fighting or arguing.
set up 1 place in position. 2 establish, *set up house.* 3 cause or start, *set up a din.*

set *noun* (*plural* sets)
1 a group of people or things that belong together. 2 a radio or television receiver. 3 the way something is placed, *the set of his jaw*. 4 a badger's burrow. 5 the scenery or stage for a play or film. 6 a group of games in a tennis match. [from Old English]

setback *noun* (*plural* setbacks)
something that stops progress or slows it down.

set book *noun* (*plural* set books)
a book that must be studied for a literature examination.

set square (*plural* set squares)
a device shaped like a right-angled triangle, used in drawing lines parallel to each other etc.

settee *noun* (*plural* settees)
a long soft seat with a back and arms.

setter *noun* (*plural* setters)
a dog of a long-haired breed that can be trained to stand rigid when it scents game.

setting *noun* (*plural* settings)
1 the way or place in which something is set. 2 music for the words of a song etc.

settle *verb* (settles, settling, settled)
1 arrange; decide or solve something, *That settles the problem.* 2 make or become calm or comfortable or orderly; stop being restless, *Stop chattering and settle down!* 3 go and live somewhere, *They settled in Canada.* 4 sink; come to rest on something, *Dust had settled on his books.* 5 pay a bill or debt.

settlement *noun* (*plural* settlements)
1 settling something. 2 the way something is settled. 3 a small number of people or houses established in a new area.

set-up *noun* (*informal*)
the way something is organized or arranged.

seven *noun* (*plural* sevens) & *adjective*
the number 7. **seventh** *adjective* & *noun*

seventeen *noun* & *adjective*
the number 17. **seventeenth** *adjective* & *noun*

seventy *noun* (*plural* seventies) & *adjective*
the number 70. **seventieth** *adjective* & *noun*

several *adjective* & *noun*
more than two but not many. [from *sever*]

severe *adjective*
1 strict; not gentle or kind. 2 intense or forceful, *severe gales.* 3 very plain, *a severe style of dress.* **severely** *adverb*, **severity** *noun*

sew *verb* (sews, sewing, sewed, sewn or sewed)
1 join things together by using a needle and thread. 2 work with a needle and thread or with a sewing machine.
[from Old English]

USAGE: Do not confuse with *sow*.

sewage (*say* soo-ij) *noun*
liquid waste matter carried away in drains.

sewer (*say* soo-er) *noun* (*plural* sewers)
a large underground drain for carrying away sewage. [from old French]

sewing machine *noun* (*plural* sewing machines)
a machine for sewing things.

sex *noun* (*plural* sexes)
1 each of the two groups (*male* and *female*) into which living things are placed according to their functions in the process of reproduction. 2 the instinct that causes members of the two sexes to be attracted to one another. 3 sexual intercourse.

sexism *noun*
discrimination against people of a particular sex, especially women.
sexist *adjective* & *noun*

sexual *adjective*
1 to do with sex or the sexes. 2 (of reproduction) happening by the fusion of male and female cells.
sexually *adverb*, **sexuality** *noun*

sexual intercourse *noun*
an intimate act between two people, in which the man puts his penis into the woman's vagina, to express love, for pleasure, or to conceive a child.

sexy *adjective* (sexier, sexiest) (*informal*)
1 sexually attractive. 2 concerned with sex.

SF *abbreviation*
science fiction.

shabby *adjective* (shabbier, shabbiest)
1 in a poor or worn-out condition; dilapidated. 2 poorly dressed. 3 unfair or dishonourable, *a shabby trick.*
shabbily *adverb*, **shabbiness** *noun*
[from Old English *sceabb* = scab]

shack *noun* (*plural* shacks)
a roughly-built hut.
[probably from a Mexican word]

shackle *noun* (*plural* shackles)
an iron ring for fastening a prisoner's wrist or ankle to something.
shackle *verb* (shackles, shackling, shackled)
put shackles on a prisoner.

shade *noun* (*plural* shades)
1 slight darkness produced where something blocks the sun's light. 2 a device that reduces or shuts out bright light. 3 a colour; how light or dark a colour is. 4 a slight difference, *The word had several shades of meaning.* 5 (*poetical*) a ghost.
shade *verb* (shades, shading, shaded)
1 shelter something from bright light. 2 make part of a drawing darker than the rest. 3 move gradually from one state or quality to another, *evening shading into night.* [from Old English *sceadu*]

shadow *noun* (*plural* **shadows**)
1 the dark shape that falls on a surface when something is between the surface and a light. 2 an area of shade.
shadowy *adjective*
shadow *verb* (**shadows, shadowing, shadowed**)
1 cast a shadow on something. 2 follow a person secretly. [same origin as *shade*]

Shadow Cabinet *noun*
members of the Opposition in Parliament who act as spokesmen on important matters.

shady *adjective* (**shadier, shadiest**)
1 giving shade, *a shady tree*. 2 in the shade, *a shady place*. 3 not completely honest; disreputable, *a shady deal*.

shaft *noun* (*plural* **shafts**)
1 a long slender rod or straight part, *the shaft of an arrow*. 2 a ray of light. 3 a deep narrow hole, *a mine shaft*.

shaggy *adjective* (**shaggier, shaggiest**)
1 having long rough hair or fibre. 2 rough, thick, and untidy, *shaggy hair*.

shake *verb* (**shakes, shaking, shook, shaken**)
1 move quickly up and down or from side to side. 2 disturb; shock; upset, *The news shook us*. 3 tremble; be unsteady, *His voice was shaking*. **shaker** *noun*
shake hands clasp a person's right hand with yours in greeting or parting or as a sign of agreement.
shake *noun* (*plural* **shakes**)
1 shaking; a shaking movement. 2 (*informal*) a moment, *I'll be there in two shakes*.
shaky *adjective*, **shakily** *adverb*

shall *auxiliary verb*
1 used with *I* and *we* to express the ordinary future tense, e.g. *I shall arrive tomorrow*, and in questions, e.g. *Shall I shut the door?* (but *will* is used with other words, e.g. *they will arrive*; *will you shut the door?*). 2 used with words other than *I* and *we* in promises, e.g. *Cinderella, you shall go to the ball!* (but *I will go* = I promise or intend to go). [from Old English]

USAGE: If you want to be strictly correct, keep to the rules given here, but nowadays many people use *will* after *I* and *we* and it is not usually regarded as wrong.

shallow *adjective* (**shallower, shallowest**)
1 not deep, *shallow water*. 2 not capable of deep feelings, *a shallow character*. **shallowness** *noun* [origin unknown]

sham *noun* (*plural* **shams**)
something that is not genuine; a pretence.
sham *adjective*
sham *verb* (**shams, shamming, shammed**)
pretend. [probably from *shame*]

shamble *verb* (**shambles, shambling, shambled**)
walk or run in a lazy or awkward way.

shame *noun*
1 a feeling of great sorrow or guilt because you have done wrong. 2 dishonour or disgrace. 3 something you regret, *It's a shame that it rained*.
shameful *adjective*, **shamefully** *adverb*
shame *verb* (**shames, shaming, shamed**)
make a person feel ashamed.

shameless *adjective*
not feeling or looking ashamed.
shamelessly *adverb*

shampoo *noun* (*plural* **shampoos**)
1 a liquid substance for washing the hair. 2 a substance for cleaning a carpet etc. or washing a car. 3 a wash with shampoo, *a shampoo and set*.
shampoo *verb* (**shampoos, shampooing, shampooed**)
wash or clean with a shampoo. [originally = to massage: from Hindi *champo* = press!]

shan't (*mainly spoken*)
shall not.

shanty[1] *noun* (*plural* **shanties**)
a shack. [from Canadian French]

shanty[2] *noun* (*plural* **shanties**)
a sailors' song with a chorus.
[probably from French *chanter* = sing]

shanty town *noun* (*plural* **shanty towns**)
a settlement consisting of shanties.

shape *noun* (*plural* **shapes**)
1 a thing's outline; the appearance an outline produces. 2 proper form or condition, *Get it into shape*. 3 the general form or condition of something, *the shape of British industry*.
shape *verb* (**shapes, shaping, shaped**)
1 make into a particular shape. 2 develop, *It's shaping up nicely*. [from Old English]

shapeless *adjective*
having no definite shape.

shapely *adjective* (**shapelier, shapeliest**)
having an attractive shape.

share *noun* (*plural* **shares**)
1 a part given to one person or thing out of something that is being divided. 2 each of the equal parts forming a business company's capital, giving the person who holds it the right to receive a portion (a *dividend*) of the company's profits.
share *verb* (**shares, sharing, shared**)
1 give portions of something to two or more people. 2 have or use or experience something that others have too, *share a room*; *share the responsibility*.

shark *noun* (*plural* **sharks**)
a large sea fish with sharp teeth.

sharp *adjective*
1 with an edge or point that can cut or make holes. 2 quick at noticing or learning things, *sharp eyes*. 3 steep or pointed; not gradual, *a*

sharp bend. **4** forceful or severe, *a sharp frost.*
5 distinct; loud and shrill, *a sharp cry.*
6 slightly sour. **7** (in music) one semitone
higher than the natural note, *C sharp.* **sharply**
adverb, **sharpness** *noun*
sharp *adverb*
1 sharply, *turn sharp right.* **2** punctually, *at six
o'clock sharp.* **3** (in music) above the correct
pitch, *You were singing sharp.*
sharp *noun* (*plural* **sharps**)
(in music) a note one semitone higher than the
natural note; the sign (♯) that indicates this.
[from Old English]

sharpen *verb* (**sharpens, sharpening, sharpened**)
make or become sharp. **sharpener** *noun*

sharp practice *noun*
dishonest or barely honest dealings in
business.

shatter *verb* (**shatters, shattering, shattered**)
1 break violently into small pieces. **2** destroy,
It shattered our hopes. **3** upset greatly, *We were
shattered by the news.*

shave *verb* (**shaves, shaving, shaved**)
1 scrape growing hair off the skin. **2** cut or
scrape a thin slice off something.
shaver *noun*
shave *noun* (*plural* **shaves**)
the act of shaving the face.
close shave (*informal*) a narrow escape.

shavings *plural noun*
thin strips shaved off a piece of wood or metal.

shawl *noun* (*plural* **shawls**)
a large piece of material worn round the
shoulders or head or wrapped round a baby.
[from Persian or Urdu]

she *pronoun*
the female person or animal being talked
about. [Middle English; related to *he*]

sheaf *noun* (*plural* **sheaves**)
1 a bundle of cornstalks tied together. **2** a
bundle of arrows, papers, etc. held together.
[from Old English]

shear *verb* (**shears, shearing, sheared, sheared or,
in sense 1, shorn**)
1 cut or trim; cut the wool off a sheep. **2** break
because of a sideways or twisting force, *the
bolts sheared off.* **shearer** *noun* [from Old
English]

USAGE: Do not confuse with *sheer.*

shears *plural noun*
a cutting tool shaped like a very large pair of
scissors and worked with both hands.

sheath *noun* (*plural* **sheaths**)
1 a close-fitting cover. **2** a cover for the blade of
a knife or sword etc. **3** a condom.

shed[1] *noun* (*plural* **sheds**)
a simply-made building used for storing things
or sheltering animals, or as a workshop. [from
shade]

shed[2] *verb* (**sheds, shedding, shed**)
1 let something fall or flow, *The tree shed its
leaves. We shed tears.* **2** give off, *A heater sheds
warmth.* **3** get rid of, *The company has shed 200
workers.* [from Old English]

sheen *noun*
a shine or gloss.
[from Old English *sciene* = beautiful]

sheep *noun* (*plural* **sheep**)
an animal that eats grass and has a thick fleecy
coat, kept in flocks for its wool and its meat.
[from Old English]

sheepdog *noun* (*plural* **sheepdogs**)
a dog trained to guard and herd sheep.

sheepish *adjective*
1 bashful. **2** embarrassed or shamefaced.
sheepishly *adverb,* **sheepishness** *noun*
[originally = innocent or silly: from *sheep*
+ *-ish*]

sheer[1] *adjective*
1 complete or thorough, *sheer stupidity.*
2 vertical, with almost no slope, *a sheer drop.*
3 (of material) very thin; transparent. [from
Old English *scir* = shining, noble, or pure]

sheer[2] *verb* (**sheers, sheering, sheered**)
swerve; move sharply away.
[probably from old German]

USAGE: Do not confuse with *shear.*

sheet *noun* (*plural* **sheets**)
1 a large piece of lightweight material used on
a bed in pairs for a person to sleep between. **2** a
whole flat piece of paper, glass, or metal. **3** a
wide area of water, ice, flame, etc.
[from Old English *scete*]

sheikh (*say* shayk *or* sheek) *noun* (*plural*
sheikhs)
the leader of an Arab tribe or village.
[from Arabic *shaykh* = elder, old man]

shelf *noun* (*plural* **shelves**)
1 a flat piece of wood, metal, or glass etc. fixed
to a wall or in a piece of furniture so that
things can be placed on it. **2** a flat level surface
that sticks out; a ledge.

shell *noun* (*plural* **shells**)
1 the hard outer covering of a nut, egg, snail,
tortoise, etc. **2** the walls or framework of a
building, ship, etc. **3** a metal case filled with
explosive, fired from a large gun.
shell *verb* (**shells, shelling, shelled**)
1 take something out of its shell. **2** fire
explosive shells at something.
shell out (*informal*) pay out money.

shellfish *noun* (*plural* **shellfish**)
a sea animal that has a shell.

shelter *noun* (*plural* shelters)
1 something that protects people from rain, wind, danger, etc. 2 protection, *Seek shelter from the rain.*
shelter *verb* (shelters, sheltering, sheltered)
1 provide with shelter. 2 protect. 3 find a shelter, *They sheltered under the trees.*

shelve *verb* (shelves, shelving, shelved)
1 put things on a shelf or shelves. 2 fit a wall or cupboard etc. with shelves. 3 postpone or reject a plan etc. 4 slope, *The bed of the river shelves steeply.* [from *shelf*]

shepherd *noun* (*plural* shepherds)
a person whose job is to look after sheep.
shepherd *verb* (shepherds, shepherding, shepherded)
guide or direct people. [from *sheep* + *herd*]

sheriff *noun* (*plural* sheriffs)
the chief law officer of a county, whose duties vary in different countries. [from Old English *scir* = shire + *refa* = officer]

sherry *noun* (*plural* sherries)
a kind of strong wine.
[named after Jerez de la Frontera, a town in Spain, where it was first made]

Shetland pony *noun* (*plural* Shetland ponies)
a kind of small, strong, shaggy pony, originally from the Shetland Isles.

shield *noun* (*plural* shields)
1 a large piece of metal, wood, etc. carried to protect the body. 2 a model of a triangular shield used as a trophy. 3 a protection.
shield *verb* (shields, shielding, shielded)
protect from harm or from being discovered.

shift *verb* (shifts, shifting, shifted)
1 move or cause to move. 2 (of an opinion or situation) change slightly.
shift for yourself manage without help; rely on your own efforts.
shift *noun* (*plural* shifts)
1 a change of position or condition etc. 2 a group of workers who start work as another group finishes; the time when they work, *the night shift.* 3 a straight dress with no waist. [from Old English]

shifty *adjective*
evasive, not straightforward; untrustworthy.
shiftily *adverb*, **shiftiness** *noun*

shilling *noun* (*plural* shillings)
a former British coin, = 5p.

shilly-shally *verb* (shilly-shallies, shilly-shallying, shilly-shallied)
be unable to make up your mind.
[from *shall I? shall I?*]

shimmer *verb* (shimmers, shimmering, shimmered)
shine with a quivering light, *The sea shimmered in the moonlight.* **shimmer** *noun*

shin *noun* (*plural* shins)
the front of the leg between the knee and the ankle.
shin *verb* (shins, shinning, shinned)
climb by using the arms and legs, not on a ladder. [from Old English]

shine *verb* (shines, shining, shone, in sense 4 shined)
1 give out or reflect light; be bright. 2 be excellent, *He doesn't shine in maths.* 3 aim a light, *Shine your torch on it.* 4 polish, *Have you shined your shoes?*

shingle *noun*
pebbles on a beach. [origin unknown]

shiny *adjective* (shinier, shiniest)
shining or glossy.

ship *noun* (*plural* ships)
a large boat, especially one that goes to sea.
ship *verb* (ships, shipping, shipped)
transport goods etc., especially by ship.

-ship *suffix*
forms nouns meaning 'condition' (e.g. *friendship, hardship*), position (e.g. *chairmanship*), or skill (e.g. *seamanship*). [from Old English]

shipping *noun*
1 ships, *Britain's shipping.* 2 transporting goods by ship.

shipshape *adjective*
in good order; tidy.

shipwreck *noun* (*plural* shipwrecks)
1 the wrecking of a ship by storm or accident. 2 a wrecked ship.
shipwrecked *adjective*

shipyard *noun* (*plural* shipyards)
a place where ships are built or repaired.

shire *noun* (*plural* shires)
a county.
the Shires the country areas of (especially central) England, away from the cities.

shirk *verb* (shirks, shirking, shirked)
avoid a duty or work etc. selfishly or unfairly.
shirker *noun* [probably from German *Schurke* = scoundrel]

shirt *noun* (*plural* shirts)
a piece of clothing for the top half of the body, made of light material and with a collar and sleeves.
in your shirtsleeves not wearing a jacket over your shirt.

shiver *verb* (shivers, shivering, shivered)
tremble with cold or fear. **shiver** *noun*, **shivery** *adjective* [origin unknown]

shoal[1] *noun* (*plural* shoals)
a large number of fish swimming together. [same origin as *school*[2]]

shoal^2 *noun* (*plural* shoals)
1 a shallow place. 2 an underwater sandbank.
[from Old English]

shock^1 *noun* (*plural* shocks)
1 a sudden unpleasant surprise. 2 great
weakness caused by pain or injury etc. 3 the
effect of a violent shake or knock. 4 an effect
caused by electric current passing through the
body.
shock *verb* (shocks, shocking, shocked)
1 give someone a shock; surprise or upset a
person greatly. 2 seem very improper or
scandalous to a person. [from French]

shock^2 *noun* (*plural* shocks)
a bushy mass of hair. [origin unknown]

shocking *adjective*
1 causing indignation or disgust. 2 (*informal*)
very bad, *shocking weather*.

shock wave *noun* (*plural* shock waves)
a sharp change in pressure in the air around
an explosion or an object moving very quickly.

shod *past tense* of shoe.

shoddy *adjective* (shoddier, shoddiest)
of poor quality; badly made or done, *shoddy
work*. **shoddily** *adverb*, **shoddiness** *noun*

shoe *noun* (*plural* shoes)
1 a strong covering for the foot. 2 a horseshoe.
3 something shaped or used like a shoe.
be in somebody's shoes be in his or her
situation.
shoe *verb* (shoes, shoeing, shod)
fit with a shoe or shoes. [from Old English]

shoelace *noun* (*plural* shoelaces)
a cord for lacing up and fastening a shoe.

shoot *verb* (shoots, shooting, shot)
1 fire a gun or missile etc. 2 hurt or kill by
shooting. 3 move or send very quickly, *The car
shot past us*. 4 kick or hit a ball at a goal. 5 (of a
plant) put out buds or shoots. 6 slide the bolt of
a door into or out of its fastening. 7 film or
photograph something, *They shot the film in
Africa*.
shoot *noun* (*plural* shoots)
1 a young branch or new growth of a plant.
2 an expedition for shooting animals.

shooting star *noun* (*plural* shooting stars)
a meteor.

shop *noun* (*plural* shops)
1 a building or room where goods or services
are on sale to the public. 2 a workshop. 3 talk
that is about your own work or job, *She is
always talking shop*.
shop *verb* (shops, shopping, shopped)
go and buy things at shops. **shopper** *noun*
shop around compare goods and prices in
several shops before buying.

shop floor *noun*
1 the workers in a factory, not the managers.
2 the place where they work.

shopkeeper *noun* (*plural* shopkeepers)
a person who owns or manages a shop.

shoplifter *noun* (*plural* shoplifters)
a person who steals goods from a shop after
entering as a customer.
shoplifting *noun*

shopping *noun*
1 buying goods in shops. 2 the goods bought.

shore^1 *noun* (*plural* shores)
the land along the edge of a sea or of a lake.
[from old German or old Dutch *schore*]

shore^2 *verb* (shores, shoring, shored)
prop something up with a piece of wood etc.
[from old German or old Dutch *schoren*]

shorn *past participle* of shear.

short *adjective*
1 not long; occupying a small distance or time,
a short walk. 2 not tall, *a short person*. 3 not
enough; not having enough of something, *We
are short of water*. 4 curt. 5 (of pastry) rich and
crumbly because it contains a lot of fat.
shortness *noun*
for short as an abbreviation, *Raymond is called
Ray for short*.
short for an abbreviation of, *'Ray' is short for
Raymond*.
short *adverb*
suddenly, *She stopped short*.

shortage *noun* (*plural* shortages)
lack or scarcity of something; insufficiency.

shortbread *noun*
a rich sweet biscuit, made with butter.

short circuit *noun* (*plural* short circuits)
a fault in an electrical circuit in which current
flows along a shorter route than the normal
one. **short-circuit** *verb*

shortcoming *noun* (*plural* shortcomings)
a fault or failure to reach a good standard.

short cut *noun* (*plural* short cuts)
a route or method that is quicker than the
usual one.

shorten *verb* (shortens, shortening, shortened)
make or become shorter.

shorthand *noun*
a set of special signs for writing words down as
quickly as people say them.

short-handed *adjective*
not having enough workers or staff.

shortly *adverb*
1 in a short time; soon, *They will arrive shortly*.
2 in a few words. 3 curtly.

shorts *plural noun*
trousers with legs that do not reach to the
knee.

short-sighted *adjective*
1 unable to see things clearly. 2 lacking
imagination or foresight.

short-tempered *adjective*
easily becoming angry.

shot[1] *past tense* of shoot.

shot[2] *noun* (*plural* shots)
1 the firing of a gun or missile etc.; the sound of this. 2 something fired from a gun; lead pellets for firing from small guns. 3 a person judged by skill in shooting, *He's a good shot.* 4 a heavy metal ball thrown as a sport. 5 a stroke in tennis, cricket, billiards, etc. 6 a photograph; a filmed scene. 7 an attempt, *Have a shot at the crossword.* 8 an injection of a drug or vaccine.
shot *adjective*
(of fabric) woven so that different colours show at different angles, *shot silk.*

should *auxiliary verb*
used to express 1 obligation or duty,
= ought to (*You should have told me*),
2 something expected (*They should be here by ten o'clock*), 3 a possible event (*if you should happen to see him*), 4 with *I* and *we* to make a polite statement (*I should like to come*) or in a conditional clause (*If they had supported us we should have won*).
[past tense of *shall*]

USAGE: In sense 4, although *should* is strictly correct, many people nowadays use *would* and this is not regarded as wrong.

shoulder *noun* (*plural* shoulders)
1 the part of the body between the neck and the arm, foreleg, or wing. 2 a side that juts out, *the shoulder of the bottle.*
shoulder *verb* (shoulders, shouldering, shouldered)
1 take something on your shoulder or shoulders. 2 push with your shoulder. 3 accept responsibility or blame.

shoulder blade *noun* (*plural* shoulder blades)
either of the two large flat bones at the top of your back.

shouldn't (*mainly spoken*)
should not.

shout *noun* (*plural* shouts)
a loud cry or call.
shout *verb* (shouts, shouting, shouted)
give a shout; speak or call loudly.

shove *verb* (shoves, shoving, shoved)
push roughly. **shove** *noun*
shove off (*informal*) go away.

shovel *noun* (*plural* shovels)
a tool like a spade with the sides turned up, used for lifting coal, earth, snow, etc.
shovel *verb* (shovels, shovelling, shovelled)
1 move or clear with a shovel. 2 scoop or push roughly, *He was shovelling food into his mouth.*
[from Old English]

show *verb* (shows, showing, showed, shown)
1 allow or cause something to be seen, *Show me your new bike.* 2 make a person understand; demonstrate, *Show me how to use it.* 3 guide, *Show him in.* 4 treat in a certain way, *She showed us much kindness.* 5 be visible, *That scratch won't show.* 6 prove your ability to someone, *We'll show them!*
show off 1 show something proudly. 2 try to impress people.
show up 1 make or be clearly visible; reveal a fault etc. 2 (*informal*) arrive.
show *noun* (*plural* shows)
1 a display or exhibition, *a flower show.* 2 an entertainment. 3 (*slang*) something that happens or is done, *He runs the whole show.*
[from Old English]

showdown *noun* (*plural* showdowns)
a final test or confrontation.

shower *noun* (*plural* showers)
1 a brief fall of rain or snow. 2 a lot of small things coming or falling like rain, *a shower of stones.* 3 a device or cabinet for spraying water to wash a person's body; a wash in this.
shower *verb* (showers, showering, showered)
1 fall or send things in a shower. 2 wash under a shower. [from Old English]

showman *noun* (*plural* showmen)
1 a person who presents entertainments.
2 someone who is good at attracting attention.
showmanship *noun*

showpiece *noun* (*plural* showpieces)
a fine example of something for people to see and admire.

showy *adjective* (showier, showiest)
likely to attract attention; brightly or highly decorated.
showily *adverb*, **showiness** *noun*

shrapnel *noun*
pieces of metal scattered from an exploding shell. [named after H. Shrapnel, a British officer who invented it in about 1806]

shred *noun* (*plural* shreds)
1 a tiny piece torn or cut off something. 2 a small amount, *There is not a shred of evidence.*
shred *verb* (shreds, shredding, shredded)
cut into shreds. **shredder** *noun*

shrew *noun* (*plural* shrews)
1 a small mouse-like animal. 2 (*old use*) a bad-tempered woman who is constantly scolding people. **shrewish** *adjective*

shrewd *adjective*
having common sense and good judgement; clever. **shrewdly** *adverb*, **shrewdness** *noun*
[from old sense of *shrew* = spiteful or cunning person]

shriek *noun* (*plural* shrieks)
a shrill cry or scream.
shriek *verb* (shrieks, shrieking, shrieked)
give a shriek. [imitating the sound]

shrill *adjective*
sounding very high and piercing.
shrilly *adverb,* **shrillness** *noun*

shrimp *noun* (*plural* **shrimps**)
a small shellfish, pink when boiled.

shrine *noun* (*plural* **shrines**)
an altar, chapel, or other sacred place.
[originally = a container for holy relics: via Old
English from Latin *scrinium* = a case or chest]

shrink *verb* (**shrinks, shrinking, shrank, shrunk**)
1 make or become smaller. 2 move back to
avoid something. 3 avoid doing something
because of fear, conscience, embarrassment,
etc. **shrinkage** *noun,* **shrunken** *adjective*

shrivel *verb* (**shrivels, shrivelling, shrivelled**)
make or become dry and wrinkled.

shroud *noun* (*plural* **shrouds**)
1 a cloth in which a dead body is wrapped.
2 each of a set of ropes supporting a ship's
mast.

shrub *noun* (*plural* **shrubs**)
a woody plant smaller than a tree; a bush.
shrubby *adjective* [from Old English]

shrubbery *noun* (*plural* **shrubberies**)
an area planted with shrubs.

shrug *verb* (**shrugs, shrugging, shrugged**)
raise your shoulders as a sign that you do not
care, do not know, etc. **shrug** *noun*
shrug something off treat it as unimportant.

shudder *verb* (**shudders, shuddering, shuddered**)
1 shiver violently with horror, fear, or cold.
2 make a strong shaking movement.
shudder *noun*

shuffle *verb* (**shuffles, shuffling, shuffled**)
1 walk without lifting the feet from the ground.
2 slide playing cards over each other to get
them into random order. 3 shift or rearrange.
shuffle *noun*

shun *verb* (**shuns, shunning, shunned**)
avoid; deliberately keep away from something.
[from Old English]

shunt *verb* (**shunts, shunting, shunted**)
move a train or wagons on to another track;
divert. **shunt** *noun,* **shunter** *noun*

shut *verb* (**shuts, shutting, shut**)
1 move a door, lid, or cover etc. so that it
blocks an opening; make or become closed.
2 bring or fold parts together, *Shut the book.*
shut down 1 stop something working. 2 stop
business.
shut up 1 shut securely. 2 (*informal*) stop
talking or making a noise.

shutter *noun* (*plural* **shutters**)
1 a panel or screen that can be closed over a
window. 2 the device in a camera that opens
and closes to let light fall on the film.
shuttered *adjective* [from *shut*]

shuttle *noun* (*plural* **shuttles**)
1 a holder carrying the weft-thread across a
loom in weaving. 2 a train, bus, or aircraft that
makes frequent short journeys between two
points.
shuttle *verb* (**shuttles, shuttling, shuttled**)
move, travel, or send backwards and forwards.
[from Old English]

shy *adjective* (**shyer, shyest**)
afraid to meet or talk to other people; timid.
shyly *adverb,* **shyness** *noun*

SI *noun*
an internationally recognized system of metric
units of measurement, including the metre and
kilogram.
[short for French *Système International
d'Unités* = International System of Units]

Siamese twins *plural noun*
twins who are born with their bodies joined
together. [after two famous twins born in Siam
(now called Thailand), who were joined near
the waist]

sick *adjective*
1 ill; physically or mentally unwell. 2 vomiting
or likely to vomit, *I feel sick.* 3 distressed or
disgusted. 4 making fun of death, disability, or
misfortune in an unpleasant way.
sick of tired of.

sicken *verb* (**sickens, sickening, sickened**)
1 begin to be ill. 2 make or become distressed
or disgusted, *Vandalism sickens us all.*
sickening *adjective*

sickle *noun* (*plural* **sickles**)
1 a tool with a narrow curved blade, used for
cutting corn etc. 2 something shaped like this
blade, e.g. the crescent moon.

sickly *adjective*
1 often ill; unhealthy. 2 making people feel
sick, *a sickly smell.* 3 weak, *a sickly smile.*

sickness *noun* (*plural* **sicknesses**)
1 illness. 2 a disease. 3 vomiting.

side *noun* (*plural* **sides**)
1 a surface, especially one joining the top and
bottom of something. 2 a line that forms part of
the boundary of a triangle, square, etc. 3 either
of the two halves into which something can be
divided by a line down its centre. 4 the part
near the edge and away from the centre. 5 the
place or region next to a person or thing, *He
stood at my side.* 6 one aspect or view of
something, *Study all sides of the problem.* 7 one
of two groups or teams etc. who oppose each
other.
on the side as a sideline.
side by side next to each other.
side *verb* (**sides, siding, sided**)
side with take a person's side in an argument.

side effect noun (plural side effects)
an effect, especially an unpleasant one, that a medicine has on you as well as the effect intended.

sidelight noun (plural sidelights)
1 a light at the side of a vehicle or ship. 2 light from one side.

sideline noun (plural sidelines)
1 something done in addition to the main work or activity. 2 a line at the side of a football pitch etc.; the area just outside this.

sidelong adjective
towards one side; sideways, a sidelong glance. [from side + Old English -ling = extending in a certain direction]

sidetrack verb (sidetracks, sidetracking, sidetracked)
take someone's attention away from the main subject or problem.

sideways adverb & adjective
1 to or from one side, Move it sideways. 2 with one side facing forwards, We sat sideways in the bus.

siding noun (plural sidings)
a short railway line by the side of a main line.

siege noun (plural sieges)
the besieging of a place.
lay siege to begin besieging.

sieve (say siv) noun (plural sieves)
a device made of mesh or perforated metal or plastic, used to separate the smaller or soft parts of something from the larger or hard parts.
sieve verb (sieves, sieving, sieved)
put something through a sieve.

sift verb (sifts, sifting, sifted)
1 sieve. 2 examine and analyse facts or evidence etc. carefully. **sifter** noun

sigh noun (plural sighs)
a sound made by breathing out heavily when you are sad, tired, relieved, etc.
sigh verb (sighs, sighing, sighed)
make a sigh. [probably from Old English]

sight noun (plural sights)
1 the ability to see. 2 a thing that can be seen or is worth seeing, Our roses are a wonderful sight. 3 an unsightly thing, You do look a sight in those clothes! 4 a device looked through to help aim a gun or telescope etc.
at sight or **on sight** as soon as a person or thing has been seen.
in sight 1 visible. 2 clearly near, Victory was in sight.

USAGE: Do not confuse with site.

sight verb (sights, sighting, sighted)
1 see or observe something. 2 aim a gun or telescope etc.

sight-reading noun
playing or singing music at sight, without preparation.

sightseeing noun
visiting interesting places in a town etc.
sightseer noun

sign noun (plural signs)
1 something that shows that a thing exists, There are signs of decay. 2 a mark, device, or notice etc. that gives a special meaning, a road sign. 3 an action or movement giving information or a command etc. 4 any of the twelve divisions of the zodiac, represented by a symbol.
sign verb (signs, signing, signed)
1 make a sign or signal. 2 write your signature on something; accept a contract etc. by doing this. 3 use signing.
sign on 1 accept a job etc. by signing a contract. 2 sign a form to say that you are unemployed and want to claim benefit. [from Latin signum = sign]

signal noun (plural signals)
1 a device, gesture, or sound etc. that gives information or a command. 2 a message made up of such things. 3 a sequence of electrical impulses or radio waves.
signal verb (signals, signalling, signalled)
make a signal to somebody. **signaller** noun

USAGE: Do not use this word in mistake for single in the phrase to single out.

signal box noun (plural signal boxes)
a building from which railway signals, points, etc. are controlled.

signature noun (plural signatures)
a person's name written by himself or herself. [from Latin signare = make a mark]

signature tune (plural signature tunes)
a special tune always used to announce a particular programme, performer, etc.

significant adjective
1 having a meaning; full of meaning. 2 important, a significant event.
significantly adverb, **significance** noun

signpost noun (plural signposts)
a sign at a road junction etc. showing the names and distances of places down each road.

Sikh (say seek) noun (plural Sikhs)
a member of a religion founded in northern India, believing in one God and accepting some Hindu and some Islamic beliefs. **Sikhism** noun [from Sanskrit sisya = disciple]

silence noun (plural silences)
absence of sound or talk.
silence verb (silences, silencing, silenced)
make a person or thing silent.

silencer *noun* (*plural* silencers)
a device for reducing the sound made by a gun
or a vehicle's exhaust system etc.

silent *adjective*
1 without any sound. 2 not speaking.
silently *adverb*
[from Latin *silere* = to be silent]

silhouette (*say* sil-oo-et) *noun* (*plural*
silhouettes)
a dark shadow seen against a light
background. **silhouette** *verb*
[named after a French author, É. de Silhouette,
who made paper cut-outs of people's profiles
from their shadows]

silicon *noun*
a substance found in many rocks, used in
making transistors, chips for microprocessors,
etc.
[from Latin *silex* = flint or quartz]

silk *noun* (*plural* silks)
1 a fine soft thread or cloth made from the
fibre produced by silkworm caterpillars for
making their cocoons. 2 a length of silk thread
used for embroidery.
silken *adjective*, **silky** *adjective*
[from Old English, probably from Latin]

silly *adjective* (sillier, silliest)
foolish or unwise. **silliness** *noun*
[from Old English *saelig* = happy, blessed by
God, later = innocent, helpless]

silt *noun*
sediment laid down by a river or sea etc.
silt *verb* (silts, silting, silted)
silt up block or clog or become blocked with silt.

silver *noun*
1 a shiny white precious metal. 2 the colour of
silver. 3 coins or objects made of silver or
silver-coloured metal. 4 a silver medal, usually
given as second prize.
silver *adjective*, **silvery** *adjective*
silver *verb* (silvers, silvering, silvered)
make or become silvery.

silver wedding *noun* (*plural* silver weddings)
a couple's 25th wedding anniversary.

similar *adjective*
nearly the same as another person or thing; of
the same kind. **similarly** *adverb*, **similarity** *noun*
[from Latin *similis* = like]

simile (*say* sim-il-ee) *noun* (*plural* similes)
a comparison of one thing with another, e.g. *He
is as strong as a horse. We ran like the wind.*
[same origin as *similar*]

simmer *verb* (simmers, simmering, simmered)
boil very gently.
simmer down calm down.

simper *verb* (simpers, simpering, simpered)
smile in a silly affected way. **simper** *noun*

simple *adjective* (simpler, simplest)
1 easy, *a simple question.* 2 not complicated or
elaborate. 3 plain, not showy, *a simple cottage.*
4 without much sense or intelligence. 5 not of
high rank; ordinary, *a simple countryman.*
simplicity *noun*

simple-minded *adjective*
naive or foolish.

simplify *verb* (simplifies, simplifying, simplified)
make a thing simple or easy to understand.
simplification *noun*

simply *adverb*
1 in a simple way, *Explain it simply.* 2 without
doubt; completely, *It's simply marvellous.*
3 only or merely, *It's simply a question of time.*

simulator *noun* (*plural* simulators)
a machine or device for simulating actual
conditions or events, often used for training, *a
flight simulator.*

simultaneous (*say* sim-ul-tay-nee-us) *adjective*
happening at the same time.
simultaneously *adverb* [from Latin]

sin *noun* (*plural* sins)
1 the breaking of a religious or moral law. 2 a
very bad action.
sin *verb* (sins, sinning, sinned)
commit a sin. **sinner** *noun*

since *conjunction*
1 from the time when, *Where have you been
since I last saw you?* 2 because, *Since we have
missed the bus we must walk home.*
since *preposition*
from a certain time, *She has been here since
Christmas.*
since *adverb*
between then and now, *He ran away and hasn't
been seen since.*
[from Old English *sithon* = then]

sincere *adjective*
without pretence; truly felt or meant, *my
sincere thanks.*
sincerely *adverb*, **sincerity** *noun*
Yours sincerely see *yours.*
[from Latin *sincerus* = clean or pure]

sine *noun* (*plural* sines)
(in a right-angled triangle) the ratio of the
length of a side opposite one of the acute angles
to the length of the hypotenuse. (Compare
cosine.) [same origin as *sinus*]

sinewy *adjective*
slim, muscular, and strong.

sinful *adjective*
1 guilty of sin. 2 wicked.
sinfully *adverb*, **sinfulness** *noun*

sing *verb* (sings, singing, sang, sung)
1 make musical sounds with the voice.
2 perform a song. **singer** *noun*

singe (*say* sinj) *verb* (singes, singeing, singed)
burn something slightly.

single *adjective*
1 one only; not double or multiple. 2 suitable for one person, *single beds*. 3 separate, *We sold every single thing*. 4 not married. 5 for the journey to a place but not back again, *a single ticket*. **singly** *adverb*
single *noun* (*plural* singles)
1 a single person or thing. 2 a single ticket. 3 a record with one short piece of music on each side.
single *verb* (singles, singling, singled)
single out pick out or distinguish from other people or things.

single file *nouns*
in **single file** in a line, one behind the other.

single-handed *adjective*
without help.

single-minded *adjective*
with your mind set on one purpose only.

singsong *adjective*
having a monotonous tone or rhythm, *a singsong voice*.

singular *noun* (*plural* singulars)
the form of a noun or verb used when it stands for only one person or thing, *The singular is 'man', the plural is 'men'*.
singular *adjective*
1 to do with the singular. 2 uncommon or extraordinary, *a woman of singular courage*. **singularly** *adverb*, **singularity** *noun* [from Latin *singulus* = single]

sinister *adjective*
1 looking evil or harmful. 2 wicked, *a sinister motive*. [from Latin, = on the left (which was thought to be unlucky)]

sink *verb* (sinks, sinking, sank, sunk)
1 go or cause to go under the surface or to the bottom of the sea etc., *The ship sank. They sank the ship*. 2 go or fall slowly downwards, *He sank to his knees*. 3 dig or drill, *They sank a well*. 4 invest money in something.
sink in become understood.
sink *noun* (*plural* sinks)
a fixed basin with a drainpipe and usually a tap or taps to supply water.

-sion *suffix* see **-ion**.

sip *verb* (sips, sipping, sipped)
drink in small mouthfuls. **sip** *noun*

siphon *noun* (*plural* siphons)
1 a pipe or tube in the form of an upside-down U, arranged so that liquid is forced up it and down to a lower level. 2 a bottle containing soda water which is released through a tube.
siphon *verb* (siphons, siphoning, siphoned)
flow or draw out through a siphon.
[Greek, = pipe]

sir *noun*
1 a word used when speaking politely to a man, *Please sir, may I go?* 2 **Sir** the title given to a knight or baronet, *Sir John Moore*. [from French; related to *senior*]

siren *noun* (*plural* sirens)
1 a device that makes a long loud sound as a signal. 2 a dangerously attractive woman. [named after the Sirens in Greek legend, women who by their sweet singing lured seafarers to shipwreck on the rocks]

sissy *noun* (*plural* sissies)
a timid or cowardly person.
[from *sis* = sister]

sister *noun* (*plural* sisters)
1 a daughter of the same parents as another person. 2 a woman who is a fellow member of an association etc. 3 a nun. 4 a female hospital nurse in charge of others. **sisterly** *adjective* [from Old English]

sister-in-law *noun* (*plural* sisters-in-law)
1 the sister of a married person's husband or wife. 2 the wife of a person's brother.

sit *verb* (sits, sitting, sat)
1 rest with your body supported on the buttocks; occupy a seat, *We were sitting in the front row*. 2 seat; cause someone to sit. 3 (of birds) perch; stay on the nest to hatch eggs. 4 be a candidate for an examination. 5 be situated; stay. 6 (of Parliament or a lawcourt etc.) be assembled for business.

site *noun* (*plural* sites)
the place where something happens or happened or is built etc., *a camping site*. [from Latin *situs* = position]

USAGE: Do not confuse with *sight*.

sit-in *noun* (*plural* sit-ins)
a protest in which people sit down or occupy a public place and refuse to move.

sitting room *noun* (*plural* sitting rooms)
a room with comfortable chairs for sitting in.

situation *noun*
1 a position, with its surroundings. 2 a state of affairs at a certain time, *The police faced a difficult situation*. 3 a job.
[same origin as *site*]

six *noun* (*plural* sixes) & *adjective*
the number 6. **sixth** *adjective* & *noun*
at sixes and sevens in disorder or disagreement.

sixteen *noun* & *adjective*
the number 16. **sixteenth** *adjective* & *noun*

sixty *noun* (*plural* sixties) & *adjective*
the number 60. **sixtieth** *adjective* & *noun*

size *noun* (*plural* sizes)
1 the measurements or extent of something.

2 any of the series of standard measurements in which certain things are made, *a size eight shoe.*
size *verb* (sizes, sizing, sized)
arrange things according to their size.
size up 1 estimate the size of something. **2** form an opinion or judgement about a person or thing.
[originally, a law fixing the amount of a tax: from old French *assise* = law, court session]

sizeable *adjective*
large or fairly large.

sizzle *verb* (sizzles, sizzling, sizzled)
make a crackling or hissing sound.

skate *noun* (*plural* skates)
1 a boot with a steel blade attached to the sole, used for sliding smoothly over ice. **2** a roller-skate.
skate *verb* (skates, skating, skated)
move on skates. **skater** *noun* [from Dutch]

skateboard *noun* (*plural* skateboards)
a small board with wheels, used for riding on (as a sport) while standing. **skateboarder,** **skateboarding** *nouns*

skein *noun* (*plural* skeins)
a coil of yarn or thread. [from old French]

skeleton *noun* (*plural* skeletons)
1 the framework of bones of the body. **2** the shell or other hard part of a crab etc. **3** a framework, e.g. of a building. **skeletal** *adjective*
[from Greek *skeletos* = dried-up]

sketch *noun* (*plural* sketches)
1 a rough drawing or painting. **2** a short account of something. **3** a short amusing play.
sketch *verb* (sketches, sketching, sketched)
make a sketch. [from Greek *schedios* = done without practice or preparation]

sketchy *adjective*
rough and not detailed or careful.

skewer *noun* (*plural* skewers)
a long pin pushed through meat to hold it together while it is being cooked. **skewer** *verb*
[origin unknown]

ski (*say* skee) *noun* (*plural* skis)
each of a pair of long narrow strips of wood, metal, or plastic fixed under the feet for moving quickly over snow.
ski *verb* (skies, skiing, skied)
travel on skis. **skier** *noun*
[Norwegian]

skid *verb* (skids, skidding, skidded)
slide accidentally.
skid *noun* (*plural* skids)
1 a skidding movement. **2** a runner on a helicopter, for use in landing.
[probably from Old Norse *skith* = ski]

skilful *adjective*
having or showing great skill.
skilfully *adverb*

skill *noun* (*plural* skills)
the ability to do something well.
skilled *adjective* [from Old Norse]

skim *verb* (skims, skimming, skimmed)
1 remove something from the surface of a liquid; take the cream off milk. **2** move quickly over a surface or through the air. **3** read something quickly.
[from old French *escume* = scum]

skimp *verb* (skimps, skimping, skimped)
supply or use less than is needed, *Don't skimp on the food.* [origin unknown]

skimpy *adjective* (skimpier, skimpiest)
scanty or too small.

skin *noun* (*plural* skins)
1 the flexible outer covering of a person's or animal's body. **2** an outer layer or covering, e.g. of a fruit. **3** a skin-like film formed on the surface of a liquid.
skin *verb* (skins, skinning, skinned)
take the skin off something.

skinny *adjective* (skinnier, skinniest)
very thin.

skip[1] (skips, skipping, skipped)
1 move along lightly, especially by hopping on each foot in turn. **2** jump with a skipping rope. **3** go quickly from one subject to another. **4** miss something out, *You can skip chapter six.*
skip *noun* (*plural* skips)
a skipping movement.

skip[2] *noun* (*plural* skips)
a large metal container for taking away builders' rubbish etc.
[from Old Norse *skeppa* = basket]

skipping rope *noun* (*plural* skipping ropes)
a rope, usually with a handle at each end, that is swung over your head and under your feet as you jump.

skirt *noun* (*plural* skirts)
1 a piece of clothing for a woman or girl that hangs down from the waist. **2** the part of a dress below the waist.
skirt *verb* (skirts, skirting, skirted)
go round the edge of something.

skittish *adjective*
frisky; lively and excitable.

skulk *verb* (skulks, skulking, skulked)
loiter stealthily.

skull *noun* (*plural* skulls)
the framework of bones of the head.

skunk *noun* (*plural* skunks)
a North American animal with black and white fur that can spray a bad-smelling fluid. [a Native American word]

sky *noun* (*plural* skies)
the space above the earth, appearing blue in daylight on fine days. [from Old Norse]

skylight *noun* (*plural* skylights)
a window in a roof.

skyline *noun* (*plural* skylines)
1 the horizon, where earth and sky appear to meet. 2 the outline of buildings etc. against the sky.

skyscraper *noun* (*plural* skyscrapers)
a very tall building.

slab *noun* (*plural* slabs)
a thick flat piece. [origin unknown]

slack *adjective*
1 not pulled tight. 2 not busy; not working hard. **slackly** *adverb*, **slackness** *noun*
slack *verb* (slacks, slacking, slacked)
avoid work; be lazy. **slacker** *noun*

slacken *verb* (slackens, slackening, slackened)
make or become slack.

slacks *plural noun*
trousers for informal occasions.

slag *noun*
waste material separated from metal in smelting. [from old German]

slag heap *noun* (*plural* slag heaps)
a mound of waste matter from a mine etc.

slain *past participle* of **slay**.

slake *verb* (slakes, slaking, slaked)
quench, *slake your thirst*.

slam *verb* (slams, slamming, slammed)
1 shut loudly. 2 hit violently. **slam** *noun*

slander *noun* (*plural* slanders)
a spoken statement that damages a person's reputation and is untrue. (Compare *libel*.)
slanderous *adjective*
slander *verb* (slanders, slandering, slandered)
make a slander against someone.
slanderer *noun*
[from old French; related to *scandal*]

slang *noun*
words that are used very informally to add vividness or humour to what is said, especially those used only by a particular group of people, *teenage slang*.
slangy *adjective* [origin unknown]

slant *verb* (slants, slanting, slanted)
1 slope. 2 present news or information etc. from a particular point of view.

slap *verb* (slaps, slapping, slapped)
1 hit with the palm of the hand or with something flat. 2 put forcefully or carelessly, *We slapped paint on the walls*. **slap** *noun*
[imitating the sound]

slapdash *adjective*
hasty and careless.

slapstick *noun*
comedy with people hitting each other, falling over, etc. [from *slap* + *stick*[1]]

slash *verb* (slashes, slashing, slashed)
1 make large cuts in something. 2 cut or strike with a long sweeping movement. 3 reduce greatly, *Prices were slashed*.
slash *noun* (*plural* slashes)
a slashing cut. [probably from old French]

slate *noun* (*plural* slates)
1 a kind of grey rock that is easily split into flat plates. 2 a piece of this rock used in covering a roof or (formerly) for writing on. **slaty** *adjective*
slate *verb* (slates, slating, slated)
1 cover a roof with slates. 2 (*informal*) criticize severely.

slaughter *verb* (slaughters, slaughtering, slaughtered)
1 kill an animal for food. 2 kill people or animals ruthlessly or in great numbers.
slaughter *noun* [from Old Norse]

slaughterhouse *noun* (*plural* slaughterhouses)
a place where animals are killed for food.

slave *noun* (*plural* slaves)
a person who is owned by another and obliged to work for him or her without being paid.
slavery *noun*
slave *verb* (slaves, slaving, slaved)
work very hard.
[from Latin *sclavus* = captive]

slavish *adjective*
1 like a slave. 2 showing no independence or originality.

slay *verb* (slays, slaying, slew, slain) (*poetical*)
kill. [from Old English]

sledge *noun* (*plural* sledges)
a vehicle for travelling over snow, with strips of metal or wood instead of wheels. **sledging** *noun*
[from old Dutch; related to *sled*]

sledgehammer *noun* (*plural* sledgehammers)
a very large heavy hammer.
[from Old English *slecg* = sledgehammer, + *hammer*]

sleek *adjective*
smooth and shiny.
[a different spelling of *slick*]

sleep *noun*
the condition or time of rest in which the eyes are closed, the body relaxed, and the mind unconscious. **sleepy** *adjective*,
sleepily *adverb*, **sleepiness** *noun*
sleep *verb* (sleeps, sleeping, slept)
have a sleep.

sleeper *noun* (*plural* sleepers)
1 someone who is asleep. 2 each of the wooden or concrete beams on which the rails of a railway rest. 3 a railway carriage with beds or berths for passengers to sleep in; a place in this.

sleepwalker *noun* (*plural* sleepwalkers)
a person who walks about while asleep.
sleepwalking *noun*

sleet *noun*
a mixture of rain and snow or hail.

sleeve *noun* (*plural* **sleeves**)
1 the part of a garment that covers the arm.
2 the cover of a record.
up your sleeve hidden but ready for you to use.

sleight (*say as* slight) *noun*
sleight of hand skill in using the hands to do conjuring tricks etc.

slender *adjective*
slim. **slenderness** *noun* [origin unknown]

sleuth (*say* slooth) *noun* (*plural* **sleuths**)
a detective.
[from Old Norse *sloth* = a track or trail]

slew *past tense* of **slay**.

slice *noun* (*plural* **slices**)
1 a thin piece cut off something. 2 a portion.
slice *verb* (**slices, slicing, sliced**)
1 cut into slices. 2 cut from a larger piece, *Slice the top off the egg.* 3 cut cleanly, *The knife sliced through the apple.*

slick *adjective*
1 quick and clever or cunning. 2 slippery.
slick *noun* (*plural* **slicks**)
1 a large patch of oil floating on water. 2 a slippery place. [from Old English]

slide *verb* (**slides, sliding, slid**)
1 move or cause to move smoothly on a surface. 2 move quietly or secretly, *The thief slid behind a bush.*
slide *noun* (*plural* **slides**)
1 a sliding movement. 2 a smooth surface or structure on which people or things can slide.
3 a photograph that can be projected on a screen. 4 a small glass plate on which things are placed to be examined under a microscope.
5 a fastener to keep hair tidy.
[from Old English]

slight *adjective*
very small; not serious or important. **slightly** *adverb*, **slightness** *noun*

slim *adjective* (**slimmer, slimmest**)
1 thin and graceful. 2 small, *a slim chance.* **slimness** *noun*
slim *verb* (**slims, slimming, slimmed**)
make yourself thinner. **slimmer** *noun*

slime *noun*
unpleasant wet slippery stuff. **slimy** *adjective*, **sliminess** *noun* [from Old English]

sling *noun* (*plural* **slings**)
1 a loop or band placed round something to support or lift it. 2 a looped strap used to throw a stone etc.
sling *verb* (**slings, slinging, slung**)
1 support or lift with a sling. 2 (*informal*) throw. [from old Dutch or Old Norse]

slink *verb* (**slinks, slinking, slunk**)
move in a stealthy or guilty way.
slinky *adjective* [from Old English]

slip *verb* (**slips, slipping, slipped**)
1 slide accidentally; lose your balance by sliding. 2 move or put quickly and quietly, *Slip it in your pocket. We slipped away from the party.* 3 escape from, *The dog slipped its leash. It slipped my memory.*
slip up make a mistake.
slip *noun* (*plural* **slips**)
1 an accidental slide or fall. 2 a mistake. 3 a small piece of paper. 4 a petticoat. 5 a pillowcase.
give someone the slip escape or avoid him or her skilfully.

slipper *noun* (*plural* **slippers**)
a soft comfortable shoe to wear indoors.

slippery *adjective*
smooth or wet so that it is difficult to stand on or hold. **slipperiness** *noun*

slipshod *adjective*
careless; not systematic.
[originally = wearing slippers or badly fitting shoes; from *slip* + *shod*]

slit *noun* (*plural* **slits**)
a narrow straight cut or opening.
slit *verb* (**slits, slitting, slit**)
make a slit or slits in something.

slither *verb* (**slithers, slithering, slithered**)
slip or slide unsteadily. [from Old English]

sliver (*say* sliv-er) *noun* (*plural* **slivers**)
a thin strip of wood or glass etc.
[from Middle English *slive* = to split or to cut a piece off]

slog *verb* (**slogs, slogging, slogged**)
1 hit hard. 2 work or walk hard and steadily.
slog *noun*, **slogger** *noun*

slogan *noun* (*plural* **slogans**)
a phrase used to advertise something or to sum up the aims of a campaign etc., *Their slogan was 'Ban the bomb!'* [from Scottish Gaelic *sluagh-ghairm* = battle-cry]

slope *verb* (**slopes, sloping, sloped**)
lie or turn at an angle; slant.
slope off (*informal*) go away.
slope *noun* (*plural* **slopes**)
1 a sloping surface. 2 the amount by which something slopes. [origin unknown]

sloppy *adjective* (**sloppier, sloppiest**)
1 liquid and splashing easily. 2 careless or slipshod, *sloppy work.* 3 weakly sentimental, *a sloppy story.* **sloppily** *adverb*, **sloppiness** *noun*
[from *slop*]

slot *noun* (*plural* **slots**)
a narrow opening to put things in. **slotted** *adjective* [from old French]

sloth (rhymes with *both*) *noun* (*plural* **sloths**)
1 laziness. 2 a South American animal that lives in trees and moves very slowly.
slothful *adjective* [from *slow*]

slot machine *noun* (*plural* slot machines)
a machine worked by putting a coin in the slot.

slouch *verb* (slouches, slouching, slouched)
stand, sit, or move in a lazy awkward way, not with an upright posture. **slouch** *noun*

slovenly (*say* sluv-en-lee) *adjective*
careless or untidy. **slovenliness** *noun*

slow *adjective*
1 not quick; taking more time than is usual.
2 showing a time earlier than the correct time, *Your watch is slow.* 3 not clever; not able to understand quickly or easily. **slowly** *adverb*, **slowness** *noun*
slow *adverb*
slowly, *Go slow.*
slow *verb* (slows, slowing, slowed)
go more slowly; cause to go more slowly, *The storm slowed us down.*

slow-worm *noun* (*plural* slow-worms)
a small European legless lizard that looks like a snake, and gives birth to live young.

sludge *noun*
thick mud. [origin unknown]

slug *noun* (*plural* slugs)
1 a small slimy animal like a snail without a shell. 2 a pellet for firing from a gun.

sluggish *adjective*
slow-moving; not alert or lively. [from *slug*]

sluice-gate *noun* (*plural* sluice-gates)
a sliding barrier for controlling a flow of water.

slum *noun* (*plural* slums)
an area of dirty overcrowded houses.

slumber *verb* (slumbers, slumbering, slumbered)
sleep. **slumber** *noun*, **slumberer** *noun*, **slumberous** or **slumbrous** *adjective*

slump *verb* (slumps, slumping, slumped)
fall heavily or suddenly.
slump *noun* (*plural* slumps)
a sudden great fall in prices or trade.

slur *verb* (slurs, slurring, slurred)
1 pronounce words indistinctly by running the sounds together. 2 mark with a slur in music.
slur *noun* (*plural* slurs)
1 a slurred sound. 2 discredit, *It casts a slur on his reputation.* 3 a curved line placed over notes in music to show that they are to be sung or played smoothly without a break.

slush *noun*
partly melted snow on the ground.
slushy *adjective*
[imitating the sound when you walk in it]

sly *adjective* (slyer, slyest)
1 unpleasantly cunning or secret.
2 mischievous, *a sly smile.*
slyly *adverb*, **slyness** *noun* [from Old Norse]

smack[1] *noun* (*plural* smacks)
1 a slap. 2 a loud sharp sound, *It hit the wall with a smack.* 3 (*informal*) a hard hit or blow.

smack *verb* (smacks, smacking, smacked)
1 slap. 2 hit hard.
smack your lips close and then part them noisily in enjoyment.
smack *adverb* (*informal*)
forcefully or directly, *The ball went smack through the window.*
[from old German or old Dutch]

smack[2] *noun* (*plural* smacks)
a slight flavour of something; a trace.
smack *verb* (smacks, smacking, smacked)
have a slight flavour or trace, *His manner smacks of conceit.*
[from Old English]

small *adjective*
not large; less than the usual size.
smallness *noun*
the small of the back the smallest part of the back (at the waist).

smallholding *noun* (*plural* smallholdings)
a small area of land used for farming.
smallholder *noun*

small hours *plural noun*
the early hours of the morning, after midnight.

small-minded *adjective*
selfish; petty.

small print *noun*
the details of a contract, especially if in very small letters or difficult to understand.

small talk *noun*
conversation about unimportant things.

smart *adjective*
1 neat and elegant; dressed well. 2 clever.
3 forceful; brisk, *She ran at a smart pace.*
smartly *adverb*, **smartness** *noun*

smarten *verb* (smartens, smartening, smartened)
make or become smarter.

smash *verb* (smashes, smashing, smashed)
1 break noisily into pieces. 2 hit or move with great force. 3 destroy or defeat completely.
smash *noun* (*plural* smashes)
1 the action or sound of smashing. 2 a collision. 3 a disaster.

smashing *adjective* (*informal*)
excellent or beautiful. **smasher** *noun*

smear *verb* (smears, smearing, smeared)
1 rub something greasy or sticky or dirty on a surface. 2 try to damage someone's reputation.
smeary *adjective*
smear *noun* (*plural* smears)
1 smearing; something smeared. 2 material smeared on a slide to be examined under a microscope. 3 a smear test. [from Old English]

smell *verb* (smells, smelling, smelt or smelled)
1 be aware of something by means of the sense organs of the nose, *I can smell smoke.* 2 give out a smell.

smell *noun* (*plural* smells)
1 something you can smell; a quality in something that makes people able to smell it. **2** an unpleasant quality of this kind. **3** the ability to smell things. **smelly** *adjective* [origin unknown]

smile *noun* (*plural* smiles)
an expression on the face that shows pleasure or amusement, with the lips stretched and turning upwards at the ends.
smile *verb* (smiles, smiling, smiled)
give a smile.

smirk *noun* (*plural* smirks)
a self-satisfied smile.
smirk *verb* (smirks, smirking, smirked)
give a smirk. [from Old English]

smite *verb* (smites, smiting, smote, smitten)
hit hard. [from Old English]

smith *noun* (*plural* smiths)
1 a person who makes things out of metal. **2** a blacksmith. [from Old English]

smithereens *plural noun*
small fragments. [from Irish]

smock *noun* (*plural* smocks)
1 an overall shaped like a very long shirt. **2** a loose top worn by a pregnant woman.

smog *noun*
a mixture of smoke and fog.
[from *smoke* + *fog*]

smoke *noun*
1 the mixture of gas and solid particles given off by a burning substance. **2** a period of smoking tobacco, *He wanted a smoke*. **smoky** *adjective*
smoke *verb* (smokes, smoking, smoked)
1 give out smoke. **2** have a lighted cigarette, cigar, or pipe between your lips and draw its smoke into your mouth; do this as a habit. **3** preserve meat or fish by treating it with smoke, *smoked haddock*. **smoker** *noun* [from Old English]

smokescreen *noun* (*plural* smokescreens)
1 a mass of smoke used to hide the movement of troops. **2** something that conceals what is happening.

smooth *adjective*
1 having a surface without any lumps, wrinkles, roughness, etc. **2** moving without bumps or jolts etc. **3** not harsh, *a smooth flavour*. **smoothly** *adverb*, **smoothness** *noun*
smooth *verb* (smooths, smoothing, smoothed)
make a thing smooth.

smote *past tense* of smite.

smother *verb* (smothers, smothering, smothered)
1 suffocate. **2** cover thickly, *The buns were smothered in sugar*. **3** restrain or conceal, *She smothered a smile*. [from Old English]

smoulder *verb* (smoulders, smouldering, smouldered)
1 burn slowly without a flame. **2** continue to exist inwardly, *Their anger smouldered*.

smudge *noun* (*plural* smudges)
a dirty mark made by rubbing something. **smudgy** *adjective*
smudge *verb* (smudges, smudging, smudged)
make a smudge on something; become smudged. [origin unknown]

smug *adjective*
self-satisfied; too pleased with your own good fortune or abilities. **smugly** *adverb*, **smugness** *noun* [from old German *smuk* = pretty]

smuggle *verb* (smuggles, smuggling, smuggled)
bring something into a country etc. secretly or illegally. **smuggler** *noun*

snack *noun* (*plural* snacks)
1 a small meal. **2** food eaten between meals. [from old Dutch]

snag *noun* (*plural* snags)
1 a difficulty. **2** a sharp projection. **3** a tear in material that has been caught on something sharp.

snail *noun* (*plural* snails)
a small animal with a soft body and a shell. [from Old English]

snake *noun* (*plural* snakes)
a reptile with a long narrow body and no legs. **snaky** *adjective* [from Old English]

snap *verb* (snaps, snapping, snapped)
1 break suddenly or with a sharp sound. **2** bite suddenly or quickly. **3** say something quickly and angrily. **4** take something or move quickly. **5** take a snapshot of something.
snap *noun* (*plural* snaps)
1 the action or sound of snapping. **2** a snapshot. **3** **Snap** *noun* a card game in which players shout 'Snap!' when they see two similar cards.

snappy *adjective*
1 snapping at people. **2** quick and lively. **snappily** *adverb*

snapshot *noun* (*plural* snapshots)
an informal photograph.

snare *noun* (*plural* snares)
a trap for catching birds or animals.
snare *verb* (snares, snaring, snared)
catch in a snare. [from Old English]

snarl *verb* (snarls, snarling, snarled)
1 growl angrily. **2** speak in a bad-tempered way. **snarl** *noun* [imitating the sound]

snatch *verb* (snatches, snatching, snatched)
seize; take quickly, eagerly, or by force.
snatch *noun* (*plural* snatches)
1 snatching. **2** a short and incomplete part of a song, conversation, etc

sneak *verb* (sneaks, sneaking, sneaked)
1 move quietly and secretly. 2 (*informal*) take secretly, *He sneaked a biscuit from the tin.*
3 (*slang*) tell tales.
sneak *noun* (*plural* sneaks)
a tell-tale. **sneaky** *adjective*, **sneakily** *adverb*

sneer *verb* (sneers, sneering, sneered)
speak or behave in a scornful way. **sneer** *noun*
[probably from Old English]

sneeze *verb* (sneezes, sneezing, sneezed)
send out air suddenly and uncontrollably through the nose and mouth in order to get rid of something irritating the nostrils.
sneeze *noun* [from Old English *fneosan*, imitating the sound]

sniff *verb* (sniffs, sniffing, sniffed)
1 make a sound by drawing in air through the nose. 2 smell something.
sniff *noun*, **sniffer** *noun*
[imitating the sound]

sniffle *verb* (sniffles, sniffling, sniffled)
1 sniff slightly. 2 keep on sniffing. **sniffle** *noun*
[imitating the sound]

snigger *verb* (sniggers, sniggering, sniggered)
giggle slyly. **snigger** *noun*

snip *verb* (snips, snipping, snipped)
cut with scissors or shears in small quick cuts.
snip *noun*

snipe *verb* (snipes, sniping, sniped)
shoot at people from a hiding place.
sniper *noun*

snippet *noun* (*plural* snippets)
a small piece of news, information, etc.
[from *snip*]

snivel *verb* (snivels, snivelling, snivelled)
cry or complain in a whining way.

snob *noun* (*plural* snobs)
a person who despises those who have not got wealth, power, or particular tastes or interests.
snobbery *noun*, **snobbish** *adjective*

snooker *noun*
a game played with cues and 21 balls on a special cloth-covered table.

snoop *verb* (snoops, snooping, snooped)
pry; ask or look around secretly. **snooper** *noun*
[from Dutch]

snooze *noun* (*plural* snoozes)
a nap. **snooze** *verb* [origin unknown]

snore *verb* (snores, snoring, snored)
breathe very noisily while sleeping. **snore** *noun*
[imitating the sound]

snort *verb* (snorts, snorting, snorted)
make a rough sound by breathing forcefully through the nose. **snort** *noun*

snout *noun* (*plural* snouts)
an animal's projecting nose, or nose and jaws.
[from old German or old Dutch]

snow *noun*
frozen drops of water that fall from the sky in small white flakes.
snow *verb* (snows, snowing, snowed)
send down snow.
be snowed under be overwhelmed with a mass of letters or work etc.

snowdrop *noun* (*plural* snowdrops)
a small white flower that blooms in early spring.

snowdrift *noun* (*plural* snowdrifts)
a large heap or bank of snow piled up by the wind.

snowflake *noun* (*plural* snowflakes)
a flake of snow.

snowshoe *noun* (*plural* snowshoes)
a frame rather like a tennis racket for walking on soft snow.

snowstorm *noun* (*plural* snowstorms)
a storm in which snow falls.

snub *verb* (snubs, snubbing, snubbed)
treat in a scornful or unfriendly way.
snub *noun* (*plural* snubs)
scornful or unfriendly treatment.

snub-nosed *adjective*
having a short turned-up nose.

snuff[1] *noun*
powdered tobacco for taking into the nose by sniffing.
[from old Dutch *snuffen* = snuffle]

snuff[2] *verb* (snuffs, snuffing, snuffed)
put out a candle by covering or pinching the flame. **snuffer** *noun* [origin unknown]

snuffle *verb* (snuffles, snuffling, snuffled)
sniff in a noisy way. **snuffle** *noun*
[same origin as *snuff*[1]]

snug *adjective* (snugger, snuggest)
1 cosy. 2 fitting closely. **snugly** *adverb*,
snugness *noun* [probably from Dutch]

snuggle *verb* (snuggles, snuggling, snuggled)
press closely and comfortably; nestle.
[from *snug*]

so *adverb*
1 in this way; to such an extent, *Why are you so cross?* 2 very, *Cricket is so boring.* 3 also, *I was wrong but so were you.*
or so or about that number.
so far up to now.
so long! (*informal*) goodbye.
so what? (*informal*) that is not important.
so *conjunction*
for that reason, *They threw me out, so I came here.* [from Old English]

soak *verb* (soaks, soaking, soaked)
make a person or thing very wet. **soak** *noun*
soak up take in a liquid in the way that a sponge does.

soap *noun* (*plural* **soaps**)
1 a substance used with water for washing and cleaning things. 2 a soap opera.
soapy *adjective*

soap opera *noun* (*plural* **soap operas**)
a television serial about the everyday lives of a group of people.
[originally American, where they were sponsored by soap manufacturers]

soar *verb* (**soars, soaring, soared**)
1 rise high in the air. 2 rise very high, *Prices were soaring.*
[from old French; related to *aura*]

sob *verb* (**sobs, sobbing, sobbed**)
make a gasping sound when crying.
sob *noun* [probably from old Dutch]

sober *adjective*
1 not drunk. 2 serious and calm. 3 (of colour) not bright.
soberly *adverb*, **sobriety** (*say* so-bry-it-ee) *noun*
sober *verb* (**sobers, sobering, sobered**)
make or become more sober. [from Latin]

so-called *adjective*
named in what may be the wrong way, *This so-called gentleman slammed the door.*

soccer *noun*
Association football. [short for *Association*]

sociable *adjective*
liking to be with other people; friendly.
sociably *adverb*, **sociability** *noun*
[same origin as *social*]

social *adjective*
1 living in a community, not alone, *Bees are social insects.* 2 of life in a community, *social science.* 3 concerned with people's welfare, *social worker.* 4 helping people to meet each other, *a social club.* 5 sociable. **socially** *adverb*
[from Latin *sociare* = unite, associate]

socialism *noun*
a political system where wealth is shared equally between people, and the main industries and trade etc. are controlled by the government. (Compare *capitalism.*)
[from French; related to *social*]

socialist *noun* (*plural* **socialists**)
a person who believes in socialism.

social security *noun*
money and other assistance provided by the government for those in need through being ill, disabled, unemployed, etc.

social services *plural noun*
welfare services provided by the government, including schools, hospitals, and pensions.

society *noun* (*plural* **societies**)
1 a community; people living together in a group or nation. 2 a group of people organized for a particular purpose, *the school dramatic society.* 3 company; companionship, *We enjoy the society of our friends.* [same origin as *social*]

sock *noun* (*plural* **socks**)
a short stocking reaching only to the ankle or below the knee. [from Old English]

socket *noun* (*plural* **sockets**)
1 a hollow into which something fits, *a tooth-socket.* 2 a device into which an electric plug or bulb is put to make a connection.
[from old French]

soda water *noun*
water made fizzy with carbon dioxide, used in drinks.

sodden *adjective*
made very wet.
[the old past participle of *seethe*]

sodium *noun*
a soft white metal.

sofa *noun* (*plural* **sofas**)
a kind of settee.
[from Arabic *suffa* = long stone bench]

soft *adjective*
1 not hard or firm; easily pressed. 2 smooth, not rough or stiff. 3 gentle; not loud.
softly *adverb*, **softness** *noun*

soft drink *noun* (*plural* **soft drinks**)
a cold drink that is not alcoholic.

soften *verb* (**softens, softening, softened**)
make or become soft or softer.
softener *noun*

software *noun*
computer programs, disks, etc. (Compare *hardware.*)

soggy *adjective* (**soggier, soggiest**)
very wet and heavy, *soggy ground.*
[from dialect *sog* = swamp]

soil *noun* (*plural* **soils**)
1 the loose earth in which plants grow.
2 territory, *on British soil.* [old French *soil*]

solar panel *noun* (*plural* **solar panels**)
a panel designed to catch the sun's rays and use their energy for heating or to make electricity.

solar power *noun*
electricity or other forms of power derived from the sun's rays.

solar system *noun*
the sun and the planets that revolve round it.
[from Latin *sol* = sun]

soldier *noun* (*plural* **soldiers**)
a member of an army. [from old French]

sole¹ *noun* (*plural* **soles**)
1 the bottom surface of a foot or shoe. 2 a flat edible sea fish.
sole *verb* (**soles, soling, soled**)
put a sole on a shoe. [from Latin *solum*]

sole² *adjective*
single; only, *She was the sole survivor.*
solely *adverb* [from Latin *solus*]

solemn *adjective*
1 not smiling or cheerful. 2 dignified or formal. **solemnly** *adverb*, **solemnity** *noun*

solicitor *noun* (*plural* **solicitors**)
a lawyer who advises clients, prepares legal documents, etc.

solid *adjective*
1 not hollow; with no space inside. 2 keeping its shape; not liquid or gas. 3 continuous, *for two solid hours*. 4 firm or strongly made; not flimsy, *a solid foundation*. 5 showing solidarity; unanimous.
solidly *adverb*, **solidity** *noun*
solid *noun* (*plural* **solids**)
1 a solid thing. 2 a shape that has three dimensions (length, width, and height or depth). [from Latin]

solids *plural noun*
solid food; food that is not liquid, *Is your baby eating solids yet?*

soliloquy (*say* sol-il-ok-wee) *noun* (*plural* **soliloquies**)
a speech in which a person speaks his or her thoughts aloud without addressing anyone. **soliloquize** *verb*
[from Latin *solus* = alone + *loqui* = speak]

solitary *adjective*
1 alone, without companions. 2 single, *a solitary example*. 3 lonely, *a solitary valley*. [from Latin *solus* = alone]

solitary confinement *noun*
a form of punishment in which a prisoner is kept alone in a cell and not allowed to talk to others.

solo *noun* (*plural* **solos**)
something sung, played, danced, or done by one person. **solo** *adjective* & *adverb*, **soloist** *noun*
[Italian, = alone]

soluble *adjective*
1 able to be dissolved. 2 able to be solved. **solubility** *noun* [same origin as *solve*]

solution *noun* (*plural* **solutions**)
1 a liquid in which something is dissolved.
2 the answer to a problem or puzzle. [same origin as *solve*]

solve *verb* (**solves**, **solving**, **solved**)
find the answer to a problem or puzzle. [from Latin *solvere* = unfasten]

solvent *adjective*
1 having enough money to pay all your debts.
2 able to dissolve another substance. **solvency** *noun*
solvent *noun* (*plural* **solvents**)
a liquid used for dissolving something.

sombre *adjective*
dark and gloomy.
[from *sub-* + Latin *umbra* = shade]

some *adjective*
1 a few; a little, *some apples*; *some sugar*. 2 an unknown person or thing, *Some fool left the door open*. 3 about, *We waited some 20 minutes*. **some time** at some point in time, *Come and see me some time* (not 'sometime'). *They left some time ago*.

some *pronoun*
a certain number or amount that is less than the whole, *Some of them were late*.

-some *suffix*
forms 1 adjectives meaning 'quality or manner' (e.g. *handsome*, *quarrelsome*), 2 nouns from numbers, meaning 'a group of this many' (e.g. *foursome*).
[from Old English]

somebody *pronoun*
1 some person. 2 an important or impressive person.

somehow *adverb*
in some way.

someone *pronoun*
somebody.

somersault *noun* (*plural* **somersaults**)
a movement in which you turn head over heels before landing on your feet. **somersault** *verb*
[from Latin *supra* = above + *saltus* = a leap]

something *noun*
some thing; a thing which you cannot or do not want to name.
something like rather like, *It's something like a rabbit*; approximately, *It cost something like £10*.

sometimes *adverb*
at some times but not always, *We sometimes walk to school*.

somewhat *adverb*
to some extent, *He was somewhat annoyed*.

somewhere *adverb*
in or to some place.

son *noun* (*plural* **sons**)
a boy or man who is someone's child.

sonata *noun* (*plural* **sonatas**)
a piece of music for one instrument or two, in several movements.
[from Italian *sonare* = to sound]

song *noun* (*plural* **songs**)
1 a tune for singing. 2 singing, *He burst into song*.
a song and dance (*informal*) a great fuss.
for a song bought or sold very cheaply.

sonic boom *noun* (*plural* **sonic booms**)
a loud noise caused by the shock wave of an aircraft travelling faster than the speed of sound. [from Latin *sonus* = sound]

son-in-law *noun* (*plural* **sons-in-law**)
a daughter's husband.

sonnet *noun* (*plural* **sonnets**)
a kind of poem with 14 lines.
[from Italian *sonetto* = a little sound]

soon *adverb*
1 in a short time from now. 2 not long after something.
as soon as willingly, *I'd just as soon stay here.*
as soon as at the moment that.
sooner or later at some time in the future.

soot *noun*
the black powder left by smoke in a chimney or on a building etc. **sooty** *adjective* [from Old English]

soothe *verb* (**soothes, soothing, soothed**)
1 calm. 2 ease pain or distress.
soothingly *adverb* [from Old English]

sop *verb* (**sops, sopping, sopped**)
sop up soak up liquid like a sponge.

sophisticated *adjective*
1 of or accustomed to fashionable life and its ways. 2 complicated, *a sophisticated machine.*
sophistication *noun*
[from Latin *sophisticare* = tamper with, mix with something]

sopping *adjective*
very wet; drenched. [from *sop*]

soppy *adjective*
1 very wet. 2 (*informal*) sentimental in a silly way. [from *sop*]

soprano *noun* (*plural* **sopranos**)
a woman, girl, or boy with a high singing voice. [Italian, from *sopra* = above]

sorcerer *noun* (*plural* **sorcerers**)
a wizard. **sorceress** *noun*, **sorcery** *noun*

sordid *adjective*
1 dirty and nasty. 2 dishonourable; selfish and mercenary, *sordid motives.* **sordidly** *adverb*,
sordidness *noun*
[from Latin]

sore *adjective*
1 painful or smarting. 2 (*informal*) annoyed or offended. 3 serious or distressing, *in sore need.*
soreness *noun*
sore *noun* (*plural* **sores**)
a sore place.
[from Old English]

sorrow *noun* (*plural* **sorrows**)
unhappiness or regret caused by loss or disappointment.
sorrowful *adjective*, **sorrowfully** *adverb*

sorry *adjective* (**sorrier, sorriest**)
1 feeling pity, regret, or sympathy. 2 wretched, *His clothes were in a sorry state.*

sort *noun* (*plural* **sorts**)
a group of things or people that are similar; a kind or variety.
out of sorts slightly unwell or depressed.

sort of (*informal*) rather; to some extent, *I sort of expected it.*

USAGE: Correct use is *this sort of thing* or *these sorts of things* (not 'these sort of things').

sort *verb* (**sorts, sorting, sorted**)
arrange things in groups according to their size, kind, etc. **sorter** *noun*
sort out disentangle; select; (*slang*) deal with and punish someone.

sortie *noun* (*plural* **sorties**)
1 an attack by troops coming out of a besieged place. 2 an attacking expedition by a military aircraft.
[from French *sortir* = go out]

SOS *noun* (*plural* **SOSs**)
an urgent appeal for help.
[the international Morse code signal of extreme distress, chosen because it is easy to recognize, but often said to stand for Save Our Souls]

sought *past tense* of **seek**.

soul *noun* (*plural* **souls**)
1 the invisible part of a person that is believed to go on living after the body has died. 2 a person's mind and emotions etc. 3 a person, *There isn't a soul about.*

sound¹ *noun* (*plural* **sounds**)
1 vibrations that travel through the air and can be detected by the ear; the sensation they produce. 2 sound reproduced in a film etc. 3 a mental impression, *We don't like the sound of his plans.*
sound *verb* (**sounds, sounding, sounded**)
1 produce or cause to produce a sound. 2 give an impression when heard, *He sounds angry.*
3 test by noting the sounds heard, *A doctor sounds a patient's lungs with a stethoscope.*
[from Latin]

sound² *verb* (**sounds, sounding, sounded**)
test the depth of water beneath a ship.
sound out try to find out what a person thinks or feels about something.
[from *sub-* + Latin *unda* = a wave]

sound³ *adjective*
1 in good condition; not damaged. 2 healthy; not diseased. 3 reasonable; correct, *His ideas are sound.* 4 reliable; secure, *a sound investment.* 5 thorough; deep, *a sound sleep.*
soundly *adverb*, **soundness** *noun*
[from Old English *gesund* = healthy]

sound barrier *noun*
the resistance of the air to objects moving at nearly supersonic speed.

sound effects *plural noun*
sounds produced artificially to make a play, film, etc. seem more realistic.

soundtrack *noun* (*plural* **soundtracks**)
the sound that goes with a cinema film.

soup *noun* (*plural* **soups**)
liquid food made from stewed bones, meat,
fish, vegetables, etc.
in the soup (*informal*) in trouble.

sour *adjective*
1 tasting sharp like unripe fruit. 2 stale and
unpleasant, not fresh, *sour milk*. 3 bad-
tempered. **sourly** *adverb*, **sourness** *noun*

source *noun* (*plural* **sources**)
the place from which something comes. [from
old French; related to *surge*]

south *noun*
1 the direction to the right of a person who
faces east. 2 the southern part of a country,
city, etc.
south *adjective & adverb*
towards or in the south. **southerly** (*say* su**th**-er-
lee) *adjective*, **southern** *adjective*,
southerner *noun*, **southernmost** *adjective*

south-east *noun, adjective, & adverb*
midway between south and east.
south-easterly *adjective*, **south-eastern** *adjective*

southward *adjective & adverb*
towards the south. **southwards** *adverb*

south-west *noun, adjective, & adverb*
midway between south and west.
south-westerly *adjective*, **south-western** *adjective*

souvenir (*say* soo-ven-eer) *noun* (*plural*
souvenirs)
something that you keep to remind you of a
person, place, or event.
[from French *se souvenir* = remember]

sovereign *noun* (*plural* **sovereigns**)
1 a king or queen who is the ruler of a country;
a monarch. 2 an old British gold coin,
originally worth £1.
[from old French; related to *super-*]

sow[1] (rhymes with *go*) *verb* (**sows, sowing,
sowed, sown** or **sowed**)
put seeds into the ground so that they will
grow into plants. **sower** *noun*
[from Old English *sawan*]

sow[2] (rhymes with *cow*) *noun* (*plural* **sows**)
a female pig. [from Old English *sugu*]

space *noun* (*plural* **spaces**)
1 the whole area outside the earth, where the
stars and planets are. 2 an area or volume,
This table takes too much space. 3 an empty
area; a gap. 4 an interval of time, *within the
space of an hour.*
space *verb* (**spaces, spacing, spaced**)
arrange things with spaces between, *Space
them out.* [from Latin *spatium* = a space]

spacecraft *noun* (*plural* **spacecraft**)
a vehicle for travelling in outer space.

spaceship *noun* (*plural* **spaceships**)
a spacecraft.

space shuttle *noun* (*plural* **space shuttles**)
a spacecraft for repeated use to and from outer
space.

space station *noun* (*plural* **space stations**)
a satellite which orbits the earth and is used as
a base by scientists and astronauts.

spacious *adjective*
providing a lot of space; roomy.
spaciousness *noun*

spade[1] *noun* (*plural* **spades**)
a tool with a long handle and a wide blade for
digging. [from Old English *spadu*]

spade[2] *noun* (*plural* **spades**)
a playing card with black shapes like upside-
down hearts on it, each with a short stem.
[from Italian *spada* = sword]

spaghetti *noun*
pasta made in long thin sticks.
[Italian, = little strings]

span *noun* (*plural* **spans**)
1 the length from end to end or across
something. 2 the distance from the tip of the
thumb to the tip of the little finger when the
hand is spread out. 3 the part between two
uprights of an arch or bridge. 4 the length of a
period of time.

spaniel *noun* (*plural* **spaniels**)
a kind of dog with long ears and silky fur.
[from old French *espaigneul* = Spanish
(because it originated in Spain)]

spank *verb* (**spanks, spanking, spanked**)
smack a person on the bottom as a
punishment. [imitating the sound]

spanner *noun* (*plural* **spanners**)
a tool for gripping and turning the nut on a bolt
etc. [German, from *spannen* = tighten]

spar[1] *noun* (*plural* **spars**)
a strong pole used for a mast or boom etc. on a
ship. [from Old Norse]

spar[2] *verb* (**spars, sparring, sparred**)
1 practise boxing. 2 quarrel or argue. [from
Old English]

spare *verb* (**spares, sparing, spared**)
1 afford to give something, *Can you spare a
moment?* 2 be merciful towards someone; not
hurt or harm a person or thing. 3 use or treat
economically, *No expense will be spared. Spare
the rod and spoil the child!*
spare *adjective*
1 not used but kept ready in case it is needed;
extra, *a spare wheel.* 2 thin; lean.
sparely *adverb*, **spareness** *noun*
go spare (*slang*) become very annoyed.

spare time *noun*
time not needed for work.

sparing (*say* spair-ing) *adjective*
economical; grudging. **sparingly** *adverb*
[from *spare*]

spark *noun* (*plural* sparks)
1 a tiny glowing particle. 2 a flash produced electrically.
spark *verb* (sparks, sparking, sparked)
give off a spark or sparks.

sparkle *verb* (sparkles, sparkling, sparkled)
1 shine with tiny flashes of light. 2 show brilliant wit or liveliness. **sparkle** *noun*
[from *spark*]

sparkler *noun* (*plural* sparklers)
a sparking firework.

spark plug *noun* (*plural* spark plugs)
a device that makes a spark to ignite the fuel in an engine.

sparrow *noun* (*plural* sparrows)
a small brown bird. [from Old English]

sparse *adjective*
thinly scattered; not numerous, *a sparse population.* **sparsely** *adverb*, **sparseness** *noun*
[from Latin *sparsum* = scattered]

spasm *noun* (*plural* spasms)
1 a sudden involuntary movement of a muscle. 2 a sudden brief spell of activity etc.
[from Greek]

spasmodic *adjective*
1 to do with or caused by a spasm. 2 happening or done at irregular intervals.
spasmodically *adverb*

spastic *noun* (*plural* spastics)
a person suffering from spasms of the muscles and jerky movements, especially caused by cerebral palsy.

USAGE: Do not use this word to mean a clumsy or stupid person.

spat *past tense* of **spit**[1].

spate *noun* (*plural* spates)
a sudden flood or rush. [origin unknown]

spatter *verb* (spatters, spattering, spattered)
1 scatter in small drops. 2 splash, *spattered with mud.* **spatter** *noun* [origin unknown]

spawn *noun*
1 the eggs of fish, frogs, toads, or shellfish. 2 the thread-like matter from which fungi grow.
spawn *verb* (spawns, spawning, spawned)
1 produce spawn. 2 be produced from spawn. 3 produce something in great quantities.
[from old French]

speak *verb* (speaks, speaking, spoke, spoken)
1 say something; talk. 2 talk or be able to talk in a foreign language, *Do you speak French?*
speak up 1 speak more loudly. 2 give your opinion.

speaker *noun* (*plural* speakers)
1 a person who is speaking. 2 someone who makes a speech. 3 a loudspeaker.

the Speaker the person who controls the debates in the House of Commons or a similar assembly.

spear *noun* (*plural* spears)
a weapon for throwing or stabbing, with a long shaft and a pointed tip.

special *adjective*
1 of a particular kind; for some purpose, not general, *special training.* 2 exceptional, *Take special care of it.*
[same origin as *species*]

special effects *plural noun*
illusions created for films or television by using props, trick photography, or computer images.

specialist *noun* (*plural* specialists)
an expert in one subject, *a skin specialist.*

speciality *noun* (*plural* specialities)
1 a special quality or product. 2 something in which a person specializes.

specialize *verb* (specializes, specializing, specialized)
give particular attention or study to one subject or thing, *She specialized in biology.*
specialization *noun*

species (*say* spee-shiz) *noun* (*plural* species)
1 a group of animals or plants that are very similar. 2 a kind or sort, *a species of sledge.*
[Latin, = appearance, form, or kind]

specific *adjective*
definite or precise; of or for a particular thing, *The money was given for a specific purpose.*
specifically *adverb*
[same origin as *species*]

specific gravity *noun*
the weight of something as compared with the same volume of water or air.

specimen *noun* (*plural* specimens)
1 a sample. 2 an example, *a fine specimen of an oak tree.* [Latin, from *specere* = to look]

speck *noun* (*plural* specks)
a small spot or particle. [from Old English]

speckle *noun* (*plural* speckles)
a small spot or mark. **speckled** *adjective*

spectacle *noun* (*plural* spectacles)
1 an impressive sight or display. 2 a ridiculous sight.
[from Latin *spectaculum* = a public show]

spectacles *plural noun*
a pair of lenses set in a frame, worn in front of the eyes to help the wearer to see clearly.
spectacled *adjective*

spectacular *adjective*
impressive. [same origin as *spectacle*]

spectator *noun* (*plural* spectators)
a person who watches a game, show, incident, etc. [from Latin *spectare* = to look at]

spectre *noun* (*plural* **spectres**)
a ghost. **spectral** *adjective*
[same origin as *spectrum*]

spectrum *noun* (*plural* **spectra**)
1 the bands of colours seen in a rainbow. 2 a wide range of things, ideas, etc.
[Latin, = image]

speculate *verb* (**speculates, speculating, speculated**)
1 form opinions without having any definite evidence. 2 make investments in the hope of making a profit but risking a loss.
speculation *noun*, **speculator** *noun*, **speculative** *adjective*
[from Latin *speculari* = spy out]

sped *past tense* of **speed**.

speech *noun* (*plural* **speeches**)
1 the action or power of speaking. 2 words spoken. 3 a talk to an audience.

speechless *adjective*
unable to speak because of great emotion.

speed *noun* (*plural* **speeds**)
1 a measure of the time in which something moves or happens. 2 quickness or swiftness.
at speed quickly.
speed *verb* (**speeds, speeding, sped** (in senses 3 and 4 **speeded**))
1 go quickly, *The train sped by.* 2 send quickly, *to speed you on your way.* 3 travel too fast. 4 make or become quicker, *This will speed things up.* [from Old English]

speed limit *noun* (*plural* **speed limits**)
the maximum speed at which vehicles may legally travel on a particular road.

speedometer *noun* (*plural* **speedometers**)
a device in a vehicle, showing its speed.
[from *speed* + *meter*]

speedy *adjective* (**speedier, speediest**)
quick or swift. **speedily** *adverb*

spell[1] *noun* (*plural* **spells**)
a saying or action etc. supposed to have magical power.
[from Old English *spel* = speech, story]

spell[2] *noun* (*plural* **spells**)
1 a period of time. 2 a period of a certain work or activity etc. [from Old English *spelian* = take someone's place, take over a task]

spell[3] *verb* (**spells, spelling, spelled** or **spelt**)
1 put letters in the right order to make a word or words. 2 have as a result, *Wet weather spells ruin for crops.* **speller** *noun* [via old French from Germanic]

spellbound *adjective*
entranced as if by a magic spell.

spend *verb* (**spends, spending, spent**)
1 use money to pay for things. 2 use up, *Don't spend too much time on it.* 3 pass time, *We spent a holiday in Spain.*

sperm *noun* (*plural* **sperms** or **sperm**)
the male cell that fuses with an ovum. [from Greek *sperma* = seed]

sphere *noun* (*plural* **spheres**)
1 a perfectly round solid shape; the shape of a ball. 2 a field of action or interest etc., *That country is in Russia's sphere of influence.*
spherical *adjective*
[from Greek *sphaira* = ball]

spice *noun* (*plural* **spices**)
a substance used to flavour food, often made from dried parts of plants. **spicy** *adjective*
[from old French]

spick and span *adjective*
neat and clean. [*span* is from Old Norse; *spick* is probably from old Dutch]

spider *noun* (*plural* **spiders**)
a small animal with eight legs that spins webs to catch insects on which it feeds.
[from Old English *spithra* = spinner]

spike *noun* (*plural* **spikes**)
1 a pointed piece of metal; a sharp point. 2 a long narrow projecting part.
spiky *adjective*

spill *verb* (**spills, spilling, spilt** or **spilled**)
1 let something fall out of a container. 2 become spilt, *The coins came spilling out.*
spillage *noun*

spin *verb* (**spins, spinning, spun**)
1 turn round and round quickly. 2 make raw wool or cotton into threads by pulling and twisting its fibres. 3 (of a spider or silkworm) make a web or cocoon out of threads from its body.
spin a yarn tell a story.
spin out cause to last a long time.

spinach *noun*
a vegetable with dark green leaves.
[via Spanish and Arabic from Persian]

spinal cord *noun* (*plural* **spinal cords**)
the thick cord of nerves enclosed in the spine, that carries impulses to and from the brain.

spindly *adjective*
thin and long or tall. [from *spindle*]

spine *noun* (*plural* **spines**)
1 the line of bones down the middle of the back. 2 a thorn or prickle. 3 the back part of a book where the pages are joined together.
[from Latin]

spineless *adjective*
1 without a backbone. 2 lacking in determination or strength of character.

spinney *noun* (*plural* **spinneys**)
a small wood or thicket. [from old French]

spin-off *noun* (*plural* **spin-offs**)
a by-product.

spinster *noun* (*plural* spinsters)
a woman who has not married.
[the original meaning was 'one who spins' (because many unmarried women used to earn their living by spinning, which could be done at home)]

spiny *adjective*
covered with spines; prickly.

spiral *adjective*
going round and round a central point and becoming gradually closer to it or further from it; twisting continually round a central line or cylinder etc. **spirally** *adverb*
spiral *noun* (*plural* spirals)
a spiral line or course.
spiral *verb* (spirals, spiralling, spiralled)
move in a spiral.
[from Greek *speira* = winding]

spire *noun* (*plural* spires)
a tall pointed part on top of a church tower.

spirit *noun* (*plural* spirits)
1 the soul. 2 a person's mood or mind and feelings, *He was in good spirits.* 3 a ghost or a supernatural being. 4 courage or liveliness, *She answered with spirit.* 5 a kind of quality in something, *the romantic spirit of the book.* 6 a strong distilled alcoholic drink.
spirit *verb* (spirits, spiriting, spirited)
carry off quickly and secretly, *They spirited her away.*
[from Latin *spiritus* = breath]

spirit level *noun* (*plural* spirit levels)
a device consisting of a tube of liquid with an air bubble in it, used to find out whether something is level.

spiritual *adjective*
1 to do with the human soul; not physical. 2 to do with the Church or religion.
spiritually *adverb*, **spirituality** *noun*
spiritual *noun* (*plural* spirituals)
a religious folk song, especially of Black people in America.

spiritualism *noun*
the belief that the spirits of dead people communicate with living people.
spiritualist *noun*

spit[1] *verb* (spits, spitting, spat or spit)
1 send out drops of liquid etc. forcibly from the mouth, *He spat at me.* 2 fall lightly, *It's spitting with rain.*
spit *noun*
saliva. [from Old English *spittan*]

spit[2] *noun* (*plural* spits)
1 a long thin metal spike put through meat to hold it while it is being roasted. 2 a narrow strip of land sticking out into the sea.
[from Old English *spitu*]

spite *noun*
a desire to hurt or annoy somebody. **spiteful** *adjective*, **spitefully** *adverb*, **spitefulness** *noun*

in spite of not being prevented by, *We went out in spite of the rain.*
[same origin as *despite*]

spitting image *noun*
an exact likeness.

splash *verb* (splashes, splashing, splashed)
1 make liquid fly about in drops. 2 (of liquid) be splashed. 3 wet by splashing, *The bus splashed us.*
splash *noun* (*plural* splashes)
1 the action or sound or mark of splashing. 2 a striking display or effect.

splay *verb* (splays, splaying, splayed)
spread or slope apart. [from *display*]

splendid *adjective*
1 magnificent; full of splendour. 2 excellent.
splendidly *adverb*
[from Latin *splendidus* = shining]

splendour *noun*
a brilliant display or appearance.
[from Latin *splendere* = shine brightly]

splint *noun* (*plural* splints)
a straight piece of wood or metal etc. tied to a broken arm or leg to hold it firm.

splinter *noun* (*plural* splinters)
a thin sharp piece of wood, glass, stone, etc. broken off a larger piece.
splinter *verb* (splinters, splintering, splintered)
break into splinters.

splinter group *noun* (*plural* splinter groups)
a group of people that has broken away from a larger group or movement.

split *verb* (splits, splitting, split)
1 break into parts; divide. 2 (*slang*) reveal a secret.
split *noun* (*plural* splits)
1 the splitting or dividing of something. 2 a place where something has split.
the splits an acrobatic position in which the legs are stretched widely in opposite directions.

split second *noun* a very brief moment of time; an instant.

splutter *verb* (splutters, spluttering, spluttered)
1 make a quick series of spitting sounds. 2 speak quickly but not clearly. **splutter** *noun*
[imitating the sound]

spoil *verb* (spoils, spoiling, spoilt or spoiled)
1 damage something and make it useless or unsatisfactory. 2 make someone selfish by always letting them have what they want.

spoke[1] (*plural* spokes)
each of the bars or rods that go from the centre of a wheel to its rim.

spoke[2] *past tense* of speak.

spokesperson *noun* (*plural* spokespersons)
a person who speaks on behalf of a group of people. **spokesman** *noun*, **spokeswoman** *noun*

sponge *noun* (*plural* sponges)
1 a sea creature with a soft porous body. 2 the skeleton of this creature, or a piece of a similar substance, used for washing or padding things. 3 a soft lightweight cake or pudding.
spongy *adjective*
sponge *verb* (sponges, sponging, sponged)
1 wipe or wash something with a sponge. 2 live by cadging from people, *He sponged on his friends.* **sponger** *noun*

sponsor *noun* (*plural* sponsors)
someone who provides money or help etc. for a person or thing, or who gives money to a charity in return for something achieved by another person.
sponsorship *noun*
sponsor *verb* (sponsors, sponsoring, sponsored)
be a sponsor for a person or thing.
[from Latin *sponsum* = promised]

spontaneous (*say* spon-tay-nee-us) *adjective*
happening or done naturally; not forced or suggested by someone else.
spontaneously *adverb*, **spontaneity** *noun*
[from Latin *sponte* = of your own accord]

spool *noun* (*plural* spools)
a rod or cylinder on which something is wound. [via old French from Germanic]

spoon *noun* (*plural* spoons)
a small device with a rounded bowl on a handle, used for lifting things to the mouth or for stirring or measuring things. **spoonful** *noun* (*plural* spoonfuls)

spoonerism *noun* (*plural* spoonerisms)
an accidental exchange of the initial letters of two words, e.g. by saying *a boiled sprat* instead of *a spoiled brat.*
[named after Canon Spooner (1844–1930), who made mistakes of this kind]

spore *noun* (*plural* spores)
a tiny reproductive cell of a plant such as a fungus or fern. [from Greek *spora* = seed]

sport *noun* (*plural* sports)
1 an athletic activity; a game or pastime, especially outdoors. 2 games of this kind, *Are you keen on sport?* 3 (*informal*) a person who behaves fairly and generously, *Come on, be a sport!*

sporting chance *noun*
a reasonable chance of success.

sports car *noun* (*plural* sports cars)
an open low-built fast car.

sportsman *noun* (*plural* sportsmen)
1 a man who takes part in sport. 2 a person who shows sportsmanship.

sportsmanship *noun*
sporting behaviour; behaving fairly and generously to rivals.

sportswoman *noun* (*plural* sportswomen)
1 a woman who takes part in sport. 2 a woman who shows sportsmanship.

spot *noun* (*plural* spots)
1 a small round mark. 2 a pimple. 3 a small amount, *We had a spot of trouble.* 4 a place. 5 a drop, *a few spots of rain.*
on the spot without delay or change of place; under pressure to take action, *This really puts him on the spot!*
spot *verb* (spots, spotting, spotted)
1 mark with spots. 2 (*informal*) notice, *We spotted her in the crowd.* 3 watch for and take note of, *train-spotting.* **spotter** *noun*

spotlight *noun* (*plural* spotlights)
1 a strong light that can shine on one small area. 2 public attention, *The Royal Family are used to being in the spotlight.*

spotty *adjective*
marked with spots.

spouse *noun* (*plural* spouses)
a person's husband or wife.
[from old French; related to *sponsor*]

spout *noun* (*plural* spouts)
1 a pipe or similar opening from which liquid can pour. 2 a jet of liquid.
spout *verb* (spouts, spouting, spouted)
1 come or send out as a jet of liquid. 2 (*informal*) speak for a long time.

sprain *verb* (sprains, spraining, sprained)
injure a joint by twisting it. **sprain** *noun*

sprawl *verb* (sprawls, sprawling, sprawled)
1 sit or lie with the arms and legs spread out loosely. 2 spread out loosely or untidily.
sprawl *noun* [from Old English]

spray[1] *verb* (sprays, spraying, sprayed)
scatter tiny drops of liquid over something.
spray *noun* (*plural* sprays)
1 tiny drops of liquid sprayed. 2 a device for spraying liquid. [origin unknown]

spray[2] *noun* (*plural* sprays)
1 a single shoot with its leaves and flowers. 2 a small bunch of flowers.
[from Old English]

spread *verb* (spreads, spreading, spread)
1 open or stretch something out to its full size, *The bird spread its wings.* 2 make something cover a surface, *We spread jam on the bread.* 3 become longer or wider, *The stain was spreading.* 4 make or become more widely known or felt or distributed etc., *We spread the news. Panic spread.*
spread *noun* (*plural* spreads)
1 the action or result of spreading. 2 a thing's breadth or extent. 3 a paste for spreading on bread. 4 (*informal*) a large or grand meal.
[from Old English]

spreadeagled *adjective*
with arms and legs stretched out, *He lay spreadeagled on the bed.*
[originally = a picture of an eagle with legs and wings stretched out, used as an emblem on a knight's shield, inn sign, etc.]

spree *noun* (*plural* **sprees**)
a lively outing. [origin unknown]

sprig *noun* (*plural* **sprigs**)
a small branch; a shoot. [from old German]

sprightly *adjective* (**sprightlier, sprightliest**)
lively and full of energy. [from *sprite*]

spring *verb* (**springs, springing, sprang, sprung**)
1 jump; move quickly or suddenly, *He sprang to his feet.* 2 originate or arise, *The trouble has sprung from carelessness.* 3 present or produce suddenly, *They sprang a surprise on us.*

spring *noun* (*plural* **springs**)
1 a springy coil or bent piece of metal. 2 a springing movement. 3 a place where water comes up naturally from the ground. 4 the season when most plants begin to grow. [from Old English]

springboard *noun* (*plural* **springboards**)
a springy board from which people jump in diving and gymnastics.

spring-clean *verb* (**spring-cleans, spring-cleaning, spring-cleaned**)
clean a house thoroughly in springtime.

springy *adjective* (**springier, springiest**)
able to spring back easily after being bent or squeezed. **springiness** *noun*

sprinkle *verb* (**sprinkles, sprinkling, sprinkled**)
make tiny drops or pieces fall on something. **sprinkler** *noun*

sprint *verb* (**sprints, sprinting, sprinted**)
run very fast for a short distance. **sprint** *noun*, **sprinter** *noun* [from Old Norse]

sprout *verb* (**sprouts, sprouting, sprouted**)
start to grow; put out shoots.

sprout *noun* (*plural* **sprouts**)
1 a shoot of a plant. 2 a Brussels sprout.

spruce[1] *noun* (*plural* **spruces**)
a kind of fir tree. [from *Pruce*, the old name of Prussia, an area in central Europe, where it was grown]

spruce[2] *adjective*
neat and trim; smart.

spruce *verb* (**spruces, sprucing, spruced**)
smarten, *Spruce yourself up.*
[probably from *spruce jerkin*, made of leather from Prussia (see **spruce**[1])]

spry *adjective* (**spryer, spryest**)
active, nimble, and lively.

spur *noun* (*plural* **spurs**)
1 a sharp device worn on the heel of a rider's boot to urge a horse to go faster. 2 a stimulus

or incentive. 3 a projecting part.
on the spur of the moment on an impulse; without planning.

spur *verb* (**spurs, spurring, spurred**)
urge on; encourage. [from Old English]

spurious *adjective*
not genuine. [from Latin]

spurn *verb* (**spurns, spurning, spurned**)
reject scornfully. [from Old English]

spurt *verb* (**spurts, spurting, spurted**)
1 gush out. 2 increase your speed suddenly.

spurt *noun* (*plural* **spurts**)
1 a sudden gush. 2 a sudden increase in speed or effort. [origin unknown]

spy *noun* (*plural* **spies**)
someone who works secretly for one country, person, etc. to find out things about another.

spy *verb* (**spies, spying, spied**)
1 be a spy. 2 keep watch secretly. 3 see or notice, *She spied a house.* 4 pry.
[from old French *espier* = espy]

squabble *verb* (**squabbles, squabbling, squabbled**)
quarrel or bicker. **squabble** *noun*

squad *noun* (*plural* **squads**)
a small group of people working or being trained together.
[from old French; related to *squadron*]

squadron *noun* (*plural* **squadrons**)
part of an army, navy, or air force.
[from Italian; related to *squad*]

squalid *adjective*
dirty and unpleasant.
squalidly *adverb*, **squalor** *noun*
[from Latin *squalidus* = rough, dirty]

squall *noun* (*plural* **squalls**)
1 a sudden storm or gust of wind. 2 a baby's loud cry.

squall *verb* (**squalls, squalling, squalled**)
(of a baby) cry loudly.
[probably from *squeal* and *bawl*]

squander *verb* (**squanders, squandering, squandered**)
spend money or time etc. wastefully.

square *noun* (*plural* **squares**)
1 a flat shape with four equal sides and four right angles. 2 an area surrounded by buildings, *Leicester Square.* 3 the number produced by multiplying something by itself, *9 is the square of 3* $(9 = 3 \times 3)$.

square *adjective*
1 having the shape of a square. 2 forming a right angle, *The desk has square corners.* 3 equal or even, *The teams are all square with six points each.*
squarely *adverb*, **squareness** *noun*

square foot, square metre, etc., the area of a surface with sides that are one foot or one metre etc. long.

square *verb* (squares, squaring, squared)
1 make a thing square. 2 multiply a number by itself, *5 squared is 25.* 3 match; make or be consistent, *His story doesn't square with yours.* 4 (*informal*) bribe.
[from old French; related to *quadrant*]
square deal *noun*
one that is honest and fair.
square meal *noun* (*plural* square meals)
a good satisfying meal.
square root *noun* (*plural* square roots)
the number that gives a particular number if it is multiplied by itself, *3 is the square root of 9* (3 × 3 = 9).
squash *verb* (squashes, squashing, squashed)
1 press something so that it loses its shape; crush. 2 pack tightly. 3 suppress or quash.
squash *noun* (*plural* squashes)
1 a crowded condition. 2 a fruit-flavoured soft drink. 3 a game played with rackets and a soft ball in a special indoor court.
squat *verb* (squats, squatting, squatted)
1 sit on your heels; crouch. 2 use an unoccupied building for living in without permission. **squat** *noun*, **squatter** *noun*
squat *adjective*
short and fat. [from *ex-* + old French *quatir* = press down, crouch]
squawk *verb* (squawks, squawking, squawked)
make a loud harsh cry. **squawk** *noun*
squeak *verb* (squeaks, squeaking, squeaked)
make a short high-pitched cry or sound. **squeak** *noun*, **squeaky** *adjective*, **squeakily** *adverb*
[imitating the sound]
squeal *verb* (squeals, squealing, squealed)
make a long shrill cry or sound. **squeal** *noun*
[imitating the sound]
squeamish *adjective*
easily disgusted or shocked. **squeamishness** *noun* [from old French]
squeeze *verb* (squeezes, squeezing, squeezed)
1 press something from opposite sides, especially to get liquid out of it. 2 force into or through a place, *We squeezed through a gap in the hedge.* **squeezer** *noun*
squeeze *noun* (*plural* squeezes)
1 the action of squeezing. 2 a drop of liquid squeezed out, *Add a squeeze of lemon.* 3 a time when money is difficult to get or borrow.
[origin unknown]
squelch *verb* (squelches, squelching, squelched)
make a sound like someone treading in thick mud. **squelch** *noun*
squid *noun* (*plural* squids)
a sea animal with eight short tentacles and two long ones. [origin unknown]
squint *verb* (squints, squinting, squinted)
1 be cross-eyed. 2 peer; look with half-shut eyes at something. **squint** *noun*

squire *noun* (*plural* squires)
1 the man who owns most of the land in a country parish or district. 2 a young nobleman in the Middle Ages who served a knight. [from *esquire*]
squirm *verb* (squirms, squirming, squirmed)
wriggle. [origin unknown]
squirrel *noun* (*plural* squirrels)
a small animal with a bushy tail and red or grey fur, living in trees. [from Greek]
squirt *verb* (squirts, squirting, squirted)
send or come out in a jet of liquid. **squirt** *noun* [imitating the sound]
St. or **St** *abbreviation*
1 Saint. 2 Street.
stab *verb* (stabs, stabbing, stabbed)
pierce or wound with something sharp.
stab *noun* (*plural* stabs)
1 the action of stabbing. 2 a sudden sharp pain, *She felt a stab of fear.* 3 (*informal*) an attempt, *I'll have a stab at it.*
stability *noun*
being stable.
stable[1] *adjective*
1 steady or firmly fixed; not likely to move or change. 2 sensible and dependable. **stably** *adverb* [from Latin *stare* = to stand]
stable[2] *noun* (*plural* stables)
a building where horses are kept.
stable *verb* (stables, stabling, stabled)
put or keep in a stable.
[from old French; related to *stable*[1]]
stack *noun* (*plural* stacks)
1 a neat pile. 2 a haystack. 3 (*informal*) a large amount, *a stack of work.* 4 a single tall chimney; a group of small chimneys.
stack *verb* (stacks, stacking, stacked)
pile things up. [from Old Norse]
stadium *noun* (*plural* stadiums)
a sports ground surrounded by seats for spectators. [Latin]
staff *noun* (*plural* staffs or, in sense 4, staves)
1 the people who work in an office, shop, etc. 2 the teachers in a school or college. 3 a stick or pole used as a weapon or support or as a symbol of authority. 4 a set of five horizontal lines on which music is written.
staff *verb* (staffs, staffing, staffed)
provide with a staff of people, *The centre is staffed by volunteers.* [from Old English]
stag *noun* (*plural* stags)
a male deer. [probably from Old English]
stage *noun* (*plural* stages)
1 a platform for performances in a theatre or hall. 2 a point or part of a process, journey, etc., *the final stage.*
stage *verb* (stages, staging, staged)
1 present a performance on a stage. 2 organize, *We decided to stage a protest.*

stagecoach *noun* (*plural* **stagecoaches**)
a horse-drawn coach that formerly ran regularly from one point to another along the same route.

stage-manage *verb* (**stage-manages, stage-managing, stage-managed**)
1 be stage manager. 2 organize and control an event so that it has a particular effect.

stage manager *noun* (*plural* **stage managers**)
the person in charge of the scenery, lighting, sound, etc. during a performance.

stage-struck *adjective*
fascinated by the theatre and longing to be an actor.

stagger *verb* (**staggers, staggering, staggered**)
1 walk unsteadily. 2 shock deeply; amaze, *We were staggered at the price.* 3 arrange things so that they do not coincide, *Please stagger your holidays so that there is always someone here.*
stagger *noun*

stagnant *adjective*
1 not flowing. 2 not active or developing, *business is stagnant.*
[from Latin *stagnum* = a pool]

stain *noun* (*plural* **stains**)
1 a dirty mark on something. 2 a blemish on someone's character or past record. 3 a liquid used for staining things.
stain *verb* (**stains, staining, stained**)
1 make a stain on something. 2 colour with a liquid that sinks into the surface.
[from an old word *distain* = dye]

stained glass *noun*
pieces of coloured glass held together in a lead framework to make a picture or pattern.

stainless steel *noun*
steel that does not rust easily.

stair *noun* (*plural* **stairs**)
each of the fixed steps in a series that lead from one level or floor to another in a building.
[from Old English]

staircase *noun* (*plural* **staircases**)
a flight of stairs.

stake *noun* (*plural* **stakes**)
1 a thick pointed stick to be driven into the ground. 2 the post to which people used to be tied for execution by being burnt alive. 3 an amount of money bet on something. 4 an investment that gives a person a share or interest in an enterprise.
at stake being risked.
stake *verb* (**stakes, staking, staked**)
1 fasten, support, or mark out with stakes. 2 bet or risk money etc. on an event.
stake a claim claim or obtain a right to something.

stalactite *noun* (*plural* **stalactites**)
a stony spike hanging like an icicle from the roof of a cave.
[from Greek *stalaktos* = dripping]

USAGE: See note at *stalagmite.*

stalagmite *noun* (*plural* **stalagmites**)
a stony spike standing like a pillar on the floor of a cave.
[from Greek *stalagma* = a drop]

USAGE: Remember that a *stalagmite* stands up from the ground, while a *stalactite* hangs down from the ceiling.

stale *adjective*
not fresh. **staleness** *noun*
[old French, = at a standstill]

stalemate *noun*
1 a drawn position in chess when a player cannot make a move without putting his or her king in check. 2 a deadlock; a situation in which neither side in an argument will give way. [from old French *stale* = at a standstill, + *mate²*]

stalk¹ *noun* (*plural* **stalks**)
a stem of a plant etc.
[from Old English *stalu*]

stalk² *verb* (**stalks, stalking, stalked**)
1 track or hunt stealthily. 2 walk in a stiff or dignified way.
[from Old English *stealcian*]

stall¹ *noun* (*plural* **stalls**)
1 a table or counter from which things are sold. 2 a place for one animal in a stable or shed.
stall *verb* (**stalls, stalling, stalled**)
1 stop suddenly, *The car engine stalled.* 2 put an animal into a stall.
[from Old English]

stall² *verb* (**stalls, stalling, stalled**)
delay things deliberately so as to avoid having to take action. [from an old word *stall* = a decoy or a pickpocket's helper]

stallion *noun* (*plural* **stallions**)
a male horse. [from old French]

stalls *plural noun*
the seats in the lowest level of a theatre.

stalwart *adjective*
sturdy; strong and faithful, *my stalwart supporters.* [from Old English]

stamen *noun* (*plural* **stamens**)
the part of a flower bearing pollen.
[Latin, = thread]

stamina *noun*
strength and ability to endure things for a long time.
[Latin, plural of *stamen* (referring to the threads of life spun by the fates)]

stammer *verb* (stammers, stammering, stammered)
keep repeating the same syllables when you speak. **stammer** *noun*

stamp *noun* (*plural* stamps)
1 a small piece of gummed paper with a special design on it; a postage stamp. **2** a small device for pressing words or marks on something; the words or marks made by this. **3** a distinctive characteristic, *His story bears the stamp of truth.*
stamp *verb* (stamps, stamping, stamped)
1 bang a foot heavily on the ground. **2** walk with loud heavy steps. **3** stick a stamp on something. **4** press a mark or design etc. on something.
stamp out put out a fire etc. by stamping; stop something, *stamp out cruelty.*

stampede *noun* (*plural* stampedes)
a sudden rush by animals or people.
stampede *verb*
[from Spanish *estampida* = crash, uproar]

stand *verb* (stands, standing, stood)
1 be on your feet without moving, *We were standing at the back of the hall.* **2** set or be upright; place, *We stood the vase on the table.* **3** stay the same, *My offer still stands.* **4** be a candidate for election, *She stood for Parliament.* **5** tolerate or endure, *I can't stand that noise.* **6** provide and pay for, *I'll stand you a drink.*
it stands to reason it is reasonable or obvious.
stand by be ready for action.
stand for 1 represent. **2** tolerate.
stand up for support or defend.
stand up to 1 resist bravely. **2** stay in good condition in hard use.
stand *noun* (*plural* stands)
1 something made for putting things on, *a music stand.* **2** a stall where things are sold or displayed. **3** a grandstand. **4** a stationary condition or position, *He took his stand near the door.* **5** resistance to attack, *We made a stand.*

standard *noun* (*plural* standards)
1 how good something is, *a high standard of work.* **2** a thing used to measure or judge something else. **3** a special flag, *the royal standard.* **4** an upright support.
standard *adjective*
1 of the usual or average quality or kind. **2** regarded as the best and widely used, *the standard book on spiders.* [from old French]

stand-in *noun* (*plural* stand-ins)
a deputy or substitute.

standing order *noun* (*plural* standing orders)
an instruction to a bank to make regular payments, or to a trader to supply something regularly.

stand-offish *adjective*
cold and formal; not friendly.

standpoint *noun* (*plural* standpoints)
a point of view.

standstill *noun*
a stop; an end to movement or activity.

staple[1] *noun* (*plural* staples)
1 a small piece of metal pushed through papers and clenched to fasten them together. **2** a U-shaped nail. **staple** *verb*, **stapler** *noun*
[from Old English]

staple[2] *adjective*
main or usual, *Rice is their staple food.*
staple *noun* [from old French]

star *noun* (*plural* stars)
1 a large mass of burning gas that is seen as a speck of light in the sky at night. **2** a shape with rays from it; an asterisk. **3** an object or mark of this shape showing rank or quality, *a five-star hotel.* **4** a famous performer; one of the chief performers in a play or show etc.
star *verb* (stars, starring, starred)
1 perform or present as a star in a show etc. **2** mark with an asterisk or star symbol.
[from Old English]

starboard *noun*
the right-hand side of a ship or aircraft when you are facing forward. (Compare *port*[1].) [from Old English *steor* = paddle for steering (usually mounted on the right-hand side), + *board*]

starch *noun* (*plural* starches)
1 a white carbohydrate in bread, potatoes, etc. **2** this or a similar substance used to stiffen clothes. **starchy** *adjective*
starch *verb* (starches, starching, starched)
stiffen with starch. [from Old English]

stare *verb* (stares, staring, stared)
look at something intensely. **stare** *noun*

starfish *noun* (*plural* starfish or starfishes)
a sea animal shaped like a star with five points.

stark *adjective*
1 complete or unmistakable, *stark nonsense.* **2** desolate and bare; without cheerfulness, *the stark lunar landscape.*
starkly *adverb*, **starkness** *noun*
stark *adverb*
completely, *stark naked.*

starling *noun* (*plural* starlings)
a noisy black bird with speckled feathers.

starry *adjective*
full of stars.

starry-eyed *adjective*
made happy by foolish dreams or unrealistic hopes.

start *verb* (starts, starting, started)
1 begin or cause to begin. **2** begin a journey. **3** make a sudden movement because of pain or surprise. **starter** *noun*

start *noun* (*plural* **starts**)
1 the beginning; the place where a race starts.
2 an advantage that someone starts with, *We gave the young ones ten minutes' start.* 3 a sudden movement.

startle *verb* (**startles, startling, startled**)
surprise or alarm someone.

starve *verb* (**starves, starving, starved**)
1 suffer or die from lack of food; cause to do this. 2 (*informal*) be very hungry.
starvation *noun* [from Old English]

state *noun* (*plural* **states**)
1 the quality of a person's or thing's characteristics or circumstances; condition.
2 a grand style, *She arrived in state.* 3 an organized community under one government (*the State of Israel*) or forming part of a republic (*the 50 States of the USA*). 4 a country's government, *Help for the earthquake victims was provided by the state.* 5 (*informal*) an excited or upset condition, *Don't get into a state about the robbery.*

state *verb* (**states, stating, stated**)
express something in spoken or written words.
[same origin as *stable*¹]

stately *adjective* (**statelier, stateliest**)
dignified, imposing, or grand. **stateliness** *noun*
[from *state*]

statement *noun* (*plural* **statements**)
1 words stating something. 2 a formal account of facts, *The witness made a statement to the police.* 3 a written report of a financial account, *a bank statement.*

state school *noun* (*plural* **state schools**)
a school which is funded by the government and which does not charge fees to pupils.

statesman *noun* (*plural* **statesmen**)
a person, especially a man, who is important or skilled in governing a country.
statesmanship *noun*, **stateswoman** *noun*

static *adjective*
not moving or changing. [from Greek]

static electricity *noun*
electricity that is present in something, not flowing as current.

station *noun* (*plural* **stations**)
1 a place where a person or thing stands or is stationed; a position. 2 a stopping place on a railway with buildings for passengers and goods. 3 a building equipped for people who serve the public or for certain activities, *the police station.* 4 a broadcasting establishment with its own frequency.
[from Latin *statio* = a stand, standing]

stationary *adjective*
not moving, *The car was stationary when the van hit it.*

USAGE: Do not confuse with *stationery.*

stationery *noun*
paper, envelopes, and other articles used in writing or typing.

USAGE: Do not confuse with *stationary.*

statistician (*say* stat-is-**tish**-an) *noun* (*plural* **statisticians**)
an expert in statistics.

statistics *noun*
the study of information based on the numbers of things.

statue *noun* (*plural* **statues**)
a model made of stone or metal etc. to look like a person or animal.
[same origin as *stable*¹]

statuette *noun* (*plural* **statuettes**)
a small statue.

stature *noun*
1 the natural height of the body. 2 greatness because of ability or achievement.
[same origin as *stable*¹]

status (*say* **stay**-tus) *noun* (*plural* **statuses**)
1 a person's or thing's position or rank in relation to others. 2 high rank or prestige.
[same origin as *stable*¹]

statute *noun* (*plural* **statutes**)
a law passed by a parliament.
statutory *adjective*
[from Latin *statuere* = set up, decree; related to *stable*¹]

staunch *adjective*
firm and loyal, *our staunch supporters.*
staunchly *adverb*
[from old French]

stave *verb* (**staves, staving, staved** or **stove**)
dent or break a hole in something, *The collision stove in the front of the ship.*
stave off keep something away, *We staved off the disaster.*

stay *verb* (**stays, staying, stayed**)
1 continue to be in the same place or condition; remain. 2 spend time in a place as a visitor.
3 satisfy temporarily, *We stayed our hunger with a sandwich.* 4 pause. 5 show endurance in a race or task.
stay put (*informal*) remain in place.
stay *noun* (*plural* **stays**)
1 a time spent somewhere, *We made a short stay in Rome.* 2 a postponement, *a stay of execution.*
[same origin as *stable*¹]

stead *noun*
in a person's or **thing's stead** instead of this person or thing.
stand a person in good stead be very useful to him or her.

steadfast *adjective*
firm and not changing, *a steadfast refusal.*

steady *adjective* (steadier, steadiest)
1 not shaking or moving; firm. 2 regular; continuing the same, *a steady pace.*
steadily *adverb*, **steadiness** *noun* [from *stead*]

steak *noun* (*plural* steaks)
a thick slice of meat (especially beef) or fish. [from Old Norse]

steal *verb* (steals, stealing, stole, stolen)
1 take and keep something that does not belong to you; take secretly or dishonestly. 2 move secretly or without being noticed, *He stole out of the room.* [from Old English]

stealthy (*say* stelth-ee) *adjective* (stealthier, stealthiest)
quiet and secret, so as not to be noticed.
stealth *noun*, **stealthily** *adverb*, **stealthiness** *noun* [probably from Old English and related to *steal*]

steam *noun*
1 the gas or vapour that comes from boiling water; this used to drive machinery. 2 energy, *He ran out of steam.* **steamy** *adjective*
steam *verb* (steams, steaming, steamed)
1 give out steam. 2 cook or treat by steam, *a steamed pudding.* 3 move by the power of steam, *The ship steamed down the river.*

steam engine *noun* (*plural* steam engines)
an engine driven by steam.

steamroller *noun* (*plural* steamrollers)
a heavy vehicle with a large roller used to flatten surfaces when making roads. [because the first ones were powered by steam]

steed *noun* (*plural* steeds) (*poetical*)
a horse.
[from Old English]

steel *noun* (*plural* steels)
1 a strong metal made from iron and carbon. 2 a steel rod for sharpening knives.
[from Old English]

steely *adjective*
1 like or to do with steel. 2 cold, hard, and severe, *a steely glare.*

steep[1] *adjective*
1 sloping very sharply, not gradually.
2 (*informal*) unreasonably high, *a steep price.*
steeply *adverb*, **steepness** *noun*

steep[2] *verb* (steeps, steeping, steeped)
soak thoroughly; saturate.
[probably from a Scandinavian language]

steepen *verb* (steepens, steepening, steepened)
make or become steeper.

steeple *noun* (*plural* steeples)
a church tower with a spire on top.

steer *verb* (steers, steering, steered)
make a car, ship, or bicycle etc. go in the direction you want; guide. **steersman** *noun*
[from Old English *stieran*]

steering wheel *noun* (*plural* steering wheels)
a wheel for steering a car, boat, etc.

stem[1] *noun* (*plural* stems)
1 the main central part of a tree, shrub, or plant. 2 a thin part on which a leaf, flower, or fruit is supported. 3 a thin upright part, e.g. the thin part of a wineglass between the bowl and the foot. 4 the main part of a verb or other word, to which endings are attached. 5 the front part of a ship, *from stem to stern.*
stem *verb* (stems, stemming, stemmed)
stem from arise from; have as its source. [from Old English]

stem[2] *verb* (stems, stemming, stemmed)
stop the flow of something.
[from Old Norse]

stench *noun* (*plural* stenches)
a very unpleasant smell.

stencil *noun* (*plural* stencils)
a piece of card, metal, or plastic with pieces cut out of it, used to produce a picture, design, etc.

step *noun* (*plural* steps)
1 a movement made by lifting the foot and setting it down. 2 the sound or rhythm of stepping. 3 a level surface for placing the foot on in climbing up or down. 4 each of a series of things done in some process or action, *The first step is to find somewhere to practise.*
in step 1 stepping in time with others in marching or dancing. 2 in agreement.
watch your step be careful.
step *verb* (steps, stepping, stepped)
tread or walk.
step in intervene.
step on it (*informal*) hurry.
step up increase something.
[from Old English *steppan*]

step- *prefix*
related through remarriage of one parent.
[from Old English *steop-*]

stepfather *noun* (*plural* stepfathers)
a man who is married to your mother but was not your natural father.

stepladder *noun* (*plural* stepladders)
a folding ladder with flat treads.

stepmother *noun* (*plural* stepmothers)
a woman who is married to your father but was not your natural mother.

stepping stone *noun* (*plural* stepping stones)
1 each of a line of stones put into a shallow stream so that people can walk across. 2 a way of achieving something, or a stage in achieving it, *good exam results can be a stepping stone to a career.*

stereo *noun* (*plural* stereos)
1 stereophonic sound or recording. 2 a stereophonic record player or radio.
[from *stereophonic*]

stereophonic *adjective*
using sound that comes from two different directions so as to give a natural effect.
[from Greek *stereos* = solid, three-dimensional + *phone* = sound]

stereotype *noun* (*plural* stereotypes)
a standardized character; a fixed idea etc., *The stereotype of a hero is one who is tall, strong, brave, and good-looking.*
[originally = a kind of printing which appeared three-dimensional: from Greek *stereos* = solid, three-dimensional, + *type*]

sterile *adjective*
1 not fertile; barren. 2 free from germs.
sterility *noun* [from Latin]

sterilize *verb* (sterilizes, sterilizing, sterilized)
1 make a thing free from germs, e.g. by heating it. 2 make a person or animal unable to reproduce.
sterilization *noun*, **sterilizer** *noun*

sterling *noun*
British money.
sterling *adjective*
1 genuine, *sterling silver.* 2 excellent; of great worth, *her sterling qualities.*
[probably from Old English *steorra* = star + *-ling* (because some early coins had a star on them)]

stern[1] *adjective*
strict and severe, not lenient or kindly.
sternly *adverb*, **sternness** *noun*

stern[2] *noun* (*plural* sterns)
the back part of a ship.
[from Old Norse]

stew *verb* (stews, stewing, stewed)
cook slowly in liquid.
stew *noun* (*plural* stews)
a dish of stewed food, especially meat and vegetables.
in a stew (*informal*) very worried or agitated.

steward *noun* (*plural* stewards)
1 a man whose job is to look after the passengers on a ship or aircraft. 2 an official who keeps order or supervises the arrangements at an event.
[from Old English *stig* = house or hall, + *ward*]

stewardess *noun* (*plural* stewardesses)
a woman whose job is to look after the passengers on a ship or aircraft.

stick[1] *noun* (*plural* sticks)
1 a long thin piece of wood. 2 a walking stick. 3 the implement used to hit the ball in hockey, polo, etc. 4 a long thin piece of something, *a stick of rock.*
[from Old English *sticca*]

stick[2] *verb* (sticks, sticking, stuck)
1 push a thing into something, *Stick a pin in it.* 2 fix or be fixed by glue or as if by this, *Stick stamps on the parcel.* 3 become fixed and

unable to move, *The boat stuck on a sandbank.* 4 (*informal*) endure or tolerate, *I can't stick that noise!* 5 (*informal*) impose a task on someone, *We were stuck with the clearing up.*
stick out 1 come or push out from a surface; stand out from the surrounding area. 2 be very noticeable.
stick to 1 remain faithful to a friend or promise etc. 2 keep to and not alter, *He stuck to his story.*
stick together 1 stay together. 2 support each other.
stick up for (*informal*) stand up for.

stickler *noun* (*plural* sticklers)
a person who insists on something, *a stickler for punctuality.*
[from Old English *stihtan* = put in order]

sticky *adjective* (stickier, stickiest)
1 able or likely to stick to things. 2 (of weather) hot and humid, causing perspiration. 3 (*informal*) uncooperative, *She was very sticky about letting me come.*
stickily *adverb*, **stickiness** *noun*
come to a sticky end die or end in a painful or unpleasant way.

stiff *adjective*
1 not bending or moving or changing its shape easily. 2 not fluid; hard to stir, *a stiff dough.* 3 difficult, *a stiff examination.* 4 formal in manner; not friendly. 5 severe or strong, *a stiff breeze.* **stiffly** *adverb*, **stiffness** *noun*
[from Old English]

stiffen *verb* (stiffens, stiffening, stiffened)
make or become stiff. **stiffener** *noun*

stifle *verb* (stifles, stifling, stifled)
1 suffocate. 2 suppress, *She stifled a yawn.*

stile *noun* (*plural* stiles)
an arrangement of steps or bars for people to climb over a fence. [from Old English]

stiletto heel *noun* (*plural* stiletto heels)
a high pointed shoe-heel.

still *adjective*
1 not moving, *still water.* 2 silent. 3 not fizzy.
stillness *noun*
still *adverb*
1 without moving, *Stand still.* 2 up to this or that time, *He was still there.* 3 in a greater amount or degree, *You can do still better.* 4 nevertheless, *They've lost. Still, they tried, and that was good.*

stillborn *adjective*
born dead. [from *still*[1] + *born*]

still life *noun* (*plural* still lifes)
a painting of lifeless things such as ornaments and fruit.

stilted *adjective*
stiffly formal. [originally = raised on stilts]

stilts *plural noun*
a pair of poles with supports for the feet so that the user can walk high above the ground.

stimulate *verb* (stimulates, stimulating, stimulated)
1 make more lively or active. 2 excite or interest. **stimulation** *noun*

sting *noun* (*plural* stings)
1 a sharp-pointed part of an animal or plant, often containing a poison, that can cause a wound. 2 a painful wound caused by this part.
sting *verb* (stings, stinging, stung)
1 wound or hurt with a sting. 2 feel a sharp pain. 3 stimulate sharply, *I was stung into answering rudely.* 4 (*slang*) cheat a person by overcharging; extort money from someone. [from Old English]

stingy (*say* stin-jee) *adjective* (stingier, stingiest)
mean, not generous; giving or given in small amounts. **stingily** *adverb*, **stinginess** *noun* [from *sting*]

stink *noun* (*plural* stinks)
1 an unpleasant smell. 2 (*informal*) an unpleasant fuss or protest.
stink *verb* (stinks, stinking, stank or stunk, stunk)
have an unpleasant smell.

stint *noun* (*plural* stints)
1 a fixed amount of work to be done. 2 limitation of a supply or effort, *They gave help without stint.*
stint *verb* (stints, stinting, stinted)
limit; be niggardly, *Don't stint them of food.*

stir *verb* (stirs, stirring, stirred)
1 mix a liquid or soft mixture by moving a spoon etc. round and round in it. 2 move slightly; start to move. 3 excite or stimulate, *They stirred up trouble.*
stir *noun*
1 the action of stirring. 2 a disturbance; excitement, *The news caused a stir.*

stirrup *noun* (*plural* stirrups)
a metal part that hangs from each side of a horse's saddle, for a rider to put his or her foot in. [from Old English]

stitch *noun* (*plural* stitches)
1 a loop of thread made in sewing or knitting. 2 a method of arranging the threads, *cross stitch.* 3 a sudden sharp pain in the side of the body, caused by running.
stitch *verb* (stitches, stitching, stitched)
sew or fasten with stitches.

stoat *noun* (*plural* stoats)
a kind of weasel also called an ermine.

stock *noun* (*plural* stocks)
1 a number of things kept ready to be sold or used. 2 livestock. 3 a line of ancestors, *a man of Irish stock.* 4 liquid made by stewing meat, fish, or vegetables, used for making soup etc. 5 a garden flower with a sweet smell. 6 shares in a business company's capital (see *share* 2). 7 the main stem of a tree or plant. 8 the base, holder, or handle of an implement etc. 9 a kind of cravat.

stock *verb* (stocks, stocking, stocked)
1 keep goods in stock. 2 provide a place with a stock of something.

stockade *noun* (*plural* stockades)
a fence made of stakes. [from Spanish]

stockbroker *noun* (*plural* stockbrokers)
a broker who deals in stocks and shares.

stock exchange *noun* (*plural* stock exchanges)
a place where stocks and shares are bought and sold.

stocking *noun* (*plural* stockings)
a garment covering the foot and part or all of the leg. [from *stock*]

stock market *noun* (*plural* stock markets)
1 a stock exchange. 2 the buying and selling of stocks and shares.

stockpile *noun* (*plural* stockpiles)
a large stock of things kept in reserve.
stockpile *verb*

stocks *plural noun*
a wooden framework with holes for a seated person's legs, used like the pillory. [from *stock*]

stock-still *adjective*
quite still.

stocktaking *noun*
the counting, listing, and checking of a shop's stock or a company's goods and resources.

stocky *adjective* (stockier, stockiest)
short and solidly built, *a stocky man.* [from *stock*]

stodgy *adjective* (stodgier, stodgiest)
1 (of food) heavy and filling. 2 dull and boring, *a stodgy book.* **stodginess** *noun*

stoical (*say* stoh-ik-al) *adjective*
bearing pain or difficulties etc. calmly without complaining. **stoically** *adverb*, **stoicism** *noun* [named after ancient Greek philosophers called *Stoics*]

stoke *verb* (stokes, stoking, stoked)
put fuel in a furnace or on a fire. **stoker** *noun* [from Dutch]

stole *past tense* of steal.

stolid *adjective*
not excitable; not feeling or showing emotion. **stolidly** *adverb*, **stolidity** *noun*

stomach *noun* (*plural* stomachs)
1 the part of the body where food starts to be digested. 2 the abdomen.
stomach *verb* (stomachs, stomaching, stomached)
endure or tolerate. [from Greek]

stone *noun* (*plural* stones)
1 a piece of rock. 2 stones or rock as material, e.g. for building. 3 a jewel. 4 the hard case round the kernel of plums, cherries, etc. 5 a unit of weight equal to 14 pounds, *She weighs 6 stone.*

stone *verb* (stones, stoning, stoned)
1 throw stones at somebody. 2 remove the stones from fruit. [from Old English]

stone- *prefix*
completely, *stone-cold*.

Stone Age *noun*
the earliest period of human history, when tools and weapons were made of stone.

stone-cold *adjective*
extremely cold; completely without warmth.

stone-deaf *adjective*
completely deaf.

stony *adjective*
1 full of stones. 2 like stone; hard. 3 not answering, *a stony silence*.

stool *noun* (*plural* stools)
1 a movable seat without arms or a back. 2 a footstool. 3 a lump of faeces.

stoop *verb* (stoops, stooping, stooped)
1 bend your body forwards and down. 2 lower yourself, *He would not stoop to cheating*.
stoop *noun* [from Old English]

stop *verb* (stops, stopping, stopped)
1 bring or come to an end; not continue working or moving. 2 stay. 3 prevent or obstruct something. 4 fill a hole, especially in a tooth.
stop *noun* (*plural* stops)
1 stopping; a pause or end. 2 a place where a bus or train etc. regularly stops. 3 a punctuation mark, especially a full stop. 4 a lever or knob that controls pitch in a wind instrument or allows organ pipes to sound. [from Old English]

stopcock *noun* (*plural* stopcocks)
a valve controlling the flow of liquid or gas in a pipe.

stopgap *noun* (*plural* stopgaps)
a temporary substitute.

stoppage *noun* (*plural* stoppages)
1 an interruption in the work of a factory etc. 2 an amount taken off someone's wages. 3 a blockage.

stopper *noun* (*plural* stoppers)
a plug for closing a bottle etc.

stopwatch *noun* (*plural* stopwatches)
a watch that can be started and stopped when you wish, used for timing races etc.

store *noun* (*plural* stores)
1 a stock of things kept for future use; a place where these are kept. 2 a shop, especially a large one.
in store 1 being stored. 2 going to happen, *There's a surprise in store for you*.
set store by something value it greatly.
store *verb* (stores, storing, stored)
keep things until they are needed. **storage** *noun*

storey *noun* (*plural* storeys)
one whole floor of a building. [from Latin]

USAGE: Do not confuse with *story*.

stork *noun* (*plural* storks)
a large bird with long legs and a long beak.

storm *noun* (*plural* storms)
1 a very strong wind usually with rain, snow, etc. 2 a violent attack or outburst, *a storm of protest*. **stormy** *adjective*
storm in a teacup a great fuss over something unimportant.
storm *verb* (storms, storming, stormed)
1 move or behave violently or angrily, *He stormed out of the room*. 2 attack or capture by a sudden assault, *They stormed the castle*.

story *noun* (*plural* stories)
1 an account of a real or imaginary event. 2 the plot of a play or novel etc. 3 (*informal*) a lie, *Don't tell stories!*
[from Latin *historia* = history]

USAGE: Do not confuse with *storey*.

stout *adjective*
1 rather fat. 2 thick and strong. 3 brave and determined, *a stout defender of human rights*.
stoutly *adverb*, **stoutness** *noun*

stove[1] *noun* (*plural* stoves)
1 a device containing an oven or ovens. 2 a device for heating a room.
[from old German or old Dutch]

stove[2] *past tense* of **stave**.

stow *verb* (stows, stowing, stowed)
pack or store something away.
stowage *noun*
stow away hide on a ship or aircraft so as to travel without paying. **stowaway** *noun*

straddle *verb* (straddles, straddling, straddled)
be astride; sit or stand across something, *A long bridge straddles the river*.

straggle *verb* (straggles, straggling, straggled)
1 grow or spread in an untidy way. 2 lag behind; wander on your own. **straggler** *noun*, **straggly** *adjective* [origin unknown]

straight *adjective*
1 going continuously in one direction; not curving or bending. 2 tidy; in proper order. 3 honest and frank, *a straight answer*.
straightness *noun*
straight *adverb*
1 in a straight line or manner. 2 directly; without delay, *Go straight home*.
straight away immediately.
[old past participle of *stretch*]

USAGE: Do not confuse with *strait*.

straight away *adverb*
immediately.

straighten *verb* (straightens, straightening, straightened)
make or become straight.

straightforward *adjective*
1 easy, not complicated. 2 honest and frank.

strain[1] *verb* (strains, straining, strained)
1 stretch tightly. 2 injure or weaken something by stretching or working it too hard. 3 make a great effort. 4 put something through a sieve or filter to separate liquid from solid matter.
strain *noun* (*plural* strains)
1 straining; the force of straining. 2 an injury caused by straining. 3 something that uses up strength, patience, resources, etc. 4 exhaustion. 5 a part of a tune.

strain[2] *noun* (*plural* strains)
1 a breed or variety of animals, plants, etc.; a line of descent. 2 an inherited characteristic, *There's an artistic strain in the family.* [from Old English]

strait *noun* (*plural* straits)
a narrow stretch of water connecting two seas. [from Latin *strictus* = tightened]

USAGE: Do not confuse with *straight*.

straits *plural noun*
1 a strait, *the Straits of Dover.* 2 a difficult condition, *We were in dire straits when we lost our money.*

strand[1] *noun* (*plural* strands)
1 each of the threads or wires etc. twisted together to form a rope, yarn, or cable. 2 a single thread. 3 a lock of hair.

strand[2] *verb* (strands, stranding, stranded)
1 run or cause to run onto sand or rocks in shallow water. 2 leave in a difficult or helpless position, *We were stranded when our car broke down.* [from Old English]

strange *adjective*
1 unusual or surprising. 2 not known or seen or experienced before.
strangely *adverb*, **strangeness** *noun*
[from Latin *extraneus* = extraneous]

stranger *noun* (*plural* strangers)
1 a person you do not know. 2 a person who is in a place or company that he or she does not know.

strangle *verb* (strangles, strangling, strangled)
1 kill by squeezing the throat to prevent breathing. 2 restrict something so that it does not develop. **strangler** *noun*

strap *noun* (*plural* straps)
a flat strip of leather or cloth etc. for fastening things or holding them in place.
strap *verb* (straps, strapping, strapped)
fasten with a strap or straps; bind.

strapping *adjective*
tall and healthy-looking, *a strapping lad.*

strategy *noun* (*plural* strategies)
1 a plan or policy to achieve something, *our economic strategy.* 2 the planning of a war or campaign. (Compare *tactics.*)
[from Greek *strategos* = a general]

stratosphere *noun*
a layer of the atmosphere between about 10 and 60 kilometres above the earth's surface. [from *stratum* + *sphere*]

straw *noun* (*plural* straws)
1 dry cut stalks of corn. 2 a narrow tube for drinking through. [from Old English]

strawberry *noun* (*plural* strawberries)
a small red juicy fruit, with its seeds on the outside. [probably because straw is put around the plants to keep slugs away]

stray *verb* (strays, straying, strayed)
leave a group or proper place and wander; get lost.
stray *adjective*
that has strayed; wandering around lost, *a stray cat.* **stray** *noun* [from old French]

streak *noun* (*plural* streaks)
1 a long thin line or mark. 2 a trace, *a streak of cruelty.* **streaky** *adjective*
streak *verb* (streaks, streaking, streaked)
1 mark with streaks. 2 move very quickly. 3 run naked in a public place for fun or to get attention. [from Old English]

stream *noun* (*plural* streams)
1 water flowing in a channel; a brook or small river. 2 a flow of liquid or of things or people. 3 a group in which children of similar ability are placed in a school.
stream *verb* (streams, streaming, streamed)
1 move in or like a stream. 2 produce a stream of liquid. 3 arrange schoolchildren in streams according to their ability.

streamline *verb* (streamlines, streamlining, streamlined)
1 give something a smooth shape that helps it to move easily through air or water. 2 organize something so that it works more efficiently.
streamlined *adjective*

street *noun* (*plural* streets)
a road with houses beside it in a city or village. [via Old English from Latin *strata via* = paved way]

strength *noun* (*plural* strengths)
1 how strong a person or thing is; being strong. 2 an ability or good quality, *Patience is your great strength.*

strengthen *verb* (strengthens, strengthening, strengthened)
make or become stronger.

stress *noun* (*plural* stresses)
1 a force that acts on something, e.g. by pressing, pulling, or twisting it; strain. 2 emphasis, especially the extra force with

which you pronounce part of a word or phrase. **3** distress caused by having too many problems or too much to do.
stress *verb* (**stresses, stressing, stressed**) put a stress on something; emphasize. [from *distress*]

stretch *verb* (**stretches, stretching, stretched**) **1** pull something or be pulled so that it becomes longer or wider or larger. **2** be continuous, *The wall stretches right round the estate.* **3** push out your arms and legs etc.
stretch *noun* (*plural* **stretches**) **1** the action of stretching. **2** a continuous period of time or area of land or water.

stretcher *noun* (*plural* **stretchers**) a framework for carrying a sick or injured person.

strict *adjective* **1** demanding obedience and good behaviour, *a strict teacher.* **2** complete or exact, *the strict truth.* **strictly** *adverb*, **strictness** *noun* [same origin as *strait*]

stride *verb* (**strides, striding, strode, stridden**) walk with long steps.
stride *noun* (*plural* **strides**) **1** a long step when walking or running. **2** progress.
get into your stride settle into a fast and steady pace of working.
take something in your stride manage or deal with something without difficulty.

strife *noun* conflict; fighting or quarrelling.

strike *verb* (**strikes, striking, struck**) **1** hit. **2** attack suddenly. **3** produce by pressing or stamping something, *They are striking some special coins.* **4** light a match by rubbing it against a rough surface. **5** sound, *The clock struck ten.* **6** make an impression on someone's mind, *She strikes me as truthful.* **7** find gold or oil etc. by digging or drilling. **8** stop work until the people in charge agree to improve wages or conditions etc. **9** go in a certain direction, *We struck north through the forest.*
strike off or **out** cross out.
strike up begin playing or singing; start a friendship etc.
strike *noun* (*plural* **strikes**) **1** a hit. **2** an attack. **3** a stoppage of work, as a way of making a protest (see sense 8 of the verb). **4** a sudden discovery of gold or oil etc.
on strike (of workers) striking.

striking *adjective* **1** that strikes. **2** noticeable.
strikingly *adverb*

string *noun* (*plural* **strings**) **1** cord used to fasten or tie things; a piece of this or similar material. **2** a piece of wire or

cord etc. stretched and vibrated to produce sounds in a musical instrument. **3** a line or series of things, *a string of buses.*
string *verb* (**strings, stringing, strung**) **1** fit or fasten with string. **2** thread on a string. **3** remove the tough fibre from beans.
string out 1 spread out in a line. **2** cause something to last a long time.
strings *plural noun* musical instruments with strings.

stringy *adjective* **1** like string. **2** containing tough fibres.

strip[1] *verb* (**strips, stripping, stripped**) **1** take a covering or layer off something. **2** undress. **3** deprive a person of something.
strip *noun* the distinctive clothes worn by a sports team while playing. [probably from Old English]

strip[2] *noun* (*plural* **strips**) a long narrow piece or area. [from old German]

strip cartoon *noun* (*plural* **strip cartoons**) a comic strip (see *comic*).

stripe *noun* (*plural* **stripes**) **1** a long narrow band of colour. **2** a strip of cloth worn on the sleeve of a uniform to show the wearer's rank. **striped** *adjective*, **stripy** *adjective* [probably from old German and related to *strip*[2]]

striptease *noun* (*plural* **stripteases**) an entertainment in which a person slowly undresses.

strive *verb* (**strives, striving, strove, striven**) **1** try hard to do something. **2** carry on a conflict. [from old French]

stroke[1] *noun* (*plural* **strokes**) **1** a hit. **2** a movement or action. **3** the sound made by a clock striking. **4** a sudden illness that often causes paralysis. [from *strike*]

stroke[2] *verb* (**strokes, stroking, stroked**) move your hand gently along something.
stroke *noun* [from Old English]

stroll *verb* (**strolls, strolling, strolled**) walk in a leisurely way. **stroll** *noun*, **stroller** *noun* [from German]

strong *adjective* **1** having great power, energy, effect, flavour, etc. **2** not easy to break, damage, or defeat. **3** having a certain number of members, *an army 5,000 strong.* **strongly** *adverb*

stronghold *noun* (*plural* **strongholds**) **1** a fortified place. **2** an area where many people live or think in a particular way, *a Tory stronghold.*

strove *past tense* of **strive**.

structure *noun* (*plural* **structures**) **1** something that has been constructed or built. **2** the way something is constructed or organized.

structural *adjective,* **structurally** *adverb*
[from Latin *struere* = build]

struggle *verb* (struggles, struggling, struggled)
1 move your arms, legs, etc. in trying to get free. 2 make strong efforts to do something. 3 try to overcome an opponent or a problem etc.

struggle *noun* (*plural* struggles)
the action of struggling; a hard fight or great effort. [origin unknown]

strum *verb* (strums, strumming, strummed)
1 sound a guitar by running your fingers across its strings. 2 play badly or casually on a musical instrument.

strut *verb* (struts, strutting, strutted)
walk proudly or stiffly.

strut *noun* (*plural* struts)
1 a bar of wood or metal strengthening a framework. 2 a strutting walk.
[probably from old German]

stub *noun* (*plural* stubs)
1 a short stump left when the rest has been used or worn down. 2 a counterfoil.

stub *verb* (stubs, stubbing, stubbed)
bump your toe painfully.
stub out put out a cigarette by pressing it against something hard.

stubble *noun*
1 the short stalks of corn left in the ground after the harvest is cut. 2 short hairs growing after shaving. [from old French]

stubborn *adjective*
obstinate. **stubbornly** *adverb,*
stubbornness *noun* [origin unknown]

stubby *adjective*
short and thick.

stuck-up *adjective* (*informal*)
conceited or snobbish.

stud *noun* (*plural* studs)
1 a small curved lump or knob. 2 a device like a button on a stalk, used to fasten a detachable collar to a shirt.

student *noun* (*plural* students)
a person who studies a subject, especially at a college or university.
[from Latin *studere* = to study]

studio *noun* (*plural* studios)
1 the room where a painter or photographer etc. works. 2 a place where cinema films are made. 3 a room from which radio or television broadcasts are made or recorded.
[Italian; related to *study*]

studious *adjective*
1 keen on studying. 2 deliberate, *with studious politeness.*
studiously *adverb,* **studiousness** *noun*

study *verb* (studies, studying, studied)
1 spend time learning about something. 2 look at something carefully.

study *noun* (*plural* studies)
1 the process of studying. 2 a subject studied; a piece of research. 3 a room where someone studies. 4 a piece of music for playing as an exercise.
[from Latin *studium* = zeal]

stuff *noun*
1 a substance or material. 2 things, *Leave your stuff outside.* 3 valueless matter, *stuff and nonsense!*

stuff *verb* (stuffs, stuffing, stuffed)
1 fill tightly. 2 fill with stuffing. 3 push a thing into something, *He stuffed the notebook into his pocket.* 4 (*informal*) eat greedily.
[from old French]

stuffing *noun*
1 material used to fill the inside of something; padding. 2 a savoury mixture put into meat or poultry etc. before cooking.

stuffy *adjective* (stuffier, stuffiest)
1 badly ventilated; without fresh air. 2 with blocked breathing passages, *a stuffy nose.* 3 formal and boring.
stuffily *adverb,* **stuffiness** *noun*

stumble *verb* (stumbles, stumbling, stumbled)
1 trip and lose your balance. 2 speak or do something hesitantly or uncertainly.

stumble *noun*
stumble across or **on** find accidentally.

stumbling block *noun* (*plural* stumbling blocks)
an obstacle; something that causes difficulty.

stump *noun* (*plural* stumps)
1 the bottom of a tree trunk left in the ground when the rest has fallen or been cut down. 2 something left when the main part is cut off or worn down. 3 each of the three upright sticks of a wicket in cricket.

stump *verb* (stumps, stumping, stumped)
1 walk stiffly or noisily. 2 put a batsman out by knocking the bails off the stumps while he or she is out of the crease. 3 (of a question or problem) be too difficult for somebody.
stump up (*informal*) produce the money to pay for something.

stumpy *adjective*
short and thick. **stumpiness** *noun*

stun *verb* (stuns, stunning, stunned)
1 knock a person unconscious. 2 daze or shock, *She was stunned by the news.*

stunt[1] *verb*
prevent a thing from growing or developing normally, *a stunted tree.* [probably from Old English]

stunt[2] *noun* (*plural* stunts)
something unusual or difficult done as a performance or to attract attention.
[originally American: origin unknown]

stupendous *adjective*
amazing or tremendous. **stupendously** *adverb*

stupid *adjective*
1 not clever or thoughtful. 2 without reason or common sense.
stupidly *adverb*, **stupidity** *noun*
[from Latin *stupidus* = dazed]

sturdy *adjective* (sturdier, sturdiest)
strong and vigorous or solid. **sturdily** *adverb*, **sturdiness** *noun* [from old French]

stutter *verb* (stutters, stuttering, stuttered)
stammer. **stutter** *noun*

style *noun* (*plural* styles)
1 the way something is done, made, said, or written etc. 2 elegance. 3 the part of a pistil that supports the stigma in a plant.
stylistic *adjective*

stylish *adjective*
in a fashionable style.

sub- *prefix* (often changing to **suc-**, **suf-**, **sum-**, **sup-**, **sur-**, **sus-** before certain consonants)
1 under (as in *submarine*). 2 subordinate, secondary (as in *subsection*).
[from Latin *sub* = under]

subconscious *adjective*
to do with our own mental activities of which we are not fully aware.
subconscious *noun*

subdivide *verb* (subdivides, subdividing, subdivided)
divide again or into smaller parts.
subdivision *noun*

subdue *verb* (subdues, subduing, subdued)
1 overcome; bring under control. 2 make quieter or gentler. [from old French]

subject *noun* (*plural* subjects)
1 the person or thing being talked about or written about etc. 2 something that is studied. 3 (in grammar) the word or words naming who or what does the action of a verb, e.g. '*the book*' in *the book fell off the table*. 4 someone who is ruled by a particular king, government, etc.
subject *adjective*
ruled by a king or government etc.; not independent.
subject to 1 having to obey. 2 liable to, *Trains are subject to delays during fog.* 3 depending upon, *Our decision is subject to your approval.*
subject (*say* sub-jekt) *verb* (subjects, subjecting, subjected)
1 make a person or thing undergo something, *They subjected him to torture.* 2 bring a country under your control. **subjection** *noun*
[from *sub-* + Latin *-jectum* = thrown]

subjective *adjective*
1 existing in a person's mind and not produced by things outside it. 2 depending on a person's own taste or opinions etc. (Compare *objective*.)

subjunctive *noun* (*plural* subjunctives)
the form of a verb used to indicate what is imagined or wished or possible. There are only a few cases where it is commonly used in English, e.g. '*were*' in *if I were you* and '*save*' in *God save the Queen*.
[from *sub-* + Latin *junctum* = joined]

sublime *adjective*
1 noble or impressive. 2 extreme; not caring about the consequences, *with sublime carelessness.* [from Latin]

submarine *adjective*
under the sea, *We laid a submarine cable.*
submarine *noun* (*plural* submarines)
a ship that can travel under water.

submerge *verb* (submerges, submerging, submerged)
go under or put under water or other liquid.
submergence *noun*, **submersion** *noun* [from *sub-* + Latin *mergere* = dip]

submit *verb* (submits, submitting, submitted)
1 let someone have authority over you; surrender. 2 put forward for consideration, testing, etc., *Submit your plans to the committee.*
submission *noun*
[from *sub-* + Latin *mittere* = send]

subnormal *adjective*
below normal.

subordinate *adjective*
1 less important. 2 lower in rank.
subordinate *noun* (*plural* subordinates)
a person working under someone's authority or control.
subordinate *verb* (subordinates, subordinating, subordinated)
treat as being less important than another person or thing. **subordination** *noun*
[from *sub-* + Latin *ordinare* = arrange]

subordinate clause *noun* (*plural* subordinate clauses)
a clause which adds details to the main clause of the sentence, but cannot be used as a sentence by itself.

sub-plot *noun* (*plural* sub-plots)
a secondary plot in a play etc.

subscribe *verb* (subscribes, subscribing, subscribed)
1 contribute money to a project or charity etc. 2 pay regularly so as to be a member of a society, get a periodical, have the use of a telephone, etc. 3 sign, *subscribe your name.* 4 say that you agree, *We cannot subscribe to this theory.* **subscriber** *noun*, **subscription** *noun*
[from *sub-* + Latin *scribere* = write]

subsequent *adjective*
coming after in time or order; later.
subsequently *adverb*
[from *sub-* + Latin *sequens* = following]

subside *verb* (subsides, subsiding, subsided)
1 sink. 2 become less intense, *Her fear subsided.* **subsidence** *noun*
[from *sub-* + Latin *sidere* = settle]

subsidiary *adjective*
1 less important; secondary. 2 (of a business) controlled by another, *a subsidiary company.*
[same origin as *subsidy*]

subsidize *verb* (subsidizes, subsidizing, subsidized)
pay a subsidy to a person or firm etc.

subsidy *noun* (*plural* subsidies)
money paid to an industry etc. that needs help, or to keep down the price at which its goods etc. are sold to the public.
[from Latin *subsidium* = assistance]

subsoil *noun*
soil lying just below the surface layer.

substance *noun* (*plural* substances)
1 matter of a particular kind. 2 the main or essential part of something, *We agree with the substance of your report but not with its details.*
[from Latin *substantia* = essence]

substantial *adjective*
1 of great size, value, or importance, *a substantial fee.* 2 solidly built, *substantial houses.* 3 actually existing. **substantially** *adverb*
[same origin as *substance*]

substitute *noun* (*plural* substitutes)
a person or thing that acts or is used instead of another.
substitute *verb* (substitutes, substituting, substituted)
put or use a person or thing as a substitute. **substitution** *noun*
[from *sub-* + Latin *statuere* = to set up]

subterranean *adjective*
underground.
[from *sub-* + Latin *terra* = ground]

subtitle *noun* (*plural* subtitles)
1 a secondary or additional title. 2 words shown on the screen during a film, e.g. to translate a foreign language.

subtle (*say* sut-el) *adjective*
1 slight and delicate, *a subtle perfume.* 2 ingenious; not immediately obvious, *a subtle joke.* **subtly** *adverb*, **subtlety** *noun*

subtract *verb* (subtracts, subtracting, subtracted)
deduct; take away a part, quantity, or number from a greater one. **subtraction** *noun*
[from *sub-* + Latin *tractum* = pulled]

suburb *noun* (*plural* suburbs)
a district with houses that is outside the central part of a city. **suburban** *adjective*
[from *sub-* + Latin *urbs* = city]

subway *noun* (*plural* subways)
an underground passage.

suc- *prefix*
1 under. 2 subordinate, secondary. see **sub-**.

succeed *verb* (succeeds, succeeding, succeeded)
1 be successful. 2 come after another person or thing; become the next king or queen, *She succeeded to the throne; Edward VII succeeded Queen Victoria.*
[from *suc-* + Latin *cedere* = go]

success *noun* (*plural* successes)
1 doing or getting what you wanted or intended. 2 a person or thing that does well, *The show was a great success.*
[same origin as *succeed*]

successful *adjective*
having success; being a success. **successfully** *adverb*

succession *noun* (*plural* successions)
1 a series of people or things. 2 the process of following in order. 3 succeeding to the throne; the right of doing this.
[same origin as *succeed*]

successive *adjective*
following one after another, *on five successive days.* **successively** *adverb*

succumb (*say* suk-um) *verb* (succumbs, succumbing, succumbed)
give way to something overpowering.
[from *suc-* + Latin *cumbere* = to lie]

such *adjective*
1 of the same kind; similar, *Cakes, biscuits, and all such foods are fattening.* 2 of the kind described, *There's no such person.* 3 so great or intense, *It gave me such a fright!*

such-and-such *adjective*
particular but not now named, *He promises to come at such-and-such a time but is always late.*

suck *verb* (sucks, sucking, sucked)
1 take in liquid or air through almost-closed lips. 2 squeeze something in your mouth by using your tongue, *sucking a toffee.* 3 draw in, *The canoe was sucked into the whirlpool.*
suck *noun*
suck up to (*informal*) flatter someone in the hope of winning their favour.

suckle *verb* (suckles, suckling, suckled)
feed on milk at the mother's breast or udder.

suction *noun*
1 sucking. 2 producing a vacuum so that things are sucked into the empty space, *Vacuum cleaners work by suction.*

sudden *adjective*
happening or done quickly or without warning. **suddenly** *adverb*, **suddenness** *noun*

suds *plural noun*
froth on soapy water.

sue *verb* (sues, suing, sued)
start a lawsuit to claim money from somebody.
[from old French]

suet *noun*
hard fat from cattle and sheep, used in cooking.

suf- *prefix*
1 under. 2 subordinate, secondary. see **sub-**.

suffer *verb* (**suffers, suffering, suffered**)
1 feel pain or sadness. 2 experience something bad, *suffer damage*. 3 (*old use*) allow or tolerate. **sufferer** *noun*, **suffering** *noun*
[from *suf-* + Latin *ferre* = to bear]

suffice *verb* (**suffices, sufficing, sufficed**)
be enough for someone's needs.
[from *suf-* + Latin *facere* = make or do]

sufficient *adjective*
enough. **sufficiently** *adverb*, **sufficiency** *noun*
[same origin as *suffice*]

suffix *noun* (*plural* **suffixes**)
a letter or set of letters joined to the end of a word to make another word (e.g. in forget*ful*, lion*ess*, rust*y*) or a form of a verb (e.g. sing*ing*, wait*ed*).
[from *suf-* + Latin *figere* = fix]

suffocate *verb* (**suffocates, suffocating, suffocated**)
1 make it difficult or impossible for someone to breathe. 2 suffer or die because breathing is prevented. **suffocation** *noun*
[from *suf-* + Latin *fauces* = throat]

sugar *noun*
a sweet food obtained from the juices of various plants (e.g. sugar cane, sugar beet). **sugar** *verb*, **sugary** *adjective*

suggest *verb* (**suggests, suggesting, suggested**)
1 give somebody an idea that you think is useful. 2 cause an idea or possibility to come into the mind. **suggestion** *noun*, **suggestive** *adjective* [from Latin]

suicide *noun* (*plural* **suicides**)
1 killing yourself deliberately, *commit suicide*. 2 a person who deliberately kills himself or herself. **suicidal** *adjective*
[from Latin *sui* = of yourself, + *-cide*]

suit *noun* (*plural* **suits**)
1 a matching jacket and trousers, or a jacket and skirt, that are meant to be worn together. 2 clothing for a particular activity, *a diving suit*. 3 any of the four sets of cards (clubs, hearts, diamonds, spades) in a pack of playing cards. 4 a lawsuit.

USAGE: Do not confuse with *suite*.

suit *verb* (**suits, suiting, suited**)
1 be suitable or convenient for a person or thing. 2 make a person look attractive.
[from Latin *sequi* = to go together or follow]

suitable *adjective*
satisfactory or right for a particular person, purpose, or occasion etc. **suitably** *adverb*, **suitability** *noun*

suitcase *noun* (*plural* **suitcases**)
a rectangular container for carrying clothes, usually with a hinged lid and a handle.

suite (*say as* sweet) *noun* (*plural* **suites**)
1 a set of furniture. 2 a set of rooms. 3 a set of attendants. 4 a set of short pieces of music.
[French; related to *suit*]

USAGE: Do not confuse with *suit*.

sulk *verb* (**sulks, sulking, sulked**)
be silent and bad-tempered because you are not pleased. **sulks** *plural noun*, **sulky** *adjective*, **sulkily** *adverb*, **sulkiness** *noun*

sullen *adjective*
sulking and gloomy.
sullenly *adverb*, **sullenness** *noun*
[from old French; related to *sole*[2]]

sulphur *noun*
a yellow chemical used in industry and in medicine. **sulphurous** *adjective* [from Latin]

sultry *adjective*
1 hot and humid, *sultry weather*. 2 suggesting passion or sexual desire, *her sultry smile*. **sultriness** *noun*

sum *noun* (*plural* **sums**)
1 a total. 2 a problem in arithmetic. 3 an amount of money.

sum *verb* (**sums, summing, summed**)
sum up 1 summarize, especially at the end of a talk etc. 2 form an opinion of a person, *sum him up*. [from Latin *summa* = main thing]

sum- *prefix*
1 under. 2 subordinate, secondary. see **sub-**.

summarize *verb* (**summarizes, summarizing, summarized**)
make or give a summary of something.

summary *noun* (*plural* **summaries**)
a statement of the main points of something said or written.

summary *adjective*
1 brief. 2 done or given hastily, without delay, *summary punishment*. **summarily** *adverb*
[same origin as *sum*]

summer *noun* (*plural* **summers**)
the warm season between spring and autumn. **summery** *adjective*

summer house *noun* (*plural* **summer houses**)
a small building providing shade in a garden or park.

summit *noun* (*plural* **summits**)
1 the top of a mountain or hill. 2 a meeting between the leaders of powerful countries, *a summit conference*.
[from Latin *summus* = highest]

summon *verb* (**summons, summoning, summoned**)
1 order someone to come or appear. 2 request firmly, *He summoned the rebels to surrender*.

summon up gather or prepare, *Can you summon up the energy to get out of bed?* [from *sum-* + Latin *monere* = warn]

sumptuous *adjective*
splendid and expensive-looking. **sumptuously** *adverb* [from Latin *sumptus* = cost, expense]

sun *noun* (*plural* **suns**)
1 the star round which the earth travels. 2 light and warmth from the sun, *Go and sit in the sun.* 3 any star in the universe round which planets travel.
sun *verb* (**suns, sunning, sunned**)
warm something in the sun, *sunning ourselves on the beach.* [from Old English]

sunbathe *verb* (**sunbathes, sunbathing, sunbathed**)
expose your body to the sun, especially to get a tan.

sunbeam *noun* (*plural* **sunbeams**)
a ray of sun.

sunburn *noun*
redness of the skin caused by the sun. **sunburnt** *adjective*

sundae (*say* **sun**-day) *noun* (*plural* **sundaes**)
a mixture of ice cream and fruit, nuts, cream, etc. [from *Sunday* (because sundaes were originally sold then, possibly to use up ice cream not sold during the week)]

sundial *noun* (*plural* **sundials**)
a device that shows the time by a shadow on a dial.

sundry *adjective*
various or several.
all and sundry everyone.

sunglasses *plural noun*
dark glasses to protect your eyes from strong sunlight.

sunken *adjective*
sunk deeply into a surface, *Their cheeks were pale and sunken.*

sunlamp *noun* (*plural* **sunlamps**)
a lamp which uses ultraviolet light to give people an artificial tan.

sunlight *noun*
light from the sun. **sunlit** *adjective*

sunny *adjective* (**sunnier, sunniest**)
1 full of sunshine. 2 cheerful, *She was in a sunny mood.* **sunnily** *adverb*

sunrise *noun* (*plural* **sunrises**)
the rising of the sun; dawn.

sunset *noun* (*plural* **sunsets**)
the setting of the sun.

sunshade *noun* (*plural* **sunshades**)
a parasol or other device to protect people from the sun.

sunshine *noun*
sunlight with no cloud between the sun and the earth.

sunstroke *noun*
illness caused by being in the sun too long.

sup- *prefix*
1 under. 2 subordinate, secondary. see **sub-**.

super *adjective* (*slang*)
excellent or superb. [from *super-*]

super- *prefix*
1 over or on top (as in *superstructure*). 2 of greater size or quality etc. (as in *supermarket*). 3 extremely (as in *superabundant*). 4 beyond (as in *supernatural*). [from Latin *super* = over]

superb *adjective*
magnificent or excellent. **superbly** *adverb* [from Latin *superbus* = proud]

superficial *adjective*
on the surface; not deep or thorough. **superficially** *adverb*, **superficiality** *noun* [from *super-* + Latin *facies* = face]

superfluous *adjective*
more than is needed. **superfluity** *noun* [from *super-* + Latin *fluere* = flow]

superhuman *adjective*
1 beyond ordinary human ability, *superhuman strength.* 2 higher than human; divine.

superimpose *verb* (**superimposes, superimposing, superimposed**)
place a thing on top of something else. **superimposition** *noun*

superintend *verb* (**superintends, superintending, superintended**)
supervise. [from *super-* + Latin *intendere* = direct, intend]

superintendent *noun* (*plural* **superintendents**)
1 a supervisor. 2 a police officer above the rank of inspector.

superior *adjective*
1 higher in position or rank, *She is your superior officer.* 2 better than another person or thing. 3 conceited. **superiority** *noun*
superior *noun* (*plural* **superiors**)
a person or thing that is superior to another. [Latin, = higher]

superlative *adjective*
of the highest degree or quality, *superlative skill.* **superlatively** *adverb*
superlative *noun* (*plural* **superlatives**)
the form of an adjective or adverb that expresses 'most', *The superlative of 'great' is 'greatest'.* (Compare *positive* and *comparative.*) [from Latin *superlatum* = carried above]

supermarket *noun* (*plural* **supermarkets**)
a large self-service shop that sells food and other goods.

supernatural *adjective*
not belonging to the natural world,
supernatural beings such as ghosts.

supersonic *adjective*
faster than the speed of sound.

superstition *noun* (*plural* **superstitions**)
a belief or action that is not based on reason or
evidence, e.g. the belief that it is unlucky to
walk under a ladder. **superstitious** *adjective*
[from Latin *superstare* = stand over]

supervise *verb* (**supervises, supervising,**
supervised)
be in charge of a person or thing and inspect
what is done.
supervision *noun*, **supervisor** *noun*,
supervisory *adjective*
[from *super-* + Latin *visum* = seen]

supper *noun* (*plural* **suppers**)
a meal eaten in the evening.
[from old French *soper* = sup]

supple *adjective*
bending easily; flexible.
supplely *adverb*, **suppleness** *noun*
[from *sup-* + Latin *plicare* = to fold, bend]

supplement *noun* (*plural* **supplements**)
1 something added as an extra. 2 an extra
section added to a book or newspaper, *the*
colour supplement.
supplementary *adjective*
supplement *verb* (**supplements, supplementing,**
supplemented)
add to something, *She supplements her pocket*
money by working on Saturdays.
[same origin as *supply*]

supply *verb* (**supplies, supplying, supplied**)
give or sell or provide what is needed or
wanted. **supplier** *noun*
supply *noun* (*plural* **supplies**)
1 an amount of something that is available for
use when needed. 2 the action of supplying
something.
[from *sup-* + Latin *-plere* = fill]

support *verb* (**supports, supporting, supported**)
1 keep a person or thing from falling or
sinking. 2 give strength, help, or
encouragement to someone, *Support your local*
team. 3 provide with the necessities of life, *She*
has two children to support. **supporter** *noun*,
supportive *adjective*
support *noun* (*plural* **supports**)
1 the action of supporting. 2 a person or thing
that supports.
[from *sup-* + Latin *portare* = carry]

suppose *verb* (**supposes, supposing, supposed**)
think that something is likely to happen or be
true.
supposedly *adverb*, **supposition** *noun*
be supposed to be expected to do something;
have as a duty.

suppress *verb* (**suppresses, suppressing,**
suppressed)
1 put an end to something forcibly or by
authority, *Troops suppressed the rebellion.*
2 keep something from being known or seen,
They suppressed the truth.
suppression *noun*, **suppressor** *noun*
[from *sup-* + Latin *pressus* = pressed]

supreme *adjective*
1 most important or highest in rank.
2 greatest, *supreme courage.*
supremely *adverb*, **supremacy** *noun*
[from Latin *supremus* = highest]

sur-^{1} *prefix*
1 under. 2 subordinate, secondary. see **sub-**.

sur-^{2} *prefix*
= super- (as in *surcharge, surface*).
[from old French]

sure *adjective*
1 convinced; feeling no doubt. 2 certain to
happen or do something, *Our team is sure to*
win. 3 reliable; undoubtedly true.
sureness *noun*
for sure definitely.
make sure 1 find out exactly. 2 make something
happen or be true, *Make sure the door is locked.*
[from old French; related to *secure*]

surf *noun*
the white foam of waves breaking on a rock or
shore. [origin unknown]

surface *noun* (*plural* **surfaces**)
1 the outside of something. 2 any of the sides of
an object, especially the top part. 3 an outward
appearance, *On the surface he was a kindly*
man.

surfboard *noun* (*plural* **surfboards**)
a board used in surfing.

surfeit (*say* **ser**-fit) *noun*
too much of something. **surfeited** *adjective*
[from *sur-*^{2} + Latin *facere* = do]

surfing *noun*
balancing yourself on a board that is carried to
the shore on the waves.
surfer *noun*

surf-riding *noun*
surfing. **surf-rider** *noun*

surge *verb* (**surges, surging, surged**)
move forwards or upwards like waves.
surge *noun* [from Latin *surgere* = rise]

surgeon *noun* (*plural* **surgeons**)
a doctor who treats disease or injury by cutting
or repairing the affected parts of the body.

surgery *noun* (*plural* **surgeries**)
1 the place where a doctor or dentist etc.
regularly gives advice and treatment to
patients. 2 the time when patients can visit the

doctor etc. **3** the work of a surgeon.
surgical *adjective*, **surgically** *adverb*
[from Greek *cheirourgia* = handiwork]

surly *adjective* (**surlier, surliest**)
bad-tempered and unfriendly. **surliness** *noun*
[originally = majestic, haughty: from *sir* + *-ly*]

surname *noun* (*plural* **surnames**)
the name held by all members of a family.

surpass *verb* (**surpasses, surpassing, surpassed**)
do or be better than all others; excel.

surplus *noun* (*plural* **surpluses**)
an amount left over after spending or using all
that was needed.
[from *sur²-* + Latin *plus* = more]

surprise *noun* (*plural* **surprises**)
1 something unexpected. **2** the feeling caused
by something that was not expected.
surprise *verb* (**surprises, surprising, surprised**)
1 be a surprise to somebody. **2** come upon or
attack somebody unexpectedly.
surprisingly *adverb* [from old French]

surrender *verb* (**surrenders, surrendering,
surrendered**)
1 give yourself up to an enemy. **2** hand
something over to another person, especially
when compelled to do so. **surrender** *noun*
[from *sur²-* + French *rendre* = give, deliver]

surreptitious (*say* su-rep-tish-us) *adjective*
stealthy. **surreptitiously** *adverb* [from Latin
surrepticius = stolen, taken secretly]

surrogate mother *noun* (*plural* **surrogate
mothers**)
a woman who agrees to conceive and give birth
to a baby for a woman who cannot do so
herself, using a fertilized egg of the other
woman or sperm from the other woman's
partner.

surround *verb* (**surrounds, surrounding,
surrounded**)
come or be all round a person or thing;
encircle.
[from *sur²-* + Latin *undare* = rise in waves]

surroundings *plural noun*
the things or conditions round a person or
thing.

survey (*say* ser-vay) *noun* (*plural* **surveys**)
1 a general look at something. **2** an inspection
of an area, building, etc.
survey (*say* ser-vay) *verb* (**surveys, surveying,
surveyed**)
make a survey of something; inspect.
surveyor *noun*
[from *sur²-* + Latin *videre* = see]

survival *noun* (*plural* **survivals**)
1 surviving; the likelihood of surviving.
2 something that has survived from an earlier
time; a relic.

survive *verb* (**survives, surviving, survived**)
stay alive; go on living or existing after
someone has died or after a disaster.
survivor *noun*
[from *sur²-* + Latin *vivere* = to live]

sus- *prefix*
1 under. **2** subordinate, secondary. see **sub-**.

susceptible (*say* sus-ept-ib-ul) *adjective*
likely to be affected by something, *She is
susceptible to colds.* **susceptibility** *noun* [from
Latin *susceptum* = caught up]

suspect (*say* sus-pekt) *verb* (**suspects, suspecting,
suspected**)
1 think that a person is not to be trusted or has
committed a crime; distrust. **2** have a feeling
that something is likely or possible.
suspect (*say* sus-pekt) *noun* (*plural* **suspects**)
a person who is suspected of a crime etc.
suspect *adjective*
[from *sus-* + Latin *specere* = to look]

suspend *verb* (**suspends, suspending, suspended**)
1 hang something up. **2** postpone; stop
something temporarily. **3** deprive a person of a
job or position etc. for a time.
[from *sus-* + Latin *pendere* = hang]

suspender *noun* (*plural* **suspenders**)
a fastener to hold up a sock or stocking by its
top.

suspense *noun*
an anxious or uncertain feeling while waiting
for something to happen or become known.
[same origin as *suspend*]

suspension *noun*
1 suspending. **2** the springs etc. in a vehicle
that lessen the effect of rough road surfaces.
3 a liquid containing small pieces of solid
material which do not dissolve.

suspicion *noun* (*plural* **suspicions**)
1 suspecting or being suspected; distrust. **2** a
slight belief. [same origin as *suspect*]

suspicious *adjective*
feeling or causing suspicion.
suspiciously *adverb*

sustain *verb* (**sustains, sustaining, sustained**)
1 support. **2** keep someone alive. **3** keep
something happening. **4** undergo; suffer, *We
sustained a defeat.*
[from *sus-* + Latin *tenere* = hold, keep]

SW *abbreviation*
1 south-west. **2** south-western.

swab (*say* swob) *noun* (*plural* **swabs**)
1 a mop or pad for cleaning or wiping
something; a small pad for cleaning a wound.
2 a specimen of fluid from the body taken on a
swab for testing.
swab *verb* (**swabs, swabbing, swabbed**)
clean or wipe with a swab. [from Dutch]

swagger *verb* (swaggers, swaggering, swaggered)
walk or behave in a conceited way; strut. **swagger** *noun*

swallow[1] *verb* (swallows, swallowing, swallowed)
1 make something go down your throat. 2 believe something that ought not to be believed. **swallow** *noun*
swallow up take in and cover; engulf, *She was swallowed up in the crowd.*
[from Old English *swelgan*]

swallow[2] *noun* (*plural* swallows)
a small bird with a forked tail and pointed wings. [from Old English *swealwe*]

swamp *noun* (*plural* swamps)
a marsh. **swampy** *adjective*
swamp *verb* (swamps, swamping, swamped)
1 flood. 2 overwhelm with a great mass or number of things. [origin unknown]

swan *noun* (*plural* swans)
a large usually white swimming bird with a long neck. [from Old English]

swank *verb* (swanks, swanking, swanked) (*informal*)
boast or swagger; show off.
swank *noun* (*informal*)
showing yourself or your possessions off in a conceited way. [origin unknown]

swansong *noun* (*plural* swansongs)
a person's last performance or work. [from the old belief that a swan sang sweetly when about to die]

swap *verb* (swaps, swapping, swapped) (*informal*)
exchange. **swap** *noun*
[formerly = seal a bargain by slapping each other's hands; imitating the sound]

swarm *noun* (*plural* swarms)
a large number of insects or birds etc. flying or moving about together.
swarm *verb* (swarms, swarming, swarmed)
1 gather or move in a swarm. 2 be crowded or overrun with insects, people, etc. [from Old English]

swarthy *adjective*
having a dark complexion. **swarthiness** *noun*
[from Old English]

swastika *noun* (*plural* swastikas)
an ancient symbol formed by a cross with its ends bent at right angles, adopted by the Nazis as their sign.
[from Sanskrit *svasti* = well-being, luck]

swat *verb* (swats, swatting, swatted)
hit or crush a fly etc. **swatter** *noun* [originally American, a different spelling of *squat*]

swathe *verb* (swathes, swathing, swathed)
wrap in layers of bandages, paper, or clothes etc. [from Old English]

sway *verb* (sways, swaying, swayed)
1 swing gently; move from side to side. 2 influence, *His speech swayed the crowd.*
sway *noun* [origin unknown]

swear *verb* (swears, swearing, swore, sworn)
1 make a solemn promise, *She swore to tell the truth.* 2 make a person take an oath, *We swore him to secrecy.* 3 use curses or coarse words in anger or surprise etc.
swear by have great confidence in something.

sweat (*say* swet) *noun*
moisture given off by the body through the pores of the skin; perspiration.
sweaty *adjective*
sweat *verb* (sweats, sweating, sweated)
give off sweat; perspire. [from Old English]

sweater *noun* (*plural* sweaters)
a jersey or pullover.

sweatshirt *noun* (*plural* sweatshirts)
a thick cotton jersey worn for sports or casual wear.

sweep *verb* (sweeps, sweeping, swept)
1 clean or clear with a broom or brush etc. 2 move or remove quickly, *The floods swept away the bridge.* 3 go smoothly, quickly, or proudly, *She swept out of the room.*
sweeper *noun*
sweep *noun* (*plural* sweeps)
1 the process of sweeping, *Give this room a good sweep.* 2 a chimney sweep. 3 a sweepstake. [from Old English]

sweeping *adjective*
general or wide-ranging, *He made sweeping changes.*

sweet *adjective*
1 tasting as if it contains sugar; not bitter. 2 very pleasant, *a sweet smell.* 3 charming or delightful.
sweetly *adverb*, **sweetness** *noun*
sweet *noun* (*plural* sweets)
1 a small shaped piece of sweet food made with sugar, chocolate, etc. 2 a pudding; the sweet course in a meal. 3 a beloved person.

sweeten *verb* (sweetens, sweetening, sweetened)
make or become sweet. **sweetener** *noun*

sweetheart *noun* (*plural* sweethearts)
a person you love very much.

swell *verb* (swells, swelling, swelled, swollen or swelled)
make or become larger in size or amount or force.
swell *noun* (*plural* swells)
1 the process of swelling. 2 the rise and fall of the sea's surface.

swelling *noun* (*plural* swellings)
a swollen place.

swerve *verb* (swerves, swerving, swerved)
turn to one side suddenly. **swerve** *noun*

swift *adjective*
quick or rapid.
swiftly *adverb*, **swiftness** *noun*
swift *noun* (*plural* **swifts**)
a small bird rather like a swallow.

swill *verb* (**swills, swilling, swilled**)
pour water over or through something; wash
or rinse.

swim *verb* (**swims, swimming, swam, swum**)
1 move the body through the water; be in the
water for pleasure. **2** cross by swimming, *She
swam the Channel.* **3** float. **4** be covered with or
full of liquid, *Our eyes were swimming in tears.*
5 feel dizzy, *His head swam.* **swimmer** *noun*
swim *noun* (*plural* **swims**)
the action of swimming, *We went for a swim.*
swimsuit *noun* [from Old English]

swimming bath *noun* (*plural* **swimming baths**)
a public swimming pool.

swimming pool *noun* (*plural* **swimming pools**)
an artificial pool for swimming in.

swindle *verb* (**swindles, swindling, swindled**)
cheat a person in business etc.
swindle *noun*, **swindler** *noun*
[from German *Schwindler* = a fool, a cheat]

swine *noun* (*plural* **swine**)
1 a pig. **2** a very unpleasant person.
3 (*informal*) a difficult thing, *This crossword's
a real swine!*

swing *verb* (**swings, swinging, swung**)
1 move to and fro while hanging; move or turn
in a curve, *The door swung open.* **2** change from
one opinion or mood etc. to another.
swing *noun* (*plural* **swings**)
1 a swinging movement. **2** a seat hung on
chains or ropes etc. so that it can be moved
backwards and forwards. **3** the amount by
which votes or opinions etc. change from one
side to another. **4** a kind of jazz music.
in full swing full of activity; working fully.

swirl *verb* (**swirls, swirling, swirled**)
move round quickly in circles; whirl.
swirl *noun* [probably from old Dutch]

swish *verb* (**swishes, swishing, swished**)
move with a hissing sound. **swish** *noun*

Swiss roll *noun* (*plural* **Swiss rolls**)
a thin sponge cake spread with jam or cream
and rolled up.

switch *noun* (*plural* **switches**)
1 a device that is pressed or turned to start or
stop something working, especially by
electricity. **2** a change of opinion, policy, or
methods. **3** mechanism for moving the points
on a railway track. **4** a flexible rod or whip.
switch *verb* (**switches, switching, switched**)
1 turn something on or off by means of a
switch. **2** change or transfer or divert
something. [probably from old German]

switchback *noun* (*plural* **switchbacks**)
a railway at a fair, with steep slopes up and
down alternately.

switchboard *noun* (*plural* **switchboards**)
a panel with switches etc. for making
telephone connections or operating electric
circuits.

swivel *verb* (**swivels, swivelling, swivelled**)
turn round.
swivel *noun* (*plural* **swivels**)
a device joining two things so that one can
revolve without turning the other.

swollen *past participle* of **swell**.

swoon *verb* (**swoons, swooning, swooned**) (*old
use* or *poetical*)
faint. **swoon** *noun* [from Old English]

swoop *verb* (**swoops, swooping, swooped**)
come down with a rushing movement; make a
sudden attack. **swoop** *noun* [probably from
sweep]

sword (*say* sord) *noun* (*plural* **swords**)
a weapon with a long pointed blade fixed in a
handle or hilt. **swordsman** *noun*

swot *verb* (**swots, swotting, swotted**) (*slang*)
study hard. **swot** *noun*
[a dialect word for *sweat*]

sycamore *noun* (*plural* **sycamores**)
a tall tree with winged seeds, often grown for
its timber. [from Greek]

syl- *prefix*
1 with, together. **2** alike. see **syn-**.

syllable *noun* (*plural* **syllables**)
a word or part of a word that has one vowel
sound when you say it, *'Cat' has one syllable,
'el-e-phant' has three syllables.* **syllabic** *adjective*
[from *syl-* + Greek *lambanein* = take]

syllabus *noun* (*plural* **syllabuses**)
a summary of the things to be studied by a
class or for an examination etc.
[from Greek]

sym- *prefix*
1 with, together. **2** alike. see **syn-**.

symbol *noun* (*plural* **symbols**)
1 a thing used as a sign, *The cross is a symbol of
Christianity.* **2** a mark or sign with a special
meaning (e.g. +, −, and ÷ in mathematics).
symbolic *adjective*, **symbolical** *adjective*,
symbolically *adverb*
[from Greek *symbolon* = token]

USAGE: Do not confuse with *cymbal.*

symbolize *verb* (**symbolizes, symbolizing,
symbolized**)
make or be a symbol of something.

symmetrical *adjective*
able to be divided into two halves which are
exactly the same but the opposite way round,

Wheels and butterflies are symmetrical.
symmetrically *adverb*, **symmetry** *noun*
[from *sym-* + Greek *metron* = a measure]

sympathize *verb* (sympathizes, sympathizing, sympathized)
show or feel sympathy. **sympathizer** *noun*

sympathy *noun* (*plural* sympathies)
1 the sharing or understanding of other people's feelings, opinions, etc. 2 a feeling of pity or tenderness towards someone who is hurt, sad, or in trouble. **sympathetic** *adjective*, **sympathetically** *adverb*
[from *sym-* + Greek *pathos* = feeling]

symphony *noun* (*plural* symphonies)
a long piece of music for an orchestra.
symphonic *adjective*
[from *sym-* + Greek *phone* = sound]

symptom *noun* (*plural* symptoms)
a sign that a disease or condition exists, *Red spots are a symptom of measles.*
symptomatic *adjective*
[from Greek *symptoma* = chance, accident]

syn- *prefix* (changing to **syl-** or **sym-** before certain consonants)
1 with, together (as in *synchronize*). 2 alike (as in *synonym*). [from Greek]

synagogue (*say* sin-a-gog) *noun* (*plural* synagogues)
a place where Jews meet for worship.
[from Greek *synagoge* = assembly]

syndicate *noun* (*plural* syndicates)
1 a group of people or firms who work together in business. 2 a group of people who buy something together, or who gamble together, sharing the cost and any gains.
[from *syn-* + Greek *dike* = judgement]

synonym (*say* sin-o-nim) *noun* (*plural* synonyms)
a word that means the same or almost the same as another word, *'Large' and 'great' are synonyms of 'big'.*
synonymous (*say* sin-on-im-us) *adjective*
[from *syn-* + Greek *onyma* = name]

syntax (*say* sin-taks) *noun*
the way words are arranged to make phrases or sentences.
syntactic *adjective*, **syntactically** *adverb*
[from *syn-* + Greek *taxis* = arrangement]

synthesizer *noun* (*plural* synthesizers)
an electronic musical instrument that can make a large variety of sounds.

synthetic *adjective*
artificially made; not natural.
synthetically *adverb*
[same origin as *synthesis*]

syringe *noun* (*plural* syringes)
a device for sucking in a liquid and squirting it out.
[from Greek *syrinx* = pipe, tube]

syrup *noun*
a thick sweet liquid. **syrupy** *adjective*
[from Arabic *sharab* = a drink]

system *noun* (*plural* systems)
1 a set of parts, things, or ideas that are organized to work together. 2 a way of doing something, *a new system of training motorcyclists.* [from Greek]

systematic *adjective*
methodical; carefully planned.
systematically *adverb*

tab *noun* (*plural* tabs)
a small flap or strip that sticks out.

tabby *noun* (*plural* tabbies)
a grey or brown cat with dark stripes.
[originally = a kind of striped silk material: named after al-Attabiyya, a district of Baghdad where it was made]

table *noun* (*plural* tables)
1 a piece of furniture with a flat top supported on legs. 2 a list of facts or figures arranged in order. 3 a list of the results of multiplying a number by other numbers, *multiplication tables.*
[from Latin *tabula* = plank, tablet, or list]

tablecloth *noun* (*plural* tablecloths)
a cloth for covering a table, especially at meals.

tablespoon *noun* (*plural* tablespoons)
a large spoon for serving food.
tablespoonful *noun*

tablet *noun* (*plural* tablets)
1 a pill. 2 a solid piece of soap. 3 a flat piece of stone or wood etc. with words carved or written on it.
[from old French *tablete* = small table or slab]

table tennis *noun*
a game played on a table divided by a net, over which you hit a small ball with bats.

taboo *adjective*
not to be done or used or talked about.
taboo *noun* [from Tongan *tabu* = sacred]

tack[1] *noun* (*plural* tacks)
1 a short nail with a flat top. 2 a tacking stitch. 3 (in sailing) the direction taken when tacking.
tack *verb* (tacks, tacking, tacked)
1 nail something down with tacks. 2 fasten material together with long stitches. 3 sail a zigzag course to take advantage of what wind there is.
tack on (*informal*) add an extra thing.

tack² *noun*
harness, saddles, etc.
[from *tackle* = equipment]

tackle *verb* (tackles, tackling, tackled)
1 try to do something that needs doing. **2** try to get the ball from someone else in a game of football or hockey.

tackle *noun* (*plural* tackles)
1 equipment, especially for fishing. **2** a set of ropes and pulleys. **3** tackling someone in football or hockey.

tacky *adjective*
sticky, not quite dry, *The paint is still tacky.*
tackiness *noun*
[from *tack¹* = a fastening]

tact *noun*
skill in not offending people.
tactful *adjective*, **tactfully** *adverb*,
tactless *adjective*, **tactlessly** *adverb*
[from Latin *tactus* = sense of touch]

tactics *noun*
1 the method of arranging troops etc. skilfully for a battle. **2** the methods you use to achieve something or gain an advantage.
tactical *adjective*, **tactically** *adverb*,
tactician *noun*
[from Greek *taktika* = things arranged]

USAGE: *Strategy* is a general plan for a whole campaign, *tactics* is for one part of this.

tadpole *noun* (*plural* tadpoles)
a young frog or toad that has developed from the egg and lives entirely in water.
[from *toad* + *poll* = head]

tag¹ *noun* (*plural* tags)
1 a label tied on or stuck into something. **2** a metal or plastic point at the end of a shoelace.
tag *verb* (tags, tagging, tagged)
1 label something with a tag. **2** add as an extra thing, *A postscript was tagged on to her letter.*
3 (*informal*) go with other people, *Her sister tagged along.*
[origin unknown]

tag² *noun*
a game in which one person chases the others.
[origin unknown]

tail *noun* (*plural* tails)
1 the part that sticks out from the rear end of the body of a bird, fish, or animal. **2** the part at the end or rear of something. **3** the side of a coin opposite the head, *Heads or tails?*
tail *verb* (tails, tailing, tailed)
1 remove stalks etc. from fruit, *top and tail gooseberries.* **2** (*informal*) follow a person or thing.
tail off become fewer, smaller, or slighter etc.; cease gradually.

tailor *noun* (*plural* tailors)
a person who makes men's clothes.

taint *noun* (*plural* taints)
a small amount of decay, pollution, or a bad quality that spoils something.
taint *verb* (taints, tainting, tainted)
give something a taint.
[from old French; related to *tint*]

take *verb* (takes, taking, took, taken)
This word has many uses, including **1** get something into your hands or possession or control etc. (*take this cup*; *we took many prisoners*), **2** make use of (*take a taxi*) or indulge in (*take a holiday*), **3** carry or convey (*Take this parcel to the post*), **4** perform or deal with (*When do you take your music exam?*), **5** study or teach a subject (*Who takes you for maths?*), **6** make an effort (*take trouble*) or experience a feeling (*Don't take offence*), **7** accept; endure (*I'll take a risk*), **8** require (*It takes a strong man to lift this*), **9** write down (*take notes*), **10** make a photograph, **11** subtract (*take 4 from 10*), **12** assume (*I take it that you agree*). **taker** *noun*
take after be like a parent etc.
take in deceive somebody.
take leave of say goodbye to.
take off (of an aircraft) leave the ground and become airborne. **take-off** *noun*
take on 1 begin to employ someone. **2** play or fight against someone. **3** (*informal*) show that you are upset.
take over take control. **takeover** *noun*
take place happen or occur.
take up 1 start something. **2** occupy space or time etc. **3** accept an offer.

takeaway *noun* (*plural* takeaways)
1 a place that sells cooked meals for customers to take away. **2** a meal from this.

tale *noun* (*plural* tales)
a story. [from Old English]

talent *noun* (*plural* talents)
a special or very great ability.
talented *adjective*
[from Greek *talanton* = sum of money]

talk *verb* (talks, talking, talked)
speak; have a conversation. **talker** *noun*
talk *noun* (*plural* talks)
1 talking; a conversation. **2** an informal lecture.
[from Middle English; related to *tale*]

talkative *adjective*
talking a lot.

tall *adjective*
1 higher than the average, *a tall tree.*
2 measured from the bottom to the top, *It is 10 metres tall.* **tallness** *noun*

tall story *noun* (*plural* tall stories)
(*informal*) a story that is hard to believe.

tally *verb* (tallies, tallying, tallied)
correspond or agree with something else, *Does your list tally with mine?*

talon *noun* (*plural* **talons**)
a strong claw. [from Latin]

tambourine *noun* (*plural* **tambourines**)
a circular musical instrument with metal discs
round it, tapped or shaken to make it jingle.
[from French]

tame *adjective*
1 (of animals) gentle and not afraid of people;
not wild or dangerous. **2** not exciting; dull.
tamely *adverb*, **tameness** *noun*
tame *verb* (**tames, taming, tamed**)
make an animal become tame. **tamer** *noun*

tamper *verb* (**tampers, tampering, tampered**)
meddle or interfere with something.
[from *temper*]

tampon *noun* (*plural* **tampons**)
a plug of soft material that a woman puts into
her vagina to absorb the blood during her
period. [French]

tan *noun* (*plural* **tans**)
1 light brown colour. **2** brown colour in skin
that has been exposed to sun.
tan *verb* (**tans, tanning, tanned**)
1 make or become brown by exposing skin to
the sun. **2** make an animal's skin into leather
by treating it with chemicals.
[probably from Latin]

tandem *noun* (*plural* **tandems**)
a bicycle for two riders, one behind the other.
[Latin, = at length]

tang *noun* (*plural* **tangs**)
a strong flavour or smell. [from Old Norse]

tangent *noun* (*plural* **tangents**)
a straight line that touches the outside of a
curve or circle.
[from Latin *tangens* = touching]

tangerine *noun* (*plural* **tangerines**)
a kind of small orange from Tangier in
Morocco. [named after Tangier]

tangle *verb* (**tangles, tangling, tangled**)
make or become twisted into a confused mass.
tangle *noun*

tango *noun* (*plural* **tangos**)
a ballroom dance with gliding steps.

tank *noun* (*plural* **tanks**)
1 a large container for a liquid or gas. **2** a
heavy armoured vehicle used in war.
[from Gujarati or Marathi, languages spoken
in India]

tankard *noun* (*plural* **tankards**)
a large mug for drinking beer from, usually
made of silver or pewter. [origin unknown]

tanker *noun* (*plural* **tankers**)
1 a large ship for carrying oil. **2** a large lorry
for carrying a liquid. [from *tank*]

tantalize *verb* (**tantalizes, tantalizing, tantalized**)
tease or torment a person by showing him or

her something good but keeping it out of reach.
[from the name of Tantalus in Greek
mythology, who was punished by being made
to stand near water and fruit which moved
away when he tried to reach them]

tantrum *noun* (*plural* **tantrums**)
an outburst of bad temper.

tap[1] *noun* (*plural* **taps**)
a device for letting out liquid or gas in a
controlled flow.
tap *verb* (**taps, tapping, tapped**)
1 take liquid out of something, especially
through a tap. **2** obtain supplies or information
etc. from a source. **3** fix a device to a telephone
line so that you can overhear conversations on
it. [from Old English]

tap[2] *noun* (*plural* **taps**)
1 a quick light hit; the sound of this.
2 tap-dancing.
tap *verb* (**taps, tapping, tapped**)
hit a person or thing quickly and lightly.
[from French]

tape *noun* (*plural* **tapes**)
1 a narrow strip of cloth, paper, plastic, etc. **2** a
narrow plastic strip coated with a magnetic
substance and used for making recordings. **3** a
tape recording. **4** a tape-measure.
tape *verb* (**tapes, taping, taped**)
1 fix, cover, or surround something with tape.
2 record something on magnetic tape.
get or **have something taped** (*slang*) know or
understand it; be able to deal with it.

tape-measure *noun* (*plural* **tape-measures**)
a long strip marked in centimetres or inches
for measuring things.

taper *verb* (**tapers, tapering, tapered**)
1 make or become thinner towards one end.
2 make or become gradually less.

tape recorder *noun* (*plural* **tape recorders**)
a machine for recording sounds or computer
data on magnetic tape and reproducing them.
tape recording *noun*

tapestry *noun* (*plural* **tapestries**)
a piece of strong cloth with pictures or patterns
woven or embroidered on it.
[from French *tapis* = carpet]

tapeworm *noun* (*plural* **tapeworms**)
a long flat worm that can live as a parasite in
the intestines of people and animals.

tar *noun*
a thick black liquid made from coal or wood
etc. and used in making roads.

target *noun* (*plural* **targets**)
something aimed at; a thing that someone tries
to hit or reach.

tariff *noun* (*plural* **tariffs**)
a list of prices or charges.
[via French and Italian from Arabic]

tarmac *noun*
an area surfaced with tarmacadam, especially on an airfield.
[*Tarmac* is a trade mark]

tarnish *verb* (tarnishes, tarnishing, tarnished)
1 make or become less shiny, *The silver had tarnished.* 2 spoil or blemish, *The scandal tarnished his reputation.* **tarnish** *noun*
[from French *terne* = dark, dull]

tarpaulin *noun* (*plural* **tarpaulins**)
a large sheet of waterproof canvas.
[from *tar* + *pall*[1]]

tarry[1] (*say* tar-ee) *adjective*
covered with or like tar.

tarry[2] (*say* ta-ree) *verb* (tarries, tarrying, tarried) (*old use*)
stay for a while longer; linger.
[origin unknown]

tart[1] *noun* (*plural* **tarts**)
1 a pie containing fruit or sweet filling. 2 a piece of pastry with jam etc. on top.
[from Latin]

tart[2] *adjective*
1 sour. 2 sharp in manner, *a tart reply.*
tartly *adverb*, **tartness** *noun*
[origin unknown]

tartan *noun*
a pattern with coloured stripes crossing each other, especially one that is used by a Scottish clan. [probably from old French *tiretaine*, a kind of material]

tartar[1] *noun* (*plural* **tartars**)
a person who is fierce or difficult to deal with.
[named after the Tartars, warriors from central Asia in the 13th century]

tartar[2] *noun* (*plural* **tartars**)
a hard chalky deposit that forms on teeth.
[from Latin]

task *noun* (*plural* **tasks**)
a piece of work to be done.
take a person to task rebuke him or her.
[from old French; related to *tax*]

tassel *noun* (*plural* **tassels**)
a bundle of threads tied together at the top and used to decorate something. **tasselled** *adjective*
[from old French]

taste *verb* (tastes, tasting, tasted)
1 take a small amount of food or drink to try its flavour. 2 be able to perceive flavours. 3 have a certain flavour.
taste *noun* (*plural* **tastes**)
1 the feeling caused in the tongue by something placed on it. 2 the ability to taste things. 3 the ability to enjoy beautiful things or to choose what is suitable, *Her choice of clothes shows her good taste.* 4 a liking, *I've developed quite a taste for skiing.* 5 a very small amount of food or drink.

tasteful *adjective*
showing good taste.
tastefully *adverb*, **tastefulness** *noun*

tasteless *adjective*
1 having no flavour. 2 showing poor taste.
tastelessly *adverb*, **tastelessness** *noun*

tasty *adjective* (tastier, tastiest)
having a strong pleasant taste.

tattered *adjective*
badly torn; ragged.
[from *tatters*]

tatters *plural noun*
rags; badly torn pieces.
in tatters torn to pieces, *My coat was in tatters.*

tattoo[1] *verb* (tattoos, tattooing, tattooed)
mark a person's skin with a picture or pattern by using a needle and some dye.
tattoo *noun* (*plural* **tattoos**)
a tattooed picture or pattern.
[from a Polynesian language]

tattoo[2] *noun* (*plural* **tattoos**)
1 a drumming or tapping sound. 2 an entertainment consisting of military music, marching, etc.
[from Dutch]

taunt *verb* (taunts, taunting, taunted)
jeer at or insult someone. **taunt** *noun*
[from French *tant pour tant* = tit for tat]

taut *adjective*
stretched tightly. **tautly** *adverb*, **tautness** *noun*
[probably from *tough*]

tautology *noun* (*plural* **tautologies**)
saying the same thing again in different words, e.g. *You can get the book free for nothing* (where *free* and *for nothing* mean the same).
[from Greek *tauto* = the same + *logos* = word]

tavern *noun* (*plural* **taverns**) (*old use*)
an inn or public house. [from Latin]

tawny *adjective*
brownish-yellow.
[from old French; related to *tan*]

tax *noun* (*plural* **taxes**)
1 money that people or business firms have to pay to the government, to be used for public purposes. 2 a strain or burden, *The long walk was a tax on his strength.*
tax *verb* (taxes, taxing, taxed)
1 put a tax on something. 2 charge someone a tax. 3 pay the tax on something, *I have taxed the car up to June.* 4 put a strain or burden on a person or thing, *Will it tax your strength?* 5 accuse, *I taxed him with leaving the door open.*
taxable *adjective*, **taxation** *noun*
[from Latin *taxare* = calculate]

taxi *noun* (*plural* **taxis**)
a car that carries passengers for payment, usually with a meter to record the fare to be paid. **taxicab** *noun*

taxi *verb* (taxies, taxiing, taxied)
(of an aircraft) move along the ground or water, especially before or after flying. [short for *taximeter cab*, from French *taxe* = tariff, charge + *mètre* = meter]

tea *noun* (*plural* teas)
1 a drink made by pouring hot water on the dried leaves of an evergreen shrub (the *tea-plant*). 2 these dried leaves. 3 a meal in the afternoon or early evening.
teacup *noun*, **tea leaf** *noun*, **tea table** *noun*, **teatime** *noun* [via Dutch from Chinese]

tea bag *noun* (*plural* tea bags)
a small bag holding about a teaspoonful of tea.

teach *verb* (teaches, teaching, taught)
1 give a person knowledge or skill; train. 2 give lessons, especially in a particular subject. 3 show someone what to do or avoid, *That will teach you not to meddle!*

teacher *noun* (*plural* teachers)
a person who teaches others, especially in a school.

team *noun* (*plural* teams)
1 a set of players forming one side in certain games and sports. 2 a set of people working together. 3 two or more animals harnessed to pull a vehicle or a plough etc.

teapot *noun* (*plural* teapots)
a pot with a lid and a handle, for making and pouring tea.

tear[1] (*say* teer) *noun* (*plural* tears)
a drop of the water that comes from the eyes when a person cries. **teardrop** *noun*
in tears crying.
[from Old English *taeher*]

tear[2] (*say* tair) *verb* (tears, tearing, tore, torn)
1 pull something apart, away, or into pieces. 2 become torn, *Newspaper tears easily.* 3 run or travel hurriedly.
tear *noun* (*plural* tears)
a split made by tearing.
[from Old English *teran*]

tear gas *noun*
a gas that makes people's eyes water painfully.

tease *verb* (teases, teasing, teased)
1 amuse yourself by deliberately annoying or making fun of someone. 2 pick threads apart into separate strands.
tease *noun* (*plural* teases)
a person who often teases others.

teaspoon *noun* (*plural* teaspoons)
a small spoon for stirring tea etc.
teaspoonful *noun*

tea towel *noun* (*plural* tea towels)
a cloth for drying washed dishes, cutlery, etc.

technical *adjective*
1 to do with technology. 2 to do with a particular subject and its methods, *the*

technical terms of chemistry. **technically** *adverb*
[from Greek *technikos* = skilled in an art or craft]

technical college *noun* (*plural* technical colleges)
a college where technical subjects are taught.

technicality *noun* (*plural* technicalities)
1 being technical. 2 a technical word or phrase; a special detail.

technician *noun* (*plural* technicians)
a person whose job is to look after scientific equipment and do practical work in a laboratory.

technique *noun* (*plural* techniques)
the method of doing something skilfully.
[French, related to *technical*]

technology *noun* (*plural* technologies)
the study of machinery, engineering, and how things work.
technological *adjective*, **technologist** *noun*
[from Greek *techne* = craft, skill, + *-ology*]

teddy bear *noun* (*plural* teddy bears)
a soft furry toy bear. [named after US President Theodore ('Teddy') Roosevelt, who liked hunting bears]

tedious *adjective*
annoyingly slow or long; boring.
tediously *adverb*, **tediousness** *noun*, **tedium** *noun*
[from Latin *taedium* = tiredness]

tee *noun* (*plural* tees)
1 the flat area from which golfers strike the ball at the start of play for each hole. 2 a small piece of wood or plastic on which a golf ball is placed for being struck.
[origin unknown]

teem *verb* (teems, teeming, teemed)
be full of something, *The river was teeming with fish.* [from Old English]

-teen *suffix*
a form of 'ten' added to numbers from *three* to *nine* to form *thirteen* to *nineteen*.

teenage *adjective*
to do with teenagers.

teenager *noun* (*plural* teenagers)
a person in his or her teens.

teens *plural noun*
the time of life between 13 and 19 years of age.

teething *noun*
(of a baby) having its first teeth beginning to grow through the gums.

teetotal *adjective*
never drinking alcohol. **teetotaller** *noun*
[from *total* with *tee* added for emphasis]

tele- *prefix*
far; at a distance (as in *telescope*).
[from Greek]

telecommunications *plural noun*
communications over a long distance, e.g. by telephone, telegraph, radio, or television.

telegram *noun* (*plural* **telegrams**)
a message sent by telegraph.

telegraph *noun*
a way of sending messages by using electric current along wires or by radio.
telegraphic *adjective*, **telegraphy** *noun*

telepathy (*say* til-ep-ath-ee) *noun*
communication of thoughts from one person's mind to another without speaking, writing, or gestures.
telepathic *adjective*
[from *tele-* + Greek *pathos* = feeling]

telephone *noun* (*plural* **telephones**)
a device or system using electric wires or radio etc. to enable one person to speak to another who is some distance away.
telephone *verb* (**telephones, telephoning, telephoned**)
speak to a person on the telephone.
[from *tele-* + Greek *phone* = sound, voice]

telescope *noun* (*plural* **telescopes**)
an instrument using lenses to magnify distant objects. **telescopic** *adjective*
telescope *verb* (**telescopes, telescoping, telescoped**)
1 make or become shorter by sliding overlapping sections into each other.
2 compress or condense something so that it takes less space or time.
[from *tele-* + Greek *skopein* = look at]

television *noun* (*plural* **televisions**)
1 a system using radio waves to reproduce a view of scenes, events, or plays etc. on a screen.
2 an apparatus for receiving these pictures.
3 televised programmes. **televise** *verb*

tell *verb* (**tells, telling, told**)
1 make a thing known to someone, especially by words. 2 speak, *Tell the truth.* 3 order, *Tell them to wait.* 4 reveal a secret, *Promise you won't tell.* 5 decide or distinguish, *Can you tell the difference between butter and margarine?*
6 produce an effect, *The strain began to tell on him.* 7 count, *There are ten of them, all told.*
tell off (*informal*) reprimand.
tell tales report something naughty or bad that someone has done.

telling *adjective*
having a strong effect, *a very telling reply.*

tell-tale *adjective*
revealing or indicating something, *There was a tell-tale spot of jam on his chin.*

temper *noun* (*plural* **tempers**)
1 a person's mood, *He is in a good temper.* 2 an angry mood, *She was in a temper.*
lose your temper lose your calmness and become angry.

temper *verb* (**tempers, tempering, tempered**)
1 harden or strengthen metal etc. by heating and cooling it. 2 moderate or soften the effects of something, *tempering justice with mercy.*
[via Old English from Latin *temperare* = mix]

temperament *noun* (*plural* **temperaments**)
a person's nature as shown in the way he or she usually behaves, *a nervous temperament.*
[same origin as *temper*]

temperamental *adjective*
1 likely to become excitable or moody suddenly. 2 to do with a person's temperament.
temperamentally *adverb*

temperate *adjective*
neither extremely hot nor extremely cold, *Britain has a temperate climate.*
[originally = not affected by strong emotions: same origin as *temper*]

temperature *noun* (*plural* **temperatures**)
1 how hot or cold a person or thing is. 2 an abnormally high temperature of the body.
[from Latin *temperatus* = tempered]

tempest *noun* (*plural* **tempests**)
a violent storm.
[from Latin *tempestas* = weather]

temple[1] *noun* (*plural* **temples**)
a building where a god is worshipped. [from Latin *templum* = consecrated place]

temple[2] *noun* (*plural* **temples**)
the part of the head between the forehead and the ear.
[from Latin *tempora* = sides of the head]

tempo *noun* (*plural* **tempos** or **tempi**)
the speed or rhythm of something, especially of a piece of music.
[Italian, from Latin *tempus* = time]

temporary *adjective*
lasting for a limited time only; not permanent.
temporarily (*say* tem-per-er-il-ee) *adverb* [from Latin *temporis* = of a time]

tempt *verb* (**tempts, tempting, tempted**)
try to persuade or attract someone, especially into doing something wrong or unwise.
temptation *noun*, **tempter** *noun*, **temptress** *noun*
[from Latin *temptare* = test]

ten *noun* (*plural* **tens**) & *adjective*
the number 10. [from Old English]

tenacious (*say* ten-ay-shus) *adjective*
1 holding or clinging firmly to something.
2 obstinate and persistent.
tenaciously *adverb*, **tenacity** *noun*
[from Latin *tenere* = to hold]

tenant *noun* (*plural* **tenants**)
a person who rents a house, building, or land etc. from a landlord. **tenancy** *noun*
[French, = holding]

tend¹ *verb* (tends, tending, tended)
have a certain tendency, *Prices tend to rise.*
[same origin as *tender*²]

tend² *verb* (tends, tending, tended)
look after, *Shepherds were tending their sheep.*
[from *attend*]

tendency *noun* (*plural* tendencies)
the way a person or thing is likely to behave,
She has a tendency to be lazy.

tender¹ *adjective*
1 easy to chew; not tough or hard. 2 easily hurt
or damaged; sensitive or delicate, *tender plants.*
3 gentle and loving, *a tender smile.*
tenderly *adverb*, **tenderness** *noun*
[from Latin *tener* = soft]

tender² *verb* (tenders, tendering, tendered)
offer something formally, *He tendered his
resignation.*
tender *noun* (*plural* tenders)
a formal offer to supply goods or carry out
work at a stated price, *The council asked for
tenders to build a school.*
legal tender kinds of money that are legal for
making payments, *Are pound notes still legal
tender?*
[from Latin *tendere* = stretch, hold out]

tendril *noun* (*plural* tendrils)
1 a thread-like part by which a climbing plant
clings to a support. 2 a thin curl of hair etc.
[from French; related to *tender*¹]

tennis *noun*
a game played with rackets and a ball on a
court with a net across the middle.

tenor *noun* (*plural* tenors)
a male singer with a high voice.

tense¹ *noun* (*plural* tenses)
the form of a verb that shows when something
happens, e.g. he *came* (**past tense**), he *comes* or
is coming (**present tense**), he *will come* (**future
tense**).
[from Latin *tempus* = time]

tense² *adjective*
1 tightly stretched. 2 nervous or worried and
unable to relax.
tensely *adverb*, **tenseness** *noun*
tense *verb* (tenses, tensing, tensed)
make or become tense.
[from Latin *tensum* = stretched]

tension *noun* (*plural* tensions)
1 how tightly stretched a rope or wire is. 2 a
feeling of anxiety or nervousness about
something that is just about to happen.
3 voltage, *high-tension cables.*
[from Latin *tensio* = stretching]

tent *noun* (*plural* tents)
a shelter made of canvas or other material.
[from French; related to *tense*²]

tentacle *noun* (*plural* tentacles)
a long flexible part of the body of certain
animals (e.g. snails, octopuses), used for feeling
or grasping things or for moving. [from Latin]

tentative *adjective*
cautious; trying something out, *a tentative
suggestion.* **tentatively** *adverb*
[same origin as *tempt*]

tenth *adjective* & *noun*
next after the ninth. [from Old English]

tenuous *adjective*
very slight or thin, *tenuous threads; a tenuous
connection.*
[from Latin *tenuis* = thin]

tepid *adjective*
only slightly warm; lukewarm, *tepid water.*
[from Latin *tepere* = to be warm]

term *noun* (*plural* terms)
1 the period of weeks when a school or college
is open. 2 a definite period, *a term of
imprisonment.* 3 a word or expression,
technical terms.
term *verb* (terms, terming, termed)
name; call something by a certain term, *This
music is termed jazz.*
[from French; related to *terminus*]

terminal *noun* (*plural* terminals)
1 the place where something ends; a terminus.
2 a building where air passengers arrive or
depart. 3 a place where a wire is connected in
an electric circuit or battery etc. 4 a device for
sending information to a computer, or for
receiving it.
terminal *adjective*
1 to do with or at the end or boundary of
something. 2 in the last stage of a fatal disease,
terminal cancer. **terminally** *adverb*
[same origin as *terminus*]

terminate *verb* (terminates, terminating,
terminated)
end; stop finally. **termination** *noun*
[same origin as *terminus*]

terminology *noun* (*plural* terminologies)
the technical terms of a subject.
terminological *adjective*
[via German from Latin]

terminus *noun* (*plural* termini)
the end of something; the last station on a
railway or bus route.
[Latin, = end, limit, or boundary]

termite *noun* (*plural* termites)
a small insect that is very destructive to
timber. [from Latin]

terms *plural noun*
1 a relationship between people, *They are on
friendly terms.* 2 conditions offered or accepted,
peace terms.

terrace *noun* (*plural* **terraces**)
1 a level area on a slope or hillside. 2 a paved area beside a house. 3 a row of houses joined together. **terraced** *adjective*

terrestrial *adjective*
to do with the earth or land.
[same origin as *terrain*]

terrible *adjective*
very bad; distressing. **terribly** *adverb*
[same origin as *terror*]

terrier *noun* (*plural* **terriers**)
a kind of small lively dog.
[from old French *chien terrier* = earth-dog (because they were used to dig out foxes from their earths)]

terrific *adjective* (*informal*)
1 very great, *a terrific storm.* 2 excellent.
terrifically *adverb*
[from Latin *terrificus* = frightening]

terrify *verb* (**terrifies, terrifying, terrified**)
fill someone with terror.
[same origin as *terrific*]

territory *noun* (*plural* **territories**)
an area of land, especially one that belongs to a country or person. **territorial** *adjective* [same origin as *terrain*]

terror *noun* (*plural* **terrors**)
1 very great fear. 2 a terrifying person or thing. [from Latin *terrere* = frighten]

terrorist *noun* (*plural* **terrorists**)
a person who uses violence for political purposes.
terrorism *noun*

terrorize *verb* (**terrorizes, terrorizing, terrorized**)
fill someone with terror; frighten someone by threatening them. **terrorization** *noun*

test *noun* (*plural* **tests**)
1 a short examination. 2 a way of discovering the qualities, abilities, or presence of a person or thing, *a test for radioactivity.* 3 (*informal*) a test match.
test *verb* (**tests, testing, tested**)
carry out a test on a person or thing.
tester *noun* [from Latin]

testament *noun* (*plural* **testaments**)
1 a written statement. 2 either of the two main parts of the Bible, the Old Testament or the New Testament. [from Latin *testari* = act as a witness, make a will]

testicle *noun* (*plural* **testicles**)
either of the two glands in the scrotum where semen is produced. [from Latin]

testify *verb* (**testifies, testifying, testified**)
give evidence; swear that something is true.
[from Latin *testis* = witness]

testimonial *noun* (*plural* **testimonials**)
1 a letter describing someone's abilities, character, etc. 2 a gift presented to someone as a mark of respect.
[same origin as *testify*]

test match *noun* (*plural* **test matches**)
a cricket or Rugby match between teams from different countries.

test tube *noun* (*plural* **test tubes**)
a tube of thin glass with one end closed, used for experiments in chemistry etc.

tether *verb* (**tethers, tethering, tethered**)
tie an animal so that it cannot move far.
tether *noun* (*plural* **tethers**)
a rope for tethering an animal.
at the end of your tether unable to endure something any more.

tetra- *prefix*
four. [from Greek]

tetrahedron *noun* (*plural* **tetrahedrons**)
a solid with four sides (i.e. a pyramid with a triangular base).
[from *tetra-* + Greek *hedra* = base]

text *noun* (*plural* **texts**)
1 the words of something written or printed. 2 a sentence from the Bible used as the subject of a sermon etc.
[from Latin *textus* = literary style]

textbook *noun* (*plural* **textbooks**)
a book that teaches you about a subject.

texture *noun* (*plural* **textures**)
the way that the surface of something feels.
[from Latin *textura* = weaving]

than *conjunction*
compared with another person or thing, *His brother is taller than he is* or *taller than him.*
[from Old English]

thank *verb* (**thanks, thanking, thanked**)
tell someone that you are grateful to him or her.
thank you I thank you.

thankful *adjective*
grateful.

thankfully *adverb*
1 in a grateful way. 2 I am grateful that; fortunately, *Thankfully, John remembered to lock the door.*

USAGE: Some people say it is incorrect to use *thankfully* to mean 'I am grateful that' or 'fortunately', and say that it should only be used to mean 'in a grateful way'. This first use is very common in informal language but you should probably avoid it when you are writing or speaking formally.

thankless *adjective*
not likely to win thanks from people, *a thankless task.*

thanks *plural noun*
1 statements of gratitude. 2 (*informal*) thank you.
thanks to as a result of; because of, *Thanks to your help, we succeeded.*

that *adjective & pronoun* (*plural* **those**)
the one there, *That book is mine. Whose is that?*
that *adverb*
to such an extent, *I'll come that far but no further.*
that *relative pronoun*
which, who, or whom, *This is the record that I wanted. We liked the people that we met on holiday.*
that *conjunction*
used to introduce a wish, reason, result, etc., *I hope that you are well. The puzzle was so hard that no one could solve it.*

thatch *noun*
straw or reeds used to make a roof.
thatch *verb* (**thatches, thatching, thatched**)
make a roof with thatch. **thatcher** *noun*

thaw *verb* (**thaws, thawing, thawed**)
melt; stop being frozen.
thaw *noun* (*plural* **thaws**)
a period of warm weather that thaws ice and snow. [from Old English]

the *adjective* (called the *definite article*)
a particular one; that or those.

theatre *noun* (*plural* **theatres**)
1 a building where plays etc. are performed to an audience. 2 a special room where surgical operations are done, *the operating theatre.*
[from Greek *theatron* = place for seeing things]

theatrical *adjective*
to do with plays or acting.
theatrically *adverb*

thee *pronoun* (*old use*)
the form of *thou* used as the object of a verb or after a preposition. [from Old English]

theft *noun* (*plural* **thefts**)
stealing. [from Old English]

their *adjective*
1 belonging to them, *Their coats are over there.*
2 (*informal*) belonging to a person, *Somebody has left their coat on the bus.*
[from Old Norse]

USAGE: Do not confuse with *there*.

theirs *possessive pronoun*
belonging to them, *These coats are theirs.*

USAGE: It is incorrect to write *their's*.

them *pronoun*
the form of *they* used as the object of a verb or after a preposition, *We saw them.*

theme *noun* (*plural* **themes**)
1 the subject about which a person speaks, writes, or thinks. 2 a melody. [from Greek]

themselves *pronoun*
they or them and nobody else. (Compare *herself.*)

then *adverb*
1 at that time, *We were younger then.* 2 after that; next, *Make the tea, then pour it out.* 3 in that case, *If this is yours, then this must be mine.*
[from Old English]

theology *noun*
the study of religion.
theological *adjective*, **theologian** *noun*
[from Greek *theos* = a god, + -*logy*]

theorem *noun* (*plural* **theorems**)
a mathematical statement that can be proved by reasoning.
[from Greek *theorema* = theory]

theoretical *adjective*
based on theory not on experience.
theoretically *adverb*

theory *noun* (*plural* **theories**)
1 an idea or set of ideas put forward to explain something. 2 the principles of a subject rather than its practice.
in theory according to what should happen rather than what may in fact happen.
[from Greek *theoria* = thinking about, considering]

therapy *noun* (*plural* **therapies**)
treatment to cure a disease etc. **therapeutic** *adjective* [from Greek *therapeia* = healing]

there *adverb*
1 in or to that place etc. 2 used to call attention to something (*There's a good boy!*) or to introduce a sentence where the verb comes before its subject (*There was plenty to eat*).
[from Old English]

USAGE: Do not confuse with *their*.

thereabouts *adverb*
near there.

therefore *adverb*
for that reason. [from *there* + *fore*]

thermo- *prefix*
heat. [same origin as *therm*]

thermodynamics *noun*
the science dealing with the relation between heat and other forms of energy.

thermometer *noun* (*plural* **thermometers**)
a device for measuring temperature.

thermostat *noun* (*plural* **thermostats**)
a piece of equipment that automatically keeps the temperature of a room or piece of equipment steady. **thermostatic** *adjective*, **thermostatically** *adverb*
[from *thermo-* + Greek *statos* = standing]

thesaurus (*say* thi-sor-us) *noun* (*plural* **thesauruses** or **thesauri**) a kind of dictionary containing sets of words grouped according to their meaning. [from Greek *thesauros* = storehouse, treasury]

these *plural* of **this**.

they *pronoun*
1 the people or things being talked about. 2 people in general, *They say the show is a great success*. 3 (*informal*) he or she; a person, *I am never angry with anyone unless they deserve it*. [from Old Norse]

they're (*mainly spoken*) they are.

USAGE: Do not confuse with *their* and *there*.

thick *adjective*
1 measuring a lot or a certain amount between opposite surfaces. 2 (of a line) broad, not fine. 3 crowded with things; dense, *a thick forest*; *thick fog*. 4 fairly stiff, *thick cream*. 5 (*informal*) stupid. **thickly** *adverb*, **thickness** *noun* [from Old English]

thicken *verb* (**thickens, thickening, thickened**) make or become thicker.

thicket *noun* (*plural* **thickets**) a number of shrubs and small trees etc. growing close together. [from Old English]

thief *noun* (*plural* **thieves**) a person who steals things. **thievish** *adjective*, **thievery** *noun*, **thieving** *noun* [from Old English]

thigh *noun* (*plural* **thighs**) the part of the leg between the hip and the knee. [from Old English]

thimble *noun* (*plural* **thimbles**) a small metal or plastic cap worn on the end of the finger to push the needle in sewing. [from Old English]

thin *adjective* (**thinner, thinnest**)
1 not thick; not fat. 2 feeble, *a thin excuse*. **thinly** *adverb*, **thinness** *noun*
thin *verb* (**thins, thinning, thinned**) make or become less thick. **thinner** *noun*

thine *adjective* & *possessive pronoun* (*old use*) belonging to thee. [from Old English]

thing *noun* (*plural* **things**) an object; something which can be seen, touched, thought about, etc.

think *verb* (**thinks, thinking, thought**)
1 use your mind; form connected ideas. 2 have as an idea or opinion, *We think we shall win*. **thinker** *noun* [from Old English]

third *adjective* next after the second. **thirdly** *adverb*
third *noun* (*plural* **thirds**)
1 the third person or thing. 2 one of three equal parts of something.

Third World *noun* the poorer countries of Asia, Africa, and South America, also called 'developing countries'.

thirst *noun*
1 a feeling of dryness in the mouth and throat, causing a desire to drink. 2 a strong desire, *a thirst for adventure*. **thirsty** *adjective*, **thirstily** *adverb*

thirteen *noun* & *adjective* the number 13. **thirteenth** *adjective* & *noun*

thirty *noun* (*plural* **thirties**) & *adjective* the number 30. **thirtieth** *adjective* & *noun*

this *adjective* & *pronoun* (*plural* **these**) the one here, *This house is ours. Whose is this?*
this *adverb* to such an extent, *I'm surprised he got this far*. [from Old English]

thistle *noun* (*plural* **thistles**) a prickly wild plant with purple, white, or yellow flowers. [from Old English]

thong *noun* (*plural* **thongs**) a narrow strip of leather etc. used for fastening things. [from Old English]

thorn *noun* (*plural* **thorns**)
1 a small pointed growth on the stem of a plant. 2 a thorny tree or shrub.

thorny *adjective* (**thornier, thorniest**)
1 having many thorns. 2 like a thorn. 3 difficult, *a thorny problem*.

thorough *adjective*
1 done or doing things carefully and in detail. 2 complete in every way, *a thorough mess*. **thoroughly** *adverb*, **thoroughness** *noun* [a different spelling of *through*]

thoroughbred *adjective* bred of pure or pedigree stock. **thoroughbred** *noun*

thoroughfare *noun* (*plural* **thoroughfares**) a public road or path that is open at both ends. [from an old sense of *thorough* = through, + *fare* = to progress]

those *plural* of **that**.

thou *pronoun* (*old use*, in speaking to one person) you. [from Old English]

though *conjunction* in spite of the fact that; even if, *We must look for it, though we probably shan't find it*.
though *adverb* however, *She's right, though*.

thought[1] *noun* (*plural* **thoughts**)
1 something that you think; an idea or opinion. 2 the process of thinking, *She was deep in thought*. [from Old English; related to *think*]

thought[2] *past tense* of **think**.

thoughtful *adjective*
1 thinking a lot. 2 showing thought for other people's needs; considerate.
thoughtfully *adverb*, **thoughtfulness** *noun*

thoughtless *adjective*
1 careless; not thinking of what may happen. 2 inconsiderate.
thoughtlessly *adverb*, **thoughtlessness** *noun*

thousand *noun* (*plural* **thousands**) & *adjective*
the number 1,000. **thousandth** *adjective* & *noun* [from Old English]

thrash *verb* (**thrashes**, **thrashing**, **thrashed**)
1 beat someone with a stick or whip; keep hitting very hard. 2 defeat someone thoroughly. 3 move violently, *The crocodile thrashed its tail.*

thread *noun* (*plural* **threads**)
1 a thin length of any substance. 2 a length of spun cotton, wool, or nylon etc. used for making cloth or in sewing or knitting. 3 the spiral ridge round a screw.
thread *verb* (**threads**, **threading**, **threaded**)
1 put a thread through the eye of a needle. 2 pass a strip of film etc. through or round something. 3 put beads on a thread.

threadbare *adjective*
(of cloth) with the surface worn away so that the threads show.

threat *noun* (*plural* **threats**)
1 a warning that you will punish, hurt, or harm a person or thing. 2 a sign of something undesirable. 3 a person or thing causing danger. [from Old English]

threaten *verb* (**threatens**, **threatening**, **threatened**)
1 make threats against someone. 2 be a threat or danger to a person or thing.

three *noun* (*plural* **threes**) & *adjective*
the number 3. [from Old English]

three-dimensional *adjective*
having three dimensions (length, width, and height or depth).

threshold *noun* (*plural* **thresholds**)
1 a slab of stone or board etc. forming the bottom of a doorway; the entrance. 2 the beginning, *We are on the threshold of a great discovery.* [from Old English]

thrift *noun*
1 careful spending or management of money or resources. 2 a plant with pink flowers.
thrifty *adjective*, **thriftily** *adverb* [Old Norse, = thriving]

thrill *noun* (*plural* **thrills**)
a feeling of excitement.
thrill *verb* (**thrills**, **thrilling**, **thrilled**)
have or give a feeling of excitement.
thrilling *adjective* [from Old English]

thriller *noun* (*plural* **thrillers**)
an exciting story, play, or film, usually about crime.

thrive *verb* (**thrives**, **thriving**, **throve**, **thrived** or **thriven**)
grow strongly; prosper or be successful.

throat *noun* (*plural* **throats**)
1 the tube in the neck that takes food and drink down into the body. 2 the front of the neck. [from Old English]

throb *verb* (**throbs**, **throbbing**, **throbbed**)
beat or vibrate with a strong rhythm, *My heart throbbed.* **throb** *noun*

thrombosis *noun*
the formation of a clot of blood in the body. [from Greek *thrombos* = lump]

throne *noun* (*plural* **thrones**)
a special chair for a king, queen, or bishop at ceremonies.
[from Greek *thronos* = high seat]

throng *noun* (*plural* **throngs**)
a crowd of people.
throng *verb* (**throngs**, **thronging**, **thronged**)
crowd, *People thronged the streets.*

throttle *noun* (*plural* **throttles**)
a device that controls the flow of fuel to an engine; an accelerator.
throttle *verb* (**throttles**, **throttling**, **throttled**)
strangle.
throttle back or **down** reduce the speed of an engine by partially closing the throttle. [from *throat*]

through *preposition*
1 from one end or side to the other end or side of, *Climb through the window.* 2 by means of; because of, *We lost it through carelessness.* 3 at the end of; having finished successfully, *He is through his exam.*
through *adverb*
1 through something, *We squeezed through.* 2 with a telephone connection made, *I'll put you through to the president.* 3 finished, *Wait till I'm through with these papers.*
through *adjective*
1 going through something, *No through road.* 2 going all the way to a destination, *a through train.* [from Old English]

throughout *preposition* & *adverb*
all the way through.

throve *past tense* of **thrive**.

throw *verb* (**throws**, **throwing**, **threw**, **thrown**)
1 send a person or thing through the air. 2 put something in a place carelessly or hastily. 3 move part of your body quickly, *He threw his head back.* 4 put someone in a certain condition etc., *It threw us into confusion.* 5 move a switch or lever in order to operate it. 6 shape a pot on a potter's wheel. **throw** *noun*, **thrower** *noun*

throw away 1 get rid of something because it is useless or unwanted. **2** waste, *You threw away an opportunity.*

thrush *noun* (*plural* **thrushes**)
a songbird with a speckled breast.
[from Old English]

thrust *verb* (**thrusts, thrusting, thrust**)
push hard. **thrust** *noun* [from Old Norse]

thud *verb* (**thuds, thudding, thudded**)
make the dull sound of a heavy knock or fall.
thud *noun* [originally Scots; probably from Old English]

thug *noun* (*plural* **thugs**)
a rough and violent person. **thuggery** *noun*
[from Hindi: the Thugs were robbers and murderers in India in the 17th–19th centuries]

thumb *noun* (*plural* **thumbs**)
the short thick finger set apart from the other four.
be under a person's thumb be completely under his or her influence.

thump *verb* (**thumps, thumping, thumped**)
1 hit or knock something heavily. **2** punch.
3 thud. **4** throb or beat strongly, *My heart was thumping.* **thump** *noun*

thunder *noun*
1 the loud noise that is heard with lightning.
2 a similar noise, *a thunder of applause.*
thunderous *adjective*, **thunderstorm** *noun*,
thundery *adjective*
thunder *verb* (**thunders, thundering, thundered**)
1 sound with thunder. **2** make a noise like thunder; speak loudly. [from Old English]

thunderbolt *noun* (*plural* **thunderbolts**)
a lightning flash thought of as a destructive missile.

thus *adverb*
1 in this way, *Hold the wheel thus.* **2** therefore.
[from Old English]

thwart *verb* (**thwarts, thwarting, thwarted**)
frustrate; prevent someone from achieving something. [from Old Norse]

thy *adjective* (*old use*)
belonging to thee. [from *thine*]

tiara (*say* tee-ar-a) *noun* (*plural* **tiaras**)
a woman's jewelled crescent-shaped ornament worn like a crown. [from Greek]

tic *noun* (*plural* **tics**)
an unintentional twitch of a muscle, especially of the face.

tick[1] *noun* (*plural* **ticks**)
1 a small mark (usually ✓) put by something to show that it is correct or has been checked. **2** a regular clicking sound, especially that made by a clock or watch. **3** (*informal*) a moment, *Back in a tick.*

tick *verb* (**ticks, ticking, ticked**)
1 put a tick by something. **2** make the sound of a tick.
tick off (*informal*) reprimand someone.
[probably from old German or old Dutch]

tick[2] *noun* (*plural* **ticks**)
a bloodsucking insect. [from Old English]

ticket *noun* (*plural* **tickets**)
1 a printed piece of paper or card that allows a person to travel on a bus or train, see a show, etc. **2** a label showing a thing's price. [via French from old Dutch]

tickle *verb* (**tickles, tickling, tickled**)
1 touch a person's skin lightly in order to produce a slight tingling feeling and laughter.
2 (of a part of the body) have a slight tingling or itching feeling. **3** amuse or please somebody.
[origin unknown]

ticklish *adjective*
1 likely to laugh or wriggle when tickled.
2 awkward or difficult, *a ticklish situation.*

tidal wave *noun* (*plural* **tidal waves**)
a huge sea wave.

tide *noun* (*plural* **tides**)
1 the regular rise and fall in the level of the sea which usually happens twice a day. **2** (*old use*) a time or season, *Christmas-tide.*
tide *verb* (**tides, tiding, tided**)
tide a person over provide him or her with what is needed, for a short time.

tidy *adjective* (**tidier, tidiest**)
1 with everything in its right place; neat and orderly. **2** (*informal*) fairly large, *It costs a tidy amount.*
tidily *adverb*, **tidiness** *noun*
tidy *verb* (**tidies, tidying, tidied**)
make a place tidy. [originally = at the right time or season: from *tide*]

tie *verb* (**ties, tying, tied**)
1 fasten something with string, ribbon, etc.
2 arrange something into a knot or bow.
3 make the same score as another competitor.
tie *noun* (*plural* **ties**)
1 a strip of material worn passing under the collar of a shirt and knotted in front. **2** a result when two or more competitors have equal scores. [from Old English]

tier (*say* teer) *noun* (*plural* **tiers**)
each of a series of rows or levels etc. placed one above the other. **tiered** *adjective*
[from French *tire* = rank[1]]

tiff *noun* (*plural* **tiffs**)
a slight quarrel. [origin unknown]

tiger *noun* (*plural* **tigers**)
a large wild animal of the cat family, with yellow and black stripes. [from Greek]

tight *adjective*
1 fitting very closely. **2** firmly fastened. **3** fully stretched; tense. **4** in short supply, *Money is*

tight at the moment. **5** stingy, *He is very tight with his money.* **6** (*slang*) drunk. **tightly** *adverb,* **tightness** *noun*

tighten *verb* (**tightens, tightening, tightened**)
make or become tighter.

tightrope *noun* (*plural* **tightropes**)
a tightly stretched rope high above the ground, on which acrobats perform.

tights *plural noun*
a garment that fits tightly over the feet, legs, and lower part of the body.

tile *noun* (*plural* **tiles**)
a thin square piece of baked clay or other hard material, used in rows for covering roofs, walls, or floors. **tiled** *adjective*

till¹ *preposition & conjunction*
until. [from Old English *til* = to]

USAGE: It is better to use *until* rather than *till* when the word stands first in a sentence (e.g. *Until last year we had never been abroad*) or when you are speaking or writing formally.

till² *noun* (*plural* **tills**)
a drawer or box for money in a shop; a cash register. [origin unknown]

tilt *verb* (**tilts, tilting, tilted**)
move into a sloping position.
tilt *noun*
a sloping position.
at full tilt at full speed or force.

timber *noun* (*plural* **timbers**)
1 wood for building or making things. **2** a wooden beam. [from Old English]

time *noun* (*plural* **times**)
1 all the years of the past, present, and future; the continuous existence of the universe. **2** a particular point or portion of time. **3** an occasion, *the first time I saw him.* **4** a period suitable or available for something, *Is there time for a cup of tea?* **5** a system of measuring time, *Greenwich Mean Time.* **6** (in music) rhythm depending on the number and stress of beats in the bar. **7** (in mathematics) **times** multiplied by, *Five times three is 15* ($5 \times 3 = 15$).
in time 1 not late. **2** eventually.
on time punctual.
time *verb* (**times, timing, timed**)
1 measure how long something takes.
2 arrange when something is to happen.
timer *noun* [from Old English]

timeless *adjective*
not affected by the passage of time; eternal.

timely *adjective*
happening at a suitable or useful time, *a timely warning.*

timetable *noun* (*plural* **timetables**)
a list showing the times when things will happen, e.g. when buses or trains will arrive and depart, or when school lessons will take place.

timid *adjective*
easily frightened. **timidly** *adverb,* **timidity** *noun*
[from Latin *timidus* = nervous]

timpani *plural noun*
kettledrums. [Italian]

tin *noun* (*plural* **tins**)
1 a silvery-white metal. **2** a metal container for food.

tinge *verb* (**tinges, tingeing, tinged**)
colour something slightly; tint. **tinge** *noun*
[same origin as *tint*]

tingle *verb* (**tingles, tingling, tingled**)
have a slight pricking or stinging feeling.
tingle *noun* [probably from *tinkle*]

tinker *verb* (**tinkers, tinkering, tinkered**)
work at something casually, trying to improve or mend it. [origin unknown]

tinkle *verb* (**tinkles, tinkling, tinkled**)
make a gentle ringing sound. **tinkle** *noun*

tinny *adjective*
1 like tin. **2** (of a sound) unpleasantly thin and high-pitched.

tinsel *noun*
strips of glittering material used for decoration.
[from old French; related to *scintillate*]

tint *noun* (*plural* **tints**)
a shade of colour, especially a pale one.
tint *verb* (**tints, tinting, tinted**)
colour something slightly.
[from Latin *tingere* = to dye or stain]

tiny *adjective* (**tinier, tiniest**)
very small. [origin unknown]

-tion *suffix* see **-ion**.

tip¹ *noun* (*plural* **tips**)
the part right at the top or end of something.
tip *verb* (**tips, tipping, tipped**)
put a tip on something. [from Old Norse]

tip² *noun* (*plural* **tips**)
1 a small amount of money given to someone who has helped you. **2** a small but useful piece of advice; a hint. **3** a slight push.
tip *verb* (**tips, tipping, tipped**)
1 give a person a tip. **2** name someone as a likely winner, *Which team would you tip to win the championship?* **tipper** *noun*
[probably from *tip*¹]

tip³ *verb* (**tips, tipping, tipped**)
1 tilt or topple. **2** empty rubbish somewhere.
tip *noun* (*plural* **tips**)
1 the action of tipping something. **2** a place where rubbish etc. is tipped.
[probably from a Scandinavian language]

tipsy *adjective*
slightly drunk. [from *tip³*]

tiptoe *verb* (tiptoes, tiptoeing, tiptoed)
walk on your toes very quietly or carefully.
on tiptoe walking or standing on your toes.

tired *adjective*
feeling that you need to sleep or rest.
tired of having had enough of something and
impatient or bored with it.

tiresome *adjective*
annoying.

tissue *noun* (*plural* **tissues**)
1 tissue paper. 2 a paper handkerchief. 3 the
substance forming any part of the body of an
animal or plant, *bone tissue*. [from old French;
related to *textiles*]

tissue paper *noun*
very thin soft paper used for wrapping and
packing things.

tit¹ *noun* (*plural* **tits**)
a kind of small bird. [probably from a
Scandinavian language]

tit² *noun*
tit for tat something equal given in return;
retaliation.
[originally 'tip for tap': from *tip²* + *tap²*]

titbit *noun* (*plural* **titbits**)
a nice little piece of something, e.g. of food,
gossip, or information.
[from a dialect word *tid* = tender, + *bit¹*]

titillate *verb* (titillates, titillating, titillated)
stimulate or excite you pleasantly. **titillation**
noun
[from Latin *titillare* = to tickle]

title *noun* (*plural* **titles**)
1 the name of a book, film, song, etc. 2 a word
used to show a person's rank or position, e.g.
Dr, Lord, Mrs. 3 a championship in sport, *the
world heavyweight title*. 4 a legal right to
something. [from Latin]

titter *verb* (titters, tittering, tittered)
giggle. **titter** *noun* [imitating the sound]

to *preposition*
This word is used to show 1 direction or
arrival at a position (*We walked to school. He
rose to power*), 2 limit (*from noon to two o'clock*),
3 comparison (*We won by six goals to three*),
4 receiving or being affected by something
(*Give it to me. Be kind to animals*).
Also used before a verb to form an infinitive (*I
want to see him*) or to show purpose etc. (*He
does that to annoy us*), or alone when the verb is
understood (*We meant to go but forgot to*).

to *adverb*
1 to or in the proper or closed position or
condition, *Push the door to*. 2 into a state of
activity, *We set to and cleaned the kitchen*.
to and fro backwards and forwards.
[from Old English]

toad *noun* (*plural* **toads**)
a frog-like animal that lives mainly on land.
[from Old English]

toadstool *noun* (*plural* **toadstools**)
a fungus (usually poisonous) with a round top
on a stalk.

toast *verb* (toasts, toasting, toasted)
1 heat bread etc. to make it brown and crisp.
2 warm something in front of a fire etc. 3 drink
in honour of someone.

toast *noun* (*plural* **toasts**)
1 toasted bread. 2 the call to drink in honour of
someone; the person honoured in this way.
[from Latin *tostum* = dried up]

tobacco *noun*
the dried leaves of certain plants prepared for
smoking in cigarettes, cigars, or pipes or for
making snuff. [via Spanish from a Central
American language]

toboggan *noun* (*plural* **toboggans**)
a small sledge used for sliding downhill.
tobogganing *noun* [via Canadian French from
a Native American language]

today *noun*
this present day, *Today is Monday*.
today *adverb*
on this day, *Have you seen him today?*
[from *to* (preposition) + *day*]

toddler *noun* (*plural* **toddlers**)
a young child who has only recently learnt to
walk. **toddle** *verb* [origin unknown]

to-do *noun* (*plural* **to-dos**)
a fuss or commotion.

toe *noun* (*plural* **toes**)
1 any of the separate parts (five in humans) at
the end of each foot. 2 the part of a shoe or sock
etc. that covers the toes.

toffee *noun* (*plural* **toffees**)
a sticky sweet made from heated butter and
sugar. [origin unknown]

together *adverb*
with another person or thing; with each other,
They went to the party together.

toil *verb* (toils, toiling, toiled)
1 work hard. 2 move slowly and with
difficulty. **toiler** *noun*
toil *noun*
hard work. [from old French]

toilet *noun* (*plural* **toilets**)
1 a bowl-like object, connected by pipes to a
drain, which you use to get rid of urine and
faeces. 2 a room containing a toilet. 3 the
process of washing, dressing, and tidying
yourself.

token *noun* (*plural* **tokens**)
1 a piece of metal or plastic that can be used
instead of money. 2 a voucher or coupon that
can be exchanged for goods. 3 a sign or signal
of something, *a token of our friendship*.

tolerable *adjective*
able to be tolerated. **tolerably** *adverb*

tolerant *adjective*
tolerating things, especially other people's
behaviour, beliefs, etc.
tolerantly *adverb*, **tolerance** *noun*

tolerate *verb* (**tolerates, tolerating, tolerated**)
allow something without protesting or
interfering. **toleration** *noun*
[from Latin *tolerare* = endure]

toll¹ (rhymes with *hole*) *noun* (*plural* **tolls**)
1 a charge made for using a road, bridge, etc.
2 loss or damage caused, *The death toll in the
earthquake is rising*. [via Old English and Latin
from Greek *telos* = a tax]

toll² (rhymes with *hole*) *verb* (**tolls, tolling, tolled**)
ring a bell slowly. **toll** *noun*
[probably from Old English]

tom *noun* (*plural* **toms**)
a male cat. **tomcat** *noun* [short for *Thomas*]

tomato *noun* (*plural* **tomatoes**)
a soft round red or yellow fruit eaten as a
vegetable. [via French, Spanish, or Portuguese
from Nahuatl (a Central American language)]

tomb (*say* toom) *noun* (*plural* **tombs**)
a place where someone is buried; a monument
built over this. [from Greek]

tomboy *noun* (*plural* **tomboys**)
a girl who enjoys rough noisy games etc.
[from *tom* (short for *Thomas*) + *boy*]

tombstone *noun* (*plural* **tombstones**)
a memorial stone set up over a grave.

tomorrow *noun* & *adverb*
the day after today.
[from *to* (preposition) + *morrow*]

ton *noun* (*plural* **tons**)
1 a unit of weight equal to 2,240 pounds or
about 1,016 kilograms. 2 a large amount,
There's tons of room. 3 (*slang*) a speed of 100
miles per hour. [a different spelling of *tun*]

tone *noun* (*plural* **tones**)
1 a sound in music or of the voice. 2 each of the
five larger intervals between notes in a
musical scale (the smaller intervals are
semitones). 3 a shade of a colour. 4 the quality
or character of something, *a cheerful tone*.
tonal *adjective*, **tonally** *adverb*
tone *verb* (**tones, toning, toned**)
1 give a particular tone or quality to
something. 2 be harmonious in colour.
tone down make a thing quieter or less bright
or less harsh.
tone up make a thing brighter or stronger.
[from Greek *tonos* = tension]

tongs *plural noun*
a tool with two arms joined at one end, used to
pick up or hold things.

tongue *noun* (*plural* **tongues**)
1 the long soft muscular part that moves about
inside the mouth. 2 a language. 3 the leather
flap on a shoe or boot underneath the laces. 4 a
pointed flame.

tongue-tied *adjective*
too shy to speak.

tonic *noun* (*plural* **tonics**)
1 a medicine etc. that makes a person healthier
or stronger. 2 a keynote in music. **tonic**
adjective [same origin as *tone*]

tonight *noun* & *adverb*
this evening or night.
[from *to* (preposition) + *night*]

tonne *noun* (*plural* **tonnes**)
a metric ton (1,000 kilograms). [French]

too *adverb*
1 also, *Take the others too*. 2 more than is
wanted or allowed etc., *That's too much sugar
for me*. [from Old English]

tool *noun* (*plural* **tools**)
an object that helps you to do a particular job,
A saw is a tool for cutting wood or metal. [from
Old English]

tooth *noun* (*plural* **teeth**)
1 one of the hard white bony parts that are
rooted in the gums, used for biting and
chewing things. 2 one of a row of sharp parts,
the teeth of a saw.
toothache *noun*, **toothbrush** *noun*, **toothed**
adjective
fight tooth and nail fight very fiercely.

toothpaste *noun* (*plural* **toothpastes**)
a paste for cleaning your teeth.

top¹ *noun* (*plural* **tops**)
1 the highest part of something. 2 the upper
surface. 3 the covering or stopper of a bottle,
jar, etc. 4 a piece of clothing for the upper part
of the body.
on top of in addition to something.
top *adjective*
highest, *at top speed*.
top *verb* (**tops, topping, topped**)
1 put a top on something. 2 be at the top of
something, *She tops the list*. 3 remove the top of
something.
top up fill up something that is half empty.
[from Old English]

top² *noun* (*plural* **tops**)
a toy that can be made to spin on its point.
[origin unknown]

top hat *noun* (*plural* **top hats**)
a man's tall stiff black or grey hat worn with
formal clothes.

top-heavy *adjective*
too heavy at the top and likely to overbalance.

topic *noun* (*plural* **topics**)
a subject to write, learn, or talk about.
[from Greek *topos* = place]

topical *adjective*
connected with things that are happening now, *a topical film*. **topically** *adverb*, **topicality** *noun*
[originally = covering a particular place or topic]

topmost *adjective*
highest.

topple *verb* (**topples, toppling, toppled**)
1 fall over; totter and fall. 2 make something fall; overthrow. [from *top*¹]

top secret *adjective*
extremely secret, *top secret information*.

topsy-turvy *adverb* & *adjective*
upside down; muddled. [probably from *top*¹ + Middle English *terve* = turn upside down]

torch *noun* (*plural* **torches**)
1 a small electric lamp that you can carry in your hand. 2 a stick with burning material on the end, used as a light.

torment *verb* (**torments, tormenting, tormented**)
1 make someone suffer greatly. 2 tease; keep annoying someone. **tormentor** *noun*
torment *noun* (*plural* **torments**)
great suffering.
[from old French; related to *torture*]

tornado (*say* tor-**nay**-doh) *noun* (*plural* **tornadoes**)
a violent storm or whirlwind.
[from Spanish *tronada* = thunderstorm]

torpedo *noun* (*plural* **torpedoes**)
a long tube-shaped missile that can be fired under water to destroy ships. [Latin, = a large sea fish that can give an electric shock which causes numbness]

torrent *noun* (*plural* **torrents**)
1 a rushing stream; a great flow. 2 a heavy downpour of rain. **torrential** *adjective*
[from Latin]

torso *noun* (*plural* **torsos**)
the trunk of the human body.
[Italian, = stump]

tortoise *noun* (*plural* **tortoises**)
a slow-moving animal with a shell over its body. [from Latin]

tortoiseshell (*say* tort-a-shell) *noun* (*plural* **tortoiseshells**)
1 the mottled brown and yellow shell of certain turtles, used for making combs etc. 2 a cat or butterfly with mottled brown colouring.

torture *verb* (**tortures, torturing, tortured**)
make a person feel great pain or worry.
torture *noun*, **torturer** *noun*

Tory *noun* (*plural* **Tories**)
a Conservative. **Tory** *adjective*
[from Irish *toraidhe* = an outlaw]

toss *verb* (**tosses, tossing, tossed**)
1 throw something, especially up into the air. 2 spin a coin to decide something according to

which side of it is upwards after it falls. 3 move restlessly or unevenly from side to side.
toss *noun*

toss-up *noun* (*plural* **toss-ups**)
1 the tossing of a coin. 2 an even chance.

tot¹ *noun* (*plural* **tots**)
1 a small child. 2 (*informal*) a small amount of spirits, *a tot of rum*.
[originally a dialect word]

tot² *verb* (**tots, totting, totted**)
tot up (*informal*) add up.
[from *total*]

total *adjective*
1 including everything, *the total amount*. 2 complete, *total darkness*. **totally** *adverb*
total *noun* (*plural* **totals**)
the amount you get by adding everything together.
total *verb* (**totals, totalling, totalled**)
1 add up the total. 2 amount to something, *The cost of the damage totalled £500.*
[from Latin *totum* = the whole]

totalitarian *adjective*
using a form of government where people are not allowed to form rival political parties.
[from *total*]

totem pole *noun* (*plural* **totem poles**)
a pole carved or painted by Native Americans with the symbols (*totems*) of their tribes or families. [from Ojibwa, a Native American language]

totter *verb* (**totters, tottering, tottered**)
walk unsteadily; wobble. **tottery** *adjective*

touch *verb* (**touches, touching, touched**)
1 put your hand or fingers etc. on something lightly. 2 be or come together so that there is no space between. 3 hit something gently. 4 move or meddle with something. 5 reach, *The thermometer touched 30° Celsius*. 6 affect someone's feelings, e.g. by making them feel sympathy, *The sad story touched our hearts*. 7 (*slang*) persuade someone to give or lend you money.
touch and go an uncertain situation.
touch down 1 (of an aircraft) land. 2 (in Rugby football) touch the ball on the ground behind the goal line.
touch up improve something by making small additions or changes.
touch *noun* (*plural* **touches**)
1 the action of touching. 2 the ability to feel things by touching them. 3 a small amount; a small thing done, *the finishing touches*. 4 a special skill or style of workmanship, *She hasn't lost her touch*. 5 communication with someone, *We lost touch with him*. 6 the part of a football field outside the playing area.
[from old French]

touching *adjective*
causing you to have kindly feelings such as pity or sympathy.

touchline *noun* (*plural* **touchlines**)
one of the lines that mark the side of a sports pitch.

touchstone *noun* (*plural* **touchstones**)
a test by which the quality of something is judged. [formerly, a kind of stone against which gold and silver were rubbed to test their purity]

touchy *adjective* (**touchier, touchiest**)
easily offended.
touchily *adverb*, **touchiness** *noun*
[origin unknown]

tough *adjective*
1 strong; difficult to break or damage. 2 difficult to chew. 3 firm or stubborn; able to stand hardship. 4 difficult, *a tough decision.*
toughly *adverb*, **toughness** *noun*

toughen *verb* (**toughens, toughening, toughened**)
make or become tough.

tour *noun* (*plural* **tours**)
a journey visiting several places.
tour *verb* (**tours, touring, toured**)
make a tour.
[from old French; related to *turn*]

tourism *noun*
the industry of providing services for people on holiday in a place.

tourist *noun* (*plural* **tourists**)
a person who makes a tour or visits a place for pleasure.

tournament *noun* (*plural* **tournaments**)
a series of contests.
[from old French; related to *turn*]

tow (rhymes with *go*) *verb* (**tows, towing, towed**)
pull something along behind you. **tow** *noun*
[from Old English *togian*]

toward *preposition*
towards.

towards *preposition*
1 in the direction of, *She walked towards the sea.* 2 in relation to; regarding, *He behaved kindly towards his children.* 3 as a contribution to, *Put the money towards a new bicycle.* 4 near, *towards four o'clock.*

towel *noun* (*plural* **towels**)
a piece of absorbent cloth for drying things.
towelling *noun*

tower *noun* (*plural* **towers**)
a tall narrow building.
tower *verb* (**towers, towering, towered**)
be very high; be taller than others, *Skyscrapers towered over the city.*
[from Greek]

town *noun* (*plural* **towns**)
a place with many houses, shops, offices, and other buildings.
[from Old English *tun* = enclosure]

town hall *noun* (*plural* **town halls**)
a building with offices for the local council and usually a hall for public events.

towpath *noun* (*plural* **towpaths**)
a path beside a canal or river, originally for use when a horse was towing a barge etc.

toxic *adjective*
poisonous; caused by poison. **toxicity** *noun*

toy *noun* (*plural* **toys**)
a thing to play with.
toy *adjective*
1 made as a toy. 2 (of a dog) of a very small breed kept as a pet, *a toy poodle.*
toy *verb* (**toys, toying, toyed**)
toy with handle a thing or consider an idea casually.

trace *noun* (*plural* **traces**)
1 a mark left by a person or thing; a sign, *There was no trace of the thief.* 2 a very small amount.
trace *verb* (**traces, tracing, traced**)
1 copy a picture or map etc. by drawing over it on transparent paper. 2 follow the traces of a person or thing; find, *The police have been trying to trace her.* **tracer** *noun* [from old French; related to *tract*¹]

tracery *noun*
a decorative pattern of holes in stone, e.g. in a church window. [from *trace*]

track *noun* (*plural* **tracks**)
1 a mark or marks left by a moving person or thing. 2 a rough path made by being used. 3 a road or area of ground specially prepared for something (e.g. racing). 4 a set of rails for trains or trams etc. 5 one of the songs or pieces of music on a CD, tape, etc. 6 a continuous band round the wheels of a tank or tractor etc.
keep track of keep yourself informed about where something is or what someone is doing.
track *verb* (**tracks, tracking, tracked**)
1 follow the tracks left by a person or animal. 2 follow or observe something as it moves.
tracker *noun*
track down find a person or thing by searching.

tract¹ *noun* (*plural* **tracts**)
1 an area of land. 2 a series of connected parts along which something passes, *the digestive tract.*
[from Latin *tractus* = drawing, draught]

tract² *noun* (*plural* **tracts**)
a pamphlet containing a short essay, especially about religion.
[via Old English from Latin]

tractor *noun* (*plural* **tractors**)
a motor vehicle for pulling farm machinery or other heavy loads.

trade *noun* (*plural* **trades**)
1 buying, selling, or exchanging goods.
2 business of a particular kind; the people working in this. 3 an occupation, especially a skilled craft.
trade *verb* (**trades, trading, traded**)
buy, sell, or exchange things. **trader** *noun*
trade in give a thing as part of the payment for something new, *He traded in his motorcycle for a car.*

trade mark *noun* (*plural* **trade marks**)
a firm's registered symbol or name used to distinguish its goods etc. from those of other firms.

tradesman *noun* (*plural* **tradesmen**)
a person employed in trade, especially one who sells or delivers goods.

trade union *noun* (*plural* **trade unions**)
a group of workers organized to help and protect workers in their own trade or industry.

tradition *noun* (*plural* **traditions**)
1 the passing down of beliefs or customs etc. from one generation to another. 2 something passed on in this way. **traditional** *adjective*, **traditionally** *adverb* [from Latin *tradere* = to hand on, deliver, or betray]

traffic *noun*
1 vehicles, ships, or aircraft moving along a route. 2 trading, especially when it is illegal or wrong, *drug traffic.*

traffic lights *plural noun*
coloured lights used as a signal to traffic at road junctions etc.

traffic warden *noun* (*plural* **traffic wardens**)
an official who assists police to control the movement and parking of vehicles.

tragedy *noun* (*plural* **tragedies**)
1 a play with unhappy events or a sad ending.
2 a very sad or distressing event.

tragic *adjective*
1 very sad or distressing. 2 to do with tragedies, *a great tragic actor.*
tragically *adverb*

trail *noun* (*plural* **trails**)
1 a track, scent, or other sign left where something has passed. 2 a path or track made through a wild region.
trail *verb* (**trails, trailing, trailed**)
1 follow the trail of something; track. 2 drag or be dragged along behind; lag behind. 3 hang down or float loosely.
[from Latin *tragula* = net for dragging a river]

trailer *noun* (*plural* **trailers**)
1 a truck or other container pulled along by a vehicle. 2 a short piece from a film or television programme, shown in advance to advertise it. [from *trail*]

train *noun* (*plural* **trains**)
1 a railway engine pulling a line of carriages or trucks that are linked together. 2 a number of people or animals moving in a line, *a camel train.* 3 a series of things, *a train of events.* 4 part of a long dress or robe that trails on the ground at the back.
train *verb* (**trains, training, trained**)
1 give a person instruction or practice so that he or she becomes skilled. 2 practise, *She was training for the race.* 3 make something grow in a particular direction. 4 aim a gun etc., *Train that gun on the bridge.* [from French; related to *traction*]

trainer *noun* (*plural* **trainers**)
1 a person who trains people or animals. 2 a soft rubber-soled shoe of the kind worn for running or by athletes etc. while exercising.

traitor *noun* (*plural* **traitors**)
a person who betrays his or her country or friends. **traitorous** *adjective*
[from old French; related to *tradition*]

tram *noun* (*plural* **trams**)
a public passenger vehicle running on rails in the road. [from old German or old Dutch *trame* = plank, shaft of a cart]

tramp *noun* (*plural* **tramps**)
1 a person without a home or job who walks from place to place. 2 a long walk. 3 the sound of heavy footsteps.
tramp *verb* (**tramps, tramping, tramped**)
1 walk with heavy footsteps. 2 walk for a long distance. [probably from old Dutch]

trample *verb* (**tramples, trampling, trampled**)
tread heavily on something; crush something by treading on it. [from *tramp*]

trampoline *noun* (*plural* **trampolines**)
a large piece of canvas joined to a frame by springs, used by gymnasts for jumping on.

trance *noun* (*plural* **trances**)
a dreamy or unconscious state rather like sleep.

tranquil *adjective*
calm and quiet.
tranquilly *adverb*, **tranquillity** *noun*
[from Latin]

tranquillizer *noun* (*plural* **tranquillizers**)
a medicine used to make a person feel calm.

trans- *prefix*
1 across; through. 2 beyond.
[from Latin *trans* = across]

transatlantic *adjective*
across or on the other side of the Atlantic Ocean.

transcript *noun* (*plural* **transcripts**)
a written copy.
[from Latin *transcriptum* = written out]

transfer *verb* (transfers, transferring, transferred)
1 move a person or thing to another place.
2 hand over.
transferable *adjective*, **transference** *noun*
transfer *noun* (*plural* transfers)
1 the transferring of a person or thing. 2 a picture or design that can be transferred onto another surface.
[from *trans-* + Latin *ferre* = carry]

transfigure *verb* (transfigures, transfiguring, transfigured)
change the appearance of something greatly.
transfiguration *noun*
[from *trans-* + Latin *figura* = figure]

transfix *verb* (transfixes, transfixing, transfixed)
1 make a person or animal unable to move because of fear or surprise etc. 2 pierce and fix with something pointed.
[from *trans-* + Latin *fixum* = fixed]

transform *verb* (transforms, transforming, transformed)
change the form or appearance or character of a person or thing. **transformation** *noun*
[from *trans-* + Latin *formare* = to form]

transformer *noun* (*plural* transformers)
a device used to change the voltage of an electric current.

transfusion *noun* (*plural* transfusions)
putting blood taken from one person into another person's body. **transfuse** *verb*
[from *trans-* + Latin *fusum* = poured]

transistor *noun* (*plural* transistors)
1 a tiny semiconductor device that controls a flow of electricity. 2 (also **transistor radio**) a portable radio that uses transistors.
transistorized *adjective*
[from *transfer* + *resistor*]

transition *noun* (*plural* transitions)
the process of changing from one condition or form etc. to another. **transitional** *adjective* [from *trans-* + Latin *itum* = gone]

transitive *adjective*
(of a verb) used with a direct object after it, e.g. *change* in *change your shoes* (but not in *change into dry shoes*). (Compare *intransitive*.)
transitively *adverb*
[from Latin *transitivus* = passing over]

translate *verb* (translates, translating, translated)
put something into another language.
translatable *adjective*, **translation** *noun*, **translator** *noun*
[from *trans-* + Latin *latum* = carried]

transliterate *verb* (transliterates, transliterating, transliterated)
write a word in the letters of a different alphabet or language. **transliteration** *noun*
[from *trans-* + Latin *littera* = letter]

translucent (*say* tranz-loo-sent) *adjective*
allowing light to shine through but not transparent.
[from *trans-* + Latin *lucens* = shining]

transmission *noun* (*plural* transmissions)
1 transmitting something. 2 a broadcast. 3 the gears by which power is transmitted from the engine to the wheels of a vehicle.

transmit *verb* (transmits, transmitting, transmitted)
1 send or pass on from one person or place to another. 2 send out a signal or broadcast etc.
transmitter *noun*
[from *trans-* + Latin *mittere* = send]

transmute *verb* (transmutes, transmuting, transmuted)
change something from one form or substance into another.
transmutation *noun*
[from *trans-* + Latin *mutare* = to change]

transparent *adjective*
able to be seen through.
[from *trans-* + Latin *parens* = appearing]

transplant *verb* (transplants, transplanting, transplanted)
1 remove a plant and put it to grow somewhere else. 2 transfer a part of the body to another person or animal. **transplantation** *noun*
transplant *noun* (*plural* transplants)
1 the process of transplanting. 2 something transplanted.
[from *trans-* + Latin *plantare* = to plant]

transport *verb* (transports, transporting, transported)
take a person, animal, or thing from one place to another.
transportation *noun*, **transporter** *noun*
transport *noun*
the action or means of transporting people, animals, or things, *The city has a good system of public transport.*
[from *trans-* + Latin *portare* = carry]

transpose *verb* (transposes, transposing, transposed)
1 change the position or order of something. 2 put a piece of music into a different key.
transposition *noun*
[from *trans-* + Latin *positum* = placed]

trap *noun* (*plural* traps)
1 a device for catching and holding animals. 2 a plan or trick for capturing, detecting, or cheating someone. 3 a device for collecting water etc. or preventing it from passing. 4 a two-wheeled carriage pulled by a horse.
trap *verb* (traps, trapping, trapped)
catch or hold a person or animal in a trap.
trapper *noun* [from Old English]

trapdoor *noun* (*plural* trapdoors)
a door in a floor, ceiling, or roof.

trapeze *noun* (*plural* **trapezes**)
a bar hanging from two ropes as a swing for acrobats. [French; related to *trapezium*]

trapezium *noun* (*plural* **trapeziums** or **trapezia**)
a quadrilateral in which two opposite sides are parallel and the other two are not.
[from Greek *trapeza* = table]

trash *noun*
rubbish or nonsense. **trashy** *adjective*

trauma (*say* traw-ma) *noun* (*plural* **traumas**)
a shock that produces a lasting effect on a person's mind.
traumatic *adjective*, **traumatize** *verb*
[Greek, = a wound]

travel *verb* (**travels, travelling, travelled**)
move from place to place.
travel *noun*, **traveller** *noun*

traveller's cheque *noun* (*plural* **traveller's cheques**)
a cheque for a fixed amount of money that is sold by banks and that can be exchanged for money in foreign countries.

trawl *verb* (**trawls, trawling, trawled**)
fish by dragging a large net along the seabed.
[from old Dutch; related to *trail*]

trawler *noun* (*plural* **trawlers**)
a boat used in trawling.

tray *noun* (*plural* **trays**)
1 a flat piece of wood, metal, or plastic, usually with raised edges, for carrying cups, plates, food, etc. 2 an open container for holding letters etc. in an office.

treacherous *adjective*
1 betraying someone; disloyal. 2 not to be relied on; dangerous, *It's snowing and the roads are treacherous*.
treacherously *adverb*, **treachery** *noun*
[from old French *trechier* = to trick or deceive]

treacle *noun*
a thick sticky liquid produced when sugar is purified. **treacly** *adjective* [originally = ointment for an animal bite; from Greek *therion* = wild or poisonous animal]

tread *verb* (**treads, treading, trod, trodden**)
walk or put your foot on something.
tread *noun* (*plural* **treads**)
1 a sound or way of walking. 2 the top surface of a stair; the part you put your foot on. 3 the part of a tyre that touches the ground.

treadmill *noun* (*plural* **treadmills**)
1 a wide mill-wheel turned by the weight of people or animals treading on steps fixed round its edge. 2 monotonous routine work.

treason *noun*
betraying your country.
treasonable *adjective*, **treasonous** *adjective*
[from old French; related to *tradition*]

treasure *noun* (*plural* **treasures**)
1 a store of precious metals or jewels. 2 a precious thing or person.
treasure *verb* (**treasures, treasuring, treasured**)
value greatly something that you have.

treasurer *noun* (*plural* **treasurers**)
a person in charge of the money of a club, society, etc.

treasury *noun* (*plural* **treasuries**)
a place where money and valuables are kept.
the Treasury the government department in charge of a country's income.

treat *verb* (**treats, treating, treated**)
1 behave in a certain way towards a person or thing. 2 deal with a subject etc. 3 give medical care in order to cure a person or animal. 4 put something through a chemical or other process, *The fabric has been treated to make it waterproof*. 5 pay for someone else's food, drink, or entertainment, *I'll treat you to an ice cream*.
treat *noun* (*plural* **treats**)
1 something special that gives pleasure. 2 the process of treating someone to food, drink, or entertainment.
[from Latin *tractare* = to handle or manage]

treatment *noun* (*plural* **treatments**)
the process or manner of dealing with a person, animal, or thing.

treaty *noun* (*plural* **treaties**)
a formal agreement between two or more countries. [from French; related to *treat*]

treble *adjective*
three times as much or as many.
treble *noun* (*plural* **trebles**)
1 a treble amount. 2 a person with a high-pitched or soprano voice.
treble *verb* (**trebles, trebling, trebled**)
make or become three times as much or as many. [from old French; related to *triple*]

tree *noun* (*plural* **trees**)
a tall plant with a single very thick hard stem or trunk that is usually without branches for some distance above the ground. [from Old English]

trek *noun* (*plural* **treks**)
a long walk or journey.
trek *verb* (**treks, trekking, trekked**)
go on a long walk or journey.
[from Dutch *trekken* = pull]

trellis *noun* (*plural* **trellises**)
a framework with crossing bars of wood or metal etc. to support climbing plants.

tremble *verb* (**trembles, trembling, trembled**)
shake gently, especially with fear. **tremble** *noun*
[from French; related to *tremulous*]

tremendous *adjective*
1 very large; huge. 2 excellent.
tremendously *adverb* [from Latin *tremendus* = making someone tremble]

trench *noun* (*plural* **trenches**)
a long narrow hole cut in the ground.
trench *verb* (**trenches, trenching, trenched**)
dig a trench or trenches.

trend *noun* (*plural* **trends**)
the general direction in which something is
going. [from Old English]

trendy *adjective* (*informal*)
fashionable; following the latest trends.
trendily *adverb*, **trendiness** *noun*

trespass *verb* (**trespasses, trespassing, trespassed**)
1 go on someone's land or property unlawfully.
2 (*old use*) do wrong; sin. **trespasser** *noun*
trespass *noun* (*plural* **trespasses**) (*old use*)
wrongdoing; sin.
[from old French *trespasser* = go beyond]

tress *noun* (*plural* **tresses**)
a lock of hair. [from French]

trestle *noun* (*plural* **trestles**)
each of a set of supports on which a board is
rested to form a table. **trestle-table** *noun*
[from old French, = small beam]

tri- *prefix*
three (as in *triangle*). [from Latin or Greek]

trial *noun* (*plural* **trials**)
1 the trying of a person in a lawcourt. 2 testing
a thing to see how good it is. 3 a test of qualities
or ability. 4 an annoying person or thing; a
hardship.
on trial 1 being tried in a lawcourt. 2 being
tested.
trial and error trying out different methods of
doing something until you find one that works.
[from old French; related to *try*]

triangle *noun* (*plural* **triangles**)
1 a flat shape with three sides and three angles.
2 a percussion instrument made from a metal
rod bent into a triangle. **triangular** *adjective*
[from *tri-* + Latin *angulus* = angle]

tribe *noun* (*plural* **tribes**)
1 a group of families living in one area as a
community, ruled by a chief. 2 a set of people.
tribal *adjective*, **tribally** *adverb*, **tribesman** *noun*
[from Latin]

tribunal (*say* try-bew-nal) *noun* (*plural* **tribunals**)
a committee appointed to hear evidence and
give judgements when there is a dispute.
[from Latin *tribunale* = tribune's seat]

tributary *noun* (*plural* **tributaries**)
a river or stream that flows into a larger one or
into a lake. [same origin as *tribute*]

tribute *noun* (*plural* **tributes**)
1 something said, done, or given to show
respect or admiration. 2 payment that one
country or ruler was formerly obliged to pay to
a more powerful one.
[from Latin *tribuere* = assign, grant, share]

trice *noun* (*old use*)
in a trice in a moment.
[from old Dutch *trisen* = pull quickly, tug]

trick *noun* (*plural* **tricks**)
1 a crafty or deceitful action; a practical joke,
Let's play a trick on Jo. 2 a skilful action,
especially one done for entertainment, *magic
tricks.* 3 the cards picked up by the winner
after one round of a card game such as whist.
trick *verb* (**tricks, tricking, tricked**)
1 deceive or cheat someone by a trick.
2 decorate, *The building was tricked out with
little flags.* [from old French]

trickery *noun*
the use of tricks; deception.

trickle *verb* (**trickles, trickling, trickled**)
flow or move slowly. **trickle** *noun*
[imitating the sound]

tricky *adjective* (**trickier, trickiest**)
1 difficult; needing skill, *a tricky job.* 2 cunning
or deceitful. **trickiness** *noun*

tricycle *noun* (*plural* **tricycles**)
a vehicle like a bicycle but with three wheels.

trifle *noun* (*plural* **trifles**)
1 a pudding made of sponge cake covered in
custard, fruit, cream, etc. 2 a very small
amount. 3 something that has very little
importance or value.
trifle *verb* (**trifles, trifling, trifled**)
treat a person or thing without seriousness or
respect, *She is not a woman to be trifled with.*
[from old French]

trifling *adjective*
small in value or importance.

trigger *noun* (*plural* **triggers**)
a lever that is pulled to fire a gun.
trigger *verb* (**triggers, triggering, triggered**)
trigger off start something happening.
[from Dutch *trekker* = puller]

trigonometry (*say* trig-on-**om**-it-ree) *noun*
the calculation of distances and angles by
using triangles. [from Greek *trigonon*
= triangle + *metria* = measurement]

trill *verb* (**trills, trilling, trilled**)
make a quivering musical sound. **trill** *noun*
[from Italian]

trim *adjective*
neat and orderly.
trimly *adverb*, **trimness** *noun*
trim *verb* (**trims, trimming, trimmed**)
1 cut the edges or unwanted parts off
something. 2 decorate a hat or piece of clothing
by adding lace, ribbons, etc. 3 arrange sails to
suit the wind.
trim *noun* (*plural* **trims**)
1 condition, *in good trim.* 2 cutting or
trimming, *Your beard needs a trim.* 3 lace,
ribbons, etc. used to decorate something.

Trinity *noun*
God regarded as three persons (Father, Son, and Holy Spirit). [from Latin]

trinket *noun* (*plural* **trinkets**)
a small ornament or piece of jewellery.

trio *noun* (*plural* **trios**)
1 a group of three people or things.
2 a group of three musicians or singers.
3 a piece of music for three musicians.
[Italian, from Latin *tres* = three]

trip *verb* (**trips, tripping, tripped**)
1 catch your foot on something and fall; make someone do this. 2 move with quick light steps. 3 operate a switch.
trip up 1 stumble. 2 make a slip or blunder. 3 cause a person to do either of these.

trip *noun* (*plural* **trips**)
1 a journey or outing. 2 the action of tripping; a stumble. 3 (*informal*) hallucinations caused by taking a drug.

tripe *noun*
1 part of an ox's stomach used as food. 2 (*slang*) nonsense. [French]

triple *adjective*
1 consisting of three parts. 2 involving three people or groups, *a triple alliance*. 3 three times as much or as many.
triply *adverb*
triple *verb* (**triples, tripling, tripled**)
treble.
[from Latin *triplus* = three times as much]

triplet *noun* (*plural* **triplets**)
each of three children or animals born to the same mother at one time. [from *triple*]

triplicate *noun*
in **triplicate** as three identical copies.
[from *tri-* + Latin *plicare* = to fold]

tripod (*say* **try**-pod) *noun* (*plural* **tripods**)
a stand with three legs, e.g. to support a camera.
[from *tri-* + Greek *podes* = feet]

trite (rhymes with *kite*) *adjective*
worn out by constant repetition; hackneyed, *a few trite remarks*.
[from Latin *tritum* = worn by use]

triumph *noun* (*plural* **triumphs**)
1 a great success or victory; a feeling of joy at this. 2 a celebration of a victory.
triumphal *adjective*, **triumphant** *adjective*, **triumphantly** *adverb*
triumph *verb* (**triumphs, triumphing, triumphed**)
1 be successful or victorious. 2 rejoice in success or victory. [from Latin]

trivia *plural noun*
unimportant details or pieces of information.
[same origin as *trivial*]

trivial *adjective*
small in value or importance.
trivially *adverb*, **triviality** *noun*
[from Latin *trivialis* = commonplace]

troll (rhymes with *hole*) *noun* (*plural* **trolls**)
(in Scandinavian mythology) a supernatural being, either a giant or a friendly but mischievous dwarf.

trolley *noun* (*plural* **trolleys**)
1 a small table on wheels or castors. 2 a small cart or truck.
[probably from dialect *troll* = to roll or flow]

trombone *noun* (*plural* **trombones**)
a large brass musical instrument with a sliding tube.
[from Italian *tromba* = trumpet]

troop *noun* (*plural* **troops**)
1 an organized group of soldiers, Scouts, etc.
2 a number of people moving along together.

USAGE: Do not confuse with *troupe*.

troop *verb* (**troops, trooping, trooped**)
move along as a group or in large numbers, *They all trooped in*.
[from Latin *troppus* = herd]

trooper *noun* (*plural* **troopers**)
a soldier in the cavalry or in an armoured unit.
[from *troop*]

troops *plural noun*
armed forces.

trophy *noun* (*plural* **trophies**)
a prize or souvenir for a victory or other success. [from Greek]

tropic *noun* (*plural* **tropics**)
a line of latitude about $23\frac{1}{2}°$ north of the equator (**tropic of Cancer**) or $23\frac{1}{2}°$ south of the equator (**tropic of Capricorn**).
the tropics the hot regions between these two latitudes.
[from Greek *trope* = turning (because the sun seems to turn back when it reaches these points)]

tropical *adjective*
to do with the tropics, *tropical fish*.

trot *verb* (**trots, trotting, trotted**)
1 (of a horse) run, going faster than when walking but more slowly than when cantering.
2 (*informal*) go, *Trot round to the chemist*.
trot out (*informal*) produce or repeat, *He trotted out the usual excuses*.
trot *noun*
a trotting run.
on the trot (*informal*) one after the other without a break, *She worked for ten days on the trot*.

trouble *noun* (*plural* **troubles**)
1 difficulty, inconvenience, or distress.
2 a cause of any of these.
take trouble take great care in doing something.

trouble verb (troubles, troubling, troubled)
1 cause trouble to someone. 2 give yourself trouble or inconvenience etc., *Don't trouble to reply*. [from old French]
troublesome adjective
causing trouble or annoyance.

trough (say trof) noun (plural troughs)
1 a long narrow open container, especially one holding water or food for animals. 2 a channel for liquid. 3 the low part between two waves or ridges. 4 a long region of low air pressure. [from Old English]

troupe (say as troop) noun (plural troupes)
a company of actors or other performers. [French, = troop]

USAGE: Do not confuse with *troop*.

trousers plural noun
a piece of clothing worn over the lower half of the body, with a separate part for each leg. [from Irish or Scottish Gaelic]

trout noun (plural trout)
a freshwater fish that is caught as a sport and for food. [from Greek]

trowel noun (plural trowels)
1 a small garden tool with a curved blade for lifting plants or scooping things. 2 a small tool with a flat blade for spreading mortar etc. [from Latin *trulla* = scoop]

truant noun (plural truants)
a child who stays away from school without permission. **truancy** noun
play truant be a truant.
[old French, = criminal, probably of Celtic origin]

truce noun (plural truces)
an agreement to stop fighting for a while.

truck¹ noun (plural trucks)
1 a lorry. 2 an open container on wheels for transporting loads; an open railway wagon. 3 an axle with wheels attached, fitted under a skateboard.
[probably from *truckle* = a pulley or castor]

truck² noun
have no truck with refuse to have dealings with, *I'll have no truck with fortune-tellers!*
[origin unknown]

trudge verb (trudges, trudging, trudged)
walk slowly and heavily. [origin unknown]

true adjective (truer, truest)
1 representing what has really happened or exists, *a true story*. 2 genuine or proper; not false, *He was the true heir*. 3 accurate. 4 loyal or faithful, *Be true to your friends*. **trueness** noun
[from Old English]

truffle noun (plural truffles)
1 a soft sweet made with chocolate. 2 a fungus that grows underground and is valued as food because of its rich flavour. [probably from Dutch]

truly adverb
1 truthfully. 2 sincerely or genuinely, *We are truly grateful*. 3 accurately. 4 loyally or faithfully.
Yours truly see *yours*.

trump noun (plural trumps)
a playing card of a suit that ranks above the others for one game.
trump verb (trumps, trumping, trumped)
beat a card by playing a trump.
trump up invent an excuse or an accusation etc.
[from *triumph*]

trumpet noun (plural trumpets)
1 a metal wind instrument with a narrow tube that widens near the end. 2 something shaped like this.
trumpet verb (trumpets, trumpeting, trumpeted)
1 blow a trumpet. 2 (of an elephant) make a loud sound with its trunk. 3 shout or announce something loudly. **trumpeter** noun

truncheon noun (plural truncheons)
a short thick stick carried as a weapon, especially by police.
[from old French; related to *trunk*]

trundle verb (trundles, trundling, trundled)
roll along heavily, *He was trundling a wheelbarrow. A bus trundled up.*
[related to Old English *trendel* = ball]

trunk noun (plural trunks)
1 the main stem of a tree. 2 an elephant's long flexible nose. 3 a large box with a hinged lid for transporting or storing clothes etc. 4 the human body except for the head, arms, and legs. [from Latin]

trunk road noun (plural trunk roads)
an important main road.
[regarded as a 'trunk' from which smaller roads branch off]

trunks plural noun
shorts worn by men and boys for swimming, boxing, etc.

truss noun (plural trusses)
1 a framework of beams or bars supporting a roof or bridge etc. 2 a bundle of hay etc. 3 a type of padded belt worn to support a hernia.
truss verb (trusses, trussing, trussed)
1 tie up a person or thing securely. 2 support a roof or bridge etc. with trusses.

trust verb (trusts, trusting, trusted)
1 believe that a person or thing is good, truthful, or strong. 2 let a person have or use something in the belief that he or she will

behave responsibly, *Don't trust him with your CD player!* **3** hope, *I trust that you are well.* **trust to** rely on, *trusting to luck.*

trust *noun* (*plural* **trusts**)
1 the belief that a person or thing can be trusted. **2** responsibility; being trusted, *Being a prefect is a position of trust.* **3** money legally entrusted to a person with instructions about how to use it.
trustful *adjective*, **trustfully** *adverb*, **trustworthy** *adjective*

trusty *adjective* (*old use*)
trustworthy or reliable, *my trusty sword.*

truth *noun* (*plural* **truths**)
1 something that is true. **2** the quality of being true.

truthful *adjective*
1 telling the truth, *a truthful boy.* **2** true, *a truthful account of what happened.*
truthfully *adverb*, **truthfulness** *noun*

try *verb* (**tries, trying, tried**)
1 attempt. **2** test something by using or doing it, *Try sleeping on your back.* **3** examine the accusations against someone in a lawcourt. **4** be a strain on, *Very small print tries your eyes.*
try on put on clothes etc. to see if they fit.

try *noun* (*plural* **tries**)
1 an attempt. **2** (in Rugby football) putting the ball down behind the opponents' goal line in order to score points.

trying *adjective*
putting a strain on someone's patience; annoying.

tub *noun* (*plural* **tubs**)
a round open container holding liquid, ice cream, soil for plants, etc.

tubby *adjective* (**tubbier, tubbiest**)
short and fat. **tubbiness** *noun* [from *tub*]

tube *noun* (*plural* **tubes**)
1 a long hollow piece of metal, plastic, rubber, glass, etc., especially for liquids or air etc. to pass along. **2** a container made of flexible material with a screw cap, *a tube of toothpaste.* **3** the underground railway in London.
[from Latin]

tuber *noun* (*plural* **tubers**)
a short thick rounded root (e.g. of a dahlia) or underground stem (e.g. of a potato) that produces buds from which new plants will grow. [Latin, = a swelling]

tuberculosis *noun*
a disease of people and animals, producing small swellings in the parts affected by it, especially in the lungs. **tubercular** *adjective* [from Latin *tuberculum* = little swelling]

tuck *verb* (**tucks, tucking, tucked**)
1 push a loose edge into something so that it is hidden or held in place. **2** put something away in a small space, *Tuck this in your pocket.*
tuck in (*informal*) eat heartily.

tuck *noun* (*plural* **tucks**)
1 a flat fold stitched in a garment. **2** (*slang*) food, especially sweets and cakes etc. that children enjoy. **tuck shop** *noun*

-tude *suffix*
forms nouns meaning 'quality or condition' (e.g. *altitude, solitude*).
[from French]

tuft *noun* (*plural* **tufts**)
a bunch of threads, grass, hair, or feathers etc. growing close together. **tufted** *adjective*

tug *verb* (**tugs, tugging, tugged**)
1 pull something hard or suddenly. **2** tow a ship.

tug *noun* (*plural* **tugs**)
1 a hard or sudden pull. **2** a small powerful boat used for towing others.
[Middle English; related to *tow*]

tug of war *noun*
a contest between two teams pulling a rope from opposite ends.

tulip *noun* (*plural* **tulips**)
a large cup-shaped flower on a tall stem growing from a bulb.
[from Persian *dulband* = turban (because the flowers are this shape)]

tumble *verb* (**tumbles, tumbling, tumbled**)
1 fall or roll over suddenly or clumsily. **2** move or push quickly and carelessly. **tumble** *noun*
tumble to (*informal*) realize what something means.

tumbler *noun* (*plural* **tumblers**)
1 a drinking glass with no stem or handle. **2** a part of a lock that is lifted when a key is turned to open it. **3** an acrobat.

tummy *noun* (*plural* **tummies**) (*informal*)
the stomach. [imitating a small child trying to say 'stomach']

tumour (*say* tew-mer) *noun* (*plural* **tumours**)
an abnormal lump growing on or in the body.
[from Latin *tumere* = to swell]

tumult (*say* tew-mult) *noun*
an uproar; a state of noisy confusion and agitation. [from Latin]

tune *noun* (*plural* **tunes**)
a short piece of music; a pleasant series of musical notes.
tuneful *adjective*, **tunefully** *adverb*
in tune at the correct musical pitch.

tune *verb* (**tunes, tuning, tuned**)
1 put a musical instrument in tune. **2** adjust a radio or television set to receive a certain channel. **3** adjust an engine so that it runs smoothly. **tuner** *noun*
[a different spelling of *tone*]

tunic *noun* (*plural* **tunics**)
1 a jacket worn as part of a uniform. 2 a garment reaching from the shoulders to the hips or knees. [from Latin]

tunnel *noun* (*plural* **tunnels**)
an underground passage.
tunnel *verb* (**tunnels, tunnelling, tunnelled**)
make a tunnel.
[from old French *tonel* = barrel]

turban *noun* (*plural* **turbans**)
a covering for the head made by wrapping a strip of cloth round a cap. [from Persian]

turbine *noun* (*plural* **turbines**)
a machine or motor driven by a flow of water, steam, or gas. [from Latin *turbo* = whirlwind, spinning top]

turbulent *adjective*
1 moving violently and unevenly, *turbulent seas*. 2 unruly.
turbulently *adverb*, **turbulence** *noun*
[same origin as *turbid*]

turf *noun* (*plural* **turfs** or **turves**)
1 short grass and the earth round its roots. 2 a piece of this cut from the ground.
the turf horse racing.

turkey *noun* (*plural* **turkeys**)
a large bird kept for its meat.
[originally the name of a different bird which was imported from Turkey]

turmoil *noun*
wild confusion or agitation, *Her mind was in turmoil*. [origin unknown]

turn *verb* (**turns, turning, turned**)
1 move round; move to a new direction. 2 change in appearance etc.; become, *He turned pale*. 3 make something change, *You can turn milk into butter*. 4 move a switch or tap etc. to control something, *Turn that radio off*. 5 pass a certain time, *It has turned midnight*. 6 shape something on a lathe.
turn down 1 fold down. 2 reduce the flow or sound of something. 3 reject, *We offered her a job but she turned it down*.
turn out 1 send out. 2 empty something, especially to search or clean it. 3 happen. 4 prove to be, *The visitor turned out to be my uncle*.
turn up 1 appear or arrive. 2 increase the flow or sound of something.
turn *noun* (*plural* **turns**)
1 the action of turning; a turning movement. 2 a change; the point where something turns. 3 an opportunity or duty etc. that comes to each person in succession, *It's your turn to wash up*. 4 a short performance in an entertainment. 5 (*informal*) an attack of illness; a nervous shock, *It gave me a nasty turn*.

good turn a helpful action.
in turn in succession; one after another.
[from Greek *tornos* = lathe]

turning *noun* (*plural* **turnings**)
a place where one road meets another, forming a corner.

turnip *noun* (*plural* **turnips**)
a plant with a large round white root used as a vegetable. [from Latin]

turnout *noun* (*plural* **turnouts**)
the number of people who attend a meeting, vote at an election, etc., *Despite the rain, there was a pretty good turnout*.

turnover *noun* (*plural* **turnovers**)
1 the amount of money received by a firm selling things. 2 the rate at which goods are sold or workers leave and are replaced. 3 a small pie made by folding pastry over fruit, jam, etc.

turnstile *noun* (*plural* **turnstiles**)
a revolving gate that lets one person in at a time.

turntable *noun* (*plural* **turntables**)
a circular revolving platform or support, e.g. for the record in a record player.

turquoise *noun* (*plural* **turquoises**)
1 a sky-blue or greenish-blue colour. 2 a blue jewel. [from French *pierre turquoise* = Turkish stone]

turret *noun* (*plural* **turrets**)
1 a small tower on a castle or other building. 2 a revolving structure containing a gun.
turreted *adjective*
[from old French *tourete* = small tower]

turtle *noun* (*plural* **turtles**)
a sea animal that looks like a tortoise.
turn turtle capsize.
[probably from French *tortue* = tortoise]

turtle-dove *noun* (*plural* **turtle-doves**)
a wild dove. [from Old English]

tusk *noun* (*plural* **tusks**)
a long pointed tooth that sticks out from the mouth of an elephant, walrus, etc.

tussle *noun* (*plural* **tussles**)
a struggle or conflict over something.

tussock *noun* (*plural* **tussocks**)
a tuft or clump of grass. [origin unknown]

tutor *noun* (*plural* **tutors**)
1 a teacher who teaches one person or small group, not in a school. 2 a teacher of students in a college or university.
[Latin, = guardian]

TV *abbreviation*
television.

twain *noun* & *adjective* (*old use*)
two. [from Old English *twegen* = two]

twang *verb* (twangs, twanging, twanged)
1 play a guitar etc. by plucking its strings.
2 make a sharp sound like that of a wire when
plucked. **twang** *noun*

tweak *verb* (tweaks, tweaking, tweaked)
pinch and twist or pull something sharply.
tweak *noun*

tweed *noun*
thick woollen twill, often woven of mixed
colours.
[originally a mistake; the Scottish word *tweel*
(= twill) was wrongly read as *tweed* by being
confused with the River Tweed]

tweezers *plural noun*
small pincers for picking up or pulling very
small things. [from French *étui* = prison, in
English = a case of surgical instruments,
including tweezers]

twelve *noun* & *adjective*
the number 12. **twelfth** *adjective* & *noun*

twenty *noun* (*plural* twenties) & *adjective*
the number 20. **twentieth** *adjective* & *noun*

twice *adverb*
1 two times; on two occasions. 2 double the
amount. [from Old English]

twiddle *verb* (twiddles, twiddling, twiddled)
twirl or finger something in an idle way; twist
something quickly to and fro.
twiddle *noun*, **twiddly** *adjective*
[origin unknown]

twig *noun* (*plural* twigs)
a small shoot on a branch or stem of a tree or
shrub. [from Old English]

twilight *noun*
dim light from the sky just after sunset or just
before sunrise.
[from Old English *twi-* = twice, double, + *light*]

twin *noun* (*plural* twins)
1 either of two children or animals born to the
same mother at one time. 2 either of two things
that are exactly alike.
twin *verb* (twins, twinning, twinned)
1 put things together as a pair. 2 if a town is
twinned with a town in a different country, the
two towns exchange visits and organize
cultural events together.

twine *verb* (twines, twining, twined)
twist or wind together or round something.

twinge *noun* (*plural* twinges)
a sudden pain; a pang. [from Old English]

twinkle *verb* (twinkles, twinkling, twinkled)
shine with tiny flashes of light; sparkle.
twinkle *noun*
[from Old English]

twirl *verb* (twirls, twirling, twirled)
twist quickly. **twirl** *noun*
[origin unknown]

twist *verb* (twists, twisting, twisted)
1 pass threads or strands round something or
round each other. 2 turn the ends of something
in opposite directions. 3 turn round or from
side to side, *The road twisted through the hills.*
4 bend something out of its proper shape.
5 (*informal*) swindle somebody. **twister** *noun*
twist *noun* (*plural* twists)
a twisting movement or action. **twisty** *adjective*
[from Old English]

twitch *verb* (twitches, twitching, twitched)
move or pull with a slight jerk. **twitch** *noun*

twitter *verb* (twitters, twittering, twittered)
make quick chirping sounds. **twitter** *noun*

two *noun* (*plural* twos) & *adjective*
the number 2.
be in two minds be undecided about something.

two-faced *adjective*
insincere or deceitful.

tycoon *noun* (*plural* tycoons)
a rich and influential business person.
[from Japanese *taikun* = great prince]

tying *present participle* of **tie**.

type *noun* (*plural* types)
1 a kind or sort. 2 letters or figures etc.
designed for use in printing.
type *verb* (types, typing, typed)
write something by using a typewriter.
typist *noun* [from Greek *typos* = impression]

typewriter *noun* (*plural* typewriters)
a machine with keys that are pressed to print
letters or figures etc. on a piece of paper.
typewritten *adjective*
[the word *typewriter* at first meant the person
using the machine, as well as the machine
itself]

typhoon *noun* (*plural* typhoons)
a violent hurricane in the western Pacific or
East Asian seas.
[from Chinese *tai fung* = great wind]

typical *adjective*
1 having the usual characteristics or qualities
of a particular type of person or thing, *a typical
school playground.* 2 usual in a particular
person or thing, *He worked with typical
carefulness.* **typically** *adverb*
[same origin as *type*]

tyranny (*say* tirran-ee) *noun* (*plural* tyrannies)
1 government by a tyrant. 2 the way a tyrant
behaves towards people.
tyrannical *adjective*, **tyrannous** *adjective*

tyrant (*say* ty-rant) *noun* (*plural* tyrants)
a person who rules cruelly and unjustly;
someone who insists on being obeyed.
[from Greek *tyrannos* = ruler with full power]

tyre *noun* (*plural* tyres)
a covering of rubber fitted round a wheel to
make it grip the road and run more smoothly.
[from *attire*]

Uu

ubiquitous (*say* yoo-**bik**-wit-us) *adjective*
found everywhere, *The ubiquitous television
aerials spoil the view.* **ubiquity** *noun* [from Latin
ubique = everywhere]

-uble *prefix* see **-able**.

udder *noun* (*plural* **udders**)
the bag-like part of a cow, ewe, female goat, etc.
from which milk is taken.

ugly *adjective* (**uglier, ugliest**)
1 unpleasant to look at; not beautiful. **2** hostile
and threatening, *The crowd was in an ugly
mood.* **ugliness** *noun*
[from Old Norse *uggligr* = frightening]

UK *abbreviation*
United Kingdom.

ulcer *noun* (*plural* **ulcers**)
a sore on the inside or outside of the body.
ulcerated *adjective*, **ulceration** *noun*

ulterior *adjective*
beyond what is obvious or stated, *an ulterior
motive.* [Latin, = further]

ultimate *adjective*
furthest in a series of things; final, *Our
ultimate destination is London.*
ultimately *adverb* [from Latin *ultimus* = last]

ultimatum (*say* ul-tim-**ay**-tum) *noun* (*plural*
ultimatums)
a final demand or statement that unless
something is done by a certain time action will
be taken or war will be declared.
[same origin as *ultimate*]

ultra- *prefix*
1 beyond (as in *ultraviolet*). **2** extremely;
excessively (as in *ultramodern*).
[from Latin *ultra* = beyond]

ultramarine *noun*
deep bright blue. [from *ultra-* + Latin *mare*
= sea (because it was originally imported
'across the sea' from the East)]

ultraviolet *adjective*
(of light-rays) beyond the violet end of the
spectrum and so not visible to the human eye.

umbilical cord *noun* (*plural* **umbilical cords**)
the tube through which a baby receives
nourishment before it is born, connecting its
body with the mother's womb.

umbrella *noun* (*plural* **umbrellas**)
1 a circular piece of material stretched over a
folding frame with a central stick used as a
handle, or a central pole, which you open to
protect yourself from rain or sun. **2** a general
protection.
[from Italian *ombrella* = a little shade]

umpire *noun* (*plural* **umpires**)
a referee in cricket, tennis, and some other
games.
umpire *verb* (**umpires, umpiring, umpired**)
act as an umpire.
[from French *non* = not + *per* = an equal, peer[2]]

UN *abbreviation*
United Nations.

un- *prefix*
1 not (as in *uncertain*). **2** (before a verb)
reversing the action (as in *unlock* = release
from being locked). [from Old English]

NOTE: Many words beginning with this
prefix are not listed here if their meaning is
obvious.

unable *adjective*
not able to do something.

unaccountable *adjective*
1 unable to be explained, *For some
unaccountable reason I completely forgot your
birthday.* **2** not accountable for what you do.
unaccountably *adverb*

unanimous (*say* yoo-**nan**-im-us) *adjective*
with everyone agreeing, *a unanimous decision.*
unanimously *adverb*,
unanimity (*say* yoo-nan-**im**-it-ee) *noun*
[from Latin *unus* = one + *animus* = mind]

unassuming *adjective*
modest; not arrogant or pretentious.
[from *un-* + *assume*]

unavoidable *adjective*
not able to be avoided.

unawares *adverb*
unexpectedly; without warning, *His question
caught me unawares.*

unbearable *adjective*
not able to be endured. **unbearably** *adverb*

unbecoming *adjective*
1 not making a person look attractive. **2** not
suitable or fitting.
[from *un-* + *become* (sense 2)]

unbelievable *adjective*
not able to be believed; incredible.
unbelievably *adverb*

unbend *verb* (**unbends, unbending, unbent**)
1 change from a bent position; straighten up.
2 relax and become friendly.

unblock *verb* (**unblocks, unblocking, unblocked**)
remove an obstruction from something.

unborn *adjective*
not yet born.

unbroken *adjective*
not broken or interrupted.

uncalled for *adjective*
not justified; impertinent.

uncanny *adjective* (uncannier, uncanniest)
strange or mysterious, *an uncanny coincidence.*
uncannily *adverb*, **uncanniness** *noun*
[from *un-* + an old sense of *canny* = knowing,
able to be known]

uncertain *adjective*
1 not certain. 2 not reliable, *His aim is rather
uncertain.* **uncertainly** *adverb*, **uncertainty** *noun*
in no uncertain terms clearly and forcefully.

uncharitable *adjective*
making unkind judgements of people or
actions. **uncharitably** *adverb*

uncle *noun* (*plural* uncles)
the brother of your father or mother; your
aunt's husband.
[from Latin *avunculus* = uncle]

uncomfortable *adjective*
not comfortable. **uncomfortably** *adverb*

uncommon *adjective*
not common; unusual.

uncompromising (*say* un-komp-rom-I-zing)
adjective
not allowing a compromise; inflexible.

unconcerned *adjective*
not caring about something; not worried.

unconditional *adjective*
without any conditions; absolute,
unconditional surrender.
unconditionally *adverb*

unconscious *adjective*
not conscious; not aware of things.
unconsciously *adverb*, **unconsciousness** *noun*

uncouth (*say* un-kooth) *adjective*
rude and rough in manner; boorish.
[from *un-* + Old English *cuth* = known]

uncover *verb* (uncovers, uncovering, uncovered)
1 remove the covering from something.
2 reveal or expose, *They uncovered a plot to kill
the king.*

undecided *adjective*
1 not yet settled; not certain. 2 not having
made up your mind yet.

undeniable *adjective*
impossible to deny; undoubtedly true.
undeniably *adverb*

under *preposition*
1 below or beneath, *Hide it under the desk.*
2 less than, *under 5 years old.* 3 governed or
controlled by, *The country prospered under his
rule.* 4 in the process of; undergoing, *The road
is under repair.* 5 using, *He writes under the
name of 'Lewis Carroll'.* 6 according to the
rules of, *This is permitted under our agreement.*
under way in motion or in progress.
under *adverb*
in or to a lower place or level or condition,
Slowly the diver went under.

under *adjective*
lower, *the under layers.* [from Old English]

under- *prefix*
1 below or beneath (as in *underwear*). 2 lower;
subordinate (as in *under-manager*). 3 not
enough; incompletely (as in *undercooked*).

undercarriage *noun* (*plural* undercarriages)
an aircraft's landing wheels and their
supports.

undercover *adjective*
done or doing things secretly, *an undercover
agent.*

undercurrent *noun* (*plural* undercurrents)
1 a current that is below the surface or below
another current. 2 an underlying feeling or
influence, *an undercurrent of fear.*

undercut *verb* (undercuts, undercutting,
undercut)
sell something for a lower price than someone
else sells it.

underdone *adjective*
not thoroughly done; undercooked.

underestimate *verb* (underestimates,
underestimating, underestimated)
make too low an estimate of a person or thing.

undergo *verb* (undergoes, undergoing,
underwent, undergone)
experience or endure something; be subjected
to, *The new aircraft underwent intensive tests.*

undergraduate *noun* (*plural* undergraduates)
a student at a university who has not yet taken
a degree.

underground *adjective* & *adverb*
1 under the ground. 2 done or working in
secret.
underground *noun*
a railway that runs through tunnels under the
ground.

undergrowth *noun*
bushes and other plants growing closely,
especially under trees.

underhand *adjective*
done or doing things in a sly or secret way.

underline *verb* (underlines, underlining,
underlined)
1 draw a line under a word etc. 2 emphasize
something.

underlying *adjective*
1 forming the basis or explanation of
something, *the underlying causes of the trouble.*
2 lying under something, *the underlying rocks.*

undermine *verb* (undermines, undermining,
undermined)
weaken something gradually.

underneath *preposition* & *adverb*
below or beneath.
[from *under-* + Old English *neothan* = beneath]

underpants *plural noun*
a piece of men's underwear covering the lower part of the body, worn under trousers.

underprivileged *adjective*
having less than the normal standard of living or rights in a community.

understand *verb* (**understands, understanding, understood**)
1 know what something means or how it works or why it exists. 2 know and tolerate a person's ways. 3 have been told, *I understand that you would like to speak to me.* 4 take something for granted, *Your expenses will be paid, that's understood.* **understandable** *adjective*, **understandably** *adverb*
[from Old English]

understanding *noun*
1 the power to understand or think; intelligence. 2 sympathy or tolerance.
3 agreement in opinion or feeling, *a better understanding between nations.*

understatement *noun* (*plural* **understatements**)
an incomplete or very restrained statement of facts or truth, *To say they disagreed is an understatement; they had a violent quarrel.*

understudy *noun* (*plural* **understudies**)
an actor who learns a part in order to be able to play it if the usual performer is ill or absent.

undertake *verb* (**undertakes, undertaking, undertook, undertaken**)
agree or promise to do something.

undertaker *noun* (*plural* **undertakers**)
a person whose job is to arrange funerals and burials or cremations.

undertone *noun* (*plural* **undertones**)
1 a low or quiet tone, *They spoke in undertones.*
2 an underlying quality or feeling etc., *His letter has a threatening undertone.*

underwear *noun*
clothes worn next to the skin, under indoor clothing.

underweight *adjective*
not heavy enough.

underwent *past tense* of **undergo**.

underworld *noun*
1 the people who are regularly involved in crime. 2 (in myths and legends) the place for the spirits of the dead, under the earth.

undeveloped *adjective*
not yet developed.

undo *verb* (**undoes, undoing, undid, undone**)
1 unfasten or unwrap. 2 cancel the effect of something, *He has undone all our careful work.*

undoing *noun*
be someone's **undoing** be the cause of their ruin or failure.

undress *verb* (**undresses, undressing, undressed**)
take your clothes off.

undue *adjective*
excessive; too great. **unduly** *adverb*

undulate *verb* (**undulates, undulating, undulated**)
move like a wave or waves; have a wavy appearance. **undulation** *noun*
[from Latin *unda* = a wave]

undying *adjective*
everlasting.

unearth *verb* (**unearths, unearthing, unearthed**)
1 dig something up; uncover something by digging. 2 find something by searching.

unearthly *adjective*
1 unnatural; strange and frightening.
2 (*informal*) very early or inconvenient, *We had to get up at an unearthly hour.*

uneasy *adjective*
1 worried or anxious. 2 uncomfortable.
uneasily *adverb*, **uneasiness** *noun*

unemployed *adjective*
without a job. **unemployment** *noun*

unerring (*say* un-er-ing) *adjective*
making no mistake, *unerring accuracy.*
[from *un-* + *err*]

uneven *adjective*
1 not level or regular. 2 unequal.
unevenly *adverb*, **unevenness** *noun*

unfair *adjective*
not fair; unjust.
unfairly *adverb*, **unfairness** *noun*

unfaithful *adjective*
not faithful; disloyal.

unfamiliar *adjective*
not familiar. **unfamiliarity** *noun*

unfasten *verb* (**unfastens, unfastening, unfastened**)
open the fastenings of something.

unfavourable *adjective*
not favourable. **unfavourably** *adverb*

unfeeling *adjective*
not caring about other people's feelings; unsympathetic.

unfit *adjective*
1 unsuitable. 2 not in perfect health because you do not take enough exercise.

unfit *verb* (**unfits, unfitting, unfitted**)
make a person or thing unsuitable.

unfold *verb* (**unfolds, unfolding, unfolded**)
1 open; spread out. 2 make or become known slowly, *as the story unfolds.*

unfortunate *adjective*
1 unlucky. 2 unsuitable or regrettable, *an unfortunate remark.* **unfortunately** *adverb*

unfounded *adjective*
not based on facts. [from *un-* + *found*^{2}]

unfriendly *adjective*
not friendly. **unfriendliness** *noun*

unfurl *verb* (**unfurls, unfurling, unfurled**)
unroll; spread out, *They unfurled a large flag.*

ungainly *adjective*
awkward-looking or clumsy; ungraceful.
ungainliness *noun*
[from *un-* + Middle English *gainly* = graceful]

ungodly *adjective*
1 not giving reverence to God; not religious.
2 (*informal*) outrageous; very inconvenient,
She woke me at an ungodly hour.
ungodliness *noun*

ungovernable *adjective*
uncontrollable.

unguarded *adjective*
1 not guarded. 2 without thought or caution;
indiscreet, *He said this in an unguarded
moment.*

unhappy *adjective*
1 not happy; sad. 2 unfortunate or unsuitable,
an unhappy coincidence. **unhappily** *adverb*,
unhappiness *noun*

unhealthy *adjective*
not healthy. **unhealthiness** *noun*

unheard-of *adjective*
never known or done before; extraordinary.

unhinge *verb* (**unhinges, unhinging, unhinged**)
cause a person's mind to become unbalanced.

uni- *prefix*
one; single (as in *unicorn*).
[from Latin *unus* = one]

unicorn *noun* (*plural* **unicorns**)
(in legends) an animal that is like a horse with
one long straight horn growing from its
forehead.
[from *uni-* + Latin *cornu* = horn]

uniform *noun* (*plural* **uniforms**)
special clothes showing that the wearer
is a member of a certain organization, school,
etc.
uniform *adjective*
always the same; not varying, *The desks are of
uniform size.*
uniformly *adverb*, **uniformity** *noun*
[from *uni-* + Latin *forma* = form]

unilateral *adjective*
done by one person or group or country etc., *a
unilateral decision.*
[from *uni-* + *lateral*]

uninhabitable *adjective*
unfit to live in.

union *noun* (*plural* **unions**)
1 the joining of things together; uniting. 2 a
trade union. [from Latin *unio* = unity]

Union Jack *noun* (*plural* **Union Jacks**)
the British flag.

unique (*say* yoo-**neek**) *adjective*
being the only one of its kind, *This jewel is
unique.* **uniquely** *adverb*
[French, from Latin *unicus* = one and only]

USAGE: *Unique* does not mean 'unusual' or
'remarkable', so avoid saying things like *very
unique* or *most unique.*

unison *noun*
in unison 1 with all sounding or singing the
same tune etc. together, or speaking in chorus.
2 in agreement.
[from *uni-* + Latin *sonus* = sound]

unit *noun* (*plural* **units**)
1 an amount used as a standard in measuring
or counting things, *Centimetres are units of
length*; *pence are units of money.* 2 a group,
device, piece of furniture, etc. regarded as a
single thing but forming part of a larger group
or whole, *an army unit*;
a sink unit. [from Latin *unus* = one]

unite *verb* (**unites, uniting, united**)
join together; make or become one thing. [same
origin as *unit*]

United Kingdom *noun*
Great Britain and Northern Ireland.

USAGE: See note at *Britain.*

unity *noun*
1 being united; being in agreement.
2 something whole that is made up of parts.
3 (in mathematics) the number one.

universal *adjective*
to do with or including or done by everyone or
everything. **universally** *adverb*

universe *noun*
everything that exists, including the earth and
living things and all the heavenly bodies. [from
Latin *universus* = combined into one]

university *noun* (*plural* **universities**)
a place where people go to study at an
advanced level after leaving school.
[from Latin *universitas*, literally = the
universe, later = a community or group of
people (i.e. the teachers and students)]

unjust *adjective*
not fair or just.

unkempt *adjective*
looking untidy or neglected.
[from *un-* + an old word *kempt* = combed]

unkind *adjective*
not kind. **unkindly** *adverb*, **unkindness** *noun*

unleaded *adjective*
(of petrol) without added lead.

unleash *verb* (**unleashes, unleashing, unleashed**)
1 set a dog free from a leash. 2 let a strong
feeling or force be released.

unless *conjunction*
except when; if ... not, *We cannot go unless we are invited.*

unlike *preposition*
not like, *Unlike me, she enjoys cricket.*

unlike *adjective*
not alike; different, *The two children are very unlike.*

unlikely *adjective* (unlikelier, unlikeliest)
not likely to happen or be true.

unlimited *adjective*
not limited; very great or very many.

unload *verb* (unloads, unloading, unloaded)
remove the load of things carried by a ship, aircraft, vehicle, etc.

unlock *verb* (unlocks, unlocking, unlocked)
open something by undoing a lock.

unlucky *adjective*
not lucky; having or bringing bad luck.
unluckily *adverb*

unmask *verb* (unmasks, unmasking, unmasked)
1 remove a person's mask. 2 reveal what a person or thing really is.

unmentionable *adjective*
too bad or embarrassing to be spoken of.

unmistakable *adjective*
not able to be mistaken for another person or thing. **unmistakably** *adverb*

unmitigated *adjective*
absolute, *an unmitigated disaster.*
[from *un-* + *mitigate*]

unnatural *adjective*
not natural or normal. **unnaturally** *adverb*

unnecessary *adjective*
not necessary; more than is necessary.

unorthodox *adjective*
not generally accepted, *an unorthodox method.*

unpack *verb* (unpacks, unpacking, unpacked)
take things out of a suitcase, bag, box, etc.

unparliamentary *adjective*
impolite or abusive.

USAGE: It is a rule of debates in Parliament that speakers must be polite to each other. Impolite language is 'unparliamentary'.

unpick *verb* (unpicks, unpicking, unpicked)
undo the stitching of something.

unpleasant *adjective*
not pleasant.
unpleasantly *adverb*, **unpleasantness** *noun*

unpopular *adjective*
not popular.

unprecedented (*say* un-press-id-en-tid) *adjective*
that has never happened before.
[from *un-* + *precedent*]

unprepared *adjective*
not prepared beforehand; not ready or equipped.

unprintable *adjective*
too rude or indecent to be printed.

unprofessional *adjective*
not professional; not worthy of a member of a profession.

unqualified *adjective*
1 not officially qualified to do something. 2 not limited, *We gave it our unqualified approval.*

unravel *verb* (unravels, unravelling, unravelled)
1 disentangle. 2 undo something that is knitted. 3 investigate and solve a mystery etc.
[from *un-* + an old word *ravel* = tangle]

unready *adjective*
not ready; hesitating.

USAGE: In the title of the English king *Ethelred the Unready* the word means 'lacking good advice or wisdom'.

unreal *adjective*
not real; existing in the imagination only.
unreality *noun*

unreasonable *adjective*
1 not reasonable. 2 excessive or unjust.
unreasonably *adverb*

unrelieved *adjective*
without anything to vary it, *unrelieved gloom.*

unreserved *adjective*
1 not reserved. 2 without restriction; complete, *unreserved loyalty.*
unreservedly *adverb*

unrest *noun*
restlessness; trouble caused because people are dissatisfied.

unroll *verb* (unrolls, unrolling, unrolled)
open something that has been rolled up.

unruly *adjective*
difficult to control; disorderly.
unruliness *noun*
[from *un-* + *rule*]

unsavoury *adjective*
unpleasant or disgusting.

unscrew *verb* (unscrews, unscrewing, unscrewed)
undo something that has been screwed up.

unscrupulous *adjective*
having no scruples about wrongdoing.

unseemly *adjective*
not proper or suitable; indecent.

unseen *adjective*
not seen; invisible.

unseen *noun* (*plural* unseens)
a passage for translation without previous preparation.

unsettled *adjective*
1 not settled or calm. 2 (of weather) likely to change.

unshakeable *adjective*
not able to be shaken; firm.

unshaven *adjective*
(of a man) not recently shaved.

unsightly *adjective*
not pleasant to look at; ugly.
unsightliness *noun*

unskilled *adjective*
not having or not needing special skill or training.

unsolicited *adjective*
not asked for, *unsolicited advice.*
[from *un-* + *solicit*]

unsound *adjective*
not sound; damaged, unhealthy, unreasonable, or unreliable.
[from *un-*+ *sound*³]

unspeakable *adjective*
too bad to be described; very objectionable.

unstable *adjective*
not stable; likely to change or become unbalanced.

unstuck *adjective*
come unstuck 1 cease to stick. 2 (*informal*) fail or go wrong.

unthinkable *adjective*
too bad or too unlikely to be worth considering.

unthinking *adjective*
thoughtless.

untidy *adjective* (untidier, untidiest)
not tidy. **untidily** *adverb*, **untidiness** *noun*

untie *verb* (unties, untying, untied)
undo something that has been tied.

until *preposition* & *conjunction*
up to a particular time or event.

USAGE: See the note on *till*¹.

untold *adjective*
1 not told. 2 too much or too many to be counted, *untold wealth* or *wealth untold.*

untruth *noun* (*plural* untruths)
an untrue statement; a lie.
untruthful *adjective*, **untruthfully** *adverb*

unused *adjective*
1 (*say* un-yoozd) not yet used, *an unused stamp.*
2 (*say* un-yoost) not accustomed, *He is unused to eating meat.*

unusual *adjective*
not usual; strange or exceptional.
unusually *adverb*

unveil *verb* (unveils, unveiling, unveiled)
1 remove a veil or covering from something.
2 reveal.

unwarranted *adjective*
not justified; uncalled for.

unwell *adjective*
not in good health.

unwholesome *adjective*
not wholesome.

unwieldy *adjective*
awkward to move or control because of its size, shape, or weight.
unwieldiness *noun* [from *un-* + *wield*]

unwind *verb* (unwinds, unwinding, unwound)
1 unroll. 2 (*informal*) relax after a time of work or strain.

unwise *adjective*
not wise; foolish. **unwisely** *adverb*

unwrap *verb* (unwraps, unwrapping, unwrapped)
open something that is wrapped.

up *adverb*
1 to or in a higher place or position or level, *Prices went up.* 2 so as to be upright, *Stand up.*
3 out of bed, *It's time to get up.* 4 completely, *Eat up your carrots.* 5 finished, *Your time is up.*
6 (*informal*) happening, *Something is up.*
up against 1 close to. 2 (*informal*) faced with difficulties, dangers, etc.
ups and downs 1 ascents and descents.
2 alternate good and bad luck.
up to 1 until. 2 busy with or doing something, *What are you up to?* 3 capable of, *I don't think I'm up to it.* 4 needed from, *It's up to us to help her.*
up to date 1 modern or fashionable. 2 giving recent information etc.

USAGE: Use hyphens when this is used as an adjective before a noun, e.g. *up-to-date information* (but *The information is up to date*).

up *preposition*
upwards through or along or into, *Water came up the pipes.*
[from Old English]

upbringing *noun*
the way someone is trained during childhood.

update *verb* (updates, updating, updated)
bring a thing up to date.

upheaval *noun* (*plural* upheavals)
a sudden violent change or disturbance.
[from *up-* + *heave*]

uphill *adverb*
up a slope.
uphill *adjective*
1 going up a slope. 2 difficult, *It was an uphill struggle.*

uphold *verb* (upholds, upholding, upheld)
support or maintain a decision or belief etc.

upholster *verb* (upholsters, upholstering, upholstered)
put covers, padding, and springs etc. on furniture. **upholstery** *noun*
[from *uphold* = maintain and repair]

upkeep *noun*
keeping something in good condition; the cost of this.

uplifting *adjective*
making you feel more cheerful.

upon *preposition*
on. [from *up* (adverb) + *on* (preposition)]

upper *adjective*
higher in place or rank etc.

upper class *noun* (*plural* upper classes)
the highest class in society, especially the aristocracy. **upper-class** *adjective*

uppermost *adjective*
highest.
uppermost *adverb*
on or to the top or the highest place, *Keep the painted side uppermost.*
[from *upper* + *most*]

upright *adjective*
1 vertical or erect. 2 strictly honest or honourable.
upright *noun* (*plural* uprights)
a post or rod etc. placed upright, especially as a support.

uprising *noun* (*plural* uprisings)
a rebellion or revolt.

uproar *noun*
an outburst of noise or excitement or anger.

uproot *verb* (uproots, uprooting, uprooted)
1 remove a plant and its roots from the ground.
2 make someone leave the place where he or she has lived for a long time.

upset *verb* (upsets, upsetting, upset)
1 overturn; knock something over. 2 make a person unhappy or distressed. 3 disturb the normal working of something; disrupt, *This has really upset my plans.*
upset *adjective*
1 unhappy or distressed. 2 slightly ill, *an upset stomach.*
upset *noun* (*plural* upsets)
1 a slight illness, *a stomach upset.* 2 an unexpected result or setback, *There has been a major upset in the quarter-finals.*

upshot *noun* (*plural* upshots)
an outcome. [originally = the final shot in an archery contest]

upside down *adverb* & *adjective*
1 with the upper part underneath instead of on top. 2 in great disorder; very untidy, *Everything had been turned upside down.*

upstairs *adverb* & *adjective*
to or on a higher floor.

upstart *noun* (*plural* upstarts)
a person who has risen suddenly to a high position, especially one who then behaves arrogantly. [from an old verb *upstart* = to spring up suddenly]

uptake *noun*
quick on the uptake quick to understand.
slow on the uptake slow to understand.

uptight *adjective* (*informal*)
tense and nervous or annoyed.

upward *adjective* & *adverb*
going towards what is higher. **upwards** *adverb*
[from *up* + *-ward*]

uranium *noun*
a heavy radioactive grey metal used as a source of nuclear energy.
[named after the planet Uranus]

urban *adjective*
to do with a town or city.
[from Latin *urbis* = of a city]

urchin *noun* (*plural* urchins)
1 a poorly dressed or mischievous boy. 2 a sea urchin. [from Latin *ericius* = hedgehog]

urge *verb* (urges, urging, urged)
1 try to persuade a person to do something.
2 drive people or animals onward.
urge *noun* (*plural* urges)
a strong desire. [from Latin]

urgent *adjective*
needing to be done or dealt with immediately.
urgently *adverb*, **urgency** *noun* [from Latin *urgens* = urging]

urinate (*say* yoor-in-ayt) *verb* (urinates, urinating, urinated)
pass urine out of your body. **urination** *noun*

urine (*say* yoor-in) *noun*
waste liquid that collects in the bladder and is passed out of the body. **urinary** *adjective*
[from Latin]

urn *noun* (*plural* urns)
1 a large metal container with a tap, in which water is heated. 2 a container shaped like a vase, usually with a foot, especially a container for holding the ashes of a cremated person.
[from Latin]

US *abbreviation*
United States (of America).

us *pronoun*
the form of *we* used when it is the object of a verb or after a preposition.

USA *abbreviation*
United States of America.

use (*say* yooz) *verb* (uses, using, used)
perform an action or job with something, *Use soap for washing.* **user** *noun*
used to 1 was or were in the habit of doing, *We*

used to go by train. **2** accustomed to or familiar with, *I'm used to his strange behaviour.*
use up use all of something.
use (*say* yooss) *noun* (*plural* **uses**)
1 the action of using something; being used, *the use of computers in schools.* **2** the purpose for which something is used, *Can you find a use for this crate?* **3** the quality of being useful, *These scissors are no use at all.* [from Latin]

used *adjective*
not new; second-hand, *used cars.*

useful *adjective*
able to be used a lot or to do something that needs doing.
usefully *adverb*, **usefulness** *noun*

useless *adjective*
not useful; producing no effect, *Their efforts were useless.*
uselessly *adverb*, **uselessness** *noun*

usher *noun* (*plural* **ushers**)
a person who shows people to their seats in a public hall or church etc.
usher *verb* (**ushers, ushering, ushered**)
lead someone in or out; escort someone as an usher.
[from Latin *ostiarius* = doorkeeper]

usherette *noun* (*plural* **usherettes**)
a woman who shows people to their seats in a cinema or theatre.

usual *adjective*
such as happens or is done or used etc. always or most of the time. **usually** *adverb*
[from Latin *usum* = used]

utensil (*say* yoo-ten-sil) *noun* (*plural* **utensils**)
a tool, device, or container, especially one for use in the house, *cooking utensils.*
[from Latin *utensilis* = fit for use]

utilitarian *adjective*
designed to be useful rather than decorative or luxurious; practical.
[from *utility*]

utility *noun* (*plural* **utilities**)
1 usefulness. **2** an organization that supplies water, gas, electricity, etc. to the community.
[from Latin *utilis* = useful]

utilize *verb* (**utilizes, utilizing, utilized**)
use; find a use for something. **utilization** *noun*
[from French]

utmost *adjective*
extreme or greatest, *Look after it with the utmost care.* **utmost** *noun*
[from Old English *utemest* = furthest out]

Utopia (*say* yoo-toh-pee-a) *noun* (*plural* **Utopias**)
an imaginary place or state of things where everything is perfect. **Utopian** *adjective* [Latin, = nowhere; used in 1516 as the title of a book by Sir Thomas More, in which he describes an ideal society]

utter[1] *verb* (**utters, uttering, uttered**)
say or speak; make a sound with your mouth.
utterance *noun* [from old Dutch]

utter[2] *adjective*
complete or absolute, *utter misery.*
utterly *adverb*
[from Old English *uttra* = outer]

uttermost *adjective* & *noun*
utmost.

U-turn *noun* (*plural* **U-turns**)
1 a U-shaped turn made in a vehicle so that it then travels in the opposite direction. **2** a complete change of policy.

Vv

vacant *adjective*
1 empty; not filled or occupied. **2** without expression; blank, *a vacant stare.*
vacantly *adverb*, **vacancy** *noun*
[from Latin *vacans* = being empty]

vacation (*say* vak-**ay**-shon) *noun* (*plural* **vacations**)
1 a holiday, especially between the terms at a university. **2** vacating a place etc.

vaccinate (*say* vak-sin-ayt) *verb* (**vaccinates, vaccinating, vaccinated**)
inoculate someone with a vaccine.
vaccination *noun*

vaccine (*say* vak-seen) *noun* (*plural* **vaccines**)
a substance used to immunize a person against a disease. [from Latin *vacca* = cow (because serum from cows was used to protect people from the disease smallpox)]

vacuum *noun* (*plural* **vacuums**)
1 a completely empty space; a space without any air in it. **2** (*informal*) a vacuum cleaner.
vacuum *verb*
[from Latin *vacuus* = empty]

vacuum cleaner *noun* (*plural* **vacuum cleaners**)
an electrical device that sucks up dust and dirt etc.

vagabond *noun* (*plural* **vagabonds**)
a person with no settled home or regular work; a vagrant.

vagina (*say* va-**jy**-na) *noun* (*plural* **vaginas**)
the passage that leads from the vulva to the womb. [Latin, = sheath]

vagrant (*say* **vay**-grant) *noun* (*plural* **vagrants**)
a person with no settled home or regular work; a tramp. **vagrancy** *noun*

vague *adjective*
not definite or clear.
vaguely *adverb*, **vagueness** *noun*
[from Latin *vagus* = wandering]

vain *adjective*
1 conceited, especially about your appearance.
2 useless, *They made vain attempts to save her*.
vainly *adverb*
in vain with no result; uselessly.
[from Latin *vanus* = empty]

USAGE: Do not confuse with *vane* or *vein*.

valency *noun* (*plural* **valencies**)
the power of an atom to combine with other
atoms, measured by the number of hydrogen
atoms it is capable of combining with.
[from Latin *valentia* = power]

valiant *adjective*
brave or courageous. **valiantly** *adverb*
[from old French; related to *value*]

valid *adjective*
1 legally able to be used or accepted, *This
passport is out of date and not valid*. 2 (of
reasoning) sound and logical. **validity** *noun*
[from Latin *validus* = strong]

valley *noun* (*plural* **valleys**)
1 a long low area between hills. 2 an area
through which a river flows, *the Nile valley*.
[from Latin]

valuable *adjective*
worth a lot of money; of great value.
valuably *adverb*

valuables *plural noun*
valuable things.

value *noun* (*plural* **values**)
1 the amount of money etc. that is considered
to be the equivalent of something, or for which
it can be exchanged. 2 how useful or important
something is, *They learnt the value of regular
exercise*.
value *verb* (**values, valuing, valued**)
1 think that something is valuable. 2 estimate
the value of a thing.
valuation *noun*, **valuer** *noun*
[from Latin *valere* = be strong]

valve *noun* (*plural* **valves**)
1 a device for controlling the flow of gas or
liquid through a pipe or tube. 2 a device that
controls the flow of electricity in old
televisions, radios, etc. 3 each piece of the shell
of oysters etc. **valvular** *adjective*
[from Latin *valva* = a panel of a folding door]

vampire *noun* (*plural* **vampires**)
a ghost or revived corpse supposed to leave a
grave at night and suck blood from living
people. [from Serbo-Croat (a Slavonic language
spoken in the Balkan countries)]

van *noun* (*plural* **vans**)
1 a covered vehicle for carrying goods.
2 a railway carriage for luggage or goods, or
for the use of the guard.
[short for *caravan*]

vandal *noun* (*plural* **vandals**)
a person who deliberately breaks or damages
things, especially public property. **vandalism**
noun [named after the Vandals, a Germanic
tribe who invaded the Roman Empire in the
5th century, destroying many books and works
of art]

vandalize *verb* (**vandalizes, vandalizing,
vandalized**)
damage things as a vandal.

vane *noun* (*plural* **vanes**)
1 a weathervane. 2 the blade of a propeller, sail
of a windmill, or other device that acts on or is
moved by wind or water. [from Old English]

USAGE: Do not confuse with *vain* or *vein*.

vanilla *noun*
a flavouring obtained from the pods of a
tropical plant.
[from Spanish *vainilla* = little pod]

vanish *verb* (**vanishes, vanishing, vanished**)
disappear completely. [from Latin]

vanity *noun*
conceit; being vain.

vanquish *verb* (**vanquishes, vanquishing,
vanquished**)
conquer. [from Latin *vincere* = conquer]

vantage point *noun* (*plural* **vantage points**)
a place from which you have a good view of
something.
[from Middle English *vantage* = advantage]

vaporize *verb* (**vaporizes, vaporizing, vaporized**)
change or be changed into vapour.
vaporization *noun*, **vaporizer** *noun*

vapour *noun* (*plural* **vapours**)
a visible gas to which some substances can be
converted by heat; steam or mist.
[from Latin *vapor* = steam]

variable *adjective*
likely to vary; changeable.
variably *adverb*, **variability** *noun*
variable *noun* (*plural* **variables**)
something that varies or can vary;
a variable quantity.

variant *adjective*
differing from something, *'Gipsy' is a variant
spelling of 'gypsy'*. **variant** *noun*
[same origin as *variance*]

variation *noun* (*plural* **variations**)
1 varying; the amount by which something
varies. 2 a different form of something.

varied *adjective*
of different sorts; full of variety.

variegated (*say* vair-ig-ay-tid) *adjective*
with patches of different colours.
variegation *noun* [same origin as *various*]

variety adjective (plural **varieties**)
1 a quantity of different kinds of things. 2 the quality of not always being the same; variation. 3 a particular kind of something, There are several varieties of spaniel. 4 an entertainment that includes short performances of various kinds.
[same origin as various]

various adjective
1 of several kinds; unlike one another, for various reasons. 2 several, We met various people. **variously** adverb
[from Latin varius = changing]

varnish noun (plural **varnishes**)
a liquid that dries to form a hard shiny usually transparent coating.
varnish verb (varnishes, varnishing, varnished)
coat something with varnish.

vary verb (varies, varying, varied)
1 make or become different; change. 2 be different. [same origin as various]

vase noun (plural **vases**)
an open usually tall container used for holding cut flowers or as an ornament.
[from Latin vas = vessel]

vast adjective
very great, especially in area, a vast expanse of water.
vastly adverb, **vastness** noun
[from Latin vastus = unoccupied, desert]

VAT abbreviation
value added tax; a tax on goods and services.

vat noun (plural **vats**)
a very large container for holding liquid.

vault verb (vaults, vaulting, vaulted)
jump over something, especially while supporting yourself on your hands or with the help of a pole.
vault noun (plural **vaults**)
1 a vaulting jump. 2 an arched roof. 3 an underground room used to store things. 4 a room for storing money or valuables. 5 a burial chamber.
[from Latin volvere = to roll]

vaulted adjective
having an arched roof.

vaunt verb (vaunts, vaunting, vaunted) (old use or poetical)
boast. **vaunt** noun
[from Latin vanus = vain]

VDU abbreviation
visual display unit.

veal noun
calf's flesh used as food.
[from Latin vitulus = calf]

vector noun (plural **vectors**)
(in mathematics) a quantity that has size and direction (e.g. velocity, = speed in a certain direction). **vectorial** adjective
[Latin, = carrier, traveller]

veer verb (veers, veering, veered)
change direction; swerve.

vegetable noun (plural **vegetables**)
a plant that can be used as food.
[from Latin vegetare = enliven, animate]

vegetarian noun (plural **vegetarians**)
a person who does not eat meat.
vegetarianism noun
[from vegetable + -arian]

vegetation noun
1 plants that are growing. 2 vegetating.
[from Latin vegetatio = the power to grow]

vehement (say vee-im-ent) adjective
showing strong feeling, a vehement refusal.
vehemently adverb, **vehemence** noun

vehicle noun (plural **vehicles**)
a means of transporting people or goods, especially on land.
[from Latin vehere = carry]

veil noun (plural **veils**)
a piece of thin material worn to cover the face or head.
take the veil become a nun.
veil verb (veils, veiling, veiled)
1 cover something with a veil. 2 partially conceal something, veiled threats.

vein noun (plural **veins**)
1 any of the tubes that carry blood from all parts of the body to the heart. (Compare artery.) 2 a line or streak on a leaf, rock, insect's wing, etc. 3 a long deposit of mineral or ore in the middle of a rock. 4 a mood or manner, She spoke in a serious vein. [from Latin]

USAGE: Do not confuse with vain or vane.

velocity noun (plural **velocities**)
speed in a given direction.
[from Latin velox = swift]

velvet noun
a woven material with very short soft furry fibres on one side. **velvety** adjective
[from Latin villus = soft fur]

vendetta noun (plural **vendettas**)
a long-lasting bitter quarrel; a feud. [Italian, from Latin vindicta = vengeance]

vending machine noun (plural **vending machines**)
a slot machine from which you can obtain drinks, chocolate, cigarettes, etc.

veneer noun (plural **veneers**)
1 a thin layer of good wood covering the surface of a cheaper wood in furniture etc. 2 an

outward show of some good quality, *a veneer of politeness.*
[via German from French *fournir* = furnish]
venerable *adjective*
worthy of being venerated, especially because of great age.
venerate *verb* (venerates, venerating, venerated)
honour with great respect or reverence.
veneration *noun*
[from Latin *venerari* = revere]
venereal disease *noun* (*plural* venereal diseases)
a disease passed on by sexual intercourse.
vengeance *noun*
revenge.
with a vengeance very strongly or effectively.
[from old French; related to *vindictive*]
venison *noun*
deer's flesh as food.
[old French, from Latin *venatio* = hunting]
Venn diagram *noun* (*plural* **Venn diagrams**)
(*in mathematics*) a diagram in which circles are used to show the relationships between different sets of things.
[named after an English mathematician, John Venn]
venom *noun*
1 the poisonous fluid produced by snakes, scorpions, etc. 2 very bitter feeling towards somebody; hatred. **venomous** *adjective*
[from Latin *venenum* = poison]
vent *noun* (*plural* vents)
an opening in something, especially to let out smoke or gas etc.
give vent to express your feelings openly.
vent *verb* (vents, venting, vented)
1 make a vent in something. 2 give vent to feelings. [from Latin *ventus* = wind]
ventilate *verb* (ventilates, ventilating, ventilated)
let air move freely in and out of a room etc.
ventilation *noun*, **ventilator** *noun*
[same origin as *vent*]
ventriloquist *noun* (*plural* ventriloquists)
an entertainer who makes his or her voice sound as if it comes from another source.
ventriloquism *noun* [from Latin *venter* = abdomen + *loqui* = speak]
venture *noun* (*plural* ventures)
something you decide to do that is risky.
venture *verb* (ventures, venturing, ventured)
risk; dare to do or say something or to go somewhere, *We ventured out into the snow.*
[from *adventure*]
venturesome *adjective*
ready to take risks; daring.
veracity (*say* ver-**as**-it-ee) *noun*
truth. **veracious** (*say* ver-**ay**-shus) *adjective*
[from Latin *verus* = true]

veranda *noun* (*plural* verandas)
a terrace with a roof along the side of a house.
[via Hindi from Portuguese *varanda* = railing, balcony]
verb *noun* (*plural* verbs)
a word that shows what a person or thing is doing, e.g. *bring, came, sing, were.*
[from Latin *verbum* = word]
verbal *adjective*
1 to do with or in words; spoken, not written, *a verbal statement.* 2 to do with verbs.
verbally *adverb* [same origin as *verb*]
verdict *noun* (*plural* verdicts)
a judgement or decision made after considering something, especially that made by a jury.
[from Latin *verus* = true + *dictum* = said]
verge *noun* (*plural* verges)
1 the extreme edge or brink of something, *on the verge of madness.* 2 a strip of grass along the edge of a road or path etc.
verge *verb* (verges, verging, verged)
verge on border on something; be close to something, *This puzzle verges on the impossible.*
veritable *adjective*
real; rightly named, *a veritable villain.*
veritably *adverb* [French; related to *verity*]
vermin *plural noun*
1 pests (e.g. foxes, rats, mice) regarded as harmful to domestic animals, crops, or food. 2 unpleasant or parasitic insects, e.g. lice.
verminous *adjective*
[from Latin *vermis* = worm]
vernacular (*say* ver-**nak**-yoo-ler) *noun* (*plural* vernaculars)
the language of a country or district, as distinct from an official or formal language.
[from Latin *vernaculus* = domestic]
versatile *adjective*
able to do or be used for many different things.
versatility *noun* [from Latin *versare* = to turn]
verse *noun* (*plural* verses)
1 writing arranged in short lines, usually with a particular rhythm and often with rhymes; poetry. 2 a group of lines forming a unit in a poem or song. 3 each of the short numbered sections of a chapter in the Bible. [via Old English from Latin *versus* = a line of writing]
version *noun* (*plural* versions)
1 a particular person's account of something that happened. 2 a translation, *modern versions of the Bible.* 3 a special or different form of something, *the latest version of this car.*
[from Latin *versum* = turned, transformed]
versus *preposition*
against; competing with, *Arsenal versus Liverpool.* [Latin, = against]

vertebra *noun* (*plural* **vertebrae**)
each of the bones that form the backbone.

vertebrate *noun* (*plural* **vertebrates**)
an animal that has a backbone. (The opposite is *invertebrate*.) [from *vertebra*]

vertical *adjective*
at right angles to something horizontal; upright. **vertically** *adverb*

vertigo *noun*
a feeling of dizziness and loss of balance, especially when you are very high up.
[Latin, = whirling around]

verve (*say* verv) *noun*
enthusiasm and liveliness.
[French, = vigour]

very *adverb*
1 to a great amount or intensity; extremely, *It was very cold.* 2 (used to emphasize something), *on the very next day; the very last drop.*
very *adjective*
1 exact or actual, *It's the very thing we need.* 2 extreme, *at the very end.*
[from old French *verai* = true]

vessel *noun* (*plural* **vessels**)
1 a ship or boat. 2 a container, especially for liquid. 3 a tube carrying blood or other liquid in the body of an animal or plant.
[from old French; related to *vase*]

vest *noun* (*plural* **vests**)
a piece of underwear covering the trunk of the body.
vest *verb* (**vests, vesting, vested**)
1 give something as a right, *The power to make laws is vested in Parliament.* 2 (*old use*) clothe.
[from Latin *vestis* = a piece of clothing]

vested interest *noun* (*plural* **vested interests**)
a strong reason for wanting something to happen, usually because you will benefit from it.

vet *noun* (*plural* **vets**)
a person trained to give medical and surgical treatment to animals.
vet *verb* (**vets, vetting, vetted**)
check a thing to see if it has any mistakes or faults. [short for *veterinary surgeon*]

veteran *noun* (*plural* **veterans**)
a person who has had long service or experience in something, *a war veteran.*
[from Latin *vetus* = old]

veterinary (*say* vet-rin-ree) *adjective*
to do with the medical and surgical treatment of animals, *a veterinary surgeon.*
[from Latin *veterinae* = cattle]

veto (*say* vee-toh) *noun* (*plural* **vetoes**)
1 a refusal to let something happen. 2 the right to prohibit something.
veto *verb* (**vetoes, vetoing, vetoed**)
refuse or prohibit something.
[Latin, = I forbid]

vex *verb* (**vexes, vexing, vexed**)
annoy; cause somebody worry.
vexation *noun*, **vexatious** *adjective*
[from Latin *vexare* = to shake]

VHF *abbreviation*
very high frequency.

via (*say* vy-a) *preposition*
through; by way of, *The train goes from London to Exeter via Bristol.*
[Latin, = by way of]

viable *adjective*
able to work or exist successfully; practicable, *a viable plan.* **viability** *noun*
[French, from *vie* = life]

viaduct *noun* (*plural* **viaducts**)
a long bridge, usually with many arches, carrying a road or railway over a valley or low ground.
[from Latin *via* = road + *ducere* = to lead]

vibrant *adjective*
full of energy; lively.
[same origin as *vibrate*]

vibrate *verb* (**vibrates, vibrating, vibrated**)
1 shake very quickly to and fro. 2 make a throbbing sound. **vibration** *noun*
[from Latin *vibrare* = shake]

vicar *noun* (*plural* **vicars**)
a member of the clergy who is in charge of a parish. [same origin as *vicarious* (because originally a vicar looked after a parish for another clergyman, or for a monastery)]

vice[1] *noun* (*plural* **vices**)
1 evil or wickedness. 2 an evil or bad habit; a bad fault. [from Latin *vitium* = fault]

vice[2] *noun* (*plural* **vices**)
a device for gripping something and holding it firmly while you work on it.
[from Latin *vitis* = vine]

vice- *prefix*
1 authorized to act as a deputy or substitute (as in *vice-captain*, *vice-president*). 2 next in rank to someone (as in *vice-admiral*).
[Latin, = in place of, by a change]

vice versa *adverb*
the other way round, *which do you prefer—blue spots on a yellow background or vice versa?*
[Latin, = the position being reversed]

vicious *adjective*
1 cruel and aggressive. 2 severe or violent.
viciously *adverb*, **viciousness** *noun*
[same origin as *vice*[1]]

vicious circle *noun* (*plural* **vicious circles**)
a situation where a problem produces an effect which itself produces the original problem or makes it worse.

victim *noun* (*plural* victims)
someone who is injured, killed, robbed, etc.
[from Latin *victima* = a person or animal
sacrificed to a god]

victimize *verb* (victimizes, victimizing, victimized)
make a victim of someone; punish a person
unfairly. **victimization** *noun*

victor *noun* (*plural* victors)
the winner. [same origin as *victory*]

Victorian *adjective*
belonging to the time of Queen Victoria
(1837–1901). **Victorian** *noun*

victory *noun* (*plural* victories)
success won against an opponent in a battle,
contest, or game. **victorious** *adjective*
[from Latin *victum* = conquered]

video *noun* (*plural* videos)
1 recorded or broadcast pictures. 2 a video
recorder or recording. 3 a visual display unit.
[Latin, = I see]

video recorder *noun* (*plural* video recorders)
a machine for recording a television
programme etc. on magnetic tape for playing
back later.

videotape *noun* (*plural* videotapes)
magnetic tape suitable for recording television
programmes.

vie *verb* (vies, vying, vied)
compete; carry on a rivalry, *vying with each
other*. [probably from *envy*]

view *noun* (*plural* views)
1 what can be seen from one place, e.g.
beautiful scenery. 2 sight; range of vision, *The
ship sailed into view*. 3 an opinion, *She has
strong views about politics*.
in view of because of.
on view displayed for inspection.
with a view to with the hope or intention of.
view *verb* (views, viewing, viewed)
1 look at something. 2 consider.
viewer *noun*
[from Latin *videre* = to see]

viewpoint *noun* (*plural* viewpoints)
a point of view.

vigorous *adjective*
full of strength and energy.
vigorously *adverb*

Viking *noun* (*plural* Vikings)
a Scandinavian trader and pirate in the 8th–
10th centuries. [from Old Norse]

vile *adjective*
1 extremely disgusting. 2 very bad or wicked.
vilely *adverb*, **vileness** *noun*
[from Latin *vilis* = cheap, unworthy]

villa *noun* (*plural* villas)
a house, especially a holiday home abroad.
[Latin, = country house]

village *noun* (*plural* villages)
a group of houses and other buildings in a
country district, smaller than a town and
usually having a church. **villager** *noun*
[old French; related to *villa*]

villain *noun* (*plural* villains)
a wicked person or a criminal.
villainous *adjective*, **villainy** *noun*
[from Latin *villanus* = villager]

vindicate *verb* (vindicates, vindicating,
vindicated)
1 clear a person of blame or suspicion. 2 prove
something to be true or worth while.
vindication *noun*
[from Latin *vindicare* = set free]

vine *noun* (*plural* vines)
a climbing or trailing plant whose fruit is the
grape. [from Latin *vinum* = wine]

vinegar *noun*
a sour liquid used to flavour food or in
pickling.
[from Latin *vinum* = wine + *acer* = sour]

vintage *noun* (*plural* vintages)
1 the harvest of a season's grapes; the wine
made from this. 2 the period from which
something comes.
[from French; related to *vine*]

vintage car *noun* (*plural* vintage cars)
a car made between 1917 and 1930.

viola (*say* vee-oh-la) *noun* (*plural* violas)
a musical instrument like a violin but slightly
larger and with a lower pitch. [Spanish or
Italian]

violate *verb* (violates, violating, violated)
1 break a promise, law, or treaty etc. 2 break
into somewhere; treat a person or place
without respect.
violation *noun*, **violator** *noun*
[from Latin *violare* = treat violently]

violence *noun*
force that does harm or damage. **violent**
adjective, **violently** *adverb* [from Latin]

violet *noun* (*plural* violets)
1 a small plant that often has purple flowers.
2 purple.

violin *noun* (*plural* violins)
a musical instrument with four strings, played
with a bow. **violinist** *noun*
[from Italian *violino* = small viola]

viper *noun* (*plural* vipers)
a small poisonous snake.
[from Latin *vipera* = snake]

virgin *noun* (*plural* virgins)
a person, especially a girl or woman, who has
never had sexual intercourse.
virginal *adjective*, **virginity** *noun*
virgin *adjective*
not yet touched or used, *virgin snow*.

virtual *adjective*
being something in effect though not strictly in
fact, *His silence was a virtual admission of guilt.*
[same origin as *virtue*]
virtually *adverb*
nearly or almost.

virtue *noun* (*plural* virtues)
1 moral goodness; a particular form of this,
Honesty is a virtue. 2 a good quality or
advantage, *Jamie's plan has the virtue of
simplicity.*
virtuous *adjective*, **virtuously** *adverb*
in virtue of because of.
[from Latin *virtus* = worth]

virtuoso (*say* ver-tew-oh-soh) *noun* (*plural*
virtuosos or virtuosi)
a person with outstanding skill, especially in
singing or playing music. **virtuosity** *noun*
[Italian, = skilful]

virus *noun* (*plural* viruses)
1 a very tiny living thing, smaller than a
bacterium, that can cause disease. 2 a disease
caused by a virus. 3 a hidden set of
instructions in a computer program that is
designed to destroy data. [Latin, = poison]

visa (*say* vee-za) *noun* (*plural* visas)
an official mark put on someone's passport by
officials of a foreign country to show that the
holder has permission to enter that country.
[Latin, = things seen]

viscount (*say* vy-kownt) *noun* (*plural* viscounts)
a nobleman ranking below an earl and above a
baron. **viscountess** *noun*
[from old French *visconte* = vice-count]

visible *adjective*
able to be seen or noticed, *The ship was visible
on the horizon.* **visibly** *adverb*, **visibility** *noun*
[from Latin]

USAGE: Do not confuse with *visual.*

vision *noun* (*plural* visions)
1 the ability to see; sight. 2 something seen in a
person's imagination or in a dream. 3 foresight
and wisdom in planning things. 4 a person or
thing that is beautiful to see.
[from old French; related to *visible* and *visual*]

visionary *adjective*
extremely imaginative or fanciful.
visionary *noun* (*plural* visionaries)
a person with extremely imaginative ideas and
plans.

visit *verb* (visits, visiting, visited)
1 go to see a person or place. 2 stay somewhere
for a while. **visitor** *noun*
visit *noun* (*plural* visits)
1 going to see a person or place. 2 a short stay
somewhere.
[from Latin *visitare* = go to see]

vista *noun* (*plural* vistas)
a long view. [Italian, = view]

visual *adjective*
to do with or used in seeing; to do with sight.
visually *adverb*
[from Latin *visus* = sight]

USAGE: Do not confuse with *visible.*

visual aid *noun* (*plural* visual aids)
a picture, slide, film, etc. used as an aid in
teaching.

visual display unit *noun* (*plural* visual display
units)
a device that looks like a television screen and
displays data being received from a computer
or fed into it.

visualize *verb* (visualizes, visualizing, visualized)
form a mental picture of something.
visualization *noun*

vital *adjective*
1 connected with life; necessary for life to
continue, *vital functions such as breathing.*
2 essential; very important.
vitally *adverb*
[from Latin *vita* = life]

vitality *noun*
liveliness or energy.

vitamin (*say* vit-a-min or vy-ta-min) *noun* (*plural*
vitamins)
any of a number of substances that are present
in various foods and are essential to keep
people and animals healthy.
[from Latin *vita* = life + *amine*, a kind of
chemical related to amino acids, which
vitamins were once thought to contain]

vivacious (*say* viv-ay-shus) *adjective*
happy and lively. **vivaciously** *adverb*,
vivacity *noun*
[from Latin *vivus* = alive]

vivid *adjective*
1 bright and strong or clear, *vivid colours*; *a
vivid description.* 2 active and lively, *a vivid
imagination.* **vividly** *adverb*, **vividness** *noun*
[from Latin *vividus* = full of life]

vivisection *noun*
doing surgical experiments on live animals.
[from Latin *vivus* = alive + *sectio* = cutting]

vixen *noun* (*plural* vixens)
a female fox. [from Old English]

vocabulary *noun* (*plural* vocabularies)
1 a list of words with their meanings. 2 the
words known to a person or used in a
particular book or subject etc.
[from Latin *vocabulum* = name]

vocal cords *plural noun*
two strap-like membranes in the throat that
can be made to vibrate and produce sounds.
[from Latin *vocis* = of the voice]

vocalist *noun* (*plural* vocalists)
a singer, especially in a pop group.

vocation *noun* (*plural* vocations)
1 a person's job or occupation. 2 a strong
desire to do a particular kind of work, or a
feeling of being called by God to do something.
[from Latin *vocare* = to call]

vocational *adjective*
teaching you the skills you need for a
particular job or profession, *vocational
training*.

vodka *noun* (*plural* vodkas)
a strong alcoholic drink very popular in
Russia. [from Russian *voda* = water]

vogue *noun* (*plural* vogues)
the current fashion, *Very short hair for women
seems to be the vogue*.
in vogue in fashion, *Stripy dresses are definitely
in vogue*.

voice *noun* (*plural* voices)
1 sounds formed by the vocal cords and uttered
by the mouth, especially in speaking, singing,
etc. 2 the ability to speak or sing, *She has lost
her voice*. 3 someone expressing a particular
opinion about something, *Emma's the only
dissenting voice*. 4 the right to express an
opinion or desire, *I have no voice in this matter*.

void *adjective*
1 empty. 2 having no legal validity.
void *noun* (*plural* voids)
an empty space or hole.
[from old French; related to *vacant*]

volatile (*say* vol-a-tyl) *adjective*
1 evaporating quickly, *a volatile liquid*.
2 changing quickly from one mood or interest
to another. **volatility** *noun*
[from Latin *volatilis* = flying]

volcano *noun* (*plural* volcanoes)
a mountain with an opening at the top from
which lava and hot gases etc. flow.
volcanic *adjective* [Italian, from *Vulcan*, the
ancient Roman god of fire]

vole *noun* (*plural* voles)
a small animal rather like a rat.

volley *noun* (*plural* volleys)
1 a number of bullets or shells etc. fired at the
same time. 2 hitting back the ball in tennis etc.
before it touches the ground.
volley *verb* (volleys, volleying, volleyed)
send or hit something in a volley or volleys.
[from Latin *volare* = to fly]

volt *noun* (*plural* volts)
a unit for measuring electric force.
[named after an Italian scientist, A. Volta, who
discovered how to produce electricity by a
chemical reaction]

voltage *noun* (*plural* voltages)
electric force measured in volts.

volume *noun* (*plural* volumes)
1 the amount of space filled by something. 2 an
amount or quantity, *The volume of work has
increased*. 3 the strength or power of sound. 4 a
book, especially one of a set. [from Latin
volumen = a roll (because ancient books were
made in a rolled form)]

voluntary *adjective*
1 done or doing something willingly, not
because you are forced to do it. 2 unpaid,
voluntary work. **voluntarily** *adverb*
voluntary *noun* (*plural* voluntaries)
an organ solo, often improvised, played before
or after a church service.
[from Latin *voluntas* = the will]

volunteer *verb* (volunteers, volunteering,
volunteered)
give or offer something of your own accord,
without being forced to.
volunteer *noun* (*plural* volunteers)
a person who volunteers to do something, e.g.
to serve in the armed forces.
[from French; related to *voluntary*]

vomit *verb* (vomits, vomiting, vomited)
bring up food etc. from the stomach and out
through the mouth; be sick. **vomit** *noun*

voodoo *noun*
a form of witchcraft and magical rites,
especially in the West Indies.
[via American French from a West African
language]

-vore *suffix*
forms nouns meaning 'eating or feeding on
something' (e.g. *carnivore*).
[same origin as *voracious*]

-vorous *suffix*
forms adjectives corresponding to nouns in
-vore (e.g. *carnivorous*).

vote *verb* (votes, voting, voted)
show which person or thing you prefer by
putting up your hand, making a mark on a
paper, etc. **voter** *noun*
vote *noun* (*plural* votes)
1 the action of voting. 2 the right to vote.
[from Latin *votum* = a wish or vow]

vouch *verb* (vouches, vouching, vouched)
vouch for guarantee that something is true or
certain, *I will vouch for his honesty*.
[from old French; related to *vocation*]

voucher *noun* (*plural* vouchers)
a piece of paper that can be exchanged for
certain goods or services; a receipt.
[from *vouch*]

vow *noun* (*plural* vows)
a solemn promise, especially to God or a saint.
vow *verb* (vows, vowing, vowed)
make a vow.
[from old French; related to *vote*]

vowel *noun* (*plural* **vowels**)
any of the letters a, e, i, o, u, and sometimes y, which represent sounds in which breath comes out freely. (Compare *consonant*.)
[from Latin *vocalis littera* = vocal letter]

voyage *noun* (*plural* **voyages**)
a long journey on water or in space.
voyage *verb* (**voyages, voyaging, voyaged**)
make a voyage. **voyager** *noun*
[from old French]

vulgar *adjective*
rude; without good manners. **vulgarly** *adverb*, **vulgarity** *noun* [from Latin *vulgus* = the common or ordinary people]

vulnerable *adjective*
able to be hurt or harmed or attacked.
vulnerability *noun*
[from Latin *vulnus* = wound]

vulture *noun* (*plural* **vultures**)
a large bird that feeds on dead animals.

vulva *noun* (*plural* **vulvas**)
the outer parts of the female genitals.

vying *present participle* of **vie**.

Ww

W. *abbreviation*
1 west. 2 western.

wad (*say* wod) *noun* (*plural* **wads**)
a pad or bundle of soft material or banknotes, papers, etc. [from Dutch]

waddle *verb* (**waddles, waddling, waddled**)
walk with short steps, swaying from side to side. **waddle** *noun* [probably from *wade*]

wade *verb* (**wades, wading, waded**)
walk through water or mud etc. **wader** *noun*
[from Old English]

wafer *noun* (*plural* **wafers**)
a kind of thin biscuit.
[from old French; related to *waffle*[1]]

waffle[1] (*say* wof-el) *noun* (*plural* **waffles**)
a small cake made of batter and eaten hot.
[from Dutch]

waffle[2] (*say* wof-el) *noun* (*informal*)
vague wordy talk or writing. **waffle** *verb*
[from an old word *waff* = to bark or yelp]

waft (*say* woft) *verb* (**wafts, wafting, wafted**)
carry or float gently through the air or over water. [from old German or Dutch]

wag[1] *verb* (**wags, wagging, wagged**)
move quickly to and fro, *a dog wagging its tail*.
wag *noun* [from Old English]

wag[2] *noun* (*plural* **wags**)
a person who makes jokes.
[from an old word *waghalter* = someone likely to be hanged]

wage *noun* or **wages** *plural noun*
a regular payment to someone in return for his or her work.
wage *verb* (**wages, waging, waged**)
carry on a war or campaign.

wager (*say* way-jer) *noun* (*plural* **wagers**)
a bet. **wager** *verb*
[from old French; related to *wage*]

waggle *verb* (**waggles, waggling, waggled**)
move quickly to and fro; wag. **waggle** *noun*
[from *wag*]

wagon *noun* (*plural* **wagons**)
1 a cart with four wheels, pulled by a horse or an ox. 2 an open railway truck, e.g. for coal.
[from Dutch]

waif *noun* (*plural* **waifs**)
a homeless and helpless person, especially a child. [from old French]

wail *verb* (**wails, wailing, wailed**)
make a long sad cry. **wail** *noun*

waist *noun* (*plural* **waists**)
the narrow part in the middle of your body.

USAGE: Do not confuse with *waste*.

waistcoat *noun* (*plural* **waistcoats**)
a short close-fitting jacket without sleeves, worn over a shirt and under a jacket.

waistline *noun* (*plural* **waistlines**)
the amount you measure around your waist, which indicates how fat or thin you are.

wait *verb* (**waits, waiting, waited**)
1 stay somewhere or postpone an action until something happens; pause. 2 be postponed, *This question must wait until our next meeting.* 3 wait on people.
wait on 1 hand food and drink to people at a meal. 2 be an attendant to someone.
wait *noun*
an act or time of waiting, *We had a long wait for the train.*
[from old French; related to *wake*[1]]

waiter *noun* (*plural* **waiters**)
a man who serves people with food and drink in a restaurant.

waiting list *noun* (*plural* **waiting lists**)
a list of people waiting for something to become available.

waiting room *noun* (*plural* **waiting rooms**)
a room provided for people who are waiting for something.

waitress *noun* (*plural* **waitresses**)
a woman who serves people with food and drink in a restaurant.

wake[1] *verb* (wakes, waking, woke, woken)
1 stop sleeping, *Wake up! I woke when I heard the bell.* 2 stop someone sleeping, *You have woken the baby.*
wake *noun* (*plural* wakes)
(in Ireland) a party held after a funeral.
[from Old English]

wake[2] *noun* (*plural* wakes)
1 the track left on the water by a moving ship. 2 currents of air left behind a moving aircraft.
in the wake of following.
[probably from Old Norse]

wakeful *adjective*
unable to sleep.

waken *verb* (wakens, wakening, wakened)
wake.

walk *verb* (walks, walking, walked)
move along on your feet at an ordinary speed.
walker *noun*
walk *noun* (*plural* walks)
1 a journey on foot. 2 the manner of walking. 3 a path or route for walking.

walking stick *noun* (*plural* walking sticks)
a stick used as a support while walking.

walk of life *noun* (*plural* walks of life)
a person's occupation or social position.

walkover *noun* (*plural* walkovers)
an easy victory.

wall *noun* (*plural* walls)
1 a continuous upright structure, usually made of brick or stone, forming one of the sides of a building or room or supporting something or enclosing an area. 2 the outside part of something, *the stomach wall.*
wall *verb* (walls, walling, walled)
enclose or block something with a wall, *a walled garden.*

wallet *noun* (*plural* wallets)
a small flat folding case for holding banknotes, documents, etc.

wallflower *noun* (*plural* wallflowers)
a garden plant with fragrant flowers, blooming in spring. [because it is often found growing on old walls]

wallow *verb* (wallows, wallowing, wallowed)
1 roll about in water, mud, etc. 2 get great pleasure by being surrounded by something, *wallowing in luxury.*
wallow *noun* [from Old English]

wallpaper *noun* (*plural* wallpapers)
paper used to cover the inside walls of rooms.

walnut *noun* (*plural* walnuts)
an edible nut with a wrinkled surface.

walrus *noun* (*plural* walruses)
a large Arctic sea animal with two long tusks.
[probably from Dutch]

waltz *noun* (*plural* waltzes)
a dance with three beats to a bar.

waltz *verb* (waltzes, waltzing, waltzed)
dance a waltz.
[from German *walzen* = revolve]

wand *noun* (*plural* wands)
a thin rod, especially one used by a magician.
[from Old Norse]

wander *verb* (wanders, wandering, wandered)
1 go about without trying to reach a particular place. 2 leave the right path or direction; stray.
wanderer *noun*

wane *verb* (wanes, waning, waned)
1 (of the moon) show a bright area that becomes gradually smaller after being full. (The opposite is *wax*.) 2 become less, smaller, or weaker, *His popularity waned.*

want *verb* (wants, wanting, wanted)
1 wish to have something. 2 need, *Your hair wants cutting.* 3 be without something; lack.
want *noun* (*plural* wants)
1 a wish to have something. 2 lack or need of something. [from Old Norse]

wanted *adjective*
(of a suspected criminal) that the police wish to find or arrest.

war *noun* (*plural* wars)
1 fighting between nations or groups, especially using armed forces. 2 a serious struggle or effort against crime, disease, poverty, etc.
at war taking part in a war.

warble *verb* (warbles, warbling, warbled)
sing with a trilling sound, as some birds do.
warble *noun*

ward *noun* (*plural* wards)
1 a room with beds for patients in a hospital. 2 a child looked after by a guardian. 3 an area electing a councillor to represent it.
ward *verb* (wards, warding, warded)
ward off keep something away.

-ward *suffix*
forms adjectives and adverbs showing direction (e.g. *backward, forward, homeward*).
[from Old English]

warden *noun* (*plural* wardens)
an official who is in charge of a hostel, college, etc., or who supervises something.
[from old French; related to *guardian*]

warder *noun* (*plural* warders) (*old use*)
an official in charge of prisoners in a prison.
[from old French; related to *guard*]

wardrobe *noun* (*plural* wardrobes)
1 a cupboard to hang clothes in. 2 a stock of clothes or costumes.
[from old French *warder* = to guard, + *robe*]

-wards *suffix*
forms adverbs showing direction (e.g. *backwards, forwards*).
[from Old English *-weardes* = -ward]

warhead *noun* (*plural* **warheads**)
the head of a missile or torpedo etc., containing explosives.

warlike *adjective*
1 fond of making war. 2 threatening war.

warm *adjective*
1 fairly hot; not cold or cool. 2 friendly or enthusiastic, *a warm welcome*. **warmly** *adverb*, **warmness** *noun*, **warmth** *noun*
warm *verb* (**warms, warming, warmed**)
make or become warm.
[from Old English]

warm-blooded *adjective*
having blood that remains warm permanently.

warn *verb* (**warns, warning, warned**)
tell someone about a danger etc. that may affect them, or about what they should do, *I warned you to take your wellingtons.* **warning** *noun* [from Old English]

warp (*say* worp) *verb* (**warps, warping, warped**)
1 bend or twist out of shape, e.g. by dampness. 2 distort a person's ideas, judgement, etc., *Jealousy warped his mind.*

warrant *noun* (*plural* **warrants**)
a document that authorizes a person to do something (e.g. to search a place) or to receive something.
warrant *verb* (**warrants, warranting, warranted**)
1 justify, *Nothing can warrant such rudeness.* 2 guarantee.
[from old French; related to *guarantee*]

warren *noun* (*plural* **warrens**)
1 a piece of ground where there are many burrows in which rabbits live and breed. 2 a building or place with many winding passages.
[from old French]

warrior *noun* (*plural* **warriors**)
a person who fights in battle; a soldier.

warship *noun* (*plural* **warships**)
a ship used in war.

wart *noun* (*plural* **warts**)
a small hard lump on the skin, caused by a virus. [from Old English]

wary (*say* wair-ee) *adjective*
cautious; looking carefully for possible danger or difficulty. **warily** *adverb*, **wariness** *noun*
[from Old English]

wash *verb* (**washes, washing, washed**)
1 clean something with water or other liquid. 2 be washable, *Cotton washes easily.* 3 flow against or over something, *Waves washed over the deck.* 4 carry along by a moving liquid, *A wave washed him overboard.* 5 (*informal*) be accepted or believed, *That excuse won't wash.*
wash out (*informal*) if an event is washed out, it is abandoned because of rain.
wash up wash dishes and cutlery etc. after use.
washing-up *noun*

wash *noun* (*plural* **washes**)
1 the action of washing. 2 clothes etc. being washed. 3 the disturbed water behind a moving ship. 4 a thin coating of colour.

washable *adjective*
able to be washed without becoming damaged.

washbasin *noun* (*plural* **washbasins**)
a small sink for washing your hands etc.

washer *noun* (*plural* **washers**)
1 a small ring of rubber or metal etc. placed between two surfaces (e.g. under a bolt or screw) to fit them tightly together. 2 a washing machine.

washing *noun*
clothes etc. being washed.

washing machine *noun* (*plural* **washing machines**)
a machine for washing clothes etc.

wasn't (*mainly spoken*)
was not.

wasp *noun* (*plural* **wasps**)
a stinging insect with black and yellow stripes round its body.
[from Old English]

wastage *noun*
loss of something by waste.

waste *verb* (**wastes, wasting, wasted**)
1 use something in an extravagant way or without getting enough results. 2 fail to use something, *You wasted an opportunity.* 3 make or become gradually weaker or useless.
waste *adjective*
1 left over or thrown away because it is not wanted. 2 not used; not usable, *waste land.*
lay waste destroy the crops and buildings etc. of an area.
waste *noun* (*plural* **wastes**)
1 wasting a thing, not using it well, *a waste of time.* 2 things that are not wanted or not used. 3 an area of waste land, *the wastes of the Sahara Desert.*
wasteful *adjective*, **wastefully** *noun*, **wastefulness** *noun*
[from Latin *vastus* = empty]

USAGE: Do not confuse with *waist.*

watch *verb* (**watches, watching, watched**)
1 look at a person or thing for some time. 2 be on guard or ready for something to happen, *Watch for the traffic lights to turn green.* 3 take care of something.
watcher *noun*
watch *noun* (*plural* **watches**)
1 the action of watching. 2 a turn of being on duty in a ship. 3 a device like a small clock, usually worn on the wrist.

watchful *adjective*
watching closely; alert.
watchfully *adverb*, **watchfulness** *noun*

watchman *noun* (*plural* **watchmen**)
a person employed to look after an empty building etc., especially at night.

water *noun* (*plural* **waters**)
1 a colourless odourless tasteless liquid that is a compound of hydrogen and oxygen. 2 a lake or sea etc. 3 the tide, *at high water*.
pass water urinate.
water *verb* (**waters, watering, watered**)
1 sprinkle or supply something with water.
2 produce tears or saliva, *It makes my mouth water*.
water down dilute.

watercolour *noun* (*plural* **watercolours**)
1 paint made with pigment and water (not oil).
2 a painting done with this kind of paint.

waterfall *noun* (*plural* **waterfalls**)
a stream flowing over the edge of a cliff or large rock.

waterlogged *adjective*
completely soaked or swamped in water. [from *water* + *log*¹ (because water was said to 'lie like a log' in the hold of a waterlogged ship]

waterproof *adjective*
that keeps out water, *a waterproof jacket*.
waterproof *verb*

water-skiing *noun*
the sport of skimming over the surface of water on a pair of flat boards (**water-skis**) while being towed by a motor boat.

watertight *adjective*
1 made or fastened so that water cannot get in or out. 2 that cannot be changed or set aside or proved to be untrue, *a watertight excuse*.

waterworks *noun*
a place with pumping machinery etc. for supplying water to a district.

watery *adjective*
1 like water. 2 full of water. 3 containing too much water.

watt *noun* (*plural* **watts**)
a unit of electric power.
[named after James Watt, a Scottish engineer, who studied energy]

wave *noun* (*plural* **waves**)
1 a ridge moving along the surface of the sea etc. or breaking on the shore. 2 a wave-like curve, e.g. in hair. 3 the wave-like movement by which heat, light, sound, or electricity etc. travels. 4 the action of waving.
wave *verb* (**waves, waving, waved**)
1 move loosely to and fro or up and down.
2 move your hand to and fro as a signal or greeting etc. 3 make a thing wavy. 4 be wavy.
[from Old English]

wavelength *noun* (*plural* **wavelengths**)
the size of a sound wave or electromagnetic wave.

waver *verb* (**wavers, wavering, wavered**)
1 be unsteady; move unsteadily. 2 hesitate; be uncertain. [from Old Norse]

wavy *adjective*
full of waves or curves.
wavily *adverb*, **waviness** *noun*

wax¹ *noun* (*plural* **waxes**)
1 a soft substance that melts easily, used to make candles, crayons, and polish. 2 beeswax.
waxy *adjective*
wax *verb* (**waxes, waxing, waxed**)
coat or polish something with wax.
[from Old English *waex*]

wax² *verb* (**waxes, waxing, waxed**)
1 (of the moon) show a bright area that becomes gradually larger. (The opposite is *wane*.) 2 become stronger or more important.
[from Old English *weaxan*]

waxwork *noun* (*plural* **waxworks**)
a model of a person etc. made in wax.

way *noun* (*plural* **ways**)
1 a line of communication between places, e.g. a path or road. 2 a route or direction. 3 a distance to be travelled. 4 how something is done; a method or style.
5 a respect, *It's a good idea in some ways*. 6 a condition or state, *Things were in a bad way*.
get or **have your own way** make people let you do what you want.
give way 1 collapse. 2 let somebody else move first. 3 yield.
in the way forming an obstacle or hindrance.
no way (*informal*) that is impossible!
under way see *under*.

waylay *verb* (**waylays, waylaying, waylaid**)
lie in wait for a person or people, especially in order to talk to them or rob them.

-ways *suffix*
forms adverbs showing direction or manner (e.g. *sideways*). [from *way*]

wayside *noun*
fall by the wayside fail to continue doing something.

wayward *adjective*
disobedient; wilfully doing what you want.
[from *away* + *-ward*]

we *pronoun*
a word used by a person to refer to himself or herself and another or others.

weak *adjective*
not strong; easy to break, bend, defeat, etc.
weakness *noun* [from Old English]

weaken *verb* (**weakens, weakening, weakened**)
make or become weaker.

weakling *noun* (*plural* **weaklings**)
a weak person or animal.

wealth *noun*
1 a lot of money or property; riches. 2 a large quantity, *The book has a wealth of illustrations.* [from Old English]

wealthy *adjective* (wealthier, wealthiest) having wealth; rich. **wealthiness** *noun*

wean *verb* (weans, weaning, weaned) make a baby take food other than its mother's milk. [from Old English]

weapon *noun* (*plural* weapons) something used to harm or kill people in a battle or fight. **weaponry** *noun*

wear *verb* (wears, wearing, wore, worn)
1 have clothes, jewellery, etc. on your body. 2 damage something by rubbing or using it often; become damaged in this way, *The carpet has worn thin.* 3 last while in use, *It has worn well.*
wearable *adjective*, **wearer** *noun*
wear off 1 be removed by wear or use. 2 become less intense.
wear on pass gradually, *The night wore on.*
wear out 1 use or be used until it becomes weak or useless. 2 exhaust.

weary *adjective* (wearier, weariest)
1 tired. 2 tiring, *It's weary work.*
wearily *adverb*, **weariness** *noun*
weary *verb* (wearies, wearying, wearied) tire. [from Old English]

weasel *noun* (*plural* weasels) a small fierce animal with a slender body and reddish-brown fur. [from Old English]

weather *noun* the rain, snow, wind, sunshine etc. at a particular time or place.
under the weather feeling ill or depressed.
weather *verb* (weathers, weathering, weathered)
1 expose something to the effects of the weather. 2 come through something successfully, *The ship weathered the storm.*

weathercock or **weathervane** *noun* (*plural* weathercocks, weathervanes) a pointer, often shaped like a cockerel, that turns in the wind and shows from which direction it is blowing.

weave *verb* (weaves, weaving, wove, woven)
1 make material or baskets etc. by crossing threads or strips under and over each other. 2 put a story together, *She wove a thrilling tale.* 3 (*past tense & past participle* weaved) twist and turn, *He weaved through the traffic.*
weaver *noun*
weave *noun* (*plural* weaves) a style of weaving, *a loose weave.*

web *noun* (*plural* webs)
1 a cobweb. 2 a network. [from Old English *webb* = a piece of woven cloth]

webbed or **web-footed** *adjective* having toes joined by pieces of skin, *Ducks have webbed feet; they are web-footed.* [from *web*]

wed *verb* (weds, wedding, wedded)
1 marry. 2 unite two different things.

wedding *noun* (*plural* weddings) the ceremony when a man and woman get married.

wedge *noun* (*plural* wedges)
1 a piece of wood or metal etc. that is thick at one end and thin at the other. It is pushed between things to force them apart or prevent something from moving. 2 a wedge-shaped thing.
wedge *verb* (wedges, wedging, wedged)
1 keep something in place with a wedge. 2 pack tightly together, *Ten of us were wedged in the lift.*

weed *noun* (*plural* weeds) a wild plant that grows where it is not wanted.
weed *verb* (weeds, weeding, weeded) remove weeds from the ground. [from Old English *weod*]

weedy *adjective* (weedier, weediest)
1 full of weeds. 2 thin and weak.

week *noun* (*plural* weeks) a period of seven days, especially from Sunday to the following Saturday. [from Old English]

weekday *noun* (*plural* weekdays) a day other than Saturday or Sunday.

weekend *noun* (*plural* weekends) Saturday and Sunday.

weekly *adjective* & *adverb* happening or done once a week.

weep *verb* (weeps, weeping, wept)
1 shed tears; cry. 2 ooze moisture in drops.
weep *noun*, **weepy** *adjective*

weeping *adjective* (of a tree) having drooping branches, *a weeping willow.*

weigh *verb* (weighs, weighing, weighed)
1 measure the weight of something. 2 have a certain weight, *What do you weigh?* 3 be important; have influence, *Her evidence weighed with the jury.*
weigh anchor raise the anchor and start a voyage.
weigh down 1 keep something down by its weight. 2 depress or trouble somebody.
weigh up estimate or assess something. [from Old English]

weight *noun* (*plural* weights)
1 how heavy something is; an object's mass expressed as a number according to a scale of units. (Compare *mass* 3.) 2 a piece of metal of known weight, especially one used on scales to

weigh things. **3** a heavy object. **4** importance or influence.
weighty *adjective*, **weightless** *adjective*
weight *verb* (weights, weighting, weighted)
put a weight on something.

weir (*say* weer) *noun* (*plural* weirs)
a small dam across a river or canal to control the flow of water.

weird *adjective*
very strange; uncanny. **weirdly** *adverb*,
weirdness *noun* [from Old English]

USAGE: When spelling this word, note that the 'e' comes before the 'i', not the other way round.

welcome *noun* (*plural* welcomes)
a greeting or reception, especially a kindly one.
welcome *adjective*
1 that you are glad to receive or see, *a welcome gift.* **2** gladly allowed, *You are welcome to come.*
welcome *verb* (welcomes, welcoming, welcomed)
show that you are pleased when a person or thing arrives. [from *well²* + *come*]

weld *verb* (welds, welding, welded)
1 join pieces of metal or plastic by heating and pressing or hammering them together. **2** unite people or things into a whole.

welfare *noun*
people's health, happiness, and comfort.
[from *well²* + *fare*]

welfare state *noun*
a system in which a country's government provides money to pay for health care, social services, benefits, etc.

well¹ *noun* (*plural* wells)
1 a deep hole dug to bring up water or oil from underground. **2** a deep space, e.g. containing a staircase.
well *verb* (wells, welling, welled)
rise or flow up, *Tears welled up in our eyes.*
[from Old English *wella* = spring of water]

well² *adverb* (better, best)
1 in a good or suitable way, *She swims well.*
2 thoroughly, *Polish it well.* **3** probably or reasonably, *This may well be our last chance.*
well off 1 fairly rich. **2** in a good situation.
well *adjective*
1 in good health, *He is not well.* **2** satisfactory, *All is well.*
[from Old English *wel* = prosperously]

well-being *noun*
good health, happiness, and comfort.

wellingtons *plural noun*
rubber or plastic waterproof boots.
wellies *plural noun* (*informal*)
[named after the first Duke of Wellington, who wore long leather boots]

well-known *adjective*
1 known to many people. **2** known thoroughly.

well-mannered *adjective*
having good manners.

well-meaning *adjective*
having good intentions.

well-read *adjective*
having read a lot of good books.

well-to-do *adjective*
fairly rich.

weren't (*mainly spoken*)
were not.

werewolf *noun* (*plural* werewolves)
(in legends) a person who sometimes changes into a wolf.
[from Old English *wer* = man, + *wolf*]

west *noun*
1 the direction where the sun sets, opposite east. **2** the western part of a country, city, etc.
west *adjective*
1 situated in the west, *the west coast.* **2** coming from the west, *a west wind.*
west *adverb*
towards the west, *We sailed west.*

westerly *adjective*
to or from the west.

western *adjective*
of or in the west.
western *noun* (*plural* westerns)
a film or story about cowboys or American Indians in western North America during the 19th and early 20th centuries.

westward *adjective* & *adverb*
towards the west. **westwards** *adverb*

wet *adjective* (wetter, wettest)
1 soaked or covered in water or other liquid.
2 not yet dry, *wet paint.* **3** rainy, *wet weather.*
wetly *adverb*, **wetness** *noun*
wet *verb* (wets, wetting, wet or wetted)
make a thing wet. [from Old English]

whale *noun* (*plural* whales)
a very large sea animal. **a whale of a** (*informal*)
very good or great, *We had a whale of a time.*

whaling *noun*
hunting whales.

what *adjective*
used to ask the amount or kind of something
(*What kind of bike have you got?*) or to say how strange or great a person or thing is (*What a fool you are!*).
what *pronoun*
1 what thing or things, *What did you say?* **2** the thing that, *This is what you must do.*
what's what (*informal*) which things are important or useful.

whatever *pronoun*
1 anything or everything, *Do whatever you like.*
2 no matter what, *Keep calm, whatever happens.*

whatever *adjective*
of any kind or amount, *Take whatever books you need. There is no doubt whatever.*

wheat *noun*
a cereal plant from which flour is made. **wheaten** *adjective* [from Old English]

wheedle *verb* (wheedles, wheedling, wheedled)
coax. [probably from German]

wheel *noun* (*plural* wheels)
1 a round device that turns on a shaft that passes through its centre. **2** a horizontal revolving disc on which clay is made into a pot.
wheel *verb* (wheels, wheeling, wheeled)
1 push a bicycle or trolley etc. along on its wheels. **2** move in a curve or circle; change direction and face another way, *He wheeled round in astonishment.* [from Old English]

wheelbarrow *noun* (*plural* wheelbarrows)
a small cart with one wheel at the front and legs at the back, pushed by handles.

wheelchair *noun* (*plural* wheelchairs)
a chair on wheels for a person who cannot walk.

wheeze *verb* (wheezes, wheezing, wheezed)
make a hoarse whistling sound as you breathe. **wheeze** *noun*, **wheezy** *adjective*

when *adverb*
at what time; at which time, *When can you come to tea?*
when *conjunction*
1 at the time that, *The bird flew away when I moved.* **2** although; considering that, *Why do you smoke when you know it's dangerous?* [from Old English]

whence *adverb & conjunction*
from where; from which.

whenever *conjunction*
at whatever time; every time, *Whenever I see it, I smile.*

where *adverb & conjunction*
in or to what place or that place, *Where did you put it? Leave it where it is.*
where *pronoun*
what place, *Where does she come from?*

whereabouts *adverb*
in or near what place, *Whereabouts are you going?*
whereabouts *plural noun*
the place where something is, *Do you know the whereabouts of my radio?*

whereas *conjunction*
but in contrast, *Some people enjoy sport, whereas others hate it.*

whereupon *conjunction*
after which; and then.

wherever *adverb*
in or to whatever place.

whet *verb* (whets, whetting, whetted)
whet your appetite stimulate it.
[from Old English *hwettan* = sharpen]

USAGE: Do not confuse with *wet.*

whether *conjunction*
as one possibility; if, *I don't know whether to believe her or not.* [from Old English]

which *adjective*
what particular, *Which way did he go?*
which *pronoun*
1 what person or thing, *Which is your desk?*
2 the person or thing referred to, *The film, which is a western, will be shown on Saturday.* [from Old English]

whichever *pronoun & adjective*
no matter which; any which, *Take whichever you like.*

whiff *noun* (*plural* whiffs)
a puff or slight smell of smoke, gas, etc. [imitating the sound of a puff]

while *conjunction*
1 during the time that; as long as, *Whistle while you work.* **2** although; but, *She is dark, while her sister is fair.*
while *noun*
a period of time, *a long while.*
while *verb* (whiles, whiling, whiled)
while away pass time, *We whiled away the afternoon on the river.* [from Old English]

whim *noun* (*plural* whims)
a sudden wish to do or have something.

whimper *verb* (whimpers, whimpering, whimpered)
cry or whine softly. **whimper** *noun*

whimsical *adjective*
impulsive and playful. **whimsically** *adverb*, **whimsicality** *noun* [from *whim*]

whine *verb* (whines, whining, whined)
1 make a long high miserable cry or a shrill sound. **2** complain in a petty or feeble way. **whine** *noun* [from Old English]

whip *noun* (*plural* whips)
1 a cord or strip of leather fixed to a handle and used for hitting people or animals. **2** an official of a political party in Parliament. **3** a pudding made of whipped cream and fruit or flavouring.
whip *verb* (whips, whipping, whipped)
1 hit a person or animal with a whip. **2** beat cream until it becomes thick. **3** move or take something suddenly, *He whipped out a gun.* **4** (*informal*) steal something.
whip up stir up people's feelings etc., *She whipped up support for her plans.*
[from old German or old Dutch]

whirl *verb* (whirls, whirling, whirled)
turn or spin very quickly. **whirl** *noun*

whirlpool *noun* (*plural* whirlpools)
a whirling current of water.

whirlwind *noun* (*plural* whirlwinds)
a strong wind that whirls round a central point.

whirr *verb* (whirrs, whirring, whirred)
make a continuous buzzing sound. **whirr** *noun* [imitating the sound]

whisk *verb* (whisks, whisking, whisked)
1 move or brush something away quickly and lightly. 2 beat eggs etc. until they are frothy.
whisk *noun* (*plural* whisks)
1 a kitchen tool used for whisking things. 2 a whisking movement. [from Old Norse]

whisker *noun* (*plural* whiskers)
1 a hair of those growing on a man's face, forming a beard or moustache if not shaved off. 2 a long bristle growing near the mouth of a cat etc. **whiskery** *adjective* [from *whisk*]

whisky *noun* (*plural* whiskies)
a strong alcoholic drink. [from Scottish Gaelic *uisge beatha* = water of life]

whisper *verb* (whispers, whispering, whispered)
1 speak very softly. 2 talk secretly.
whisper *noun* [from Old English]

whist *noun*
a card game usually for four people.

whistle *verb* (whistles, whistling, whistled)
make a shrill or musical sound, especially by blowing through your lips.
whistler *noun*
whistle *noun* (*plural* whistles)
1 a whistling sound. 2 a device that makes a shrill sound when air or steam is blown through it. [from Old English]

White *noun* (*plural* Whites)
a person with a light-coloured skin.
White *adjective*

white *noun* (*plural* whites)
1 the very lightest colour, like snow or salt. 2 the transparent substance (*albumen*) round the yolk of an egg, which turns white when it is cooked.
white *adjective*
1 of the colour white. 2 very pale from the effects of illness or fear etc. 3 (of coffee) with milk.
whiteness *noun*

white elephant *noun* (*plural* white elephants)
a useless possession.

white-hot *adjective*
extremely hot; so hot that heated metal looks white.

white lie *noun* (*plural* white lies)
a harmless or trivial lie that you tell in order to avoid hurting someone's feelings.

whiten *verb* (whitens, whitening, whitened)
make or become whiter.

whitewash *noun*
1 a white liquid containing lime or powdered chalk, used for painting walls and ceilings etc. 2 concealing mistakes or other unpleasant facts so that someone will not be punished.
whitewash *verb*

whither *adverb* & *conjunction* (*old use*)
to what place. [from Old English]

USAGE: Do not confuse with *wither*.

whittle *verb* (whittles, whittling, whittled)
1 shape wood by trimming thin slices off the surface. 2 reduce something by removing various things from it, *whittle down the cost*. [from Old English]

whiz *verb* (whizzes, whizzing, whizzed)
1 move very quickly. 2 sound like something rushing through the air.

who *pronoun*
which person or people; the particular person or people, *This is the boy who stole the apples*. [from Old English]

whoever *pronoun*
1 any or every person who. 2 no matter who.

whole *adjective*
1 complete. 2 not injured or broken.
whole *noun*
1 the full amount. 2 a complete thing.
on the whole considering everything; mainly.

wholemeal *adjective*
made from the whole grain of wheat etc. [from *whole* + *meal*^{2}]

whole number *noun* (*plural* whole numbers)
a number without fractions.

wholesale *noun*
selling goods in large quantities to be resold by others. (Compare *retail*.) **wholesaler** *noun*
wholesale *adjective* & *adverb*
1 on a large scale; including everybody or everything, *wholesale destruction*. 2 in the wholesale trade.

wholesome *adjective*
good for health; healthy, *wholesome food*.
wholesomeness *noun*
[from an old sense of *whole* = healthy, + *-some*]

wholly *adverb*
completely or entirely.

whom *pronoun*
the form of *who* used when it is the object of a verb or comes after a preposition, as in *the boy whom I saw* or *to whom we spoke*.

whoop (*say* woop) *noun* (*plural* whoops)
a loud cry of excitement. **whoop** *verb*

whooping cough (*say* hoop-ing) *noun*
an infectious disease that causes spasms of coughing and gasping for breath. [because of the sound the person makes gasping for breath]

whopper noun (plural **whoppers**) (slang)
something very large.
[from Middle English whop = to strike or beat]

whopping adjective (slang)
very large or remarkable, a whopping lie.
[from whopper]

who's (mainly spoken)
who is; who has.

USAGE: Do not confuse with whose.

whose pronoun
belonging to what person or persons; of whom;
of which, Whose house is that?
[from Old English]

USAGE: Do not confuse with who's.

why adverb
for what reason or purpose; the particular
reason on account of which, This is why I came.
[from Old English]

wick noun (plural **wicks**)
1 the string that goes through the middle of a
candle and is lit. 2 the strip of material that
you light in a lamp or heater etc. that uses oil.
[from Old English]

wicked adjective
1 morally bad or cruel. 2 very bad; severe, a
wicked blow. 3 mischievous, a wicked smile.
wickedly adverb, **wickedness** noun
[from Old English wicca = witch]

wicket noun (plural **wickets**)
1 a set of three stumps and two bails used in
cricket. 2 the part of a cricket ground between
the wickets.
[via old French from Germanic]

wicketkeeper noun (plural **wicketkeepers**)
the fielder in cricket who stands behind the
batsman's wicket.

wide adjective
1 measuring a lot from side to side; not
narrow. 2 measuring from side to side, The
cloth is one metre wide. 3 covering a great
range, a wide knowledge of birds. 4 fully open,
staring with wide eyes. 5 far from the target,
The shot was wide of the mark. **widely** adverb,
wideness noun
wide adverb
1 widely. 2 completely or fully, wide awake.
3 far from the target, The shot went wide.
[from Old English]

widen verb (widens, widening, widened)
make or become wider.

widespread adjective
existing in many places or over a wide area, a
widespread belief.

widow noun (plural **widows**)
a woman whose husband has died.
widowed adjective [from Old English]

widower noun (plural **widowers**)
a man whose wife has died. [from widow]

width noun (plural **widths**)
how wide something is; wideness.
[from wide]

wield verb (wields, wielding, wielded)
hold something and use it, wielding a sword.
[from Old English]

wife noun (plural **wives**)
the woman to whom a man is married.
[from Old English wif = woman]

wig noun (plural **wigs**)
a covering made of real or artificial hair, worn
on the head.
[short for periwig, from old French perruque]

wigwam noun (plural **wigwams**)
a tent formerly used by Native Americans,
made by fastening skins or mats over poles.
[a Native American word]

wild adjective
1 living or growing in its natural state, not
looked after by people. 2 not cultivated, a wild
landscape. 3 not civilized, the Wild West. 4 not
controlled; very violent or excited. 5 very
foolish or unreasonable, these wild ideas.
wildly adverb, **wildness** noun [from Old English]

wilderness noun (plural **wildernesses**)
a wild uncultivated area; a desert. [from Old
English wild deor = wild deer, + -ness]

wildlife noun
wild animals.

wilful adjective
1 obstinately determined to do what you want,
a wilful child. 2 deliberate, wilful murder.
wilfully adverb, **wilfulness** noun
[from will² + -ful]

will¹ auxiliary verb
used to express the future tense, questions, or
promises. [from Old English wyllan]

USAGE: See the entry for shall.

will² noun (plural **wills**)
1 the mental power to decide and control what
you do. 2 a desire; a chosen decision, I went to
the party against my will. 3 determination to do
something, They set to work with a will. 4 a
written statement of how a person's
possessions are to be disposed of after his or
her death.
at will whenever you like, You can come and go
at will.
will verb (wills, willing, willed)
use your will-power; influence something by
doing this, I was willing you to win!
[from Old English willa]

willing adjective
ready and happy to do what is wanted.
willingly adverb, **willingness** noun
[from will²]

willow *noun* (*plural* **willows**)
a tree or shrub with flexible branches, usually growing near water.

will-power *noun*
strength of mind to control what you do.

willy-nilly *adverb*
whether you want to or not.
[from *will I, nill I* (= will I, will I not)]

wilt *verb* (**wilts, wilting, wilted**)
lose freshness or strength; droop.
[originally dialect; probably from old Dutch]

wily (*say* wy-lee) *adjective*
cunning or crafty. **wiliness** *noun*
[from *wile*]

win *verb* (**wins, winning, won**)
1 defeat your opponents in a battle, game, or contest. **2** get or achieve something by a victory or by using effort or skill etc., *She won the prize.*
win *noun* (*plural* **wins**)
a victory. [from Old English]

wince *verb* (**winces, wincing, winced**)
make a slight movement because of pain or embarrassment etc.
[from old French]

wind¹ (rhymes with *tinned*) *noun* (*plural* **winds**)
1 a current of air. **2** gas in the stomach or intestines that makes you feel uncomfortable. **3** breath used for a purpose, e.g. for running or speaking. **4** the wind instruments of an orchestra.
get or **have the wind up** (*slang*) feel frightened.
wind *verb* (**winds, winding, winded**)
put a person out of breath, *The climb had winded us.* [from Old English *wind*]

wind² (rhymes with *find*) *verb* (**winds, winding, wound**)
1 go or turn something in twists, curves, or circles. **2** wind up a watch or clock etc.
winder *noun*
wind up 1 make a clock or watch work by tightening its spring. **2** close a business. **3** (*informal*) end up in a place or condition, *He wound up in jail.*
[from Old English *windan*]

windfall *noun* (*plural* **windfalls**)
1 a piece of unexpected good luck, especially a sum of money. **2** a fruit blown off a tree by the wind.

wind instrument *noun* (*plural* **wind instruments**)
a musical instrument played by blowing, e.g. a trumpet.

windmill *noun* (*plural* **windmills**)
a mill worked by the wind turning its sails.

window *noun* (*plural* **windows**)
1 an opening in a wall or roof etc. to let in light and often air, usually filled with glass. **2** the

glass in this opening. **3** an area on a VDU screen used for a particular purpose.
[from Old Norse *vind* = wind, air + *auga* = eye]

windpipe *noun* (*plural* **windpipes**)
the tube by which air passes from the throat to the lungs.

windscreen *noun* (*plural* **windscreens**)
the window at the front of a motor vehicle.

windy *adjective*
with much wind, *It's windy outside.*

wine *noun* (*plural* **wines**)
1 an alcoholic drink made from grapes or other plants. **2** dark red colour.
[same origin as *vine*]

wing *noun* (*plural* **wings**)
1 one of the pair of parts of a bird, bat, or insect, that it uses for flying. **2** one of the pair of long flat parts that stick out from the side of an aircraft and support it while it flies. **3** a part that sticks out at one end or side of something; **the wings** the sides of a theatre stage out of sight of the audience. **4** the part of a motor vehicle's body above a wheel. **5** a player at either end of the forward line in football or hockey etc. **6** a section of a political party, with more extreme opinions than the others.
on the wing flying.
take wing fly away.
wing *verb* (**wings, winging, winged**)
1 fly; travel by means of wings, *The bird winged its way home.* **2** wound a bird in the wing or a person in the arm.

winged *adjective*
having wings.

wink *verb* (**winks, winking, winked**)
1 close and open your eye quickly, especially as a signal to someone. **2** (of a light) flicker or twinkle.
wink *noun* (*plural* **winks**)
1 the action of winking. **2** a very short period of sleep, *I didn't sleep a wink.*

winkle *verb* (**winkles, winkling, winkled**)
winkle out extract; prise a thing out, *I managed to winkle out some information.*

winner *noun* (*plural* **winners**)
1 a person or animal etc. that wins.
2 something very successful, *Her latest book is a winner.*

winnings *plural noun*
money won.

winter *noun* (*plural* **winters**)
the coldest season of the year, between autumn and spring.
wintry *adjective*

wipe *verb* (**wipes, wiping, wiped**)
dry or clean something by rubbing it.
wiper *noun*
wipe out 1 cancel, *wipe out the debt.* **2** destroy something completely.

wire *noun* (*plural* **wires**)
1 a strand or thin flexible rod of metal. 2 a piece of wire used to carry electric current. 3 a fence etc. made from wire. 4 a telegram.
wire *verb* (**wires, wiring, wired**)
1 fasten or strengthen something with wire. 2 fit or connect something with wires to carry electric current.

wireless *noun* (*plural* **wirelesses**) (*old use*)
a radio. [because it does not need wires to conduct sound]

wiry *adjective*
1 like wire. 2 lean and strong.

wisdom *noun*
1 being wise. 2 wise sayings.
[from Old English *wis* = wise, + *-dom*]

wisdom tooth *noun* (*plural* **wisdom teeth**)
a molar tooth that may grow at the back of the jaw of a person aged about 20 or more.

wise *adjective*
knowing or understanding many things; judging well. **wisely** *adverb*
[from Old English *wis*]

-wise *suffix*
forms adverbs meaning 'in this manner or direction' (e.g. *otherwise, clockwise*).
[from Old English *wise* = way or manner]

wish *verb* (**wishes, wishing, wished**)
1 feel or say that you would like to have or do something or would like something to happen. 2 say that you hope someone will get something, *Wish me luck!*
wish *noun* (*plural* **wishes**)
1 something you wish for; a desire. 2 the action of wishing, *Make a wish when you blow out the candles.* [from Old English]

wishbone *noun* (*plural* **wishbones**)
a forked bone between the neck and breast of a bird (sometimes pulled apart by two people; the person who gets the bigger part can make a wish).

wishful thinking *noun*
believing something because you wish it were true rather than on the facts.

wisp *noun* (*plural* **wisps**)
1 a few strands of hair or bits of straw etc. 2 a small streak of smoke or cloud etc.
wispy *adjective* [origin unknown]

wistful *adjective*
sadly longing for something. **wistfully** *adverb*, **wistfulness** *noun*
[from Middle English *whist* = quiet, + *-ful*]

wit *noun* (*plural* **wits**)
1 intelligence or cleverness, *Use your wits.* 2 a clever kind of humour. 3 a witty person.
at your wits' end not knowing what to do.
[from Old English]

witch *noun* (*plural* **witches**)
a person, especially a woman, who uses magic to do things. [from Old English]

witchcraft *noun*
the use of magic, especially for evil purposes.

witch-hunt *noun* (*plural* **witch-hunts**)
a campaign to find and punish people who hold views that are considered to be unacceptable or dangerous.

with *preposition*
used to indicate 1 being in the company or care etc. of (*Come with me*), 2 having (*a man with a beard*), 3 using (*Hit it with a hammer*), 4 because of (*shaking with laughter*), 5 feeling or showing (*We heard it with pleasure*), 6 towards or concerning (*I was angry with him*), 7 in opposition to; against (*Don't argue with your father*), 8 being separated from (*We had to part with it*). [from Old English]

withdraw *verb* (**withdraws, withdrawing, withdrew, withdrawn**)
1 take back or away; remove, *She withdrew money from the bank.* 2 go away from a place or people, *The troops withdrew from the frontier.*
withdrawal *noun*
[from Old English *with-* = away, back, + *draw*]

wither *verb* (**withers, withering, withered**)
1 shrivel or wilt. 2 make something shrivel or wilt. [a different spelling of *weather*]

USAGE: Do not confuse with *whither*.

withering *adjective*
scornful or sarcastic, *a withering remark.*

within *preposition* & *adverb*
inside; not beyond something.

without *preposition*
1 not having, *without food.* 2 free from, *without fear.* 3 (*old use*) outside, *without the city wall.*
without *adverb* (*old use*)
outside, *We looked at the house from within and without.* [from Old English]

withstand *verb* (**withstands, withstanding, withstood**)
endure something successfully; resist.
[from Old English *with-* = against, + *stand*]

witness *noun* (*plural* **witnesses**)
1 a person who sees or hears something happen, *There were no witnesses to the accident.* 2 a person who gives evidence in a lawcourt.
witness *verb* (**witnesses, witnessing, witnessed**)
1 be a witness of something, *Did anyone witness the accident?* 2 sign a document to confirm that it is genuine. [from *wit*]

witticism *noun* (*plural* **witticisms**)
a witty remark.

witty *adjective* (**wittier, wittiest**)
clever and amusing; full of wit.
wittily *adverb*, **wittiness** *noun*

wizard *noun* (*plural* **wizards**)
1 a male witch; a magician. **2** a person with amazing abilities. **wizardry** *noun*
[from an old sense of *wise* = a wise person]

wobble *verb* (**wobbles, wobbling, wobbled**)
stand or move unsteadily; shake slightly.
wobble *noun*, **wobbly** *adjective*

woe *noun* (*plural* **woes**)
1 sorrow. **2** misfortune. **woeful** *adjective*,
woefully *adverb* [from Old English]

woebegone *adjective*
looking unhappy. [from *woe* + an old word *bego*
= attack, surround]

wok *noun* (*plural* **woks**)
a Chinese cooking pan shaped like a large
bowl. [from Chinese]

wolf *noun* (*plural* **wolves**)
a fierce wild animal of the dog family.
wolf *verb* (**wolfs, wolfing, wolfed**)
eat something greedily. [from Old English]

woman *noun* (*plural* **women**)
a grown-up female human being.
womanhood *noun* [from Old English]

womanly *adjective*
having qualities that are thought to be typical
of women.

womb (*say* woom) *noun* (*plural* **wombs**)
the hollow organ in a female's body where
babies develop before they are born.
[from Old English]

women's lib or **women's liberation** *noun*
the freedom of women to have the same rights,
opportunities, and status as men.

wonder *noun* (*plural* **wonders**)
1 a feeling of surprise and admiration or
curiosity. **2** something that causes this feeling;
a marvel.
no wonder it is not surprising.
wonder *verb* (**wonders, wondering, wondered**)
1 feel that you want to know; try to form an
opinion, *We are still wondering what to do next.*
2 feel wonder. [from Old English]

wonderful *adjective*
marvellous or excellent.
wonderfully *adverb*

won't (*mainly spoken*)
will not.

woo *verb* (**woos, wooing, wooed**) (*old use*)
1 court a woman. **2** seek someone's favour.
wooer *noun* [from Old English]

wood *noun* (*plural* **woods**)
1 the substance of which trees are made.
2 many trees growing close together.

wooded *adjective*
covered with growing trees.

wooden *adjective*
1 made of wood. **2** stiff and showing no
expression or liveliness. **woodenly** *adverb*

woodpecker *noun* (*plural* **woodpeckers**)
a bird that taps tree trunks with its beak to
find insects.

woodwind *noun*
wind instruments that are usually made of
wood, e.g. the clarinet and oboe.

woodwork *noun*
1 making things out of wood. **2** things made
out of wood.

woody *adjective*
1 like wood; consisting of wood. **2** full of trees.

wool *noun* (*plural* **wools**)
1 the thick soft hair of sheep and goats etc.
2 thread or cloth made from this.

woollen *adjective*
made of wool.

woolly *adjective*
1 covered with wool or wool-like hair. **2** like
wool; woollen. **3** not thinking clearly; vague or
confused, *woolly ideas.* **woolliness** *noun*

word *noun* (*plural* **words**)
1 a set of sounds or letters that has a meaning,
and when written or printed has no spaces
between the letters. **2** a promise, *He kept his
word.* **3** a command or spoken signal, *Run
when I give the word.* **4** a message; information,
We sent word of our safe arrival.
word for word in exactly the same words.
word *verb* (**words, wording, worded**)
express something in words, *Word the question
carefully.*

word class *noun* (*plural* **word classes**)
any of the groups into which words are divided
in grammar (noun, pronoun, adjective, verb,
adverb, preposition, conjunction, interjection).
Also know as part of speech.

wording *noun*
the way something is worded.

word of honour *noun*
a solemn promise.

word-perfect *adjective*
having memorized every word perfectly, *He
was word-perfect at the rehearsal.*

word processor *noun* (*plural* **word processors**)
a kind of computer used for editing and
printing words typed into it.

wordy *adjective*
using too many words; not concise.

wore *past tense* of **wear**.

work *noun* (*plural* **works**)
1 something you have to do that needs effort or
energy, *Digging is hard work.* **2** the use of
effort or energy to do something (contrasted
with *play* or *recreation*). **3** a job; employment.
4 something produced by work, *The teacher
marked our work.* **5** a piece of writing,
painting, music, etc., *the works of William
Shakespeare.*

at work working.

out of work having no work; unable to find paid employment.

work *verb* (**works, working, worked**)
1 do work. 2 have a job; be employed, *She works in a bank.* 3 act or operate correctly or successfully, *Is the lift working?* 4 make something act; operate, *Can you work the lift?* 5 shape or press etc., *Work the mixture into a paste.* 6 make a way; pass, *The grub works its way into timber.*

work out 1 find an answer by thinking or calculating. 2 have a particular result.

work up make people become excited; arouse.

workable *adjective*
that can be used or will work.

worker *noun* (*plural* **workers**)
1 a person who works. 2 a member of the working class. 3 a bee or ant etc. that does the work in a hive or colony but does not produce eggs.

working class *noun* (*plural* **working classes**)
people who work for wages, especially in manual or industrial work.

workman *noun* (*plural* **workmen**)
a man employed to do manual labour; a worker.

workmanship *noun*
a person's skill in working; the result of this.

work of art *noun* (*plural* **works of art**)
a fine picture, building, etc.

workshop *noun* (*plural* **workshops**)
a place where things are made or mended.

world *noun* (*plural* **worlds**)
1 the earth with all its countries and peoples. 2 a planet, *creatures from another world.* 3 the people or things belonging to a certain activity, *the world of sport.* 4 a very great amount, *It will do him a world of good. She is worlds better today.*

worm *noun* (*plural* **worms**)
1 an animal with a long small soft rounded or flat body and no backbone or limbs. 2 an unimportant or unpleasant person. **wormy** *adjective*

worm *verb* (**worms, worming, wormed**)
move along by wriggling or crawling.

worm out gradually get someone to tell you something by constantly and cleverly questioning them, *We eventually managed to worm the truth out of them.*

worn *past participle* of **wear.**

worn-out *adjective*
1 exhausted. 2 damaged by too much use.

worried *adjective*
feeling or showing worry.

worry *verb* (**worries, worrying, worried**)
1 be troublesome to someone; make a person feel slightly afraid. 2 feel anxious. 3 hold something in the teeth and shake it, *The dog was worrying a rat.* **worrier** *noun*

worry *noun* (*plural* **worries**)
1 the condition of worrying; being uneasy. 2 something that makes a person worry.

worse *adjective & adverb*
more bad or more badly; less good or less well.
[from Old English; related to *war*]

worship *verb* (**worships, worshipping, worshipped**)
1 give praise or respect to God or a god. 2 love or respect a person or thing greatly.
worshipper *noun*

worship *noun* (*plural* **worships**)
1 worshipping; religious ceremonies. 2 a title of respect for a mayor or certain magistrates, *his worship the mayor.*
[from Old English *weorth* = worth, + *-ship*]

worst *adjective & adverb*
most bad or most badly; least good or least well.
[from Old English]

worth *adjective*
1 having a certain value, *This stamp is worth £100.* 2 deserving something; good or important enough for something, *That book is worth reading.*

worthwhile *adjective*
important or good enough to deserve the time or effort needed, *a worthwhile job.*
[from *worth the while* = worth the time]

worthy *adjective*
having great merit; deserving respect or support, *a worthy cause.* **worthiness** *noun*
worthy of deserving, *This charity is worthy of your support.*
[from *worth*]

would *auxiliary verb*
used 1 as the past tense of *will*[1] (*We said we would do it*), in questions (*Would you like to come?*), and in polite requests (*Would you come in, please?*), 2 with *I* and *we* and the verbs *like, prefer, be glad,* etc. (e.g. *I would like to come, we would be glad to help*), where the strictly correct use is *should,* 3 of something to be expected (*That's just what he would do!*).

USAGE: For sense 2, see the note on *should* 4.

would-be *adjective*
wanting or pretending to be, *a would-be comedian.*

wouldn't (*mainly spoken*)
would not.

wound[1] (*say* woond) *noun* (*plural* **wounds**)
1 an injury done by a cut, stab, or hit. 2 a hurt to a person's feelings.

wound *verb* (**wounds, wounding, wounded**)
1 cause a wound to a person or animal. 2 hurt a person's feelings, *She was wounded by these remarks.*

wound[2] (*say* wownd) *past tense* of **wind**[2].

wrap *verb* (**wraps, wrapping, wrapped**)
put paper or cloth etc. round something as a covering.

wrapper *noun* (*plural* **wrappers**)
a piece of paper etc. wrapped round something.

wreath (*say* reeth) *noun* (*plural* **wreaths**)
1 flowers or leaves etc. fastened into a circle, *wreaths of holly.* 2 a curving line of mist or smoke.
[from Old English *writhan* = writhe]

wreathe (*say* reeth) *verb* (**wreathes, wreathing, wreathed**)
1 surround or decorate something with a wreath. 2 cover, *Their faces were wreathed in smiles.* 3 move in a curve, *Smoke wreathed upwards.*
[from *wreath* and *writhe*]

wreck *verb* (**wrecks, wrecking, wrecked**)
damage or ruin something so badly that it cannot be used again.
wreck *noun* (*plural* **wrecks**)
1 a wrecked ship or building or car etc. 2 a person who is left very weak, *a nervous wreck.* 3 the wrecking of something.

wreckage *noun*
the pieces of a wreck.

wren *noun* (*plural* **wrens**)
a very small brown bird.

wrench *verb* (**wrenches, wrenching, wrenched**)
twist or pull something violently.
wrench *noun* (*plural* **wrenches**)
1 a wrenching movement. 2 pain caused by parting, *Leaving home was a great wrench.* 3 an adjustable tool rather like a spanner, used for gripping and turning bolts, nuts, etc.
[from Old English]

wrestle *verb* (**wrestles, wrestling, wrestled**)
1 fight by grasping your opponent and trying to throw him or her to the ground. 2 struggle with a problem etc. **wrestle** *noun*, **wrestler** *noun*
[from Old English]

wretch *noun* (*plural* **wretches**)
1 a person who is very unhappy or who you pity. 2 a person who is disliked; a rascal.
[from Old English]

wretched *adjective*
1 miserable or unhappy. 2 of bad quality. 3 not satisfactory; causing a nuisance, *This wretched car won't start.* **wretchedly** *adverb*,
wretchedness *noun* [from *wretch*]

wriggle *verb* (**wriggles, wriggling, wriggled**)
move with short twisting movements.
wriggle *noun*, **wriggly** *adjective*
wriggle out of avoid work or blame etc. cunningly.

wring *verb* (**wrings, wringing, wrung**)
1 twist and squeeze a wet thing to get water etc. out of it. 2 squeeze something firmly or forcibly. 3 get something by a great effort, *We wrung a promise out of him.* **wring** *noun*
wringing wet so wet that water can be squeezed out of it.

wrinkle *noun* (*plural* **wrinkles**)
1 a small furrow or ridge in the skin. 2 a small crease in something.
wrinkle *verb* (**wrinkles, wrinkling, wrinkled**)
make wrinkles in something; form wrinkles.
[origin unknown]

wrist *noun* (*plural* **wrists**)
the joint that connects the hand and arm.

wristwatch *noun* (*plural* **wristwatches**)
a watch for wearing on the wrist.

write *verb* (**writes, writing, wrote, written**)
1 put letters or words etc. on paper or another surface. 2 be the author or composer of something, *write books* or *music.* 3 send a letter to somebody. **writer** *noun*, **writing** *noun*
[from Old English]

writhe *verb* (**writhes, writhing, writhed**)
1 twist your body because of pain. 2 wriggle. 3 suffer because of great shame.

wrong *adjective*
1 incorrect; not true, *the wrong answer.* 2 morally bad; unfair; unjust, *It is wrong to cheat.* 3 not working properly, *There's something wrong with the engine.*
wrongly *adverb*, **wrongness** *noun*
wrong *adverb*
wrongly, *You guessed wrong.*
wrong *noun* (*plural* **wrongs**)
something morally wrong; an injustice.
in the wrong having done or said something wrong.
wrong *verb* (**wrongs, wronging, wronged**)
do wrong to someone; treat a person unfairly.
[probably from Old Norse]

wrought *adjective*
(of metal) worked by being beaten out or shaped by hammering or rolling etc., *wrought iron.*
[the old past participle of *work*]

wry *adjective* (**wryer, wryest**)
1 slightly mocking or ironic, *a wry smile.* 2 twisted or bent out of shape. (Compare *awry.*)
wryly *adverb*, **wryness** *noun*

Xx

-xion *suffix* see -ion.

Xmas *noun*
Christmas.
[the X represents the Greek letter called chi, the first letter of *Christos* = Christ]

X-ray *noun* (*plural* X-rays)
a photograph or examination of the inside of something, especially a part of the body, made by a kind of radiation (called **X-rays**) that can penetrate solid things.
X-ray *verb* (X-rays, X-raying, X-rayed)
make an X-ray of something.

xylophone (*say* zy-lo-fohn) *noun* (*plural* xylophones)
a musical instrument made of wooden bars that you hit with small hammers.
[from Greek *xylon* = wood + *phone* = sound]

Yy

-y^1 and **-ie** *suffixes*
form names showing fondness, or diminutives (e.g. *daddy, pussy*).
[origin unknown]

-y^2 *suffix*
forms adjectives meaning 'to do with' or 'like' (e.g. *angry, horsy, messy, sticky*).
[from Old English]

yacht (*say* yot) *noun* (*plural* yachts)
1 a sailing boat used for racing or cruising. 2 a private ship. **yachting** *noun*, **yachtsman** *noun*, **yachtswoman** *noun*
[from Dutch *jaghtschip* = fast pirate ship]

yak *noun* (*plural* yaks)
an ox with long hair, found in central Asia.
[from Tibetan]

yank *verb* (yanks, yanking, yanked) (*informal*)
pull something strongly and suddenly.
yank *noun* [origin unknown]

Yankee *noun* (*plural* Yankees)
an American, especially of the northern USA.
[probably from Dutch *Janke* = Johnny]

yap *verb* (yaps, yapping, yapped)
bark shrilly. yap *noun*

yard^1 *noun* (*plural* yards)
1 a measure of length, 36 inches or about 91 centimetres. 2 a long pole stretched out from a mast to support a sail.
[from Old English *gerd*]

yard^2 *noun* (*plural* yards)
an enclosed area beside a building or used for a certain kind of work, *a timber yard*.
[from Old English *geard*]

yarn *noun* (*plural* yarns)
1 thread spun by twisting fibres together, used in knitting etc. 2 (*informal*) a tale or story.
[from Old English]

yawn *verb* (yawns, yawning, yawned)
1 open the mouth wide and breathe in deeply when feeling sleepy or bored. 2 form a wide opening, *A pit yawned in front of us*. yawn *noun*
[from Old English]

ye *pronoun* (*old use*, in speaking to two or more people)
you. [from Old English]

year *noun* (*plural* years)
1 the time the earth takes to go right round the sun, about 365¼ days. 2 the time from 1 January to 31 December; any period of twelve months. **yearly** *adjective* & *adverb*

yearn *verb* (yearns, yearning, yearned)
long for something. [from Old English]

yeast *noun*
a substance that causes alcohol and carbon dioxide to form as it develops, used in making beer and wine and in baking bread etc.
[from Old English]

yell *verb* (yells, yelling, yelled)
give a loud cry; shout. yell *noun*

yellow *noun* (*plural* yellows)
the colour of buttercups and ripe lemons.
yellow *adjective*
1 of yellow colour. 2 (*informal*) cowardly.
yellowness *noun*
[from Old English]

yellow pages *plural noun*
a special telephone directory giving addresses and telephone numbers of businesses, arranged according to what services they provide.

yelp *verb* (yelps, yelping, yelped)
give a shrill bark or cry. yelp *noun*
[from Old English *gielpan* = to boast]

yen^1 *noun* (*plural* yen)
a unit of money in Japan.
[from Japanese *en* = round]

yen^2 *noun* (*plural* yens)
a longing for something. [from Chinese]

yes *adverb*
used to agree to something (= the statement is correct) or as an answer (= I am here).
[from Old English]

yesterday *noun* & *adverb*
the day before today. [from Old English]

yet *adverb*
1 up to this time; by this time, *The post hasn't come yet.* 2 eventually, *I'll get even with him yet!* 3 in addition; even, *She became yet more excited.*
yet *conjunction*
nevertheless, *It is strange, yet it is true.*

yew *noun* (*plural* **yews**)
an evergreen tree with dark green needle-like leaves and red berries.

yield *verb* (**yields, yielding, yielded**)
1 give in or surrender. 2 agree to do what is asked or ordered; give way, *He yielded to persuasion.* 3 produce as a crop or as profit etc.

yoga (*say* yoh-ga) *noun*
a Hindu system of meditation and self-control. [Sanskrit, literally = union]

yoghurt (*say* yog-ert) *noun*
milk thickened by the action of certain bacteria, giving it a sharp taste. [from Turkish]

yoke *noun* (*plural* **yokes**)
1 a curved piece of wood put across the necks of animals pulling a cart or plough etc. 2 a shaped piece of wood fitted across a person's shoulders, with a pail or load hung at each end. 3 a close-fitting upper part of a piece of clothing, from which the rest hangs.
yoke *verb* (**yokes, yoking, yoked**)
harness or join things by means of a yoke. [from Old English]

USAGE: Do not confuse with *yolk*.

yolk (rhymes with *coke*) *noun* (*plural* **yolks**)
the round yellow part inside an egg. [from Old English *geolu* = yellow]

USAGE: Do not confuse with *yoke*.

yonder *adjective* & *adverb*
over there.

you *pronoun*
1 the person or people being spoken to, *Who are you?* 2 anyone or everyone; one, *You can't tell what will happen next.*

young *adjective*
having lived or existed for only a short time; not old.

youngster *noun* (*plural* **youngsters**)
a young person; a child.

your *adjective*
belonging to you. [from Old English]

USAGE: Do not confuse with *you're*.

you're (*mainly spoken*)
you are.

USAGE: Do not confuse with *your*.

yours *possessive pronoun*
belonging to you.
Yours faithfully, Yours sincerely, Yours truly ways of ending a letter before you sign it. (*Yours faithfully* and *Yours truly* are more formal than *Yours sincerely*.)

USAGE: It is incorrect to write *your's*.

yourself *pronoun* (*plural* **yourselves**)
you and nobody else. (Compare *herself*.)

youth *noun* (*plural* **youths**)
1 being young; the time when you are young. 2 a young man. 3 young people.
youthful *adjective*, **youthfulness** *noun*

youth hostel *noun* (*plural* **youth hostels**)
a place, often in the countryside, where young people can stay cheaply when they are on holiday.

yo-yo *noun* (*plural* **yo-yos**)
a round wooden or plastic toy that moves up and down on a string that you hold. [probably from a language spoken in the Philippines]

Yule *noun* (*old use*)
the Christmas festival, also called **Yuletide**.

Zz

zap *verb* (**zaps, zapping, zapped**) (*slang*)
1 attack or destroy something forcefully. 2 change quickly from one section of a videotape etc. to another. [imitating the sound of a blow or shot]

zeal *noun*
enthusiasm or keenness.
zealous (*say* zel-us) *adjective*, **zealously** *adverb* [from Greek]

zebra (*say* zeb-ra) *noun* (*plural* **zebras**)
an African animal of the horse family, with black and white stripes all over its body. [Italian, Spanish, or Portuguese]

zebra crossing *noun* (*plural* **zebra crossings**)
a place for pedestrians to cross a road safely, marked with broad white stripes.

zero *noun* (*plural* **zeros**)
1 nought; the figure 0. 2 the point marked 0 on a thermometer etc. [from Arabic *sifr* = cipher]

zero hour *noun*
the time when something is planned to start.

zest *noun*
great enjoyment or interest.
zestful *adjective*, **zestfully** *adverb*

zigzag *noun* (*plural* **zigzags**)
a line or route that turns sharply from side to side.

zigzag *verb* (**zigzags, zigzagging, zigzagged**)
move in a zigzag.
[via French from German]

zinc *noun*
a white metal. [from German]

zip *noun* (*plural* **zips**)
1 a zip fastener. **2** a sharp sound like a bullet going through the air. **3** liveliness or vigour.
zippy *adjective*
zip *verb* (**zips, zipping, zipped**)
1 fasten something with a zip fastener. **2** move quickly with a sharp sound.
[imitating the sound]

zip fastener or **zipper** *noun* (*plural* **zip fasteners, zippers**)
a fastener consisting of two strips of material, each with rows of small teeth that interlock when a sliding tab brings them together.

zodiac (*say* zoh-dee-ak) *noun*
a strip of sky where the sun, moon, and main planets are found, divided into twelve equal parts (called **signs of the zodiac**), each named after a constellation.
[from Greek *zoidion* = image of an animal]

zone *noun* (*plural* **zones**)
an area of a special kind or for a particular purpose, *a war zone*; *a no-parking zone*.
[Greek, = girdle]

zoo *noun* (*plural* **zoos**)
a place where wild animals are kept so that people can look at them or study them.
[short for *zoological gardens*]

zoology (*say* zoh-ol-o-jee) *noun*
the study of animals. **zoological** *adjective*,
zoologist *noun*
[from Greek *zoion* = animal, + *-logy*]

zoom *verb* (**zooms, zooming, zoomed**)
1 move very quickly, especially with a buzzing sound. **2** rise quickly, *Prices had zoomed*.
zoom *noun*
[imitating the sound]

Appendices

APPENDIX 1

Prefixes and suffixes

Prefixes

A prefix is placed at the beginning of a word to change its meaning or to form a new word. The following prefixes have entries at their alphabetical places in the dictionary.

a-	apo-	contra-	equi-	infra-	octa-	pro-	sur-
ab-	ar-	cor-	eu-	inter-	octo-	proto-	sus-
abs-	arch-	counter-	ex-	intra-	of-	pseudo-	syl-
ac-	as-	cross-	extra-	intro-	omni-	psycho-	sym-
ad-	at-	de-	for-	ir-	op-	quadri-	syn-
aero-	aut-	deca-	fore-	iso-	ortho-	quasi-	tele-
af-	auto-	deci-	geo-	kilo-	out-	radio-	tetra-
Afro-	be-	demi-	hecto-	mal-	over-	re-	thermo-
ag-	bene-	di-	hepta-	mega-	pan-	retro-	trans-
al-	bi-	dia-	hetero-	micro-	para-	se-	tri-
ambi-	bio-	dif-	hexa-	milli-	penta-	self-	ultra-
amphi-	cata-	dis-	homo-	mini-	per-	semi-	un-
an-	cath-	dys-	hydr-	mis-	peri-	step-	under-
ana-	centi-	e-	hydro-	mono-	phil-	sub-	uni-
Anglo-	circum-	ef-	hyper-	multi-	philo-	suc-	vice-
ant-	co-	electro-	hypo-	neo-	photo-	suf-	
ante-	col-	em-	il-	non-	poly-	sum-	
anti-	com-	en-	im-	ob-	post-	sup-	
ap-	con-	epi-	in-	oc-	pre-	super-	

Suffixes

A suffix is placed at the end of a word to form another word or to form a plural, past tense, comparative, superlative, etc. The following suffixes have entries at their alphabetical places in the dictionary.

-able	-cracy	-ette	-hood	-ification	-kin	-or	-vorous
-arch	-crat	-faction	-ible	-ing	-less	-pathy	-ward
-archy	-cule	-ferous	-ic	-ion	-ling	-phobia	-wards
-arian	-cy	-fold	-ical	-ise	-logical	-ship	-ways
-ary	-dom	-ful	-ician	-ish	-logist	-sion	-wise
-ate	-ed	-fy	-icity	-ism	-logy	-some	-xion
-ation	-ee	-gen	-ics	-ist	-ly	-teen	-y
-bility	-er	-gon	-ie	-ite	-most	-tion	
-ble	-esque	-gram	-ier	-itis	-ness	-tude	
-cide	-ess	-graph	-iest	-ive	-oid	-uble	
-cle	-est	-graphy	-iferous	-ize	-ology	-vore	

APPENDIX 2

Some foreign words and phrases used in English

ad hoc done or arranged only when necessary and not planned in advance. [Latin, = for this]

ad infinitum (*say* in-fin-I-tum)
without limit; for ever.
[Latin, = to infinity]

ad nauseam (*say* naw-see-am)
until people are sick of it.
[Latin, = to sickness]

aide-de-camp (*say* ayd-der-**kahm**)
a military officer who is the assistant to a senior officer.
[French, = camp-helper]

à la carte ordered and paid for as separate items from a menu. (Compare *table d'hôte.*) [French, = from the menu]

alfresco *adjective* & *adverb*
in the open air, *an alfresco meal.*
[from Italian *al fresco* = in the fresh air]

alter ego another, very different, side of someone's personality. [Latin, = other self]

au fait (*say* oh **fay**)
knowing a subject or procedure etc. well.
[French, = to the point]

au gratin (*say* oh **grat**-an)
cooked with a crisp topping of breadcrumbs or grated cheese. [French]

au revoir (*say* oh rev-**wahr**)
goodbye for the moment.
[French, = to be seeing again]

avant-garde (*say* av-ahn-**gard**) *noun*
people who use a very modern style in art or literature etc. [French, = vanguard]

bête noire (*say* bayt **nwahr**)
a person or thing you greatly dislike. [French, = black beast]

bona fide (*say* **boh**-na **fy**-dee)
genuine; without fraud, *Are they bona fide tourists or spies?* [Latin, = in good faith]

bona fides (*say* **boh**-na **fy**-deez)
honest intention; sincerity, *We do not doubt his bona fides.* [Latin, = good faith]

bon voyage (*say* bawn vwah-**yah**z)
pleasant journey! [French]

carte blanche (*say* kart **blahnsh**)
freedom to act as you think best.
[French, = blank paper]

c'est la vie (*say* sel la **vee**)
life is like that. [French, = that is life]

chef-d'oeuvre (*say* shay **dervr**)
a masterpiece. [French, = chief work]

compos mentis in your right mind; sane. (The opposite is **non compos mentis**.) [Latin, = having control of the mind]

cordon bleu (*say* kor-dawn **bler**)
(of cooks and cookery) first-class.
[French, = blue ribbon]

corps de ballet (*say* kor der **bal**-ay)
the whole group of dancers (not the soloists) in a ballet. [French]

corps diplomatique (*say* kor dip-lom-at-**eek**)
the diplomatic service. [French]

coup de grâce (*say* koo der **grahs**)
a stroke or blow that puts an end to something.
[French, = mercy-blow]

coup d'état (*say* koo day-**tah**)
the sudden overthrow of a government.
[French, = blow of State]

crème de la crème (*say* krem der la krem)
the very best of something.
[French, = cream of the cream]

curriculum vitae (*say* veet-I)
a brief account of a person's education, career, etc. [Latin, = course of life]

déjà vu (*say* day-zha vew)
a feeling that you have already experienced what is happening now. [French, = already seen]

de rigueur (*say* der rig-er)
proper; required by custom or etiquette.
[French, = of strictness]

de trop (*say* der **troh**)
not wanted; unwelcome.
[French, = too much]

doppelgänger (*say* **dop**-el-geng-er)
noun
the ghost of a living person.
[German, = double-goer]

dramatis personae (*say* dram-a-tis per-**sohn**-I)
the characters in a play.
[Latin, = persons of the drama]

en bloc (*say* ahn **blok**)
all at the same time; in a block. [French]

en masse (*say* ahn **mass**)
all together. [French, = in a mass]

en passant (*say* ahn pas-ahn)
by the way. [French, = in passing]

en route (*say* ahn **root**)
on the way. [French]

entente (*say* ahn-**tahnt** *or* on-**tont**)
noun
a friendly understanding between nations.
[French]

esprit de corps (*say* es-pree der **kor**)
loyalty to your group.
[French, = spirit of the body]

eureka (*say* yoor-**eek**-a)
interjection
I have found it! [Greek]

exeunt (*say* eks-ee-unt)
verb
they leave the stage. [Latin, = they go out]

ex gratia (*say* eks **gray**-sha)
given without being legally obliged to be given,
an ex gratia payment.
[Latin, = from favour]

faux pas (*say* foh **pah**)
an embarrassing blunder.
[French, = false step]

hara-kiri *noun*
a form of suicide formerly used by Japanese
officers when in disgrace.
[from Japanese *hara* = belly, *kiri* = cutting]

hoi polloi the ordinary people; the masses.
[Greek, = the many]

Homo sapiens human beings regarded as a
species of animal. [Latin, = wise man]

hors-d'oeuvre (*say* or-**dervr**)
noun
food served as an appetizer at the start of a
meal. [French, = outside the work]

in camera in a judge's private room, not in
public. [Latin, = in the room]

in extremis (*say* eks-**treem**-iss)
at the point of death; in very great difficulties.
[Latin, = in the greatest danger]

in memoriam in memory (of). [Latin]

in situ (*say* sit-yoo)
in its original place. [Latin]

joie de vivre (*say* zhwah der **veevr**)
a feeling of great enjoyment of life. [French, =
joy of life]

laissez-faire (*say* lay-say-**fair**) *noun*
a government's policy of not interfering.
[French, = let (them) act]

maître d'hôtel (*say* metr doh-**tel**)
a head waiter. [French, = master of house]

milieu (*say* **meel**-yer) *noun*
environment; surroundings.
[French, from *mi* = mid + *lieu* = place]

modus operandi (*say* moh-dus op-er-**and**-ee)
1 a person's way of working. **2** the way a thing
works. [Latin, = way of working]

nem. con. *abbreviation*
unanimously. [short for Latin *nemine
contradicente* = with nobody disagreeing]

nom de plume a writer's pseudonym. [French, =
pen-name (this phrase is not used in France)]

non sequitur (*say* non sek-**wit**-er)
a conclusion that does not follow from the
evidence given. [Latin, = it does not follow]

nota bene (*say* noh-ta **ben**-ee)
(usually shortened to NB) note carefully.
[Latin, = note well]

nouveau riche (*say* noo-voh **reesh**)
a person who has only recently become rich.
[French, = new rich]

objet d'art (*say* ob-zhay **dar**)
a small artistic object.
[French, = object of art]

par excellence (*say* par eks-el-**ahns**)
more than all the others; to the greatest degree.
[French, = because of special excellence]

pas de deux (*say* pah der **der**)
a dance (e.g. in a ballet) for two persons.
[French, = step of two]

pâté de foie gras (*say* pat-ay der fwah **grah**)
a paste or pie of goose-liver.
[French, = paste of fat liver]

per annum for each year; yearly. [Latin]

per capita (*say* **kap**-it-a)
for each person. [Latin, = for heads]

persona grata (*say* per-soh-na **grah**-ta)
a person who is acceptable to someone,
especially a diplomat acceptable to a foreign
government. (The opposite is **persona non
grata**.)
[Latin, = pleasing person]

pièce de résistance (*say* pee-ess der ray-zees-
tahns)
the most important item. [French]

placebo (*say* plas-ee-boh)
noun (*plural* **placebos**) a harmless substance
given as if it were medicine, usually to
reassure a patient.
[Latin, = I shall be pleasing]

poste restante (*say* rest-**ahnt**)
a part of a post office where letters etc. are kept
until called for.
[French, = letters remaining]

prima facie (*say* pry-ma **fay**-shee)
at first sight; judging by the first impression.
[Latin, = on first appearance]

quid pro quo (*say* kwoh)
something given or done in return for
something.
[Latin, = something for something]

raison d'être (*say* ray-zawn **detr**)
the purpose of a thing's existence.
[French, = reason for being]

rigor mortis (*say* ry-ger **mor**-tis)
stiffening of the body after death.
[Latin, = stiffness of death]

RIP *abbreviation*
may he or she (or they) rest in peace.
[short for Latin *requiescat* (or *requiescant*) *in pace*]

sang-froid (*say* sahn-**frwah**)
noun
calmness in danger or difficulty.
[French, = cold blood]

savoir faire (*say* sav-wahr **fair**)
noun
knowledge of how to behave socially. [French, = knowing how to do]

sotto voce (*say* sot-oh **voh**-chee)
in a very quiet voice.
[Italian, = under the voice]

status quo (*say* stay-tus **kwoh**)
the state of affairs as it was before a change.
[Latin, = the state in which]

sub judice (*say* joo-dis-ee)
being decided by a judge or lawcourt. [Latin, = under a judge]

table d'hôte (*say* tahbl **doht**)
a restaurant meal served at a fixed inclusive price. (Compare **à la carte**.) [French, = host's table]

terra firma dry land; the ground.
[Latin, = firm land]

tête-à-tête (*say* tayt-ah-**tayt**)
noun
a private conversation, especially between two people. [French, = head to head]

vis-à-vis (*say* veez-ah-**vee**) *adverb* & *preposition*
1 in a position facing one another; opposite to.
2 as compared with.
[French, = face to face]

viva voce (*say* vy-va **voh**-chee)
in a spoken test or examination.
[Latin, = with the living voice]

volte-face (*say* volt-**fahs**) *noun*
a complete change in your attitude towards something. [French]

APPENDIX 3

Days of the week

The days of the week were named more than a thousand years ago, in Anglo-Saxon times, and the English names are based on those given by the ancient Romans. They are named after the planets, taking the order of these from ancient astronomy.

Sunday from Old English *sunnandaeg* = day of the sun; the Latin name was *solis dies*.

Monday from Old English *monandaeg* = day of the moon; the Latin name was *lunae dies*. Compare French *lundi*.

Tuesday from Old English *Tiwesdaeg* = day of Tiw, the Old English name of the Norse god of war, whose name was substituted for that of Mars, the Roman god of war; the Latin name was *Martis dies* = day of Mars. Compare French *mardi*.

Wednesday from Old English *Wodnesdaeg* = day of Woden or Odin, the chief Norse god, whose name was substituted for that of Mercury, the Roman messenger-god; the Latin name was *Mercurii dies*. Compare French *mercredi*.

Thursday from Old English *thuresdaeg* = day of thunder, named after Thor, the Norse god of thunder, whose name was substituted for that of Jove or Jupiter, the Roman god who controlled thunder and lightning; the Latin name was *Jovis dies* = day of Jupiter. Compare French *jeudi*.

Friday from Old English *Frigedaeg* = day of Frigg, wife of the god Odin (see *Wednesday*); the Latin name was *Veneris dies* = day of Venus. Compare French *vendredi*.

Saturday from the Old English *Saeternesdaeg* = day of Saturn, a Roman god; the Latin name was *Saturni dies*. Compare French *samedi*.

Months of the year

The names of the months go back to ancient Roman times, and some are named after Roman gods and goddesses.

January is named after Janus, god of gates and beginnings, who faced two ways (past and future), whose festival was held on 9 January.

February is named after *februa*, an ancient Roman feast of purification held in this month.

March is named after Mars, god of war, several of whose festivals were held in this month. It was originally the first month of the year and the months September–December were counted from here.

April is from its Latin name *Aprilis*. The Romans considered this month to be sacred to Venus, goddess of love, and its name may be taken from that of her Greek equivalent Aphrodite.

May is named after the goddess Maia, who was worshipped in this month.

June is named after Juno, queen of the gods.

July is named after Julius Caesar, who was born in this month.

August is named after Augustus Caesar, the first Roman emperor, who was given the name Augustus (Latin, = majestic) in 27 BC.

September is from Latin *septem* = seven, because it was the seventh month in the ancient Roman calendar (see the note on *March*).

October is from Latin *octo* = eight (eighth month).

November is from Latin *novem* = nine (ninth month).

December is from Latin *decem* = ten (tenth month).

Signs of the zodiac

The strip of sky called the *zodiac* is divided into twelve equal sections, each named after a group of stars (its *sign*) that was formerly situated in it. When seen from the Earth, the sun appears to move through each section in turn during one year. The dates given below are the approximate times when it enters and leaves each sign.

In ancient times, people believed that stars and planets influenced the entire world and all that happened in it, including crops, medicine, and people's lives. The key to a person's whole life was thought to lie in the way the planets were arranged (called a *horoscope*) at his or her birth. Many newspapers and magazines print forecasts of what is about to happen to those born under each sign, but only a few people treat them seriously.

The names of the signs are derived from the Latin word with the same meaning.

Aries	the Ram	21 March–20 April
Taurus	the Bull	21 April–20 May
Gemini	the Twins	21 May–20 June
Cancer	the Crab	21 June–21 July
Leo	the Lion	22 July–22 August
Virgo	the Virgin	23 August–21 September
Libra	the Scales	22 September–22 October
Scorpio	the Scorpion	23 October–21 November
Sagittarius	the Archer	22 November–21 December
Capricorn	the Goat	22 December–20 January
Aquarius	the Water-carrier	21 January–19 February
Pisces	the Fishes	20 February–20 March

APPENDIX 4

Countries of the world

Country	People	Adjective
Afghanistan	Afghans	Afghan
Albania	Albanians	Albanian
Algeria	Algerians	Algerian
Andorra	Andorrans	Andorran
Angola	Angolans	Angolan
Antigua and Barbuda	Antiguans, Barbudans	Antiguan, Barbudan
Argentina	Argentinians	Argentinian or Argentine
Armenia	Armenians	Armenian
Australia	Australians	Australian
Austria	Austrians	Austrian
Azerbaijan	Azerbaijanis or Azeris	Azerbaijani
Bahamas	Bahamians	Bahamian
Bahrain	Bahrainis	Bahraini
Bangladesh	Bangladeshis	Bangladeshi
Barbados	Barbadians	Barbadian
Belarus	Belorussians	Belorussian
Belgium	Belgians	Belgian
Belize	Belizians	Belizian
Benin	Beninese	Beninese
Bermuda	Bermudans	Bermudan
Bhutan	Bhutanese	Bhutanese
Bolivia	Bolivians	Bolivian
Bosnia-Herzegovina	Bosnians	Bosnian
Botswana	Batswana or Citizens of Botswana	Botswanan
Brazil	Brazilians	Brazilian
Brunei Darussalam	People of Brunei	Bruneian or Brunei
Bulgaria	Bulgarians	Bulgarian
Burkina Faso	Burkinans	Burkinan or Burkina
Burundi	People of Burundi	Burundi
Cambodia	Cambodians	Cambodian
Cameroon	Cameroonians	Cameroonian
Canada	Canadians	Canadian
Cape Verde	Cape Verdeans	Cape Verdean
Central African Republic	People of the Central African Republic	Central African Republic
Chad	Chadians	Chadian
Chile	Chileans	Chilean
China, People's Republic of	Chinese	Chinese
Colombia	Colombians	Colombian
Comoros	Comorans	Comoran
Congo, Democratic Republic of the	Congolese	Congolese
Congo, Republic of the	Congolese	Congolese
Costa Rica	Costa Ricans	Costa Rican
Côte d'Ivoire	People of the Côte d'Ivoire	of the Côte d'Ivoire
Croatia	Croats	Croatian
Cuba	Cubans	Cuban
Cyprus	Cypriots	Cypriot
Czech Republic	Czechs	Czech
Denmark	Danes	Danish
Djibouti	Djiboutians	Djiboutian
Dominica	Dominicans	Dominican
Dominican Republic	Dominicans	Dominican
East Timor	East Timorese	East Timorean
Ecuador	Ecuadoreans	Ecuadorean
Egypt	Egyptians	Egyptian

Country	People	Adjective
El Salvador	Salvadoreans	Salvadorean
Equatorial Guinea	Equatorial Guineans	of Equatorial Guinea
Eritrea	Eritreans	Eritrean
Estonia	Estonians	Estonian
Ethiopia	Ethiopians	Ethiopian
Fiji	Fijians	Fijian
Finland	Finns	Finnish
France	French	French
Gabon	Gabonese	Gabonese
Gambia, The	Gambians	Gambian
Georgia	Georgians	Georgian
Germany	Germans	German
Ghana	Ghanaians	Ghanaian
Greece	Greeks	Greek
Grenada	Grenadians	Grenadian
Guatemala	Guatemalans	Guatemalan
Guinea	Guineans	Guinean
Guinea-Bissau	People of Guinea-Bissau	Guinea-Bissau
Guyana	Guyanese	Guyanese
Haiti	Haitians	Haitian
Honduras	Hondurans	Honduran
Hungary	Hungarians	Hungarian
Iceland	Icelanders	Icelandic
India	Indians	Indian
Indonesia	Indonesians	Indonesian
Iran	Iranians	Iranian
Iraq	Iraqis	Iraqi
Ireland, Republic of	Irish	Irish
Israel	Israelis	Israeli
Italy	Italians	Italian
Jamaica	Jamaicans	Jamaican
Japan	Japanese	Japanese
Jordan	Jordanians	Jordanian
Kazakhstan	Kazakhs	Kazakh
Kenya	Kenyans	Kenyan
Kiribati	Kiribatians	Kiribatian
Kuwait	Kuwaitis	Kuwaiti
Kyrgyzstan	Kyrgyz	Kyrgyz
Laos	Laotians	Laotian
Latvia	Latvians	Latvians
Lebanon	Lebanese	Lebanese
Lesotho	Basotho	Lesotho
Liberia	Liberians	Liberian
Libya	Libyans	Libyan
Liechtenstein	Liechtensteiners	Liechtenstein
Lithuania	Lithuanians	Lithuanian
Luxembourg	Luxembourgers	Luxembourgian
Macedonia (former Yugoslav Republic of Macedonia)	Macedonians	Macedonian
Madagascar	Malagasies	Malagasy
Malawi	Malawians	Malawian
Malaysia	Malaysians	Malaysian
Maldives	Maldivians	Maldivian
Mali	Malians	Malian
Malta	Maltese	Maltese
Marshall Islands	Marshall Islanders	Marshall Islands
Mauritania	Mauritanians	Mauritanian
Mauritius	Mauritians	Mauritian

Country	People	Adjective
Mexico	Mexicans	Mexican
Micronesia	Micronesians	Micronesian
Moldava	Moldavans	Moldovan
Monaco	Monégasques	Monégasque
Mongolia	Mongolians	Mongolian
Morocco	Moroccans	Moroccan
Mozambique	Mozambicans	Mozambican
Myanmar (Burma)		
Namibia	Namibians	Namibian
Nauru	Nauruans	Nauruan
Nepal	Nepalese	Nepalese
Netherlands	Dutch	Dutch
New Zealand	New Zealanders	New Zealand
Nicaragua	Nicaraguans	Nicaraguan
Niger	Nigeriens	Nigerien
Nigeria	Nigerians	Nigerian
North Korea (People's Democratic Republic of Korea)	North Koreans	North Korean
Norway	Norwegians	Norwegian
Oman	Omanis	Omani
Pakistan	Pakistanis	Pakistani
Palau	Palauans	Palauan
Panama	Panamanians	Panamanian
Papua New Guinea	Papua New Guineans	Papua New Guinean
Paraguay	Paraguayans	Paraguayan
Peru	Peruvians	Peruvian
Philippines	Filipinos	Philippine
Poland	Poles	Polish
Portugal	Portuguese	Portuguese
Qatar	Qataris	Qatari
Romania	Romanians	Romanian
Russia (Russian Federation)	Russians	Russian
Rwanda	Rwandans	Rwandan
St Kitts-Nevis	People of St Kitts-Nevis	Kittian, Nevisian
St Lucia	St Lucians	St Lucian
St Vincent and the Grenadines	St Vincentians	St Vincent
St Lucia	St Lucians	St Lucian
Samoa	Samoans	Samoan
São Tomé and Principe	People of São Tomé and Principe	of São Tomé and Principe
Saudi Arabia	Saudi Arabians	Saudi Arabian
Scotland (part of the United Kingdom)	Scots	Scottish, Scots, or Scotch
Senegal	Senegalese	Senegalese
Seychelles	Seychellois	Seychellois
Sierra Leone	Sierra Leoneans	Sierra Leonean
Singapore	Singaporeans	Singaporean
Slovakia	Slovaks	Slovak
Slovenia	Slovenes	Slovenian
Solomon Islands	Solomon Islanders	Solomon Islands
Somalia	Somalis	Somali
South Africa	South Africans	South African
South Korea (Republic of Korea)	South Koreans	South Korean
Spain	Spaniards	Spanish
Sri Lanka	Sri Lankans	Sri Lankan
Sudan	Sudanese	Sudanese
Suriname	Surinamers	Surinamese
Swaziland	Swazis	Swazi
Sweden	Swedes	Swedish
Switzerland	Swiss	Swiss

Country	People	Adjective
Syria	Syrians	Syrian
Taiwan	Taiwanese	Taiwanese
Tajikistan	Tajiks	Tajik
Tanzania	Tanzanians	Tanzanian
Thailand	Thais	Thai
Togo	Togolese	Togolese
Tonga	Tongans	Tongan
Trinidad and Tobago	Trinidadians and Tobagans or Tobagonians	Trinidadian, Tobagan or Tobagonian
Tunisia	Tunisians	Tunisian
Turkey	Turks	Turkish
Turkmenistan	Turkmens	Turkmen
Tuvalu	Tuvaluans	Tuvaluan
Uganda	Ugandans	Ugandan
Ukraine	Ukrainians	Ukrainian
United Arab Emirates	People of the United Arab Emirates	of the United Arab Emirates
United Kingdom	British	British
United States of America	Americans	American
Uruguay	Uruguayans	Uruguayan
Uzbekistan	Uzbeks	Uzbek
Vanuatu	People of Vanuatu	Vanuatu
Vatican City	Vatican citizens	Vatican
Venezuela	Venezuelans	Venezuelan
Vietnam	Vietnamese	Vietnamese
Yemen	Yemenis	Yemeni
Yugoslavia (Montenegro and Serbia)	Yugoslavs (Montenegrins and Serbians)	Yugoslav (Montenegrin and Serbian)
Zambia	Zambians	Zambian
Zimbabwe	Zimbabweans	Zimbabwean

APPENDIX 5

Weights and Measures

Note The conversion factors are not exact unless so marked. They are given only to the accuracy likely to be needed in everyday calculations.

1. METRIC, WITH BRITISH EQUIVALENTS

Linear Measure

1 millimetre	= 0.039 inch
1 centimetre = 10 mm	= 0.394 inch
1 decimetre = 10 cm	= 3.94 inches
1 metre = 10 dm	= 1.094 yards
1 decametre = 10 m	= 10.94 yards
1 hectometre = 100 m	= 109.4 yards
1 kilometre = 1,000 m	= 0.6214 mile

Square Measure

1 square centimetre	= 0.155 sq. inch
1 square metre = 10,000 sq. cm	= 1.196 sq. yards
1 are = 100 sq. metres	= 119.6 sq. yards
1 hectare = 100 ares	= 2.471 acres
1 square kilometre = 100 hectares	
	= 0.386 sq. mile

Cubic Measure

1 cubic centimetre	= 0.061 cu. inch
1 cubic metre = 1,000,000 cu. cm	
	= 1.308 cu. yards

Capacity Measure

1 millilitre	= 0.002 pint
	(British)
1 centilitre = 10 ml	= 0.018 pint
1 decilitre = 10 cl	= 0.176 pint
1 litre = 10 dl	= 1.76 pints
1 decalitre = 10 l	= 2.20 gallons
1 hectolitre = 100 l	= 2.75 bushels
1 kilolitre = 1,000 l	= 3.44 quarters

Weight

1 milligram	= 0.015 grain
1 centigram = 10 mg	= 0.154 grain
1 decigram = 10 cg	= 1.543 grains
1 gram = 10 dg	= 15.43 grains
1 decagram = 10 g	= 5.63 drams
1 hectogram = 100 g	= 3.527 ounces
1 kilogram = 1,000 g	= 2.205 pounds
1 tonne (metric ton) = 1,000 kg	
	= 0.984 (long) ton

2. BRITISH AND AMERICAN, WITH METRIC EQUIVALENTS

Linear Measure

1 inch	= 25.4 mm exactly	
1 foot = 12 inches	= 0.3048 metre	
1 yard = 3 feet	= 0.9144 metre exactly	
1 (statute) mile	= 1,760 yards	= 1.609 km

Square Measure

1 square inch	= 6.45 sq. cm	
1 square foot	= 144 sq. in.	= 9.29 sq. dm
1 square yard	= 9 sq. ft.	= 0.836 sq. metre
1 acre	= 4,840 sq. yd.	= 0.405 hectare
1 square mile	= 640 acres	= 259 hectares

Cubic Measure

1 cubic inch	= 16.4 cu. cm	
1 cubic foot	= 1,728 cu. in.	= 0.0283 cu. metre
1 cubic yard	= 27 cu. ft.	= 0.765 cu. metre

Capacity Measure

British

1 pint	= 20 fluid oz.
= 34.68 cu. in.	= 0.568 litre
1 quart = 2 pints	= 1.136 litres
1 gallon = 4 quarts	= 4.546 litres
1 peck = 2 gallons	= 9.092 litres
1 bushel = 4 pecks	= 36.4 litres
1 quarter = 8 bushels	= 2.91 hectolitres

American dry

1 pint = 33.60 cu. in.	= 0.550 litre
1 quart = 2 pints	= 1.101 litres
1 peck = 8 quarts	= 8.81 litres
1 bushel = 4 pecks	= 35.3 litres

American liquid

1 pint = 16 fluid oz.	= 0.473 litre
= 28.88 cu. in.	
1 quart = 2 pints	= 0.946 litre
1 gallon = 4 quarts	= 3.785 litres

Avoirdupois Weight

1 grain	= 0.065 gram	
1 dram	= 1.772 grams	
1 ounce	= 16 drams	= 28.35 grams
1 pound	= 16 ounces	= 7,000 grains
	= 0.4536 kilogram (0.45359237 exactly)	
1 stone	= 14 pounds	= 6.35 kilograms
1 quarter	= 2 stones	= 12.70 kilograms

1 hundredweight	= 4 quarters	= 50.80 kilograms
1 (long) ton	= 20 hundredweight	
		= 1.016 tonnes
1 short ton	= 2,000 pounds	
		= 0.907 tonne

3. POWER NOTATION

This expresses concisely any power of ten (any number that is composed of factors 10), and is sometimes used in the dictionary. 10^2 or ten squared = 10×10 = 100; 10^3 or ten cubed = $10 \times 10 \times 10$ = 1,000. Similarly, 10^4 = 10,000 and 10^{10} = 1 followed by ten noughts = 10,000,000,000. Proceeding in the opposite direction, dividing by ten and subtracting one from the index, we have 10^2 = 100, 10^1 = 10, 10^0 = 1, $10^{-1} = \frac{1}{10}$, $10^{-2} = \frac{1}{100}$, and so on; $10^{-10} = 1/10^{10}$ = 1/10,000,000,000.

4. TEMPERATURE

Fahrenheit: Water boils (under standard conditions) at 212° and freezes at 32°.
Celsius or Centigrade: Water boils at 100° and freezes at 0°.
Kelvin: Water boils at 373.15 K and freezes at 273.15 K.

Celsius	Fahrenheit	Celsius	Fahrenheit
−17.8°	0°	50°	122°
−10°	14°	60°	140°
0°	32°	70°	158°
10°	50°	80°	176°
20°	68°	90°	194°
30°	86°	100°	212°
40°	104°		

To convert Celsius into Fahrenheit: multiply by 9, divide by 5, and add 32.
To convert Fahrenheit into Celsius: subtract 32, multiply by 5, and divide by 9.

5. METRIC PREFIXES

	Abbreviation or symbol	Factor		Abbreviation or symbol	Factor
deca-	da	10	deci-	d	10^{-1}
hecto-	h	10^2	centi-	c	10^{-2}
kilo-	k	10^3	milli-	m	10^{-3}
mega-	M	10^6	micro-	μ	10^{-6}
giga-	G	10^9	nano-	n	10^{-9}
tera-	T	10^{12}	pico-	p	10^{-12}
peta-	P	10^{15}	femto-	f	10^{-15}
exa-	E	10^{18}	atto-	a	10^{-18}

These prefixes may be applied to any units of the metric system: hectogram (abbreviated hg) = 100 grams; kilowatt (abbreviated kW) = 1,000 watts.

6. SI UNITS

Basic SI units

Quantity	Unit	Symbol
Length	Metre	m
Mass	Kilogram	kg
Time	Second	s
Electric current	Ampere	A
Temperature	Kelvin	K
Light intensity	Candela	cd
Amount of substance	Mole	mol

Derived SI units

Quantity	Unit	Symbol
Area	Square metre	m^2
Volume	Cubic metre	m^3
Frequency	Hertz	Hz
Force	Newton	N
Pressure	Pascal	Pa
Energy	Joule	J
Power	Watt	W
Electric potential	Volt	V
Electrical resistance	Ohm	Ω
Electric charge	Coulomb	C
Radioactivity	Becquerel	Bq

Basic SI units and derived SI units

The seven basic SI units have scientific standards that define the size of the units with great precision. All derived units are related to the basic SI units. Each unit has its own entry in the dictionary.

Note: SI stands for Système International, the international system of units of measurement.

OXFORD
Dictionaries and Thesauruses
for home and school

Oxford Very First Dictionary
Oxford First Dictionary
Oxford First Thesaurus

Oxford Illustrated Junior Dictionary
Oxford Illustrated Junior Thesaurus
Oxford Junior Dictionary
Oxford Junior Thesaurus

Oxford Primary Dictionary
Oxford Primary Thesaurus
Oxford Children's Dictionary
Oxford Children's Thesaurus

Oxford Practical School Dictionary
Oxford Concise School Dictionary
Oxford Concise School Thesaurus
Oxford School Dictionary
Oxford School Thesaurus
Oxford Pocket School Dictionary
Oxford Pocket School Thesaurus
Oxford Mini School Dictionary
Oxford Mini School Thesaurus

Oxford Student's Dictionary

Large Print
Oxford Young Readers' Dictionary
Oxford Young Readers' Thesaurus